Resource Book on TRIPS and Development

The Resource Book, conceived as a guide to the TRIPS Agreement, provides detailed analysis of each of the provisions of the Agreement, aiming at a sound understanding of WTO Members' rights and obligations. The purpose is to clarify the implications of the Agreement, especially highlighting the areas in which the treaty leaves leeway to Members for the pursuit of the their own policy objectives, according to their respective levels of development. In doing so, the book does not produce tailor-made prescriptions but gives guidance on the implications of specific issues and on the options available. The book is not limited to the analysis of the TRIPS Agreement but also considers related questions and developments at the national, regional, and international level.

The United Nations Conference on Trade and Development (UNCTAD) and the International Centre for Trade and Sustainable Development (ICTSD) have come together to implement the UNCTAD-ICTSD Project on Intellectual Property Rights and Sustainable Development. The Project aims to improve understanding of the development implications of the TRIPS Agreement. The Resource Book is a contribution to this effort.

Resource Book on
TRIPS and
Development

UNCTAD-ICTSD

ICTSD

International Centre for Trade
and Sustainable Development

UNCTAD

CAMBRIDGE
UNIVERSITY PRESS

CAMBRIDGE UNIVERSITY PRESS
Cambridge, New York, Melbourne, Madrid, Cape Town, Singapore, São Paulo

Cambridge University Press
40 West 20th Street, New York, NY 10011-4211, USA

www.cambridge.org
Information on this title: www.cambridge.org/9780521850445

First published 2005

Printed in the United States of America

A catalog record for this publication is available from the British Library.

Library of Congress Cataloging in Publication Data

ISBN-13   978-0-521-85044-5 hardback
ISBN-10   0-521-85044-4 hardback

Contents

Preface

Intellectual Property (IP) was until recently the domain of specialists and producers of Intellectual Property Rights (IPRs). The Agreement on Trade-Related Aspects of Intellectual Property Rights (the TRIPS Agreement) concluded during the Uruguay Round negotiations has in this regard signalled a major shift. The incorporation of IP into the multilateral trading system and its relationship with a wide area of key public policy issues has elicited great concern over its pervasive role in people's lives and in society in general. Developing country Members of the World Trade Organization (WTO) no longer have the policy options and flexibilities developed countries had in using IPRs to support their national development. But TRIPS is not the end of the story. Significant new developments have taken place at the international, regional and bilateral level that build on and strengthen the minimum TRIPS standards through the progressive harmonization of policies along standards of technologically advanced countries. The challenges ahead in designing and implementing IP-policy at the national and international levels are considerable.

This book has been conceived as a guide offering background and technical information on the TRIPS Agreement. It provides legal and economic analysis on each treaty provision with a view to identifying development-friendly policy options for the implementation of the Agreement. From this point of view, the book, because of its contents and coverage, should be of interest to a wider audience including practitioners, academics, diplomats and policy-makers in general.

The book is a major output of the UNCTAD-ICTSD Project on Intellectual Property Rights and Sustainable Development[1] launched in 2001. The central objective of the Project is to contribute to the emergence of a critical mass of a well-informed IP community – decision makers, negotiators, private sector and civil society, particularly in developing countries – able to define their own development objectives and effectively advance those objectives at the national and international levels.

Rubens Ricupero
Secretary-General, UNCTAD

Ricardo Meléndez Ortiz
Executive Director, ICTSD
September 2004

---

[1] For information on the activities and outputs of the UNCTAD-ICTSD Project, see <http://www.iprsonline.org/unctadictsd/description.htm>.

Acknowledgments

This Resource Book has been prepared under the responsibility of the UNCTAD-ICTSD Project on Intellectual Property Rights and Sustainable Development but is the result of the collective effort of the persons listed below who have been involved in different stages and degrees.

The work has been carried out under the direct responsibility of Pedro Roffe (Project Director, ICTSD) and Christoph Spennemann (Project Assistant, UNCTAD).[2] Graham Dutfield (Senior Research Fellow, Queen Mary Intellectual Property Research Institute, Queen Mary, University of London) was responsible for the substantive review, editing and polishing of the manuscript.

Frederick Abbott (Edward Ball Eminent Scholar Professor, Florida State University College of Law)[3] and Carlos M. Correa (Professor, Director of the Masters Programme on Science and Technology Policy and Management, University of Buenos Aires)[4] were the principal consultants and overall advisers.

The following resource persons made specific contributions to this work: John N. Adams (Professor, Faculty of Law, University of Sheffield);[5] Michael Blakeney (Professor, Director of the Centre for Commercial Law Studies, Queen Mary, University of London);[6] Mariano Garcia-Rubio (Teaching and Research Assistant, Law Department, Graduate Institute of International Studies, Geneva);[7] Mohan Kumar (Trade Diplomat, India);[8] Peter Muchlinski (Professor, Kent Law School, University of Kent);[9] Ruth G. Okediji (William L. Prosser Professor of Law, University of Minnesota);[10] Marino Porzio (Attorney at law, Santiago de Chile);[11] Uma Suthersanen (Senior Lecturer, Queen Mary Intellectual Property Research

[2] C. Spennemann also prepared specific inputs to various chapters of the book and particularly to Chapter 32.

[3] Besides his overall responsibility to this work, F. Abbott contributed with the original texts of Part 1 and Chapters 14, 15, 25 and 36.

[4] Besides his overall responsibility to this work, C. Correa contributed with the original texts of Chapters 17, 21–24, 27, 28 and 30.

[5] J. Adams contributed with inputs to Chapters 17–20 and 26.

[6] M. Blakeney contributed with inputs to Chapters 14 and 15.

[7] M. Garcia Rubio contributed with inputs to Chapters 32, 37 and 39.

[8] M. Kumar contributed with inputs to Chapters 31–33, 35 and 36.

[9] P. Muchlinski contributed with inputs to Chapter 34.

[10] R. Okediji contributed with the original chapters on copyright in Part 2.

[11] M. Porzio contributed with inputs to Chapter 30.

Institute, Queen Mary, University of London);[12] Geoff Tansey (Writer and Consultant, UK);[13] and Hanns Ullrich (Professor of Law, European University Institute, Florence).[14]

The members of the UNCTAD-ICTSD core team are: Christophe Bellman (Programmes Director, ICTSD), Johanna von Braun (Programme Officer, Intellectual Property, ICTSD), Khalil Hamdani (Head, Policy and Capacity-building Branch, UNCTAD), Ricardo Melendez (Executive Director, ICTSD), Assad Omer (former staff, UNCTAD), Pedro Roffe (Project Director, ICTSD), Christoph Spennemann (Project Assistant, UNCTAD), Taffere Tesfachew (Special Assistant to the Deputy Secretary-General, UNCTAD), David Vivas Eugui (Programme Manager, Intellectual Property, Technology and Services, ICTSD) and James Zhan (Chief, International Arrangements Section, UNCTAD). The core team is grateful to all people involved in the preparation of the book but is solely responsible for its contents.

This activity benefited from the generous support of the Department for International Development (DFID) of the United Kingdom and the Swedish International Development Cooperation Agency (SIDA).

---

[12] U. Suthersanen contributed with the original text of Chapter 16.

[13] G. Tansey provided valuable comments on all chapters of the book.

[14] H. Ullrich contributed with the original text of Chapter 29.

Explanatory Note: The Methodology

The Resource Book, conceived as a practical guide to the TRIPS Agreement, provides detailed analysis of each of its provisions, aiming at a sound understanding of WTO Members' rights and obligations. The purpose is to clarify the implications of the Agreement, especially highlighting the areas in which the treaty leaves leeway to Members for the pursuit of their own policy objectives, according to their respective levels of development. In doing so, the book does not produce tailor-made prescriptions but gives guidance on the implications of specific issues and on the options available. The book is not limited to the analysis of the TRIPS Agreement but also considers related questions and developments at the national, regional and international level.

The preparation of this book was completed in May 2004. It will be periodically updated. The latest versions will be made available on the project website at <http://www.iprsonline.org/unctadictsd/ResourceBookIndex.htm>.

Structure and general contents

The Resource Book is divided into six parts, basically following the structure of the TRIPS Agreement. In synthesis it covers:

Part One: Nature of Obligations, Principles and Objectives
Articles 1 to 8, including the characterization of the TRIPS rules as minimum standards; the discretion of Members as to the method of implementation; the categories of intellectual property rights embraced by TRIPS; the national treatment and most-favoured-nation treatment obligations; the exhaustion of IPRs and the TRIPS objectives and principles.

Part Two: Substantive Obligations
Part Two corresponds to Sections 1–7 of Part II of the TRIPS Agreement. It deals in detail with all substantive rights covered by TRIPS, especially sensitive issues such as patents and related matters like the access to medicines and the Doha Declaration on the TRIPS Agreement and Public Health. Another patent issue concerns the ongoing negotiations under Article 27.3(b) on the patentability of life forms, where a thorough analysis of implementing options is presented, accompanied by a summary of Members' respective positions on the review of this provision. Moreover, the reader is provided with a detailed analysis of the TRIPS provisions on geographical indications, facilitating the understanding of the ongoing

negotiations in the Council for TRIPS. Other chapters concern copyright (including the WIPO "Internet Treaties"); trademarks; industrial designs; integrated circuits and undisclosed information.

Part Three: Intellectual Property Rights and Competition
Part Three covers Articles 8.2 and 40 of the Agreement. It deals in the main with measures needed to prevent the abuse of intellectual property rights.

Part Four: Enforcement, Acquisition and Maintenance of Rights
This part comprises Parts III and IV of the TRIPS Agreement. In this area WTO Members face considerable implementation challenges concerning the establishment of appropriate enforcement procedures.

Part Five: Interpretation and Dispute Prevention and Settlement
It deals with Part V of the TRIPS Agreement on transparency and dispute settlement and on the methods of interpretation employed by the WTO panels and the Appellate Body. The section on dispute settlement explains in detail the WTO dispute settlement system under the DSU and provides insight into the problems of a possible introduction of "non-violation complaints" to TRIPS-related disputes.

Part Six: Transitional and Institutional Arrangements
The final part of the book covers Parts VI and VII of the TRIPS Agreement. The main areas of interest for developing countries are the chapters on transitional periods, on technical cooperation and transfer of technology, especially on the obligation to provide for "mailbox" applications and exclusive marketing rights under Article 70.8 and 9.

The analysis of the individual TRIPS provisions

In the consideration and analysis of each of the TRIPS provisions, the book follows a common structure[15] so that each chapter consists of the following sections and subsections:

1. Introduction: terminology, definition and scope
This section contains general introductory observations on the issue under consideration.

2. History of the provision
This section is divided into two subsections dealing respectively with:

2.1 Situation pre-TRIPS
This subsection shows whether and to what extent the issue or subject-matter in question was dealt with prior to the TRIPS Agreement.

---

[15] The reader should note that while the book follows a common structure, due to its collective nature including resource persons from different legal traditions, some chapters treat certain issues favouring either a continental or a common law approach.

2.2 Negotiating history

This subsection explains the different negotiating positions adopted during the Uruguay Round and provides the historical background to the understanding of the TRIPS provision under consideration.

This negotiating history follows, in general, a common pattern that describes, as necessary, the national positions of principal actors in the negotiations and a) the Anell Draft; b) the Brussels Draft; and, where appropriate, c) the Dunkel Draft.

a) The Anell Draft. In his 23 July 1990 Report to the General Negotiating Group (GNG) on the status of work in the TRIPS Negotiating Group, the Chairman (Lars E. R. Anell) presented alternative draft texts: an A and B proposal. These proposals differed not only with respect to the particular draft provisions, but also as far as the overall approach to a future agreement on trade-related IPRs was concerned.[16] The main body of the report included "A" (developed country supported) and "B" (developing country supported) proposals that consolidated draft texts previously submitted by different delegations and included revisions based on consultations among the parties.[17] There was also an Annex to the report that reproduced proposals previously submitted by delegations, which provisions had not been the subject of detailed consultations. The Annex did not attribute "A" and "B" proposals in the same way as the main report, and also referred to "C" proposals. Therefore, the distinction in the main report between developed country proposals on the one hand and developing country proposals on the other hand may not be made in the context of the Annex. While the main report of the Anell Draft contained Parts II (general provisions and basic principles), III (substantive IPR standards), IV (enforcement), V (acquisition of IPRs), and IX (trade in counterfeit and pirated goods), the Annex reproduced Parts I (preambular provision and objectives), VI (dispute prevention and settlement), VII (transitional arrangements), and VIII (institutional arrangements, final provisions).

b) The Brussels Draft corresponds to the Ministerial Text of December 1990 containing the Draft Final Act Embodying the Results of the Uruguay Round of

---

[16] Chairman's Report to the GNG, Status of Work in the Negotiating Group, Negotiating Group on Trade-Related Aspects of Intellectual Property Rights, including Trade in Counterfeit Goods, MTN.GNG/NG11/W/76, 23 July 1990.

[17] See the Chairman's Report to the GNG, MTN.GNG/NG11/W/76, 23 July 1990: "[...] The two basic approaches to the negotiations on TRIPS are identified in the text by the letters A and B. These approaches differ not only in substance but also in structure. In broad terms, approach A envisages a single TRIPS agreement encompassing all the areas of negotiation and dealing with all seven categories of intellectual property on which proposals have been made; this agreement would be implemented as an integral part of the General Agreement. Approach B provides for two parts, one on trade in pirated and counterfeit goods (reflected in Part IX of the attached text) and the other on standards and principles concerning the availability, scope and use of intellectual property rights (reflected in Parts I–VIII). Under this approach, the latter part would cover the same categories of intellectual property as approach A, with the exception of the protection of trade secrets, which its proponents do not accept as a category of intellectual property; this part would be implemented in the 'relevant international organisation, account being taken of the multidisciplinary and overall aspects of the issues involved.' Options within an approach, A or B, are indicated by the use of square brackets or little "a"s, "b"s etc. [...]"

Multilateral Trade Negotiations, Revision, Trade-Related Aspects of Intellectual Property Rights, Including Trade in Counterfeit Goods.[18] *This draft text was prepared by Chairman Anell on his own responsibility and was said to reflect the results of negotiations through 22 November 1990. The Chairman submitted the draft text to the Brussels Ministerial Conference scheduled for 3–7 December 1990.*

c) The Dunkel Draft refers to then GATT Director General who proposed in December 1991 his Draft Final Act Embodying the Results of the Uruguay Round of Multilateral Trade Negotiations.[19]

3. Possible interpretations
Section 3 contains a technical analysis of the respective provision, providing legal arguments in favour of a development-friendly interpretation.

4. WTO jurisprudence
This section summarizes and analyses, in the light of the previous section, those parts of panel and Appellate Body reports dealing with the TRIPS provision under analysis.

5. Relationship with other international instruments
This section specifies how the respective subject matter is dealt with under other relevant agreements and how this could have implications for the TRIPS Agreement. The analysis is divided into two subsections:

5.1 WTO Agreements

5.2 Other international instruments

6. New developments
Section 6 provides for a comparison of the approaches taken by various legislations and provides further, where possible, an outlook on new and emerging issues. The common structure describes, as far as possible, developments in the following areas:

6.1 National laws

6.2 International instruments

6.3 Regional and bilateral contexts

6.4 Proposals for review
This subsection provides information on the latest stage of WTO negotiations on the respective subject matter.

7. Comments, including economic and social implications
Finally, section 7 of the common structure of the book highlights development-oriented policy issues and provides, in general, broad considerations on possible economic and social implications.

---

[18] MTN.TNC/W/35/Rev. 1, 3 Dec. 1990.

[19] MTN.TNG/W/FA, 20 Dec. 1991.

List of Acronyms

AB	Appellate Body
ARIPO	African Regional Industrial Property Organization
CAFTA	Central American Free Trade Agreement
CBD	Convention on Biological Diversity
CTM	Community Trade Mark
DMCA	Digital Millennium Copyright Act
DSB	Dispute Settlement Body
DSU	Dispute Settlement Understanding
EC	European Community
ECJ	European Court of Justice
EFTA	European Free Trade Area
EMRs	Exclusive Marketing Rights
EPC	European Patent Convention
EPO	European Patent Office
EU	European Union
FTAA	Free Trade Area of the Americas
GATS	General Agreement on Trade in Services
GATT	General Agreement on Tariffs and Trade
GIs	Geographical Indications
ICJ	International Court of Justice
IGC	(WIPO) Intergovernmental Committee on Intellectual Property and Genetic Resources, Traditional Knowledge and Folklore
IP	Intellectual Property
IPIC Treaty	Treaty on Intellectual Property in Respect of Integrated Circuits
IPRs	Intellectual Property rights
ITC	International Trade Commission
ITPGRFA	International Treaty on Plant Genetic Resources for Food and Agriculture
IU	International Undertaking on Plant Genetic Resources
LDC	Least-developed country
MFN	Most-favoured Nation
NAFTA	North American Free Trade Agreement
OAPI	Organisation Africaine de la Propriété Intellectuelle (African Intellectual Property Organization)
OECD	Organisation for Economic Co-operation and Development
OHIM	(European) Office for Harmonization in the Internal Market
SCP	(WIPO) Standing Committee on the Law of Patents
SCT	(WIPO) Standing Committee on the Law of Trademarks, Industrial Designs and Geographical Indications

TBT Agreement	Agreement on Technical Barriers to Trade
TK	Traditional Knowledge
TNC	Transnational Corporation
TNC	Trade Negotiations Committee
TNG	TRIPS Negotiating Group
TRIMS	Trade-related Investment Measures
TRIPS	Agreement on Trade-related Aspects of Intellectual Property Rights
UPOV	Union Internationale pour la Protection des Obtentions Végétales (International Union for the Protection of New Varieties of Plants)
URAA	Uruguay Round Agreements Act
VCLT	Vienna Convention on the Law of Treaties
WCT	WIPO Copyright Treaty
WHO	World Health Organization
WIPO	World Intellectual Property Organization
WPPT	WIPO Performances and Phonograms Treaty
WTO	World Trade Organization

PART 1: NATURE OF OBLIGATIONS, PRINCIPLES AND OBJECTIVES

1: Preamble

Members,

Desiring to reduce distortions and impediments to international trade, and taking into account the need to promote effective and adequate protection of intellectual property rights, and to ensure that measures and procedures to enforce intellectual property rights do not themselves become barriers to legitimate trade;

Recognizing, to this end, the need for new rules and disciplines concerning:

(a) the applicability of the basic principles of GATT 1994 and of relevant international intellectual property agreements or conventions;

(b) the provision of adequate standards and principles concerning the availability, scope and use of trade-related intellectual property rights;

(c) the provision of effective and appropriate means for the enforcement of trade-related intellectual property rights, taking into account differences in national legal systems;

(d) the provision of effective and expeditious procedures for the multilateral prevention and settlement of disputes between governments; and

(e) transitional arrangements aiming at the fullest participation in the results of the negotiations;

Recognizing the need for a multilateral framework of principles, rules and disciplines dealing with international trade in counterfeit goods;

Recognizing that intellectual property rights are private rights;

Recognizing the underlying public policy objectives of national systems for the protection of intellectual property, including developmental and technological objectives;

Recognizing also the special needs of the least-developed country Members in respect of maximum flexibility in the domestic implementation of laws and regulations in order to enable them to create a sound and viable technological base;

Emphasizing the importance of reducing tensions by reaching strengthened commitments to resolve disputes on trade-related intellectual property issues through multilateral procedures;

> Desiring to establish a mutually supportive relationship between the WTO and the World Intellectual Property Organization (referred to in this Agreement as "WIPO") as well as other relevant international organizations;
>
> Hereby agree as follows:

1. Introduction: terminology, definition and scope

The preamble of the TRIPS Agreement reflects the contentious nature of the negotiations and the differences in perspective among the negotiating WTO Members.

Government officials and judges may use the preamble of a treaty as a source of interpretative guidance in the process of implementation and dispute settlement. The statements contained in preambles are not intended to be *operative* provisions in the sense of creating specific rights or obligations. A preamble is designed to establish a definitive record of the intention or purpose of the parties in entering into the agreement.

Article 31 of the Vienna Convention on the Law of Treaties (VCLT)[1] provides that the preamble forms part of the treaty text and, as such, part of the terms and "context" of the treaty for purposes of interpretation.[2] In this sense, the preamble should be distinguished from the negotiating history of the treaty that is a "supplementary means of interpretation" that should be used when the express terms are ambiguous, or to confirm an interpretation (Article 32, VCLT).[3]

2. History of the provision

2.1 Situation pre-TRIPS

TRIPS is a "new instrument" on IPRs in international trade. It is the result of "new area" negotiations in the Uruguay Round.[4] Its preamble reflects a particular

---

[1] The Convention was adopted on 22 May 1969 and entered into force on 27 January 1980. Text: United Nations, *Treaty Series*, vol. 1155, p.331.

[2] Article 31 of the Vienna Convention on the Law of Treaties (VCLT) provides in relevant part:
"1. A treaty shall be interpreted in good faith in accordance with the ordinary meaning to be given to the terms of the treaty in their context and in the light of its object and purpose.
2. The context for the purpose of the interpretation of a treaty shall comprise, in addition to the text, including its preamble and annexes:" [underlining added]

[3] Article 32 of the VCLT provides:
"Recourse may be had to supplementary means of interpretation, including the preparatory work of the treaty and the circumstances of its conclusion, in order to confirm the meaning resulting from the application of article 31, or to determine the meaning when the interpretation according to article 31:
(a) leaves the meaning ambiguous or obscure; or
(b) leads to a result which is manifestly absurd or unreasonable."
The terms "treaty" and "international agreement" are largely synonymous, and are used interchangeably in this chapter. In some national legal systems (such as that of the United States), the terms are sometimes used to distinguish the type of domestic ratification procedure that must be followed for approval.

[4] The other principle "new area" of negotiations concerned trade in services, resulting in the General Agreement on Trade in Services, or GATS. While trade-related investment measures (or TRIMS) also covered a "new area", the resulting agreement in that area largely restated existing GATT 1947 rules.

balance of rights and obligations unique to the Agreement. In this sense, there is no "pre-TRIPS situation" for the preamble since the Agreement was designed to fill a perceived gap in the GATT 1947 legal system. The preamble reflects the views of the parties regarding the outcome of the negotiations and the object and purposes of the new instrument. Yet, the object and purposes of a new legal instrument do not arise in a historical vacuum. It is therefore useful to refer briefly to the factors that brought the new instrument about.

Prior to negotiation of TRIPS, IPRs were principally regulated at the international level by a number of treaties administered by the World Intellectual Property Organization (WIPO). These treaties included the Paris Convention on Industrial Property and the Berne Convention on Literary and Artistic Works. Starting in the late 1970s, developed countries expressed increasing concern that the treaty system administered by WIPO failed to adequately protect the interests of their technology-based and expressive industries. The major concerns were that WIPO treaties did not in some cases establish adequate substantive standards of IPR protection and that the WIPO system did not provide adequate mechanisms for enforcing obligations.

In the 1970s, the developing countries sought to establish new rules on a New International Economic Order (NIEO) that would include among its objectives mechanisms to facilitate the transfer of technology from developed to developing countries. Part of this initiative entailed securing greater access to technology protected by IPRs in the developed countries by limiting the scope of protection in developing countries and by closely regulating the exercise of rights.[5] The objectives of the NIEO were perceived by the developed countries as conflicting with their own interests in strengthening protection of IPRs, first in WIPO and later in the GATT. Through the early 1980s developing countries were not persuaded that altering the WIPO system to strengthen IPR protection was necessary or appropriate.

In the lead-up to negotiations on a mandate for the Uruguay Round, developed country industry groups successfully created a coalition of governments that would pursue the objective of moving IPRs regulation from WIPO to the GATT. At the GATT, the dual objectives of establishing high standards of IPR protection and a strong multilateral enforcement mechanism would be pursued.

The GATT was founded with the goal of liberalizing world trade.[6] It was not concerned with intellectual property as such. One of the major issues confronting GATT negotiators prior to launching the Uruguay Round was whether IPRs should be considered sufficiently "trade-related" to be brought within the subject matter covered by the institution. Since WIPO existed as a specialized agency of the United Nations with the role of defining and administering international IPRs

---

[5] Such efforts were exemplified by the technology regulations put in place by the Andean Community in the early 1970s through Decision 24 of the Andean Group. See, Frederick M. Abbott, *Bargaining Power and Strategy in the Foreign Investment Process: A Current Andean Code Analysis*, 3 SYRACUSE J. OF INT'L L. & COMM. 319 (1975); Susan Sell, *Power of Ideas: North South Politics of Intellectual Property and Antitrust* (1998), State University of New York Press; and S.J. Patel. P. Roffe, A. Yusuf, *International Technology Transfer: The Origins and Aftermath of the United Nations Negotiations on a Draft Code of Conduct*. 2001, Kluwer Law International, The Hague.

[6] See the preamble to the GATT 1947.

standards, it was not clear whether or why the GATT should take on an overlapping mandate.

The subject of TRIPS was included in the Uruguay Round mandate without prejudgment regarding the substance or form of any resulting agreement. In fact, there was expectation at the outset of the negotiations that only a Tokyo Round type "code" among the developed countries and a select few developing countries might be achieved in a first round of negotiations on this subject matter.[7]

From the outset of the Uruguay Round negotiations in 1986, and until early 1989, developing countries were opposed to incorporating substantive standards of IPR protection in the GATT (although there was sympathy for affording basic protection against trademark counterfeiting and copyright piracy).[8] However, the resistance of developing countries was overcome through a combination of concessions offered by developed countries in other areas (principally agriculture and textiles), and by threats of trade sanctions and, implicitly at least, dismantling of the GATT. [9]

Although the major developed country actors – the United States, European Community, Japan and Switzerland – took somewhat different approaches to TRIPS during the Uruguay Round, the coalition essentially remained firm on broad strategic objectives throughout the negotiations.

2.2 Negotiating history

2.2.1 Early proposals

2.2.1.1 The USA. The initial November 1987 United States "Proposal for Negotiations on Trade-Related Aspects of Intellectual Property Rights" included a section that addressed the objectives of the agreement:

> "Objective. The objective of a GATT intellectual property agreement would be to reduce distortions of and impediments to legitimate trade in goods and services caused by deficient levels of protection and enforcement of intellectual property rights. In order to realize that objective all participants should agree to undertake the following:
>
> – Create an effective economic deterrent to international trade in goods and services which infringe intellectual property rights through implementation of border measures;

---

[7] See the 1987 U.S. proposal quoted in the next Section that, in its final clause, assumes the adoption of a code among a limited group of GATT contracting parties.

[8] See, Frederick M. Abbott, *Protecting First World Assets in the Third World: Intellectual Property Negotiations in the GATT Multilateral Framework*, 22 VAND. J. OF TRANSNAT'L L. 689 (1989), J.H. Reichman, *From Free Riders to Fair Followers: Global Competition Under the TRIPS Agreement.*, 29 New York University Journal of International Law and Politics 11 (1996) and UNCTAD, *The TRIPS Agreement and Developing Countries* (1996), United Nations Publication, Sales No. E.96.II.D.10.

[9] See UNCTAD-ICTSD Policy Discussion Paper, *Intellectual Property Rights: Implications for Development* (2003), Geneva [hereinafter UNCTAD-ICTSD Policy Discussion Paper].

– Recognize and implement standards and norms that provide adequate means of obtaining and maintaining intellectual property rights and provide a basis for effective enforcement of those rights;

– Ensure that such measures to protect intellectual property rights do not create barriers to legitimate trade;

– Extend international notification, consultation, surveillance and dispute settlement procedures to protection of intellectual property and enforcement of intellectual property rights;

– Encourage non-signatory governments to achieve, adopt and enforce the recognized standards for protection of intellectual property and join the agreement."[10]

2.2.1.2 The EC. A proposal of Guidelines and Objectives submitted by the European Community to the TRIPS Negotiating Group in July 1988 also addressed the general purposes of an agreement, stating *inter alia*:

"... the Community suggests that the negotiations on substantive standards be conducted with the following guidelines in mind:

– they should address trade-related substantive standards in respect of issues where the growing importance of intellectual property rights for international trade requires a basic degree of convergence as regards the principles and the basic features of protection;

– GATT negotiations on trade related aspects of substantive standards of intellectual property rights should not attempt to elaborate rules which would substitute for existing specific conventions on intellectual property matters; contracting parties, could, however, when this was deemed necessary, elaborate further principles in order to reduce trade distortions or impediments. The exercise should largely be limited to an identification of an agreement on the principles of protection which should be respected by all parties; the negotiations should not aim at the harmonization of national laws;

– the GATT negotiations should be without prejudices to initiatives that may be taken in WIPO or elsewhere...."[11]

The EC proposal stated that it was not intended to indicate a preference for a "code" approach.[12]

---

[10] Suggestion by the United States for Achieving the Negotiating Objective, United States Proposal for Negotiations on Trade-Related Aspects of Intellectual Property Rights, Negotiating Group on Trade-Related Aspects of Intellectual Property Rights, including Trade in Counterfeit Goods, MTN.GNG/NG11/W/14, 20 Oct. 1987, Nov. 3, 1987.

[11] Guidelines and Objectives Proposed by the European Community for the Negotiations on Trade Related Aspects of Substantive Standards of Intellectual Property Rights, Negotiating Group on Trade-Related Aspects of Intellectual Property Rights, including Trade in Counterfeit Goods, MTN.GNG/NG11/W/26, July 1988, at II.

[12] *Id.*, at note 1.

2.2.1.3 India. In July 1989, India submitted a detailed paper that elaborated a developing country perspective on the negotiations. It concluded:

> "It would...not be appropriate to establish within the framework of the General Agreement on Tariffs and Trade any new rules and disciplines pertaining to standards and principles concerning the availability, scope and use of intellectual property rights."[13]

At a meeting of the TRIPS Negotiating Group in July 1989, the objectives and principles of the agreement were discussed. As reported by the Secretariat, India was among those countries that made a fairly detailed intervention:

> "5. In his statement introducing the Indian paper, the representative of India first referred to recent action by the United States under its trade law and recalled the serious reservations of his delegation about the relevance and utility of the TRIPS negotiations as long as measures of bilateral coercion and threat continued. Subject to this reservation, his delegation submitted the paper circulated as document NG11/W/37, setting out the views of India on this agenda item. At the outset, he emphasised three points. First, India was of the view that it was only the restrictive and anti-competitive practices of the owners of the IPRs that could be considered to be trade-related because they alone distorted or impeded international trade. Although India did not regard the other aspects of IPRs dealt with in the paper to be trade-related, it had examined these other aspects in the paper for two reasons: they had been raised in the various submissions made to the Negotiating Group by some other participants; and, more importantly, they had to be seen in the wider developmental and technological context to which they properly belonged. India was of the view that by merely placing the label "trade-related" on them, such issues could not be brought within the ambit of international trade. Secondly, paragraphs 4(b) and 5 of the TNC decision of April 1989 were inextricably interlinked. The discussions on paragraph 4(b) should unambiguously be governed by the socio-economic, developmental, technological and public interest needs of developing countries. Any principle or standard relating to IPRs should be carefully tested against these needs of developing countries, and it would not be appropriate for the discussions to focus merely on the protection of the monopoly rights of the owners of intellectual property. Thirdly, he emphasised that any discussion on the intellectual property system should keep in perspective that the essence of the system was its monopolistic and restrictive character. This had special implications for developing countries, because more than 99 per cent of the world's stock of patents was owned by the nationals of the industrialised countries. Recognising the extraordinary rights granted by the system and their implications, international conventions on this subject incorporated, as a central philosophy, the freedom of member States to attune their intellectual property protection system to their own needs and conditions. This freedom of host countries should be recognised as a fundamental principle and should guide all of the discussions in the Negotiating Group. ... Substantive standards on intellectual property were really related to socio-economic, industrial and technological development, especially

---

[13] Communication from India, Standards and Principles Concerning the Availability, Scope and Use of Trade-Related Intellectual Property Rights, MTN.GNG/NG11/W/37, 10 July 1989.

in the case of developing countries. It was for this reason that GATT had so far played only a peripheral role in this area and the international community had established other specialised agencies to deal with substantive issues of IPRs. The Group should therefore focus on the restrictive and anti-competitive practices of the owners of IPRs and evolve standards and principles for their elimination so that international trade was not distorted or impeded by such practices."[14]

The Indian position was debated extensively, with a substantial number of developing delegations lending their support.

2.2.2 The Anell Draft

The preamble draft texts (as well as drafts regarding objectives and principles) appeared in the Annex to the 23 July 1990 Anell Report to the General Negotiating Group (GNG) on the status of work in the TRIPS Negotiating Group.[15] The source of each Annex proposal is indicated by numerical reference to the country source document:

> "This Annex reproduces tel quel Parts I, VI, VII and VIII of the composite draft text which was circulated informally by the Chairman of the Negotiating Group on 12 June 1990. The text was prepared on the basis of the draft legal texts submitted by the European Communities (NG11/W/68), the United States (NG11/W/70), Argentina, Brazil, Chile, China, Colombia, Cuba, Egypt, India, Nigeria, Peru, Tanzania and Uruguay, and subsequently also sponsored by Pakistan and Zimbabwe (NG11/W/71), Switzerland (NG11/W/73), Japan (NG11/W/74) and Australia (NG11/W/75)."

Because features of the preamble originated from drafts on objectives and principles, the draft texts on objectives and principles are also reproduced here:

> "PART I: PREAMBULAR PROVISIONS; OBJECTIVES
>
> 1. Preamble (71); Objectives (73)
>
> 1.1 Recalling the Ministerial Declaration of Punta del Este of 20 September 1986; (73)
>
> 1.2 Desiring to strengthen the role of GATT and its basic principles and to bring about a wider coverage of world trade under agreed, effective and enforceable multilateral disciplines; (73)
>
> 1.3 Recognizing that the lack of protection, or insufficient or excessive protection, of intellectual property rights causes nullification and impairment of advantages and benefits of the General Agreement on Tariffs and Trade and distortions detrimental to international trade, and that such nullification and impairment may be caused both by substantive and procedural deficiencies, including ineffective enforcement of existing laws, as well as by unjustifiable discrimination of foreign persons, legal entities, goods and services; (73)

---

[14] Note by the Secretariat, Meeting of Negotiating Group of 12–14 July 1989, Negotiating Group on Trade-Related Aspects of Intellectual Property Rights, including Trade in Counterfeit Goods, MTN.GNG/NG11/14, 12 September 1989.

[15] For an explanation of the Anell Draft, see the explanatory note on the methodology at the beginning of this volume.

1.4 Recognizing that adequate protection of intellectual property rights is an essential condition to foster international investment and transfer of technology; (73)

1.5 Recognizing the importance of protection of intellectual property rights for promoting innovation and creativity; (71)

1.6 Recognizing that adequate protection of intellectual property rights both internally and at the border is necessary to deter and persecute piracy and counterfeiting; (73)

1.7 Taking into account development, technological and public interest objectives of developing countries; (71)

1.8 Recognizing also the special needs of the least developed countries in respect of maximum flexibility in the application of this Agreement in order to enable them to create a sound and viable technological base; (71)

1.9 Recognizing the need for appropriate transitional arrangements for developing countries and least developed countries with a view to achieve successfully strengthened protection and enforcement of intellectual property rights; (73)

1.10 Recognizing the need to prevent disputes by providing adequate means of transparency of national laws, regulations and requirements regarding protection and enforcement of intellectual property rights; (73)

1.11 Recognizing the need to settle disputes on matters related to the protection of intellectual property rights on the basis of effective multilateral mechanisms and procedures, and to refrain from applying unilateral measures inconsistent with such procedures to PARTIES to this PART of the General Agreement; (73)

1.12 Recognizing the efforts to harmonize and promote intellectual property laws by international organizations specialized in the field of intellectual property law and that this PART of the General Agreement aims at further encouragement of such efforts; (73)

2. Objective of the Agreement (74)

2A The PARTIES agree to provide effective and adequate protection of intellectual property rights in order to ensure the reduction of distortions and impediments to [international (68)] [legitimate (70)] trade. The protection of intellectual property rights shall not itself create barriers to legitimate trade. (68, 70)

2B The objective of the present Agreement is to establish adequate standards for the protection of, and effective and appropriate means for the enforcement of intellectual property rights; thereby eliminating distortions and impediments to international trade related to intellectual property rights and foster its sound development. (74)

2C With respect to standards and principles concerning the availability, scope and use of intellectual property rights, PARTIES agree on the following objectives:

(i) To give full recognition to the needs for economic, social and technological development of all countries and the sovereign right of all States, when enacting national legislation, to ensure a proper balance between these needs and the rights granted to IPR holders and thus to determine the scope and level of protection of such rights, particularly in sectors of special public concern, such as health, nutrition, agriculture and national security. (71)

(ii) To set forth the principal rights and obligations of IP owners, taking into account the important inter-relationships between the scope of such rights and obligations and the promotion of social welfare and economic development. (71)

(iii) To facilitate the diffusion of technological knowledge and to enhance international transfer of technology, and thus contribute to a more active participation of all countries in world production and trade. (71)

(iv) To encourage technological innovation and promote inventiveness in all countries. (71)

(v) To enable participants to take all appropriate measures to prevent the abuses which might result from the exercise of IPRs and to ensure intergovernmental co-operation in this regard. (71)"[16]

The Anell text included in its main body (i.e., not in the Annex) a "B" provision with respect to "Principles" that is mainly reflected in Articles 7 and 8 of TRIPS. It is, however, relevant to the preamble:

"8. Principles

8B.1 PARTIES recognize that intellectual property rights are granted not only in acknowledgement of the contributions of inventors and creators, but also to assist in the diffusion of technological knowledge and its dissemination to those who could benefit from it in a manner conducive to social and economic welfare and agree that this balance of rights and obligations inherent in all systems of intellectual property rights should be observed.

8B.2 In formulating or amending their national laws and regulations on IPRs, PARTIES have the right to adopt appropriate measures to protect public morality, national security, public health and nutrition, or to promote public interest in sectors of vital importance to their socio-economic and technological development.

8B.3 PARTIES agree that the protection and enforcement of intellectual property rights should contribute to the promotion of technological innovation and enhance the international transfer of technology to the mutual advantage of producers and users of technological knowledge.

8B.4 Each PARTY will take the measures it deems appropriate with a view to preventing the abuse of intellectual property rights or the resort to practices which unreasonably restrain trade or adversely affect the international transfer of technology. PARTIES undertake to consult each other and to co-operate in this regard."[17]

The difference in perspectives among developed and developing countries is evident in the Annex to the Anell text. Much of the ultimately concluded TRIPS Agreement preamble can be found in proposals from Japan and Switzerland from the developed country side. A more modest influence is seen from proposals by the group of developing countries. The first paragraph of the TRIPS preamble principally emerges from proposals of the United States, European Community and Japan (*see* paragraphs 2A and 2B of "Objective of the Agreement", above). The structure and terms of the preamble reflect the generally successful

---

[16] Chairman's Report to the GNG, Status of Work in the Negotiating Group, Negotiating Group on Trade-Related Aspects of Intellectual Property Rights, including Trade in Counterfeit Goods, MTN.GNG/NG11/W/76, 23 July 1990.

[17] *Id.*

effort of developed countries to incorporate protection of IPRs in the WTO legal system.

2.2.3 The Brussels and Dunkel Drafts

The draft text of the TRIPS Agreement transmitted to the Brussels Ministerial Conference on Chairman Anell's initiative in December 1990 substantially reorganized the July 1990 proposals into the form of a preamble, and Articles 7 ("Objectives") and 8 ("Principles").[18] The Brussels Draft text on the preamble was essentially the same as the final TRIPS text, with no significant changes made in the Dunkel Draft.[19]

3. Possible interpretations

As noted earlier, the preamble of TRIPS may be used as a source for interpretation of the operative provisions of the agreement.[20] Since the preamble is not directed to establishing specific rights or obligations, it is difficult to predict the circumstances in which its provisions may be relied upon. Many or most TRIPS Agreement articles leave some room for interpretation, and in this sense the preamble may be relevant in many interpretative contexts. Some general observations may nevertheless be useful.

The first clause of the preamble indicates that the main objective of the Agreement is "to reduce distortions and impediments to international trade". This objective is to be accomplished "taking into account" the need to protect and enforce IPRs. The protection of IPRs is not an end in itself, but rather the means to an end. This is a critical point, because interest groups often lose sight of the basic mission of the WTO which, as stated in the preamble of the WTO Agreement, is to promote trade and economic development, not to protect the interests of particular private IPR-holding interest groups.

The first clause of the preamble also recognizes that measures to enforce IPRs may become obstacles to trade. Border measures, for example, might be implemented in ways that allow IPRs holders to inhibit legitimate trade opportunities of producers.

Subparagraph (b) of the second clause refers to the need to provide "adequate" IPR standards. The intention of the drafters was not to create the system of IPR protection that would be considered "optimum" by particular right holders groups, but one that is adequate to protect the basic integrity of the trading system. The development and implementation of IPR laws involves balancing the interests of the public in access to information and technology, and the interests of those creating new works and inventions in securing return on their investments. It is often possible to expand the protection of private right holders and increase

---

[18] Draft Final Act Embodying the Results of the Uruguay Round of Multilateral Trade Negotiations, Revision, Trade-Related Aspects of Intellectual Property Rights, Including Trade in Counterfeit Goods, MTN.TNC/W/35/Rev. 1, 3 Dec. 1990.

[19] Trade Negotiations Committee, Draft Final Act Embodying the Results of the Uruguay Round of Multilateral Trade Negotiations, MTN.TNG/W/FA, 20 Dec. 1991 (generally referred to as the "Dunkel Draft").

[20] See Section 1 above and references to the VCLT therein.

their investment returns, but this expansion of rights may have an adverse impact on the welfare of a wider public. The objective of IPR laws is not to provide the maximum possible return to right holders, but to strike the proper balance of private and public interests. In the trade context, the objective (as stated in the first paragraph of the preamble) is to avoid distortion of the system. WTO Members may argue that TRIPS substantive standards and enforcement measures become trade-related issues only when they are operating inadequately at an aggregate level materially affecting trade flows in a negative way.

Subparagraph (c) recognizes that enforcement measures may take into account differences in national legal systems. This recognizes an important element of flexibility in enforcement.

The fourth clause of the preamble refers to intellectual property rights as "private rights." The reference to IPRs as "private rights" in the preamble was not intended to exclude the possibility of government or public ownership of IPRs.[21] Most likely, the reference to IPRs as private rights was inserted in the preamble because of the unique characteristic of TRIPS in regulating national laws governing privately held interests (e.g., patents), in specifying remedies that are to be provided under national law for protecting such interests, and in clarifying that governments would not be responsible for policing IPR infringements on behalf of private right holders.

The fifth clause of the preamble recognizes "the underlying public policy objectives of national systems for the protection of intellectual property, including developmental and technological objectives." Developing country delegations had strongly promoted the importance of recognizing the public policy objectives of IPRs during the TRIPS negotiations, and that such policy objectives called for moderating the demands of right holders. Public policy objectives are further dealt with in Articles 7 and 8.

The sixth clause emphasizes the need for "maximum flexibility" in favour of least developed countries. This is addressed more specifically in Article 66,[22] but it is important that it is stated in the preamble in terms of "maximum" flexibility, as the term "maximum" does not appear in Article 66.

The eighth clause of the preamble emphasizes the importance of dealing with TRIPS issues through multilateral procedures. This was included in the preamble to address frequently articulated concerns of the developing countries about use of bilateral threats and enforcement measures to address alleged deficiencies in IPR protection.

The ninth clause recognizes the intention to pursue mutually supportive relationships with WIPO and other "relevant" international organizations. To a certain

---

[21] Public ownership of IPRs was and is a fairly common practice. According to a senior member of the WTO Secretariat who participated in the TRIPS negotiations, the reference to "private rights" was included at the insistence of the Hong Kong delegation, which wanted clarification that the enforcement of IPRs is the responsibility of private rights holders, and not of governments. See Frederick M. Abbott, *Technology and State Enterprise in the WTO*, in 1 World Trade Forum: State Trading in the Twenty-First Century 121 (Thomas Cottier and Petros Mavroidis eds. 1998). Assuming that this accurately reflects the genesis of the relevant language, other delegations may have attached different significance to the "private rights" language.

[22] See Chapter 33.

extent, the emphasis on WIPO downplays the significant role that other multilateral organizations play in the field of IPR protection, such as the United Nations Conference on Trade and Development (UNCTAD). As such, the lack of specific reference to other international organizations may reflect a general lack of attention among trade negotiators to the wider effects that TRIPS would have on international public policy.

4. WTO jurisprudence

4.1 Shrimp-Turtles

The potential importance of the preamble to TRIPS is demonstrated by reference to the decision of the WTO Appellate Body in the Shrimp-Turtles case.[23] In that case, reference in the WTO Agreement to the objective of "sustainable development" fundamentally influenced the approach of the AB to interpretation of the GATT 1994. This is not to suggest that particular terms of the preamble to TRIPS will necessarily play a role of comparable importance to that of "sustainable development" in the WTO Agreement, but rather to illustrate that the preamble *might* play an important role in the interpretative process.

In the Shrimp-Turtles case, the AB rejected a narrow interpretation of Article XX of the GATT 1947 adopted by the panel, which had placed a strong emphasis on protecting against threats to "the multilateral trading system". The AB said:

"An environmental purpose is fundamental to the application of Article XX, and such a purpose cannot be ignored, especially since the preamble to the *Marrakesh Agreement Establishing the World Trade Organization*[24] (the "*WTO Agreement*") acknowledges that the rules of trade should be 'in accordance with the objective of sustainable development', and should seek to 'protect and preserve the environment'." (at para. 12)

It added:

"Furthermore, the Panel failed to recognize that most treaties have no single, undiluted object and purpose but rather a variety of different, and possibly conflicting, objects and purposes. This is certainly true of the *WTO Agreement*. Thus, while the first clause of the preamble to the *WTO Agreement* calls for the expansion of trade in goods and services, this same clause also recognizes that international trade and economic relations under the *WTO Agreement* should allow for 'optimal use of the world's resources in accordance with the objective of sustainable development', and should seek 'to protect and preserve the environment'. The Panel in effect took a one-sided view of the object and purpose of the *WTO Agreement* when it fashioned a new test not found in the text of the Agreement." (at para. 17)

The AB also observed that:

"While Article XX was not modified in the Uruguay Round, the preamble attached to the *WTO Agreement* shows that the signatories to that Agreement were, in 1994,

---

[23] *United States – Import Prohibition on Certain Shrimp and Shrimp Products*, AB-1998-4 WT/DS58/AB/R, 12 Oct. 1998.

[24] Done at Marrakesh, 15 April 1994.

fully aware of the importance and legitimacy of environmental protection as a goal of national and international policy. The preamble of the *WTO Agreement* – which informs not only the GATT 1994, but also the other covered agreements – explicitly acknowledges 'the objective of *sustainable development*':" (at para. 129)

"From the perspective embodied in the preamble of the *WTO Agreement*, we note that the generic term "natural resources" in Article XX(g) is not "static" in its content or reference but is rather 'by definition, evolutionary'." [at para. 130 footnotes omitted, italics in the original]

It would not be an exaggeration to say that the preamble of the WTO Agreement not only played a key role in determining the result of the *Shrimp-Turtles* case, in which the AB provided a much more nuanced approach to evaluating claims of trade discrimination than the panel; but, moreover, it provided the foundation for what may be the single most important development in the interpretative approach of the AB since the inception of the WTO – that is, the notion of "evolutionary" interpretation.[25]

As noted earlier, because there is a wide variety of dispute that may arise under TRIPS, it is not practicable to predict the circumstances in which the preamble may be employed as an interpretative source. What the Shrimp-Turtles case makes evident is that the potential role of the preamble should not be discounted.

5. Relationship with other international instruments

5.1 WTO Agreements

The preamble of TRIPS should be read in conjunction with the preamble of the WTO Agreement that sets out the objectives of the organization. These objectives are to reduce barriers and discrimination in trade in order to promote economic development and improve standards of living, with attention to sustainable development, and with special attention to the needs of developing countries. The TRIPS Agreement was added to the GATT – now WTO – framework to assure that adequate protection of IPRs promoted world trade in goods and services; and that the under- and over-protection of IPRs did not undermine the economic strategy and ultimate objectives of the organization. The protection of IPRs is part of the means to an end – to be "taken into account" within a larger strategy to promote economic growth. The core objective of the WTO is to improve worldwide standards of living.

5.2 Other international instruments

The preamble of TRIPS in its last paragraph (see quotation in Section 1, above) makes specific reference to establishing a mutually supportive relationship between the WTO and WIPO and other relevant international organizations. Although discussing how to establish such a relationship was not given much consideration during the Uruguay Round, developing Members may rely on this provision in the context of urging greater cooperation with UNCTAD, the World Health

---

[25] For more details on the interpretation of the TRIPS Agreement, including the concept of "evolutionary interpretation", see Annex II to Chapter 32.

Organization (WHO) and other institutions that pursue broad developmental interests.

6. New developments

6.1 National laws

6.2 International instruments

6.2.1 The Doha Declaration on the TRIPS Agreement and Public Health
The Declaration on the TRIPS Agreement and Public Health adopted by Ministers at Doha on 14 November 2001 includes important statements regarding the objectives of TRIPS.[26] The Doha Declaration includes recitals or preambular provisions (paragraphs 1–3) that precede and provide context for its operative provisions (paragraphs 4–7).[27] The role of the Doha Declaration in the interpretation of TRIPS is discussed in Chapter 6 (Objectives and principles).

6.3 Regional and bilateral contexts

6.4 Proposals for review

7. Comments, including economic and social implications

The preamble of TRIPS refers to the general purposes and objectives of the Agreement. This raises the questions whether the agreement as a whole is in the interests of developing Members of the WTO, and whether parts of the agreement may reflect an inappropriate balance from a developing country standpoint.

There is wide acceptance among international economists and other policy specialists concerned with the role of IPRs in the economic development process that our collective understanding of this role is substantially incomplete. This incompleteness derives from the nature of IP itself and from the measurement problems associated with it.[28]

As a basic proposition, and leaving aside for the moment issues relating to the situation of IPRs in various developmental contexts, to empirically determine the role IPRs play in the economic development process, we would need to

---

[26] See WT/MIN(01)/DEC/W/2 of 14 November 2001.

[27] The Doha Declaration in paras. 1–3 provides:

"1. We recognize the gravity of the public health problems afflicting many developing and least-developed countries, especially those resulting from HIV/AIDS, tuberculosis, malaria and other epidemics.

2. We stress the need for the WTO Agreement on Trade-Related Aspects of Intellectual Property Rights (TRIPS Agreement) to be part of the wider national and international action to address these problems.

3. We recognize that intellectual property protection is important for the development of new medicines. We also recognize the concerns about its effects on prices."

[28] This section is based on Frederick M. Abbott, *The Enduring Enigma of TRIPS: A Challenge for the World Economic System*, 1 Journal of International Economic Law 497 (1998) (Oxford Univ. Press). See also the Report of the Commission on Intellectual Property Rights, *Integrating Intellectual Property Rights and Development Policy*, London, 2002, in particular Chapter 1 [hereinafter IPR Commission]; see also the UNCTAD-ICTSD Policy Discussion Paper, in particular Part I.

measure the cause and effect relationship between creating knowledge and creative works on the one hand, and restricting their diffusion and use for a certain duration on the other. Though economists and other policy specialists have endeavoured to create mechanisms for such measurement, this task has so far proven impracticable.

For any nation or region, IPRs are only one factor that will determine the course of development. Other factors include natural resource endowment, labour force characteristics, availability of capital, the size of markets and conditions of competition, and the form of government management/intervention in society. The difficulties inherent in disaggregating IPRs from other determinants of economic development have so far precluded meaningful measurement of the role of IPRs in the economic development process.

Though policy specialists may not be able to make precise measurements about the role of IPRs in economic development, there is an emerging consensus that the impact of IPRs is likely to be quite case sensitive. There are sound reasons to conclude, for example, that the role of patents in the process of development of an automotive sector is quite different to the role of patents in the development of a pharmaceutical sector. Similarly, there are sound reasons to conclude that the role of IPRs will be different in the economies of industrialized, developing and least-developed countries (LDCs), and that even among these broad categories of economic development there will be variations depending on a number of factors such as market size, local capacity for innovation, and so forth.[29]

Among international IPR specialists there is certainly a range of views as to the value of introducing higher levels of IPR protection in newly industrializing, developing and least-developed countries. Some are strong advocates of introducing such systems on the grounds that they are preconditions of long-term economic growth, and are necessary complements to other facets of commercial law. It has been suggested that sound governance structures are central to improving economic welfare in developing countries, and that the introduction and improvement of IPRs-related legal rules and institutions may have a positive general impact on governance within these countries.

Other specialists are rather sceptical of introducing IPR systems on the grounds that rent transfer effects are likely to predominate, or that time and energy are better spent in areas (such as water and sanitation infrastructure) more likely to yield tangible benefits. There are those who would advocate a nuanced approach that would take into account the industry-specific and country-specific factors elaborated above.

Despite this range of perspectives, these specialists might nevertheless agree that (a) there are substantial gaps in our understanding based on the inherent nature of IP and difficulties in measuring its effects; (b) that the role of IPRs in economic development is likely to be industry and country case sensitive; and (c) that international IPR policy-makers are seeking to strike a balance between interests in

---

[29] See Lall, *Indicators of the Relative Importance of Intellectual Property Rights to Developing Countries*, UNCTAD-ICTSD, Geneva, 2003; also available at <http://www.iprsonline.org/index.htm>.

knowledge creation and knowledge diffusion under conditions in which drawing welfare-maximizing boundaries is difficult.

Regarding TRIPS balance, some points seem clear. There are cases in which private interests in IPRs must be subordinated to more compelling public interests. For example, developing countries are facing increasing social, political and financial difficulties as a consequence of epidemic disease. Although research-based pharmaceutical enterprises in the developed countries may require high rates of return on investment in order to finance research into new treatments, the developing and least developed WTO Members cannot be expected to bear the burden of paying for this research.

Whether and to what extent there are other circumstances in which IPRs must give way to more compelling public interests can be taken up as these questions present themselves. The TRIPS Agreement can only survive as an instrument of international public policy if it is able to appropriately balance potentially competing interests.

2: Nature and Scope of Obligations

> ### Article 1   Nature and Scope of Obligations
>
> 1. Members shall give effect to the provisions of this Agreement. Members may, but shall not be obliged to, implement in their law more extensive protection than is required by this Agreement, provided that such protection does not contravene the provisions of this Agreement. Members shall be free to determine the appropriate method of implementing the provisions of this Agreement within their own legal system and practice.

1. Introduction: terminology, definition and scope

The requirement to implement an international agreement is implicit in the obligation to perform it in good faith. The obligation to perform in good faith (*"pacta sunt servanda"*) is established by Article 26 of the Vienna Convention on the Law of Treaties (VCLT), which substantially codifies customary international law. Article 1.1 of TRIPS provides that Members will "give effect to the provisions" of the Agreement, restating the basic international legal obligation.

Article 1.1 adds two rules to this basic affirmation of the law of treaties. First, Members may, but need not, adopt more extensive protection of intellectual property (IP) than is required by the agreement and, second, "Members shall be free to determine the appropriate method of implementing the provisions of this Agreement within their own legal system and practice".

By stating that Members may adopt protection "more extensive" than that provided for in the agreement, Article 1.1 establishes its rules as the base (or floor) of protection often referred to as TRIPS "minimum standards". Article 1.1 makes clear that Members are not obligated to adopt more extensive than TRIPS Agreement standards, so-called "TRIPS-plus" levels of protection.

The third sentence of Article 1.1 concerning freedom of implementation method is important in at least two senses. First, in addressing the relationship between TRIPS and domestic legal systems of Members, it does not establish an express rule regarding "direct effect" or "self-executing effect", leaving this to a determination by each Member. Each Member decides whether it will adopt specific statutes or administrative rules to implement TRIPS, or instead rely on the text of the Agreement as part of national law (see below, Section 3).

Second, it acknowledges the flexibility inherent in the express text of the TRIPS Agreement and intellectual property law more generally, authorizing each Member to implement the rules in the manner most appropriate for itself, provided that implementation is in accord with the terms of the agreement.

2. History of the provision

2.1 Situation pre-TRIPS

2.1.1 "Give effect"

Prior to TRIPS the rules governing the protection of intellectual property at the multilateral level were established primarily by the World Intellectual Property Organization (WIPO) conventions.[30] The factors that led certain governments to propose the negotiation of the TRIPS Agreement are considered in Chapter 6 regarding the objectives and principles of the Agreement.

As noted above, international law requires state parties to a treaty or international agreement to "give effect" to that agreement as a matter of good faith performance. The VCLT, recognizing the obligation to perform in good faith, was adopted in 1969, and entered into force in 1980. Thus prior to the TRIPS Agreement negotiations the obligation to "give effect" to a treaty was accepted in international law.

2.1.2 Minimum standards and more extensive protections

A treaty or international agreement might provide that its rules are intended to embody the sole set of norms for a particular subject matter, and effectively preclude a state party from adopting an alternative set of rules with more (or less) extensive protection. The parties negotiating the TRIPS Agreement had the option to decide that a uniform set of negotiated rules would represent the upper and lower boundary of IPR protection. Whether or not a treaty is intended to be the sole source of norms is determined by applying general principles of treaty interpretation. It is not the subject of a general rule. It bears noting that states are sovereign within their own territories and generally have the right to legislate in the manner they consider appropriate, unless discretion has been limited by a treaty or other rule of international law.[31]

The General Agreement on Tariffs and Trade 1947 (GATT 1947) provided the rules for the multilateral trading system prior to entry into force of the WTO Agreement. The GATT 1947 set certain maximum or upper boundaries in areas such as tariffs and quotas. Thus, under Article II, GATT 1947, Contracting Parties committed themselves to tariff bindings that constituted the upper threshold they might impose (on an MFN basis). It was not left to the discretion of each

---

[30] These treaties, principally the Paris Convention on the Protection of Industrial Property and the Berne Convention on the Protection of Literary and Artistic Works, are introduced in Chapter 3.

[31] Article 1.1, TRIPS Agreement, recognizes that, absent an agreed upon restriction or peremptory norm, states retain sovereign rights to govern within their territories. In this case, they retain the right to adopt more extensive protection.

Contracting Party to adopt more extensive tariff protection than that to which it bound itself, but it was open to each Contracting Party to provide less tariff protection.

The WIPO Conventions did not attempt to establish the sole set of norms for the protection of IPRs, although they limited state discretion in a number of ways (for example, by requiring national treatment). Generally speaking, state parties to the WIPO conventions remained free to adopt more extensive protections than those specifically mandated by the agreements. While the Berne Convention established minimum standards of copyright protection, the Paris Convention did not define the principal substantive standards of patent protection, essentially leaving this to each state party.

IPRs may act as trade barriers and/or cause trade distortions.[32] If a government grants patents without adequate attention to whether true novelty and inventive step are involved, it may create unjustified impediments to market entry for products both of local and foreign origin. The U.S. Federal Trade Commission has observed that weak patents pose a threat to competitive markets and has urged greater vigilance on the part of patent officials, as well as improved mechanisms for challenging such patents.[33] Although concern about potential overprotection of IPRs was evidenced by various WTO Members throughout the TRIPS Agreement negotiations, and the potential problem of overprotection is referred to in the preamble, upper boundaries of protection are not well defined by the agreement.

2.1.3 Determining method of implementation

The VCLT and customary international law regarding treaties do not mandate particular means by which state parties should implement their obligations. The national (or regional) constitution of each state provides the interface between treaty obligations and domestic law. There are significant differences between the ways that national constitutions treat the relationship between treaties and domestic law.[34]

---

[32] As acknowledged in the first recital of the TRIPS preamble: "[...], and to ensure that measures and procedures to enforce intellectual property rights do not themselves become barriers to legitimate trade; [...]"

[33] A 2003 Federal Trade Commission (FTC) study of competition and patents in the United States focused on anticompetitive risks of overprotection, including through grant of patents of suspect quality. Proliferation of patents may threaten innovation by creating obstacles to competitive R & D, and impose costs on consumers. Recommendations included creation of opposition procedure, reducing litigation presumptions favouring patent holders, tightening standards and increasing resources for examining patent applications, exercising caution in expanding scope of patentable subject matter, and increasing federal agency competition vigilance regarding operation of patent system. U.S. Federal Trade Commission, *To Promote Innovation: The Proper Balance of Competition and Patent Law and Policy*, October 2003.

[34] There are generally three approaches. Under the "monist" approach the treaty is essentially treated as part of national law without any action needed by the national government other than to accept the treaty (*e.g.*, in Argentina, France and the Netherlands). Under the "dualist" approach the treaty and national law are considered separate, except to the extent that the national government takes specific steps to transform all or part of the treaty into national law (*e.g.*, in the United Kingdom). There is a middle ground approach in which treaties may be given direct effect, but the rights and obligations may also be modified by the legislature (*e.g.*, in the United States).

2.1.3.1 Direct effect. A treaty may or may not be intended to have "direct effect" (or "self-executing effect") in the domestic law of states that are parties to it and whose national constitutions allow for this possibility. Generally speaking, if a treaty is directly effective, persons (whether natural persons, i.e. individuals, or enterprises) may rely on it as a source of law before national courts. If a treaty is directly effective, the national government does not need to take additional steps to implement it beyond those involved in approving or adhering to the treaty. If the national government does not alter the terms of a directly effective treaty in the implementation process, this may limit the range of options open to the executive or legislative authorities in controlling how it is implemented.[35] Interpretation moves into the hands of judges who are called upon to apply it in specific cases or controversies.

The WIPO conventions do not expressly address the issue of direct application. Some national courts have directly applied the Berne[36] and Paris[37] Conventions as domestic law.

The GATT 1947 did not expressly state whether it was intended to be directly effective. The question was left for national authorities to decide based on interpreting its terms and context, and this question remained controversial throughout the GATT 1947 period. In a series of decisions addressing this question, the European Court of Justice (ECJ) decided that it was not, based on the general nature of its obligations and the fact that Contracting Parties often settled disputes by political negotiation rather than through the more legalized dispute settlement process.[38]

The negotiators of the TRIPS Agreement had the option to expressly indicate whether or not its terms would be directly effective, or to leave this as a matter for interpretation by national authorities or subject to constitutional law.

2.1.3.2 Legal systems and practice. As with ordinary domestic legislation, the terms of a treaty may be more or less detailed or precise. When legislation is drafted in general terms, it often requires more specific regulations in order to

---

[35] The law concerning direct effect of treaties is complex. If a treaty is directly effective, this does not necessarily preclude the government from adopting legislation to implement it, or even to modify its terms for domestic legal purposes. In the U.S. constitutional system, for example, the Congress may adopt "later in time" legislation that modifies the terms of the treaty for domestic purposes, even though this may not be consistent with U.S. international legal obligations. On the other hand, in the Netherlands, a directly effective treaty adopted by the legislative body may not be modified by subsequent legislation. If domestic law is to be altered, the treaty must be amended, or adherence withdrawn. See generally, *Parliamentary Participation in the Making and Operation of Treaties: A Comparative Study* (S.A. Riesenfeld & F.M. Abbott, eds. 1994: Martinus Nijhoff/Kluwer), and country chapters therein [hereinafter "Parliamentary Participation"].

[36] See, e.g., *SUISA v. Rediffusion AG*, Bundesgericht (Switzerland), [1982] ECC 481, Jan. 20, 1981, referring also to other European judgments. In the SUISA decision, the court refers to both Swiss federal law and the Berne Convention as the source of applicable legal rules.

[37] See, e.g, *Cuno v. Pall*, 729 F. Supp. 234 (EDNY 1989), U.S. federal district court applying Article 4*bis* of the Paris Convention directly.

[38] Beginning with Joined Cases 21 to 24/72 *International Fruit Company N.V. v. Produktschap voor Groenten en Fruit (No. 3)* [1972], ECR 1219. As to the ECJ's jurisprudence with respect to a possible direct effect of the *WTO Agreements*, see below, Section 6.3; as well as Chapter 32.

give it effect. Similarly, when treaties are drafted in more general terms, they may require more specific national legislation to produce effects in local law.

The WIPO conventions did not provide specific rules regarding how state parties should implement them in national law. Each state party was left to determine the appropriate method of implementation in the domestic legal system.

The level of specificity in the GATT 1947 varied among its provisions, though most of its rules were stated in a fairly general way. The Tokyo Round Codes added substantial specificity in areas such as regulation of dumping and subsidies, in part to address a perception that the more general rules of the GATT 1947 provided too much flexibility regarding the manner in which Contracting Parties interpreted those rules.

Intellectual property has traditionally been a highly sensitive policy area, and prior to the Uruguay Round states took rather different approaches to IPR regulation, even when addressing the same subject matter. In approaching the TRIPS negotiations, GATT Contracting Parties had the option of adopting very specific rules intended to remove discretion that states traditionally enjoyed in regulating IPRs, or adopt more general rules and leave greater discretion in the method of implementation. On the whole, the TRIPS Agreement that was concluded allows substantial flexibility in the specific implementation of IPR rules, while broadly demanding subject matter coverage for traditionally sensitive areas. The result is thus a mixed one: flexibility as to the finer aspects of implementation, yet starting from a broad scope of coverage.

2.2 Negotiating history

2.2.1 The 1987 U.S. proposal

Discussions concerning the extent to which TRIPS would provide more general guidelines or instead seek to "harmonize" national IPR legislation are evident throughout the negotiating history. In its initial 1987 proposal, the United States suggested consistency with a defined set of standards, stating:

> "In adhering to a GATT Agreement on trade-related aspects of intellectual property rights, Parties would agree to provide in their national laws for the protection of intellectual property at a level consistent with agreed norms attached in an annex to the Agreement."[39]

2.2.2 The 1988 E.C. proposal

The European Community stressed in 1988 the importance of allowing for different national approaches:

> "[Negotiations] should address trade-related substantive standards in respect of issues where the growing importance of intellectual property rights for international

---

[39] Suggestion by the United States for Achieving the Negotiating Objective, United States Proposal for Negotiations on Trade-Related Aspects of Intellectual Property Rights, Negotiating Group on Trade-Related Aspects of Intellectual Property Rights, including Trade in Counterfeit Goods, MTN.GNG/NG11/W/14, 20 Oct. 1987, Nov. 3, 1987, at Norms.

trade requires a basic degree of convergence as regards the principles and the basic features of protection; GATT negotiations on trade related aspects of substantive standards of intellectual property rights should not attempt to elaborate rules which would substitute for existing specific conventions on intellectual property matters; contracting parties could, however, when this was deemed necessary, elaborate further principles in order to reduce trade distortions or impediments. *The exercise should largely be limited to an identification of and agreement on the principles of protection which should be respected by all parties; the negotiations should not aim at the harmonization of national laws."* [40] [italics added]

2.2.3 The 1989 Australian proposal

Other industrialized country delegations highlighted that the TRIPS negotiations should focus on basic principles and trade effects. For example, in 1989, the Australian delegation adopted the following approach:

"Introducing his country's proposal (NG11/W/35), the representative of Australia said that the paper was intended to address the key issue of what standards and principles concerning the availability, scope and use of IPRs were appropriate to avoid inadequate or excessive protection of intellectual property in trade. Noting the use of the word "adequate" in paragraph 4(b) of the April TNC decision, he said that this suggested to his authorities that the Group was not necessarily looking for the highest possible standards or the broadest scope of protection."[41]

2.2.4 The 1988 Swiss proposal

The Swiss proposal for a TRIPS Agreement was centred on the notion that governments would maintain flexibility to adopt IPR laws they considered appropriate, provided that those laws did not conflict with an indicative list of practices that would be presumed to nullify or impair GATT rights.[42]

2.2.5 The Indian position in 1989

Reflecting the importance that the Indian delegation attached to the question of discretion regarding standards, in 1989 its delegate observed:

"Recognising the extraordinary rights granted by the system and their implications, international conventions on this subject incorporated, as a central philosophy, the freedom of member States to attune their intellectual property protection system to their own needs and conditions. *This freedom of host countries should be recognised as a fundamental principle and should guide all of the discussions in the Negotiating Group."* [43] [Italics added]

---

[40] Guidelines and Objectives Proposed by the European Community for the Negotiations on Trade Related Aspects of Substantive Standards of Intellectual Property Rights, Negotiating Group on Trade-Related Aspects of Intellectual Property Rights, including Trade in Counterfeit Goods, MTN.GNG/NG11/W/26, July 1988, at II.

[41] Note by the Secretariat, Meeting of Negotiating Group of 12-14 July 1989, Negotiating Group on Trade-Related Aspects of Intellectual Property Rights, including Trade in Counterfeit Goods, MTN.GNG/NG11/14, 12 September 1989, at para. 6 [hereinafter July 1989 meeting].

[42] Proposition de la Suisse, MTN.GNG/NG11/W/25, 29 June 1988.

[43] Note on July 1989 meeting, at para. 5.

2.2.6 The Anell Draft

At the meeting of TRIPS negotiators in October – November 1989, a number of interventions by delegations indicated a widely held perception that TRIPS should reflect a set of minimum substantive standards that would not be intended to harmonize national law.[44]

The composite text circulated by the Chairman (Lars E. R. Anell) of the TRIPS Negotiating Group in a July 23 1990 report on the status of work referred to implementation in the following way:

> "3A. Unless expressly stated otherwise, nothing in Parts III-V of this agreement shall prevent PARTIES from granting more extensive protection to intellectual property rights than that provided in this agreement."

2.2.7 The Brussels and Dunkel Drafts

Article 1.1 appeared in the draft text transmitted on the Chairman's initiative to the Brussels Ministerial Conference in December 1990, and in its final form in the Dunkel Draft text. Both texts were essentially similar to the current provision under TRIPS.

The years during which the TRIPS negotiations took place witnessed a great deal of attention among trade scholars to the question whether the GATT 1947, and the ultimately adopted WTO Agreement, should be given "direct effect" by Members.[45] The focus of this inquiry was on whether persons (individual or enterprise) should be given the right to invoke WTO rights and obligations before their national courts. Despite this substantial amount of activity in the academic arena, and bearing in mind that a number of leading trade scholars substantially influenced the Uruguay Round negotiations, the question of direct effect was not a subject that drew the express attention of the TRIPS negotiators, at least as reflected in the minutes of the negotiating sessions.

3. Possible interpretations

3.1 Article 1.1, First sentence

> Members shall give effect to the provisions of this Agreement.

The interpretation of the first sentence of Article 1.1 that Members shall "give effect" to its provisions, is not a likely subject of dispute, in light of the third

---

[44] For example, the delegate from New Zealand said that the New Zealand proposal was presented as a basis for adequate minimum standards; it did not seek to constrain countries from going further than the minimum standards. Given the limited amount of time left for negotiation, his delegation felt that the Group should not attempt to be over-ambitious, either in the level of detail of commitments or through attempting to invent a whole new system. Note by the Secretariat, Meeting of Negotiating Group of 30 October-2 November 1989, Negotiating Group on Trade-Related Aspects of Intellectual Property Rights, including Trade in Counterfeit Goods, MTN.GNG/NG11/16, 4 December 1989, at para. 3.

[45] See generally, *National Constitutions and International Economic Law, Studies in Transnational Economic Law* (M. Hilf, E.-U. Petersmann, ed.), Deventer, 1993.

sentence that elaborates on the "method" for giving effect. In the absence of the third sentence, argument might well be had over how the giving of effect is to be accomplished. Since the question is more specifically addressed by the third sentence, the first should be understood as serving to state the general treaty obligation to perform in good faith.

As stated above (Section 1), the obligation to "give effect" may be discharged not only through the adoption of specific statutes or administrative rules to implement TRIPS, but also where a Member elects to rely directly on the text of the Agreement as part of national law. In this case, however, it should be noted that some of the TRIPS provisions, in order to be applied to a particular case, require further concretisation through domestic legislation or case law.[46]

3.2 Article 1.1, Second sentence

> Members may, but shall not be obliged to, implement in their law more extensive protection than is required by this Agreement, provided that such protection does not contravene the provisions of this Agreement.

There are several interpretative issues raised by this sentence.

It appears reasonable to conclude that this provision signifies that the rules of TRIPS are intended as "minimum" standards of IPR protection. Members may adopt more extensive protection, but not less extensive protection. Note, however, that the minimum standard of protection is that "required" by the Agreement, and that the express requirements of the Agreement are often framed in rather flexible terms. In this sense, the minimum standards are subject to differential application.

The second sentence also provides that Members "shall not be obliged to" implement more extensive protection. Some Members have made demands in the context of bilateral or regional negotiations that other Members adopt so-called "TRIPS-plus" standards of protection. The express language of this second sentence makes clear that no Member is obligated by the TRIPS Agreement to adopt such TRIPS-plus standards.

An important interpretative question is whether a Member that *demands* the adoption of TRIPS-plus standards in the bilateral or regional context might be failing to perform its TRIPS Agreement obligations in good faith. The argument on behalf of a Member's being subjected to such demands would be that it accepted its TRIPS obligations as part of a set of reciprocally negotiated commitments that represent a balance of rights and obligations on which that Member is entitled to rely. Bilateral pressure to exceed the agreed upon commitments is contrary to

---

[46] For instance, the TRIPS provisions on exceptions to exclusive rights, such as Article 30 with respect to patents, which reads: "Members may provide limited exceptions to the exclusive rights conferred by a patent, provided that such exceptions do not unreasonably conflict with a normal exploitation of the patent and do not unreasonably prejudice the legitimate interests of the patent owner, taking account of the legitimate interests of third parties." For details on Article 30 see below, Chapter 23.

the object and purpose of the WTO Agreement and TRIPS Agreement to provide a secure framework for the conduct of international trade relations.

A counter-argument is that each Member is sovereign and free to accept or reject additional commitments in the bilateral or regional context. Diplomacy often involves the application of pressure in some form, and the application of pressure cannot inherently be ruled out in international relations.

The WTO Appellate Body and Dispute Settlement Body (DSB) might well have to consider whether there are forms of bilateral or regional pressure that exceed the limits of good faith performance of TRIPS. Recall that in negotiations surrounding the adoption of the Doha Declaration on the TRIPS Agreement and Public Health, developing countries sought a commitment from developed Members that bilateral and regional pressures to forego TRIPS Agreement options, and to adopt TRIPS-plus measures, would be halted.[47] The question from a TRIPS Agreement interpretative standpoint is the threshold at which a Member would be considered "obliged" to adopt more extensive protection as the result of bilateral pressure. At what point would the pressured Member be relinquishing its sovereign capacity to freely bargain?[48]

Another important interpretative question raised by Article 1.1, second sentence, is at what stage more extensive protection contravenes TRIPS? The preamble of the Agreement, discussed in Chapter 1, recognizes that "measures and procedures to enforce intellectual property rights" may constitute "barriers to legitimate trade". Yet the express text of TRIPS on substantive matters is largely devoted to setting forth minimum standards of protection, not maximum levels or upper limits. In this sense, the text of the Agreement appears to provide limited guidance regarding the kinds of more extensive IPRs substantive measures that might "contravene the Agreement". On the other hand, the enforcement provisions of TRIPS provide that certain rights must be accorded to parties alleged to be engaged in infringing acts. So, for example, Article 42 prescribes that defendants be accorded due process rights in IPR enforcement proceedings. The adoption of more extensive protection that diminished these due process rights would contravene TRIPS. In this regard, more extensive protections should not include reducing the rights of those asserted to be engaged in infringing acts. Since the reduction of procedural rights would contravene specific provisions of TRIPS, the reference in Article 1.1 may not add very much in this regard.

3.3 Article 1.1, Third sentence

> Members shall be free to determine the appropriate method of implementing the provisions of this Agreement within their own legal system and practice.

---

[47] See Non-paper (Africa Group et al.), "Ministerial Declaration on the TRIPS Agreement and Public Health", 19 Sept. 2001.

[48] There is an analogy to the common law contract doctrine of "unconscionability" that examines whether a bargain should be voided because of undue pressure placed by one party on another.

A narrow construction of this provision might suggest that the words "appropriate method"[49] refer only to the legal procedure by which a Member implements its TRIPS obligations. So, for example, a Member could choose to implement TRIPS by adopting either a statute or administrative regulation, or allow the TRIPS Agreement direct effect and rely on judicial application of the Agreement.

A broader construction of this provision acknowledges the flexibility inherent in the text of TRIPS. It refers not only to method, but also to the "legal system and practice" of each Member. The method of implementation therefore may take into account each Member's system of laws, and its practice regarding the application of those laws. Throughout the historical development of IPR law, countries have taken different approaches within their legal systems and practice to basic issues such as the scope of permissible exceptions, including the means by which exceptions are recognized. In some countries, for example, exceptions to patent rights are adopted as part of the statutory framework. In others, courts have crafted the exceptions as a matter of judicial application.[50] The acknowledgement that courts may be responsible for determining the permissible scope of exceptions is an inherent acknowledgement that IPR protection will vary among Members, and that Members maintain flexibility in implementing TRIPS.

There are limits to TRIPS Agreement flexibility in the sense that its rules cannot be stretched beyond reasonable good faith interpretation.[51]

In acknowledging the freedom of each Member to determine the appropriate method of implementing the Agreement, Article 1.1, third sentence, does not mandate that Members give it "direct" or "self-executing" effect. At the same time, that sentence does not appear to indicate that the Agreement should not be considered directly effective in countries where this is permitted. Instead, the matter is left to the constitutional system and practice of each Member state to determine.

It might be argued that because all Members need not apply TRIPS directly, it is not intended to be applied directly by any Member. This argument, which is based on reciprocity of obligation, has not traditionally persuaded courts where direct effect is practiced. Some states, such as the United Kingdom, do not allow direct effect for any treaty, and if reciprocity determined the directly applicable character of a treaty, then no treaty to which the UK is a party could be directly effective. This is not the accepted practice. The most reasonable interpretation of Article 1.1, third sentence, would appear to be that each Member is free to determine whether it will apply the Agreement directly, and that this will depend on its legal system and practice.

Where direct effect is possible, courts tend to look at whether the terms of the agreement are sufficiently precise to be applied by a court in a concrete case or controversy, and in light of the object and purpose of the agreement. The question of direct effect thus involves a "contextual analysis". If TRIPS is given direct effect, this will provide entitlements to right holders, as well as entitlements to those

---

[49] The New Shorter Oxford English Dictionary defines "method" as a noun as "I Procedure for attaining an object."

[50] See, e.g., Annex 5 to the *Canada-Generics* decision describing national approaches to regulatory review exceptions. (Canada – Patent Protection of Pharmaceutical Products, Report of the Panel, WT/DS114/R, 17 March 2000.)

[51] See discussion of the *India-Mailbox* case, Section 4, below.

defending against claims brought by right holders (for example, by allowing "fair use" defences). If the national legislature wants to exercise greater control over the way the TRIPS Agreement is locally applied, it may well decide not to rely on principles of direct effect that leaves issues of specific implementation up to the courts.

4. WTO jurisprudence

4.1 India-Mailbox

Article 1.1 was most notably discussed by the WTO Appellate Body ("AB") in the *India-Mailbox* case.[52] In that case, India argued that because Article 1.1 allowed it to implement the requirement of establishing a mechanism for the receipt and preservation of patent applications (the so-called "mailbox") in the manner it determined to be appropriate, the AB should accept its representation that the mechanism it had established was adequate within its own legal system. The AB acknowledged India's freedom to choose the appropriate method of implementation within its own legal system, but did not accept that this precluded examining whether the means chosen by India were in fact adequate to fulfil its obligation. The AB said:

"58. . . . [W]e do *not* agree with the Panel that Article 70.8(a) requires a Member to establish a means 'so as to eliminate any reasonable doubts regarding whether mailbox applications and eventual patents based on them could be rejected or invalidated because, at the filing or priority date, the matter for which protection was sought was unpatentable in the country in question' . . . . In our view, India is obliged, by Article 70.8(a), to provide a legal mechanism for the filing of mailbox applications that provides a sound legal basis to preserve both the novelty of the inventions and the priority of the applications as of the relevant filing and priority dates. No more.

59. But what constitutes such a sound legal basis in Indian law? To answer this question, we must recall first an important general rule in the *TRIPS Agreement*. Article 1.1 of the *TRIPS Agreement* states, in pertinent part:

. . . Members shall be free to determine the appropriate method of implementing the provisions of this Agreement within their own legal system and practice.

Members, therefore, are free to determine how best to meet their obligations under the *TRIPS Agreement* within the context of their own legal systems. And, as a Member, India is 'free to determine the appropriate method of implementing' its obligations under the *TRIPS Agreement* within the context of its own legal system.

60. India insists that it has done that. India contends that it has established, through 'administrative instructions', a 'means' consistent with Article 70.8(a) of the *TRIPS Agreement*. According to India, these 'administrative instructions' establish a mechanism that provides a sound legal basis . . .

[. . .]

---

[52] *India – Patent Protection for Pharmaceutical and Agricultural Chemical Products*, Report of the Appellate Body, WT/DS50/AB/R, 19 December 1997 ("India – Mailbox"). For more details on the factual background, see Chapter 36.

64. India asserts that the Panel erred in its treatment of India's municipal law because municipal law is a fact that must be established before an international tribunal by the party relying on it. In India's view, the Panel did not assess the Indian law as a fact to be established by the United States, but rather as a law to be interpreted by the Panel. India argues that the Panel should have given India the benefit of the doubt as to the status of its mailbox system under Indian domestic law. India claims, furthermore, that the Panel should have sought guidance from India on matters relating to the interpretation of Indian law.

65. In public international law, an international tribunal may treat municipal law in several ways. Municipal law may serve as evidence of facts and may provide evidence of state practice. However, municipal law may also constitute evidence of compliance or non-compliance with international obligations [...].

66. In this case, the Panel was simply performing its task in determining whether India's 'administrative instructions' for receiving mailbox applications were in conformity with India's obligations under Article 70.8(a) of the *TRIPS Agreement*. It is clear that an examination of the relevant aspects of Indian municipal law and, in particular, the relevant provisions of the Patents Act as they relate to the 'administrative instructions', is essential to determining whether India has complied with its obligations under Article 70.8(a). There was simply no way for the Panel to make this determination without engaging in an examination of Indian law. But, as in the case cited above before the Permanent Court of International Justice, in this case, the Panel was not interpreting Indian law 'as such'; rather, the Panel was examining Indian law solely for the purpose of determining whether India had met its obligations under the *TRIPS Agreement*. To say that the Panel should have done otherwise would be to say that only India can assess whether Indian law is consistent with India's obligations under the *WTO Agreement*. This, clearly, cannot be so.

[...]

70. We are not persuaded by India's explanation of . . . seeming contradictions. Accordingly, we are not persuaded that India's 'administrative instructions' would survive a legal challenge under the Patents Act. And, consequently, we are not persuaded that India's 'administrative instructions' provide a sound legal basis to preserve novelty of inventions and priority of applications as of the relevant filing and priority dates."

The AB decided that freedom to determine appropriate method is not the equivalent of a right to self-certify compliance with TRIPS obligations. Compliance requires demonstration of a legally sound basis of implementation.

4.2 Canada-Generics

In the *Canada-Generics* case,[53] Canada argued that Article 1.1, third sentence, provided it with substantial discretion in determining the scope of exceptions to patent rights, particularly when read in conjunction with Articles 7 and 8.1.

---

[53] *Canada – Patent Protection of Pharmaceutical Products*, Report of the Panel, WT/DS114/R, 17 March 2000 ("Canada–Generics").

According to the panel report, Canada argued:

"The existence of such a discretion was consistent with the provision of Article 1.1 that Members should be free to determine the appropriate method of implementing the provisions of the TRIPS Agreement, which provisions of course included Articles 7 and 30 as well as Articles 27, 28 and 33.

The provision of this discretion, in the interests of achieving an appropriate balance in each of the national legal systems, reflected Members' desire to ensure that the limitations on the scope of patent rights that existed within – or were contemplated for – their own intellectual property laws at the time the Agreement was being negotiated would be taken into account." (para. 4.13) (argument of Canada)

The European Communities argued in response:

"Article 1.1 of the TRIPS Agreement was invoked by Canada in order to establish that it had a broad *discretion* as to how to implement its obligations under the Agreement. However, Canada was wrong to consider that this provision provided a general discretion for Members to *adjust* obligations under the Agreement. It clearly stated that the protection of intellectual property under the TRIPS Agreement was to be considered a *minimum level of protection*. The flexibility which was allowed related to the *means* by which this minimum level of protection was secured in each Member's legal system." (para. 4.29)(argument of the EC)

In its determination, the Panel did not attribute significance to Article 1.1, instead focusing on Articles 7 and 8. It said:

"7.23 Canada called attention to a number of other provisions of the TRIPS Agreement as relevant to the purpose and objective of Article 30. Primary attention [footnote 385] was given to Articles 7 and 8.1 . . . [footnote 385: Attention was also called to the text of the first recital in the Preamble to the TRIPS Agreement and to part of the text of Article 1.1. The Preamble text in question reads: 'Desiring to reduce distortions and impediments to international trade, and taking into account the need to promote effective and adequate protection of intellectual property rights, *and to ensure that measures and procedures to enforce intellectual property rights do not themselves become barriers to legitimate trade*,' (emphasis added by Canada)]

[. . .]

7.25 The EC also referred to the provisions of first consideration of the Preamble and Article 1.1 as demonstrating that the basic purpose of the TRIPS Agreement was to lay down minimum requirements for the protection and enforcement of intellectual property rights.

[. . .]

7.26 Both the goals and the limitations stated in Articles 7 and 8.1 must obviously be borne in mind when doing so as well as those of other provisions of the TRIPS Agreement which indicate its object and purposes."

The panel in the *Canada-Generics* case did not specifically rely on Articles 7 and 8.1 or Article 1.1 in its determination regarding Canada's stockpiling and regulatory review exceptions.

4.3 U.S. – Copyright (Homestyle Exemption)

The decision of the panel in the *U.S. – Copyright (Homestyle Exemption)* case refers to the argument of the United States in its written submission concerning Article 1.1.[54] In its written submission, the United States said:

> "Article 1.1 of TRIPS also *emphasizes flexibility*, and provides that 'Members shall be free to determine the appropriate method of implementing the provisions of this Agreement within their own legal system and practice'."[55] (Italics added)

It is notable that the United States acknowledged that Article 1.1 "emphasizes flexibility" in defending its implementation of Article 13, TRIPS Agreement, which deals with limitations and exceptions to copyright.

5. Relationship with other international instruments

As noted earlier, the obligation on states to implement treaties is implicit in the obligation to perform in good faith recognized in the VCLT. The manner in which each state undertakes this obligation depends on its national constitutional arrangement and on the terms, context and object and purpose of the treaty in question.

6. New developments

6.1 National laws

Article 1.1 addresses the method of implementing the Agreement. Since all WTO Members were required to implement at least certain parts of the Agreement upon its entry into force on 1 January 1995, a large body of national experience has already accumulated. Additional implementation obligations arose on 1 January 1996 and 1 January 2000, depending on the level of development of Members.[56]

Inquiry regarding national experience in the implementation of TRIPS should include studying the means by which Members have chosen to give effect to the flexibility inherent in the rules, for example, in the adoption of exceptions to general obligations. Such exceptions have already been the subject of WTO dispute settlement in the fields of patent (*Canada-Generics*) and copyright (*U.S. – Copyright (Homestyle Exemption)*).[57]

There have been notable instances of Members being challenged in national courts regarding compliance with TRIPS Agreement obligations. The most significant and widely reported was the case brought by 39 pharmaceutical companies against the government of South Africa regarding the Medicines and Related Substances Control Amendment Act of 1997. The legal arguments of the pharmaceutical companies included that parallel importation of medicines was not allowed

---

[54] *United States – Section 110(5) of the US Copyright Act*, Report of the Panel, WT/DS160/R, 15 June 2000 (*"U.S. – Copyright (Homestyle Exemption)"*), at para. 6.189, note 167.

[55] *Id.*, Annex 2.1, First Written Submission of the United States, 26 Oct. 1999, para. 21.

[56] For details on the TRIPS transitional periods, see Chapter 33.

[57] There is limited discussion of the trademark exceptions in *U.S. – Havana Club*, but that treatment was not a significant element in the AB decision.

pursuant to Article 28. The pharmaceutical companies eventually withdrew their complaint.[58]

In view of the extensive national experience in implementing TRIPS, it is not feasible to provide a systematic review here. It is, however, possible to describe a few approaches Members have taken regarding whether TRIPS is directly effective (or self-executing) in domestic law. The experience of Argentina, South Africa and the United States is representative of the variety of potential approaches. The situation in the European Communities is described below in relation to regional arrangements.

6.1.1 Argentina

The Constitution of Argentina has been interpreted by courts as allowing the direct application of international treaties, provided that their particular provisions are precise and complete enough to be applied without further legislative developments. This doctrine has been applied in several cases where plaintiffs invoked provisions of the TRIPS Agreement, particularly articles 33 and 50 of the Agreement.[59] The Supreme Court confirmed this monist interpretation in several rulings,[60] indicating that in case of contradiction between a provision of the domestic law and a provision of TRIPS, the latter overrides and replaces the former.

6.1.2 South Africa

The South African Constitution has undergone several recent revisions that have affected the manner in which treaties may be given effect in national law.[61] The Constitution under which the Uruguay Round Agreements were approved for ratification by the South African Parliament required that a treaty be expressly adopted as part of national law to have direct effect.[62] The South African Parliament approved the ratification of the Uruguay Round Agreements in 1995, and did not stipulate that those agreements would have direct effect.[63] The subsequent

---

[58] For a description of the legal arguments in the South Africa pharmaceuticals case, see Frederick M. Abbott, *WTO TRIPS Agreement and Its Implications for Access to Medicines in Developing Countries*, Study Paper 2a for the British Commission on Intellectual Property Rights, Feb. 2002, available at <http://www.iprscommission.org>. For an analysis of the interplay of parallel imports and Article 28, TRIPS Agreement, see below, Chapter 5.

[59] See, e.g., *S.C. Johnson & Son Inc.c/Clorox Argentina S.A.s/medidas cautelares*, Cam.Fed.Civ. y Com. Sala II, 30 April 1998; *Lionel's S.R.L s/ medidas cautelares*, Cam.Fed.Civ.y Com. Sala II, 24 November 1998.

[60] See *Unilever NV c/Instituto Nacional de la propiedad Industrial s/denegatoria de patente*, 24.10.2000; *Dr. Karl Thomae Gesellschaft mit Beschränkter Haftung c/Instituto Nacional de la Propiedad Industrial s/denegatoria de patente*, 13.2.01. See also Correa, Carlos (2001) "El régimen de patentes tras la adopción del Acuerdo sobre los Derechos de la Propiedad Intelectual Relacionados con el Comercio", Jurisprudencia Argentina, No. 6239, Buenos Aires.

[61] See, e.g., John Dugard and Iain Currie, *International Law and Foreign Relations*, in Annual Survey of South African Law 1995, at 76 et seq. (Juta & Co., Limited) [hereinafter Dugard and Currie].

[62] This text largely followed the British model and required legislative action to give treaty provisions direct effect in national law. See Azanian Peoples Organization v. President of the Republic, Constitutional Court of South Africa, Case CCT17/96, decided July 25, 1996, at paras. 26–27.

[63] See Dugard and Currie, referring to approval of ratification of "Marrakesh Final Agreement establishing the World Trade Organization and incorporating the General Agreement on Tariffs

and present text of the Constitution allows for the possibility of direct effect without express statement when a self-executing treaty provision is not inconsistent with the Constitution or an act of Parliament.[64]

There is an interesting and as yet unresolved question under South African law whether a treaty adopted prior to the change in the constitutional treatment of direct effect, including TRIPS, will be evaluated under the new or old constitutional rule.

In any case, the South African Parliament adopted legislation to bring national law into compliance with the WTO Agreements, including TRIPS.[65] This is consistent with the type of dualist approach followed in the United States, which permits direct effect, but allows the legislature to control even directly effective treaties by subsequent legislation. The one approach does not exclude the other. That is, a treaty may be directly effective as to some issues, but controlled by legislation as to others.

6.1.3 United States

In the U.S. constitutional framework, the Congress has primary authority in the conduct of external trade relations, and the President and executive branch act in the field of international trade relations under both general and specific grants of authority from the Congress.[66] Congress authorized U.S. adherence to the WTO Agreement, including TRIPS, in the Uruguay Round Agreements Act (URAA), which also implemented the WTO Agreement in U.S. domestic law.[67] In connection with the congressional fast-track approval process that was used for the URAA, the executive branch submitted to the Congress a Statement of Administrative Action that was and is intended to represent the authoritative interpretation of the WTO Agreement by the executive branch both for purposes of U.S. international obligation and domestic law.[68] The Statement of Administrative Action was

---

and Trade (GATT) – *National Assembly Debates* col 653 (6 April 1995); *Senate Debates* col 554 (6 April 1995)", at page 77, and exclusion from list of treaties resolved to have direct effect by Parliament, at page 79.

[64] Article 231 of the Constitution of South Africa, adopted 8 May 1996, amended 11 Oct 1996 and in force from 7 Feb 1997, provides in relevant part:
Section 231 International agreements
    "(4) Any international agreement becomes law in the Republic when it is enacted in law by national legislation; but a self-executing provision of an agreement that has been approved by Parliament is law in the Republic unless it is inconsistent with the Constitution or an Act of Parliament.
    (5) The Republic is bound by international agreements which were binding on the Republic when this Constitution took effect."

[65] For a discussion of the interface between the South African Constitution, trade agreements and national trade law, see Gerhard Erasmus, *The Incorporation of International Trade Agreements into South African Law: The Extent of Constitutional Guidance*, 28 SOUTH AFRICAN YEARBOOK OF INTERNATIONAL LAW, 2003 at pgs.157–181.

[66] See generally, Riesenfeld and Abbott, *The Scope of U.S. Senate Control over the Conclusion and Operation of Treaties, in* Parliamentary Participation at 302.

[67] Uruguay Round Agreements Act [hereinafter URAA], Pub. L. 103-465, 108 Stat 4809 (1994), sec. 101(a)(1).

[68] Office of the U.S. Trade Representative, The Uruguay Round Agreements Act Statement of Administrative Action, at introduction. URAA, sec. 101(d).

approved by Congress in connection with approval of the URAA.[69] The President accepted the WTO Agreement and related Uruguay Round Agreements following approval by Congress[70] and in accordance with the procedures prescribed in Article XIV of the WTO Agreement. The WTO Agreement and related agreements entered into force for the United States on January 1, 1995.[71]

Congress in the URAA followed a pattern that it had established in connection with the GATT Tokyo Round Agreements, by denying self-executing or direct effect to the WTO Agreement.[72]

The provisions of the URAA which deny the WTO Agreement self-executing or direct effect apply to all constituent components of the agreement, and so encompass TRIPS. These provisions preclude a private party's direct reliance on the WTO Agreement as the basis for civil action against a private party, or as the basis for action against the federal or state governments.

6.2 International instruments

6.3 Regional and bilateral contexts

6.3.1 Regional

In an advisory opinion of 1994, the ECJ decided that the TRIPS Agreement must be adopted jointly by the member states and the EC because the member states and EC shared competence in the regulations of IPRs.[73] When the Council of the European Communities subsequently approved adherence to the Uruguay Round

---

[69] URAA, sec. 101(a)(2).

[70] URAA, sec. 101(b).

[71] See 19 USCA §3511 (1996).

[72] Section 102 of the URAA provides "(a) Relationship of Agreements to United States Law.- (1) United States Law to Prevail in Conflict.- No provision of any of the Uruguay Round Agreements, nor the application of any such provisions to any person or circumstance, that is inconsistent with any law of the United States shall have effect." Section 102 of the URAA further provides:
  "(c) Effect of Agreement With Respect to Private Remedies.–
  (1) Limitations.– No person other than the United States–
  (A) shall have any cause of action or defense under any of the Uruguay Round Agreements or by virtue of congressional approval of such an agreement, or
  (B) may challenge, in any action brought under any provision of law, any action or inaction by any department, agency, or other instrumentality of the United States, any State, or any political subdivision of a State on the ground that such action or inaction is inconsistent with such agreement.
  (2) Intent of congress.– It is the intention of the Congress through paragraph (1) to occupy the field with respect to any cause of action or defense under or in connection with any of the Uruguay Round Agreements, including by precluding any person other than the United States from bringing any action against any State or political subdivision thereof or raising any defense to the application of State law under or in connection with any of the Uruguay Round Agreements–
  (A) on the basis of a judgment obtained by the United States in an action brought under any such agreement; or
  (B) on any other basis."
The Statement of Administrative Action is perhaps more categorical than the statute concerning the preclusion of direct effect, particularly as it might relate to actions as between private parties. It says, *inter alia*:
  "A private party thus could not sue (or defend suit against) the United States, a state or a private party on grounds of consistency (or inconsistency) with those [WTO] agreements." *Id.* at 20.

[73] Opinion 1/94 of 15 November 1994 [1994] ECR I-5267, para 105.

Agreements, the decision expressing that approval included a recital that it was understood the WTO Agreement would not be considered directly effective for the EC.[74] A recital would not ordinarily have the same legal effect as an operative provision of a decision, but would nonetheless be expected to have some influence in the interpretation of that decision and the subject treaty by the EC organs.

In 1999, the ECJ in *Portugal v. Council* decided that the WTO Agreements were not directly effective in the law of the EC.[75] The ECJ relied on essentially the same arguments that persuaded it in 1972 (in the *International Fruit* case) that the GATT 1947 was not directly effective in Community law.[76] In 2000, the ECJ decided in *Parfums Christian Dior v. Tuk Consultancy*[77] that its decision in *Portugal v. Council* extended to TRIPS, and that TRIPS is not directly effective as a matter of Community law.[78] The ECJ added, however, that because TRIPS is an international obligation of the EC, the courts should endeavour to interpret EC law consistently with TRIPS.[79]

For the EC, the matter is complex because it does not enjoy exclusive competence *vis-à-vis* the member states in the field of IPRs. The ECJ therefore said that the question of direct effect must be resolved as a matter of member state law as to those areas in which the member state retains exclusive competence.[80]

---

[74] Council Decision (of 22 December 1994) concerning the conclusion on behalf of the European Community, as regards matters within its competence, of the agreements reached in the Uruguay Round multilateral negotiations (1986-1994) *Official Journal of the European Communities L 336, 23/12/1994 p. 1–2.*

[75] See Case C-149/96 *Portuguese Republic v Council of the European Union*, [1999] ECR I-8395, at para. 47: "It follows from all those considerations that, having regard to their nature and structure, the WTO agreements are not in principle among the rules in the light of which the Court is to review the legality of measures adopted by the Community institutions." [hereinafter *Portugal v Council*].

[76] See Joined Cases 21 to 24/72 *International Fruit Company N.V. v. Produktschap voor Groenten en Fruit* (No. 3) [1972] ECR 1219.

[77] See joined cases C-300/98 and C-392/98 *Parfums Christian Dior SA and Tuk Consultancy BV*, [2000] ECR I-11307. While in *Portugal v Council* the ECJ refused the *EU member states* the possibility to invoke the WTO Agreements against EC legislation, the *Christian Dior* decision concerned the denial of direct effect in favour of *individuals* (i.e. EU citizens).

[78] The ECJ said:
"44. For the same reasons as those set out by the Court in paragraphs 42 to 46 of the judgment in *Portugal v Council*, the provisions of TRIPs, an annex to the WTO Agreement, are not such as to create rights upon which individuals may rely directly before the courts by virtue of Community law."

[79] The ECJ said:
"49. [...] in a field to which TRIPs applies and in respect of which the Community has already legislated, the judicial authorities of the Member States are required by virtue of Community law, when called upon to apply national rules with a view to ordering provisional measures for the protection of rights falling within such a field, to do so as far as possible in the light of the wording and purpose of Article 50 of TRIPs, [...]"

[80] The ECJ said:
"49. [...] in a field in respect of which the Community has not yet legislated and which consequently falls within the competence of the Member States, the protection of intellectual property rights, and measures adopted for that purpose by the judicial authorities, do not fall within the scope of Community law. Accordingly, Community law neither requires nor forbids that the legal order of a Member State should accord to individuals the right to rely directly on the rule laid down by Article 50(6) of TRIPs or that it should oblige the courts to apply that rule of their own motion."

In *Christian Dior*, this meant that the courts of the Netherlands would decide whether Article 50.6, TRIPS Agreement, regarding provisional measures, would be directly applied in Dutch law. The ECJ has in effect acknowledged that the question whether TRIPS is directly effective is to be determined by each WTO Member (bearing in mind that in the case of the EC the identity of that Member may differ depending on the context).

6.4 Proposals for review

As part of its authority under Article 68, TRIPS Agreement, (see Chapter 35 of this book) to monitor implementation of obligations and afford Members the opportunity to consult with respect to IPRs, the Council for TRIPS is reviewing implementation of TRIPS Agreement obligations. These reviews began with respect to developed Members following their general implementation deadline of 1 January 1996, and with respect to developing Members following their general implementation deadline of 1 January 2000.[81]

A number of developing Members have suggested an amendment or interpretation of TRIPS that would preclude the exercise of bilateral or regional pressure against Members that propose to act to take advantage of flexibility inherent in TRIPS, such as the right to issue compulsory licenses.[82] This type of amendment or interpretation would address Article 1.1, second sentence, providing that Members are not obliged to adopt TRIPS-plus protection.

7. Comments, including economic and social implications

TRIPS established minimum standards of IPR protection that are consistent with the prevailing standards in the most highly industrialized countries. Highly industrialized countries such as the United States and Japan went through prolonged periods of providing weak IPR protection to achieve their present levels of development.[83] TRIPS to some extent precludes today's developing countries from relying on this same model of economic transformation by setting minimum standards at levels tailored for later stages of growth. Moreover, by setting minimum standards, but not maximum standards, TRIPS leaves an opening for bilateral and regional agreements that may significantly shift the balance of economic interests to the more powerful WTO Members, thereby further exacerbating problems in the global distribution of wealth. With hindsight, developing Members might have insisted more strongly that TRIPS reflect not only the minimum standards of IPR protection, but also that any increase in those standards be negotiated only within the multilateral framework of the WTO (where developing Members have a higher degree of control over outcomes). Developing Members have a certain margin of flexibility in the implementation of TRIPS Agreement standards

---

[81] This review process is discussed in Chapter 35.

[82] See, e.g., proposal of developing country group for a Declaration on the TRIPS Agreement and Public Health, Section 3 above.

[83] See UNCTAD-ICTSD Policy Discussion Paper, Chapter 1.

which they should take great care to use and preserve.[84] This may not be the optimal way to address development priorities, but it is for now the one provided by TRIPS.

[84] The importance of understanding the flexible nature of TRIPS Agreement provisions is elaborated in various works by Profs. Carlos Correa and Jerome Reichman, see, e.g., Carlos Correa, *Integrating Public Health Concerns into Patent Legislation in Developing Countries* (South Centre 2000), and; Jerome H. Reichman, *Securing Compliance with the TRIPS Agreement After U.S. v. India*, 1 J. INT'L ECON. L. 585 (1998).

3: Categories of Intellectual Property Embraced by TRIPS

Article 1 Nature and Scope of Obligations

1. [...]

2. For the purposes of this Agreement, the term "intellectual property" refers to all categories of intellectual property that are the subject of Sections 1 through 7 of Part II.

3. [...][footnote 2: In this Agreement, "Paris Convention" refers to the Paris Convention for the Protection of Industrial Property; "Paris Convention (1967)" refers to the Stockholm Act of this Convention of 14 July 1967. "Berne Convention" refers to the Berne Convention for the Protection of Literary and Artistic Works; "Berne Convention (1971)" refers to the Paris Act of this Convention of 24 July 1971. "Rome Convention" refers to the International Convention for the Protection of Performers, Producers of Phonograms and Broadcasting Organizations, adopted at Rome on 26 October 1961. "Treaty on Intellectual Property in Respect of Integrated Circuits" (IPIC Treaty) refers to the Treaty on Intellectual Property in Respect of Integrated Circuits, adopted at Washington on 26 May 1989. "WTO Agreement" refers to the Agreement Establishing the WTO.]

Article 2 Intellectual Property Conventions

1. In respect of Parts II, III and IV of this Agreement, Members shall comply with Articles 1 through 12, and Article 19, of the Paris Convention (1967).

2. Nothing in Parts I to IV of this Agreement shall derogate from existing obligations that Members may have to each other under the Paris Convention, the Berne Convention, the Rome Convention and the Treaty on Intellectual Property in Respect of Integrated Circuits.

---

1. Introduction: terminology, definition and scope

The term "intellectual property" is capable of being defined in different ways. Article 1.2 does not define "intellectual property" as a concept, but instead refers to sections of the agreement that address "categories".

The term "intellectual property" (and "intellectual property rights") appears mainly in the preamble and in Part III, TRIPS Agreement (relating to enforcement measures). As used in the preamble, the term refers to the general subject matter scope of the Agreement, and helps shape the context of the operative provisions of the Agreement. Part III requires Members to make available certain types of enforcement measures with respect to "intellectual property" or "intellectual property rights". The WTO Appellate Body and the European Court of Justice have already rendered decisions that interpret "intellectual property" as used in the TRIPS Agreement.

TRIPS incorporates provisions of treaties (or conventions) that were negotiated and concluded and are now administered in the framework of WIPO. Parts of that incorporation are accomplished in Article 2. The WIPO conventions are also referenced within Part II concerning substantive obligations. TRIPS supplements and modifies certain terms of the WIPO conventions, and establishes new rules outside the existing scope of those conventions.

A number of proposals have been made to expand the subject matter scope of TRIPS, most of them coming from developing countries. These proposals would include the fields of traditional knowledge, folklore and genetic resources within the scope of TRIPS Agreement coverage.[85]

This chapter focuses on the overall approach of TRIPS to defining the subject matter scope of intellectual property.

2. History of the provision

2.1 Situation pre-TRIPS

Until the middle part of the twentieth century, a distinction was customarily drawn between "industrial property", and the works of authors and artists. "Industrial property" was the province of business, and generally referred to patents and trademarks. The domain of the author and artist was protected by copyright and related rights. This distinction is reflected in the names of the two earliest multilateral agreements on the protection of intellectual property, the Paris Convention on the Protection of Industrial Property (1883) and the Berne Convention on the Protection of Literary and Artistic Works (1886).[86]

While this distinction was at one time grounded in commerce, the dawning of the so-called "post-industrial" era loosened the tie. The author became, for example, the computer programmer whose work underpinned a new generation of businesses. The boundaries between the industrial and artistic blurred, and the inclusive term "intellectual property" became commonly used to refer to the results of creative human endeavour protected by law.

---

[85] See Chapter 21.

[86] The coining of the term "intellectual property" is usually attributed to Josef Kohler and Edmond Picard in the late nineteenth century. This usage did not, however, become common for some years. See J.H. Reichman, *Charting the Collapse of the Patent-Copyright Dichotomy: Premises for a Restructured International Intellectual Property System*, 13 Cardozo Arts & Ent. L.J. 475, 480 (1995), citing among others, 1 Stephen P. Ladas, *The International Protection of Literary and Artistic Property* 9–10 (1938).

The Convention Establishing the World Intellectual Property Organization (adopted 1967, entered into force 1970), defined "intellectual property" at Article 2, stating:

"(viii) 'intellectual property' shall include the rights relating to:
– literary, artistic and scientific works,
– performances of performing artists, phonograms, and broadcasts,
– inventions in all fields of human endeavor,
– scientific discoveries,
– industrial designs,
– trademarks, service marks, and commercial names and designations,
– protection against unfair competition, and all other rights resulting from intellectual activity in the industrial, scientific, literary or artistic fields."

This definition is very broad. It encompasses subject matter not traditionally protected as industrial or intellectual property (for example, scientific discoveries are generally excluded from patent protection), and it does not evidence a limitation based on creativity.[87] However, this definition is used in the context of establishing the objectives of a specialized agency of the United Nations, and not in the operative context of defining the scope of rights. In this sense, the WIPO Convention definition is useful as an indication of how broadly the concept of intellectual property may be extended. It provides a basis for comparison with the more limited definition adopted in the TRIPS Agreement.

The principal WIPO conventions, Paris and Berne, took substantially different approaches to defining the subject matter of the interests they regulated. Article 2 of the Berne Convention includes a detailed and comprehensive definition of authors' and artists' expression that is generally subject to copyright. The Paris Convention, on the other hand, contains no definition of the subject matter, including patent or trademark.[88]

---

[87] In its final phrase, the Convention refers to the results of "intellectual activity". This may refer to intellectual effort, as well as creation.

[88] Commencing in 1985, a WIPO Committee of Experts on the Harmonization of Certain Provisions in Law for the Protection of Inventions was established under the authority of the International (Paris) Union for the Protection of Intellectual Property. As the name of this Committee implies, it was charged with seeking to establish common rules in the field of patents. See *WIPO Experts Make Progress On Patent Harmonization Draft*, BNA's Patent, Trademark & Copyright Journal, Analysis, January 10, 1991, 41 PTCJ 231 (Issue No. 1013), Lexis/Nexis Database, at Introduction. The scope of this project was initially broad, as governments sought to agree upon harmonized substantive provisions of patent law. In late 1992, the scope of this project was limited by the removal of a number of basic articles from the negotiations. See Paris Union Assembly, Nineteenth Session, WIPO doc. P/A/XIX/3, July 31, 1992. There are a number of explanations for the shift in scope of the negotiations. Some governments had expressed the view that conclusion of the TRIPS Agreement would reduce the need for a patent harmonization agreement. It was also apparent that the United States was unwilling at that point to agree to a core demand of other governments; that it adopt a "first-to-file" approach to patenting. An agreement could not be reached without this concession from the United States. Further negotiation of an agreement of broad scope appeared futile, and in subsequent years this exercise (which culminated in the adoption of the Patent Law Treaty) was devoted to technical administrative matters.

2.2 Negotiating history

2.2.1 The involvement of WIPO

From the very outset of the TRIPS negotiations the question of the relationship between a GATT-negotiated agreement and the existing body of WIPO conventions was the subject of extensive discussion. This was closely related to the institutional question whether intellectual property rights regulation should be moved into the GATT, the answer to which was not self-evident to many delegations. There were technical questions regarding the scope and nature of the protection of IPRs afforded by the WIPO Conventions, and conceptual questions regarding the nature of the relationship between GATT and WIPO once the TRIPS negotiations were concluded.

On 13 October 1986, shortly following the adoption of the Uruguay Round mandate (15 September 1986), the Director General of WIPO Arpad Bogsch sent to the Director General of the GATT Arthur Dunkel a request that,

> "WIPO . . . be fully associated in all activities that GATT will undertake in the field of intellectual property, including the question of counterfeit goods, and, in particular, that WIPO be invited to all the meetings of the Trade Negotiations Committee as well as to those of the different Committees or Working Groups that may be entrusted to deal with intellectual property questions."[89]

WIPO was subsequently invited to participate as observer in the formal meetings of the TRIPS Negotiating Group (TNG), a level of participation less than had been requested.[90]

Subsequently, the TNG requested that WIPO prepare comprehensive reports on the treatment of IPRs by existing multilateral conventions, on the status of negotiations within the WIPO framework, and on the existing treatment of IPRs within national legal systems.[91] In this respect, the participation-in-fact by WIPO in the activities of the TRIPS Negotiating Group was significant.

---

[89] MTN.GNG/NG11/W/1, 25 February 1987, Communication from the Director General of the World Intellectual Property Organization.

[90] "1. The Negotiating Group agreed to recommend to the GNG [Group of Negotiations on Goods] to invite to formal meetings of the Group international organizations which could facilitate the work of the Group by providing appropriate technical support in the field of their expertise to complement the expertise primarily available from participants. This support might take the form of oral responses during the meetings to requests through the Chairman for factual information on and clarification of matters concerning the relevant instruments and activities of any such organization, and factual papers to be prepared at the request of the Group." Note by the Secretariat, Meeting of the Negotiating Group of 10 June 1987, MTN.GNG/NG11/2, 23 June 1987.

[91] See, e.g., Meeting of the Negotiating Group of 23–24 Nov. 1987, MTN.GNG/NG11/5, 14 December 1987:
"37. After discussion of various suggestions for documentation for its next meeting, the Group agreed to:
1. Authorize the Chairman to invite the WIPO Secretariat:
(A) to prepare with respect to conventions administered by WIPO a factual statement providing a reference to provisions of existing international conventions providing protection for types of intellectual property included in MTN.GNG/NG11/W/12 (Section II, sub-paragraphs (i) through (vi));

There was discussion throughout the TRIPS negotiating process concerning the extent to which the WIPO conventions would form the basis of TRIPS rules and how such conventions would be integrated. At the meeting of the TNG of 29 February – 3 March 1988, these issues were discussed in some detail, leading to a request for factual information from WIPO. The meeting notes indicate:

"22. Referring to documents MTN.GNG/NG11/W/19 and 21, some participants said that efforts in the Group to deal with trade problems arising in the area of norms should build on the long history of work in this area in other organizations, in particular WIPO. While international standards or norms for the protection of intellectual property rights existed in some areas, they were absent or limited in other areas. For example, it was said that, whereas the Berne Convention for the Protection of Literary and Artistic Works contained rather precise norms, those in the Paris Convention for the Protection of Industrial Property were less complete. The existing international rules did not appear sufficient to forestall the trade problems that were arising from the inadequate provision of basic intellectual property rights in many countries. There was need for further study of the provisions of existing international conventions as they related to trade problems arising, of their implementation in member countries and of the reasons why some countries had not acceded to them. Some participants wished to have further information on existing international law and on how the norms provided therein compared to norms in national legislation and the issues and suggestions put forward in the Group; for example, was the level of protection accorded under international norms based on a concept of "sufficient profit" and, if so, how was this assessed? A number of questions were put to the representative of the World Intellectual Property Organization. Suggestions were also made about papers that the WIPO Secretariat might be invited to prepare in this connection (see paragraph 39 below for the decision of the Group).

[. . .]

39. On the basis of a proposal put forward by Mexico and two other participants, the Negotiating Group took the annexed Decision, inviting the Secretariat of the World Intellectual Property Organization to prepare a document for it. The Chairman said that the document would be a factual document, independent of the other documents before the Group, aimed at increasing understanding and would be without prejudice to the position of any participant in the negotiations and to the scope of the Group's Negotiating Objective. It was expected that the Chairman and the GATT secretariat would keep in contact with the Secretariat of WIPO during the preparation of the document. . . .

40. The representative of the World Intellectual Property Organization welcomed the decision of the Group to request a major contribution from WIPO. It would be difficult for WIPO to present all the information requested in the brief time before the next meeting of the Group. WIPO would do all it could to provide the

(B) to prepare the same kind of factual information as asked for in paragraph 1(A) as far as ongoing work in WIPO is concerned for updating the Note for the Chairman on 'Activities in Other International Organizations of Possible Interest in Relation to Matters Raised in the Group'.

maximum amount of information for the next meeting and would provide the rest as soon as possible thereafter."[92]

The meeting of the TNG of 16–19 May 1988 was largely devoted to discussion of a WIPO-prepared document on the Existence, Scope and Form of Generally Internationally Accepted and Applied Standards/Norms of the Protection of Intellectual Property (MTN.GNG/NG11/W/24). In this discussion, delegates expressed views concerning the extent to which the Paris and Berne Conventions provided adequate levels of IPR protection, and on whether negotiation of changes to the rules provided by those Conventions was better undertaken in the GATT or WIPO.[93]

By the TNG meeting of 12–14 July 1989, delegations were engaged in detailed discussion of their perceptions regarding the adequacy of the regulatory standards found in the existing WIPO conventions.[94] Although there were questions raised regarding the need for rules to supplement the existing provisions of the Berne Convention, for the most part it was accepted that the Berne Convention established adequate substantive standards of copyright protection.[95] Discussions regarding the Paris Convention regarding patents reflected sharply divergent perspectives, largely as between developed and developing country delegations.[96]

2.2.2 The Anell Draft

The composite text prepared by the Chairman of the TNG (Lars Anell) in July 1990[97] included draft provisions on categories of IPRs and the relationship of the WIPO Conventions. The Anell text provided:

"PART II: GENERAL PROVISIONS AND BASIC PRINCIPLES

1. Scope and Coverage

For the purposes of this agreement, the term "intellectual property" refers to all categories of intellectual property that are the subject of Sections . . . to . . . of Part III. This definition is without prejudice to whether the protection given to that subject matter takes the form of an intellectual property right.

5. Intellectual Property Conventions

5A. PARTIES shall comply with the [substantive] provisions [on economic rights] of the Paris Convention (1967), of the Berne Convention (1971) [and of the Rome Convention].

---

[92] Meeting of the Negotiating Group of 29 Feb.–3 Mar. 1988 MTN.GNG/NG11/6, 8 April 1988.

[93] At this stage in the TRIPS negotiations, the Secretariat notes of meetings generally did not refer to the specific delegation intervening, but usually to a "participant" or "participants". For later meetings the intervening delegations were sometimes, though not always, identified.

[94] Meeting of Negotiating Group of 12–14 July 1989, MTN.GNG/NG11/14, 12 Sept. 1989.

[95] See, e.g., paras. 23–34, *id.*

[96] See paras. 67–85, *id.*

[97] Status of Work in the Negotiating Group, Chairman's Report to the GNG, MTN.GNG/NG11/W/76, 23 July 1990. For more details on this draft see the explanatory note on the methodology at the beginning of this volume.

PART III: STANDARDS CONCERNING THE AVAILABILITY, SCOPE AND USE OF INTELLECTUAL PROPERTY RIGHTS

SECTION 1: COPYRIGHT AND RELATED RIGHTS

1. Relation to Berne Convention

1A PARTIES shall grant to authors and their successors in title the [economic] rights provided in the Berne Convention (1971), subject to the provisions set forth below.

1B PARTIES shall provide to the nationals of other PARTIES the rights which their respective laws do now or may hereafter grant, consistently with the rights specially granted by the Berne Convention."

With respect to the Rome Convention for the Protection of Performers, Producers of Phonograms and Broadcasting Organizations, the Anell Draft contained a proposal that would have gone beyond the corresponding obligation under the current TRIPS Agreement (see above, bracketed text under proposal 5A). This proposal would have rendered substantive obligations under the Rome Convention mandatory for all WTO Members, which is not the case under Article 2, TRIPS Agreement (see below, Section 3, for details).

2.2.3 The Brussels Draft

The Anell composite text emerged with modification in the Brussels Ministerial Text in December 1990. Article 1.2 (regarding the term "intellectual property") of the Brussels Ministerial Text and the final TRIPS Agreement text are essentially identical (although the Brussels text does not identify the relevant Section numbers).

Article 2.1 of the Brussels Ministerial Text provided:

"1. In respect of Parts II, III and IV of this Agreement, PARTIES shall not depart from the relevant provisions of the Paris Convention (1967)."

At this stage, the Paris Convention is still referenced in general terms, contrasting to the subsequent introduction of reference to specific articles. Also a "shall not depart" from formula is used, instead of the later "shall comply with".[98]

Article 2.2 of the Brussels Ministerial Text provided:

"2. Nothing in this Agreement shall derogate from existing obligations that PARTIES may have to each other under the Paris Convention, the Berne Convention, the Rome Convention and the Treaty on Intellectual Property in Respect of Integrated Circuits."

The transition from the Anell composite text to the Brussels Ministerial Text is important. For example, the predecessor to Article 1.2 in the Anell composite text contained an additional sentence implicitly acknowledging that some of the rights regulated by the agreement might not be considered "intellectual property" in the customary sense in which that term was used (see above, Anell Draft, under paragraph 1, "Scope and Coverage"). Also, Article 2.2 of the Brussels Ministerial Text

---

[98] For an interpretation of the current TRIPS obligation to "comply" with Paris Convention provisions and the question of a possible hierarchy between the TRIPS Agreement and the Paris Convention, see below, Section 3 (Possible interpretations).

(see above) added an important provision referring to derogation from *obligations* under the WIPO Conventions, but without reference to *rights* under those Conventions (as to the differentiation in this context between "rights" on the one hand and "obligations" on the other hand, see Section 3).

2.2.4 The Dunkel Draft

The only change in the Dunkel Draft and final TRIPS Agreement text is introduction in Article 2.2 of the limiting reference to "Parts I to IV" of the TRIPS Agreement as occasioning no derogation.[99] In practical terms, this limitation does not substantially alter the provision; the Parts not referenced under the current Article 2.2 concern provisions on dispute prevention and settlement (Part V); transitional arrangements (Part VI); and institutional arrangements and final provisions (Part VII). These provisions are unique to TRIPS and are thus unlikely to affect Members' obligations under the referenced conventions.

3. Possible interpretations

3.1 Article 1.2, TRIPS Agreement

> For the purposes of this Agreement, the term "intellectual property" refers to all categories of intellectual property that are the subject of Sections 1 through 7 of Part II.

As will be evident from the discussion that follows, "categories of intellectual property" is not synonymous with the headings of Sections 1 through 7, Part II of TRIPS. It is useful, nonetheless, to list those headings to provide a reference point for further discussion.

"Part II – Standards Concerning the Availability, Scope and Use of Intellectual Property Rights

Section 1 – Copyright and Related Rights

Section 2 – Trademarks

Section 3 – Geographical Indications

Section 4 – Industrial Designs

Section 5 – Patents

---

[99] The Dunkel Draft texts of Articles 1.2 and 2, TRIPS Agreement, are almost identical to the finally adopted versions, with the only changes clarifying the section numbers referenced. The Dunkel Draft text of Article 1.2, TRIPS Agreement, referred to "Sections 1 *to* 7 of Part II", whereas the final TRIPS Agreement in Article 1.2 text refers to "Sections 1 *through* 7 of Part II" (italics added). The Dunkel Draft text of Article 2.1, TRIPS Agreement, referred to "Articles 1–12 and 19 of the Paris Convention (1967), whereas the final TRIPS Agreement text in Article 2.1 refers to "Articles 1 through 12, and Article 19, of the Paris Convention (1967)". Similarly, Article 9.1 of the Dunkel Draft text and the TRIPS Agreement regarding Berne Convention rules are essentially identical, with only clarifying changes involving numbering. Negotiating history regarding references to WIPO Conventions for other forms of intellectual property is addressed in the relevant chapters of this book.

Section 6 – Layout-Designs (Topographies) of Integrated Circuits

Section 7 – Protection of Undisclosed Information"

The scope of the intellectual property rights subject matter covered by TRIPS determines the extent of each Member's obligation to implement and enforce the agreement. The text indicates that Article 1.2 is intended to limit the subject matter scope of "intellectual property". By defining "intellectual property" by reference to "all categories" of intellectual property that are the subject of certain sections of the Agreement, the definition excludes other potential categories of intellectual property that are not the subject of those sections.[100]

The question arises, what is meant by a "category"? "Category" is defined as a set or subset of things.[101] The term is inherently ambiguous because sets and subsets may be defined more broadly or narrowly depending on the intent of the creator of the set or subset. So, for example, when reference is made to the "category" of "Copyright and related rights", that reference could be understood to refer only to the specific types of protection referred to in Section 1 of Part II, or it could be understood to refer to any type of right that "relates" to expressive works (bearing in mind that "neighbouring rights" to copyright has its own customary meaning).[102]

Furthermore, since the reference in Article 1.2 is to categories that "are the subject" of Sections 1 through 7, the scope of the covered matter may not be strictly limited by the general category headings of the sections. Within the sections there are references to subject matters not traditionally considered to be within those general categories. For example, *sui generis* plant variety protection is provided as an optional form of protection under Section 5 on patents. Such protection does not involve patents as such. As discussed in detail below (Section 4), the Appellate Body in its *Havana Club* case has endorsed this interpretation.

Since Article 1.2 is expressed in the form of limitation, there is good reason to conclude that the categories of intellectual property should bear a reasonably close relationship to the subject matters enumerated in Sections 1 through 7 of Part II, especially as the negotiating history of TRIPS reflects an intention to regulate those subject matter areas that were agreed upon, and not areas as to which the parties did not agree.

There are certain subject matter areas "at the border" of existing forms of intellectual property. One notable area is database protection. In this respect, it is decisive whether the database at issue, *by reason of the selection or arrangement of its contents*, constitutes an *intellectual creation*. If this is the case, it is covered

---

[100] The definition of "intellectual property" in the Convention Establishing WIPO (referred to above), by way of contrast, includes not only a list of subject matter areas designated as intellectual property, but also a general reference to "all other rights resulting from intellectual activity in the industrial, scientific, literary or artistic fields." The list in the Convention Establishing WIPO includes subject matter that is not expressly covered by the TRIPS Agreement, for example, "scientific discoveries", which are different from "inventions" that are subject to patent protection (see Article 27.1, TRIPS Agreement).

[101] The New Shorter Oxford English Dictionary defines "category" as "Any of a possibly exhaustive set of basic classes among which all things might be distributed".

[102] See Chapter 13.

as intellectual property under Article 10.2, TRIPS Agreement.[103] If, on the other hand, the selection or arrangement of the contents of the database is *not creative* (e.g. a telephone book), it cannot be considered "intellectual property" in the customary sense because such compilation reflects only the expenditure of effort. The EC Database Directive provides protection of databases as a *sui generis* right distinct from interests protected by copyright.[104] The U.S. Supreme Court has denied copyright protection to non-creative databases. Yet such databases might be protectable to some extent by unfair competition law, and the question arises whether an interest in a database protected by unfair competition law might be considered an intellectual property right. Since non-creative databases are not the subject of Sections 1 through 7 of Part II of TRIPS, it seems that they should not be considered, for the purpose of the Agreement, "intellectual property", even if they may be protected by unfair competition law.[105]

The incorporation of provisions of the WIPO conventions also raises interpretative issues regarding the categories of intellectual property covered by TRIPS. For example, Article 2.1 provides that Members shall comply with Articles 1 through 12 and 19 of the Paris Convention (in respect of Parts II, III and IV, TRIPS Agreement). TRIPS thus incorporates a definition of "industrial property" in Article 1, Paris Convention, which plays an uncertain role in respect both to interpretation of the Paris Convention and TRIPS.[106] According to the WTO Appellate Body (see discussion of *Havana Club* case, Section 4 below), even though trade names are not expressly addressed by any "category" of Sections 1 through 7, Part II, the TRIPS Agreement covers them because it incorporates an obligation to comply with Article 8, Paris Convention.[107]

Sections 1 through 7 of Part II of TRIPS are drafted with a moderate degree of specificity concerning the subject matter of intellectual property protection, and the application of TRIPS to some subject matter areas is fairly clear. However, Sections 1 through 7 are not uniformly precise, and Article 1.1 grants discretion to Members regarding the way in which subject matter may be protected. Members have some discretion in determining what types of legal entitlements will

---

[103] For details, see Chapter 9. Note that TRIPS does not provide any definition of what constitutes an "intellectual creation" within the meaning of Article 10.2.

[104] Under the EC Directive, such protection is granted in addition to, but independent of, copyright protection. For details on the EC Database Directive, see Chapter 9, Section 6.3 (regional contexts).

[105] On the other hand, as noted above, databases that do constitute an intellectual creation are covered by Article 10.2, TRIPS Agreement and therefore qualify as "intellectual property" within the meaning of Article 1.2.

[106] To illustrate the potential interpretative issues, Article 1(3), Paris Convention, states that:
"Industrial property shall be understood in the broadest sense and shall apply not only to industry and commerce proper, but likewise to agricultural and extractive industries and to all manufactured or natural products, for example, wines, grain, tobacco leaf, fruit, cattle, minerals, mineral waters, beer, flowers, and flour."
If this definition were considered in connection with Article 27:2–3, TRIPS Agreement, it might be argued to inform the types of exclusions from patentability that could be adopted. It seems doubtful that such a role for Article 1(3), Paris Convention, was intended.

[107] In Section 6.4 below (proposals for review), the situation regarding traditional knowledge (TK) and folklore, as matters presumably outside the scope of the existing categories of intellectual property, is briefly examined. For more details, see Chapter 21.

be considered "intellectual property" and will ultimately determine the scope of "intellectual property" within their own legal systems and practice.

3.2 Article 2, TRIPS Agreement and other cross-referencing provisions

---

Article 2

1. In respect of Parts II, III and IV of this Agreement, Members shall comply with Articles 1 through 12, and Article 19, of the Paris Convention (1967).

2. Nothing in Parts I to IV of this Agreement shall derogate from existing obligations that Members may have to each other under the Paris Convention, the Berne Convention, the Rome Convention and the Treaty on Intellectual Property in Respect of Integrated Circuits.

The web of relationships between TRIPS and the various WIPO conventions is complex. It is established by a number of TRIPS provisions, including but not limited to Article 2.[108] The provisions of each category of intellectual property refer directly or indirectly to one or more of the WIPO conventions. Details concerning the relationships between the sets of norms are better dealt with in those chapters that address specific intellectual property subject matter. However, some general observations may be made here.

Article 2.1 provides that Members "shall comply" with Articles 1 through 12 and 19, Paris Convention, in respect to Parts II, III and IV.[109] The obligation to comply with the relevant Paris Convention provisions thus applies in respect to the substantive standards relating to the categories of intellectual property, to the enforcement of intellectual property rights, and to the mechanisms for acquiring those rights.[110]

---

[108] Footnote 2 to Article 1.3, TRIPS Agreement, as quoted above (Section 1), describes the particular version of the relevant WIPO convention to which the other provisions refer. This is necessary because the WIPO conventions are typically subject to revisions that may not be accepted by all parties to the prior version in force. In some cases, WTO Members may be parties to different revisions of the WIPO conventions. In fact, there are few instances in which Members are not parties to the versions referenced in Article 1.2, TRIPS Agreement. Article 1.3, TRIPS Agreement, also establishes rules regarding how nationals of Members are defined, in accordance with various agreements administered by WIPO.

[109] Part II, TRIPS Agreement, addresses "Standards Concerning the Availability, Scope and Use of Intellectual Property Rights", Part III deals with "Enforcement of Intellectual Property Rights", and Part IV concerns "Acquisition and Maintenance of Intellectual Property Rights and Related *Inter-Partes* Procedures".

[110] Articles 1 through 12 and 19, Paris Convention, include rules regarding the basic national treatment obligation (Article 2), filing and priority rules for patents, utility models, industrial designs and trademarks (Article 4), independence of patents (Article 4bis), compulsory licensing (Article 5), protection of industrial designs (Article 5quinquies), registration and independence of trademarks (Article 6), well known marks (Article 6bis), service marks (Article 6sexies), trade names (Article 8), seizure of trademark or trade name infringing imports (Article 9), unfair competition (Article 10bis), right to enforce trademark, trade name and unfair competition in national law (Article 10ter), establishment of intellectual property offices (Article 12), and right to make special agreements (Article 19).

The parts of TRIPS not subject to Paris Convention compliance obligations relate to the general provisions and basic principles, dispute settlement, transitional arrangements and institutional arrangements.[111]

There is some ambiguity as to whether by obligating Members to "comply", Article 2.1 is subjecting TRIPS to the provisions of the Paris Convention. The ordinary meaning of "comply" is to conform or obey.[112]

The Vienna Convention on the Law of Treaties provides at Article 30:

> "1. [...]
>
> 2. When a treaty specifies that it is subject to, or that it is not to be considered as incompatible with, an earlier or later treaty, the provisions of that other treaty prevail.
>
> 3. When all the parties to the earlier treaty are parties also to the later treaty but the earlier treaty is not terminated or suspended in operation under article 59, the earlier treaty applies only to the extent that its provisions are compatible with those of the latter treaty."

TRIPS does not provide a general hierarchy of norms as between its rules and those of the Paris Convention. The directive that WTO Members should "comply" with relevant provisions of the Paris Convention may imply that Paris Convention rules should take priority in the event of a conflict in the sense of Article 30(2), VCLT. The alternative under Article 30(3), VCLT, that TRIPS should be considered a later in time treaty the provisions of which prevail over the Paris Convention does not appear satisfactory because of the specific incorporation of Paris Convention provisions, the obligation to "comply" with them, and the lack of express indication that Paris Convention rules are intended to be superseded by TRIPS. However, Article 2.2 needs to be considered. Article 2.2 provides:

> "Nothing in Parts I to IV of this Agreement shall derogate from existing obligations that Members may have to each other under the Paris Convention, the Berne Convention, the Rome Convention and the Treaty on Intellectual Property in Respect of Integrated Circuits."

By stating that nothing in Parts I to IV "shall derogate from existing obligations" under the Paris Convention, Article 2.2 might imply that TRIPS provisions may derogate from existing "rights" (but not obligations) under the Paris Convention. On the other hand, the Article 2.2 text might only be an affirmation that TRIPS was not intended to affect specific entitlements that private right holders may have obtained by virtue of operation of the Paris Convention, and not be intended to more generally address the hierarchy of norms. There was no draft text of Article 2.2 prior to the Brussels Draft, and the negotiating history offers little in the way of guidance regarding the drafters' intent.

---

[111] Part I, TRIPS Agreement, addresses "General Provisions and Basic Principles", Part V addresses "Dispute Prevention and Settlement", Part VI addresses "Transitional Arrangements" and Part VII addresses "Institutional Arrangements; Final Provisions".

[112] The New Oxford Shorter English dictionary defines "comply" as "1. fulfill, accomplish" and "5. act in accordance with ... "

Provisions of the Paris Convention are referenced elsewhere in TRIPS in different ways to accomplish different results. For example, Article 16.2–3, TRIPS Agreement, applies Article 6*bis*, Paris Convention, regarding well known trademarks to service marks, and modifies its application to goods and services, using a *mutatis mutandis* formula. Article 22.2(b), TRIPS Agreement, regarding geographical indications of origin incorporates Article 10*bis*, Paris Convention, regarding unfair competition as one of its basic standards of protection. Article 39.1, TRIPS Agreement, refers to Article 10*bis*, Paris Convention, as the basis for providing protection for undisclosed information, stating that the specific rules in Article 39.2–3 apply "In the course of ensuring effective protection . . . as provided in Article 10*bis*". Each of these formulas may have different legal consequences.

The formula for incorporation of Berne Convention rules is similar to that used for the Paris Convention, and is found at Article 9.1, TRIPS Agreement:

> "Members shall comply with Articles 1 through 21 of the Berne Convention (1971) and the Appendix thereto. However, Members shall not have rights or obligations under this Agreement in respect of the rights conferred under Article 6bis of that Convention or of the rights derived therefrom."[113]

The methods by which provisions of other WIPO conventions are incorporated vary. For example, certain conditions, limitations and exceptions permitted by the Rome Convention are incorporated in Article 14, TRIPS Agreement (regarding performance and broadcast rights), by reference to the Rome Convention as a whole. Article 35, TRIPS, incorporates specific articles and paragraphs of the Treaty on Intellectual Property in Respect of Integrated Circuits (IPIC Treaty) and refers to additional rules of Articles 36–38, TRIPS Agreement.

The Berne, Rome and IPIC Conventions are all subject to Article 2.2, so that Members shall not derogate from existing obligations under those Conventions. Just as with respect to the Paris Convention, derogation from existing "rights" under the Paris, Rome and IPIC are not referenced, but this may not imply a general hierarchy that differentiates as between rights and obligations.

All or virtually all Members of the WTO are also parties to the Paris and Berne Conventions. As regards these two Conventions, Article 2.2 effectively states a rule of general application as among all WTO Members.[114] The Rome Convention has limited membership (77 members as of July 15, 2004[115]) and the IPIC Convention (as of August 2004) has not entered into force.[116] The obligation not to derogate

---

[113] The specific provisions of the Berne Convention for which a compliance obligation is established are elaborated in Chapters 7–13. Articles 1 through 21, Berne Convention, however, encompass all the substantive provisions regarding copyright subject matter. The Appendix establishes special provisions in favour of developing countries. The articles that are not referenced concern institutional arrangements. Article 6*bis*, which is excluded by operation of the second sentence, establishes certain moral rights in favour of authors and artists.

[114] It is conceivable that a state first acceding to the WTO and TRIPS Agreement, and later joining one of the four listed Conventions, might be argued not to fall within the terms of Article 2.2, TRIPS Agreement because its other obligations were not "existing" when it acceded to the WTO or TRIPS Agreement. The prospects of this situation arising, with meaningful consequences attached, appears sufficiently remote as not to warrant treatment here.

[115] See <http://www.wipo.int/treaties/en/documents/pdf/k-rome.pdf>.

[116] For more details on the IPIC Convention, see Chapter 27.

from existing obligations applies only among parties to the relevant agreements. In this respect, Article 2.2 differs from Article 2.1: the obligation under the first paragraph to comply with certain obligations under the Paris Convention extends even to those WTO Members that are not parties to the Paris Convention. The same approach applies to Articles 1–21 of the Berne Convention and its Appendix (see Article 9.1, TRIPS, as quoted above) and Articles 2–7 (except Article 6.3), Article 12 and 16.3 of the IPIC Treaty (see Article 35, TRIPS). With respect to the Rome Convention, TRIPS does not contain a comparable reference to non-WTO obligations. As stated above, Article 14.6, TRIPS, declares certain *exceptions* to copyright as permitted by the Rome Convention to be applicable in the TRIPS context.[117] But there is no such reference to any *obligations* under the Rome Convention. Note that in this respect, one proposal under the Anell Draft sought to include a reference to the Rome Convention in the predecessor to Article 2.1 (see above, Section 2.2). This would have rendered the Rome obligations generally mandatory for all WTO Members.

As opposed to the mandatory extension of non-WTO obligations to all WTO Members under the first paragraph of Article 2, the second paragraph of the same Article applies only between those Members that are parties to the enumerated agreements. The purpose of this provision is to make sure that parties to these agreements do not take TRIPS as an excuse to no longer respect their non-WTO commitments where those go beyond the TRIPS minimum standards. In *EC-Bananas*, the arbitration award concerning, *inter alia*, the level of suspension of concessions applied to the EC, also referred to Article 2.2. In this respect, the arbitrators said:

> "This provision can be understood to refer to the obligations that the contracting parties of the Paris, Berne and Rome Conventions and the IPIC Treaty, who are also WTO Members, have between themselves under these four treaties. This would mean that, by virtue of the conclusion of the WTO Agreement, e.g. Berne Union members cannot derogate from existing obligations between each other under the Berne Convention. For example, the fact that Article 9.1 of the TRIPS Agreement incorporates into that Agreement Articles 1–21 of the Berne Convention with the exception of Article 6bis does not mean that Berne Union members would henceforth be exonerated from this obligation to guarantee moral rights under the Berne Convention."[118]

In the final analysis, the relationship between TRIPS, the Paris Convention and the other WIPO conventions may require the development of treaty jurisprudence specific to this set of circumstances in which the various sets of rules appear to "inform" each other.

---

[117] Article 14.6, TRIPS Agreement reads in relevant part: "Any Member may, in relation to the rights conferred under paragraphs 1, 2 and 3, provide for conditions, limitations, exceptions and reservations to the extent permitted by the Rome Convention."

[118] See *European Communities – Regime for the Importation, Sale and Distribution of Bananas – Recourse to Arbitration by the European Communities under Article 22.6 of the DSU* – Decision by the Arbitrators, WT/DS27/ARB/ECU, at para. 149. For the development implications of the dispute settlement system in general and the *EC-Bananas* case in particular, see Chapter 32, Section 7.

3.3 State practice

One of the most important issues raised in regard to the relationship between TRIPS and WIPO conventions is the extent to which "state practice" under the WIPO conventions will be considered relevant to interpretation of TRIPS. Article 31(3)(b), VCLT, provides that together with the context, the following should be taken into account in the process of treaty interpretation:

> "(b) any subsequent practice in the application of the treaty which establishes the agreement of the parties regarding its interpretation."

The Paris and Berne Conventions have been in force for more than a century and a great deal of state practice under these conventions has accumulated. An argument in favour of taking such state practice into account in interpreting TRIPS is that such practice provides a substantial amount of legal texture or context to otherwise general terms. Moreover, by adopting the rules of these Conventions, TRIPS negotiators signalled that they were not intending to make a sharp break with pre-existing intellectual property legal development, albeit they did choose to modify various rules. Finally, the Paris and Berne Conventions were subject to fairly wide adherence by WTO Members even prior to conclusion of TRIPS.

On the other hand, a number of WTO Members were not parties to the Paris and Berne Conventions for much of the historical evolution of these treaties. A number of developing and least-developed WTO Members were subject to foreign rule for a good part of the period during which the Paris and Berne Conventions were evolving. The developing and least-developed Members might argue in favour of being allowed to develop their own state practice before the practices of developed Members are used to interpret TRIPS.

The VCLT rule on the use of state practice as an interpretative source does not directly address the issue whether prior practice applies to later adherents to the treaty. Under ordinary circumstances, it might be assumed that prior state practice will be taken into account since the meaning of a treaty develops over time as its parties implement it, and thereby agree on its interpretation. Each party joining the treaty would not expect to find a "blank slate" on which no prior state practice was written.

The question may well be asked, however, whether the TRIPS Agreement relationship to the Paris and Berne Conventions involves a unique situation that should lead treaty interpreters to develop a particularized jurisprudence to address this case. At a point in time, a substantial group of countries that was not party to the Paris and Berne Conventions accepted the application of the rules of those Conventions in the new TRIPS context. The object and purpose of TRIPS is different from the object and purpose of the WIPO conventions. The first has as its object and purpose the prevention of trade distortions attributable to intellectual property rules (i.e., under- and over-protection of IPRs). The latter have the purpose of promoting the protection of intellectual property. Only taken together with TRIPS can the WIPO conventions be understood in the TRIPS context. State practice under the WIPO conventions prior to application of TRIPS Agreement rules may have some relevance in the TRIPS interpretative process, but not without a second lens through which prior WIPO state practice is viewed.

State practice is always evolving, and the practices of developing and least-developed WTO Members subsequent to application of TRIPS Agreement rules will also inform interpretation of the Paris and Berne Convention rules.

In a number of instances TRIPS either supplements[119] or modifies[120] the terms of the WIPO conventions. In such cases, prior state practice under the WIPO conventions would only be relevant to the extent that TRIPS does not set out to modify that state practice.

4. WTO jurisprudence

4.1 Havana Club

The subject matter scope of TRIPS, including its relationship to the WIPO Conventions, is considered in some detail by the WTO Appellate Body (AB) in the *United States – Section 211 Omnibus Appropriations Act of 1998* ("*Havana Club*")[121] case.

The panel in the *Havana Club* case decided that trade names were not "intellectual property" within the meaning of Article 1.2 because they were not a "category" of Sections 1 through 7, Part II.[122] The panel said:

> "We interpret the terms 'intellectual property' and 'intellectual property rights' with reference to the definition of 'intellectual property' in Article 1.2 of the TRIPS Agreement. The textual reading of Article 1.2 is that it establishes an inclusive definition and this is confirmed by the words 'all categories'; the word 'all' indicates that this is an exhaustive list. Thus, for example, the national and most-favoured-nation treatment obligations contained in Articles 3 and 4 of the TRIPS Agreement that refer to the 'protection of intellectual property' would be interpreted to mean the categories covered by Article 1.2 of the TRIPS Agreement. We consider the correct interpretation to be that there are no obligations under those Articles in relation to categories of intellectual property not set forth in Article 1.2, e.g., trade names, consistent with Article 31 of the Vienna Convention." (para. 8.26)

The panel went on to consider whether Article 2.1, by incorporating Article 8, Paris Convention (obligating parties to provide trade name protection), brought trade names within the scope of intellectual property covered by the agreement. The panel reasoned that since Article 2.1 provided that the referenced Paris Convention articles were to be complied with "in respect of" Parts II, III and IV of TRIPS, and since those parts did not refer to trade names, Article 8, Paris Convention did not add obligations regarding trade names. The panel referred to negotiating history

---

[119] For example, Article 10.1, TRIPS Agreement, provides that computer programs are protected by copyright. Prior state practice under the Berne Convention had accepted this view prior to conclusion of the TRIPS Agreement, so this article supplements the Convention by confirming that practice.

[120] For example, Article 16.2, TRIPS Agreement, provides new rules regarding the meaning of well-known trademarks which arguably modify Article 6*bis*, Paris Convention. To the extent that Article 16.2, TRIPS Agreement, creates new rules, prior state practice under Article 6*bis*, Paris Convention, would not be relevant to its interpretation.

[121] AB-2001-7, WT/DS176/AB/R, Report of the Appellate Body, 2 Jan. 2002.

[122] *United States – Section 211 Omnibus Appropriations Act of 1998*, WT/DS176/R, Report of the Panel, 6 Aug. 2001.

to confirm its conclusion, though the references are somewhat tangential to its reasoning.

The AB disagreed with the panel. It said:

"333. We disagree with the Panel's reasoning and with the Panel's conclusion on the scope of the *TRIPS Agreement* as it relates to trade names.

334. To explain, we turn first to the Panel's interpretation of Article 1.2 of the *TRIPS Agreement*, which, we recall, provides:

For the purposes of this Agreement, the term 'intellectual property' refers to all categories of intellectual property that are the subject of Sections 1 through 7 of Part II.

335. The Panel interpreted the phrase ' "intellectual property" refers to all categories of intellectual property that are the *subject* of Sections 1 through 7 of Part II' (emphasis added) as if that phrase read 'intellectual property means those categories of intellectual property appearing in the *titles* of Sections 1 through 7 of Part II.' To our mind, the Panel's interpretation ignores the plain words of Article 1.2, for it fails to take into account that the phrase 'the subject of Sections 1 through 7 of Part II' deals not only with the categories of intellectual property indicated in each section *title*, but with other *subjects* as well. For example, in Section 5 of Part II, entitled 'Patents', Article 27(3)(b) provides that Members have the option of protecting inventions of plant varieties by *sui generis* rights (such as breeder's rights) instead of through patents. Under the Panel's theory, such *sui generic* rights would not be covered by the *TRIPS Agreement*. The option provided by Article 27(3)(b) would be read out of the *TRIPS Agreement*.

336. Moreover, we do not believe that the Panel's interpretation of Article 1.2 can be reconciled with the plain words of Article 2.1. Article 2.1 explicitly incorporates Article 8 of the Paris Convention (1967) into the *TRIPS Agreement*.

337. The Panel was of the view that the words 'in respect of' in Article 2.1 have the effect of 'conditioning' Members' obligations under the Articles of the Paris Convention (1967) incorporated into the *TRIPS Agreement*, with the result that trade names are not covered. We disagree.

338. Article 8 of the Paris Convention (1967) covers only the protection of trade names; Article 8 has no other subject. If the intention of the negotiators had been to exclude trade names from protection, there would have been no purpose whatsoever in including Article 8 in the list of Paris Convention (1967) provisions that were specifically incorporated into the *TRIPS Agreement*. To adopt the Panel's approach would be to deprive Article 8 of the Paris Convention (1967), as incorporated into the *TRIPS Agreement* by virtue of Article 2.1 of that Agreement, of any and all meaning and effect. As we have stated previously:

One of the corollaries of the "general rule of interpretation" in the *Vienna Convention* is that interpretation must give meaning and effect to all the terms of a treaty. An interpreter is not free to adopt a reading that would result in reducing whole clauses or paragraphs of a treaty to redundancy or inutility.

339. As for the import of the negotiating history, we do not see it as in any way decisive to the issue before us. The documents on which the Panel relied are not conclusive of whether the *TRIPS Agreement* covers trade names. The passages

quoted by the Panel from the negotiating history of Article 1.2 do not even refer to trade names. There is nothing at all in those passages to suggest that Members were either for or against their inclusion. Indeed, the only reference to a debate about the categories for coverage in the *TRIPS Agreement* relates, not to trade names, but to trade secrets. The Panel itself acknowledged that '[t]he records do not contain information on the purpose of the addition' of the words 'in respect of' at the beginning of Article 2.1. Therefore, we do not consider that any conclusions may be drawn from these records about the interpretation of the words 'in respect of' in Article 2.1 as regards trade names.

340. Thus, in our view, the Panel's interpretation of Articles 1.2 and 2.1 of the *TRIPS Agreement* is contrary to the ordinary meaning of the terms of those provisions and is, therefore, not in accordance with the customary rules of interpretation prescribed in Article 31 of the *Vienna Convention*. Moreover, we do not believe that the negotiating history confirms, within the meaning of Article 32 of the *Vienna Convention*, the Panel's interpretation of Articles 1.2 and 2.1.

341. For all these reasons, we reverse the Panel's finding in paragraph 8.41 of the Panel Report that trade names are not covered under the *TRIPS Agreement* and find that WTO Members do have an obligation under the *TRIPS Agreement* to provide protection to trade names." [footnotes omitted, italics in the original]

The AB's analysis confirms the view that the broad subject matter headings of Sections 1 through 7, Part II, do not strictly limit the subject matter scope of "intellectual property". This does not mean that the subject matter of "intellectual property" is unlimited. In the case of trade names, they are covered subject matter because they are specifically incorporated by Article 8, Paris Convention. Nonetheless, to some extent the AB has adopted a broader rather than narrower view of the interpretation of "intellectual property" in Article 1.2.

In *Havana Club*, the AB also explained the legal relationship between TRIPS and the Paris Convention. There is nothing surprising about this explanation but, as it comes from the AB, it is worth setting out.

"123. Article *6quinquies* [the 'as is' or 'telle quelle' rule regarding trademarks] forms part of the Stockholm Act of the Paris Convention, dated 14 July 1967. The Stockholm Act is a revision of the original *Paris Convention for the Protection of Industrial Property*, which entered into force on 7 July 1884. The parties to the Paris Convention, who are commonly described as the 'countries of the Paris Union', are obliged to implement the provisions of that Convention.

124. Article 2.1 of the *TRIPS Agreement* provides that: '[i]n respect of Parts II, III and IV of this Agreement, Members shall comply with Articles 1 through 12, and Article 19, of the Paris Convention (1967).' Thus, Article *6quinquies* of the Paris Convention (1967), as well as certain other specified provisions of the Paris Convention (1967), have been incorporated by reference into the *TRIPS Agreement* and, thus, the *WTO Agreement*.

125. Consequently, WTO Members, whether they are countries of the Paris Union or not, are obliged, under the *WTO Agreement*, to implement those provisions of the Paris Convention (1967) that are incorporated into the *TRIPS Agreement*. As

we have already stated, Article *6quinquies* of the Paris Convention (1967) is one such provision."

4.2 EC – Bananas
For the interpretation of Article 2.2 in this case see above, Section 3.

5. Relationship with other international instruments

5.1 WTO agreements
The general question of the proper interpretation of terms such as "intellectual property" is common to all WTO Agreements. The term "intellectual property" is unique in the sense that it is the subject of an extensive history of regulation by multilateral instruments outside the WTO context. There are analogies, nonetheless, in terms such as "national treatment" that were used in various treaty contexts (including in the Paris and Berne Conventions) well before the GATT 1947.

The determination of the subject matter scope of "intellectual property" under Article 1.2 might be relevant to other WTO agreements in the sense that subject matter not covered by TRIPS might be principally regulated by another WTO agreement.

The extensive incorporation and cross-referencing of TRIPS to the WIPO conventions is distinctive to TRIPS (among the WTO agreements).

5.2 Other international instruments
While TRIPS incorporates and cross-references WIPO conventions, the WIPO conventions do not in their text incorporate or cross-reference the TRIPS Agreement. However, the 1996 WIPO Copyright Treaty[123] includes a number of "Agreed Statements", and among these are three that refer to TRIPS.[124] In each case, the presumed objective of the agreed statement is to clarify that the rules adopted at WIPO are consistent with the rules of TRIPS. However, the language used to express this consistency does little to resolve ambiguity.

As example, Article 4, WIPO Copyright Treaty and Article 10.1, TRIPS Agreement, each provide that computer software is protected by copyright, but the agreements describe the subject matter of "computer programs" differently. The WIPO definition is framed more broadly ("whatever may be the mode or form

---

[123] Adopted in Geneva on 20 December 1996. The treaty is available at <http://www.wipo.int/clea/docs/en/wo/wo033en.htm>.

[124] These agreed statements are as follows:

"Agreed statements concerning Article 4: The scope of protection for computer programs under Article 4 of this Treaty, read with Article 2, is consistent with Article 2 of the Berne Convention and on a par with the relevant provisions of the TRIPS Agreement."

"Agreed statements concerning Article 5: The scope of protection for compilations of data (databases) under Article 5 of this Treaty, read with Article 2, is consistent with Article 2 of the Berne Convention and on a par with the relevant provisions of the TRIPS Agreement."

"Agreed statements concerning Article 7: It is understood that the obligation under Article 7(1) does not require a Contracting Party to provide an exclusive right of commercial rental to authors who, under that Contracting Party's law, are not granted rights in respect of phonograms. It is understood that this obligation is consistent with Article 14(4) of the TRIPS Agreement."

of their expression"), apparently providing a greater scope for the evolution of technologies that may eventually make obsolete the TRIPS Agreement reference ("whether in source or object code"). The agreed statement to Article 4, WIPO Copyright Treaty provides that the "scope of protection" under the WIPO Copyright Treaty (and the Berne Convention) is "on a par with the relevant provisions of the TRIPS Agreement". This might be interpreted to mean that the WIPO rule does not cover evolutionary technologies otherwise not captured within the TRIPS Agreement reference to source or object code, thereby leaving any adjustments based on technological evolution in the hands of the WTO.

In addition to these recently adopted cross-references in the WIPO Copyright Treaty, there is a close and ongoing working relationship established between the TRIPS Council and WIPO. WIPO has been delegated the tasks of receiving notifications of WTO Member intellectual property laws, and of providing assistance to Members in the preparation of TRIPS-compliant legislation. In addition, WTO Members pay close attention to rule-making activities at WIPO that may affect their rights and obligations under TRIPS. These latter relationships between WIPO and the WTO are considered later in this book in the context of the Council for TRIPS.[125]

6. New developments

6.1 National laws

6.2 International instruments

6.2.1 The Convention on Biological Diversity

TRIPS does not incorporate or cross-reference the Convention on Biological Diversity (CBD),[126] adopted prior to its conclusion (i.e. in 1992). Following proposals on this subject by a number of developing Members, WTO Ministers at the Doha Ministerial agreed that the Council for TRIPS should examine the relationship between the TRIPS Agreement and the CBD. Ministers instructed the Council for TRIPS,

> "in pursuing its work programme including under the review of Article 27.3(b), the review of the implementation of the TRIPS Agreement under Article 71.1 and the work foreseen pursuant to paragraph 12 of this Declaration, to examine, *inter alia*, the relationship between the TRIPS Agreement and the Convention on Biological Diversity, the protection of traditional knowledge and folklore, and other relevant new developments raised by Members pursuant to Article 71.1. In undertaking this work, the TRIPS Council shall be guided by the objectives and principles set out in Articles 7 and 8 of the TRIPS Agreement and shall take fully into account the development dimension."[127]

---

[125] See Section 3 of Chapter 35.

[126] The English text of the Convention is available at <http://www.biodiv.org/doc/legal/cbd-en.pdf>.

[127] See the Ministerial Declaration of 14 November 2001, WT/MIN(01)/DEC/W/1, paragraph 19.

Substantive aspects of the TRIPS-CBD relationship are discussed later in this book.[128] Since this work programme is at its initial stages, it is premature to indicate the legal mechanism by which the CBD ultimately may be incorporated or cross-referenced by the TRIPS Agreement.

6.2.2 WIPO patent and trademark activities

WIPO has initiated a significant set of activities (the WIPO Patent Agenda) regarding the international patent system with the objective of determining whether amendments or supplements to existing patent rules would be necessary or useful. This project might lead to proposals for revision of the Patent Cooperation Treaty (PCT).[129] Perhaps more likely such changes would be proposed as a new agreement concerning the approximation or harmonization of substantive patent law. Whatever form such developments in the field of patents might take, they will have implications for the TRIPS Agreement, potentially of a far reaching nature. There are Standing Committees on the Law of Patents and Trademarks at WIPO, each of which is considering the proposal of new substantive rules. It is premature at this stage to offer concrete observation on how the results of these work programmes might be integrated, either formally or informally, with TRIPS.

6.3 Regional and bilateral contexts

6.3.1 Regional

The European Court of Justice (ECJ) directly addressed interpretation of "intellectual property" in Article 1.2 in its *Parfums Christian Dior* decision.[130] It was called upon to decide whether EU member state (national) legislation that protects industrial designs through general civil "unlawful competition" rules is within the scope of Article 50 that applies to "intellectual property rights". Only if the unlawful competition rules establish an "intellectual property right" would the enforcement rules of TRIPS (in this case, Article 50.1) be applicable in the member state court. The ECJ held that "industrial design" protection was clearly a category of "intellectual property" because it is enumerated as such in Section 4, Part II, and that it was for WTO Members to decide what national rules would be used to protect that intellectual property (and so establish an "intellectual property right") in the context of implementing TRIPS in their own legal systems (in the sense of Article 1.1, TRIPS). It said:

> "Interpretation of the term 'intellectual property right'
>
> 50. The third question in Case C-392/98 is designed to ascertain whether the right to sue under general provisions of national law concerning wrongful acts, in particular unlawful competition, in order to protect an industrial design against

---

[128] For details on the various proposals submitted in this respect to the Council for TRIPS see Chapter 21, Section 3.5.

[129] See Correa and Musungu, *The WIPO Patent Agenda: The Risks for Developing Countries*, Working Paper no. 12, South Centre, 2002.

[130] See joined cases C-300/98 and C-392/98 *Parfums Christian Dior SA and Tuk Consultancy BV*, [2000] ECR I-11307. On this decision, see also Chapter 2, Section 6.3.

copying is to be classified as an 'intellectual property right' within the meaning of Article 50(1) of TRIPs.

51. Thus defined, the question falls into two parts. The first issue is whether an industrial design, such as that in question in the main proceedings, falls within the scope of TRIPs. If it does, it must then be determined whether the right to sue under general provisions of national law, such as those relied on in the main proceedings, in order to protect a design against copying constitutes an "intellectual property right" within the meaning of Article 50 of TRIPs.

52. As regards the first issue, the national court has correctly pointed out that, according to Article 1(2) of TRIPs, the term 'intellectual property' in Article 50 refers to all categories of intellectual property that are the subject of Sections 1 to 7 of Part II of that agreement. Section 4 concerns "industrial designs".

53. Article 25 sets out the conditions for protection of an industrial design under TRIPs. Article 26 concerns the nature of the protection, possible exceptions and the duration of the protection.

54. It is for the national court to determine whether the industrial design at issue in the main proceedings satisfies the requirements laid down in Article 25.

55. As to the second issue, TRIPs contains no express definition of what constitutes an 'intellectual property right' for the purpose of that agreement. It is therefore necessary to interpret this term, which appears many times in the preamble and in the main body of TRIPs, in its context and in the light of its objectives and purpose.

56. According to the first recital in its preamble, the objectives of TRIPs are to 'reduce distortions and impediments to international trade, . . . taking into account the need to promote effective and adequate protection of intellectual property rights, and to ensure that measures and procedures to enforce intellectual property rights do not themselves become barriers to legitimate trade'. In the second recital, the Contracting Parties recognise the need for new rules and disciplines concerning:

'(a) [. . .]

(b) the provision of adequate standards and principles concerning the availability, scope and use of trade-related intellectual property rights;

(c) the provision of effective and appropriate means for the enforcement of trade-related intellectual property rights, taking into account differences in national legal systems;

[. . .]'

57. In the third and fourth recitals, the Contracting Parties recognise 'the need for a multilateral framework of principles, rules and disciplines dealing with international trade in counterfeit goods and the fact that 'intellectual property rights are private rights'.

58. Article 1(1), concerning the 'nature and scope of obligations', provides that members are to be free to determine the appropriate method of implementing the provisions of TRIPs within their own legal system and practice.

59. Article 62, which constitutes Part IV of TRIPs, entitled 'Acquisition and maintenance of intellectual property rights and related *inter partes* procedures', provides in the first and second paragraphs that the Contracting Parties may make the

acquisition or maintenance of intellectual property rights conditional on compliance with reasonable procedures and formalities, including procedures for grant or registration. Such procedures are not, however, an essential requirement for the acquisition or maintenance of an intellectual property right within the meaning of TRIPs.

60. It is apparent from the foregoing provisions as a whole that TRIPs leaves to the Contracting Parties, within the framework of their own legal systems and in particular their rules of private law, the task of specifying in detail the interests which will be protected under TRIPs as 'intellectual property rights' and the method of protection, provided always, first, that the protection is effective, particularly in preventing trade in counterfeit goods and, second, that it does not lead to distortions of or impediments to international trade.

61. Legal proceedings to prevent alleged copying of an industrial design may serve to prevent trade in counterfeit goods and may also impede international trade.

62. It follows that a right to sue under general provisions of national law concerning wrongful acts, in particular unlawful competition, in order to protect an industrial design against copying may qualify as an 'intellectual property right' within the meaning of Article 50(1) of TRIPs.

63. It follows from all of the foregoing considerations that the answer to the third question in Case C-392/98 must be that Article 50 of TRIPs leaves to the Contracting Parties, within the framework of their own legal systems, the task of specifying whether the right to sue under general provisions of national law concerning wrongful acts, in particular unlawful competition, in order to protect an industrial design against copying is to be classified as an 'intellectual property right' within the meaning of Article 50(1) of TRIPs."

6.4 Proposals for review

A number of developing countries are pressing to expand the subject matter scope of TRIPS to include fields such as traditional knowledge (TK), folklore and related interests. In addition, a number of developing countries are pressing to expand the recognition by TRIPS of their interests in genetic resources. The latter question is related to negotiations concerning the relationship between TRIPS and the CBD (see above, Section 6.2).

TK such as medicinal uses of plant varieties is often considered not to fall within the existing "categories" of intellectual property protection. For example, such knowledge may have been known to some portion of the public and therefore not qualify for patent protection (because of the absence of novelty). Folklore has often been known within a culture for many years, and therefore may not be considered to be newly subject to copyright. If these kinds of interests are to be covered by TRIPS, it may be necessary to expand the categories of intellectual property, or at least expand the subject matter addressed by the existing categories.[131]

---

[131] For a detailed analysis of possible ways of protecting TK and folklore, see G. Dutfield, *Protecting Traditional Knowledge and Folklore – A review of progress in diplomacy and policy formulation*, UNCTAD-ICTSD, Geneva, June 2003. The paper is also available at <http://www.ictsd.org/pubs/ictsd_series/iprs/CS_dutfield.pdf>.

At the Doha Ministerial in November 2001, Ministers instructed the TRIPS Council to examine the protection of traditional knowledge and folklore (see above, Section 6.2).

As noted above, the TRIPS Council is considering the relationship between TRIPS and the CBD. There are no present proposals to review the categories of intellectual property covered by the TRIPS Agreement, or the relationship between TRIPS and the WIPO conventions.

7. Comments, including economic and social implications

It is not easy to generalize regarding the effects on developing countries of expanding or limiting the subject matters falling within the scope of TRIPS. Generally speaking, as the preponderance of intellectual property rights are held by developed country actors, the developing countries are economically disadvantaged by increased rent payments arising when such intellectual property falls within the scope of protection.[132] In this regard, an approach limiting the subject matter scope of intellectual property is favourable to developing country interests. However, the principal forms of intellectual property in which developed country persons have ownership interest already are within the scope of Article 1.2. The developing countries are already subject to broad subject matter coverage in fields of intellectual property where developed country ownership predominates.

The fields of traditional knowledge and folklore, and genetic resources, are ones in which developing countries have significant strength. The argument might well be made that developing countries have an interest in expanding the existing categories of intellectual property protection in TRIPS to cover such fields. However, there are risks to ventures such as this. Once the door is open to expanding TRIPS Agreement coverage, it may be difficult to limit the accretion of rights.

The TRIPS Agreement might have repeated the rules of the WIPO Conventions, rather than incorporating or cross-referencing them. Yet it is doubtful that the choice of incorporation or cross-reference in itself had significant implications for developing country interests. It is possible that by maintaining WIPO as a forum for the progressive development of intellectual property law, the developed countries left an avenue for ratcheting-up levels of protection in the absence of a WTO consensus. This, however, is more a question of institutional organization and competence than of the relationship among legal agreements.

---

[132] One of the arguments advanced by developed countries is that developing countries may have access to a larger pool of creative matter because their increased rent payments result in a higher level of investment in the developed countries. However, in the absence of providing intellectual property protection for creative activity undertaken in the developed countries, they would have access to the pool of creative matter from the developed countries, less whatever increment might be generated as a result of their own increased rent payments.

4: Basic Principles

Article 3   National Treatment

1. Each Member shall accord to the nationals of other Members treatment no less favourable than that it accords to its own nationals with regard to the protection* of intellectual property, subject to the exceptions already provided in, respectively, the Paris Convention (1967), the Berne Convention (1971), the Rome Convention or the Treaty on Intellectual Property in Respect of Integrated Circuits. In respect of performers, producers of phonograms and broadcasting organizations, this obligation only applies in respect of the rights provided under this Agreement. Any Member availing itself of the possibilities provided in Article 6 of the Berne Convention (1971) or paragraph 1(b) of Article 16 of the Rome Convention shall make a notification as foreseen in those provisions to the Council for TRIPS.

2. Members may avail themselves of the exceptions permitted under paragraph 1 in relation to judicial and administrative procedures, including the designation of an address for service or the appointment of an agent within the jurisdiction of a Member, only where such exceptions are necessary to secure compliance with laws and regulations which are not inconsistent with the provisions of this Agreement and where such practices are not applied in a manner which would constitute a disguised restriction on trade.

[Footnote]*: For the purposes of Articles 3 and 4, "protection" shall include matters affecting the availability, acquisition, scope, maintenance and enforcement of intellectual property rights as well as those matters affecting the use of intellectual property rights specifically addressed in this Agreement.

Article 4   Most-Favoured-Nation Treatment

With regard to the protection of intellectual property, any advantage, favour, privilege or immunity granted by a Member to the nationals of any other country shall be accorded immediately and unconditionally to the nationals of all other Members. Exempted from this obligation are any advantage, favour, privilege or immunity accorded by a Member:

(a) deriving from international agreements on judicial assistance or law enforcement of a general nature and not particularly confined to the protection of intellectual property;

(b) granted in accordance with the provisions of the Berne Convention (1971) or the Rome Convention authorizing that the treatment accorded be a function not of national treatment but of the treatment accorded in another country;

(c) in respect of the rights of performers, producers of phonograms and broadcasting organizations not provided under this Agreement;

(d) deriving from international agreements related to the protection of intellectual property which entered into force prior to the entry into force of the WTO Agreement, provided that such agreements are notified to the Council for TRIPS and do not constitute an arbitrary or unjustifiable discrimination against nationals of other Members.

Article 5   Multilateral Agreements on Acquisition or Maintenance of Protection

The obligations under Articles 3 and 4 do not apply to procedures provided in multilateral agreements concluded under the auspices of WIPO relating to the acquisition or maintenance of intellectual property rights.

---

1. Introduction: terminology, definition and scope

The national treatment and most favoured nation (MFN) principles have as their objective the creation of non-discriminatory international legal arrangements. The national treatment and MFN principles are cornerstones of the WTO legal system, including TRIPS. The national treatment principle is also at the core of the Paris and Berne Conventions.

1.1 National treatment

Briefly stated, the national treatment principle requires each WTO Member to treat nationals of other Members at least as well as it treats its own nationals in relation to the protection of intellectual property. National treatment obligations in TRIPS differ from the national treatment obligations established by Article III, GATT 1994. The GATT addresses trade in goods, and in that context national treatment requires non-discriminatory treatment of "like products", or tangible things. Intellectual property rights are held by persons (whether natural or juridical), and TRIPS Agreement national treatment rules require non-discriminatory treatment of persons. In this regard, the national treatment principle of the TRIPS Agreement is analogous to that of the General Agreement on Trade in Services (GATS) (Article XVII) which applies to service suppliers (that is, persons providing services). Note, however, that the GATS national treatment rules operate in a different manner than those of TRIPS.[133]

Application of the national treatment principle is not so straightforward. Much of GATT 1947 jurisprudence was devoted to refining national treatment rules, including ways to determine what constitutes a "like product". Dispute settlement under GATT 1994 continues to address complex national treatment questions in relation to trade in goods.

GATT-WTO jurisprudence has recognized two types of discrimination: *de jure* and *de facto*. When legal rules distinguish in their express terms between foreign and local nationals, this may constitute discrimination as a matter of law, or *de jure* discrimination (if the distinctions are not justified by non-discriminatory purposes). On the other hand, legal rules that use identical terms to address foreign and local nationals may appear neutral, but in fact produce discriminatory results through operation in practice. When facially neutral legal rules are discriminatory in effect, this is referred to as *de facto* discrimination. The TRIPS Agreement national treatment provisions encompass both *de jure* and *de facto* discrimination.

The national treatment principle is set out in TRIPS using a different legal formula than is used in the WIPO conventions (see Section 3.1.2, below). The national treatment provisions in the WIPO conventions are incorporated by reference in TRIPS. The differences are not great, and their practical significance is uncertain. There are several relatively complex exceptions from national treatment in the various WIPO conventions, and these are largely incorporated in TRIPS.

1.2 Most-favoured-nation treatment

The MFN principle requires each Member to treat nationals of all other Members on an equivalent basis in relation to intellectual property protection. The MFN principle was not traditionally incorporated in the WIPO Conventions. It was assumed that WIPO members would not grant intellectual property rights protection to foreign nationals more extensive than the protection granted to local nationals. In this setting, a national treatment obligation would place all foreigners on the same plane. As bilateral pressures mounted in the late 1980s to increase IPR protection, Uruguay Round negotiators became concerned that some countries were indeed granting IPR privileges to foreign nationals more extensive than the rights granted to their own nationals. This focused attention on incorporating an MFN principle in TRIPS, so that all Members would obtain an equivalent level of protection when more extensive protection was granted to foreigners.

The MFN principle in TRIPS is particularly important because of its relationship to regional integration arrangements. Article 4 was drafted in a manner that was intended to accommodate the interests of certain pre-existing regional arrangements. However, the legal formula used in Article 4 (d) to establish that accommodation is oddly suited to such a purpose (see Section 3.2, below). The regional arrangements affected by it have notified the Council for TRIPS of potentially

---

[133] Under the GATS a Member's national treatment obligations are defined by its Schedule of Commitments that may include exceptions and limitations on a sector by sector basis.

broad claims of exemption, though the effect of these claims in practice remains to be determined.

Articles 3, 4 and 5 were not subject to the transition arrangements in favour of developing country and least developed country Members, and so became applicable to them on January 1, 1996 (see Articles 65.2 and 66.1, TRIPS Agreement).[134]

2. History of the provision

2.1 Situation pre-TRIPS

The national treatment principle was incorporated in bilateral friendship and commerce agreements during the nineteenth century, prior to negotiation of the Paris and Berne Conventions.[135] The most favoured nation treatment principle appeared in trade agreements during the eighteenth century.[136] In the trade and investment context, these two principles provide the foundation for liberal market access by prohibiting discrimination against imports and investment from countries in whose favour they operate. In the intellectual property context, these principles promote market access in favour of foreigners by providing that their legal interests should be protected at least as well as nationals of the host country, and by attempting to assure an equality of protection among trade and investment partners.

National treatment and "unconditional" MFN treatment do not require the grant of equivalent rights or favours in exchange for non-discriminatory treatment.[137] However, it is possible to grant national treatment subject to exceptions,[138] and it is possible to place conditions on MFN treatment (such that a country may agree to provide equal treatment to all its trading partners, but only if those partners agree to match concessions it provides).

The concepts of national treatment and MFN may be usefully compared with the concept of "reciprocity". When legal relations are based on reciprocity, a state is expected to grant rights or favours only in exchange for rights or favours from other states. A privilege may be denied in the absence of equivalent or reciprocal treatment. There are a few provisions in the WIPO conventions that allow for

---

[134] For a detailed analysis of the TRIPS transitional periods, see Chapter 33.

[135] See, e.g. Belgian-American Diplomacy Treaty of Commerce and Navigation: November 10, 1845, at art. 1; Swiss-American Diplomacy Convention of Friendship, Commerce and Extradition Between the United States and Switzerland; November 25, 1850, at art. 1. http://www.yale.edu/lawweb/avalon/. National treatment provisions were also incorporated in bilateral copyright treaties pre-dating the Berne Convention. See Samuel Ricketson, The Birth of the Berne Union, THE CENTENARY OF THE BERNE CONVENTION, CONFERENCE (Intellectual Property Law Unit, Queen Mary College, University of London and British Literary and Artistic Copyright Association London, April 17–18, 1986).

[136] See, e.g., Treaty of Amity and Commerce Between The United States and France; February 6, 1778, at arts. 3 & 4. See also Convention to Regulate Commerce between the United States and Great Britain (1815), at Article 2; <http://www.yale.edu/lawweb/avalon/>.

[137] "Conditional MFN" means that a country accepts to provide equivalent treatment to each of its trading partners, provided that those trading partners agree to provide equivalent concessions to it ("reciprocity", see below). By way of contrast, it is one of the core elements of unconditional MFN and national treatment to operate on a non-reciprocity basis.

[138] As is done in the General Agreement on Trade in Services (GATS).

differential treatment of foreigners based on "material reciprocity".[139] It is of some interest that trade negotiating rounds in the GATT 1947 and WTO are conducted on the basis of reciprocity, while the results of those negotiations are embodied in agreements that operate on principles of non-discrimination.

2.2 Negotiating history

2.2.1 Overview of the initial U.S. and EC positions

The initial U.S. proposal for negotiation of a TRIPS Agreement did not explicitly discuss the national and MFN principles, although it did refer to examining the existing international agreements concerning the protection of intellectual property.[140] The first proposal from the EC regarding substantive standards, however, made significant reference to the national treatment and MFN principles.[141]

The EC proposal stated:

"6.(ii) Two fundamental principles are those of most favoured nation treatment and of national treatment. These GATT principles concern the treatment given to goods whereas an agreement on intellectual property rights would be concerned with the protection of the rights held by persons. Bearing this difference in mind, these principles should constitute essential elements of a GATT Agreement on trade related aspects of intellectual property rights.[142]

---

[139] For example, Article 7(8), Berne Convention, limits the term of copyright to that of the country of origin of the work, unless the country where protection is claimed authorizes longer protection. Article 14*ter*, Berne Convention, limits the obligation to protect "droit de suite" depending on the extent of protection in the artist's country of origin.

[140] Suggestion by the United States for Achieving the Negotiating Objective, United States Proposal for Negotiations on Trade-Related Aspects of Intellectual Property Rights, Negotiating Group on Trade-Related Aspects of Intellectual Property Rights, including Trade in Counterfeit Goods, MTN.GNG/NG11/W/14, 20 Oct. 1987, Nov. 3, 1987.

[141] Guidelines and Objectives Proposed by the European Community for the Negotiations on Trade Related Aspects of Substantive Standards of Intellectual Property Rights, Negotiating Group on Trade-Related Aspects of Intellectual Property Rights, including Trade in Counterfeit Goods, MTN.GNG/NG11/W/26, July 1988, at III.D.6.

[142] The EC proposal continued:

"– under the most favoured nation treatment principle, parties would be obliged to accord nationals and residents of other parties any advantage relating to the protection and enforcement of intellectual property rights granted to the nationals and residents of any other country.

It will however, be necessary to define certain implications and limitations of the MFN principle. In particular, advantages which accrue to a party by virtue of an intellectual property convention and which have not been incorporated in the GATT Agreement should only have to be granted to nationals or residents of signatories of such conventions. . . .

– the national treatment principle would require that nationals or residents of another signatory of the GATT Agreement should be granted protection which would not be less favourable that the one granted under like circumstances to nationals or residents of the importing country. This principle would not have to be granted with regard to aspects of protection exclusively based on an intellectual property rights convention to which the other party concerned had not adhered.

In applying these GATT principles, account must be taken of the fact that the Paris Convention for the Protection of Industrial Property and the Berne Convention for the Protection of Literary and Artistic Works also provide for the national treatment for nationals of signatories of those conventions. The application of these GATT principles should be without prejudice to the full application of this fundamental principle of the Paris and Berne Conventions." *Id*.

2.2.2 National treatment

2.2.2.1 The Anell Draft. The proposition to include a national treatment standard in TRIPS was not in itself contentious. Negotiations rather focused on more
detailed aspects of the mechanics of incorporation. It was noted, for example,
that the national treatment standard in the Paris Convention (Article 2(1) and
Article 3)[143] requires equivalent treatment for foreign nationals, and the Berne
Convention appears to do the same (Article 5(1) and (3)).[144] On the other hand,
the GATT Article III national treatment is based on a "no less favourable" standard,[145] implying that imported products may be treated preferably to local products. Some negotiators pointed out that adoption of a strict equivalent treatment
standard in TRIPS might eliminate the need for an MFN provision since each
member would be required to treat nationals of all Members the same.[146] However, it appears that most negotiators supported the formula used in the GATT
1947 that would allow preferential treatment of foreign nationals.[147]

There was discussion of the extent to which the national treatment principle
would extend to government regulation of the "use" of intellectual property, in addition to regulation of the grant and enforcement of rights.[148] This discussion was
inconclusive. Negotiators appeared to agree that the national treatment standard

---

[143] The Paris Convention provides in relevant part:

Article 2

(1) Nationals of any country of the Union shall, as regards the protection of industrial property,
enjoy in all the other countries of the Union the advantages that their respective laws now grant, or
may hereafter grant, to nationals; all without prejudice to the rights specially provided for by this
Convention. Consequently, *they shall have the same protection as the latter*, and the same legal remedy
against any infringement of their rights, provided that the conditions and formalities imposed upon
nationals are complied with.

. . .

Article 3

Nationals of countries outside the Union who are domiciled or who have real and effective industrial
or commercial establishments in the territory of one of the countries of the Union shall be *treated
in the same manner* as nationals of the countries of the Union. [italics added]

[144] Article 5, Berne Convention, provides:

(1) Authors shall enjoy, in respect of works for which they are protected under this Convention, in
countries of the Union other than the country of origin, *the rights which their respective laws do now
or may hereafter grant to their nationals*, as well as the rights specially granted by this Convention.

. . .

(2) Protection in the country of origin is governed by domestic law. However, when the author is
not a national of the country of origin of the work for which he is protected under this Convention,
he shall enjoy in that country *the same rights as national authors*. [italics added]

[145] GATT 1947 Article III provides, for example:

4. The products of the territory of any contracting party imported into the territory of any other
contracting party shall be accorded treatment *no less favourable* than that accorded to like products
of national origin in respect of all laws, regulations and requirements . . . [emphasis added]

[146] Meeting of Negotiating Group of 5–6 January 1990, Note of the Secretariat, MTN.GNG/
NG11/18, 27 February 1990, at para. 20.

[147] *Id.*, at para. 19.

[148] *Id.*

should apply at least to those intellectual property rights covered by TRIPS, and also that existing exceptions to national treatment found in the WIPO conventions should be recognized.[149] The view was expressed that *de facto* discrimination should be covered as well as *de jure* discrimination.

The draft composite text prepared by TNG Chairman Anell reflected the points made in the discussions. It provided:

"6. National Treatment

6.1 Each PARTY shall accord to the nationals of other PARTIES [treatment no less favourable than] [the same treatment as] that accorded to the PARTY's nationals with regard to the protection of intellectual property, [subject to the exceptions already provided in, respectively,] [without prejudice to the rights and obligations specifically provided in] the Paris Convention [(1967)], the Berne Convention [(1971)], [the Rome Convention] and the Treaty on Intellectual Property in Respect of Integrated Circuits (note 2). [Any PARTY not a party to the Rome Convention and availing itself of the possibilities as provided in Article 16(1)(a)(iii) or (iv) or Article 16(1)(b) of that Convention shall make the notification foreseen in that provision to (the committee administering this agreement).]

(note 2) For the first two and the last of these conventions, the exceptions have been listed by WIPO in document NG11/W/66. For the Rome Convention, the relevant provisions would appear to be Articles 15, 16(1)(a)(iii) and (iv) and (b), and 17."[150]

2.2.2.2 The Brussels Draft. The draft text of the TRIPS Agreement transmitted to the Brussels Ministerial Conference on the Chairman Anell's initiative in December 1990 included a draft national treatment provision approximating the Dunkel Draft text (see below), and the finally adopted TRIPS Agreement.[151] The Brussels

---

[149] *Id.*

[150] Status of Work in the Negotiating Group, Chairman's Report to the GNG, MTN.GNG/NG11/W/76, 23 July 1990. The Anell text continued:

"6.2A Any exceptions invoked in respect of procedural requirements imposed on beneficiaries of national treatment, including the designation of an address for service or the appointment of an agent within the jurisdiction of a PARTY, shall not have the effect of impairing access to, and equality of opportunity on, the market of such PARTY and shall be limited to what is necessary to secure reasonably efficient administration and security of the law.

6.3A Where the acquisition of an intellectual property right covered by this agreement is subject to the intellectual property right being granted or registered, PARTIES shall provide granting or registration procedures not constituting any de jure or de facto discrimination in respect of laws, regulations and requirements between nationals of the PARTIES.

6.4A With respect to the protection of intellectual property, PARTIES shall comply with the provisions of Article III of the General Agreement on Tariffs and Trade, subject to the exceptions provided in that Agreement. [note 3]

[note 3] This provision would not be necessary if, as proposed by some participants, the results of the negotiations were to be an integral part of the General Agreement on Tariffs and Trade."

[151] The Brussels text did not include the final TRIPS text, "In respect of performers, producers of phonograms and broadcasting organizations, this obligation only applies in respect of rights provided under this Agreement" (Article 3.1, second sentence). As noted in the text below, footnote 3 was added at the Dunkel Draft stage. Draft Final Act Embodying the Results of the Uruguay Round

Draft on national treatment adopted the "no less favourable" treatment option, and the "subject to" language regarding existing exceptions.

2.2.2.3 The Dunkel Draft. The Dunkel Draft text added a sentence concerning the rights of performers, producers of phonograms and broadcast organisations.[152] It also added footnote 2 (which then became footnote 3 under the final version of TRIPS) following the word "protection", stating:

> "For the purposes of Articles 3 and 4 of this Agreement, protection shall include matters affecting the availability, acquisition, scope, maintenance and enforcement of intellectual property rights as well as those matters affecting the use of intellectual property rights specifically addressed in this Agreement."

The added footnote is significant in that it extends the scope of the national treatment obligation to the use of intellectual property rights, and in that sense addresses the subject of market access. WTO Members are obligated not only to allow foreign nationals to obtain and maintain IPRs, but must also allow them to exercise those rights at least as favourably as local nationals.

The final TRIPS Agreement text of Article 3 made no material changes to the Dunkel Draft text.

2.2.3 MFN treatment

2.2.3.1 The EC and U.S. proposals. Although a number of developing countries questioned the need for including an MFN obligation in the TRIPS Agreement, particularly as the prospective list of exceptions expanded,[153] its inclusion was not a major source of controversy. The main points of discussion concerned whether and how exceptions to the basic concept would be included.

There was some support for an approach to MFN that would have provided for a "weaker" standard that would have prohibited only arbitrary or unjustifiable discrimination among Members, but without additional exceptions.[154] Most Members, however, appeared to share the view that the basic MFN principle in TRIPS should reflect the approach taken in the GATT 1947, that is, that rights or concessions granted to one Member should immediately and unconditionally be granted to all WTO Members, with limited exceptions.[155]

---

of Multilateral Trade Negotiations, Revision, Trade-Related Aspects of Intellectual Property Rights, Including Trade in Counterfeit Goods, MTN.TNC/W/35/Rev. 1, 3 Dec. 1990.

[152] *Id.* The Dunkel Draft referred to "broadcast organizations" rather than "broadcasters".

[153] See, e.g., Meeting of the Negotiating Group of 1 November 1990, Note of the Secretariat, MTN.GNG/NG11/27,14 November 1990, at para. 4, at which a delegate speaking on behalf of a number of developing countries "said that he was still not convinced of the need to include the mfn principle in the text, since it was alien to the intellectual property system, and would in any case be rendered meaningless by the growing list of exceptions written into it."

[154] Meeting of Negotiating Group of 5-6 January 1990, Note of the Secretariat, MTN.GNG/NG11/18, 27 February 1990, at para. 20.

[155] *Id.*

A principal point of debate concerned the extent to which regional arrangements such as customs unions and free trade areas might be exempt from MFN obligations, as well as how existing bilateral agreements (particularly in the field of geographical indications) would be addressed. The European Community had a particular interest in this subject matter as it was progressively attempting to integrate its internal intellectual property framework. However, it was not alone in expressing concern regarding the prospective relationship between regional integration efforts and TRIPS rules.

The EC's March 1990 proposal for a regional integration exception was drafted to provide extensive rights to discriminate.[156] Its proposal on MFN and exceptions stated:

> "Article 3 Most Favoured Nation Treatment/Non-Discrimination
> In addition to the full application of Article I of the General Agreement, contracting parties shall ensure that the protection of intellectual property rights is not carried out in a manner which would constitute an arbitrary or unjustifiable discrimination between nationals of a contracting party and those of any other country or which would constitute a disguised restriction on international trade.
>
> Article 4 Customs Unions and Free Trade Areas
>
> Contracting parties which constitute a customs union or free trade area within the meaning of Article XXIV of the General Agreement may apply to one another measures relating to the protection of intellectual property rights without extending them to other contracting parties, in order to facilitate trade between their territories."

There was little apparent support for an open-ended Article XXIV-based provision such as the EC suggested. At the TNG meeting of 14–16 May 1990, most delegations that expressed a view did not support the EC approach.[157] The United States offered a proposal regarding MFN and the customs union issue that began to approximate the solution eventually framed in Article 4.[158] The U.S. proposal provided:

> "Any advantage, favour, privilege, or immunity affecting the protection or enforcement of intellectual property rights which is given by a contracting party to the right-holders of another contracting party shall be accorded immediately and unconditionally to the right-holders of all other contracting parties except for any advantage, favor, privilege, or immunity which exceeds the requirements of this Agreement and which is provided for in an international agreement to which the contracting party belongs, so long as such agreement is open for accession by any contracting party of this Agreement."

---

[156] Draft Agreement on Trade-Related Aspects of Intellectual Property Rights (received from the European Communities 27 March 1990) MTN.GNG/NG11/W/68, 29 March 1990.

[157] Meeting of Negotiating Group of 14–16 May 1990, Note by the Secretariat, MTN.GNG/NG11/21, 22 June 1990, at paras. 17 & 38.

[158] Communication from the United States, Draft Agreement on the Trade-Related Aspects of Intellectual Property Rights, MTN.CNG/NG11/W/70, 11 May 1990, referenced *id.*, para. 11.

In this regard, reaction to the U.S. proposal is noteworthy:

"Article 3: Most Favoured Nation Treatment/Non-discrimination. Some participants stated they would have preferred a stricter MFN obligation along the lines
of that found in Article I of the General Agreement, which was particularly important for small and medium size countries. It was also said that from this point of
view it was an improvement over the formulation proposed by the European Communities. A number of participants sought clarification of the meaning and scope
of the exception in the last few lines of the Article; would it cover Article XXIV
agreements and existing bilateral agreements; would accession be on the same
terms as the original parties and would it be automatic or subject to successful
negotiations? Some delegations doubted that a right of accession would necessarily prevent or remedy discrimination resulting from certain bilateral agreements,
since this might depend on how those agreements were drafted. The absence of
an explicit reference to customs unions was also noted."[159]

2.2.3.2 The Anell Draft. The Anell composite text regarding MFN provided:

7. Most-Favoured-Nation Treatment/Non-Discrimination

7.1aA PARTIES shall ensure that the protection of intellectual property is not
carried out in a manner [which would constitute an arbitrary or unjustifiable
discrimination between nationals of a PARTY and those of any other country or which would constitute a disguised restriction on international trade]
[that has the effect of impairing access to and equality of opportunity on their
markets].

7.1b.1 With regard to the protection of intellectual property, any advantage,
favour, privilege or immunity granted by a PARTY to the nationals of any other
[country] [PARTY] shall be accorded [immediately and unconditionally] to the
nationals of all other PARTIES.

7.1b.2 Exempted from this obligation are any advantage, favour, privilege or immunity accorded by a PARTY:

– Deriving from international agreements on judicial assistance and law enforcement of a general nature and not particularly confined to the protection of intellectual property rights.

– Concerning procedures provided under international agreements relating to
the acquisition and maintenance of protection for intellectual property in several
countries, provided that accession to such agreements is open to all PARTIES.

– Granted in accordance with the provisions of the Berne Convention (1971)
[and the Rome Convention] authorising that the treatment accorded be a function not of national treatment but of the treatment accorded in another country.
(Note 4)

– Deriving from international agreements related to intellectual property law
which entered into force prior to the entry into force of this agreement, provided
that such agreements do not constitute an arbitrary and unjustifiable discrimination against nationals of other PARTIES and provided that any such exception in

---

[159] Meeting of the Negotiating Group of 1 November 1990, Note of the Secretariat, MTN.GNG/
NG11/27,14 November 1990, at para. 17.

respect of another PARTY does not remain in force for longer than [X] years after the coming into force of this agreement between the two PARTIES in question.

(Note 4) The relevant provisions would appear to be Articles 2(7), 6(1), 7(8), 14ter(1) and (2), 18 and 30(2)(b) of the Berne Convention and Articles 15 and 16(1)(a)(iv) and (b) of the Rome Convention.

– Exceeding the requirements of this agreement and which is provided in an international agreement to which the PARTY belongs, provided that [such agreement is open for accession by all PARTIES to this agreement] [any such PARTY shall be ready to extend such advantage, favour, privilege or immunity, on terms equivalent to those under the agreement, to any other PARTY so requesting and to enter into good faith negotiations to this end.]

7.2A With respect to the protection of intellectual property, PARTIES shall comply with the provisions of Article I of the General Agreement on Tariffs and Trade, subject to the exceptions provided in that Agreement. (Note 5)

(Note 5) This provision would not be necessary if, as proposed by some participants, the results of the negotiations were to be an integral part of the General Agreement on Tariffs and Trade.

2.2.3.3 The Brussels Draft. The Brussels Ministerial Text of December 1990 incorporated an Article 4 draft that is identical to the Dunkel Draft and final TRIPS Agreement text in so far as the basic MFN obligation and the exceptions in subparagraphs (a) and (b) are concerned. The Brussels Ministerial Text also provided for two other exemptions for MFN obligations:

"(c) deriving from international agreements related to the protection of intellectual property which entered into force prior to the entry into force of this agreement, provided that such agreements are notified to the Committee established under Part VII below and do not constitute an arbitrary or unjustifiable discrimination against nationals of other PARTIES;

(d) exceeding the requirements of this Agreement and provided in an international agreement to which the PARTY belongs, provided that such agreement is open for accession by all PARTIES to this Agreement, or provided that such PARTY shall be ready to extend such advantage, favour, privilege or immunity, on terms equivalent to those under the agreement, to the nationals of any other PARTY so requesting and to enter into good faith negotiations to this end."

It is important to note that Article 6 of the Brussels Ministerial Text on the subject of exhaustion of rights, discussed in Chapter 5, included a footnote 3 reference stating: "For purposes of exhaustion, the European Communities shall be considered a single Party." To the extent that the EC was attempting to protect its intra-Community exhaustion rule in the Brussels Draft Article 4 (c) (see above), it was also seeking to protect it elsewhere. Footnote 3 to Article 6 was dropped by the Dunkel Draft stage.

Subparagraph (d) of the Brussels Ministerial Text was dropped in the Dunkel Draft, and subparagraph (c) was modified to form the Dunkel Draft and final TRIPS Agreement subparagraph (d). Note that the Brussels subparagraph (d) would have provided a wider exemption to MFN than subparagraph (d) of

Article 4, TRIPS. The latter makes an exemption dependent on the existence of international agreements specifically "related to the protection of intellectual property", whereas the Brussels subparagraph (d) as quoted above referred to any sort of agreement containing "TRIPS-plus" provisions. Also, the Brussels Draft in the above subparagraph (d) did not require the respective international agreement to have entered into force prior to the TRIPS Agreement, as does Article 4 (d), TRIPS Agreement.

TRIPS subparagraph (c) (Article 4) relating to performers, producers of phonograms and broadcasters (ultimately "broadcast organizations") was added at the Dunkel Draft stage.

The Brussels Ministerial Text of Article 4 reflected a substantial change from the Anell composite text, both in terms of the basic MFN obligation and the exceptions. Regarding the basic MFN obligation, the use of unjustifiable discrimination as the benchmark (as initially proposed by the EC), and direct reference to impairing market access, were dropped. The idea that the exception for pre-existing agreements would be of a limited duration (see above, subparagraph 7.1b.2) was eliminated. Chairman Anell's transmittal Commentary to the Ministers said:

> "Turning to the major outstanding issues on points of substance, there is, in Part I on General Provisions and Basic Principles, a need for further work on Article 4 on Most-Favoured-Nation Treatment, in particular sub-paragraph (d)."[160]

2.2.3.4 The Dunkel Draft.

There are no significant differences between the Dunkel Draft text of Article 4 and the final text of Article 4 of TRIPS.

Subparagraph (d) of the Brussels Draft as quoted above was eliminated in the Dunkel Draft and final TRIPS Agreement text.

Note that footnote 2 of the Dunkel Draft (which then became footnote 3 to Article 3 under the TRIPS final text) addressing "use" of IPRs also applies to Article 4, and to that extent the market access issue is covered (see the discussion above with respect to the Dunkel Draft provision on national treatment).

2.2.4 Exception for WIPO Acquisition and Maintenance Agreements

In the course of the TRIPS negotiations, the WTO Secretariat and WIPO prepared a number of reports concerning existing international agreements relating to intellectual property,[161] including those relating to the acquisition and maintenance

---

[160] See Brussels Ministerial Text as quoted above.

[161] See, e.g., International Conventions Regarding Intellectual Property and Their Membership, Note by the Secretariat, MTN.GNG/NG11/W/13, 2 Sept. 1987, and Provisions of Existing International Conventions Providing Protection for Intellectual Property, Communication from the WIPO Secretariat, MTN.GNG/NG11/W/21, 12 February 1988. The latter report notes that because it describes substantive provisions, it does not include description of the agreements relating to acquisition of rights, "the Madrid Agreement Concerning the International Registration of Marks, the Hague Agreement Concerning the International Deposit of Industrial Designs, the Patent Cooperation Treaty, the Trademark Registration Treaty and the Budapest Treaty on the International Recognition of the Deposit of Microorganisms for the Purposes of Patent Procedure. For the same reason, the present document does not cover those provisions of the Lisbon Agreement for the

of IPRs.[162] Negotiators recognized that Members that are party to multilateral agreements for the acquisition and maintenance of IPRs would enjoy certain rights or privileges as compared with those Members that were not party to those agreements.[163] Although the negotiating record of the TRIPS Agreement does not reflect extensive discussion on this matter, it is apparent that preserving the differential rights of Members under agreements such as the Patent Cooperation Treaty would require an exception from the national treatment and MFN principles of TRIPS. Without such an exception, Members that were not party to the agreements on acquisition and maintenance of rights would be assumed to enjoy the benefits of those agreements without joining them (and assuming obligations).

One important question was whether the exclusion from national and MFN treatment would apply to all international agreements governing the acquisition and maintenance of rights, or only to specified agreements. The composite text prepared by TNG Chairman Anell included an express exception for acquisition-related agreements as part of its MFN proposal. This would have provided an MFN exemption:

> "Concerning procedures provided under international agreements relating to the acquisition and maintenance of protection for intellectual property in several countries, provided that accession to such agreements is open to all PARTIES." (*see above*, at 7.1b.2)

This broadly formulated exemption would presumably have encompassed the European Patent Convention, to give one example.

The Brussels Ministerial Text and the Dunkel Draft text included Article 5, which was adopted without material change as Article 5, TRIPS Agreement. Article 5 provides an exemption from the requirements of Articles 3 (national treatment) and 4 (MFN), but is limited to acquisition and maintenance agreements concluded under WIPO auspices.

3. Possible interpretations

3.1 National treatment

3.1.1 General observations
The basic obligation of each Member under Article 3 is to treat nationals of other Members at least as favourably as it treats its own nationals in respect to the protection of intellectual property. Under traditional GATT 1947 jurisprudence, the national treatment principle was understood to permit express or formal legal distinctions between the treatment of imported and locally produced goods, provided

---

Protection of Appellations of Origin and their International Registration which deal with the international registration of appellations of origin", at para. 4.

[162] See particularly, Existence, Scope and Form of Generally Internationally Accepted and Applied Standards/Norms for the Protection of Intellectual Property, Note Prepared by the International Bureau of WIPO, MTN.GNG/NG11/W/24/Rev.1, 15 Sept. 1988.

[163] See, e.g., Compilation of Written Submissions and Oral Statements, Prepared by the Secretariat, MTN.GNG/NG11/W/12/Rev.1, 5 February 1988, at 66.

that there was no discriminatory effect in their treatment. For example, sanitary inspections of imported cattle might be conducted in a different way than sanitary inspections of locally raised cattle. Imported cattle might be inspected on entering the country, while local cattle might be inspected through periodic visits to ranches. In each case, the objective of assuring food safety would be the same. Formally different treatment would be justified by the circumstances. There is nothing in the negotiating history or text of Article 3 to suggest that Members intended to modify this approach. Thus, TRIPS permits express or formal distinctions among local and foreign nationals, provided the effects are non-discriminatory.

Generally speaking, the Paris and Berne Convention national treatment provisions also appear to permit formal differences in rules, provided that the level of protection provided to local and foreign nationals is equivalent (See Articles 2(1) and 3, Paris Convention, and Article 5(1) and (3), Berne Convention).

3.1.2 No less favourable and equivalent treatment

The Paris and Berne Conventions each require that state parties provide equivalent treatment to local and foreign nationals. The Paris Convention formula (in Article 2(1)) is specific on the subject of infringement, stating that foreign nationals "shall have the same legal remedy against any infringement of their rights, provided that the conditions and formalities imposed upon nationals are complied with."[164]

A Member might act inconsistently with the Paris or Berne Convention requirement of equivalence while providing more favourable treatment in accord with Article 3. Yet, as noted in Chapter 3, a WTO Member may not derogate from its obligations under the Paris and Berne Conventions, including their national treatment obligations (Article 2.2, TRIPS). Thus, while Article 3 may grant the flexibility to treat foreign nationals more favourably than local nationals, the incorporated provisions of the Paris and Berne Conventions might be interpreted to take this flexibility away. The apparent conflict might be resolved from the standpoint of TRIPS by interpreting the Paris and Berne requirements of equivalence not to establish an "obligation" in regard to foreign nationals, since application of Paris and Berne rules of equivalence may in fact diminish the potential rights of foreign nationals.

The possibility that a WTO Member would treat foreign nationals more favourably than its own nationals (and, problematically, selectively discriminating among nationals of different countries) led to incorporation of the MFN principle in TRIPS. Given the lack of apparent incentive for doing so, it may be the exceptional case in which a Member will choose to grant preferential treatment to foreigners (this assumption having underlain the WIPO Convention system). Thus, the potential inconsistency between TRIPS and the Paris and Berne Convention national treatment provisions may become an issue only in an exceptional context.

---

[164] Yet, under Article 2(3), Paris Convention, "provisions . . . relating to judicial and administrative procedure and to jurisdiction . . . which may be required by the laws on industrial property are expressly reserved." The distinction between a "remedy" that must be the "same", and a "procedure" that is "reserved" or exempt may be difficult to draw, and in this sense the Paris Convention is not a model of clarity.

3.1.3 *De jure* discrimination

National treatment controversies may arise from formal differences in legal rules that Members claim to provide "no less favourable" (or equivalent) treatment to foreign nationals (*de jure* differentiation).

GATT 1947 and WTO jurisprudence is substantially devoted to interpretation of the national treatment obligation in respect to trade in goods. As a general proposition, formally different rules are said to contravene the national treatment obligation when they unfavourably affect "conditions of competition" between imported and locally produced goods, making it *potentially* more difficult for imported goods to compete. Whether and how conditions of competition are affected significantly depends on the factual setting, and this makes generalization difficult. What is clear, however, in the trade in goods context is that adverse effects-in-fact on imports need *not* be demonstrated. It need only be demonstrated that the *economic environment* for imports has been unfavourably altered by the rules that are challenged.[165]

If a WTO Member drafts its IPR rules in a way that differentiates between local and foreign nationals, there is of course a possibility that such rules may discriminate against foreign nationals. The issue under Article 3 is whether the rules are in fact discriminatory in the sense of making it more difficult for foreign nationals to obtain or enforce IPR protection.

Article 3.2 provides some guidance regarding the adoption of formally different rules. It provides that exceptions from national treatment allowed under the WIPO Conventions specified in Article 3.1 may be used regarding:

> judicial and administrative procedures, including the designation of an address for service or the appointment of an agent within the jurisdiction of a Member, only where such exceptions *are necessary to secure compliance with laws and regulations which are not inconsistent with the provisions of this Agreement and where such practices are not applied in a manner which would constitute a disguised restriction on trade.* [emphasis added]

Article 2(3), Paris Convention reserves (or exempts) from its national treatment obligation laws on judicial and administrative procedure. Article 3.2, TRIPS Agreement, significantly cuts down on the scope of that Paris Convention exception from the national treatment obligation. Exceptions must be "necessary", and must not be "applied in a manner which would constitute a disguised restriction on trade".

If Article 3.2 establishes rigorous standards in respect to differential treatment of foreign nationals as to judicial and administrative procedures, this suggests that formally (or expressly) different substantive rules may also be examined rigorously, both in regard to form and practice. The decision of the WTO Appellate Body in the *U.S. – Havana Club* case, discussed below, appears to confirm a rigorous approach to application of the TRIPS Agreement national treatment standard.

Allocation of the burden of proof may play a substantial role in dispute settlement concerning formally different rules. Does the fact that a Member has elected to draft different IPR rules for local and foreign nationals place the burden of

---

[165] See also Chapter 32, Section 3.

proof on that Member to justify the formal difference in treatment? Article 3 does not expressly address this issue. On the one hand, Members have the discretion to draft laws in the manner they determine to be appropriate (see Chapter 2 on Article 1.1).[166] It could be argued that taking advantage of this right should not have any negative effects such as the reversal of the burden of proof. On the other hand, formal differences in the treatment of foreign nationals would certainly aid in establishing a *prima facie* case of inconsistency with the national treatment standard, and increase the likelihood that the burden would be shifted to the Member adopting the differential treatment to justify the differences.[167]

3.1.4 *De facto* discrimination

Discriminatory treatment in the national treatment context may occur not only on the basis of expressly or formally different legal rules, but also when rules that are the same on their face in fact operate in a discriminatory manner (*de facto* discrimination). This principle was long recognized as a matter of GATT 1947 jurisprudence, and reflects also long-standing jurisprudence of the European Court of Justice.

The paradigm case of *de facto* discrimination in GATT 1947 law happened to involve the protection of U.S. intellectual property rights holders under Section 337 of the U.S. Tariff Act of 1930.[168] Section 337 made it easier for a patent holder in the United States to block imports alleged to infringe a patent than to proceed against comparable infringing goods already within the United States.[169] The former could be accomplished through an expeditious administrative proceeding that eliminated rights to counterclaim, while the latter required a more complex and time-consuming court trial. Section 337 treated all imported products on an equivalent basis in a formal sense. On its face, the legislation was non-discriminatory as between foreign and U.S. nationals. However, the panel observed that the preponderance of imports into the United States was produced by foreign nationals, so the legislation would in fact affect foreign nationals routinely, while affecting U.S. nationals perhaps rarely. The panel concluded that Section 337 violated U.S. national treatment obligations under Article III, GATT 1947, in an operational or *de facto* sense.

The negotiating record of the TRIPS Agreement indicates that Members were well aware of the doctrine of *de facto* discrimination in the national treatment context. There is no indication that Members intended to alter this doctrine in adopting Article 3.

---

[166] See discussion of the importance of Member sovereignty in implementation of WTO obligations in *EC Measures Concerning Meat and Meat Products (Hormones)*, Report of the Appellate Body, WT/DS26/AB/R; WT/DS48/AB/R of 16 January 1998 [hereinafter "EC – Beef Hormones"].

[167] See discussion of U.S. – Havana Club case, below, in which the WTO AB indicates that the EC, having shown that the U.S. legislation distinguished on its face between U.S. and foreign nationals, had established a *prima facie* case of discrimination, at para. 281. This put the U.S. in the position of rebutting the *prima facie* case, and in essence constituted a shift in the burden of proof.

[168] See *United States – Section 337 of the Tariff Act of 1930*, Report of the Panel, adopted 7 November 1989, BISD 36S/345 [hereinafter "U.S. – Section 337"].

[169] See discussion below (Section 4) in respect to *U.S. – Havana Club* decision.

3.1.5 Exceptions from national treatment under the WIPO Conventions

The exceptions referred to by Article 3 under the Paris, Berne and IPIC Conventions were compiled by WIPO during the TRIPS negotiations and cross-referenced in the Anell draft of a national treatment provision. For ease of reference, that listing by WIPO is appended to this Chapter as Annex 1. The Rome Convention is not exclusively administered by WIPO, and was not addressed in its report. However, the Anell text noted that:

> "For the Rome Convention, the relevant provisions would appear to be Articles 15, 16(1)(a)(iii) and (iv) and (b), and 17."[170]

Another limitation of the national treatment obligation exists with respect to the rights of performers, producers of phonograms and broadcasting organizations: the second sentence of Article 3.1 states that:

> "In respect of performers, producers of phonograms and broadcasting organizations, this obligation [i.e. national treatment] only applies in respect of the rights provided under this Agreement."

This means that any additional rights provided under other international agreements[171] do not have to be extended to nationals of WTO Members that are not parties to this other agreement.[172]

3.2 MFN treatment

Application of an MFN standard in the context of IPR protection is an innovation in the multilateral context, and precedent is therefore limited. Article 4

---

[170] Article 15, Rome Convention, allows for certain fair use exceptions to protection; Article 16(1)(a)(iii) and (iv), allows for limitations on the obligation to pay equitable remuneration for secondary uses of phonograms based, *inter alia*, on reciprocity. Article 16(1)(b) allows contracting states to exempt protection of television broadcasts in public places, permitting affected states to withdraw such protection. Article 17 allows contracting states which granted protection of producers of phonograms solely on the basis of fixation on October 26, 1961, to maintain that criterion for certain purposes. As noted below in regard to notification practice, some WTO Members have notified the TRIPS Council of exceptions from application of Article 5, para. 1(b) or (c), Rome Convention, regarding the criterion of fixation or publication in another contracting state for granting national treatment to producers of phonograms. "Fixation" is not defined in the Rome Convention, but it is defined in the later WIPO Performances and Phonograms Treaty (WPPT) as "the embodiment of sounds, or of the representations thereof, from which they can be perceived, reproduced or communicated through a device." (WPPT, Article 2(c)). In a more colloquial sense, "fixation" refers to recording music (or other expression) on to a CD or other tangible medium.

[171] An international agreement providing additional rights in this respect is the WIPO Performances and Phonograms Treaty (WPPT), adopted in Geneva on 20 December 1996. Available at <http://www.wipo.int/clea/docs/en/wo/wo034en.htm>. Due to its **post**-TRIPS adoption, however, obligations particular to this treaty would in any case not have to be extended to WTO Members that are not parties to the WPPT. A **pre**-TRIPS international agreement in this respect is the Rome Convention for the Protection of Performers, Producers of Phonograms and Broadcasting Organizations. This Convention is equally not mandatory for those WTO Members that are not parties to it (see Chapter 3).

[172] The purpose of this limitation is to avoid "free riding" of those latter Members. For instance, those Members not parties to the WPPT or the Rome Convention cannot claim that their nationals be accorded the rights that are not guaranteed in their own territory. The national treatment obligation is limited to the minimum rights provided under Article 14, TRIPS Agreement (for details on Article 14, TRIPS Agreement, see Chapter 13).

provides for the immediate and unconditional extension to nationals of all Members "any advantage, favour, privilege or immunity" granted with respect to the protection of intellectual property to nationals of any country (including a non-Member of the WTO). This article is modelled on Article I of the GATT 1947 and 1994.

What constitutes an advantage or concession in the protection of intellectual property is not necessarily clear. Granting to nationals of another Member more extensive protection of rights would likely be considered an advantage that must be extended to nationals of all Members. But if a country decides to provide more extensive exceptions, for example, in the area of fair use of copyrighted materials, and decides to extend those exceptions to foreign nationals of only certain WTO Members, might other "unaffected" Members consider this an "advantage" regarding protection that should automatically apply to them? Some "unaffected" foreign nationals might wish to take advantage of the exceptions, and find they are unable to do so. This could well have negative commercial implications for those foreign nationals.[173] The question what constitutes an advantage as a matter of intellectual property protection and the extension of MFN treatment becomes rather important when the Article 4(d) exemption and its application to regional markets is considered.

Article 4 refers to advantages in respect to "intellectual property". Recall here the discussion in Chapter 3 regarding the definition and scope of the term "intellectual property", and that the MFN obligation applies only to such subject matter.

The exceptions to MFN treatment in Article 4 are complex. Article 4(d) in particular leaves considerable room for interpretation. Pursuant to Article 4, MFN treatment need not be provided regarding advantages, favours, privileges and immunities:

> "(a) deriving from international agreements on judicial assistance or law enforcement of a general nature and not particularly confined to the protection of intellectual property;
>
> (b) granted in accordance with the provisions of the Berne Convention (1971) or the Rome Convention authorizing that the treatment accorded be a function not of national treatment but of the treatment accorded in another country;
>
> (c) in respect of the rights of performers, producers of phonograms and broadcasting organizations not provided under this Agreement;
>
> (d) deriving from international agreements related to the protection of intellectual property which entered into force prior to the entry into force of the WTO Agreement, provided that such agreements are notified to the Council for TRIPS and do not constitute an arbitrary or unjustifiable discrimination against nationals of other Members."

Regarding Article 4(a), there are numerous international agreements – bilateral, regional and multilateral – that deal with judicial assistance and law enforcement.

---

[173] Consider, for example, television broadcasters, and the situation in which some foreign broadcasters are permitted to rebroadcast newsworthy events, while others are not. For those that are not, their audience might decline, depriving them of an economic benefit. Thus, an "exception" may confer a benefit.

This would include agreements regarding obtaining evidence, extradition, investigation of anticompetitive activity, and enforcement of judgments. Most of these agreements may have some application in the field of intellectual property. Many of the commitments that countries make to each other in these agreements are based explicitly or implicitly on reciprocity. That is, a country agrees to furnish aid in obtaining evidence to another country in exchange for a commitment by that other country to do likewise. It was beyond the scope of the TRIPS negotiations to attempt to rationalize all of these arrangements so that each Member treated all other Members on the same basis under these various agreements, and a general exemption is provided.

As noted in previous sections regarding national treatment, there are certain provisions of the Berne and Rome Conventions that allow for differential treatment of foreign nationals based on reciprocity. For example, the Berne Convention allows a party to limit the term of protection for a work of foreign origin to the term of protection granted in the country of origin. Article 4(b) allows for these differences in the treatment of foreign nationals in the MFN context.

The rights of performers, producers of phonograms and broadcast organizations are governed by a patchwork of multilateral, regional and bilateral agreements. The WIPO Performances and Phonograms Treaty (WPPT) concluded in 1996 attempts to rationalize this arrangement, but it is not part of the TRIPS framework. TRIPS establishes minimum rights in favour of performers, producers of phonograms and broadcast organizations (see Article 14), but a deliberate choice was made not to require each Member to extend its complete basket of protective rights to all other Members. Article 4(c) acknowledges this decision, thus constituting a parallel to the second sentence of Article 3 on national treatment for performers, producers of phonograms and broadcast organizations (see above, Section 3.1).

Article 4(d) addresses one of the most difficult sets of issues reflected in TRIPS, and does so in a way that does not provide clarity or certainty. Two elements, however, reduce the uncertainty: first, the exception is limited to agreements that entered into force before the TRIPS Agreement, and second, Members are required to notify the Council for TRIPS of such agreements.

The express text of Article 4(d) refers to advantages "deriving from international agreements related to the protection of intellectual property". In light of the negotiating history of this provision, it is noteworthy that no express reference is made to customs unions or free trade areas (under Article XXIV, GATT 1994) or regional services arrangements (under Article V, GATS). Presumably this was done so that preferences under "pure" intellectual property arrangements such as the European Patent Convention, the once-contemplated Community Patent Convention, ARIPO, OAPI, and similar arrangements might fall within its scope. At the same time, it is doubtful that many persons familiar with the charter documents of the European Community, Andean Pact, Mercosur/l[174] or NAFTA would ordinarily understand these agreements as "related to the protection of intellectual

---

[174] The acronym for this organization in Spanish is "Mercosur" and in Portuguese is "Mercosul". Most commonly it is referred to in English as "Mercosur". In this text, the form "Mercosur/l" is used to reflect both languages.

property". While indeed each of these regional arrangements has intellectual property protection within its subject matter scope, it is only a part of each arrangement; and it is as if to say that the Constitution of Brazil or the United States is a charter document related to the protection of intellectual property because it refers to that subject matter in a few places.

The use of the phrase "deriving from" is also significant, because it suggests that the advantages, favours, etc. that are exempted from MFN treatment are not static, but rather may develop over time based on the underlying pre-existing agreement. This is particularly important because it would seem to leave a very large space for regional arrangements such as the EC to increase the scope of MFN derogations based on the earlier-adopted EC Treaty.

While the negotiating history of Article 4(d) does indicate an awareness of the EC's concerns to establish a space in which its intellectual property regime would enjoy certain privileges, there was also concern expressed by a number of negotiating Members that the MFN exemption be narrowly constructed. In this context, there is reason to ask whether Article 4(d) was truly intended as an open-ended exclusion from the MFN obligation that would encompass any future actions contemplated by the EC or similar regional arrangements.

Having made this point, the fact that Article 3 mandates national treatment significantly reduces the possibilities for abuse of the MFN exemption. That is, preferential treatment among members of a regional arrangement should not adversely affect third country nationals to the extent they are provided national treatment within each Member of the regional group, except in the unlikely event that one of those Members grants "better than national treatment" to other Members of the group.

What then, does Article 4(d) accomplish? The EC had an interest in protection of its "intra-Community exhaustion" doctrine. When goods are placed on the market with the consent of the IP right holder in one member state they enjoy free circulation in other member states of the Community.[175] In the EC's view, this treatment of goods placed on the market within the Community does not necessarily extend to goods placed on the market outside the Community. However, since each EC member state is depriving its local IP right holder of protection with respect to goods placed on the market within the Community, it is difficult to see how this is an "advantage, favour, privilege or immunity" granted to Community nationals that the EC should be exempted from extending to non-EC nationals, though this appears to be the position taken by the EC.[176]

With this background, let us consider some of the notifications so far made under Article 4(d). The EC notification states:

> "We hereby notify on behalf of the European Community and its Member States to the Council for Trade-Related Aspects of Intellectual Property Rights, pursuant to Article 4, paragraph (d) of the Agreement on Trade-Related Aspects of

---

[175] The same (or an economically linked) IP right holder may not prevent importation into a second member state.

[176] In this sense, IP right holders outside EC territory are treated "better than" IP right holders within EC territory because the external IP right holders are not subject to exhaustion of their rights based on placing their goods on an external market.

Intellectual Property Rights, both the Treaty establishing the European Community and the Agreement establishing the European Economic Area. Notification of these agreements covers not only those provisions directly contained therein, as interpreted by the relevant jurisprudence, but also existing or future acts adopted by the Community as such and/or by the Member States which conform with these agreements following the process of regional integration."[177]

The Andean Pact notification states:

"In accordance with Article 4(d) of the Agreement on Trade-Related Aspects of Intellectual Property Rights (TRIPS), the Governments of the Republics of Bolivia, Colombia, Ecuador, Peru and Venezuela, Members of the Andean Community, hereby notify the Council for TRIPS of the Cartagena Agreement.

This notification of the Cartagena Agreement relates not only to the provisions directly included therein, as interpreted and applied in the relevant law, but also to the regulations which have been or may in the future be adopted by the Andean Community or its Member Countries, in accordance with the Agreement in the course of the process of regional integration."[178]

The Mercosul/r notification states:

"The Common Market Group requested the Pro Tempore Chairman to notify to the Council for the WTO Agreement on Trade-Related Aspects of Intellectual Property Rights (TRIPS), the Treaty of Asunción and the Ouro Preto Protocol, with reference not only to the provisions contained therein but also all agreements, protocols, decisions, resolutions and guidelines adopted or to be adopted in the future by MERCOSUR or its States Parties in the course of the regional integration process that are of relevance to TRIPS, pursuant to the Agreement.

By virtue of the above and in keeping with the terms of Article 4(d) of the TRIPS Agreement, I hereby notify the texts of the Treaty of Asunción of 26 March 1991 establishing MERCOSUR and the Ouro Preto Protocol signed on 17 December 1994."[179]

The U.S. NAFTA notification states:

"Pursuant to Article 4(d) of the Agreement on Trade-Related Aspects of Intellectual Property Rights (TRIPS), the United States hereby notifies Article 1709, paragraph (7), of the North American Free Trade Agreement (NAFTA) as being exempt from the most-favoured-nation treatment obligations of the TRIPS Agreement."[180]

---

[177] Notification under Article 4(d) of the Agreement, European Communities and their Member States, IP/N/4/EEC/1, 29 January 1996.

[178] Notification under Article 4(d) of the Agreement, Bolivia, Colombia, Ecuador, Peru, Venezuela, IP/N/4/BOL/1, IP/N/4/COL/1, IP/N/4/ECU/1, IP/N/4/PER/1, IP/N/4/VEN/2, 19 August 1997.

[179] Notification under Article 4(d) of the Agreement, Argentina, Brazil, Paraguay, Uruguay, IP/N/4/ARG/1, IP/N/4/BRA/1, IP/N/4/PRY/1, IP/N/4/URY/1, 14 July 1998.

[180] Notification under Article 4(d) of the Agreement, United States, IP/N/4/USA/1, 29 February 1996. Article 1709(7), NAFTA, provides: "Subject to paragraphs 2 and 3 [reproducing the TRIPS Article 27(a)(2) and (3) rights of exclusion from patentability], patents shall be available and patent rights enjoyable without discrimination as to the field of technology, the territory of the Party where the invention was made and whether the products are imported or locally produced."

The notifications, and particularly for the EC, Andean Pact and Mercosul/r, are drafted in a way that suggests a wide scope of exemption authority. The EC, for example, includes "relevant jurisprudence" and "future acts" . . . "following the process of regional integration". Were the same regional groups and their member countries not bound by national treatment obligations, the exemptions would appear to permit almost any grant of preferences to countries within the group that would not be extended to foreign nationals. Yet because the EC as a regional arrangement (and the member states of the EC) and each of the other arrangements must provide national treatment to nationals of third countries, the scope for exemption by virtue of derogation from MFN treatment may in fact be rather limited.

3.3 WIPO Acquisition and Maintenance Treaties

Article 5 provides an exemption from TRIPS national and MFN treatment obligations for IPRs acquisition and maintenance agreements established under WIPO auspices. The referenced agreements, for example, may require authorities in each state party to accept certain forms of registration, certification and other data from applicants in other state parties. Such requirements generally are not extended to applications that do not originate from non-party states (though rights may accrue to persons who have a sufficient connection to a party state, but are not nationals of that state). In the absence of an exemption from national treatment and MFN, rights under the WIPO acquisition and maintenance treaties would automatically be extended to all WTO Members (and their nationals) without corresponding obligations.

The WIPO acquisition and maintenance agreements would be understood to encompass the Madrid Agreement (and Protocol) Concerning the International Registration of Marks, the Hague Agreement Concerning the International Deposit of Industrial Designs, the Patent Cooperation Treaty, the Patent Law Treaty, the Trademark Law Treaty and the Budapest Treaty on the International Recognition of the Deposit of Microorganisms for the Purposes of Patent Procedure, and certain provisions of the Lisbon Agreement for the Protection of Appellations of Origin and their International Registration. The list of such agreements is not fixed, and new multilateral acquisition and maintenance agreements adopted under WIPO auspices would also qualify for national and MFN treatment exemption under Article 5.

Since the Paris and Berne Conventions and the IPIC Treaty are multilateral agreements concluded under WIPO auspices, and contain provisions addressing acquisition and maintenance of patents, trademarks, industrial designs, copyright and integrated circuit lay-out designs, an argument might be made that these agreements, at least in so far as provisions relevant to acquisition and maintenance are concerned, also fall within the scope of the Article 5 exemption. However, since these agreements are otherwise specifically incorporated by reference in TRIPS,[181] such an interpretation would appear inconsistent with the apparent intention of the TRIPS Agreement drafters.

---

[181] See TRIPS Article 2.1 for the Paris Convention; Article 9.1 for the Berne Convention; and Article 35 for the IPIC Treaty. For more details, see Chapter 3.

4. WTO jurisprudence

4.1 U.S. – Havana Club

In the *U.S. – Havana Club* case,[182] the WTO Appellate Body (AB) applied the national treatment rules of TRIPS and the Paris Convention. The AB observed that the national treatment obligation of the Paris Convention extended back to the 1880s, and that the parties to the case before it would be subject to the Paris Convention national treatment rule even were they not parties to TRIPS. While the AB referenced both the TRIPS and Paris Convention rules, it did not refer to the different legal formulas used, instead highlighting that the decision to include a national treatment provision in the TRIPS Agreement indicated the "fundamental significance of the obligation of national treatment to [the framers'] purposes in the *TRIPS Agreement*".[183] The AB also addressed the relevance of jurisprudence regarding the GATT national treatment provision, saying:

> "As we see it, the national treatment obligation is a fundamental principle under-lying the *TRIPS Agreement*, just as it has been in what is now the GATT 1994. The Panel was correct in concluding that, as the language of Article 3.1 of the *TRIPS Agreement*, in particular, is similar to that of Article III:4 of the GATT 1994, the jurisprudence on Article III:4 of the GATT 1994 may be useful in interpreting the national treatment obligation in the *TRIPS Agreement*." (*Id.*, at para. 242)

The panel in the *U.S. – Havana Club* case decided that U.S. legislation regulating trademarks that had been confiscated by the Cuban government was not incon-sistent with Article 3. While there were in fact formal legal differences between the way U.S. nationals and foreign nationals were addressed by the relevant legis-lation, the panel found that as a practical matter the possibility was extremely re-mote that a U.S. national would receive preferential treatment. Certain favourable treatment of U.S. nationals would require affirmative administrative action by U.S. regulatory authorities (contrary to the longstanding practice of the authorities to refuse such action), and the U.S. indicated that its regulatory authorities would not in fact act in a way that such preferential treatment would be provided.

The AB rejected the legal analysis of the panel, referring to the *U.S. – Section 337* decision regarding Article III:4, GATT 1947.[184] In that earlier decision, the panel said that even though the possibility for a certain type of discrimination to take place under a legislative arrangement was small, the fact that the possibility was present constituted sufficient discrimination to present a national treatment in-consistency. In *U.S. – Havana Club*, the AB said:

> "The United States may be right that the likelihood of having to overcome the hurdles of both Section 515.201 of Title 31 CFR and Section 211(a)(2) may, echoing the panel in *US – Section 337*, be *small*. But, again echoing that panel, even the *possibility* that non-United States successors-in-interest face two hurdles is

---

[182] *United States – Section 211 Omnibus Appropriations Act of 1998*, WT/DS176/AB/R, Report of the Appellate Body, 2 January 2002 [hereinafter "U.S. – Havana Club"].

[183] *Id.*, at para. 240.

[184] See above, Section 3 on *de facto* discrimination.

inherently less favourable than the undisputed fact that United States successors-in-interest face only one." (AB Report, Havana Club, at para. 265)

The AB's approach may strike those familiar with the *U.S. – Section 337* decision as strained. In that case, the United States had adopted a comprehensive administrative mechanism for patent (and other IP right) holders to seek remedies against infringing imports. That Section 337 mechanism contained a number of features making it easier to obtain remedies against imports than to obtain remedies (in domestic infringement proceedings) against goods circulating in the United States. One element of the Section 337 arrangement (though not the most important one from a discrimination standpoint) was that an importer might in theory be subject to simultaneous proceedings at the U.S. International Trade Commission (ITC) and in federal court regarding the same allegedly infringing conduct. (From a practical standpoint, the major discriminatory feature of the ITC procedure was its failure to allow for alleged infringers to assert patent counterclaims. Also, the ITC procedure was substantially more time-compressed than court proceedings.) From the standpoint of importers, the prospects for discriminatory application of U.S. patent law were real and ever-present. It was not surprising in this context that the Section 337 panel rejected U.S. suggestions that the discriminatory features of the legislation were of no practical consequence.

The situation in *U.S. – Havana Club* was significantly different. In *Havana Club* the AB was faced with a consistent U.S. practice of refusing to grant licenses of the type with which the EC expressed concern and a stated commitment by the U.S. not to grant such licenses in the future. Moreover, factual scenarios posited by the EC in which discrimination issues might arise were extremely unlikely. In this sense, the AB effectively decided that any formal differences in legal procedures would not withstand national treatment scrutiny, even if the practical consequences were extremely remote, and if the government adopting the procedures accepted not to use them.

The AB also applied Article 4 in *U.S. – Havana Club*. It said:

> "Like the national treatment obligation, the obligation to provide most-favoured-nation treatment has long been one of the cornerstones of the world trading system. For more than fifty years, the obligation to provide most-favoured-nation treatment in Article I of the GATT 1994 has been both central and essential to assuring the success of a global rules-based system for trade in goods. Unlike the national treatment principle, there is no provision in the Paris Convention (1967) that establishes a most-favoured-nation obligation with respect to rights in trademarks or other industrial property. However, the framers of the *TRIPS Agreement* decided to extend the most-favoured-nation obligation to the protection of intellectual property rights covered by that Agreement. As a cornerstone of the world trading system, the most-favoured-nation obligation must be accorded the same significance with respect to intellectual property rights under the *TRIPS Agreement* that it has long been accorded with respect to trade in goods under the GATT. It is, in a word, fundamental." (*Id.*, at para. 297)

The U.S. legislation at issue provided formally different treatment on its face as respects nationals of Cuba and other foreign countries ("non-Cuban foreign nationals"). The AB noted again that this established a *prima facie* inconsistency. The

U.S. had attempted to rebut this inconsistency by demonstrating that as a practical matter there would be no discrimination among nationals of different foreign countries. The panel had accepted the U.S. position. The AB rejected the panel's holding in reliance on a remote set of hypothetical circumstances suggested by the EC regarding differential treatment of non-U.S. national trademark holders. The AB established an extremely rigorous standard for application of the MFN principle which few formal differences in treatment of nationals from different foreign Members are likely to survive.

4.2 EC – Protection of Trademarks and GIs

Following separate requests by Australia[185] and the USA,[186] the WTO Dispute Settlement Body (DSB) at its meeting on 2 October 2003 established a single panel to examine complaints with respect to EC Council Regulation (EEC) No. 2081/92 of 14 July 1992 (published in the EU's Official Journal L 208 of 24 July 1992, pages 1-8) on the protection of geographical indications and designations of origin for agricultural products and foodstuffs.[187] The complaints are based, *inter alia*, on alleged violations of the TRIPS national treatment and most-favoured-nation treatment obligations (Articles 3.1 and 4) through the above EC Regulation.[188] The contested provision in this respect is Article 12 of the Regulation on the protection of geographical indications for foreign products.[189] Article 12 provides:

"Article 12

1. Without prejudice to international agreements, this Regulation may apply to an agricultural product or foodstuff from a third country provided that:

– the third country is able to give guarantees identical or equivalent to those referred to in Article 4,

– the third country concerned has inspection arrangements equivalent to those laid down in Article 10,

– the third country concerned is prepared to provide protection equivalent to that available in the Community to corresponding agricultural products for foodstuffs coming from the Community.

2. If a protected name of a third country is identical to a Community protected name, registration shall be granted with due regard for local and traditional usage and the practical risks of confusion.

Use of such names shall be authorized only if the country of origin of the product is clearly and visibly indicated on the label."

---

[185] WT/DS290/18 of 19 August 2003.

[186] WT/DS174/20 of 19 August 2003.

[187] *European Communities – Protection of Trademarks and Geographical Indications for Agricultural Products and Foodstuffs* [hereinafter "EC – Protection of Trademarks and GIs"], WT/DS174/21 and WT/DS290/19 of 24 February 2004, Constitution of the Panel Established at the Requests of the United States and Australia.

[188] See the above requests by Australia and the USA for the establishment of a panel. Note that the same complaint is also based on other TRIPS provisions, in particular relating to the protection of trademarks and geographical indications. See Chapters 14 and 15.

[189] For an analysis of this EC legislation on GIs see also Chapter 15, Section 2.1.

5. Relationship with other international instruments

5.1 WTO Agreements

As the AB observed in the *U.S. – Havana Club* decision, interpretation of the national treatment and MFN principles of TRIPS will be informed by interpretation of comparable provisions in the other WTO agreements. The extent to which the comparable provisions inform TRIPS will depend on the specific context of their application in these other settings. The GATT 1994 and GATS each contain express national treatment and MFN obligations, and the TBT and TRIMS Agreements incorporate national treatment provisions. Caution will necessarily be required in drawing analogies among the various agreements as the treatment, for example, of imported goods might imply different results than the treatment of foreign rights holders. In any case, it is difficult to suggest general principles as to the relationship among the various agreements and their application of non-discrimination rules beyond that suggested by the AB, that is, that they may inform each other.

One question that is squarely presented by the notifications of the EC, Andean Pact and Mercosur/l under Article 4(d)[190] is the extent to which the formation of a customs union or free trade area (under Article XXIV, GATT 1994) or regional services arrangement (under Article V, GATS) provides leeway for discrimination in favour of persons or enterprises within those arrangements. There is a very long history in GATT jurisprudence and practice, and in the academic literature, on the place of regional arrangements within the multilateral trading system, and this history suggests that such regional arrangements tend to stake claims to broad exclusions from multilateral rules. These claims have encompassed derogation from national treatment as well as MFN obligations, even though Article XXIV, GATT 1994, appears to contemplate only exception from the requirement of MFN treatment.[191] Such assertions may arise as well in the TRIPS context, despite the lack of express reference to such possibilities.

5.2 Other international instruments

The relationship of the TRIPS national and MFN treatment provisions to the WIPO conventions has already been discussed (see above, Section 3).

The national and MFN treatment provisions of TRIPS may play a role in determining its relationship to the Convention on Biological Diversity (CBD). If a WTO Member adopts rules to implement its obligations under the CBD, those rules may be related to IP protection, for example, to patent protection. The rules that are adopted would apply to nationals of other Members based on application of the national treatment principle.

6. New developments

6.1 National laws

Articles 3, 4 and 5 became applicable to all WTO Members on January 1, 1996. Since most Members were party to the Paris and Berne Conventions that already

---

[190] The U.S. NAFTA notification is more limited than these others.

[191] The claims to exemption from national treatment are described and analyzed in Frederick M. Abbott, *GATT and the European Community: A Formula for Peaceful Coexistence*, 12 Mich. J. Int'l. L. 1 (1990).

mandated national treatment in respect to patents, trademarks and copyright, the national treatment requirement of TRIPS should not have imposed any special implementation burdens on these Members. Nonetheless, many WTO Members modified their intellectual property legislation to take into account TRIPS Agreement requirements, and those that maintained inconsistencies from national treatment should have altered their legislation.

6.2 International instruments

6.3 Regional and bilateral contexts

6.3.1 Regional
The notifications from regional groups have been discussed above (see Section 3).

The European Court of Justice (ECJ) has perhaps more than any other judicial body had occasion to analyze the national treatment principle in the context of the integration of markets. While GATT 1947 panel reports relating to national treatment dealt almost exclusively with the treatment of imported goods, the case law of the ECJ has frequently dealt with the treatment of persons. From the standpoint of TRIPS national treatment analysis, it may be useful to analyze and compare decisions of the ECJ for insight into how the WTO AB might evaluate differential treatment of persons to determine whether discrimination exists.[192]

Specifically on the subject of national treatment, the adoption by the EC of the Database Directive in 1995[193] raised interesting issues concerning the EC's understanding of the national treatment and MFN principles in TRIPS. In the Database Directive the EC established a *sui generis* data protection right (in Article 7) that is more extensive than that required by TRIPS.[194] In addressing the beneficiaries of that new right, the Directive states at Article 11:

> "1. The right provided for in Article 7 shall apply to databases whose makers or successors in title are nationals of a Member State or who have their habitual residence in the territory of the Community.
>
> 2. Paragraph 1 shall also apply to companies and firms formed in accordance with the law of a Member State [...].
>
> 3. Agreements extending the right provided for in Article 7 to databases manufactured in third countries and falling outside the provisions of paragraphs 1 and 2 shall be concluded by the Council acting on a proposal from the Commission. [...]."

The Database Directive clearly denies national treatment to persons in non-EC member states. That is, in order to benefit from database protection, a person must be a national of a member state (or habitually reside there). Article 11(3) foresees the denial of MFN treatment to countries outside the EC, as it authorizes

---

[192] Current ECJ case law and doctrine on national treatment may be found in Paul Craig and Grainne de Burca, *EU Law*, 2nd edition, Oxford, 1998.

[193] Common Position (EC) No 20/95 adopted by the Council on 10 July 1995 with a view to adopting Directive 95/EC of the European Parliament and of the Council...on the legal protection of databases (OJ C 288, 30 October 1995, p. 14).

[194] For a detailed analysis of the EC Database Directive, see Chapter 9, Section 6.3.

the Communities to extend the benefits of database protection on a country-by-country basis.

The only plausible justification for the expressly discriminatory features of the Database Directive is that the EC does not consider database protection to constitute "intellectual property" within the meaning of Article 1.2.[195] Assuming that the EC is correct in this view, the Database Directive shows that, at least in the opinion of the EC, advantages regarding the protection of information not strictly within the definition of intellectual property may be treated without regard to the fundamental principles of national and MFN treatment.

6.3.2 Bilateral

Developing WTO Members are often encouraged by developed Members to adopt so-called "TRIPS-plus" standards of intellectual property rights protection.[196] National and MFN treatment are relevant to the establishment of TRIPS-plus standards.[197] The consequences of importing increasingly high standards of IPR protection in regional and bilateral trade agreements has yet to be adequately studied from the standpoint of the MFN principle. Are members of regional and bilateral agreements that adopt TRIPS-plus standards obligated to provide those higher standards of protection to WTO Members not part of the arrangement? Since there is no exception for differential IPR treatment within arrangements negotiated after TRIPS (see Article 4(d)), this may appear to be the case. But if these higher standards make it more difficult for imports to penetrate the market (because of internal barriers), is this a "concession" as to which Members are benefiting as a consequence of MFN, or does this represent a withdrawal of concessions and a fundamental alteration of the conditions of competition as to third countries? The answer to this question may have broad systemic ramifications for the WTO.

6.4 Proposals for review

There are no formal proposals for review of the national treatment and MFN principles before the TRIPS Council. However, as part of the agenda of the working party on regional integration the place of the TRIPS Agreement is being evaluated along with other aspects of regional integration. Moreover, implicit in the Doha agenda discussions on improving the treatment of developing Members within the WTO framework is consideration of the extent to which national and MFN treatment may need to be adjusted in the interests of promoting development. For example, one of the main issues being addressed by the Working Group on Trade and Competition is the extent to which national competition policy in

[195] For an analysis of whether databases constitute "intellectual property" in the sense of Article 1.2, see Chapter 3, Section 3.1.

[196] This aspect of the TRIPS dynamic is addressed in Chapter 2, Section 3.2.

[197] On the implications of TRIPS-plus agreements in the context of the MFN treatment obligation, see also D. Vivas-Eugui, *Regional and bilateral agreements and a TRIPS-plus world: the Free Trade Area of the Americas (FTAA)*, TRIPS Issues Papers 1, Quaker United Nations Office (QUNO), Geneva; Quaker International Affairs Programme (QIAP), Ottawa; International Centre for Trade and Sustainable Development (ICTSD), Geneva, 2003 (available at <http://www.geneva. quno.info/pdf/FTAA%20(A4).pdf >).

developing Members may accommodate preferences for local enterprises (e.g., small and medium enterprises (SMEs)), and whether a national treatment provision in a WTO competition agreement might adversely affect such preferences.[198] IPRs are the subject of general competition policy and decisions regarding national treatment in the competition context would have an impact on the competition provisions of TRIPS.

7. Comments, including economic and social implications

The Appellate Body has characterized the national treatment and MFN principles as fundamental to the WTO legal system, including TRIPS. The centrality of these principles to the GATT 1947 and the WTO multilateral trading system is unarguable. The MFN principle was adopted not only as a trade liberalization device, but perhaps even more importantly as a political instrument to reduce the tendency of governments to form alliances based on economic considerations. In the first half of the twentieth century, these political alliances had formed the backdrop of war. There was (and remains) a compelling justification for seeking to minimize potentially dangerous fragmentation of the global economy.

National treatment and MFN are not, however, an unalloyed benefit from the standpoint of developing Members of the WTO. Principles that require foreign economic actors to be treated on the same basis as local economic actors may place individuals and enterprises within developing countries at a distinct disadvantage in respect to more globally competitive foreign operators. Developing Members may "gain" from improved access to developed country markets to the extent their products are competitive. They may "lose" if local enterprises are unable to compete at home against more highly capitalized and efficient foreign operators. In some cases, the gains from access to foreign markets will not offset the losses to local enterprises in terms of lost profits and employment.[199] Care should therefore be taken not to oversell the benefits of national treatment and MFN from the standpoint of developing WTO Members.

This potential skewing of benefits is particularly significant in the TRIPS context. Developed Members of the WTO maintain tremendous advantages over developing Members in regard to existing stocks of technological assets, and the capacity for future research and development. By agreeing to treat foreign patent holders on the same basis as local patent holders, developing Members establish a level playing field on which the teams are of rather unequal strength.

The response of developed Members is that transfer of technology and capacity building will improve the developing country technology "teams". This concept, while elegant in theory, has seen only minimal implementation in practice.[200] If developing Members are sceptical, so far it is with good reason.

---

[198] See, e.g., Report of the Working Group on the Interaction Between, Trade and Competition Policy to the General Council, WT/WGTCP/6, 9 Dec. 2002, at para. 44.

[199] See Joseph Stiglitz, *Globalization and Its Discontents* (2002).

[200] For a deeper analysis of the interplay between IPR protection and technology transfer, see UNCTAD-ICTSD, *Intellectual Property Rights: Implications for Development*. Policy Discussion Paper, Geneva, 2003, Chapter 5 (Technology Transfer). For an analysis of Article 66.2, TRIPS Agreement (concerning the promotion of technology transfer to LDC Members), see Chapter 34.

Annex Beneficiaries of and Exceptions to National Treatment under Treaties Administered By WIPO, Communication from the World Intellectual Property Organization, MTN.GNG/NG11/W/66, 28 February 1990

II. LIST OF EXCEPTIONS TO NATIONAL TREATMENT

(a) under the Paris Convention

6. The following exceptions to national treatment are contained in the Paris Convention:

i) the provisions of the laws of each of the countries party to the Paris Convention relating to judicial or administrative procedure and to jurisdiction, which may be required by the laws on industrial property, are expressly reserved (Paris Convention, Article 2(3));

ii) the provisions of the laws of each of the countries party to the Paris Convention relating to the designation of an address for service or the appointment of an agent, which may be required by the laws on industrial property, are expressly reserved (Paris Convention, Article 2(3)).

(b) under the Berne Convention

7. The following exceptions to national treatment are contained in the Berne Convention:

i) where a work is protected in the country or origin solely as an industrial design – and not (also) as a work of applied art, i.e., by copyright law – that work is entitled in another country party to the Berne Convention only to such special protection as is granted in that country to industrial designs – even though copyright protection is available in that country (Berne Convention, Article 2(7), second sentence, first part);

ii) where a country not party to the Berne Convention fails to protect in an adequate manner the works of authors who are nationals of one of the countries party to the Berne Convention, the latter country may restrict the protection given – on the basis of their first publication in that country – to the works of authors who are, at the date of the first publication thereof, nationals of the other country and are not habitually resident in one of the countries party to the Berne Convention; if the country of first publication avails itself of this right, the other countries party to the Berne Convention are not required to grant to works thus subjected to special treatment a wider protection than that granted to them in the country of first publication (Berne Convention, Article 6(1));

iii) in the country where protection is claimed, the term of protection shall not, unless the legislation of that country otherwise provides, exceed the term fixed in the country of origin of the work (Berne Convention, Article 7(8));

iv) the right ("droit de suite"), enjoyed by the author, or, after his death, by the persons or institutions authorized by national legislation, to an interest in any sale of the work – which is either an original work of art or an original manuscript of a writer or composer – subsequent to the first transfer by the author of the work may be claimed in a country party to the Berne Convention only if legislation in the country to which the author belongs so permits, and to the extent permitted by the country where this right is claimed (Berne Convention, Article 14ter(1) and (2));

v) in relation to the right of translation of works whose country of origin is a country – other than certain developing countries – which, having used the limited possibility of reservations available in that respect*, has declared its intention to apply the provisions on the right of translation contained in the Berne Convention of 1886 as completed by the Additional Act of Paris of 1896 (concerning the restriction, under certain conditions, of the term of protection of the right of translation to ten years from the first publication of the work), any country has the right to apply a protection which is equivalent to the protection granted by the country of origin (Berne Convention, Article 30(2)(b), second sentence).

(c) under the IPIC Treaty

8. The following exceptions to national treatment are contained in the IPIC Treaty:

i) any Contracting Party is free not to apply national treatment as far as any obligations to appoint an agent or to designate an address for service are concerned (IPIC Treaty, Article 5(2));

ii) any Contracting Party is free not to apply national treatment as far as the special rules applicable to foreigners in court proceedings are concerned (IPIC Treaty, Article 5(2)).

---

* Only four States have maintained such a reservation.

5: Exhaustion of Rights

Article 6   Exhaustion

For the purposes of dispute settlement under this Agreement, subject to the provisions of Articles 3 and 4 nothing in this Agreement shall be used to address the issue of the exhaustion of intellectual property rights.

Paragraph 5 of the Doha Declaration on the TRIPS Agreement and Public Health

5. Accordingly and in the light of paragraph 4 above, while maintaining our commitments in the TRIPS Agreement, we recognize that these flexibilities include:

[. . .]

(d) The effect of the provisions in the TRIPS Agreement that are relevant to the exhaustion of intellectual property rights is to leave each Member free to establish its own regime for such exhaustion without challenge, subject to the MFN and national treatment provisions of Articles 3 and 4.

---

1. Introduction: terminology, definition and scope

Article 6 addresses the exhaustion of intellectual property rights. The concept of exhaustion plays an enormously important role in determining the way that intellectual property rules affect the movement of goods and services in international trade.

An intellectual property right, such as patent, trademark or copyright, is typically defined in terms of rights granted to the holder to prevent others from making use of it. For example, a patent grants to an inventor the right to prevent others from making, using, selling, offering for sale, or importing the invention without his or her consent. The trademark grants to its holder the right to prevent others from using a protected sign on identical or similar goods where such use is likely to cause consumer confusion. The copyright grants to its holder the right to prevent others from reproducing or distributing the work.

The doctrine of exhaustion addresses the point at which the IPR holder's control over the good or service ceases. This termination of control is critical to the functioning of any market economy because it permits the free transfer of goods and services. Without an exhaustion doctrine, the original IPR holder would perpetually exercise control over the sale, transfer or use of a good or service embodying an IPR, and would control economic life.

An IPR is typically exhausted by the "first sale" (U.S. doctrine) or "placing on the market" of the good or service embodying it. The basic idea is that once the right holder has been able to obtain an economic return from the first sale or placing on the market, the purchaser or transferee of the good or service is entitled to use and dispose of it without further restriction.

As illustration, consider a can of soda labelled with the famous "Coca-Cola" trademark. Because the Coca-Cola Company holds rights to that mark, it may prevent others from first-selling the can of soda without its consent. If you buy the can of soda from an authorized first-seller, the Coca-Cola Company's right in its trademark is exhausted, and it cannot prevent you from drinking the soda, or from giving or selling the can of soda to someone else. The trademark holder has lost its right to control further disposition of the product. Your purchase of the can of Coca-Cola does not authorize you to begin making your own cans of Coca-Cola, or licensing the mark to others. In other words, the first sale does not grant you rights in the trademark, but rather it extinguishes the Coca Cola Company's entitlement to control movement of that particular can of soda.

From the standpoint of the international trading system, the focus of the exhaustion question is whether it operates on a national, regional or international basis. IPRs are typically granted by national authorities. With the grant of an IPR, the patent, trademark or copyright holder obtains a "bundle of rights" that it may exercise within the territory of the granting authority. When a good or service is first sold or marketed in a country, this exhausts the IPR embodied in it.[201] Yet the same IPR holder may hold equivalent or "parallel" rights in many countries. The Coca-Cola Company, again for illustrative purposes, may hold trademark registrations for the Coca-Cola mark in every country of the world.

A country may choose to recognize that exhaustion of an IPR occurs when a good or service is first sold or marketed outside its own borders. That is, the first sale or marketing under a "parallel" patent, trademark or copyright abroad exhausts the IPR holder's rights within that country. If exhaustion occurs when a good or service is first sold or marketed outside a country, the IPR holder within the country may not oppose importation on the basis of its IPR. The importation of a good or service as to which exhaustion of an IPR has occurred abroad is commonly referred to as "parallel importation", and the goods and services subject to such trade are commonly referred to as "parallel imports". Since goods and services

---

[201] The manner in which IPRs are affected by exhaustion doctrine may vary depending on the characteristics of the form of protection. For example, while the first sale of a book will exhaust the copyright holder's right to control distribution of the book, the first showing of a film may not exhaust the right to control further showing of the film. For a discussion of the rental right in cinematographic works under Article 11, TRIPS, see Chapter 10.

subject to exhaustion of IPRs are exported as well as imported, the subject matter of trade in such goods is commonly referred to as "parallel trade".

If a country recognizes a doctrine of "national" exhaustion, an IPR holder's right to control movement of a good or service is only extinguished by the first sale or marketing of a good or service within the territory of that country. If a country recognizes a doctrine of "regional" exhaustion, an IPR holder's right to control movement is extinguished when a good or service is first sold or marketed in any country of the region. If a country recognizes a doctrine of "international exhaustion", an IPR holder's right to control movement is extinguished when a good or service is first sold or marketed anywhere in the world.

The flow of goods and services across borders is significantly affected by the exhaustion doctrine that WTO Members choose to adopt. Under a doctrine of international exhaustion, goods and services flow freely across borders after they have been first sold or placed on the market under certain conditions anywhere in the world. Under a doctrine of national exhaustion, the movement of goods and services may be blocked by IPR holders. Under national exhaustion, IPR holders have the power to segregate markets.

There is considerable debate concerning whether granting IPR holders the power to segregate markets is good or bad from various perspectives – economic, social, political and cultural. From the standpoint of those favouring open markets and competition, it may appear fundamentally inconsistent to permit intellectual property to serve as a mechanism to inhibit trade. Yet IPR holders argue that there are positive dimensions to market segregation, and corollary price discrimination.

During the GATT TRIPS negotiations, there was fairly extensive discussion of the exhaustion issue, but governments did not come close to agreeing upon a single set of exhaustion rules for the new WTO. They instead agreed that each WTO Member would be entitled to adopt its own exhaustion policy and rules. This agreement was embodied in Article 6, precluding anything in that agreement from being used to address the exhaustion of rights in dispute settlement, subject to the TRIPS provisions on national and MFN treatment.

2. History of the provision

2.1 Situation pre-TRIPS

Prior to negotiation of the TRIPS Agreement governments maintained different policies and rules on the subject of exhaustion of intellectual property rights in so far as those policies and rules affected international trade.[202] The situation in Europe and in the United States was rather complicated, as countries not only

---

[202] The first clear articulation of the concept of exhaustion of IPRs is sometimes traced to an 1873 U.S. Supreme Court decision, *Adams v. Burke* U.S. (17 Wall) 453 (1873). This case involved an attempt by the holder of a patent on a funeral casket lid to impose territorial restrictions on a purchaser's resale of caskets incorporating that lid. The Supreme Court held that the patent holder's control over the invention was exhausted on the first sale. It said:

"in the essential nature of things, when the patentee, or the person having his rights, sells a machine or instrument whose sole value is in its use, he receives the consideration for its use and he parts with the right to restrict that use. The article, in the language of the court, passes without the limit of the monopoly. That is to say, the patentee or his assignee having in the act of sale received all the royalty or consideration which he claims for the use of his invention in that particular machine

followed different approaches to the questions of national, regional and international exhaustion, but often differentiated their policies and rules depending upon the type of IPR affected.

In the United States, for example, the Supreme Court had addressed the issue of exhaustion in the field of trademarks, and interpreted domestic law to establish a "common control" doctrine.[203] If a product protected by a U.S. trademark was first sold abroad by a company owned or under common control with a company in the United States, the U.S. trademark could not be invoked to prevent parallel imports. However, if the product was first sold abroad by an independent company, or a licensee of the U.S. trademark holder, parallel imports could be blocked.

The Supreme Court had never expressly addressed the question of parallel importation in the field of patents.[204] Several important Court of Appeals decisions held in favour of international exhaustion of patent rights.[205] There was some contrary opinion at the district court level.[206] In the field of copyright, there was little in the way of judicial decision regarding national and international exhaustion prior to TRIPS, although this subject matter has been addressed with some frequency following its negotiation.

The European Court of Justice (ECJ) pioneered the exhaustion question in so far as it affected the movement of goods across borders. In 1964, shortly following the formation of the European Community, the ECJ was confronted in *Consten and Grundig* with an attempt by a manufacturer of audio equipment to prevent trade in its products among the member states by invoking parallel trademark rights.[207] The ECJ immediately recognized that the goal of European market integration would be inhibited if trademark holders could block the free movement of goods, and at that early stage invoked competition law principles to preclude such action. Subsequently, the ECJ framed its jurisprudence on this subject, fashioning an "intra-Community exhaustion doctrine", on the basis of the prohibition in the EC Treaty against quantitative restrictions and measures with equivalent effects (Article 28, EC Treaty, 1999 numbering).[208]

---

or instrument, it is open to the use of the purchaser without further restriction on account of the monopoly of the patentees." (453 U.S., at 456)[footnote omitted]

[203] *Kmart v. Cartier*, 486 U.S. 281 (1988).

[204] A case sometimes cited to the effect that the U.S. prohibited parallel importation in patented goods is *Boesch v. Graff* 133 U.S. 697 (1890). That case, however, involved goods first sold outside the United States under a "prior user's" exception to patent rights, and without the consent of the patent holder. (According to the prior user exception, a third person using the invention in good faith prior to the filing of the patent may continue the use of the invention in spite of the granting of the patent.) The potential implications of this decision are analyzed below.

[205] See most notably *Curtiss Aeroplane & Motor Corp. v. United Aircraft Engineering Corp.*, 266 F. 71 (2d Cir. 1920) and further cases discussed in Margreth Barrett, *The United States' Doctrine of Exhaustion: Parallel Imports of Patented Goods*, 27 N. Ky. L. Rev. 911 (2000).

[206] See, e.g., *Griffin v. Keystone Mushroom Farm, Inc.*, 453 F. Supp. 1283 (E.D. Pa. 1978).

[207] *Consten and Grundig v. Commission*, Cases 56, 58/64, [1966] ECR 299.

[208] The entire early history of ECJ jurisprudence on the subject of exhaustion is framed in terms of the tension between Article 30, EC Treaty (prohibiting quantitative restrictions and measures with equivalent effect) and Article 36, EC Treaty (allowing measures to protect IPRs). The EC Treaty was renumbered in 1999, so that former Article 30 is now Article 28, and former Article 36 is now Article 30. This makes for considerable confusion when discussing ECJ jurisprudence in this field.

Prior to the TRIPS Agreement negotiations all EC member states were subject to the "intra-Community" exhaustion rule in all fields of IPR protection.[209] There was an extensive body of case law in which the ECJ had refined this rule in particular contexts. For example, the Court recognized that the showing or broadcast of films presented special circumstances that required certain limitations on the general "placing on the market" rule.[210] In the field of trademarks, the Court allowed parallel traders flexibility in repackaging and labelling pharmaceuticals so long as this did not present a threat to consumer safety.[211] The ECJ further indicated in the context of a decision on rental rights that a certain level of approximation of IPR laws among the member states was necessary to protect the interests of rights holders.[212] EC member states were thus subject to a uniform rule of "intra-Community" or "regional" exhaustion across all fields of IP (or at least those with a sufficient level of approximation).

Though not free from doubt, the EC rule on patents appeared to contemplate that only goods placed on the market in a member state would be subject to the rule of exhaustion.[213] Thus, while the placing of a patented good on the market within the territory of the Community exhausted the patent holder's rights and allowed free movement within the Community, the placing of a patented good on the market outside the Community did not affect the patent holder's rights within the Community, and parallel importation could be blocked. EC member states maintained different approaches to international exhaustion in the field of trademarks, and until the adoption of the First Trade Marks Directive in 1988 the ECJ had not sought to impose a uniform approach. EC member states differed on the question whether the Directive mandated a uniform approach to the international exhaustion question.[214] Prior to the TRIPS Agreement negotiations, member states also maintained different approaches to the international exhaustion question in the field of copyright.[215] At the outset of the TRIPS negotiations in 1986, the EC did not approach the exhaustion question with a "single voice".

---

[209] Regarding patents, the leading case was *Centrafarm v. Sterling Drug*, Case 15/74, 1974 ECR 1147.

[210] See *Coditel SA v. Cine-Vog Films*, Case 62/79, [1980] ECR 881, [1981] CMLR 362, decision of Mar. 18, 1980 (Coditel I); see also *Coditel SA v. Cine-Vog Films*, Case 262/81, [1982] ECR 3381, [1983] 1 CMLR 49, decision of Oct. 6, 1982 (Coditel II) [regarding the potential applicability of former Article 85 EC Treaty on anti-competitive inter-firm agreements to the same facts].

[211] See *Pharmacia & Upjohn SA v. Paranova A/S*, Case C-379/97, 12 Oct. 1999.

[212] See *Warner Brothers v. Christiansen*, Case 158/86, [1988] ECR 2605, [1990] 3 CMLR 684.

[213] See, e.g., *Merck v. Stephar*, Case 187/80, [1981] ECR 2063, [1981] 3 CMLR 463 and *Polydor v. Harlequin Record Shops*, Case 270/80, [1982] ECR 329, [1982] 1 CMLR 677, Feb. 9, 1982 [broadly referring to industrial property rights]; cf. W.R. Cornish, INTELLECTUAL PROPERTY, 4th ed. 1999, at 6-15/6-16 [hereinafter Cornish].

[214] First Council Directive of 21 December 1988 to approximate the laws of the Member States relating to trade marks (89/104/EEC), OJ L 040, 11/02/1989 P.0001-0007. These differences were not settled until the ECJ's decision in *Silhouette v. Hartlauer* in 1998, in which it imposed a mandatory "intra-Community exhaustion" rule in trademarks, to the exclusion of international exhaustion. See discussion below, Section 6.3.

[215] Cf. Cornish, at 1-59.

Other countries and regions had also considered the question of national or international exhaustion. Japan[216] and Switzerland[217] each had substantial jurisprudence on the subject. The countries of Latin America appeared largely to favour international exhaustion. Decision 85 on Industrial Property of the Andean Commission excluded the right to prevent importation from patent holders, effectively providing for international exhaustion.[218] Decision 85 established an express rule of regional exhaustion in respect of trademarks.[219] South Africa maintained a rule of international exhaustion in the fields of patent[220] and trademark.[221]

Prior to the TRIPS negotiations there had been little in the way of systematic investigation of the potential impact of various exhaustion regimes on international trade and/or economic development. The European Court of Justice had identified that enforcement of national IPRs rules might play an important role in European efforts to integrate markets.

2.2 Negotiating history

2.2.1 Initial proposals

The subject of exhaustion of rights and parallel importation was discussed in the TRIPS Negotiating Group (TNG) on a substantial number of occasions during the Uruguay Round. It is evident from those discussions that delegations perceived the subject matter of importance, and had different views regarding the appropriate outcome. It is important to note that contemporaneous discussions on this subject matter were taking place at WIPO in the context of patent law harmonization negotiations throughout much of the TRIPS negotiations. In neither forum

---

[216] Report of Mitsuo Matsushita to Committee on International Trade Law of the International Law Association, noted in Abbott, First Report, Frederick M. Abbott, *First Report (Final) to the Committee on International Trade Law of the International Law Association on the Subject of Parallel Importation*, 1 J. Int'l Econ. L. 607 (1998).

[217] See Thomas Cottier and Marc Stucki, *Parallelimporte im Patent-, Urheber- und Muster-und Modellrecht aus europarechtlicher und völkerrechtlicher Sicht*, in B. Dutoit (edit.), Conflits entre importations parallèles et propriété intellectuelle?, Librairie Droz, Geneva 1996, p. 29 et seq.

[218] Article 28, Decision 85, provided:
"Article 28. With the limitations stipulated in the present Regulation, the patent shall confer on its owner the right to exploit the invention itself in an exclusive manner, to grant one or more licenses for its exploitation, and to receive royalties or compensation deriving from its exploitation by third persons.

The patent shall not confer an exclusive right to import the patented product or one manufactured under his patented process." [13 Int'l Legal Matl's 1478, 1492 (1974)]

See Frederick M. Abbott, *Bargaining Power and Strategy in the Foreign Investment Process; A Current Andean Code Analysis*, 3 SYR. J, INT'L L & COMM. 320, 346–51 (1975).

[219] Article 75, Decision 85, provided:
"Article 75. The owner of a trademark may not object to the importation or entry of merchandise or products originating in another Member Nation, which carry the same trademark. The competent national authorities shall require that the imported goods be clearly and adequately distinguished with an indication of the Member Nation where they were produced." [13 Int'l L. Matl's 1478, (1974)].

[It is not clear whether this rule was intended to exclude international exhaustion in the field of trademarks.]

[220] See *Stauffer Chemical Company v. Agricura Limited* 1979 BP 168.

[221] See Trade Marks Act 1993, Article 34(2)(d).

did governments come close to agreeing on uniform treatment of the exhaustion question.

The initial 1987 U.S. proposal for a TRIPS Agreement did not reference the subject of exhaustion.[222]

A compilation of written and oral submissions regarding trade in counterfeit goods circulated by the GATT Secretariat in April 1988 noted concerns regarding parallel imports. It said:

> "27. The question has been raised as to what would be the substantive intellectual property norms by reference to which counterfeit goods should be defined. In this regard the following points have been made:
>
> . . .
>
> – parallel imports are not counterfeit goods and a multilateral framework should not oblige parties to provide means of action against such goods."[223]

This compilation noted similar observations concerning the need to preserve rights of parallel importation in connection with border measures and safeguards to protect legitimate trade.[224]

The first EC proposal on substantive standards of July 1988 acknowledged the subject matter of exhaustion in regard to trademarks, though not specifically in the import context.[225]

Through the course of negotiations in 1989, a number of comments were directed at assuring that any rules developed in regard to border enforcement measures not be applied to parallel import goods, both in respect to copyright and trademark.[226] The Indian delegation specifically objected to a U.S. proposal to provide for national exhaustion in respect of trademarks:

> "The representative of India said that he disagreed with the United States proposal in relation to the exhaustion of rights. Referring to paragraph 38 of the Indian paper, he said that the principle of international exhaustion of rights should apply to trademarks."[227]

---

[222] United States Proposal for Negotiations on Trade-Related Aspects of Intellectual Property Rights, Nov. 3, 1987, at Patents (text reprinted in *U.S. Framework Proposal to GATT Concerning Intellectual Property Rights*, 4 BNA INT'L TR REPTR 1371 (Nov. 4, 1987)).

[223] Trade in Counterfeit Goods: Compilation of Written Submissions and Oral Statements, Prepared by the Secretariat, MTN.GNG/NG11/W/23, 26 April 1988.

[224] *Id.*, para. 38(iii).

[225] The EC proposal stated:
"Limited exceptions to the exclusive rights conferred by a trademark, which take account of the legitimate interests of the proprietor of the trademark and of third parties, may be made, such as fair use of descriptive terms and exhaustion of rights." Guidelines and Objectives Proposed by the European Community for the Negotiations on Trade Related Aspects of Substantive Standards of Intellectual Property Rights, Negotiating Group on Trade-Related Aspects of Intellectual Property Rights, including Trade in Counterfeit Goods, MTN.GNG/NG11/W/26, July 1988, at III.D.3.b(i).

[226] Note by the Secretariat, Meeting of Negotiating Group of 3–4 July 1989, MTN.GNG/NG11/13, 16 August 1989, e.g., at para. D7; Note by the Secretariat, Meeting of Negotiating Group of 12–14 July 1989, MTN.GNG/NG11/14, 12 September 1989, at para. 26.

[227] *Id.*, Meeting of 3–4 July 1989, at para. 45.

In 1989, Canada made a proposal to specifically provide for international exhaustion of rights in respect to the protection of layout-designs of integrated circuits.[228]

In March 1990, the EC tabled a draft text for a TRIPS Agreement[229] that provoked substantial comment from other delegations on the subject of exhaustion. As stated in a note by the GATT Secretariat:

> "Article 4: Customs Unions and Free Trade Areas. . . . The representative of the Community said that the underlying purpose of the Article was to enable the Community to continue to apply the principle of Community exhaustion in respect of trade among the member States.
>
> . . .
>
> Trademarks. A participant expressed concern that provisions on the very important concepts of parallel imports and exhaustion of rights were absent in the proposed draft agreement. Another participant asked if, under the Community proposal, trademark rights could or could not be used to prevent parallel imports. A further participant was of the view that the proposed Articles on trademarks would enable parallel imports of genuine goods to be prohibited; this conflicted with the Paris Convention and might lead to a division of markets, thus resulting in impediments and distortions of trade.
>
> . . .
>
> [Patents] Article 24: Rights Conferred. A participant expressed the view that the proposed provisions on rights conferred were not in line with the principles of intellectual property protection, for example because they tried to invalidate parallel imports and the doctrine of exhaustion of rights. . . . [230]

A proposal from the United States[231] shortly following the EC proposal likewise elicited a significant number of concerns regarding the exhaustion question. According to the GATT Secretariat:

> Article 2. [Copyright] . . . In answer to a question, he [i.e. the U.S. delegate] said paragraph (2)(b) could be clarified at a later stage, but the intent was that exhaustion of rights in one territory would not exhaust rights elsewhere. In that light, if goods put on the market in one country were exported to another country where exhaustion had not taken place, it would not undermine the rights established by paragraph (2)(a). Some participants said that they were concerned about the introduction of a right of importation, both here and in Article 9(b), since it could affect the right to effect parallel importations; such a right was not called for by the Berne Convention and could in itself give rise to trade distortions, especially in small countries. Another participant felt the relationship between the right of importation and the right of first distribution was not clear, the latter seeming to

---

[228] Note by the Secretariat, Meeting of Negotiating Group of 30 October-2 November 1989, MTN.GNG/NG11/16, 4 December 1989, at discussion of paragraph 13 of proposal.

[229] European Communities, Draft Agreement on Trade-Related Aspects of Intellectual Property Rights, MTN.GNG/NG11/W/68, 29 March 1990.

[230] Note by the Secretariat, Meeting of Negotiating Group of 2, 4 and 5 April 1990, MTN.GNG/NG11/20, 24 April 1990.

[231] Communication from the United States (NG11/W/70).

cover the former. In response to a question, the representative of the United States indicated that paragraph (2)(a) would not prevent imports of legitimate goods.

19. In relation to the proposed provisions on trademarks, a participant expressed concern about the absence of provisions . . . on parallel imports and exhaustion of rights. The following specific points were made in relation to the United States proposal on trademarks:

. . .

Article 12: Rights Conferred. Answering a query, the representative of the United States said that the last sentence of the first paragraph did not refer to parallel imports. The reason for this formulation was that his delegation had a difficulty with the comparable statement in the Community text which suggested that confusion should not be required where an identical sign was used on an identical good, because it had some difficulty in providing rights in the trademark area where confusion did not exist. The proposal that confusion would be presumed to exist in such cases was aimed at bridging this difference. A participant wondered if "use" of a mark included advertising and distribution and whether it could be presumed that exhaustion of rights would be left to national legislation. Some participants felt that the balance in the second paragraph leant perhaps too strongly towards the interests of international companies and could create uncertainty for domestic industry. . . ."[232]

2.2.2 The Anell Draft

The text prepared and distributed by Chairman Anell in July 1990 contained limited reference to the subject of exhaustion.[233] It provided:

"4. Exceptions

4A Limited exceptions to the exclusive rights conferred by a trademark, such as fair use of descriptive terms, may be made, provided that they take account of the legitimate interests of the proprietor of the trademark and of third parties.

4B Rights shall be subject to exhaustion if the trademarked goods or services are marketed by or with the consent of the owner in the territories of the PARTIES.

. . .

SECTION 4: SPECIAL REQUIREMENTS RELATED
TO BORDER MEASURES[1]

15. Suspension of Release by Customs Authorities

15A Without prejudice to point 21 of this Part, PARTIES shall, in conformity with the provisions set out below, establish procedures according to which a right holder, who has valid grounds for suspecting that the importation of [goods which infringe his intellectual property right] [counterfeit trademark or pirated copyright goods] may take place, may lodge an application in writing with the competent authorities, administrative or judicial, for the suspension by the customs authorities of the release into free circulation of such goods. [This provision does not create an obligation to apply such procedures to parallel imports]."

---

[232] Note by the Secretariat, Meeting of Negotiating Group of 14–16 May 1990 MTN.GNG/NG11/21, 22 June 1990.

[233] Status of Work in the Negotiating Group, Chairman's Report to the GNG, MTN.GNG/NG11/ W/76, 23 July 1990 [hereinafter Anell Draft].

[. . .]

[Note 1]: It will be made clear at an appropriate place in any agreement that, for the European Communities and for the purposes of this Section, the term "border" is understood to mean the external border of the European Communities with third countries.

2.2.3 The revised Anell Draft

However, subsequent to formal distribution of the July 1990 text, Chairman Anell distributed in October 1990 an informal text that incorporated a revised provision on exhaustion. Although that informal text has not yet been made publicly available, it was commented upon in a TNG meeting of 1 November 1990.

"3. Speaking on behalf of a number of developing countries, a participant welcomed the structure of the paper which, he said, was in line with the mandate provided in the Mid-term Review. By separating the text into two distinct agreements respectively dealing with trade-related aspects of intellectual property rights and trade in counterfeit and pirated goods, the paper conformed to the intent of the Punta del Este negotiating mandate..... Regarding its substantive contents, he wished to put on record the view that the paper did not adequately take into account the special needs and problems of developing countries. Flexibility in favour of developing countries was required in any TRIPS agreement, in view of their special developmental and technological needs....

4. Continuing, he then highlighted some provisions of the text which differed from other provisions because the problems involved were of a more fundamental character, while emphasising that this should not be interpreted as an acceptance of provisions he would not mention..... He welcomed the inclusion in the text of a general provision on exhaustion, which was a basic principle relating to intellectual property rights and as such should not be subject to any exceptions or conditions which might weaken or invalidate its application. In this connection, he said that it should be clarified throughout the text that any references to exclusive rights of importation implied a right to exclude only infringing goods. Alternatively, the grant of this right should be left to the discretion of Parties."[234]

2.2.4 The Brussels Draft

The Brussels Draft began to approximate the final text of Article 6, but the differences are important and instructive.

"Article 6: Exhaustion[3]

Subject to the provisions of Articles 3 and 4 above, nothing in this Agreement imposes any obligation on, or limits the freedom of, PARTIES with respect to the determination of their respective regimes regarding the exhaustion of any intellectual property rights conferred in respect of the use, sale, importation or other distribution of goods once those goods have been put on the market by or with the consent of the right holder.

[Footnote 3]: For the purposes of exhaustion, the European Communities shall be considered a single Party."

---

[234] Meeting of the Negotiating Group of 1 Nov. 1990, MTN.GNG/NG11/27,14 Nov. 1990.

It may first be noted that the Brussels text was framed in terms of substantive obligations under TRIPS and not as a limitation on dispute settlement on the subject of exhaustion. The later move toward preclusion of dispute settlement is emblematic of the inability of the parties to reach any substantive agreement on the exhaustion issue.

That inability to reach any substantive conclusion may at least in part be explained by the phrase "once those goods have been put on the market by or with the consent of the right holder". There was considerable debate concerning the scope of the exhaustion doctrine throughout the Uruguay Round. A number of developing countries did not wish to limit application of the doctrine to circumstances in which the IPR holder had consented to placing goods on the market, because there are other circumstances that were considered potentially to exhaust rights, such as sales under compulsory license.

In addition, reference to exhaustion of "rights conferred in respect of the use, sale, importation or other distribution of goods" differed substantially from the formula on exhaustion of rights contemporaneously under negotiation at WIPO in the patent law harmonization context, which is discussed in the next paragraphs.

It is also important to observe that at this stage the EC's intra-Community exhaustion doctrine would have been expressly addressed in a footnote to Article 6, and this was subsequently dropped.

The negotiating parties ultimately rejected a formula that would have essentially defined the scope of exhaustion doctrine.

Commencing in 1985,[235] a Committee of Experts on the Harmonization of Certain Provisions in Law for the Protection of Inventions was established under the authority of the International (Paris) Union for the Protection of Intellectual Property. As the name of this Committee implies, it was charged with seeking to establish common rules in the field of patents. The scope of this project was initially broad, as governments sought to agree upon harmonized substantive provisions of patent law. In late 1992, the scope of this project was limited by the removal of a number of basic articles from the negotiations.[236]

Article 19 of the Committee of Experts Draft Treaty on the Harmonization of Patent Laws (Eighth Session, June 11 to 22, 1990) concerns Rights Conferred by the Patent. The first two paragraphs of the proposal are directed at establishing basic rights in respect to product and process patents. The third paragraph concerns permissible exceptions to patent rights, and the fourth deals with the subject of contributory infringement (not relevant here). The text provides:

"Article 19

(formerly Article 302 [of prior draft text])

Rights Conferred by the Patent

Alternative A

---

[235] See *WIPO Experts Make Progress On Patent Harmonization Draft*, BNA's Patent, Trademark & Copyright Journal, Analysis, January 10, 1991, 41 PTCJ 231 (Issue No. 1013), Lexis/Nexis Database, at Introduction.

[236] See Paris Union Assembly, Nineteenth Session, WIPO doc. P/A/XIX/3, July 31, 1992.

[Products] Where the subject matter of the patent concerns a product, the owner of the patent shall have the right to prevent third parties from performing, without his authorization, at least the following acts:

the making of the product,

the offering or the putting on the market of the product, the using of the product, or the importing or stocking of the product for such offering or putting on the market or for such use.

[Processes] . . .

[Exceptions to Paragraphs (1) and (2)] (a) Notwithstanding paragraphs (1) and (2), any Contracting Party shall be free to provide that the owner of a patent has no right to prevent third parties from performing, without his authorization, the acts referred to in paragraphs (1) and (2) in the following circumstances:

where the act concerns a product which has been put on the market by the owner of the patent, or with his express consent, insofar as such an act is performed after that product has been put on the market in the territory of that Contracting Party, or, in the case of a regional market, in the territory of one of the members States of such group."

The WIPO draft text would have permitted a state to adopt national or regional exhaustion, but not international exhaustion. This was in fact an issue that remained controversial within the WIPO negotiations until the time the negotiations were suspended. The important aspect for present purposes is that the WIPO text uses a formula for substantively defining the exhaustion principle that is different than that under discussion at the GATT. The WIPO text refers to permitting "acts" in relation to patented products, with reference back to rights otherwise ascribed to the patent holder.

2.2.5 The Dunkel Draft
The Dunkel Draft text of Article 6 distributed in late 1991 is identical to Article 6, TRIPS Agreement.

At a 1998 meeting on the subject of exhaustion of rights and parallel importation, Mr. Adrian Otten, Director of the WTO Intellectual Property Division, who served as Secretary to the Trade Negotiating Group during the Uruguay Round negotiations, presented an oral description of the negotiations. That presentation was summarized in a report on the 1998 meeting:

"Adrian Otten (WTO) – Mr. Otten pointed out that the treatment of exhaustion of rights in the TRIPS Agreement was the subject of difficult and intensive negotiations during the Uruguay Round. The formula in Article 6, TRIPS Agreement, reflects a compromise between governments favoring an explicit recognition of national discretion in regard to exhaustion practices, including the choice of national or international exhaustion, and governments not wanting to provide such recognition although not seeking to regulate such practices specifically. The penultimately proposed formula would have indicated that the TRIPS Agreement did not address the issue of exhaustion of rights, while the final formula indicates that for purposes of dispute settlement under the TRIPS Agreement, nothing in that Agreement (subject to articles 3 and 4) will be used to address the issue of exhaustion. Both sides to the negotiations preferred the final formula. Mr. Otten observed that earlier proposals, on the one hand, for a provision restricting the scope for parallel imports in situations where prices had been influenced by government measures such as price controls and for a specific rule providing rights against parallel imports in the copyright area and, on the other hand, a provision requiring international exhaustion, at least in the trademark area, were rejected during these negotiations. In a subsequent comment from the floor, Mr. Otten indicated that he remains to be convinced that provisions of WTO agreements outside the TRIPS Agreement may not be used to address national laws on the exhaustion of IPRs, where the treatment accorded depends on the geographical origin of the goods rather than the nationality of the persons involved."[237]

3. Possible interpretations

Interpretation of Article 6 is among those aspects of TRIPS that have been most intensively discussed and written about. There are two main areas of controversy, although one of these has been definitively resolved by the Doha Declaration on the TRIPS Agreement and Public Health (see discussion below).

> "For the purposes of dispute settlement under this Agreement..."

The first clause refers specifically to "dispute settlement under this Agreement." Rights in intellectual property may have effects in other areas of WTO regulation. For example, technology protected by IPRs may be part of a technical standard that is regulated by the Agreement on Technical Barriers to Trade (TBT Agreement). The conformity of a technical standard with the TBT Agreement may be challenged in dispute settlement. The plain language of Article 6 suggests that rules of TRIPS might be used to address an exhaustion of IPRs issue in dispute settlement under the TBT. Moreover, the question of exhaustion is intricately connected with the free movement of goods, as recognized early on by the European Court of Justice. An IPR may have the same effects as a quota. There is a possibility for a Member to assert that a rule of national exhaustion that permitted IPRs holders to block importation of goods is inconsistent with Article XI, GATT 1994, that provides:

"1. No prohibitions or restrictions other than duties, taxes or other charges, whether made effective through quotas, import or export licences or other measures, shall be instituted or maintained [...]"

The plain language of Article 6 appears to allow a GATT panel to evaluate an IPR as a measure with the equivalent effect of a quota. This possibility is acknowledged

---

[237] Remarks of Adrian Otten in Frederick M. Abbott, *Second Report (Final) to the Committee on International Trade Law of the International Law Association on the Subject of the Exhaustion of Intellectual Property Rights and Parallel Importation*, presented in London, July 2000, at the 69th Conference of the International Law Association, rev. 1.1 [hereinafter "Second Report"] (posted at http://www.ballchair.org).

by several leading TRIPS experts who were closely involved in the Uruguay Round negotiations.[238]

Other TRIPS experts have argued that the Agreement constitutes a "lex specialis" or self-contained set of rules applicable to IPRs and trade regulation, and that the exhaustion question could not be examined by a GATT panel.[239] There is no WTO DSB jurisprudence on this issue, and for the time being the subject matter is open. However, the Appellate Body has placed great reliance on the plain language and meaning of the WTO Agreements, and the plain meaning certainly appears to support the view that the issue of exhaustion and relevant TRIPS rules could be examined in a dispute under an agreement other than TRIPS.

Another aspect of the first clause is that it is directed to WTO dispute settlement, and so does not directly preclude actions before national courts on exhaustion issues. This limitation was argued by certain Members and their industry groups to be synonymous with saying that Members are not permitted to adopt their own policies and rules on the subject of exhaustion, but rather that rules on this subject are established by TRIPS. Most prominently, pharmaceutical industry associations argued that Article 28, TRIPS Agreement, establishing the rights of patent holders, including to prevent importation, precluded adoption of an international exhaustion policy in the field of patents.

The argument that TRIPS precludes Members from adopting their own policies and rules on the subject of exhaustion is inconsistent with the terms of the Agreement, the practice of WTO Members, and the negotiating history of the Agreement.

Article 6 says that the rules of the Agreement may not be used to address the subject of exhaustion for purposes of WTO dispute settlement. This suggests that the rules of the Agreement may be used to address the subject in national court proceedings. It does not, however, say that Members are restricted in their choice of exhaustion policies, and these are very different matters.

Article 28, for example, grants patent holders the right to prevent third parties from importing patent protected goods without their consent. It does not, however, prescribe a rule as to how their consent will be determined. In Members that have adopted a rule of national exhaustion, consent only exhausts rights as to goods placed on the market within the territory of that Member. In Members that have adopted a rule of regional exhaustion, consent affects goods placed on the market in any Member within the regional group. In Members that have adopted a rule of international exhaustion, consent affects goods placed on the market anywhere in the world. TRIPS does not prescribe a rule regarding the geographic basis on which consent is determined, and clearly allows for international exhaustion.

---

[238] See Thomas Cottier, *The WTO System and the Exhaustion of Rights*, draft of November 6, 1998, for Conference on Exhaustion of Intellectual Property Rights and Parallel Importation in World Trade, Geneva, Nov. 6-7, 1998, Committee on International Trade Law, and Remarks of Thomas Cottier, in Second Report, and Remarks of Adrian Otten in Second Report, taking the position that Article 6 does not preclude application of the GATT 1994 or GATS to issues involving parallel importation.

[239] See Marco C.E.J. Bronckers, *The Exhaustion of Patent Rights under World Trade Organization Law*, 32 J. WORLD TR. L. 32 (1998) and Remarks of Marco Bronckers and Remarks of William Cornish, Second Report.

Footnote 6 to Article 28, TRIPS Agreement, provides: "This right, like all other rights conferred under this Agreement in respect of the use, sale, importation or other distribution of goods, is subject to the provisions of Article 6." This indicates that the right of importation granted to patent holders under Article 28 may not be used to address the subject matter of exhaustion in dispute settlement under TRIPS. In other words, no Member may be challenged in the WTO for adopting an international exhaustion rule based on the word "import" in Article 28.

At the time TRIPS was negotiated, GATT Contracting Parties applied different rules of exhaustion, often varying with the field of IPR protection.[240] There is no suggestion in the negotiating history of the TRIPS Agreement that Members reached agreement on uniform exhaustion rules at the time of its conclusion. Moreover, as noted later, since TRIPS entered into force, Members have continued to adopt and apply different exhaustion policies.[241]

If there was any doubt whether Article 6 prevents Members from adopting their own policies and rules on the subject of exhaustion of IPRs, this doubt was firmly eliminated by paragraph 5(d) of the Doha Declaration on the TRIPS Agreement and Public Health, which provides:

> "(d) The effect of the provisions in the TRIPS Agreement that are relevant to the exhaustion of intellectual property rights is to leave each Member free to establish its own regime for such exhaustion without challenge, subject to the MFN and national treatment provisions of Articles 3 and 4."[242]

The express recognition that Members may establish their own exhaustion regime does not, however, resolve all interpretative issues under Article 6. The main question remaining "on the table" involves whether Members must limit their recognition of the basis for exhaustion to IPR protected goods or services placed on the market with the "consent" of the right holder.

IPRs generally confer on right holders the right to prevent others from taking acts in relation to the IPR, such as selling an IPR protected product. The rationale behind basing exhaustion on the consent of the right holder is that the right holder has voluntarily surrendered its right to prevent the undertaking of the relevant act. Once the right holder "consents", it may no longer "prevent". The concept of exhaustion of IPRs is that the right holder is not granted a perpetual or indefinite right of consent, but rather a limited right.

IPR holders may suggest that limiting or interfering with their right to consent is a violation of fundamental rights in property. Since exhaustion signals an end to control over the good or service protected by the IPR, to exhaust without consent is an impermissible taking of rights in property.

Governments do not, however, confer absolute rights in IPRs. All IPRs are subject to exceptions in the public interest. Some exceptions are potentially more intrusive than others.

One circumstance that is often suggested as a basis for exhaustion without the consent of the IPRs holder is compulsory licensing. TRIPS acknowledges that

---

[240] See discussion above, Section 2.1.

[241] See, e.g., discussion of the domestic legislation of various WTO Members, below, Section 6.1.

[242] See WT/MIN(01)/DEC/W/2 of 14 November 2001.

governments may grant compulsory licenses, and establishes controls on terms and processes involved in granting them. Some TRIPS experts take the view that the first sale or marketing of an IPR protected good exhausts the IPR in the same manner as consent to the first sale or marketing, and that WTO Members may adopt international exhaustion rules that recognize compulsory licensing as the basis for exhaustion. Other TRIPS experts take the view that consent of the IPR holder is the only acceptable basis for an international exhaustion policy. The latter view is largely rooted in the concept of territoriality. The suggestion is that IPR holders outside the Member that grants a compulsory license should not have their right to prevent a first sale (that is, their "property right") affected by that Member's decision. To allow one Member to make exhaustion decisions that affects other Members would place too much power in the hands of the first Member.[243]

Although allowing international exhaustion based on compulsory licensing does place power in the hands of the granting Member, since TRIPS permits each Member to determine its own policy and rules on the exhaustion issue, it is not clear why there is a threat to importing Members. They are not required to recognize compulsory licensing as the basis for exhaustion, but they may do so.

A liberal approach to international exhaustion would recognize the "lawful" or "legitimate" placing of IPR protected goods or services on the market anywhere in the world as exhausting the right of importation. As noted earlier, there are exceptions to IPR protection other than provided by compulsory licensing, such as those recognized under Article 30, TRIPS Agreement. Consider a product placed on the market in the European Community under a so-called prior user's exception to patent rights.[244] The prior user of the invention acts without the consent of the patent holder, but the goods placed on the market are treated for internal market purposes just as if the patent holder had authorized the marketing. Should WTO Members outside the EC be required to differentiate in their exhaustion policies as between goods first marketed by the patent holder and goods first marketed by the prior user?

The text of Article 6 does not provide a definitive answer to the scope that Members may give to their doctrine of exhaustion, and this may argue in favour of allowing recognition of compulsory licensing, for example, as a basis.

Although Article 6 provides that nothing in TRIPS should be used to address exhaustion of IPRs, it does not define "exhaustion". If a Member adopts an exhaustion policy or rules that another Member considers to extend the concept beyond reasonable limits, there would not appear to be a bar to challenging that interpretation in dispute settlement.

> . . . subject to the provisions of Articles 3 and 4. . . .

---

[243] As with other aspects of IPRs and exhaustion policy, the rules respecting compulsory licensing might differ depending on the form of protection.

[244] According to the prior user exception, a third person using the invention in good faith prior to the filing of the patent may continue the use of the invention in spite of the granting of the patent.

Article 6 is not without express limitations. The exhaustion policy and rules of Members is subject to Articles 3 and 4, TRIPS Agreement.[245]

Application of the TRIPS national treatment provision to exhaustion doctrine suggests that Members must treat foreign nationals on at least an equivalent basis as local nationals regarding protection of IPRs by exhaustion rules. From a right holder's perspective, this would suggest that a Member may not apply a doctrine of international exhaustion that allows importation as regards foreign IPRs holders, and apply a doctrine of national exhaustion that prevents importation as regards local IPRs holders. This would assure that foreign nationals do not face greater competition from lower priced products than local nationals.

Application of the TRIPS MFN principle to exhaustion doctrine suggests that Members must not apply different exhaustion rules to nationals of different Members. Thus, for example, if the United States applies a doctrine of international exhaustion to IPRs held by Chinese nationals, it must apply the same rule to IPRs held by nationals of the EC. On the assumption that the nationals of Members are most likely to hold the IPRs relating to goods produced in their countries of origin, as a practical matter this means that imports from China and imports from the EU should be subject to the same U.S. rules on exhaustion.

Regional exhaustion doctrines could be considered not consistent with the basic MFN principle in TRIPS because they accord a different status in practical effect to goods imported from countries within the region than to countries from outside the region. In this case, right holders within Members that are part of the region may suffer *vis-à-vis* right holders in Members outside the region. A right holder whose good is first placed on the market outside the region may be able to block import into a Member of the region (and control the distribution of its product), while a right holder within the region could not prevent an importation from another Member within the region. This raises the interesting question whether a national of an EC member state or another regional arrangement could succeed on a claim that it was subject to less protection of IPRs than a national residing outside the EC. The EC claims that Article 4(d) allows it to discriminate against IPR holders residing within the region by precluding them from preventing the intra-Community free movement of goods and services.

4. WTO jurisprudence

None of the WTO Dispute Settlement Body, Appellate Body nor any panel has been asked to interpret Article 6. There are no dispute settlement decisions that discuss it.

However, as noted above, Ministers meeting in Doha adopted the Declaration on the TRIPS Agreement and Public Health that expressly addresses "the provisions in the TRIPS Agreement that are relevant to the exhaustion of intellectual property." Paragraph 5(d) of the Doha Declaration does not limit its reference to Article 6 precisely to account for arguments from some Members and industry groups that other Articles (such as Article 28) override it by implication.

---

[245] For a consideration of the purpose and effect of these Articles addressing national and MFN treatment, respectively, see Chapter 4.

Although there is some debate among legal experts as to precisely the character that should be ascribed to the Doha Declaration, there is no doubt that it will be taken into account by decision-making bodies in the context of dispute settlement. The Ministers clearly acted in Doha with a purpose, and there would be no reason to "recognize" an interpretation of the TRIPS Agreement if they did not intend this recognition to influence interpretation of the Agreement. The legal character of the Doha Declaration is discussed further in Chapters 6 and 33.[246]

5. Relationship with other international instruments

5.1 WTO Agreements

As discussed earlier, Article 6 specifically refers to settlement of disputes under the TRIPS Agreement. This leaves open the possibility that provisions of TRIPS relevant to the issue of exhaustion of rights will be applied in dispute settlement under other WTO Agreements.

As also mentioned, a claim might arise under the GATT 1994 that enforcement of IPRs to prevent importation of goods involves application of measures equivalent to quotas. If a Member permitted the adoption of a technical standard that incorporates IPR-protected subject matter, questions might arise regarding the extent to which the IPR-holder could control use or modification of the standard, implicating TRIPS rules relevant to exhaustion under the TBT Agreement. Since audio-visual services, as example, frequently incorporate IPR protected elements, it is certainly possible that a GATS dispute could implicate provisions of TRIPS relevant to exhaustion.

The relationship between TRIPS provisions relevant to exhaustion, including Article 6, and other WTO Agreements, remains to be determined in dispute settlement. There are different views among legal experts regarding whether Article 6 precludes exhaustion issues from being considered under other WTO Agreements. The "plain text" of Article 6 does not appear to preclude TRIPS rules relevant to exhaustion from being applied in dispute settlement under other agreements, but this does not exclude the possibility that TRIPS will be found to "occupy the field" of exhaustion subject matter as a special agreement governing trade and IPRs subject matter, or *lex specialis*.

5.2 Other international instruments

In December 1996 two new treaties with respect to intellectual property rights were adopted at WIPO: the Copyright Treaty (WCT) and the Performances and Phonograms Treaty (WPPT).[247] These two treaties include provisions with respect

---

[246] See Section 6.2 (International instruments) of both Chapters; see also F. Abbott, *The Doha Declaration on the TRIPS Agreement and Public Health: Lighting A Dark Corner at the WTO*, in: Journal of International Economic Law (2002), 469–505.

[247] World Intellectual Property Organization: Copyright Treaty [adopted in Geneva, Dec. 20, 1996], 36 I.L.M. 65 (1997) and World Intellectual Property Organization: Performances and Phonograms Treaty [adopted in Geneva, Dec. 20, 1996], 36 I.L.M. 76 (1997).

to the exhaustion of rights that, like Article 6,[248] reflect lack of agreement among governments on a unified approach to exhaustion of rights issues.[249] Several of the "agreed statements" to each of the WIPO Copyright Treaty and the WPPT address issues related to the issue of exhaustion, for example, by attempting to clarify distinctions between rights to redistribute physical copies of protected works and digital copies of such works.[250]

The WCT and WPPT are not incorporated in TRIPS, and their rules (including agreed statements) are not subject to WTO dispute settlement. At present, there are a limited number of state parties to these agreements. However, it is possible that in the future these agreements will have sufficiently wide adherence among WTO Members that a dispute settlement panel or the AB might look to them as evidence of state practice in interpreting related copyright provisions of TRIPS.

6. New developments

6.1 National laws
There have been a considerable number of national and regional court decisions on the subject of exhaustion of rights since the entry into force of TRIPS.

6.1.1 Australia and New Zealand
Australia and New Zealand each adopted legislation permitting parallel importation of works protected by copyright. The legislation adopted by Australia distinguishes among different types of copyrighted works.[251] In June 2000, the

---

[248] Article 6 of the Copyright Treaty provides:

(1) Authors of literary and artistic works shall enjoy the exclusive right of authorizing the making available to the public of the original and copies of their works through sale or other transfer of ownership.

(2) *Nothing in this Treaty shall affect the freedom of Contracting Parties to determine the conditions, if any, under which the exhaustion of the right in paragraph (1) applies after the first sale or other transfer of ownership of the original or a copy of the work with the authorization of the author.* [italics added]

Article 8 of the Performances and Phonograms Treaty provides:

(1) Performers shall enjoy the exclusive right of authorizing the making available to the public of the original and copies of their performances fixed in phonograms through sale or other transfer of ownership.

(2) *Nothing in this Treaty shall affect the freedom of Contracting Parties to determine the conditions, if any, under which the exhaustion of the right in paragraph (1) applies after the first sale or other transfer of ownership of the original or a copy of the fixed performance with the authorization of the performer.* [italics added]

[249] The Committee of Experts that prepared proposals for the treaties offered two alternative draft provisions: one that would have excluded international exhaustion, and one that would have permitted each treaty party to adopt an international exhaustion rule. See Chairman of the Committee of Experts, Basic Proposal for the Substantive Provisions of the Treaty on Certain Questions Concerning the Protection of Literary and Artistic Works to be Considered by the Diplomatic Conference, WIPO Doc. CRNR/DC/4, Aug. 30, 1996, at Article 8.

[250] For example, with respect to Article 6 of the Copyright Treaty as quoted above there was adopted an "Agreed statement concerning Articles 6 and 7", providing: "As used in these Articles, the expressions 'copies' and 'original and copies,' being subject to the right of distribution and the right of rental under the said Articles, refer exclusively to fixed copies that can be put into circulation as tangible objects."

[251] See Chris Creswell, *Recent Developments in Australia and New Zealand*, paper [furnished following Committee meeting of November 6–7, 1998]. See also, Abraham Van Melle, *Parallel*

government of Australia announced, following the recommendation of its Intellectual Property and Competition Review Committee, that it would further liberalize its rule of international exhaustion in the field of copyright by eliminating a requirement that importers await the Australian copyright holder's release of the work on the local market.[252]

6.1.2 Japan

In 1997 in the *BBS* case,[253] the Japanese Supreme Court held that the right under the Japanese Patent Act of a patent holder in Japan to block importation of a patented product was exhausted when the product was first sold abroad, subject to the possible imposition of contractual restrictions to the contrary.

6.1.3 South Africa

The South Africa Medicines and Related Substances Control Amendment Act of 1997 included a provision permitting the Minister of Health to establish the conditions under which parallel importation of patented medicines would be authorized. Since South Africa recognized international exhaustion as to patents as a matter of its common law, and since there was no indication that the parliament intended to change this rule when it amended the Patent Act to implement TRIPS, it is unlikely that Section 15C of the Medicines Amendment Act made new law in South Africa, except to provide regulatory authority to the Health Minister. Nonetheless, this legislation regarding parallel importation provoked intense diplomatic protest from the United States and European Community, and a lawsuit by 39 pharmaceutical companies (which also addressed other provisions of the Medicines Amendments Act). The challenges to the Medicines Amendment Act were withdrawn in 2001.

6.1.4 Other developing countries

A recent WIPO report identifies developing countries with regard to whether their legislation (a) allows for compulsory licensing and (b) adopts national or international exhaustion in respect to IPRs.[254]

Importing in New Zealand: Historical Origins, Recent Developments, and Future Directions, [1999] EIPR 63.

[252] See Fourteenth Copyright Newsletter of the Intellectual Property Branch of the Attorney-General's Department, <http://law.gov.au/copyright_enews>, June 29, 2000:

"The Government announced on 27 June 2000 that it will amend the Copyright Act 1968 to allow for parallel importation of legitimately produced books, periodicals, printed music, and software products including computer-based games. When implemented, this decision will remove the legal impediment imposed by the Copyright Act on Australian importers obtaining these products and making them available to consumers as soon as they are released anywhere in the world. They will not be obliged to wait for the Australian copyright owners to release them in Australia."

[253] *BBS Kraftfahrzeugtechnik AG and BBS Japan, Inc. v. Rasimex Japan, Inc.*, Supreme Court Heisei 7 (o) No. 1988 (July 1, 1997), J. of S. Ct., No. 1198 (July 15, 1997).

[254] See Legislative Assistance provided by the World Intellectual Property Organization (WIPO) in relation to the Implementation of the Agreement on Trade-Related Aspects of Intellectual Property Rights (the TRIPS Agreement) and the Doha Declaration, at <http://www.wipo.int/cfdiplaw/en/trips/index.htm>, visited 8 April 2004.

6.1.5 Switzerland

A 1999 decision, *Kodak v. Jumbo-Markt*,[255] by the Swiss Federal Supreme Court specifically addressed the question whether Article 6 permitted each WTO Member to adopt its own exhaustion regime in the field of patents, and found that it did.[256] The Swiss Supreme Court decided in favour of national exhaustion (rather than international exhaustion) for patents in Switzerland (based on its interpretation of existing national legislation), although it has adopted a rule of international exhaustion for copyright and trademark.

In 1998 the Swiss Federal Supreme Court in the *Nintendo*[257] case extended Switzerland's rule of international exhaustion in the field of trademarks[258] to the field of copyrighted works. In the *Nintendo* case, a producer of video games holding parallel copyright protection in Switzerland and the United States sought to block the importation into Switzerland of games first placed on the market in the United States with its consent. The Swiss Federal Court found no basis for adopting a different approach with regard to copyright than it had adopted in respect to trademarks in the *Chanel* case (decided in 1996). It said that the holder of parallel copyrights made the decision upon which market to first place its work, and that it received its economic return from this first marketing.[259]

6.1.6 United States

The weight of expert opinion during the Uruguay Round and after was that the United States followed a doctrine of international exhaustion in the field of

---

[255] *Kodak SA v. Jumbo-Markt AG*, 4C.24/1999/rnd, December 7, 1999.

[256] In the *Kodak* case, the Swiss Supreme Court found:

"3 b) Pursuant to Article 28 of the TRIPs Agreement, the patent holder has inter alia the right to prevent third parties selling patented objects and importing such for this purpose. This provision with its protection of imports merely lays down that the import of products that infringe the patent must be prohibited, without itself laying down a prohibition on parallel imports. This follows not only from Article 6 of the TRIPs Agreement but is also clarified in a reference to Article 6 in a footnote to Article 28 of the Agreement (GATT Message 1, 1994 Federal Gazette IV, p. 301/2; cf. also Bollinger, Die Regelung der Parallelimporte im Recht der WTO, sic! 1998, p. 548; Alesch Staehelin, Das TRIPs-Abkommen, 2nd ed., Bern 1999, p. 57 et seq. and 148/9; Cottier & Stucki, loc. cit., p. 52; Cohen Jehoram, International Exhaustion versus Importation Right: a Murky Area of Intellectual Property Law, 1996 GRUR Int., p. 284). The claim expressed occasionally in the literature that the substantive protection of importation practically requires national exhaustion through the TRIPs Agreement is not, on the other hand, convincing (argued by Straus, Bedeutung des TRIPs für das Patentrecht, 1996 GRUR Int., p. 193/4); for the attempt to derive the exclusive application of national exhaustion from this agreement ignores and misinterprets the objectives of the agreement to establish the World Trade Organisation dated April 15, 1994, one element of which is the TRIPs Agreement, namely to eliminate all kinds of trade restrictions. On the contrary, TRIPs is intended to balance two sets of interests, namely the demand for the freedom of trade on the one hand and an increased protection of intellectual property rights on the other hand (Bronckers, The Exhaustion of Patent Rights under WTO Law, Journal of World Trade 1998, p. 144). Exhaustion, and hence the question of whether in particular parallel imports can be prohibited by the party entitled to the patent, is not, however, regulated by Article 28 of TRIPs, but expressly reserved to national law pursuant to Article 6 of the Agreement (cf. also Kunz-Hallstein, Zur Frage der Parallelimporte im internationalen gewerblichen Rechtsschutz, 1998 GRUR, p. 269/70)."

[257] *Imprafot AG v. Nintendo Co. et al.*, Swiss Federal Supreme Court, No. 4C.45/1998/zus, July 20, 1998.

[258] *Chanel SA, Geneva and Chanel SA, Glarus v. EPA SA*, BGE 122 II 469, Oct. 23, 1996.

[259] See Carl Baudenbacher, *Trademark Law and Parallel Imports in a Globalized World – Recent Developments in Europe with Special Regard to the Legal Situation in the United States*, 22 Fordham Int'l L. J. 645 (1999), at 688 [hereinafter Baudenbacher].

patents. However, in late 2001, the Court of Appeals for the Federal Circuit (CAFC) rendered a decision, *Jazz Photo v. ITC*, (CAFC 2001) 264 F.3d 1094, that appears to overrule earlier precedent on this subject, and pending future developments before the Supreme Court, may be understood to reflect the current rule.

The case involved an appeal to the U.S. Court of Appeals for the Federal Circuit of a decision by the International Trade Commission in a Section 337 action initiated by Fuji Photo. Fuji sought to prevent importation of used disposable cameras in which third parties had replaced film. Some of those disposable cameras were first sold in the United States (and exported for film replacement), and some were first sold abroad. Fuji holds a number of patents on the disposable cameras in the United States and elsewhere.

The CAFC held that Fuji exhausted its patent rights concerning the disposable cameras when they were first sold, and it could not prevent third parties from refurbishing and reselling them. However, it went on to hold (in a brief conclusory statement) that exhaustion of the patent holder's rights only took place regarding products that had been first sold in the United States,[260] saying:

> "Fuji states that some of the imported LFFP cameras originated and were sold only overseas, but are included in the refurbished importations by some of the respondents. The record supports this statement, which does not appear to be disputed. United States patent rights are not exhausted by products of foreign provenance. To invoke the protection of the first sale doctrine, the authorized first sale must have occurred under the United States patent. See Boesch v. Graff, 133 U.S. 697, 701–703, 33 L. Ed. 787, 10 S. Ct. 378 (1890) (a lawful foreign purchase does not obviate the need for license from the United States patentee before importation into and sale in the United States). Our decision applies only to LFFPs for which the United States patent right has been exhausted by first sale in the United States. Imported LFFPs of solely foreign provenance are not immunized from infringement of United States patents by the nature of their refurbishment." (264 F.3d 1094,1105)

The CAFC held that Fuji could not prevent importation of cameras that had first been sold in the United States, exported for repair, then re-imported. However, since U.S. patent rights as to cameras first sold outside the United States were not exhausted, importation of cameras first sold and repaired outside the United States could be blocked.[261]

---

[260] Much of the CAFC decision involves the question whether the actions by third parties constitute "repair" or "reconstruction" as a matter of U.S. patent law. Under existing doctrine, a patent holder may not prevent a third party from "repairing" a patented product that has been first sold, but may prevent the "reconstruction" of a product. Reconstruction is treated as the equivalent of "making" a new product, and therefore to be within the acts the patent holder may prevent.

The ITC decided that the acts performed by third parties constituted reconstruction, and that importation of the used and reconstructed disposable cameras should be generally prohibited. The CAFC disagreed with the ITC's legal analysis, holding that the acts performed by third parties constituted "repair", and therefore were permitted as to disposable cameras that had been first sold. That is, the rights of the patent holders to exercise control over repair of the cameras had been "exhausted" when they were first sold.

[261] This analysis by the CAFC may not adequately address pre-existing U.S. law on patents and parallel importation. As is well known among those familiar with U.S. case law on the question of exhaustion, the Supreme Court's decision in *Boesch v. Graff* in 1890 involved limited and different

6.2 International instruments

See discussion of WIPO treaties, Section 5.2, above.

6.3 Regional and bilateral contexts

6.3.1 Regional

In 1998 the European Free Trade Area (EFTA) Court decided the *Maglite* case.[262] In this case, the holder of parallel trademarks in Norway and the United States sought to block the importation into Norway (by an unrelated party) of a product initially placed on the U.S. market with the trademark holder's consent.[263] The EFTA Court recognized that European Economic Area (EEA) countries are generally bound to follow European Union jurisprudence regarding intellectual property, including the rule of intra-EEA exhaustion. The EFTA Court held, however, that since EFTA is a free trade area lacking a common external commercial policy, while the EU is a customs union adhering to a common external commercial policy, that each EFTA country is entitled to adopt its own rule with respect to the international exhaustion of trademark rights. Norway was thus entitled to follow its longstanding rule in favour of international exhaustion.

circumstances than those in the present case. In Boesch, the inventor of a lamp burner held parallel patents in Germany and the United States. Under German law, there was a "prior use" exception that allowed a third party to lawfully manufacture and sell a patented product in Germany. The goods (lamp burners) that were sold in Germany and sent to the United States were made and sold by a party other than the patent holder under the prior use exception. The U.S. patent holder had not placed the goods on the market in Germany, and had not exhausted its U.S. patent rights with respect to those goods.

Since Boesch, there have been several important Court of Appeals decisions holding that the United States follows a doctrine of international exhaustion of patent rights. Among the most important of these is the decision of the Court of Appeals for the Second Circuit in *Curtiss Aeroplane v. United Aircraft*, 266 F. 71 (2d. Cir. 1920). In that case, a holder of U.S. patents on aircraft components had licensed the British government to produce aircraft in Canada (for use in the First World War). After the war, the British government sold some of the aircraft it had produced to a third party that imported them into the United States for resale. The Second Circuit held that the U.S. patent holder, in consenting to the use of its patent for the manufacture of airplanes in Canada, had exhausted its right to control the importation of the resulting aircraft into the United States.

While there has been some conflicting case law at the district court level on the question of international exhaustion of patent rights, the most comprehensive analysis of the case law finds that the U.S. follows a doctrine of international exhaustion in respect to patents (see Margreth Barrett, above), that is, at least until *Jazz Photo*. In *Jazz Photo*, the CAFC states a principle which it derives from *Boesch v. Graff*, but that case has previously and properly been limited and distinguished by other Courts of Appeal. The CAFC fails to take note of this contrary pre-existing case law.

[262] *MAG Instrument Inc. v. California Trading Co. Norway, Ulsteen*, Case E-2/97, 1997 Rep. EFTA Ct. 127, [1998] 1 C.M.L.R. 331.

[263] According to Prof. Baudenbacher:

The plaintiff in the proceedings before the Fredrikstad City Court (Fredrikstad Byrett), Mag Instrument, Inc., was a U.S. company that produces and sells the so-called Maglite lights. In Norway, Viking International Products A/S, Oslo, was the authorized sole importer and sole distributor for those products. The trademark was registered in Norway in the plaintiff's name. The defendant, California Trading Company Norway, Ulsteen, had imported Maglite lights directly from the United States into Norway for sale in Norway, without the consent of the plaintiff. The plaintiff brought proceedings against the defendant before the national court, arguing that the imports infringed its exclusive trademark rights. (Baudenbacher, at 650)

In *Silhouette v. Hartlauer*,[264] decided in 1998, the European Court of Justice (ECJ) considered whether the First Trade Marks directive prescribed a uniform rule of intra-EC exhaustion in the field of trade marks. This case involved an action by an Austrian trademark holder to prevent the importation into Austria of goods that it had exported and sold to an unrelated purchaser in Bulgaria (outside the EEA). A third party sought to export the same goods from Bulgaria and resell them in Austria without the consent of the Austrian trademark holder. The ECJ interpreted Article 7(1) of the First Trade Marks Directive to mandate that member states of the EU (and EEA) follow a rule of intra-EU exhaustion of trademark rights, and that the Directive precluded the member states from adopting a rule of international exhaustion. Austria was therefore precluded by the Trade Marks Directive from continuing to follow its rule of international exhaustion in the field of trademarks.[265]

Since EC directives and regulations regarding IPRs adopted before and after conclusion of TRIPS generally include the same legal formula regarding intra-Community exhaustion of rights as is found in the First Trade Marks Directive, it is most likely that those directives and regulations will be determined to mandate that EC member states exclusively apply rules of regional exhaustion.[266]

6.3.2 Bilateral

Paragraph 5(d) of the Doha Declaration on the TRIPS Agreement and Public Health confirmed the right of WTO Members to adopt their own policies and rules on the subject of exhaustion of rights. However, since the adoption of the Declaration several countries have entered into bilateral "free trade" agreements that obligate them to prevent parallel importation of patented products, at least when the patent holder has included a territorial limitation on the distribution of the product by contract or "other means".[267] As discussed in Chapter 2, TRIPS establishes minimum standards of IPR protection, but leaves Members discretion

---

[264] *Silhouette International Schmied Gesellschaft mbH & Co. KG v. Hartlauer Handelsgesellschaft mbH*, Case C-355/96, [1998] E.C.R. I-4799, [1998] 2 C.M.L.R. 953. Advocate General Francis Jacobs recommended to the ECJ that it decide the First Trade Marks Directive required EEA member states to exclusively follow a rule of intra-Union exhaustion. The opinion of the Advocate General was critically analyzed in Frederick M. Abbott and D.W. Feer Verkade, *The Silhouette of a Trojan Horse: Reflections on the Advocate General Jacobs' Opinion in Silhouette v. Hartlauer*, Bijblad bij De Industriële Eigendom 111, Apr. 16, 1998 and W. R. Cornish, *Trade Marks: Portcullis for the EEA?*, 20 EIPR 172, May 1998.

[265] In a follow on decision to Silhouette, the ECJ held that a trademark holder placing goods on the market outside the EC might by implication authorize parallel importation into the EC market (that is, relinquish its right to prevent importation), but that consent by implication must be unequivocally demonstrated. *Davidoff v. Levi Strauss and Tesco Stores v. Levi Strauss*, Joined Cases C-414/99 to C-416/99.

[266] See, e.g.,the Copyright Directive, Biotechnology Directive, Rental Rights Directive, Database Directive.

[267] For example, the U.S.– Morocco FTA provides at Article 15.9: PATENTS
"15.9 (4) Each Party shall provide that the exclusive right of the patent owner to prevent importation of a patented product, or a product that results from patented process, without the consent of the patent owner shall not be limited by the sale or distribution of that product outside its territory [footnote 9][fn. 9 – A Party may limit application of this paragraph to cases where the patent owner has placed restrictions on import by contract or other means.]"
See also, a comparable provision in the U.S.-Australia FTA, at Article 17.9(4).

to adopt higher standards. TRIPS does not preclude Members from agreeing to relinquish rights to permit parallel importation. Yet, it seems inconsistent with the spirit of the Doha Declaration that Members that have agreed on the multilateral level to national autonomy in the determination of exhaustion policy would have been asked to relinquish that autonomy as part of a package of bilateral trade concessions.

6.4 Proposals for review

The adoption of the Doha Declaration on the TRIPS Agreement and Public Health resolved the question whether WTO Members are permitted to adopt their own regimes regarding exhaustion of rights (see above, Section 3). There are no present proposals to reopen this issue.

However, the relationship between rules on exhaustion of patent rights and proposals to facilitate price discrimination in favour of developing countries to address public health needs has resulted in renewed discussion concerning the extent to which restrictions on parallel trade may be desirable in certain contexts. These issues are being considered in the context of continuing negotiations regarding implementation of paragraph 6 of the Doha Declaration.

7. Comments, including economic and social implications

There is considerable debate regarding the economic and social implications of different exhaustion of rights regimes.[268] It is important to acknowledge at the outset that the same conclusions may not apply to all forms of IPRs, or for that matter to different goods and services protected by these different forms. There may or may not be a single optimum exhaustion rule. With that said, there are a few general observations that can be made.

First, rules of exhaustion are designed to foster competition among producers, and to benefit consumers. Exhaustion of IPRs limits the legal capacity of producers to control the movement of goods and services after the first sale or lawful placing on the market, and reduces the potential for trade-restrictive (including anti-competitive) behaviours. As a "first principle", it is to the consumer's advantage that exhaustion of rights is accepted.

In the international setting, there are two main arguments made by proponents of limiting exhaustion and parallel importation. The first is that by allowing IPR holders to segregate markets and charge different prices, producers can achieve higher rates of return on their investments in intellectual property. This will permit producers to reinvest greater amounts in the creation of new and better goods and services, which is to the benefit of consumers.

---

[268] See, e.g., Frederick M. Abbott, *First Report (Final) to the Committee on International Trade Law of the International Law Association on the Subject of Parallel Importation*, 1 J. Int'l Econ. L. 607 (1998); Keith Maskus, *Parallel Imports in Pharmaceuticals: Implications for Competition and Prices in Developing Countries*, Final Report to the World Intellectual Property Organization, draft of April 2001; Commission on Macroeconomics and Health, CMH Working Paper Series, Paper No. WG4:1 – Scherer, F.M. and Watal, Jayashree, *Post-TRIPS Options for Access to Patented Medicines in Developing Countries*, June 2001.

Similar arguments are often made to promote higher levels of IPR protection generally, and there is good reason to be sceptical about the need for higher levels of protection and increasing returns to IPR-holders at a cost to the public of higher prices.

A second argument is that parallel imports hurt developing country interests because, if goods placed on the market in developing countries can freely flow to developed countries, producers will refrain from charging lower prices in developing countries.

It is curious that some developed countries that are the most aggressive promoters of liberal trade – which is about maintaining free movement of goods and services, competitive markets and operation of comparative advantage – favour market segregation and differential pricing when it comes to IPRs and parallel trade. It is difficult to reconcile the view that open markets benefit developing countries by allowing them access to developed markets for their low-production cost products, and the view that low-priced goods must remain in developing countries. If it is correct that price discrimination as a general proposition favours developing countries, this might imply that liberal trade rules are not the most beneficial for them.

As a general proposition, international exhaustion of IPRs may be the principle most consistent with fostering competition, specialization and global economic welfare (assuming that economists would not advocate a rethinking of the foundations of the WTO system). Yet does this mean that price discrimination will never benefit developing countries? Probably not. There are circumstances in which it may be desirable to limit inter-country price competition to promote the interests of consumers in developing countries, such as when the prospects for developing countries to establish their own globally competitive sources of supply are limited.[269] There may not be many such cases, and even those cases may result from IPR protection granted to developed country technologies. The point is, however, that there may be exceptional cases in which the advantages of an international exhaustion regime would be outweighed by competing developing country consumer interests. In such cases it may be possible to grant an exception to the otherwise applicable rules, rather than opting for a closed exhaustion regime that on the whole disadvantages developing countries.

The argument by some developed countries that rules allowing parallel trade harm developing country interests because such rules inhibit the sale of lower priced goods in many cases proceeds from a false factual premise. Perhaps paradoxically, goods and services are often sold in developing countries at prices higher than in developed countries, and developing country consumers will benefit from importing from the developed countries.

---

[269] For example, the Commission on Intellectual Property Rights established by the British government recommended that supply of patented pharmaceuticals to developing countries at lower differential prices might be facilitated if developed countries prevented parallel importation of those medicines. The Commission, however, recommended that developing countries continue to allow parallel importation of patented medicines to assure the lowest cost source of supply. IPR Commission, at Chpt. 2.

6: Objectives and Principles

> ## Article 7 Objectives
>
> The protection and enforcement of intellectual property rights should contribute to the promotion of technological innovation and to the transfer and dissemination of technology, to the mutual advantage of producers and users of technological knowledge and in a manner conducive to social and economic welfare, and to a balance of rights and obligations.

> ## Article 8 Principles
>
> 1. Members may, in formulating or amending their laws and regulations, adopt measures necessary to protect public health and nutrition, and to promote the public interest in sectors of vital importance to their socio-economic and technological development, provided that such measures are consistent with the provisions of this Agreement.
>
> 2. Appropriate measures, provided that they are consistent with the provisions of this Agreement, may be needed to prevent the abuse of intellectual property rights by right holders or the resort to practices which unreasonably restrain trade or adversely affect the international transfer of technology.

1. Introduction: terminology, definition and scope

An article of a treaty establishes rights and obligations for the parties. A general principle of treaty interpretation is that terms are presumed not to be surplus. Words are in a treaty for a reason and should be given their ordinary meaning in its context.[270] When the negotiators of the TRIPS Agreement

---

[270] See, e.g., the decision of the WTO Appellate Body in *United States – Standards for Reformulated and Conventional Gasoline*, WT/DS2/9 20 May 1996, in which the AB said:

"Applying the basic principle of interpretation that the words of a treaty, like the *General Agreement*, are to be given their ordinary meaning, in their context and in the light of the treaty's object and purpose, the Appellate Body observes that the Panel Report failed to take adequate account of the words actually used by Article XX in its several paragraphs." *Id.*, at page 18.

decided to include specific articles on "Objectives" and "Principles" in the agreement, they presumable did so with the goal of establishing rights and/or obligations.

Articles 7 and 8 have been invoked by Members to support rather different views of the purposes of TRIPS. The articles reflect the tensions inherent in the negotiations. Developing country Members have expressed considerable concern that only one side of the Agreement's objectives are pursued by developed Members, these being the objectives relating to the protection of technology "assets", while the stated objectives "that the protection and enforcement of intellectual property rights should contribute to the promotion" of transferring technology and actively promoting developmental interests are relegated to a secondary, and perhaps even illusory, status.

On 14 November 2001, WTO Members meeting in Doha adopted a Ministerial Declaration on the TRIPS Agreement and Public Health that bears directly on Articles 7 and 8. The implications of this Declaration for these provisions is described and analysed in Section 6.2.1, below.

2. History of the provision

2.1 Situation pre-TRIPS

Articles 7 and 8 of TRIPS establish the objectives and principles of this particular Agreement. Since TRIPS brought the regulation of intellectual property rights into the GATT, and now WTO, multilateral trading system for the first time,[271] there is no pre-TRIPS situation in respect to the objectives and principles of the Agreement. In other words, the objectives and principles of the TRIPS are unique to the Agreement.

The pre-TRIPS Agreement situation with respect to international governance of IPRs involved treaties administered by WIPO and other institutions. Even with respect to more detailed treaties like the Berne Convention, the pre-TRIPS international situation largely left discretion to regulate IPRs in the hands of each state, taking into account the domestic regulatory interests of the state. TRIPS represented a dramatic shift in that situation, taking away a great deal of internal regulatory discretion, and potentially shifting the pre-existing balance of internal interests. In light of this rather dramatic shift, the elaboration of objectives and principles in Articles 7 and 8 may well be viewed as a means to establish a balancing of interests at the multilateral level to substitute for the balancing traditionally undertaken at the national level.

Neither the Paris nor Berne Convention included provisions analogous to Articles 7 and 8. That is, there are no provisions that act to establish an overarching set of principles regarding the interpretation and implementation of the agreement.

---

[271] As noted elsewhere in this book, there were a few provisions in the GATT 1947 that concerned unfair competition, and Article XX(d) provided an exception for measures taken to protect IP. There was, however, no attempt in the agreement to establish substantive IPRs standards.

2.2 Negotiating history

2.2.1 Early proposals[272]

2.2.1.1 The USA. The initial November 1987 United States "Proposal for Negotiations on Trade-Related Aspects of Intellectual Property Rights" included a section that addressed the objectives of the agreement:

"Objective. The objective of a GATT intellectual property agreement would be to reduce distortions of and impediments to legitimate trade in goods and services caused by deficient levels of protection and enforcement of intellectual property rights. In order to realize that objective all participants should agree to undertake the following:

– Create an effective economic deterrent to international trade in goods and services which infringe intellectual property rights through implementation of border measures;

– Recognize and implement standards and norms that provide adequate means of obtaining and maintaining intellectual property rights and provide a basis for effective enforcement of those rights;

– Ensure that such measure to protect intellectual property rights do not create barriers to legitimate trade;

– Extend international notification, consultation, surveillance and dispute settlement procedures to protection of intellectual property and enforcement of intellectual property rights;

– Encourage non-signatory governments to achieve, adopt and enforce the recognized standards for protection of intellectual property and join the agreement."[273]

2.2.1.2 The EC. A proposal of Guidelines and Objectives submitted by the European Community to the TRIPS Negotiating Group in July 1988 also addressed the general purposes of an agreement, stating *inter alia*:

"... the Community suggests that the negotiations on substantive standards be conducted with the following guidelines in mind:

– they should address trade-related substantive standards in respect of issues where the growing importance of intellectual property rights for international trade requires a basic degree of convergence as regards the principles and the basic features of protection;

– GATT negotiations on trade related aspects of substantive standards of intellectual property rights should not attempt to elaborate rules which would substitute

---

[272] The proposals from the United States and European Community, as well as the statement by the Indian delegate that follow, also are reproduced in Chapter 1 regarding the preamble to the TRIPS Agreement. However, these elements of the negotiating history bear directly on the development of Articles 7 and 8, as well as the Preamble, and are repeated here for the convenience of the reader.

[273] Suggestion by the United States for Achieving the Negotiating Objective, United States Proposal for Negotiations on Trade-Related Aspects of Intellectual Property Rights, Negotiating Group on Trade-Related Aspects of Intellectual Property Rights, including Trade in Counterfeit Goods, MTN.GNG/NG11/W/14, 20 Oct. 1987, Nov. 3, 1987.

for existing specific conventions on intellectual property matters; contracting parties, could, however, when this was deemed necessary, elaborate further principles in order to reduce trade distortions or impediments. The exercise should largely be limited to an identification of an agreement on the principles of protection which should be respected by all parties; the negotiations should not aim at the harmonization of national laws;

– the GATT negotiations should be without prejudices to initiatives that may be taken in WIPO or elsewhere. . . ."[274]

2.2.1.3 India. In July 1989, India submitted a detailed paper that elaborated a developing country perspective on the objective of the negotiations. It concluded:

"It would . . . not be appropriate to establish within the framework of the General Agreement on Tariffs and Trade any new rules and disciplines pertaining to standards and principles concerning the availability, scope and use of intellectual property rights."[275]

At a meeting of the TRIPS Negotiating Group in July 1989, the objectives and principles of the agreement were discussed. As reported by the Secretariat, India was among those countries that made a fairly detailed intervention:

"5. In his statement introducing the Indian paper, the representative of India first referred to recent action by the United States under its trade law and recalled the serious reservations of his delegation about the relevance and utility of the TRIPS negotiations as long as measures of bilateral coercion and threat continued. Subject to this reservation, his delegation submitted the paper circulated as document NG11/W/37, setting out the views of India on this agenda item. At the outset, he emphasised three points. First, India was of the view that it was only the restrictive and anti-competitive practices of the owners of the IPRs that could be considered to be trade-related because they alone distorted or impeded international trade. Although India did not regard the other aspects of IPRs dealt with in the paper to be trade-related, it had examined these other aspects in the paper for two reasons: they had been raised in the various submissions made to the Negotiating Group by some other participants; and, more importantly, they had to be seen in the wider developmental and technological context to which they properly belonged. India was of the view that by merely placing the label "trade-related" on them, such issues could not be brought within the ambit of international trade. Secondly, paragraphs 4(b) and 5 of the TNC decision of April 1989 were inextricably inter-linked. The discussions on paragraph 4(b) should unambiguously be governed by the socio-economic, developmental, technological and public interest needs of developing countries. Any principle or standard relating to IPRs should be carefully tested against these needs of developing countries, and it would not be appropriate

---

[274] Guidelines and Objectives Proposed by the European Community for the Negotiations on Trade Related Aspects of Substantive Standards of Intellectual Property Rights, Negotiating Group on Trade-Related Aspects of Intellectual Property Rights, including Trade in Counterfeit Goods, MTN.GNG/NG11/W/26, July 1988, at II. The EC proposal stated that it was not intended to indicate a preference for a "code" approach. *Id.*, at note 1.

[275] Communication from India, Standards and Principles Concerning the Availability, Scope and Use of Trade-Related Intellectual Property Rights, MTN.GNG/NG11/W/37, 10 July 1989.

for the discussions to focus merely on the protection of the monopoly rights of the owners of intellectual property. Thirdly, he emphasised that any discussion on the intellectual property system should keep in perspective that the essence of the system was its monopolistic and restrictive character. This had special implications for developing countries, because more than 99 per cent of the world's stock of patents was owned by the nationals of the industrialised countries. Recognising the extraordinary rights granted by the system and their implications, international conventions on this subject incorporated, as a central philosophy, the freedom of member States to attune their intellectual property protection system to their own needs and conditions. This freedom of host countries should be recognised as a fundamental principle and should guide all of the discussions in the Negotiating Group. . . . Substantive standards on intellectual property were really related to socio-economic, industrial and technological development, especially in the case of developing countries. It was for this reason that GATT had so far played only a peripheral role in this area and the international community had established other specialised agencies to deal with substantive issues of IPRs. The Group should therefore focus on the restrictive and anti-competitive practices of the owners of IPRs and evolve standards and principles for their elimination so that international trade was not distorted or impeded by such practices."[276]

The Indian position was debated extensively, with a substantial number of developing delegations lending their support.

2.2.2 The Anell Draft
The main body of the Anell text (as opposed to its Annex)[277] included a draft with respect to "Principles", which is a "B" text (i.e. developing country-supported).

"8. Principles

8B.1 PARTIES recognize that intellectual property rights are granted not only in acknowledgement of the contributions of inventors and creators, but also to assist in the diffusion of technological knowledge and its dissemination to those who could benefit from it in a manner conducive to social and economic welfare and agree that this balance of rights and obligations inherent in all systems of intellectual property rights should be observed.

8B.2 In formulating or amending their national laws and regulations on IPRs, PARTIES have the right to adopt appropriate measures to protect public morality, national security, public health and nutrition, or to promote public interest in sectors of vital importance to their socio-economic and technological development.

8B.3 PARTIES agree that the protection and enforcement of intellectual property rights should contribute to the promotion of technological innovation and enhance the international transfer of technology to the mutual advantage of producers and users of technological knowledge.

---

[276] Note by the Secretariat, Meeting of Negotiating Group of 12–14 July 1989, Negotiating Group on Trade-Related Aspects of Intellectual Property Rights, including Trade in Counterfeit Goods, MTN.GNG/NG11/14, 12 September 1989.

[277] For an explanation of the Anell Draft, see the explanatory note on the methodology at the beginning of this volume.

8B.4 Each PARTY will take the measures it deems appropriate with a view to preventing the abuse of intellectual property rights or the resort to practices which unreasonably restrain trade or adversely affect the international transfer of technology. PARTIES undertake to consult each other and to co-operate in this regard."[278]

Most of the elements of Articles 7 and 8 can be identified in Article 8B, above, although some elements of Articles 7 and 8 can also be found in the Annex.[279] It is significant that the developing country proposal for objectives and principles

---

[278] Chairman's Report to the GNG, Status of Work in the Negotiating Group, Negotiating Group on Trade-Related Aspects of Intellectual Property Rights, including Trade in Counterfeit Goods, MTN.GNG/NG11/W/76, 23 July 1990.

[279] The Annex (see also Chapter 1) provided:

"This Annex reproduces tel quel Parts I, VI, VII and VIII of the composite draft text which was circulated informally by the Chairman of the Negotiating Group on 12 June 1990. The text was prepared on the basis of the draft legal texts submitted by the European Communities (NG11/W/68), the United States (NG11/W/70), Argentina, Brazil, Chile, China, Colombia, Cuba, Egypt, India, Nigeria, Peru, Tanzania and Uruguay, and subsequently also sponsored by Pakistan and Zimbabwe (NG11/W/71), Switzerland (NG11/W/73), Japan (NG11/W/74) and Australia (NG11/W/75).

"PART I: PREAMBULAR PROVISIONS; OBJECTIVES

1. Preamble (71); Objectives (73)

1.1 Recalling the Ministerial Declaration of Punta del Este of 20 September 1986; (73)

1.2 Desiring to strengthen the role of GATT and its basic principles and to bring about a wider coverage of world trade under agreed, effective and enforceable multilateral disciplines; (73)

1.3 Recognizing that the lack of protection, or insufficient or excessive protection, of intellectual property rights causes nullification and impairment of advantages and benefits of the General Agreement on Tariffs and Trade and distortions detrimental to international trade, and that such nullification and impairment may be caused both by substantive and procedural deficiencies, including ineffective enforcement of existing laws, as well as by unjustifiable discrimination of foreign persons, legal entities, goods and services; (73)

1.4 Recognizing that adequate protection of intellectual property rights is an essential condition to foster international investment and transfer of technology; (73)

1.5 Recognizing the importance of protection of intellectual property rights for promoting innovation and creativity; (71)

1.6 Recognizing that adequate protection of intellectual property rights both internally and at the border is necessary to deter and persecute piracy and counterfeiting; (73)

1.7 Taking into account development, technological and public interest objectives of developing countries; (71)

1.8 Recognizing also the special needs of the least developed countries in respect of maximum flexibility in the application of this Agreement in order to enable them to create a sound and viable technological base; (71)

1.9 Recognizing the need for appropriate transitional arrangements for developing countries and least developed countries with a view to achieve successfully strengthened protection and enforcement of intellectual property rights; (73)

1.10 Recognizing the need to prevent disputes by providing adequate means of transparency of national laws, regulations and requirements regarding protection and enforcement of intellectual property rights; (73)

1.11 Recognizing the need to settle disputes on matters related to the protection of intellectual property rights on the basis of effective multilateral mechanisms and procedures, and to refrain from applying unilateral measures inconsistent with such procedures to PARTIES to this PART of the General Agreement; (73)

1.12 Recognizing the efforts to harmonize and promote intellectual property laws by international organizations specialized in the field of intellectual property law and that this PART of the General Agreement aims at further encouragement of such efforts; (73)

became operative provisions of TRIPS (i.e., Articles 7 and 8), while the largely developed country proposals set out in the Annex were reflected in the more general statement of intent (i.e., the Preamble). Because articles of a treaty are intended to establish rights and obligations, Articles 7 and 8 should carry greater weight in the process of implementation and interpretation.

2.2.3 The Brussels Draft

The draft text of the TRIPS Agreement transmitted to the Brussels Ministerial Conference on the Chairman Anell's initiative in December 1990 reorganized the July 1990 proposal on "Principles" into Articles 7 ("Objectives") and 8 ("Principles").[280] The Brussels Draft retained significant portions of the developing country proposals, but in doing so added language that limited the range of public policy options. This was accomplished through the use of a "do not derogate" formula in Articles 8.1 and 8.2.

On Article 7, the Brussels Draft provided:

> "The protection and enforcement of intellectual property rights should contribute to the promotion of technological innovation and to the transfer and dissemination of technology, to the mutual advantage of producers and users of technological knowledge and in a manner conducive to social and economic welfare, and to a balance of rights and obligations."

2. Objective of the Agreement (74)

2A The PARTIES agree to provide effective and adequate protection of intellectual property rights in order to ensure the reduction of distortions and impediments to [international (68)] [legitimate (70)] trade. The protection of intellectual property rights shall not itself create barriers to legitimate trade. (68, 70)

2B The objective of the present Agreement is to establish adequate standards for the protection of, and effective and appropriate means for the enforcement of intellectual property rights; thereby eliminating distortions and impediments to international trade related to intellectual property rights and foster its sound development. (74)

2C With respect to standards and principles concerning the availability, scope and use of intellectual property rights, PARTIES agree on the following objectives:

(i) To give full recognition to the needs for economic, social and technological development of all countries and the sovereign right of all States, when enacting national legislation, to ensure a proper balance between these needs and the rights granted to IPR holders and thus to determine the scope and level of protection of such rights, particularly in sectors of special public concern, such as health, nutrition, agriculture and national security. (71)

(ii) To set forth the principal rights and obligations of IP owners, taking into account the important inter-relationships between the scope of such rights and obligations and the promotion of social welfare and economic development. (71)

(iii) To facilitate the diffusion of technological knowledge and to enhance international transfer of technology, and thus contribute to a more active participation of all countries in world production and trade. (71)

(iv) To encourage technological innovation and promote inventiveness in all countries. (71)

(v) To enable participants to take all appropriate measures to prevent the abuses which might result from the exercise of IPRs and to ensure intergovernmental co-operation in this regard. (71)"
Chairman's Report to the GNG, Status of Work in the Negotiating Group, Negotiating Group on Trade-Related Aspects of Intellectual Property Rights, including Trade in Counterfeit Goods, MTN.GNG/NG11/W/76, 23 July 1990.

[280] Draft Final Act Embodying the Results of the Uruguay Round of Multilateral Trade Negotiations, Revision, Trade-Related Aspects of Intellectual Property Rights, Including Trade in Counterfeit Goods, MTN.TNC/W/35/Rev. 1, 3 Dec. 1990.

With respect to Article 8.1, the Brussels Draft provided:

> "1. Provided that PARTIES do not derogate from the obligations arising under this Agreement, they may, in formulating or amending their national laws and regulations, adopt measures necessary to protect public health and nutrition, and to promote the public interest in sectors of vital importance to their socio-economic and technological development."

With respect to Article 8.2, the Brussels Draft provided:[281]

> "2. Appropriate measures, provided that they do not derogate from the obligations arising under this Agreement, may be needed to prevent the abuse of intellectual property rights by right holders or the resort to practices which unreasonably restrain trade or adversely affect the international transfer of technology."

2.2.4 The Dunkel Draft

With respect to Article 7, there was no change from the Brussels to the Dunkel Draft and the final TRIPS text.

With respect to Article 8.1, there was only one change to the Brussels Draft made in the Dunkel Draft text, and that was adopted in the final TRIPS Agreement. The Dunkel Draft of late 1991 and final TRIPS Agreement texts move the first clause of the Brussels Draft Article 8.1 (as quoted above) to the end of the paragraph, and use the legal formula, "provided that such measures are consistent with the provisions of this Agreement." The difference between an undertaking not to derogate, on the one hand, and to act consistently, on the other, is difficult to discern. Regarding Article 8.2, the "do not derogate" formula of the Brussels Draft was also modified in the Dunkel Draft text to a "consistent with" formula.

No significant changes to the Dunkel Draft texts were made in the TRIPS Agreement.

3. Possible interpretations

3.1 Article 7 (Objectives)

Article 7 of TRIPS provides:

> The protection and enforcement of intellectual property rights should contribute to the promotion of technological innovation and to the transfer and dissemination of technology, to the mutual advantage of producers and users of technological knowledge and in a manner conducive to social and economic welfare, and to a balance of rights and obligations.

IPRs have been designed to benefit society by providing incentives to introduce new inventions and creations.[282] Article 7 makes it clear that IPRs are not an end

---

[281] For the negotiating history of Article 8.2, TRIPS Agreement, see also Part 3 (IPRs and Competition), Section 2.2.

[282] Correa, Carlos, *Formulating Effective Pro-development National Intellectual Property Policies*, Trading in Knowledge. Bellmann, C., Dutfield, G. and Meléndez-Ortiz, R., London, 2003, Earthscan: 9, 209.

in themselves. It sets out the objectives that member countries should be able to reach through the protection and enforcement of such rights. The wording of Article 7 ("The protection . . . should contribute . . .") suggests that such a protection does not automatically lead to the effects described therein. In introducing IPR protection, countries should frame the applicable rules so as to promote technological innovation and the transfer and dissemination of technology "in a manner conducive to social and economic welfare".[283] IPRs are unlikely to promote innovation in countries with low scientific and technological capabilities, or where capital to finance innovative activities is lacking. The concept of "mutual advantage of producers and users of technological knowledge" is of particular importance in this context, since developing countries are largely *users* of technologies produced abroad.[284]

Article 7 provides guidance for the interpreter of the Agreement, emphasizing that it is designed to strike a balance among desirable objectives. It provides support for efforts to encourage technology transfer, with reference also to Articles 66 and 67. In litigation concerning intellectual property rights, courts commonly seek the underlying objectives of the national legislator, asking the purpose behind establishing a particular right. Article 7 makes clear that TRIPS negotiators did not mean to abandon a balanced perspective on the role of intellectual property in society. TRIPS is not intended only to protect the interests of right holders. It is intended to strike a balance that more widely promotes social and economic welfare.

3.2 Article 8 (Principles)
Article 8.1 provides:

> 1. Members may, in formulating or amending their laws and regulations, adopt measures necessary to protect public health and nutrition, and to promote the public interest in sectors of vital importance to their socio-economic and technological development, provided that such measures are consistent with the provisions of this Agreement.

Article 8.1 establishes a basis for the adoption of internal measures in language similar to that used in Article XX(b) of the GATT 1994. However, Article XX(b) of the GATT 1994 is used to justify internal measures which are necessary yet otherwise inconsistent with the GATT 1994. Article 8.1, by way of contrast, provides that necessary measures must be "consistent with" the Agreement.

Since language of a treaty is presumed not to be surplus, it would appear that Article 8.1 is to be read as a statement of TRIPS interpretative principle: it advises that Members were expected to have the discretion to adopt internal measures they consider necessary to protect public health and nutrition, and to promote the

---

[283] "Transfer" generally refers to the *transmission* of technology in a bilateral context (e.g. a licensing agreement), while "dissemination" rather alludes to the *diffusion* of innovation. IPRs normally reduce the diffusion of innovations as the title-holder charges prices above marginal costs in order to take advantage from the exclusive rights he enjoys.

[284] Interestingly, although TRIPS covers trademarks and copyrights, it only refers in Article 7 to "technological" knowledge.

public interest in sectors of vital importance to their socio-economic and technological development. The constraint is that the measures they adopt should not
violate the terms of the agreement. This suggests that measures adopted by Members to address public health, nutrition and matters of vital socio-economic importance should be presumed to be consistent with TRIPS, and that any Member
seeking to challenge the exercise of discretion should bear the burden of proving
inconsistency. Discretion to adopt measures is built into the agreement. Chal-
lengers should bear the burden of establishing that discretion has been abused.

The reference to "promot[ing] the public interest in sectors of vital importance
to their socio-economic and technological development" places substantial discretion in the hands of WTO Members regarding the kinds and subject matter
of measures that may be adopted in the context of Article 8.1. Sectors of vital
importance may vary from country to country and region to region, and the provision is not limited to implementation by developing countries. So long as sectors
and measures are identified in good faith, the sovereign discretion of the Member
adopting such measures should be accepted.

This statement of principle in Article 8.1 should prove important in limiting
the potential range of non-violation nullification or impairment causes of action
that might be pursued under TRIPS.[285] Article 8.1 indicates that Members were
reasonably expected to adopt such TRIPS-consistent measures. In this regard,
developed Members may not succeed with claims that their expectations as to the
balance of concessions have been frustrated.

Article 8.2 provides:

> 2. Appropriate measures, provided that they are consistent with the provisions
> of this Agreement, may be needed to prevent the abuse of intellectual property
> rights by right holders or the resort to practices which unreasonably restrain trade
> or adversely affect the international transfer of technology.

This Article to a large extent reflects the view advanced by the Indian delegation,
among others, during the Uruguay Round negotiations that a main objective of
TRIPS should be to provide mechanisms to restrain competitive abuses brought
about by reliance on IPR protection.

Like Article 8.1, Article 8.2 includes the requirement that measures taken should
be "consistent with" TRIPS. It is complementary to Article 40 that addresses
anticompetitive licensing practices or conditions that restrain trade.[286] Article 31,
regarding compulsory licensing of patents, also deals specifically with the application of measures to remedy anticompetitive practices.[287]

---

[285] Note that the moratorium concerning the applicability of non-violation complaints under
TRIPS has been extended to the Sixth Ministerial Conference in December 2005. See Chapter 32, providing interpretation favourable to a continuing exclusion of such complaints in the
TRIPS context. The same Chapter analyzes in detail the implications of non-violation complaints
in the TRIPS context.

[286] For a detailed analysis of both Article 8.2 and Article 40, see Chapter 29.

[287] For details, see Chapter 25.

TRIPS does not place significant limitations on the authority of WTO Members to take steps to control anticompetitive practices.[288]

4. WTO jurisprudence

The Preamble and Articles 7 and 8 were given modest attention by the parties (including third countries) and panel in the *Canada – Generics* dispute.[289] The panel said:

"(b) Object and Purpose

7.23 Canada called attention to a number of other provisions of the TRIPS Agreement as relevant to the purpose and objective of Article 30. Primary attention [footnote] was given to Articles 7 and 8.1....

In the view of Canada,... Article 7 above declares that one of the key goals of the TRIPS Agreement was a balance between the intellectual property rights created by the Agreement and other important socio-economic policies of WTO Member governments. Article 8 elaborates the socio-economic policies in question, with particular attention to health and nutritional policies. With respect to patent rights, Canada argued, these purposes call for a liberal interpretation of the three conditions stated in Article 30 of the Agreement, so that governments would have the necessary flexibility to adjust patent rights to maintain the desired balance with other important national policies.

The EC did not dispute the stated goal of achieving a balance within the intellectual property rights system between important national policies. But, in the view of the EC, Articles 7 and 8 are statements that describe the balancing of goals that had already taken place in negotiating the final texts of the TRIPS Agreement. According to the EC, to view Article 30 as an authorization for governments to 'renegotiate' the overall balance of the Agreement would involve a double counting of such socio-economic policies. In particular, the EC pointed to the last phrase of Article 8.1 requiring that government measures to protect important socio-economic policies be consistent with the obligations of the TRIPS Agreement. The EC also referred to the provisions of first consideration of the Preamble and Article 1.1 as demonstrating that the basic purpose of the TRIPS Agreement was to lay down minimum requirements for the protection and enforcement of intellectual property rights.

In the Panel's view, Article 30's very existence amounts to a recognition that the definition of patent rights contained in Article 28 would need certain adjustments. On the other hand, the three limiting conditions attached to Article 30 testify strongly that the negotiators of the Agreement did not intend Article 30 to bring about what would be equivalent to a renegotiation of the basic balance of the Agreement. Obviously, the exact scope of Article 30's authority will depend on the specific meaning given to its limiting conditions. The words of those conditions

---

[288] See Frederick M. Abbott, *Are the Competition Rules in the WTO TRIPS Agreement Adequate?*, 7 J Int'l Econ. L No. 3, 2004, at 687–703.

[289] *Canada – Patent Protection of Pharmaceutical Products*, Report of the Panel, WT/DS114/R, March 17, 2000 (hereinafter "Canada-Generics").

must be examined with particular care on this point. Both the goals and the limitations stated in Articles 7 and 8.1 must obviously be borne in mind when doing so as well as those of other provisions of the TRIPS Agreement which indicate its object and purposes."

[Footnote]: Attention was also called to the text of the first recital in the Preamble to the TRIPS Agreement and to part of the text of Article 1.1. The Preamble text in question reads:

'Desiring to reduce distortions and impediments to international trade, and taking into account the need to promote effective and adequate protection of intellectual property rights, *and to ensure that measures and procedures to enforce intellectual property rights do not themselves become barriers to legitimate trade*.' (emphasis added by Canada)

Part of the Article 1.1 text referred to reads:

'Members shall be free to determine the appropriate method of implementing the provisions of this Agreement within their own legal systems and practice.'

When it analyzed the relationship between Article 27.1 and Article 30 of the TRIPS Agreement, the panel employed Articles 7 and 8.1 in its analysis, stating:

"7.92 ... Beyond that, it is not true that Article 27 requires all Article 30 exceptions to be applied to all products. Article 27 prohibits only discrimination as to the place of invention, the field of technology, and whether products are imported or produced locally. Article 27 does not prohibit bona fide exceptions to deal with problems that may exist only in certain product areas. Moreover, to the extent the prohibition of discrimination does limit the ability to target certain products in dealing with certain of the important national policies referred to in Articles 7 and 8.1, that fact may well constitute a deliberate limitation rather than a frustration of purpose. It is quite plausible, as the EC argued, that the TRIPS Agreement would want to require governments to apply exceptions in a non-discriminatory manner, in order to ensure that governments do not succumb to domestic pressures to limit exceptions to areas where right holders tend to be foreign producers." [emphasis added]

The panel suggests that Articles 7 and 8.1, and the policies reflected in those articles, are bounded by the principle of non-discrimination in Article 27.1 with respect to patents. Presumably the panel is invoking the specific non-discrimination requirement of Article 27.1 as a control on the more general policies stated in Articles 7 and 8.1, and also invoking the consistency requirement of Article 8.1. It is not clear how far this idea of giving precedence to specific obligations over more general policies should be extended.[290]

---

[290] It is also important to recall that the panel in the same paragraph says that *bona fide* exceptions may apply to certain product areas (i.e. fields of technology), thus establishing the critical distinction between bad faith "discrimination" on one hand, and good faith "differentiation" on the other.

5. Relationship with other international instruments

5.1 WTO Agreements

The objectives and principles of TRIPS must be considered in relation to the objectives of the WTO Agreement, which is reflected in its preamble. In addition to promoting general economic growth compatible with sustainable development, the preamble of the WTO Agreement:

> "*Recogniz[es]* further that there is need for positive efforts designed to ensure that developing countries, and especially the least developed among them, secure a share in the growth in international trade commensurate with the needs of their economic development,"

In fact, most of the WTO agreements include provisions regarding special and differential treatment for developing countries. Since Articles 7 and 8 refer to development objectives, it may be useful in the context of dispute settlement to cross-reference developmental objectives and principles of the appropriate agreements.

5.2 Other international instruments

The objectives and principles set forth in Articles 7 and 8 are supported by a myriad of other international instruments that promote economic development, transfer of technology, social welfare (including nutritional and health needs), and so forth. Human rights instruments, such as the International Covenant on Economic, Social and Cultural Rights, support a number of the same objectives and principles as Articles 7 and 8. The various agreements of the International Labour Organization, and the charter of the World Health Organization, support the development-oriented objectives and principles of TRIPS. In the implementation of TRIPS and in any dispute settlement proceedings it will be useful to establish the supportive links between the objectives and principles stated in Articles 7 and 8, and the objectives and principles of other international instruments. The Appellate Body, as noted in Chapter 1 (Section 4 on the "Shrimp-Turtles" case), has moved firmly away from the notion of the WTO as a "self-contained" legal regime, and the establishment of support in other international instruments may help persuade the AB to recognize and give effect to developmental priorities.

6. New developments

6.1 National laws

6.2 International instruments

6.2.1 The Doha Declaration on the TRIPS Agreement and Public Health

The Declaration on the TRIPS Agreement and Public Health adopted by Ministers at Doha on 14 November 2001 includes important statements regarding the objectives and principles of TRIPS.[291]

---

[291] See WT/MIN(01)/DEC/W/2 of 14 November 2001.

Operative paragraph 4 of the Doha Declaration can be understood as directed to elaborating on the meaning of Article 8.1. It provides:

> "4. We agree that the TRIPS Agreement does not and should not prevent Members from taking measures to protect public health. Accordingly, while reiterating our commitment to the TRIPS Agreement, we affirm that the Agreement can and should be interpreted and implemented in a manner supportive of WTO Members' right to protect public health and, in particular, to promote access to medicines for all.
>
> In this connection, we reaffirm the right of WTO Members to use, to the full, the provisions in the TRIPS Agreement, which provide flexibility for this purpose."

The first important point regarding this paragraph is that it is stated in the form of an agreement (i.e., "we agree"). Since this statement was adopted by consensus of the Ministers, and since the operative language is in the form of an agreement, this may be interpreted as a "decision" of the Members under Article IX.1 of the WTO Agreement. Although paragraph 4 is not an "interpretation" in the formal sense since it was not based on a recommendation of the TRIPS Council pursuant to Article IX:2 of the WTO Agreement, a decision that states a meaning of the Agreement should be considered as a very close approximation of an interpretation and, from a functional standpoint, may be indistinguishable.

The statement that TRIPS "does not . . . prevent Members . . . from taking measures to protect public health" might be interpreted as a broad mandate to developing and least developed Members to take whatever steps they consider appropriate to addressing public health concerns. An aggressive interpretation would be that developing Members are free, for example, to override patent protection as the situation demands, without constraint by TRIPS. However, the broad mandate is qualified by the second clause of this paragraph that reaffirms the right of Members to use the existing flexibility in TRIPS "for this purpose". It can be argued that the opening statement merely affirms that TRIPS allows Members to address public health concerns within the framework of the rules established by the Agreement. This is reinforced by the opening phrase of paragraph 5 (see below).

The second sentence of paragraph 4 indicates that TRIPS "can and should be interpreted and implemented . . . to promote access to medicines for all". This would imply that the Agreement should not be used to maintain prices that are unaffordable to the poor. This again would imply that patent protection may be limited in order to provide lower priced access to medicines, but is qualified by the second sentence of paragraph 4 (and paragraph 5).

In the second sentence of paragraph 4, Members reiterate their commitment to TRIPS, and in the third sentence Members indicate that the Agreement contains certain flexibilities. This suggests that the existing language of TRIPS is not intended to be overridden or superseded by the Declaration, despite the strong first sentence of paragraph 4.

The first part of paragraph 5 of the Declaration provides:

> "5. Accordingly and in the light of paragraph 4 above, while maintaining our commitments in the TRIPS Agreement, we recognize that these flexibilities include:

(a) In applying the customary rules of interpretation of public international law, each provision of the TRIPS Agreement shall be read in the light of the object and purpose of the Agreement as expressed, in particular, in its objectives and principles."

Paragraph 5(a) states an interpretative principle that has already been enunciated by the panel in the Canada-Generics case, and that would already be understood by operation of Article 31 of the Vienna Convention on the Law of Treaties. By particularizing reference to objectives and principles, the Declaration appears indirectly to reference Articles 7 and 8 and this may have the effect of elevating those provisions above the preamble of TRIPS for interpretative purposes.[292]

6.3 Regional and bilateral contexts

6.4 Proposals for review

The Doha Declaration on the TRIPS Agreement and Public Health (see above) followed meetings of the Council for TRIPS that included substantial discussion of the objectives and principles of TRIPS. It is understood that those initial meetings are part of a continuing process of examining the impact of TRIPS on public health.[293]

A number of developing countries have indicated that the implementation of Article 7 should be examined in the Council for TRIPS in the context of determining whether TRIPS is fulfilling the objective of contributing to the dissemination and transfer of technology.[294]

7. Comments, including economic and social implications

Article 7 recognizes that IPRs are intended to achieve a balance among social welfare interests, including interests in the transfer of technology, and the interests of producers.

TRIPS does not contain a general safeguard measure comparable to Article XX of the GATT 1994 or Article XIV of the GATS. For those other Multilateral Trade Agreements (MTAs), the necessity to protect human life or health may take priority over the generally applicable rules of the agreement, subject only to general principles of non-discrimination. Yet when it comes to intellectual property, the "exceptions" are circumscribed with various procedural or compensatory encumbrances, making their use more difficult. Article 8.1 contains language similar to

---

[292] The TRIPS Agreement preamble might be understood to place a somewhat greater weight on the interests of intellectual property rights holders than on public interests.

[293] A number of developing countries have suggested that Article 8.1 of the TRIPS Agreement might be made consistent with Article XX(b) of the GATT 1994 that permits exceptional measures that are otherwise inconsistent with the agreement. Although it is not clear whether the Council for TRIPS will consider this issue since it was at least partially addressed in the Doha Declaration, it is a potential agenda item.

[294] While reference to reaffirming commitments under Article 66.2 was made in the Doha Declaration, this reference relates to encouraging actions by enterprises and institutions in favour of least developed Members. For more details on Article 66.2, see Chapter 34.

that of GATT Articles XX and GATS Article XIV, yet it demands consistency rather than tolerating inconsistency. What accounts for this difference in approach? Proponents of high levels of IPR protection argue this is necessary to protect against abuse of exceptions, and that IPRs such as patents represent a special case. Article XX of GATT has been invoked to prevent fleets of fishing vessels from operating in ways injurious to dolphins and sea turtles. Yet there is no comparable provision in TRIPS that allows Members to generally suspend IPR protection to allow the manufacture and distribution of vitally needed medicines to save human lives. This distinction poses a fundamental question regarding the nature of the WTO. One that is unlikely to go away soon.

7: Copyright Works

Article 9   Relation to the Berne Convention

1. Members shall comply with Articles 1 through 21 of the Berne Convention (1971) and the Appendix thereto. However, Members shall not have rights or obligations under this Agreement in respect of the rights conferred under Article 6*bis* of that Convention or of the rights derived therefrom.

2. Copyright protection shall extend to expressions and not to ideas, procedures, methods of operation or mathematical concepts as such.

---

1. Introduction: overview, terminology, definition and scope

1.1 Overview of copyright in general, and in TRIPS[1]

The law of copyright is addressed to creative expression. Copyright protection includes a number of enumerated rights that initially are vested in the author[2] of the copyrighted work.

---

[1] See UNCTAD, *The TRIPS Agreement and Developing Countries*, Geneva, 1996 [hereinafter UNCTAD 1996].

[2] The notion of "authorship" received quite a bit of attention during the TRIPS negotiations. The Motion Picture Association of America (MPAA) wanted a definition of authorship that would recognize corporations as authors. Historically, civil law countries have emphasized authors as "flesh and blood" creators only. While common law countries also tend to identify the author as the natural person who created the work, copyright tradition in these countries is less wedded to this notion. In terms of identifying the author, Article 15(1) of the Berne Convention (Paris Act) states a rule that the name appearing on the work "in the usual manner" is the author – at least for the purposes of instituting an infringement proceeding. National laws may customize this concept to reflect their own policies and many countries have in fact done so. For example, in France and the United Kingdom, the author is presumed to be the person whose name appears on *published* copies of the work. See France, Intellectual Property Code Art. L 113-1; United Kingdom, Copyright Designs Patent Act 1988 §104(2). In the United States, the presumption of authorship is based on the information stated on the certificate of copyright registration. Section 410(c) of the Copyright Act provides that when a work is registered within five years of publication the certificate "shall" constitute presumptive evidence of the validity of the copyright, stated therein. In general, the Berne Convention gives considerable flexibility to national law to define who an author is and how to identify the author. See WIPO, *Guide to the Berne Convention for the Protection of Literary and Artistic Works (Paris Act, 1971)* 93 (1978). The TRIPS Agreement should be interpreted to have incorporated this deference to national definitions of authorship given the assimilation of Berne Convention Articles 1-21 into the TRIPS Agreement. See TRIPS Agreement Article 9(1).

Copyright law protects a variety of works that are generally characterized as literary or artistic. Traditionally, such works were limited to novels, poems, dramas, musical compositions, paintings and drawings. Technological developments, however, continued to transform the ways in which creativity could be expressed and exploited, thus giving rise to a corresponding need to stretch the boundaries of the traditional concept of "literary and artistic works." Today, copyright extends to utilitarian works such as computer programs, databases and architectural works. Indeed, there will likely be an ongoing expansion of what constitutes "literature" and "art" as technology continues to transform the way creativity is expressed, disseminated and managed. The advent of digital computing and demands for protection of industrially applicable "expression" has made more difficult the historical distinction between "industrial property" and "artistic expression".

As the corpus of protected works was expanded to accommodate new technological developments, new rights were added to accommodate the variety of ways that the work could be exploited in the marketplace.[3] Hence, copyright remains a dynamic body of law, responding to multiple changes in the incentive structure that has historically characterized investments in creative endeavours. At the same time, new norms and principles are being established to address the challenges posed by the information age.

Seen from a development perspective, **TRIPS** Agreement patent rules may favour enterprises that are already the holders of most patented technology and are in a better position to undertake new research and development. Copyright-dependent enterprises in the developed countries certainly have important advantages over developing country enterprises because they have greater access to capital and better developed distribution networks. Yet in copyright there is a somewhat more level playing field among developed and developing countries since many expressive works can be created with little capital, are protected automatically under copyright law (unlike the case of patents), and may not require an expensive distribution network to be marketed. While it may cost a great deal to invent and patent a new jet engine or radar system, a large part of the world population can write a story or record a song. The Internet makes distribution of new expressive works inexpensive, even if for the moment it may not be so easy to protect copyrighted material on a digital network. The more equal playing field in copyright is reflected in a lower level of controversy so far between developed and developing countries regarding copyright protection than is evident in some other areas regulated by **TRIPS**.

Generally speaking, copyright protection provides exclusive rights to make and distribute copies of a particular expression and also of derivative works, such as adaptations and translations. The right extends for a limited time period, with TRIPS and the Berne Convention generally prescribing a minimum term of the life of the creator plus 50 years. The protection is more limited in scope than patent

---

[3] See, for example, the provisions of the two WIPO treaties designed specifically to deal with the unique issues associated with digital communications technologies. These two treaties are the WIPO Copyright Treaty and the WIPO Performers and Phonograms Treaty. Both were adopted by the Diplomatic Conference in Geneva, Switzerland, on December 20, 1996.

protection, particularly in the sense that copyright does not preclude "independent creation" of an identical work. The period of protection, while substantially longer than that for patents, is nevertheless limited so that society can ultimately gain from having artistic works become freely available. The copyright gives the author-creator the right to assign at least his or her economic rights to a more efficient distributor, such as a publisher or music company, in return for royalties. Copyright also protects certain "moral rights" of authors, which in some circumstances may not be assignable or transferable.

Copyright protection is intended to provide incentives for the creation of new works of art, music, literature, cinema and other forms of expression. Protection is generally considered necessary because, without copyright, it is relatively easy to free ride on these creative efforts and the price of expressive goods would be reduced to the costs of copying them.[4] Copyright is also required because there is great uncertainty about the likely success of new creations and in some cases the cost of development is substantial, such as with a film or symphonic work. Free riders are able to tell with greater certainty than creators which works are worth copying, thereby avoiding the financial risks assumed by creators. There are important limits on the scope of copyright. The principal limitation consists, in common law jurisdictions, of the fair use or fair dealing doctrines, or, in continental law jurisdictions, of specific statutory exceptions. Both kinds of limitations acknowledge the importance to society of education, news and commentary, as well as social criticism. In consequence, they allow some unauthorized copying for limited purposes.[5] Reverse engineering of more industrially-applicable copyrighted works such as computer software has been permitted under fair use doctrine under conditions that have varied among countries. In summary, copyright involves

---

[4] Most intellectual goods share characteristics that require intervention in the form of copyright (or patent) laws. Imagine, for example, that it costs X+1 dollars to produce a book. Once published, the book is sold for X+2. After publication, however, it costs considerably less to reproduce copies of the book. For example, photocopying the entire book may cost only "X" or even less. Consumers are likely to pay the lesser price which may be a short term positive outcome for the public. In the long term, however, it will harm the public because the rate of book writing will decrease due to an author's inability to prevent unauthorized reproduction of the work. In economic terms this is referred to as the "public goods" problem associated with intangibles such as ideas, which are protected under patent laws, and expressions of ideas protected by copyright. The cost of creating a public good is typically high while the cost of reproduction is low. Further, reproduction does not deplete the original. In other words, a photocopy of the book is just as good, in terms of content, as any other copy of the same book. This characteristic is referred to as "non-rivalrous" and it distinguishes intellectual property from other types of property. Public goods also are "non-excludable." In other words once the good is produced, there is no way to prevent others from enjoying its benefits. Once a copyrightable song is released, it is impossible to keep non-paying members from hearing and enjoying the music, whether they hear it at a friend's home or at a party. One rationale for copyright law is that it solves the public goods problem. Implicit in this view, however, is that the production of copyrightable works at optimal levels is a desirable objective for society. Other views of copyright include a human rights philosophy, which posits that the protection of intellectual goods is an intrinsic aspect of recognizing human dignity. Whatever the philosophical basis for copyright, however, it is clear that the existence of a mechanism for protecting creative work has positive gains for economic growth and development. The fact that other, non-economic, goals are also satisfied makes copyright even more valuable than a purely economic justification might otherwise suggest.

[5] For more details on these exceptions to copyright, including the fair use and fair dealing doctrines, see Chapter 12, in the introduction.

providing exclusive rights in respect to creative expression, subject to some public-interest limitations.

TRIPS (Part II, Section 1) sets forth standards for the protection of authors, broadcasting organizations, performers and phonogram producers. The main obligations imposed by TRIPS in the area of copyright and related rights include: (i) protection of works covered by the Berne Convention,[6] excluding moral rights, with respect to the expression and not the ideas, procedures, methods of operation or mathematical concepts as such (Article 9); (ii) protection of computer programs as literary works and of compilations of data (Article 10); (iii) recognition of rental rights, at least for phonograms, computer programs, and for cinematographic works (except if rental has not led to widespread copying that impairs the reproduction right) (Article 11); (iv) recognition of rights of performers, producers of phonograms and broadcasting organizations (Article 14).

In addition, the Agreement (Article 51) obliges Members to take measures at the border with regard to suspected pirated copyright goods and requires criminal procedures and penalties to be applied in cases of copyright piracy[7] on a commercial scale (Article 61). As with other matters covered by the Agreement, developing and least-developed countries enjoy transitional periods to implement their obligations relating to copyright and related rights.[8]

From a development perspective, it is common to all forms of copyright that enhanced protection may in the long term stimulate the establishment of local cultural industries in developing countries, provided that other obstacles to such development are avoided. However, in the short and medium term, stronger copyright protection does give rise to some concern. Since copyrights are exclusive, they create access barriers to the protected subject matter, such as books, computer software and scientific information.[9] It is thus essential to developing country policy makers to strike the right balance between incentives for creativity on the one hand and ways to enable their societies to close the knowledge gap vis-à-vis developed countries, on the other hand. For this purpose, the copyright provisions of TRIPS provide for some flexibility, which will be analysed in detail in the subsequent chapters.

Another important development issue concerns the direct costs of implementation of the TRIPS copyright provisions.[10] Since there are no formalities for the

---

[6] See Berne Convention for the Protection of Literary and Artistic Works, September 9, 1886, completed at Paris on May 4, 1896, revised at Berlin on November 13, 1908, completed at Berne on March 20, 1914, revised at Rome on June 2, 1928, at Brussels on June 26, 1948, at Stockholm on July 14, 1967, and at Paris on July 24, 1971, and amended on September 28, 1979 [hereinafter Berne Convention].

[7] For the purposes of TRIPS, "pirated copyright goods shall mean any goods made without the consent of the right-holder or person duly authorized by the right-holder in the country of production and which are made directly or indirectly from an article where the making of that copy would have constituted an infringement of a copyright or a related right under the law of the country of importation" (footnote to Article 51).

[8] UNCTAD 1996, paras. 161, 162.

[9] See IPR Commission p. 99. The report can be consulted at http://www.iprcommission.org/graphic/documents/final_report.htm. Page numbers refer to the pdf and hard copy versions of this report.

[10] For the following, see UNCTAD 1996, paras. 185, 186.

acquisition of copyrights and related rights, the expansion and strengthening of protection shall not necessarily lead to increased administrative costs. However, deposit of works is required in some countries for specific legal purposes, or is convenient for the purposes of proof in eventual litigation. TRIPS may, therefore, have an impact on the volume of work of copyright offices and may require additional resources (mainly personnel and computer facilities).

The main direct costs for implementing the TRIPS copyright provisions may stem from enforcement. Administrative (police and customs) and judicial authorities may be increasingly involved in procedures regarding injunctions and other remedies, suspension of release of products into circulation, and other enforcement-related procedures. This may imply significant costs – yet to be estimated – that, in principle, will be only partially absorbed by the title-holders.

The following and the subsequent copyright chapters deal in detail with the following issues: copyright works (copyrightable subject matter); computer programs; databases; the rental right; term of protection; limitations and exceptions; and rights related to copyright.

1.2 Terminology, definition and scope

Article 9 does not provide a definition of copyright works but instead defers to the provisions of the Berne Convention for Literary and Artistic Works.[11] Thus, it is the provisions of the Berne Convention that determine what constitutes copyrightable works under TRIPS.[12] However, TRIPS Article 9.2 makes explicit what is *not* protectable by copyright. There must be protection for expressions, but not for "ideas, procedures, methods of operation or mathematical concepts as such."[13] This invokes what is often described as the "idea/expression dichotomy" in many common law countries.[14] As a matter of fact, however, the rule that copyright protection extends only to expressions and not to the underlying ideas is generally recognized in all countries.[15]

Under TRIPS, distinguishing between the idea and the expression, for purposes of ascertaining what exactly is copyrightable in a particular work is a function implicitly left to the legislature and/or judiciary of a Member. However, the explicit incorporation of the idea/expression dichotomy in an international agreement is precedential, and sets an important boundary for the scope of proprietary rights in

---

[11] TRIPS Article 9 incorporates by reference the Berne Convention (Paris Text) of 1971. Thus, all WTO Members are bound by the Paris Text.

[12] See Article 2 of the Berne Convention, as quoted under Section 3, below.

[13] For more details on the protectable subject matter, see Section 3, below.

[14] This doctrine was well articulated by the Supreme Court of the United States in *Baker v. Selden* (101 U.S. 99,1879: "A treatise on the composition and use of medicines, be they old or new; on the construction and use of ploughs, or watches, or churns; or on the application of colors for painting or dyeing; or on the mode of drawing lines to produce the effect of perspective, would be the subject of copyright; but no one would contend that the copyright of the treatise would give the exclusive right to the art or manufacture described therein.... The use of the art is a totally different thing from a publication of the book explaining it. The copyright of a book on bookkeeping cannot secure the exclusive right to make, sell, and use account-books prepared upon the plan set forth in such book."

[15] Claude Masouye, *Guide to the Berne Convention for the Protection of Literary Artistic Works*, 12 (1978).

creative works. Ideas are the basic building blocks of creative works and reserving them from the scope of copyright is an important policy strategy to ensure that copyright protection does not operate to confer monopoly rights on the basic elements of creative endeavours. The delimitation is also important because it serves to channel certain creative works into the realm of copyright and others into the realm of patent law. Finally, the idea/expression dichotomy ensures that future authors are not hindered from engaging in creative activity due to a monopoly by previous authors on the underlying ideas of their work.[16]

Thus, the idea/expression dichotomy helps to sustain the public domain – that all important store of resources that sustains future creativity and from which the public at large may freely use and obtain entire works (such as those in which copyright protection has expired) or aspects of works free from copyright claims (such as underlying ideas, procedures, etc.). One leading copyright scholar notes that "a vigorous public domain is a crucial buttress to the copyright system" and that without it, copyright might not be tolerable.[17]

To amplify the idea/expression dichotomy, Article 9.2 also excludes methods of operation and mathematical concepts from copyright protection. It should be noted that in addition to the exceptions listed in Article 9.2, the Berne Convention adds "news of the day" and "miscellaneous facts having the character of mere items of press information."[18] Accordingly, these two additional categories of works are also non-copyrightable under TRIPS.

As expressly stated in Article 9.1, second sentence, TRIPS does not obligate WTO Members to provide protection of moral rights as provided under Article 6*bis* of the Berne Convention. The moral right is of a non-economic character being the author's right to "claim authorship of the work and to object to any distortion, mutilation or other modification of, or other derogatory action in relation to, the said work, which would be prejudicial to his honour or reputation."[19]

Finally, Article 9.1 expressly obligates Members to comply with the Appendix to the Berne Convention. This Appendix contains special provisions regarding developing countries. Most importantly, it provides developing countries with the

---

[16] A simple example might be useful here. If an author writes a book describing a beautiful castle in Spain, it will not preclude a subsequent writer from writing a book about the same castle. The idea of writing a book about the castle is not protected by copyright. Only the expression of the idea is protected – that is, what the novel actually says about the castle. Further, what copyright offers is protection against *copying* of the expression, but not against a third party's *independent creation* of similar expressions. Thus, if the second author writes the same things about the castle, perhaps even using the same words and phrases, the first author does not have a claim of copyright violation unless the second author copied his work. The task of distinguishing idea from expression may be relatively simple with regard to certain categories of works such as the book used in this example. However, with regard to more functional works such as computer programs, distinguishing the "idea" from the "expression" can be quite complex. In most countries, application of the idea/expression dichotomy is the task of the judiciary which makes the determination on a case by case basis.

[17] Jessica Litman, *The Public Domain*, 39 Emory L.J. 965 (1990).

[18] Berne Convention, Article 2(8).

[19] See Article 6*bis* of the Berne Convention.

possibility to issue, on certain conditions, compulsory licenses for the reproduction of copyrighted materials (Article III of the Appendix) and for the translation of copyrighted materials into a language in general use in the authorizing country.[20]

2. History of the provision

2.1 Situation pre-TRIPS

Article 9.1 does not establish a new standard of international copyright *per se*, but simply codifies what had been the practice in most countries prior to the negotiation of TRIPS. Instead, Article 9.2 clarifies the provisions of Article 2 of the Berne Convention, which establishes the scope of copyrightable subject matter. Further, through the explicit codification of the idea/expression dichotomy, Article 9.2 advances an important social objective at the international level, namely, encouraging the development of a robust public domain for the benefit of the public at large and ensuring the security of this resource for future generations of authors.

By way of a definition, Article 2(1) of the Berne Convention provides a non-exhaustive list of works that must be protected by copyright. These include

> "every production in the literary, scientific and artistic domain, whatever may be the mode or form of its expression, such as books, pamphlets and other writings; lectures, addresses, sermons and other works of the same nature; dramatic or dramatico-musical works; choreographic works and entertainments in dumb show; musical compositions with or without words; cinematographic works...; works of drawing, painting, architecture, sculpture, engraving and lithography; photographic works...; works of applied art; illustrations, maps, plans, sketches and three-dimensional works relative to geography, topography, architecture or science."

In addition to these "first generation" works, the Berne Convention in Article 2(3) requires copyright protection for translations, adaptations, arrangements of music and other alterations of a literary or artistic work. Essentially, this provision requires that works that are derived from first generation works be equally protected by copyright without prejudicing the copyright in the earlier works. For example, an English translation of a Portuguese novel must be protected by copyright, distinct from the copyright in the underlying Portuguese novel. Similarly, a movie that is based on a novel, or a new arrangement of a musical composition, must also be protected by copyright distinct from the first work. These "derivative works," as they are called in certain jurisdictions, enjoy copyright status as "original" works independent of the copyright on the works on which they were based or from which they were derived.

---

[20] On the Appendix to the Berne Convention, see also Chapter 12.

2.2 Negotiating history

2.2.1 The Anell Draft

On what is now Article 9, the Anell Draft of 23 July 1990[21] included the following proposals:

> 1A "PARTIES shall grant to authors and their successors in title the [economic] rights provided in the Berne Convention (1971), subject to the provisions set forth below."

> 1B "PARTIES shall provide to the nationals of other parties the rights which their respective laws do now or may hereafter grant, consistently with the rights specially granted by the Berne Convention."

The bracketed reference in the developed countries' proposal to "economic" rights indicates some negotiators' intention to exclude moral rights from the new copyright obligations. Apart from that, however, the scope of Article 9 was intended by delegations to conform substantially to the Berne Convention.

2.2.2 The Brussels Draft

The Brussels Ministerial Text[22] on what is now Article 9.1 was quite similar to the current Article 9.1. It provided that

> "PARTIES shall comply with the substantive provisions [on economic rights] of the Berne Convention (1971). [However, PARTIES shall not have rights or obligations under this Agreement in respect of the rights conferred under Article 6*bis* of that Convention or of the rights derived therefrom]."

The main difference was that the Brussels Draft referred to the "substantive provisions" of the Berne Convention, instead of providing for an explicit list as now under Article 9.1. This modification through the final version of Article 9 has been welcomed as a means of avoiding confusion about the exact scope of the reference to the Berne Convention.[23]

The reason for the exclusion of moral rights from the scope of Article 9 was the concern of some countries from the Anglo-American copyright system that strengthened moral rights could possibly represent obstacles to the full enjoyment by a purchaser of a legally obtained licence.[24] Civil law countries would have preferred the inclusion in Article 9.1 of moral rights.[25]

---

[21] Chairman's report to the Group of Negotiation on Goods, document MTN.GNG/NG11/W/76, of 23 July 1990 [hereinafter Anell Draft].

[22] Draft Final Act Embodying the Results of the Uruguay Round of Multilateral Trade Negotiations, Revision, Trade-Related Aspects of Intellectual Property Rights, Including Trade in Counterfeit Goods, MTN.TNC/W/35/Rev. 1, 3 Dec. 1990 [hereinafter Brussels Draft].

[23] See Daniel Gervais, *The TRIPS Agreement: Drafting History and Analysis* (1998) [hereinafter Gervais], p. 72, para. 2.51, with examples of possible confusion.

[24] Ibid., para. 2.52. This position is based on the view that moral rights cannot be waived by the author.

[25] Ibid., rejecting the above Anglo-American concern about moral rights by arguing that those rights may be waived under the Berne Convention. According to this author, it is up to domestic legislation to determine whether moral rights may be waived, see paras. 2.52, 2.53.

As far as Article 9.2 is concerned, it originated in a Japanese proposal reserved to computer programs.[26] In July 1990, still in the framework of specific rules on computer programs, the Anell Draft proposal provided that

"Such protection shall not extend to ideas, procedures, methods [, algorithms] or systems."

This language is in essence similar to the current Article 9.2, which for the first time in an international agreement provides for a list of uncopyrightable subject matter. In the Brussels Draft, this proposal was still contained in the draft provision specifically related to computer programs.[27] The draft was subsequently taken out of the computer-specific provision and enlarged in scope to apply to copyrights in general. Thus, the pertinent provision of the Dunkel Draft of December 1991 read as follows: "Copyright protection shall extend to expressions and not to ideas, procedures, methods of operation or mathematical concepts as such."[28]

3. Possible interpretations

3.1 Literary and artistic works

Article 2 of the Berne Convention-explicitly assimilated to TRIPS through Article 9 – provides that:

"(1) The expression "literary and artistic works" shall include every production in the literary, scientific and artistic domain, whatever may be the mode or form of its expression, such as books, pamphlets and other writings; lectures, addresses, sermons and other works of the same nature; dramatic or dramatico-musical works; choreographic works and entertainments in dumb show; musical compositions with or without words; cinematographic works to which are assimilated works expressed by a process analogous to cinematography; works of drawing, painting, architecture, sculpture, engraving and lithography; photographic works to which are assimilated works expressed by a process analogous to photography; works of applied art; illustrations, maps, plans, sketches and three-dimensional works relative to geography, topography, architecture or science.

(2) It shall, however, be a matter for legislation in the countries of the Union to prescribe that works in general or any specified categories of works shall not be protected unless they have been fixed in some material form.

(3) Translations, adaptations, arrangements of music and other alterations of a literary or artistic work shall be protected as original works without prejudice to the copyright in the original work.

(4) It shall be a matter for legislation in the countries of the Union to determine the protection to be granted to official texts of a legislative, administrative and legal nature, and to official translations of such texts.

(5) Collections of literary or artistic works such as encyclopaedias and anthologies which, by reason of the selection and arrangement of their contents, constitute

---

[26] Ibid., para. 2.56.

[27] See the Brussels Draft on what is now Article 10.2 (Chapter 8).

[28] See Article 9.2 of the Dunkel Draft, document MTN.TNC/W/FA of 20 December 1991.

intellectual creations shall be protected as such, without prejudice to the copyright in each of the works forming part of such collections.

(6) The works mentioned in this article shall enjoy protection in all countries of the Union. This protection shall operate for the benefit of the author and his successors in title.

(7) Subject to the provisions of Article 7(4) of this Convention, it shall be a matter for legislation in the countries of the Union to determine the extent of the application of their laws to works of applied art and industrial designs and models, as well as the conditions under which such works, designs and models shall be protected. Works protected in the country of origin solely as designs and models shall be entitled in another country of the Union only to such special protection as is granted in that country to designs and models; however, if no such special protection is granted in that country, such works shall be protected as artistic works.

(8) The protection of this Convention shall not apply to news of the day or to miscellaneous facts having the character of mere items of press information."

An overview of the works enumerated in this Article 2, and by assimilation TRIPS Article 9, suggests at least seven categories of works that must be protected under national copyright systems. These are (i) literary works, which cover all forms of writings, whether by words or numbers or symbols; (ii) dramatico-musical works such as plays, mimes, choreography, operas and musical comedies; (iii) cinematographic works, which include film or videotaped dramatic works and other forms of content fixed in film; (iv) works of music with or without words; (v) visual art works in two and three-dimensional forms, including applied art (for example, this category would include architecture, sculptures, engravings, lithography, maps, plans and photographic works); (vi) derivative works, which include translations, adaptations, and arrangements; (vii) compilations and collective works such as encyclopedias and, more recently, databases. For each of these categories, the particular manner in which copyright protection is extended differs across countries.

In the United States, for example, the right to protect translations, adaptations and alterations of pre-existing works is granted to the author of the underlying work as part of the initial copyright grant[29] that precludes others from making derivative works without the permission of the copyright owner. Failure to obtain such permission before adapting or altering the work will lead to claims of infringement. In other jurisdictions, notably in European countries, moral rights, which constitute an inextricable part of the copyright grant, effectively limit what third parties can do to alter or modify copyrighted works. The objective of these two approaches is similar: to limit by copyright the freedom of a party, other than the author of the first generation work, to alter or modify the work.

Neither the U.S. nor the European approach to derivative works is dictated by TRIPS. While the Berne Convention requires protection for moral rights, TRIPS

---

[29] 17 U.S.C. §106(2). U.S. copyright law includes specific provisions addressing some traditional moral rights interests, such as preventing the destruction of well-known artistic works. In other respects, U.S. law addresses traditional moral rights interests through derivative rights and unfair competition rules.

specifically excludes such a requirement.[30] Consequently, under TRIPS, a Member may choose to grant the right to make these works to the author of the first work, or may simply allow others to make the adaptations and translations. TRIPS only requires that when such works are produced, national copyright legislation must extend protection to them. A country is free to determine how and to whom the protection should be directed. Note, however, that with regard to collections the Berne Convention requires that an author be given the right to make compilations of his or her own work.[31]

One possible interpretation of Article 9.2 is that it requires protection of all qualifying "expressions" in the context of Article 9.1 which would, in theory, widen the scope of copyright works.[32] In practice, however, it would appear that there are very few works which could not qualify for copyright protection, subject of course to the explicit exceptions recognized by the Berne Convention. Since TRIPS assimilates the Berne Convention standard for what constitutes copyrightable subject matter, there is a need to understand the scope of works eligible for protection under Berne Convention Article 2.

3.2 Official texts, lectures, addresses

The Berne Convention also gives Member States the discretion to determine whether official government texts, such as judicial opinions, legislative enactments and administrative rules, will be protected by copyright.[33] Countries such as the United Kingdom and Canada and other British Commonwealth countries protect such works by copyright (typically referred to as "Crown Copyright" or "Parliamentary Copyright") but with generous provisions for free use by the public. Other countries, such as the United States, Germany and Japan,[34] explicitly exclude federal government works from copyright protection.[35] Additional areas of national discretion in regard to copyright protection are political speeches, speeches given in the course of legal proceedings, the conditions under which lectures, addresses or speeches to the public may be reproduced by the press, broadcast, communicated to the public by wire and made the subject of public communication when the use is justified by an informatory purpose.[36] The discretion granted by Berne Convention Article 2bis in this regard is circumscribed by Berne Convention Article 11bis which requires that countries grant authors of literary and artistic works the exclusive right to communicate their work to the public. Consequently, a country can determine the conditions under which this right may be exercised,

---

[30] See TRIPS Agreement, Article 9.1.

[31] Berne Convention, Article 2bis(3).

[32] See Gervais, at 78.

[33] See Berne Convention, Article 2(4).

[34] 17 U.S.C. §101, §105; German Copyright Act, §5(1), 2004; Japan Copyright Act, Art. 13.

[35] See 17 U.S.C. §§101, 105. It is unclear whether state government materials may be the proper subjects of copyright since the statute only explicitly excludes works of the federal government. The weight of scholarly opinion suggests that, for the same policy reasons that underlie the exclusion of federal government works, state government works should also be excluded. However, there has been no determinative ruling on this matter by a court.

[36] See Berne Convention, Article 2bis.

but this should not prejudice the author's right to obtain equitable remuneration for such broadcasts.

3.3 Creativity and originality requirements

It is important to note that the works listed in Article 2(1) are mere illustrations of the kind of works that qualify as "literary and artistic works." Thus, it is quite possible to extend copyright protection to works that are not enumerated in Article 2(1), so long as the work can reasonably qualify as "productions in the literary, scientific and artistic domain." The Berne Convention does not offer much insight into a precise definition for this phrase. However, the history of the Berne negotiations indicate that delegates agreed that some element of creative activity must be present in the work.[37] In other words, the work protected must be considered an intellectual creation. As the German law puts it, the work must be a "personal intellectual creation."[38] The substantive quality of the work is typically of no relevance to the question of eligibility for protection; thus, the first poem of a new author is entitled to copyright protection as much as a poem by an accomplished and renowned poet. This is, in effect, an agreement that neutrality (or indifference) to the aesthetic value of a work is a standard principle of copyright regulation. As an international matter, aesthetic neutrality has the benefit of avoiding contestable determinations of culturally subjective evaluations of the merit of literary and artistic works from different parts of the world. At the same time, aesthetic neutrality from a national perspective allows judicial enforcement of copyright to be based on legal standards and not the aesthetic judgment (or preference) of the judge.[39] It is not surprising, then, that the vast majority of countries have adopted this approach, requiring that a work be creative or "original" meaning that the work should demonstrate intellectual investment but not requiring any standard of quality for the purposes of copyright protection. In this regard, Berne Convention Article 2(5) mandates protection for collections of works which *by reason of the selection and arrangement* of their contents constitute intellectual creations. Examples of such collective works include encyclopaedias, academic journals and anthologies.[40]

While it has generally been agreed upon by member countries that the work be original (i.e., it should be the product of independent human intellect and creativity), levels of the originality requirement may differ from country to country. In the United States, originality is a fairly low standard requiring "only that the

---

[37] See Sam Ricketson, *The Berne Convention for the Protection of Literary and Artistic Works: 1886–1986*, Queen Mary, Univ. of London, 1987, 229–230 [hereinafter Ricketson].

[38] See German Copyright Act, §2(2).

[39] Although in common law countries in particular, judicial authorities are inevitably susceptible to making aesthetic judgements even when they claim to be neutral enforcers of the copyright standard. See generally, Alfred Yen, *Copyright Opinions and Aesthetic Theory*, 71 S. Cal. L. Rev. 247 (1998).

[40] Note that the basis for copyright protection in such works is the intellectual creativity evident in the selection of the works and how the works are arranged to form a collection. Further, each work in the collection enjoys copyright protection separate from the copyright in the whole collective work. Thus, reproducing the entire collection by photocopying a journal is a violation of the copyright in the collective work, while reproducing an article in a journal is a violation of the copyright in that particular article.

work was independently created by the author and that it possesses at least a minimal degree of creativity."[41] In Japan the originality standard is relatively higher, requiring that "thoughts and sentiments are expressed in a creative way."[42] The originality requirement with respect to works based primarily on factual materials tends to incorporate an element of creativity. In *Feist Publ'ns v. Rural Tel. Serv. Co.*,[43] the U.S. Supreme Court held that originality in the case of such works requires some modicum of creativity. This decision was followed by the Canadian Court of Appeal in *Tele-Direct (Publ'ns) Inc. v. American Bus. Infor. Inc.* [44] The Court in this case stated that "the basis of copyright is the originality of the work in question so long as work, taste, and discretion have entered in to the composition, that originality is established." It concluded that the defendant had "arranged its information, the vast majority of which is not subject to copyright, according to accepted, commonplace standards of selection in the industry. In doing so, it exercised only a minimal degree of skill, judgment or labour in its overall arrangement which is insufficient to support a claim of originality in the compilation so as to warrant copyright protection."

In Europe, standards of originality varied between countries. For example, Germany represented a country that required a high level of originality, *inter alia* in compilations of factual works while, in the United Kingdom and Ireland, the originality requirement was more comparable to that of the United States.[45] However the EC Copyright Directives have constrained the degree of divergence on this standard and the trend now is toward a uniform standard.[46] These sample definitions of the originality standard illustrate the convergence of the creativity requirement with the originality requirement; in many countries, creativity simply constitutes a part of the originality requirement.

3.4 The fixation requirement

Berne Convention Article 2(2) permits countries to prescribe that works will not be protected by copyright "unless they have been fixed in some material form". In the United States, for example, a literary and artistic work must be "fixed in

---

[41] 499 U.S. 340.

[42] See Japanese Copyright Law, Arts. 1 and 2(1)(i), translated in Dennis S. Karjala & Keiji Sugiyama, *Fundamental Concepts in Japanese and American Copyright Law*, 36 Am. J. Comp. L. 613 (1988), reprinted in Comparative Law: Law and the Legal Process in Japan, 717 (Kenneth L. Port ed., 1996).

[43] *Feist Publ'ns Inc. v. Rural Tel. Serv. Co.*, 449 U.S. 340 (1991) [hereinafter "Feist"].

[44] 76 C.P.R. 3d 296 (1997).

[45] Herman Cohen Jeroham, *The EC Copyright Directives, Economics and Authors' Rights*, 25 Int'l Rev. Indus. Prop. & Copyright Law 821 (1994) (providing comparisons of the originality requirement in different European countries).

[46] See Gerhard Schricker, *Farewell to the "Level of Creativity" (Schöpfungshöhe) in German Copyright Law?* 26 Int. Rev. of Industrial Property and Copyright Law, 1995 (noting the effect of the EC Directive on the Legal Protection of Computer Programs on the high level of creativity required in German Copyright Law. He states that the German implementation of the Directive incorporates the exclusion of the qualitative and aesthetic criteria in the Recitals of the Directive.) See also, Paul Goldstein, *International Copyright*, 164, 2001. Finally, it should be noted that TRIPS and the WCT require a standard of "intellectual creation" for databases. See TRIPS Article 10.2; WCT, Article 5. There is some possibility that this standard will eventually be generalized for all categories of copyright works.

a tangible medium of expression" to qualify for copyright protection.[47] In many other countries such as Belgium, Germany, France, Brazil, and Italy, a work is eligible for copyright protection as long as it is in a form that others can perceive it, but regardless of whether it is "fixed" in a tangible medium of expression. The Berne Convention grants Members the discretion to make a choice about whether fixation will be a required element of copyright protection in their respective countries.[48] Some reasons why fixation may be a useful requirement include: (i) fixation allows the public to have sustained access to the work by requiring that creative works exist in a form that facilitates such access (e.g., how can one own the copy of a song, or a book if they are not fixed?);[49] (ii) fixation may facilitate making distinctions between works that are copyrightable and works that are not, by requiring authors to do something "extra" to show their interest in the rewards that underlie copyright; (iii) fixation may serve a public policy goal of facilitating the length of time that copyright protection exists in the work – if the work is not in a stable form, it may be more difficult to determine when protection starts and (importantly for public policy concerns) when it ends. As one author has noted, however, the modern trajectory is to abandon the fixation requirement.[50] Since under TRIPS such a requirement is not mandatory (Article 9.1 only refers to the option under Article 2.2, Berne Convention), it should be considered only if a country has identifiable public policy objectives that would best be served by a requirement of fixation.

4. WTO jurisprudence

There has been no panel decision dealing mainly with the subject of copyrightable works. However, in *US – Section 110(5) of the Copyright Act*, the panel briefly clarified the contents of Articles 11 and 11*bis* of the Berne Convention.[51] These provisions are among those referred to under Article 9 of TRIPS and specify the author's rights with respect to dramatic and musical works (Article 11 Berne) and in relation to broadcasting and related rights (Article 11*bis* Berne).[52] The EC had asserted a violation of Articles 9.1 TRIPS, 11 (1)(ii) and 11*bis*(1)(iii) of the

---

[47] 17 U.S.C. §102(a). Under U.S. copyright law, a work satisfies the fixation requirement if its embodiment in a copy or phonorecord, by or under the authority of the author, is sufficiently permanent or stable to permit it to be perceived, reproduced, or otherwise communicated for a period of more than transitory duration.

[48] See Berne Convention, Article 2(2).

[49] This possibility is not quite as unimaginable today given the capabilities of communications technology such as the Internet.

[50] Ysolde Gendreau, *The Criteria of Fixation in Copyright Law*, 159 R.I.D.A. 100, 126 (1994).

[51] See *US – Section 110(5) of the Copyright Act*, Complaint by the European Communities, WT/DS160/R June 15, 2000, paras. 6.18-6.29. Note that this dispute focused on another issue, namely the analysis of Article 13 of the TRIPS Agreement (i.e. limitations and exceptions to exclusive copyrights). For details see Chapter 12.

[52] See Article 11 (1) of the Berne Convention: "Authors of dramatic, dramatico-musical and musical works shall enjoy the exclusive right of authorizing:

(i) the public performance of their works, including such public performance by any means or process;

(ii) any communication to the public of the performance of their works."

Berne Convention.[53] The panel distinguished the two Berne provisions by stating that:

> "Regarding the relationship between Articles 11 and 11bis, we note that the rights conferred in Article 11(1)(ii) concern the communication to the public of performances of works in general. Article 11bis(1)(iii) is a specific rule conferring exclusive rights concerning the public communication by loudspeaker or any other analogous instrument transmitting, by signs, sounds or images, the broadcast of a work."[54]

In addition, the panel stressed that both provisions are only implicated if the protected works are communicated to the public, because purely private performances do not need any authorization from the right holder.[55]

5. Relationship with other international instruments

5.1 WTO Agreements

There are no other WTO Agreements dealing with the issue of copyrightable subject matter. Consequently, there is no particular relationship between the TRIPS/Berne copyright provisions and other WTO Agreements. Under Article XX GATT, there is, however, a reference to intellectual property rights and more specifically, copyrights: for the purpose of copyright protection, and provided that certain conditions are met, WTO Members may deviate from the basic GATT obligations of most-favoured nation treatment, national treatment and the prohibition of quantitative restrictions.[56] As opposed to TRIPS and the Berne Convention, the GATT thus treats the protection of intellectual property rights as an exception. Article XX GATT does not however address the issue of copyrightable material.

Article 11bis (1) of the Berne Convention provides: "Authors of literary and artistic works shall enjoy the exclusive right of authorizing:

(i) the broadcasting of their works or the communication thereof to the public by any other means of wireless diffusion of signs, sounds or images;

(ii) any communication to the public by wire or by rebroadcasting of the broadcast of the work, when this communication is made by an organization other than the original one;

(iii) the public communication by loudspeaker or any other analogous instrument transmitting, by signs, sounds or images, the broadcast of the work."

Both articles thus concern the rights of the *author* and are therefore to be distinguished from Article 14 TRIPS, which deals with the rights of performers, producers of sound recordings and broadcasting organizations.

[53] See US – Section 110(5) of the Copyright Act, para. 6.26.

[54] Ibid., para. 6.25.

[55] Ibid., paras. 6.24, 6.28. The USA did not contest that its legislation affected the above-mentioned provisions of the Berne Convention, and thus Article 9.1 of the TRIPS Agreement (see para. 6.29). The main issue of the dispute was therefore whether this violation of the Berne Convention was justified under Article 13 of the TRIPS Agreement.

[56] See Article XX (d) GATT, which reads in its relevant part: "Subject to the requirement that such measures are not applied in a manner which would constitute a means of arbitrary or unjustifiable discrimination between countries where the same conditions prevail, or a disguised restriction on international trade, nothing in this Agreement shall be construed to prevent the adoption or enforcement by any contracting party of measures: ... (d) necessary to secure compliance with laws or regulations which are not inconsistent with the provisions of this Agreement, including those relating to [...] the protection of patents, trade marks and copyrights, [...]."

5.2 Other international instruments

The incorporation of the Berne Convention into TRIPS means that the negotiating context of the Berne Convention is an important interpretive resource for WTO Members. The initial TRIPS copyright dispute already demonstrates the significant reliance dispute panels will place on Berne history when interpreting TRIPS.[57] Further, the WIPO Copyright Treaty (WCT) tracks the language of TRIPS Article 9.2 and excludes "ideas, procedures, methods of operation or mathematical concepts as such" from protection.[58] Accordingly, the interpretation of TRIPS Article 9.2 will undoubtedly inform the interpretation of the WCT.

6. New developments

6.1 National laws

The overwhelming majority of national laws adopt the scope of copyrightable works provided under the Berne Convention and TRIPS. Some countries have included additional categories of works, such as folklore, in their copyright laws.

7. Comments, including economic and social implications

The preceding discussion on the TRIPS requirements for copyright works raises some important economic and social issues. As a point of initial observation, Article 9 contemplates some discretion for countries in prescribing the conditions of protectable subject matter. The extent to which intellectual works are copyrightable determines the balance between incentives for creativity on the one hand and the possibilities for the general public to accede to knowledge-based products on the other hand. TRIPS in some degree provides Members with the freedom to strike this balance according to their particular needs and economic development. Members may choose to require a certain level of creativity and originality; Members may choose whether or not government publications will be protected by copyright and; copyright protection does not extend to ideas, or to mere facts, news of the day or items of press information. Members may also determine the copyright status of political speeches and speeches delivered in the course of legal proceedings. Of course, because TRIPS imposes a *minimum* standard of protection, countries that wish to extend protection to works not required under TRIPS may exercise the discretion to do so. However, in each of the areas where TRIPS does not mandate a specific rule of protection, important social objectives are implicated. For example, the explicit exclusion of ideas from the ambit of copyright protection serves an important public policy objective mentioned earlier, namely, preserving and enriching a public domain of materials and resources which the public can freely draw upon. The copyright status of political speeches implicates sociopolitical issues such as freedom of the press and freedom of speech. Similarly, the decision to extend copyright to government works has implications for the public

---

[57] See *US – Section 110(5) of the Copyright Act*, Complaint by the European Communities, WT/DS160/R June 15, 2000.

[58] See WCT, Article 2.

in terms of the accessibility to the laws by which they are governed.[59] The exercise of national discretion in these areas is of great importance to the economic and social objectives that underlie the copyright system. In this context, the Commission on Intellectual Property Rights has referred to evidence from the past showing that in certain cases, diffusion of knowledge throughout developing countries has been positively affected by weak levels of copyright enforcement. The Commission then expresses the view that many poor people in developing countries have only been able to access certain knowledge-based products through the use of unauthorized copies at much lower prices.[60]

Copyright serves to provide an incentive so that creative activity will be encouraged. Such creative activity is ultimately directed at benefiting the public. The determination of what works are protected and the conditions of such protection should be carefully considered in light of the rich variety of approaches that have been experimented with in the past, and with particular regard to the goals of economic development. A careful balance is necessary in implementing all of the required standards to ensure that the public welfare is not compromised by rules that only consider the incentive aspect. Conversely, implementation should consider what is necessary to encourage optimal production of copyrightable works. For example, a high creativity standard may not be as effective in encouraging the production of a wide range of works, as a low standard has proven to be in countries such as the United States. Alternatively, one might opt for a high standard of creativity in certain categories of works, such as computer programs, and a low standard in others. Since the originality/creativity requirement is a matter of national discretion, it is unlikely that adopting different standards for different works can be said to violate any TRIPS mandate.

In sum, the scope of protectable copyright works has important implications for the social objectives that are inextricably bound to the copyright system. Some of these include freedom of expression, the facilitation of creativity by future generations, the opportunity for the public to access certain kinds of works and the political importance of certain civil freedoms. All of these must be taken into account in adopting a particular model of implementation of the negotiated standards in TRIPS with respect to copyright works. They should also be accounted for in future negotiations about the scope of copyright works.

---

[59] Indeed the policy reason for the exclusion of government works in the U.S. copyright law is the significant concern that in a democratic society under the rule of law, laws must be freely available to the public.

[60] See the report of the IPR Commission, p. 101. The report (ibid.) also states that in the past, certain developed countries used to refuse to grant any copyright protection to foreign authors, driven by the concern to satisfy the country's need for knowledge. This may be seen as an encouragement of nationals of the respective country to make use of unauthorized copies of works belonging to foreign authors. Nowadays, such practice would obviously violate Articles 3 (national treatment) and 9.1 of the TRIPS Agreement. It is noteworthy that some developed countries are seeking to deny to developing countries the right to adopt the very public policies they have used in the past.

8: Computer Programs

Article 10.1 Computer Programs and Compilations of Data

Computer programs, whether in source or object code, shall be protected as literary works under the Berne Convention (1971).

---

1. Introduction: terminology, definition and scope

Article 10.1 requires Member States to recognize computer programs as literary works under the Berne Convention. The Berne Convention itself does not explicitly provide that computer programs constitute copyrightable subject matter; however, works enumerated in Article 2 of the Berne Convention are mere illustrations of the kinds of works to which copyright might extend. Further, these illustrations are not exhaustive. Consequently works such as computer programs that exhibit utilitarian characteristics but also contain expressive elements are legitimate candidates for copyright protection.[61]

Since TRIPS does not provide any definition of the term "computer program", Members may keep the definitions they adopted under their domestic laws prior to the entry into force of TRIPS.[62] For example, under the 1976 U.S. Copyright Act, a computer program is defined as "a set of statements or instructions to be used directly or indirectly in a computer in order to bring about a certain result."[63] The Japanese Copyright Law states that a computer program is "an expression of combined instructions given to a computer so as to make it function and obtain a certain result."[64] While the U.K. law does not provide a definition of computer programs, it extends copyright protection both to the program as well as drawings, stories and other traditional works that are generated by the program.[65]

Article 10.1 requires copyright protection for computer programs whether in "source code" or in "object code." Source code is a level of computer language

---

[61] Note that computer programs must satisfy all the requirements, such as originality, of other copyright works.

[62] See also Section 6.1 of this chapter, below.

[63] 17 U.S.C. §101.

[64] Japan, Copyright Act, Article2(1)(Xbis).

[65] United Kingdom, Copyright, Designs and Patents Act 1988, §178.

consisting of words, symbols and alphanumeric labels. It is a "high level" language and is intelligible to human beings. Object code is another level of computer language that, unlike source code, is incomprehensible to human beings. Object code is a machine language that employs binary numbers consisting of a string of "0's" and "1's." Many computer programs are written in source code but then distributed in object code form. A computer program known as a "compiler" is used to translate or convert source code into object code.

The object of such copyright protection is, as follows from Article 9.2, not the idea on which the computer software is based, but the expression of that idea through the object code or source code.

2. History of the provision

2.1 Situation pre-TRIPS

Prior to TRIPS, computer programs already enjoyed copyright protection in a significant number of countries. For example, in the United States, computer programs have been protected by copyright, as confirmed in 1976 when the Copyright Act was amended to expressly acknowledge that computer programs are within the subject matter scope of protection. Similarly, in 1991 the European Community Directive on the Legal Protection of Computer Programs[66] ("EC Software Directive") required member countries to extend copyright protection to computer programs.[67] Indeed, by 1991, at least 54 countries recognized copyright protection in computer programs. While most did so through legislative amendment, a few took place through executive proclamations or judicial decisions that extended the existing copyright laws to computer programs.[68]

2.2 Negotiating History

As with other provisions, Article 10 was the subject of several different proposals. With regard to computer programs, earlier drafts of Article 10.1 reflected a struggle over a compromise agreement on what precisely the scope of such a provision might be.

2.2.1 The Anell Draft

"2. Protectable Subject Matter

2.1 PARTIES shall provide protection to computer programs [,as literary works for the purposes of point 1 above,] [and to databases]. Such protection shall not extend to ideas, procedures, methods [, algorithms] or systems.

2.2B.1 For the purpose of protecting computer programs, PARTIES shall determine in their national legislation the nature, scope and term of protection to be granted to such works.

---

[66] Council Directive of 14 May 1991 on the Legal Protection of Computer Programs, 1991 O.J. (L-122) 42.

[67] Article 1(1).

[68] See Michael S. Keplinger, *International Protection for Computer Programs* 315 PLI/Pat 457 (1991).

2.2B.2 In view of the complex legal and technical issues raised by the protection of computer programs, PARTIES undertake to cooperate with each other to identify a suitable method of protection and to evolve international rules governing such protection."

In the above draft, there was no independent provision on databases, unlike under the current Article 10 (see Chapter 9). The first paragraph had its origin in a Japanese proposal suggesting the following language:

"The copyright protection for computer program works under the present Agreement shall not extend to any programming language, rule or algorithm use for making such works."[69]

This proposal was modified later to conform more closely to Section 102 of the 1976 U.S. Copyright Act which provides that

"copyright protection for an original work of authorship [does not] extend to any idea, procedure, process, system, method of operation, concept, principle, or discovery regardless of the form in which it is described, explained, illustrated, or embodied in such work."

The former Japanese proposal was taken over into the Brussels Draft (as quoted below), but ultimately removed from the context of computer programs and interposed, instead, as a general rule distinguishing copyrightable and non-copyrightable subject matter. This is the rule now embodied in Article 9.2 discussed in Chapter 7.

2.2.2 The Brussels Draft
This draft in its first paragraph contained essentially the same language as the current Article 10.1, but the term "literary" was still bracketed. The final agreement to protect computer programs as "literary" works has important implications for the scope of protection. Without such express reference, Members would be free to qualify computer software as works of applied art or an equivalent thereof, instead.[70] As such, the protection of computer programs could be less wide than the protection of "literary" works in the narrow sense of the term. The reason for this is that Article 2(7) of the Berne Convention makes the protection of works of applied art dependent on domestic legislation, which may determine the extent to which and the conditions under which such works are to be protected. In addition to that, Article 7(4) of the Berne Convention exempts, *inter alia*, works of applied art from the general term of protection (i.e. the author's life plus 50 years) and sets up a minimum term of only 25 years from the making of the work.

In addition to that, the first paragraph of the draft contained a bracketed second sentence providing that:

"[Such protection shall not extend to ideas, procedures, methods of operation or mathematical concepts.]"

---

[69] See Teruo Doi, *The TRIPS Agreement and the Copyright Law of Japan: A Comparative Analysis*, Journal of the Japanese Group of AIPPI (1996).
[70] See Gervais, p. 81, para. 2.60.

This was an amended version of the former Japanese proposal as referred to above, which was subsequently (i.e. after the Brussels Draft) taken out of the computer-related draft provision and put into a more general form under Article 9.2.

The third difference with respect to the current Article 10.1 was that paragraph 1 of the Brussels Draft proposal contained a second sub-paragraph on the compliance with certain procedures as a requirement for the protection of computer programs. This bracketed provision read as follows:

"[This shall not prevent PARTIES from requiring, as a condition of protection of computer programs, compliance with procedures and formalities consistent with the principles of Part IV of this Agreement or from making adjustments to the rights of reproduction and adaptation and to moral rights necessary to permit normal exploitation of a computer program, provided that this does not unreasonably prejudice the legitimate interests of the right holder.]"

This proposal was not taken over into the final version of Article 10.1. Its first semi-sentence is very similar to the current Article 62, which is however not limited to copyrights in computer programs but applicable to all categories of IPRs covered by TRIPS.[71] The second part of the proposed paragraph, referring to adjustments to certain rights for the normal exploitation of a computer program, was entirely dropped.

3. Possible interpretations

The public policy interest in encouraging the creation of computer programs does not necessarily require protection solely in the form of copyright. Article 10 requires that copyright protection be extended to computer programs. However, TRIPS does not preclude additional forms of protection for computer programs. Thus, under TRIPS, a Member could offer patent, copyright and trade secret protection for computer programs.[72] In such a case, the author can choose which form of protection is most desirable assuming of course that, in the case of software patents, the higher standards of creativity required by patent law are also satisfied.

It should be noted that the possibility of alternative forms of protection for computer programs were contemplated prior to TRIPS, and such alternatives do exist in some national laws.[73] What TRIPS does require, though, is that one of the options for legal protection is in the form of copyright law.

---

[71] For more details on Article 62 of the TRIPS Agreement, see Chapter 30.

[72] One could argue that TRIPS Article 27.1, which prohibits field specific exclusions of patentable subject matter, requires that Member States recognize patent protection for software related invention so long as the invention satisfies the other requirements for patentability. See J.H. Reichman, *Universal Minimum Standards of Intellectual Property Protection Under the TRIPS Component of the WTO Agreement*, 29 International Lawyer 345, 360 (1995). More clearly, TRIPS Article 39, which requires protection for undisclosed information, offers a trade secret regime as an alternative to copyright protection for software. Note that because of the mandatory language of Article 10.1, Member States must provide copyright protection for computer programs. However, an innovator may opt for protection under the trade secret laws instead. This outcome is acceptable under TRIPS.

[73] See the U.S. Supreme Court decision *Diamond v. Diehr*, 450 U.S. 175 (1981) which paved the way for legal recognition of the patentability of software. Most recently, the controversial decision

TRIPS does not define, however, the eligibility criteria that Members must apply to computer programs, nor, apart from a generalized exclusion of ideas, procedures, methods of operation or mathematical concepts as such (Article 9.2), does the Agreement concern itself with the scope of copyright protection for this subject matter. Meanwhile, the software industry keeps evolving at a rapid pace, as does litigation in some countries concerning copyright protection of computer programs.[74]

TRIPS allows for reverse engineering of computer programs by honest avenues. This means that, although wholesale copying of computer programs is prohibited, the practice of re-implementing functional components of a protected program in "clones" is not. Programs that are independently coded and that yet deliver essentially the same functional performance or behaviour as the originator's own software do not infringe the latter's rights.[75] This may boost competition and innovation by firms in all countries, including in developing countries where some capabilities for the production of software already exist.

This distinction in Article 9.2 between protectable expressions on the one hand, and non-protectable ideas on the other, has been implemented differently at the national level, as may be illustrated by the U.S. approach to computer programs and the EC Software Directive. Under the Directive, the licensor cannot restrict a person's right to observe, study or test the way a program functions in order to obtain an understanding of the ideas embodied in the program, so long as the person doing so is engaging in permitted activity. In certain circumstances, the Directive also recognizes the right of a person who is a rightful owner of the work to decompile (i.e., translate object code into source code) the program to obtain information for purposes of ensuring interoperability with another computer program.[76] This right is circumscribed by the caveat that the information is not available elsewhere.[77] These rights do not have counterparts in the U.S. copyright law, although judicial decisions have often resulted in the same outcome. Inevitably, the scope of copyright protection for computer programs will, for the time being, continue to remain flexible and dependent on the interpretation and application given by national courts.

With respect to limitations or exceptions on the scope of protection for computer programs, there is some considerable divergence in the practices of major producers of software such as the United States and the European Union. The

---

in *State Street Bank & Trust Co. v. Signature Fin. Group*, 149 F. 3d 1368 (Fed. Cir. 1998) confirmed the patentability of business method software patents.

[74] On this and the following two paragraphs, see UNCTAD, *The TRIPS Agreement and Developing Countries*, New York and Geneva, 1996, paras. 181–183.

[75] Recall that the object of copyright protection in a computer program is not the underlying idea, but the computer language (i.e. source code or object code, see above, Section 1.) used to express that idea. The critical issue is that the coding of the program was carried out *independently*. In that case, the idea underlying the program is expressed in a way that differs from the way in which the originator of the program has expressed this idea. The new code thus constitutes the expression (of the underlying idea) that may only be attributed to the person having reverse engineered the original program. It is thus the independence of the expression (i.e. the code) that matters, not the similarity of the result.

[76] See EC Software Directive, Article 6.

[77] *Id*. Article 6(1).

differences are most evident with regard to the issue of reverse engineering. Reverse engineering may take place for a variety of purposes including research and the facilitation of compatibility (interoperability) to produce competing software, or software related products. Regardless of its purpose, the process of reverse engineering implicates the reproduction rights of the owner of the original computer program. In the United States, the appropriateness of a particular act of reverse engineering is a matter of judicial determination. U.S. domestic courts examine this practice on a case-by-case basis. In the European Union, however, reverse engineering is regulated by the Software Directive. This has led to distinct policies.

In the United States, for example, courts have held that reverse engineering of software is permissible under certain conditions.[78] These conditions are evaluated under the rubric of general limitations to copyright such as the fair use doctrine. Consequently, the underlying purpose of the use is of considerable importance in these cases. Reverse engineering for purposes of research is likely to yield favourable decisions to the defendant. Indeed, many commentators view this as an important policy tool in copyright law and that such purposes animate the objectives of having a copyright system in the first place.[79] Reverse engineering in efforts to create compatible software has also been deemed permissible by courts in the United States.[80]

By contrast, Article 6 of the EC Software Directive conditions decompilation (reverse engineering) for compatibility purposes on the fact that the information necessary to accomplish compatibility must not have been previously readily available. Further, decompilation is to be confined to the aspects of the program related to the need for compatibility. Reverse engineering for purposes of creating competing products is prohibited. There is no specific exception for research, and the limited scope of decompilation permitted by the terms of the Directive is not to be construed in a manner that would unreasonably interfere with the owner's normal exploitation of the computer program.

It could be concluded that once the issue of copyrightable elements of a program has been decided, some deference to domestic policies that permit activities such as reverse engineering or "back-up" or "archival" copies will be acceptable under TRIPS so long as these exceptions are reasonably consistent with the mandate for protection. The scope of these limitations arguably could be challenged under TRIPS Article 13 (see Chapter 12), which requires that WTO Members limit the nature and scope of exceptions to copyright. However, Article 13 does not relate to the question of what is copyrightable but, instead, to the exceptions and limitations to the copyright in the protected work. In terms of what aspects of a computer program are copyrightable, domestic courts still have the task of distinguishing idea from expression; TRIPS does not provide any explicit rules on

[78] See e.g., *Sega Enterprises Ltd. v. Accolade, Inc.*, 977 F.2d 1510 (9th Cir. 1992).

[79] See Lawrence D. Graham & Richard O. Zerbe, Jr., *Economically Efficient Treatment of Computer Software: Reverse Engineering, Protection and Disclosure*, 22 Rutgers Computer & Tech. L. J. 61, 67 (1996).

[80] See *Sega Enterprises*, 77 F. 2d 1510; *Atari Games Corp. v. Nintendo of America Inc.*, 30 U.S.P.Q. 2d 1401 (N.D. Cal. 1993).

what constitutes "expression" in computer programs. Consequently, there is some flexibility available to countries to determine the extent of copyright protection in a particular computer program.

Finally, software producers may also benefit from provisions in TRIPS requiring WTO Members to protect undisclosed information and to repress unfair competition. For example, once domestic laws to protect undisclosed information are enacted in conformity with Article 39, a local competitor whose conduct violates its provisions may become unable to profit from the improper acquisition of know-how that copyright laws may otherwise have left unprotected.[81] Similarly, the unfair competition norms incorporated into TRIPS through Article 10*bis* of the Paris Convention prevent competitors from copying trademarks or trade dress even though they may otherwise imitate non-copyrightable components of foreign computer programs.

4. WTO jurisprudence

To date, there is no WTO panel decision on this subject.

5. Relationship with other international instruments

The Berne Convention does not explicitly mention computer programs in its illustrative list of copyright works. Consequently, the first international treaty to do so is TRIPS. In 1996, two additional copyright treaties were negotiated under the auspices of the World Intellectual Property Organization (WIPO). These treaties, namely the WIPO Copyright Treaty (WCT) and the WIPO Performances and Phonograms Treaty (WPPT), were directed specifically to the effects of the digital revolution on copyright.

The WCT is a special agreement as defined in Berne Convention Article 20 ("The Governments of the countries of the Union reserve the right to enter into special agreements among themselves, in so far as such agreements grant to authors more extensive rights than those granted by the Convention, or contain other provisions not contrary to this Convention . . . "). By its own terms, the WCT has no connection with any other treaties but the Berne Convention.[82] Nonetheless, the WCT is not to be interpreted as prejudicing any rights and obligations under other treaties.[83] This suggests that for nations that have ratified both the WCT and TRIPS, the two agreements should be implemented and interpreted consistently.

With regard to computer programs, the WCT is the second international treaty to explicitly address copyright protection. WCT Article 4 states: "Computer programs are protected as literary works within the meaning of Article 2 of the Berne Convention. Such protection applies to computer programs, whatever may be the mode or form of their expression." The reference to the Berne Convention suggests that, as a matter of international law, the requirements for copyright works under Berne Convention Article 2 will apply, *mutatis mutandis*, to computer programs

---

[81] Know-how is not an expression, but an idea, and thus not eligible for copyright protection.
[82] See WCT, Article 1(1).
[83] Id.

protected under the provisions of the WCT. Thus, even though the WCT does not explicitly mention the idea/expression dichotomy, it is reasonable to assume that the idea/expression principle extends to the scope of copyright protection recognized for computer programs by WCT Article 2. The combined legal force of TRIPS Article 10 and WCT Article 4 confirms that computer programs are firmly established as copyrightable subject matter under international copyright law. As the previous discussion indicates, however, this confirmation does not mean that all countries protect computer programs in the same way and to the same extent.

6. New developments

6.1 National laws

A large cross-section of countries had already extended copyright protection to computer programs prior to the negotiation of TRIPS. Consequently, many countries were already in compliance with Article 10 with respect to the availability of copyright protection for computer programs. However, differences in protection remain, as is particularly evident in the scope of exceptions or limitations to protection. For example, judicial decisions in the United States suggest that software structure, sequence and organization are protectable under copyright law.[84] Other countries have not clearly determined that this is the case under their legislation. In addition, TRIPS requires that computer programs be protected as literary works for a term of the life of the author plus 50 years.[85] Those countries which, prior to TRIPS, accorded a lesser term of protection for computer programs must modify their laws to be compliant with the term requirements of TRIPS.

An issue not addressed under TRIPS is the use by copyright holders of encryption technologies.[86] In this context, it is noteworthy that the U.S. 1998 Digital Millennium Copyright Act (DMCA), implementing the WCT, makes illegal those acts circumventing encryption technologies, even in cases traditionally considered legal under the fair use exception.[87] This kind of approach to encryption is by no means mandatory either under TRIPS or under the WCT. Developing countries are free to deny protection to encryption technologies when these are used to prevent certain public policy goals, such as distance learning.

In addition to the move to support encryption practices through copyright, some industries in certain countries are pressing their governments to pass legislation even *requiring* computer manufacturers to integrate into their products particular devices technically preventing the copying of protected works without the author's consent.[88] However, no such legislation has so far been enacted.

---

[84] *Whelan v. Jaslow*, 797 F. 2d 1222 (3d Cir. 1986). See also Dennis S. Karjala, *The Relative Roles of Patent and Copyright in the Protection of Computer Programs*, 17 John Marshall J. of Computer & Information L., 41, 53 (1998) hereinafter Karjala.

[85] As required by the Berne Convention, Article 7(1).

[86] "Encryption" is "a procedure that renders the contents of a computer message or file unintelligible to anyone not authorized to read it. The message is encoded mathematically with a string of characters called a *data encryption key*. [. . .]" (See J. Friedman (ed.), *Dictionary of Business Terms*, third edition 2000, p. 220).

[87] See IPR Commission report, p. 107, referring to the above U.S. law.

[88] See the IPR Commission report, p. 107.

6.2 International instruments

As opposed to TRIPS, the WCT does address the issue of encryption: Article 11 WCT (Obligations concerning Technological Measures) provides that:

> "Contracting Parties shall provide adequate legal protection and effective legal remedies against the circumvention of effective technological measures that are used by authors in connection with the exercise of their rights under this Treaty or the Berne Convention and that restrict acts, in respect of their works, which are not authorized by the authors concerned or permitted by law."

The language employed in this provision offers quite a bit of flexibility as to implementation. What is "adequate" legal protection is to be determined by national legislation, according to national preferences. It is important to note that this provision does not obligate countries to protect encryption technologies in any given case. The last part of Article 11 makes clear that the case of unauthorized use (i.e. without agreement from the author) is not the only one in which encryption may be supported by national copyright law. Instead, countries may limit such support to cases where the use of the protected material is not permitted by law, irrespective of the will of the author. It is thus up to the domestic legislator and national preferences to judge in which degree encryption technologies are justified, and to which extent cases of fair use should prevail.[89] Countries may opt for quasi-absolute copyright protection by condoning encryption technologies whenever the author does not wish to provide free access to certain works. Alternatively, they may deny the support of encryption technologies through copyright law if circumvention serves certain public policy objectives such as education and technology transfer.

7. Comments, including economic and social implications

The market for computer programs is characterized by what many economic commentators refer to as network effects. Simply put, this means that the software market is one where the value of the product increases as the number of people who purchase it also increases. For example, communication technologies such as the telephone or fax machine are generally very susceptible to network effects. Consider that if only one person purchased a telephone or a fax machine, the value of either product would increase as other people purchased the same products. Conversely, the values could decline to nothing if only one person owned a telephone or a fax machine.

Similarly, the market for software that runs on a computer operating system is subject to network effects. This problem has important implications for the diffusion of computer programs. Operating systems have an "interface" that encompasses the way in which computer modules communicate. Computer programs for an application must be written in a way that allows it to run on a particular operating system. The more applications that run on a particular operating system, the more valuable that system becomes. As more applications are written by software developers, more consumers are likely to purchase it because of the variety

---

[89] On fair use see Chapter 12, Article 13, TRIPS Agreement.

of applications available for that particular operating system. As more consumers purchase it, more applications will be developed, and so on. This positive feedback effect gives some understanding of why dominant software firms emerge. To encourage competition in the software industry, there must be careful attention paid to the precise features of software that are protected by copyright.

For example, some commentators argue that certain "internal" interfaces should not be protected by copyright because they are essentially nothing more than "industrial compilations of applied know-how."[90] The central focus of arguments against the copyrightability of computer interfaces is that interfaces *must* be used for computer programmers to write programs that can run on the operating system. If these kinds of interfaces are excluded from copyright, then competitors will be free to use the interface to develop a competitive product, which is an important aspect of promoting the public interest. User interfaces that produce computer screen displays are more likely to be subject to copyright under a number of different categories. Such displays might constitute pictorial works (e.g., video game characters) or literary works (e.g., help screens).[91]

The importance of computer programs to modern life makes the economic and social implications of protection an important issue for all countries. As discussed above, the important issue is to "abstract" the idea of the program from its expression to ensure that copyright protection is not being used to acquire more rights than the system otherwise permits. Additionally, some countries recognize three general limitations or exceptions to the copyright in computer programs. These are (i) exceptions for "back-up copies"[92]; (ii) exceptions to foster access to the non-copyrightable elements of the computer program such as "reverse engineering";[93] (iii) exceptions to facilitate interoperability. Properly delineated exceptions in the last two categories have important ramifications for competition and diffusion.

A country with a young software industry may wish to consider strong protection for copyrightable elements to encourage investment in the development of software. As the industry matures, however, it is important to foster competition by allowing certain uses that would facilitate further research and development and ensure that the market is not unduly dominated by the first mover. Such market dominance may have particularly serious repercussions in developing countries,

---

[90] See Pamela Samuelson et al., *A Manifesto Concerning the Legal Protection of Computer Programs*, 94 Columbia Law Review, 2308 (1994).

[91] See Karjala, at 55.

[92] For example, under the EC Software Directive, a person has the right to make a back-up copy of the computer program. Also, the Czechoslovakian copyright law of 1990 permitted users to make back-up copies of a computer program without permission from the owner and without a duty to pay remuneration. Finally, Article 7 of the Brazilian Law of 1987 excluded from infringement, "the integration of the program within an application solely for the use of the person making the integration".

[93] As to the legality of reverse engineering under TRIPS and as to its domestic implementation, see above, under Section 3. Note, however, that *independent* efforts to develop computer programs that meet local industrial and administrative needs may sometimes pay bigger dividends than re-implementing foreign products, which is generally a costly endeavour requiring high technical skills. The potential benefits of obtaining the most up-to-date software by means of direct investment, licensing or other arrangements should always be weighed against re-implementation (in the sense of reverse engineering) of existing software. See UNCTAD, 1996, para. 184.

where high prices charged by a monopolist would exclude most parts of the
population from the purchase of the copyrighted software. In this respect, the
Commission on Intellectual Property Rights favours an active promotion through
developing country governments and their donor partners of low-cost software
products.[94]

On the positive side, computer software offers important opportunities for countries already having acquired a certain level of technological capacity to close the
knowledge gap *vis-à-vis* industrialized countries. Computer-related technologies
are the principal means of accessing information and furthering technology transfer.[95] The possibility of charging higher prices for copyrighted computer software
may also have the positive effect of encouraging the development of local industries producing software that is better adapted to local conditions. This may eventually increase developing countries' participation in the world market of computer software, which is currently very modest.[96] Thus, the cost-benefit ratio of
reinforced protection would have to be judged both in terms of impact on the diffusion of computer technology, including in particular for educational purposes –
and on the improved opportunities given to local producers, who would not be
able to start up and grow if they were victims of the inexpensive and easy-to-make
copying of their products.[97]

The problem of access barriers through strengthened copyright protection
arises in particular with respect to the Internet. The world wide web is a major
medium for distance learning, considering that providing Internet access is less
costly than the setting up of entire libraries.[98] On the other hand, works published
on the Internet (e.g. scientific articles) are increasingly protected from free access
through new technologies such as encryption. This practice denies Internet users
the access to certain websites, even if such access would be limited to private (e.g.
learning) purposes.[99]

Therefore, developing countries should be very careful about condoning encryption technologies which would prevent free access to on-line documents essential
to the dissemination of knowledge, including distance learning. This would inhibit developing countries' efforts to close the technology gap towards developed

---

[94] See IPR Commission report, p. 105. For this purpose, the Commission recommends that developing countries and their donor partners review their software procurement policies "with a view
to ensuring that options for using low-cost and/or open source software products are properly
considered and their costs and benefits are carefully evaluated." (ibid.). "Open source" software
refers to the source code of a computer program, which is, other than the object code, comprehen-
sible to human beings (see above, Section 3.). According to the IPR Commission, another way of
promoting competition with a view to ensuring affordable software prices is to limit the protection
of computer programs to the object code, making the source code available to developing country
software industries.

[95] See IPR Commission report, p. 104.

[96] See UNCTAD, 1996 (paras. 170-172), responding to the concern that due to actual market shares,
strengthened software protection is likely to improve developed countries' market positions *vis-à-
vis* developing countries.

[97] Ibid., para. 172.

[98] See IPR Commission report p. 107.

[99] See IPR Commission report, p. 106.

countries. Accordingly, the Commission on Intellectual Property Rights has recommended that:

> "Users of information available on the Internet in the developing nations should be entitled to 'fair use' rights such as making and distributing printed copies from electronic sources in reasonable numbers for educational and research purposes, and using reasonable excerpts in commentary and criticism. Where suppliers of digital information or software attempt to restrict 'fair use' rights by contract provisions associated with the distribution of digital material, the relevant contract provision may be treated as void. Where the same restriction is attempted through technological means, measures to defeat the technological means of protection in such circumstances should not be regarded as illegal. Developing countries should think very carefully before joining the WIPO Copyright Treaty and other countries should not follow the lead of the US and the EU by implementing legislation on the lines of the DMCA or the Database Directive."[100]

In addition to specific legislative exceptions, such as those in the EC Software Directive, it is possible that other general copyright limitations could also be extended to computer programs. Thus, a country could choose to identify explicit limitations in its copyright law, while also allowing courts to extend the generalized limitations on other copyright works to computer programs as well.

In sum, copyright protection of computer programs, like copyright protection in general, gives rise to the same concern about striking the right balance between the encouragement of intellectual activity on the one hand and the free availability of certain documents for public policy purposes on the other.

[100] See IPR Commission report, p. 109.

9: Databases

> ### Article 10.2 Computer Programs and Compilations of Data
>
> 2. Compilations of data or other material, whether in machine readable or other form, which by reason of the selection or arrangement of their contents constitute intellectual creations shall be protected as such. Such protection, which shall not extend to the data or material itself, shall be without prejudice to any copyright subsisting in the data or material itself.

1. Introduction: terminology, definition and scope

A database may be defined simply as a collection of data. For the purpose of determining whether a collection of data qualifies for copyright protection, other elements are incorporated into this definition. The Berne Convention does not use the word "database", but instead specifies in Article 2(5) that "collections" of literary and artistic works which "by reason of the selection and arrangement of their contents constitute intellectual creations shall be protected as such."

Thus, a collection of short stories, or anthologies, or a collection of scholarly works, would be eligible for copyright protection under the Berne Convention, independent of the copyright status in the stories or scholarly works, so long as the "selection and arrangement" of the contents reflect some intellectual creativity. This is, in essence, a requirement for originality.

TRIPS Article 10.2 broadens the concept of a database. It provides that "compilations of data or other material, whether in machine readable or other form, which by reason of the selection or arrangement of their contents constitute intellectual creations shall be protected as such. Such protection, which shall not extend to the data or material itself, shall be without prejudice to any copyright subsisting in the data or material itself." Consequently, under TRIPS, compilations of copyrightable and non-copyrightable material should be protected so long as the requisite level of originality in the selection *or* arrangement is satisfied.[101]

---

[101] It is important to specify the difference in requirements under TRIPS and Berne. TRIPS Article 10.2 requires originality in either the selection or arrangement of the material. The Berne Convention requires originality in the selection "and" arrangement. In effect, the TRIPS Agreement relaxes the Berne Convention standard for originality. This interpretation is consistent with

The incorporation of fundamental copyright requirements, such as originality, suggests that the rights granted to authors of databases should correspond to those granted to other copyright works. The protection of moral rights is, however, not required under TRIPS.[102]

2. History of the provision

2.1 Situation pre-TRIPS

Article 2*bis*(3) of the Berne Convention requires that authors be granted the exclusive right to make collections of their works. Thus, all Parties to the Berne Convention were required to recognize protection for collections, and to vest in authors the right to make such collections of their own works. Collections or compilations of merely factual material, however, were susceptible to little or no protection in several countries for reasons that centred primarily on a failure to satisfy the originality requirement.[103] The originality requirement, combined with the Berne Convention's own exclusion of news of the day and "miscellaneous facts" from copyright protection served to reinforce policy decisions not to extend protection to works that, although reflective of economic and labour-intensive investment, lack the requisite creative element.

2.2 Negotiating history

2.2.1 The Anell Draft

"2. Protectable Subject Matter

2.1 PARTIES shall provide protection to computer programs [, as literary works for the purposes of point 1 above,] [and to databases]. Such protection shall not extend to ideas, procedures, methods [, algorithms] or systems."[104]

The brief reference to databases indicates that delegations at this stage of the negotiations had not yet focused on the specific issue of databases, but rather on the conditions of protection to be accorded to computer programs. This changed radically with the Brussels Draft, providing a detailed proposal on databases, which was separated from the draft provision on computer programs.

2.2.2 The Brussels Draft

"2. Compilations of data or other material, whether in machine readable or other form, which by reason of the selection and arrangement of their contents constitute intellectual creations shall be protected as such. Such protection, which

---

the broad language employed by TRIPS Article 10 that defines the subject of a compilation as "data" and "other material" in any form.

[102] TRIPS, Article 9.1. Of course, countries that choose to grant moral rights to authors may do so under TRIPS. The point is that moral rights are not mandated by TRIPS.

[103] See U.S. Supreme Court decision in *Feist*, 499 U.S. 340, and the Canadian decision of *Tele-Direct* that followed the principles enunciated in *Feist*. See also the discussion on originality in Chapter 7.

[104] The above quotation is limited to the part of the draft referring to databases.

shall not extend to the data or material itself, shall be without prejudice to any copyright subsisting in the data or material itself."

This proposal is identical to the current Article 10.2 of TRIPS, with one exception: contrary to Article 10.2, TRIPS, the draft required both the selection *and* the arrangement of the data compilations to constitute intellectual creations (see above, Section 1). It thereby reproduced the similar provision of the Berne Convention (i.e. Article 2(5) on collections of literary and artistic works),[105] which equally refers to the originality of both the selection and the arrangement.

3. Possible interpretations

Article 10.2 extends the Berne Convention notion of compilations (Article 2(5)) to include databases as well as "other material". In other words, as long as the originality requirement is met, TRIPS requires protection for works that are compilations of any material, not just literary and artistic works.[106] This material does not have to constitute a database or data, as is made clear by the reference to "data or other material". However, Article 10.2 still requires that the compilation of data or other material satisfy the standard of originality. As a consequence, qualifying compilations shall be protected as "intellectual creations". The protection to be accorded is thus similar to the one provided for computer programs.

With regards to literary or artistic works, there is no internationally uniform standard of originality. Thus, Members are free to determine, according to their domestic policy preferences, the criteria to be met for a data compilation to qualify as an "intellectual creation". As a general rule in the case of compilations, reference may be made, for example, to the "Feist" decision of the U.S. Supreme Court[107] and the "Tele-Direct" judgment of the Canadian Court of Appeal,[108] according to which the arrangement of information in a compilation has to imply more than just the exercise of a minimal degree of skill, judgment or labour.

The extensive membership of the Berne Convention meant that many countries already accorded protection to collection as defined by the Berne Convention. However, given the expansive definition of "compilations" in Article 10.2, it is likely that the scope of protection afforded will now be significantly broadened. This observation is even more important in view of the provisions of the WCT on the protection of databases that are addressed below.

Finally, the database creator needs authorization from copyright owners whose works are reproduced in the database.

---

[105] This Article provides that: "(5) Collections of literary or artistic works such as encyclopedias and anthologies which, by reason of the selection and arrangement of their contents, constitute intellectual creations shall be protected as such, without prejudice to the copyright in each of the works forming part of such collections."

[106] Gervais (p. 82, para. 2.61) refers to the view expressed by the WIPO secretariat and some commentators that even the protection under the Berne Convention is not limited to collections of literary and artistic works. This view is based on a conjunctive reading of paragraphs 1 and 5 of Article 2 of the Berne Convention.

[107] *Feist Publ'ns Inc. v. Rural Tel. Serv. Co.*, 449 U.S. 340 (1991).

[108] *Tele-Direct (Publ'ns) Inc. v. American Bus. Infor. Inc.* 76 C.P.R. 3d 296 (1997).

4. WTO jurisprudence

There is no panel decision on this subject.

5. Relationship with other international instruments

5.1 WTO Agreements

5.2 Other international instruments

5.2.1 The Berne Convention

Article 2(5) of the Berne Convention provides for the protection of collections of "literary or artistic works" in a similar way as Article 10.2 of TRIPS with respect to compilations of "data or other material". The common aspect of the two provisions is that the collection for which protection is sought has to constitute an intellectual creation.[109] The first difference between the two is that the Berne Convention requires originality in both the selection and arrangement of the collection, whereas under TRIPS, it is either the selection or the arrangement of the compilation that has to be original.[110]

The second difference is that protection under the Berne Convention is limited to collections of "literary or artistic works". In other words, the elements making up the collection have to be eligible as copyrightable materials themselves (in the sense of Article 2(1) of the Berne Convention). As opposed to that, TRIPS refers to "data or other material", which do not necessarily benefit from copyright protection.[111] Consequently, the elements making up the compilation are not required to constitute copyrightable subject matter themselves. TRIPS in comparison with the Berne Convention thus enlarges the scope of protection for compilations of works.

6. New developments

6.1 National laws

6.2 International instruments

6.2.1 The WCT

WCT Article 5 is substantially similar to the provisions of TRIPS Article 10.2. It provides that "compilations of data or other material, in any form, which by reason of the selection or arrangement of their contents constitute intellectual creations, are protected as such. This protection does not extend to the data or the material

---

[109] See the *Feist* decision by the U.S. Supreme Court (above), according to which works based on factual material without incorporating a sufficient degree of creativity do not qualify for copyrightable subject matter.

[110] See above, Section 1 (Introduction).

[111] Recall that Articles 9 TRIPS and 2 of the Berne Convention leave WTO Members considerable flexibility with respect to the creativity requirement in copyright protection (see Chapter 7). Members are thus not required to afford copyright protection to data, when they consider that the latter do not meet a sufficient standard of creativity. Nevertheless, they would have to grant protection to collections of such data, provided the conditions of Article 10.2 are met.

itself and is without prejudice to any copyright subsisting in the data or material contained in the compilation." Like TRIPS, the WCT extends protection to "data" broadly defined to include both copyrightable and non-copyrightable material. Further, like Article 10.2, the WCT premises such protection on the presence of some intellectual creativity or originality as manifested in the author's selection of the materials or in their arrangement. The WCT, by closely tracking the language in TRIPS, effectively relaxed the standard for originality in the Berne Convention as suggested earlier.

6.3 Regional contexts: The EC Database Directive

The protection of compilations is not, in itself, a recent or revolutionary development in the copyright laws of most countries. What is clear from both TRIPS and the WCT is that the concept of "compilations" has been expanded to include data of any type. But by reserving copyright protection only to the selection or arrangement of the data compiled, and not to the underlying data, copyright protection for compilations is limited to the results of the creative effort exerted by the author.

Recently, however, databases have been the subject of a different *sui generis* form of protection. One model for database protection is the EC Directive on the Legal Protection of Databases ("EC Database Directive")[112]. This model is distinguishable from the copyright model for compilations in some very important ways. First, copyright protection is based on creative input (originality) in the selection or arrangement of pre-existing works. The EC Database Directive is intended, instead, to protect investments made in creating the database, what has been called the "sweat of the brow" in the United States.[113] In essence, this model of protection is not intended to stimulate intellectual creativity in creating new works, but to encourage and protect economic investments in the development of a database. Article 1(2) of the EC Database Directive defines a database as "a collection of independent works, data or other materials arranged in a systematic or methodical way and individually accessible by electronic or other means." This definition includes "hard copy" or paper databases, but specifically excludes computer programs used to make or operate a database.[114]

Under the EC Database Directive, a database that satisfies the creativity requirement of copyright must be protected by copyright.[115] Owners of qualifying databases are granted specific and exclusive copyright rights. These rights are: the right to make or to authorize temporary or permanent reproductions; translations, adaptations, arrangements and any other alteration; the right to make any form of distribution to the public of the database or of copies thereof; the right to make any communication, display or performance to the public; and the right to any reproduction distribution, communication, display or performance to the public of the results of any translation, adaptation, arrangement or other alteration of

---

[112] See Directive 96/9/EC of the European Parliament and of the Council of March 11, 1996 on the Legal Protection of Databases, 1996 O.J. (L77) 20.

[113] See Feist, 499 U.S. 340.

[114] See Database Directive, Article 1(3).

[115] See Database Directive, Article 3.

the database.[116] There is, however, no mention of a moral right for the author of a database.

In addition to the copyright scheme, the EC Database Directive also created a new *sui generis* right to prevent the unauthorized extraction or re-utilization of the contents of the database.[117] This right gives the author of the database absolute control over any use of the information contained in the database. According to Article 7(4) of the Directive, this right is granted in addition to the copyright protection required by Article 3;[118] the exclusive right to extract/re-utilize the contents of the database is granted in addition to, but independent of, copyright protection. This means, in effect, that the conceptual approach of the EC Database Directive is one of a strong property rights regime which recognizes few if any exceptions to the exclusive rights that it grants the author of a database. The objective of rewarding economic investment rather than intellectual creativity is reflected in the conditions for protection under the EC Database Directive. For example, Article 7(1) of the Directive provides that the *sui generis* right must be granted to the maker of a database "which shows that there has been qualitatively and/or quantitatively a substantial investment in either the obtaining, verification or presentation of the contents."

The EC Database Directive provides a few exceptions to the database right. These exceptions are: exceptions for the use of non-electronic databases for private purposes; extraction for purposes of illustration and teaching so long as the source is indicated and the use is justified by a non-commercial purpose; and extraction or re-utilization that occurs for the purposes of public security or an administrative or judicial procedure.[119] Finally, the *sui generis* database protection will be extended internationally on a reciprocal basis.

In reaction to the EC Database Directive, private industry in the United States also began to express interests in a *sui generis* right similar to what the EC provided. Of particular concern was the fact that the EU would not protect American database producers in Europe, unless the United States offered reciprocal protection for European database owners. (Such denial of national treatment does not infringe Article 3, TRIPS, if databases under the Database Directive are not considered "intellectual property" in the sense of Article 1.2, TRIPS. See Chapter 4, Section 6.3.1.) The strong property rights approach adopted by the EU has, however, generated significant public concern in the United States. While there has been recognition of the need to encourage the creation of databases, public

---

[116] *Id.* See Article 5.

[117] See EC Database Directive, Article 7(1).

[118] Article 7(4) provides that the *sui generis* right "shall apply irrespective of the eligibility of the database for protection by copyright or other rights. Moreover, it shall apply irrespective of eligibility of the contents of that database for protection by copyright or by other rights. Protection of databases under the right provided for ... shall be without prejudice to rights existing in respect of their contents." The difference of this concept *vis-à-vis* the scheme for the protection of collected works under the Berne Convention, the TRIPS Agreement and the WCT is reflected in the first sentence of the quoted provision: all three of those international instruments require a creative element in the arrangement or/and the selection of the compilation. The EC Directive waives this requirement, because it is not meant to further creativity, but to protect investment in databases.

[119] See Database Directive, Article 9.

interest groups including educational institutions, research institutions and libraries, have protested the property rights model in the initial proposals considered by Congress. Concerns that were expressed included how to determine the appropriate term of protection for the database right, the perceived need for a fair use provision to facilitate research, the fear of high transaction costs for data use, free speech implications of the property model and concerns about potential anti-competitive effects of such a strong right in the use of data.

Some opponents to the strong property rights approach have instead advocated a misappropriation/unfair competition model as an alternative approach to the property model.[120] Such an approach would condition liability for unauthorized data use on a notion of substantial harm to the actual or neighbouring market of the database owner. Thus far, a law protecting solely economic or laborious investment in creating a database is yet to be passed in the United States.

7. Comments, including economic and social implications

Copyright protection for compilations of data has different economic and social implications to the *sui generis* right currently in place in the European Union, and under consideration in the United States. Like the copyright model for the protection of compilations in TRIPS and in the WCT, a *sui generis* model for databases is designed to protect a particular kind of investment (i.e., primarily economic) with a view to encouraging optimal levels of production of databases. The difference is that a *sui generis* model is limited to such protection, whereas the mentioned copyright schemes also seek to protect creative activity.

As mentioned above, with regard to computer programs, rights might encourage increased levels of production of these works, provided the market and technological conditions are present. However, the level of protection offered in law must be counterbalanced with limitations or exceptions to ensure that there is adequate competition in database production. An important consideration is that a *sui generis* right extends to material that is not protected by copyright law. Consequently, what has been considered a deliberate "leak" in the copyright system – one intended to give second generation innovators "raw materials" to work with – will be plugged by a database protection model like that of the EC. The potentially high costs to the public of obtaining information under this type of system, and the effects on competition, must be balanced with the goal of protection for databases. A database protection system should attempt to balance the competing interests at stake to ensure that economic welfare goals are maximized.[121]

---

[120] See J.H. Reichman and P. Samuelson, *Intellectual Property Right and Data?*, 50 Vanderbilt Law Review, 51 (1997).

[121] The IPR Commission has even gone so far as to recommend that developing countries should not establish a *sui generis* system similar to the EC Database Directive. See IPR Commission report, p. 109 (quoted in Chapter 8, Section 7).

10: The Rental Right

> ## Article 11   Rental Rights
>
> In respect of at least computer programs and cinematographic works, a Member shall provide authors and their successors in title the right to authorize or to prohibit the commercial rental to the public of originals or copies of their copyright works. A Member shall be excepted from this obligation in respect of cinematographic works unless such rental has led to widespread copying of such works which is materially impairing the exclusive right of reproduction conferred in that Member on authors and their successors in title. In respect of computer programs, this obligation does not apply to rentals where the program itself is not the essential object of the rental.

1. Introduction: terminology, definition and scope

A rental right, in general, is a subset of the right of distribution that is more commonly recognized in a variety of different forms in domestic and international agreements. Broadly speaking, the distribution right encompasses rental, lending and resale rights. Under a rental right, the copyright holder may collect royalties from third parties engaged in the commercial rental of their copyrighted works. TRIPS establishes a rental right in respect of computer programs and cinematographic works. Under the terms of the Agreement, owners of these two categories of works must be granted the right to "authorize or prohibit the commercial rental to the public of originals or copies of their copyright works." With respect to cinematographic works, a Member may choose not to grant a rental right unless commercial rental has led to widespread copying such that the exclusive right of the owner to reproduce the work is materially impaired. The rental right is also not applicable to objects that contain computer programs, where the program is not itself the essential object of the rental.

The brief history of this provision suggests that its inclusion in TRIPS was a significant, if challenging, accomplishment.

2. History of the provision

2.1 Situation pre-TRIPS

Many countries already had right of distribution in place prior to the TRIPS negotiations. For instance, the U.S. copyright law recognizes rental rights in phonorecords and computer programs notwithstanding the first sale doctrine (see Section 3, below). The prohibition of the unauthorized rental of these works is accompanied by several conditions and exceptions. With regard to phonorecords, (i) the owner of the phonorecord must have disposed of it without authorization from the owners of the copyright in the sound recording and any musical works embodied in the phonorecord; (ii) such disposition must be for the purposes of direct or indirect commercial advantage and; (iii) such disposition must be "by rental, lease, or lending, or by any other act or practice in the nature of rental, lease or lending."[122] With regard to computer programs, the prohibition on unauthorized rental is inapplicable to (i) "a computer program which is embodied in a machine or product and which cannot be copied during the ordinary operation or use of the machine or product"[123]; (ii) "a computer program embodied in or used in conjunction with a limited purpose computer that is designed for playing video games and may be designed for other purposes"[124]; (iii) "the lending of a computer program for non-profit purposes by a non-profit library."[125] Transfers by non-profit educational institutions are also exempted.

Another example is the EU, which in 1992 adopted a Rental Right and Lending Right Directive[126] ("EC Rental Right Directive") regulating the rental, lease, or lending of all types of copyrighted works. The EC Rental Right Directive establishes an exclusive right to authorize or prohibit such rental or lending of all works except buildings and works of applied art. The EC Software Directive also provides a right to control the rental of computer programs.[127]

2.2 Negotiating history

2.2.1 The Anell Draft

(Rental Rights)

"3A.2.1 [At least in the case of computer programs [, cinematographic works] [and musical works,]] PARTIES shall provide authors and their successors in title the [right to authorise or prohibit the rental of the originals or copies of their copyright works] [or, alternatively,] [the right to obtain an equitable remuneration] [corresponding to the economic value of such a use] [whenever originals or copies are rented or otherwise made available against payment]. [It is understood that granting to authors the right to authorise or prohibit the rental of their works for

---

[122] 17 U.S.C. § 109(b)(1)(A).

[123] 17 U.S.C. § 109(b)(1)(B)(i).

[124] *Id.* at § 109(b)(1) (B)(ii).

[125] *Id.* at § 109(b)(2)(A).

[126] EC Directive on Rental Right and Lending Right and on Certain Rights Related to Copyright in the Field of Intellectual Property, Council Directive 92/100 of 19 November 1992 O.J. (L346) 61.

[127] See EC Software Directive, Article 4(c).

a certain period of time and to claim an equitable remuneration for the remaining period is sufficient to fulfil this provision.]

3A.2.2 For the purposes of the previous point, rental shall mean the disposal [for a limited period of time] of the possession of the original or copies for [direct profit-making purposes] [direct or indirect commercial advantage].

3A.2.3 There shall be no obligation to provide for a rental right in respect of works of applied art or architecture."[128]

The Anell Draft also contained a provision dealing more generally with distribution and importation rights:

"(Right of Importation and Distribution)

3A.1 Economic rights shall include:

3A.1.1 the right to import or authorize the importation into the territory of the PARTY of lawfully made copies of the work as well as the right to prevent the importation into the territory of the PARTY of copies of the work made without the authorization of the right-holder;

3A.1.2 the right to make the first public distribution of the original or each authorized copy of a work by sale, rental, or otherwise except that the first sale of the original or such copy of, at a minimum, a computer program shall not exhaust the rental or importation right therein.1 [note]

[note] 1 It is understood that, unless expressly provided to the contrary in this agreement, nothing in this agreement shall limit the freedom of PARTIES to provide that any intellectual property rights conferred in respect of the use, sale, importation and other distribution of goods are exhausted once those goods have been put on the market by or with the consent of the right holder."

Prior to the TRIPS negotiations (see situation pre-TRIPS, above), some countries already recognized a right of distribution for copyright owners, but there had never been an explicit global agreement on such a right,[129] and countries have historically adopted a variety of approaches to the notion of a discrete distribution right. It is clear from the above draft provisions that some delegations sought to introduce, on the international level, a general right of importation and distribution of copyrighted material. This would necessarily have implied an agreement on the controversial issue of exhaustion, because the right to import and distribute certain copyrighted works is usually exhausted after the first sale of the particular product.[130] Delegations were unable to reach agreement in this respect. However, they did agree on a subset of the distribution right, i.e. the rental right; not as to copyrighted works in general, but as to two categories, namely computer programs and cinematographic works. In comparison to a general right of importation and distribution, this rental right is therefore limited. It is designed to give owners of computer programs the right to control the rental of their works and sets up a conditional obligation for Members to recognize a rental right in

---

[128] MTN.GNG/NG11/W/76, 23 July 1990.

[129] The WCT introduced a distribution right for literary and artistic works. See WCT, Article 6(1).

[130] See Section 3, below. For a detailed analysis of the principle of exhaustion (or "first-sale-doctrine"), see Chapter 5.

respect of audiovisual works. The Brussels Draft represented the first step into this direction.

2.2.2 The Brussels Draft

"In respect of at least computer programs and cinematographic works, a PARTY shall provide authors and their successors in title the right to authorise or prohibit the commercial rental to the public of originals or copies of their copyright works [, or alternatively the right to obtain an equitable remuneration corresponding to the economic value of such use] [, where circumstances arise by which the commercial rental of originals or copies of copyright works has led to [unauthorised] copying of such works which is materially impairing the exclusive right of reproduction conferred in that PARTY on authors and their successors in title]."[131]

By the time of the Brussels Draft, the proposals for a general right of importation and distribution of copyrighted materials had disappeared and given way to the above provision. This was limited to the rental right in computer programs and cinematographic works and was thus very close to the current Article 11 of TRIPS.

The Brussels Draft still contained a bracketed reference to a remuneration right as an alternative to the right to prohibit or authorize the commercial rental of copyright works. This alternative was not taken over into TRIPS.

The current second sentence of Article 11, referring to the material impairment of the reproduction right through widespread copying, was already part of the Brussels Draft provision, but it was bracketed and did not seem to be limited to cinematographic works, as under TRIPS.[132]

Also, it did not refer to "widespread", but to "unauthorised" copying (in brackets). Thus, the current approach taken under TRIPS is more economic: what really causes a "material impairment" of the exclusive reproduction right is not so much the illegality of the copying but rather the economic fact that such copying is "widespread", thus preventing the right holder from selling his own copies. It is self-evident that in those cases, most of the copying will be "unauthorized". A particular reference to such term would therefore appear superfluous.

The final difference between the Brussels and the current texts is the addition under TRIPS that with respect to computer programs, the obligation to grant an exclusive rental right does not arise in case the program itself is not the essential object of the rental (see Section 3 below).

3. Possible interpretations

Countries recognize and provide different forms of protection for the different ways that an author's work could be circulated in the market. For example,

---

[131] See Draft Final Act Embodying the Results of the Uruguay Round of Multilateral Trade Negotiations, Revision, Trade-Related Aspects of Intellectual Property Rights, Including Trade in Counterfeit Goods, MTN.TNC/W/35/Rev. 1, 3 Dec. 1990.

[132] One commentator on the negotiating history states that the current Article 11, second sentence was drafted in a manner that would exclude the United States, where a rental right with respect to cinematographic works has been contested, while at the same time imposing such right on as many countries as possible. See Gervais, at 84–85, para. 2.65.

the 1976 U.S. Copyright Act provides an exclusive right to distribute "copies or phonorecords of the copyrighted work to the public by sale or other transfer of ownership, or by rental, lease or lending."[133] The U.S. first sale doctrine (referred to as the principle of "exhaustion" in other countries) is an important limitation to this right. This doctrine effectively terminates the author's control over the distribution of the work upon the first sale. However, there are exceptions to the first sale doctrine that preserve an author's control with respect to specific categories of works, notwithstanding the first sale doctrine. The widely divergent views and practices on when and how an author's control over a work should be regulated once the work has entered the stream of commerce, made international agreement over the doctrine of first sale/exhaustion infeasible. Consequently, both TRIPS and the WCT permit member countries to determine the scope of this exception in their respective national laws.[134]

Article 11 reflects the areas where countries have agreed to an exception to these limitations to the distribution right, namely with respect to computer programs and cinematographic works. In addition, Article 14.4, TRIPS, obligates Members to apply Article 11 with respect to computer programs to producers of phonograms and any other right holders in phonograms (see Chapter 13). For computer programs, Article 11, first sentence, grants an unconditional right to the author to authorize or prohibit the commercial rental of her/his work. With respect to cinematographic works, however, the phrasing of the second sentence of Article 11 ("A Member shall be excepted from this obligation in respect of cinematographic works unless such rental has led to widespread copying...") makes clear that the obligation to grant an exclusive rental right is to be considered as an exception. The use of the term "unless" indicates a reversal of the burden of proof; it is thus up to the right holder to establish evidence that the rental by third persons of his work has resulted in "widespread copying" of his work, which is "materially impairing the exclusive right of reproduction". Unless the right holder is able to submit such proof, a WTO Member is free to choose whether or not to grant such exclusive rental right with respect to cinematographic works. This leaves open a question of interpretation as to when these conditions are met, and the criteria that might be used to determine when a specific country is obligated to grant rental rights in audiovisual works. It appears to be in the discretion of domestic legislators to determine, for instance, on which conditions the right of reproduction is materially impaired in its exclusiveness.[135] Nonetheless, evidence of widespread piracy in a particular Member is likely to trigger the obligation of that Member to grant the exclusive rental right.

Finally, with respect to computer programs, the obligation to grant an exclusive rental right does not arise in case the program itself is not the essential object of the rental.[136]

---

[133] 17 U.S.C. § 106(3).

[134] See TRIPS Article 6; WCT Article 6(2).

[135] Gervais, p. 85, para. 2.66, expresses the view that the right holder for the purpose of proving material impairment has to show that the copying of his works affects both his ability to authorize and to prohibit reproduction.

[136] For example, in case of the rental of a car incorporating software-operated devices such as fuel injection.

4. WTO jurisprudence

There has been no WTO panel decision on this subject.

5. Relationship with other international instruments

5.1 WTO Agreements

5.2 Other international instruments

The WCT, like TRIPS, extends commercial rental rights to "authors of (i) computer programs; (ii) cinematographic works; (iii) works embodied in phonograms, as determined in the national law of contracting parties."[137] With regard to phonograms, however, the WCT adopts a different approach than TRIPS. The WCT grants the rental right to *authors* of works embodied in the phonograms (such authorship being defined by national law) while TRIPS Article 14.4 recognizes such a rental right for "producers of phonograms and any other right holders in phonograms as determined by domestic law." One possible way to reconcile these two approaches is to provide a joint right to authors and producers with respect to the rental right for phonograms. Of course, one could simply view the author or composer of the work as the rightful owner of the right since, in the first instance, the author has rights to prohibit unauthorized duplication of the underlying work.

Like TRIPS, the WCT recognizes some limitations with regard to the rental right for computer programs. First, the rental right does not apply to cases "where the program itself is not the essential object of the rental; as for cinematographic works, a country can choose not to extend the rental right to these works unless commercial rental has led to widespread copying of such works thus "materially impairing the exclusive right of reproduction." (WCT Art. 7(2)(i)(ii).) With regard to pre-existing national practices dealing with record rentals, the WCT grandfathers[138] those practices subject to the same conditions as audiovisual works, namely that "the commercial rental of the works embodied in the phonograms is not giving rise to the material impairment of the exclusive right of reproduction of authors."[139] Again, this test is open to interpretation in terms of how it is to be applied. The grandfathering of pre-existing schemes was necessary to respond to concerns raised by Japan during the negotiations.

6. New developments

6.1 National laws

6.2 International instruments

6.3 Regional contexts

7. Comments, including economic and social implications

Article 11 leaves considerable flexibility for the establishment and implementation of rental rights. While these rights are generally recognized under continental law

---

[137] See WCT Article 7(1) and TRIPS Article 14.4, first sentence in conjunction with Article 11.

[138] A "grandfather clause" allows countries acceding to an agreement to maintain pre-existing domestic legislation otherwise inconsistent with the relevant agreement.

[139] *Id.* at Article 7(3).

as one component of the author's rights, it may need to be specifically spelled out in some jurisdictions. Though the rental of computer programs has not become generalized practice, and, hence, this provision has little economic impact, the rental of cinematographic works has become widespread in many countries. The control over the distribution of copies of films for individual use may add to the rents generated by other forms of exploitation of such works. However, the enforcement of rental rights often faces significant obstacles, due to the ease with which copies can be reproduced and the cost and difficulty involved in detecting and bringing legal action against infringers.

One of the most important issues with respect to the lending right is how non-profit institutions such as libraries might fare under a comprehensive rental rights system. The EC Rental Right Directive authorizes states to allow public lending so long as authors receive some compensation for the rental of their works.[140] This approach is best characterized as a "liability rule" rather than a property rule. While there is no obligation under TRIPS to grant such a right, there appears to be a definite trend in some countries outside of the EU to adopt the public lending right. Certainly, for countries that have a comprehensive rental rights system, there must be some deliberation as to how to ensure that public services that facilitate access to and use of copyrighted works are available to society. In addition, as traditional copyright works such as books and other written material are increasingly embodied in digital form, the regulation of the rental right will play an important role in balancing the interests of owners and the importance of access by members of the public to copyrighted works.

[140] See EC Rental Right Directive, Art. 5.

11: Term of Protection

> ### Article 12 Term of Protection
>
> Whenever the term of protection of a work, other than a photographic work or a work of applied art, is calculated on a basis other than the life of a natural person, such a term shall be no less than fifty years from the end of the calendar year of authorized publication, or, failing such authorized publication within fifty years from the making of the work, fifty years from the end of the calendar year of making.

1. Introduction: terminology, definition and scope

TRIPS suggests that there is no uniformly applicable term of protection for all categories of copyrighted works. Article 7(1) of the Berne Convention prescribes a minimum term of copyright protection which is the life of the author plus fifty years. This is incorporated in TRIPS Article 9.1 through reference to the Berne Convention. Article 12 addresses those cases where the life of a natural person is not the basis for measuring the term of protection. It is directed at works of corporate authorship or, to put it more directly, works where the identified author is not a natural person. Examples of such works include sound recordings and films under U.S. law, and collective works under French law.

2. History of the provision

2.1 Situation pre-TRIPS

Prior to TRIPS, the term of copyright duration was addressed in Article 7 of the Berne Convention, prescribing in paragraph (1) a minimum term of protection of the author's life plus fifty years. Even under the Berne Convention, however, the use of the life of the author as a basis for determining the length of copyright protection is not applicable to all categories of works. The key point is that for works where the life of a natural person is not the basis for measuring the term of copyright protection, other indicators must be used.

The provisions of the Berne Convention dealing with cinematographic works and pseudonymous and anonymous works provide good examples of such indicators. Article 7(2) of the Berne Convention provides that in the case of cinematographic works, countries "may" provide a term of protection that shall expire fifty years after the work has been made available to the public with the consent of the author. If the work is not made public with the consent of the author within fifty years after the work was first made, then the term of protection is simply fifty years calculated from when the work was made.

With regard to anonymous and pseudonymous works, Article 7(3) of the Berne Convention provides a term of protection for fifty years after the work has been lawfully made available to the public. However, if the author of the work discloses his or her identity, Article 7(3) provides a term of protection that is consistent with the general standard namely, life of the author plus fifty years. The same result occurs when the pseudonym of the author "leaves no doubts" as to the identity of the author. In such a case, the term of protection reverts to the standard term of life plus fifty years.

Berne Convention Article 7(4) provides that countries have the discretion to determine the term of protection for photographic works and works of applied art if such works are protected as "artistic works." However, the minimum term of protection for these categories of works is twenty-five years from their making. As explicitly stated in Berne Convention Article 7(6), for all categories of works, countries are free to grant terms of protection greater than the minimum imposed.

Finally, the Berne Convention is silent on a specific term of protection for the works of non-natural (i.e., corporate) authors.

Although other copyright treaties such as the Universal Copyright Convention also established a minimum term of protection,[141] Article 12 is a direct derivation from Berne Convention Article 7 as discussed above.

2.2 Negotiating history

2.2.1 The Anell Draft

"7. Term of Protection

7A.1 The term of protection of a work whose author is a legal entity shall be no less than 50 years from the end of the year of authorised publication, or, failing such authorised publication within 50 years from the making of the work, 50 years from the end of the year of making.

7A.2 The term of protection of computer programs shall be no less than 50 years after the end of the year of creation."

While this draft provision already provided the same term of protection as the current Article 12, it differs in two important aspects: first, it contained an extra paragraph on computer programs, which is not present in the current TRIPS text; second, it expressly referred, in its first paragraph, to "legal entities" as the author of the protected work.

With regard to the extra paragraph on computer programs, it has to be recalled that at the time of the Anell Draft, the protection of computer programs as literary

---

[141] Life of the author plus twenty-five years. See Universal Copyright Convention, Paris Text, 1971, Article IV(2)(a).

works had not yet been agreed upon.[142] The second paragraph of the above draft appears to represent some delegations' objective to ensure, for computer programs, the same term of protection as accorded to literary works under Article 7(1) of the Berne Convention, independently of their qualification as such works. Otherwise, computer programs, as not expressly considered "literary works", could have been interpreted by Members to qualify for "works of applied art" in the sense of Article 7(4) of the Berne Convention, for which the mandatory term of protection is only 25 years from the making. With the final acceptance, under Article 10.1 of TRIPS, of computer programs as literary works, this special term of protection for computer programs is no longer necessary: they either fall directly under Article 7(1) of the Berne Convention (in case the author of the software is a natural person), or they benefit from the term of protection provided for under Article 12 TRIPS (in case the author of the software is a corporate entity). In both cases, the term is 50 years (from the death of the natural author or from the authorized publication or the end of the calendar year of the making).

With regard to the second difference (i.e. the express reference to a "legal entity" as the author of the work), the 1990 draft reflects the desire of U.S. film producers for explicit recognition of corporate authors. U.S. film-makers, under the aegis of the Motion Picture Association of America (MPAA),[143] were concerned about discrimination in countries that only recognized natural "flesh and blood" authors. In countries generally identified with the author's rights tradition, non-natural persons are recognized as first right holders (as opposed to "authors") of a work. In these countries there is a preference for recognizing authorship only in natural persons. A U.S. proposal during the TRIPS negotiations to accomplish the goal of expressly recognizing corporate authorship was not successful. Article 12 affords an implicit recognition of the concept of a non-natural author, but, as opposed to the Anell Draft, it does not explicitly say so.

2.2.2 The Brussels Draft

The text of the Brussels Draft was essentially identical to the final version under TRIPS. The only difference was that under the Brussels Draft, there was a proposal to except computer programs from the mandatory term of 50 years, as is currently the case under TRIPS with respect to photographic works and works of applied art (Article 7(4), Berne Convention). This exemption of computer programs reflects the delegations' disagreement, at the time of the Brussels Draft, whether to protect computer programs as "literary works". Interestingly, the Brussels Draft thus adopted the opposite approach to computer programs vis-à -vis the earlier Anell Draft. The latter had proposed to secure a minimum protection of 50 years for software products, whereas the Brussels Draft proposed to except computer programs from the 50-year term.

With regard to the Anell Draft, the Brussels Draft had already eliminated the express reference to a "legal entity" as the author of the protected works.

---

[142] See Chapter 8.

[143] This organization is now known as the Motion Picture Association (MPA).

3. **Possible interpretations**

As stated earlier, Article 12 is very similar to Article 7(2) and 7(3) of the Berne Convention. Article 12 requires that where the life of a natural person is not the basis for calculating the copyright term, the minimum term of protection for a copyrighted work is fifty years from the end of the calendar year of authorized publication. In the absence of an authorized publication of the work within fifty years from its making, then the term of protection is fifty years from the end of the calendar year of its making. For example, if a work is authored by a non-natural person in 1999 and publication is authorized in the year 2000, the minimum term of protection for the work is fifty years. This means that the work is protected by copyright until the end of the year 2050. However, if there is no authorized publication between 1999 (the year of its making) and 2049 (fifty years from the year of its making), then the term of protection is calculated from the end of the year of its making (1999); thus copyright in the work would expire at the end of 2049.

It should be noted that the absence of authorized publication results in a term of protection that is one year less than the scenario where protection is authorized in the year 2000. Of course, if the work is created in 1999 *and* authorized for publication in 1999, then for all practical purposes the end result is the same as though there were no authorized publication. In other words, the copyright term of such a work will expire at the end of 2049.

The above analysis suggests that the later in time an authorized publication takes place, the longer the work may, for all practical purposes, be protected by copyright. For example, if a work created in 1999 is authorized for publication in 2030 (i.e., 31 years after creation), calculation of the copyright term will start at the end of the year 2030. Thus, the copyright term will not expire until the end of 2080. By conditioning the term of copyright protection on "authorized publication," Article 12 changed the Berne Convention standard that required calculation of the term of copyright protection once the work is "made available to the public."[144] The term "publication" is narrower than "making available to the public". A work may be made available to the public in various ways, not only through publication. TRIPS does not define the term "publication" so it is most likely that the definition employed in the Berne Convention (Article 3(3)) will be used to interpret this language in TRIPS.[145] Thus, any of the acts excluded from the definition of "publication" under Article 3(3) of the Berne Convention constitute acts of "making available to the public". This is the case referred to in the last part of Article 12 ("... or, failing such authorized publication ..."). Therefore, the term

---

[144] See Berne Convention, Article 7(2) and 7(3).

[145] See Gervais, at 87. The incorporation of the Berne Convention into TRIPS lends support to this position. Article 3 (3) of the Berne Convention defines a "published work" as one in which copies have been manufactured with the consent of the author and that the copies are made available to satisfy the reasonable requirements of the public. This provision states that "the performance of a dramatic, dramatico-musical, cinematographic or musical work, the public recitation of a literary work, the communication by wire or the broadcasting of literary and artistic works, the exhibition of a work of art and the construction of a work of architecture shall not constitute publication."

of protection would then be calculated on the basis of the calendar year of making (i.e. fifty years after the end of that year).

Finally, Article 12 retains the exceptions to copyright term that have been historic features of the Berne Convention. In effect, Article 12 does not extend to photographic works and works of applied art. The copyright term provided for such works remains the standard set in Article 7(4) of the Berne Convention, namely a minimum of 25 years.[146]

4. WTO jurisprudence

There has been no WTO panel decision on this subject.

5. Relationship with other international instruments

5.1 WTO Agreements

5.2 Other international instruments

Article 12 simply establishes a minimum standard for the term of copyright protection with regard to works in which the measure of the term is not the life of a natural person. Outside of these works, the term of copyright protection is as provided in the Berne Convention. Thus, for a majority of copyrighted works, the provisions of Article 7 of the Berne Convention will remain the applicable law regarding duration of copyright protection. With regard to photographic works, the WCT provides that countries "shall not apply the provision of Article 7(4) of the Berne Convention" (i.e. a minimum duration of 25 years from the making of the work).[147] This suggests that the WCT mandates an upgrade of the term of protection for photographic works to the Berne Convention minimum of life of the author plus fifty years.[148]

6. New developments

6.1 National laws

For most copyrighted works authored by individuals (natural persons), a majority of countries adhere to a specified period of time after the death of the author. Article 7(1) of the Berne Convention specifies the minimum term of protection as the life of the author plus fifty years and this standard has been incorporated into TRIPS. This term requirement is, however, merely a minimum; countries are free to adopt longer terms of protection and many countries have done so. The EC Term of Protection Directive[149] requires a term of protection for the life of the author plus seventy years (Art. 1(1)). In 1998, the United States followed the

---

[146] Note, however, that in respect of photographic works, this was modified by the 1996 WCT. See below, Section 5.2.

[147] See WCT, Article 9.

[148] See Goldstein, *International Copyright*, at 235 (2001). This is so because the exclusion by the WCT of Article 7(4) of the Berne Convention results in the applicability of Article 7(1) of the Berne Convention, providing the general term of protection of the life of the author plus fifty years.

[149] Council Directive 93/98 of 29 October 1993 Harmonizing the Term of Protection of Copyright and Certain Related Rights O.J. (L290) 9.

European example and extended the general term of copyright to life of the author plus seventy years.[150] However, as far as copyrighted works of *corporate* authors are concerned, the same U.S. law extended the term of protection to 95 years, whereas the above mentioned EC legislation limits that term to 50 years only.

Several Latin American countries have extended the terms of copyright protection to higher standards than required under the Berne Convention, such as Mexico (life of the author plus 75 years), Brazil, Ecuador and Peru (life of the author plus 70 years).[151]

In a recent dispute involving big entertainment companies on the one hand and a coalition of Internet publishers on the other, the U.S. Supreme Court upheld the above U.S. law against allegations of unconstitutionality.[152] Internet publishers seeking to publish, *inter alia* , early Mickey Mouse cartoons, jazz classics and novels of F. Scott Fitzgerald had argued that the extension of all copyright terms by 20 years violated a clause in Article I, Section 8 of the U.S. Constitution. According to this provision, copyrights may be issued "for limited times". The principal argument of the opponents of copyright term extension was that the extension had the effect of delaying entry into the public domain of works created under a previous (shorter term) regime. Since the authors of existing copyrighted works were not being given any new incentive to create, the extension had the primary effect of limiting works in the public domain, and this was contrary to the objectives of the copyright clause of the Constitution.[153] In the opinion of the majority of the judges, Congressional power to grant copyright protection implies the right to extend the term of protection for all existing copyrights. As stated in the decision:

> "History reveals an unbroken congressional practice of granting to authors of works with existing copyrights the benefit of term extensions so that all under copyright protection will be governed evenhandedly under the same regime."[154]

On the other hand, the 1998 U.S. legislation was severely criticized by the dissenting judges. They warned in particular that the extension of the term of

---

[150] The rules of duration in the United States are much more complex than this statement suggests. Indeed, the same is true for other countries such as the United Kingdom. This is because extensions of the copyright term can be retroactive. Thus, for works in existence and eligible for protection at the time of the extension, the calculation of the term of protection requires careful reading of the earlier statutes under which the work was protected and how the extension of term should be calculated. See e.g., 1976 U.S. Copyright Act § 302–§ 305; John N. Adams & Michael Edenborough, *The Duration of Copyright in the United Kingdom after the 1995 Regulations*, 11 E.I.P.R. 590 (1996).

[151] See Roffe, Pedro (2004), *Bilateral Agreements and a TRIPS-plus World: the Chile – USA Free Trade Agreement*, TRIPS Issues Papers – No 4, Quaker International Affairs Programme, Ottawa, Section 3.3.1 [hereinafter Roffe, 2004]. In the cases of Brazil and Mexico, the author explains these extensions with those countries' important cultural industries.

[152] *Eldred v. Ashcroft*, 123 S. Ct. 769 (2003).

[153] The opponents of the above law also argued that the extension of the copyright term by 20 years amounted to a perpetual right, and not one for limited times. However, from a constitutional standpoint this was not the argument relied upon since the opponents tacitly acknowledged that the Supreme Court would find it difficult to interfere in the judgement of Congress whether 50 or 70 years after the death of the author was an appropriate copyright term. The decision was taken by a 7-to-2 majority.

[154] Majority opinion, written by Justice Ginsburg, 123 S. Ct. 769, 778.

protection would harm education and research, due to the impediments to access for copyrighted materials.[155]

With regard to works authored by non-natural persons or, in some cases, particular categories of works, countries have enacted different laws. Thus with regard to copyright term under TRIPS, the requirements of the Berne Convention remain the standard with the exception of the changes introduced by Article 12. Other than the well-known term of protection for individually authored works, there is discretion under the Berne Convention with regard to the term for other categories of works. The chart in Annex 1 at the end of this Chapter depicts copyright terms with respect to different categories of works.

Finally, it is important to observe that countries do have some discretion in determining whether the term of protection will be based on the life of a natural person. For example, in the United States works made for hire are protected for 95 years from the year of the work's first publication, or 120 years from creation whichever expires first. This term applies whether the employer is a natural or corporate person. In the United Kingdom the copyright term in a computer-generated work lasts for fifty years from the end of the year in which the work was made.[156] The key issue is that where national legislation bases the copyright term on a measure other than the life of a natural person, then TRIPS Article 12 is implicated. The question of whether authorship is vested in a natural person is likely to be determined by the particular view of authorship that the country subscribes to.

6.2 International instruments

6.3 Regional and bilateral contexts

At the bilateral context, recent free trade agreements signed by the USA with a number of developing countries have adhered to the trend in developed countries, as outlined above, to expand the terms of protection for most works to 70 years compared to 50 under TRIPS.[157]

7. Comments, including economic and social implications

Longer copyright terms prolong the author's control over the use and disposition of the copyrighted work. Accordingly, public policy issues are implicated each time the copyright term is extended. For example, the public domain is comprised of, among other things, expired copyrighted works. The longer the copyright term, the slower the growth of the public domain with respect to works in which the copyright term has expired. Concerns over the effect of longer copyright terms on the public interest prompted criticism in the United States over Congress's extension of the copyright term. Indeed, there have already been challenges to the constitutionality of this legislation. One important argument that has been put forth by critics of the extension in the United States is that retroactive application

---

[155] See the dissenting opinions of Justices Stephens and Breyer, 123 S. Ct. 769, 790 et seq.

[156] See § 12(3), United Kingdom, Copyright, Designs and Patents Act 1988.

[157] See Roffe, 2004.

of extension is not consistent with the goals of copyright given the fact that authors of existing works do not need the extra twenty years of protection as an incentive for these works. Consequently, the extension is more of a cost imposed on the public. What is important for any country is that the term of protection should provide sufficient time for authors to recoup their investments, while also preserving public interest by facilitating a sustained growth of the public domain.

Annex 1: Copyright term under the TRIPS Agreement

Category of work	Required minimum term of protection (incorporated from Berne Convention Article 7)
Traditional copyright work authored by a natural person	life of the author plus fifty years (Berne Convention, Art. 7(1)).
Collective works	life plus fifty years for each author's contribution. If the selection and organization of the contributions constitute an original expression, the collective work as a whole is also entitled to copyright protection for the life of the author (editor) plus fifty years.
Joint works	life plus fifty years, calculated from the death of the last surviving author.
Anonymous and pseudonymous works	fifty years after the work has been lawfully made available to the public. If the identity of the author is known (despite the pseudonym) or disclosed the term of protection reverts to life plus fifty. (Berne Convention, Art. 7(3)).
Cinematographic works	fifty years after the work has been made available to the public with the consent of the author OR if it is not made available to the public within fifty years of the making of the work, then the term of protection shall be fifty years after the making of the work. (Berne Convention Art. 7(2)).
Photographs and works of applied art	twenty-five years from the making of such a work. (Berne Convention, Art. 7(4))[158]
Works whose term is calculated other than by the life of a natural person (TRIPS Art. 12)	fifty years from the end of the calendar year of authorized publication, OR if there is no authorized publication within fifty years that the work was made, then the term of protection shall be fifty years from the making of the work.

Note that each of these terms of protection is the minimum required by TRIPS; countries are free to establish longer terms of protection for any of these works.

---

[158] Recall that countries that are members of the WCT are effectively required to protect photographs for longer than the term in Article 7(4) of the Berne Convention. See WCT, Art. 9, rendering applicable the general term of protection under Article 7(1) of the Berne Convention (i.e. the life of the author plus fifty years). Note that the United States protects eligible photographs for life plus seventy years as does the EC.

12: Limitations and Exceptions

> ## Article 13   Limitations and Exceptions
> Members shall confine limitations or exceptions to exclusive rights to certain special cases which do not conflict with a normal exploitation of the work and do not unreasonably prejudice the legitimate interests of the right holder.

1. Introduction: terminology, definition and scope

The question of exceptions and limitations to copyright strikes directly at the issue of the appropriate balance between the rights of creators and the public interest in access to copyrighted works. If a country adopts too many exceptions and limitations (this would likely be inconsistent with TRIPS Article 13) it could adversely affect the incentives to create by reducing the economic rewards to right holders. Conversely, some limitations are necessary to effectuate copyright's broader purpose of advancing the public good. Thus, limitations to facilitate private use, teaching, research and other socially valuable purposes are generally considered to be an important aspect of copyright regulation. In continental law jurisdictions, national copyright laws provide case-specific exceptions to copyright in the above areas.[159] Common law jurisdictions follow the fair use or the fair dealing doctrines, on the basis of which similar exceptions have been developed through case law.[160]

---

[159] See, for instance, Part 1, Section 6, §§ 44a *et seq.* of the German Copyright Act, providing detailed exceptions to copyright in clearly defined areas.

[160] See C. Correa, *Fair use in the digital era*, International Review of Industrial Property and Copyright Law (IIC), vol. 33, No. 5/2002. For an analysis of this doctrine in the U.S. legal system, see R. Okediji, *Toward an International Fair Use Doctrine*, Columbia Journal of Transnational Law, vol. 39, 2000–2001, pp. 75 *et seq.* Many cases of fair use relate to copying for non-commercial purposes such as education, research, personal use, archival and library uses, and news reporting (see below, Section 3, and the report of the IPR Commission, p. 173). On the fair dealing doctrine, see W. Cornish and D. Llewelyn, *Intellectual Property: Patents, Copyright, Trade Marks and Allied Rights* (5th ed. 2003), pp. 440–443. In addition, both international and domestic continental and common law recognize other exemptions and immunities for educational and social purposes as well as, in some countries, compulsory licences for recorded musical work and broadcasts. Still other limitations arise from the states' general exercise of its police powers and from abuses of the statutory monopoly, whether or not rising to the level of antitrust violations. In some countries, even the protection of moral rights assumes a public-interest character by enabling State authorities

The fair use and fair dealing doctrines as well as codified case-specific exceptions under continental law permit certain unauthorized but socially beneficial uses, either because transaction costs might otherwise stand in the way of negotiated licences, or because the resulting public benefit is thought to outweigh the loss of private gain.

2. History of the provision

2.1 Situation pre-TRIPS

Before the entry into force of TRIPS, exceptions to and limitations of copyrights were contained in the Berne Convention.

There is explicit mention under the Berne Convention that countries may provide exceptions for the following activities:

• Reproduction by the press or broadcasters of lectures, addresses and other works of the same nature. (Article 2*bis*(2));

• Reproduction of works in certain special cases, provided that the reproduction does not unreasonably prejudice the legitimate interests of the author. (Article 9(2));[161]

• Quotations from a work that has already been lawfully made available to the public, so long as the quoting is compatible with fair practice and its extent does not exceed the justified purpose of the quotation. (Article 10(1));

• Use of literary or artistic works for teaching provided that the use is compatible with fair practice. (Article 10(2));

• Reproduction by the press, the broadcasting or communication to the public of articles published in newspapers or periodicals on current economic, political or religious topics. The source of the work must always be clearly indicated. (Article 10*bis*(1));

• Reproduction of works for the purpose of reporting current events to the extent justified by the informatory purpose. (Article 10*bis* (2)).

Article 9(2), Berne Convention, represents a general exception (which language resembles Article 13, TRIPS Agreement), while the other above provisions refer to specific exceptions for certain uses of a copyrighted work. All these exceptions are incorporated into TRIPS by way of reference under Article 9.1. The pivotal issue is whether Article 13 enlarges upon these exceptions, codifies the *status quo* or limits the exceptions.

In this context, the history of the general exception embodied in Berne Convention Article 9(2) is useful since the language of TRIPS Article 13 is derived from this provision.

---

to preserve the integrity of cultural goods beyond the lifetimes of their creator or, in the case of folklore, in the absence of a specifically identifiable author (see UNCTAD 1996, para. 178).

[161] This provision reads as follows: "(2) It shall be a matter for legislation in the countries of the Union to permit the reproduction of such [i.e. literary and artistic] works in certain special cases, provided that such reproduction does not conflict with a normal exploitation of the work and does not unreasonably prejudice the legitimate interests of the author."

Article 9(2) was introduced into the Berne Convention during the 1967 revision, and then adopted in the 1971 Paris Text. Many states had different exceptions to the reproduction right; consequently, an agreement on the acceptable scope of limitations was difficult to negotiate. The problem facing the negotiators was how best to accommodate all the existing exceptions in Member States and at the same time impose constraints on the creation of additional exceptions. Evidence from a report of the Swedish government and the Bureau for the Protection of Intellectual Property (BIRPI)[162] regarding an initial proposal for the scope of Berne Convention Article 9(2) indicates that a major consideration for exceptions in national laws was that such exceptions not enter into economic competition with the right holder. Berne Convention Article 9(2) requires a three-step analysis to evaluate the Berne consistency of any exception to copyright contained in national laws.

First, is the exception limited to "certain special cases"? Second, does the exception conflict with the "normal exploitation" of the copyrighted work? And third, does the exception "unreasonably prejudice the legitimate interests" of the right holder? These three important clauses are reproduced in Article 13, reinforcing the argument that the interpretation of Berne Convention Article 9(2) must have an effect on the interpretive scope of Article 13.

2.2 Negotiating history

2.2.1 The Anell Draft

"8. Limitations, Exemptions and Compulsory Licensing

8A.1 In respect of the rights provided for at point 3, the limitations and exemptions, including compulsory licensing, recognised under the Berne Convention (1971) shall also apply mutatis mutandis. [Limitations made to the rights in favour of private use shall not apply to computer software.] [PARTIES may also provide for other limited exceptions to rights in respect of computer programs, consistent with the special nature of these works.]

8A.2 PARTIES shall confine any limitations or exemptions to exclusive rights (including any limitations or exceptions that restrict such rights to "public" activity) to clearly and carefully defined special cases which do not impair an actual or potential market for or the value of a protected work.

8A.3 Translation and reproduction licensing systems permitted in the Appendix to the Berne Convention (1971):

8A.3.1 shall not be established where legitimate local needs are being met by voluntary actions of copyright owners or could be met by such action but for intervening factors outside the copyright owner's control; and

8A.3.2 shall provide an effective opportunity for the copyright owner to be heard prior to the grant of any such licences.

8A.4 Any compulsory licence (or any restriction of exclusive rights to a right of remuneration) shall provide mechanisms to ensure prompt payment and

---

[162] BIRPI was the predecessor organization to WIPO.

remittance of royalties at a level consistent with what would be negotiated on a voluntary basis.

8B (See Sections 8 and 9 below.)"

2.2.2 The Brussels Draft

"1. [essentially identical to Article 13 TRIPS]

[2. Translation and reproduction licences permitted under the Appendix to the Berne Convention (1971) shall not be granted where the legitimate local needs of a PARTY could be met by voluntary actions of right holders but for obstacles resulting from measures taken by the government of that PARTY.]"

The bracketed second paragraph is very similar to proposal 8A.3.1 under the Anell Draft, as quoted above. This provision would have limited developing countries' possibilities to have recourse to the compulsory licensing systems provided for in the Appendix to the Berne Convention, in particular with respect to the reproduction of copyrighted works and their translation into local languages. This limitation was, however, not taken over into the final version of Article 13. As made obvious in Article 9.1, Members agreed to make the Appendix available without any limitations (except of course for the requirements made in the Appendix itself).

3. Possible interpretations

The terminology employed in Article 13 is substantially similar to Berne Convention Article 9(2) which prescribes the scope of limitations to the right of reproduction. Given the incorporation of Articles 1–21 of the Berne Convention in TRIPS, any interpretation of Article 13 requires consistency with Berne Convention provisions that regulate limitations and exceptions to copyright.

> Article 9 of the Berne Convention: [*Right of Reproduction*: 1. Generally; 2. Possible exceptions; Sound and visual recordings]
> "(1) Authors of literary and artistic works protected by this Convention shall have the exclusive right of authorizing the reproduction of these works, in any manner or form.
> (2) It shall be a matter for legislation in the countries of the Union to permit the reproduction of such works in certain special cases, provided that such reproduction does not conflict with a normal exploitation of the work and does not unreasonably prejudice the legitimate interests of the author.
> (3) [...]."

In the following, the three separate conditions of legality of copyright exceptions as provided under Article 13 will be examined.

3.1 Certain special cases

> Members shall confine limitations or exceptions to exclusive rights to certain special cases. . .

According to Professor Ricketson, in particular regard to the first step of the test, the phrase "certain special cases" should be interpreted as requiring an exception for a specific purpose.[163] Broad exceptions covering a wide range of subject matter or uses would not be consistent with the provision. In addition, the exception should be justified by a clear public policy or other exceptional circumstances.[164] With regard to this latter element proposed by Professor Ricketson, a WTO panel has rejected this interpretation.[165] The WTO panel held that with respect to the first step, TRIPS Article 13 prohibits broad exceptions of general application, rejecting an interpretation based on the subjective goals of the national legislation.

A panel decision has effect only between the parties to the dispute and does not constitute a binding precedent in the relations between other WTO Members.[166] Because the Appellate Body might disagree with the legal analysis of a panel, a non-appealed panel report should be treated with some caution. It is nevertheless important to note that the above panel treated a dispute between two developed Members, the U.S. and the EC. Even though it refused to take any public policy considerations into account, it would not have neglected the Appendix to the Berne Convention in case the dispute had involved a developing country Member. This Appendix has become an integral part of TRIPS, by way of reference in Article 9.1. The Appendix *inter alia* permits developing countries to issue compulsory licenses for the reproduction of copyrighted material. The conditions are that the respective Member has notified the other Members of its intention to avail itself of the facilities provided under the Appendix.[167] In addition, compulsory licenses are only authorized if the respective work has not been distributed after a certain period of time to the general public of the affected country "at a price reasonably related to that normally charged in the country for comparable works".[168] The required time period normally amounts to five years, but only three years in respect of natural and physical sciences, mathematics and technology.[169]

---

[163] See Ricketson. Note that this interpretation referred to Article 9(2), Berne Convention. Since both Article 9(2) of the Berne Convention and Article 13 of the TRIPS Agreement rely on the same three conditions, the following analysis will be subsumed under the pertinent parts of Article 13 of the TRIPS Agreement.

[164] *Id.* at para. 9.6.

[165] See WTO panel report, Section 110(5) of the U.S. Copyright Act, June 15, 2000, NT/DS160/R, para. 6. 111–112.

[166] Another panel would thus be free to adopt a different interpretation of Article 13 of the TRIPS Agreement.

[167] See Article I (1) of the Appendix to the Berne Convention.

[168] See Article III (2) (a) (i) of the Appendix.

[169] See Article III (3) (i) of the Appendix.

Under such circumstances, "any national" of the affected country "may obtain a license to reproduce and publish such edition [i.e. meeting the above criteria] at that or a lower price for use in connection with systematic instructional activities."[170]

This possibility must not be denied to developing countries via an overly strict interpretation of Article 13. This would be contrary to Members' obligation under Article 9.2 to give full effect to the Berne Appendix. Also, a domestic legislation that conditioned the unauthorized printing of schoolbooks and other teaching material on the respect of the criteria referred to under the Berne Appendix would actually be confined to "certain special cases" within the meaning of Article 13.

In addition, it should be noted that despite the rather narrow scope of Article 13, developed countries also provide for the unauthorized use of copyrighted material. In that respect, several approaches exist. Countries may list exceptions and limitations, or they may choose to utilize a broad statement that defines when and under what circumstances a right holder's rights will be limited. A third possibility is that a country may combine both approaches. In most countries, this is the dominant model.[171] For example, the 1976 U.S. Copyright Act contains explicit limitations on a copyright owner's rights[172] as well as a general "fair use" provision that may be used as a defence to a claim of infringement by a right holder. The United Kingdom as well as the French and German copyright legislations adopt this model.

Examples of limitations to the reproduction and adaptation right commonly found in domestic legislation include:

• Copies made for the purposes of scholarly and private use. With regard to software, Articles 5(3) and 6 of the EC Software Directive specifically exempt back up copies, black box analyses and decompilation. The 1976 U.S. Copyright Act does not have a specific exemption for software decompilation (or "reverse engineering") but the fair use provision has been extended to such activity:[173]

• Parody;

• Media (press) uses for current events or news of the day;

• Uses in educational institutions, including for teaching;[174]

• Research;[175]

---

[170] See Article III (2) (a) (ii) of the Appendix.

[171] This approach is also reflected in the Berne Convention. Recall for example that Article 10 lists some specific exceptions while Art. 9(2) contains a general clause dealing with exceptions to the rights of reproduction.

[172] See e.g.,U.S. Copyright Act, § 114(d) which permits certain types of digital audio transmissions of sound recordings; § 111 which allows for certain broadcast retransmissions; § 512 which allows certain temporary copies to be created by on-line service providers.

[173] See *Sega Enterprises Ltd. v. Accolade, Inc.*, 977 F. 2d 1510 (9th Cir. 1993); *Sony Computer Entertainment, Inc. v. Connectix Corp.*, 203 F. 3d 596 (9th Cir. 2000).

[174] See, e.g., the recent U.S. TEACH Act. For details, see under Section 6.1 of this chapter.

[175] See, e.g., § 52a of the German Copyright Act, providing for the unauthorized use of copyrighted works for purposes of research and university teaching (as opposed to teaching in primary and secondary schools).

- Quotation;

- Ephemeral copies.

The copyright laws of some countries, such as the United States, include significant mechanisms for the compulsory licensing of copyrighted works. For example, the U.S. Copyright Act, Section 114, establishes an arrangement under which digital audio transmissions of sound recordings are authorized under statutory license subject, in some cases, to payment of a royalty. Section 115 establishes an arrangement under which copyrighted non-dramatic musical works may be recorded on phonograms and distributed, also subject to payment of a royalty.

3.2 Conflict with the normal exploitation of the work

> which do not conflict with a normal exploitation of the work . . .

With regard to the second step of the test, the WTO panel held that "normal" includes both an empirical and a normative component. Thus, the evaluation of an exception under this second step requires an analysis of the way a work is in fact exploited as well as whether the nature of the exploitation is permissible or desirable.[176] The panel held that, while not every commercial use of a work is necessarily in conflict with a normal exploitation, such a conflict will arise if uses of the work pursuant to the exception or limitation "enter into competition with the ways that right holders normally extract economic value from that right."[177]

This second step should not pose too much of a burden to any development policy seeking to promote the dissemination of knowledge through the free availability of copyrighted material. One of the main characteristics of fair dealing provisions or statutory exceptions is that they are limited to non-commercial uses. In case documents are copied for private, research or teaching purposes in less advanced countries, these copies will not "enter into competition with the ways that right holders extract economic value" from that copyright, as expressed in the terms of the panel. Copies made for the above purposes will not be sold in the market, cutting off sales opportunities for the copyright holder. It could of course be argued that fair dealing provisions prevent the right holder from selling the needed material to those people or institutions using them for learning purposes. But such argumentation neglects the fact that the people benefiting from the free availability of unauthorized copies do not dispose of the financial means to purchase these copies. From the right holder's perspective, there is thus no lost opportunity. Such opportunity simply does not exist.

---

[176] See the panel report at paragraph 6.166.
[177] *Id.* at paragraph 6.183.

3.3 Unreasonable prejudice to the legitimate interests of the right holder

> and do not unreasonably prejudice the legitimate interests of the right holder.

As to the meaning of "interests," the above panel determined that both economic and non-economic advantage or detriment are covered. With regard to "legitimate" the panel noted that this means an interest authorized by law in the legal positivist sense, as well as a normative concern for protecting those interests that are justifiable in light of the objectives that motivate copyright protection.[178] This suggests that there could be some public policy interests that potentially might weigh in the analysis of what constitutes a "legitimate" interest of the right holder. For example, the free speech objectives that underlie copyright in many countries might suggest that a right holder who wants to use copyright to suppress the communication of certain works may not be exercising the right in a legitimate way. In other words, such an author may not have a "legitimate" right to suppress the communication of his works. Likewise, it could be argued that a right holder who wishes to prevent the free distribution of copies of his work for non-commercial purposes lacks any legitimacy in doing so. While in the case of non-commercial use, the right holder does not run the risk of important economic losses, she/he would at the same time prevent the implementation of a policy that offers a promising potential for the development of a knowledge-based society in less advanced countries.

Finally, with regard to the term "prejudice" the panel held that an exception or limitation that "has the potential to cause an unreasonable loss of income to the copyright owner"[179] is unreasonable and rises to the level of prejudice against the author.

In the case of fair use exceptions that are limited to teaching or research purposes, the chances of the right holder's encountering an "unreasonable loss" appear rather low. However, this condition depends on a careful case-by-case examination.

The three-step test of TRIPS Article 13 (and Berne Convention Article 9(2)) is cumulative. In other words, the exception or limitation in question must satisfy each of the three elements before it can be held to be consistent with TRIPS.[180]

---

[178] *Id*. at paragraph 6.224.

[179] *Id*. at paragraph 6.229.

[180] Note that Article 13 is very similar to Article 30, the exception to patent rights. The wording being slightly different, the three-step analysis appears to be almost identical under both provisions. The first step under Article 30 is to examine if the exception at issue is "limited". This is similar to the Article 13 condition of "certain special cases", which equally denotes the limited character of a possible exception. The second condition under Article 30 refers to the "normal exploitation" of the patent right, the only difference with Article 13 being that the exception shall not "unreasonably" conflict with such exploitation. At this point, the copyrights exception appears stricter, prohibiting any conflict whatsoever, arguably including reasonable ones. Finally, the third condition under both provisions refers to the legitimate interests of the right holder, which must not be unreasonably prejudiced. However, the patents exception contains a fourth condition which is not part of the express language of TRIPS Article 13 or Berne Convention Article 9(2): the legitimate interests of third parties have to be taken into account when examining the interests of the patent

Thus, if an exception or limitation is found to be broad or general (i.e., not limited to "certain special cases") there is no practical need to continue the analysis. The exception or limitation would be in that case inconsistent with Article 13.

4. WTO jurisprudence

On January 29, 1999, the WTO Secretariat received notification from the European Communities requesting consultations with the United States pursuant to Article 4 of the Dispute Settlement Understanding (DSU) and Article 64 of TRIPS, contending that Section 110(5) of the U.S. Copyright Act is inconsistent with Article 9.1 of TRIPS which requires Members to comply with Articles 1-21 of the Berne Convention. On April 15, 1999, the European Communities requested the establishment of a WTO panel under Article 6 of the DSU and Article 64.1 of TRIPS, alleging that Section 110(5), also known as the Fairness in Music Licensing Act (FIMLA), violates U.S. obligations under TRIPS and cannot be justified under any of the permitted exceptions or limitations.[181] In its defence, the United States argued, *inter alia*, that FIMLA is fully consistent with TRIPS and that it meets the standard of Article 13.[182]

In evaluating the scope of Article 13, the panel noted two differences between this provision and Berne Convention Article 9(2).[183] First, the latter provides that countries may in their national legislation "permit" the reproduction of works, while TRIPS Article 13 states that Members should "confine" limitations and exceptions.[184] The EC argued in part that this language should be read as a restriction on the permissible exceptions under the Berne Convention, since the principal objective of TRIPS is to heighten intellectual property protection.[185] The panel held that the application of Article 13 need not lead to different standards from those applicable under the Berne Convention.[186] In other words, it did not follow the EC's view that Article 13 is intended to restrict the exceptions permitted under the Berne Convention.

holder. However, the same test is arguably implied in examining, under Article 13, whether any prejudice to the right holder's interests is unreasonable. In this sense, the practical differences in the application of both exceptions appear to be marginal. For a thorough analysis of the Article 30 exception, see Chapter 23.

[181] See First Submission of the European Communities and Their Member States to the Panel, United States–Section 110(5) of the U.S. Copyright Act, Oct. 5, 1999, WTO Doc. WT/DS. See also panel report on Section 110(5), para. 3.1 (see above, Section 3 of this chapter). The European Community challenged both the "business exemption" (see 17 U.S.C. § 110(5)(B)) and the "home style exemption" (see 17 U.S.C. § 110(5)(A)).

[182] See First Submission of the United States of America, United States–Section 110(5) of the U.S. Copyright Act, Oct. 26, 1999, WTO Doc. WT/DS. See also panel report on Section 110(5), para. 3.3.

[183] Panel report on Section 110(5), at 27.

[184] *Id*. at 26, para. 6.71–6.72.

[185] *Id*. at 28, para. 6.78.

[186] *Id*., at para. 6.81. The EC had also contested the general applicability of Article 13 TRIPS to the provisions of the Berne Convention (id., at para. 6.75). The panel rejected this argument by stating that nothing in the express language of Article 13 TRIPS (or any other provision of the TRIPS Agreement) leads to a conclusion that the scope of Article 13 is limited to the new rights under the TRIPS Agreement (id., at para. 6.80).

The second distinction the panel noted between the Berne Convention and TRIPS is that the exceptions permitted under Berne Convention Article 9(2) are limited to the reproduction right while Article 13 is potentially applicable to all the copyright rights.[187] In all other respects the two provisions mirror each other in that limitations or exceptions are to be confined to (i) special cases; (ii) which do not conflict with a normal exploitation of the work, and (iii) do not unreasonably prejudice the legitimate interests of the right holder.[188] Both the EU and the United States agreed that these three conditions apply cumulatively under Article 13.[189] This cumulative interpretation has also been generally accepted with regard to Article 9(2) of the Berne Convention.[190]

5. Relationship with other international instruments

5.1 WTO Agreements
Among the WTO Agreements, TRIPS is the only one dealing with exceptions to copyright. Under GATT Article XX, there is a reference to copyright, but not to any exception thereto.[191]

5.2 Other international instruments
As stated earlier, Article 13 is derived substantially from Article 9(2), Berne Convention. Both the WCT[192] and the WIPO Performances and Phonograms Treaty[193] have incorporated this same three-step test as the standard for evaluating limitations and exceptions to the exclusive rights recognized in those treaties. It is expected that the interpretation of the three-step test will be consistent under all of the treaties that have incorporated it.

The Rome Convention, as partly incorporated by reference into TRIPS,[194] allows the domestic laws to exempt both private use and uses for the purpose of teaching or scientific research.[195] Such exemptions also extend to computer programs "as literary works" under the Berne Convention.

Finally, the concessions granted to developing countries under the Appendix to the Berne Convention (i.e. the possibility to issue compulsory licenses for the

---

[187] *Id*. at 27, para. 6.74.

[188] *Id*. See Berne Convention, Article 9(2); TRIPS Agreement, Article 13.

[189] Panel report on Section 110(5), para. 6.74.

[190] *See* Ricketson. The panel accepted this interpretation and noted that both parties agreed to this standard. Panel report on Section 110(5), para. 6.74.

[191] This is because the GATT follows a different approach towards intellectual property rights: they are considered as exceptions to the basic GATT rules. See Chapter 7.

[192] *See* Article 10.

[193] *See* Article 16(2).

[194] See Article 2.2 of the TRIPS Agreement, which obligates WTO Members not to take their TRIPS obligations as an excuse to derogate from obligations existing among them under, *inter alia*, the Rome Convention. As opposed to the Paris Convention (see Article 2.1 TRIPS), the Berne Convention (see Article 9.1 TRIPS), and the Washington Treaty (see Article 35 TRIPS), the TRIPS Agreement does not make the provisions of the Rome Convention mandatory for those WTO Members that are no parties to the Rome Convention. For this reason, the Rome Convention is only "partly incorporated" into TRIPS. For details, see Chapter 3.

[195] See Article 15.1(a) and (d).

reproduction of copyrighted material) require express renewals by qualifying developing countries at periodic intervals. New adherents to the Berne Convention remain entitled to these concessions, if they so request.[196]

6. New developments

6.1 National laws
In 2002, the U.S. Congress enacted the TEACH Act, extending the possibilities for unauthorized use of copyrighted material from conventional classroom teaching to distance learning activities. Provided a range of requirements is respected, the TEACH Act authorizes non-profit educational institutions to use copyrighted materials in distance education without permission from the copyright holder and without payment of royalties.[197]

6.2 International instruments

6.3 Regional and bilateral contexts

7. Comments, including economic and social implications

Limited exceptions to the minimum levels of copyright protection required by TRIPS are permitted. Such exceptions serve the purpose of ensuring that the protection of exclusive rights in copyrighted works does not harm the public interest. The exclusivity granted to authors reflects the necessity to provide creators of expressions with financial incentives for their activity. However, the ultimate purpose of copyright is not to ensure the material wealth of authors, but rather to promote intellectual creativity for the cultural enrichment of society. The author is conferred an exclusive right for the marketing of his works in exchange for his cultural contribution to society. In case society cannot benefit from the author's works to a satisfying degree, e.g. because the author charges excessive prices, this would disturb the mutual exchange between the author on the one hand and society on the other. This justifies the authorization of third parties to reproduce the copyrighted materials without the author's consent. On the other hand, in order to keep up the incentive for the author to engage in creative expression, the exception should be limited to what is absolutely required in the public interest, and the economic interests of the right holder should not be affected. This requires a delicate balancing test between the competing interests of the public and the author.

From a development perspective, it is essential to construe exceptions to copyright in a way allowing governments to pursue the policy objective of closing the knowledge gap *vis-à-vis* developed countries. Fair use provisions or statutory exceptions determine the extent to which third parties may make unauthorized use of protected copyright works. This is particularly important for the purposes of teaching, research, private use and technology transfer. Through the recourse to fair use provisions or specific exceptions, domestic legislators seek to strike an

---

[196] See UNCTAD 1996, para. 179.

[197] See the "Technology, Education and Copyright Harmonization Act" (the "TEACH Act"). For a summary of this legislation, see <http://www.ala.org/Template.cfm?Section=Distance_Education_and_the_TEACH_Act&Template=/ContentManagement/ContentDisplay.cfm&ContentID=25939>.

appropriate balance between the encouragement of creative activity on the one hand and the dissemination of knowledge to the public on the other hand.

In this context, the IPR Commission equally considered the importance of copyright exceptions to development goals by recommending that:

"In order to improve access to copyrighted works and achieve their goals for education and knowledge transfer, developing countries should adopt pro-competitive measures under copyright laws. Developing countries should be allowed to maintain or adopt broad exemptions for educational, research and library uses in their national copyright laws. The implementation of international copyright standards in the developing world must be undertaken with a proper appreciation of the continuing high level of need for improving the availability of these products, and their crucial importance for social and economic development."[198]

While a country may enact very narrow exceptions or limitations, calibrating the interests of rights holders and the public is typically the responsibility of domestic courts who must interpret the limitations in a manner that reflects that country's copyright policy keeping in mind, of course, international obligations such as those imposed by Article 13.

Finally, it is important to note that compulsory licensing with regard to the right of reproduction continues to be a possibility under TRIPS.[199]

---

[198] See the IPR Commission report, p. 104. The Commission also encourages free on-line access to all academic journals, see ibid., p. 102.

[199] However countries wishing to preserve their right to invoke the Appendix were required to take steps to preserve the possibility of doing so. Thailand was the first country to do so in 1996. Note that this Appendix to the Berne Convention *inter alia* allows for limited compulsory licensing to enable the translation of works into local languages. However, this option has not been very successful, with only a few developing countries having made use of it (see the IPR Commission report, p. 99).

13: Related Rights

Article 14   Protection of Performers, Producers of Phonograms (Sound Recordings) and Broadcasting Organizations

1. In respect of a fixation of their performance on a phonogram, performers shall have the possibility of preventing the following acts when undertaken without their authorization: the fixation of their unfixed performance and the reproduction of such fixation. Performers shall also have the possibility of preventing the following acts when undertaken without their authorization: the broadcasting by wireless means and the communication to the public of their live performance.

2. Producers of phonograms shall enjoy the right to authorize or prohibit the direct or indirect reproduction of their phonograms.

3. Broadcasting organizations shall have the right to prohibit the following acts when undertaken without their authorization: the fixation, the reproduction of fixations, and the rebroadcasting by wireless means of broadcasts, as well as the communication to the public of television broadcasts of the same. Where Members do not grant such rights to broadcasting organizations, they shall provide owners of copyright in the subject matter of broadcasts with the possibility of preventing the above acts, subject to the provisions of the Berne Convention (1971).

4. The provisions of Article 11 in respect of computer programs shall apply *mutatis mutandis* to producers of phonograms and any other right holders in phonograms as determined in a Member s law. If, on 15 April 1994, a Member has in force a system of equitable remuneration of right holders in respect of the rental of phonograms, it may maintain such system provided that the commercial rental of phonograms is not giving rise to the material impairment of the exclusive rights of reproduction of right holders.

5. The term of the protection available under this Agreement to performers and producers of phonograms shall last at least until the end of a period of 50 years computed from the end of the calendar year in which the fixation was made or the performance took place. The term of protection granted pursuant to paragraph 3 shall last for at least 20 years from the end of the calendar year in which the broadcast took place.

6. Any Member may, in relation to the rights conferred under paragraphs 1, 2 and 3, provide for conditions, limitations, exceptions and reservations to the extent

permitted by the Rome Convention. However, the provisions of Article 18 of the Berne Convention (1971) shall also apply, *mutatis mutandis*, to the rights of performers and producers of phonograms in phonograms.

1. Introduction: terminology, definition and scope

"Related rights" refers to the category of rights granted to performers, phonogram producers and broadcasters. In some countries such as the United States and the United Kingdom, these rights are simply incorporated under the general rubric of copyright. Other countries, such as Germany and France, protect these rights under the separate category called "neighbouring rights." The reason for this differentiation is the perception in those countries that works protected under related rights do not meet the same requirement of personal intellectual creativity as literary and artistic works.[200] For instance, the production of a broadcast or a compact disk is considered to be an activity of technical and organizational character, rather than the expression of personal intellectual creativity.[201] Protection of such works is nevertheless required, considering their economic value and the fact that they are easy to imitate.

TRIPS leaves Members free to protect these works under copyright proper or as a separate category of related rights. In the following, the rights of performers, phonogram producers and broadcasting organizations as covered by Article 14 will be referred to as "related rights".[202]

Article 14 does not define what "performers" are. Aid in interpretation might be found in the definition of that term under Article 3 (a) of the Rome Convention, and in the later WIPO Perfomances and Phonograms Treaty (WPPT), according to which "performers" are:

"actors, singers, musicians, dancers, and other persons who act, sing, deliver, declaim, play in, or otherwise perform literary or artistic works [or expressions of folklore]". [bracketed portion from Article 2, WPPT]

"Phonograms" and "sound recordings" are used coextensively in Article 14, in an effort to ensure that this Article clearly encompasses countries that use related rights systems to provide protection for phonograms, and those, most notably the United States, that protect sound recordings as copyright works. In general, the definition of a phonogram has been extended in related rights countries so that the term may reasonably encompass sound recordings. This trend is reinforced by Article 2(b) of the WPPT, which defines a phonogram as the "fixation of the sounds of a performance or of other sounds, or of a representation of sounds other than

---

[200] On the creativity and originality requirement under copyright law, see Chapter 7, Section 3. As opposed to originality, copyright law does not require the work to meet certain quality standards (ibid.).

[201] This is the approach taken under German copyright law. See J. Ensthaler, *Gewerblicher Rechtsschutz und Urheberrecht*, 2. edition 2003, Berlin, Heidelberg, New York.

[202] It is not in the purpose of this Book to decide whether these rights are to be protected under copyright proper (as in e.g. the USA and the UK) or as a separate category of "neighbouring rights" (as in e.g. France and Germany).

in the form of a fixation incorporated in a cinematographic or other audiovisual work." In any event, to the extent that definitions differ across jurisdictions, the provisions of Article 14 cover both these categories of works.

2. History of the provision

2.1 Situation pre-TRIPS

The protection of related rights has been a much slower and uneven development in national laws (see below), notwithstanding negotiation of an international convention in 1961. The International Convention for the Protection of Performers, Producers of Phonograms and Broadcasting Organisations (Rome Convention) entered into force in 1964.[203] The scope of protection afforded to related rights under the Rome Convention is generally lower than the protection offered under the Berne Convention. For example, the term of protection under the Rome Convention is twenty years,[204] compared to life of the author plus fifty years under the Berne Convention. Prior to TRIPS, the different forms of protecting related rights had the practical effect of relaxing a country's Berne Convention obligations with regard to certain works (such as broadcasts) that, due to the separate related rights system, were not considered literary works. In respect of broadcasts, TRIPS will have little impact on this, considering that the level of harmonization reflected in Article 14 is very low. Indeed, Article 14 contemplates a very high degree of flexibility in what a country is obligated to protect and the conditions under which such protection must take place.[205]

In the United States, there is a recognised unitary public performance right that includes live performance as well as performance by transmission. The right is granted to copyright owners of "literary, musical, dramatic, and choreographic works, pantomimes, and motion pictures and other audiovisual works."[206] Owners of sound recordings (i.e., phonograms) are not granted this public performance right, but instead have a separate public performance right limited to digital audio transmissions.[207] In addition performers are granted the right to prevent the unauthorized fixation of live performances.[208] The U.S. approach is one model of how a country might assimilate related rights within the copyright system, as distinct from the two-system approach utilized by many European countries.

The EC Rental Right Directive requires that performers be granted the exclusive right to authorize or prohibit the rental or lending of fixations of their performances.[209] Under the Directive, a performer may transfer the rental right

---

[203] However, the Rome Convention has not been ratified by the United States.

[204] *See* Rome Convention, Article 14.

[205] For example, Article 14.5, TRIPS Agreement requires a minimum term of protection of 50 years for performers and phonogram producers and 20 years for broadcasting organizations (counted from the end of the respective calendar year, see Section 3 of this chapter). This leaves Members distinguishing between copyright and related rights free to afford longer protection to literary and artistic works (life of the author plus at least 50 years).

[206] 17 U.S.C. §106(4).

[207] Id. at §106(6).

[208] Id. at §1101(a).

[209] EC Rental Right Directive, Article 2(1).

but the right to an equitable remuneration for the rental is inalienable.[210] The Directive also requires that broadcasting organizations have the exclusive right to fix their broadcasts, as well as to reproduce the fixations, directly or indirectly.[211] Public rebroadcast and communication rights[212] as well as public distribution rights for broadcasters[213] are also recognized by the Directive.

2.2 Negotiating history

Article 14.1 provides that performers shall have "the possibility of preventing" the unauthorized fixation of their unfixed performances and the reproduction of such fixation. In addition, performers shall have the right to prevent the "unauthorized broadcasting by wireless means and the communication to the public of their live performance." Protection for the rights of performers has historically been the province of the Rome Convention. The fact that Article 14.1 simply requires that countries grant "the possibility" of the rights in question flows from the negotiating conditions that characterized the Rome Convention, where the United Kingdom dealt with unauthorized fixation under the penal code. Phrasing the right in this way facilitated ratification of the Rome Convention by the United Kingdom.[214] In general, the Rome Convention provides a significant amount of the context for the provisions of Article 14. Consequently, the interpretation of the full scope of Article 14 is directly related to the Rome Convention and its own negotiating history.

2.2.1 The Anell Draft

"10. Relation to Rome Convention

10A PARTIES shall, as minimum substantive standards for the protection of performers, broadcasting organisations and producers of phonograms, provide protection consistent with the substantive provisions of the Rome Convention. [Articles 1 to 20 of the Rome Convention could be considered to constitute the substantive provisions.]

11. Rights of Producers of Phonograms (Sound Recordings)

11A.1 PARTIES shall extend to producers of phonograms the right to authorise or prohibit the direct or indirect reproduction of their phonograms [by any means or process, in whole or in part].

11A.2a [In regard to the rental of phonograms,] the provisions of point 3 in respect of computer programs shall apply mutatis mutandis in respect of producers of phonograms [or performers or both].

11A.2b The protection provided to producers of phonograms shall include the right to prevent all third parties not having their consent from putting on the market, from selling, or from otherwise distributing copies of such phonograms.

11A.3 The provisions of point 4A shall apply mutatis mutandis to the producers of phonograms.

12. Rights of Performers

---

[210] Id. at Article 4(1), (2).
[211] Id. at Article 7(1).
[212] Id. at Article 8(3).
[213] Id. at Article 9(1).
[214] Gervais, p. 96/97.

12A The protection provided for performers shall include the possibility of preventing:

12A.1 the broadcasting [by any technical means or process such as by radio wave, by cable or by other devices] [by wireless means and the communication to the public of their live performance];

12A.2 the fixation of their unfixed performance [on phonograms or data carriers and from reproducing such fixations];

12A.3 the reproduction of a fixation of their performance;

12A.4 the production of their performance in any place other than that of the performance;

12A.5 the offering to the public, selling, or otherwise distributing copies of the fixation containing the performance.

13. Rights of Broadcasting Organisations

13.1 Broadcasting organisations shall have the possibility of preventing:

13A.1 the fixation of their broadcasts [on phonograms or data carriers, and from reproducing such fixations];

13A.2 the reproduction of fixations;

13A.3 the communication to the public of their [television] broadcasts;

13A.4 the rebroadcasting by wireless means of their broadcasts;

13A.5 the retransmitting of their broadcast;

13A.6 the putting on the market, sale, or other distribution of copies of the broadcast.

14. Public Communication of Phonograms

14A If a phonogram published for commercial purposes, or a reproduction of such a phonogram, is used directly for broadcasting or for any communication to the public, a single equitable remuneration shall be paid by the user to the performers, or to the producers of the phonogram, or to both.

15. Term of Protection

15A.1a The term of protection granted to producers of phonograms, performers and broadcasting organisations shall last at least until the end of a period of [20] [50] years computed from the end of the year in which the fixation was made or the performance or broadcast took place.

15A.2a PARTIES may, however, provide for a period of protection of less than 50 years provided that the period of protection lasts at least for 25 years and that they otherwise assume a substantially equivalent protection against piracy for an equivalent period.

15Ab Point 7 shall apply mutatis mutandis to the producers of phonograms.

16. Exceptions

16Aa PARTIES may, in relation to the rights conferred by points 11, 12, 13 and 14, provide for limitations, exceptions and reservations to the extent permitted by the Rome Convention.

16Ab Points 8A.2-4 of this Part shall apply mutatis mutandis to phonograms.

16B (See Section 8 of this Part.)

17. Acquisition of Rights

17A.1 The provisions of points 6 and 9 of this Part shall apply mutatis mutandis to the producers of phonograms.

17A.2 PARTIES shall protect phonograms first fixed or published in the territory of another PARTY, including phonograms published in the territory of a PARTY within thirty days of their publication elsewhere; and phonograms the producer of which is a national of a PARTY, or is a company headquartered in the territory of a PARTY.

17A.3 The acquisition and validity of intellectual property rights in phonograms shall not be subject to any formalities, and protection shall arise automatically upon their creation."

With respect to substantive protection, performers' rights under the current Article 14 correspond more or less to the performers' rights as listed under paragraph 12 of the Anell Draft. The same is true with respect to producers' rights under Article 14.2 and paragraph 11 of the Anell Draft, and to the rights of broadcasting organizations under Article 14.3 and paragraph 13 of the Anell Draft. The difference between the scope of protection between the draft and the final version is that the final version does not refer to any distribution rights as does paragraph 12A.5 (for performers) and paragraph 13A.6 (for broadcasting organizations). The reason for this is that at the time of the Anell Draft, some delegations were still attempting to introduce a general right of distribution of copyrighted material.[215] This idea was then abandoned, and so was the reference to any distribution rights under the subsequent (Brussels) draft, as quoted below.

TRIPS does not refer either to paragraphs 12A.4 or 13A.5 of the Anell Draft.[216] Paragraph 17A.2 above refers to a national treatment obligation. In view of the general national treatment provision under Article 3 TRIPS, such specification was no longer required in the final version of the Agreement.

Finally, paragraph 17A.3 of the Anell Draft was not taken over into Article 14, but is now included in Article 62.1 of TRIPS, which authorizes Members to condition the acquisition and maintenance of the rights under Sections 2 through 6 (of Part II) on reasonable procedures and formalities. Thus, such authorization is not given with respect to copyrights under Section 1 (of Part II of the Agreement). This corresponds to the general rule that a copyright automatically comes into existence with the creation of the work.

2.2.2 The Brussels Draft

["1. In respect of a fixation of their performance on a phonogram, performers shall have the possibility of preventing: the fixation of their unfixed performance; and the reproduction of such fixation. Performers shall also have the possibility of preventing the broadcasting by wireless means and the communication to the public of their live performance.]

2. Producers of phonograms shall enjoy the right to authorize or prohibit the direct or indirect reproduction of their phonograms.

---

[215] See Chapter 10, Section 2.2.

[216] Regarding paragraph 13A.5, the retransmission right was framed without reference to public communication, and this may have been viewed as potentially imposing excessive liability on common carriers. Paragraph 12A.4 was, at the least, inelegantly drafted.

[3. Broadcasting organizations shall have the right to authorise or prohibit the fixation, the reproduction of fixations, and the rebroadcasting by wireless means of broadcasts, as well as the communication to the public of television broadcasts of the same. Where PARTIES do not grant such rights to broadcasting organizations, they shall provide right holders in the subject matter of broadcasts with the possibility of preventing the above acts.]

4. The provisions of Article 11 shall apply *mutatis mutandis* to right holders in phonograms.

5. The term of the protection available under this Agreement to performers and producers of phonograms shall last at least until the end of a period of [50] years computed from the end of the calendar year in which the fixation was made or the performance or broadcast took place. The term of protection granted pursuant to paragraph 3 above shall last for at least [25] years from the end of the calendar year in which the broadcast took place.

6. Any PARTY to this Agreement may, in relation to the rights conferred under paragraphs 1-3 above, provide for conditions, limitations, exceptions and reservations to the extent permitted by the Rome Convention. [However, the provisions of Article [–217] of this Section shall also apply *mutatis mutandis* to the rights of performers and producers of phonograms in phonograms.]"

The Brussels Draft was essentially similar to the current version of Article 14. As opposed to the Brussels Draft, the current version in its paragraphs 1 and 3 specifies that the enumerated rights of performers and broadcasting organizations apply only to situations where third persons make use of their protected materials without the right holders' authorization.

Paragraph 3 was quite controversial during the negotiations:[218] A number of countries supported the inclusion of a copyright of broadcasting organizations with respect to their broadcasts. Other countries opposed such right, agreeing only to provide broadcasting organizations with copyrights concerning the audiovisual productions themselves (as opposed to the broadcasting of these productions). As a compromise, the Brussels Draft (like the current Article 14.3) left it up to Members to decide whether to grant the enumerated rights to broadcasting organizations. In case a Member refuses to do so, it remains obligated to grant the same rights more generally to owners of copyright (possibly including broadcasters) in the subject matter of broadcasts (see below, Section 3).

Paragraph 4 of the Brussels Draft version made the rental right (Article 11) applicable to performers, producers and broadcasting organizations. It did not, however, distinguish between computer programs and cinematographic works. This was so because under the Brussels Draft article on rental rights, there was no distinction between those categories of works, either.[219]

Paragraph 4 of the Brussels Draft article on related rights did not refer to a remuneration right as does the current Article 14.4, second sentence. The reason for this was that under the Brussels Draft, there was a reference to remuneration rights in what is now Article 11.[220] This right was construed as an alternative to

---

[217] This was the provision on protection of works existing at time of entry into force.

[218] For the following, see Gervais, p. 99, para. 2.80.

[219] See above, Chapter 10.

[220] Ibid., Section 2.2 (negotiating history).

the exclusive rental right. Since paragraph 4 of Brussels Article 14 referred to Article 11 and thus to the remuneration right, any additional, express reference under draft Article 14 was not required. However, when the reference in Article 11 to a remuneration right was deleted under the final TRIPS version, such reference had to be inserted into the TRIPS version of Article 14, applying specifically to the rental of phonograms.

Finally, the proposed minimum term of protection provided to the rights of broadcasting organizations was 25 years (paragraph 5). Under TRIPS, this term was reduced to 20 years.

3. Possible interpretations

3.1 Article 14.1 TRIPS (Rights of performers)

> 1. In respect of a fixation of their performance on a phonogram, performers shall have the possibility of preventing the following acts when undertaken without their authorization: the fixation of their unfixed performance and the reproduction of such fixation. Performers shall also have the possibility of preventing the following acts when undertaken without their authorization: the broadcasting by wireless means and the communication to the public of their live performance.

The first sentence of this paragraph corresponds to Article 7.1 (b) and (c) of the Rome Convention. The right accorded to performers is not construed as a full right to *authorize* or to prohibit, but merely as a negative right, i.e. as the possibility of preventing unauthorized acts. This provision leaves Members some freedom as to the means by which they choose to grant such right to performers. Under the Rome Convention, Article 7.1 has traditionally been interpreted as giving parties to the Convention the freedom to exclude civil judicial proceedings from the scope of performers' rights, thus limiting right holders' possibilities to the invocation of criminal sanctions or administrative procedures.[221] Since the Rome Convention is referred to under Article 14.6 of TRIPS, the question has been raised whether the same flexibility is permitted under TRIPS.[222] This appears doubtful, considering that under Article 42 of TRIPS, Members "shall make available to right holders civil judicial procedures concerning the enforcement of any intellectual property right covered by this Agreement". This obligation is expressly waived in the case of geographical indications, as made clear in footnote 4 to Article 23.1. Such explicit waiver does not exist, however, with respect to Article 14.1.[223]

As far as the scope of the first paragraph is concerned, it is limited to the fixation of the protected work on a phonogram. Thus, the first paragraph does not cover audiovisual fixations.

---

[221] Gervais, p. 98, para. 2.79.

[222] Ibid, qualifying such flexibility as a possible "exception" permitted under the Rome Convention, as referred to in Article 14.6.

[223] Ibid. However, it may be argued that by using the same language as the Rome Convention, Article 14.1 would arguably have "imported" the traditional interpretation of the Rome Convention, irrespective of Article 42 of TRIPS.

3.2 Article 14.2 TRIPS (Rights of producers of phonograms and sound recordings)

> 2. Producers of phonograms shall enjoy the right to authorize or prohibit the direct or indirect reproduction of their phonograms.

Article 14.2 parallels Article 10 of the Rome Convention. It grants producers of phonograms the right to authorize or prohibit the direct or indirect reproduction of their phonograms. While the direct reproduction refers to the copying of the music, etc. directly from the phonogram, "indirect" reproduction of a phonogram is done, e.g., by recording a radio or television programme containing the music that is fixed on the phonogram.

3.3 Article 14.3 TRIPS (Rights of broadcasting organizations)

> 3. Broadcasting organizations shall have the right to prohibit the following acts when undertaken without their authorization: the fixation, the reproduction of fixations, and the rebroadcasting by wireless means of broadcasts, as well as the communication to the public of television broadcasts of the same. Where Members do not grant such rights to broadcasting organizations, they shall provide owners of copyright in the subject matter of broadcasts with the possibility of preventing the above acts, subject to the provisions of the Berne Convention (1971).

This paragraph leaves it up to Members to grant special rights to broadcasting organizations, as long as they provide the above rights in the subject matter of broadcasts to owners of copyright in general. While there must be a right given to someone to prevent the enumerated acts, Members have flexibility as to who that person(s) should be. Members may want to avoid the situation in which two different parties are granted rights in respect to the same broadcast, that is, the creator/owner of the "content" (i.e., the traditional copyright holder), and the broadcast organization that merely makes the content available to the public in a broadcast form. If both the traditional copyright holder and the broadcast organization have rights in the same transmission, this can lead to conflicts, for example, regarding re-use of the content.

3.4 Article 14.4 TRIPS (Rental rights)

> 4. The provisions of Article 11 in respect of computer programs shall apply mutatis mutandis to producers of phonograms and any other right holders in phonograms as determined in a Member's law. If, on 15 April 1994, a Member has in force a system of equitable remuneration of right holders in respect of the rental of phonograms, it may maintain such system provided that the commercial rental of phonograms is not giving rise to the material impairment of the exclusive rights of reproduction of right holders.

In addition to the exclusive reproduction right conferred by Article 14.2, Article 14.4 grants producers an exclusive rental right with regard to their phonograms. This was accomplished by extending the provisions of Article 11 "to producers of phonograms and any other right holders as determined in domestic law." Thus, under the terms of a domestic law, the rental right shall apply both to producers and other right holders in the phonogram contemplated by domestic law. If the domestic law does not determine other right holders in the phonogram, Article 14 still mandates a rental right for producers of phonograms.

3.5 Article 14.5 TRIPS (Term of protection)

> 5. The term of the protection available under this Agreement to performers and producers of phonograms shall last at least until the end of a period of 50 years computed from the end of the calendar year in which the fixation was made or the performance took place. The term of protection granted pursuant to paragraph 3 shall last for at least 20 years from the end of the calendar year in which the broadcast took place.

This paragraph is largely self-explanatory. An important distinction is made between performers and producers on the one hand, and broadcasting organizations on the other.

If, under Article 14.3, a Member chooses to not grant special rights to broadcasting organizations, it has to grant rights to the creator of the subject-matter of the broadcast, which is eligible for protection under general copyright law as literary or artistic work. In that case, the general term of protection for copyright under the Berne Convention applies.

3.6 Article 14.6 TRIPS (Conditions, limitations, exceptions and reservations)

> 6. Any Member may, in relation to the rights conferred under paragraphs 1, 2 and 3, provide for conditions, limitations, exceptions and reservations to the extent permitted by the Rome Convention. However, the provisions of Article 18 of the Berne Convention (1971) shall also apply, *mutatis mutandis*, to the rights of performers and producers of phonograms in phonograms.

The first sentence makes applicable compulsory licenses for broadcasts, as far as permitted under the Rome Convention, and as far as rights in the broadcast are granted. Under the Rome Convention, compulsory licenses are authorized under Article 13 (d), which provides that

> "Broadcasting organisations shall enjoy the right to authorize or prohibit: [...]
> (d) the communication to the public of their television broadcasts if such communication is made in places accessible to the public against payment of an entrance

fee; it shall be a matter for the domestic law of the State where protection of this right is claimed to determine the conditions under which it may be exercised."[224]

The second sentence refers to Article 18 of the Berne Convention. This provision provides that:

"(1) This Convention shall apply to all works which, at the moment of its coming into force, have not yet fallen into the public domain in the country of origin through the expiry of the term of protection.

(2) If, however, through the expiry of the term of protection which was previously granted, a work has fallen into the public domain of the country where protection is claimed, that work shall not be protected anew.

(3) The application of this principle shall be subject to any provisions contained in special conventions to that effect existing or to be concluded between countries of the Union. In the absence of such provisions, the respective countries shall determine, each in so far as it is concerned, the conditions of application of this principle.

(4) The preceding provisions shall also apply in the case of new accessions to the Union and to cases in which protection is extended by the application of Article 7 or by the abandonment of reservations."

One of the "special conventions" under the first sentence of paragraph 3 is the TRIPS Agreement itself, which provides in Article 70(5):

"A Member is not obliged to apply the provisions of Article 11 and of paragraph 4 of Article 14 with respect to originals or copies purchased prior to the date of application of this Agreement for that Member."

4. WTO jurisprudence

There has been no WTO panel decision on this subject.

5. Relationship with other international instruments

5.1 WTO Agreements

5.2 Other international instruments

The scope of the import of the level of protection for related rights in TRIPS can only be fully appreciated in light of the other international agreements that deal with the protection of related rights. Indeed TRIPS explicitly mentions that nothing in its provisions shall derogate from existing obligations under the Rome Convention.[225] However, several treaties deal with protection of different related rights. In addition to TRIPS the major ones include the Rome Convention and

---

[224] This last part of the provision may be interpreted as giving parties the right to authorize compulsory licenses.

[225] See TRIPS Article 1.3.

the WPPT. In many respects, these treaties incorporate substantially similar rules and principles. However, there are some areas of distinction as made evident in the summary table below.

A Comparative Overview of Related Rights Protection

	ROME CONVENTION(RC)	TRIPS AGREEMENT	WIPO PERFORMANCES AND PHONOGRAMS TREATY (WPPT)
Rights of Performers	Art. 7.1(b) (c) ["possibility of preventing" unauthorized broadcast and communication to the public of unfixed performance; reproduction of an unauthorized fixation of a performance.]	Art. 14.1 [in respect of unfixed works, "possibility of preventing" unauthorized fixation and reproduction of the unauthorized fixation; possibility of preventing unauthorized broadcasting by wireless means and communication to public of live performances.]	Art. 6 [grants exclusive rights in unfixed performances as to broadcasting communication to the public and fixation; Art. 7 grants an exclusive right to reproduce as to fixed performances; Art. 8 grants an exclusive right of distribution; Art. 9 grants an exclusive rental rights; Art. 10 grants an exclusive right to make the work available through an interactive system. The obvious example would be the Internet. Note, also that WPPT, Art. 5., requires moral rights for performers.]

(continued)

A Comparative Overview of Related Rights Protection (continued)

	ROME CONVENTION(RC)	TRIPS AGREEMENT	WIPO PERFORMANCES AND PHONOGRAMS TREATY (WPPT)
Rights of Producers of Phonograms and Sound Recordings	Art. 10 [right to authorize or prohibit direct or indirect reproduction of phonograms] The Rome Convention provides for a performance right. See Art. 12. The Geneva Phonograms Convention provides for a public distribution right.	Art 14.2 [right to authorize or prohibit direct or indirect reproduction of their phonograms] Note that, unlike the Rome Convention, TRIPS requires fixation on a phonogram alone. Other forms of fixation are not covered. Protection for such works will have to be covered by other provisions. Thus, for example, audiovisual works could be protected under Article 19 of the Rome Convention or Article 2 of the WPPT.	Art. 11 [exclusive right to authorize direct or indirect reproduction of their phonograms in any manner or form.] Art. 12 establishes a public distribution right; Art. 13 establishes a commercial rental right; Art. 14 establishes an exclusive right to make their phonograms available to the public by wire or wireless means.; Art. 15 establishes a right to a single equitable remuneration for the direct or indirect use of phonograms published for commercial purposes for broadcasting or any communication to the public.

	ROME CONVENTION(RC)	TRIPS AGREEMENT	WIPO PERFORMANCES AND PHONOGRAMS TREATY (WPPT)
Rights of Broadcasting Organizations	Art. 13 [right to authorize or prohibit (a) rebroadcasting of their broadcasts; (b) fixation of their broadcasts (c) reproductions of unauthorized fixations of their broadcasts; (d) communication to the public of their television broadcasts.]	Art. 14.3 [right to prohibit unauthorized fixations, reproduction of fixations, rebroadcasting of wireless means of broadcasts and communication to the public of television broadcasts of the same. TRIPS gives countries the option of giving these rights to broadcasting organizations or to owners of copyright in the subject matter of the broadcast, subject to the Berne Convention.]	

Article 14.5 requires that rights granted to performers and producers of phonograms "shall" last at least until the end of fifty years from the date of fixation or date of the performance. The rights of broadcasting organizations must last a minimum of twenty years from the end of the calendar year in which the broadcast took place.[226] Conditions, limitations, exceptions and reservations are permitted under TRIPS with respect to the rights granted in paragraphs 1–3 of Article 14 on the same terms as provided in the Rome Convention.[227] Article 18 of the Berne Convention is also invoked to apply to the rights of performers and producers of phonograms in the phonograms themselves.[228] It is important to note that compulsory licensing is allowed under the Rome Convention to the extent that it is compatible with the Convention.

[226] *See* TRIPS, Article 14.5.
[227] *See* Article 14.6.
[228] Id.

6. New developments

6.1 National laws

6.2 International instruments

6.3 Regional contexts

7. Comments, including economic and social implications

The rights of performers, producers of phonograms and broadcasting organizations arguably are tangential to the incentive structure of the copyright system. In other words these categories relate more to the exploitation of underlying literary and artistic works, which means that strong proprietary rights may not be needed to encourage their development. The reality is that most of the works that are covered by a related rights regime do not need the full term of copyright protection as their economic value is likely to be exhausted long before such term expires. TRIPS provides a framework for the protection of these related rights that allows much room for Members to tailor the protection of such rights to suit domestic economic and political realities. It is important to note that because these categories of works are designed to exploit copyrighted works, the real issue for regulation is how rights administration (through collecting societies, as discussed below) will be designed to facilitate the ability of producers and broadcasting organizations to bring these works to the public. Thus, the economic and social concerns relating to related rights must be examined in the domestic context with a view to balancing the efficient mechanism of collecting societies with the need to ensure that the owners of underlying copyright works are not unduly taken advantage of. It is in respect of the regulation of collecting societies vis-a-vis rights owners that the protection of related rights may affect the incentive to authors.

From a development perspective,[229] related rights may be of particular interest to countries endowed with oral traditions and culture, in the representation of which authors are usually performers as well. Expressions of folklore that often fail to qualify for copyright protection can thus indirectly obtain protection from rights in performances, fixations and broadcasts. Similarly, the protection of phonogram producers may contribute to developing countries' efforts to establish their own sound-recording industries which promote the dissemination of national culture, both within and outside the country, and also foster export opportunities.[230] In the same vein, broadcasting organizations in developing countries can benefit from protecting costly programmes against unauthorized reproduction, and rebroadcasts of major culture and sports programmes abroad are potential sources of foreign exchange.

To these ends, developing countries need to establish an institutional framework, including national collecting societies, in order to ensure that public and private funds invested in the production of cultural goods bear fruit on both

---

[229] As to the following, see UNCTAD, 1996, paras. 168, 169.

[230] On the relevance of the music sector for developing countries, see UNCTAD-ICTSD, *Intellectual Property Rights: Implications for Development*, Policy Discussion Paper, Geneva, 2003, Chapter 3 (in particular pp. 70/71).

domestic and foreign markets. These agencies may also assist local authors and artists in restoring copyrights or related rights protection to any works of national origin that foreign authorities must now remove from the public domain by virtue of the Berne Convention and relevant provisions of TRIPS.

On the other hand, developing countries should take appropriate measures to ensure that collecting societies, due to their market power, do not themselves prevent the competition required to keep prices of copyrighted materials at affordable levels. This means that a country should not promote collecting societies without at the same time ensuring a workable set of competition rules, including the establishment of the competent authorities to administer these rules.[231]

---

[231] The IPR Commission has cautioned against an uncritical promotion of collecting societies (see the report, pp. 98, 99). The Commission advances two reasons for this view. First, it states that collecting societies operating in developing countries tend to collect "far more" royalties for foreign rights holders from industrialized countries than for domestic rights holders from developing countries. This tendency might, however, just reflect the economic reality in developing countries, i.e. that most holders of copyrights are nationals from developed countries. The second argument brought forward by the IPR Commission concerns the above-mentioned problem of collecting societies acquiring considerable market power and thus presenting a threat to competition and affordable prices. The IPR Commission concludes that collecting societies should not be established before the respective country has set up the institutions and the regulatory framework necessary for the protection of competition in the software market. The Commission also expresses the view that the benefit to the local population of collecting societies will be more direct in large markets, considering the modest absolute number of local copyright holders in small developing countries. According to the Commission, copyright holders as the immediate beneficiaries should bear the costs of setting up and running collecting societies.

14: Trademarks

Article 15   Protectable Subject Matter

1. Any sign, or any combination of signs, capable of distinguishing the goods or services of one undertaking from those of other undertakings, shall be capable of constituting a trademark. Such signs, in particular words including personal names, letters, numerals, figurative elements and combinations of colours as well as any combination of such signs, shall be eligible for registration as trademarks. Where signs are not inherently capable of distinguishing the relevant goods or services, Members may make registrability depend on distinctiveness acquired through use. Members may require, as a condition of registration, that signs be visually perceptible.

2. Paragraph 1 shall not be understood to prevent a Member from denying registration of a trademark on other grounds, provided that they do not derogate from the provisions of the Paris Convention (1967).

3. Members may make registrability depend on use. However, actual use of a trademark shall not be a condition for filing an application for registration. An application shall not be refused solely on the ground that intended use has not taken place before the expiry of a period of three years from the date of application.

4. The nature of the goods or services to which a trademark is to be applied shall in no case form an obstacle to registration of the trademark.

5. Members shall publish each trademark either before it is registered or promptly after it is registered and shall afford a reasonable opportunity for petitions to cancel the registration. In addition, Members may afford an opportunity for the registration of a trademark to be opposed.

Article 16   Rights Conferred

1. The owner of a registered trademark shall have the exclusive right to prevent all third parties not having the owner's consent from using in the course of trade identical or similar signs for goods or services which are identical or similar to those in respect of which the trademark is registered where such use would

result in a likelihood of confusion. In case of the use of an identical sign for identical goods or services, a likelihood of confusion shall be presumed. The rights described above shall not prejudice any existing prior rights, nor shall they affect the possibility of Members making rights available on the basis of use.

2. Article 6bis of the Paris Convention (1967) shall apply, mutatis mutandis, to services. In determining whether a trademark is well-known, Members shall take account of the knowledge of the trademark in the relevant sector of the public, including knowledge in the Member concerned which has been obtained as a result of the promotion of the trademark.

3. Article 6bis of the Paris Convention (1967) shall apply, mutatis mutandis, to goods or services which are not similar to those in respect of which a trademark is registered, provided that use of that trademark in relation to those goods or services would indicate a connection between those goods or services and the owner of the registered trademark and provided that the interests of the owner of the registered trademark are likely to be damaged by such use.

Article 17   Exceptions

Members may provide limited exceptions to the rights conferred by a trademark, such as fair use of descriptive terms, provided that such exceptions take account of the legitimate interests of the owner of the trademark and of third parties.

Article 18   Term of Protection

Initial registration, and each renewal of registration, of a trademark shall be for a term of no less than seven years. The registration of a trademark shall be renewable indefinitely.

Article 19   Requirement of Use

1. If use is required to maintain a registration, the registration may be cancelled only after an uninterrupted period of at least three years of non-use, unless valid reasons based on the existence of obstacles to such use are shown by the trademark owner. Circumstances arising independently of the will of the owner of the trademark which constitute an obstacle to the use of the trademark, such as import restrictions on or other government requirements for goods or services protected by the trademark, shall be recognized as valid reasons for non-use.

2. When subject to the control of its owner, use of a trademark by another person shall be recognized as use of the trademark for the purpose of maintaining the registration.

Article 20   Other Requirements

The use of a trademark in the course of trade shall not be unjustifiably encumbered by special requirements, such as use with another trademark, use in a special form or use in a manner detrimental to its capability to distinguish the goods or services of one undertaking from those of other undertakings. This will not preclude a requirement prescribing the use of the trademark identifying the undertaking producing the goods or services along with, but without linking it to, the trademark distinguishing the specific goods or services in question of that undertaking.

Article 21   Licensing and Assignment

Members may determine conditions on the licensing and assignment of trademarks, it being understood that the compulsory licensing of trademarks shall not be permitted and that the owner of a registered trademark shall have the right to assign the trademark with or without the transfer of the business to which the trademark belongs.

---

1. Introduction: terminology, definition and scope

Trademarks (or trade marks)[232] are signs that distinguish the goods or services of one enterprise from those of another. They are identifiers intended to rapidly convey information to consumers. The conventional and largely uncontroversial wisdom regarding trademarks is that they reduce consumer transaction costs by allowing individuals to scan product displays and make purchasing decisions by associating signs with known qualities or characteristics of goods or services, including the reputation of producers. A secondary role of the trademark – more controversial from a legal and economic standpoint – is to facilitate producer investment in advertising and promotion in order to stimulate consumer demand; that is, to generate goodwill by self-promotion.

Part of the impetus for the overall TRIPS negotiating effort was concern over trademark counterfeiting, the straightforward misappropriation of the persona of a producing enterprise.[233] Although trademark counterfeiting may have benefits for consumers in a limited set of circumstances,[234] the practice was not defended by any group of countries during the TRIPS negotiations. In fact, many developing countries that generally opposed substantive negotiation of IPRs in the GATT as an

---

[232] U.S.-English uses the single word "trademark" and U.K.-Commonwealth English uses the separate words "trade mark" for the same subject matter.

[233] According to footnote 14 to Article 51 of TRIPS, counterfeit trademarked goods "shall mean any goods, including packaging, bearing without authorization a trademark which is identical to the trademark validly registered in respect of such goods, or which cannot be distinguished in its essential aspects from such a trademark, and which thereby infringes the rights of the owner of the trademark in question under the law of the country of importation".

[234] That is, for example, when the counterfeiter offers high quality substitute goods at lower prices.

alternative pressed to limit the scope of negotiations to trademark "counterfeiting" and copyright "piracy".

While the basic role of trademarks is generally accepted, important questions regarding the scope of protection remain. One set of issues concerns whether trademarks can and should be used to inhibit parallel trade in goods or services. Recognizing that a very high percentage of goods in international trade are identified by a trademark, rules preventing parallel importation based on trademark rights may significantly affect trade flows. Another set of issues concerns the fair use of trademarks. In what circumstances may journalists or competitors use a trademark to refer to goods or services? Does the colouring of a medicine give its producer the right to prevent others from using the same colour for another version of that medicine?

TRIPS represented a significant step in the evolution of trademark law. Just as for patents, the Paris Convention for the Protection of Industrial Property includes rules regulating the grant and use of trademarks, but it does not define the subject matter of protection. Although the European Community, in particular, had taken significant steps in the approximation of trademark law at the regional level, TRIPS for the first time defined the subject matter of trademark protection at the multilateral level.

2. History of the provision

2.1 Situation pre-TRIPS

Prior to negotiation of TRIPS, most countries granted and enforced rights in trademarks, although there were significant differences in the subject matter scope of protection, the application of conditions of use, and in procedural aspects such as renewal periods.

2.1.1 The Paris Convention

The Paris Convention (1883, as revised) establishes a rule of national treatment for trademark applicants and owners (Article 2). It provides a right of priority for trademark applicants, although the period of six months is shorter than that for patent applicants (Article 4). The Convention establishes a "reasonable" period before cancellation of a mark for non-use (Article 5.C(1)). It recognizes that conditions for application will be established by national legislation (Article 6(1)) and confirms the independence of marks (Article 6(3)). The Convention addresses in a rather general way the subject of "well-known marks" (Article 6*bis*). It includes rules on assignment, allowing assignment of a mark along with transfer of the portion of the business within the country that manufactures or sells the subject goods (Article 6*quater*). The Convention establishes the "telle quelle" or "as is" rule, providing that marks must be accepted for registration in the same form as registered in the country of origin (Article 6*quinquies*). It provides that countries must protect "service marks", but does not require that they be subject to registration (Article 6*sexies*). The Convention includes an undertaking to protect "collective marks" (Article 7*bis*) and "trade names" (Article 8). It includes an obligation on countries to seize infringing goods, either on importation or approximate thereto (Article 9), and a provision requiring similar remedies with respect to goods bearing false indication of source (Article 10). The Convention requires countries to protect against "unfair competition " (Article 10*bis*), which includes acts of a nature to create confusion concerning the goods of a competitor, and to provide appropriate legal remedies to nationals of other countries (as well as associations) to effectively repress the acts referred to in Articles 9, 10 and 10*bis* (Article 10*ter*).

2.1.2 The GATT 1947

The GATT 1947 included several provisions addressing trademarks. Article XII:3 (c)(iii) required that in the application of balance of payment measures, Contracting Parties would not "prevent compliance with patent, trade mark, copyright, or similar procedures". Article XVIII, Section B(10), providing safeguard flexibility for low income countries, similarly precluded interference with trademark procedures. Article XX, General Exceptions, permits measures:

> "(d) necessary to secure compliance with laws or regulations which are not inconsistent with the provisions of this Agreement, including those relating to . . . the protection of . . . trade marks, and the prevention of deceptive practices."

As discussed in Chapter 15, Article IX addresses "marks of origin" that, however, are different than trademarks.[235]

2.1.3 The Nice Agreement

The Nice Agreement Concerning the International Classification of Goods and Services for the Purposes of Registration of Marks (1957), provides a framework for designating classes of goods and services, and is in wide use.[236]

2.1.4 Regional laws

Effort at the regional level to approximate trademark law had begun in the Andean Group in the early 1970s, and the European Community adopted the First Trade Marks Directive in 1988, shortly after commencement of the Uruguay Round.

2.2 Negotiating history

Concerns among U.S. and European industry groups with trademark counterfeiting were a significant factor in the launch of the TRIPS negotiations in the Uruguay Round.[237] Although there was a dearth of hard data concerning the phenomenon, there was a wide perception within developed country industry circles that sales

---

[235] As opposed to trademarks that indicate the *producer*, marks of origin under the GATT 1947 indicate the *territorial origin* of products. Thus, they share basic features with the more refined concept of geographical indications under Articles 22–24 of TRIPS. For a detailed explanation of the differences between trademarks and geographical indications, see Chapter 15.

[236] For a list of the current Parties to the Agreement, see <http://www.wipo.org/treaties/documents/english/pdf/i-nice.pdf>.

[237] On the original motivations to negotiate the TRIPS Agreement, see *Intellectual Property Rights: Implications for Development*, Policy Discussion Paper, UNCTAD-ICTSD, Geneva, 2003, p. 44 et seq. ("The emergence of TRIPS") (also available at <http://www.ictsd.org/iprsonline/unctadictsd/projectoutputs.htm#policy>) [hereinafter Policy Paper].

and profits, particularly in developing countries, were being eroded by such misappropriation.

2.2.1 Tokyo Round developments

Towards the end of the Tokyo Round, the United States floated a proposal for an Anti-Counterfeiting Code, though this proposal was not actively pursued.[238] A Ministerial Declaration adopted 29 November 1982 included a Decision on Trade in Counterfeit Goods that instructed the GATT Council to "examine the question of counterfeit goods with a view to determining the appropriateness of joint action in the GATT framework on trade aspects of commercial counterfeiting and, if such action is found to be appropriate, the modalities of such action." At the 40th Session of the Contracting Parties, in November 1984, a Group of Experts on Trade in Counterfeit Goods was convened to examine the issue. The Group met on six occasions in 1985, tabling its report on 9 October 1985. The report observed that:

"(a) while all intellectual property rights were affected, goods bearing protected trade marks were more directly affected;

(b) a growing problem of trade in counterfeit goods existed;

(c) existing provisions in international law [...] particularly the Paris Convention were very useful yet insufficient instruments to prevent trade in counterfeit goods....

...

(f) any measures taken to prevent trade in counterfeit goods should not become an obstacle to trade in genuine goods."

2.2.2 The 1987 U.S. proposal

The 1987 United States Proposal for Negotiations on Trade-Related Aspects of Intellectual Property Rights addressed trademarks as follows:

"Trademarks

A trademark should consist of any word, symbol, design or device, including any distinctively shaped three-dimensional object, except the generic name of the goods and services or words descriptive thereof. The term trademark should include service mark.

Exclusive rights to a trademark should derive from use or registration. Well-known marks should be protected. Trademarks which offend national symbols, policies or sensibilities should not give rise to exclusive rights.

Systems for registration of trademarks and service marks should be provided on equal terms and at reasonable costs. Owners of marks identical or confusingly similar to a mark for which registration is sought should be given the opportunity to challenge promptly such registration.

Trademarks should be registered for no less than 5 years and should be renewable indefinitely for similar terms. The trademark right should lapse if the trademark has not been used for a period of years and no special circumstances can be shown

---

[238] Frederick M. Abbott, *Protecting First World Assets in the Third World: Intellectual Property Negotiations in the GATT Multilateral Framework*, 22 Vand. J. Transnat'l L. 689 (1989).

to justify such non-use. The use of a trademark should not be encumbered by any special requirements.

Licensing of trademarks, with provision for adequate compensation for the licensor, should be permitted. No compulsory licensing of trademarks shall be permitted Assignments of trademarks should not be unnecessarily encumbered."[239]

2.2.3 The 1988 EC proposal

The European Communities' 1988 submission of Guidelines and Objectives Proposed by the European Community for the Negotiations on Trade Related Aspects of Substantive Standards of Intellectual Property Rights said:

"D.3.b. trademarks

(i) The registration of a trademark shall confer on the proprietor exclusive rights therein. The proprietor shall be entitled to prevent all third parties not having his consent from using in the course of trade identical or similar signs for goods or services which are identical or similar to those for which the trademark is registered. In case of the use of an identical sign for identical goods or services, a likelihood of confusion shall not be required.

Protection shall, as far as possible, also extend under trademark law or other law to the use in the course of trade of any sign which is identical with, or similar to, the trademark in relation to goods or services which are not similar to those for which the trademark is registered, where the latter has a reputation and where use of that sign without due cause takes unfair advantage of or is detrimental to the distinctive character or the repute of the trademark.

Limited exceptions to the exclusive rights conferred by a trademark, which take account of the legitimate interests of the proprietor of the trademark and of third parties, may be made, such as fair use of descriptive terms and exhaustion of rights. The term trademarks shall include service marks and collective marks

(ii) Protection shall be granted for any signs capable of being represented graphically, particularly words, including personal names, designs, letters, numerals, the shape of goods or of their packaging, provided that such signs are capable of distinguishing the goods or services of one undertaking from those of other undertakings Protection shall, in particular, be denied to marks which are (i) devoid of any distinctive character, (ii) contrary to public policy or to accepted principles of morality, (iii) of such a nature as to deceive the public, for instance as to the nature, quality or geographical origin of the goods or services, and (iv) in conflict with earlier rights.

(iii) A trademark right may be acquired by registration or by use, in particular by use resulting in a reputation of the trademark. A system for the registration of trademarks shall be maintained. Use of a trademark prior to registration shall not be a condition for registration.

(iv) Registration of a trademark may be renewed indefinitely.

(v) If use of a registered mark is required to maintain trademark rights, the registration may be cancelled only after an uninterrupted period of at least five

---

[239] Suggestion by the United States for Achieving the Negotiating Objective dated 19 Oct. 1987, MTN.GNG/NG11/W/14, 20 Nov. 1987, at Annex.

years of non-use, unless legitimate reasons for non-use exist. Circumstances arising independently of the will of the proprietor of a trademark which constitute a
serious obstacle to the use of the mark (such as e.g. import restrictions on products protected by the trademark) are sufficient to constitute legitimate reasons for
non-use.

The compulsory licensing of trademarks shall not be permitted. Trademarks may
be transferred with or without the transfer of the undertaking to which they belong."[240]

The EC had introduced a number of concepts not found in the U.S. proposal. These
included exceptions for fair use and exhaustion of rights, and the possibility for
"naked" transfers (that is, transfers unaccompanied by assets of the business), as
well as explicit recognition that use of a trademark should not be a precondition
for registration.

2.2.4 The 1989 Brazilian proposal

In December 1989, Brazil made the following proposal on trademarks:

"TRADEMARKS

(a) Definition

31. Protection should be granted to distinctive signs, such as names, words, denominations, monograms, emblems, and symbols which allow the differentiation
of goods and services for commercial purposes.

32. A trademark should also enable the distinction between the goods or services
of two undertakings and assure quality to the consumer.

33. Those signs which contain some elements that form part of an existing registration or conflicts therewith or are prohibited by law or by the Paris Convention
shall not be registerable as trademarks.

(b) Derivation of rights

34. Protection for trademarks should derive from registration. The use of a trademark should not be a pre-requisite for registration.

(c) Rights conferred

33. The registration of a trademark shall confer on the owner exclusive rights
therein.

36. The use, reproduction, manufacturing and non-authorised imitation by third
parties, which would result in error or confusion, should be considered as a violation of the rights conferred to trademark owners.

(d) Protection of well-known marks

37. Protection should be provided for trademarks which are well-known in the
country where such protection is granted. For that purpose, countries should examine the adoption of internal rules of protection, according to their interests and
needs. Such rules may establish, for example, that well-known trademarks should
be given protection in all classes and be kept on a special register so as to prevent
the registration of another mark which reproduces or imitates the well-known

---

[240] MTN.GNG/NG11/W/26, 7 July 1988.

mark, when confusion may arise as to the origin of-the goods or services or when the reputation-of the well-known mark is damaged.

38. It is incumbent on the owner of the mark to have recourse to means provided in domestic legislation against violation of well-known marks.

(e) Exceptions to rights conferred

39. Exceptions to rights conferred by a mark, which take account of rights of third parties as well as of public interest, should be allowed. The principle of international exhaustion of rights should be applied in the case of parallel imports.

(f) National registration systems

40. Countries should maintain a system for the registration of marks, with a view to administering existing trademark rights under conditions of fullest possible transparency. Such system should include provisions allowing third parties to raise objections to the granting of a registration, among other procedures which permit the safeguarding of rights of third parties in the country, the enforcement of law, as well as facilitate the administrative control by interested third parties of the local use of marks, including well-known marks.

(g) Term of protection

41. The term of protection as well as the conditions for renewal of registration should be defined by national legislations.

(h) Use requirements

42. National legislations which establish compulsory use of a mark should include provisions for forfeiture of a mark due to non-use or interrupted use, after a reasonable period of time and in cases where the owner does not present valid justifications. –

43. National legislations could establish the following criteria for the use of a mark: (i) a licensing agreement per se is not an evidence of the use of a mark; (ii) evidence of use by third parties requires the registration with the relevant government authority of the licence granted by the owner of the mark.

(i) Licensing and assignment

44. National legislations should be able to establish the terms and conditions for the assignment of a mark.

(j) Non-discriminatory treatment

45. The principle of national treatment, as contained in the Paris Convention, should be strictly observed by national legislations.

(k) Obligations of trademark owners

45. In order to avoid abuse, trademark owners should have the following obligations:

(i) to use a mark in the host country lest the registration of the mark be declared forfeited;

(ii) to avoid anti-competitive use of a mark;

(iii) to avoid engaging in restrictive business practices in connection with licensing agreements, such as tied purchases of inputs, prohibition or restrictions on exports from the host country; restrictions on the use after the expiry of an agreement; and others;

(iv) contribute to the transfer of technology to the host country through transparent and more favourable licensing agreement conditions.

47. Participants assume the obligation to control and punish national trademark owners which engage in restrictive business practices adversely affecting the rights of third parties."[241]

2.2.5 A 1990 developing country joint proposal

A 14 May 1990 submission of Argentina, Brazil, Chile, China, Colombia, Cuba, Egypt, India, Nigeria, Peru, Tanzania and Uruguay included the following with respect to trademarks:

"Article 7: Marks

(1) Parties shall provide protection for trademarks and service marks registered in their territories in compliance with the formalities and requirements laid down in their respective national legislation.

(2) The registration of a trademark or a service mark shall confer upon its registered owner the right to preclude others from the use of the mark or a similar mark for goods or services which are identical or similar to those in respect of which the registration was granted where such use would result in a likelihood of confusion. Rights shall be subject to exhaustion if the trademark goods or services are marketed by or with the consent of the owner in the territories of the Parties to the present Agreement.

(3) It shall be a matter for national legislation to determine the conditions for the use of a mark as well as the duration of the protection granted."[242]

This proposal called for a uniform rule of international exhaustion of trademark rights, and would have left to each Contracting Party the duration of protection.

2.2.6 The Anell Draft

The consolidated text of Chairman Anell (June 1990) included the following provision on the subject of trademarks (identified by "A" as developed and "B" as developing country proposals):

"SECTION 2: TRADEMARKS

1. Protectable Subject Matter

1A.1 A trademark is a sign capable of distinguishing goods or services of one undertaking from those of other undertakings. It may in particular consist of words and personal names, letters, numerals, the shape of goods and of their packaging, combinations of colours, other graphical representations, or any combination of such signs.

1A.2 Trademarks which are:

(i) devoid of any distinctive character;

(ii) of such a nature as to deceive the public, for instance as to the nature, quality or geographical origin of the goods or services; or

---

[241] MTN.GNG/NG11/W/57, 11 Dec. 1989.
[242] MTN.GNG/NG11/W/71, 14 May 1990.

(iii) in conflict with earlier rights,

[shall not be protected] [cannot be validly registered]. Protection may also be denied in particular to trademarks contrary to morality or public order.

1A.3 The term "trademark" shall include service marks, as well as collective [and] [or] certification marks.

1B PARTIES shall provide protection for trademarks and service marks registered in their territories in compliance with the formalities and requirements laid down in their respective national legislation.

2. Acquisition of the Right and Procedures

2A.1 PARTIES shall enable the right to a trademark to be acquired by registration or by use. For the acquisition of the right to a trademark by use, a PARTY may require that the trademark is well-known among consumers or traders of the PARTY.

2A.2 A system for the registration of trademarks shall be provided. The nature of the goods [or services] to which a trademark is to be applied shall in no case form an obstacle to registration of the trademark.

2A.3 [[Actual] use of a trademark prior to [the application for] registration shall not be a condition for registration.] [Use of a trademark may be required as a prerequisite for registration.]

2A.4 PARTIES are encouraged to participate in a system for the international registration of trademarks.

2A.5 PARTIES shall publish each trademark either before it is registered or promptly after it is registered and shall afford other parties a reasonable opportunity to petition to cancel the registration. In addition, PARTIES may afford an opportunity for other parties to oppose the registration of a trademark.

2B Parties shall provide protection for trademarks and service marks registered in their territories in compliance with the formalities and requirements incorporated or laid down in their respective national law.

3. Rights Conferred

3.1 [The owner of a registered trademark shall have exclusive rights therein.] The owner of a registered trademark [or service mark] shall be entitled to prevent all third parties not having his consent from using in the course of trade identical or similar signs for goods or services which are identical or similar to those in respect of which the trademark registration has been granted [where such use would result in a likelihood of confusion.] [However, in case of the use of an identical sign for identical goods or services, a likelihood of confusion shall be presumed.]

3.2A Protection for registered or unregistered trademarks shall extend under trademark law or other law to the use in the course of trade of any sign which is identical with, or similar to, the trademark in relation to goods or services which are not similar to those in respect of which the right to the trademark has been acquired, where the latter has a reputation and where use of that sign without due cause takes unfair advantage of, or is detrimental to, the distinctive character or the repute of the trademark.

3.3A PARTIES shall refuse to register or shall cancel the registration and prohibit use of a trademark likely to cause confusion with a trademark of another which is considered to be well-known [in that country]. [This protection shall be extended inter alia against the use of such marks for goods or services which are dissimilar to original goods or services.] [In determining whether a trademark is well-known, the extent of the trademark's use and promotion in international trade must be taken into consideration. A PARTY may not require that the reputation extend beyond the sector of the public which normally deals with the relevant products or services.]

3.4A The owner of a trademark shall be entitled to take action against any unauthorised use which constitutes an act of unfair competition.

4. Exceptions

4A Limited exceptions to the exclusive rights conferred by a trademark, such as fair use of descriptive terms, may be made, provided that they take account of the legitimate interests of the proprietor of the trademark and of third parties.

4B Rights shall be subject to exhaustion if the trademarked goods or services are marketed by or with the consent of the owner in the territories of the PARTIES.

5. Term of Protection

5A Initial registration of a trademark shall be for a term of no less than ten years. The registration of a trademark shall be renewable indefinitely.

5B It shall be a matter for national legislation to determine the duration of the protection granted.

6. Requirement of Use

6.1 If use of a registered trademark is required to maintain the right to a trademark, the registration may be cancelled only after [an uninterrupted period of at least [five years] [three years]] [a reasonable period] of non-use, unless valid reasons based on the existence of obstacles to such use are shown by the trademark owner.

6.2A Use of the trademark by another person with the consent of the owner shall be recognized as use of the trademark for the purpose of maintaining the registration.

6.3A Valid reasons for non-use shall include non-use due to circumstances arising independently of the will of the proprietor of a trademark which constitute an obstacle to the use of the trademark, such as import restrictions on or other governmental requirements for products protected by the trademark.

7. Other Requirements

7A The use of a trademark in commerce shall not be [unjustifiably] encumbered by special requirements, such as use with another trademark, a use requirement which reduces the function of the trademark as an indication of source, [or use in a special form].

7B It shall be a matter for national legislation to determine the conditions for the use of a mark.

8. Licensing and Compulsory Licensing

8A Compulsory licensing of trademarks shall not be permitted.

8B It will be a matter for national legislation to determine the conditions for the use of a mark. (See also Section 8)

9. Assignment

9A The right to a [registered] trademark may be assigned with or without the transfer of the undertaking to which the trademark belongs. [PARTIES may require that the goodwill to which the trademark belongs be transferred with the right to the trademark.] [PARTIES may prohibit the assignment of a registered trademark which is identical with, or similar to, a famous mark indicating a state or a local public entity or an agency thereof or a non-profit organisation or enterprise working in the public interest.]

9B It will be a matter for national legislation to determine the conditions for the use or assignment of a mark. (See also Section 8 below)"[243]

The position of developing country Members included demands for international exhaustion of trademarks and national determinations regarding the duration of protection. In addition, developing country Members wanted to preserve the right to determine the conditions of use of marks. Trademarks are defined at this stage to include service marks. Among the developed country proposals, there was question whether use could be retained as a pre-condition of registration. A specific provision acknowledging fair use was included, although limitations were introduced.

2.2.7 The Brussels Draft

The Brussels Ministerial Text of December 1990 follows. At that stage, the Chairman's Commentary that accompanied the text said regarding trademarks "In Section 2 of Part II on Trademarks, there is an outstanding issue concerning special requirements regarding the use of a mark (Article 22)."[244]

"SECTION 2: TRADEMARKS

Article 17: Protectable Subject Matter

1. Any sign, or any combination of signs, capable of distinguishing the goods or services of one undertaking from those of other undertakings, shall be capable of constituting a trademark. Such signs, in particular words including personal names, letters, numerals, figurative elements and combinations of colours as well as any combination of such signs, shall be eligible for registration as trademarks. Where signs are not inherently capable of distinguishing the relevant goods or services, PARTIES may make registrability depend on distinctiveness acquired through use. PARTIES may require, as a condition of registration, that signs be capable of graphical representation.

2. Paragraph 1 above shall not be understood to prevent a PARTY from denying registration of a trademark on other grounds, provided that they do not derogate from the provisions of the Paris Convention (1967).

3. PARTIES may make registrability depend on use. However, actual use of a trademark shall not be a condition for filing an application for registration. An application shall not be refused solely on the ground that intended use has not taken place before the expiry of a period of 3 years from the date of application.

---

[243] MTN.GNG/NG11/W/76, 23 July 1990.
[244] MTN.TNC/W/35/Rev.1, 3 Dec. 1990.

4. The nature of the goods or services to which a trademark is to be applied shall in no case form an obstacle to registration of the trademark.

5. PARTIES shall publish each trademark either before it is registered or promptly after it is registered and shall afford a reasonable opportunity for petitions to cancel the registration. In addition, PARTIES may afford an opportunity for the registration of a trademark to be opposed.

Article 18: Rights Conferred

1. The owner of a registered trademark shall have the exclusive right to prevent all third parties not having his consent from using in the course of trade identical or similar signs for goods or services which are identical or similar to those in respect of which the trademark is registered where such use would result in a likelihood of confusion. In case of the use of an identical sign for identical goods or services, a likelihood of confusion shall be presumed.

2. Article 6bis of the Paris Convention shall apply, mutatis mutandis, to services. In determining whether a trademark is well-known, account shall be taken of the knowledge of the trademark in the relevant sector of the public including knowledge in that PARTY obtained as a result of the promotion of the trademark in international trade.

3. Article 6bis of the Paris Convention shall apply, mutatis mutandis, to goods or services which are not similar to those in respect of which a trademark is registered, provided that use of that trademark in relation to those goods or services would unfairly indicate a connection between those goods or services and the owner of the registered trademark.

Article 19: Exceptions

PARTIES may provide limited exceptions to the rights conferred by a trademark, such as fair use of descriptive terms, provided that such exceptions take account of the legitimate interests of the owner of the trademark and of third parties.

Article 20: Term of Protection

Initial registration, and each renewal of registration, of a trademark shall be for a term of no less than seven years. The registration of a trademark shall be renewable indefinitely.

Article 21: Requirement of Use

1. If use is required to maintain a registration, the registration may be cancelled only after an uninterrupted period of at least three years of non-use, unless valid reasons based on the existence of obstacles to such use are shown by the trademark owner. Circumstances arising independently of the will of the owner of the trademark which constitute an obstacle to the use of the trademark, such as import restrictions on or other government requirements for goods or services protected by the trademark, shall be recognised as valid reasons for non-use.

2. When subject to the control of its owner, use of a trademark by another person shall be recognised as use of the trademark for the purpose of maintaining the registration.

Article 22: Other Requirements

A. The use of a trademark in commerce shall not be unjustifiably encumbered by special requirements, such as use with another trademark, use in a special form or use in a manner detrimental to its capability to distinguish the goods or services of one undertaking from those of other undertakings.

B. It shall be a matter for national legislation to determine the conditions for the use of a mark.

Article 23: Licensing and Assignment

PARTIES may determine conditions on the licensing and assignment of trademarks, it being understood that the compulsory licensing of trademarks shall not be permitted and that the owner of a registered trademark shall have the right to assign his trademark with or without the transfer of the business to which the trademark belongs."[245]

It is rather interesting to note that only under the Brussels Draft a more detailed treatment of well-known marks was introduced. These rules represented a fairly substantial innovation in the law of trademarks. The duration of the mark is now recognized as indefinite. Renewals are now set with a minimum term of seven years. Reference to exhaustion has been moved to the more generally applicable Article 6. As noted by the Chairman, differences remain over conditions on the use of marks.

2.2.8 The Dunkel Draft

There was no material difference between the Dunkel Draft text (20 December 1991) and the final TRIPS Agreement text with respect to Articles 15–21.

3. Possible interpretations

3.1 Article 15

3.1.1 Article 15.1: definition

Article 15:   Protectable Subject Matter

1. Any sign, or any combination of signs, capable of distinguishing the goods or services of one undertaking from those of other undertakings, shall be capable of constituting a trademark. Such signs, in particular words including personal names, letters, numerals, figurative elements and combinations of colours as well as any combination of such signs, shall be eligible for registration as trademarks. Where signs are not inherently capable of distinguishing the relevant goods or services, Members may make registrability depend on distinctiveness acquired through use. Members may require, as a condition of registration, that signs be visually perceptible.

The definition of the subject matter of trademark protection, while relatively brief, carries with it a great deal of content. The first sentence indicates that "any sign" ... "shall be capable of constituting a trademark". This definition would include anything perceptible to a human being that could serve as a signalling device,

---

[245] MTN.TNC/W/35/Rev.1, 3 Dec. 1990.

including not only visually perceptible words and designs, but also sounds, scents, tastes and textures. In fact, sounds and scents have been determined to qualify for trademark protection in a number of jurisdictions, and the first sentence of Article 15.1 does not exclude this. However, the second sentence says that "in particular" the listed subject matter "shall be eligible for registration as trademarks" (i.e., "personal names, letters, numerals, figurative elements and combinations of colours as well as any combination of such signs"). The list does not include signs that are not visually perceptible. It also limits the reference to colours to "combinations", whereas single colours have in some jurisdictions been held to qualify for trademark protection. The fourth sentence permits Members to condition registration on visual perceptibility.[246] This now makes clear that sounds, scents, tastes and textures need not be accorded protection, even though they may well qualify as "signs". Thus the broad reference of the first sentence is intended to permit Members to adopt an extensive scope of trademark subject matter protection, the second sentence is intended to set out a list of obligatory subject matter and the fourth sentence permits the exclusion of certain subject matter.

It was earlier observed that the function of the trademark is not entirely settled. Traditionally, it is well accepted that trademarks serve the function of identifying the source of goods. A can of soda, for example, with the well-known trademark "Coca-Cola" is the product of the Coca-Cola Company. Yet source identification is not the only potential function of the trademark, and the traditionally accepted "source identification" function to some extent has been diluted by the express provisions of TRIPS.

In addition to source identification, the trademark may also serve to protect the so-called "goodwill" of an enterprise. In a trademark sense, the term "goodwill" is used to capture an intangible: the reputation of an enterprise that it has built up.[247] This reputation is not earned solely by the quality or other characteristics of products placed on the market. A business may specifically invest in the reputation of its products or services without in fact doing anything to modify or improve them. This is investment in advertising or promotion that is intended to give consumers a certain impression of the products or services, even if they have never purchased them. It is artificially created reputation. To the producer there is a real financial value to advertising and promotion. There is also a potential economic and social cost. Consumers may be encouraged to purchase products they do not need, and may purchase products of inferior quality as a result of advertising.

Should trademark law protect the investment of enterprises in promoting their goods and services, even if that investment is not directly correlated to the quality or other characteristics of the goods and services? While this may seem an esoteric question, the answer may have quite significant implications for trademark litigation, both in terms of the capability of an enterprise to enforce a mark against an alleged infringer, and in terms of remedies (including damages). If a

---

[246] On the question of visual perceptibility or graphic representability of *olfactory signs*, see the approach taken under EC law, below, Section 6.3.1.

[247] The term "goodwill" also has a financial accounting meaning, generally referring to the difference between the value of a company's hard assets and its market value (or the premium a buyer may be willing to pay over its hard asset value).

third party is understood to contravene the rights of the trademark holder only by misrepresenting the source of goods or services, this might permit the third party to avoid infringement by clearly indicating the true source of its goods or services, even if the trademark is referenced by it on the goods (or, for example, in comparative advertisement). If, on the other hand, a third party is understood to contravene the rights of the trademark owner by taking advantage of its goodwill, then any reference to the mark may be sufficient to give the third party a reputation benefit (that is, by attracting the attention of consumers), even if the true source of the goods or services is clear. This effectively lowers the threshold for infringement. Moreover, when calculating damages, there may be a significant difference between determining injury based on consumer confusion as to the true source of goods, and determining injury based on the effect on the trademark owner's goodwill.

Article 15.1 provides that trademarks are signs "capable of distinguishing the goods or services of one undertaking from those of other undertakings". A sign that allows consumers to distinguish or differentiate among undertakings is not the same thing as a sign that identifies a particular undertaking as the source of goods or services. Article 15.1, first sentence, does not require that the consumer be able to identify the specific source of the goods or services. The consumer should be able to determine that goods or services identified by the mark are distinct from other goods or services.[248]

It is doubtful that the text of Article 15.1, first sentence, lays to rest the question whether trademark protection must extend to goodwill as an essential feature, in addition to providing protection for source identification. On the other hand, Article 15.1, first sentence, appears to allow Members to extend trademark protection to goodwill.

Article 15.1 specifically refers to signs distinguishing "services" as being subject to registration. This is a significant change from Article 6*sexies* of the Paris Convention that requires states to provide protection for service marks, but does not mandate that they be subject to registration.[249] However, it is doubtful that inclusion of a registration requirement for service marks engendered a significant change in the practice of Members since most would have permitted the registration of service marks prior to the conclusion of TRIPS. Just as the subject matter of "services" is not defined in the General Agreement on Trade in Services (GATS), it is not defined in TRIPS.

The third sentence of Article 15.1 provides that "Where signs are not inherently capable of distinguishing the relevant goods or services, Members may make registrability depend on distinctiveness acquired through use." Trademarks are generally understood to fall into the following categories. "Arbitrary" or "fanciful" marks, such as "Exxon", have no inherent meaning. They are created by the enterprises that use them. "Suggestive" marks may have a meaning in common

---

[248] For example, Article 15.1 does not require that soda carrying the Coca-Cola trademark is manufactured by the Coca-Cola Company. It requires only that consumers are able to distinguish Coca-Cola from Pepsi and other cola products.

[249] "Article 6sexies Marks: Service Marks

The countries of the Union undertake to protect service marks. They shall not be required to provide for the registration of such marks." (Paris Convention)

language, but the common meaning is not ordinarily associated with the goods or services. Thus "Sunrise", for example, has a common meaning with reference to a planetary phenomenon. Yet "Sunrise" can be used in connection with marketing a dishwashing liquid to suggest light and cleanliness. It is a suggestive mark. "Descriptive" marks rely on the common meaning of terms to identify the goods or services. In their common meaning, the terms do not identify or distinguish between undertakings. Consider, for example, "General Electric" for electrical appliances, or "Volkswagen" (i.e., "people's car") for automobiles. In both cases, the words used to form the mark convey a meaning that, even if somewhat indirectly, describe the goods of the business. Trademark law generally permits descriptive terms to acquire trademark status, but in many jurisdictions this depends on the terms having achieved a certain level of recognition among consumers as associating goods or services with an enterprise. This is what Article 15.1, third sentence, means when it refers to "distinctiveness acquired through use." Thus, Members may condition registration of "descriptive" marks on their having achieved some level of distinctiveness in the minds of consumers. The tests for when sufficient recognition has been achieved vary among countries.[250]

3.1.2 Article 15.2

> 2. Paragraph 1 shall not be understood to prevent a Member from denying registration of a trademark on other grounds, provided that they do not derogate from the provisions of the Paris Convention (1967).

A Member might elect to refuse registration of a trademark on grounds other than that it does not distinguish the goods or services of an undertaking. For example, in the *U.S. – Havana Club* case decided by the WTO Appellate Body (AB), the United States had refused to register a mark on grounds that the party claiming ownership of the mark was not its rightful owner. The U.S. refusal was upheld by the AB as being within U.S. discretion to make determinations regarding the lawful holders of marks.[251]

Article *6quinquies* of the Paris Convention, which was at issue in the *U.S. – Havana Club* case, obliges Members to accept marks for registration in the same form ("as is", or *telle quelle*") as registered in the country of origin. This rule was designed to prevent trademark registration authorities from requiring translations or other adaptations of marks to meet local preferences or rules. Under Article 15.2, a Member must comply with the "as is" obligation, and in that way it may not derogate from the Paris Convention. There are exceptions even to the "as is"

---

[250] It should be noted that "generic" terms may not serve as trademarks for the goods they identify. A "generic" term is that which is used for a type or class (a "genus") of products or services, such as "bed" or "car". So, a maker of beds could not use "bed" standing alone as its trademark. However, generic terms sometimes form part of combination term trademarks, and can be protected only as used in the combination. Moreover, a generic term may be used in its non-generic sense as a trademark, *e.g.*, "Apple" for computers.

[251] The *U.S. – Havana Club* decision of the AB is discussed in detail, *infra* at Section 4.1.

obligation. That is, Article 6*quinquies*, Paris Convention, recognizes certain bases even for refusing to accept the same form of the mark. These are:

"B. . . . 1. when they are of such a nature as to infringe rights acquired by third parties in the country where protection is claimed;

2. when they are devoid of any distinctive character, or consist exclusively of signs or indications which may serve, in trade, to designate the kind, quality, quantity, intended purpose, value, place of origin, of the goods, or the time of production, or have become customary in the current language or in the bona fide and established practices of the trade of the country where protection is claimed;

3. when they are contrary to morality or public order and, in particular, of such a nature as to deceive the public. It is understood that a mark may not be considered contrary to public order for the sole reason that it does not conform to a provision of the legislation on marks, except if such provision itself relates to public order. This provision is subject, however, to the application of Article 10*bis*."

The Paris Convention enumerates other bases on which the registration of trademarks may be denied (Article 6*bis* and 6*ter*). Article 6*bis* establishes an obligation to refuse third party registration of well-known marks. Treatment of well-known marks is addressed in Subsection 3.2.2 below. Article 6*ter* creates obligations to refuse trademark registration for state flags and symbols.

3.1.3 Article 15.3: use of trademarks

> 3. Members may make registrability depend on use. However, actual use of a trademark shall not be a condition for filing an application for registration. An application shall not be refused solely on the ground that intended use has not taken place before the expiry of a period of three years from the date of application.

Trademark protection originated as a form of unfair competition law. The tort of "passing off" in Commonwealth jurisdictions evolved to address claims of taking unfair advantage of another person's trademark or business name. This cause of action did not depend on the registration of a mark. The concept is broader than trademark infringement, and could encompass misuse of trade names as well as other distinctive characteristics of a business. It was and remains the subject matter of common law.[252] Protection of trademarks developed in the United States as a part of the law of unfair competition. Although trademarks long ago came to benefit from registration in the Commonwealth and U.S. legal systems, there remains the possibility to establish and enforce "common law" trademarks from use in commerce.

Before TRIPS was negotiated, the United States required use of a trademark in commerce as a precondition to federal registration. This precondition was intended to assure that trademarks were associated only with real goods or services.

---

[252] On the common law doctrine of "passing off", see W.R. Cornish, *Intellectual Property: Patents, Copyright, Trade Marks and Allied Rights* (4th ed. 1999), at Chapter 16.

Among other objectives, this would avoid a proliferation of unused marks on the records of the Patent and Trademark Office (USPTO). The use precondition also served as a reward to business enterprises that acted swiftly to put their goods and services on the market.

However, even without the complications that this use-based registration system created at the international level (since there was a basic incompatibility with most other countries that allowed registration without use), the precondition came to be seen as an impediment to more modern marketing strategies that involved the advertisement to the public of new goods and services before they were actually placed on the market. If use were a precondition for registration, business enterprises would face risks by advertising in advance of product and service introduction. Other businesses might actually use a mark on a good or service before the enterprise advertising it placed its own good or service on the market.

The USA moved to a modified use-based registration during the Uruguay Round as the advantages of a more globally-integrated trademark registration system became apparent to U.S. businesses. A Madrid Protocol-based registration system (administered by WIPO) could be employed to reduce registration inefficiencies, and some of the domestic difficulties that the use-based system presented for marketing strategies could be overcome. The U.S. system remains grounded in "use" as a condition of registration, but it is now acceptable to file for registration declaring "intent to use" a mark, and subsequently filing within a prescribed period a verification that the mark has actually been used in commerce.[253] Formal registration of the mark does not occur until the applicant submits verification of actual use to the USPTO. In the meantime, the applicant benefits from priority "constructive use" of the mark that in effect precludes a third party from acquiring competing federal trademark rights during the intent-to-use period, and also allows infringement claims based on that constructive use.[254]

Article 15.3, third sentence, provides that registration may not be denied during a three-year application period solely on the grounds of non-use. This in effect requires that a form of priority be established for unused marks included in filed applications since for a period of three years the mark should be treated (for application purposes) as if it is being used. However, this does not appear to require that an applicant be given rights as against an alleged infringer of an unused mark during the "priority" period since it refers only to the ultimate grant of registration, not to the interim period. It is for each Member to determine the effect of an application under national law. Article 4 of the Paris Convention provides a six-month right of priority in respect to the filing of trademark applications outside the country of first application. This prevents the intervening use of a mark or filing of an application from interfering with the rights of the priority holder.

---

[253] See 15 U.S.C. §1051(b)–(d). The prescribed period for filing a verification of use is within six months of a "notice of allowance", extendable by an additional 24 months. Because a notice of allowance is issued after examination, period for response, publication and an opposition period, it is very doubtful that registration would be denied for non-use within the three-year period prescribed by Article 15.3, TRIPS Agreement.

[254] See 15 U.S.C. §1057(c). The benefits of "constructive use" do not arise until registration is granted, but can be applied with retroactive effect.

Article 15.3 accommodates the U.S.-style registration system that continues to require use as a precondition to completion of registration, but permits an application to be filed prior to actual use. It is of interest that non-use cannot be the sole grounds for refusing registration during a three-year period, but otherwise the effects of an application are not stated.

3.1.4 Article 15.4

> 4. The nature of the goods or services to which a trademark is to be applied shall in no case form an obstacle to registration of the trademark.

Article 15.4 essentially restates Article 7 of the Paris Convention, adding express reference to service marks.[255] As noted elsewhere in this book, IPRs are not market access rights. The fact that Article 15.4 states that trademark registration must be granted in connection with all kinds of goods and services does not require that a Member allow such goods and services to be sold.

Article 6*quinquies* of the Paris Convention ("as is" or "*telle quelle*") permits trademark registration to be refused on grounds that the mark is "contrary to morality or public order and, in particular, of such a nature as to deceive the public". Note that reference is to the mark itself, and not to associated goods or services.

The question of morality or public order might arise in connection with goods such as cigarettes that are known to be harmful to health, the advertising or sale of which Members might choose to heavily regulate or even ban. Article 15.4 suggests that a mark used in connection with, for example, cigarettes may not be refused registration because of the product with which it is associated. This appears to create a tension with Article 6*quinquies* that permits refusal of registration of a mark on morality and public order grounds. This apparent tension might be resolved by interpreting Article 6*quinquies* to be limited to refusals for signs or symbols that are offensive "as such". Yet this is a difficult line to draw since a sign or symbol inherently acts to draw (or stimulate) a connection in the public mind to some good, service, activity or belief. A Member might argue that it is entitled to block the registration of a mark used on cigarettes not because of the product, but because promotion of the mark itself has adverse consequences for the public; that is, the mark "as such" is injurious to public order because it encourages a type of behaviour known to cause serious injury (and the behaviour is not linked or limited to the products of a particular enterprise). Whether or not this argument is persuasive, the critical point from a public policy perspective is that allowing registration of a trademark or service mark does not impair the government's authority to regulate the product associated with the mark. Even if a Member must allow registration of trademarks for cigarettes, it may ban (or limit) the sale of the cigarettes on public health grounds.

---

[255] Article 7 of the Paris Convention provides:
"The nature of the goods to which a trademark is to be applied shall in no case form an obstacle to the registration of the mark."

3.1.5 Article 15.5

> 5. Members shall publish each trademark either before it is registered or promptly after it is registered and shall afford a reasonable opportunity for petitions to cancel the registration. In addition, Members may afford an opportunity for the registration of a trademark to be opposed.

Article 15.5 addresses the procedural issues of publication, cancellation and opposition. It is fairly straightforward. Marks should be published so that third persons who may have an interest in objecting to their registration may have notice of them. Members are required to provide a procedure for seeking cancellation, and may (but need not) implement an opposition system. An opposition system would allow the prevention of registration, whereas cancellation would take place after registration.

Questions may arise regarding what types of publication satisfy the requirement. Article 15.5 does not limit publication to hard text, and presumably Internet publication would suffice. This might certainly save costs for trademark offices. Questions may also arise as to how quickly "prompt" publication must occur, and what a "reasonable opportunity" for presenting a cancellation petition is. Terms such as "prompt" and "reasonable" by definition give some leeway to the Member interpreting them. It does not seem productive to explore the potential limits of those terms here. Undoubtedly there are many variations on procedures complying with these requirements.

3.2 Article 16

3.2.1 Article 16.1: exclusive rights

> 1. The owner of a registered trademark shall have the exclusive right to prevent all third parties not having the owner's consent from using in the course of trade identical or similar signs for goods or services which are identical or similar to those in respect of which the trademark is registered where such use would result in a likelihood of confusion. In case of the use of an identical sign for identical goods or services, a likelihood of confusion shall be presumed. The rights described above shall not prejudice any existing prior rights, nor shall they affect the possibility of Members making rights available on the basis of use.

These few sentences of Article 16.1 alone can provide the subject matter for a book on the law of trademarks, and it is necessary to limit discussion here to some key elements.

The rights are attributable to owners of "registered" trademarks. Members may, but need not, protect "common law" trademarks. In the *U.S. – Havana Club* case the United States was defending its right to determine who the "owner" of the subject trademark was, as a condition predicate to determining what the rights of that owner might be.

As with other IPRs, the trademark right is a "negative right" entitling the owner to "prevent all third parties". If the owner has "consent[ed]" to use of the mark, it is no longer entitled to block its use. The owner consents to use of the mark by affixing it to a good it places on the market and it thereby authorizes third persons to resell or otherwise transfer the good. This consent underlies the principle of exhaustion of rights.

The owner's right to prevent extends to "using [the mark] in the course of trade". This implies that uses of the mark other than in the "course of trade" may not be prevented. So, for example, a newspaper article concerning a good's qualities or other characteristics that is intended to inform readers, but not to promote or discourage sales of the good (as an advertisement), might not be prevented by the mark owner as a use in the "course of trade". (Such uses are also permitted as a limited exception to trademark rights.)

The preventable use is connected with "identical or similar signs for goods or services which are identical or similar to those in respect of which the trademark is registered where such use would result in a likelihood of confusion." There is relatively little room for divergent interpretation of trademark infringement when an "identical" trademark is used without consent in the course of trade on "identical" goods or services. This is the basic case of trademark counterfeiting. The questions: (1) when are trademarks "similar", (2) when are goods or services "similar", and (3) when would "likelihood of confusion" exist, form much of the subject matter of trademark law. The basic idea is that a competitor should not be able to take advantage of the identity of the trademark owner by using a sufficiently similar sign such that consumers will be misled into believing that there is a connection between the trademark owner and the similar goods being offered by the competitor.

There are theoretically an unlimited number of signs that might be used as trademarks and to distinguish goods and services in commerce. As a practical matter the number is much more limited. Ordinary descriptive terms are often used in trademarks. There are a limited number of such terms in each language, and among those terms a more limited number is familiar to the average consumer. As a practical matter when enterprises are preparing to launch products on the market, it is not at all uncommon for them to come up with the same or similar ideas about what to call them.

The question whether two signs or trademarks are sufficiently similar such that use of one would infringe rights in the other is basically one of fact. The judge, administrator or jury must compare the two marks and determine whether they convey a similar impression. A TRIPS Agreement interpretative issue might arise if a Member decided to apply very strict standards of comparison between allegedly infringing marks such as to make it very difficult for a trademark owner to prove infringement by similar, but not identical, signs. Purely for illustrative purposes, a Member could adopt a rule under which "Coco-Cola" was not considered similar to "Coca-Cola", and allow a local producer to take advantage of the well-known mark. While the concept of *similarity* is flexible, as with many other IPRs concepts there are limits beyond which it may not be stretched.

There is an analogous issue regarding the similarity of goods or services. Is a powerboat similar to a sailboat for trademark confusion purposes? Is a refrigerator similar to an automobile? The rule of Article 16.1 is that an identical or similar mark may not be used on similar goods or services. This implies that an identical or similar mark may be used on goods that are *not* similar. The question is one of fact. The judge, administrator or jury must determine whether in the mind of the consumer there will be a sufficient connection between two goods or services such that an assumption is likely to be made that these are produced by the same enterprise.

Ultimately the question is asked whether "such use would result in a likelihood of confusion". The term "likelihood" means that there is a significant probability that consumers will in fact be confused. There is, however, no common trademark law standard as to what percentage of consumers have been or might be confused, and courts even within the same national jurisdiction may apply rather different standards. If it can be demonstrated that consumers have *in fact* been confused by purchasing a good or service assumed to be offered by one enterprise, but in reality offered by another, that typically is strong evidence of "likelihood" of confusion. However, confusion *in fact* is often difficult to prove.

There are almost certain to be significant variations among Members with respect to the standards applied in determining "likelihood of confusion". It would be difficult to set out limits to what would be considered a reasonable good faith approach, recognizing that these determinations are highly context-specific. In the final analysis, likelihood of confusion is determined by a finder of fact based on an overall impression drawn from a mix of elements. Courts have established various multi-pronged approaches that identify elements to be considered (in the USA perhaps the best known is the eight-element "Sleekcraft" analysis[256]), but even here the elements may be weighted differently depending on the setting.[257]

The second sentence of Article 16.1 provides that, "In case of the use of an identical sign for identical goods or services, a likelihood of confusion shall be presumed." This provision should facilitate the successful prosecution of infringement claims where the intent to directly take advantage of the trademark owner is evident (e.g., straightforward trademark counterfeiting). By establishing a presumption of likelihood of confusion where the signs and goods/services are identical, the burden is shifted to the alleged infringer to prove the absence of likelihood. This removes a significant evidentiary task from the trademark owner. It is, however, possible to rebut the presumption. Professor T. Cottier has noted that in cases of parallel importation (in countries following a rule of international exhaustion of trademarks), the presumption may be rebutted by showing that the goods were put on the market with the trademark owner's consent in another country.[258]

---

[256] *AMF Inc. v. Sleekcraft Boats*, 599 F.2d 341 (9th Cir. 1979).

[257] For example, whether an infringer acts with bad intent bears significant weight even though this does not directly affect the perception of the consumer.

[258] Thomas Cottier, *Das Problem der Parallelimporte im Freihandelsabkommen Schweiz-EG und im Recht der WTO-GATT*, Revue Suisse de la Propriété Intellectuelle, I/1995, 37, 53–56 [hereinafter

The third sentence of Article 16.1 refers to non-prejudice to existing prior rights. The intent of this phrase is not entirely clear. On one hand, it may refer to a rather typical situation in which two parties have used potentially conflicting trademarks within the same national territory, perhaps in different locations, and national jurisprudence has recognized that identical or similar trademarks may be used concurrently by different owners. Even if one of the trademarks is or becomes registered, the concurrent use may be allowed to continue. This concept of non-prejudice would allow prior or concurrent use rights on an ongoing basis, regardless of whether conduct pre- or post-dates TRIPS. On the other hand, the phrase might be interpreted to the effect that the rules of Article 16.1 are not intended to have an effect on trademark rights that arose prior to its entry into force, and that such uses might continue. However, similar situations would not be permitted to arise after TRIPS Agreement rules became applicable. This would in effect modify the rule of Article 70.2, establishing an obligation to extend new TRIPS Agreement rights to existing subject matter, unless otherwise provided. The third sentence of Article 16.1 was added after the Brussels Ministerial.

The second phrase of Article 16.1 ("nor shall they affect the possibility of Members making rights available on the basis of use"), is not ambiguous. It makes clear that the institution of common law trademark rights may continue in Members that choose to continue or newly adopt it. However, the rights prescribed under the first and second sentences of Article 16.1 are not automatically applicable to common law trademarks, which may enjoy a different set of rights than registered marks.

3.2.2 Article 16.2: well-known trademarks

2. Article 6bis of the Paris Convention (1967) shall apply, mutatis mutandis, to services. In determining whether a trademark is well-known, Members shall take account of the knowledge of the trademark in the relevant sector of the public, including knowledge in the Member concerned which has been obtained as a result of the promotion of the trademark.

Article 6bis of the Paris Convention addresses the subject of so-called "well-known" trademarks.[259] A special regime for such marks has the objective of

---

Cottier]. Note that these cases have to be distinguished from the above example of trademark counterfeiting: in the case of parallel imports, the identical sign originates from the same trademark holder; whereas in the case of counterfeiting, a person different from the right holder uses the latter's trademark for his own products.

[259] "Article 6bis Marks: Well-Known Marks

(1) The countries of the Union undertake, ex officio if their legislation so permits, or at the request of an interested party, to refuse or to cancel the registration, and to prohibit the use, of a trademark which constitutes a reproduction, an imitation, or a translation, liable to create confusion, of a mark considered by the competent authority of the country of registration or use to be well known in that country as being already the mark of a person entitled to the benefits of this Convention and used for identical or similar goods. These provisions shall also apply when the essential part of the mark constitutes a reproduction of any such well-known mark or an imitation liable to create confusion therewith.

providing protection for trademarks that are well known in a country as already belonging to a certain person, even though they are not, or not yet, protected in that country through a registration. In the absence of registration of the well-known mark, the conflicting mark could theoretically be registered and enforced to the detriment of the well-known mark, which would in most cases result in consumer confusion. Such practice is widely regarded as constituting an act of unfair competition,[260] thus requiring the protection of the well-known trademark.

The necessity of protection of well-known marks usually arises in new markets, i.e. in countries previously closed to foreign traders or which, through an increase in economic development become attractive for the suppliers of branded products. In those cases, the owner of the well-known, but unregistered trademark is considered as worth of protection as if she/he had actually registered the mark. This shows that registration is not considered the ultimate criterion of protection. It is considered more important that the registration of the same or a similar mark by a third person could lead to confusion of the public, who would automatically associate the registered mark with the non-registered, but well-known owner or his products.

To make clear that well-known service marks are subject to protection on the same basis as trademarks (for goods), Article 16.2, first sentence, explicitly extends the protection of Article 6*bis*, Paris Convention, to service marks.

Article 6*bis*, Paris Convention, has been understood to leave substantial uncertainty regarding the standards states should apply in determining whether a mark is well known.[261] Article 16.2, TRIPS, second sentence, addresses one aspect of that uncertainty. It establishes that the question whether a mark is well known should be determined in respect to the "relevant sector of the public". Assume, for example, that an enterprise is the leading manufacturer of sophisticated equipment used by scientific laboratories to determine the chemical composition of materials. The trademark of that enterprise might be very well known among all technical specialists in the field of chemical composition, but would likely be more or less completely unknown to the general public. Article 16.2 indicates that a mark should be considered well known based on the "relevant" sector of the public, which in such circumstances would be the technical specialists. There

(2) A period of at least five years from the date of registration shall be allowed for requesting the cancellation of such a mark. The countries of the Union may provide for a period within which the prohibition of use must be requested.

(3) No time limit shall be fixed for requesting the cancellation or the prohibition of the use of marks registered or used in bad faith."

As noted earlier, the Paris Convention differentiates between trademarks and service marks. States, for example, are not required to provide for registration of service marks. The TRIPS Agreement requires that registration be made available for service marks.

[260] See G.H.C. Bodenhausen, *Guide to the Application of the Paris Convention for the Protection of Industrial Property as revised at Stockholm in 1967*, BIRPI, Geneva, 1968, p. 90 (on Article 6*bis*, under (d)).

[261] In September 1999 WIPO members adopted a Joint Resolution setting out guidance on various aspects of well-known marks, including criteria that might be used in making determinations. See below, Subsection 6.2.2. See, e.g., *Joint Recommendation Concerning Provisions on the Protection of Well-Known Marks*, adopted by the WIPO General Assembly and the Assembly of the Paris Union, Sept. 1999.

is a risk that defining "well known" in terms of the relevant sector of the public will lead to a proliferation of well known marks. This risk can be addressed by imposing a relatively high standard regarding the degree of knowledge of the mark among the relevant sector, which possibility is within the scope of the provision.

Article 16.2, second sentence, adds to its relevant sector clarification the phrase, "including knowledge in the Member concerned which has been obtained as a result of the promotion of the trademark".[262] Ordinarily, the level of advertisement of a mark is one ground upon which knowledge among the public is evaluated by a finder of fact in determining whether a descriptive mark has acquired "secondary meaning". The TRIPS text clarifies that a mark may be well known even if it has not been used on goods and services within the Member concerned, but has become known there through advertisement. As indicated above, one of the principal reasons the Paris Convention provided special protection for well-known marks was to prevent their registration by third parties in markets that foreign mark holders had not yet entered (and to allow cancellation of registrations so obtained). Third parties would often register well-known marks and seek "ransom" from their foreign holders wanting to obtain registration in the new market. Yet Article 6bis, Paris Convention, does not explicitly address the question whether a mark should be protected even if goods were not yet placed on the market. Article 16.2, second sentence, now makes clear that having goods or services on the market in a Member is not a prerequisite to holding interests there in a well-known mark.

3.2.3 Article 16.3: well-known trademarks

> 3. Article 6bis of the Paris Convention (1967) shall apply, *mutatis mutandis*, to goods or services which are not similar to those in respect of which a trademark is registered, provided that use of that trademark in relation to those goods or services would indicate a connection between those goods or services and the owner of the registered trademark and provided that the interests of the owner of the registered trademark are likely to be damaged by such use.

Article 16.3 addresses the situation in which a third party uses a well-known mark in connection with goods or services for which the mark holder is not well known. This provision differs from Article 16.2. in three respects. First, the well-known mark in question is *registered*, as follows from the language of the provision (see quotation above). Second, the goods or services for which the confusingly similar trademark is used are different from those goods or services that are covered by the well-known mark.[263] Third, this provision emphasizes protection of

---

[262] The Brussels Ministerial Text (December 1990) referred to "including knowledge in that PARTY obtained as a result of the promotion of the trademark in international trade".

[263] This is also what distinguishes this provision from the *first* paragraph of Article 16, which applies in case of identical or similar goods or services protected by a registered trademark (referred to below as "*ordinary* trademark confusion").

the *reputation* of the well-known mark. This is indicated by the last part of the paragraph, requiring that the "interests of the owner of the registered trademark are likely to be damaged" by the use of the third party's trademark (see below for details). Articles 16.2 of TRIPS and 6*bis* of the Paris Convention do not contain such reference to the interests of the right holder, but focus on the likelihood of confusion of the public. Nevertheless, it has been observed that Article 16.3, by referring to Article 6*bis* of the Paris Convention, also takes account of the concern about confusion of the public.[264]

To illustrate the operation of Article 16.3, consider, for example, the situation in which the well-known automobile trademark "AUDI" was used by a third party in connection with the marketing of television sets. To begin with, there would be a difficult question whether television sets might be part of the natural product line expansion of an automobile manufacturer in an ordinary trademark confusion sense (i.e., under Article 16.1). If so, there would be similarity between the television sets potentially covered by the registered trademark and the third party's television sets. Thus, the question of well-known marks might not arise since there may already be a likelihood of confusion between similar goods. However, if there is no likelihood of confusion in the *ordinary* trademark sense, Article 16.3 indicates that the finder of fact should proceed to ask whether a consumer would consider there to be a connection between the goods, even if not part of a natural product line expansion (i.e. the case of non-similarity of the goods). Would a consumer seeing the term "AUDI" on a television set think that there was a connection with the automobile company? In recent years there has been an increasing tendency for producers well known in one area of commerce to market into unrelated lines of commerce. Would it have been anticipated, for example, that the "Marlboro" and "Camel" cigarette marks would be used on clothing and shoes? In this context, Article 16.3 addresses a significant question regarding well-known marks.

Article 16.3 contains an important qualifier. The interests of the owner of the well known trademark must be "likely to be damaged by such use". There are two ways such damage might be foreseen. First, the well known trademark holder might itself have been planning to enter the same market as the third party using the mark. It would therefore be injured by the loss of a revenue opportunity. Second, the third party using the mark might be doing so in a way that would tarnish or injure the reputation of the trademark holder. The burden should presumably be on the trademark holder to establish the likelihood of damage since third party use of a mark in connection with a dissimilar product would not ordinarily be assumed to cause damage.

Subjective questions such as those involving the likelihood of damage from use of a mark on dissimilar goods may be answered differently in various Members. This is to be expected. In the application of TRIPS Agreement provisions such as Articles 16.2 and 16.3, the issue from a WTO legal standpoint is whether the rules are applied reasonably and in good faith, not whether an exact methodology is used to reach a definitive result.

---

[264] See Gervais, p. 111.

3.3 Article 17: exceptions

> Exceptions
>
> Members may provide limited exceptions to the rights conferred by a trademark, such as fair use of descriptive terms, provided that such exceptions take account of the legitimate interests of the owner of the trademark and of third parties.

Trademark rights involve exclusivity in signs or symbols. In effect a sign or symbol may be taken out of public usage and reserved to private control. When trademarks involve arbitrary combinations of letters and/or designs the effects on the public may be relatively inconsequential. However, there are a variety of contexts in which the effect on the public may be substantial.

When a descriptive word becomes the subject of trademark protection the capacity for expression is restricted. Even though the rights of the trademark holder are nominally limited to use with respect to certain goods or services in the course of trade, there is a chilling effect around the use of the word that discourages others from using it. The impact, both direct and indirect, of granting private rights in words is what motivates the prohibition on the grant of trademark rights in "generic" terms.

It is difficult for one enterprise to compare its goods with those of another without referring to the latter's goods by their trademark name. For this reason, the use of a competitor's mark in comparative advertising is typically allowed as an exception to the rights of the holder.

There are a number of other contexts in which trademarks are referred to without the consent of the owner. A common type of reference is in news reporting and commentary. It is often difficult to make reference to the goods or services of an enterprise without referring to the trademark name. Again consider the example of the "AUDI" trademark. It would be difficult for the publishers of a magazine directed to auto enthusiasts to review the performance of AUDI automobiles without using the term "AUDI". The publisher could, of course, refer to an automobile manufacturer based in Germany with product lines known by certain characteristics, but this would strain writers and the reading public alike. The use by the publisher of the term "AUDI" in this context is a form of fair use of a trademark, sometimes referred to as "nominative fair use".

Like copyright, trademark protects only the identification of the product and not its function. Pharmaceutical manufacturers market drugs in coloured capsules or tablets. Doctors, pharmacists and consumer-patients come to identify those drugs by their distinctive colouring. The users of the drugs come to rely on the colour as a principal means for determining what to ingest. The colour serves a critical function from a public health standpoint. When generic versions of a drug are produced by second-comers, significant problems for consumer-patients may arise if they are unable to identify the same medication by the same colour. Colour has taken on an important functional characteristic. The use by third parties of the same colour on equivalent drugs may be justified on either of two bases. First, it might be said that the colour is not serving a trademark function because it is functional, and thus not protected. Second, it might be said that use of the colour is a limited exception to the rights of the trademark owner as a fair use in the public interest.[265]

The Paris Convention does not expressly address the subject of exceptions to trademark rights, and from that standpoint Article 17 does not have a textual precedent at the multilateral level. This is similar to the circumstances of Article 30 with respect to patents. (By way of contrast, Article 13, with respect to copyright derives from Article 9(2), Berne Convention, and has a history of prior application.) As of mid-2004, WTO panels (but not so far the Appellate Body) have rendered decisions interpreting Article 13 and Article 30, but not Article 17. While there may be a temptation to analogize because of the similar language of the three exception provisions, it is important to be aware that the forms of IPRs perform very different roles and that the public and private interests in each may be rather different.

The term "limited exception" is capable of different reasonable interpretations. In the *Canada – Generic Pharmaceuticals* case,[266] the panel construed the language to refer to a narrow derogation.[267] Canada had argued that a "limited exception" is an exception with defined boundaries. The text is susceptible to both interpretations.

Article 17 gives "fair use of descriptive terms" as illustration of a limited exception, but clearly not in an exclusive way, as is made clear by the use of the terms "such as". As noted above, there are a number of other types of limited exception that have been recognized in different legal systems.

Article 17 further provides that a limited exception should "take account of the legitimate interests of the owner of the trademark and of third parties". Application of this language will of necessity involve subjective judgments regarding the balance of public and private interests in trademarks. The panel in *Canada-Generic*

---

[265] Note that use by third parties of the same colour on equivalent drugs has been admitted by the Court of the European Free Trade Association (EFTA, comprising Iceland, Liechtenstein, Norway, and Switzerland. With the exception of Switzerland, the EFTA countries have concluded with the EC and its member states the Treaty on the European Economic Area (EEA), resulting in their participation in the EC's common market and their being bound by EC law). See case E-3/02, *Merck v. Paranova* of 8 July 2003, EFTA Court: one of the biggest European parallel importers, Paranova, imported pharmaceutical products into Norway that the pharmaceutical company Merck had sold before under its trademark in Southern Europe. Before selling the drugs in Norway, Paranova repacked them, leaving the tablets as such untouched. The new packings displayed Merck's name and trademark, and the colours used on Merck's own packings. However, those colours were not in the same place as on Merck's original packings; instead of placing them in the center, Paranova had moved them to the corners of the packings. In response to trademark infringement proceedings initiated by Merck, the EFTA Court decided that under EC law, the holder of a trademark may prevent parallel importers from using a certain design only if such design damages the reputation of the right holder or his mark. The use by the parallel trader of the original colours in a different place with a view to facilitating the identification by consumers of the parallel trader's own product line does not amount to such damage. Contrary to the modelling of a new packing as such, the parallel importer in creating its own design on the packing may go beyond minimum modifications required by the importing country.

[266] WT/DS114/R, 17 March 2000. For a detailed discussion, see Chapter 23.

[267] *Canada – Generic Pharmaceuticals case*, para. 7.30.

Pharmaceuticals found that "legitimate interests" was to be understood more broadly than "legal interests" and to take into account broader social interests.[268] Each of the trademark exceptions discussed above should be permissible within the scope of subjective balancing implicit in taking account of the legitimate interests of owners and third parties.

3.4 Article 18: term of protection

> Term of Protection
>
> Initial registration, and each renewal of registration, of a trademark shall be for a term of no less than seven years. The registration of a trademark shall be renewable indefinitely.

Prior to TRIPS, WTO Members maintained significantly disparate renewal periods. Many trademark offices were (and remain) dependent on renewal fees to maintain their operations, and not surprisingly are anxious to collect fees. The seven-year minimum initial and renewal registration period was a compromise between the United States proposal for a minimum ten-year period and a developing country proposal to leave the question of duration to each Member (see 2.2.5, above).

Trademarks are capable of indefinite duration. This does not mean that trademark rights last indefinitely based on the mere payment of renewal fees. Trademarks are subject to cancellation on grounds such as non-use (see Article 19 below). Article 18, however, makes clear that there is no temporal limit to how long a trademark may remain valid if requirements for maintaining rights are satisfied.

3.5 Article 19: requirement of use

> Requirement of Use
>
> 1. If use is required to maintain a registration, the registration may be cancelled only after an uninterrupted period of at least three years of non-use, unless valid reasons based on the existence of obstacles to such use are shown by the trademark owner. Circumstances arising independently of the will of the owner of the trademark which constitute an obstacle to the use of the trademark, such as import restrictions on or other government requirements for goods or services protected by the trademark, shall be recognized as valid reasons for non-use.
>
> 2. When subject to the control of its owner, use of a trademark by another person shall be recognized as use of the trademark for the purpose of maintaining the registration.

[268] Ibid., paras. 7.68 and 7.73.

Article 19.1, first sentence, sets a three-year (uninterrupted) minimum term prior to which a registered mark may not be cancelled for non-use. The Paris Convention, at Article 5.C(1), provides that "the registration may be cancelled only after a reasonable period."[269] TRIPS, thus, effectively defines the "reasonable period" of the Paris Convention.

Article 5.C(1), Paris Convention, and Article 19.1, TRIPS, first sentence, each provide a basis upon which the trademark owner can prevent cancellation. The Paris Convention permits the trademark owner to "justify his inaction". TRIPS refers to the "existence of obstacles to such use". Neither formulation is clear as to what types of facts or circumstances might justify non-use, leaving substantial discretion to Members to delimit the scope of the grounds. They might be quite broad, for example, allowing the registered holder to justify non-use on grounds that it was unable to put a good into production for technical reasons. On the other hand, they might be narrow, for example, referring only to obstacles arising outside the trademark holder's control, such as a government ban on sales of the subject good.

The Paris Convention rule allowing owners to "justify" non-use might be construed not to provide an excuse when the government acted. The government's action might be construed to de-legitimize the trademark owner's excuse. Article 19.2, second sentence, makes clear that indeed the obstacle may arise from outside the trademark owner's control, including government-imposed restrictions on the subject goods or services. Thus, an excuse based on a legitimately-imposed government restriction should still constitute a legitimate excuse.

Article 19.2 provides for the situation in which the trademark is licensed by its owner to a third party. Use by the licensee is equivalent to use by the owner for purposes of preventing cancellation for non-use. However, the licensee's use of the mark is only covered "When subject to the control of its owner". It would appear that a "naked license", that is, a license under which the trademark holder merely collects royalties but does not supervise the licensee, may not constitute use under this provision. This is the logical import of the language and supported by the negotiating history which shows the language concerning control replacing an earlier text according to which only the owner's consent to use of the mark was required.[270] It might alternatively be argued that so long as the trademark owner holds a contractual interest in the mark the licensee is under its control (however loose) and that this may suffice for "control" within the meaning of Article 19.2. This does not seem very persuasive in light of the express language and negotiating history.

---

[269] Article 5 of the Paris Convention provides:
"C. (1) If, in any country, use of the registered mark is compulsory, the registration may be cancelled only after a reasonable period, and then only if the person concerned does not justify his inaction."

[270] Note that the "A" proposal under the Anell Draft did not include a requirement of control, providing:
"6.2A Use of the trademark by another person with the consent of the owner shall be recognized as use of the trademark for the purpose of maintaining the registration." See text *supra*, Section 2.2.

3.6 Article 20: other requirements

> Other Requirements
>
> The use of a trademark in the course of trade shall not be unjustifiably encumbered by special requirements, such as use with another trademark, use in a special form or use in a manner detrimental to its capability to distinguish the goods or services of one undertaking from those of other undertakings. This will not preclude a requirement prescribing the use of the trademark identifying the undertaking producing the goods or services along with, but without linking it to, the trademark distinguishing the specific goods or services in question of that undertaking.

Prior to negotiation of TRIPS, it was not unusual for national trademark legislation, particularly in developing countries, to include requirements concerning the manner in which trademarks could be used. The domestic licensee of a foreign-origin trademark might be required to use its own trademark alongside that of the licensor. Additional rules might prescribe the relative placement of local and foreign-origin marks on goods. Despite the "telle quelle" or "as is" rule regarding registration in the same form, a foreign-origin trademark owner might be required to transform its mark into a more locally-friendly form, such as by providing a translated version of descriptive terms. The development-oriented objective of such requirements, *inter alia*, was to assure that some name or trademark recognition was established in favour of a local enterprise, assuming that the foreign licensor's presence in the market might be transitory. By requiring the foreign licensor to link its mark with that of a local enterprise, developing country authorities encouraged continuity in business relationships since the licensor might be more reluctant to discontinue its association with a business with whose name or products it had been linked in the public mind. From the perspective of the foreign-origin licensor, this type of requirement presented obstacles to business planning. If the mark or name of a licensee (such as a distributor) was to be linked with the licensor's mark, the licensor risked injury to its own reputation based on actions of the licensee. Also, as the special requirements might discourage foreign-origin licensors from changing or discontinuing business relationships, this was not viewed positively by the licensors.

Article 20 precludes the imposition of "special requirements, such as use with another trademark, use in a special form or use in a manner detrimental to its capability to distinguish the goods or services of one undertaking from those of other undertakings". The first reference is clear, that is "with another trademark". The meaning of "special form" might refer either to a standard format prescribed for all trademark owners (such as "in translation", or in a particular size or colour scheme), or to a case-by-case determination by a trademark authority. It is less clear what is intended by "use in a manner detrimental to its capability to distinguish". Such a result might come about if a mark-owner is required to reduce the size or placement of its mark to a point that consumers would have difficulty recognizing it, or to place it alongside information or materials that likewise would reduce its impact on consumers. Thus, for example, a requirement to include the generic name of a product alongside a trademark might be argued to have such an effect. However, the legal formulation leaves substantial flexibility to the interpreter.

However, Article 20 specifically authorizes rules that require the mark or name of the producing enterprise to be included with that of the trademark owner. Such requirements are intended to serve a development objective by indicating to the public that a local producer is the *de facto* supplier of the goods or services, with the expectation that the local public will gain assurance regarding the capacity of local suppliers. At the same time, Article 20 provides that the local enterprise will use its mark "without linking it to, the trademark" of the subject owner. This is presumably intended to prevent the local enterprise from taking "unfair advantage" of the foreign-origin mark. There should be some form of differentiation, though Article 20 does not provide or suggest a specific means. Although this provision was negotiated in response to developing country insistence that they should be allowed to facilitate awareness of local production capacity, the text does not distinguish between local undertaking-producers and foreign undertaking-producers. If a Chinese producer is making a product on which a U.S. trademark is placed, and the product is being sold in Indonesia, the mark of the Chinese producer should just as well be required to appear (based on the principle of national treatment) as that of an Indonesian producer putting the U.S. mark on the product for sale in Indonesia.

3.7 Article 21: licensing and assignment

Licensing and Assignment

Members may determine conditions on the licensing and assignment of trademarks, it being understood that the compulsory licensing of trademarks shall not be permitted and that the owner of a registered trademark shall have the right to assign the trademark with or without the transfer of the business to which the trademark belongs.

Trademarks were traditionally understood to serve as identifiers of the source of goods. The consumer expected that goods placed on the market by a particular producer would conform to the quality standards that the trademark, and thus the producer or source, represented. Consequently, in many legal systems it was not permitted to license a trademark to a third party or, if licensing was permitted (and this was largely a development of mid-20th century trademark law), the licensor was required to exercise control over the licensee so as to assure the consumer that the trademark continued to represent an equivalent product.

If a trademark was owned by a business, and the business was sold, there was generally not a legal obstacle to transfer of the mark along with the business. As businesses became more multinational, as well as subdivided into separate operating units, it became commonplace to sell and transfer part of the business, or business operations in a particular country, as opposed to selling and transferring an entire combined enterprise. National trademark laws, as well as Article 6*quater*(1) of the Paris Convention, acknowledged that assignment and transfer of a mark should be permitted to take place if at least "the portion of the business or goodwill located in that country be transferred to the assignee, together with the exclusive right to manufacture in the said country, or to sell therein, the goods bearing the mark assigned".[271]

Article 21 acknowledges the right of Members to continue to impose restrictions on the licensing and assignment of trademarks.[272] Members may, for example, continue to require that trademark licensors exercise adequate control over the activities of licensees so as to protect the source indication function of the mark (that is, the integrity of the mark from the standpoint of the consumer). The terms of the first clause are not restricted, "Members may determine conditions" on licensing and transfer. The limitations are set out in the second clause.

First, compulsory licensing of trademarks is not permitted. While Article 5.A of the Paris Convention authorizes the compulsory licensing of patents, Article 5.C does not specifically address compulsory licensing of trademarks. It provides that cancellation for non-use should only take place after a "reasonable period" (see Subsection 2.1.1, supra). If a mark is cancelled, it becomes available for use by third parties. In an indirect way cancellation might be viewed as a form of compulsory licensing, but the two concepts are different.

Since trademarks are intended to indicate the source of products, it might seem contradictory to that basic function to permit compulsory licensing to third parties. The source of products would by definition change, and consumers might be misled. Yet there is perhaps more to this question than first meets the eye. Consider the situation in which a compulsory patent license is issued for a medicine. Prior to the introduction of the third-party version of medicine under compulsory license, it is marketed to doctor-pharmacist-consumers under the trademark of the patent holder company. The patent holder asserts that its trademark rights extend to the colour of the medicine tablet. If the colour of the tablet is not licensed along with the patent, this might lead to a situation of confusion in the consuming community (i.e. among doctors, patients and pharmacists). As a practical matter, under TRIPS a compulsory license for the claimed mark – which is

---

[271] Article 6*quater*
"Marks: Assignment of Marks

(1) When, in accordance with the law of a country of the Union, the assignment of a mark is valid only if it takes place at the same time as the transfer of the business or goodwill to which the mark belongs, it shall suffice for the recognition of such validity that the portion of the business or goodwill located in that country be transferred to the assignee, together with the exclusive right to manufacture in the said country, or to sell therein, the goods bearing the mark assigned.

(2) The foregoing provision does not impose upon the countries of the Union any obligation to regard as valid the assignment of any mark the use of which by the assignee would, in fact, be of such a nature as to mislead the public, particularly as regards the origin, nature, or essential qualities, of the goods to which the mark is applied."

[272] A "license" is generally understood to refer to a legal arrangement in which a person is given permission to use something owned by another person, but without transfer of ownership interest in the subject matter of the license. An "assignment" is generally understood to refer to a legal arrangement in which ownership interest is effectively transferred from one person to another. However, because the law sometimes imposes restrictions on the formal transfer of ownership of things, an "assignment" of rights might not in all cases involve a formal recordation of change in ownership. For this reason, the words "assignment" and "transfer" are often used to refer first to the change in legal interest in a thing, and second to the formal act involved in recording a change in ownership.

prohibited by Article 21 – is not necessary for two reasons. Trademarks do not cover "function", and if the colour of a medicine tablet is performing a function for doctors, patients and pharmacists, the colour cannot be exclusively reserved to a trademark holder. In addition, Article 17 permits limited exceptions to trademark rights, and a Member may recognize a "fair use" right in the mark in these circumstances.[273]

Second, "the owner of a registered trademark shall have the right to assign the trademark with or without the transfer of the business to which the trademark belongs". This formula represents a break with the traditional view of the trademark as an indication of source. There is now permitted the "naked assignment" of marks. The trademark has in essence become a stand-alone commodity that can be traded just as lumber. This acknowledges a major change in the general principles underlying trademark law.

However, the fact that trademarks may be sold and transferred as commodities does not dispense with the basic requirements for the maintenance of marks. In countries where use is required to maintain marks, the new owner must assure that some use in connection with the covered goods or services is made so as to avoid cancellation after the minimum prescribed period has elapsed. Likewise, the mark cannot be allowed to become "generic" and thereby lose its trademark function. (Even a fanciful mark may become generic if it is widely used in reference to a product and the trademark owner does not take steps to assert its rights and control over the term.)

4. WTO jurisprudence

4.1 United States – Havana Club

4.1.1 Factual background

United States – Section 211 Omnibus Appropriations Act of 1998 ("U.S. – Havana Club")[274] is the first decision in which the Appellate Body (AB) interprets substantive intellectual property rights rules of TRIPS and the Paris Convention for the Protection of Industrial Property. It is also the first case that applies the national and most favoured nation (MFN) treatment provisions of TRIPS.

The factual setting is complex, but may be briefly summarized. Prior to the coming to power of the revolutionary government in Cuba, a family-owned Cuban enterprise made and sold rum under the trademark "Havana Club". That enterprise registered the Havana Club mark in Cuba and the United States. The revolutionary government confiscated the assets of the family-owned business, including the trademarks, and did not compensate the former owners. The former owners

---

[273] As noted in the text, when medicines are identified by a single colour, that colour is often functionally used by consumers as the means to identify it. In these circumstances, there are strong grounds for either (a) denying trademark rights in a single colour as it serves a functional (and therefore non-trademark) purpose, or (b) recognizing a fair use right on behalf of third party producers. Even a limited reference to the "brand name" of the trademark holder may be permitted as fair use when done in a way that does not suggest endorsement of the third party product by the trademark holder.

[274] WTO Appellate Body, *United States – Section 211 Omnibus Appropriations Act of 1998*, WT/DS176/AB/R, 2 January 2002 ("U.S. – Havana Club").

did not attempt to renew their trademark registration in the United States, and it lapsed. Subsequently, the Cuban state enterprise that succeeded to the mark in Cuba registered the mark in the United States.

In the 1990s, a France-based multinational liquor manufacturer and distributor (Pernod Ricard) entered into a joint venture with the Cuban state enterprise to sell Havana Club rum worldwide. The joint venture took assignment of the U.S.-registered trademark. In the same period, a U.S.-based (Bermuda incorporated) liquor manufacturer and distributor (Bacardi) purchased the residual interests of the former Cuban-family owners of the Havana Club mark, and began to sell rum under the Havana Club mark in the United States. The Cuban-French joint venture was precluded from selling into the U.S. market because of U.S. legislation and regulations that prevented Cuba and its nationals from doing business in and with the United States. Nonetheless, the Cuban-French joint venture sued the U.S. distributor in federal court in the United States for infringement of its trademark and trade name (and related unfair competition claims) to preserve its rights in the U.S. market.

While the infringement litigation was proceeding, the U.S. Congress passed legislation directed at trademarks and trade names that had been confiscated from Cuban nationals. This legislation retroactively invalidated the assignment of the Havana Club trademark registration to the Cuban-French joint venture, and denied Cuba the right to renew its registration of the Havana Club mark in the United States. In addition, the legislation instructed U.S. courts not to enforce rights in trademarks and trade names asserted by Cuban nationals or their successors-in-interest based on earlier confiscations. The federal court in which the Cuban-French joint venture brought its infringement and unfair competition action rejected the claims based on the newly adopted legislation. This decision was upheld by a federal appeals court, and the U.S. Supreme Court refused to grant a further right of appeal.

4.1.2 The EC position

The EC initiated a dispute settlement action under the DSU based on a number of asserted TRIPS inconsistent actions by the United States. The principal claims involved alleged inconsistencies with U.S. obligations under trademark provisions of TRIPS and incorporated rules of the Paris Convention. The most heavily relied upon was Article 6*quinquies*, Paris Convention, which embodies the so-called "telle quelle" or "as is" rule (see 3.1.2, above). This rule generally provides that the trademark registration authorities of a party must accept for registration a mark in the same form it has been previously registered in the trademark holder's country of origin. This rule was designed to prevent trademark authorities from demanding changes to the form or appearance of marks to conform with national preferences, and to allow for the use of marks on a uniform basis throughout the Paris Convention system. The EC took this rule a step further, arguing not only must the mark be accepted for registration in the same form, but the mark must be accepted for registration, thereby attempting to convert a rule relating to form to a rule relating to conditions of registration.

The panel and the AB accepted that the rules of the Paris Convention are incorporated by reference in TRIPS, and treated the task of interpreting the Paris

Convention as equivalent to interpreting the TRIPS Agreement. It is notable that the panel requested and received an extensive factual report from the WIPO International Bureau (or Secretariat) regarding the negotiating history of Article 6 *quinquies*, Paris Convention.[275] The panel relied on this negotiating history to confirm its interpretation of the Paris Convention.[276] The AB also relied on the WIPO-furnished report, as well as Professor Bodenhausen's Guide to the Paris Convention (1967) for interpretative guidance.[277]

4.1.3 The Appellate Body's interpretation of the *telle quelle* rule under the Paris Convention

The panel and the AB both rejected the EC's claim concerning the *telle quelle* rule in Article 6*quinquies* of the Paris Convention. Contrary to the view expressed by the EC, the AB interpreted the *telle quelle* rule as being limited to the *form* of a trademark. WTO Members are thus free to determine, through domestic legislation, the requirements for the filing and the registration of trademarks. The AB relied on Article 6(1) of the Paris Convention, which provides that

> "The conditions for the filing and registration of trademarks shall be determined in each country of the Union by its domestic legislation."

According to the AB, this provision would be undermined if Article 6 *quinquies* required Members to accept not only the form of a foreign mark, but equally another country's substantive conditions for the filing and registration of trademarks.[278]

---

[275] *United States – Section 211 Omnibus Appropriations Act of 1998*, Report of the Panel, WT/DS176/R, 6 Aug. 2001, at VI. The panel referred to its request and the reply (having furnished a summary of the reply), as follows:

"8.11 As mentioned previously, at the first substantive meeting, we informed the parties of our intention to seek information from the International Bureau of the World Intellectual Property Organization ('WIPO') pursuant to Article 13 of the DSU. The International Bureau of WIPO is responsible for the administration of the Paris Convention (1967) for the Protection of Industrial Property.

8.12 Article 13.1 of the DSU states that a panel has 'the right to seek information and technical advice from any individual or body which it deems appropriate.' Article 13.2 further provides that panels may 'seek information from any relevant source and may consult experts to obtain their opinion on certain aspects of the matter.'

8.13 Pursuant to this authority vested in panels under Article 13, we requested, in a letter dated 1 February 2001, the International Bureau of WIPO to provide us with factual information, in particular the negotiating history and subsequent developments, concerning the provisions of the Paris Convention (1967) relevant to the dispute, including Articles 2(1), 6, 6*bis*, 6*quinquies* and 8 of the Paris Convention (1967). With respect to Article 6*quinquies*, we requested any factual information on its intended scope. We also requested the International Bureau of WIPO to provide any factual information on whether the provisions of the Paris Convention (1967) regulate how the owner of a trademark is to be determined under domestic law of the Paris Union members. The International Bureau of WIPO responded to our request on 2 March 2001." [footnote omitted]

[276] *Id.*, at para. 8.82.

[277] AB, *U.S. – Havana Club*, paras. 122–48 (see, *e.g.*, footnote 81). The United States made extensive reference in its pleadings as an interpretative source to the guide to the Paris Convention prepared by Prof. Bodenhausen, a former senior WIPO official, during his tenure at WIPO.

[278] Ibid., at paras. 139 *et seq.*

4.1.4 The Appellate Body's interpretation of Articles 15 and 16 of the TRIPS Agreement

The panel and AB also rejected the EC's claims that Articles 15 and 16 mandated that the United States accept for registration a mark that its legislature had determined not to be lawfully owned by the party asserting ownership. The EC had argued that Article 15, which defines the nature of signs that are eligible for trademark protection, and Article 16, which defines the rights that must be accorded to trademark holders, require that the United States accept marks for registration. The USA argued that questions as to whether a mark qualifies for registration, and as to the rights of trademark owners, are distinct from the more primordial question as to who is the legitimate holder or owner of the mark. According to the U.S. view, Articles 15 and 16 do not purport to regulate the question of ownership.

In essence, the panel and AB endorsed this interpretation. They confirmed the authority of the United States to determine that it would not recognize claims to ownership based on foreign confiscations that offended the public policy of the forum state.

The panel and AB relied mainly on the plain language of Articles 15 and 16 to reject the EC's claim, and in confirming that interpretation noted the absence of TRIPS negotiating history that would support the EC's more expansive view of those provisions.

a) With respect to Article 15.1, the AB observed that trademarks "eligible" for registration are not *entitled* to protection; they only *qualify* for protection. In other words, the fact that a trademark meets all the distinctiveness requirements under Article 15.1 does not impose on Members the obligation to *automatically* provide for the registration of such mark. Registration may still be denied on the basis of other requirements (such as the question of trademark ownership) that each country may determine in its domestic legislation (see above).[279]

The AB supported this textual interpretation with several arguments relating to the context of Article 15.1. In particular, the AB stressed the significance of Article 15.2, authorizing Members to deny registration of trademarks on other grounds than those provided in Article 15.1. This implies, according to the AB, that Members are not obligated to register every sign meeting the distinctiveness requirements under Article 15.1.[280] Another contextual argument advanced by the AB was based on Article 6(1) of the Paris Convention. As under Article 6*quinquies* of the Paris Convention (see above), the AB observed that the EC's interpretation of Article 15.1 would deprive WTO Members of the legislative discretion accorded to them by Article 6(1). If Members were obliged to automatically register any trademark meeting the distinctiveness criteria in Article 15.1, there would be no room for additional criteria set up in Members' domestic laws.[281]

Concerning Article 15.2, the EC had argued that the relevant U.S. legislation, besides violating Article 15.1, could not be justified on "other grounds" within the

---

[279] See report of the AB, at paras. 155 *et seq.*

[280] Ibid., paras. 157–159.

[281] Ibid., para. 165. The AB further relied on paragraphs 3 and 4 of Article 15 TRIPS to support its above interpretation of Article 15.1. See ibid., paras. 160–164.

meaning of Article 15.2.[282] In this context, the EC contended that those "other grounds" referred to in Article 15.2 were only those exceptions *expressly foreseen* in the Paris Convention or in TRIPS. Since neither the Paris Convention nor TRIPS expressly provided for a rule requiring, as a precondition for registration, a proof of ownership of the kind stipulated under the relevant U.S. legislation, such requirement could not be considered as being justified on "other grounds" within the meaning of Article 15.2.[283] The AB refused this interpretation, relying on Article 6(1) of the Paris Convention. The discretion of Paris Union countries to determine the conditions for the registration of trademarks include, according to the AB, the right to also determine the conditions to *refuse* a registration. The only limits to this latter right are those grounds explicitly prohibited by the Paris Convention.[284]

The AB thus expressed a view contrary to the EC's interpretation: WTO Members may freely determine the grounds for the denial of trademark registration according to their domestic rules, unless those grounds are expressly prohibited by the Paris Convention or by TRIPS.

As to Article 16, the AB stated that neither this nor any other TRIPS provision contains a definition of trademark ownership.[285] The AB inferred from Article 6(1) of the Paris Convention (see above) that WTO Members have kept the discretion to regulate in their domestic laws the conditions for ownership of a trademark.[286]

4.1.5 Points of disagreement between the panel and the AB in the *Havana Club* case

The AB overruled the panel on four aspects of its decision. For the purposes of the present chapter, the most important one concerned the question whether "trade names" are to be considered "intellectual property" in the sense of Article 1.2 of TRIPS.

The panel decided that "trade names" were not "intellectual property" within the meaning of Article 1.2, TRIPS Agreement, because they were not a "category" of Sections 1 through 7, Part II.[287] The panel went on to consider whether Article 2.1, TRIPS, by incorporating Article 8, Paris Convention (obligating parties to provide trade name protection), brought trade names within the scope of intellectual property covered by the Agreement. The panel reasoned that since Article 2.1 provided that the referenced Paris Convention articles were to be complied with "in respect of" Parts II, III and IV of TRIPS, and since those parts did not refer to trade names,

---

[282] See ibid., para. 169. The AB, even though noting that *without a violation* of Article. 15.1 TRIPS, an examination whether the relevant U.S. legislation would be justified on "other grounds" within the meaning of Article 15.2 would not be necessary, nevertheless decided to do so, referring to its obligation under Article 17.6 of the DSU to rule on alleged legal misinterpretations by a panel.

[283] Ibid.

[284] Ibid., para. 176. For such explicit prohibition, see Article 6(2) of the Paris Convention, according to which a registration may not be refused or invalidated on the ground that filing, registration, or renewal, has not been effected in the country of origin.

[285] See the AB report at paras. 187 and 195.

[286] Ibid., at para. 189.

[287] *United States – Section 211 Omnibus Appropriations Act of 1998*, Report of the Panel, WT/DS176/R, 6 Aug. 2001, at paras. 823–40.

Article 8, Paris Convention did not add obligations regarding trade names. The panel referred to the negotiating history to confirm its conclusion, though the references are somewhat tangential to its reasoning.

The AB disagreed with the panel. It said that the panel's interpretation of Article 1.2, TRIPS, was too restrictive, and essentially assumed that "intellectual property" was limited to the specific subject matter set out in the titles of the relevant sections of the agreement, ignoring that other subject matter is addressed within those sections.[288] Perhaps more importantly, the AB said that the panel's interpretation would effectively render useless the incorporation through Article 2.1 TRIPS of Article 8 of the Paris Convention (dealing exclusively with trade names), thus depriving Article 8 of "any and all meaning and effect".[289]

In addition to this interpretation concerning trade names, the AB reversed the panel's findings in three other respects, concerning the compatibility of the relevant U.S. legislation with TRIPS Articles 3 (national treatment obligation), 4 (most-favoured nation obligation), and 42 (fair and equitable judicial proceedings for the enforcement of IPRs).[290]

In sum, the *Havana Club* case illustrates the outstanding importance of the Paris Convention for the interpretation of TRIPS: most of the trademark-related arguments advanced by the AB are more or less directly based on the interpretation of Article 6(1) of the Paris Convention. This provision in turn indicates the WTO Members' large discretion as far as filing and registration conditions are concerned.

4.2 Indonesia – Certain Measures Affecting the Automobile Industry

For the sake of completeness, it should be noted that the United States made certain trademark claims against Indonesia in the *"Indonesia – Cars"* case.[291] U.S., EC and Japanese claims in this case were primarily asserted under the Agreement on Subsidies and Countervailing Measures. However, as part of its National Car Programme, Indonesia required a joint venture or national company to acquire and maintain an Indonesian-registered trademark intended for that purpose. The idea was that the cars produced in the program would have an Indonesian character not dependent on a foreign brand name. The USA argued that this was inconsistent with the TRIPS national treatment rule because it provided a preference for Indonesian nationals in acquiring marks. The panel rejected this on ground that foreigners were entitled to register marks as well as Indonesians, even if

---

[288] In this context, the AB mentioned Part II, Section 5 of the TRIPS Agreement, the title of which only refers to "patents", although Articles 27(3)b also covers *sui generis* protection systems for plant varieties (see para. 335 of the AB's report).

[289] Ibid., para. 338.

[290] For a detailed analysis of the AB's interpretation of these provisions, see Chapter 4 and 30, respectively. The AB's arguments with respect to Articles 3 and 4 TRIPS are also presented by F. Abbott, *WTO Dispute Settlement Practice Relating to the TRIPS Agreement*, in: WTO Jurisprudence 1995–2002 Law and Dispute Settlement Practice of the World Trade Organization, Kluwer Publishers, Studies in Transnational Economic Law, 2003, under I. C. See also UNCTAD, *Course on Dispute Settlement*, Module 3.14 (TRIPS) (F. Abbott), Section 5.5 (available at <http://www.unctad.org/en/docs/edmmisc232add18_en.pdf>).

[291] Report of the Panel, WT/DS54/R, WT/DS55/R, WT/DS59/R, WT/DS64/R, 2 July 1998.

Indonesian-owned marks had a preference in respect to a subsidy program. The USA also argued that the Indonesian program discriminated against foreigners in the maintenance of marks since it did not allow foreign holders to use their globally-recognized marks in the local market on the same basis as Indonesian-owned marks. Again, the panel noted that foreign owners were entitled to maintain and use their marks in Indonesia, but only to not have the benefits of a particular subsidized program. Finally, the USA argued that the Indonesian program was inconsistent with Article 20, TRIPS Agreement (as well as the Article 65.5 requirement not to lessen the degree of consistency with TRIPS rules), because Indonesia was imposing special requirements on the use of marks in connection with participation in its program. It said that if a mark was used in the program, it could not be used elsewhere, and this would deprive the owner of the mark's potential value. The panel said that the developer and owner of a mark used in the program would be well aware at the outset that the subject mark would be restricted in its use, and thus the Indonesian rule did not amount to a "requirement" for use of the mark in the sense of Article 20. The panel also said that while only Indonesia-owned marks would benefit from the program, this was not a fact tied to the mark as such, but rather was a condition of participating in the program. This did not constitute a "requirement" regarding the use of a foreign-origin mark.

In the *Indonesia-Cars* dispute, the United States attempted to transform part of a subsidies-goods dispute (on which it had some success) into a TRIPS dispute. The Indonesian programme favoured domestic production, and it also favoured local trademark holders to the extent they were able to participate in the program. The panel avoided the suggestion to adopt a very broad view of TRIPS Agreement obligations that might effectively convert all domestic preference programmes into IPR discrimination programmes.

4.3 EC – Protection of Trademarks and GIs

Following separate requests by Australia[292] and the USA,[293] the WTO Dispute Settlement Body (DSB) at its meeting on 2 October 2003 established a single panel[294] to examine complaints with respect to EC Council Regulation (EEC) No. 2081/92 of 14 July 1992[295] on the protection of geographical indications and designations of origin for agricultural products and foodstuffs. The complaints are based, *inter alia*, on alleged violations of Articles 16 (rights conferred upon the trademark holder) and 20 (prohibition of special requirements for the use of trademarks).[296]

The pertinent EC Regulation in Article 14 provides protection against the registration of trademarks corresponding to protected geographical indications.

---

[292] WT/DS290/18 of 19 August 2003.

[293] WT/DS174/20 of 19 August 2003.

[294] *European Communities – Protection of Trademarks and Geographical Indications for Agricultural Products and Foodstuffs* [hereinafter "EC – Protection of Trademarks and GIs"], WT/DS174/21 and WT/DS290/19 of 24 February 2004, Constitution of the Panel Established at the Requests of the United States and Australia.

[295] See Official Journal of the European Communities (OJEC) L 208 of 24 July 1992, pp. 1–8.

[296] See the above requests by Australia and the USA for the establishment of a panel.

According to this provision,[297] such trademarks relating to the same product shall be refused registration or declared invalid

- in case the application for registration of the trademark was submitted *after* the application for GI registration was published;

- or in case the application for registration of the trademark was submitted *before* the application for GI registration was published, provided that that publication occurred before the trademark was registered.

In other terms, the only situation under which a corresponding trademark may remain valid is where the application for GI registration is published only after the *bona-fide* registration of the trademark. But even under those circumstances, use of the trademark will be discontinued where[298]

- the trademark consists exclusively of signs or indications which may serve, in trade, to designate the kind, quality, quantity, intended purpose, value, geographical origin, or the time of production of the goods or of rendering of the service, or other characteristics of the goods;

- or where the trademark is of such a nature as to deceive the public, for instance as to the nature, quality or geographical origin of the goods or service;

- or where the trademark, after the date on which it was registered, in consequence of the use made of it by the proprietor of the trademark or with his consent in respect of the goods or services for which it is registered, is liable to mislead the public, particularly as to the nature, quality or geographical origin of those goods or services.

Since the establishment of the panel, there has been no further WTO action in this dispute (as of July 2004).

5. Relationship with other international instruments

5.1 WTO Agreements

As noted earlier, Article XX(d) of GATT 1994 (as successor to the GATT 1947) authorizes Members to adopt measures necessary to protect trademarks (and against unfair competition), and Articles XIII and XVIII preclude interference with trademarks in connection with the adoption of certain safeguard measures.

GATT Article XI prohibits the use of measures other than duties (such as quotas or related measures) to restrict imports or exports. Some commentators have argued that GATT Article XI precludes the adoption of rules restricting the parallel importation of trademarked goods, noting that Article 6 refers only to claims regarding exhaustion arising under TRIPS (and therefore does not preclude recourse to the GATT on this question).[299] Further, it is argued that rules prohibiting parallel

---

[297] See Article 14(1) of the above EC Regulation.

[298] See Article 14(2) of the above EC Regulation, referring to the First Council Directive 89/104/EEC of 21 December 1988 to approximate the laws of the member states relating to trademarks.

[299] See Cottier. For a detailed analysis of the issue of exhaustion of IPRs and Article 6 TRIPS, see Chapter 5.

imports function as quotas and are unnecessary to protect trademarks since parallel import goods are initially placed on the market by the trademark holder or with its consent.[300] This line of reasoning has long been employed by the European Court of Justice to reject the use of national trademarks to block the free movement of goods within the EU (referring to Articles 28 and 30, EC Treaty), and it might logically be extended to the WTO context. Others have argued that TRIPS is *lex specialis* regulating IPRs within the framework of the WTO, that Article 6 allows Members to adopt their own policies with respect to exhaustion, and that this effectively precludes reference to GATT on this subject.[301]

The express text of Article 6 refers only to exhaustion claims "under this Agreement". If the Appellate Body's instruction to give effect to the words of the WTO Agreements is followed, there is no reason why the question of parallel importation of trademarked goods cannot be evaluated under the GATT. This does not necessarily lead to the conclusion that rules restricting parallel trade would be rejected as unnecessary quotas since the AB might say that (a) TRIPS permits a Member to adopt its own policy on exhaustion (b) if it exercises its discretion in favour of national exhaustion only, then in that context (c) blocking parallel imports may be necessary to protect the rights of the trademark owner. In any case, this interpretative question has yet to be addressed by a panel or the Appellate Body.

With respect to WTO Agreements other than the GATT, trademarks do not purport to be dependent for their validity on the characteristics of products or region of production (unlike geographical indications that might depend for their validity on certain objective characteristics and thereby potentially raise concerns under the TBT Agreement).[302] Trademarks are regulated by TRIPS as identifiers that permit consumers to distinguish between goods and services, and there is no specific connection between trademarks and any other WTO Agreement. As was suggested by the *Indonesia – Cars* case, this does not mean that trademark-related issues will not be raised in the context of disputes arising under other WTO Agreements. However, as the panel observed in that case, questions regarding trademarks that surface in disputes involving other WTO Agreements are likely to involve attempts to expand TRIPS into a market access agreement, which it is not.

5.2 Other international instruments

The trademark provisions of TRIPS are closely linked to various agreements administered by WIPO. The Paris Convention, directly incorporated by reference in TRIPS, differs from the latter in various respects, for example as far as the

---

[300] This is said without prejudice to the question whether parallel importation may be based on compulsory licensing of patents. There is no compulsory licensing of trademarks permitted under Article 21, TRIPS Agreement.

[301] See Marco C.E.J. Bronckers, *The Exhaustion of Patent Rights under World Trade Organization Law*, 32 J. World Tr. 137–159 (No. 5, 1998). See also Chapter 5.

[302] For more details on the potential conflict between the TBT rules and the TRIPS provisions on geographical indications, see Chapters 15 and 34.

assignment of trademarks is concerned:[303] under Article 6*quater* of the Paris Convention, it is up to the parties to decide whether a trademark assignment is valid only together with the transfer of the business to which the trademark belongs. By contrast, Article 21 obligates Members to provide for the possibility of a "naked assignment" of marks (see above, Subsection 3.7). Thus, WTO Members are denied the discretion accorded to them under the Paris Convention to make the validity of a trademark assignment dependent on the parallel transfer of the business. As to the relationship between these opposite provisions, the pertinent provision of the Vienna Convention on the Law of Treaties (Article 30.3) stipulates that a more recent treaty takes precedence over an earlier one. In the case of the Paris Convention and TRIPS, the latter therefore prevails. However, this concerns only those countries parties to both agreements, Article 30.4(a) of the Vienna Convention. When the parties to the later treaty do not include all the parties to the earlier one, Art. 30.4(b) provides that:

> (b) as between States parties to both treaties and a State party to only one of the treaties, the treaty to which both States are parties governs their mutual rights and obligations.

Consequently, the limitation of state sovereignty with respect to the transfer of the business as pronounced in Article 21 affects all Members of the WTO when dealing with trademark holders from other WTO Member countries.[304] In case a mark holder from a *non*-WTO Member[305] intends to assign her/his mark to a national from a WTO Member, however, the latter is not bound by Article 21 and may thus require, according to Article 6*quater* Paris Convention, the transfer of the business along with the trademark (provided the assigned mark is one that is registered or used in that WTO Member's territory).

Trademarks are also regulated by the Nice Agreement Concerning the Classification of Goods and Services for the Purposes of the Registration of Marks (1957) (see discussion above). The Trademark Law Treaty adopted in 1994 establishes uniform rules regarding trademark applications, prohibiting requirements other than those set out in the agreement.

WIPO also administers two agreements providing mechanisms for registration of marks in multiple jurisdictions, the Madrid Agreement Concerning the International Registration of Marks (1891, as revised) and the Protocol Relating to the Madrid Agreement Concerning the International Registration of Marks (1989). An international system for the registration of trademarks is obviously important to their acquisition and maintenance and represents a partial trend towards integration of the global IPRs framework. There is not, however, a specific correlation

---

[303] Another important difference exists with respect to the protection of service marks, see above, Subsection 3.1.1.

[304] This is in conformity with Article 2.1 TRIPS, which prohibits the derogation by WTO Members from, *inter alia*, their *obligations* under the Paris Convention. Article 21 TRIPS does not obligate Members to disregard any Paris obligation; it obliges them to waive a *right* they have under that Convention.

[305] Such as Russia, for instance, which is not (yet) a Member of the WTO, but a State party to the Paris Convention.

between the Madrid registration system and TRIPS trademark rules that merits further exploration at this stage.

6. New developments

6.1 National laws

Many WTO Members have amended their IPRs laws, including the trademark provisions, to establish consistency with TRIPS. It is not within the scope of this book to review all these developments.

In the United States, the only change to trademark law specifically made in the Uruguay Round Agreements Act was to clarify that non-use of a trademark for three consecutive years constitutes prima facie evidence of abandonment.[306] However, prior to conclusion of the TRIPS negotiations the U.S. Lanham Act regulating trademarks was amended to provide for the filing of trademark applications prior to actual use (see discussion above at Section 3), and this action was undertaken in light of the TRIPS negotiations (as well as the contemporaneous NAFTA negotiations).

In 1999 the U.S Treasury Department adopted so-called "Lever-rules" which permit the blocking of parallel import trademarked goods which are materially different from identically-marked goods marketed in the United States, *unless* the importer places a conspicuous notice on the goods indicating that they are materially different, in which case such goods *may* be parallel imported.[307] This rule must be read in the context of the general rule applicable to trademarked goods, which is that goods placed on the market outside the United States by an enterprise under "common control" with the U.S. trademark owner may be parallel imported, but goods placed on the market by a third party licensee may not be.[308] In this context, the "Lever rules" limit to a certain extent the general principle that parallel imports are allowed when commonly controlled enterprises are involved.

---

[306] URAA, §521.

[307] U.S. trademark holders may notify the Customs Service of goods which are claimed to embody "physical and material differences between the specific articles authorized for importation or sale in the United States and those not so authorized." (19 CFR §133.2 (e) ("'Lever-rule' protection")). Supporting evidence must be provided. The Customs Service will prohibit importation of "gray market" goods produced by commonly controlled enterprises which it has determined to be physically or materially different (19 CFR §133.23(a)(3)); *unless* such goods or their packaging "bears a conspicuous and legible label designed to remain on the product until the first point of sale to a retail consumer in the United States stating that: 'This product is not a product authorized by the United States trademark owner for importation and is physically and materially different from the authorized product.' The label must be in close proximity to the trademark as it appears in its most prominent location on the article itself or the retail package or container...." (19 CFR §133.23 (b)).

[308] This rule was adopted by the U.S. Supreme Court as a matter of statutory interpretation in the *K mart Corp. v. Cartier*, 486 U.S. 281 (1988). For a detailed discussion of U.S. rules in this area, see Frederick M. Abbott, *Political Economy of the U.S. Parallel Trade Experience: Toward a More Thoughtful Policy*, 4 World Trade Forum (Thomas Cottier and Petros Mavroidis eds. 2002)(University of Michigan Press).

6.2 International instruments

6.2.1 ICANN

The evolution of the Internet "domain name" has had a significant impact on the development of international trademark law. In response to complaints from trademark owners concerning the unauthorized use of marks in domain names, and especially the use of those domain names in bad faith (such as to redirect Internet users to pornographic websites, or to sell the domain name to the trademark owner for a substantial price), WIPO initiated a process that culminated in the adoption by the Internet Corporation for Assigned Names and Numbers (ICANN) of the Uniform Domain Name Dispute Resolution Policy (UDRP). The UDRP applies to all domain names registered under the main generic top level domains (such as ".com" and ".org"), as well as to a variety of country code domains. ICANN has authorized several dispute resolution service providers, including the WIPO Arbitration and Mediation Centre, to make determinations regarding whether particular domain names have been registered and used abusively. The determinations are made by administrative panellists appointed by the service providers. By almost all accounts, the system developed by WIPO and adopted by ICANN has been successful in bringing a reasonable degree of legal order to the field of Internet domain names.

What is of particular interest regarding the UDRP system is its inherently multilateral character, in the absence of a traditional international legal framework (that is, a governing treaty). ICANN is a U.S.-chartered body with a multinational governing board that establishes rules for operation of the Internet, and the UDRP functions under authority of ICANN. The relationship between the dispute settlement providers (such as the WIPO Centre) and domain name holders is established by contract (i.e., the domain name registration agreement).

Panellists deciding cases under the UDRP are not infrequently called upon to resolve trademark disputes involving parties from different countries, invoking rights under various national trademark laws. Partly as a result of the harmonizing effect of the trademark rules of TRIPS (which have been referenced in a number of UDRP decisions), panellists have been able to adopt more or less common approaches to questions involving conflicts between trademarks and domain names.

The success of the UDRP process may presage the development of other streamlined IP dispute resolution systems.

6.2.2 WIPO and Paris Union Joint Recommendations

The Paris Union Assembly and the General Assembly of WIPO have so far adopted three Joint Recommendations, concerning provisions on the protection of well-known marks, trademark licenses and provisions on the protection of marks, and other industrial property rights in signs, on the Internet.[309] Such recommendations are of non-binding character; WIPO countries are thus not obligated to adopt

---

[309] See <http://www.wipo.org/about-ip/en/index.html?wipo_content_frame=/about-ip/en/trademarks.html>.

the higher standards contained therein in their domestic laws. However, India for example has proposed to integrate the Recommendation on the protection of well-known marks into her 1999 draft trademark law.[310] Bilateral free trade agreements refer specifically to the WIPO Joint Recommendation on well-known Marks. For example, in the agreement between Chile and the U.S. the parties commit themselves to be guided by the principles contained in the Recommendation.[311]

6.3 Regional and bilateral contexts

6.3.1 Regional

6.3.1.1 Andean Group. Decision 486 of the Andean Group[312] regulates the field of trademarks in detail. National trademark authorities of the Member Countries remain responsible for implementing the Decision, including by acting as registration authorities. Decision 486 provides for the international exhaustion of trademark rights, stating:

> "Article 158. Trademark registration shall not confer on the owner the rights to prevent third parties from engaging in trade in a product protected by registration once the owner of the registered trademark or another party with the consent of or economic ties to that owner has introduced that product into the trade of any country, in particular where any such products, packaging or packing as may have been in direct contact with the product concerned have not undergone any change, alteration, or deterioration.
>
> For the purposes of the preceding paragraph, two persons shall be considered to have economic ties when one of the persons is able to exercise a decisive influence over the other, either directly or indirectly, with respect to use of the trademark right or when a third party is able to exert that influence over both persons."

Regarding the licensing of marks, Decision 486 requires the registration of licensing agreements with the competent authority of the member country concerned. Article 163 provides that,

> "The competent national authority shall not register any trademark licensing agreements or assignments or transfers that do not conform to the provisions of the Common Regime for the Treatment of Foreign Capital and for Trademarks, Patents, Licenses, and Royalties, or that do not conform to Andean Community or domestic antitrust."

6.3.1.2 European Union. The EU regulates extensively in the field of trademarks, and there is a substantial jurisprudence on the subject of marks by the European

---

[310] J. Watal, *Intellectual Property Rights in the WTO and Developing Countries*, Kluwer Law International, 2001, p. 394.

[311] See Article 17.1.9, FTA between Chile and the United States.

[312] Commission of the Andean Community, Decision 486, Common Intellectual Property Regime, 14 Sept. 2000, available at <http://www.ictsd.org/iprsonline/legalinstruments/regional.htm>.

Court of Justice (ECJ). Until adoption of the First Trade Marks Directive in 1988,[313] trademarks were almost exclusively regulated by member state legislation. The major exception involved questions relating to free movement of goods (i.e., intra-Union exhaustion) in which the ECJ took an active interest. The First Trade Marks Directive has established a set of approximated trademark rules that member states are required to reflect in national trademark law. As to protectable subject matter, the Directive obligates member states to protect as trademarks "any sign capable of being represented graphically".[314] According to the ECJ, this does *not* mean that the respective sign must be capable of being perceived visually, provided that the sign

> "can be *represented graphically*, particularly by means of images, lines or characters, and that the representation is clear, precise, self-contained, easily accessible, intelligible, durable and objective."[315]

With respect to *olfactory signs*, the requirement of graphic representability is neither satisfied by a chemical formula, nor by a description in written words, nor by a deposit of an odour sample or by a combination of these elements.[316]

Under the Trade Marks Directive, marks remain independent within each member state, and registration functions and adjudication of disputes is a national matter. In addition to the Directive, the 1993 Community Trade Mark Regulation was adopted,[317] and this created a new situation for the EU. Although member states would continue to maintain their own trademark registration systems, it would now be possible to obtain a single Community Trade Mark (CTM) extending rights throughout the EU. A Community trademark authority was established (the Office for Harmonization in the Internal Market (OHIM)) in Alicante, Spain, which performs registration functions, including the conduct of opposition proceedings. Adjudication of trademark infringement actions is somewhat complex, because an action to invalidate and cancel a mark is conducted before the OHIM, while the infringement proceeding is pending in a member state court authorized to hear infringement claims. The CTM is "indivisible" in the sense that it may

---

[313] First Council Directive of 21 December 1988 to approximate the laws of the Member States relating to trade marks (89/104/EEC).

[314] See Article 2 of the Directive: "A trade mark may consist of any sign capable of being represented graphically, particularly words, including personal names, designs, letters, numerals, the shape of goods or of their packaging, provided that such signs are capable of distinguishing the goods or services of one undertaking from those of other undertakings".

[315] *Ralf Sieckmann v Deutsches Patent- und Markenamt* (Case C-273/00), Court of Justice of the European Communities, European Court Reports 2002, p. I-11737, 12 December 2002, at para. 55 (emphasis added).

[316] Ibid., at para. 73. The ECJ argues that a chemical formula is not sufficiently intelligible to make people recognise the odour in question. In addition, a chemical formula does not represent the odour of a substance, but the substance *as such* (para. 69). The written description of an odour, even though being graphic, is not sufficiently clear, precise and objective (para. 70). The deposit of an odour sample does not constitute a graphic representation; neither is such a sample sufficiently stable or durable (para. 71). Finally, even a combination of all those elements does not satisfy the requirements of clarity and precision of the graphic representation (para. 72).

[317] Council Regulation (EC) No 40/94 of 20 December 1993 on the Community trade mark.

not be assigned and transferred in respect to a part of EU territory, although it is possible to grant licenses limited to a part of the EU.

There are many interesting aspects to the EU's trademark system, which is rather complicated owing to the integration of long-standing member state trademark systems with a unified CTM system. For present purposes, it is of particular interest to refer to the attitude of the EU with respect to exhaustion of trademarks.[318] The ECJ developed and has long recognized a doctrine of "intra-Community" or "intra-Union" exhaustion, in which it is understood that importation of a good placed on the market by or with the consent of the trademark owner in one member state may not be blocked by invocation of a parallel trademark in another member state. There are many ECJ decisions that address nuanced questions that arise in respect to this basic rule. For example, pharmaceutical trademark holders have attempted to prevent parallel trade within the EU by registering different marks for the same medicine in different member states. Unless an importer changes the trademark on the medicine to reflect the particular mark used in the importing country, pharmacists may be resistant to dispensing the "foreign" product (or medicines registration rules may even prohibit its marketing). The ECJ has decided that in these circumstances an importer has the right to re-brand the medicine since otherwise the pharmaceutical producers would be able to circumvent the intra-Union exhaustion rule, subject to the condition that this is done in a way to protect the consumer.[319]

Perhaps of most direct relevance to the WTO and TRIPS Agreement was the decision of the ECJ in *Silhouette v. Hartlauer*.[320] In that case, the ECJ interpreted the First Trade Marks Directive to adopt a rule of intra-Community exhaustion of trademarks only, and by extension to exclude a rule of international exhaustion for the Community. The Court reasoned that the member states should have only a single policy on exhaustion, and since several of them did not recognize a doctrine of international exhaustion, it would create a difficult situation to allow different policies for different members. Although this reasoning is open to question (since the situation of different policies had existed for many years without apparent trouble), the EU today maintains a single policy of intra-Community exhaustion of trademarks. Therefore, the owner of a trademark within the Community may block parallel imports from outside the Community.[321]

---

[318] See also Chapter 5.

[319] See *Bristol-Myers Squibb v. Paranova*, ECJ Joined Cases C-427/93, C-429/93 and C-436/93; *Upjohn v. Paranova*, ECJ Case C-379/97 and *Boehringer v. Swingard*, ECJ Case C-143/00, and by the EFTA Court, *Paranova Inc v. Merck & Co*, Case E-/302.

[320] *Silhouette International Schmied GmbH & Co, KG v. Hartlauer Handelsgesellschaft mbH* (Case C-355/96), Court of Justice of the European Communities, [1998] 2 CMLR 953, 16 July 1998.

[321] It is interesting to note that the EFTA Court in its interpretation of the same EU Trade Marks Directive has come to the opposite conclusion: according to the EFTA Court, the Trade Marks Directive leaves EFTA countries the freedom to maintain a system of international trademark exhaustion. See *Mag Instrument Inc./California Trading Company Norway, Ulsteen*, (Case E-2/97), in Gewerblicher Rechtsschutz und Urheberrecht (GRUR) Int. 1998, p. 309 et seq. (3 December 1997).

6.3.1.3 NAFTA. Article 1708 of the NAFTA addresses trademarks in a manner that effectively incorporates TRIPS requirements in this regional framework (that was negotiated contemporaneously with TRIPS). While there are certain minor differences (e.g., the minimum period for renewal is ten years, rather than the seven-year standard of TRIPS), none appear to raise any issues of particular interest from a TRIPS implementation standpoint.

6.3.1.4 MERCOSUL/R. On 5 August 1995, the Mercosul/r Council adopted a Protocol on the Harmonization of Norms regarding Intellectual Property in the Mercosul/r in Matters of Trademarks, Indications of Source and Appellations of Origin.[322] In that Protocol, the state parties commit themselves to observing the rules of the Paris Convention and TRIPS (Article 2). There are additional common rules concerning the subject matter of protection (Articles 5–6), the rights conferred by registration (Article 11), procedures for registration and cancellation (Articles 7–10, 15) and use of marks (Article 16). For the most part, however, the details of trademark law in the Mercosul/r are left to the national authorities.

6.4 Proposals for review

There are no pending proposals for review of the trademark provisions of TRIPS.

7. Comments, including economic and social implications

7.1 The opportunities

Economists are confident that there are significant net benefits to a well-functioning trademark system in market economies.[323] It is generally acknowledged that trademarks serve a useful social and economic function by providing consumers with information that assists them to sort through a complex marketplace. Indeed, trademark protection could be particularly valuable in developing countries because of the potential to develop brand recognition for high-quality crafts, clothing, and music.[324] Enterprises in developing countries may establish their own market identities through appropriate trademarks and offer products that can be distinguished from those already on the market. Subject to the respect of Article 20 (special requirements, see above), governments in some developing countries may consider policies and incentives that encourage foreign firms to allow licensees to adapt more of the licensed products for both domestic and export needs and promote the use of local trademarks. The success of Japanese industry in importing foreign technology while developing indigenous marks constitutes an example for other countries to emulate, even if countries at lower stages of development may have less bargaining power when formulating appropriate regulations and may, therefore, remain more dependent on the introduction of foreign marks.

---

[322] MERCOSUR/CMC/DEC. No. 8/95, available at
<http://www.mercosur.org.uy/espanol.snor/normativa/decisiones/DEC895.htm>.

[323] See *The TRIPS Agreement and Developing Countries*, UNCTAD 1996, paras. 188 et seq. [hereinafter UNCTAD 1996].

[324] See UNCTAD 1996, para. 189; see also Policy Discussion Paper, p. 69.

Apart from the promotion of local marks, strengthened trademark regimes may also encourage both direct investment and licensing by foreign producers who seek to monitor quality and to maintain brand names and goodwill in the international market generally. On the whole, more technology will be licensed to domestic firms when the licensor can both lower transaction costs by recourse to standard intellectual property norms and maintain quality controls through trademark licence agreements. Local production under licence again reduces the need for imports and helps to build an industrial infrastructure.

There are few grounds on which to quarrel with the proposition that businesses should be able to protect their identity in the marketplace. For this reason, the basic proposition that trademarks should be protected against misappropriation was subject to little controversy during the Uruguay Round negotiations, and that basic proposition is similarly non-controversial today. In an integrated world market where products of different countries circulate freely and prices are determined by open competition, it is hard to see any social benefits resulting from a toleration of trade in counterfeit goods to any country, at least in the medium and long term. Border controls are thus a logical outgrowth of both the provisions on trademarks in general and the provisions that incorporate the international standards of unfair competition law set out in Article 10*bis* of the Paris Convention into TRIPS. Hence, the imposition of border controls to repress imports of counterfeit goods represents one significant result of TRIPS, provided that countries implement these measures in a genuinely non-discriminatory fashion and do not erect disguised barriers to trade.[325]

7.2 The challenges

TRIPS may require changes in legislation with regard to several aspects of trademark law, including strengthening protection of service-marks and of well-known marks. In this area, however, the implementation of enforcement rules and, particularly, requirements related to border measures, may have greater implications than the provisions relating to the availability of rights as such.

In addition, as with all forms of private ownership of property, questions arise concerning the rights of ownership and where the most appropriate boundary lines are to be drawn. Next to the issue of the scope of fair use rights, the question of whether mark holders should be permitted to block parallel trade that acquires particular importance in this context.

TRIPS allows each Member to determine its own policy with respect to parallel imports. Such imports, if allowed by national legislation, are one of the instruments that may be used to tackle excessive pricing or other unreasonable commercial conditions eventually imposed by trademark owners. Parallel trade may foster sound competition, to the extent that it permits access to legitimate products commercialized under more favourable conditions abroad. This may avoid price discrimination to the detriment of the consumer and increase the social gains of the protection. The realization of these gains, however, may be impaired if the use of trademarks on parallel imported products creates confusion for the public about the quality and other characteristics of the protected products or

---

[325] UNCTAD 1996, para. 194.

services. In addition, there is a need to assure coherence between domestic exhaustion regimes in trademark law and patent law. Parallel importation of trademarked goods such as pharmaceuticals will be most efficient as a remedy against excessive pricing if the WTO Member in question follows the rule of international exhaustion in respect of both trademarks and patents.[326]

Whether there will be trademark-related problems from the standpoint of developing country interests depends on whether the Appellate Body will allow a reasonable level of discretion to each Member to define its own interests in trademark protection. So far, the Appellate Body has stressed that Members are required to comply with the terms of the Agreement, but are not obligated to fulfil the expectations of other Members regarding what the agreement might have said, but did not.

Of course, large multinational enterprises use trademarks to promote their goods, and those trademarks have themselves become associated with the process referred to by some in a pejorative sense as "globalization". As a visible symbol of capitalism, well-known trademarks may be the subject of popular attack. Yet it might be wise to resist the temptation to associate the identifier with the underlying problem. Trademarks may be an instrument of powerful multinational corporations, but they are also an instrument of the small businessperson. Trademarks are a form of intangible property that is capable of being abused. From the standpoint of promoting and protecting developing country interests, it is a matter of exercising vigilance over the misuse of trademarks and other IPRs. Accordingly, strengthened trademark regimes should be complemented with up-to-date regulations dealing directly with the abusive licensing practices that may flow from market power.[327]

---

[326] In case a country has adopted the rule of international exhaustion in the field of trademarks, but follows a national exhaustion regime in the patent area, companies holding a domestic trademark and patent on the same pharmaceutical product cannot oppose parallel imports of such product on the basis of their domestic trademark, but may do so on the basis of their domestic patent. This does leave open the possibility to import other drugs not covered by the patent, but nevertheless seriously limits the efficacy of price control (in particular where there are no generic alternatives to a patented drug).

[327] See UNCTAD 1996, at para. 193.

15: Geographical Indications

Article 22   Protection of Geographical Indications

1. Geographical indications are, for the purposes of this Agreement, indications which identify a good as originating in the territory of a Member, or a region or locality in that territory, where a given quality, reputation or other characteristic of the good is essentially attributable to its geographical origin.

2. In respect of geographical indications, Members shall provide the legal means for interested parties to prevent:

(a) the use of any means in the designation or presentation of a good that indicates or suggests that the good in question originates in a geographical area other than the true place of origin in a manner which misleads the public as to the geographical origin of the good;

(b) any use which constitutes an act of unfair competition within the meaning of Article 10*bis* of the Paris Convention (1967).

3. A Member shall, ex officio if its legislation so permits or at the request of an interested party, refuse or invalidate the registration of a trademark which contains or consists of a geographical indication with respect to goods not originating in the territory indicated, if use of the indication in the trademark for such goods in that Member is of such a nature as to mislead the public as to the true place of origin.

4. The protection under paragraphs 1, 2 and 3 shall be applicable against a geographical indication which, although literally true as to the territory, region or locality in which the goods originate, falsely represents to the public that the goods originate in another territory.

Article 23   Additional Protection for Geographical Indications for Wines and Spirits

1. Each Member shall provide the legal means for interested parties to prevent use of a geographical indication identifying wines for wines not originating in the place indicated by the geographical indication in question or identifying spirits for spirits not originating in the place indicated by the geographical indication in question, even where the true origin of the goods is indicated or the geographical

---

indication is used in translation or accompanied by expressions such as "kind", "type", "style", "imitation" or the like.*

2. The registration of a trademark for wines which contains or consists of a geographical indication identifying wines or for spirits which contains or consists of a geographical indication identifying spirits shall be refused or invalidated, ex officio if a Member's legislation so permits or at the request of an interested party, with respect to such wines or spirits not having this origin.

3. In the case of homonymous geographical indications for wines, protection shall be accorded to each indication, subject to the provisions of paragraph 4 of Article 22. Each Member shall determine the practical conditions under which the homonymous indications in question will be differentiated from each other, taking into account the need to ensure equitable treatment of the producers concerned and that consumers are not misled.

4. In order to facilitate the protection of geographical indications for wines, negotiations shall be undertaken in the Council for TRIPS concerning the establishment of a multilateral system of notification and registration of geographical indications for wines eligible for protection in those Members participating in the system.

[Footnote]* Notwithstanding the first sentence of Article 42, Members may, with respect to these obligations, instead provide for enforcement by administrative action.

Article 24   International Negotiations; Exceptions

1. Members agree to enter into negotiations aimed at increasing the protection of individual geographical indications under Article 23. The provisions of paragraphs 4 through 8 below shall not be used by a Member to refuse to conduct negotiations or to conclude bilateral or multilateral agreements. In the context of such negotiations, Members shall be willing to consider the continued applicability of these provisions to individual geographical indications whose use was the subject of such negotiations.

2. The Council for TRIPS shall keep under review the application of the provisions of this Section; the first such review shall take place within two years of the entry into force of the WTO Agreement. Any matter affecting the compliance with the obligations under these provisions may be drawn to the attention of the Council, which, at the request of a Member, shall consult with any Member or Members in respect of such matter in respect of which it has not been possible to find a satisfactory solution through bilateral or plurilateral consultations between the Members concerned. The Council shall take such action as may be agreed to facilitate the operation and further the objectives of this Section.

3. In implementing this Section, a Member shall not diminish the protection of geographical indications that existed in that Member immediately prior to the date of entry into force of the WTO Agreement.

4. Nothing in this Section shall require a Member to prevent continued and similar use of a particular geographical indication of another Member identifying

wines or spirits in connection with goods or services by any of its nationals or domiciliaries who have used that geographical indication in a continuous manner with regard to the same or related goods or services in the territory of that Member either (a) for at least 10 years preceding 15 April 1994 or (b) in good faith preceding that date.

5. Where a trademark has been applied for or registered in good faith, or where rights to a trademark have been acquired through use in good faith either:

(a) before the date of application of these provisions in that Member as defined in Part VI; or

(b) before the geographical indication is protected in its country of origin; measures adopted to implement this Section shall not prejudice eligibility for or the validity of the registration of a trademark, or the right to use a trademark, on the basis that such a trademark is identical with, or similar to, a geographical indication.

6. Nothing in this Section shall require a Member to apply its provisions in respect of a geographical indication of any other Member with respect to goods or services for which the relevant indication is identical with the term customary in common language as the common name for such goods or services in the territory of that Member. Nothing in this Section shall require a Member to apply its provisions in respect of a geographical indication of any other Member with respect to products of the vine for which the relevant indication is identical with the customary name of a grape variety existing in the territory of that Member as of the date of entry into force of the WTO Agreement.

7. A Member may provide that any request made under this Section in connection with the use or registration of a trademark must be presented within five years after the adverse use of the protected indication has become generally known in that Member or after the date of registration of the trademark in that Member provided that the trademark has been published by that date, if such date is earlier than the date on which the adverse use became generally known in that Member, provided that the geographical indication is not used or registered in bad faith.

8. The provisions of this Section shall in no way prejudice the right of any person to use, in the course of trade, that person's name or the name of that person's predecessor in business, except where such name is used in such a manner as to mislead the public.

9. There shall be no obligation under this Agreement to protect geographical indications which are not or cease to be protected in their country of origin, or which have fallen into disuse in that country.

1. Introduction: terminology, definition and scope

The term "geographical indication" came into use in WIPO negotiations in the mid-1970s and effectively entered into common usage with the conclusion of TRIPS. Although the protection of product names associated with places was long embodied in various legal doctrines, use of the term "geographical indication" in TRIPS was intended to help bring coherence to an unsettled area.

TRIPS defines "geographical indications" in Article 22.1 as "indications which identify a good as originating in the territory of a Member, or a region or locality in that territory, where a given quality, reputation or other characteristic of the good is essentially attributable to its geographic origin." There are a number of important elements in this legal formulation. The "indication" is not expressly limited to the name of a place, so that a product name known to be associated with a place may qualify for protection. While a good's association with a place may be based on a "given quality", which would be understood as some objectively identifiable characteristic, this is not a requirement for protection. The place identifier may instead have a reputational or goodwill association with consumers. This criterion for protection would not be an objectively measurable characteristic of the good, but instead a determination regarding consumer association of a good with a place.

The geographical indication is distinguished from most other forms of IPR represented in TRIPS by its shared character. A geographical indication is not the property of a single right holder, but is rather an identifier that is used by producers in a place. This characteristic – that is, the absence of a particular owner – distinguishes the geographical indication from the trademark.[328]

Although TRIPS obligates WTO Members to protect rights in geographical indications, it leaves substantial discretion to each Member to determine the manner in which such protection will be afforded.

2. History of the provision

2.1 Situation pre-TRIPS

Identifiers of the geographical origin of goods have long been protected against commercial misuse.[329] The common law doctrine of passing off, based on protection against the tort of unfair competition, was used to protect merchants against deceptive geographic claims.[330] In U.S. and U.K. law, for example, geographic origin was protected by collective marks and certification marks.[331] In civil law jurisdictions, the appellation of origin was used to protect against false claims of geographic origin. Moreover, laws regulating international trade typically required importers to identify the geographic origin of goods to allow for the appropriate application of customs duties, quota regulations and so forth.

---

[328] Collective trademarks involve shared ownership, but typically in respect to a defined group of owners. A geographical indication is typically available to all producers within a region, although the group of producers in a region entitled to use the indication may be restricted by various forms of regulation.

[329] See Document Sct/6/3 Rev. *On Geographical Indications: Historical Background, Nature Of Rights, Existing Systems for Protection and Obtaining Protection in Other Countries*, Prepared by the Secretariat, WIPO Standing Committee On The Law Of Trademarks, Industrial Designs And Geographical Indications, SCT/8/4, April 2, 2002.

[330] On the common law doctrine of passing off, see W.R. Cornish, *Intellectual Property: Patents, Copyright, Trade Marks and Allied Rights* (4th ed. 1999), at Chapter 16.

[331] In the U.K., for example, Stilton cheese and Harris Tweed are protected by certification trade marks. The Harris Tweed mark was first registered in 1909, and is now owned by the Harris Tweed Authority, which was established by a 1993 Act of Parliament.

2.1.1 Multilateral rules

2.1.1.1 The Paris Convention. The basic principle of protection against unfair competition is set out in Article 10*bis* of the Paris Convention, which is both generally incorporated in TRIPS at Article 2 (see Chapter 3), and specifically incorporated as a foundation for protection of geographical indications at Article 22.2(b). Article 10*bis* of the Paris Convention states:

"Unfair Competition

(1) The countries of the Union are bound to assure to nationals of such countries effective protection against unfair competition.

(2) Any act of competition contrary to honest practices in industrial or commercial matters constitutes an act of unfair competition.

(3) The following in particular shall be prohibited:

1. all acts of such a nature as to create confusion by any means whatever with the establishment, the goods, or the industrial or commercial activities, of a competitor;

2. false allegations in the course of trade of such a nature as to discredit the establishment, the goods, or the industrial or commercial activities, of a competitor;

3. indications or allegations the use of which in the course of trade is liable to mislead the public as to the nature, the manufacturing process, the characteristics, the suitability for their purpose, or the quantity, of the goods."

In addition, the Paris Convention, at Article 10(1), includes provision (cross-referenced to Article 9), obligating state parties to provide for the seizure of imports "in cases of direct or indirect use of a false indication of the source of the good or the identity of the producer, manufacturer, or merchant". Article 10(2) provides that a right to prevent such imports should be accorded to "Any producer, manufacturer, or merchant, whether a natural person or a legal entity, engaged in the production or manufacture of or trade in such goods and established either in the locality falsely indicated as the source, or in the region where such locality is situated, or in the country falsely indicated, or in the country where the false indication of source is used".

2.1.1.2 The Madrid Agreement. The Madrid Agreement for the Repression of False or Deceptive Indications of Source on Goods of April 14, 1891, incorporated a limited extension to Article 10 of the Paris Convention, addressing not only "false" indications of source, but also "deceptive" indications, providing at Article 1(1):

"All goods bearing a false or deceptive indication by which one of the countries to which this Agreement applies, or a place situated therein, is directly or indirectly indicated as being the country or place of origin shall be seized on importation into any of the said countries."

The additional reference to deceptive indications was viewed by its proponents as a way to address the practice of accompanying a geographic name with a form of qualifier or disclaimer (e.g., California Burgundy or California Chablis), when such combination-indication might nonetheless cause consumer confusion.

Adherence to the Madrid Agreement was and remains limited.[332]

2.1.1.3 The GATT 1947. Article IX of the GATT 1947 addressed marks of origin,[333] *inter alia*, at Article IX:1 requiring MFN treatment for such marks. The concept of the geographical indication is previewed at Article IX:6, providing:

> "The contracting parties shall co-operate with each other with a view to preventing the use of trade names in such manner as to misrepresent the true origin of a product, to the detriment of such distinctive regional or geographical names of products of the territory of a contracting party as are protected by its legislation. Each contracting party shall accord full and sympathetic consideration to such requests or representations as may be made by any other contracting party regarding the application of the undertaking set forth in the preceding sentence to names of products which have been communicated to it by the other contracting party."

Article IX:6, GATT 1947, was not framed in terms of strict obligation, but rather in terms of cooperation with a view to prevent misrepresentation. Also, the duty to cooperate is based on protection of a distinctive regional or geographic name by legislation in the country requesting cooperation, and further based on notification of the applicable names.

Article IX:6, GATT 1947, was subject to interpretation by a panel in the *Japan – Alcoholic Beverages* case.[334] The panel in that case found that Japan's requirement

---

[332] For a list of the Contracting Parties, see <http://www.wipo.int/treaties/en/documents/pdf/f-mdrd-o.pdf>.

[333] Article IX, GATT 1947:

"Marks of Origin

1. Each contracting party shall accord to the products of the territories of other contracting parties treatment with regard to marking requirements no less favourable than the treatment accorded to like products of any third country.

2. The contracting parties recognize that, in adopting and enforcing laws and regulations relating to marks of origin, the difficulties and inconveniences which such measures may cause to the commerce and industry of exporting countries should be reduced to a minimum, due regard being had to the necessity of protecting consumers against fraudulent or misleading indications.

3. Whenever it is administratively practicable to do so, contracting parties should permit required marks of origin to be affixed at the time of importation.

4. The laws and regulations of contracting parties relating to the marking of imported products shall be such as to permit compliance without seriously damaging the products, or materially reducing their value, or unreasonably increasing their cost.

5. As a general rule, no special duty or penalty should be imposed by any contracting party for failure to comply with marking requirements prior to importation unless corrective marking is unreasonably delayed or deceptive marks have been affixed or the required marking has been intentionally omitted.

6. [see text above]."

[334] *Japan – Customs Duties, Taxes and Labelling Practices on Imported Wines and Alcoholic Beverages*, Report of the Panel adopted on 10 November 1987, (L/6216 – 34S/83).

of the disclosure of the actual origin of goods on product labels effectively dispelled potential consumer confusion as to the origin of the products, if such confusion might have been present.[335]

2.1.1.4 The Lisbon Agreement. "Appellations of Origin" were addressed in the Lisbon Agreement for the Protection of Appellations of Origin and their International Registration (adopted in 1958). This agreement extends substantially greater protection for geographical names than prior agreements, but depends on

---

[335] Relevant excerpts from the panel report, *id.*, state:
"The Panel noted from the drafting history relating to Article IX:6 that it had been agreed that the text of Article IX:6
'should not have the effect of prejudicing the present situation as regards certain distinctive names of products, provided always that the names affixed to the products cannot misrepresent their true origin. This is particularly the case when the name of the producing country is clearly indicated. It will rest with the governments concerned to proceed to a joint examination of particular cases which might arise if disputes occur as a result of the use of distinctive names of products which may have lost their original significance through constant use permitted by law in the country where they are used'. (Reports of Committees and Principal Sub-Committees, UN Conference on Trade and Employment, 1948, p. 79).
The Panel noted that the Japanese Law and Cabinet Order concerning Liquor Business Association and Measures for Securing Revenue of Liquor Tax stipulated that 'Any manufacturer of liquors must indicate, at a legible location of the container of liquors…which are shipped out from the manufacturing premise…, the name of the manufacturer, the place of the manufacturing premise…, the capacity of the container…, the category of liquors…, the grade of liquors and the following matters according to the category of liquors, in a conspicuous manner', including the alcohol content in the case of wine, whisky, brandy, spirits and liqueurs. The Panel examined a large number of labels, photos, wine bottles and packages submitted by the EEC as evidence. The Panel found that this evidence seemed to confirm the Japanese submission to the Panel that the labels on liquor bottles manufactured in Japan indicated their Japanese origin.
5.15 The Panel examined the view of the European Community that the use of French words, French names, of other European languages and European label styles or symbols by Japanese manufacturers continued to mislead Japanese consumers as to the origin of the liquors, and that the indication of a Japanese manufacturer did not clarify his precise activities because, for instance, wines bottled in Japan could contain as much as 95 per cent imported bulk wine. The Panel inferred from the wording of Article IX:6 that it was confined to an obligation to 'cooperate with each other with a view to preventing the use of trade names in such manner as to misrepresent the true origin of a product, to the detriment of such distinctive regional or geographical names of products of the territory of a contracting party as are protected by its legislation'. The Panel noted that there was no definition of a 'trade name' in the General Agreement, and that there were differences in the laws of various countries as to what might constitute a trade name. The Panel did not consider it necessary to define the term 'trade name' in this case for the following reasons: Article IX:6 was designed to protect 'distinctive regional or geographical names of products of the territory of a contracting party as are protected by its legislation'. The Panel did not dispose of evidence and was unable to find that the use by Japanese manufacturers of labels written partly in English (in the case of whisky and brandy) or in French (in the case of wine), the use of the names of varieties of grapes (such as 'Riesling' or 'Semillon), or the use of foreign terms to describe Japanese spirits ('whisky', 'brandy') or Japanese wines ('chateau', 'reserve', 'vin rose') had actually been to the detriment of 'distinctive regional or geographical names of products' produced and legally protected in the EEC. Nor could the Panel find that Japan – given, for example, its participation in the Madrid Agreement for the Repression of False or Deceptive Indications of Source on Goods and its internal laws and regulations on labelling and on the protection of distinctive regional or geographical names (such as 'Armagnac' or 'Chianti') – had failed to meet its obligation to cooperate pursuant to GATT Article IX:6."

an initial grant of registration for an appellation in the country of origin,[336] as well as registration at WIPO which may be rejected by each country where protection is intended.[337] Article 2(1), setting out the subject matter, provides:

> "In this Agreement, 'appellation of origin' means the geographical name of a country, region, or locality, which serves to designate a product originating therein, the quality and characteristics of which are due exclusively or essentially to the geographical environment, including natural and human factors."

The scope of protection extends beyond the literally registered geographical name. Article 3 provides:

> "Protection shall be ensured against any usurpation or imitation, even if the true origin of the product is indicated or if the appellation is used in translated form or accompanied by terms such as 'kind,' 'type,' 'make,' 'imitation,' or the like."

Protection is included against a registered appellation becoming "generic" (Article 6). Adherence to the Lisbon Agreement was and remains quite limited.[338]

2.1.1.5 WIPO initiatives.

In 1974 and 1975, WIPO pursued preparation of a new multilateral treaty on the protection of geographical indications. Once it became apparent that efforts would be undertaken to revise the Paris Convention, and that such revision would consider further elaboration of provisions relevant to geographical indications, work on preparation of the new multilateral treaty was ended.[339]

As part of negotiations on revisions to the Paris Convention in the 1980s and early 1990s, WIPO member states considered adopting an additional Article *10quater* addressing geographical indications.[340] The substance of these discussions was summarized by the WIPO International Bureau in a report prepared for the Standing Committee on the Law of Trademarks, Industrial Designs and Geographical Indications (SCT/8/4) and the relevant portions of the report are set out in Annex 1 to this chapter.

2.1.2 National and regional rules

As noted in the just-referenced report by the WIPO International Bureau,[341] the approaches taken to the protection of geographical indications have been varied, and have basically fallen into four legal categories: (1) unfair competition and passing off, (2) collective and certification marks, (3) protected appellations of origin and registered geographical indications, and (4) administrative schemes for protection.

---

[336] Article 1(2), Lisbon Agreement.

[337] Article 5(3), *id.*

[338] For a list of the Contracting Parties, see <http://www.wipo.int/treaties/en/documents/pdf/j-lisbon.pdf>.

[339] WIPO Standing Committee on the Law of Trademarks, Industrial Designs and Geographical Indications, SCT/8/4, April 2, 2002, at paras. 66–71.

[340] One of the reasons for this was the fact that the Paris Convention in Article 10(1) protected only against false geographical indications, but not against deceptive ones.

[341] SCT/8/4, April 2, 2002.

2.1.2.1 Unfair competition and passing off. The treatment of geographical indications under the common law principles of unfair competition and passing off
is based on the injury that is suffered by a business through a false representation
by a competitor that its product comes from the same source. One aspect of the
unfairness involves taking advantage of the reputation of the injured party (which
has been built up through its labours). A second aspect of the unfairness involves
the harm that may come to the indication-holder if the goods placed on the market
are of inferior quality, thus causing damage to its reputation. A third aspect of the
unfairness goes to the injury to the public being deceived into purchasing goods
other than those for which it bargained.

In order to make out a claim of unfair competition or passing off with respect to
the geographic origin of goods, the claimant typically would need to demonstrate
that the public had formed a sufficient identification or association between the
subject goods and the territorial name, and that the public was misled by the
complained-against party's use of the name. Protection of geographical indications
using an unfair competition or passing off theory was exemplified in a line of
"Champagne" cases in which common law courts provided protection for the
name of the French wine producing region.[342]

Protection of trademarks is grounded in unfair competition law, though it has
evolved in many regions to rely in substantial part on a registration system. The
geographical indication is not protected by trademark as such because the trademark is used to identify the goods of an undertaking or enterprise, and is not
generally associated with a collective or community (except, of course, in the
case of collective marks, discussed below). In addition, a trademark is not limited by territory. It is limited by identification to an undertaking or enterprise.
Trademarks have become increasingly assignable in the nature of property. Because geographical indications are based on a link to territory, they are non-
assignable (in the sense of being attributed to persons outside the geographic
territory).

2.1.2.2 Collective and certification marks. Some countries used the collective
mark and/or certification mark to overcome the obstacles inherent in according trademark protection to geographical names. A collective mark would belong
to an association or group whose members are entitled to use that mark, and

---

[342] See, *e.g.*, *Wineworths Group Ltd. v. Comite Interprofessionel du Vin de Champagne*, 2 NZLR 327
[1991] ("*Wineworths v. CIVC*"), decided by the New Zealand Court of Appeal. Judge J. Gault stated:
  "Champagne is a geographical name. When used in relation to wine the primary significance it
  would convey to persons who know that would be as the geographical origin of the product. If the
  name conveys something of the characteristics of the wine it is because those familiar with wine sold
  by reference to the name associate those characteristics with it. . . . For suppliers the attracting force
  in the name constitutes a part of the goodwill of their business. That will be so whether the name
  is associated solely with one supplier or with a class of suppliers who stand in the same position to
  the name. The goodwill may be enjoyed among the whole population or among a particular market
  segment.

  That goodwill will be damaged if someone else uses the name in relation to a product in such
  a manner as to deceive purchasers into believing the product has the characteristics of products
  normally associated with the name when it does not. The damage may give rise to a claim for
  'passing off' although deceptive trading would be a more accurate designation." (2 NZLR 327, 336)

could (depending on the jurisdiction) incorporate a geographical name. A certification mark would belong to a certifying person or body which, by affixing or allowing the affixing of the mark, would provide assurance with a set of rules or qualifications.[343]

There were and remain substantial differences in the way that collective and certification marks are regulated by national law. The Paris Convention provides:

"Article 7*bis*

Marks: Collective Marks

(1) The countries of the Union undertake to accept for filing and to protect collective marks belonging to associations the existence of which is not contrary to the law of the country of origin, even if such associations do not possess an industrial or commercial establishment.

(2) Each country shall be the judge of the particular conditions under which a collective mark shall be protected and may refuse protection if the mark is contrary to the public interest.

(3) Nevertheless, the protection of these marks shall not be refused to any association the existence of which is not contrary to the law of the country of origin, on the ground that such association is not established in the country where protection is sought or is not constituted according to the law of the latter country."

Article 7*bis*(2) provides considerable latitude regarding the protection that a country might accord to a collective mark incorporating a geographic name. In theory such protection could be denied on grounds that geographical names are "generic" in a trademark law sense.

2.1.2.3 Appellations of origin and geographical indications.

Another approach to geographical indications is protection through the "appellation of origin", which form of protection is typically defined by national statute. The appellation of origin is distinguished from the later-developed concept of the geographical indication in that the former requires a specific link between the territory and some quality or characteristic of the good, including by the contribution of human labour. The concept of the geographical indication, as later developed, dispenses with the requirement of a link to a quality or characteristic of the good, and allows the reputation of the good to serve as the basis for the link to the territory. From the standpoint of the producer, the requirement of affirmatively demonstrating a differentiating quality or characteristic of a good linked in some way to a territory could be problematic.[344] The appellation of origin is typically based on a registration system.

---

[343] In the United States, collective and certification marks are defined in the Trademark (Lanham) Act, 15 USC §1127. The Trademark Manual of Examining Procedure (TMEP) refers to the following judicial decisions regarding the protection of names of geographic regions as certification marks: "*Community of Roquefort v. William Faehndrich, Inc.*, 303 F.2d 494, 133 USPQ 633 (2d Cir. 1962); *State of Florida, Department of Citrus v. Real Juices, Inc.*, 330 F. Supp. 428, 171 USPQ 66 (M.D. Fla. 1971) (SUNSHINE TREE for citrus from Florida); *Bureau National Interprofessionnel Du Cognac v. International Better Drinks Corp.*, 6 USPQ2d 1610 (TTAB 1988) (COGNAC for distilled brandy from a region in France)" (TMEP §1306.01).

[344] Can wine tasters, for example, be counted on to consistently distinguish the products of different regions in blind taste tests?

The Council of the European Communities adopted Regulation (EEC) No. 2081/92 of 14 July 1992 on the protection of geographical indications and designations of origin for agricultural products and foodstuffs.[345] This Regulation provides a common system for the registration and protection of geographical indications in the field of agriculture, but not including wines and spirit drinks.[346] It calls for the Commission to maintain a "register of protected designations of origin and protected geographical indications",[347] and incorporates provisions relating to Commission review of applications,[348] publication[349] and opportunity for objection to the registration of a geographical indication.[350] The Regulation also provides for a list of specifications that protected geographical indications (PGIs) are expected to comply with, and for member states to establish inspection structures to ensure that the specifications are met.[351]

The protection to be afforded is set out in Article 13, which provides, *inter alia*:

"Article 13

1. Registered names shall be protected against:

(a) any direct or indirect commercial use of a name registered in respect of products not covered by the registration in so far as those products are comparable to the products registered under that name or insofar as using the name exploits the reputation of the protected name;

(b) any misuse, imitation or evocation, even if the true origin of the product is indicated or if the protected name is translated or accompanied by an expression such as 'style', 'type', 'method', 'as produced in', 'imitation' or similar;

(c) any other false or misleading indication as to the provenance, origin, nature or essential qualities of the product, on the inner or outer packaging, advertising material or documents relating to the product concerned, and the packing of the product in a container liable to convey a false impression as to its origin;

(d) any other practice liable to mislead the public as to the true origin of the product. Where a registered name contains within it the name of an agricultural product or foodstuff which is considered generic, the use of that generic name on the appropriate agricultural product or foodstuff shall not be considered to be contrary to (a) or (b) in the first subparagraph.

2. By way of derogation from paragraph 1 (a) and (b), Member States may maintain national systems that permit the use of names registered under Article 17 for a period of not more than five years after the date of publication of registration, provided that:

– the products have been marketed legally using such names for at least five years before the date of publication of this Regulation,

– the undertakings have legally marketed the products concerned using those names continuously during the period referred to in the first indent,

---

[345] OJ L 208, 24.7.1992, p.1. On this regulation, see also below, Section 4 of this chapter.
[346] *Id.*, Article 1.
[347] *Id.*, Article 6(3).
[348] *Id.*, Article 6(1).
[349] *Id.*, Article 6(2).
[350] *Id.*, Article 7.
[351] *Id.*, Article 10.

– the labelling clearly indicates the true origin of the product.

However, this derogation may not lead to the marketing of products freely within the territory of a Member State where such names were prohibited.

3. Protected names may not become generic.

[...]"

Article 14 provides protection against the registration of trademarks corresponding to protected geographical indications.

Article 12 of the 1992 Regulation includes a provision regarding protection of geographical indications for foreign products. It provides:

"Article 12

1. Without prejudice to international agreements, this Regulation may apply to an agricultural product or foodstuff from a third country provided that:

– the third country is able to give guarantees identical or equivalent to those referred to in Article 4,

– the third country concerned has inspection arrangements equivalent to those laid down in Article 10,

– the third country concerned is prepared to provide protection equivalent to that available in the Community to corresponding agricultural products for foodstuffs coming from the Community.

2. If a protected name of a third country is identical to a Community protected name, registration shall be granted with due regard for local and traditional usage and the practical risks of confusion.

Use of such names shall be authorized only if the country of origin of the product is clearly and visibly indicated on the label."

The requirement in Article 12(1) that "the third country concerned is prepared to provide protection equivalent to that available in the Community to corresponding agricultural products for foodstuffs coming from the Community" arguably constitutes a material reciprocity requirement and has been at the source of a dispute initiated against the EC by Australia and the USA as allegedly infringing the TRIPS obligations of national treatment and most-favoured nation treatment.[352]

In addition to the Regulation on agricultural products and foodstuffs, the EC has also passed specific legislation governing GIs for wines and spirits. The EC's regulation of the names of wines and spirits dates back at least as early as Council Regulation (EEC) No 817/70 of 28 April 1970 laying down special provisions relating to quality wines produced in specified regions. This was repealed and replaced by Council Regulation (EEC) No 338/79 of 5 February 1979 laying down special provisions relating to quality wines produced in specified regions.[353] The 1979 regulatory system was extremely complicated, relying on authorities of the member states to lay out the conditions for qualifying as a quality wine produced in a

---

[352] See Chapter 4. The same dispute also refers to alleged violations of some of the TRIPS provisions on GIs; see below, Section 4.

[353] OJ L 054, 05/03/1979 p. 0048-0056.

specified region, and indicating that the right to a designation was to be based on a number of factors of production, including cultivation and wine-making methods, and analysis of growing conditions.[354] Wines were to be subject to analytic testing to justify their listing on registers maintained by the member states. The 1979 regulation was replaced by Council Regulation (EEC) No 823/87 of 16 March 1987 laying down special provisions relating to quality wines produced in specified regions.[355] The 1987 Regulation was based on the same basic principles as the 1979 Regulation, and relied on member states to maintain lists of wines meeting established criteria, and to perform analytic testing. This system of regulation, as will be discussed in Section 6.3.1 of this Chapter, was revised following the entry into force of TRIPS. It remains complex.[356]

2.1.2.4 Administrative schemes. The WIPO International Bureau report for the SCT (see below, Annex 1) also refers to administrative schemes for protection which would include national regulations that govern labelling and other administrative aspects of wine production and marketing. These schemes may include the application of penalties for false or misleading labelling of products, including with respect to the geographical origin of the goods.

It is apparent that the concept of the "geographical indication" was unsettled in the period prior to and during the TRIPS Agreement negotiations. The highest level of attention to the subject was paid by the European Community, in particular as a feature of the common agricultural policy.

2.2 Negotiating history

Whereas at the outset of the TRIPS negotiations the United States proposals contained no mention of geographical indications,[357] the initial substantive submission by the European Community of July 1988 included a detailed provision on the protection of geographical indications in which can already be seen the outlines of the TRIPS Agreement rules.[358]

2.2.1 The EC proposal

"3. f. Geographical indications including appellations of origin

(i) Geographical indications are, for the purpose of this agreement, those which designate a product as originating from a country, region or locality where a given quality, reputation or other characteristic of the product is attributable to its geographical origin, including natural and human factors.

---

[354] *Id.*, Article 2.

[355] OJ L 084, 27/03/1987 p. 0059-0068.

[356] See, e.g., Council Regulation (EC) No 1493/1999 of 17 May 1999 on the common organization of the market in wine.

[357] Suggestion by the United States for Achieving the Negotiating Objective, MTN.GNG/NG11/W/14 (October 1987), and Revision, 17 October 1988, MTN.GNG/NG11/W/14/Rev. 1.

[358] Guidelines and Objectives Proposed by the European Community for the Negotiations on Trade Related Aspects of Substantive Standards of Intellectual Property Rights, MTN.GNG/NG11/W/26.

(ii) Geographical indications shall be protected against any use which constitutes an act of unfair competition, including use which is susceptible to mislead the public as to the true origin of the product. Shall notably be considered to constitute such use:

– any direct or indirect use in trade in respect of products not coming from the place indicated or evoked by the geographical indication in question;

– any usurpation, imitation or evocation, even where the true origin of the product is indicated or the appellation or designation is used in translation or accompanied by expressions such as 'kind', 'type', 'style', 'imitation' or the like;

– the use of any means in the designation or presentation of the product likely to suggest a link between the product and any geographical area other than the true place of origin.

(iii) Where appropriate, protection should be accorded to appellations of origin, in particular for products of the vine, to the extent that it is accorded in the country of origin.

(iv) Appropriate measures shall be taken under national law for interested parties to prevent a geographical indication from developing into a designation of generic character as a result of the use in trade for products from a different origin, it being understood that appellations of origin for products of the vine shall not be susceptible to develop into generic designations.

The registration of a trademark which contains or consists of a geographical or other indication denominating or suggesting a country, region or locality with respect to goods not having this origin shall be refused or invalidated. National laws shall provide the possibility for interested parties to oppose the use of such a trademark.

(v) In order to facilitate the protection of geographical indications including appellations of origin, the establishment of an international register for protected indications should be provided for. In appropriate cases the use of documents certifying the right to use the relevant geographical indication should be provided for."

2.2.2 The Swiss proposal

The Swiss proposal of July 1989 also contained a fairly well elaborated provision regarding geographical indications.[359] Note that the Swiss text contemplates that services will be included among the scope of subject matter coverage:

"III. GEOGRAPHICAL INDICATIONS –

Definition of Geographical Indications

14. A geographical indication is any designation, expression or sign which aims at indicating that a product is originating from a country, a region or a locality.

The norms on geographical indications also relate to services.

[359] Standards and Principles Concerning the Availability, Scope and Use of Trade-Related Intellectual Property Rights, Communication from Switzerland, MTN.GNG/NG11/W/38, 11 July 1989.

Use of Geographical Indications

15. Geographical indications shall be protected against use which is likely to mislead the public as to the true origin of the products. Shall notably be considered to constitute such use:

– any direct or indirect use in trade in respect of products not originating from the place indicated or evoked in the geographical indication in question;
– any evocation, even where the true origin of the product is indicated or the designation is used in translation or accompanied by expressions such as 'kind', 'type', 'style' or 'imitation';
– the use of any means in the designation or presentation of the product likely to suggest a link between the product and any geographical area other than the true place of origin.

Appropriate measures shall be taken so as to prevent a geographical indication from developing into a designation of a generic character as a result of the use in trade for products of a different origin.

The registration of a trademark which contains or consists of a geographical or other indication designating or suggesting a country, region or locality with respect to products not having this origin shall be refused or invalidated, if the use of such indication is likely to mislead the public as to the true geographical origin of the product."

2.2.3 The US proposal
Even as of its fully articulated May 1990 proposal to the TNG,[360] the United States appeared sceptical of extending the scope of protection afforded to geographical indications:

"C. Geographical Indications Including Appellations of Origin

Article 18

Contracting parties shall protect geographic indications that certify regional origin by providing for their registration as certification or collective marks.

Article 19

Contracting parties shall provide protection for non-generic appellations of origin for wine by prohibiting their use when such use would mislead the public as to the true geographic origin of the wine. To aid in providing this protection, contracting parties are encouraged to submit to other contracting parties evidence to show that each such appellation of origin is a country, state, province, territory, or similar political subdivision of a country equivalent to a state or county; or a viticultural area."

2.2.4 The proposal by a group of developing countries
While India's submission of July 1989 did not discuss geographical indications,[361] the proposal from the group of Argentina, Brazil, Chile, China, Colombia, Cuba,

[360] Draft Agreement on the Trade-Related Aspects of Intellectual Property Rights, Communication from the United States, MTN.GNG/NG11/W/70, 11 May 1990.
[361] Standards and Principles Concerning the Availability, Scope and Use of Trade-Related Intellectual Property Rights, Communication from India, MTN.GNG/NG11/W/37, 10 July 1989.

Egypt, India, Nigeria, Peru, Tanzania and Uruguay of May 1990[362] largely relied on unfair competition principles to address the protection of geographical indications, providing:

> "Chapter III
>
> GEOGRAPHICAL INDICATIONS
>
> Article 9: Protection of Geographical Indications Including Appellations of Origin*
> Parties undertake to provide protection for geographical indications including appellations of origin against any use which is likely to confuse or mislead the public as to the true origin of the product.
>
> [Footnote]* Geographical indications are any designation, expression or sign which aims at indicating that a product originates from a country, region or locality."

2.2.5 The Anell Draft

The Anell Draft of July 1990 ("A" developed and "B" developing country proposals) included detailed treatment of geographical indications, providing:[363]

> "SECTION 3: GEOGRAPHICAL INDICATIONS
>
> 1.   Definition
>
> 1.1 Geographical indications are any designation, expression or sign which [aims at indicating] [directly or indirectly indicates] that a product [or service] originates from a country, region or locality.
>
> 1.2 [Geographical indications] [Appellations of origin] are for the purpose of this agreement [geographical] indications which designate a product as originating from the territory of a PARTY, a region or locality in that territory where a given quality, reputation or other characteristic of the products is attributable [exclusively or essentially] to its geographical origin, including natural [and] [or] human factors. [A denomination which has acquired a geographical character in relation to a product which has such qualities, reputation or characteristics is also deemed to be an appellation of origin.]
>
> 1.3 PARTIES agree that the provisions at point 2b.1 and 2b.2 below shall also apply to a geographical indication which, although literally true as to the territory, region or locality in which the goods originate, falsely represents to the public that the goods originate in the territory of another PARTY.
>
> 2. Protection
>
> 2a PARTIES shall provide protection for geographical indications by complying with the provisions under the Madrid Agreement for the Repression of False or Deceptive Indications of Source on Goods of 1891, as last revised in 1967.
>
> 2b.1 PARTIES shall protect [, at the request of an interested party,] geographical [or other] indications [denominating or suggesting the territory of a PARTY, a region or a locality in that territory] against use with respect to products not originating in that territory if that use [constitutes an act of unfair competition

---

[362] Communication from Argentina, Brazil, Chile, China, Colombia, Cuba, Egypt, India, Nigeria, Peru, Tanzania and Uruguay, MTN.GNG/NG11/W/71, 14 May 1990.

[363] See MTN.GNG/NG11/W/76 of 23 July 1990.

in the sense of Article 10*bis* of the Paris Convention (1967), including use which] [might mislead] [misleads] the public as to the true origin of the product.

[Such protection shall notably be afforded against:

– any direct or indirect use in trade in respect of products not originating from the place indicated or evoked by the geographical indication in question;

– any usurpation, imitation or evocation, even where the true origin of the product is indicated or the appellation or designation is used in translation or accompanied by expressions such as 'kind', 'type', 'style', 'imitation' or the like;

– the use of any means in the designation or presentation of products likely to suggest a link between those products and any geographical area other than the true place of origin.]

2b.2 PARTIES shall [, at the request of an interested party,] refuse or invalidate the registration of a trademark which contains or consists of:

[an indication denominating or suggesting a geographical indication,]

[a geographical or other indication denominating or suggesting the territory of a PARTY, or a region or locality in that territory,]

with respect to products not originating in the territory indicated [, if use of such indication [for such products] is of such a nature as to mislead or confuse the public [as to the true place of origin]]. [National laws shall provide the possibility for interested parties to oppose the use of such a trademark.]

2b.3 Appropriate measures shall be provided by PARTIES to enable interested parties to impede a geographical indication [, generally known in the territory of the PARTY to consumers of given products or of similar products as designating the origin of such products manufactured or produced in the territory of another PARTY,] from developing, as a result of its use in trade for [identical or similar] products of a different origin, into a designation of generic character [for these products or for similar products] [, it being understood that appellations of origin for products of the vine shall not be susceptible to develop into generic designations].

2c.1 PARTIES shall protect geographical indications that certify regional origin by providing for their registration as certification or collective marks.

2c.2 PARTIES shall provide protection for non-generic appellations of origin for wine by prohibiting their use when such use would mislead the public as to the true geographic origin of the wine. To aid in providing this protection, PARTIES are encouraged to submit to other PARTIES evidence to show that each such appellation of origin is a country, state, province, territory, or similar political subdivision of a country equivalent to a state or country; or a viticultural area.

2d PARTIES undertake to provide protection for geographical indications including appellations of origin against any use which is likely to confuse or mislead the public as to the true origin of the product.

3. International Register

PARTIES agree to cooperate with a view to establishing an international register for protected geographical indications, in order to facilitate the protection of geographical indications including appellations of origin. In appropriate cases the use of documents certifying the right to use the relevant geographical indication should be provided for.

4. Exceptions

4.1 No PARTY shall be required to apply the provisions for the protection of geographical indications:

(a) to the prejudice of holders of rights relating to an indication identical with or similar to a geographical indication or name and used or filed in good faith before the date of the entry into force of this agreement in the PARTY;

(b) with regard to goods for which the geographical indication or name is in the common language the common name of goods in the territory of that PARTY, or is identical with a term customary in common language.

4.2a PARTIES agree that the preceding paragraphs shall not prevent the conclusion pursuant to Article 19 of the Paris Convention (1967) of bilateral or multilateral agreements concerning the rights under those paragraphs, with a view to increasing the protection for specific geographical or other indications, and further agree that any advantage, favour, privilege or immunity deriving from such agreements are exempted from the obligations under point 7 of Part II of this agreement.

4.2b Given the country specific nature of [geographical indications] [appellations of origin], it is understood that in connection with any advantage, favour, privilege or immunity stemming from bilateral agreements on such [indications] [appellations] and exceeding the requirements of this agreement, the most-favoured nation treatment obligations under point 7 of Part II of this agreement shall be understood to require each PARTY belonging to such an agreement to be ready to extend such advantage, favour, privilege or immunity, on terms equivalent to those under the agreement, to any other PARTY so requesting and to enter into good faith negotiations to this end."

This draft revealed the delegations' disagreement over several issues. The draft definitions of geographical indication (see above, Section 1 "Definition") varied considerably. Whereas one proposal was very general, not even referring to the link between the characteristics of the product and its geographical origin (paragraph 1.1), an alternative draft definition came close to what is today Article 22.1 (paragraph 1.2). Both draft definitions used the term "product" instead of "good". This could be an indication of some delegations' intention to include services in the scope of protection. On the other hand, the draft definition in paragraph 1.1 referred to "product [or service]". In that context, the term "product" was considered to be limited to "good", whereas the ordinary meaning of "product" would arguably also cover services. The final version under Article 22.1 refers to "goods", thus excluding services (for details, see Section 3, below).

As far as the scope of protection was concerned, the Anell Draft contained a bracketed proposal (under paragraph 2b.1, above), according to which protection was to be afforded against

"any usurpation, imitation or evocation, even where the true origin of the product is indicated or the appellation or designation is used in translation or accompanied by expressions such as 'kind', 'type', 'style', 'imitation' or the like".

The language used in this proposal is almost identical to the terms of the current Article 23.1. It provides for protection even where the public is not misled as to the origin of the products. However, in one important aspect, this proposal went beyond the scope of the current Article 23.1: it applied to *all* products and was not limited to wines and spirits. The proposal was not retained in the subsequent Brussels Draft (see below).

The Anell Draft under paragraph 2c.1 expressly refers to the U.S. system of protecting geographical indications as certification or collective marks. This reference was not retained in the Brussels Draft or in TRIPS. Instead, both obligate Members to provide the "legal means" for protection.

As far as the establishment of a multilateral register for geographical indications was concerned, the Anell Draft under Section 3 went beyond the scope of the current Article 23.4: it was not limited to wines, but referred to geographical indications in general. This approach was kept under the Brussels Draft (see below), but was limited to wines in the subsequent Dunkel Draft of December 1991.[364]

Concerning the provisions on exceptions from protection, the Anell Draft already contained some of the elements of the current version of Article 24, although it was much shorter than this latter provision. In particular, it referred to the exception of generic names (paragraph 4.1(b); now Article 24.6) and of the continuous prior use of an indication identical with or similar to a protected geographical indication (paragraph 4.1(a); now Article 24.4). As to continuous prior use, this draft provided a substantially wider exception than the current version of Article 24, applying to geographical indications for all kinds of products, whereas Article 24.4 applies only to geographical indications "identifying wines or spirits in connection with goods or services". Second, it would be permissible to allow parties that had registered or used a geographical indication in good faith prior to entry into force of TRIPS in a Party to continue such use. In one respect, however, the Anell Draft provided for a stricter exception than the current Article 24.4: under Article 24.4, continuous use does not depend on a good faith requirement, if such use occurred for at least 10 years preceding 15 April 1994 (see Section 3 for details).

In addition to these two exceptions, the Anell Draft contained two opposing proposals concerning bilateral agreements for the increased protection of geographical indications (see paragraphs 4.2a and 4.2b, above; now Article 24.1). Whilst the delegations agreed on the general admissibility of such bilateral agreements, it was not clear whether the increased protection resulting from those would have to be extended to all the other Members of the WTO, according to the most-favoured nation (MFN) principle. One proposal (4.2a) advocated the exemption of bilateral TRIPS-plus protection from the MFN principle, the other (4.2b) proposed to subject these TRIPS-plus provisions to the MFN rule. Under the Brussels Draft and the final text of TRIPS, this express reference to MFN was dropped (see below).[365]

2.2.6 The Brussels Draft
The Chairman's Note to the December 1990 Brussels Ministerial Text indicated, "In regard to Section 3 of Part II on Geographical Indications, it should be made

---

[364] See Article 23.4 of the Draft Agreement on Trade-Related Aspects of Intellectual Property Rights, Including Trade in Counterfeit Goods. Included in the "Dunkel Draft" of December 1991 (part of document MTN.TNC/W/FA, dated 20 December 1991).

[365] For more details on the relationship between bilateral TRIPS-plus provisions on geographical indications and the MFN obligation, see below, Section 3 of this chapter (regarding Article 24.1 TRIPS).

clear that there are still considerable differences on Articles 25, 26 and 27". The text provided:[366]

"SECTION 3: GEOGRAPHICAL INDICATIONS

Article 24: Protection of Geographical Indications

1. Geographical indications are, for the purposes of this Agreement, indications which identify a good as originating in the territory of a PARTY, or a region or locality in that territory, where a given quality or other characteristic on which its reputation is based is essentially attributable to its geographical origin.

2. In respect of geographical indications, PARTIES shall provide in their domestic law the legal means for interested parties to prevent:

(a) the use of any means in the designation or presentation of a good that indicates or suggests that the good in question originates in a geographical area other than the true place of origin in a manner which misleads the public as to the geographical origin of the good;

(b) any use which constitutes an act of unfair competition within the meaning of Article 10bis of the Paris Convention (1967).

3. A PARTY shall, at the request of an interested party, refuse or invalidate the registration of a trademark which contains or consists of a geographical indication with respect to goods not originating in the territory indicated, if use of the indication in the trademark for such goods in that PARTY is of such a nature as to mislead the public as to the true place of origin.

4. The provisions of the preceding paragraphs of this Article shall apply to a geographical indication which, although literally true as to the territory, region or locality in which the goods originate, falsely represents to the public that the goods originate in another territory.

Article 25: Additional Protection for Geographical Indications for Wines

1. Each PARTY shall provide in its domestic law the legal means for interested parties to prevent use of a geographical indication identifying wines for wines not originating in the place indicated by the geographical indication in question, even where the true origin of the goods is indicated or the geographical indication is used in translation or accompanied by expressions such as 'kind', 'type', 'style', 'imitation' or the like.

2. The registration of a trademark for wines which contains or consists of a geographical indication identifying wines shall be refused or invalidated at the request of an interested party with respect to such wines not having this origin.

3. In the case of homonymous geographical indications for wine, protection shall be accorded to each indication, subject to the provisions of paragraph 4 of Article 24 above. Each PARTY shall determine the practical conditions under which the homonymous indications in question will be differentiated from each other, taking into account the need to ensure equitable treatment of the producers concerned and that consumers are not misled.

[366] See Draft Final Act Embodying the Results of the Uruguay Round of Multilateral Trade Negotiations, Revision, Trade-Related Aspects of Intellectual Property Rights, Including Trade in Counterfeit Goods, MTN.TNC/W/35/Rev. 1, 3 Dec. 1990.

Article 26: Exceptions

1. Where a geographical indication of a PARTY has been used with regard to goods originating outside the territory of that PARTY in good faith and in a widespread and continuous manner by nationals or domiciliaries of another PARTY, including use as a trademark, before the date of application of these provisions in the other PARTY as defined in Article 68 below, nothing in this Agreement shall prevent such continued use of the geographical indication by those nationals or domiciliaries of the said other PARTY.

2. A PARTY shall not take action to refuse or invalidate registration of a trademark first applied for or registered:

(a) before the date of application of these provisions in that PARTY as defined in Article 68 below;

(b) before the geographical indication is protected in its country of origin; on the basis that the trademark is identical with, or similar to, a geographical indication.

3. No PARTY shall be required to apply the provisions of this Article in respect of a geographical indication of any other PARTY with respect to goods for which the relevant indication is identical with the term customary in common language as the common name for such goods or of the process for their production in the territory of that PARTY, or where the goods are products of the vine, is the name of a grape variety."

4. There shall be no obligation under this Agreement to protect geographical indications which are not or cease to be protected in their country of origin, or which have fallen into disuse in that country.

5. On the request of a PARTY, each PARTY shall be willing to enter into good faith negotiations aimed at [sic] The provisions of the preceding paragraphs shall not prevent PARTIES from concluding bilateral and multilateral agreements concerning the protection under this Section, with a view to increasing the protection for specific geographical indications.

Article 27: Notification of Geographical Indications

In order to facilitate the protection of geographical indications, the Committee shall examine the establishment of [sic] establish a multilateral system of notification and registration of geographical indications eligible for protection in the PARTIES participating in the system."

Like the final text of **TRIPS**, this draft made a clear distinction between a basic protection for all goods (Article 24) and an additional protection for wines (Article 25). The additional protection for spirits was only added in the subsequent Dunkel Draft of December 1991.

2.2.6.1 Draft Article 24. As far as the Brussels Draft Article 24 is concerned, there were two differences with respect to the current Article 22: first, Article 22.1 stipulates that one of the grounds for protection of the indication is the reputation of a good, which is attributable to its geographical origin ("... where a given quality, reputation, or other characteristic of the good is essentially attributable to its geographical origin".). In the Brussels Draft, the link between the reputation on the one hand and the geographical origin on the other hand was more indirect, the relevant part of the provision reading: "... where a given quality or other characteristic *on which its reputation is based* is essentially attributable to its geographical origin." (emphasis added). In other words, it was not the reputation itself which was directly based on the geographical origin, but the goods' quality or characteristics, which in turn created the reputation. The final version considers the reputation itself to constitute a characteristic of the good. This was probably clarified in order to highlight the difference with respect to the Lisbon Agreement, which does not protect the pure reputation of a good.

The second difference between the Brussels Draft and the final TRIPS text concerns the provision dealing with the refusal or invalidation of trademarks containing or consisting of geographical indications (Article 24.3 of the Brussels Draft; Article 22.3 of TRIPS). While the Brussels Draft authorized such action only at the request of an interested party, Article 22.3 also permits Members to provide for *ex officio* refusals or invalidations. This option was introduced with the 1991 Dunkel Draft (Article 22.3).

2.2.6.2 Draft Article 25. The Brussels Draft in Article 25.1 provided for an additional protection of geographical indications for wines (as the current Article 23.1). Like Article 23.2 TRIPS, Article 25.2 of the Brussels Draft also obligated the Parties to invalidate any trademarks containing or consisting of a geographical indication where the wine did not have the indicated origin. The *main differences* were the following:

a) The Brussels Draft did not refer to spirits, only to wines.

b) In case the geographical indication used in a trademark indicates a place different from the true place of origin, the Brussels Draft (Article 25.2) only provided for a refusal of the trademark registration or its invalidation at the request of an interested party. In addition to that, Article 23.2 accords the right to Members to provide for these remedies *ex officio*.

c) Under the draft provision, there was no fourth paragraph (as there is now under Article 23) calling for international negotiations on the establishment of a multilateral system for the notification and the registration of geographical indications for wines and spirits. However, both the Brussels Draft in Article 27 and the Anell Draft (see above) provided for a separate provision on this issue which covered not only geographical indications for wines, but all products. This was limited to wines through the Dunkel Draft of December 1991 (Article 23.4). Later on, the negotiations on the multilateral register were extended (see Section 6.4).

2.2.6.3 Draft Article 26. Compared to the Anell Draft, the Brussels Draft provision on exceptions (Article 26, above; now Article 24 TRIPS) contained two additional elements: Article 26 paragraphs 2 and 4 covered what is today Article 24 paragraphs 5 and 9.[367] Article 26.4 of the Brussels Draft already had the same wording as Article 24.9 TRIPS, and draft Article 26.2 was retained in almost identical form in Article 24.5 TRIPS.

---

[367] I.e. an exception in favour of trademarks applied for, registered in good faith or acquired through use in good faith before the obligation to protect a similar or identical geographical indication arises; and an exception to the protection of geographical indications that lack protection in their country of origin.

Article 26, paragraphs 1 & 2 of the Brussels Draft (continued and good faith use of protected indications by third parties) substantially altered the Anell Draft's approach by making the defence of good faith use (paragraph 1) or registration (paragraph 2) available for third parties that had acted prior to the entry into force of the respective Member's substantive obligations (per the then-Article 68 transition arrangements). The Brussels Draft, like the Anell Draft, made this exception entirely dependent on good faith. Under Article 24.4(a) TRIPS, there is provision for exception in circumstances not dependent on good faith (see Section 3).

Article 26.1 of the Brussels Draft, like the Anell Draft, referred to geographical indications in general and not only to those identifying wines and spirits, as does Article 24.4.

Finally, paragraphs 3 and 5 of the Brussels Draft Article 26 contained proposals essentially similar to the current paragraphs 6 and 1 of Article 24 (i.e. provisions on generic names and on bilateral or multilateral TRIPS-plus negotiations).

2.2.7 The Dunkel Draft text of December 1991

Articles 22–24 of this draft were essentially the same as the final text of Articles 22–24 of TRIPS.[368] The only substantive difference was the more limited scope of the continued and similar use exception under Article 24.4 of the Dunkel Draft: while the latter referred only to geographical indications identifying wines, TRIPS extended this exemption to spirits.

3. Possible interpretations

3.1 Article 22 (Geographical indications in general)

3.1.1 Article 22.1

> Geographical indications are, for the purposes of this Agreement, indications which identify a good as originating in the territory of a Member, or a region or locality in that territory, where a given quality, reputation or other characteristic of the good is essentially attributable to its geographical origin.

The definition of geographical indications in Article 22.1 avoids specifying the kind of "indications" that are within its scope. A word may serve as a geographical indication without itself being the name of a territory, and so may "evoke" the territory. While a word may be an indication, other types of symbols, such as pictorial images, might also serve as identifiers.

The definition is limited to a "good", indicating that the negotiators rejected the proposal that services also be attributed to territories. This does not preclude the possibility that Members may under national law allow claims for unfair competition based on misleading attribution of the source of services, but such protection is not required by this section of TRIPS.

---

[368] Note that the numbering of the provisions on geographical indications is the same in the Dunkel Draft and the TRIPS Agreement.

While the reference to a "good" is limiting in the sense of excluding services, it is broad in the sense of applying to all goods for which an appropriate geographical link is made. All agricultural products, for example, and not only wines and spirits as more specifically addressed in Article 23, are potentially the subject of geographical indications.

The geographical indication identifies a good "originating" in the territory of a Member. This means that the good must be mined, grown or manufactured in that territory. As a consequence, there is no possibility for assigning the right to affix a geographical indication to a party outside that territory. Note, however, that there may be some flexibility in the term "originating". Some portion of the work involved in creating a good might take place outside the territory without undermining its "originating" character. The permissible extent of such outside work is a question common to the area of rules of origin elsewhere in GATT-WTO law. Because the law applicable to geographical indications is unsettled, there may well be dispute regarding the extent of the flexibility as to permissible outside work.

The definition in Article 22.1 refers to "a given quality, reputation or other characteristic of the good . . . essentially attributable to its geographical origin". The notion of "quality" would encompass physical characteristics of the good, that is, attributes of the good that can be objectively measured. By separate reference to "reputation", however, the definition makes clear that identification of a particular objective attribute of a good is not a prerequisite to conferring protection. It is enough that the public associates a good with a territory because the public believes the good to have desirable characteristics, *i.e.*, that the good enjoys a "reputation" linked to the identifier of the place.

Geographical indications, like trademarks, may be built up through investment in advertising. This leads to the possibility that the public will in fact be deceived as to the quality of goods and its territorial link through false or misleading advertisement.

Article 22.1 refers to "other characteristic" of the good. If quality is commonly understood as implying a positive attribute, and reputation is commonly understood to imply a favourable impression, the term "other characteristic" may imply that a good may have an attribute such as colour, texture or fragrance that might be considered more neutral or even unfavourable in the perception of consumers, yet still entitle the producing territory to protect its name in respect of that good.

The quality, etc., must be "essentially attributable" to the geographic territory.[369] This term or phrase is intended to establish the "link" between the product and the relevant territory. In large measure, the question whether product characteristics or reputation are attributable to a territory is at the root of debate concerning the potential scope of coverage for geographical indications. A literal reading of "territory" would suggest that the link must be physical, that is, that the product must embody certain characteristics because of the soil conditions, weather or

---

[369] The Oxford New Shorter English Dictionary defines "attributable" as an adjective as "able to be attributed *to*, owing *to*". As a noun, "attribute" is defined as
"2 A quality or character ascribed (esp. in common estimation) to a person or thing. Also, an epithet denoting this...4 An inherent characteristic quality or feature of a person or thing; a property; in *Statistics* etc., a non-quantifiable property."

other physical elements in a place. This might be demonstrable, for example, in respect to wines the grapes for which are harvested in certain locations. However, because the notion of "essentially attributable" to geographic territory is extended by other terms in the Article 22.1 definition to refer to reputation, this implies that the link to territory may be based on human labour in the place. It might even extend to goodwill created by advertisement in respect to the place, although such an interpretation might at some point strain the definition of "attributable" which appears to require that the characteristic or reputation be inherent in the place, and not be solely the figment of a product marketer's imagination. This is not to suggest that national authorities in each WTO Member must adopt a broad reading of "reputation" or "essentially attributable", but rather to suggest that the language has some inherent flexibility.

3.1.2 Article 22.2

> In respect of geographical indications, Members shall provide the legal means for interested parties to prevent:
>
> (a) the use of any means in the designation or presentation of a good that indicates or suggests that the good in question originates in a geographical area other than the true place of origin in a manner which misleads the public as to the geographical origin of the good;
>
> (b) any use which constitutes an act of unfair competition within the meaning of Article 10*bis* of the Paris Convention (1967).

Article 22.2 establishes the basic standard of protection for geographical indications. It is a non-specific standard leaving to Members substantial flexibility. It should be noted at the outset of this discussion that Article 23, TRIPS Agreement, eliminates a significant degree of this flexibility for geographical indications pertaining to wines and sprits, and the following discussion may be helpful in explaining why Article 23 was adopted.

A Member must "provide the legal means". The "legal means" could refer to a wide variety of statutory, administrative and/or common law methods of protection, and appears to encompass all the possibilities for protection in use by Members when TRIPS entered into force. As described earlier, this includes protection under common law doctrines of unfair competition, passing off, registration of collective and certification marks, registration of geographical indications and appellations of origin, and administrative mechanisms.

The legal means must be provided to "interested parties". This would extend beyond governmental authorities to persons with rights in the geographical indication in question, but again leaves substantial flexibility as to how the requirement might be implemented. For example, in respect of a region, the party interested in a geographical indication might be an organization or collective of producers that exercises control over use of the relevant term, and the "interested party" might be limited to the organization or collective. In this context, national law may limit access to the legal means for protection to what is defined as an "interested party" for this purpose. Article 22.2 does not appear to require that all persons who might conceivably assert an interest in a geographical indication be entitled to prosecute a claim of protection.[370]

The scope of protection in Article 22.2(a) extends to "the use of any means in the designation or presentation of a good that indicates or suggests that the good in question" originates in a place. The reference to "any means in the designation or presentation" is rather broad, and appears to encompass the notion that the designation or presentation need only "evoke" the territory, and thus not be limited to a geographic name. For example, the name of a cheese may often not be that of a geographic location as such, but rather be associated with a particular locality where it is produced. The Article 22.2(a) reference to "designation or presentation" does not exclude the names of cheeses that evoke a locality. Moreover, the reference to "any means" may extend to graphical or pictorial representations of a region. When the terms "any means" are read in combination with "indicates or suggests", the definition appears to be open to a wide potential range of signifiers that would evoke a connection between a good and a place.

Having noted that the potential range of signifiers is very broad, the definition is qualified by the terms "originates in a geographical area other than the true place of origin in a manner which misleads the public as to the geographical origin of the good". The "true place of origin" refers to the place where the good is actually grown, mined or manufactured, as opposed to the geographic location where, in view of the interested party, it should have been made. The key limitation in the Article 22.2(a) definition is that the designation *"misleads the public as to the geographical origin of the good"* [italics added].

Under what circumstances will a designation be understood to "mislead the public"? The "public" might be understood as the general consumer with limited knowledge as to the origin of products, or it might be understood as a more specialized group of consumers who regularly purchase the products in question. By way of illustration, many cheeses are marketed in the United States under names of European origin. However, it is very doubtful that a significant part of the consuming public in the United States draws a link between these cheeses and any geographic location. Assuming solely for argument's sake that American consumers have some vague sense that a type of cheese at some point was made in Europe, specific knowledge as to a geographical link is likely to be limited to a very small portion of consumers.[371] If only a small part of American consumers might be confused as to the geographic origin of their purchases, does that small part constitute the "public"?

---

[370] Note that Article 10(2) of the Paris Convention enumerates parties who should be accorded the right to prevent imports under Article 10. However, there are substantial differences between the substantive obligations under Article 10 of the Paris Convention and under Article 22.2 of the TRIPS Agreement, and it is not clear what conclusions might be drawn from such reference. *See also* Section 2.1.1.1 *supra*.

[371] In U.S. trademark law, establishing consumer confusion generally requires that some significant portion of the relevant consuming public identifies a mark with a good, and not only a few with specialized knowledge. In European trademark law, it may be more accepted that specialized consumers, even though small in number, will be considered to form a sufficient target of confusion.

National authorities might determine that consumers will not be misled if there is sufficient information regarding the actual (or true) origin of the product on labelling or packaging, even if a geographical indication appears on the labelling or packaging as well. Of course, whether adequate labelling might serve to dispel potential confusion would depend on the way it is presented. Even accurate information can be presented in a misleading way.

The term "Champagne" is often used as the paradigm geographical indication that has earned protection against use by producers outside a region. It is doubtful that interested parties of most other geographical terms can establish close to the level of association that consumers make between the Champagne region of France and quality sparkling wine. Even in light of that strong association, German producers of "Sekt" argued vigorously before the European Court of Justice that consumers would *not* be confused by a label referring to the "champagne-method" of production, provided that a bottle disclosed the true origination of the product in Germany.[372] (The ECJ rejected the petition of the German producers on grounds, *inter alia*, that the Community had not acted in a manifestly inappropriate way. Its regulations were within the permissible scope of Community regulation.)

The requirement that a geographical indication mislead the public as to the origin of a good places considerable discretion in the hands of national authorities to determine how the "public" will be defined and how strong an association there must be to establish that the public is "misled".

Article 22.2(b) refers to "any use which constitutes an act of unfair competition within the meaning of Article 10*bis* of the Paris Convention (1967)."[373] As noted in Section 2.1.1.1 of this chapter, the Paris Convention establishes a general frame of reference regarding the doctrine of unfair competition, rules on which are found in all legal systems, though legislated and implemented in different ways. As noted in the introductory discussion, common law systems allowed causes of action against the misleading use of geographical names under the doctrine of "passing off" (or, in essence, representing that goods were those of a competitor), or as a tort of unfair competition. Since unfair competition is not a rigidly defined concept, Article 22.2(b) appears primarily intended to bring forward the causes of action previously found in common and civil law legal systems with respect to geographical indications, but without attempting to more precisely regulate how those causes of action are defined or implemented. For example, Article 10*bis*(3)(3), Paris Convention, provides that acts prohibited under the doctrine of unfair competition shall include "indications or allegations the use of which in the course of trade is liable to mislead the public as to the nature, the manufacturing process, the characteristics, the suitability for their purpose, or the quantity, of the goods." It is not clear the extent to which this provision adds to the obligation established by Article 22.2(a) of TRIPS to prevent the use of geographical indications in a way that would mislead the public as to the origin of goods,

---

[372] See *SMW Winzersekt GmbH v. Land Rheinland-Pfalz*, ECJ, (C-306/93), [1995] 2 CMLR 718.

[373] The subject of unfair competition is also treated in this book in respect to trade secrets, which rely on Article 10*bis* as the legal ground for protection in Article 39.1, TRIPS Agreement. See Chapter 28.

especially since the protectable characteristics include the quality, reputation or "other characteristics" associated with the goods. The reference to Article 10*bis* may be intended to indicate that Article 22.2(a) should not be understood as a limitation on causes of action previously available under Article 10*bis*, Paris Convention, regarding geographical indications. It may also be argued that Article 22.2(b) extends the scope of protection provided under Article 22.2(a) because it protects against misleading the public regarding the "nature or characteristics of goods", thus encompassing more directly the situation where a geographic indication is used along with a qualifier or disclaimer (e.g., California Chablis). This situation may already be within the scope of potentially misleading consumers concerning "origin", because qualifiers and disclaimers in trademark law (by way of analogy) are not necessarily a barrier to a finding of consumer confusion. The fact that a consumer may ultimately recognize that "California Chablis" does not originate in a region in France does not mean that the consumer's initial interest was not attracted by a misleading suggestion of origin. Ultimately this is a question of fact.

As noted earlier, Article 23 provides additional protection for wines and spirits and expressly limits the flexibilities inherent in Article 22. Moreover, Article 22.2 must be read in connection with Article 24 that establishes exceptions to some generally applicable rules.

3.1.3 Article 22.3

A Member shall, *ex officio* if its legislation so permits or at the request of an interested party, refuse or invalidate the registration of a trademark which contains or consists of a geographical indication with respect to goods not originating in the territory indicated, if use of the indication in the trademark for such goods in that Member is of such a nature as to mislead the public as to the true place of origin.

Article 22.3 should be read in conjunction with Article 24.5. The practical effect of Article 22.3 is substantially affected by Article 24.5.

Article 22.3 essentially establishes that trademarks should not be registered if they contain or consist of a geographical indication in a manner "as to" mislead the public as to the origin of goods. It refers both to future applications for registration, which should be denied, and to existing registrations, which should be invalidated. Article 22.3 relies on the "mislead the public" language of Article 22.2(a). It is not clear why the drafters of Article 22.3 chose not to refer back to Article 22.2(a) as the definitional context for marks that should be precluded from registration or should be invalidated, though perhaps it was thought that Article 22.2(b) would expand the potential range of indications that should be subject to Article 22.3.

Article 22.3 places substantial discretion in the hands of trademark registration authorities since (a) it provides that they should act *ex officio* if permitted under national law and (b) it places in their hands at least an initial determination whether the public will be misled by use of a geographical term. Article 22.3 appears to place an affirmative duty on trademark registration authorities to examine the records of issued trademarks for evidence of conflict with geographical indications for purposes of potential purging of misleading marks, though it seems unlikely that trademark authorities would in fact be prepared to undertake such a retroactive review of registered marks. Moreover, since Article 24.5 excludes marks registered or acquired by use in good faith prior to entry into force of TRIPS Agreement provisions in the respective Member, there would be grounds only to look back at trademarks acquired in "bad faith". The actions of trademark authorities are in any event subject to the requirements of Part IV, TRIPS Agreement, regarding the acquisition and maintenance of rights (see Part 4 of this book).

3.1.4 Article 22.4

> The protection under paragraphs 1, 2 and 3 shall be applicable against a geographical indication which, although literally true as to the territory, region or locality in which the goods originate, falsely represents to the public that the goods originate in another territory.

Article 22.4 is directed to the circumstance in which a territory or locality in Member A has taken the same name as a territory or locality in Member B, and a person in Member A uses a corresponding geographical indication to take advantage of the reputation of a good built up in Member B. This might, for example, apply to a locality in the Americas that used the name of a European locality when it was established. It is in effect an anti-circumvention measure. It may be argued that producers of an identically-named region should not be precluded from using their own geographical name in commerce, provided that they adequately indicate the actual geographical origin of goods through labelling.

3.2 Article 23 (Wines and Spirits)

3.2.1 Article 23.1

> Each Member shall provide the legal means for interested parties to prevent use of a geographical indication identifying wines for wines not originating in the place indicated by the geographical indication in question or identifying spirits for spirits not originating in the place indicated by the geographical indication in question, even where the true origin of the goods is indicated or the geographical indication is used in translation or accompanied by expressions such as 'kind', 'type', 'style', 'imitation' or the like.*
>
> [Footnote]* Notwithstanding the first sentence of Article 42, Members may, with respect to these obligations, instead provide for enforcement by administrative action.

It is important to observe at the outset of discussion of Article 23 that obligations under it are significantly qualified by exceptions set out in Article 24. These exceptions are detailed in discussion of Article 24 (see below, Section 3.3 of this chapter).

Article 23 is limited in its scope of application to "wines"[374] and "spirits".[375] There is considerable scope for defining wines and spirits more and less inclusively. Although the most common reference to "wine" is to a product made from grapes, there are other distilled alcoholic beverages that use the term "wine", including "rice wine" and wines made from various fruits other than grapes (for example, "peach wine"). Uruguay Round negotiators manifested their understanding that wine may include more products than grape-derived wine when in Article 24.6 they specifically referred to "products of the vine" and "grape varieties". The term "spirits" may be limited to beverages with a higher alcoholic content which is perhaps the most common understanding of that term. A narrow definition of "wines" and "spirits" may exclude certain intermediate alcoholic beverages between wines (which generally have a lower alcohol content) and spirits (which generally have a higher alcoholic content), such as certain liqueurs. It appears that the text of Article 23.1 does not include "beer",[376] which is certainly not wine, nor is it within the common understanding of "spirits" (because, *inter alia*, the alcohol content of beer is typically low). The intention of the drafters as regard the scope of "wines" and "spirits" is not clear from the text of Article 23.1, leaving to Members some discretion as to the scope of coverage for these terms.

As with respect to Article 22.2, the use of the term "legal means" in Article 23.1 leaves to the discretion of each Member the manner in which it will implement its obligation to allow "interested parties" to prevent use. Also, the "interested parties" who are entitled to bring an action may be defined in national law. Because wine growing regions commonly impose conditions on local producers to be considered authorized users of the regional denomination, this may account for restrictions in some national laws regarding who is entitled to bring an action as an "interested party".

Unlike Article 22.2(a), Article 23.1 does not impose the requirement that use of the geographical indication mislead the public. The difficulties inherent in demonstrating consumer association between the product and the place are dispensed with. Furthermore, Article 23.1 goes a step further and addresses the potential cure by labelling. Neither indicating the true origin of the good, nor use of the terms "kind", "type", "style", "imitation" or "the like", in conjunction with the geographical indication is acceptable as a cure for use of the indication.

The preclusion of cure by accurate labelling is not so unusual in the context of protection of identifiers. In trademark law, for example, use of a third person's mark for commercialization purposes is not generally cured if accompanied by

---

[374] The New Shorter Oxford English Dictionary defines wine, as a noun: "1 Alcoholic liquor produced from fermented grape juice; (with specifying wd) a type of this; a drink of this. 2 Alcoholic liquor resembling wine made from the fermented juice of other fruits, or from grain, flowers, the sap of various trees, etc. Usu. w. specifying wd".

[375] The New Shorter Oxford English Dictionary defines "spirit", as a noun: "13c Strong distilled alcoholic liquor for drinking".

[376] The New Shorter Oxford English Dictionary defines "beer", as a noun: "1 Alcoholic liquor produced by fermentation of malt etc. and flavoured with hops or other bitters, *esp.* the lighter kind of liquor so produced; a type of this; a drink of this".

an indication of the actual producer of the good. This is because the consumer is drawn to the good by the mark. The mark has confused the consumer, even if that confusion is eventually dispelled.

Yet the preclusion of cure by additional labelling does not resolve all questions relating to association between a product and a place. The definition of "geographical indication" in Article 22.1, which also applies to Article 23, requires that there be a link between the product – whether by quality, reputation or other characteristic – and the place. While under Article 23.1 the person asserting rights in a geographical indication for wines or spirits need not demonstrate that consumers have been misled by a third party's use, the person asserting rights must still demonstrate that there is a link between the wine or spirit and the territory – to the exclusion of the other's potential claim to a *bona fide* use (although, as noted below, homonymous indications may be enforced, raising the possibility that more than one claimant may have rights to prevent use). That is, the capacity to enforce a geographical indication depends on holding a geographical indication to the exclusion of others.

Footnote 4 provides that Members may enforce the obligation under Article 23.1 through administrative action, despite the first sentence of Article 42. The latter provides:

> "Members shall make available to right holders* civil judicial procedures concerning the enforcement of any intellectual property right covered by this Agreement".

> [Footnote] "*For the purpose of this Part, the term 'right holder' includes federations and associations having legal standing to assert such rights."

This suggests that holders of geographical indications in wines and spirits may have a more limited set of judicial remedies available than other IPR holders under TRIPS. However, this should not be understood to reduce the protections afforded to defendants to protect their interests, as already provided in Article 49 regarding administrative procedures, which states:

> "To the extent that any civil remedy can be ordered as a result of administrative procedures on the merits of a case, such procedures shall conform to principles equivalent in substance to those set forth in this Section."[377]

3.2.2 Article 23.2

> The registration of a trademark for wines which contains or consists of a geographical indication identifying wines or for spirits which contains or consists of a geographical indication identifying spirits shall be refused or invalidated, *ex officio* if a Member's legislation so permits or at the request of an interested party, with respect to such wines or spirits not having this origin.

Article 23.2 should be read in conjunction with Article 24.5. The practical effect of Article 23.2 is substantially affected by Article 24.5.

---

[377] For more details on this provision, see Chapter 30.

Article 23.2 is similar to Article 22.3, except it dispenses with "if use of the indication in the trademark for such goods in that Member is of such a nature as to mislead the public as to the true place of origin". In this regard, the scope of inquiry by the trademark registration authorities under Article 23.2 should be significantly more limited than under Article 22.3. Again, however, it remains for the claimant to demonstrate that it is the holder of a geographical indication – linking a product to a place – and this imposes a burden of proof on the claimant.

3.2.3 Article 23.3

> In the case of homonymous geographical indications for wines, protection shall be accorded to each indication, subject to the provisions of paragraph 4 of Article 22. Each Member shall determine the practical conditions under which the homonymous indications in question will be differentiated from each other, taking into account the need to ensure equitable treatment of the producers concerned and that consumers are not misled.

"Homonymous" is defined by the New Shorter Oxford English Dictionary (as an adjective) as

> "1 Employing the same name for different things, equivocal, ambiguous 2 Having the same name".

Article 23.3 addresses the situation in which two different geographic regions use the same name for a wine or spirit, and where each such use is *bona fide*. (The reference back to Article 22.4 excludes the circumstance in which a second-user has adopted a geographic name to take unfair advantage of the original user of that name.) It is left to each Member to determine "practical conditions under which the homonymous indications in question will be differentiated from each other". This instruction is decidedly vague and leaves each Member with substantial discretion as to how it might require producing regions to distinguish their products. This might include, for example, requiring that the country of origin be stated on the label in a particular way (in addition to the more specific geographical indication). The direction to take into account equitable treatment of producers suggests that measures should not be used to discriminate in favour of producers of one region over another. The direction to protect consumers suggests that whatever system is adopted should clearly inform the consumer.

3.2.4 Article 23.4

> In order to facilitate the protection of geographical indications for wines, negotiations shall be undertaken in the Council for TRIPS concerning the establishment of a multilateral system of notification and registration of geographical indications for wines eligible for protection in those Members participating in the system.

Article 23.4 placed on the built-in agenda of the TRIPS Council a negotiation limited to the subject matter of wines.[378] This paragraph refers to Members "participating in the system", and it might well be understood as envisioning the possibility of a plurilateral agreement.[379] Alternatively, it might be suggested that since not all Members are wine producers, even if there is true multilateral agreement on a register, not all Members would be understood to "participate" in the system. (This interpretation suffers from the fact that protection for wine exporters depends on recognition of rights in importing Members, so that Members without producers would still be required to "participate" in the system if it is to work on a multilateral basis.) Or, the negotiations might result in a multilateral agreement as to which Members could choose to participate or not, although this would seem mainly in the nature of a plurilateral agreement.

The term "notification" indicates that part of the negotiations should concern only a system for providing information. Of course, notification may have a beneficial effect for those seeking to protect geographical indications since, for example, trademark authorities may be required under Article 23.2 to take *ex officio* action to revoke trademarks that consist of geographical indications. With a notification system in place, trademark authorities might avoid a search for potentially relevant geographical indications.

The term "registration" implies steps toward a more enforcement-oriented system, since registration of IP rights generally establishes a presumption in favour of the registered right holder. Whether registration creates a presumption of rights might depend on whether registration is predicated upon substantive review by relevant authorities, or is automatic based on application. If registration is automatic, a good case can be made for denying such act a presumption-creating effect.

In the TRIPS Council, Members have expressed differing views on the interpretation of this provision.[380]

In any event, Article 23.4 does not obligate Members to do anything other than to undertake negotiations in the TRIPS Council.

3.3 Article 24 (International negotiations; exceptions)

3.3.1 Article 24.1

Members agree to enter into negotiations aimed at increasing the protection of individual geographical indications under Article 23. The provisions of paragraphs 4 through 8 below shall not be used by a Member to refuse to conduct negotiations or to conclude bilateral or multilateral agreements. In the context

---

[378] Note that the scope of these negotiations was later extended to cover also spirits. See Section 6.4, below.

[379] Under WTO law, a plurilateral agreement is an agreement to which not every WTO Member is a party. Adherence is optional (e.g. the WTO Agreement on Government Procurement). Most of the WTO Agreements are multilateral agreements: participation is mandatory and an integral part of a country's membership in the WTO ("single undertaking").

[380] See below, Section 6.4 of this chapter.

> of such negotiations, Members shall be willing to consider the continued appli-
> cability of these provisions to individual geographical indications whose use was
> the subject of such negotiations.

Article 24.1 provides a basis for future negotiations. The reference in the first sentence to "individual geographical indications" suggests that Members intended
to address indications on an identifier-by-identifier basis, as opposed to a product class-by-product class basis. The term "individual" is an adjective or noun
referring to a single item.[381] It would be difficult to construe the term "individual
geographical indications" as referring to something other than particular names
suggesting territories.

The latter issue being uncontested, the interpretation of this provision has nevertheless been the source of considerable controversy in the TRIPS Council. Delegations disagree on the question whether Article 24.1 is limited to geographical
indications for wines and spirits, or whether it authorizes negotiations to extend
the additional protection available under Article 23 TRIPS to goods other than
wines and spirits.[382]

Members opposing such extension argue that the terms "individual geographical indications under Article 23" relate exclusively to the goods covered by
Article 23, i.e. wines and spirits. According to this view, the reference to increased
protection of those indications relates to the possible abolition of the current exemption under Article 24.4.[383] Consequently, the authorization for negotiations
under Article 24.1 would be limited to 'individual indications for wines and spirits'.[384] Therefore, there would be no mandate for negotiations on the extension of
the Article 23 protection to products other than wines and spirits. Such negotiations would re-open TRIPS without any legal basis.[385]

Members favouring the extension contend that "provisions of Article 24.1 are
of general application to all products and the reference to Article 23 does not relate to products contained therein but to a means of additional protection to be
provided."[386] To support their view, those Members refer to Article 24.2, which authorizes the TRIPS Council to keep under review the application of the provisions

---

[381] The New Shorter Oxford English Dictionary defines "individual" as a noun and adjective as
"3 Existing as a separate indivisible identity; numerically one; single, as distinct from others of the
same kind; particular. 4 Of, pertaining or peculiar to a single person or thing, rather than a group;
characteristic of an individual."

[382] For a detailed discussion of the opposing arguments in the TRIPS Council and an overview of
the positions taken by WTO Members, see Rangnekar, *Geographical Indications. A Review of Proposals at the TRIPS Council: Extending Article 23 to Products other than Wines and Spirits*, UNCTAD-
ICTSD, Geneva, 2003 [hereinafter Rangnekar] (also available at <http://www.iprsonline.org/
unctadictsd/projectoutputs.htm#casestudies>). The following paragraphs are based on that study.

[383] See the Communication from New Zealand (IP/C/W/205, paragraph 23).

[384] Ibid., paragraph 22; see also the TRIPS Council Minutes of Meeting of 6 March 2001 (IP/C/M/29,
point G).

[385] See the Communication from Argentina, Australia, Canada, Chile, Guatemala, New Zealand,
Paraguay, and the USA (IP/C/W/289, paragraph 3).

[386] See the Communication from Bulgaria, the Czech Republic, Egypt, Iceland, India, Kenya,
Liechtenstein, Pakistan, Slovenia, Sri Lanka, Switzerland and Turkey (IP/C/W/204, paragraph 12).

on geographical indications. With respect to this mandated review, the TRIPS Council reported to the 1996 Singapore Ministerial that inputs from delegations on the issue of scope were permitted.[387] The supporters of extension consider this reference by the TRIPS Council to the "scope" of the review to support[388] negotiations on extension in the above sense.[389]

So far, this interpretative issue has not been settled.

The second sentence of Article 24.1 refers to the exceptions of Article 24.4–8, and indicates that the exceptions should not be used as the basis for refusing to conduct future negotiations. Some Members apparently considered that other Members would argue that because certain geographical indications are not currently protected, they should not be protected in the future. That is, that an agreement to exclude those indications *ab initio* barred the future consideration of their protection. As a practical matter, allowing for the future consideration of matters initially excepted does not affect what Members might otherwise negotiate over, since future negotiations might relate to any matters already addressed by an agreement. Nonetheless, the provision appears aimed at clarifying the initial intent.

Some Members also were concerned that the exceptions would be used by some other Members to refuse negotiations on protection of geographical indications in the bilateral or multilateral context outside the WTO TRIPS Agreement framework. Although Members may pursue negotiations regarding IPRs matters not covered by TRIPS, the potential for concluding bilateral or multilateral negotiations on geographical indications outside the Council for TRIPS context raises some difficult questions under the principle of non-discrimination embodied in Article 4 regarding most favoured nation (MFN) treatment.[390] If Member A agrees on a bilateral basis to protect certain geographical indications of Member B, but does not agree to protect other geographical indications of Member C, it would appear that Member A is discriminating in favour of Member B and against Member C. From a TRIPS standpoint, failure of reciprocity is not an adequate defence to an allegation of discrimination. TRIPS Agreement rights and obligations are not based on reciprocity. Nevertheless, extending bilateral rights in geographical indications to other Members could prove to be quite complex, where bilateral protection has been negotiated for individual indications, as authorized under Article 24.1, and not for an entire product class.[391] If Member A affords TRIPS-plus protection to a particular indication from Member B, it cannot simply extend the protection of this particular indication to Member C, because the protected good is not produced in C, and producers from C must not use the indication protected in B.[392] Instead, Members A and C would have to agree, in bilateral

---

[387] See document IP/C/8, paragraph 34.

[388] Rangnekar, p. 45, with further arguments and discussion.

[389] See the Communication (Revision) from Bulgaria, the Czech Republic, Egypt, Iceland, India, Kenya, Liechtenstein, Pakistan, Slovenia, Sri Lanka, Switzerland and Turkey (IP/C/W/204/Rev.1, paragraph 14).

[390] Discussed in Chapter 4.

[391] See Article 24.1 TRIPS, which refers to "individual geographical indications". See above, the interpretation of the first sentence of Article 24.

[392] For example, the USA could not just extend the protection granted to "Champagne" to producers in Argentina, who do not and must not produce "Champagne".

negotiations, which particular geographical indication from Member C would en-joy, in Member A, a protection comparable to the one afforded to the indication from Member B.[393] It remains for Members to clarify this situation.

The final sentence of Article 24.1 essentially brings Members back to the starting point. That is, the Members who might have refused to negotiate on grounds that certain geographical indications were exempted under Articles 24.4–8 may yet de-cide that they wish to see those exemptions maintained. There is no presumption in favour of extending the scope of protection.

3.3.2 Article 24.2

> The Council for TRIPS shall keep under review the application of the provisions of this Section; the first such review shall take place within two years of the entry into force of the WTO Agreement. Any matter affecting the compliance with the obligations under these provisions may be drawn to the attention of the Council, which, at the request of a Member, shall consult with any Member or Members in respect of such matter in respect of which it has not been possible to find a satisfactory solution through bilateral or plurilateral consultations between the Members concerned. The Council shall take such action as may be agreed to facilitate the operation and further the objectives of this Section.

Article 24.2, first sentence, places review of the "application" of Part II, Section 3, on the built-in agenda of the TRIPS Council, with the first review scheduled to take place prior to December 31, 1996. The reference to "application" suggests that it is the conduct of Members in implementing provisions, rather than the provisions themselves, that are the subject of the review. The second sentence en-titles a Member with a complaint concerning compliance with the provisions to bring the matter to the attention of the TRIPS Council for consultations and, fol-lowing failed bilateral or plurilateral consultations, the Council will consult with a Member or Members that are complained about. The third sentence provides that the Council "shall take such action as may be agreed to facilitate the operation and further the objectives of this Section." This third sentence presumably relates to both of the two preceding sentences, that is, the Council's general obligation to review application of the Section and specific complaints raised by Members. There are several interesting aspects to the third sentence. First, action is limited to matters that may be "agreed". This suggests that no Member could be directed to take measures to which it objects, assuming that the Council for TRIPS con-tinues to operate by consensus. Second, the action should involve steps that may

---

[393] This is the reason why in the Anell Draft, the provision on bilateral agreements (paragraph 4.2b, see above, Section 2.2) proposed "to require each PARTY belonging to such an agreement to be ready to extend such advantage, favour, privilege or immunity, on terms equivalent to those under the agreement, to any other PARTY so requesting *and to enter into good faith negotiations to this end*." (emphasis added). This problem is particular to geographical indications. In the case of other intellectual property rights, bilateral TRIPS-plus protection is usually negotiated for an entire category of rights (i.e. patents) and not for individual products. Therefore, the extension of such protection to other WTO Members does not depend on further negotiations. If, for instance, Member A accords TRIPS-plus protection to patent holders from Member B, it can extend the same type of protection to patent holders from Member C.

"facilitate the operation and further the objectives" of the Section. Such action might be a recommendation to one or more Members regarding compliance with the agreement, or it might involve making a broader recommendation regarding amendments or modifications to the Section. Although the text is not a model of clarity, it seems doubtful that the third sentence is intended to confer authority on the Council for TRIPS to take measures regarding changes to TRIPS in a manner different than that prescribed by the WTO Agreement.

3.3.3 Article 24.3

> In implementing this Section, a Member shall not diminish the protection of geographical indications that existed in that Member immediately prior to the date of entry into force of the WTO Agreement.

This provision appears to be directed to preventing Members from taking advantage of the flexibility inherent in Section 3 to the detriment of parties claiming rights in geographical indications. Although it is similar to Article 65.5, TRIPS, precluding developing Members enjoying a transition period from reducing consistency with TRIPS provisions,[394] it is worded differently. Article 65.5 does not suggest that laws should remain unchanged, provided that the result is consistent with the Agreement. Article 24.3 implies that there is a standard by which the protection of geographical indications may be measured, and that future actions should not place geographical indications below that standard. This is an ambiguous approach or concept since it presumes a measurement of the strength of protection that is not otherwise found in TRIPS, and it is unclear what the benchmarks for such measurement would be.

3.3.4 Article 24.4

> Nothing in this Section shall require a Member to prevent continued and similar use of a particular geographical indication of another Member identifying wines or spirits in connection with goods or services by any of its nationals or domiciliaries who have used that geographical indication in a continuous manner with regard to the same or related goods or services in the territory of that Member either (a) for at least 10 years preceding 15 April 1994 or (b) in good faith preceding that date.

Article 24.4 establishes a critical exception from the scope of Article 23. A Member is not required to prevent "continued and similar use" of particular geographical indications for wines and spirits. The exclusion applies to "goods and services". This is significant because Section 3 otherwise establishes rules only respecting

---

[394] Article 65.5 provides:
"A Member availing itself of a transitional period under paragraphs 1, 2, 3 or 4 shall ensure that any changes in its laws, regulations and practice made during that period do not result in a lesser degree of consistency with the provisions of this Agreement."
For a detailed analysis of this provision, see Chapter 33.

"goods". The services might include, for example, advertising of wines and spirits, or listing them on restaurant menus. The rule applies not only to persons who are nationals, but also to persons domiciled in the Member, who have used the indication. The first of two criteria for qualifying for exception is that the indication has been used continuously, and in respect to the same or related goods and services in the territory of the Member, since at least 15 April 1984 (that is, ten years prior to 15 April 1994).[395] This first criterion is not qualified by a requirement of good faith. The similar or identical geographical indication may have been deliberately adopted to take advantage of the reputation of foreign producers.

A second (alternative) criterion is that the geographical indication has been used prior to 15 April 1994 "in good faith". The "good faith" element is a potential source of controversy. From the standpoint of the party that adopted the geographical indication, "good faith" might mean a belief that its action did not violate a legal rule, even if it knew that producers in a foreign territory used the same indication. From the standpoint of a complaining producing region, "good faith" might suggest that the party adopting the indication was not aware, or did not have reason to be aware, of the indication that was adopted. If use of a foreign geographical indication was permitted under national law prior to 15 April 1994, it may be difficult to succeed with a case that its use was in bad faith. Action in bad faith implies wrongful conduct, and in the commercial context wrongful conduct is typically that which is contrary to legal norms.[396]

The two criteria of exclusion for wines and spirits suggest that much of the protection afforded by Article 23 will be prospective in nature, rather than reaching back to practices ongoing as of the time of the Marrakesh Ministerial.

3.3.5 Article 24.5

> Where a trademark has been applied for or registered in good faith, or where rights to a trademark have been acquired through use in good faith either:
>
> (a) before the date of application of these provisions in that Member as defined in Part VI; or
>
> (b) before the geographical indication is protected in its country of origin; measures adopted to implement this Section shall not prejudice eligibility for or the validity of the registration of a trademark, or the right to use a trademark, on the basis that such a trademark is identical with, or similar to, a geographical indication.

Article 24.5 excludes from the application of Article 22.3 and Article 23.2 trademarks (i) that have been applied for or registered in good faith or (ii) that have been acquired by use in good faith. The criterion of "good faith" is not specifically

---

[395] 15 April 1994 is the date on which the Uruguay Round Agreements were adopted at the Marrakesh Ministerial. Members adopted this date in Article 24.3 presumably to prevent commercial operators from taking advantage of the delay until 1 January 1995 to initiate "good faith" use of indications.

[396] Article 39, TRIPS Agreement, refers to actions contrary to "honest commercial practices", but includes a list of practices that are contrary to legal norms.

defined, but may mean that an intention to take unfair advantage of a competitor was absent, or that the applicant or registrant had a reasonable belief that its actions were not contrary to existing legal principles within its own jurisdiction.

The exception is limited in time to two circumstances. Registration must have been applied for or granted, or use must have been commenced, prior to entry into force of this section of TRIPS for the subject country (so, for example, on 1 January 2000, for developing countries), or before the indication is protected in its country of origin. Although the text is inelegantly drafted, it would appear that the temporal limitations established by subsections (a) and (b) apply both to registered marks and common law marks because the phrases following these subsections qualify registered marks as well as common law marks, and there is no indication that common law and registered marks are to be treated differently.

3.3.6 Article 24.6

> Nothing in this Section shall require a Member to apply its provisions in respect of a geographical indication of any other Member with respect to goods or services for which the relevant indication is identical with the term customary in common language as the common name for such goods or services in the territory of that Member. Nothing in this Section shall require a Member to apply its provisions in respect of a geographical indication of any other Member with respect to products of the vine for which the relevant indication is identical with the customary name of a grape variety existing in the territory of that Member as of the date of entry into force of the WTO Agreement.

Article 24.6 recognizes that some terms claimed as geographical indications are the common name for goods and services in Members, and provides a general exception for providing protection against the usage of such names. Article 24.6 does not rely on the term "generic", which is an important term in trademark law, to describe the subject terms, but rather uses the phrase "the term customary in common language as the common name". The term "generic" (or "non-generic") was proposed for use in parts of this Section during the negotiation phase. Perhaps it was rejected because negotiators did not want the specialized trademark law meaning to be transposed to this context (recognizing that the term "generic" may be defined differently in Members), or perhaps it was rejected because the term "generic" tends to apply to the broad class of a product, while geographical indications may typically apply to a specialized product. In any case, whether a term is the common name for goods and services is a factual question that is analogous to the trademark law factual question whether a term is generic. An inquiry may rely on dictionaries, books and periodicals, consumer surveys and the knowledge of the judge.[397]

The second sentence is inelegantly drafted. The sentence is ambiguous because it uses the term "Member" three times, but it is not completely clear to which "Member" the third reference to "that Member" is intended to apply. The sentence

---

[397] In trademark cases where a term is argued to be generic, if the term is sufficiently familiar, *e.g.*, "chair", a judge may determine genericness as a matter of his or her own knowledge.

could be construed such that if, in Member A, wine is produced from and given the name of grapes that are customarily known in Member A by the name of a geographic region in Member B, protection need not be provided to the name of the geographic region in Member B. Article 26.3 of the Brussels Text (see Subsection 2.2.6 above), would suggest that this first construction is intended. Alternatively, the second sentence may provide an exception from protection in Member A as to a geographical indication for grape wine which is, as to Member B, both the geographic name associated with the wine and the customary name of the grape variety from which it is made.[398]

3.3.7 Article 24.7

> A Member may provide that any request made under this Section in connection with the use or registration of a trademark must be presented within five years after the adverse use of the protected indication has become generally known in that Member or after the date of registration of the trademark in that Member provided that the trademark has been published by that date, if such date is earlier than the date on which the adverse use became generally known in that Member, provided that the geographical indication is not used or registered in bad faith.

A request regarding a trademark under this Section would be directed to the trademark authorities asking that the mark be refused registration or invalidated because it conflicts with a protected geographical indication. A "request" might be made in connection with "use" to the extent that an application for registration is based on use in commerce, and a request for refusal is based on the use.

Article 24.7 allows a Member to provide, first, that a "request" must be made within a 5-year period after the geographical indication "has become generally known" in the Member where the request is made. The concept of "generally known" is employed because a geographical indication might be protected by unfair competition rules (rather than registration) so that knowledge would not arise as a presumption from registration.

Second, a Member may require that a request be made within five years of the registration of a trademark (so the request would be for invalidation), if that were shorter than the period during which adverse use of the geographical indication was generally known. This second option is limited to the extent that the trademark holder must not have registered the geographical indication in bad faith. A geographical indication might be registered as a trademark in bad faith, for example, as a means to prevent a competitor from entering the market without a *bona fide* intention on the part of the registrant to enter the market under that name.

The limitation on the time for requests need not be adopted by Members. It is set out as an option.

---

[398] So, for example, if in Member B wine is made in the "X" region from the "X" grape, wine growers in Member A may make and sell "X" wine because it is named for the "X" grape, even if "X" might otherwise be protected as a geographical indication.

3.3.8 Article 24.8

> The provisions of this Section shall in no way prejudice the right of any person to use, in the course of trade, that person's name or the name of that person's predecessor in business, except where such name is used in such a manner as to mislead the public.

Article 24.8 appears directed to the situation in which a personal name is also used as the name of a business or product, and such name is also a geographical indication. A person retains the right to use their name in business, but not in "such a manner as to mislead the public." This problem arises also in trademark law when a personal name is also a trademark, and the personal name is used for business purposes. It is in fact a question whether the person using the personal name is attempting to unfairly exploit the trademark.

3.3.9 Article 24.9

> There shall be no obligation under this Agreement to protect geographical indications which are not or cease to be protected in their country of origin, or which have fallen into disuse in that country.

Article 24.9 effectively provides that geographical indications, at the option of the Member where protection is sought, are dependent on their treatment in the country of origin. This is different, for example, than the treatment of patents which are independent of their treatment in the country of invention. It reflects the nature of the geographical indication which depends on a link to a territory. If the link is broken, protection is lost. The rule presents some risks to the holders of geographical indications that are dependent on the actions of administrative bodies in their territories since action or inaction by those bodies may deprive the holders of rights they might have asserted based on public association of the geographical indication with the product. The last phrase indicates that a geographical indication may be lost through disuse in the country of origin. This is analogous to the treatment of trademarks, although trademarks are generally maintained or lost in their country of registration or use (not in the country of origin).[399]

4. WTO jurisprudence

4.1 EC – Protection of Trademarks and GIs

Following separate requests by Australia[400] and the USA,[401] the WTO Dispute Settlement Body (DSB) at its meeting on 2 October 2003 established a single

---

[399] Although under the Madrid registration system a mark may during a limited period be lost based on invalidation in the country of origin.

[400] WT/DS290/18 of 19 August 2003.

[401] WT/DS174/20 of 19 August 2003.

panel[402] to examine complaints with respect to EC Council Regulation (EEC) No. 2081/92 of 14 July 1992[403] on the protection of geographical indications and designations of origin for agricultural products and foodstuffs. The complaints are based, *inter alia*, on alleged violations of TRIPS Articles 22.1 (definition of GIs), 22.2 (a) and (b) (obligation to provide the legal means for the prevention of misleading use of GIs and the prevention of any use of GIs constituting an act of unfair competition), and 24.5 (good faith application, registration or use of trademarks).[404]

Article 2 of the above EC Regulation provides definitions for "designations of origin" and "geographical indications".[405] The former appears to be narrower than the latter: as opposed to "geographical indications", "designations of origin" does not refer to a product's reputation as an independent element of protectable subject matter. In addition, the requirement of the link between the product's characteristics and its origin appears to be stricter under "designations of origin": the reference to a particular geographical environment includes a reference to the "inherent natural and human factors", which is not the case for "geographical indications".

The definition of "geographical indications" under Article 22.1 refers to "indications which identify a good as originating in the territory of a Member, or a region or locality..." The above EC Regulation defines "geographical indications" as "the name of a region, a specific place or, in exceptional cases, a country..."

As to the rights conferred by a GI, Article 22.2 (a) establishes the requirement of consumer confusion ("...in a manner which misleads the public as to the

---

[402] *European Communities – Protection of Trademarks and Geographical Indications for Agricultural Products and Foodstuffs* [hereinafter "*EC – Protection of Trademarks and GIs*"], WT/DS174/21 and WT/DS290/19 of 24 February 2004, Constitution of the Panel Established at the Requests of the United States and Australia.

[403] See above, Section 2.1.

[404] See the above requests by Australia and the USA for the establishment of a panel. The alleged violation of Article 22.1 (definition of GIs) was invoked solely by the USA. Australia, on the other hand, asserted a violation of both letters (a) and (b) under Article 22, whereas the USA referred expressly only to misleading use of GIs (letter (a) of the same provision). Note that the same complaint was also based on other TRIPS provisions, in particular relating to the national treatment and most-favoured nation treatment obligations and to trademark protection. See Chapters 4 and 14.

[405] The provision provides in part: "2. For the purposes of this Regulation: (a) designation of origin: means the name of a region, a specific place or, in exceptional cases, a country, used to describe an agricultural product or a foodstuff:
– originating in that region, specific place or country, and
– the quality or characteristics of which are essentially or exclusively due to a particular geographical environment with its inherent natural and human factors, and the production, processing and preparation of which take place in the defined geographical area;
(b) geographical indication: means the name of a region, a specific place or, in exceptional cases, a country, used to describe an agricultural product or a foodstuff:
– originating in that region, specific place or country, and
– which possesses a specific quality, reputation or other characteristics attributable to that geographical origin and the production and/or processing and/or preparation of which take place in the defined geographical area.
3. Certain traditional geographical or non-geographical names designating an agricultural product or a foodstuff originating in a region or a specific place, which fulfil the conditions referred to in the second indent of paragraph 2 (a) shall also be considered as designations of origin. [...]"

geographical origin of the good"). The EC Regulation in Article 13.1 (b) provides that names registered as a "geographical indication" or a "designation of origin" shall be protected against

> "(b) any misuse, imitation or evocation, even if the true origin of the product is indicated or if the protected name is translated or accompanied by an expression such as 'style', 'type', 'method', 'as produced in', 'imitation' or similar"

This provision makes the exercise of the rights conferred independent of actual consumer confusion.[406]

The above EC Regulation in Article 14 provides protection against the registration of trademarks corresponding to protected geographical indications. According to this provision,[407] such trademarks relating to the same product shall be refused registration or declared invalid

- in case the application for registration of the trademark was submitted after the application for GI registration was published;
- or in case the application for registration of the trademark was submitted before the application for GI registration was published, provided that that publication occurred before the trademark was registered.

Thus, the only situation under which a corresponding trademark may remain valid is where the application for GI registration is published only after the *bona-fide* registration of the trademark. But even under those circumstances, use of the trademark will be discontinued where[408]

- the trademark consists exclusively of signs or indications which may serve, in trade, to designate the kind, quality, quantity, intended purpose, value, geographical origin, or the time of production of the goods or of rendering of the service, or other characteristics of the goods;
- or where the trademark is of such a nature as to deceive the public, for instance as to the nature, quality or geographical origin of the goods or service;
- or where the trademark, after the date on which it was registered, in consequence of the use made of it by the proprietor of the trademark or with his consent in respect of the goods or services for which it is registered, is liable to mislead the public, particularly as to the nature, quality or geographical origin of those goods or services.

4.2 Japan – Alcoholic Beverages
As noted in Section 2.1, above, Article IX, GATT 1947, was interpreted by a panel in the *Japan – Alcoholic Beverages* case.

---

[406] Note that in this respect, the above provision is similar to Article 23.1, TRIPS Agreement, which provides an enhanced form of protection for GIs for wines and spirits.

[407] See Article 14.1 of the above EC Regulation.

[408] See Article 14.2 of the above EC Regulation, referring to the First Council Directive 89/104/EEC of 21 December 1988 to approximate the laws of the Member States relating to trademarks.

5. Relationship with other international instruments

5.1 WTO Agreements

5.1.1 The GATT

In Section 2.1, *supra*, it was noted that Article IX, GATT 1947, addressed geographical indications in a non-obligatory manner, and Article IX continues in force as part of GATT 1994. In light of the non-obligatory character of Article IX, and the more specific treatment of geographical indications in TRIPS, it is doubtful that there will be any conflict in operation of the relevant provisions.

5.1.2 The TBT Agreement

The Agreement on Technical Barriers to Trade ("TBT Agreement"), on the other hand, may have more concrete application to geographical indications, and it raises the possibility for potential conflict of norms. Annex 1, paragraph 1, of the TBT Agreement defines a "technical regulation" as a:

> "Document which lays down product characteristics or their related processes and production methods, including the applicable administrative provisions, with which compliance is mandatory. It may also include or deal exclusively with terminology, symbols, packaging, marking or labelling requirements as they apply to a product, process or production method."

Annex 1, para. 2, of the TBT Agreement defines a "standard" as a:

> "Document approved by a recognized body, that provides, for common and repeated use, rules, guidelines or characteristics for products or related processes and production methods, with which compliance is not mandatory. It may also include or deal exclusively with terminology, symbols, packaging, marking or labelling requirements as they apply to a product, process or production method."

Provisions by which WTO Members have regulated entitlement to appellations of origin,[409] geographical indications[410] and certification marks[411] commonly set forth quality standards that producers within a territory must satisfy in order to use the identifier.

---

[409] As discussed, *supra* Section 2.1.2.3, appellations of origin typically are allowed to be affixed only on the basis of meeting quality or characteristic standards.

[410] For example, the EC Council Regulation on the common organization of the market for wine, discussed *infra*, Section 6.3.1, includes details on wine quality standards.

[411] For example, the U.S. Trademark (Lanham) Act, 15 U.S.C. §1127, defines "certification mark" as follows:
"The term 'certification mark' means any word, name, symbol, or device, or any combination thereof–
(1) used by a person other than its owner, or
(2) which its owner has a bona fide intention to permit a person other than the owner to use in commerce and files an application to register on the principal register established by this Act, to certify regional or other origin, material, mode of manufacture, quality, accuracy, or other characteristics of such person's goods or services or that the work or labor on the goods or services was performed by members of a union or other organization."

The TBT Agreement regulates technical regulations, standards, certification procedures and related matters in a comprehensive way. It applies in different ways to governmental and non-governmental bodies. The basic objective is avoidance of use of technical regulations and standards as disguised barriers to trade. It is possible that rules adopted in a Member governing the recognition of geographical indications could discriminate against producers from other Members in a manner inconsistent with the TBT Agreement, whether or not such rules are compatible with TRIPS. It will therefore be important to consider potentially applicable rules of the TBT Agreement in adopting, implementing and enforcing rules concerning the protection of geographical indications.

5.2 Other international instruments

WIPO conventions that contain provisions relevant to geographical indications are discussed in Section 2.1, above, including the Paris Convention, the Madrid Agreement for the Repression of False or Deceptive Indications of Source on Goods and the Lisbon Agreement for the Protection of Appellations of Origin and their International Registration. Each of these agreements remains in force. Provisions of the Paris Convention relevant to geographical indications are incorporated by reference in TRIPS (see Chapter 3).

6. New developments

6.1 National laws

6.2 International instruments

The WIPO Standing Committee on the Law of Trademarks, Industrial Designs and Geographical Indications is pursuing an active work program on geographical indications largely directed toward identifying common legal principles that might be recommended for adoption in national law.[412]

6.3 Regional and bilateral contexts

6.3.1 Regional

6.3.1.1 European Union. The EC has regulated extensively on the subject of geographical indications. As noted in Section 2.1, prior to conclusion of TRIPS, the EC adopted Council Regulation (EEC) No. 2081/92 of 14 July 1992 on the protection of geographical indications of origin for agricultural products and foodstuffs.

In addition, in 1999 the EC adopted a detailed Council Regulation (EC) No 1493/1999 of 17 May 1999 on the common organization of the market in wine. The 1992 Regulation (dealing with products other than wine and spirits) is essentially limited to protection of identifiers. The 1999 Regulation, in contrast, deals broadly with the wine industry, and includes the protection of geographical indications as one major element of a broader regulatory framework. Chapter II (Description, Designation, Presentation and Protection of Certain Products), along

---

[412] See, e.g., Standing Committee on the Law of Trademarks, Industrial Designs and Geographical Indications, SCT 8/4, 9/4 & 9/5.

with Annexes VII and VIII, deal *inter alia* with geographical indications and labelling (see Article 47(e) and (f)). Article 48 establishes the basic standard of protection for geographical indications, providing:

"Article 48

The description and presentation of the products referred to in this Regulation, and any form of advertising for such products, must not be incorrect or likely to cause confusion or to mislead the persons to whom they are addressed, particularly as regards:

– the information provided for in Article 47. This shall apply even if the information is used in translation or with a reference to the actual provenance or with additions such as 'kind', 'type', 'style', 'imitation', 'brand' or the like;

– the characteristics of the products, and in particular, their nature, composition, alcoholic strength by volume, colour, origin or provenance, quality, the vine variety, vintage year or nominal volume of the containers,

– the identity and status of the natural or legal persons or group of persons who have been or are involved in the production or distribution of the product in question, in particular the bottler."

Article 49 provides a rule against marketing non-conforming wines, stating, *inter alia*:

"Article 49

1. Products whose description or presentation does not conform to the provisions of this Regulation or the detailed rules adopted for its implementation may not be held for sale or put on the market in the Community or exported." [provision for derogation through export is later addressed]

Article 50 provides the rule for treatment of imports:

"1. Member States shall take all necessary measures to enable interested parties to prevent, on the terms set out in Articles 23 and 24 of the Agreement on Trade-Related Aspects of Intellectual Property Rights, the use in the Community of a geographical indication attached to the products referred to in Article 1(2)(b) for products not originating in the place indicated by the geographical indication in question, even where the true origin of the goods is indicated or the geographical indication is used in translation or accompanied by expressions such as "kind", "type", "style", "imitation" or the like.

2. For the purposes of this Article, "geographical indications" is taken to mean indications which identify a product as originating in the territory of a third country which is a member of the World Trade Organisation or in a region or locality within that territory, in cases where a certain quality, reputation or other given characteristic of the product may be attributed essentially to that geographical place of origin.

3. Paragraphs 1 and 2 shall apply notwithstanding other specific provisions in Community legislation laying down rules for the designation and presentation of the products covered by this Regulation."

Article 50, unlike Article 12 of the 1992 Regulation, does not include a material reciprocity requirement (see above, Section 2.1). It is interesting to note, however, that wines which comply with the EC's internal regulatory scheme for geographical indications for wines are directly protected against competitors being placed on the market, whereas third country wines are subject to rules to be adopted by the member states. It is an interesting question whether EU and third country producers of wine are receiving equivalent treatment in terms of protection.

According to two recent judgements of the European Court of Justice (ECJ), not only the production of a protected good, but equally its further preparation (such as the grating of certain protected cheeses, the cutting of certain protected hams, and the packing of those products) has to take place in the indicated region, if this is expressly provided in the specification of the protected indication. The Court reasoned that those processes, if done incorrectly, could negatively affect the quality of the respective products and thus endanger their genuineness.[413]

6.3.1.2 NAFTA. Article 1721, "Definitions", of NAFTA Chapter Seventeen on Intellectual Property defines geographical indication in a manner essentially identical to that of Article 21, TRIPS Agreement, providing:

> "geographical indication means any indication that identifies a good as originating in the territory of a Party, or a region or locality in that territory, where a particular quality, reputation or other characteristic of the good is essentially attributable to its geographical origin."

Article 1712 addresses the rights of interested persons with respect to geographical indications, stating *inter alia*:

> "Article 1712: Geographical Indications
>
> 1. Each Party shall provide, in respect of geographical indications, the legal means for interested persons to prevent:
>
> (a) the use of any means in the designation or presentation of a good that indicates or suggests that the good in question originates in a territory, region or locality other than the true place of origin, in a manner that misleads the public as to the geographical origin of the good;
>
> (b) any use that constitutes an act of unfair competition within the meaning of Article 10*bis* of the Paris Convention.
>
> [....]"

In addition, NAFTA Chapter Three on National Treatment and Market Access of Goods includes the following:

> "Article 314: Distinctive Products
>
> Each Party shall comply with Annex 314 respecting standards and labelling of the distinctive products set out therein."

---

[413] See ECJ cases C-469/00 and C-108/01 (concerning "Grana Padano" cheese and "Prosciutto di Parma"/Parma ham), and *Belgium v. Spain*, C-388-95 [2000] ECR 1-3123 (concerning "Rioja").

"ANNEX 314

Distinctive Products

1. Mexico and Canada shall recognize Bourbon Whiskey and Tennessee Whiskey, which is a straight Bourbon Whiskey authorized to be produced only in the State of Tennessee, as distinctive products of the United States. Accordingly, Mexico and Canada shall not permit the sale of any product as Bourbon Whiskey or Tennessee Whiskey, unless it has been manufactured in the United States in accordance with the laws and regulations of the United States governing the manufacture of Bourbon Whiskey and Tennessee Whiskey.

2. The United States and Mexico shall recognize Canadian Whiskey as a distinctive product of Canada. Accordingly, the United States and Mexico shall not permit the sale of any product as Canadian Whiskey, unless it has been manufactured in Canada in accordance with the laws and regulations of Canada governing the manufacture of Canadian Whiskey for consumption in Canada.

3. The United States and Canada shall recognize Tequila and Mezcal as distinctive products of Mexico. Accordingly, the United States and Canada shall not permit the sale of any product as Tequila or Mezcal, unless it has been manufactured in Mexico in accordance with the laws and regulations of Mexico governing the manufacture of Tequila and Mezcal. This provision shall apply to Mezcal, either on the date of entry into force of this Agreement, or 90 days after the date when the official standard for this product is made obligatory by the Government of Mexico, whichever is later."

6.3.1.3 The Andean Group. The Andean Group Decision 486 provides for the protection of the exclusive right to make use of officially recognized "appellations of origin".[414]

6.3.1.4 The Bangui Agreement. This Agreement of 1977, which was revised in 1999, relates to the creation of the African Intellectual Property Organization (OAPI). It includes regional protection for different categories of intellectual property rights including appellations of origin.

6.3.1.5 The Group of Three[415]. The Agreement establishing the Group of Three lays down the right of member countries to protect "designations of origin"[416] and geographical indications. However, it is left to domestic legislation to determine the conditions for protection.[417]

---

[414] See Title XII, Chapter I of Decision 486 of 2000.

[415] This is a free trade agreement between Colombia, Venezuela and Mexico. It aims to achieve a free trade area by 2005. The full text of the agreement in English is available at <http://www.sice.oas.org/Trade/G3_E/G3EC1.asp>.

[416] This term is often used instead of "appellation of origin".

[417] See C. Correa, *Protection of Geographical Indications in the CARICOM Countries*, September 2002 (manuscript).

6.3.1.6 MERCOSUL/R. A 1995 Protocol on Harmonization of Rules on Intellectual Property in Relation to Trademarks, Geographical Indications and Denominations of Origin contains a general obligation for parties to protect both geographical indications and appellations of origin. However, the Protocol does not determine the scope of protection.[418]

6.3.1.7 The Revised Central American Convention for the Protection of Industrial Property. This 1994 Convention requires the protection of geographical indications, using the same definition of that notion as employed by Article 22.1.[419]

6.3.2 Bilateral

The protection of geographical indications has increasingly become the subject matter of bilateral trade and investment agreements. Particularly by creating an agreed register of protected indications, countries avoid subsequent disputes as to particular terms. It is not so clear the extent to which such bilateral agreements serve the interests of consumers since they are likely to reflect the influence of producers in the negotiating process. Moreover, to the extent that such bilateral agreements establish protection for producers from one country, they may effectively foreclose producers from another country to challenge the decision to confer protection. In this way, bilateral protection agreements may undermine the MFN principle by conferring more extensive protections to some Members over others.[420]

There are a large number of bilateral and mini-lateral agreements that incorporate protection of geographical indications, either in a general provision or through the acceptance of an agreed-upon register. It is in particular the EC that has been very active in this respect. Recently, the EC has concluded several bilateral agreements referring to the protection of GIs, in particular with Australia, Chile, Mexico and South Africa. A more detailed discussion of these agreements would, however, go beyond the scope of this book.

6.4 Proposals for review

As discussed earlier, Part II, Section 3 of TRIPS places further negotiation regarding geographical indications on the work program of the TRIPS Council in two ways. First, Article 23.4 refers to a multilateral system for notification and registration for wines. Second, pursuant to Article 24.1, "Members agree to enter into negotiations aimed at increasing the protection of individual geographical indications under Article 23". In addition to further negotiations, Article 24.2 calls for continuing review of the application of provisions under this Section.

---

[418] Ibid.

[419] Ibid.

[420] As to the complex relationship between the MFN obligation and bilateral TRIPS-plus provisions on individual geographical indications, see above, Section 3.

Both Articles 23.4 and 24.1 were reflected in the Ministerial Declaration adopted in Doha on 14 November 2001,[421] which stated:

> "18. With a view to completing the work started in the Council for Trade-Related Aspects of Intellectual Property Rights (Council for TRIPS) on the implementation of Article 23.4, we agree to negotiate the establishment of a multilateral system of notification and registration of geographical indications for wines and spirits by the Fifth Session of the Ministerial Conference. We note that issues related to the extension of the protection of geographical indications provided for in Article 23 to products other than wines and spirits will be addressed in the Council for TRIPS pursuant to paragraph 12 of this Declaration."

Prior to and following the Doha Ministerial, Members have made extensive submissions to the TRIPS Council regarding the establishment of a register and extending protection under Article 23 to additional geographical indications.

6.4.1 The Multilateral Register

The WTO Secretariat prepared a Note of 18 February 2003 (TN/IP/W/7) on *Discussions on the Establishment of a Multilateral System of Notification and Registration of Geographical Indications for Wines and Spirits: Compilation of Issues and Points*. That Note illustrates that Members disagreed on virtually all aspects of establishing a multilateral system, especially with respect to the legal effects of registration. In particular, some points of discussion included: (1) the meaning of the terms "notification" and "registration", (2) the procedures that might be followed in using a system, including whether and how an "opposition" procedure might operate, (3) whether disputes at the registration or opposition phase might be resolved by an arbitration mechanism of some kind, (4) the effect that registration would have in terms of establishing presumptions, (5) how the costs of a new system would be borne, in the contexts of costs to governments, costs to producers, costs to consumers, and costs to an administering body, and (6) what role WIPO might play in the administration of a new system.

6.4.2 The Extension Debate

Following the Doha Ministerial Declaration, negotiations on the extension of protection under Article 24.1 TRIPS are considered an "outstanding implementation issue".[422] As far as the scope of those negotiations is concerned (i.e. whether or not they cover the possible extension of the Article 23 protection to products other

---

[421] WT/MIN(01)/DEC/1, 20 November 2001. Note that the Declaration expressly extended the scope of the negotiations on the multilateral register to spirits (Article 23.4 refers only to wines). Prior to this express reference to spirits, Members had disagreed whether spirits were actually covered by the negotiations. For details, see Rangnekar, p. 41.

[422] See paragraph 12 (b) of the Doha Ministerial Declaration of 20 November 2001, WTO document WT/MIN(01)/DEC/1, and *Tiret* 87 of the Compilation of Outstanding Implementation Issues. (This compilation was set up on the basis of paragraph 13 of the Ministerial Decision on Implementation-related Issues and Concerns, adopted at Doha on 14 November 2001, WTO document WT/MIN(01)/17. It is contained in WTO document Job(01)/152/Rev.1, which can be consulted at <http://www.ictsd.org/ministerial/doha/docs/imp_iss.pdf>.)

than wines and spirits), delegations have not yet been able to come to a compromise solution.[423]

7. Comments, including economic and social implications

The subject of geographical indications attracted only modest interest in the course of the Uruguay Round TRIPS negotiations. Since that time, interest has gradually intensified, so that today the subject is one of the most intensely argued in the Doha Development Round. The arc of interest may be explained by developments in the world economy over the past decade, in particular in the field of agriculture.

Although geographical indications do not pertain solely to agricultural products, the most common field of application and potential application is in regard to basic and processed agricultural products. The field of agriculture is one in which competitive advantage depends on factors that may favour highly mechanized large-scale producers, on one side, and low-cost labour intensive producers on the other.

For Members pursuing agricultural policies that favour substantial subsidization of smaller scale farming and food production, competitive advantage might be maintained by the differentiation of products based on "ephemeral" characteristics, such as names evocative of exotic locales. While consumers may be relatively indifferent to an alcoholic beverage identified as a "quality sparkling wine produced in a specified region", they are not indifferent to "Champagne", a name which can be heavily advertised and promoted. The post-Uruguay Round attention to geographical indications is occurring contemporaneously with efforts, not yet successful, to reduce or eliminate agricultural subsidies. Geographical indications might serve as a basis for competitive advantage in a newly liberalized agricultural trading environment.

For developing WTO Members the continuing negotiations on geographical indications present difficult analytic questions. At the moment, Europe stakes the greatest number of claims to geographical indications. In a static economic sense, wider acceptance of these claims is likely to result in increased IP-rent payments from developing countries to Europe, at least in the short and medium term. Yet there are some important geographical indications existing in developing Members, and over time as developing Member exporters become more sophisticated in their approaches to developed country markets, there may be increasing interest in product differentiation on the basis of locale. Predicting the economic impact on developing Members of agreeing to enhanced protection for geographical indications is rather difficult.

Much will depend on the characteristics of a given country's economy. If the country is not an agricultural producer or exporter, the possibilities for gain from providing additional protection for geographical indications is rather limited. More likely, increased costs to consumers for protected goods will be the result.

If a developing country produces agricultural products for export, it still faces a dilemma in respect to additional protection of geographical indications. If, for

---

[423] For a detailed analysis of the extension debate, see Rangnekar.

example, European wine and cheese producers are better able to protect the traditional names of products in the EU and foreign markets, one effect may be to
make it more difficult for emerging developing country exporters from entering
those markets. A grocery store has limited shelf space. If a substantial part is devoted to "speciality" goods protected by geographical indications, it is not so easy
for other producers to find marketing space.

Some developing countries presently export products they consider not to be
adequately protected in overseas markets by geographical indications. Producers
in these countries might be more aggressive in taking advantage of existing legal
opportunities to protect their identifiers.[424] In some cases, an apparent lack of protection may indicate that the right avenues for protection are not yet explored. It
should be noted, however, that in countries where the protection of geographical
indications is based on unfair competition concepts (rather than on the registration of protected names), there may be additional costs of litigation that will make
these avenues more expensive.

Over time developing country producers may generate new geographical indications that will help them penetrate foreign markets, and protect their local
markets. If developing country producers are willing and able to invest in the
creation of protectable geographical names, this would be a reason for favouring
additional protection.

On a static basis, it seems likely the major beneficiaries of extending protection
for geographical indications will be countries already having a competitive edge in
this sector. It is less certain when dynamic gains will accrue to developing country
producers.[425]

---

[424] Japan, by way of illustration, was quite critical of Section 337 of the U.S. Trade Act of 1930
until its producers learned that effective lawyers in the United States could turn Section 337 into
a strong mechanism for the protection of Japanese industry.

[425] For a detailed assessment of the economic impact of protecting geographical indications see D.
Rangnekar, *The Socio-Economics of Geographical Indications. A Review of Empirical Evidence from
Europe*, UNCTAD-ICTSD, Geneva, 2004 (also available at <http://www.iprsonline.org/unctadictsd/
projectoutputs.htm#casestudies>).

Annex 1 Excerpt from WIPO, SCT/8/4, April 2, 2002
Standing Committee on the Law of Trademarks, Industrial Designs
and Geographical Indications
Eighth Session
Geneva, May 27 to 31, 2002

DOCUMENT SCT/6/3 REV. ON GEOGRAPHICAL INDICATIONS: HISTORICAL
BACKGROUND, NATURE OF RIGHTS, EXISTING SYSTEMS FOR PROTEC-
TION AND OBTAINING PROTECTION IN OTHER COUNTRIES

III. Attempts to Revise the Multilateral System of Protection after 1958

. . .

(b) Revision of the Paris Convention

72. As indicated, during the time the WIPO draft treaty on geographical indications was being prepared, the process for the revision of the Paris Convention was
initiated. In the course of the discussions on the revision of the Paris Convention, a
working group on conflicts between an appellation of origin and a trademark prepared a proposal to include in the Paris Convention a new article on the protection
of appellations of origin and indications of source. Under the Rules of Procedure of
the Diplomatic Conference on the Revision of the Paris Convention, the said proposal became a basic proposal for the revision of the Paris Convention.[29][426] In
the proposal, the terminology used in the WIPO draft treaty of 1975 was adopted;
thus the term "geographical indication" was used. The purpose of the new article of the Paris Convention, which was provisionally numbered Article 10*quater*,
was twofold. First, the article would ensure more extensive protection of appellations of origin and indications of source against their use as trademarks. Second,
a special provision in favour of developing countries would be included, which
would allow those countries to reserve a certain number of potential geographical
indications for the future so that, even if they were not yet used as geographical
indications, they could not be used as trademarks.

73. Draft Article 10*quater* established in its paragraph (1) the principle that a
geographical indication which directly or indirectly suggested a country of the
Paris Union or a region or locality in that country with respect to goods not
originating in that country may not be used or registered as a trademark, if the
use of the indication for the goods in question was of a nature as to mislead the
public as to the country of origin. Draft paragraph (2) extended the application
of draft paragraph (1) to geographical indications which, although literally true,
falsely represented to the public that the goods originated in a particular country.

74. Draft paragraph (3) contained an additional provision in respect of geographical indications which had acquired a reputation in relation to goods originating in a country, region or locality, provided that such reputation was generally
known in the country where protection was sought by persons engaged in the production of goods of the same kind or in trade in such goods. This additional provision would have established a reinforced protection for certain generally known
geographical indications without the requirement of misleading use.

---

[426] [29][renumber following in order] PR/DC/4

75. Draft paragraph (4) allowed the continuation of use which had been begun in good faith. Draft paragraph (5) required that all factual circumstances must be considered when applying the preceding provisions. Draft paragraph (6) reserved the possibility of bilateral or multilateral negotiations between member countries of the Paris Union.

76. Finally, draft paragraph (7) provided that each developing country may notify the International Bureau of up to 200 geographical names denominating the country itself or a region or a locality on its territory, with the consequence that the International Bureau would notify all Paris Union member States and that these States would be obliged to prohibit the registration or use of trademarks containing or consisting of the notified names. The effect of the notification would last for 20 years. During this period, any developing country having made a notification would have the possibility of making known and protecting the geographical indication as referring to a geographical area in its territory from which certain goods originated so that subsequently the general provisions on protection of geographical indications would apply.

77. Draft Article 10*quater* was discussed in the four sessions of the Diplomatic Conference as well as in some of the subsequent consultative meetings. Although, initially, the Group of industrialized market economy countries was divided in respect of the protection of geographical indications which had acquired a certain reputation, in 1984, those countries agreed on a proposal for a new Article 10*quater*, which can be summarized as follows:[427]

78. Draft paragraphs (1) and (2) were similar to draft paragraphs (1) and (2) of Article 10*quater*, as contained in the basic proposals for the revision of the Paris Convention, subject to some minor changes; draft paragraph (3) dealt with the special case of any "geographical indication generally known in a country to consumers of given products or of similar products as designating the origin of such products manufactured or produced in another country of the Union," and provided that the protection would not, as in the basic proposal, be directed against the use as a trademark but against a development of such an indication to a designation of generic character for the said product or similar products;

79. Draft paragraph (4) contained an amended version of the special provisions in favour of developing countries; in contrast to the basic proposal, the number of geographical indications which could be reserved was up to 10, and they could only be reserved if the goods for which the name was or was going to be used had been indicated; draft paragraphs (5) to (7) contained slightly amended versions of the provisions of the basic proposal in respect of acquired rights, the consideration of all factual circumstances and the possibilities of concluding bilateral and multilateral agreements. However, this proposal was never discussed in the sessions of the Diplomatic Conference itself.

80. It should also be mentioned that in 1982 the competent Main Committee of the Diplomatic Conference on the Revision of the Paris Convention adopted an amendment to Article 6*ter* of the Paris Convention.[428] That Article, in its text as applicable at present, contains a prohibition on using as trademarks state emblems, official marks or emblems of intergovernmental organizations. The

[427] PR/DC/51
[428] PR/DC/INF/38Rev.

proposed amendment concerned the inclusion of the official names of States in the list of emblems, etc., which may not be used as trademarks. This would be of importance for protection of geographical indications since official names of States would always have to be excluded from use as trademarks.

81. Since the Diplomatic Conference for the Revision of the Paris Convention was never concluded, the two proposals for addressing geographical indications within that framework Convention described above were never fully discussed and remained drafts.

(c) The 1990 Committee of Experts on the International Protection of Geographical Indications

82. In 1990, the WIPO Committee of Experts on the International Protection of Geographical Indications considered the establishment of a new treaty dealing with the international protection of geographical indications.[429] The main reasons for a perceived unsatisfactory situation concerning the international protection of geographical indications were the limited scope of the provisions of the Paris Convention, and the limited acceptance of the Madrid Agreement on Indications of Source and the Lisbon Agreement. It was felt that this situation could only be overcome through the establishment of a new worldwide treaty.

83. In order to make the treaty attractive to all States party to the Paris Convention, the replacement of the concepts of "appellation of origin" and "indication of source" by the notion of "geographical indication" was evoked. It was felt that this notion could cover all existing concepts of protection. Furthermore, a need was perceived to establish a new international registration system, which would be more widely acceptable than the Lisbon Agreement. To that end, a basic principle was that Contracting Parties should be free to choose the manner of protection of a geographical indication in its country of origin, rather than requiring a specific form of protection. In addition, the new treaty should provide for effective protection of geographical indications against degeneration into generic terms, and ensure effective enforcement of protection.

84. The Committee of Experts discussed the following three groups of issues pertinent to the establishment of a new treaty, namely: What should be the subject matter of protection? What should be the general principles of protection, including the conditions of protection, its contents, and the mechanisms for its enforcement and for setting disputes arising under the new Treaty? Should there be a system of international registration and, if so, what should it consist of?[430]

85. The Committee did not reach a common position on those questions. At the end of its first session, the Chair concluded that a number of delegations had expressed the wish for the preparation of a new treaty, whereas other had expressed reservations. Those reservations concerned, in particular, whether the new treaty should provide for a registration system or for the establishment of lists of geographical indications protected by Contracting Parties.[431] The work concerning the establishment of a new treaty was not continued, since the Committee of Experts on the International Protection of Geographical Indications did not meet for any further session.

[429] GEO/CE/I/2
[430] GEO/CE/I/2, paragraph 64
[431] GEO/CE/I/3, paragraph 122

16: Industrial Designs

1. Introduction: terminology, definition and scope

The term "design" can be applied to almost any product or work. Yet, in traditional legal terms, the concept of industrial design concentrates on the appearance of a product. Thus, a "design" connotes an element or characteristic completely separate from the object it enhances or to which it is applied. It is something often added to an object, having no relation to its overall form or function, sometimes by an artist not even remotely connected with its design. Examples of such behaviour are plentiful: antique coffee mills or porcelain statues made into lamps, ashtrays with varied ornamentation and animals.

This difficulty of definition explains, in part, the complexity faced by legislators in classifying design protection. The ambiguity of "design" results in overlap with other intellectual property laws, such as copyright, unfair competition, utility model, and trademark laws. For example, the European Union legislators have determined that the more modern concept of "design", espoused by the current EU design laws, means any aspect of a product which promotes the marketability of that product. However, within the European Union, the adoption of a *sui generis* design law for the protection of designs leaves unanswered the adjacent anomaly posed by the possibility of protection under other IPRs, especially copyright law.

This problem is not alleviated by the ambivalent attitude of TRIPS to designs. TRIPS simultaneously adopts both the Paris and Berne positions and obliges Members to provide for a minimum standard of protection without specifying the nature of protection. In relation to textile designs, however, Members must protect textile designs either through design law or through copyright law.[432] Thus, Members have much flexibility in drafting local laws with local objectives in mind,[433] as long as certain elements are incorporated into the local design laws. Conversely, where Members' interests lie in protecting the domestic design industry from domestic and international piracy, it should be noted that the two provisions on designs in the Agreement do not offer much in terms of mandatory rules. Thus, this introductory section expands on broad definitional questions and comparative legal approaches to industrial designs.

1.1 Definitions

This section briefly explains terms commonly employed throughout this chapter.

Copyright: the term copyright is used here in the wider context to include both the Anglo-US concept of copyright and the European civil law concept of author's rights.

Design (*dessins et modèles*): the specific term under French and Benelux law is *"dessins et modèles"*, which roughly translates as "two-dimensional drawings or patterns and three-dimensional models" in the English language. For our purposes, we use the single term of "design". The notion of design is used widely, and can include protectable subject matter under both copyright and design laws, as well as other supplementary protection.

Sui generis design law: all references to "design law" are in relation to the *sui generis* or to the specific design law in countries which offers protection to designs either on a registration-based system or a deposit-based system.

Utility model law (petty patents, *certificat d'utilité*, *Gebrauchsmuster*, etc.): this usually refers to a second and additional type of patent protection for minor or

---

[432] Article 25.2 of the TRIPS Agreement.

[433] J.H. Reichman, *Symposium: Uruguay Round–GATT/WTO Universal Minimum Standards of Intellectual Property Protection under the TRIPS Component of the WTO Agreement*, (1995) 29 International Lawyer 345, at p. 375 [hereinafter Reichman, Symposium].

incremental inventions, with a shorter duration of protection, with little or no examination process, and a lowered threshold of protection. There is no universal consensus as to what constitutes a utility model law, and the lack of international harmonisation means that most countries refer to such protection under different names: petty patent, the small patent, utility certificates, innovation certificate and utility innovation. Other than designs, utility models concern the technical novelty of a product, and not its ornamental aspects.[434]

Work of applied art (*œuvre des arts appliqués*): this term is applied under copyright law, especially in civil law jurisdictions. Although no definition is offered under any Member's law, the term "work of applied art" is generally intended to refer to artistic works, often three-dimensional designs, which have been industrially applied to an article, which is subsequently commercially exploited. On many occasions, the term is treated as being equivalent to the notion of "industrial design", albeit in the context of copyright law. It can be analogous with the notion of "works of artistic craftsmanship", as employed under common law jurisdictions.

1.2 Terminology

As explained above, the nature of design lends itself as being considered as being protectable either as an industrial property or as a copyright work: this has led to the *sui generis* design approach versus copyright approach. This section lists the characteristics of protection under both these approaches.

1.2.1 Essential characteristics of the copyright approach

The common elements present in the copyright approach to design protection are:

• copyright is accorded automatically; thus, there are no formalities nor registration procedures;

• an anti-copying right is proffered, as opposed to an exclusive right;[435]

• the main criterion of protection is originality, which is easier to fulfil than that of novelty;[436]

• the duration of protection is much longer than under the design approach: most countries offer 50 years *post mortem auctoris*.

---

[434] See Section 3.7.4, below.

[435] This means that, if a third party *independently* creates a design that by chance resembles the protected design, the copyright in the protected design does not provide for the right to prevent the third party from making or selling his original design. Such right is only offered in case third parties *copy* the protected design. Thus, copyright provides no absolute protection, as opposed to exclusive rights (see under the following paragraph).

[436] The originality criterion is met where a piece of work is the result of independent human intellect and creativity, even if a similar product has been known to the public before. Conversely, the novelty criterion requires that no identical design must have been made available to the public prior to the date of filing of the application for registration of the design for which protection is claimed (see Article 5.1 (b) of the Council Regulation (EC) No 6/2002 of 12 December 2001 on Community designs, OJ L 3, 5.1.02, p. 1, concerning the registered Community design).

1.2.2 Essential characteristics of the *sui generis* design approach

Most *sui generis* design laws in the world are fashioned upon patent law. The common denominator in this approach is that protection is accorded upon registration or deposit of the design. Furthermore, the following features regularly appear in most *sui generis* systems:

• where protection is granted upon registration, publication usually follows registration though some countries provide for secret or deferred publication;

• upon registration, most countries confer an exclusive right. The proprietor of the design right is thus given the right to sue any person who produces an identical or similar design for infringement, even if the latter design arises from an independent creation;

• the usual criterion for protection is novelty, though the standard of novelty required varies from country to country (ranging from domestic novelty to universal novelty);

• a duration of protection shorter than copyright is usually conferred (for example, the European Community Registered Design Right confers a maximum 25-year term of protection).[437]

1.2.3 Essential characteristics of the unregistered sui generis design approach

A third possibility is the unregistered design right system, which has been adopted by the United Kingdom, Hong Kong-China, the European Union[438] and New Zealand. However, since this is a new type of right, there are no international conventions which govern this area, though it is arguable that TRIPS may be applicable, as long as the criteria for protection as spelled out in Article 25.1 and the minimum term of protection in Article 26.3 (10 years) are respected.[439] Note the particular characteristics:

• all unregistered design right systems confer automatic protection, without the need for registration or deposit;

• the term of protection is short (3 years in the European Union,[440] and 10–15 years in the United Kingdom);

• the criterion of protection under the United Kingdom and Hong Kong system is an objective standard of originality, which is lower than novelty under its patent and *sui generis* design laws;

---

[437] Article 12 of the EC Design Regulation.

[438] Note that the EC Design Regulation provides both options, i.e. a registered and an unregistered design rights system. See below, Box 5.

[439] On the other hand, note that in *Azrak-Hamway International Inc. v. Meccano SA* (1997) RPC 134 (United Kingdom), the tribunal considered the UK unregistered design rights regime as a supplementary regime of protection outside the ambit of the TRIPS Agreement.

[440] Note that this alone would not meet the TRIPS minimum term of protection of 10 years. However, the EC equally provides a registered design right with a term of protection of 25 years from the date of filing (subject to renewal by the right owner every five years, see Article 12 of the EC Design Regulation).

• the criterion of protection under the European Union system is novelty and individual character.[441]

2. History of the provision

2.1 Situation pre-TRIPS

There has always been a lack of international consensus as to the proper means of protecting designs.[442] The Berne Convention[443] and the Paris Convention[444] have both avoided the issue of the nature of design by accepting designs as being appropriate subject matter for both copyright and industrial property protection. With respect to the Hague Agreement on the international registration of industrial designs and its Geneva Act (1999), see discussions below (Section 5.2.1).

2.2 Negotiating history

2.2.1 Article 25 TRIPS

2.2.1.1 The Anell Draft[445]

"SECTION 4: INDUSTRIAL DESIGNS

1. Requirements for Protection

1.1 PARTIES shall provide for protection for industrial designs which are new [and] [or] original [, ornamental and non-obvious].

1.2 PARTIES [may] [shall] condition such protection on registration [or other formality].

1.3 PARTIES may provide that protection shall not extend to features required by technical reasons.

1.4 Such protection shall be provided without affecting any protection under copyright law [or other law].

2. Textiles Designs

2A The acquisition of industrial design rights in textiles or clothing shall not be encumbered by any special requirements such as ex officio examination of novelty before registration, compulsory publication of the design itself or disproportionate fees for multiple users of the registration."

---

[441] See Articles 5.1(a) and 6 of the EC Design Regulation. The novelty requirement is met if no identical design has been made available to the public before the date on which the design for which protection is claimed has first been made available to the public.

[442] See AIPPI Annuaire 1982/III, p. 27; 1984/I, p. 79; 1985/III, pp. 19 and 271; 1991/VIII, pp. XI–XIII. For an international perspective, L. Duncan, *Improvement of international protection of designs and models.*, (1993) AIPJ 32; U. Suthersanen, *Design Law in Europe*, Sweet & Maxwell 2000, Chapter 22 [hereinafter Suthersanen, Design Law in Europe]. See also the Australian Law Reform Commission on Designs, Report No. 74, 1995.

[443] Berne Convention for the Protection of Literary and Artistic Works of September 9, 1886, Paris (1971) version. See Article 2(7).

[444] Paris Convention for the Protection of Industrial Property of March 20, 1883, Stockholm version (October 2, 1979). See Articles 1(2), and 5*quinquies*.

[445] Document MTN.GNG/NG11/W/76, of 23 July 1990.

2.2.1.2 The Brussels Draft[446]

"1. PARTIES shall provide for the protection of industrial designs which are new [and] [or] original. PARTIES may provide that designs are not new [and] [or] original if they do not significantly differ from known designs or combinations of known design features. PARTIES may provide that such protection shall not extend to designs dictated essentially by technical or functional or technical considerations.

2. Each PARTY shall ensure that requirements for securing protection for textile designs, in particular in regard to any cost, examination or publication, do not unreasonably impair the opportunity to seek and obtain such protection. PARTIES shall be free to meet this obligation through industrial design law or through copyright."

As these draft texts illustrate, the main issue was whether the standard of protection of industrial designs should be based on the narrow United States approach or the wide European approach. The above drafts reflect the respective prior proposals made by the EC and the USA. The United States draft was narrow, and provided for protection for industrial designs which are "new, original, ornamental and non-obvious". Subsequently the term "original" was also advocated by the EC, developing countries and Japan. Delegations disagreed as to whether it should be "new or original" (EC) or "new and/or original" (Japan) or "new and original" (developing countries), with the United States still insisting on the criteria of "ornamental and non-obvious".

The main reason why the EC was eager to include the issue of designs in the TRIPS negotiations was to attempt to make the United States align its design protection with that of other developed countries, and thus expand its coverage. A major contention from the United States perspective was that design protection should not be widened to such an extent so as to protect "functional designs" such as designs for motor vehicle spare parts or "crash parts". Spare or "crash" parts manufacturers, together with consumer groups, lobbied hard to reject the EC approach.[447]

2.2.2 Article 26 TRIPS

2.2.2.1 The Anell Draft

"3. Industrial Design Rights

3. The owner of a [protected] [registered] industrial design shall have the right to prevent third parties not having his consent from:
manufacturing;
[selling] [offering, putting on the market];
using;

---

[446] Draft Final Act Embodying the Results of the Uruguay Round of Multilateral Trade Negotiations, Revision, Trade-Related Aspects of Intellectual Property Rights, Including Trade in Counterfeit Goods, MTN.TNC/W/35/Rev. 1, 3 Dec. 1990.

[447] See J. C. Ross and J. Wasserman, *Trade-Related Aspects of Intellectual Property Rights*, 1993, pp. 55–56.

or importing for commercial purposes;

[an object which is the subject matter of the industrial design right] [their industrial designs] [articles the appearance of which does not differ substantially from that of the protected design] [articles bearing a design which is a copy or substantially a copy of the protected design].

4. Obligations of Industrial Design Owners

4B With respect to the obligations of an industrial design owner, the requirements for patent inventions under point 3 of Section 5 below shall apply.

5. Term of Protection and Renewal

5A.1 The term of protection available shall be at least ten years.

5A.2 PARTIES shall provide for an initial term of protection of registered industrial designs of at least five years [from the date of application], with a possibility of renewal for [at least another period] [two consecutive periods] of five years.

5B The term of protection shall be provided under national legislation.

6. Remedial Measures under National Legislations; Compulsory Licensing of Industrial Designs

6A.1 [PARTIES shall not issue compulsory licences for industrial designs except to remedy adjudicated violations of competition law to which the conditions set out at point 3 of Section 5 below shall apply *mutatis mutandis*.] [The compulsory licensing of an industrial design shall not be permitted.]

6A.2 The protection of industrial designs shall not be subject to any forfeiture by reason of failure to exploit.

6B (See Section 8 below)"

2.2.2.2 The Brussels Draft. The first two paragraphs and the fourth paragraph of the Brussels Draft were essentially identical to the final version of Article 26.1–3. In addition, the Brussels Draft contained a developing country proposal providing that:

"3B With respect to the obligations of the owner of a protected industrial design, the provisions set forth in paragraph 3 (b) of Article [29] below shall apply."

A comparable reference to certain obligations of patent holders was already included in the Anell Draft (paragraph 4B as quoted above). Article 29.3(b) of the Brussels Draft provided:

"3. PARTIES may provide that a patent owner shall have the following obligations:

[...]

[(b) In respect of licensing contracts and contracts assigning patents, to refrain from engaging in abusive or anti-competitive practices adversely affecting the transfer of technology.]"

This draft obligation corresponded to some developing countries' concerns that exclusive intellectual property rights might actually have a negative impact on technology transfer. The reference to abusive or anti-competitive licensing practices was however not retained in the final version of Article 29 TRIPS on the obligations of patent holders, nor under the current Article 26 concerning the rights of industrial design owners. Instead, there is now Article 40 dealing specifically with the control of anti-competitive practices in contractual licences.[448]

A concession to the flexibility in design protection is reflected by the fact that the reference to "registered" industrial designs in the first paragraph of the Anell Draft was not maintained in the subsequent Brussels Draft and the final version of the Agreement. Such conditioning of protection to a registration system would have eliminated the other two available systems, i.e. the copyright system and the unregistered *sui generis* protection.

A further particularity in the Anell Draft provision is the express reference to forfeiture and compulsory licences (paragraphs 6A.1 and 6A.2, as quoted above). Such reference appears neither in the Brussels Draft nor in the final version of TRIPS. Instead, Article 26.2 TRIPS contains a general exception clause similar to the one under Article 30 concerning patent rights.[449]

3. Possible interpretations

TRIPS stipulates that Members must provide the following:

(a) independently created new or independently created original industrial designs must be protected – Article 25.1;

(b) proprietors of textile designs should not face obstacles arising from costs, examinations or publications in gaining protection – Article 25.2;

(c) design proprietors should have the right to stop third parties making, selling and importing articles which incorporate a design which is identical or substantially similar to the protected design, for commercial purposes – Article 26.1;

(d) the minimum term of protection is 10 years – Article 26.3.

3.1 Concept of industrial design

Although TRIPS states that all industrial designs must be protected, there has been no attempt to provide guidelines as to the type of subject matter which constitutes industrial designs. The concept "industrial design" in Article 25.1 can refer to all types of aesthetic, useful and functional designs including subject matter protected as "works of applied art" or "works of artistic craftsmanship" under copyright law, or as utility models. Importantly, there is no guidance as to the relationship between works of applied art (specifically referred to in Article 12) and industrial designs. Moreover, "industrial design" can be taken to include indigenous and folkloric icons, symbols and designs.

3.2 Nature of protection – copyright or *sui generis* design right (registered or unregistered)

To the extent they comply with the protection requirements under Article 25.1, Members can opt for either protection through copyright or *sui generis* design

---

[448] For more details on Article 40, see Chapter 29.

[449] See below, under Section 3 (in relation to the Annex to the Berne Convention, which applies to developing countries only).

protection, depending on the local industrial needs. Note that TRIPS follows and supplements the Berne and Paris Conventions.[450]

The major difference between the copyright approach on the one hand (including copyright proper and unregistered design right, see above, Section 1) and the *sui generis* registered design right on the other hand is the scope of protection: the registered design right protects against both deliberate copying and the independent development of a similar design. Under the copyright approach, protection is offered against deliberate copying only. Independent creations of similar designs may not be prevented.[451] Finally, the unregistered design right has characteristics similar to copyright (see above, Section 1). The main difference is the term of protection, which is usually much shorter than under copyright.[452]

A WTO Member is also free to adopt both ways of *sui generis* protection, as illustrated by the Japanese example: in addition to its registered design law, Japan now protects unregistered designs under an unfair competition regime, based on liability principles.[453]

3.2.1 Berne Convention on designs

Should WTO Members adopt copyright law as the preferred vehicle of protection for designs, Articles 1–21 of the Berne Convention must be complied with.[454] The key provision under the Berne Convention is Article 2(7), which basically leaves it to Berne Union/WTO Members to decide whether works of applied art and industrial designs should qualify for protection under copyright law, and if so, the conditions of protection. Union/WTO Members are free to expressly exclude copyright protection for works of applied art or industrial designs, and they

---

[450] One should further note that works of applied art and industrial designs are exempted from the national treatment and MFN requirements under Articles 3 and 4 of the TRIPS Agreement. See Section 3.6, below.

[451] See, for example, Article 19 of the EC Design Regulation on the rights conferred by the Community design: "1. A **registered** Community design shall confer on its holder the exclusive right to use it and to prevent any third party not having his consent from using it. The aforementioned use shall cover, in particular, the making, offering, putting on the market, importing, exporting or using of a product in which the design is incorporated or to which it is applied, or stocking such a product for those purposes.

2. An **unregistered** Community design shall, however, confer on its holder the right to prevent the acts referred to in paragraph 1 only if the contested use results from copying the protected design. The contested use shall not be deemed to result from copying the protected design if it results from an independent work of creation by a designer who may be reasonably thought not to be familiar with the design made available to the public by the holder. [...]" (emphasis added).

[452] The usual minimum term of copyright protection is the author's life plus 50 years, Article 7(1), Berne Convention, Article 9.1, TRIPS Agreement. By contrast, the EC Design Regulation provides a term of three years for the protection of unregistered designs.

[453] See UNCTAD, *The TRIPS Agreement and Developing Countries*, Geneva, 1996, para. 251 [hereinafter UNCTAD 1996]. The term of protection for unregistered designs in Japan is three years (ibid.). Note that this alone would not be consistent with TRIPS Article 26.3 (term of protection of at least 10 years).

[454] See Article 9.1 of the TRIPS Agreement, which by way of reference incorporates these provisions of the Berne Convention. See also Chapter 7.

may do so by employing a variety of statutory or judicial exclusionary devices to proscribe the following: industrially manufactured articles; non-aesthetic designs; patentable subject matter; designs where the aesthetic element cannot be separated from the utilitarian aspect (see Boxes 1 and 5, below). Nevertheless, irrespective of the mode of protection, Union/WTO Members must provide some sort of protection to works of applied art and industrial designs: where there is no *sui generis* design law, the provision clearly stipulates that such works must be protected under copyright law.[455] This corresponds to a similar obligation under the Paris Convention.

3.2.2 Paris Convention on designs

All WTO Members are subject to Articles 1–12, and Article 19 of the Paris Convention.[456] While Article 1(2) of the Paris Convention promulgates the notion that designs are to be categorised as industrial property, the Convention does not offer any guidance as to the nature or conditions of protection. Thus, industrial designs can either benefit from *sui generis* design protection (registered, unregistered, or both), copyright protection or some other sort of quasi-copyright or design protection.[457]

3.3 Conditions of protection (Article 25.1)

> 1. Members shall provide for the protection of independently created industrial designs that are new or original. Members may provide that designs are not new or original if they do not significantly differ from known designs or combinations of known design features. Members may provide that such protection shall not extend to designs dictated essentially by technical or functional considerations.

3.3.1 Independently created

It is a mandatory requirement that independently created designs must be protected. The question then is whether this is to be interpreted in the sense that the design must not be copied or whether it means the design must have some minimal amount of creativity or individuality. The more persuasive view is that the TRIPS drafters clearly intended the criterion of originality to entail more of a creative contribution than mere independent creation, due to the fact that two terms are employed to convey different meanings in the same sentence.[458] One commentator, however, suggests that it probably is meant to exclude copied or imitated

---

[455] Articles 2(7) *in fine*, and 2(1) of the Berne Convention.

[456] See Article 2.1 of the TRIPS Agreement.

[457] See Article 5*quinquies* of the Paris Convention; also see G.H.C. Bodenhausen, *Guide to the Application of the Paris Convention for the Protection of Industrial Property*, BIRPI, Geneva, 1968, p. 86 [hereinafter Bodenhausen].

[458] Reichman, Symposium, at p. 376. According to this view, the requirements of originality and of independent creation would not be one and the same criterion, but would constitute two separate requirements.

designs, in part to assuage those Members who had argued unsuccessfully for cumulative criteria of new and original.[459] Members may define this concept in local legislation to adopt either meaning.

Box 1: The U.S. regime

In the United States, protection is available under patent law for "any new, original and ornamental design for an article of manufacture." Furthermore, in order for a design to qualify for design patent protection, it must present an aesthetically pleasing appearance that is not dictated by function, and it must satisfy the general criteria of patentability i.e. full novelty and non-obviousness (§§102, 103, 171, U.S. Patents Act).

In brief, the law does not give protection to "new designs" or "original designs", but rather to designs which fulfil both criteria and requires candidates to fulfil a higher threshold of protection by requiring non-obviousness as well, a term more identified with the patent criterion of "inventive step".

Note, however, that designs are also protected in U.S. law by copyright and trade dress protection (a branch of trademark protection), so that the relatively strict criteria for design patent are mainly relevant to this strongest of the several forms of protection.

3.3.2 New or original

Members are left with the option of either implementing the criterion of novelty or originality. The history of the final formulation of "new or original" says much for the nebulous nature of "industrial design law".[460] Can Members go further and adopt both criteria of protection, i.e. that a design must be new *and* original? This is highly unlikely due to the history of the provision, and the express usage of "or", rather than "and/or", as proposed by some delegations. Are Members allowed to adopt more criteria of protection? This is apparently the case under the current U.S. design patent regime (see Box 1) and arguably also under the European Community Design Right[461] (see Box 2).

---

[459] See Gervais, para. 2.125. According to this author, those Members were concerned about the possibility that a design which was not new could still be protected on the basis of its originality. In order to prevent such possibility, those Members would have pushed, towards the end of the negotiations, for the additional criterion that the designs must have been created independently. Thus, the criterion of independent creation would not be apart from the originality criterion, but would qualify it.

[460] The concept of "new" stemmed from the compromise reached between the United States and Switzerland (new) and the EC, Japan and a group of developing countries (novel); subsequently the term "original" was advocated by the EC, the United States, developing countries and Japan. A slight tussle ensued as to whether it should be "new or original" (EC) or "new and/or original" (Japan) or "new and original" (developing countries, with the United States adding the criteria of "ornamental and non-obvious").

[461] Council Regulation EC No 6/2002 of 12 December 2001 on Community designs, OJ L 3, 5.1.02, p. 1.

Box 2: The EC design regime

The EC design regime accords protection to designs which fulfil the twin criteria of novelty and individual character. The latter could arguably constitute an additional requirement to the ones listed under Article 25.1 of TRIPS. However, the concept of "individual character" under the EC design laws may also be a reformulation of the "independently created" criterion under Article 25.1 TRIPS. A design shall be considered to have individual character if the overall impression it produces on the informed user differs from the overall impression produced on such a user by any design which has been made available to the public before the date of filing of the application for registration or, if priority is claimed, the date of priority. In assessing individual character, the degree of freedom of the designer in developing the design shall be taken into consideration.[462]

Members are offered the opportunity of anchoring their chosen criterion of protection (i.e. originality or novelty) to a prior art base constituting "known designs or combinations of known design features" (Article 25.1, second sentence). This may allow a Member to opt for an originality requirement which adopts an objective standard, rather than a copyright law standard (as under the United Kingdom unregistered design right system – see Box 3).[463]

Box 3: The UK unregistered design regime

The United Kingdom unregistered design right resembles a hybrid quasi-copyright. The right fulfils a perceived need for an automatic, short-term, quasi-copyright protection regime which would be available to both functional and non-functional three-dimensional designs. The design must be original, in the sense that it is not commonplace in the design field in question, and it must not fall foul of the exclusion provisions which bar protection to certain types of features, mainly in relation to design features of spare parts (see ss. 213 *et seq*, U.K. Copyright, Designs and Patents Act 1988).[464] Hong Kong-China has also adopted the British unregistered design right system.

---

[462] Articles 3–5, Directive 98/71/EC on the legal protection of designs, OJ L 289, 28.10.98, p. 28; Articles 4–6, Council Regulation EC No 6/2002 of 12 December 2001 on Community designs, OJ L 3, 5.1.02, p. 1.

[463] Under copyright law, the standard of originality is not an objective, but a subjective one: any product which is the result of *independent* human intellect and creativity is offered protection, even if it resembles another product. Thus, the reason for the grant of protection is the independence of the creation, rather than the difference of the resulting product from other products. Contrary to this subjective approach, the second sentence of Article 25.1 TRIPS (as quoted above) enables Members to base design protection on the difference between the resulting product and other products. Thus, an independently created design which does not significantly differ from a known design may be denied protection.

[464] For an account of the British system, see Suthersanen, *Design Law in Europe*, chapter 16.

> The British unregistered design right was partly based on the EC Directive 87/54/EEC on topography protection[465] which, in turn, was based on the United States Semiconductor Chip Protection Act 1984.

Members are also free to adopt local/regional/universal novelty, and to implement grace periods (see Box 4).

Box 4: Grace period

There is provision for a grace period for exhibition purposes under Article 11 of the Paris Convention. Union Members must grant temporary protection to patentable inventions, utility models and industrial designs in respect of goods exhibited at official or officially recognized international exhibitions held in the territory of any of them.[466] The grace period provided must not extend beyond the priority period: 12 months for utility models, and 6 months for industrial designs.

Within the European Union, both national and Community design laws offer a 12-month grace period in respect of registered designs.[467] During this period, the design proprietor will be able to claim the Community *unregistered* design right.

3.3.3 Registration

Registration or deposit is not a requirement of protection.[468] Therefore, Members have the option of adopting one or all of the following three alternative regimes:

a) copyright;

b) registered *sui generis* design right;

c) unregistered *sui generis* design right.

---

[465] Council Directive 87/54/EEC on the legal protection of topographies of semiconductor products, OJ L 24, 24.1.87, p. 36.

[466] The reason for this provision is that under the Paris Convention, the protection of the covered industrial property rights in one member State is independent of such protection in another member State (i.e. the principle of territoriality). Thus, an invention which is patented in country A, but not yet in countries B and C, could arguably lose its novelty in countries B and C when displayed to the public at an international exhibition. Subsequent patent applications in countries B and C would then have to be refused. Such approach would obviously prevent holders of a national patent to make available to international exhibitions their inventions. For this reason, Article 11 of the Paris Convention obligates member States to grant protection to exhibited goods for a limited period of time. Note that such protection may be provided through various means: by stipulating in domestic law that such exhibition will not destroy the novelty of the invention, or by granting to the right holder a temporary right of priority for subsequent applications in other States of the Paris Union (see Bodenhausen, p. 150, sub-paragraph (c)).

[467] Article 6(2), Directive 98/71/EC on the legal protection of designs, OJ L 289, 28.10.98, p. 28; Article 12, Council Regulation EC No 6/2002 of 12 December 2001 on Community designs, OJ L 3, 5.1.02, p. 1.

[468] By contrast, the Anell Draft provided that Members had the option of providing protection either upon registration or on other formalities. See above, Section 2.2.

Option c) offers an anti-copying regime, and examples of it are the United Kingdom unregistered design right (see Box 3) and the European Community Unregistered Design Right (see Box 5).[469] The United Kingdom further offers the example of a country which has all three alternative types of protection, i.e. copyright, registered design right and unregistered design right.

Box 5: Community design right

The European Community Design Regulation offers a Community Design Right (CDR). The CDR offers the design owner a two-tier system of rights. The proprietor will be entitled to quasi-copyright protection under the Unregistered CDR automatically upon the first marketing of his/her design; in the alternative, the design holder can opt for stronger, exclusive protection under the Registered CDR. The criteria of protection for both the unregistered and registered CDR will be the same: novelty and individual character. Furthermore, no protection will be accorded to certain types of design features including features solely dictated by its technical function.[470]

3.4 Textile designs (Article 25.2)

---

2. Each Member shall ensure that requirements for securing protection for textile designs, in particular in regard to any cost, examination or publication, do not unreasonably impair the opportunity to seek and obtain such protection. Members shall be free to meet this obligation through industrial design law or through copyright law.

TRIPS added Article 25.2 in response for rapid and cheap protection given by a non-registration regime, but only in the field of the textiles industry. The provision calls for a protection regime that does not "unreasonably impair the opportunity to seek and obtain such protection", and this may be hard to comply with unless a non-examination, non-registration/deposit system is adopted; the option available to Members appears to be to either allow copyright protection for textiles or to introduce a quasi-copyright, short term regime such as the unregistered design right (see Boxes 3 and 5).[471]

A final issue is whether textile designs would be classified as works of applied art or industrial designs under Article 2(7), Berne Convention, in which case Members are free to provide for a *sui generis* design protection or for copyright protection.[472]

---

[469] For more details on the different forms of protection available under Articles 25, 26, TRIPS Agreement, see above, Section 3.2 of this chapter.

[470] See Articles 4–12, Council Regulation EC No 6/2002 of 12 December 2001 on Community designs, OJ L 3, 5.1.02, p. 1.

[471] In this respect, see also Article 62.2, TRIPS Agreement, calling for Members to ensure that procedures for grant or registration permit the granting or registration of the right within a reasonable period of time.

[472] See above, Section 3.2.1.

3.5 Scope of protection (Article 26.1)

> 1. The owner of a protected industrial design shall have the right to prevent third parties not having the owner's consent from making, selling or importing articles bearing or embodying a design which is a copy, or substantially a copy, of the protected design, when such acts are undertaken for commercial purposes.

All WTO Members' legislation must ensure that the owner of a protected industrial design has the minimum right to prevent unauthorised third parties from making, selling or importing articles bearing or embodying the protected design, for commercial purposes. The provision should not affect a Member's right to award either a registration-based monopoly right or a mere anti-copying right. Nevertheless, irrespective of the nature of the right, the scope of the right must extend to designs which are either identical or are substantial copies of the protected design.

As with all rights to prevent importation under TRIPS, the right under Article 26.1 is subject to Article 6 that permits each WTO Member to adopt its own regime for exhaustion (see Chapter 5). It is therefore permissible to adopt a regime of international exhaustion for industrial design rights.

3.6 National treatment and reciprocity of protection (Article 26.1, Article 3)

It should be noted that the rules on national treatment and MFN treatment, under Articles 3 and 4, are subject to the exceptions under the Berne Convention. Works of applied art and industrial designs occupy a privileged position in being exempted from both these basic TRIPS provisions,[473] as national treatment in relation to these types of works is qualified under the Berne Convention. Works of applied art or designs are entitled to protection in other Members of the Union only to the extent of the nature of protection they are granted in the country of origin – if no such special protection is granted in that country, such works shall be protected as artistic works.[474]

Therefore, if a design is protected in State A solely under its *sui generis* design law, then such a work will only be granted similar *sui generis* protection in another Union/WTO Member State (State B), and need not be entitled to full copyright protection; the exception being that if State B does not offer special *sui generis* protection for works of applied art, such works will be entitled to full copyright protection. The wording of the provision only covers situations where a work in its country of origin is *solely* protected under design legislation; if other forms of protection are available in that country, the national treatment and MFN treatment obligations do apply. Thus, where a work of applied art in State A is protectable under both copyright and design laws, the exception under Article 2(7) of the Berne Convention does not apply. State B has no option but to offer to the work in question the same protection it offers to works of domestic right holders (be it copyright or design law or both).

---

[473] Articles 3.1 and 4(b) of the TRIPS Agreement. See discussion on these provisions in Chapter 4.
[474] Article 2(7) of the Berne Convention.

The applicability of the national treatment obligation in this context is related to the issue of cumulative protection countries versus partial protection countries. Consider the situation where the country of origin, for example, the USA, restricts copyright protection of works of applied art to such works which fulfil the separability criterion (see Box 6); can another Union/WTO state, for example, France, apply a similar restrictive approach, despite its liberal attitude to works of applied art? This would only seem possible if the other country (France, in the example) did not have to respect the national treatment obligation. This again would only be the case if the second sentence of Article 2(7) of the Berne Convention applied (i.e. if the country of origin of the works in question would provide protection solely under design law.). But since in the given example, the country of origin does provide copyright protection, Article 2(7) does not apply. Consequently, France in the above example would have to respect the national treatment obligation and thus afford copyright protection to such works in accordance with its own jurisprudence.[475]

Thus, as Reichman notes,

"exporters in both developed and developing countries should note that compliance with the requirements of domestic design laws provides no guarantees against infringements of foreign design rights based on different criteria. For example, designs legally created or copied under current U.S. law, if exported, could sometimes violate the United Kingdom's unregistered design right, which protects both functional and appearance designs, as well as, say, the French copyright law, or the new Japanese unfair competition law. "[476]

3.7 Functional designs – exceptions and limitations (Articles 25.1 and 26.2)

Article 25.1

1. Members shall provide for the protection of independently created industrial designs that are new or original. Members may provide that designs are not new or original if they do not significantly differ from known designs or combinations of known design features. Members may provide that such protection shall not extend to designs dictated essentially by technical or functional considerations.

Article 26.2

2. Members may provide limited exceptions to the protection of industrial designs, provided that such exceptions do not unreasonably conflict with the normal exploitation of protected industrial designs and do not unreasonably prejudice the legitimate interests of the owner of the protected design, taking account of the legitimate interests of third parties.

---

[475] See also Ricketson, para. 52.
[476] Reichman, Symposium, p. 377.

There are no compulsory provisions as to excluded subject matter or limitations/exceptions to protection, though Articles 25.1 and 26.2 offer Members an optional mandate. The difference between the two provisions is the following: designs under Article 25.1 do not qualify for design protection in the first place, whereas under Article 26.2, works would normally be protectable, but are excluded for some exceptional reasons (as will be analysed below). Article 25.1 contains two different sets of exclusions: under the second sentence, and on certain conditions, Members may exclude the novelty or originality of designs, thus denying to such designs the basic prerequisites for protection.[477] Under the third sentence, the reason for excluding designs from protection is the works' essentially technical or functional character (as will be analysed in the following Subsection).

3.7.1 Functional exclusions, Article 25.1, third sentence TRIPS

The third sentence of Article 25.1 allows Members, if they wish, to exclude designs dictated essentially by technical or functional considerations: since the reference to functional designs is an optional requirement, Members may also omit this provision from their domestic laws. In other words, Members can also choose the alternative of granting *sui generis* protection to both aesthetic and functional designs (for example, the United Kingdom unregistered design right system protects certain types of functional designs – see Box 3).

Since these exclusions/limitations are optional, it is up to the Member to limit the protection of designs according to the conditions and demands of its local industry. Thus, the European Union's design laws have adopted a specific "interconnections" exclusion clause, whilst the British/Hong Kong copyright laws limit copyright protection of functional design drawings and works of applied art.[478] Another example of a Member limiting its copyright protection of industrial designs is the U.S. copyright law (Box 6).

3.7.2 Article 26.2 TRIPS, analogue to Article 30

While it is not compulsory for Members to introduce exceptions to protection, Article 26.2, TRIPS places an obligation on those Members which do introduce exceptions or limitations under their domestic law; such Members must ensure that the exceptions do not conflict with the following rules:

• the exceptions have to be limited;

• the exceptions should not unreasonably conflict with the normal exploitation of protected industrial designs;

• the exceptions should not unreasonably prejudice the legitimate interests of the owners of protected industrial designs, taking into account the legitimate interests of third parties (i.e. there must be a balance between the rights of owners, on the one hand, and the rights of consumers/users/competitors, on the other hand).

---

[477] See above, concerning the conditions of protection under Article 25.1 (Section 3.3).

[478] See ss. 51 and 52, United Kingdom Copyright, Designs and Patents Act 1988.

Article 26.2 is essentially identical to Article 30 regarding exceptions to the rights of patent holders.[479] Article 13, on limitations and exceptions to copyright, which derives from Article 9(2) of the Berne Convention, uses different and more restrictive language (referring to "certain special cases" and eliminating references to "unreasonable"-ness and "interests of third parties"). In line with the Appellate Body's frequent admonition that the precise words of TRIPS were selected for a reason, it is apparent that the negotiators intended exceptions to industrial design protection to be regulated under the more flexible standards of Article 26.2 (and its analogue Article 30).

The panel in the *Canada – Generic Pharmaceuticals* case has interpreted the language of Article 30, and that decision is reviewed in Chapter 23 below. Design protection might act as an unreasonable impediment to the achievement of economic and social objectives in developing Members, for example, if used to prevent the interface of mechanical or electrical equipment of different manufacturers. It is therefore foreseeable that developing Members may wish to provide legal mechanisms for allowing the use of protected designs in such cases.

Moreover, since Article 26.2 is the only provision dealing with exceptions to industrial designs, the issuance of compulsory licenses for such designs would be encompassed by its rules. Where TRIPS intends to preclude compulsory licensing of an IPR, such a restriction (see, e.g., Article 21 on trademarks) is generally stated. Since compulsory licensing of copyrights is a fairly common practice and permitted under Article 13 in conjunction with Article 9(2), Berne, it would be anomalous if such licensing were not permitted under Article 26.2. Also, Article 5.B, Paris Convention, prevents the forfeiture of industrial designs based on non-working or importation, but does not preclude compulsory licensing.

Box 6: Designs under U.S. copyright law

Designs can be protected under the United States copyright law as "pictorial, graphic and sculptural works". These are defined as follows:

> "Pictorial, graphic, and sculptural works include two-dimensional and three-dimensional works of fine, graphic, and applied art, photographs, prints and art reproductions, maps, globes, charts, diagrams, models, and technical drawings, including architectural plans. Such works shall include works of artistic craftsmanship insofar as their form but not their mechanical or utilitarian aspects are concerned; the design of a useful article, as defined in this section, shall be considered a pictorial, graphic, or sculptural work only if, and only to the extent that, such design incorporates pictorial, graphic, or sculptural features that can be identified separately from, and are capable of existing independently of, the utilitarian aspects of the article." (s. 101, U.S. Copyright Act)

---

[479] Article 30 provides: "Members may provide limited exceptions to the exclusive rights conferred by a patent, provided that such exceptions do not unreasonably conflict with a normal exploitation of the patent and do not unreasonably prejudice the legitimate interests of the patent owner, taking account of the legitimate interests of third parties." See Chapter 23.

The "separability" criterion applies only to a "useful article", which is:

"an article having an intrinsic utilitarian function that is not merely to portray the appearance of the article or to convey information." (s. 101, U.S. Copyright Act)

3.7.4 Utility models

Utility models ("petty patents") differ from industrial designs in that the latter typically concern *ornamental aspects* of an industrial article, whereas utility models are granted for the *technical novelty* of such article.[480] Therefore, it has been observed that utility models and industrial designs rarely concern the same subject.[481] However, in the case of *functional* designs, such overlapping is possible, considering that those designs are dictated essentially by technical or functional considerations (Article 25.1). Thus, an increasing number of jurisdictions have chosen to provide for the protection of functional designs under a utility model regime as an alternative to an industrial designs system. TRIPS does not discuss utility models.[482] The relationship between industrial designs and utility models is accentuated by the Paris Convention, recognising the interdependency of priority periods between utility models and industrial designs. A period of priority can be secured for an application for an industrial design based on the filing date of a utility model.[483]

Utility model protection is said to be of great importance to developing countries. A main goal of the industrial property system is the promotion of innovation within industrial society; it is thought that a cheap and rapid utility model regime would improve the legal environment for small and medium sized companies, especially those which are engaged in an ongoing process of innovation and adaptation. This is more so in relation to certain types of product sectors which are

---

[480] Bodenhausen, p. 52. This does not mean that the outward appearance of an industrial article cannot be protected by a utility model: if besides the *ornamental* function, the outward appearance fulfils a *technical* function, it is eligible for utility model protection.

[481] Ibid.

[482] While there is no specific reference to utility model protection under the TRIPS Agreement, it is arguable that by reference in Article 2.1 TRIPS, the relevant provisions of the Paris Convention provisions (including Article 1(2) of the Convention) are extended to all WTO Members. Article 1(2) of the Paris Convention provides in relevant part: "The protection of industrial property has as its object patents, utility models, [...]"

[483] See Article 4E(1) of the Paris Convention. This means that once an application for a utility model has been filed, subsequent applications by the same person in other countries benefit from a priority right even if they do not concern a utility model, but an industrial design. However, the period of priority accorded to utility models amounts to twelve months, whereas the period for industrial designs is only six months, see Article 4C(1) of the Convention. Article 4E(1) clarifies that the priority period for applications for industrial designs that are based on a prior application for a utility model shall not benefit from the longer period for utility models. This provision applies only to the case in which the first application is filed with respect to a utility model and subsequently priority is claimed on the basis of that application for a second application concerning an industrial design. It has been observed, however, that the reverse case may be assumed to be covered as well (Bodenhausen, p. 52). In that case, a first application for an industrial design would determine the date as of which the priority period for any subsequent applications for a utility model would commence. Those later applications would then benefit from the longer term accorded to utility models (i.e. one year instead of six months as for industrial designs).

concerned not so much with revolutionary technological breakthroughs, but more so with incremental or improvement innovation.[484] For example, one cited reason for the need for a European utility model law is the need for a rapid and cheap protective regime for such minor innovations in the following industries: toy manufacturing, clock and watchmaking, optics, microtechnology and micromechanics.[485]

3.8 Term of protection (Article 26.3)

> 3. The duration of protection available shall amount to at least 10 years.

The minimum term of protection is ten years. TRIPS does not specify whether this term is to be computed from the date of filing (if any) or the date of issue. This provision is taken to refer only to situations where *sui generis* design law is the *only* means of protection. If a WTO Member opts for copyright protection of industrial designs, the duration of protection must be governed by Article 7 of the Berne Convention.[486] The general rule for copyright is that the duration of protection must be 50 years *post mortem auctoris*. The exceptions to this general rule include works of applied art – Members remain free to provide for a shorter duration of protection, as long as a minimum term of 25 years from the making of the work is granted.[487]

There are several issues which arise.

First, will all intellectual property regimes which provide for protection of designs have to confer a minimum duration of 10 years? For example, should the proposed 3-year European Unregistered Community Design Right be amended to 10 years?[488] It is submitted that Article 26.3 merely requires Members to offer at least one regime of protection which offers a minimum ten-year period of protection, whether that regime is copyright, registered design right or unregistered design right.[489] Secondly, is Article 26.3 in conflict with the 25-year minimum term secured for works of applied art under Article 7(4) of the Berne Convention? The

---

[484] U. Suthersanen, *Incremental Inventions in Europe: A Legal and Economic Appraisal of Second Tier Patents*, Journal of Business Law 2001, 319; U. Suthersanen, *The Economic Efficacy Of Utility Model Protection: A Comparative Review Of European Union, Asia-Pacific And U.S. Policy And Practice,* in: Industrial Property Rights in the Bio-tech Age – Challenges for Asia (eds. Christopher Heath and A. Kamperman Sanders), Kluwer International, 2002 (discussing the different questions policy makers need to ask prior to implementing utility model protection).

[485] EC Commission Green Paper on the Protection of Utility Models in the Single Market, COM(95) 370 final, July 19, 1995, at p. 16.

[486] Article 12 of the TRIPS Agreement does not affect works of applied art, which we must assume refer to industrial designs, as well.

[487] Article 7(4) of the Berne Convention. For the history of this provision, see Ricketson, paras. 6.33-6.43.

[488] Article 12, Council Regulation EC No 6/2002 of 12 December 2001 on Community designs, OJ L 3, 5.1.02, p. 1.

[489] See *Azrak-Hamway International Inc. v. Meccano SA* (1997) RPC 134 (United Kingdom), where it was argued that the provision relating to licenses of right under the United Kingdom unregistered design right was contrary to the minimum requirements under the TRIPS Agreement; the tribunal,

argument that the TRIPS provision only urges Members to introduce at least one 10-year protective regime falters in light of the fact that Members may choose to protect industrial designs under a copyright-only regime or the fact that there is a strong suggestion that textile designs, at least, should benefit from copyright protection. In light of this, it is submitted that where a Member opts to protect designs under an industrial property regime such as a *sui generis* design law, the minimum term of protection must be 10 years, if this is the only means of protection; however, where designs are only protected under copyright law, the minimum term of protection must be 25 years, in accordance with the Berne Convention. In cases where both copyright and *sui generis* design law protection are offered, the term applying to the copyright protection has to be 25 years. The term applying at the same time to the *sui generis* protection can be less than 10 years: the minimum term of 10 years as required under Article 26.3 is already more than respected by the 25-year copyright term.

4. WTO jurisprudence

To date, there has been no panel or Appellate Body decision concerning Article 25 or 26.

5. Relationship with other international instruments

5.1 WTO Agreements

5.2 Other international instruments

5.2.1 The Geneva Act (1999) of the Hague Agreement Concerning the International Registration of Industrial Designs[490]

If the registration approach is adopted, the registered design right is limited to the country in which protection is granted. If multi-regional protection is required, multiple filing is necessary. Under the WIPO-administered Hague Agreement Concerning the International Deposit of Industrial Designs, a procedure for an international registration is offered.

The Hague Agreement was concluded in 1925, and has been subject to two revisions: 1934 (London) and 1960 (The Hague). The objective of the Agreement is to facilitate the application for design protection in several countries by providing a mechanism for a centralised international deposit system, similar to the international registration of trademarks under the Madrid Agreement. A design proprietor can, with one application filed with WIPO, obtain protection in one or more or all the States adhering to the Agreement. The applicant is not required to obtain national registration in the country of origin. The protection accorded is strictly national and is subject to national laws and conditions in the countries

---

however, held that the United Kingdom unregistered design right was outside the ambit of the TRIPS Agreement, being a supplementary regime of protection.

[490] The Hague Agreement Concerning the International Deposit of Industrial Designs of November 6, 1925, as revised by the Hague Act of November 28, 1960; Regulations Under the Hague Agreement Concerning the International Deposit of Industrial Designs, January 1, 1998.

designated in the application. Individual countries designated in the application may refuse protection if requirements for protection of national law are not fulfilled.

The main problem arises from the fact that many major countries are not parties to the Hague Agreement. Only 29 countries are signatory to this treaty. Noticeably absent from the membership list are all the South American countries, Japan, Canada, the United States and most Asian countries.[491] A second related problem with the Hague Agreement is the fact that contracting states are either parties to the 1934 Act or the 1960 Act, and different and difficult procedural rules are applicable.

The Geneva Act 1999 has a twofold objective, namely: on the one hand, to extend the Hague system to new members by allowing or facilitating the accession of states whose legislation provides for a novelty examination;[492] on the other hand, to preserve the fundamental simplicity of the Hague system and make it more attractive to applicants. The Geneva Act also provides for the establishment of a link between the international registration system and regional systems, such as the European Community Design Office or the African Intellectual Property Organization (OAPI), by providing that intergovernmental organizations may become party to the Act.[493]

6. New developments

6.1 National laws[494]

6.1.1 Ownership of copyright and design protection
Neither TRIPS nor the Hague Agreement contains any provisions on ownership and whether local laws may make provision for authorship and/or ownership to vest in natural or legal persons. Once again, the vagueness of the provisions can work for the benefit of developing countries, should they wish to extend design protection to traditional/indigenous works of arts or local innovations. For example, under the British unregistered design right, a person can qualify for protection either as the author, employer, commissioner or the first marketer of the design work.[495]

6.1.2 Artistic designs and moral rights, including *droit de suite* (resale right)
The Berne Convention provides for certain moral rights: the right to claim authorship of the work and the right to object to any mutilation or deformation or other

---

[491] Among Asian countries, only the Democratic People's Republic of Korea (North Korea), Indonesia and Mongolia have signed the Agreement.

[492] This is so because some domestic laws subject design protection to the patentability criteria of novelty and inventive step. For an example, see above, Box 1.

[493] To date, however, no intergovernmental organization has actually adhered to the Geneva Act. For a list of the Contracting Parties see <http://www.wipo.org/treaties/documents/english/pdf/h-hague.pdf>.

[494] For the USA, the United Kingdom and the European Union, see Boxes 1 to 6, above. For Japan, see Section 3.2, above.

[495] Ss. 215, 217 *et seq.*, Copyright, Designs and Patents Act 1988 (U.K.).

modification of, or other derogatory action in relation to, the work which would be prejudicial to the author's honour or reputation.[496] Such rights may be of importance to certain Members which wish to see a cessation of works of traditional or indigenous arts being exported and exploited in other countries. Of course, one problem has always been ownership issues; however, international agreements and treaties are traditionally reluctant to offer rules on ownership of intellectual property rights.[497] Some national laws have been more explicit on this issue (see Boxes 7 and 8 below).

Box 7: The French *droit d'auteur* regime

Under the French *droit d'auteur*, there is a clear exception to the rule that an author can only be a natural person: where a work qualifies as a "collective work", authorship can vest in both natural and legal persons.[498] The category of "collective work" can arise in respect of all types of created works, including works of applied art and industrial designs. Furthermore, it has been held that technically, there is nothing in law which prevents a legal entity from claiming moral rights in a work created by a legal entity as in the case of collective works. Where a legal person is the promoter and owner of copyright in the collective work, it has the right to make modifications to the work as long as such changes are for the purpose of harmonising the work as a whole and are subject to the moral rights of individual authors who contribute to the collective work. Nonetheless, the legal owner's rights can extend further and in one decision, it was held that the publication of a design made by designers at a Citroën firm was in violation of the firm's moral right of disclosure.[499]

Moreover, certain types of works are entitled to a *droit de suite* or resale royalty right: the right is reserved for original works of art and original manuscripts of writers and composers.[500] The pre-condition of "original" refers to the uniqueness of the work, as opposed to the copyright sense of originality or creativity. The Berne Convention stipulates a proviso in respect of this right: an author can claim the *droit de suite* or resale royalty right in a Berne Union country only if the

---

[496] Article 6*bis* of the Berne Convention.

[497] As to the TRIPS Agreement, a U.S. proposal during the TRIPS negotiations to *expressly* recognize corporate authorship was unsuccessful. Instead, Article 12 TRIPS provides for a special term of copyright protection in cases where the term of protection is calculated on a basis other than the life of a natural person. This includes works of corporate authorship and thus constitutes an *implicit* recognition of the concept of a non-natural author. See Chapter 11.

[498] Articles L. 113-2, 113-5, French Intellectual Property Code 1992. See Suthersanen, *Design Law in Europe*, pp. 147–148. Another example of an express recognition of (corporate) ownership are sound recordings and films under U.S. law, see Chapter 11.

[499] Suthersanen, *ibid*, p. 157.

[500] See Article 14*ter* (1) of the Berne Convention: "The author, or after his death the persons or institutions authorized by national legislation, shall, with respect to original works of art and original manuscripts of writers and composers, enjoy the inalienable right to an interest in any sale of the work subsequent to the first transfer by the author of the work."

legislation in the country to which the author belongs so permits, and only to the extent permitted by the country where this protection is claimed.[501]

Developing countries producing highly original indigenous or folkloric art may wish to argue as to the inclusion of the *droit de suite*. Currently, several countries, including Bolivia, Chile, Kenya, Indonesia and Panama protect folkloric work under national copyright laws.[502] The provision is probably of more utility to countries which experience only few imports of foreign art or design works, but instead increasing exports of local or domestic art works or designs due to foreign interest in indigenous or folkloric art. It should be noted that many countries do deny the *droit de suite* to works of applied art or three-dimensional designs meant for industrial use.

6.2 International instruments

6.3 Regional and bilateral contexts

For the EC Directive of 2001 on the resale right for the benefit of the author of an original work of art, see Box 8.

Box 8: The EC resale right directive

Article 1(1) of the EC Resale Right Directive provides:[503]

"Member States shall provide, for the benefit of the author of an original work of art, a resale right, to be defined as an inalienable right, which cannot be waived, even in advance, to receive a royalty based on the sale price obtained for any resale of the work, subsequent to the first transfer of the work by the author."

Article 2, ibid, provides:

"(1) For the purposes of this Directive, 'original work of art' means works of graphic or plastic art such as pictures, collages, paintings, drawings, engravings, prints, lithographs, sculptures, tapestries, ceramics, glassware and photographs, provided they are made by the artist himself or are copies considered to be original works of art.

(2) Copies of works of art covered by this Directive, which have been made in limited numbers by the artist himself or under his authority, shall be considered to be original works of art for the purposes of this Directive. Such copies will normally have been numbered, signed or otherwise duly authorised by the artist."

---

[501] See Article 14*ter* (2) of the Berne Convention: "The protection provided by the preceding paragraph may be claimed in a country of the Union only if legislation in the country to which the author belongs so permits, and to the extent permitted by the country where this protection is claimed."

[502] See UNESCO/WIPO *Model Provisions for National Laws for Protection of Expressions of Folklore Against Illicit Exploitation and other Prejudicial Actions*, 1982.

[503] EC Directive 2001/84/EC of 27 September 2001 on the resale right for the benefit of the author of an original work of art, OJ L 272, 13.10.2001, p. 32.

6.4 Proposals for review

There is no formal proposal for review before the Council for TRIPS.

7. Comments, including economic and social implications

The discussion above illustrates the difficult task which legislators face in implementing the TRIPS provisions on industrial designs. The conclusion is that the different approaches are suited to different product sectors. It is, thus, important for any developing country to note which industries contribute the most to the economic development of the country, and the type of protection those industries require.

The discussion below highlights the different issues arising from such analysis.

7.1 Industries which benefit from the copyright approach

The availability of immediate and automatic protection is particularly useful for short-lived products. The lower threshold of originality (in comparison to novelty) is advantageous for industries which customarily rely on the prior state of art, for example, cultural or folkloric art. The criterion of originality allows industries to embark on market testing for their products without any loss of protection;[504] industries require a right to forestall piracy during the early and sensitive stages of market-testing. There are no application or registration costs, thus making the approach more suited for small and medium-sized enterprises. Copyright protection is not product specific, and will encompass the entire class or range of goods for which the design is used, giving a much wider scope of protection. The long duration of copyright protection corresponds to the need of some industries where product manufacture and consumer tastes are cyclical in nature. Copyright laws are increasingly being utilised to protect industrial subject matter such as computer programs and electronic databases. From the above, one can discern that copyright protection is extremely attractive to short-lived industries such as the toy, fashion and textile industries which are fast moving, quickly imitated and in need of immediate protection.

7.2 Industries which are disadvantaged under the copyright approach

Some industries, however, object to the copyright system due to the legal uncertainty which ensues from a non-registration system. Since copyright protection can arise automatically, there is no indication as to the duration of copyright protection. The absence of any examination process or public record or source of information leaves it impossible to determine which features of a product can be safely imitated. This is especially important in heavy and light manufacturing industries where new designs rely heavily on prior art or where the design is an improvement of an older design, or drawing which leaves competitors in doubt as to which elements are still in protection and which are not. The lack of registration

---

[504] This is so because a design that has been created independently will be qualified as original in the copyright sense even after the design has been made available to the public through market testing. This would be different under the *sui generis* approach, due to the novelty requirement, see below.

and public records creates problems in identifying the rights owners and their successors/licensees, and can hinder the transferability of rights. Since independent creations are outside the scope of copyright or anti-copying laws, there can be simultaneous protection of identical designs by different designers, which is not conducive to a climate of legal predictability. A low threshold of originality may lead to an erosion of the scope of protection which would provide ineffective protection. The converse argument is that some copyright laws provide over-wide protection due to their low originality threshold, their non-requirement of artistic merit, and their long duration of protection. This may lead to the protection of functional drawings and products, which is anti-competitive and would force many competitors out of the relevant product market. The protection criteria may be difficult to meet due to their subjectivity: many countries require an artistic or aesthetic element to be present in three-dimensional designs. Copyright law does not usually allow for a general compulsory licensing provision to counter anti-competitive effects.[505] Copyright only offers protection against imitation rather than an exclusive right, thus entailing evidentiary difficulties during infringement proceedings.

7.3 Industries which benefit from the *sui generis* design approach

The main advantage of this approach revolves on the single fact of registration, and the legal certainty which ensues. The registration system functions as a source of information, especially in relation to ownership, date of registration, priority applications, and the protected features (via a statement of novelty). Upon registration, competitors are placed on notice as to the existence of protection – this is a favoured factor by large manufacturing organisations and trade associations, especially in the engineering industry. There is no need to prove copying which can be difficult and often relies on circumstantial evidence such as access to works. The twin benefits of registration and an exclusive right enhances the registered design proprietor's ability to obtain remuneration either through licensing opportunities or by offering his right as a security interest or charge. The short duration conferred can be advantageous and pro-competitive, especially in relation to more utilitarian designs. Furthermore, most systems employ a renewal system thereby enabling the design proprietor the option of claiming the maximum term of protection, only when required, while ensuring that a steady number of designs will fall into the public domain before their maximum term of protection expires save for the commercially viable designs.

An illustration of how the registration of designs may be utilized for developing country concerns is the move by indigenous communities in Argentina to press for the creation of a register for their traditional knowledge.[506] Such register could include, *inter alia*, a list of traditional designs of indigenous people in South America

---

[505] As explained above (see Section 2.2), the Anell Draft did contain such a general provision, which, however, does not appear in the TRIPS final version.

[506] See "Call for Argentine register of local knowledge", at <http://www.scidev.net/frame3.asp?id=2103200311090739andt=Nandauthors=Valeria%20Romanandposted=21%20Mar%202003 andc=1andr=1>. The Argentine National Institute of Industrial Property (INPI) is currently examining such a request submitted by 44 indigenous leaders.

and thus prevent third parties from using these designs without the consent of the indigenous creators.[507]

7.4 Industries which are disadvantaged under the *sui generis* design approach

However, one should also note that the apparent advantages conferred by registration may be illusory if national industrial property offices do not carry out detailed examinations. Moreover, the registration formalities can be complex and difficult to comply with, especially in respect of details as to the dimensions of the drawings, type of photographs, etc. Small and medium-sized firms are either unaware of the registration system in respect of their creations, or do not feel that the registration system applies to their work. This can lead to premature disclosure of the design through prior use or publication in the market. The registration process is an especial burden for industries such as the toy, clothes, fashion and furniture industries where a product's life cycle is short. The concept of novelty imposes an unrealistically high threshold for designs which are, by their nature, based on the prior state of art; no allowance is given for incremental creativity. The criterion of novelty and the corresponding lack of grace period mean that market testing of products is usually denied.[508] In many industries, the product design may revolve around several basic design themes, and market testing is needed to decide which specific design collections deserve registration. The cost of registration, especially in respect of multiple design applications, can be exorbitant. This is especially difficult for small firms with no trained personnel in industrial property matters. The publication of designs can be used by imitators in producing rival or pirate products. This has been cited as an especial problem in the textile and ceramics industries. There is a decline in the rate of increase in international registration, thus proving its unpopularity with industry.

7.5 Implementation costs

As the costs of implementation are concerned, it is important to note that they will vary with the type of regime adopted.[509] Any system depending on the registration of a right (i.e. the registered *sui generis* design right approach) requires some prior examination of the submitted design with a view to deciding if it meets the conditions for protection (i.e. independent creation, novelty, or originality, Article 25.1). Such examination will entail certain costs,[510] but is justified in view of the fact that the applicant seeks to be granted an exclusive right. In case of non-registration systems (i.e. the copyright and unregistered *sui generis* design right approach), the right conferred is usually non-exclusive, and it comes into existence

---

[507] Ibid, reporting that a multitude of sandals, belts and other handicrafts sold in Buenos Aires bear the traditional designs of South American indigenous people, but are sold without the consent of those having developed the designs.

[508] This is so because once tested, the product arguably cannot be considered as novel anymore. For details on the novelty requirement, see Chapter 17.

[509] UNCTAD, 1996, para. 256.

[510] Ibid.

automatically with the creation of the design. Therefore, there is no examination, nor registration, and related costs will thus be avoided.

It is up to each government to decide how much weight will be given to the cost factor, and how much importance will be attached to the other criteria referred to above.

7.6 Summation

• TRIPS provisions on industrial designs are minimal, thus leaving Members room for implementation of any type of protective regime, including unregistered design right (see Sections 3.2 and 3.3.3 as well as Box 5).

• Members must either adopt copyright protection or *sui generis* design protection or both. Nothing under TRIPS forbids cumulative protection of industrial designs under design and copyright laws (see Section 3.2).

• The criterion of protection must include either originality or novelty (see Section 3.3.2, and Boxes 2 and 4).

• Most Members implementing TRIPS maintain the minimum standards; however, many developed Members, such as the European Community and the USA have opted for higher criteria of protection. It is unclear whether Members can opt for further more onerous criteria unless Members offer more than one type of protection for industrial designs (i.e. copyright and design laws) (see Section 3.3 and Boxes 1-3).

• At all times the mandatory requirement as to textile designs should be taken into account (see Section 3.4).

• The main problems with Articles 25 and 26 is that these provisions are not clear as to the exceptions incorporated under copyright and industrial design laws. For example, it is difficult to gain protection under U.S. and British copyright laws for three-dimensional industrial designs. Can Members go further and limit/curtail copyright protection to such an extent that no copyright protection is accorded to works of applied art, whereas the *sui generis* system requires more than novelty/originality? (see Boxes 1, 6 and Section 3.3.2)

• National treatment or reciprocity – to what extent should the Berne exceptions still apply? (see Section 3.6)

• Articles 25 and 26 allow utility model protection (see Section 3.7.4).

• In respect of indigenous or folkloric artistic works, Members should consider whether increased moral rights protection is a worthwhile approach (see Boxes 7 and 8).

Ultimately, it will be up to Members to decide whether they wish to promote certain local industries engaged in incremental innovation or designs by either adopting an anti-intellectual property market regime (for example, by excluding functional and other types of designs), or a pro-intellectual property market regime (by strengthening design protection or introducing utility model laws). In respect of other Members' laws, particular regard must be had to whether other countries which apparently have more protectionist laws, by adopting wide exclusions and limitations, actually offer much less protection than is otherwise perceived: the question for all Members is whether their laws actually diminish or neutralise the protection which must be granted under TRIPS.

In respect of Articles 25 and 26, it has been observed that developing countries should look to their own interests and view existing copyright and design regimes critically.[511] However, in negotiations with developed country Members, it may well be to the advantage of developing countries to argue for strengthened design right, copyright or moral right protection of traditional designs as a negotiating tool in response to demands for increased protection in other industrial sectors.

[511] UNCTAD, 1996, para. 252.

17: Patents: Subject Matter and Patentability Requirements

Article 27.1 Patentable Subject Matter

Subject to the provisions of paragraphs 2 and 3, patents shall be available for any inventions, whether products or processes, in all fields of technology, provided that they are new, involve an inventive step and are capable of industrial application.* Subject to paragraph 4 and Article 65, paragraph 8 of Article 70 and paragraph 3 of this Article, patents shall be available and patent rights enjoyable without discrimination as to the place of invention, the field of technology and whether products are imported or locally produced.

[Footnote]*: For the purposes of this Article, the terms "inventive step" and "capable of industrial application" may be deemed by a Member to be synonymous with the terms "non-obvious" and "useful" respectively.

---

1. Introduction: overview, terminology, definition and scope

1.1 Overview of TRIPS provisions on patents

TRIPS (Part II, Section 5) contains standards relating to patents and covers both substantive standards as well as specific issues of enforcement that are generally applicable to patents. The following provisions are noteworthy:[512]

(a) Members may not exclude any field of technology from patentability, and they may not discriminate as to fields of technology, the place of invention and whether products are imported or locally produced (Article 27);

(b) Members may exclude from patentability: inventions contrary to *ordre public* or morality; certain methods for human or animal treatment; and plants and animals, with some qualifications. Members may also provide for limited exceptions to the exclusive rights conferred by a patent, provided certain requirements are met (Articles 27, 30);

(c) The domestic patent laws must provide a minimum term of twenty years of protection from the filing date. Such protection must depend on the same

---

[512] See UNCTAD, *The TRIPS Agreement and Developing Countries*, Geneva, 1996, paras 111–114 [hereinafter UNCTAD, 1996].

conditions of eligibility though the definition of the specific standards of patentability is left to national laws (Article 33 and 27);

(d) The patentee's bundle of exclusive rights must include the right to prevent the importation of the patented products (Article 28), subject to the applicable rules of exhaustion (Article 6);

(e) Compulsory licences remain available and can be granted under the existing law of the Member country, subject to the conditions set forth in the Agreement (Article 31).

These provisions build on standards previously established by the Paris Convention,[513] such as the rights of priority, which even WTO Members who do not adhere to this Convention must now respect. Single countries may deviate from these universal patent law standards only to the extent that they make use of transitional periods, which vary with the beneficiary's status as either a developing country, an economy in transition or a least-developed country (LDC).[514] For example, developing countries could postpone implementing most of the required standards for a period of five years (Article 65). LDCs under Article 66.1 obtained a reprieve for eleven years, while a proof of hardship may qualify them for further delays and other concessions.[515] Under the Doha Declaration on the TRIPS Agreement and Public Health, this original transition period has been extended for LDCs until 2016, *inter alia* with respect to the granting of patents on pharmaceutical products.

The provisions on enforcement (Part III of the Agreement) are generally applicable to patent rights, although Member countries need not apply the special requirements of border control measures to patents. Such measures are obligatory for trademarks and copyrights. In addition, the Agreement (Articles 70.8 and 70.9) describes the procedures to be followed in case a Member country applies the transitional periods provided for under Article 65 of the Agreement to pharmaceutical products and agro-chemicals. This provision allows developing countries to delay the recognition of pharmaceutical patents for up to ten years from the date of entry into force of TRIPS. The transitional periods are automatically applicable, i.e., there is no need for prior notification or declaration by concerned Member countries. However, Members that apply the extended period of 10 years for pharmaceutical or agrochemicals are bound to accept the filing of new applications for pharmaceutical product patents during that period, and they are further bound eventually to grant exclusive marketing rights (EMRs) for a limited period (Article 70.9).[516]

This and the subsequent chapters of this book (numbers 18-26) deal in detail with the following patent issues: subject matter and patentability requirements; non-discrimination; *ordre public* and morality; therapeutic, surgical and diagnostic methods; biotechnological inventions: genetic resources, plant variety

---

[513] Paris Convention for the Protection of Industrial Property, Stockholm Act of 14 July 1967.

[514] For details on the transitional arrangements, see Chapter 33.

[515] See also WTO Agreement, Article XI(2), requiring LDCs only ... "to undertake commitments and concessions to the extent consistent with the individual development, financial and trade needs or their administrative and institutional capabilities".

[516] For details, see Chapter 36.

protection, traditional knowledge; rights and exceptions; disclosure of information; non-voluntary uses; and, process patents: burden of proof.

1.2 Terminology, definition and scope

Article 27.1 contains the overriding requirement that patents shall be available for all types of product and process inventions, subject to the principle of non-discrimination (with regard to the place of invention, the field of technology and whether products are imported or locally produced), and to certain facultative exceptions discussed below.

A patent confers an exclusive right granted by a state to an inventor for a certain period of time[517] in return for disclosure of his or her invention in a document known as the patent specification. The description of the invention in the specification must be sufficient that others skilled in the technological field ("skilled in the art") are able to read the specification and perform the invention for themselves after the patent expires. The extent of the exclusive rights is defined in the part of the patent application known as the claims. Only third parties carrying out activities that fall within the claims will commit infringement of the patent. The way in which the claims are construed varies from jurisdiction to jurisdiction. In some a fairly literal approach is adopted, and functional equivalents not claimed in the specification will not infringe the patent. Others treat functional equivalents that would be obvious to third parties skilled in the art as falling within the claims.

Under the Paris Convention for the Protection of Industrial Property, states were free to exclude areas from patentability, as well as to provide special rules for certain types of inventions. In addition, they had freedom to define the requirements for patentability. TRIPS has changed this situation. Article 27.1 includes a general obligation of patentability addressing in this manner one of the major concerns raised by the pharmaceutical industry with respect to prevailing regimes prior to TRIPS. In addition, all discrimination between sectors (as well as on the basis of the place of invention) has been banned. As discussed below,[518] Article 27.1, *in fine*, also provided a basis for limiting the power of States to differentiate the treatment conferred to products locally produced and imported. Though not explicitly mentioned in this provision, the main aim of the proponents of such a non-discrimination clause was to restrain the use of compulsory licences for lack of local exploitation. Being the result of a compromise, this aspect of Article 27.1 has been the subject of considerable controversy.[519]

2. History of the provision

2.1 Situation pre-TRIPS

At the start of the Uruguay Round, about 50 countries did not grant protection to pharmaceutical products at all, and some excluded pharmaceutical processes from protection as well. Many also excluded food and other products from patentability.[520]

---

[517] At least twenty years from the date of filing, Article 33 TRIPS – see Chapter 22 below.

[518] See Chapter 25.

[519] See Chapter 25.

[520] See UNCTAD, 1996.

The main international instrument dealing with patents before the entry into force of TRIPS was the Paris Convention. Unlike Article 27.1, though, the Convention allowed exclusions from patentability and did not establish any patentability criteria;[521] it was up to the Paris Union countries to determine these in their domestic laws.

2.2 Negotiating history

The drafting of Article 27.1 was in part based on Article 10 of the draft WIPO Patent Law Treaty of 1991. This required that patents be available for inventions in all fields of technology, subject to fulfilling the usual requirements for patentability: (1) novelty; (2) industrial applicability; and, (3) display of an inventive step. Article 27.1 establishes therefore a general principle of patentability. The same principle was codified at the time of the negotiations in Article 52(1) of the European Patent Convention[522] and in many national patent laws.

2.2.1 The Anell Draft

"SECTION 5: PATENTS

1. Patentable Subject Matter

1.1 Patents shall be [available] [granted] for [any inventions, whether products or processes, in all fields of technology,] [all products and processes] which are new, which are unobvious or involve an inventive step and which are useful or industrially applicable.

1.2 Patents shall be available according to the first-to-file principle.

1.3 Requirements such as filing of an adequate disclosure in a patent application and payment of reasonable fees shall not be considered inconsistent with the obligation to provide patent protection.

(See also point 3.1 below)[523]

1.4 The following [shall] [may] be excluded from patentability:

[...]

1.4.2 Scientific theories, mathematical methods, discoveries and materials or substances [already existing] [in the same form found] in nature.

[...]

1.4.5 [Production, application and use of] nuclear and fissionable material, [and substances manufactured through nuclear transformation].

1.5B PARTIES may exclude from patentability certain kinds of products, or processes for the manufacture of those products on grounds of public interest, national security, public health or nutrition.

[...]"[524]

---

[521] I.e. the criteria of novelty, inventive step and industrial applicability as laid down in Article 27.1 of the TRIPS Agreement.

[522] This Article reads as follows: "European patents shall be granted for any inventions which are susceptible of industrial application, which are new and which involve an inventive step".

[523] Point 3.1 of the Anell Draft concerned the disclosure obligation. See Chapter 24.

[524] See Chairman's report to the Group of Negotiation on Goods, document MTN.GNG/NG11/W/76, of 23 July 1990.

The patentability of both products and processes for inventions in all fields of technology was an unresolved issue in the Anell Draft, but opposition in this respect was dropped by the time the Brussels Draft was tabled. Paragraphs 1.4.2, 1.4.5, and 1.5B above do not appear in the final form of TRIPS. Paragraph 1.4.2 was an express recognition that for the purpose of patentability, discoveries have to be distinguished from inventions. Even though this distinction is not expressly made in the current Article 27.1, Members do have broad discretion to exclude natural substances from patentability.[525] The bracketed reference in paragraph 1.4.2 to materials or substances "in the same form found" in nature reflects some Members' practice to allow for the patentability of biological material once this has been isolated from its natural environment.[526] The reference in paragraph 1.4.5 to nuclear and fissionable material was later taken out of the patent context and inserted into the general TRIPS provision on security exceptions under Article 73.[527] Finally, the public interest clause in paragraph 1.5B above was not included as such in the final version of TRIPS. National security interests are referred to under Article 73. Public health and nutrition as well as the public interest in more general terms are included under Article 8.1 as objectives that Members may promote and protect in the formulation of domestic IPR legislation. But this provision does not authorize Members to deviate from the substantive obligations under TRIPS, as is made clear by its final phrase ("provided that such measures are consistent with the provisions of this Agreement").[528]

2.2.2 The Brussels Draft

"1. Subject to the provisions of paragraphs 2 and 3 below, patents shall be available for any inventions, whether products or processes, in all fields of technology, provided that they are new, involve an inventive step and are capable of industrial application. [note]. [Patents shall be available without discrimination as to where the inventions were made.]

[. . .]

[note]"[529] (essentially identical to the current version of TRIPS)

At the time of the Brussels Draft, the non-discrimination requirement with respect to the availability of patents, as contained in the current Article 27.1, second sentence, was still controversial. The provision took its final form under the 1991 Dunkel Draft.[530]

---

[525] See Section 3 of this chapter.

[526] See Section 3 of this chapter, with respect to the patentability of isolated micro-organisms under the European Patent Convention and under U.S. patent law.

[527] For more details, see Chapter 39.

[528] For more details on Article 8, see Chapter 6.

[529] See Draft Final Act Embodying the Results of the Uruguay Round of Multilateral Trade Negotiations, Revision, Trade-Related Aspects of Intellectual Property Rights, Including Trade in Counterfeit Goods, MTN.TNC/W/35/Rev. 1, 3 Dec. 1990.

[530] See Draft Final Act Embodying the Results of the Uruguay Round of Multilateral Trade Negotiations, MTN.TNC/W/FA, 20 December 1991.

3. Possible interpretations

3.1 Availability in all fields of technology

> Subject to the provisions of paragraphs 2 and 3, patents shall be available for any inventions, whether products or processes in all fields of technology . . .

The introductory phrase "subject to the provisions of paragraphs 2 and 3" – which provide for non-mandatory exceptions to patentability – indicates that, where established by national laws, such exceptions override the general rules contained in paragraph 1 of Article 27.

This Article explicitly obliges making patents available for both product and processes,[531] and prohibits distinctions relating to the field of technology to which the invention belongs. Thus the exclusions from patentability of pharmaceutical products that were once common in national patent laws[532] will not be permissible after full implementation of TRIPS.

An important interpretative question is whether this Article obliges Members to protect *uses* as such, for instance, new uses of known products, in addition to products and processes. Comparative law on this issue varies considerably. In the USA, the patenting of use inventions, where admitted, depends on whether the purpose of the use is novel and non-obvious. Method inventions may be judged independently of the purpose. Even if intended for a novel purpose, the key consideration in determining the patentability of a method invention is whether it could be anticipated by other methods.[533] In the United States, patents on uses are confined to a particular "method-of-use", which does not encompass protection of the product as such.[534] In Europe, the patentability of a known product for a new specific purpose is allowed under Article 54(5) of the European Patent Convention. Thus, the identification of the *first* medical indication of a known product may permit patenting of the product.[535] In cases where an application

---

[531] Process patents can confer rights not only over the use of the process in question, but also over products obtained directly by the process, see Article 28.1(b), TRIPS Agreement. However, in the latter case problems arise where the product is either a known substance or a discovery (as to the meaning of "discovery" see below, under Section 3.2.1 of the present chapter (on novelty) and under Section 7 of the present chapter). Product-by-process claims of this sort give rise to especial problems in relation to biotechnology. This is discussed in Chapter 21.

[532] Other examples of exclusions were, for instance, in the case of India, chemical processes, methods of agriculture and horticulture (including herbicides and pesticides), alloys and new uses for known products or processes. Argentina was a typical example of another approach which, while excluding pharmaceuticals from patentability, permitted process patents, except in relation to pharmaceutical products producible through a single procedure (because this was thought to be an indirect form of product patent). Such exclusions are not permissible under Article 27.1.

[533] See, e.g., Bernd Hansen and Fritjoff Hirsch, *Protecting inventions in chemistry. Commentary on chemical case law under the European Patent Convention and the German Patent Law*, WILEY-VCH, Weinheim 1997, p. 120 [hereinafter Hansen and Hirsch].

[534] See, e.g., Robert P. Merges, *Patent law and policy. Cases and materials*, Contemporary Legal Educational Series, Boston 1992, p. 489 [hereinafter Merges].

[535] The Technical Board of Appeal of the European Patent Office has ruled that such claims should be deemed as covering all therapeutic uses of the product as in the case of claims on a

refers to the *second* medical indication of a known pharmaceutical product, however, an obstacle to patentability arises. Patent applications over the therapeutic use of a known product essentially are instructions to the physician about how to employ a certain substance to treat a particular disease. Such a new use, hence, is equivalent to a *method of therapeutic treatment*, which is deemed non-patentable under European law.

In order to overcome such barrier, however, since 1984 the European Patent Office admitted, under a legal fiction, claims on the second medical indication of a known pharmaceutical product when framed under the so-called "Swiss formula".[536] The difference between this legal fiction and Article 54(5) of the European Patent Convention as discussed above is the following: Article 54(5) allows the patenting of a (known) *product* for a new specific purpose. The "Swiss formula", on the other hand, concerns the patenting of the *use* of the product, thus a method, and not a product. However, the "Swiss formula" suffers from "the logical objection that it lacks novelty, since it claims the use of the compound for preparation of a medicament, and normally the medicament itself will be the same as that already used for the first pharmaceutical indication".[537]

Under TRIPS, WTO Members are free to decide whether to allow the patentability of the uses of known products, including for therapeutic use,[538] and are certainly free to adopt the "Swiss formula" approach. The Agreement only obliges them to grant patents for products and processes (Article 27.1). Many patent laws recently adopted in developing countries make no specific reference to the availability of patents for uses, leaving unclear whether the protection for processes covers uses or methods of use.

Any application for a patent must satisfy the basic criteria of novelty, inventive step and industrial applicability. Accordingly, Article 27.1 makes it clear that patents are to be granted for inventions. TRIPS, however, does not define what an "invention" is; it only specifies the requirements that an invention should meet in order to be patentable (Article 27.1). This leaves Members considerable freedom to determine what should be deemed an invention and, if they so desire, to exclude from patentability any substance which exists in nature as being a mere discovery and not an invention. As pointed out before, the Anell Draft of Article 27[539] was explicit on the point that discoveries of things already existing in nature are, in principle, unpatentable. Article 8 of the draft Patent Law Treaty mentioned above was also explicit on this, as is the European Patent Convention.

---

pharmaceutical composition. Infringement of such claims would only take place when the product is commercialized for direct therapeutic use, and not in bulk (Philip Grubb, *Patents for chemicals, pharmaceuticals and biotechnology. Fundamentals of global law, practice and strategy*, Clarendon Press, Oxford 1999, p. 218 [hereinafter Grubb]).

[536] "Use of X for the manufacture of a medicine to treat Y".

[537] See, e.g., Grubb, p. 221.

[538] Because patents protect inventions but not discoveries, the discovery of a new purpose for a product cannot render a known product patentable *as such* under general principles of patent law. This remains the case unless in connection with the new purpose the product is forced to be present in an amended new form (Hansen and Hirsch, p. 104).

[539] See above, Section 2.2 of this chapter.

There are various other examples of specific exclusions that were present in earlier drafts of TRIPS, but which are not in the current text. For example, there is now no provision in TRIPS equivalent to Article 52.2 of the European Patent Convention which provides –

"The following in particular shall not be regarded as inventions within the meaning of paragraph 1:

(c) schemes, rules and methods for performing mental acts, playing games or doing business, and programs for computers ..."

However, this does not exempt patent applications covering such subject matter from the requirement of satisfying the basic criteria of novelty, inventive step and industrial applicability. In the case of computer programs, the reality is that the industry has advanced to the point where most "new" programs are largely assemblages of existing programs.[540] Obviously, an attempt to patent existing programs would fail because of lack of novelty. On the other hand, a new assemblage might pass the test of novelty,[541] but it could well fail the requirement of inventive step if such an assemblage would be obvious to a skilled programmer.

3.2 Patentability Criteria

> ...provided that they are new, involve an inventive step and are capable of industrial application ...[542]

This provision sets up the criteria of patentability, without however harmonizing the way in which they have to be implemented. Thus, Members have considerable leeway in applying those three criteria (novelty, inventive step and industrial applicability). As long as they respect the basic definitions of those criteria as set out below, they may implement them according to what is most appropriate for their specific level of development. For instance, the criterion of "industrial applicability" may be interpreted in a narrow or wide way. Members may require that

---

[540] These are, in principle, protected by copyright as required by the TRIPS Agreement Article 10. As far as information technology is concerned, the difference between patents and copyrights is the following: while the latter protects original computer programs as an *expression of thought* against unauthorized copying, patent protection covers the *underlying ideas*, procedures and methods of operation (cf. also Article 9.2 TRIPS). The minimum term of protection under the Berne Convention (Article 7(1)) is the life of the author plus 50 years after his death. This means that most programs are technically still in copyright. However, copyright only protects the expression of ideas, and in any case the authorship and the ownership of many basic programs is now unknown. An assembly of such programs, independently arrived at by a skilled programmer to solve a particular problem, would not infringe copyright unless the proprietors of those basic programs were to surface. In this event, which in practice seldom occurs, the offer of a reasonable royalty should suffice.

[541] The equivalent in mechanical terms would be a novel assemblage of known integers, such as the well-known "Workmate" portable workbench.

[542] A footnote to this Article states 'For the purposes of this Article, the terms "inventive step" and "capable of industrial application" may be deemed by a Member to be synonymous with the terms "non-obvious" and "useful" respectively'.

the invention result in a true industrial product; or they may settle for a wider approach, requiring only a certain degree of utility of the invention in the widest sense, i.e. without insisting on the creation of a product usable by industry.[543] In fact, there is a general opinion that OECD offices have been somewhat lax in granting some types of patents including pharmaceutical patents, and this may not be in the interest of developing countries.[544] Those relying on examination under the Patent Cooperation Treaty may experience a similar problem.

3.2.1 "Novelty"

This requirement generally means that the information must not have been available to the public prior to the original application date (the priority date).[545] Since the inventor is granted a patent for disclosing something new, it follows that if the invention has already been disclosed in literature available to the public, the applicant (the "inventor") can disclose nothing new in return for the grant, and is either not entitled to be granted a patent, or if one has been granted, is liable to have it revoked. The disclosure may have taken place within the jurisdiction or elsewhere in the world. It also follows from the nature of invention that the discovery of things already existing in nature, e.g., a new plant or mineral, is not an invention.

Prior *secret* use destroyed patentability and afforded grounds for revocation under some patent systems, for example those based on the old UK law.[546] UK law, however, had to be changed to comply with the European Patent Convention. A prior secret use is not part of the state of the art, and it is the state of the art at the time the application is filed (the "priority date") that is relevant for the purposes of satisfying the novelty requirement under Article 27.1.

3.2.2 "Inventive step"

The invention must not merely be something new; it must represent a development over prior art.[547] While under patent law in Europe and in many other countries

---

[543] Cf. infra, under Section 3.2.3 of this chapter (Industrial applicability).

[544] See, e.g., Carlos Correa, *Trends in drug patenting. Case studies*, Corregidor, Buenos Aires, 2001 [hereinafter Correa 2001b].

[545] European Patent Office case law has it that the theoretical possibility of having access to information renders it available to the public (case T 444/88), whatever the means by which the invention was made accessible, and – in the case of prior public use – irrespective of whether there were particular reasons for analysing the product (cases G 1/92,). The United States requires complete disclosure in a *single* publication to destroy novelty, despite the fact that a skilled person may have been able to derive the invention without effort from a combination of publications. In addition, under U.S. law oral disclosure of an invention *outside* the United States does not destroy novelty. This relative concept of novelty has allowed the patenting in the USA of knowledge and materials used by indigenous communities abroad. See, e.g., Carlos Correa, *Traditional knowledge and intellectual property. Issues and options surrounding the protection of traditional knowledge*, QUNO, Geneva, 2001 [hereinafter Correa, 2001a].

[546] The Patents Act 1949 s. 32(1)(l) provided for revocation of a patent on the ground that the invention claimed was secretly used in the United Kingdom before the priority date.

[547] In European Patent Office (EPO) jurisprudence, the relevance of which is discussed below, "inventive step" is distinguished from technical progress. Therefore technical progress comparisons with marketed products as alleged support for this requirement being satisfied are not

this is generally described as an "inventive step", in the United States the requirement is defined as "non-obviousness". Footnote 5 to Article 27.1 specifically permits a Member to consider that "inventive step" is synonymous with "non-obvious".

The inventive step is often evaluated by considering the "unexpected" or "surprising" effect of the claimed invention. U.S. courts, however, currently reject this approach and stress that patentable inventions may result either from painstaking research, slow trial and error, or serendipity.[548] The low standard of inventiveness applied in some countries, including in the United States, has led to the grant of a large number of patents on minor or trivial developments, often aggressively used to artificially extend the duration of protection and to block legitimate competition.[549]

Given the market disruption and costs that patents granted on low or non-inventive developments may cause, developing countries may opt for high standards of inventiveness. Thus, the World Bank has suggested that developing countries "could set high standards for the inventive step, thereby preventing routine discoveries from being patented."[550]

TRIPS, as mentioned, leaves significant freedom for Members to determine the degree of strictness to be applied for judging the inventive step. Though applying a low threshold may facilitate the patenting of incremental developments, which predominate in domestic industry in developing countries, this would be done at the cost of unduly restraining competition and increasing litigation costs in key areas such as pharmaceuticals where extensive patenting of minor developments has become normal practice.[551] In order to promote and reward minor innovations related forms of IP could be adopted, such as utility models.[552]

Both the European Patent Office (EPO) and the national courts in the member countries of the European Patent Convention have in the past expressed the view that computer-implemented inventions contributing to the state of the art in a way not obvious to a person of normal skill in the field concerned is more than just a computer program "as such" and may consequently be patented.[553] However,

---

sufficient. There must be demonstrated the presence of an inventive step with regard to the closest state of the art – see cases T 181/82; T 164/83 (also cases T 317/88 and T 385/94).

[548] See, e.g., Jay Dratler, *Intellectual property law, commercial, creative, and industrial property*, Law Journal Press 1999, §2.03[3].

[549] See, e.g., John Barton, *Reforming the patent system*, Science, vol. 287, 17 March 2000, p. 1933–1934 [hereinafter Barton].

[550] World Bank (2001), Global Economic Prospects and the Developing Countries, p. 143.

[551] See, e.g., Carlos Correa, *Trends in Drug Patenting*. Case Studies, Corregidor, Buenos Aires, 2001.

[552] Utility models protect the *functional* aspect of models and designs, generally in the mechanical field. Though novelty and inventiveness are required, the criteria for conferring protection are generally less strict than for patents. The term of protection also is shorter. Utility models are concerned with the way in which a particular configuration of an article works, unlike *industrial designs*, which are only concerned with its ornamental aspect.

[553] Cf. the document of the European Commission *Patents: Commission proposes rules for inventions using software*, available at <http://europa.eu.int/comm/internal_market/en/indprop/comp/02-277.htm>.

Members retain the right not to protect computer programs that produce no "technical effect" beyond the operation of the computer where they reside.

3.2.3 "Industrial applicability"

The invention must be capable of being used in any kind of industry (including agriculture). Industry in this sense is any physical activity of a technical character.[554]

Members considerably differ in their treatment of industrial applicability. Under U.S. law, the concept applied is "utility".[555] Hence, certain developments that do not lead to an industrial product may be patented in the USA: an invention only needs to be operable and capable of satisfying some function of benefit to humanity (i.e. be useful).[556] This concept is broader than the industrial applicability required in Europe and other countries. The U.S. rule permits the patentability of purely experimental inventions that cannot be made or used in an industry, or that do not produce a so-called technical effect,[557] as illustrated by the large number of patents granted in the United States on methods of doing business, and by the patenting of research tools, such as expression sequence tags (ESTs) and single nucleotide polymorphisms (SNPs).[558]

Surgical techniques and diagnostic procedures could arguably fail this requirement, but can in any event be specifically excluded from patentability under Article 27.3 (a) as discussed below.

4. WTO jurisprudence

On 30 April 1996, the USA requested consultations with Pakistan under the Dispute Settlement Understanding (DSU) for an alleged violation of, *inter alia*, Article 27 of TRIPS.[559] However, on 25 September 1997, the two parties to the dispute informed the Dispute Settlement Body (DSB) that they had found a common solution. Thus, a panel was never established.

---

[554] The technical character of an invention is a basic requirement of patentability (see Article 27.1 TRIPS: "...patents shall be available ...in all fields of *technology*, ..." (emphasis added)). According to the European Patent Office's Guidelines on Patentability, any physical activity of a technical character is an activity which belongs to the useful or practical arts as distinct from the aesthetic or fine arts – Guideline C-IV, 4.1. The Guidelines are available at <http://www.European-patent-office.org>.

[555] Footnote 5 to Article 27.1 specifically permits a Member to consider that "capable of industrial application" is synonymous with "useful".

[556] See, e.g., Donald S. Chisum and Michael A. Jacobs, *Understanding Intellectual Property Law*, Legal Text series, Matthew Bender, New York 1992, pp. 2–50 [hereinafter Chisum and Jacobs].

[557] It should be noted that "technical effect" has no official definition. The doctrine has its origins in German patent law (see Graham Dutfield, *Intellectual Property Rights and the Life Science Industries: A Twentieth Century History*, Ashgate, Aldershot 2003, p. 81).

[558] The guidelines for examining utility were changed in the USA in 2001, possibly leading to the exclusion from patentability of some of these matters. See USPTO Utility Examination Guidelines Federal Register Vol 66 No 4 January 5, 2001.

[559] WTO document WT/DS36.

5. Relationship with other international instruments

5.1 WTO Agreements
No specific relationships have been identified.

5.2 Other international instruments
The Paris Convention requires the protection of patents, but does not establish rules on the patentability requirements.

As noted above, Article 10.1 requires computer software to be protected as a literary work under the Berne Convention.[560]

6. New developments

6.1 National laws
Most developing countries that have amended their patent laws to implement TRIPS have adopted (often in conformity with previous domestic law and practice) *universal* novelty, inventive step and industrial applicability as requirements for protection. Given the considerable room available for the interpretation and application of these requirements, national practices may differ significantly and also evolve over time.

6.2 International instruments
In 2001 the Director General of WIPO announced a new initiative, approved by the WIPO Assembly, called the "WIPO Patent Agenda" for worldwide discussions aiming at preparing a strategic blue print that would underlie the future development of the international patent system.[561] One of the components of the Agenda is the development and harmonization of substantive patent law with the goal of adopting a new Substantive Patent Law Treaty. This Treaty, if adopted, could include rules on the patentability requirements discussed above and, thus, eliminate or limit the freedom that currently countries have to define and implement such requirements.[562] In this context, the Commission on Intellectual Property Rights [hereinafter IPR Commission] cautioned in its report:

> "Developing countries should identify a strategy for dealing with the risk that WIPO harmonisation will lead to standards that do not take account of their interests. This could be done by seeking a global standard reflecting the recommendations of this report; it could be done by seeking continued flexibility in the WIPO standards; it could be done by rejection of the WIPO process if it appears that the outcome will not be in the interests of developing countries."[563]

---

[560] The basic provision of that Convention relating to literary works is Article 2.

[561] See WIPO, *Agenda for development of the international patent system*, document A/36/14.

[562] See WIPO documents SCP/7/3 and SCP/7/4 of March 6, 2002.

[563] *Integrating Intellectual Property Rights and Development Policy*, Report of the Commission on Intellectual Property Rights, London, September 2002, p. 132. The Report can be consulted at: <http://www.iprcommission.org/graphic/documents/final_report.htm>.

6.3 Regional and bilateral contexts

6.3.1 Regional

In 2000, the European Commission proposed the creation of a Community patent to give inventors the possibility of acquiring one single patent legally valid throughout the EU.[564] Currently, patents in European countries are granted either by the national patent offices as a national right or by the European Patent Office (EPO) as a "European Patent". The latter is, however, not the same as the proposed Community patent: it is not a uniform, single right, but a bundle of national patents. Thus, even though there is just one application procedure, matters of substantive law are still regulated by the member states of the European Patent Convention (EPC), which may require the patent to be translated into their national language. In addition, the national courts remain competent to apply national patent laws, which may vary considerably across the EPC member states.

In addition to the proposal on the Community Patent, the Commission has issued a proposal for an EC Directive on the protection by patents of computer-implemented inventions.[565] This proposal distinguishes between two types of inventions. On the one hand, those involving the use of a computer program and thereby contributing to the state of the art in the technical field concerned would be eligible for patent protection. On the other hand, computer programs as such or business methods employing existing technological ideas would not be eligible as patents. However, they continue to benefit from copyright protection to be provided according to Article 10.1.[566]

The Commission's proposal still needs to be adopted by both the EU Council and the EU Parliament.[567]

7. Comments, including economic and social implications

7.1 General observations on TRIPS patent provisions, including Article 27.1

Of all the measures contained in TRIPS, the patent provisions may be the most significant in terms of economic implications for developing countries. This follows from the growing importance of patents in major industrial sectors, particularly in R&D-intensive sectors, from the number and breadth of the patent provisions that are covered and from the differences in the scope and extent of protection

---

[564] The draft Council Regulation on a Community Patent is available in a EU Council document of 8 March 2004, at <http://register.consilium.eu.int/pdf/en/04/st07/st07119.en04.pdf>.

[565] Cf. COM (2002) 92 final of 20 February 2002, available at: <http://europa.eu.int/comm/internal_market/en/indprop/comp/com02-92en.pdf>.

[566] For details, see Chapter 8.

[567] There are some remaining controversies between theses two EU bodies. In particular, the Parliament favours wide exceptions to patentability for computer-implemented inventions, covering the use of patented technology for interoperability and data handling. See <http://europa.eu.int/rapid/pressReleasesAction.do?reference=IP/04/659&format=HTML&aged=0&language=EN&guiLanguage=en>.

that will now have to be afforded by both developed and developing countries, as compared with prior law.

The major impact of the Agreement will be felt in cases where patent protection needs to be extended (after the transitional period) to new subject-matter areas, such as pharmaceuticals, agrochemicals, beverages and food, in order to implement Article 27.1 of the Agreement. Important economic effects may also arise from the obligation to extend the term of protection (20 years from application).

Many studies have been conducted on the general implications of introducing or reinforcing intellectual property protection in developing countries.[568] Particular concerns have been expressed with regard to the availability and pricing of medicines after product patents are introduced in compliance with TRIPS. The introduction of patents will normally lead to prices higher than those that would have prevailed in the absence of protection, but the quantum of the price differential will vary significantly with a number of factors, such as: (i) the length of the transitional period applied by a particular member country; (ii) the date of granting and the scope of the exclusive marketing rights (EMRs) eventually conferred; (iii) the conditions under which patents are granted and, particularly, the availability of compulsory licences, and the way in which competition law is applied; and (iv) the share of the market attributable to patented products, their price elasticity, the substitutability of products, differences between the market structure pre-TRIPS and post-TRIPS, the eventual existence of price controls, the significance of local production of pharmaceuticals, the size and technological capabilities of local firms, among other factors.

The extended period of patent protection and the strengthened exclusive rights will limit the scope for early legitimate imitation by local firms. As a result, when a given invention finally enters the public domain, the technology may already have been superseded by other protected technologies. However, local inventors will also obtain a longer period in which to recover their investments, although the aggregate amount of such investments will normally fall well below that in developed countries.

Given the lack of reliable empirical data, predictions about the likely economic effects of the patent provisions tend to vary with the general outlook of the investigators. On balance, it seems fair to say that, at least from the medium- and long-term perspective, the economic effects of the patent provisions depend largely on the levels of development of countries and sectors concerned, the speed, nature and cost of innovation, as well as on the measures developing countries may take in adopting the new framework. The introduction of patents will entail sacrifices in static efficiency[569] while benefits for most developing countries in terms of dynamic efficiency[570] are uncertain, particularly to the extent that research

---

[568] Cf. Part One of UNCTAD, 1996.

[569] *Static efficiency* is achieved when there is an optimum utilization of existing resources at the lowest possible cost. See UNCTAD, 1996.

[570] *Dynamic efficiency* is the optimal introduction of new products or products of superior quality, more efficient production processes and organization, and (eventually) lower prices over time. While patents may sacrifice static efficiency, to the extent that they stimulate innovation, they may in the long term improve dynamic efficiency. See UNCTAD, 1996.

and development of drugs for diseases prevalent in developing countries (such as malaria) continues to be neglected.

The producers able and willing to supply the world market with low-price pharmaceutical products which were under patent in developed countries have principally been situated in Brazil, China and India. Producers in these (and any other) countries are able to continue to manufacture a range of generic products while still complying with TRIPS because pharmaceuticals were not patentable under their local laws until recently. Brazil's Patent Law was amended in 1996 with effect from March 15, 1997. China became the 143rd Member of the WTO on 11 December 2001, 30 days after it had notified the Director-General that it had completed domestic ratification of its accession package. India, as a founding Member of the WTO, has been a Member of TRIPS since 1 January 1995, but has taken advantage of a transition period allowing it to delay introduction of pharmaceutical product patent protection until January 1, 2005.

At present some Members are pressing developing and least-developed countries to accelerate their adoption of patent protection for pharmaceutical products. This is not advisable. A survey of the more important economics literature on pharmaceutical protection in developing countries concluded that:

> "The preponderance of conclusions is pessimistic about the net effects of drug patents on the economic welfare of developing countries (or, more accurately, of net importers of patented drugs)."[571]

Although arguments can be made that the introduction of patents can be beneficial in stimulating innovation and attracting inward investment, there is little or no empirical evidence to confirm that this is likely to apply in the case of developing and least-developed countries:

> "It is remarkable how little is known about the potential effects of changing global policy regimes in this fundamental manner, despite the fact that the pharmaceutical sector is the most extensively studied of all IP-sector industries."[572]

Most inventions in the pharmaceutical field today are made by research teams, which require the availability of a pool of reasonably well-educated researchers. Some quite poor countries do have good educational systems, and in such cases, pharmaceutical companies may channel research (or production) facilities into those countries because of the lower labour costs. The Republic of Ireland benefited from this factor a generation ago. However, the link between the location of research and development facilities and the existence of patent protection is by no means clear-cut. India, for example, developed a significant capacity for the production of raw materials for the pharmaceutical industry, without patent protection. It was also able to attract much inward investment for software development at a time when the protection of software under Indian law was problematic. India, however, had at the relevant time a well-developed law of contract, and this can for certain purposes substitute for intellectual property law.

---

[571] Keith Maskus, *Intellectual Property Rights in the Global Economy*, IIE 2000, p. 160 [hereinafter Maskus].

[572] Maskus, p. 160.

On January 1, 2005, or January 1, 2016 (subject to any further extension), whichever is applicable, the "mailbox" applications that were submitted during the transition period will be operationalized (see Chapter 36), and patent protection will become available for such of those applications as satisfy the normal criteria of patentability set out above. Accordingly, those developing countries at present exporting off-patent pharmaceutical products will lose that capacity with regard to mailbox applications and medicines invented after the operative date in the relevant country. After the expiry of the relevant transitional period, and subject to the doctrine of exhaustion of rights,[573] the importers of such off-patent products will similarly have to cease such importation. The extent to which compulsory licensing under Article 31 might be used in this new situation is discussed below.[574]

Article 27.1 does not create the obligation to grant patents for computer programs. The refusal by the European Commission to consider computer programs as such to be patentable is motivated by the concern that otherwise the distinction between patent rights on the one side and copyrights on the other might be blurred.[575] For developing countries, this approach has an important implication: if a computer program as a whole were patentable, the practice of reverse engineering,[576] which is legal under copyright protection, could be prevented by the patent holder.[577]

Finally, it is relevant to consider here the concerns expressed by developing countries in connection with the general patentability requirement of TRIPS in relation to biological materials and traditional knowledge. Several cases of "biopiracy" or misappropriation have been identified in the past, and fears have been raised with regard to the implications of Article 27.1 in that regard. There are a number of responses to these fears. In the first place, discoveries of things already existing in nature are, in principle, unpatentable. Article 8 of the draft Patent Law Treaty mentioned above, was explicit on this, as is the European Patent Convention. So also was the Anell Draft of Article 27.[578] Article 27.1 makes it clear that patents are to be granted for inventions, and a discovery of something already existing in nature is not an invention. Unfortunately, in practice, because the applicant is not obliged to disclose the origin of the substance over which the patent is sought, the granting office will often be ignorant of whether the substance is a

---

[573] See Chapter 5.

[574] See Chapter 25.

[575] As observed above, patents cover only those *specific components* of a software application that are based on some inventive step, whereas copyrights protect the *entire* program against unauthorized copying.

[576] I.e. the dismantling of a finished product into its various components in order to examine how it was originally put together.

[577] The practice of reverse engineering of computer programs is targeted at the underlying *idea*, but not the *expression* of that idea. Consequently, reverse engineering leaves copyright untouched, but would possibly affect patents, if those were available. See also the EC Commission's document *Patents: Commission proposes rules for inventions using software*, available at: <http://europa.eu.int/comm/internal_market/en/indprop/comp/02-277.htm>.

[578] The draft in relevant part (paragraph 1.4.2) read: "Scientific theories, mathematical methods, discoveries and materials or substances [already existing] [in the same form found] in nature." See above, Section 2.2 of this chapter.

discovery. In such a case a patent could well be granted. Although such a patent would be liable to be revoked, there are obviously costs involved in obtaining expert advice and in applying for revocation, especially through national courts. Such costs may be beyond the means of those affected. There seems to be no reason, however, under TRIPS why a national patent office – which is normally given powers to regulate its own procedures – should not of its own initiative follow a complaint, carry out an investigation, and revoke a patent it has granted.[579] Such powers would, of course, have to be exercised judicially and in accordance with the requirements of TRIPS. But the conferring of judicial powers on a patent office is not inconsistent with TRIPS[580] and may offer a more attractive, quicker and cheaper solution than compelling complainants to have recourse to the courts.

[579] In the case of *R v. Comptroller-General of Patents, Designs and Trade Marks, ex parte Ash & Lacy Building Products*, 1 February 2002, Laddie J held that the Comptroller of the UK Patent Office had power to continue revocation proceedings, even though she could not compel the patentee to participate in them. In this respect UK practice differs from that of the European Patent Office.

[580] The procedure of the European Patent Office permits oppositions after grant. The UK Patent Office has quite extensive judicial powers conferred on it, including the possibility of trying alleged infringements. Re-examination can also be conducted by the U.S. Patent and Trademark Office.

18: Patents: Non-Discrimination

Article 27.1 Patentable Subject Matter

...patents shall be available and patent rights enjoyable without discrimination as to the place of invention, the field of technology and whether products are imported or locally produced.

---

1. Introduction: terminology, definition and scope

The requirement that patent rights shall be available and enjoyable without discrimination as to the field of technology follows from the general rule of patentability contained in the first sentence of Article 27.1.[581] This second sentence, however, adds an important element: while patents need to be recognized in all fields of technology (subject only to permissible exceptions as discussed in Chapters 19–21 below), the law cannot discriminate in its treatment of different fields, both in terms of availability of rights and of capacity to enjoy them. For instance, patents may not last differently depending on the field of technology involved, nor can they be subject to more stringent conditions (e.g., with regard to the acquisition of rights) in certain fields than in others. This rule may be deemed to include both positive (i.e., superior rights) and negative (i.e., inferior rights) discrimination. This rule, however, is not absolute, as discussed below (Section 3).

A provision which sought to limit the grant and enjoyment of patent rights to inventions made within a particular Member would clearly be contrary to this provision. It would also be contrary to this provision to have a requirement under which evidence of inventive acts were restricted to the territory of a particular country, and foreign applicants were not permitted to prove a date of invention which antedated their filing date in that particular country.[582]

It should be noted that there is no comparable non-discrimination clause in other sections of TRIPS, and that the obligation under Article 27.1 is limited only to discrimination based on the three elements indicated in the provision, that

---

[581] See Chapter 17.

[582] See discussion in Sections 2.1 and 6 below.

is, place of the invention, field of technology, and local production/importation. Discrimination based on other factors is not banned.[583]

2. History of the provision

2.1 Situation pre-TRIPS

Neither the Paris Convention nor national laws contained a provision comparable to Article 27.1. Hence, discrimination now banned was permissible, such as establishing different terms of patent protection according to the field of technology, as provided for under some domestic patent law.[584]

The principle that patents shall be available, and patent rights enjoyable without discrimination as to the place of invention had generally been accepted under the European Patent Convention. However, in some countries, differential treatment was granted to patents depending on the country of invention. That was the case, for instance, under the Canadian regulation on compulsory licences introduced in 1988 and in force until Bill C-91 was passed in February 1993.[585] The United States – the single country to maintain a "first-to-invent" rule concerning entitlement to a patent[586] – imposed a discriminatory burden on foreign inventors under §104 of the U.S. Patents Act. Evidence of inventive acts was restricted to the territory of the USA. Consequently, evidence by foreign applicants that the date of invention antedated their U.S. filing date was inadmissible if it were based solely on knowledge, use or other activity in a country other than the USA. This territorial limitation was later extended to Canada and Mexico under the North American Free Trade Area Treaty, and subsequently to WTO Member countries.

Similarly, national laws could treat patents differently depending on the local or imported origin of the product. Thus, Section 337 of the U.S. Tariff Act accorded to imported products challenged as infringing U.S. patents treatment less favourable than the treatment accorded to similarly challenged products of U.S. origin. This Section was found inconsistent with the GATT in *United States – Section 337 of the Tariff Act of 1930.*[587]

It has been a common feature in patent laws (of developed and developing countries) to provide for compulsory licences in cases of "non-working" (in conformity with Article 5.A (4) of the Paris Convention), and to interpret that working was only satisfied by local production (not by importation). Some commentators

---

[583] As to the difference between the general rules of non-discrimination contained in Articles 3 (national treatment) and 4 (most-favoured-nation treatment) and the patent-specific non-discrimination rule in Article 27.1, see Section 5 of this chapter, below.

[584] On the term of patent protection, Article 33, see Chapter 22.

[585] For details, see UNCTAD-ICTSD, Jerome H. Reichman and Catherine Hasenzahl (2002), *Non-Voluntary Licensing of Patented Inventions : The Canadian Experience.* Intellectual Property Rights & Sustainable Development Series, November 2002 [hereinafter Reichman, Hasenzahl, The Canadian Experience], available at <http://www.iprsonline.org/unctadictsd/docs/reichman_hasenzahl_Canada.pdf>.

[586] The rule applied in the USA is said to be in conformity with Article 1(8) of the U.S. Constitution which provides that Congress has power 'to promote the progress of science and useful arts, by securing for limited times to . . . inventors the exclusive right to their . . . discoveries.' It is also thought by many to be fair, because the patent is granted to the first inventor, and not to the first to apply.

[587] See L/6439-365-345 (1989 GATT TPD LEXIS 2).

have interpreted Article 27.1 as a ban to such differentiation but, as discussed in Chapter 25 below, such interpretation is controversial.

2.2 Negotiating history

2.2.1 The Anell Draft
The Anell Draft contained no provision comparable with the current non-discrimination clause in Article 27.1.

2.2.2 The Brussels Draft
"Patents shall be available without discrimination as to where the inventions were made."

Thus, the Brussels Draft did include a non-discrimination clause with respect to patented inventions. However, this clause covered only part of the final provision under Article 27.1. The draft referred only to non-discrimination as to the place of invention, but did not expressly prohibit discrimination as to the field of technology and as to the place where the protected product is produced. The latter has to be distinguished from the place of invention, which may not be the same as the place of production.

3. Possible interpretations

Under Article 27.1 Members are obliged to make available patents, that is to ensure the right to obtain a patent, irrespective of the place of invention, the field of technology, or whether products are imported or locally produced. Availability does not mean, however, that a patent needs to be granted in all circumstances, since this will depend on the applicant's ability to meet the patentability requirements and other conditions (such as appropriate disclosure).

An important element for the interpretation of this provision is the concept of "patent rights". While defining in Article 28 the patentee's rights as exclusive, the Agreement makes clear that patents confer a *negative* right, that is, the legal faculty to prevent others from doing certain acts relating to the invention, and not a *positive* right with regard to his/her own products or processes. Thus, the fact that a patent has been granted on a medicine does not give the patent owner the right to sell it, unless health regulations have been complied with, but he can, immediately after the patent grant, prevent others from using the invention.[588]

To "discriminate" means "be, set up, or act on the basis of, a difference ... make a distinction, especially unjustly on grounds of race or colour or sex".[589]

In the *EC-Canada* case,[590] the panel made a distinction between "discrimination" and "differentiation". It clarified that the conduct prohibited by Article 27.1 is "discrimination" as to the field of technology; that "discrimination" is not the same as "differentiation"; and, that WTO Members can adopt different rules for

---

[588] See also Chapter 22.

[589] The Concise Oxford Dictionary, p. 274.

[590] *Canada – Patent Protection for Pharmaceutical Products* [*EC – Canada*], WT/DS 114/R.

particular product areas, provided that the differences are adopted for *bona fide* purposes (see Section 4 below).

Finally, Article 27.1 prohibits discrimination based on whether the invention is locally produced or imported.[591]

4. WTO jurisprudence

4.1 EC – Canada

On 19 December 1997, the European Communities and their Member states requested consultations with Canada under the DSU for the latter's alleged violation of, *inter alia*, Article 27.1. The EC contended, *inter alia*, that under Canadian law, patent rights were not enjoyable without discrimination as to the field of technology within the meaning of Article 27.1, second sentence. The panel, however, did not find a violation of Article 27.1, since the challenged provision of the Canadian law (Section 55.2(1)) was not limited to pharmaceutical products, but was applicable to every product that was subject to marketing approval requirements.[592] Though the panel based part of its findings on Article 27.1, it refused to provide a general definition of what "discrimination" meant. It argued that

> "In considering how to address these conflicting claims of discrimination, the Panel recalled that various claims of discrimination, de jure and de facto, have been the subject of legal rulings under GATT or the WTO.[593] These rulings have addressed the question whether measures were in conflict with various GATT or WTO provisions prohibiting variously defined forms of discrimination. As the Appellate Body has repeatedly made clear, each of these rulings has necessarily been based on the precise legal text in issue, so that it is not possible to treat them as applications of a general concept of discrimination. Given the very broad range of issues that might be involved in defining the word "discrimination" in Article 27.1 of the TRIPS Agreement, the Panel decided that it would be better to defer attempting to define that term at the outset, but instead to determine which issues were raised by the record before the Panel, and to define the concept of discrimination to the extent necessary to resolve those issues".[594]

The panel also considered the applicability of the non-discrimination clause to the exceptions regulated in Article 30 of TRIPS. It held that

> "Article 27.1 prohibits discrimination as to enjoyment of "patent rights" without qualifying that term. Article 30 exceptions are explicitly described as "exceptions to the exclusive rights conferred by a patent" and contain no indication that any

---

[591] For the possible implications of this provision on the issuance of compulsory licenses, see Chapter 25.

[592] *Canada – Patent Protection for Pharmaceutical Products* [*EC – Canada*], WT/DS 114/R, at para. 7.99.

[593] See, e.g., *Japan – Taxes on Alcoholic Beverages*, WT/DS8/AB/R, WT/DS10/AB/R, WT/DS11/AB/R (adopted 1 November 1996); *European Communities – Regime for the Importation, Sale and Distribution of Bananas*, WT/DS27/AB/R (adopted 17 November 1997); *EC Measures Concerning Meat and Meat Products (Hormones)*, WT/DS26/AB/R, WT/DS48/AB/R (adopted 15 February 1998); *United States – Import Prohibition of Certain Shrimp and Shrimp Products*, WT/DS58/AB/R (adopted 6 November 1998).

[594] See *EC – Canada*, para. 7.98.

exemption from non-discrimination rules is intended. A discriminatory exception that takes away enjoyment of a patent right is discrimination as much as is discrimination in the basic rights themselves. The acknowledged fact that the Article 31 exception for compulsory licences and government use is understood to be subject to the non-discrimination rule of Article 27.1, without the need for any textual provision so providing, further strengthens the case for treating the non-discrimination rules as applicable to Article 30" (para. 7.91).

The panel added that limiting an exception to a particular field of technology does not make it acceptable under the condition of "limited exception" imposed by Article 30. The panel argued that

> "... it is not true that being able to discriminate against particular patents will make it possible to meet Article 30's requirement that the exception be "limited". An Article 30 exception cannot be made "limited" by limiting it to one field of technology, because the effects of each exception must be found to be "limited" when measured against each affected patent. Beyond that, it is not true that Article 27 requires all Article 30 exceptions to be applied to all products. Article 27 prohibits only discrimination as to the place of invention, the field of technology, and whether products are imported or produced locally. Article 27 does not prohibit bona fide exceptions to deal with problems that may exist only in certain product areas. Moreover, to the extent the prohibition of discrimination does limit the ability to target certain products in dealing with certain of the important national policies referred to in Articles 7 and 8.1, that fact may well constitute a deliberate limitation rather than a frustration of purpose. It is quite plausible, as the EC argued, that the TRIPS Agreement would want to require governments to apply exceptions in a non-discriminatory manner, in order to ensure that governments do not succumb to domestic pressures to limit exceptions to areas where right holders tend to be foreign producers." (para. 7.92)

4.2 United States – Brazil

In January 2001, the United States launched a challenge against Brazilian legislation that authorizes the granting of compulsory licences and parallel imports in instances when patents are not locally worked.[595] The dispute, however, ended several months later, when the U.S. complaint was withdrawn.[596] In a separate case Brazil asked the United States for consultations with regard to provisions of U.S. law limiting the right to use or sell any federally owned invention only to a licensee that agrees that any products embodying the invention or produced through the use of the invention will be manufactured substantially in the United States.[597]

---

[595] See *Brazil – Measures Affecting Patent Protection* [*United States – Brazil*], Request for the Establishment of a Panel by the United States, January 9, 2001, WT/DS199/3. On February 1, 2001, the DSB established a panel, however, no panel members were appointed. Cuba, the Dominican Republic, Honduras, India and Japan reserved third party rights. See also Chapter 25 (Section 4 on WTO jurisprudence).

[596] Without prejudice to their respective positions, the United States and Brazil have agreed to enter into bilateral discussions before Brazil makes use of Article 68 against a U.S. patent holder. *Brazil – Measures Affecting Patent Protection*, Notification of Mutually Agreed Solution WT/DS199/4, G/L/454, IP/D/23/Add.1, July 19, 2001. See also Joint U.S.-Brazil Statement, June 25, 2001.

[597] See WT/DS224/1, February 7, 2001. This case was not pursued.

5. Relationship with other international instruments

As mentioned above, the Paris Convention expressly authorizes, on certain conditions, compulsory licensing for the failure to work patents locally. TRIPS does not contain such a clear and express authorization. The Agreement, as opposed to the Paris Convention, applies the principle of non-discrimination on a higher, more uniform level. While both agreements contain the national treatment principle,[598] the Paris Convention does not oblige Member countries to prohibit, in their domestic legislation, the discrimination of patents as to the place of invention, the field of technology or whether products are imported or locally produced. As long as these sorts of discrimination are applied to both nationals and foreigners, the general principle of national treatment is respected. Here, TRIPS goes one step further: not only must Members ensure equal treatment of nationals and foreigners, but on top of that, they have to comply with certain minimum standards, prohibiting, in general, the above discriminations.

In this context, it should be noted that where two countries are parties to the Paris Convention, but only one is a WTO Member, TRIPS does not create any obligations.[599] It only applies (and thus, as the later treaty, supersedes the Paris Convention), where both (or all) countries are WTO Members.[600]

6. New developments

The non-discrimination clause provides for a principle that is not stated, as such, in national laws, but that should be respected while establishing the rights and obligations of patent owners. The adoption of such a clause forced Canada to eliminate differential treatment for inventions made in the country with regard to compulsory licences. It also underpinned the amendment to the above-mentioned Section 104 of the U.S. Patent law, which was revised in order to extend the right to establish priority with respect to an invention not only in NAFTA countries, but in any WTO Member.[601]

However, the main impact of the non-discrimination clause has probably been in the area of compulsory licensing. Though debatable, the interpretation of the last sentence of Article 27.1 in the sense that working of a patent can be satisfied by importation for the purposes of compulsory licences, is likely to have led many countries to consider importation as equivalent to local production for the purposes of working an invention. An important exception is Article 68 of the

---

[598] See Article 3 of the TRIPS Agreement, Articles 2 and 3, Paris Convention.

[599] See Article 30.4(b), Vienna Convention.

[600] See Article 30.4(a) in conjunction with Article 30.3, Vienna Convention. For more details on the interplay between the Paris Convention and the TRIPS Agreement in that case, see Chapter 3.

[601] The U.S. Patents Act currently provides the following –
§104 Inventions made abroad
(a) In General
    (1) Proceedings
In proceedings in the Patent and Trademark Office, in the courts, and before any other competent authority, an applicant for a patent, or a patentee, may not establish a date of invention by reference to the knowledge or use thereof, or other activity with respect thereto, in a foreign country other than a NAFTA country or a WTO member country, except as provided in §§119 and 365 of this title.

Brazilian patent law, as amended in 1996 which, as noted above, was challenged by the USA. Also, the Indonesian patent law, as revised in 2001, provides that the patent holder is obliged to make the patented products or use the patented process in Indonesia. He can be exempted from this obligation if the making of the product or the use of the process is only suitable to be implemented on a regional scale (Article 17).

7. Comments, including economic and social implications

The non-discrimination rule contained in Article 27.1 is intended to protect right-holders against arbitrary policies that undermine their rights, when such policies are adopted on grounds of the field of technology, the place of invention or the origin (locally manufactured or imported) of the products.

The need to differentiate the rights according to the types of inventions concerned has been extensively debated. Many have wondered why patent rights of equal effect and duration should be granted to inventors who have made different contributions, some of them significant and others less so.[602] Debates have largely focused on the duration of patent rights, since the rate of obsolescence of technology and the periods necessary to recover R&D investments significantly vary across sectors.[603]

In fact, patent laws in many countries currently allow for a differentiation based on the field of technology, as illustrated by the extension of protection conferred to pharmaceutical patents in the USA and Europe in order to compensate for the period required to obtain the marketing approval of a new drug.

In the light of the panel's distinction in the *EC-Canada* case between discrimination and differentiation,[604] questions arise as to the extent to which national patent laws may differentiate in the treatment of patent rights and obligations on justified, *bona fide*, grounds. The Doha Declaration on the TRIPS Agreement and Public Health gives an indication in this direction. The fact that public health and, in particular pharmaceuticals (paragraphs 6 and 7), has been singled out as an issue requiring special attention in the implementation of TRIPS, suggests that public health-related patents may deserve to be treated differently from other patents. Also, French patent law, not challenged so far by any WTO Member, differentiates in the treatment of pharmaceutical products for the purposes of granting compulsory licences.[605]

---

[602] See, e.g., Lester Thurow, *Needed: A New System of Intellectual Property Rights*, Harvard Business Review, September – October: 1997.

[603] See Chapter 22 below.

[604] See Section 3 above.

[605] The French patent law provides that: "Where the interest of public health demand, patents granted for medicines or for processes for obtaining medicines, for products necessary in obtaining such medicines or for processes for manufacturing such products may be subject to *ex officio* licences in accordance with Article L. 613-17 in the event of such medicines being made available to the public in insufficient quantity or quality or at (abnormally high prices) by order of the Minister responsible for industrial property at the request of the Minister responsible for health." (Law No. 92-597 of 1 July, 1992, Article L. 613-16).

19: Patents: Ordre Public and Morality

> ### Article 27.2 Patentable Subject Matter
>
> Members may exclude from patentability inventions, the prevention within their territory of the commercial exploitation of which is necessary to protect ordre public or morality, including to protect human, animal or plant life or health or to avoid serious prejudice to the environment, provided that such exclusion is not made merely because the exploitation is prohibited by their law.

1. Introduction: terminology, definition and scope

States have the right to protect the public interest, and patent law is not an exception to this general principle. Based on a long established tradition in patent law (particularly in the European context), TRIPS allows (but not mandates)[606] two possible exceptions to patentability, based on *ordre public* and morality. The implementation of these exceptions, which need to be provided for under national law in order to be effective, means that a WTO Member may, in certain cases, refuse to grant a patent when it deems it necessary to protect higher public interests.[607]

The term *"ordre public"*, derived from French law, is not an easy term to translate into English, and therefore the original French term is used in TRIPS. It expresses concerns about matters threatening the social structures which tie a society together, i.e., matters that threaten the structure of civil society as such.

"Morality" is "the degree of conformity to moral principles (especially good)".[608] The concept of morality is relative to the values prevailing in a society. Such values are not the same in different cultures and countries, and change over time. Some important decisions relating to patentability may depend upon the judgement about morality. It would be inadmissible that patent offices grant patents to any kind of invention, without any consideration of morality.[609]

---

[606] See the text of Article 27.2: "Members *may* exclude from patentability..." (emphasis added).

[607] Note that while Article 27.2 allows not to grant a patent, Article 30 relates to exceptions to exclusive rights, that is, it is operative only when a patent has been granted. See Chapter 23 below.

[608] The Concise Oxford Dictionary, p. 637.

[609] See, e.g., Alberto Bercovitz, *Panel Discussion on Biotechnology*, in Kraih Hill and Laraine Morse (Eds.), *Emergent Technologies and Intellectual Property. Multimedia, Biotechnology & Others Issues*, ATRIP, CASRIP Publications Series No. 2, Seattle 1996, p. 53.

Article 27.2 clarifies, unlike equivalent precedents in national laws, that protection of *ordre public* or morality includes the protection of "human, animal or plant life or health or to avoid serious prejudice to the environment", thereby explicitly allowing for exceptions to patentability when any of these interests may be negatively affected by patent grants. The concept of "health" may be deemed to encompass not only medical care, but also the satisfaction of basic requirements such as adequate food, safe water, shelter, clothing, warmth and safety.[610] The "environment" refers to the "surrounding objects, region, or conditions, especially circumstances of life of person or society".[611]

Finally, it should be noted, as examined in more detail below, that WTO Members can provide for the exceptions referred to but they are subject under Article 27.2 to one important condition: non-patentability may only be established if the commercial exploitation of the invention needs to be prevented to protect the interests referred to above. This excludes the possibility of applying such exceptions when, for instance, it would be in the interest of public health to promote the diffusion of an invention (e.g., a medicinal product), since a Member cannot refuse a patent on *ordre public* or morality grounds and, at the same time, permit the commercialisation of the invention.

2. History of the provision

2.1 Situation pre-TRIPS

Ordre public and morality considerations had been taken into account in many jurisdictions before the adoption of TRIPS. In the USA, for instance, traditionally the concept of inventions contrary to *ordre public*, as applied by the courts, referred to an invention that was "frivolous or injurious to the well-being, good policy, or sound morals of a society".[612]

European laws[613] and many other civil law jurisdictions had provided for explicit exceptions on terms comparable to Article 27.2. That was the case, in particular, of Article 53(a) of the European Patent Convention, whose wording probably inspired the drafters of TRIPS. After the adoption of Article 4*quater* in the Paris Convention,[614] many national laws were reformed so as to acknowledge that a

---

[610] See, e.g., Robert Beaglehole and Ruth Bonita, *Public Health at the Crossroads. Achievements and prospects*, Cambridge University Press, Melbourne 1999, p. 45; Fraser Mustard, *Health, health care and social cohesion*, in Daniel Drache and Terry Sullivan (editors), Health Reform. Public Success. Private Failure, Routledge, London and New York 1999.

[611] The Concise Oxford Dictionary, p. 323.

[612] See *Lowell v. Lewis*, 15 (a. 1018 No. 8568) (C.D. Mass. 1817), quoted in Chisum and Jacobs, p. 2.5. In the United States, "the trend is to restrict this subjective public policy approach to utility" (*Idem*).

[613] See, e.g. Rainer Moufang, *The Concept of "Ordre Public" and Morality in Patent Law*, in Geertrui Van Overwalle (Ed.), Patent Law, Ethics and Biotechnology, Katholieke Universiteit Brussel, Bruxelles 1998, No.13, p. 69 [hereinafter Moufang].

[614] Article 4*quater* reads as follows: "The grant of a patent shall not be refused and a patent shall not be invalidated on the ground that the sale of the patented product or of a product obtained by means of a patented process is subject to restrictions or limitations resulting from the domestic law." This provision is thus equivalent to the last part of Article 27.2 TRIPS. However, there is no comparable reference to *ordre public* or morality.

possible conflict with simple statutory law could not be regarded as a sufficient reason for rejecting a patent application.

2.2 Negotiating History

2.1 The Anell Draft

"1.4 The following [shall] [may] be excluded from patentability:

1.4.1 Inventions, [the publication or use of which would be], contrary to public order, [law,] [generally accepted standards of] morality, [public health,] [or the basic principle of human dignity] [or human values]."

[...]

2.2 The Brussels Draft

"2. PARTIES may exclude from patentability inventions, the prevention within their territory of the publication or any exploitation of which is necessary; to protect public morality or order, including to secure compliance with laws or regulations which are not inconsistent with the provisions of this Agreement; or to protect human, animal or plant life or health."

The final text is closer to that of Article 53 of the European Patent Convention. However, the latter refers to conflicts that may follow not only from the exploitation but also from the "publication" of the invention, an alternative that in the view of some authorities would be irreconcilable with Article 27.2 of TRIPS.[615]

Article 27.2 makes it clear that an exclusion from patentability cannot be grounded merely on the fact that the existing law of a Member prohibits exploitation. The present wording is a change from the Brussels Draft that read "including to secure compliance with laws or regulations which are not inconsistent with the provisions of this Agreement". In other words, an exclusion from patentability must be justified within the terms of Article 27.2 itself.

3. Possible interpretations

> Members may exclude from patentability inventions, the prevention within their territory of the commercial exploitation of which is necessary to protect ...

Article 27.2 is concerned with the exclusion of particular inventions, not categories of inventions which are dealt with in Article 27.3 (discussed in Chapter 21 below). It is clear from the wording of the provision that the risk must come from the commercial exploitation of the invention, not from the invention as such. It would also seem, given the wording of Article 27.2, that the likely impact must be within the territory concerned, not that of another Member.

An exception based on this Article can be applied only when it is necessary to prevent the "commercial exploitation" of the invention. Therefore, the condition

---

[615] See, e.g., Moufang, p. 72.

for the application of the exception would not be met if there is a need to prevent non-commercial uses of the invention (e.g., for scientific research).

It has been debated whether the exception can only be applied when there is an actual prohibition on the commercialization of the invention, or when there is need to prevent it (even if still not done by the government concerned). According to one opinion, an effective ban should exist in order to make the exception viable.[616] It has been held, however, that TRIPS "does not require an actual ban of the commercialization as a condition for exclusions; only the necessity of such a ban is required. In order to justify an exclusion under Article 27 (2) TRIPS, a Member state would therefore have to demonstrate that it is necessary to prevent – by whatever means – the commercial exploitation of the invention. Yet, the Member would not have to prove that under its national laws the commercialization of the invention was or is actually prohibited".[617]

... is necessary to protect ordre public or morality, ...

Article 27.2 introduces a "necessity test" to assess whether protection of an overriding social interest is justified. Though TRIPS constitutes the *lex specialis* for dealing with patent issues in the WTO framework, the GATT/WTO jurisprudence on Article XX of GATT is likely to play a role in the interpretation of said Article.[618]

Article XX (a) and (b) of GATT have a similar structure to Article 27.2, and it is clear that, for the purposes of these provisions exclusions must be objectively justified.[619] These provisions permit Members to make exceptions to the basic GATT free trade principle on the ground (a) that it is *necessary* to protect public morals, and (b) that it is *necessary* to protect human, animal or plant life [emphasis added]. Thus, under GATT, quarantine, sanitary and similar regulations must not constitute arbitrary or unjustifiable discrimination or a disguised restriction on trade. A measure is justified only if no reasonable alternative is available to a Member which is not inconsistent, or at least less inconsistent, with GATT.[620]

---

[616] Adrian Otten, *Viewpoint of the WTO*, (M. Swaminathan, Ed.), in Agrobiodiversity and Farmers' Rights Proceedings of a Technical Consultation on an Implementation Framework for Farmers' Rights, M.S. Swaminathan Research Foundation, Madras 1996.

[617] Dan Leskien and Michael Flitner, *Intellectual Property Rights and Plant Genetic Resources: Options for a Sui Generis System*, Issues in Genetic Resources No. 6, IPGRI, Rome 1997, p. 15.

[618] In the *India- Patent Protection for Pharmaceutical and Agricultural Chemical Products* case (WT/DS50) the panel held that the TRIPS Agreement has a "relatively self-contained, *sui generis* status within the WTO." However, it also held that the Agreement is "an integral part of the WTO system, which itself builds upon the experience of over nearly half a century under the GATT 1947" (para. 7.19).

[619] See *GATT Analytical Index*, Vol. I, p. 518 *et seq.*

[620] See 1990 Panel Report on *Thailand 'Thailand - Restrictions on Importation of and Internal Taxes on Cigarettes'* BISD 37S/200, adopted November 7, 1990. A contracting party cannot justify a measure inconsistent with GATT provisions as 'necessary' in terms of Article XX(b) if an alternative measure it could reasonably be expected to employ not inconsistent with GATT is available to it. Thus a Thai government restriction on the importation of cigarettes could not be justified in terms of the desirable objective of stopping people smoking, given that alternatives such as anti-smoking campaigns are available, and have been shown to be effective in a number of countries around the world. Similarly, a United States measure prohibiting the importation of tuna under

Ordre public encompasses, according to European law, the protection of public security and the physical integrity of individuals as part of society.[621] This concept includes also the protection of the environment, but is deemed to be narrower than 'public order', which appeared in some drafts of the Agreement. Though European law may be an important source for the interpretation of that concept, there is no generally accepted notion of *"ordre public"* and no reason for other WTO Members to follow the European approach. Members have a considerable flexibility to define which situations are covered, depending upon their own conception of the protection of public values.

Ordre public should be contrasted with the exclusion from patentability on morality grounds. Morality seems to depend, for the purposes of this Article, on the particular culture of a country or region.[622] While it is possible to give a meaning to "morality" which is not culturally dependent, it would seem likely that the provision was drafted from a more relativist viewpoint and could include, for instance, religious concerns in a particular Member. According to Ladas, morality

"... reflects customs and habits anchored in the spirit of a particular community. There is no clearly objective standard of feeling, instincts, or attitudes toward a certain conduct. Therefore, specific prescriptions involving uniform evaluation of certain acts are extremely difficult."[623]

The jurisprudence of the European Patent Office (EPO) has distinguished between *ordre public* and morality (Decision T.356/93). Under the Guidelines for Examination of the EPO, "ordre public" is linked to security reasons, such as riot or public disorder, and inventions that may lead to criminal or other generally offensive behaviour (Part C, chapter IV, 3.1). This concept also encompasses the protection of the environment.[624] Under the morality clause, the Office has to establish whether

the Marine Mammal Protection Act to save dolphin life and health (they often get caught in the nets used to catch tuna) was held not to be fully consistent with the GATT obligations, because other means of protecting dolphins were available—see *United States – Restrictions on Imports of Tuna* BISD 29S/155. On the other hand, the Appellate Body held that a French prohibition of manufacture, processing, sale, import and marketing of asbestos and asbestos containing products was "necessary" to protect human life in terms of GATT Article XX(b) (See *European Communities – Measures Affecting Asbestos or Products Containing Asbestos [EC – Asbestos]*, WT/DS135/AB/R of 12 March 2001). In particular, the Appellate Body denied the availability of alternative and equally effective measures such as "controlled use" of asbestos as advocated by Canada (see *EC – Asbestos*, para. 174. For a detailed analysis of this jurisprudence, see Jan Neumann, Elisabeth Türk, *Necessity Revisited – Proportionality in World Trade Organization Law After Korea – Beef, EC – Asbestos and EC – Sardines*, Journal of World Trade 2003, vol. 37, No. 1, pp. 199 – 233.). See also Carlos Correa, *Implementing National Public Health Policies in the Framework of the WTO Agreements*, 34 Journal of World Trade 2000, vol. 34, No. 5, 2, p. 92-96.

[621] "Ordre public" is a legal expression with a long tradition in the area of international private law, where it serves as a last resort when the application of foreign law leads to a result which would be wholly unacceptable for the national legal order. See, e.g., Moufang, p. 71.

[622] Gervais, p. 149.

[623] Stephen P. Ladas, *Patents, Trademarks, and Related Rights. National and International Protection*, Harvard University Press 1975, pp. 1685–1686.

[624] In case T 356/93 the Board of Appeal of the European Patent Office observed "It is generally accepted that the concept of 'ordre public' covers the protection of public security and the physical integrity of individuals as part of society. This concept encompasses also the protection of the environment. Accordingly, under Article 53(a) EPC, inventions the exploitation of which is likely

an invention would be so abhorrent for the public that its patenting would be inconceivable. Morality includes the totality of the accepted norms which are deeply rooted in a particular culture.

The analysis of the application of Article 53.b) of the EPC is made case-by-case. The EPO has employed two methods for that purpose: the balancing of interests at stake[625] and the opinion of the vast majority of the public.[626] In all the cases where these methods were applied, the EPO affirmed the patentability of the inventions under examination.

> . . . including to protect human, animal or plant life or health or to avoid serious prejudice to the environment, . . .

Article 27.2 includes *examples* of permissible exceptions to patentability, for the protection of human, animal or plant life or health, and avoiding serious prejudice to the environment within the relevant Member.

As mentioned, some decisions by the EPO show that the effects of an invention on the environment may constitute a valid ground for denying patentability. However, the EPO refused to assume a *regulatory role* on the introduction of genetic engineering inventions. In dealing with this issue, one of the opposition decisions argued that

> "A patent does not give a positive right to its proprietor to use the invention but rather only confers the right to exclude others from using the invention for a limited period of time. If the legislator is of the opinion that certain technical knowledge should be used under limited conditions only it is up to him to enact appropriate legislation."[627]

As noted by Moufang, patent examiners "are not specifically trained in ethics or in risk assessment. Since patents do not give a positive right to use the protected inventions, other bodies have to shoulder the responsibility for the decisions of society whether certain technology can and should be put into practice."[628]

---

to breach public peace or social order (for example, through acts of terrorism) or to seriously prejudice the environment are to be excluded from patentability as being contrary to 'ordre public'".

[625] The balancing of interests takes into consideration the advantages and disadvantages of an invention, including the possible environmental risks due to the eventual dissemination of genes in nature (Decision T.19/90). In the area of plant technology, the Board of Appeals of the EPO has argued that plant genetic engineering is not a technical domain that, as such, may be deemed contrary to morality or public order. In decision T 356/93 (Plant Genetic Systems), it reasoned that it needed to be established in each individual case whether a particular invention relates to an improper use or has destructive effects on plant biotechnology. The Board held that "inventions the exploitation of which is likely to breach public peace or social order (for example, through acts of terrorism) or to seriously prejudice the environment are to be excluded from patentability as being contrary to ordre public".

[626] The opinion of the majority of the public was considered by the Opposition Division of the EPO in a decision of 8.12.94 in the case of "Relaxin". The patent related to a DNA fragment codifying for a human protein. The Office examined whether the invention would appear immoral for the vast majority of the public.

[627] Decision T0019/90, in the "oncomouse" case.

[628] Moufang, p. 72.

> ... provided that such exclusion is not made merely because the exploitation is prohibited by their law.

The last sentence of Article 27.2 establishes that the sole fact that the exploitation is prohibited by law is not sufficient reason to exclude patentability. This is in line with Article 4*quater* of the Paris Convention, which contains a rule equivalent, though not identical, to the provision contained in the last part of Article 27.2: it stipulates that the grant of a patent shall not be refused (or the registration of a patent not be invalidated) for the sole reason that the sale of the patented product is restricted or limited under domestic law. Thus, mere marketing restrictions as such cannot justify exclusions from patentability. There has to be a specific link between the commercial exploitation of the patent and the respective Member's *ordre public* or morality: Article 27.2 requires that this commercial exploitation would represent a particular danger to either *ordre public* or morality.

4. WTO jurisprudence

There is no specific WTO jurisprudence on this provision. It might be of interest, however, noting the discussion about the concept of "exploitation" in the *EC - Canada* case. Canada took the position that "exploitation" of the patent "involves the extraction of commercial value from the patent by "working" the patent, either by selling the product in a market from which competitors are excluded, or by licensing others to do so, or by selling the patent rights outright. The European Communities also defined "exploitation" by referring to the same three ways of "working" a patent" (para. 7.51). Since the parties differed primarily on their interpretation of the term "normal", the panel defined "normal exploitation" as

> "The normal practice of exploitation by patent owners, as with owners of any other intellectual property right, is to exclude all forms of competition that could detract significantly from the economic returns anticipated from a patent's grant of market exclusivity. The specific forms of patent exploitation are not static, of course, for to be effective exploitation must adapt to changing forms of competition due to technological development and the evolution of marketing practices" (para. 7.55).

5. Relationship with other international instruments

5.1 WTO Agreements
Article XX, letters (a) and (b) of the GATT 1994 authorizes WTO Members to deviate from GATT obligations through measures necessary to protect public morals; as well as human, animal or plant life or health, subject to further requirements.[629]

---

[629] This provision reads: "Subject to the requirement that such measures are not applied in a manner which would constitute a means of arbitrary or unjustifiable discrimination between countries where the same conditions prevail, or a disguised restriction on international trade, nothing in this Agreement shall be construed to prevent the adoption or enforcement by any contracting party of measures:
(*a*) necessary to protect public morals;
(*b*) necessary to protect human, animal or plant life or health;"

5.2 Other international instruments

6. New developments

6.1 National laws

The approach expressed in Article 27.2 was retained in post-TRIPS developments in Europe,[630] and can be found in many other national laws. Moreover, some recent legislative changes in patent law have defined specific exceptions based on ethical considerations in relation to inventions consisting of parts of the human body or techniques applied to human beings. Thus, as a result of a comprehensive legislative initiative in the field of bioethics, the French domestic patent law, as amended in July 1994, provides that the human body, its elements and products as well as knowledge relating to the overall structure of a human gene or elements thereof may not, as such, form the subject matter of a patent. The Australian Patents Act stipulates that "human beings, and the biological processes for their generation, are not patentable inventions". The European Directive on Biological Inventions, similarly, provides that the human body and its elements in their natural state shall not be considered patentable inventions. However, patents over human genes or cell lines have been granted as a matter of routine by the EPO, whose Opposition Division has not found any reasons why the patenting of human genes should be intrinsically unethical.[631]

6.2 International instruments

6.3 Regional and bilateral context

A number of regional and bilateral free trade agreements such as CAFTA, USA-Jordan, USA-Singapore, and USA-Australia contain exceptions to patentability similar to Article 27.2, TRIPS. On the other hand, the USA-Chile FTA does not expressly provide for such exception.[632]

6.4 Proposals for review

There have been no proposals for review of this Article.

7. Comments, including economic and social implications

A patent is simply a grant of exclusive rights. It does not of itself authorise the exploitation of the patented invention, and this can be regulated in separate

---

[630] The 1998 European Directive on Biotechnological Inventions contains a provision (Article 9) similar to Article 53 of the European Patent Convention. See, e.g., Vandergheynst, Dominique, *La notion d'ordre public et des bonnes mœurs dans la proposition de directive européenne relative à la protection juridique des inventions biotechnologiques*, in Geertrui Van Overwalle (Ed.), Patent Law, Ethics and Biotechnology, Katholieke Universiteit Brussel, Bruxelles 1998, No. 13, pp. 82–92; Deryck Beyleveld; Roger Brownsword and Margaret Llewelyn, *The morality clauses of the Directive on the Legal Protection of Biotechnological Inventions: conflict, compromise and the patent community*, in Richard Goldberg and Julian Lonbay (Eds.), Pharmaceutical Medicine. Biotechnology, and European Law, Cambridge University Press 2000.

[631] Moufang, pp. 75–76.

[632] For details, see Roffe, 2004, who in this context discusses a TRIPS non-derogation clause contained in the U.S.-Chile FTA.

legislation provided this is consistent with Article 27.2 (that is, for example, that it is necessary to protect human, animal or plant life or health or to avoid serious prejudice to the environment). In the case of pharmaceutical inventions, for example, separate marketing approval is usually required before the invention can be prescribed by doctors for their patients. This marketing approval can sometimes take several years after the grant of the patent. A classic example of an invention contrary to *ordre public* would be a novel kind of letter bomb. It would clearly be permissible to exclude such devices from patentability under Article 27.2. The non-disclosure of the mechanism of the device in a patent specification is a necessary first step in such prevention.

One important point to be considered is the extent to which the role of a patent office in judging and eventually denying a patent on the basis of moral or public order grounds may be sufficient to prevent the harmful effects from taking place. Given the limited competence of a patent office, non-patentability would only ensure that an invention is not the subject of property rights, but by no means would this be sufficient to prevent the use of the invention by any interested person, since it would remain in the public domain.

20: Patents: Therapeutic, Surgical and Diagnostic Methods

Article 27.3 (a)   Patentable Subject Matter

Members may also exclude from patentability:

diagnostic, therapeutic and surgical methods for the treatment of humans or animals; . . .

---

1. Introduction: terminology, definition and scope

While TRIPS in Article 27.1 only requires the protection of processes and products,[633] some national laws have extended patentability to inventions consisting of methods of using certain products or performing certain steps.

Article 27.3(a) applies specifically to *methods* for the treatment of humans or animals. It makes clear that in this area, for the purpose of patentability, the (patentable) products or processes need to be differentiated from the methods of the treatment. In other words, *the way inventions are used* in order to heal humans or animals may be excluded from patentability. The reasons for this exception are various and depend on each country's perspective. While European countries advance ethical or moral considerations for this provision's equivalent in Article 52(4) of the European Patent Convention,[634] developing countries have stressed, *inter alia*, the need for local availability of treatment methods.[635]

Therapeutic, surgical and diagnostic methods produce effects on the human (or animal) body, and not an industrial effect. Therefore, they may be deemed not patentable because of non-compliance with the industrial applicability requirement provided for in most patent laws, even in the absence of a specific exception. However, in the United States[636] and other countries, such as Australia and New Zealand, patent law allows for the patenting of medical methods if they satisfy the definition of process and the other conditions of eligibility.[637]

---

[633] See Chapter 17.

[634] Set out below, Section 3 of this chapter (Possible interpretations).

[635] Gervais, p. 150.

[636] In the USA, "utility" and not industrial applicability is required, thereby allowing for a broader scope of patentability.

[637] A bill enacted in 1996 (amending U.S. patent law, 35 USC 287.c) determined, nevertheless, that the use of patented surgical procedures is protected from infringement suits. See, e.g., Grubb, p. 220.

2. History of the provision

2.1 Situation pre-TRIPS

Therapeutic, surgical and diagnostic methods were excluded from patent protection under European law, as well as the laws of many other countries before the adoption of TRIPS. Under Article 52(4) of the European Patent Convention, for instance, the exclusion of methods of treatment follows from the requirement of industrial applicability. This is spelled out in Article 52(4) which provides that

"Methods of treatment of the human or animal body by surgery or therapy and diagnostic methods practised on the human or animal body shall not be regarded as inventions which are susceptible of industrial application within the meaning of paragraph 1. This provision shall not apply to products, in particular substances or compositions, for use in any of these methods."

2.2 Negotiating History

Both the Anell Draft and the Brussels Draft included a provision similar to Article 27.3 (a).

2.2.1 The Anell Draft

"1.4 The following [shall] [may] be excluded from patentability:

[...]

1.4.3 Methods of [medical] treatment for humans [or animals]."

2.2.2 The Brussels Draft

"3. PARTIES may also exclude from patentability:

(a) [Diagnostic, therapeutic and] surgical methods for the treatment of humans and animals;"

3. Possible interpretations

> Members may also exclude from patentability: . . .

TRIPS allows Members to provide for an exclusion to patentability in the cases referred to, but does not oblige them to do so. The exclusions are facultative, or could be limited to some of the methods mentioned in Article 27.3 (a).

> (a) diagnostic, therapeutic and surgical methods for the treatment of humans or animals; . . .

The exception applies to methods of treatment; that is, to procedures designed to treat humans or animals. This possible exception does not encompass the means utilized to perform the treatment. Accordingly, while for example a novel form of surgical procedure cannot be patented, a novel form of apparatus invented to enable that procedure to be carried out is, in principle, patentable. It can be argued that pharmaceutical products constitute a therapeutic treatment for humans and animals, and therefore might be excluded from patentability. However, it would be difficult to sustain this argument in light of the negotiating history of TRIPS, which addressed at some length issues surrounding pharmaceutical patents, as well as provisions such as the Article 70.8 "mailbox" rule that expressly cover pharmaceutical patents.

4. WTO jurisprudence

There has been no specific dispute on issues covered by this provision.

5. Relationship with other international instruments

5.1 WTO Agreements

5.2 Other international instruments

As noted above, there is an equivalent of this provision in Article 52(4) of the European Patent Convention. The exclusion is consistent with the object of the Paris Convention Article 1(1) which states that the countries to which it applies constitute a Union for the protection of "industrial property". Article 1(3) provides that "industrial property" shall be understood in the broadest sense and shall apply not only to industry and commerce proper, but likewise to agricultural and extractive industries and to all manufacture or natural products such as wines, grain, tobacco leaf, fruit, cattle, minerals, mineral waters, beer, flowers and flour.[638] Broad as this definition is, it clearly does not cover methods of therapeutic treatment, surgery or diagnosis.

6. New developments

6.1 National laws

6.2 International instruments

6.3 Regional and bilateral contexts

6.4 Proposals for review

The exclusion under Article 27.3(a) is connected to the generally accepted concept of patentable subject matter, and is unlikely to be modified without a major change in international views on this matter. Nevertheless, the view has been expressed from time to time that it might be appropriate to permit the patenting of a new surgical procedure since that would ensure its disclosure and dissemination.[639]

---

[638] This list should not be read as requiring the things listed to be patentable *as such*. As noted above, patents are granted for *inventions*, and the discovery of a new plant or mineral existing in nature would not be an invention. Consequently, the above listed natural products would only be patentable if they were *modified* in a way that satisfied the patentability criteria of novelty, inventive step and industrial applicability.

[639] Jeremy Phillips and Alison Firth, *Introduction to Intellectual Property*, 4th ed., Butterworths, Witltshire 2000, p. 59, citing Cuthbert *Patent Law Reform in New Zealand: Should Methods*

However, it is very unlikely that this view will find wide acceptance in the medical profession, and without such acceptance, the exclusion is likely to remain.

7. Comments, including economic and social implications

The exclusion authorized by Article 27.3(a) is fairly narrow, and has few implications for the way in which funding for medical research is directed. For example, new devices such as scanners and fibre optic cameras to enable surgery to be carried out without the invasive techniques that were formerly necessary, are in principle patentable. On the other hand, techniques such as keyhole surgery made possible by such devices may be excluded from patentability. Similarly, pharmaceutical products and apparatus that now render surgery unnecessary, where it was necessary previously, are patentable.

Even in countries where the patentability of such methods is allowed, patents granted are relatively rare. One possible reason for this is that enforcing such patents is very problematic. The patent owner would need to monitor the activities by a more or less large number of doctors and surgeons, who generally provide their services subject to strict privacy rules. Enforcement may be more feasible when new and complex methods are applied by a small number of easily identifiable professionals. This may be the case of gene therapies, at least until they become safer and more widely diffused.

The exclusion of therapeutic methods may have significant implications in the pharmaceutical sector, in relation to the patentability of the new use of a known pharmaceutical product.[640] In effect, there is no real difference between patent claims relating to the use of a substance and those relating to a therapeutic method: in both cases a new medical activity is claimed, i.e., a new way of using one or more known products.[641] The patenting of a new therapeutic effect of a known pharmaceutical product, therefore, is contrary to the ban on patents for therapeutic methods, where applied. Some countries have overcome this problem by admitting the patentability of a new use of an existing drug under the so called "Swiss claims", under which a method claim is drafted as a claim for the use of a product to manufacture a medicine.[642] There is no obligation under TRIPS, however, to adopt this approach.

of Medical Treatment be Patentable? Patent World, May 1997; Kell, *Expanding the Frontiers of Patentability: Methods of Medical Treatment of the Human Body*, EIPR 1995, p. 202.

[640] This is an issue of increasing economic importance, in part due to the decline in the discovery of new molecules with significant therapeutic value.

[641] Bengt Domeij, *Pharmaceutical Patents in Europe*, Kluwer Law International / Norstedts Juridik, Stockholm 2000, p. 178.

[642] See Chapter 17, Section 3.

21: Patents: Biotechnological Inventions: Genetic Resources, Plant Variety Protection, Traditional Knowledge

---

Article 27.3(b)   Patentable Subject Matter

Members may also exclude from patentability:

plants and animals other than micro-organisms, and essentially biological processes for the production of plants or animals other than non-biological and microbiological processes. However, Members shall provide for the protection of plant varieties either by patents or by an effective *sui generis* system or by any combination thereof. The provisions of this subparagraph shall be reviewed four years after the date of entry into force of the WTO Agreement.

---

1. Introduction: terminology, definition and scope

Article 27.3(b) addresses one of the most controversial issues covered by TRIPS. The often called "biotechnology clause" describes subject matter that Members *may* exclude from patentability while, at the same time, specifically obliges Members to protect microorganisms and certain biotechnological processes.

The drafting of this clause – the single one in the whole TRIPS Agreement subject to an early review[643] – reflected, on the one hand, the strong interests of some developed countries in ensuring protection of biotechnological innovations and, on the other, the important differences existing among such countries with regard to the scope of protection, as well as the concerns of many developing countries about the patentability of life forms.

Since the adoption of the Agreement, the differences in the treatment of biotechnological inventions among developed countries have been reduced,[644] but not eliminated.[645] Many developing countries have indicated, in the process of review of Article 27.3(b) and in preparations for the Third WTO Ministerial Conference (December 1999), their discomfort with the implications of this provision, particularly in view of several cases of protection, in developed countries, of biological

---

[643] Which should have taken place in 1999.

[644] Particularly with the approval of the EU Directive on Biotechnological Inventions (No. 96/9/EC of March 11, 1996).

[645] Thus, plant varieties and animal races are not patentable in Europe, while they are eligible for protection in the USA.

resources or traditional knowledge (such as quinoa, ayahuasca and curative uses of turmeric)[646] originating in developing countries. In the opinion of these countries, there is need to reconcile Article 27.3(b) with the relevant provisions of the Convention on Biological Diversity, particularly on prior informed consent and benefit sharing.

Article 27.3(b) leaves considerable flexibility for Members to adopt different approaches to the patentability of inventions relating to plants and animals, but unambiguously requires the protection of micro-organisms.[647] In addition, this Article obliges Members to provide protection for "plant varieties". The distinction between a "plant", that is, a living organism that belongs to the plant kingdom, and a "plant variety"[648] must be borne in mind for the interpretation of this clause. For example, when a pest-resistant gene is introduced by means of genetic engineering in a certain number of cotton plants[649], one or more "transgenic" plants are obtained. The patentability of these plants may or may not be admitted under national law. These plants, however, do not necessarily constitute a "plant variety", unless whenever cultivated, the resulting plants retain certain predetermined characteristics and can be propagated unchanged.

In case a Member chooses to protect living organisms through patents,[650] only such organisms having undergone a certain technical modification are not

---

[646] See Correa, 2001 and UNCTAD-ICTSD, Policy Discussion Paper (2003).

[647] A "micro-organism" is "an organism not visible to naked eye" (*The Concise Oxford Dictionary*, Oxford University Press, Seventh Ed., 1982). Note, however, that in the Council for TRIPS, there is no agreement on a common definition of what constitutes a micro-organism (see Communication from the European Communities and their Member States to the Council for TRIPS of 17 October 2002, IP/C/W/383, page 1).

[648] According to the UPOV Convention (as revised in 1991) a "plant variety" is "a plant grouping within a single botanical taxon of the lowest rank, which grouping, irrespective of whether the conditions for the grant of a breeder's right are fully met, can be defined by the expression of the characteristics resulting from a given genotype or combination of genotypes, distinguished from any other plant grouping by the expression of at least one of the said characteristics and considered as a unit with regard to its suitability for being propagated unchanged". One essential element in this definition is that a plant "variety" is a *grouping* of plants which retain their distinguishing characters when reproduced from seeds or by asexual means (for example, cuttings). See National Research Council, Committee on Managing Global Genetic Resources: *Agricultural Imperatives, Managing Global Genetic Resources. Agricultural Crop Issues and Policies*, National Academy Press, Washington, D.C. 1993, p. 412. Expressed in less technical terms, a plant variety is the technical modification of a naturally existing plant. The result of this modification is a transformed plant which retains certain characteristics when reproduced from seeds or by asexual means (the latter meaning reproduction not from seeds but through methods such as cutting, division, layering, etc.).

[649] While inserting genes is the task of *biotechnologists*, developing a variety is the responsibility of *breeders*. "Plant breeding" is the science-based activity that aims to improve the quality and yield of plant varieties yield, see W. Hale and J. Margham, *The Harper Collins Dictionary: Biology*, Harper Perennial, New York 1991, p. 430 [hereinafter Hale and Margham]. Two ways of breeding have to be distinguished. "Conventional " breeding" (as opposed to genetic engineering) utilizes selection, crossing and other methods in order to obtain the expression of the desired traits in a group of plants. Genetic engineering is the general term referring to all techniques used to isolate particular genetic material (i.e. DNA) from one organism and introduce it into another organism, thus resulting in the latter being "transgenic". See Geoff Tansey, *Food Security, Biotechnology and Intellectual Property. Unpacking some issues around TRIPS*. A Discussion Paper, Quaker United Nations Office, Geneva 2002, p. 6, quoting Peter Lund.

[650] Note that under Article 27.3(b), only micro-organisms, microbiological and non-biological processes have to be protected through patent law. For plant varieties, Members may establish *sui*

pre-existent in nature and may thus be considered as new. Since the determination of the precise meaning of novelty (like the other patentability criteria) is left to the WTO Members' discretion, the degree of technical intervention required to satisfy the novelty criterion varies widely among domestic patent laws.[651]

While Article 27.3(b) is flexible about the form of protection of plant varieties, it forced the introduction of IPR protection in an area in which most developing countries had none before the adoption of the Agreement. This obligation has raised concerns in some of those countries about the impact of IPR protection on farming practices (particularly the re-use and exchange of seed by farmers), genetic diversity, and food security.

2. History of the provision

2.1 Situation pre-TRIPS

After the decision by the U.S. Supreme Court in *Diamond v. Chakrabarty* (1980),[652] which accepted for the first time a patent on a living organism *per se*,[653] the patentability of such matter expanded in industrialized countries to include cells and sub-cellular parts, including genes, as well as multicellular organisms. An accepted principle since the 1980s in those countries was that the fact that an invention consisted of, was based on or employed living matter, was not a sufficient reason to exclude patent protection, including for biological materials pre-existing in nature (provided that the latter were claimed in an isolated or purified form). Despite this trend, considerable differences remain in those countries with regard to the scope of patentability of biotechnology-related inventions. Divergences were even more profound with respect to developing countries.[654]

In the field of plant varieties, few countries (most of them developed countries) had adopted at the time of the negotiation of TRIPS specific regulations on breeders' rights and had adhered to the Convention for the Protection of New Varieties of Plants ("the UPOV Convention") of December 2, 1961, which was subsequently revised in 1972, 1978 and 1991.[655] In addition, the 1978 Act of the UPOV Convention did not permit the provision of both breeders' rights and patent protection for the same genera or species (Article 2).[656]

---

generis systems that do not rely on the same criteria for protection as patents (i.e. novelty, inventive step and industrial applicability). For details, see Sections 3 and 5 of this chapter.

[651] For more details, see Section 3 of this chapter.

[652] 447 U.S. 303 (1980).

[653] The patent, filed in 1972, related to a genetically modified microorganism. It asserted 36 claims related to the invention of "a bacterium from the genus Pseudomonas containing therein at least two stable energy-generating plasmids, each of these plasmids providing a separate hydrocarbon degradative pathway".

[654] See World Intellectual Property Organization, Memorandum on Exclusion from Patent Protection, Doc. No. HL/CE/IV/INF/1, reprinted in 27 Industrial Property, 192 (1988).

[655] UPOV is a French acronym for what is referred to in English as the International Union for the Protection of New Varieties of Plants. WIPO and UPOV are closely associated. The UPOV Convention is a shorthand for the treaty administered by that organization.

[656] This limitation was lifted by the 1991 revision of the Convention (see below, Section 5.2 of this chapter).

2.2 Negotiating history

The initial negotiating proposals by the United States, Japan, the Nordic countries and Switzerland aimed at broad patent coverage for plants and living organisms.[657] In contrast, most developing countries (joined by the European Community countries in relation to plant varieties and animal races) rejected such an approach.

2.2.1 The Anell Draft

The Anell Draft text under negotiation in July 1990 (W/76) showed how substantial the divergences among the parties were. A heavily bracketed text alluded to the possible exclusion from patentability of

"1.4.4 [Any] plant or animal [including micro-organisms] [varieties] or [essentially biological] processes for the production of plants or animals; [this does not apply to microbiological processes or the products thereof]. [As regards biotechnological inventions, further limitations should be allowed under national law]."

2.2.2 The Brussels Draft

By December 1990, the parties had not agreed on the issue of patent protection for plants and animals, and the differences were still outstanding. The Brussels Draft text provided, in bracketed language, that parties could exclude from patentability:

"[b] A. Animal varieties [and other animal inventions] and essentially biological processes for the production of animals, other than microbiological processes or the products thereof. PARTIES shall provide for the protection of plant varieties either by patents or by an effective sui generis system or by any combination thereof. This provision shall be reviewed [...] years after the entry into force of this Agreement.]

[b] B. Plants and animals, including microorganisms, and parts thereof and processes for their production. As regards biotechnological inventions, further limitations should be allowed under national law.]"

Paragraph A essentially reflected the views of developed countries, and paragraph B of developing countries. As a simple comparison with the adopted Article 27.3(b) shows, the developed countries' approach finally prevailed to a large extent.

3. Possible interpretations

3.1 Plants and animals

> Members may also exclude from patentability ... plants and animals

Article 27.3(b) allows for the exclusion from patentability of "plants and animals" in general. In the absence of any distinction, and in the light also of the second

[657] See Terence Stewart (Ed.), *The GATT Uruguay Round. A negotiating History* (1986–1992), Kluwer Law and Taxation Publishers 1993, p. 2294.

sentence of the same Article that introduces an exception for one particular classification (plant varieties), the scope of the exception under Article 27.3(b) is to be interpreted in broad terms. Consequently, Members may exclude plants as such (including transgenic plants),[658] plant varieties (including hybrids), as well as plant cells, seeds and other plant materials. They may also exclude animals (including transgenic) and animal races.

Members may opt to exclude from patentability only certain categories of plant and animal inventions. Thus, in European countries the prohibition to patent a plant "variety" does not prevent the patenting of plants as such. Similarly, the granting of a patent by the European Patent Office on the "Harvard oncomouse" (a mouse genetically modified to facilitate the testing of anti-cancer drugs) was also based on the judgment that it was not a "race" but a specifically altered "animal".[659]

3.2 Micro-organisms

> ... other than micro-organisms ...

A "micro-organism" is an organism that is not normally perceptible by the eye. The scientific concept of "micro-organism" refers to "a Member of one of the following classes: bacteria, fungi, algae, protozoa or viruses."[660]

An important question is whether microorganisms as found in nature should be patented under this provision. It is generally accepted that "to be patentable, a micro-organism cannot be as it exists in nature".[661] However, in some jurisdictions it is sufficient to isolate a microorganism and identify a use therefore to obtain a patent.

Thus, in countries that are parties to the European Patent Convention a patent may be granted when a substance found in nature can be characterized by its structure, by its process of isolation or by other criteria, if it is new in the sense that it was not previously available to the public. The European Directive on Biotechnological Inventions clarifies that "biological material which is isolated from its natural environment or processed by means of a technical process may be the subject of an invention even if it already occurred in nature" (Article 3.2).

In the United States, an isolated or purified form of a natural product is patentable. The concept of "new" under the novelty requirement does not mean "not preexisting" but "novel" in a prior art sense, so that the unknown but natural

---

[658] Note that the transgenic character alone is not sufficient for the plant to be considered a plant variety. On top of the transgenic modification, the transformed plant would have to be stable in its characteristics, i.e. retain them after reproduction. See above, under Section 1.

[659] Article 27.2 of the TRIPS Agreement allows Members not to grant patents on inventions which are contrary to *ordre public* or morality. See Chapter 19. An exception of this kind, provided for under European law, has been invoked (albeit unsuccessfully) before the European Patent Office in relation to patent applications related to transgenic plants and animals. See Frédéric Pollaud-Dulian, *La Brevetabilité des inventions. Etude comparative de jurisprudence*, France-OEB, Le Droit des Affaires, No. 16, Paris 1997.

[660] See J. Coombs, *Macmillan Dictionary of Biotechnology*, Macmillan, London and Basinstoke 1986, p. 198.

[661] U.S. Communication to the Council of TRIPS, IP/C/W/209, 3 October 2000.

existence of a product does not preclude the product from the category of statutory subject matter. Similarly, in Japan the Enforcement Standards for Substance Patents stipulated that patents can be granted on chemical substances artificially isolated from natural materials, when the presence of the substance could not be detected without prior isolation with the aid of physical or chemical methods.

Members may also opt for a narrower scope of patentability, confining it to microorganisms that have been genetically modified.[662] TRIPS, in effect, does not define what an "invention" is; it only specifies the requirements that an invention should meet in order to be patentable (Article 27.1).[663]

Another important practical issue relates to the patenting of cells, genes and other sub-cellular components. In many jurisdictions, the patenting of these materials has become common practice.[664] Though these materials are not visible to the naked eye, they do not constitute "microorganisms" and, therefore, are not subject to the obligation established in Article 27.3 (b).

3.3 Processes

> Members may also exclude from patentability . . . essentially biological processes for the production of plants or animals other than non-biological and microbiological processes.

Another possible exclusion from patentability relates to essentially biological processes for the production of plants or animals. Processes for the therapeutic treatment or utilization of plants and animals are not covered by the exception.[665]

The notion of "essentially biological process" has been defined by the European Patent Office on the basis of the degree of "technical intervention"; if the latter plays an important role in the determination of or control over the results, the process may be patentable.[666] Under this notion, conventional breeding methods are generally not patentable. In contrast, methods based on modern biotechnology (e.g., tissue culture,[667] insertion of genes in a plant) where the technical intervention is significant, would be patentable.

---

[662] See, e.g., Article 10.XI of the Brazilian Industrial Property Code (Law No. 9.279, 14 May 1996), which excludes from patentability "biological materials found in nature", even if isolated, including the "genome or germplasm" of any living being.

[663] See Chapter 17.

[664] For instance, genetic materials may be patented in many countries if claimed in a non-naturally occurring form, that is, as an isolated or purified molecule. In the United States, the doctrine of *Re Deuel* (1995) has paved the way for the patenting of DNA even when encoding known proteins, on the grounds that – due to the degeneracy of the genetic code – their structure could not have been predicted. In Europe, however, gene sequences which code for a known protein are generally now regarded as *prima facie* obvious, although such was not the case in the earliest days of molecular biology.

[665] Diagnostic, therapeutic and surgical methods for the treatment of animals may be exempted from patentability under Article 27.3 (a) of the TRIPS Agreement.

[666] Guidelines for Examination of the EPO, No. X-232.2.

[667] This is a technique in which individual cells grow and divide in a bath of sterile, nutritive fluid, used *inter alia*, in plant breeding (Hale and Margham, p. 528).

The exclusion of "essentially biological processes" does not extend to "non-biological" processes for the production of plants or animals. It does not extend either to microbiological processes which are generally patentable. It is not so simple to determine when a process is "microbiological". In principle, this concept would include any process that uses or modifies microorganisms. There are, however, processes that only include one or more steps that are "microbiological." In accordance with the European Directive on Biotechnological Inventions, such processes should be deemed as "microbiological" if at least one essential step is microbiological (Article 2.2).

3.4 Plant varieties

> However, Members shall provide for the protection of plant varieties either by patents or by an effective *sui generis* system or by any combination thereof.

TRIPS obliges Members to protect plant varieties by means of patents, an effective *sui generis* regime or a combination of both. While the granting of patents is regulated under considerably detailed standards, the only requirement with respect to a *sui generis* system is that it must confer an "effective" protection. Countries can, thus, determine the scope and contents of the rights to be granted.

The flexibility permitted by Article 27.3(b) in relation to the form of protection for plant varieties has been the reflection, to a large extent, of the lack of consensus on the matter among the industrialized countries during the TRIPS negotiations. While in the USA, Australia and Japan a plant variety may be patented as such, this is not the case in Europe, as mentioned above. The reference to a *"sui generis system"* may be deemed to suggest the breeder's rights regime, as established in the UPOV Convention. However, the possibility is open to combine the patent system with the breeders' rights regime, or to develop other *"sui-generis"* forms of protection.

Industrial property protection for plant varieties is not new. In the 1920s and 1930s several countries introduced legislation that gradually evolved into a *sui generis* system of protection ("breeders' rights") distinct from the patent system. Based on requirements of distinctness, novelty, uniformity and stability, breeders' rights have typically been permitted to control the commercialization of propagating materials (like seeds), without interfering, however, either with the use of saved seeds by farmers on their own land ("farmers' privilege") or with the development of new varieties by a third party taking as a starting point a protected variety ("breeders' exemption"). Such *sui generis* regime obtained recognition at the international level in the 1960s with the adoption of the UPOV Convention. The Convention introduced minimum standards for the recognition of breeders' rights and, as mentioned, it initially prohibited the provision of patent and *sui generis* protection for plant varieties.[668]

---

[668] The limitation contained in Article 2 of the 1978 Act was not applicable to countries that provided double protection before the expiry of the period for signature of the 1978 Act (Article 37). This allowed the United States to maintain both patents and breeders' rights for plant varieties.

Breeders' rights protect plant varieties, which are new, distinct, uniform and stable. They grant the faculty to exclude non-authorized persons from using and multiplying propagating materials of protected varieties. Several features differentiate breeders' rights from patents. The former apply to a specific variety (which must physically exist), while patents may refer to genes, cells, plants, seeds or (where allowed) the varieties as such. Another important difference is that the breeder's rights system generally allows farmers to re-use in their own exploitations the seeds they have obtained, a possibility that patents generally exclude.[669] In addition, under breeders' rights protected varieties may be used for further breeding without the authorization of the title-holder ("breeders' exemption"). This may not be possible, depending on national legislation, under patent law.

3.5 Review

> The provisions of this subparagraph shall be reviewed four years after the date of entry into force of the WTO Agreement.

TRIPS entered into force on 1 January 1995. Though the review should have taken place in 1999 there has been no agreement at the Council for TRIPS on the meaning of "review". Developed countries have held that a "review of implementation" is what is called for,[670] while for developing countries a "review" should open the possibility of revising the provision itself.[671]

The review of Article 27.3(b) was also one of the TRIPS issues dealt with at the Ministerial Meeting at Doha in 2001. In this respect, the Doha Declaration included the following mandate for the Council for TRIPS:[672]

> "19. We instruct the Council for TRIPS, in pursuing its work programme including under the review of Article 27.3(b), the review of the implementation of the TRIPS Agreement under Article 71.1 and the work foreseen pursuant to paragraph 12 of this Declaration, to examine, *inter alia*, the relationship between the TRIPS Agreement and the Convention on Biological Diversity, the protection of traditional knowledge and folklore, and other relevant new developments raised by Members pursuant to Article 71.1. In undertaking this work, the TRIPS Council shall be guided by the objectives and principles set out in Articles 7 and 8 of the TRIPS Agreement and shall take fully into account the development dimension."

---

[669] Since living organisms are self-replicating, the sale of a patented organism is at the same time the sale of the means by which the organism can be replicated. Patent rights are deemed in this case to extend to the descendants of the protected organism.

[670] See, e.g., U.S. communication IP/C/W/209; Australia communication IP/C/W/310 ("the coverage of this agenda item is relatively narrow, that is, the item is concerned with a review of the effectiveness of the operation of an optional exclusion to patentability...").

[671] This view is based on the literal text of the provision, as compared to Article 71.1 where the negotiating parties used the expression "review the implementation". According to *The Concise Oxford Dictionary* (Oxford University Press, Seventh edition, 1982, reprinted in 1989), "review" is "revision" which in turn means "to read or look over or reexamine or reconsider and correct, improve, or amend...law, constitution, etc."

[672] See paragraph 19 of the Ministerial Declaration, WT/MIN(01)/DEC/1 of 20 November 2001.

Implementing this mandate, the Council for TRIPS has been discussing, *inter alia*, the following agenda items:

(a) the review of the provisions of Article 27.3(b);

(b) the relationship between TRIPS and the Convention on Biological Diversity (CBD);

(c) the protection of traditional knowledge (TK) and folklore.[673]

The Council has addressed these items together, due to their interrelated character. Despite consultations held by the Chair, Members have so far not been able to remove their substantive differences over these issues. A number of proposals made under the three items above will be analyzed in the following paragraphs.

3.5.1 Review of Article 27.3(b)

With respect to the review of Article 27.3(b), some developing country Members, as mentioned above, interpret "review" as opening up the possibility of *amending* Article 27.3(b). In particular, the African Group in a June 2003 submission to the Council[674] proposed an amendment of Article 27.3(b):

> "The African Group maintains its reservations about patenting any life forms as explained on previous occasions by the Group and several other delegations. In this regard, the Group proposes that Article 27.3(b) be revised to prohibit patents on plants, animals, micro-organisms, essentially biological processes for the production of plants or animals, and non-biological and microbiological processes for the production of plants or animals. For plant varieties to be protected under the TRIPS Agreement, the protection must clearly, and not just implicitly or by way of exception, strike a good balance with the interests of the community as a whole and protect farmers' rights and traditional knowledge, and ensure the preservation of biological diversity.
>
> In any case, the Council for TRIPS must ensure that the exceptions for ordre public or morality in paragraph 2 of Article 27 are not rendered meaningless by any provisions in its paragraph 3(b) through requiring Members to do what is otherwise contrary to ordre public and morality in their societies. The barest minimum in this regard, would be to clarify that paragraph 3(b) does not in any manner restrict the rights of Members to resort to the exceptions in paragraph 2.
>
> [...]
>
> As pointed out above, the African Group has consistently raised serious concerns about patents on life forms and research tools and on the basis of these concerns the Group has maintained that there should not be a possibility, within the framework of the TRIPS Agreement, of patents on micro-organisms as well as on non-biological and microbiological processes for the production of plants and animals.
>
> It is the view of the Group that the distinction drawn in Article 27.3(b) for micro-organisms, and for non-biological and microbiological processes for the

---

[673] See, e.g., WTO/AIR/2322 of 27 May 2004, WTO/AIR/2246 of 5 February 2004, and WTO/AIR 2104 of 20 May 2003.

[674] See Joint Communication from the African Group, IP/C/W/404 of 26 June 2003 [hereinafter African Group June 2003].

production of plants or animals, is artificial and unwarranted, and should be removed from the TRIPS Agreement, so that the exception from patentability in paragraph 3(b) covers plants, animals, and micro-organisms, as well as essentially biological processes and the non-biological and microbiological processes for the production of plants or animals."

This proposal has been the basis of controversial debates within the Council in 2003 and 2004. Developed Members have rejected an amendment of Article 27.3(b) in the above sense, referring, *inter alia*, to their biotechnology industries.[675] The EC, for example, has proposed that those Members seeking to avoid the patenting of natural materials could make use of the TRIPS flexibilities, i.e. to define narrowly the patentability criteria. In this vein, genetic resources occurring in nature would not be patentable (failing to meet the novelty requirement).[676]

The aim of some developed countries, if a revision did take place, would be to eliminate the exception for plants and animals, and to establish that the UPOV Convention as revised in 1991 should be the *only* means of protection available for plant varieties, excluding other *sui generis* systems. Thus, according to the United States, the TRIPS Council should consider

"whether it is desirable to modify the TRIPS Agreement by eliminating the exclusion from patentability of plants and animals and incorporating key provisions of the UPOV agreement regarding plant variety protection."[677]

For many developing countries, in contrast, it would be important to maintain the exception for plants and animals, as well as the flexibility to develop *sui generis* regimes on plant varieties which are suited to the seed supply systems of the countries concerned.

3.5.2 Relationship between TRIPS and CBD

Different views on the TRIPS-CBD relationship have been expressed at the Council for TRIPS in relation to the review of Article 27.3(b). While developed countries have found no inconsistencies between the two treaties,[678] several developing countries have indicated the need to reconcile them, possibly by means of a revision of TRIPS.[679]

---

[675] This point was raised by the EC in the March 2004 Meeting of the Council.

[676] The EC expressed this view during the March 2004 Meeting of the Council. See also the Communication from the European Communities and their Member States to the Council for TRIPS of 17 October 2002, IP/C/W/383 [hereinafter EC October 2002], in which the EC rejects an amendment of Article 27.3(b), stating that this provision provides sufficient flexibility to design patent protection according to a country's needs, interests or ethical standards.

[677] Communication from the United States of 19 November 1998, WT/GC/W/115, under item II.A. See also the Communication from the European Commission to the Council and the European Parliament, *The EU approach to the Millennium Round* 1999, p. 16. Note that in recent bilateral free trade agreements, there is a trend towards qualifying UPOV as the sole possible means of plant variety protection. See Section 6.3 of this chapter.

[678] See, e.g., U.S. communication IP/C/W/209; Australia communication IP/C/W/310.

[679] See, e.g., the African Group proposal to harmonize the TRIPS Agreement with the CBD in WT/GC/W/202, and the Indian proposal in WT/GC/W/225.

The main concern of many developing countries is that TRIPS does not require patent applicants whose inventions incorporate or use genetic material or
associated knowledge to comply with certain obligations under the Convention
for Biological Diversity (CBD). This convention makes access to genetic material subject to prior informed consent of and equitable benefit sharing with the
Contracting Party providing the genetic resources.[680] Developing countries have
repeatedly voiced concern about possible misappropriation of their genetic
resources by developed country patent applicants.[681]

In order to address such concerns, developing countries have proposed in the
Council for TRIPS to amend TRIPS in a way as to require an applicant for a patent
relating to biological materials or traditional knowledge to provide, as a condition
for obtaining the patent:

- disclosure of the source and country of origin of the biological resource and of
the traditional knowledge used in the invention;

- evidence of prior informed consent through approval of authorities under the
relevant national regime; and

- evidence of fair and equitable benefit sharing under the relevant national
regime.[682]

The approach to enforce CBD obligations through the TRIPS patent system is
opposed by a number of developed countries,[683] supporting the alternative idea of
pursuing ongoing work in WIPO's Intergovernmental Committee on Intellectual

---

[680] See Article 15 CBD. For more details, see Section 5.2 of this chapter.

[681] See, e.g., African Group June 2003, p. 4.

[682] See Submission by Bolivia, Brazil, Cuba, Dominican Republic, Ecuador, India, Peru, Thailand,
Venezuela, IP/C/W/403 of 24 June 2003. These three issues were also included in a checklist submitted to the Council for TRIPS on 2 March 2004 by Brazil, Cuba, Ecuador, India, Peru, Thailand
and Venezuela (see IP/C/W/420). The African Group has made a similar proposal, advocating the
amendment of Article 29, TRIPS Agreement (conditions on patent applicants), to include an obligation to disclose the country of origin of any biological resources and traditional knowledge as
well as to provide confirmation of compliance with domestic access regulations. See African Group
June 2003, p. 6.

[683] At the March and June 2004 Council Meetings, the USA and Japan expressed particular opposition to this approach. Switzerland, on the other hand, acknowledged that these issues should
be dealt with under the patent system and has proposed to amend the WIPO Patent Cooperation
Treaty (PCT) to include, in appropriate cases, the declaration of origin of genetic material in patent
applications as a voluntary requirement (IP/C/W/400; reiterated in IP/C/W/423). The proposal includes a concrete description of when disclosure would be relevant, as well as a penalty system
for failure to comply in which case the patent would be rejected or withdrawn. Finally, the EC (see
EC October 2002) has signalled its agreement to examine and discuss the possible introduction of
a system that keeps track of all patent applications regarding genetic resources. At the same time,
however, the EC has made clear (ibid.) that legal consequences of the non-respect of a disclosure
obligation should lie outside the ambit of patent law. As opposed to the issue of disclosure of origin, the EC at the March 2004 Meeting of the Council for TRIPS expressed reluctance to engage in
discussions on the item of prior informed consent. For an overview of the June 2003 and June 2004
Meetings of the Council for TRIPS, see ICTSD Bridges Trade BioRes, 13 June 2003, *CBD-TRIPS
Discussion Picking Up Speed At the WTO* (<http://www.ictsd.org/biores/03-06-13/story1.htm>); and
ICTSD, Bridges Weekly Trade News Digest, 23 June 2004, *Quiet TRIPS Council Focuses on Health,
Biodiversity-Related Issues* (<http://www.ictsd.org/weekly/04-06-23/story3.htm>).

Property and Genetic Resources, Traditional Knowledge and Folklore (IGC).[684] Overall, the issue remains controversial.

3.5.3 The protection of traditional knowledge (TK) and folklore

Discussions in the Council for TRIPS have mainly focused on the question of the right forum for TK protection. Developing countries are almost unanimous in their firm support of the idea that TK protection should be negotiated in the WTO.[685] In these countries' view, any other forum, including WIPO, would not provide the appropriate means for the enforcement of rights.

On the other side, developed Members are opposed to treating TK in the WTO and insist that the matter be dealt with under WIPO auspices (in the IGC).[686] Some of the arguments relate to the expertise of WIPO as well as to the overloaded Doha agenda of the WTO that would not permit sufficient resources to take up a new issue such as TK.

Another controversial issue in this context is the term of protection of TK. While developing countries support the African Group's position[687] that there should be no limitation, like in the case of GIs, developed Members stress the necessity to preserve the public domain in this area.[688]

4. WTO jurisprudence

There is no WTO jurisprudence so far on this subject.[689]

5. Relationship with other international instruments

5.1 WTO Agreements

Other WTO Agreements do not have direct implications on the matters regulated under Article 27.3 (b).

---

[684] For an overview of the ongoing work in the IGC, see South Centre/CIEL IP Quarterly Update: First Quarter 2004. *Intellectual Property and Development: Overview of Developments in Multilateral, Plurilateral, and Bilateral Fora*, available at <http://www.ciel.org/Publications/IP_Update_Spring04.pdf>. See also South Centre/CIEL IP Quarterly Update: Second Quarter 2004. *Intellectual Property and Development: Overview of Developments in Multilateral, Plurilateral, and Bilateral Fora*, available at <http://www.ciel.org/Publications/IP_Update_Summer04.pdf>.

[685] See, e.g., the African Group June 2003.

[686] See, e.g., EC October 2002, p. 2: "The EC support further work towards the development of an international *sui generis* model for legal protection of TK in WIPO. At this stage, the TRIPS Council is not the right place to negotiate a protection regime for a complex new subject matter like TK or folklore. This is an issue where the WTO should ideally be able to build on the work done by the WIPO Intergovernmental Committee on Intellectual Property, Genetic Resources, Traditional Knowledge and Folklore. Depending on the outcome of the WIPO process, the TRIPS Council will have to determine whether this result warrants further work in the WTO."

[687] See the African Group June 2003, Annex Draft Decision on Traditional Knowledge, para. 4 (c).

[688] This point was raised by the EC at the March 2004 Meeting of the Council for TRIPS. The EC maintained that TK and GIs are different, the latter protecting only the name, while TK protects the knowledge incorporated in a product.

[689] The USA requested consultations under the DSU against Argentina in relation, *inter alia*, to the patentability of micro-organisms (WT/DS 196/1).

5.2 Other international instruments

5.2.1 UPOV

The International Convention for the Protection of New Varieties of Plants, administered by the Union for the Protection of New Varieties of Plants (UPOV), was established in Paris in 1961 and revised three times since then. UPOV sets forth standards, including national treatment, for the granting of "breeders' rights" as a *sui generis* form of protection for plant varieties. The last revision, which took place in 1991,[690] introduced significant reforms to the 1978 Act of the Convention.[691]

In order to be eligible for protection, a plant variety must meet the following requirements:

(i) Novelty. The variety must not – or, where the law of a state so provides, must not for more than one year – have been offered for sale or marketed with the consent of the breeder in the state where the applicant seeks protection, nor for more than four years (six years in the case of grapevines and trees, including rootstocks) in any other state. The 1991 Act makes the one-year period of grace compulsory and requires that "propagating or harvested material of the variety" must not have been "sold or otherwise disposed of to others" (Article 6 of the 1991 Act).

(ii) Distinctness. The variety must be clearly distinguishable by one or more important characteristics from any other variety whose existence is a matter of common knowledge (Article 7 of the 1991 Act).

(iii) Uniformity. Subject to the variation that may be expected from the particular features of its mode of propagation, the variety must be sufficiently uniform in its relevant characteristics (Article 8 of the 1991 Act).

(iv) Stability. Subject to the variation that may be expected from the particular features of its mode of propagation, the variety must be stable in its essential characteristics. This is the case if the latter remain unchanged after repeated propagation or, in the case of a particular cycle of propagation, at the end of each such cycle (Article 9 of the 1991 Act).

(v) Denomination. The variety must be given a denomination enabling it to be identified; the denomination must not be liable to mislead or to cause confusion as to the characteristics, value or identity of the new variety or the identity of the breeder (Article 5 (2) in conjunction with Article 20 (2) of the 1991 Act).

The Convention in Article 11 provides for the so-called right of priority. Any breeder (national or a resident of a Member state) may file a first application for

---

[690] Though new members to UPOV can only join the 1991 Act, many countries still remain obliged under the 1978 Act of the Convention.

[691] The main changes included the expansion of the coverage of protection to all plant genera and species; the extension of the breeder's exclusive rights, in certain cases, beyond reproductive material, to harvested material and products obtained through illegal use of propagating material; allowing members the option to accumulate breeders' rights and patent protection for plant varieties (a possibility excluded under the 1978 Act); and introduction of the concept of "essentially derived varieties" (For an explanation of this term, see below under this Section).

protection of a given plant variety in any of the Member states. If the breeder files an application for the same variety in any other Member state within 12 months from the filing of the first application, the breeder will enjoy a right of priority for this later application.

Protection is granted after the competent authority of the Member state in which protection is sought has ascertained that the plant variety for which protection is sought fulfils the above criteria. The examination of homogeneity and stability, as mentioned, must take into account the particularities of the mode of propagation of the variety.

According to Article 14(1)(a) of the Convention, as amended in 1991, there are seven acts of exploitation for which the breeder's authorization is required: (i) production or reproduction (multiplication); (ii) conditioning for the purpose of propagation; (iii) offering for sale; (iv) selling or other marketing; (v) exporting; (vi) importing; (vii) stocking for any of these purposes.

The above mentioned rights may be exercised in respect of the propagating material, and also in respect of the harvested material (including whole plants and parts of plants), provided that the latter has been obtained through the unauthorized use of propagating material, and that the breeder has had no reasonable opportunity to exercise his right in relation to the propagating material.

The breeder's right extends, in addition to the protected variety itself, to varieties which are not clearly distinguishable from the protected variety, which are "essentially derived" from the protected variety,[692] and those whose production requires the repeated use of the protected variety.

As in the case of UPOV 1978, according to UPOV 1991 the underlying genetic resource embodied in a protected plant variety is freely available to third parties for the purpose of breeding other varieties (breeders' exemption). This is crucial for the further improvement of existing varieties. However, Article 15(1)(iii) in conjunction with Article 14(5) of UPOV 1991 now makes clear that the breeders' exemption does not apply where the third party's breeding activities do not result in a genuinely new variety, but in one that is essentially derived from the initial, protected variety.[693] This is because the breeder's exclusive rights to the initial variety extend to those essentially derived varieties, as observed above.[694]

---

[692] See Article 14 (5)(a) of UPOV 1991. A variety which is essentially derived from a protected variety and which fulfils the criteria of novelty, distinctness, uniformity and stability, may be the subject of protection by a third party but cannot be exploited without the authorization of the breeder of the original variety. The concept of essential derivation applies to varieties which are predominantly derived from another variety and which, except for the differences that result from the act of derivation, conform to the initial variety in the expression of the essential characteristics that result from the genotype or a combination of genotypes of the initial variety (Article 14(5) of the UPOV Convention, 1991 Act).

[693] See also Biswajit Dhar, *Sui Generis Systems for Plant Variety Protection. Options under TRIPS. A Discussion Paper*, Quaker United Nations Office, Geneva 2002, p. 15 [hereinafter Dhar].

[694] In effect, this provision means that the breeder of breeders' right-protected variety A has the right to demand that the breeder of variety B secure his or her authorization to commercialise B if it was essentially derived from A. The main idea here is that breeders should not be able to acquire protection too easily for minor modifications of extant varieties or free-ride without doing any breeding of their own, problems that the increased application of biotechnology in this field appeared likely to exacerbate. Beyond resolving these particular issues, the provision was

It can thus be noted that the new concept of "essentially derived" varieties as introduced by UPOV 1991 enlarges the exclusive right of breeders, extending those rights from the initial variety to all varieties essentially derived therefrom (Article 14 (5)(a)(i)).

Under UPOV 1978, farmers were permitted to save seeds for re-use in their exploitations. UPOV 1991 made this exemption optional for Member countries, which may restrict the breeder's rights "in order to permit farmers to use for propagating purposes, on their own holdings, the product of the harvest which they have obtained by planting on their own holdings" (Article 15 (2)). This exemption, in addition, is to be applied "within reasonable limits and subject to the safeguarding of the legitimate interests of the breeder". Thus, the Diplomatic Conference that adopted the 1991 revision indicated that Article 15 (2) should not be interpreted as extending the "privilege" to sectors of agricultural or horticultural production where it is not "a common practice".[695] Here again, UPOV 1991 provided for a considerable strengthening of the exclusive breeders' rights. While under UPOV 1978, farmers were authorized to re-use in any way protected material without the obligation to pay any royalty to commercial breeders,[696] Article 15 (2) of UPOV 1991 results in an important limitation of the farmers' privilege. Farmers are not allowed to sell protected seeds, but are limited to their re-use for propagating purposes on their own land.[697]

also intended to ensure that patent rights and breeders' rights operate in a harmonious fashion in jurisdictions where plants and their parts, seeds and genes are patentable and access to these could be blocked by patent holders. Such a practice would undermine one of the main justifications for breeders' rights protection, which is that breeders should be able to secure returns on their investments but without preventing competitors from being able to freely access breeding material. An example here might be useful. Let us consider the case of a breeders' right-protected variety called A and a patented genetic element owned by a separate company. The owner of a patent on this genetic element is free to use A to produce his or her variety B and, absent of the essential derivation provision, place B on the market with no obligations to the owner of A despite the fact that B differs from A only in the addition of the patented genetic element. However, the owner of A would need a license from the producer of B to use the patented genetic element in the breeding of further varieties. In such a situation, then, patents can have the effect of blocking the breeders' exemption that breeders' rights normally provide. It should be noted here that the breeders' right-issuing office will not itself determine whether a variety is essentially derived from an earlier one. This will be left to the courts. See Graham Dutfield, *Intellectual Property Rights, Biogenetic Resources and Traditional Knowledge*, Earthscan: London 2004, p. 35; R. Jördens, *Legal and technological developments leading to this symposium: UPOV's perspective*. Paper presented at WIPO-UPOV Symposium on the Co-existence of Patents and Plant Breeders' Rights in the Promotion of Biotechnological Developments. 25 October 2002, Geneva, p. 6. It is noteworthy that the EC Directive on the Legal Protection of Biotechnological Inventions seeks to make breeders' rights and patents operate more harmoniously by providing that where the acquisition or exploitation of a breeder's right is impossible without infringing a patent, or vice versa, a compulsory license may be applied for. If issued, the licensor party will be entitled to cross-license the licensee's patent or breeder's right.

[695] It should be noted that the UPOV Convention contains minimum standards of protection and, hence, any member country may decide to provide higher protection than that resulting from the Convention rules.

[696] See Dhar, p. 15.

[697] In addition, the exercise of the farmers' privilege shall be "subject to the safeguarding of the legitimate interests of the breeder" (Article 15(2) UPOV 1991), which might be taken by some countries as an authorization to require the farmer to pay royalties to the breeder for the re-use of protected seeds.

The UPOV Convention also allows access to and the use of protected material without the consent of the title-holder in cases of public interest, against an equitable remuneration.

5.2.2 Convention on Biological Diversity

The Convention on Biological Diversity (CBD) of 1992 deals with the conservation and sustainable use of genetic resources. It recognizes the states' sovereign rights over the genetic resources residing in their jurisdictions (Article 3). The Convention requires each Contracting Party to implement several measures in order to ensure the *in-situ* and *ex-situ* conservation of genetic resources.

Article 15 of the CBD recognizes the authority of national governments to determine access to genetic resources, subject to national legislation.[698] Notwithstanding this recognition, each Contracting Party "shall endeavour to create conditions to facilitate access to genetic resources for environmentally sound uses by other Contracting Parties and not to impose restrictions that run counter to the objectives of this Convention" (Article 15.2).

According to Article 15 para. 4 and 5 of the Convention, access, where granted, shall be on mutually agreed terms and subject to prior informed consent (PIC) of the Contracting Party providing genetic resources,[699] unless otherwise determined by that Party. In addition, the CBD stipulates that each Contracting Party shall endeavour to develop and carry out scientific research based on genetic resources provided by other Contracting Parties with the full participation of, and where possible in, such Contracting Parties. Most importantly, each Contracting Party is bound to take legislative, administrative or policy measures with the aim of sharing in a fair and equitable way the results of research and development and the benefits arising from the commercial and other utilization of genetic resources with the Contracting Party providing such resources. Such sharing shall be upon mutually agreed terms (Article 1 para. 6 and 7).

Article 16 regulates the access to and transfer of technology, which are deemed "essential elements for the attainment of the objectives" of the Convention. Contracting Parties undertake to provide and/or facilitate access for and transfer to other Contracting Parties of "technologies that are relevant to the conservation and sustainable use of biological diversity or make use of genetic resources and do not cause significant damage to the environment" (Article 16.1). For the case of developing countries, access "shall be provided and/or facilitated under fair and most favourable terms, including on concessional and preferential terms

---

[698] Under the framework established by the 1983 International Undertaking on Plant Genetic Resources (IU, the predecessor of the 2001 International Treaty on Plant Genetic Resources for Food and Agriculture), plant genetic resources for food and agriculture (PGRFA) were deemed a "common heritage of mankind" and subject to a system of free exchange among the parties to the IU ("Plant genetic resources are a common heritage of mankind to be preserved, and to be freely available for use, for the benefit of present and future generations", IU Preamble).

[699] For the purpose of the Convention, the "genetic resources being provided by a Contracting Party" are only those that are provided by Contracting Parties that are countries of origin of such resources or by the Parties that have acquired the genetic resources in accordance with the Convention (Article 15.3).

where mutually agreed, and, where necessary, in accordance with the financial mechanism established by Articles 20 and 21" (Article 16.2).

The Convention addresses the case where technologies that are relevant to the conservation and sustainable use of biological diversity or make use of genetic resources are subject to intellectual property rights. In such a case, the access and transfer shall be provided on terms which recognize and are consistent with the "adequate and effective protection" of intellectual property rights (Article 16.2). However, the Contracting Parties shall cooperate "subject to national legislation and international law in order to ensure that such rights are supportive of and do not run counter to its objectives" (Article 16.5).

Moreover, each Contracting Party undertakes to take legislative, administrative or policy measures, as appropriate, with regard to intellectual property, the handling of biotechnology and the distribution of its benefits, with the aim that

- Contracting Parties, in particular those that are developing countries, which supply genetic resources are provided access to and transfer of technology which makes use of those resources, on mutually agreed terms, including technology protected by patents and other intellectual property rights, where necessary, through the provisions of Articles 20 and 21 and in accordance with international law and consistent with paragraphs 4 and 5 of Article 16 (Article 16.3).

- The private sector facilitates access to, joint development and transfer of technology referred to in Article 16.1 for the benefit of both governmental institutions and the private sector of developing countries and in this regard shall abide by the obligations included in paragraphs 2 and 3 of Article 16 (Article 16.4).

- An effective participation in biotechnological research activities is ensured to those Contracting Parties, especially developing countries, which provide the genetic resources for such research (Article 19.1).

- Priority access by Contracting Parties, especially developing countries, is promoted on a fair and equitable basis to the results and benefits arising from biotechnologies based upon genetic resources provided by those Contracting Parties. Such access shall be on mutually agreed terms (Article 19.2).

Finally, each Contracting Party shall, directly or by requiring any natural or legal person under its jurisdiction providing any living modified organism resulting from biotechnology, provide any available information about the use and safety regulations required by that Contracting Party in handling such organisms, as well as any available information on the potential adverse impact of the specific organisms concerned to the Contracting Party into which those organisms are to be introduced (Article 19.4).

The relationship between the provisions of TRIPS and the CBD has given rise to different opinions,[700] ranging from perfect harmony to collision. The collision has been associated with the possible granting of IPRs, based on or consisting of genetic resources, without observing the prior informed consent and benefit sharing obligations established by the CBD. It has also been held that a possible

---

[700] See UNCTAD-ICTSD Policy Discussion Paper. For an overview of the current discussion at the Council for TRIPS, see Section 3 of this chapter, above.

conflict may arise in the context of the *implementation* of both instruments, but not necessarily as a result of normative contradictions.[701]

6. New developments

6.1 National laws
Considerable differences exist in national laws with regard to the patentability of biotechnological inventions. The facultative exceptions allowed by Article 27.3(b) have been incorporated into the national laws of many developed and developing countries.[702] Plant and animal varieties are not patentable in the majority of countries.[703] Based on the exceptions allowed by TRIPS, some developing countries have explicitly excluded the patentability of pre-existing biological materials, including genes, unless they are genetically altered. Patents may still be granted, in these cases, for the process used to obtain a biotechnology-based product.

For most developing countries, Article 27.3(b) called for a substantial change in national law, since the majority did not protect plant varieties at the time of negotiation and adoption of the Agreement. Many developing countries have joined or are in the process of joining UPOV, while others have explored the development of non-UPOV modes of protection,[704] including the recognition of "Farmers' Rights".[705] For instance, the Parliament of India passed, on 9 August 2001, a Plant Variety Protection and Farmers' Rights Act. The Act includes provisions for farmers' varieties to be registered, with the help of governmental or non-governmental organizations. The applicant for registration of a variety must disclose information regarding the use of genetic material conserved by any tribal or rural family. Any village or local community may claim compensation for the contribution made in the evolution of a variety. A Gene Fund is created, which should be the

---

[701] "Many policy-makers and members of civil society are concerned that the TRIPS Agreement promotes private commercial interests at the expense of other important public policy objectives, such as those contained in the CBD. Specifically they are concerned that the TRIPS Agreement is creating serious challenges to the successful implementation of the CBD, including in relation to . . . access and benefit sharing, protection of traditional knowledge, technology transfer, and the conservation and sustainable use of biological diversity", WWF/CIEL, *Biodiversity & Intellectual Property Rights: Reviewing Intellectual Property Rights in Light of the Objectives of the Convention on Biological Diversity*, Joint Discussion Paper, Gland–Geneva 2001, pp. 11–12.

[702] See, e.g., the replies to the questionnaire circulated by the WTO Secretariat, IP/C/W/122 and 126; OMPI/BIOT/WG/99/1, 28 October 1999. See also OECD, *Intellectual property practices in the field of biotechnology*, Working Party of the Trade Committee, TD/TC/WP(98)15/Final, Paris 1999 [hereinafter OECD].

[703] Only in five OECD countries plants *per se*, parts of plants *and* plant varieties are patentable. In only six of such countries patents may cover animals *per se*, animal organs *and* animal varieties (OECD, p. 5). Many patent laws adopted in developing countries have excluded the patentability of plants and animals or, more narrowly, of plant varieties and animal races.

[704] See, e.g., Organization of African States (OAU), *African Model Legislation for the Protection of the Rights of Local Communities, Farmers and Breeders, and for the Regulation of Access to Biological Resources*.

[705] See on this concept, Carlos Correa, *Options for the implementation of Farmers' Rights at the national level*, South Centre, Working Paper, Geneva 2000.

recipient of all revenues payable to the farming communities. The Act also contains a provision on "Farmers Rights" according to which

> "The farmer ... shall be deemed to be entitled to save, use, sow, resow, exchange, share or sell his farm produce including seed of a variety protected under this Act in the same manner as he was entitled before the coming into force of this Act, provided that the farmer shall not be entitled to sell branded seed of a variety protected under this Act" (Section 39 (iv)).[706]

Peru has established a comprehensive legal system for the protection of traditional knowledge associated with biodiversity.[707] This law reflects the CBD requirements of prior informed consent and benefit sharing. It enables indigenous and local communities to assert their rights over collectively held knowledge. For this purpose, the law obliges interested parties to obtain the prior informed consent of those communities providing the biodiversity-related knowledge. In case of industrial or commercial use, interested parties are required to sign a contract with an organization representing the indigenous communities. According to Article 27 of the new law, such contracts (or licences) have to include, *inter alia*, the right of indigenous communities to claim a minimum compensation, i.e. 5 percent of gross sales of commercial products derived from collective knowledge.

6.2 International instruments

6.2.1 The ITPGRFA

In November 2001, the International Treaty on Plant Genetic Resources for Food and Agriculture (ITPGRFA) was agreed upon at the FAO Conference in Rome. It builds on the 1983 International Undertaking on Plant Genetic Resources for Food and Agriculture (IU) and entered into force on 29 June 2004, after ratification by 40 Parties. As opposed to the IU, the ITPGRFA contains legally-binding obligations with respect to access to and benefit-sharing of plant genetic resources in the particular area of food and agriculture. It harmonizes the earlier provisions of the IU with the CBD, recognizing both the Parties' sovereignty over their plant genetic resources and their dependence for food security on the exchange of those resources with other Parties. The ITPGRFA seeks to avoid high transaction costs resulting from bilateral exchanges of breeding material as required under the CBD (Article 15) by establishing a multilateral system to facilitate access and benefit-sharing of genetic resources.[708] This multilateral system of exchange operates by means of a standard Material Transfer Agreement to be adopted by the

---

[706] For the purpose of clause (iv) branded seed means any seed put in a package or any other container and labeled in a manner indicating that such seed is of a variety protected under this Act.

[707] Law No. 27811, in force since 10 August 2002. For more details, see M. Ruiz and I. Lapena, *New Peruvian Law Protects Indigenous Peoples' Collective Knowledge*, in: Bridges Between Trade and Sustainable Development, September 2002 (year 6, no. 6), p. 15, available at <http://www.ictsd.org/monthly/bridges/BRIDGES6-6.pdf>.

[708] See Tansey, p. 10.

ITPGRFA's Governing Body (Article 12.4). A general pool of the resources of those crops covered by the Treaty is established and made available for further research, breeding and education purposes.[709]

As far as the relationship between the ITPGRFA and TRIPS is concerned, it is in particular Article 12.3(d) of the ITPGRFA that has been subject to controversy.[710] There are several areas of possible conflict of those two agreements. Article 12.3(d) and (f), dealing with access to plant genetic resources for food and agriculture, provides that such access shall be provided, *inter alia*, according to the following conditions:

(d) Recipients shall not claim any intellectual property or other rights that limit the facilitated access to the plant genetic resources for food and agriculture, or their genetic parts or components, *in the form received* from the Multilateral System; (emphasis added)

(f) Access to plant genetic resources for food and agriculture protected by intellectual and other property rights shall be consistent with relevant international agreements, and with relevant national laws;

Paragraph (f) makes clear that the ITPGRFA is not intended to circumvent the disciplines of TRIPS. It thus informs the interpretation of paragraph (d), which cannot be seen as an authorization of the Parties to violate the TRIPS patent provisions. According to its terms, paragraph (d) does not disallow the patenting of plant genetic resources in general, but only *in the form received* from the Multilateral System. This clearly excludes the patenting of seeds as acquired from a seed bank. On the other hand, it is not clear if the provision also excludes the patenting of such genetic material that has been modified or isolated from its natural environment. A more detailed analysis of this issue would however go beyond the scope of this book.

Finally, Article 13 of the ITPGRFA provides that benefits accruing from the facilitated access to the covered plant genetic resources shall be shared fairly and equitably (Article 13.1). Four benefit-sharing mechanisms are foreseen (Article 13.2): exchange of information; access to and transfer of technology; capacity building; and sharing of the benefits arising from commercialization.

Article 13.2(b)(i) of the Treaty subjects the access to and transfers of technology to the respect of applicable property rights and access laws. Subsection (d)(ii) of the same provision specifies that the standard Material Transfer Agreement (i.e. the Treaty's standardized means of providing facilitated access to the covered genetic resources) shall include a requirement obliging recipients of material accessed from the Multilateral System to pay to a specific financial resources body an equitable share of the benefits arising from the commercialization of products incorporating such material.[711]

---

[709] For further details on the ITPGRFA, see Tansey, p. 10, as well as the UNCTAD-ICTSD Policy Discussion Paper.

[710] See UNCTAD-ICTSD Policy Discussion Paper, p. 109.

[711] For more details on the benefit-sharing provisions of the ITPGRFA see Tansey, p. 11. On the ITPGRFA's approach to Farmers' Rights see UNCTAD-ICTSD Policy Discussion Paper, p. 109.

6.2.2 The Doha Declaration

As mentioned under Section 3 of this chapter, paragraph 19 of the 2001 Doha Ministerial Declaration provides the Council for TRIPS with a mandate to examine, under the review of Article 27.3(b), issues such as the relationship between TRIPS and the Convention on Biological Diversity and the protection of traditional knowledge and folklore.

6.2.3 The COP 7

At its seventh meeting in February 2004, the Conference of the Parties (COP) to the Convention on Biological Diversity (CBD) decided to mandate its Ad Hoc Open-ended Working Group on Access and Benefit-sharing to elaborate and negotiate an international regime on access to genetic resources and benefit-sharing with the aim of adopting instruments to effectively implement the provisions in Article 15 and Article 8(j) of the Convention[712] and the three objectives of the Convention (i.e. conservation of biodiversity; sustainable use of biodiversity; and fair and equitable benefit sharing).[713] In the same context, the COP also addressed the relationship between IPRs and genetic resources and associated traditional knowledge:

> "7. *Requests* the Ad hoc Open-ended Working Group on Access and Benefit-Sharing to identify issues related to the disclosure of origin of genetic resources and associated traditional knowledge in applications for intellectual property rights, including those raised by a proposed international certificate of origin/source/legal provenance, and transmit the results of this examination to the World Intellectual Property Organization and other relevant forums.
>
> 8. *Invites* the World Intellectual Property Organization to examine, and where appropriate address, taking into account the need to ensure that this work is supportive of and does not run counter to the objectives of the Convention on Biological Diversity, issues regarding the interrelation of access to genetic resources and disclosure requirements in intellectual property rights applications, including, *inter alia*:
>
> (a) Options for model provisions on proposed disclosure requirements;
>
> (b) Practical options for intellectual property rights application procedures with regard to the triggers of disclosure requirements;
>
> (c) Options for incentive measures for applicants;
>
> (d) Identification of the implications for the functioning of disclosure requirements in various World Intellectual Property Organization-administered treaties;
>
> (e) Intellectual property-related issues raised by proposed international certificate of origin/source/legal provenance; and regularly provide reports to the Convention on Biological Diversity on its work, in particular on actions or steps proposed to

---

[712] On Article 15, CBD, see above, Section 5.2. Article 8(j), CBD provides that each Contracting Party shall, as far as possible and appropriate, "Subject to its national legislation, respect, preserve and maintain knowledge, innovations and practices of indigenous and local communities embodying traditional lifestyles relevant for the conservation and sustainable use of biological diversity and promote their wider application with the approval and involvement of the holders of such knowledge, innovations and practices and encourage the equitable sharing of the benefits arising from the utilization of such knowledge, innovations and practices".

[713] See UNEP/CBD/COP/7/L.28 of 20 February 2004.

address the above issues, in order for the Convention on Biological Diversity to provide additional information to the World Intellectual Property Organization for its consideration in the spirit of mutual supportiveness;

9. *Invites* the United Nations Conference on Trade and Development and other relevant international organisations to examine the issues in, and related to, the matters specified in paragraphs 7 and 8 in a manner supportive of the objectives of the Convention on Biological Diversity and prepare a report for submission to the on-going process of the work of the Convention on Biological Diversity on access and benefit sharing."[714]

6.3 Regional and bilateral contexts

6.3.1 Regional and bilateral

The European Directive on Biotechnological Inventions (No. 96/9/EC of March 11, 1996) has set forth, as mentioned, specific standards for the patent protection of biotechnological inventions. The Directive may be considered as essentially declaratory of long standing law throughout much of Europe.[715]

In numerous bilateral and regional agreements the issue of patentability of biotechnological inventions and of the protection of plant varieties have been addressed. In many cases such agreements require the patentability of plants and animals, and the adherence (by the developing country partner) to the UPOV Convention. In fact, the most active negotiations on TRIPS-plus provisions in the area of biotechnology have been taking place on the regional and bilateral levels. An exhaustive analysis of these agreements would go beyond the scope of this Book. Recent examples include the Central American Free Trade Agreement,[716] NAFTA, the draft Free Trade Area of the Americas (FTAA), and the free trade agreements USA – Jordan, EU – Mexico and some Euro-Mediterranean Association Agreements.[717] These agreements declare UPOV to be the appropriate vehicle for the protection of plant breeders' rights, despite Members' freedom under Article 27.3(b) to implement a non-UPOV *sui generis* system of protection. The effect of such regional and bilateral agreements is illustrated by the quickly increasing number of new Members of UPOV.[718]

---

[714] See UNEP/CBD/COP/7/L.28, pages 10/11.

[715] See, e.g., Grubb, p. 213.

[716] The negotiations between the USA and El Salvador, Guatemala, Honduras, Nicaragua and Costa Rica were concluded in January 2004.

[717] See OECD, *The Relationship Between Regional Trade Agreements and the Multilateral Trading System: Intellectual Property Rights*, TD/TC/WP(2002)28/FINAL, 2002. In the case of the free trade agreement between the USA and Chile, the latter has committed to adhere to the 1991 Act of UPOV by 1 January, 2009. In addition, the Chile – USA FTA provides a "best effort" clause in order for each Party to undertake best efforts to develop and propose legislation to make available patent protection for plants under certain circumstances. For a detailed analysis of the USA – Chile FTA, see Roffe, 2004.

[718] After 1 January 1995, Belarus, Bolivia, Brazil, Bulgaria, Chile, China, Colombia, Croatia, Ecuador, Estonia, Kenya, Kyrgyzstan, Latvia, Lithuania, Mexico, Nicaragua, Panama, Paraguay, Portugal, the Republic of Korea, the Republic of Moldova, Romania, the Russian Federation, Singapore, Slovenia, Trinidad and Tobago, Tunisia, and Ukraine became Members of UPOV 1991 or 1978.

6.4 Proposals for review

As mentioned above, several proposals have been made in relation to the review of Article 27.3(b).[719]

7. Comments, including economic and social implications

Although biotechnology was known since fermentation was used to produce beer and make bread, the economic interest in biotechnology has increased extraordinarily since "modern" biotechnology emerged in the late 1970s as a result of the development of monoclonal antibody technology and the techniques of molecular biology and recombinant DNA.[720] Since the 1980s considerable progress has been made in the development of biotechnology-based pharmaceuticals (e.g., recombinant erithropoietin, growth hormone) as well as in the application of genetic engineering to animals and plants (e.g., transgenic varieties resistant to herbicides or insects).

While genetic engineering-based industries are largely concentrated in developed countries, developing countries possess most of the biodiversity available in the world. They are the source of genetic resources of great value for agriculture and industry (e.g., medicinal plants). Traditional farmers, in particular, have contributed in the past and continue to improve plant varieties and to preserve biodiversity. They provide gene pools crucial for major food crops and other plants. Developing countries have voiced their concerns, and in some cases have taken concrete action in relation to what they consider an illegitimate appropriation by foreign companies or researchers under the patent system.[721, 722]

The recognition of IPRs, more specifically of patents, on plants has also raised significant concerns. Many, particularly in developing countries, fear that IPRs may prevent farmers from re-using saved seeds, thus limiting traditional practices that are essential for their survival. In addition, the patenting of certain traits (e.g., higher oil content, disease resistance, higher yield, etc.), genes or plant varieties may limit further research and breeding, including in crops essential for food security. Finally, according to one view, IPRs may contribute to further uniform and monoculture strategies that erode biodiversity, and to increased concentration in farming and in the seeds industry.[723] Small

---

[719] See Section 3 of this chapter.

[720] CEFI, *The Challenges of Biotechnology*, Madrid 1997, p. 218.

[721] Thus, the Council for Scientific and Industrial Research (CSIR) from India asked for a re-examination of the U.S. patent No. 5,401,5041 granted for the wound healing properties of *turmeric*. The U.S. Patent and Trademark Office (USPTO) revoked this patent after ascertaining that there was no novelty, the innovation having been used and reported on in India for centuries. India has also set up a project to document traditional medicinal knowledge in a digital form, and has proposed the inclusion of a special classification in the International Patent Classification (IPC) in order to enable the retrieval of information on traditional knowledge for patent examination.

[722] See in this regard the Communication from the USA to the Council of TRIPS, IP/C/W/209, 3 October 2000.

[723] In this context, it has been observed that the patenting of genetic material through one company may prevent other companies from further research depending on that genetic material. A frequent reaction in both developed and developing countries is an increasing number of mergers and

and medium farmers and breeders are likely to suffer the most devastating impact.[724]

In the opinion of the proponents of an expanded and reinforced, patent-based approach, however, protection is required to provide an incentive to innovate and the necessary reward for R&D high investments. In their view, the possible negative impact of IPR protection would be offset by benefits in terms of new and better plant varieties.

The possible development of *sui generis* regimes for plant varieties and for traditional knowledge[725] has also attracted considerable interest as means to do justice to traditional and indigenous communities, and to provide them with economic compensation for their contributions.[726]

Finally, attention shall be drawn to the recommendations adopted by the Commission on Intellectual Property Rights (IPR Commission) in its final report. As to plants and intellectual property protection, the Commission concluded:

> "Developing countries should generally not provide patent protection for plants and animals, as is allowed under Article 27.3(b) of TRIPS, because of the restrictions patents may place on use of seed by farmers and researchers. Rather they should consider different forms of *sui generis* systems for plant varieties.
>
> Those developing countries with limited technological capacity should restrict the application of patenting in agricultural biotechnology consistent with TRIPS, and they should adopt a restrictive definition of the term "micro-organism."
>
> Countries that have, or wish to develop, biotechnology-related industries may wish to provide certain types of patent protection in this area. If they do so, specific exceptions to the exclusive rights, for plant breeding and research, should be established. The extent to which patent rights extend to the progeny or multiplied product of the patented invention should also be examined and a clear exception provided for farmers to reuse seeds.
>
> The continuing review of Article 27.3(b) of TRIPS should also preserve the right of countries not to grant patents for plants and animals, including genes and genetically modified plants and animals, as well as to develop *sui generis* regimes for the protection of plant varieties that suit their agricultural systems. Such regimes should permit access to the protected varieties for further research and breeding, and provide at least for the right of farmers to save and plant-back seed, including the possibility of informal sale and exchange."[727]

---

acquisitions by multinational companies in order to control or benefit from other companies' patents. This again creates important entry barriers to innovative start-ups, thus raising serious concerns about the maintenance of effective competition in the agricultural industries' sector. See IPR Commission report, p. 65. The report is available at <http://www.iprcommission.org/graphic/documents/final_report.htm>. The page numbers refer to the pdf version of the full report as available on the internet and as a hard copy.

[724] For an analysis of the implications of patents on plants, see The Crucible Group, *People, plants and patents. The impact of intellectual property on trade, plant biodiversity, and rural society*, IDRC, Ottawa, 1994.

[725] See, e.g., the OAU *African Model Legislation for the Protection of the Rights of Local Communities, Farmers and Breeders, and for the Regulation of Access to Biological Resources*.

[726] For a review of the literature on this subject, see Graham Dutfield, *Literature survey on intellectual property rights and sustainable human development*, Geneva 2002.

[727] IPR Commission report, p. 66.

With regard to the issue of access to plant genetic resources and farmers' rights, the Commission recommended that:

> "Developed and developing countries should accelerate the process of ratification of the FAO International Treaty on Plant Genetic Resources for Food and Agriculture and should, in particular, implement the Treaty's provisions relating to:
>
> • Not granting IPR protection of any material transferred in the framework of the multilateral system, in the form received.
>
> • Implementation of Farmers' Rights at the national level, including (a) protection of traditional knowledge relevant to plant genetic resources for food and agriculture; (b) the right to equitably participate in sharing benefits arising from the utilisation of plant genetic resources for food and agriculture; (c) the right to participate in making decisions, at the national level, on matters related to the conservation and sustainable use of plant genetic resources for food and agriculture."[728]

The Commission also addressed the concern that overly broad patents might inhibit further research by recommending:

> "Developing countries providing patent protection for biotechnological inventions should assess whether they are effectively susceptible to industrial application, taking account of the USPTO guidelines as appropriate.
>
> Developing countries should adopt the best mode provision to ensure that the patent applicant does not withhold information that would be useful to third parties. If developing countries allow patents over genes as such, regulations or guidelines should provide that claims be limited to the uses effectively disclosed in the patent specification, so as to encourage further research and commercial application of any new uses of the gene."[729]

---

[728] Ibid, p. 69.
[729] Ibid, pp. 117/118.

22: Patents: Rights Conferred

Article 28   Rights Conferred

1. A patent shall confer on its owner the following exclusive rights:

(a) where the subject matter of a patent is a product, to prevent third parties not having the owner's consent from the acts of: making, using, offering for sale, selling, or importing* for these purposes that product;

(b) where the subject matter of a patent is a process, to prevent third parties not having the owner's consent from the act of using the process, and from the acts of: using, offering for sale, selling, or importing for these purposes at least the product obtained directly by that process.

2. Patent owners shall also have the right to assign, or transfer by succession, the patent and to conclude licensing contracts.

[Footnote]*: "This right, like all other rights conferred under this Agreement in respect of the use, sale, importation or other distribution of goods, is subject to the provisions of Article 6."[730]

Article 32   Revocation/Forfeiture

An opportunity for judicial review of any decision to revoke or forfeit a patent shall be available.

Article 33   Term of Protection

The term of protection available shall not end before the expiration of a period of twenty years counted from the filing date.*

[Footnote]*: "It is understood that those Members which do not have a system of original grant may provide that the term of protection shall be computed from the filing date in the system of original grant."

---

[730] Article 6 of TRIPS stipulates that "For the purposes of dispute settlement under this Agreement, subject to the provisions of Articles 3 and 4 nothing in this Agreement shall be used to address the issue of the exhaustion of intellectual property rights."

1. Introduction: terminology, definition and scope

Patents are granted in relation to products and processes, dealt with in paragraphs 1 and 2, respectively, of Article 28. A product is a "thing or substance produced by natural process or manufacture."[731] A process is a "series of operations in manufacture, printing, photography, etc".[732]

Article 28 obliges Members to ensure that patent owners enjoy exclusive rights, and details the minimum content of such rights, which may be exercised with regard to acts performed *during* manufacturing as well as to acts performed *after* manufacturing. The exclusive[733] nature of the rights conferred is inherent to patent grants, though not to all forms of intellectual property.[734] It permits the title-holder, if successful in the exploitation of the invention, to obtain significant rents during the lifetime of the patent, thus fulfilling one of the basic purposes of patent grants.

While defining the patentee's rights as exclusive, the Agreement makes it clear that patents confer a negative right, that is, the legal faculty to prevent others from doing certain acts relating to the invention (*ius excluendi*), rather than a positive right with regard to his products or processes.[735] This distinction is important for the interpretation of Article 28, as well of other provisions in this Section.[736]

Much of the content of Article 28.1(a) reflected the status of prior legislation on the matter. Article 28.1(b), which provides for the extension of the protection conferred on a process patent to the product directly obtained by that process, introduced in contrast a standard applied in many developed countries but generally unknown in most developing countries.

Article 32 addresses an important issue in patent law: the revocation[737] or forfeiture[738] of a patent. However, this provision only establishes a procedural requirement (the availability of judicial review), and does not stipulate the grounds or other substantive conditions for such acts to take place, thereby leaving considerable leeway to Members to legislate on the matter. In particular, Article 32

---

[731] The Concise Oxford Dictionary, p. 821.

[732] The Concise Oxford Dictionary, p. 820.

[733] "Exclusive" means "shutting out, not admitting of", *The Concise Oxford Dictionary*, p. 336.

[734] See, e.g. Articles 22.2 (geographical indications) and 39.1 (undisclosed information) of the Agreement.

[735] Thus, the acquisition of a patent right on a product does not empower the patent owner to produce it if this were contrary, for instance, to environmental regulations, or to commercialize it, if prior marketing approval were required.

[736] For example, the enjoyment of "patent rights" in Article 27.1, if strictly interpreted, should be understood in relation to products made, used, sold, etc, by a third party, and not to the own patentee's products.

[737] "Revocation" is the result of an act of repealing, annulling, withdrawing, rescinding, or cancelling a right. See *The Concise Oxford Dictionary*, p. 893. In the present context, a patent can be revoked where grounds exist that would have justified a refusal to grant the patent in the first place.

[738] "Forfeiture" takes place when a right is lost as penalty of crime, neglect, etc. See *The Concise Oxford Dictionary*, p. 384. As opposed to the *revocation* of a patent, forfeiture does not address the situation where the patent should not have been granted from the beginning, but rather where the original grant was justified, and only afterwards the patentee behaved in a way that forfeited his right.

does not limit a Member's right to determine the *grounds* for revocation and forfeiture.

The duration of patent rights is established in Article 33, which mandates a minimum term of twenty years counted from the date of filing of the application. Since under the Paris Convention for the Protection of Industrial Property members were free to determine the duration of patents, considerable diversity existed on this matter at the time of the negotiation of TRIPS. Article 33 is likely to have a powerful harmonizing effect to the extent that, as suggested by recent legislative changes, most countries tend to adopt the 20 years term. The interpretation of this provision has been addressed in one case decided under the Dispute Settlement Understanding, as discussed below.

2. History of the provisions

2.1 Situation pre-TRIPS

Article 28.1(a) reflects standards followed in many countries before TRIPS. Though under different formulations, patent laws had generally covered acts of making, selling or otherwise disposing of the invention. Some laws also covered acts of keeping or stocking a patented product, as well as acts by a third party who assisted in the preparations for infringing acts ("contributory infringement").[739] In some cases, acts of using the invention were subject to the patentee's exclusive rights, including use without making or sale.[740] In contrast, prior to TRIPS the act of importation was not generally enumerated as an exclusive right of the patent owner, though in some jurisdictions such act was indirectly covered.[741]

The extension of protection to products directly obtained by the patented process, as provided for under Article 28.1(b), had not obtained broad acceptance before TRIPS. The Paris Convention alluded to the rights in respect of products obtained by a patented process in a foreign country, but deferred to national law the option to recognize exclusive rights in respect of the imported products (Article 5*quater*).

Such extension had been applied in some developed countries, often with considerable controversy.[742] In the case of the USA, the extension was only introduced by a legislative amendment in 1988.[743] The extension was not provided, however, in the laws of most developing countries, where process patents only covered, in

---

[739] See, e.g., W. Cornish, *Intellectual property: Patents, copyright, trade marks and allied rights*, second edition, Sweet & Maxwell, New York 1989, p. 167.

[740] For example, acts of purchasing and using a machine (see, e.g., Chisum and Jacobs, pp. 2–217).

[741] See, e.g., Lionel Bently and Brad Sherman, *Intellectual property law*, Oxford University Press, New York 2001, p. 490 [hereinafter Bently and Sherman].

[742] See, e.g., Hansen and Hirsch, pp. 356–359; Joseph Straus, *Reversal of the burden of proof, the principle of 'fair and equitable procedures' and preliminary injunctions under the TRIPS Agreement*, The Journal of World Intellectual Property 2000, vol. 3, No. 6, pp. 807–823 (809) [hereinafter Straus].

[743] Process Patent Amendments Act of 1988. Prior to this amendment, a patent owner could petition the U.S. International Trade Commission for an order prohibiting importation of a product under Tariff Act 337, only if "an industry in the United States, relating to the Article protected by the patent...concerned, exists or is in the process of being established", see, e.g., Chisum and Jacobs, pp. 2–220.

general, the right to exclude others from the domestic use of the process, but not to impede the importation of products manufactured abroad with the patented process. The inclusion of this obligation in TRIPS was the outcome of a long and difficult negotiation.[744]

Great diversity existed before TRIPS in relation to the duration of patent rights. Under the Paris Convention, members had full freedom to determine the term of protection. Different terms were provided for by national laws, sometimes calculated from grant, and in other cases from filing. Thus, many developed and developing countries had patent duration of 15 to 17 years counted from the date of grant. In some countries, protection was even shorter. For instance, in India, process patents for food, drug and medicines were granted for five years from the date or sealing or seven years from the date of filing, whichever was shorter.[745]

2.2 Negotiating history

2.2.1 Exclusive rights

2.2.1.1 The Anell Draft. The Anell Draft reflected considerable differences between parties with regard to the enumeration of exclusive rights:

"2. Rights Conferred

2.1A A patent shall confer on its owner at least the following exclusive rights:

(a) to prevent third parties not having his consent from the acts of: making, using, [putting on the market, offering] [or selling] [or importing] [or importing or stocking for these purposes] the product which is the subject matter of the patent.

(b) where the subject matter of a patent is a process, to prevent third parties not having his consent from the act of using the process, and from the acts of: using, [putting on the market, offering] [selling,] [or importing,] [or importing or stocking for these purposes,] at least the product obtained directly by that process.

2.1B Once a patent has been granted, the owner of the patent shall have the following rights:

(a) The right to prevent others from making, using or selling the patented product or using the patented process for commercial or industrial purposes.

(b) The right to assign, or transfer by succession, the patent and to conclude licence contracts.

(c) The right to a reasonable remuneration when the competent authorities of a PARTY to the present agreement use a patent for government purpose or provide for the granting of a licence of right or a compulsory licence. Such reasonable remuneration will be determined having regard to the economic situation of the PARTY, the nature of the invention, the cost involved in developing the patent and other relevant factors.

(See also point 5A.3.9 below)"

---

[744] See, Gervais, p. 154.
[745] Section 53(1) of the Patent Act, 1970.

2.2.1.2 The Brussels Draft. The Brussels Draft (3 December 1990) on exclusive patent rights was essentially identical to the current version of Article 28; however, the part now contained in Article 28 concerning the rights of a process patent holder in the products directly obtained by that process was bracketed, thus indicating the negotiators' disagreement on this issue:

"Article 28: Rights Conferred

1. A patent shall confer on its owner the following exclusive rights:

(a) to prevent third parties not having his consent from the acts of: making, using, offering for sale, selling, or importing [footnote] for these purposes the product which is the subject matter of the patent;

(b) where the subject matter of a patent is a process, to prevent third parties not having his consent from the act of using the process [, and from the acts of: using, offering for sale, selling, or importing for these purposes at least the product obtained directly by that process].

2. Patent owners shall also have the right to assign, or transfer by succession, the patent and to conclude licensing contracts.

[Footnote]: "This right, like all other rights conferred under this Agreement in respect of the use, sale, importation or other distribution of goods, is subject to the provisions of Article 6."

2.2.2 Revocation/Forfeiture

2.2.2.1 The Anell Draft. The Anell Draft provided:

"6. Revocation/Forfeiture

6A.1 A patent [[may not be revoked or forfeited [merely] on grounds [of non-working] stipulated in 5A.2 above]] [may only be revoked on grounds that it fails to meet the requirements of 1.1 and 1.3 above].

6A.2 Judicial review shall be available in the case of forfeiture of a patent where applicable.

6B A patent may be revoked on grounds of public interest and where the conditions for the grant of compulsory licences are not fulfilled."

2.2.2.2 The Brussels Draft. The Brussels Draft was identical to the current version of Article 32 TRIPS.

2.2.3 Term of protection

2.2.3.1 The Anell Draft. The Anell Draft provided:

"4. Term of Protection

4A.1 The term of protection shall be [at least] [15 years from the date of filing of the application, except for inventions in the field of pharmaceuticals for which the term shall be 20 years] [20 years from the date of filing of the application] [or where other applications are invoked in the said application, 20 years from the filing date of the earliest filed of the invoked applications which is not the priority date of the said application].[746]

4A.2 PARTIES are encouraged to extend the term of patent protection in appropriate cases, to compensate for delays regarding the exploitation of the patented invention caused by regulatory approval processes.

4B It shall be a matter for national legislation to determine the duration of protection."

2.2.3.2 The Brussels Draft

"[1A The term of protection available shall not end before the expiration of a period of 20 years counted from the filing date. [footnote]]

[1B It shall be a matter for national legislation to determine the term of protection.]

[Footnote]: It is understood that those Members which do not have a system of original grant may provide that the term of protection shall be computed from the filing date in the system of original grant."

It was the former proposal (minimum term of 20 years) that was finally adopted as Article 33 of TRIPS.

3. Possible interpretations

3.1 Article 28.1 (a)

Rights Conferred

28.1. A patent shall confer on its owner the following exclusive rights:

(a) where the subject matter of a patent is a product, to prevent third parties not having the owner's consent from the acts of: making, using, offering for sale, selling, or importing [6] for these purposes that product;

Article 28.1, largely inspired by Article 19 of the WIPO draft Patent Law Treaty,[747] enumerates the exclusive rights in relation to a product in a manner substantially similar to pre-existing laws. It covers acts of:

(a) "Making", meaning constructing, framing, creating, from parts or other substances.[748] The exclusive rights may be exercised in relation to any acts resulting in the production of the product, including by manufacturing and other methods

---

[746] At the initial stages of the TRIPS negotiations, Japan proposed a term of 15 years from the date of grant, as available in its law; Australia and New Zealand 16 years from the date of filing a complete specification. The EC and USA proposed a higher standard of 20 years from the date of filing, which was finally adopted. Countries supporting a shorter term did not unite to propose any alternative and, hence, the issue was decided by default, see Jayashree Watal, *Intellectual property rights in the WTO and developing countries*, Kluwer Law International, The Hague/London/Boston 2001, p. 114.

[747] See, e.g., Gervais, p. 153.

[748] The Concise Oxford Dictionary, p. 611.

(e.g., extraction from a natural product) independently of the scale of production[749] and, most importantly, of the method of production used. This signifies that whatever the process used by a third party, an infringement would occur whenever the patented product is made, even if an independently developed and inventive process were used.[750] Similarly, it is immaterial for the purpose of establishing an infringement whether the product is made for domestic consumption or for export.[751]

In principle, the patent owner may prevent acts of "making", including where a product is made for non-commercial purposes. In order to avoid this effect, patent laws normally provide for exceptions in respect of acts done for private non-commercial purposes, and/or for scientific research and education.[752]

Few problems have arisen under national laws in determining what "making" means, except in the cases of repair or modification of a patented product, where infringement depends on the extent of repair or modification and on the circumstances of the particular case.[753]

(b) "Using", meaning utilization of the product by a third party. This concept may include a sales demonstration, but not merely possession or display,[754] acts of commercialization which do not entail a sale, such as renting or leasing, as well as the utilization of a product as part of a land vehicle, aircraft or vessel.[755] It may permit the right holder to act against the acquirer and user of an infringing product, and not only against the party who manufactured or sold it.

However, the exclusive right of the patent owner in respect of acts of "using" is subject to the principle of exhaustion of rights. According to this principle, as interpreted under most laws, the patent owner cannot control the use of the product after its first sale. National laws differ, however, with respect to the concept and geographical scope of the exhaustion principle. Exhaustion may be established at the national level (i.e., for acts taking place within the country only); at the regional level (e.g., for acts occurring in countries which are members of a common

---

[749] Many laws provide for an exception to the exclusive patentee's rights for the preparation for individual cases, in a pharmacy or by a medical doctor, of a medicine in accordance with a medical prescription.

[750] Unless a dependent patent and a compulsory licence – under the terms allowed by Article 31 (l) of the TRIPS Agreement – were obtained by the third party.

[751] In the USA, for instance, making an entire patented product for export infringes the patent (see. e.g. Chisum and Jacobs, pp. 2–219). The coverage of exports under the patentee's exclusive rights is one of the underlying problems in the discussion of paragraph 6 of the Doha Declaration on the TRIPS Agreement and Public Health, and the reason why an exception based on Article 30 of the Agreement was originally suggested. See the "Doha Ministerial Declaration on the TRIPS Agreement and Public Health" [hereinafter "the Doha Declaration"], WT/MIN(01)/DEC/W/2, 14 November 2001. See also the EU submission to the Council for TRIPS, IP/C/W/339, 4 March 2002. For more details on paragraph 6 of the Doha Declaration, see Chapter 25.

[752] See Chapter 23.

[753] See, e.g., Bently and Sherman, pp. 488.

[754] See, e.g., Chisum and Jacobs, p. 2–217.

[755] See Article 5ter of the Paris Convention.

market); or with an international scope. Several countries have followed this latter approach in recent changes of legislation.[756]

(c) "Offering for sale", including acts aimed at the commercialization of a product, even where the latter has not yet occurred. This right may be deemed partially implicit in the right of selling, but this is not necessarily the case in some jurisdictions.[757]

(d) "Selling", covering transactions for the transfer, against a price, of a patented product. It represents one of the most common modes of infringement. Acts of selling without making are covered under this right, for instance, by a person who purchases and resells a patented product, or by a person who imports it.

(e) "Importing", covering the introduction of the patented product into the country where protection is conferred, even if done for non-commercial purposes or free of cost. The importation of a product has not been generally enumerated in national patent laws as part of the exclusive rights.[758] Footnote 6 subjects the application of this provision to the principle of exhaustion of rights, as established by national law.[759]

Article 28.1 does not refer to acts by a contributory infringer, nor to acts of keeping or stocking a patented product, which are specifically contemplated under some national laws.

3.2 Article 28.1(b)

> (b) where the subject matter of a patent is a process, to prevent third parties not having the owner's consent from the act of using the process, ...

Article 28.1(b) describes the acts that can be prevented by the owner of a process patent. Process patents are generally deemed to include methods of "making" a product.[760] The patent owner may prevent the use of such method in the country of registration of the patent. If a product is obtainable by different processes, a

---

[756] See Chapter 5.

[757] For instance, in the USA, the patent law does not provide for penalties for the offer to sell a patented product. See, e.g., Richard Neff and Fran Smallson (1994), *NAFTA. Protecting and enforcing intellectual property rights in North America*, SHEPARD'S, Colorado, p. 86.

[758] In some jurisdictions it has been held that importation amounts to infringement of a patent only when a person deals with the patented invention in the course of trade or for the purposes of profit (Bently and Sherman, p. 490). In the USA, importing a patented product has not been deemed, alone, an infringement, but any subsequent sale or use of the product could infringe (see, e.g., Chisum and Jacobs, pp. 2–220).

[759] See Chapter 5.

[760] In the USA, processes also encompass "method-of-use" patents, which allow the protection of inventions consisting of the use of a product not suggested by the prior art, when the product is known and not patentable. Method-of-use patents do not entail protection of the product as such. See, e.g., Merges, p. 489. The TRIPS Agreement, however, does not oblige to follow this particular approach.

third party can legally make it, provided that it employs a different process,[761] and provided that the patentee does not also hold a patent on that product.[762]

> ...and from the acts of: using, offering for sale, selling, or importing for these purposes at least the product obtained directly by that process.

This provision also allows for the extension of the protection conferred on a process to the product "obtained directly by that process". This extension, coupled with the reversal of burden of proof,[763] implies a significant strengthening of patent rights on process inventions under TRIPS.

Without such extension, a process patent granted in country A could not be invoked in cases where the patented process has been utilized in country B and the resulting product is imported into country A. The extension of the protection to the product obtained directly by the patented process addresses this problem. It constitutes an exception to the general principle according to which the protection conferred for an invention is defined by the object of the invention.

Article 28.1(b) applies when a product has been *directly* obtained by the patented process, and not merely when it is *obtainable* by it.[764] The difference is important, since in the chemical sector the same product may, in many cases, be obtained through different processes. The extended protection only applies when it may be proven that the product was produced by the patented process.[765] In some cases, however, it may be difficult to determine whether a product has been directly obtained by a patented process, such as when the process involves different steps and only some of them are covered by the patent.[766] For the extended protection to arise there should be a direct relationship between the process and product, that is, there should be no material or important steps outside the scope of the patent claims that intervene between the process and the product in question.[767]

An important, and still open, question arises in relation to the application of this extension to cases in which the obtained products were specifically excluded

---

[761] If an infringement is invoked, courts would normally determine whether the alternative process can be deemed or not "equivalent" to the patented process. See, e.g, Harold Wegner, *Patent law in biotechnology, chemicals & pharmaceuticals*, Stockton, Chippenham 1994, p. 526 [hereinafter Wegner, 1994].

[762] In that case, the patentee may invoke his exclusive right to prevent others from *making the product*, see Article 28.1 (a). As explained above, this right prevents third parties from making the protected product through whichever process.

[763] See Chapter 26.

[764] The insertion of "at least" in the last sentence of Article 28.1(b) suggests that Members may, but are not obliged to, extend protection to products not directly obtained by the protected process.

[765] In case the conditions under Article 34 are met, the burden of proof is reversed; in that case the extended protection applies when the *alleged infringer* cannot prove that the product was made through a process different from the patented one. For details, see also Chapter 26.

[766] See, e.g., Hansen and Hirsch, p. 357.

[767] See, e.g., Bentley and Sherman, 2001, p. 493.

from patentability by the national law, such as in the case of plants and animals.[768] It may be argued that when a unique process is known, such extension would be tantamount to the protection of the product as such, thereby *de facto* overriding the prohibition to patent the product.

3.3 Article 28.2

> 28.2. Patent owners shall also have the right to assign, or transfer by succession, the patent and to conclude licensing contracts.

Intellectual property rights, like other property, can be assigned or transferred by succession. Article 28.2 makes it clear that patent owners have no restriction to assign their rights, be it on an onerous or on a cost-free basis. This Article seems to ban conditions (such as the transfer of the business or goodwill)[769] that would limit the ability to transfer the patent rights. However, measures such as requiring that the transfer be in writing and registered with the patent office would be admissible.

The "right ... to conclude licensing contracts" seems to allude to the freedom to contract, that is, to the patent owner's discretion to enter into a licensing agreement. This provision would seem to exclude any measure that would impose on the patent owner an obligation to licence his invention. However, Article 31 explicitly allows Members to provide for compulsory licences, thereby authorizing Members to grant licences without or against the consent of the patent owner.[770]

Though patent owners enjoy, in principle, the right to *determine the terms and conditions* of the licences they grant, Article 28.2 does not prevent Members from subjecting such terms and conditions to commercial and other national laws, including competition laws. Nevertheless, Article 40 of **TRIPS** circumscribes the measures that states may adopt to regulate licensing practices and conditions.[771]

3.4 Revocation (Article 32)

> Article 32 Revocation/Forfeiture
>
> An opportunity for judicial review of any decision to revoke or forfeit a patent shall be available.

This Article provides that any decision to revoke of forfeit a patent, for any reason, must be subject to a judicial review. It does not establish the grounds for revocation or forfeiture, which can be determined by national laws. Under European law,[772] for instance, revocation may take place when it is determined that

---

[768] See Chapter 21.

[769] See, e.g., Articles 21 and 31 (e) of the TRIPS Agreement.

[770] See Chapter 25.

[771] See Chapter 29.

[772] See Articles 52–7 and 138C(1) of the European Patent Convention.

(a) the invention was not patentable, because it did not meet any of the patentability requirements;

(b) the patent was granted to a person who was not entitled to that patent;

(c) the specification of the patent did not disclose the invention clearly enough and completely enough for it to be performed by a person skilled in the art; or

(d) the subject matter in the patent extends beyond the subject matter in the application as filed.

As indicated, in the negotiations concerning the Anell Draft (see above), attempts were made to limit revocation to cases where a patent had failed to meet the criteria for grant but this position did not find sufficient support. Hence, Members may contemplate, for instance, revocation on grounds of public interest.[773]

The revocation may proceed with regard to the patent as a whole, or in respect of some of the claims. In countries where the law requires that one principal and one or more subordinated claims be submitted, the invalidation of the principal claim means the revocation of the whole patent. TRIPS leaves full freedom to Members to legislate upon these issues.

Similarly, there are no specific limitations in Article 32 with regard to the grounds and conditions for forfeiture. Most patent laws provide for the forfeiture of a patent when maintenance fees are not timely paid. Such fees are charged in order to finance patent offices' activities and, in some cases, also to pursue some policy objectives, such as inducing the early termination of patent rights (see below).

The Paris Convention mandates that a period of grace of not less than six months be "allowed for the payment of the fees prescribed for the maintenance of industrial property rights, subject, if the domestic legislation so provides, to the payment of a surcharge" (Article 5*bis* (1)). In any case, the countries of the Union shall have the right to provide for the restoration of patents which have lapsed by reason of non-payment of fees (Article 5*bis* (2)). Forfeiture may also be established as a sanction for abuses by the patent holder, such as in cases of non-working. However, Article 5A (3) of the Paris Convention stipulates that "forfeiture of the patent shall not be provided for except in cases where the grant of compulsory licences would not have been sufficient to prevent the said abuses. No proceedings for the forfeiture or revocation of a patent may be instituted before the expiration of two years from the grant of the first compulsory licence."

Article 32 requires the availability of a "judicial review". It seems to be premised on the assumption that revocation or forfeiture is determined by an administrative body, and that the subsequent intervention of a judicial authority is necessary to ensure a due process of law. Under many laws, however, revocation can only be declared by judicial authorities, and the judicial review may only proceed once a final decision is reached by the highest competent court. A question also arises as

---

[773] See, e.g., Gervais, p. 168. Some developing countries' laws (e.g., Andean Group, Costa Rica) allow for the revocation of patents granted in cases where the origin of the biological materials claimed is not disclosed. The consistency of this solution with the TRIPS Agreement is currently subject to considerable debate. See Chapter 24.

to whether "judicial"[774] in this context necessarily means the intervention of a judicial court, or whether the mandated review could be made by an administrative authority, provided that it follows the formal legal procedures of a court of law.

3.5 Term of protection

Article 33   Term of Protection

The term of protection available shall not end before the expiration of a period of twenty years counted from the filing date. [Footnote 8].

[Footnote 8]: It is understood that those Members which do not have a system of original grant may provide that the term of protection shall be computed from the filing date in the system of original grant.

This provision establishes a minimum standard, that is, protection must *at least* extend for twenty years from the filing date.[775] However, during the negotiations on this provision, some developed countries attempted to determine a longer term of protection for products the marketing of which is subject to regulatory approval as established, for instance, for pharmaceutical products in the USA, Europe and other countries. This approach was not accepted by the negotiating parties; no Member, hence, may be obliged to grant a term longer than twenty years from filing in any field of technology.[776]

The content of Article 33 was clarified in the *Canada – Term of patent protection* case. Based on the ordinary meaning of "available,"[777] the panel concluded that "patent right holders are entitled, as a matter of right, to a term of protection that does not end before twenty years from the date of filing"[778] and that the use of such a word "probably reflects the fact that patent right holders must pay fees from time to time to maintain the term of protection and that patent authorities are to make those terms 'available' to patent right holders who exercise their right to maintain the exclusive rights conferred by the patent" (para. 6.110).

The Appellate Body, in reviewing the panel's report, argued that

"In our view, the words used in Article 33 present very little interpretative difficulty. The "filing date" is the date of filing of the patent application. The term of protection "shall not end" before twenty years counted from the date of filing of the patent application. The calculation of the period of "twenty years" is clear and specific. In simple terms, Article 33 defines the earliest date on which the term of

---

[774] "Judicial" is "of, done by, proper to, a court of law" (*The Concise Oxford Dictionary*, p. 543).

[775] The footnote to this Article applies in countries which give effect to patents granted in other jurisdictions, such as in the case of countries that rely on the patent law of their ex-metropolis.

[776] See Article 1.1 above which provides that "...Members may, but shall not be obliged to, implement in their law more extensive protection than is required by this Agreement...".

[777] The *Black's Law Dictionary* defines the word "available" as "having sufficient force or efficacy; effectual; valid" and the word "valid" in turn means "having legal strength or force, incapable of being rightfully overthrown or set aside".

[778] See WT/DS170/R, para. 6.103.

protection of a patent may end. This earliest date is determined by a straightforward calculation: it results from taking the date of filing of the patent application and adding twenty years. As the filing date of the patent application and the twenty-year figure are both unambiguous, so too is the resultant earliest end date of the term of patent protection."[779]

In supporting the panel's interpretation, the Appellate Body added that "in Article 33 of TRIPS, the word 'available' means 'available, as a matter of right', that is to say, available as a matter of legal right and certainty."[780]

4. WTO jurisprudence

4.1 Exclusive rights

There have been no specific decisions on Article 28. In the *Canada-Patent protection of pharmaceutical products* case, however, the panel stressed that the exclusion of "all forms of competition" is the essence of patent rights. It held that

> "The normal practice of exploitation by patent owners, as with owners of any other intellectual property right, is to exclude all forms of competition that could detract significantly from the economic returns anticipated from a patent's grant of market exclusivity . . . Patent laws establish a carefully defined period of market exclusivity as an inducement to innovation, and the policy of those laws cannot be achieved unless patent owners are permitted to take effective advantage of that inducement once it has been defined."[781]

4.2 Term of protection

As mentioned, in the *Canada – Term of patent protection* case[782] the panel and the Appellate Body addressed the interpretation of Article 33. Canada had argued that Section 45 of its Patent Act, which established a 17-year terms from the date on which the patent was issued, did not prescribe a term of protection that would end before the expiration of the 20-year period from the date of filing. Canada argued that a term of protection of at least equal to (and frequently in excess of) a period of 20 years from the date of filing was "available" under Section 45 and that this Section was, therefore, consistent with Article 33 of TRIPS. It considered that 17 years of "effective" protection for the "exclusive privilege and property rights" conferred by the Patents Act were "equivalent or superior" to the term of "exclusive privilege and property rights" provided by Article 33. Canada made such assertion based on the fact that:

> "the time-period between the filing date and issuance of patent necessarily erodes the term of patent protection in cases where, as in Article 33, the protection period is measured as of the filing date. Since the time-period between the filing date and issuance of patent is on average five years in Canada, it was Canada's

---

[779] See WT/DS170/AB/R, 18 September 2000, para. 85.

[780] Ibid., para. 90.

[781] See WT/DS/114/R, para. 7.55.

[782] See WT/DS114/R (Report of the Panel) and WT/DS170/AB/R (Report of the Appellate Body).

contention that a patent right holder will receive only 15 years of 'exclusive privilege and property rights' under a system that grants a 20-year protection term as of the filing date whereas Section 45 provides a successful patent applicant with 17 years of constant protection for the 'exclusive privilege and property rights'" (para. 6.90).

Both the panel and the Appellate Body rejected Canada's arguments. In examining what "available" in Article 33 meant in the context of this dispute, the AB stated that

"The key question for consideration with respect to the "availability" argument is, therefore, whether Section 45 of Canada's Patent Act, together with Canada's related regulatory procedures and practices, make available, as a matter of legal right and certainty, a term of protection of twenty years from the filing date for each and every patent. The answer is clearly in the negative, even without disputing the assertions made by Canada with respect to the many statutory and other informal means available to an applicant to control the patent process. The fact that the patent term required under Article 33 can be a by-product of possible delays in the patent-granting process does not imply that this term is available, as a matter of legal right and certainty, to each and every Old Act patent applicant in Canada" (para. 91).

"To demonstrate that the patent term in Article 33 is "available", it is not sufficient to point, as Canada does, to a combination of procedures that, when used in a particular sequence or in a particular way, may add up to twenty years. The opportunity to obtain a twenty-year patent term must not be "available" only to those who are somehow able to meander successfully through a maze of administrative procedures. The opportunity to obtain a twenty-year term must be a readily discernible and specific right, and it must be clearly seen as such by the patent applicant when a patent application is filed. The grant of the patent must be sufficient in itself to obtain the minimum term mandated by Article 33. The use of the word "available" in Article 33 does not undermine but, rather, underscores this obligation" (para. 92).

5. Relationship with other international instruments

5.1 WTO Agreements

5.2 Other international instruments

6. New developments

6.1 National laws

The enumeration of exclusive rights in Article 28 has been adopted, in some cases literally, by a number of developing countries that changed their patent laws in order to implement the Agreement.[783]

---

[783] See, e.g., Article 42 of the Brazilian Industrial Property Code (1996); Article 52 of the Andean Community "Common Regime on Industrial Property" (Decision 486, 2000); the Kenyan Industrial Property Act (2001) which explicitly incorporates, however, the right of "stocking" a protected product (Article 54(1)(a)(ii)).

Article 33 has had a significant impact in many developed and developing countries, which were bound to amend provisions relating to the duration of conferred rights. Thus, the USA, New Zealand, Portugal[784] and Canada were among the developed countries that changed their legislation in order to conform to the 20-year term mandated by TRIPS. Numerous developing countries that previously granted a shorter term of patent protection also modified their laws accordingly.

6.2 International instruments

6.3 Regional and bilateral contexts

6.3.1 Regional

Article 1709(5) of NAFTA enumerates the exclusive rights conferred on the patent owner. Unlike Article 28.1(a) of TRIPS, NAFTA neither enumerates the right to prevent others from offering for sale, nor the right to prevent the importation of a patented product. The NAFTA provision, however, empowers the owner of a process patent to prevent the importation of a product obtained directly by that process.

6.3.2 Bilateral

The USA-Jordan Agreement on the Establishment of a Free Trade Area (October 2000) provides for an extension of the patent term for pharmaceutical products:

> "With respect to pharmaceutical products that are subject to a patent ... each Party shall make available an extension of the patent term to compensate the patent owner for unreasonable curtailment of the patent term as a result of the marketing approval process" (Article 23 (a)).

6.4 Proposals for review

There are no proposals for review of Articles 28, 32 and 33.

7. Comments, including economic and social implications

Product patents confer broader rights than process patents. Thus, once a product is patented, third parties can be excluded from the market even in cases where they develop their own processes for obtaining the same product. This explains why some industries, such as the pharmaceutical industry, were so keen to include in TRIPS a general obligation to protect product inventions in all fields of technology, as provided for in Article 27.1. Protection of pharmaceutical process only had allowed the development in some countries of domestic industries that were able to produce and market copies of products patented elsewhere.

However, the protection given to process patents is potentially broad because all the different products that can be obtained with a single process fall within the remit of the patent and, additionally, protection may be deemed to include not

---

[784] The USA filed a WTO dispute against Portugal in 1996 for not extending the 20-year patent term to patents filed before 1 June 1995, the date of modification of the Portuguese patent law. Portugal amended this provision in 1996, and the case was dropped.

only the products that flow from the process, but also the products that are based upon such products, that is, their derivatives.[785]

Under Article 28.1(b) products manufactured abroad can be deemed infringing of a patented process in the country of importation. This extension of protection, which significantly strengthens process patents is based on economic considerations, since it is not always possible to obtain a patent for the product, or the patent thereon may have expired. However, there has to be a *direct* relationship between the process and the product. If patentees were able to regulate the use of products that only come into existence as a result of material steps that occur outside the claimed process, the ambit of the monopoly would unduly extend beyond the scope of the patented invention.[786]

Though in a post-TRIPS scenario, pharmaceutical product patents will be recognized in all WTO Members, the extension under Article 28.1(b) will still be relevant in relation to off-patent products, especially when only one process of production is economically efficient or technically viable. In fact, large pharmaceutical firms are active in the patenting of production processes in order to extend the protection beyond the expiry of the product patent, or to mitigate the lack of product patent protection in some countries.[787] The extension of process patent protection may be used by such firms to impede the formulation of pharmaceuticals by domestic firms based on imported active ingredients (if directly obtained by the patented process).

The timely revocation of wrongly granted patents protects the public domain from undue appropriation, thus facilitating the diffusion of knowledge and competition. Members may opt to broadly or narrowly define the grounds for such a revocation. Given the growing number of low quality patents granted in many jurisdictions, due to poor search of the prior art, the application of loose patentability standards, or defects in the specification or claims,[788] accessible and low cost procedures for revocation may avoid costly distortions in the operation of the patent system.[789]

Economists have extensively examined the efficiency implications of the patent system and the optimal patent life. Determining *a priori* the optimal patent life of any given invention is costly and in some cases may simply be impossible. If the patent lasts for a too long period, social costs may exceed the social benefits realized from patents. Such costs notably include a sacrifice in static efficiency[790]

---

[785] See, e.g., Bently and Sherman, p. 493.

[786] See, e.g., Bentley and Sherman, p. 494.

[787] See, e.g., Carlos Correa, *Reforming the Intellectual Property Rights System in Latin America*, The World Economy 2000, vol. 23, no.6.

[788] See, e.g., Barton, pp. 1933–1934.

[789] Pre-grant opposition mechanisms can also be considered for this purpose. See, e.g., Carlos Correa, *Integrating Public Health Concerns into Patent Legislation in Developing Countries*, South Centre 2000 [hereinafter Correa, 2000a].

[790] It is recalled (cf. supra) that *static efficiency* is achieved when there is an optimum utilization of existing resources at the lowest possible cost, whereas *dynamic efficiency* is the optimal introduction of new products or products of superior quality, more efficient production processes and organization, and (eventually) lower prices over time. While patents may sacrifice static efficiency, to the extent that they stimulate innovation, they may in the long term improve dynamic efficiency.

due to prices above marginal costs, and the costs incurred by competitors in trying to "invent around". While a long period of protection may be justifiable in the case of major inventions, for minor improvements, which nowadays constitute the bulk of patent grants, the optimal period of protection should be shorter and commensurate with the lower investment in skill, time, and resources made by the patentee.[791]

[791] The granting of utility models or "petty patents" for minor inventions may provide a way of approaching this issue (see U Suthersanen, *Incremental inventions in Europe: a legal and economic appraisal of second tier patents*. Journal of Business Law, July 2001, pp 319–343.). Another option is to establish a modest annual maintenance fee for the first several years of a patent's life which thereafter escalates at regular intervals until the patent period is exhausted. In Germany, for instance, the outcome of this approach has been that "fewer than 5% of German patents remain in force for their entire term, the average patent life being a little less than eight years. Thus, the renewal fee system reduces the social costs of patent monopolies. In addition, it has apparently had no adverse effect on inventive activity in Germany" (Robert Cooter and Thomas Ulen, *Law and Economics*, Harper Collins Publishers, USA 1988, p. 138. It should be noted that utility models are also available in Germany.

23: Patents: Exceptions to Rights Conferred

> ### Article 30   Exceptions to Rights Conferred
>
> Members may provide limited exceptions to the exclusive rights conferred by a patent, provided that such exceptions do not unreasonably conflict with a normal exploitation of the patent and do not unreasonably prejudice the legitimate interests of the patent owner, taking account of the legitimate interests of third parties.

1. Introduction: terminology, definition and scope

Patents confer an exclusive right, that is, the right to prevent others from using (in various forms) the invention, without the authorization of the patent holder. The market power conferred by patents, and the important benefits the patent owner may obtain, constitute one of the essential elements of patent grants. However, the conferred rights are not absolute. Under most patent laws, such rights may not be exercised with regard to certain acts by third parties. This means that under certain specified circumstances, there may be exceptions to the exclusive rights.[792]

The purpose of the exceptions as well as their scope may vary significantly among national laws, depending on the policy objectives pursued in each country. Such exceptions may apply in relation to non-commercial acts (e.g., private use, scientific research) or to commercial acts. In some cases, they aim at increasing static efficiency by speeding up competition (e.g., the early working exception) while in others the main concern is enhancing dynamic efficiency by avoiding barriers to future research (e.g., experimental exception).

Exceptions to patent rights operate automatically, in the sense that there is no need for a party to obtain a specific authorization from a governmental body or judicial court, as it is the case with compulsory licences, to perform the exempted act. As a result, the exceptions may be invoked as a defence in case of alleged infringement by any third party, at any time during the lifetime of the patent.

---

[792] These exceptions should not be confused with the exceptions to patentability, which exclude a given subject matter from protection and, therefore, lead to the non-granting of a patent (see Article 27, paras. 2 and 3, TRIPS). The exceptions considered here apply when a patent has been granted.

TRIPS does allow the establishment of exceptions to patent rights under specified conditions. Since no equivalent provision was found in the Paris Convention, the negotiating parties relied instead on the text of Article 9(2) of the Berne Convention.[793]

Because Article 30 does not enumerate the specific acts that may be exempted, the kind and scope of the permissible exceptions depend, as discussed below, on the interpretation of the three cumulative conditions set forth by Article 30. National lawmakers face the complex task of defining possible exceptions to patent rights in the light of such conditions. Comparative law and WTO case law may provide useful guidance in the design of this important aspect of patent laws.

2. History of the provision

2.1 Situation pre-TRIPS

Various exceptions to patent rights were provided by national laws at the time of the negotiation and adoption of TRIPS. They included, among others:

- use of the invention for teaching and research;[794]

- commercial experimentation on the invention to test or improve on it;[795]

- experiments made for the purposes of seeking regulatory approval for marketing of a product after the expiration of a patent;[796]

- preparation of medicines under individual prescriptions;

- use of the invention by a third party that had used it *bona fide* before the date of application of the patent ("prior use");

- importation of a patented product that has been lawfully marketed in a foreign country ("parallel imports").[797]

---

[793] Art. 9(2) of the Berne Convention reads as follows: "It shall be a matter for legislation in the countries of the Union to permit the reproduction of such works in certain special cases, provided that such reproduction does not conflict with a normal exploitation of the work and does not unreasonably prejudice the legitimate interests of the author."

[794] This exception has been admitted, for instance, in the USA, though in a limited manner, basically for scientific purposes (Wegner, 1994, p. 267).

[795] For instance, case law in Europe has accepted research done to find out more information about a product – provided that it is not made just to convince licensing authorities or customers about the virtues of an alternative product – and to obtain further information about the uses of a product and its possible side-effects and other consequences of its use. See W. Cornish, *Experimental Use of Patented Inventions in European Community States*, International Review of Industrial Property and Copyright Law 1998, vol. 29, No.7, p.736 [hereinafter Cornish, 1998].

[796] This is generally known as the "Bolar exception", which was introduced for the first time by the U.S. Drug Price Competition and Patent Term Restoration Act (1984) in order to permit testing of a drug for establishing the bio-equivalency of generic products before the expiration of the relevant patent. This exception is named "Bolar" after a case judged by U.S. courts in *Roche Products Inc. vs. Bolar Pharmaceutical Co.*(733 F. 2d. 858, Fed. Cir., cert. denied 469 US 856, 1984), in which the issue of the exception was dealt with. The court denied Bolar the right to begin the FDA approval process before the expiration of the patent.

[797] Parallel imports may be justified under the "exhaustion principle" as recognized in Article 6 of the TRIPS Agreement and under any national laws, provided that the domestic patent law does not follow a regime of national exhaustion. See Chapter 5.

While these exceptions limit the rights of the patent owner, the purpose and scope of the exempted acts varied considerably. TRIPS has not attempted to constrain the freedom of Members to determine the *grounds* of the possible exceptions, but has established the substantive *conditions* for their admissibility.

2.2 Negotiating history

The negotiation of this provision centred on the scope of the exceptions to be allowed, as well as the way in which it would be formulated. As indicated by the Anell Draft, some of the negotiating parties (notably the European Communities,[798] Brazil[799] and Canada[800]) were inclined to develop a non-exhaustive list of specific exceptions.[801]

2.2.1 The Anell Draft

"2.2 Exceptions to Rights Conferred

2.2 [Provided that legitimate interests of the proprietor of the patent and of third parties are taken into account,] limited exceptions to the exclusive rights conferred by a patent may be made for certain acts, such as:

2.2.1 Rights based on prior use.

2.2.2 Acts done privately and for non-commercial purposes.

2.2.3 Acts done for experimental purposes.

2.2.4 Preparation in a pharmacy in individual cases of a medicine in accordance with a prescription, or acts carried out with a medicine so prepared.

2.2.5A Acts done in reliance upon them not being prohibited by a valid claim present in a patent as initially granted, but subsequently becoming prohibited by a valid claim of that patent changed in accordance with procedures for effecting changes to patents after grant.

2.2.6B Acts done by government for purposes merely of its own use."

2.2.2 The Brussels Draft

The Brussels Draft was essentially identical to Article 30. Compared to the list of specific exceptions under the Anell Draft, both the Brussels Draft and the final TRIPS text adopted more general language, modelled on Article 9(2) of the Berne Convention, without specification of the particular acts that could be exempted.

3. Possible interpretations

3.1 The conditions of Article 30

The admissibility of exceptions to patent rights is subject, under Article 30, to three conditions which in the view of the panel in *Canada-Patent Protection of Pharmaceutical Products*[802] (hereinafter "*EC-Canada*"), are "cumulative, each

---

[798] See MTN.GNG/NGII/W/26, 7 July 1988 (Section D.a.(i)).

[799] See MTN.GNG/NGII/W/57, 11 December 1989.

[800] See MTN.GNG/NGII/W/47, 25 October 1989.

[801] The U.S. proposal did not address this issue. According to the U.S. delegation, Contracting Parties could "limit the patent owner's rights solely through compulsory licences" (see MTN.GNG/NGII/W/70, 11 May 1990).

[802] WT/DS114/R, 17 March 2000.

being a separate and independent requirement that must be satisfied. Failure to comply with any one of the three conditions results in the Article 30 exception being disallowed."[803] The panel added that

> "The three conditions must, of course, be interpreted in relation to each other. Each of the three must be presumed to mean something different from the other two, or else there would be redundancy.[804] Normally, the order of listing can be read to suggest that an exception that complies with the first condition can nevertheless violate the second or third, and that one which complies with the first and second can still violate the third. The syntax of Article 30 supports the conclusion that an exception may be "limited" and yet fail to satisfy one or both of the other two conditions. The ordering further suggests that an exception that does not "unreasonably conflict with normal exploitation" could nonetheless "unreasonably prejudice the legitimate interests of the patent owner."[805]

> Members may provide limited exceptions to the exclusive rights conferred by a patent, . . .

The first condition to be met is that the exception must be "limited". According to its ordinary meaning, "limited" is "confined within definite limits; restricted in scope, extent, amount, etc. It is also "small" in relation to an amount or number; or "low" in relation to an income.[806]

An exception may be deemed limited when it is subject to certain boundaries, for instance, with regard to the acts involved (e.g., importation, exportation, evaluation), the purpose of the use (e.g., for private purposes or education), the outcome of the invention's use (e.g., preparation of individual medicinal prescriptions), the persons that may invoke the exception, or its duration. An exception may be limited in relation to a field of technology as well (e.g., food or pharmaceuticals). While the consistency of this latter kind of limitations with the non-discrimination clause of Article 27.1 was addressed by the panel in the *EC-Canada* case, the panel did not give a definite interpretation of the issue.[807]

---

[803] Ibid., para. 7.20.

[804] See *United States – Standards for Reformulated and Conventional Gasoline*, WT/DS2/AB/R, p. 23 (adopted 20 May 1996).

[805] *EC-Canada*, WT/DS114/R, 17 March 2000, para. 7.21. The report of the drafting committee for Article 9(2) of the Berne Convention, from which this text was derived, concluded that measures not in conflict with "normal exploitation" could nonetheless prejudice the "legitimate interests" of the copyright owner. The report is quoted in paragraph 7.72 of the *EC-Canada* panel's report.

[806] New Shorter Oxford Dictionary, p. 1592.

[807] The panel held that "Article 27 prohibits only discrimination as to the place of invention, the field of technology, and whether products are imported or produced locally. Article 27 does not prohibit bona fide exceptions to deal with problems that may exist only in certain product areas. Moreover, to the extent the prohibition of discrimination does limit the ability to target certain products in dealing with certain of the important national policies referred to in Articles 7 and 8.1, that fact may well constitute a deliberate limitation rather than a frustration of purpose. It is quite plausible, as the EC argued, that the TRIPS Agreement would want to require governments to apply exceptions in a non-discriminatory manner, in order to ensure that governments do not succumb to domestic pressures to limit exceptions to areas where right holders tend to be foreign producers" (para. 7.92).

The panel provided an interpretation of what "limited" means in Article 30:

> "[...] The word 'exception' by itself connotes a limited derogation, one that does not undercut the body of rules from which it is made. When a treaty uses the term "limited exception", the word "limited" must be given a meaning separate from the limitation implicit in the word "exception" itself. The term "limited exception" must therefore be read to connote a narrow exception – one which makes only a small diminution of the rights in question.[808]

> [...] In the absence of other indications, the Panel concluded that it would be justified in reading the text literally, focusing on the extent to which legal rights have been curtailed, rather than the size or extent of the economic impact. In support of this conclusion, the Panel noted that the following two conditions of Article 30 ask more particularly about the economic impact of the exception, and provide two sets of standards by which such impact may be judged.[footnote omitted] The term "limited exceptions" is the only one of the three conditions in Article 30 under which the extent of the curtailment of rights as such is dealt with."[809]

In adopting a narrow concept of "limited", the panel has focused on the extent of the curtailment and not on the extent of the economic implications thereof. Hence, an exception with little economic effects might be disallowed under this doctrine even if the patent owner is not negatively affected in practice. In the panel's view, the economic impact of the exception must be evaluated under the other conditions of Article 30.

Given that panel reports do not create binding precedents (and the fact that this particular report was not subject to appeal), nothing would prevent future panels and the Appellate Body from adopting a broader concept in this matter, as suggested by Canada in its submission.[810]

... provided that such exceptions do not unreasonably conflict with normal exploitation of the patent ...

The second condition established by Article 30 is that the exception should not "unreasonably conflict with the normal exploitation" of the patent. This language, substantially borrowed from Article 9(2) of the Berne Convention, requires a determination of what is "unreasonable" in certain circumstances and when there is a "conflict" with the "normal" exploitation of a patent. The literal method of interpretation followed by GATT/WTO panels requires a careful understanding of these key elements.

The concept of "unreasonable" indicates acts that go "beyond the limits of what is reasonable or equitable."[811] "Conflict" means "struggle, clash, be

---

[808] *EC-Canada*, para. 7.30.

[809] *EC-Canada*, para. 7.31.

[810] See Canada's submission in the *EC-Canada* case relating to limited nature of the products, the persons that may invoke the exception and its duration, and the panel's critical position on these arguments in relation to Article 52.2(2) of the Canadian Patent law (para. 7.37).

[811] The Concise Oxford Dictionary, p. 1176.

incompatible,[812] and "normal" "conforming to standard, regular, usual, typical."[813] Finally, "exploitation" means utilization.[814]

The panel in *EC-Canada* did not address what "unreasonably" means, since its analysis led to the conclusion that there was no "conflict" with the normal exploitation of a patent, and therefore it was not necessary to elucidate whether the Canadian exception was reasonable or not. If a conflict of such kind were found, however, the way in which "unreasonably" were to be interpreted would acquire crucial importance and become a delicate issue.

Members have considerable latitude to interpret what "unreasonable" is. In the last instance, the unreasonableness of an exception will depend on the conceptual framework under which a decision is made. The panel in *EC-Canada*, for instance, took the view that

> "Patent laws establish a carefully defined period of market exclusivity as an inducement to innovation, and the policy of those laws cannot be achieved unless patent owners are permitted to take effective advantage of that inducement once it has been defined."[815]

This statement hints at the panel's conception on the role and objectives of the patent system, a subject on which different positions and theories have been elaborated.[816] It may be argued that while emphasizing stimulation to innovation, the panel's view fails to consider other equally essential objectives of the patent system. The diffusion of knowledge and its continuous improvement are equally important objectives of that system, which in the last instance was instituted to serve the public interest.[817] It is important to note in this regard that in the Doha Ministerial Declaration on the TRIPS Agreement and Public Health, Members stated that

> "In applying the customary rules of interpretation of public international law, each provision of the TRIPS Agreement shall be read in the light of the object and purpose of the Agreement as expressed, in particular, in its objectives and principles."[818]

Developing countries have, in particular, stressed the need to construe the "purpose" of the Agreement and of the protection conferred thereunder on the basis of Article 7 of the Agreement.[819]

---

[812] The Concise Oxford Dictionary, p. 197.

[813] The Concise Oxford Dictionary, p. 690.

[814] The Concise Oxford Dictionary, p. 340.

[815] *EC-Canada*, WT/DS114/R, 17 March 2000, para. 7.55.

[816] Alan Gutterman, *Innovation and competition policy: a comparative study of regulation of patent licensing and collaborative research & development in the United States and the European Community*, Kluwer Law International, London 1997.

[817] Paul Welfens; John Addison; David Audretsch; Thomas Gries and Hariolf Grupp, *Globalization, Economic Growth and Innovation Dynamics*, Springer, Berlin 1999, p. 138.

[818] Declaration on the TRIPS Agreement and Public Health, WTO document WT/MIN/(01)/DEC/2 of 20 November 2001, para. 5 (a).

[819] See the submission by the African Group, Barbados, Bolivia, Brazil, Cuba, Dominican Republic, Ecuador, Honduras, India, Indonesia, Jamaica, Pakistan, Paraguay, Philippines, Peru, Sri Lanka,

Another important issue for the interpretation of Article 30 is what is meant by "normal" exploitation. As noted by the panel in *EC-Canada*, "normal" is "regular, usual, typical, ordinary, conventional."[820] The panel also noted

> "the term can be understood to refer either to an empirical conclusion about what is common within a relevant community, or to a normative standard of entitlement. The Panel concluded that the word "normal" was being used in Article 30 in a sense that combined the two meanings."[821]

Patents confer negative rights, that is, the right to exclude any unauthorized use of the invention. In the *EC-Canada* case the panel held that

> "'exploitation' refers to the commercial activity by which patent owners employ their exclusive patent rights to extract economic value from their patent."[822] "The normal practice of exploitation by patent owners, as with owners of any other intellectual property right, is to exclude all forms of competition that could detract significantly from the economic returns anticipated from a patent's grant of market exclusivity. The specific forms of patent exploitation are not static, of course, for to be effective exploitation must adapt to changing forms of competition due to technological development and the evolution of marketing practices. Protection of all normal exploitation practices is a key element of the policy reflected in all patent laws."[823]

... and do not unreasonably prejudice the legitimate interests of the patent owner, ...

Thailand and Venezuela (IP/C/W/296) [hereinafter developing country proposal IP/C/W/296]: "Each provision of the TRIPS Agreement should be read in light of the objectives and principles set forth in Articles 7 and 8. Such an interpretation finds support in the Vienna Convention on the Law of Treaties (concluded in Vienna on 23 May, 1969), which establishes, in Article 31, that "[a] treaty shall be interpreted in good faith in accordance with the ordinary meaning to be given to the terms of the treaty in their context and in the light of its object and purpose" (para 17). "Article 7 is a key provision that defines the objectives of the TRIPS Agreement. It clearly establishes that the protection and enforcement of intellectual property rights do not exist in a vacuum. They are supposed to benefit society as a whole and do not aim at the mere protection of private rights. Some of the elements in Article 7 are particularly relevant, in order to ensure that the provisions of TRIPs do not conflict with health policies: the promotion of technological innovation and the transfer and dissemination of technology; the mutual advantage of producers and users of technological knowledge; social and economic welfare; and the balance of rights and obligations" (para. 18).

[820] The New Shorter Oxford English Dictionary, p. 1940.

[821] *EC-Canada*, WT/DS114/R, 17 March 2000, para. 7.54. It may be argued, however, that what is "normal" or not entirely depends on an empirical analysis, since the right to exclude the unauthorized making of an invention is not a just a "normal" way of operating, but a legal faculty established by law.

[822] *EC-Canada*, para. 7.54. As the panel explained, "Canada took the position that "exploitation" of the patent involves the extraction of commercial value from the patent by "working" the patent, either by selling the product in a market from which competitors are excluded, or by licensing others to do so, or by selling the patent rights outright. The European Communities also defined "exploitation" by referring to the same three ways of "working" a patent. The parties differed primarily on their interpretation of the term 'normal'" (para. 7.51).

[823] Ibid, para. 7.55.

A further condition of Article 30 requires that the exception does "not unreasonably prejudice the legitimate interests of the patent owner". To "prejudice" means to "impair validity or strength of (right, claim, statement, one's chances, etc)."[824] "Legitimate" means "lawful, proper; regular, conforming to standard type; logically admissible."[825] The *EC-Canada* panel rejected the EC interpretation that "legitimate interests" are essentially "legal" interests. It considered that

> "To make sense of the term "legitimate interests" in this context, that term must be defined in the way that it is often used in legal discourse – as a normative claim calling for protection of interests that are "justifiable" in the sense that they are supported by relevant public policies or other social norms. This is the sense of the word that often appears in statements such as "X has no legitimate interest in being able to do Y".[826]

> ... taking account of the legitimate interests of third parties.

The last condition of Article 30 was absent in the text of Berne Article 9(2) which inspired drafters of Article 30. According to the *EC-Canada* panel,

> "[A]bsent further explanation in the records of the TRIPS negotiations, however, the Panel was not able to attach a substantive meaning to this change other than what is already obvious in the text itself, namely that the reference to the 'legitimate interests of third parties' makes sense only if the term 'legitimate interests' is construed as a concept broader than legal interests."[827]

3.2 Acts that may be exempted
The specification of several particular exempted acts was considered during negotiations (see 2.1, above), but the final text of Article 30 only included a general rule. An analysis of comparative law suggests different types of exemptions that may be provided for in national legislation.

3.2.1 Research and experimentation
Exceptions may be granted for scientific research, that is, for acts made without a commercial intent but merely to generate new knowledge. It may also be possible to exempt acts of experimentation on the invention even if made with commercial purposes,[828] such as in order to "invent around", improve on the protected invention, evaluate an invention in order to request a licence, or for other legitimate purposes, such as to test whether the invention works and the patent granted is valid.

---

[824] The Concise Oxford Dictionary, p. 810.

[825] The Concise Oxford Dictionary, p. 574.

[826] *EC-Canada*, WT/DS114/R, 17 March 2000, para. 7.69.

[827] Ibid, para 7.71.

[828] The Community Patent Convention, for instance, provides that there is no infringement in case of "acts done for experimental purposes relating to the subject-matter of the patented invention" (Article 27.b).

Without providing a final judgment on the consistency of research exemptions with Article 30, in *EC-Canada*, the panel considered this exception.

"...as an illustration one of the most widely adopted Article 30-type exceptions in national patent laws – the exception under which use of the patented product for scientific experimentation, during the term of the patent and without consent, is not an infringement. It is often argued that this exception is based on the notion that a key public policy purpose underlying patent laws is to facilitate the dissemination and advancement of technical knowledge and that allowing the patent owner to prevent experimental use during the term of the patent would frustrate part of the purpose of the requirement that the nature of the invention be disclosed to the public. To the contrary, the argument concludes, under the policy of the patent laws, both society and the scientist have a 'legitimate interest' in using the patent disclosure to support the advance of science and technology."[829]

3.2.2 Early working

Another important application of Article 30 may be the "early working" or "Bolar exception".[830] Its purpose is to allow generic drug producers to place their products on the market as soon as a patent expires, and thereby allow consumers to obtain medicines at lower prices immediately thereafter. The *EC-Canada* case confirmed the consistency of an exception of this type with Article 30 (see Section 4, below).

3.2.3 Individual prescriptions

An exception allowing for the preparation of medicines under individual prescriptions also seems compatible with Article 30, and has been in fact provided for in many national laws. This type of exception is generally limited to on-demand medicines prepared for an individual case in a pharmacy or by a medical professional.

3.2.4 Prior use

The *bona fide* use of an invention by a third party before the date of application of the patent is also a common ground for exceptions to the patent exclusive rights. Given the redundancy in science and technology activities, two or more firms or researchers may obtain substantially similar results. In fact, many people are looking for solutions to the same problems, often racing to be the first in reaching a viable (and patentable) solution. The prior use was recognized as valid ground for an exception in the context of the WIPO draft treaty for the harmonization of patent law.[831] The recognition of prior user rights (as provided for, e. g., in Section 64 of the UK Patents Act 1977) has been deemed consistent with the European Patent Convention,[832] and is to be considered compatible with TRIPS.

---

[829] *EC-Canada*, para. 7.69.

[830] For an explanation of this term, see above, Section 2 of this chapter.

[831] See Article 20 of the draft treaty presented at the Diplomatic Conference held in The Hague in 1991.

[832] Some member states of the European Patent Convention recognise prior user rights, and some do not. Since this situation may inhibit the free movement of goods between member states of the European Union and the European Economic Area, the European Parliament and Council could

3.2.5 Parallel imports

Article 30 may also allow derogations with regard to the exclusive right to import, when a patented product has been lawfully marketed in a foreign country (generally called "parallel imports"). Article 28 states that a patent shall confer on its owner, where the subject matter is a product, the exclusive right to prevent unauthorized third parties from "importing" the product for the purposes of making, using, offering for sale, or selling. In a footnote, however, it is clarified that the exclusive right of importation, "like all other rights conferred under this Agreement in respect of the use, sale, importation or other distribution of goods, is subject to the provisions of Article 6."[833]

4. WTO jurisprudence

4.1 EC-Canada

In the *EC-Canada* case, the interpretation of Article 30 was extensively addressed by the panel,[834] in relation to the "Bolar exception" as contemplated in Section 55.2 of Canadian patent law, which provided:

> "(1) It is not an infringement of a patent for any person to make, construct, use or sell the patented invention solely for uses reasonably related to the development and submission of information required under any law of Canada, a province or a country other than Canada that regulates the manufacture, construction, use or sale of any product.
>
> (2) It is not an infringement of a patent for any person who makes, constructs, uses or sells a patented invention in accordance with subsection (1) to make, construct or use the invention, during the applicable period provided for by the regulations, for the manufacture and storage of Articles intended for sale after the date on which the term of the patent expires."

The panel found consistent with TRIPS obligations paragraph (1) of this Article, but inconsistent the stockpiling provision as contained in paragraph (2).

The panel noted that, in the framework of TRIPS,

> "[...] which incorporates certain provisions of the major pre-existing international instruments on intellectual property, the context to which the Panel may have recourse for purposes of interpretation of specific TRIPS provisions, in this case Articles 27 and 28, is not restricted to the text, Preamble and Annexes of the TRIPS Agreement itself, but also includes the provisions of the international instruments on intellectual property incorporated into the TRIPS Agreement [...]."[835]

legislate for their member states to remove inhibitions hindering the free movement of goods between their member States.

[833] Article 6 of the TRIPS Agreement states that: "For the purposes of dispute settlement under this Agreement, subject to the provisions of Articles 3 and 4 nothing in this Agreement shall be used to address the issue of the exhaustion of intellectual property rights." For details, see Chapter 5.

[834] *Canada – Patent Protection of Pharmaceutical Products*, WT/DS114/R, 17 March 2000. However, as mentioned, the panel did not consider necessary to examine all elements in Article 30 in order to reach its conclusion. It neither addressed when a conflict with the patent owner would be "unreasonable", nor the meaning of the final phrase of the Article (relating to the legitimate interests of third parties).

[835] *EC-Canada*, para. 7.14.

On this basis, the panel considered that Article 9(2) of the Berne Convention for the Protection of Literary and Artistic Works (1971)

"[...] is an important contextual element for the interpretation of Article 30 of the TRIPS Agreement."[836]

As a consequence of the extended context that the panel took into account, it concluded that

"the interpretation may go beyond the negotiating history of the TRIPS Agreement proper and also inquire into that of the incorporated international instruments on intellectual property."[837]

Though according to the EC, Articles 7 and 8 were to be deemed statements that describe the balancing of goals that had already taken place in negotiating the final texts of TRIPS, in the panel's view:

"Article 30's very existence amounts to a recognition that the definition of patent rights contained in Article 28 would need certain adjustments. On the other hand, the three limiting conditions attached to Article 30 testify strongly that the negotiators of the Agreement did not intend Article 30 to bring about what would be equivalent to a renegotiation of the basic balance of the Agreement. Obviously, the exact scope of Article 30's authority will depend on the specific meaning given to its limiting conditions. The words of those conditions must be examined with particular care on this point. Both the goals and the limitations stated in Articles 7 and 8.1 must obviously be borne in mind when doing so as well as those of other provisions of the TRIPS Agreement which indicate its object and purposes."[838]

The panel found that the exception contained in 55.2(1) of the Canadian law - including activities seeking product approvals in foreign countries – was "limited" within the meaning of Article 30:

"The exception is 'limited' because of the narrow scope of its curtailment of Article 28.1 rights. As long as the exception is confined to conduct needed to comply with the requirements of the regulatory approval process, the extent of the acts unauthorized by the right holder that are permitted by it will be small and narrowly bounded. Even though regulatory approval processes may require substantial amounts of test production to demonstrate reliable manufacturing, the patent owner's rights themselves are not impaired any further by the size of such production runs, as long as they are solely for regulatory purposes and no commercial use is made of resulting final products."[839]

Though the EC argued that an early working obligation, as provided by the Canadian law, should be linked to an extension of the patent term, as conferred in

---

[836] Ibid.

[837] Ibid, para. 7.15.

[838] Ibid, para. 7.26.

[839] Ibid, para. 7.45.

Europe, Switzerland and the USA, the panel dismissed this argument. It stressed that

> "the interest claimed on behalf of patent owners whose effective period of market exclusivity had been reduced by delays in marketing approval was neither so compelling nor so widely recognized that it could be regarded as a 'legitimate interest' within the meaning of Article 30 of the TRIPS Agreement. Notwithstanding the number of governments that had responded positively to that claimed interest by granting compensatory patent term extensions, the issue itself was of relatively recent standing, and the community of governments was obviously still divided over the merits of such claims. Moreover, the Panel believed that it was significant that concerns about regulatory review exceptions in general, although well known at the time of the TRIPS negotiations, were apparently not clear enough, or compelling enough, to make their way explicitly into the recorded agenda of the TRIPS negotiations. The Panel believed that Article 30's 'legitimate interests' concept should not be used to decide, through adjudication, a normative policy issue that is still obviously a matter of unresolved political debate."[840]

In relation to the "stockpiling provision", Canada argued that the curtailment of the patent owner's legal rights was "limited" just so long as the exception preserved the exclusive right to sell to the ultimate consumer during the patent term. However, in the panel's view

> "the question of whether the stockpiling exception is a 'limited' exception turns on the extent to which the patent owner's rights to exclude 'making' and 'using' the patented product have been curtailed. The right to exclude 'making' and 'using' provides protection, additional to that provided by the right to exclude sale, during the entire term of the patent by cutting off the supply of competing goods at the source and by preventing use of such products however obtained. With no limitations at all upon the quantity of production, the stockpiling exception removes that protection entirely during the last six months of the patent term, without regard to what other, subsequent, consequences it might have. By this effect alone, the stockpiling exception can be said to abrogate such rights entirely during the time it is in effect."[841]

Another important issue considered by the Panel was whether the market advantage gained by the patent owner in the months after expiration of the patent could also be considered a purpose of the patent owner's rights to exclude "making" and "using" during the term of the patent. It held that

> "[I]n both theory and practice, the Panel concluded that such additional market benefits were within the purpose of these rights. In theory, the rights of the patent owner are generally viewed as a right to prevent competitive commercial activity by others, and manufacturing for commercial sale is a quintessential competitive commercial activity, whose character is not altered by a mere delay in the commercial reward. In practical terms, it must be recognized that enforcement of the

---

[840] Ibid, para. 7.82.
[841] Ibid, para. 7.34.

right to exclude 'making' and 'using' during the patent term will necessarily give all patent owners, for all products, a short period of extended market exclusivity after the patent expires. The repeated enactment of such exclusionary rights with knowledge of their universal market effects can only be understood as an affirmation of the purpose to produce those market effects."[842]

The panel dismissed Canada's argument that the fact that the exception could only be used by those persons having utilized the regulatory review exception of Section 55.2(1) limited the scope of the exception both to those persons and to products requiring regulatory approval, and that the stockpiling exception was also "limited" because it only applied for six months before the expiry of the patent. The panel held that "each exception must be evaluated with regard to its impact on each affected patent, independently" and that the fact that the exception applied only to the last six months of the patent term obviously reduced its impact on all affected patented products. It agreed with the EC that six months was a commercially significant period of time, especially since there were no limits at all on the volume of production allowed, or the market destination of such production.

Finally, it is important to note that, in the panel's view, both Articles 30 and 31 are subject to the non-discrimination clause contained in Article 27.1.[843] This interpretation has been contested, however, by a number of developing countries.[844]

4.2 United States-Section 110(5) of the US Copyright Act

In *United States-Section 110(5) of the US Copyright Act*,[845] a panel examined the three criteria under Article 13 (the exception clause in the copyright Section of the Agreement).[846] Given that both provisions were inspired by Article 9(2) of the Berne Convention (1971), some considerations made in such analysis may also be relevant to the interpretation of exceptions under Article 30.

---

[842] Ibid, para. 7.35.

[843] "Article 27.1 prohibits discrimination as to enjoyment of 'patent rights' without qualifying that term. Article 30 exceptions are explicitly described as 'exceptions to the exclusive rights conferred by a patent' and contain no indication that any exemption from non-discrimination rules is intended. A discriminatory exception that takes away enjoyment of a patent right is discrimination as much as is discrimination in the basic rights themselves. The acknowledged fact that the Article 31 exception for compulsory licences and government use is understood to be subject to the non-discrimination rule of Article 27.1, without the need for any textual provision so providing, further strengthens the case for treating the non-discrimination rules as applicable to Article 30. Articles 30 and 31 are linked together by the opening words of Article 31 which define the scope of Article 31 in terms of exceptions not covered by Article 30" (para. 7.91 of the panel's report). The panel considered an "acknowledged fact" the application of the non-discrimination clause to Article 31, because both Canada and the EC agreed on this interpretation of Article 31. See Chapter 25.

[844] See para. 33 of developing country proposal IP/C/W/296.

[845] WT/DS160/R of 15 June 2000. For a detailed analysis of this case, see Chapter 12 of this book.

[846] This provision stipulates that: "Members shall confine limitations or exceptions to exclusive rights to certain special cases which do not conflict with a normal exploitation of the work and do not unreasonably prejudice the legitimate interests of the right holder."

5. Relationship with other international instruments

5.1 WTO Agreements

5.2 Other international instruments

As pointed out in this chapter of the book, Article 30 has a clear link with Article 9 (2) of the Bern Convention.

6. New developments

6.1 National laws

National patent laws adopted or amended after the adoption of TRIPS have established different types of exceptions to the patent holder's exclusive rights. A general review of patent laws in developing countries, however, reveals that the room left by Article 30 has only been used in a limited manner so far.

In many countries an explicit exception has been provided for research conducted for "scientific purposes".[847] In other countries, acts for experimental purposes have been specifically exempted, under different conditions. In Mongolia, for instance, it is not an infringement to make use of an invention "for scientific research or experimental purposes."[848] In Taiwan Province of China a third party is allowed to use the invention for "research or experimental purposes only, with non-profit acts or intention involved therein."[849]

The laws of many countries also included exceptions for "experimental purposes", without limiting them to non-commercial acts, such as the law of Botswana,[850] Turkey,[851] Trinidad and Tobago,[852] Bhutan,[853] El Salvador,[854] and Singapore.[855]

Argentina implemented a "Bolar exception" under Law 24.766 of 1996, allowing for experimentation and application for approval of a generic product before the expiration of the respective patent (Article 8). This exception is not linked to the extension of the patent term.

Israel introduced in 1998 provisions, modelled on the U.S. law,[856] allowing third parties to experiment, before the expiration of a patent, for obtaining registration for marketing in Israel or in a foreign country with a similar exception. The law not only permits the use of the invention to undertake local trials but the export

---

[847] E.g., Guinea-Bissau, Decreto-Ley of 1996, Article 4.c.

[848] Patent Law of 1993, as amended in 1997, Article 18.2.1.

[849] Patent Law, as amended in 1994 and 1997, Article 57.1.

[850] As amended in 1997, Article 24.3.a.iii.

[851] Law of 1996, Article 75.b.

[852] Act No. 21 of 1996, Article 42.b.

[853] The Industrial Property Regulations, 1997, Article 4.a.iii.

[854] Law No. 35, 1996, Article 19.2.

[855] Patents Act, 1994, as amended in 1995, Article 66.2.b.

[856] The U.S. Drug Price Competition and Patent Term Restoration Act of 1984, which adopted the "Bolar exception", permitted the extension of the patent term so as to compensate pharmaceutical patent owners for the time consumed by the marketing approval of a drug, up to five years.

of materials in small quantities to initiate approval procedures before the expiry of the patent in the countries that allow it. It also grants an extension of the life of the patent for up to five years (or for 14 years from first registration worldwide or upon expiration of an extension granted elsewhere, whichever terminates the earliest). Australia also adopted an exception of this kind, linked to the extension of the patent term.

The "Bolar exception" was also incorporated into Article 43 of the Brazilian Industrial Property Code by Law 10.196 of 14 February 2001.

Though in Europe this exception has not been formally introduced yet,[857] the German Federal Supreme Court accepted a "Bolar" type exception in *Boehringer Ingelheim Int. GmbH v. Dr. Rentschler Arzneimittel GmbH and others* (11.7.95). The Court stated that "... it is not contrary to the permissibility of clinical tests that the defendants are carrying out or supporting these with the further aim of licensing under the laws relating to pharmaceuticals". In another decision (*Wellcome Foundation Ltd. vs. Parexel International and others* (1.1.98)), the Paris Court of Appeal held that undertaking tests for obtaining marketing approval did not constitute infringement as such.

Explicit derogations to the exclusive right to import have been provided for in some laws under the principle of "exhaustion of rights". This is the case, for instance, of Argentina,[858] the Andean Group countries (Decision 486), South Africa (for medicines),[859] and Kenya.

6.2 International instruments

6.3 Regional and bilateral contexts

6.3.1 Regional

6.3.2 Bilateral

The USA-Jordan agreement explicitly permits the parties to adopt a "Bolar" type exception, including for exports when made to meet regulatory requirements in a foreign country. Article 19 of the agreement states that

"If a Party permits the use by a third party of a subsisting patent to support an application for marketing approval of a product, the Party shall provide that any product produced under this authority shall not be made, used or sold in the territory of the Party other than for purposes related to meeting requirements

[857] The European Parliament has expressed its opinion in favour of the admission of a "Bolar" type exception. In its resolution of 16 April 1996, paragraph 17, it stated that: "Measures should be introduced which enable pharmaceutical companies to begin, in advance of patent or supplementary protection certificate (SPC) expiry, such laboratory experiments and regulatory preparations as may be required only for the registration of generic pharmaceuticals developed in the EU, to be available on the market immediately, but only after the expiry of a patent or SPC for a proprietary product".

[858] The implementing regulation (Decree 260/96), however, significantly reduces the scope of such exception.

[859] The permission to parallel import is incorporated in the Medicines Act, which was challenged before the South African Supreme Court on this and other grounds by the pharmaceutical industry. The complaint, nevertheless, was withdrawn in April 2001.

for marketing approval, and if export is permitted, the product shall only be exported outside the territory of the Party for purposes of meeting requirements for marketing approval in the Party or in another country that permits the use by a third party of a subsisting patent to support an application for marketing approval of a product".

The same type of exception is permitted under Article 17.9.4 of the USA-Chile FTA.

6.4 Proposals for review
There have been no proposals for review of Article 30.

7. Comments, including economic and social implications

The economic and social implications of the exceptions allowed under Article 30 are significant. The exceptions mitigate the potential anti-competitive effects of the exclusive rights and may thereby increase static or dynamic efficiency.

Thus, the experimental use exception, particularly if permitted for *commercial* purposes, may speed up follow-on innovation and further technological progress. It may clearly enhance dynamic efficiency, without reducing static efficiency.

The "Bolar exception", as indicated above, permits an early introduction of competitive products, normally pharmaceuticals, as soon as the patent expires and thereby allows consumers to gain access to medicines at lower prices. In the absence of such exception, the introduction of generic copies may be delayed for several months or years, during which the patent owner might charge high prices despite the expiry of the patent. This exception increases static efficiency; since the patent holder will be able to keep its monopoly till the expiry of the patent, it is unlikely to reduce dynamic efficiency. An analysis of the welfare implications of the Act that introduced this exception in the USA indicated that

> "...from the perspective of economic welfare, the Act is the source of large potential positive gains of two types. First, it eliminated costly scientific testing which served no valid purpose. Second, the Act lowered prices to consumers with some elimination of deadweight losses and large transfers from producers to consumers."[860]

The exception of prior use is based on reasons of justice (it is not fair to prevent the use of an invention to those who possessed it and did not apply for a patent) as well as static efficiency. The existence of an alternative supply to the patent owner may drive prices down and benefit consumers.[861]

---

[860] See, e.g., W. Viscusi; John Vernon and Joseph Harrington, *Economics of regulation and antitrust*, Second Edition, The MIT Press, Cambridge 1997, p. 857.

[861] Note that several of the above exceptions were also referred to by the IPR Commission report (p. 119). In addition to those exceptions, the Commission also proposed an exception for *teaching purposes* (ibid.) and highlights the importance of such exemption, due to the increasing encroachment of patent rights into traditional copyright areas such as computer programs.

Finally, parallel imports as an exception to exclusive patent rights may be a powerful tool to increase allocative efficiency.[862] If consumers can acquire from a foreign country legitimate products at lower prices than those locally charged by the patent holder, there is an increase in static efficiency without necessarily reducing dynamic efficiency: the patent holder has been remunerated (in the foreign market) for the intellectual contribution he has made. Of course, the levels of profit obtained by the patent holder may be lower than those obtainable if he/she were able to fragment markets and charge a higher price in the importing country, but this does not mean that the owner would not be able to recover R&D expenditures.

The pharmaceutical industry has claimed that the admission of parallel imports may endanger future R&D. It has argued that the exports of drugs sold at low cost in developing countries to higher-priced markets would affect the industry's ability to fund future R&D.[863] It has been argued, however, that trade in medicines is subject to quite stringent national regulations that erect effective barriers to market access. Moreover, parallel imports would only take place where significant price differentials exist. Pharmaceutical firms may reduce such differentials or sell the patented products under different trademarks or packaging in major markets, in order to make parallel importation difficult or unattractive.[864] Developed countries that consider their industries to be jeopardized by "parallel exports" from low price countries may adopt measures to prevent parallel imports under their national legislation. Thus, the IPR Commission in its Report recommended that

> "Developed countries should maintain and strengthen their legislative regimes to prevent imports of low priced pharmaceutical products originating from developing countries."[865]

At the same time, it has been suggested that in order to keep a system of tier pricing and prevent low-priced medicines in developing countries from flowing to developed countries, the former should adopt measures to prevent their exportation.[866]

---

[862] For a general analysis of the exhaustion doctrine under the TRIPS Agreement, see Chapter 5. For a discussion of parallel imports in the trademark context, see Chapter 14.

[863] Arguments against parallel trade also include the objection that it will increase opportunities for "counterfeit and substandard products to enter the market" (Harvey Bale, *TRIPS, Pharmaceuticals and Developing Countries: Implications for Drug Access and Drug Development*, paper presented at the WHO Workshop on the TRIPS Agreement and its Impact on Pharmaceuticals, IFPMA, Jakarta 2000, p. 18), but this is essentially a problem of law enforcement that can be addressed under normal procedures.

[864] See, e.g., Jayashree Watal, *Pharmaceutical patents, prices and welfare losses: a simulation study of policy options for India under the WTO TRIPS Agreement*, Washington DC 2000 (mimeo).

[865] See IPR Commission report, p. 41. This could be done by the adoption or maintenance in developed countries of a system of national or regional exhaustion of intellectual property rights. For more details on the principle of exhaustion, see Chapter 5.

[866] Thus, the U.S. delegation held at the Council for TRIPS Special Session of June 21, 2001, that "In our view, advocates of parallel importation overlook the fact that permitting such imports discourages patent owners from pricing their products differently in different markets based upon the level of economic development because of the likelihood that, for example, products sold for low prices in a poor country will be bought up by middle men and sent to wealthiest country markets and sold at higher prices, for the benefit primarily of the middle men. The lack of parallel

Finally, as far as the situation in developing countries is concerned, the IPR Commission recommended that:

"Developing countries should not eliminate potential sources of low cost imports, from other developing or developed countries. In order to be an effective pro-competitive measure in a scenario of full compliance with TRIPS, parallel imports should be allowed whenever the patentee's rights have been exhausted in the foreign country. Since TRIPS allows countries to design their own exhaustion of rights regimes (a point restated at Doha), developing countries should aim to facilitate parallel imports in their legislation."[867]

import protection can also have significant health and safety implications. Our law enforcement and regulatory agencies, especially FDA, have commented on how very difficult it is for them to keep counterfeit and unapproved drugs out of our country even with the strong parallel import protection provided in the United States. Advocating parallel imports, therefore, could work to the disadvantage of the very people on behalf of whom the advocates purport to be speaking." As Dr. Brundtland in Oslo noted, "For differential pricing to work on a large scale, I think we can all agree that there must be watertight ways of preventing lower priced drugs from finding their way back into rich country markets."

[867] IPR Commission report, p. 42. A possible means to realize this objective would be the adoption in developing countries of an international regime of exhaustion, contrary to the national/regional exhaustion regimes recommended for developed countries, see above.

24: Patents: Disclosure Obligations

Article 29   Conditions on Patent Applicants

1. Members shall require that an applicant for a patent shall disclose the invention in a manner sufficiently clear and complete for the invention to be carried out by a person skilled in the art and may require the applicant to indicate the best mode for carrying out the invention known to the inventor at the filing date or, where priority is claimed, at the priority date of the application.

2. Members may require an applicant for a patent to provide information concerning the applicant's corresponding foreign applications and grants.

---

1. Introduction: terminology, definition and scope

A patent application includes the specification, the claims and the summary of the invention. The specification (or description) of the invention is generally written like a science or engineering report describing the problem the inventor faced, the prior art and the steps taken to solve the problem. In some jurisdictions, the applicant must also provide a characterization of the "best mode" of solving the problem, in order to facilitate others' practicing the invention upon the expiry of the patent by revealing the best-known way (at the time of the patent application) of doing so.[868]

The essential goals of the specification are to substantiate the evidence of completion of the act of invention,[869] that is, whether the inventor has effectively made a patentable invention; and to make new technical information available to the public so others are able to recreate the invention and improve upon it.[870]

---

[868] See, e.g. Jay Dratler (Jr.), *Intellectual property law: commercial, creative and industrial property*, vol. 1, Law Journal Seminars-Press, New York 1996, p. 2-85 [hereinafter Dratler, 1996].

[869] See, e.g., Mark Janis, *On courts herding cats: contending with the "written description" requirement (and other unruly patent disclosure doctrines)*, Washington University Journal of Law and Policy 2000, vol. 2, p. 68 [hereinafter Janis].

[870] See, e.g., Robert Merges and Richard Nelson, *On limiting or encouraging rivalry in technical progress: the effect of patent-scope decisions*, The Journal of Economic Behaviour and Organization 1994, No. 25, p. 129 [hereinafter Merges and Nelson].

Disclosure has historically been one of the fundamental principles of patent law. It provided one of the early justifications for the granting of patents.[871] The justification of patent rights based on disclosure was in some cases put in the form of a "social contract" theory: "society makes a contract with the inventor by which it agrees to grant him the exclusive use of the invention for a period and in return the inventor agrees to disclose technical information in order that it will later be available to society."[872]

Another part of the patent application is a set of claims which should define, in precise terms, what the inventor considers to be the specific scope of the invention.[873] The patent claims serve a quite different function from the specification: they distinguish the inventor's intellectual property from the surrounding terrain,[874] that is, they define the technological territory that cannot be invaded by third parties without risking an infringement suit. The way this is done varies from jurisdiction to jurisdiction. As explained in Chapter 17 (Section 1), some countries take a literal approach, whereas others rely on the doctrine of functional equivalents.

The specification and claims are closely related. There must be a correlation between the scope of the disclosure and the scope of the claims. The former should "support" the latter, in order to ensure that the exclusivity granted to the patent owner is justified by the actual technical contribution to the art.[875]

TRIPS includes specific obligations on the disclosure of the invention, but leaves WTO Members the freedom to determine its relationship with the claims and, in particular, the complex issue of claims interpretation.[876]

2. History of the provision

2.1 Situation pre-TRIPS

While the specific requirements of the obligation to disclose the invention and their practical enforcement (by patent offices and courts) vary among countries,

---

[871] "In the absence of protection against imitation by others, an inventor will keep his invention secret. This secret will die with the inventor and society will lose the new art. Hence, a means must be devised to induce the inventor to disclose his secret for the use of future generations. This can best be done by granting him an exclusive patent which protects him against imitation" (Edith T. Penrose, *The economics of the international patent system*, The Johns Hopkins Press, Baltimore 1951, p. 32 [hereinafter Penrose]).

[872] Penrose, p. 32. Lord Mansfield was perhaps the first jurist to formulate the social contract theory when, in a 1778 case, he pronounced that "the law relative to patents requires, as a price the individual should pay the people for his monopoly, that he should enrol, to the very best of his knowledge and judgment, the fullest and most sufficient description of all the particulars on which the effect depended, that he was at the time able to do". *Liardet v. Johnson*, [1778] 1 WPC 52 at 54.

[873] The claims are the "metes and bounds" of patent rights, see *Markman v. Westview Instruments Inc.*, 517 US, 370, 372 (1996).

[874] See, e.g., Merges and Nelson, p. 129.

[875] For a discussion on this relationship under U.S. and European law, see Janis, pp. 55–108.

[876] See, e.g., John Duffy, *On improving the legal process of claims interpretation: administrative alternatives*, Washington University Journal of Law and Policy 2000, vol. 2, reproduced in Richard R. Nelson, *The sources of economic growth*, Harvard University Press, Cambridge (USA)-London (UK), 1996, pp. 109–166; Carlos Correa, *Integrating Public health Concerns into Patent Legislation in Developing Countries*, South Centre 2000, p. 81 [hereinafter Correa, 2000a].

such obligation was a well established element in patent law at the time of the negotiation of TRIPS.

The best mode requirement (which, as discussed below, is not mandatory under the Agreement) was well established under U.S. law, despite some ambiguities,[877] but it was not provided for in the legislation of most other countries, including in Europe and Japan. Moreover, the obligation (also non-mandatory) to provide information concerning the applicant's corresponding foreign applications and grants had no significant precedents, if any.

2.2 Negotiating history

2.2.1 The Anell Draft

"3. Obligations of Patent Owners

The owner of the patent shall have the following obligations:

3.1 to disclose prior to grant the invention in a clear and complete manner to permit a person versed in the technical field to put the invention into practice [and in particular to indicate the best mode for carrying out the invention];

(See also point 1.3 above)[878]

3.2 to give information concerning corresponding foreign applications and grants;

3.3B to work the patented invention in the territory of the Party granting it within the time limits fixed by national legislation;

3.4B in respect of licence contracts and contracts assigning patents, to refrain from engaging in abusive or anticompetitive practices adversely affecting the transfer of technology, subject to the sanctions provided for in Sections 8 and 9 below."

The draft provision on "obligations of the patent owner" was one of the most controversial in the whole TRIPS negotiations, since developing countries tried to incorporate an obligation to work the patented invention locally (see paragraph 3.3B, above). Equally, developing countries sought to include a clause against abusive or anticompetitive licensing practices on the part of patent holders (see paragraph 3.4B, above).

2.2.2 The Brussels Draft

The first two draft paragraphs were essentially the same as under the current Article 29. In addition, the Brussels Draft still contained references to a local work-ing obligation and abusive or anti-competitive licensing practices. By contrast to

---

[877] See, e.g., Dratler, 1996, pp. 2–85; Charles Hauff, *The best mode requirement of the U.S. patent system*, in Michael Lechter (Ed.), *Successful Patents and Patenting for Engineers and Scientists*, IEEE Press, New York 1995, p. 219.

[878] Point 1.3 of the Anell Draft referred to patentable subject matter and provided: "Require-ments such as filing of an adequate disclosure in a patent application and payment of reasonable fees shall not be considered inconsistent with the obligation to provide patent protection." See Chapter 17.

the Anell Draft, however, these obligations were optional:

> "3. PARTIES may provide that a patent owner shall have the following obligations:
>
> (a) To ensure the [working] [exploitation] of the patented invention in order to sat-isfy the reasonable requirements of the public. [For the purposes of this Agreement the term "working" may be deemed by PARTIES normally to mean manufacture of a patented product or industrial application of a patented process and to exclude importation.]
>
> [(b) In respect of licensing contracts and contracts assigning patents, to refrain from engaging in abusive or anti-competitive practices adversely affecting the transfer of technology.]
>
> 4. PARTIES may adopt the measures referred to in Articles [31, 32 and 40][879] below to remedy the non-fulfillment of the obligations mentioned in paragraph 3 above."

In the subsequent negotiations, the working obligation disappeared from the final text of Article 29 as a result of the compromise struck in December 1991, which was reflected in the wording of Article 27.1 *in fine*. Article 29, as adopted, was finally limited to matters relating to the disclosure of the invention for purposes of examination and of execution of the invention after the expiry of the patent term. The clause on anti-competitive licensing practices was moved to the more general provision under Article 40, TRIPS, thus disconnecting it from the patent application procedure.

3. Possible interpretations

Article 29 contains one mandatory and two facultative elements. First, it requires Members to disclose the invention "in a manner sufficiently clear and complete for the invention to be carried out by a person skilled in the art". It, thus, un-surprisingly incorporates the "enablement" requirement, as usually established in national patent laws.[880] Such requirement aims at ensuring that patents per-form their informative function, by demanding that the patent specification enable those skilled in the art to make and use the full scope of the invention without undue experimentation.[881]

Second, Article 29.1 introduces, in a facultative manner, the best mode require-ment inspired by U.S. law. This requirement aims at preventing inventors from obtaining protection while concealing from the public the preferred embodiments

---

[879] As in the final TRIPS text, the referenced Articles referred to compulsory licensing, revoca-tion/forfeiture of patents and the control of anti-competitive licensing practices.

[880] Under current U.S. law, for instance, the enablement doctrine is codified in 35 U.S.C. No. 112, para. 1 (1984) which provides that "[T]he specification shall contain a written description of the invention, and of the manner and process of making and using it, in such full, clear, concise, and exact terms as to enable any person skilled in the art to which it pertains, or with which it is most nearly connected, to make and use the same, and shall set forth the best mode contemplated by the inventor of carrying out his invention".

[881] The directions given in the specification for performing the invention must be such as to enable the invention to be carried into effect without an excessive number of experiments. See, for instance, the English case of *Plimpton v Malcolmson* (1876) 3 Ch D 531, 576.

of their inventions. Unlike the enablement requirement, which requires an objective analysis, the best mode requirement is a subjective one: what constitutes the best mode of executing the invention depends upon what the inventor knew and considered to be the best way of executing his invention, at the time of the filing of the patent application[882] or the priority date.[883] This information rarely includes the actual know-how for the execution of the invention, since at the time of filing there is seldom production experience.

Third, Article 29 allows Members to require information concerning the applicant's corresponding foreign applications and grants. Such information may be important, particularly for patent offices in developing countries, in order to improve and speed up the examination process. However, such requirement does not affect the basic principle of independence of patent applications.[884] The Agreement does not refer to the consequences of the failure to comply with this requirement. However, since this requirement may be a condition imposed on patent applicants, an application may be rejected if the applicant fails to provide the referred to information.

The Agreement leaves considerable room for the implementation of the standards provided for in Article 29. WTO Members could for example strictly implement these standards with a view to facilitating competitive innovation, adapting protected inventions to local conditions, or merely practicing them once the term of protection expires.[885]

Another aspect left to WTO Members is the extent to which the applicant would be obliged, if several embodiments of the invention were claimed, to provide sufficient information to enable the reproduction of *each* embodiment for which the applicant seeks patent protection. A strict enablement requirement may mandate disclosure of each embodiment.[886] This approach would prevent excessively broad patents covering embodiments of the invention that have not been described

---

[882] See, e.g., Dratler, 1996, pp. 2–86.

[883] The priority date means the date on which the first application was made, in accordance with Article 4 of the Paris Convention. The purpose of this right is to enable someone who has filed a patent application in one country to file posterior applications for the same patent in the other countries of the Paris Union. In this scenario, it is possible that a third person in one of these other countries files an application for the same patent before the original applicant has a chance to deposit his application for that country. The priority date results in the recognition of the original filing in all the other Paris Union countries. Thus, any applications by third persons intervening between the original filing in one country and any subsequent filings by the original applicant in the other countries will be considered posterior to the original filing. The condition is, however, that the subsequent filings in the other countries be effectuated within 12 months from the date of filing of the first application. For details, see Article 4A, B, C of the Paris Convention.

[884] "Patents applied for in the various countries of the Union by nationals of countries of the Union shall be independent of patents obtained for the same invention in other countries, whether members of the Union or not" (Paris Convention for the Protection of Industrial Property, Article 4*bis*(1) (1967)).

[885] See, e.g., UNCTAD, 1996, p. 33.

[886] However, some patent offices, such as the European Patent Office, accept that, in order to be valid, the description need not include specific instructions as to how all possible variants within the claim definition can be obtained. See, e.g., Trevor Cook, Catherine Doyle, and David Jabbari, *Pharmaceuticals biotechnology & The Law*, Stockton Press, New York 1991, p. 80.

by the applicant in a form that effectively allows their reproduction by a third party.

It may also be possible for Members to introduce a written description requirement in order to determine whether patent disclosure reasonably conveys to one skilled in the art that the inventor possessed the claimed subject matter at the time of filing the application.[887]

Further, Members may define how the relationship between the specification and the claims is to be considered,[888] as well as the method of interpretation of claims. Moreover, WTO Members may decide whether such requirements would be applied during original examination of the application by the patent office and/or on occasion of post-grant opposition procedures.[889]

One important issue not addressed by TRIPS relates to the disclosure of inventions relating to micro-organisms[890] and other biological materials. In these cases, the written description is insufficient; access to the relevant knowledge is only possible through access to the biological material itself.[891] Such access may be permitted to third parties (for experimental purposes) after the publication of the patent application, as provided under European law, or after the patent grant, such as in the case of the USA.

Finally, a controversial issue is whether national laws may require that the patent applicant inform the country of origin of the biological material, and/or demonstrate that the applicant has complied with the relevant rules with regard to access to such material. This requirement[892] would help to ensure compliance with the benefit sharing provisions of the Convention on Biological Diversity, and to avoid possible misappropriation ("biopiracy") of genetic resources and associated knowledge.

The consistency of such additional requirement[893] with Articles 27.1 and 29 has been questioned, particularly if non-compliance would lead to the rejection of the patent application or the invalidation of a granted patent.[894] According to the U.S.

---

[887] The negotiating history of Article 29.1 would indicate, however, that there was not intention to incorporate a "written description" requirement. See, e.g. Janis, p. 59 and 88, fn. 133.

[888] For instance, under the European Patent Convention the claims must be "clear and concise and be supported by the description" ("support requirement") (Article 84).

[889] This means that a third party may challenge a patent granted by arguing that the disclosure is not sufficient for a person skilled in the art to carry out the invention. See Janis, p. 89.

[890] The Budapest Treaty (1977) has created a system for the international recognition of the deposit of microorganisms that facilitates the tasks of patent offices and provides guarantees to the applicants/patent holders.

[891] It is important to ensure that the scope of protection for biological material patents corresponds to the material actually deposited. If there is no correspondence between the description and the deposited material, the patent (or claim) may be deemed void.

[892] An obligation of this type was incorporated in the draft of the European Union Directive relating to patents on biotechnology, as recommended by the European Parliament in July 1997. Though it was removed from the finally approved text, Recital 27 of the Directive mentions an obligation to provide information as to geographical origin of biological material where this is known, without prejudice to patent validity. See European Directive on Biotechnological Inventions No. 96/9/EC of March 11, 1996.

[893] Which has been established in some national laws (see Section 6.1 below).

[894] "The origin of the genetic resources and of other circumstances related to their acquisition is not generally necessary for the invention to be carried out by a person skilled in the art", Pires de

government, imposing such requirement would be

> "an extremely ineffective way for countries that are the source of genetic resources or traditional knowledge … In addition, imposing additional requirements on all patent applicants only increases the cost of obtaining patents that would have a greater adverse effect on individual inventors, non-profit entities, and small and medium sized businesses, including those in developing countries."[895]

For some WTO Members, this matter would require an amendment of the Agreement (see Section 6.4 below). It has also been suggested that the acquisition and enforcement of rights in inventions, knowingly derived directly or indirectly from an illegal act, such as the unauthorized acquisition of genetic resources, may be deemed abusive. As a result, patents so obtained may be deemed valid but not enforceable.[896]

4. WTO jurisprudence

There have been no cases under the DSU on this matter.

5. Relationship with other international instruments

5.1 WTO Agreements

There are no other WTO Agreements relevant to this subject.

5.2 Other international instruments

The Budapest Treaty on the International Recognition of the Deposit of Microorganisms for the Purposes of Patent Procedure (1977), amended in 1980[897] constitutes a union for the international recognition of the deposit of micro-organisms for the purposes of patent procedure. Contracting States allowing or requiring the deposit of micro-organisms for the purposes of patent procedure shall recognize, for such purposes, the deposit of a micro-organism with any international depositary authority.

It is also interesting to note that at the meeting of the WIPO Standing Committee on the Law of Patents on September 6–14, 1999, Colombia proposed the

---

Nuno Carvalho, *Requiring disclosure of the origin of genetic resources and prior informed consent in patent applications without infringing the TRIPS Agreement: The problem and the solution*, Re-Engineering Patent Law 2000, vol. 2, p. 380 [hereinafter Pires de Carvalho].

[895] See WTO DOC. IP/C/W/162 (Oct. 29, 1999).

[896] See, e.g. Pires de Carvalho, p. 395 and 399. This option would be based on the "fraudulent procurement doctrine": "if patent applicants fail to be candid on matters that may have an impact on the final decision on patentability, such as novelty or inventiveness, then the patent may be invalidated. When the lack of candor regards matters that are not essential to the grant or rejection of the patent, then fraudulent procurement is sanctioned by non-enforceability. Enforceability is restored when the patent owner corrects the misrepresentations or other inequitable conducts-in other words, when *he cleans his hands*". (ibidem, p. 397).

[897] With a membership of 59 countries as of 15 July 2004 (see <http://www.wipo.int/treaties/en/registration/budapest/index.html>).

following language (not finally adopted) to be included in the proposed Patent Law Treaty:

> "1. All industrial property protection shall guarantee the protection of the country's biological and genetic heritage. Consequently, the grant of patents or registrations that relate to elements of that heritage shall be subject to their having been acquired legally.
>
> 2. Every document shall specify the registration number of the contract affording access to genetic resources and a copy thereof where the goods or services for which protection is sought have been manufactured or developed from genetic resources, or products thereof, of which one of the member countries is the country of origin."

6. New developments

6.1 National laws

In the Indian Patents (Second Amendment) Act, 2002, the grounds for rejection of the patent application, as well as revocation of the patent, include non-disclosure or wrongful disclosure of the source of origin of biological resource of knowledge in the patent application, and anticipation of knowledge, oral or otherwise. It has also been made incumbent upon patent applicants to disclose in their patent applications the source of origin of the biological material used in the invention.[898]

In 2000, Denmark amended the Patent Act, in part to implement the EC Directive on Biotechnological Inventions (see 6.3.1 below). Accordingly, based on the Act, the existing ministerial regulation on patents was amended by supplementing its paragraph 3 with the following provision:

> "If an invention concerns or makes use of biological material of vegetable or animal origin, the patent application shall include information on the geographical origin of the material, if known. If the applicant does not know the geographical origin of the material, this shall be indicated in the application. Lack of information on the geographical origin of the material or on the ignorance hereon does not affect the assessment of the patent application or the validity of the rights resulting from the granted patent.
>
> Breach of this provision could imply a violation of the obligation in the Danish Penal Code (par. 163) to provide correct information to a public authority."

Article 31 of Brazil's Provisional Measure No. 2.186–16 on access and benefit sharing (23 August 2001) provides that:

> "The grant of industrial property rights by the competent bodies for a process or product obtained using samples of components of the genetic heritage is

---

[898] In addition, Section 6 of the Indian Biological Diversity Act, 2002, states that anybody seeking any kind of intellectual property rights on a research based upon biological resource or knowledge obtained from India, needs to obtain prior approval of the National Biodiversity Agency (NBA). The NBA will impose benefit-sharing conditions. Section 18 (iv) stipulates that one of the functions of NBA is to take measures to oppose the grant of IPRs in any country outside India on any biological resource obtained from India or knowledge associated with such biological resource.

contingent on the observance of this Provisional Measure, the applicant being obliged to specify the origin of the genetic material and the associated traditional knowledge, as the case may be."

In a similar vein, Article 13 of the Egyptian Law on the protection of intellectual property rights, 2002, provides as follows:

"Where the invention involves biological, plant or animal product, or traditional medicinal, agricultural, industrial or handicraft knowledge, cultural or environmental heritage, the inventor should have acquired the sources in a legitimate manner."

6.2 International instruments

Article 3 of the draft Substantive Patent Law Treaty[899] contains rules on disclosure and description of the inventions. Paragraph 1 of Article 3 establishes that:

"[...] The disclosure of the invention in the application as a whole shall be adequate, if, as of the date of filing of the application, it sets forth the invention in a manner sufficiently clear and complete for the invention to be carried out by a person skilled in the art, as prescribed in the Regulations."

In addition, paragraph 2 of Article 3 establishes that

"[...] In respect of the disclosure, no requirement additional to or different from those provided for in paragraph (1) may be imposed."

6.3 Regional and bilateral contexts

6.3.1 Regional

Under the "Common Regime on Access to Genetic Resources" of the Andean Group patent applicants are obliged to provide patent offices with information concerning the origin of the genetic resource in question and some proof of prior informed consent from government authorities as well as traditional knowledge holders.[900] Any intellectual property right or other claims to resources shall not be considered valid, if they were obtained or used in violation of the terms of a permit for access to biological resources residing in any of the Andean countries, as regulated under that Decision.

---

[899] Draft 5 of 19 December 2000, available at <http://www.wipo.org/scp/en/documents/session_5/pdf/splt_5.pdf>. Note that this draft has not yet turned into any legally binding agreement. Contrary to the TRIPS Agreement, which only sets up *minimum standards* for patents, this exercise aims at the international *harmonization* of substantive patent law. On an earlier draft of 1991 see WIPO, *Records of the Diplomatic Conference for the Conclusion of a Treaty Supplementing the Paris Convention as far as Patents are Concerned*, vol. 1: "First Part of the Diplomatic Conference, the Hague", Geneva 1991, pp. 15–16 [hereinafter WIPO, 1991]. The draft Substantive Patent Law Treaty has to be distinguished from the WIPO "Patent Law Treaty", adopted on 1 June, 2000. The latter constitutes a legally binding agreement, but it is limited to *procedural* provisions and does not make any attempt to harmonize *substantive* patent law. It is available at <http://www.wipo.int/clea/docs/en/wo/wo038en.htm>.

[900] See Common Regime on Access to Genetic Resource, Andean Decision 391 of 02 July 1996. See also in this context the Biodiversity Law (No. 7788) of Costa Rica, enacted on 27 May 1998.

The EC Directive on Biotechnological Inventions[901] alludes in Recital 27 to an obligation to provide information as to the geographical origin of biological material where this is known, without prejudice to patent validity.

6.4 Proposals for review

As analyzed in Chapter 21, Members of the Council for TRIPS have been discussing ways to address the unauthorized patenting of genetic material and associated traditional knowledge. In this context, developing country Members have been advocating the amendment of TRIPS to include, as a requirement for the granting of the patent, the applicant's obligation to disclose the origin of the genetic material at issue.[902] The African Group has proposed an amendment of Article 29 that would result in a *mandatory* disclosure requirement:

"Compared to other alternatives, Article 29 of the TRIPS Agreement seems to be the most suitable for an appropriate modification to contain these rights and obligations, by including the requirements for equity, disclosure of the community of origin of the genetic resources and traditional knowledge, and a demonstration of compliance with applicable domestic procedures. These requirements would formalise what in the view of the Group should be expected of all such patent applications. Given the failure of certain domestic systems to prevent patents that constituted a misappropriation of genetic resources and traditional knowledge, these requirements would be useful in preventing or minimising the repetition or even the increase of such cases.

The Group suggests that Article 29 be modified by adding the following as paragraph 3: 3. Members shall require an applicant for a patent to disclose the country and area of origin of any biological resources and traditional knowledge used or involved in the invention, and to provide confirmation of compliance with all access regulations in the country of origin."[903]

Some developed country Members, on the other hand, have expressed their opposition to enforcing disclosure of origin of genetic resources through the patent system (see Chapter 21).[904] Switzerland, while acknowledging that a disclosure obligation should be dealt with under the patent system, has proposed to pursue the matter outside the WTO, i.e. through an amendment of the WIPO Patent

---

[901] No. 96/9/EC of March 11, 1996.

[902] Next to the disclosure of origin requirement, these proposals also include obligations for the patent applicant to prove evidence of prior informed consent and fair and equitable benefit sharing in respect of the country where the genetic material originates. See the Joint Communication from the African Group, IP/C/W/404 of 26 June 2003 [hereinafter African Group June 2003] and the Submission by Bolivia, Brazil, Cuba, Dominican Republic, Ecuador, India, Peru, Thailand, Venezuela, IP/C/W/403 of 24 June 2003. See also the checklist submitted to the Council for TRIPS on 2 March 2004 by Brazil, Cuba, Ecuador, India, Peru, Thailand and Venezuela (IP/C/W/420).

[903] See African Group June 2003, p. 6.

[904] The EC has signalled agreement to discuss a disclosure requirement, but is opposed to treating this issue under the patent system. See Communication from the European Communities and their Member States to the Council for TRIPS of 17 October 2002, IP/C/W/383.

Cooperation Treaty, making disclosure a *voluntary* requirement for the patent grant.[905]

7. Comments, including economic and social implications

The nature of the patent bargain requires the patent applicant to make a full disclosure of the matter claimed for his benefit.[906] This serves two purposes.

First, the information contained in patent specifications is an important tool for research and the advancement of technology. Access to this information, nowadays facilitated by the availability of several on-line and off-line databases, provides a useful tool to industry and scientific institutions.

Second, the technical information carried in a patent has to be put at the unrestricted disposal of the public at the expiry of the term of protection. The patent owner obtains a temporary monopoly, subject to the condition that the society at large may benefit from full use of the information once that term has elapsed.

The achievement of these two purposes critically depends on the completeness and quality of the patent description. If the applicant were able to conceal from the public the information necessary to execute the invention, these purposes would be defeated.

Moreover, the grant of a right to exclude is only justified when the inventor can prove actual possession of the information claimed to be inventive. The description, therefore, may play the dual role of ensuring full disclosure as well as limiting the scope of protection to what the applicant has actually invented.[907]

Ensuring the completeness and quality of patent disclosure, in a manner accessible to local researchers and industry, is essential in developing countries. Patent offices should pay attention to the quality of translation into the domestic language. However, the mere translation of patent applications as originally filed in other countries may not be sufficient in some developing countries to enable third parties to practice the invention.[908] Patent offices may, hence, adopt rules requiring the proper identification and description of inventions in a manner understandable to local people skilled in the art.

Compliance by Members with Article 29 does not seem problematic, since the mandatory elements contained therein are in line with well-established practice in patent law. Members are free to introduce into national laws the non-mandatory elements of that provision. They would in general benefit from incorporating the

---

[905] See IP/C/W/400l, p. 2: "Based on the PLT, national law may foresee that the validity of granted patents is affected by a lacking or incorrect declaration of the source, if this is due to fraudulent intention." Reiterated in IP/C/W/423 and the June 2004 Meeting of the TRIPS Council.

[906] See, e.g. Peter Groves, *Source Book on Intellectual Property Law*, Cavendish Publishing Limited, London 1997, p. 202.

[907] The importance of this limitation of the scope of protection was also stressed by the IPR Commission in its report, in particular with respect to the patenting of genetic material. The Commission recommended (p. 118): "If developing countries allow patents over genes as such, regulations or guidelines should provide that claims be limited to the uses effectively disclosed in the patent specification, so as to encourage further research and commercial application of any new uses of the gene."

[908] See, e.g., UNCTAD, 1996, para. 132.

best mode requirement,[909] as well as the obligation to provide information about foreign applications and grants. In addition, Members enjoy considerable room to determine the specific contours of the disclosure obligations, as well as the relationship between description and claims and the form of interpretation of the latter.

Wherever this is possible, manufacturers prefer to keep processes secret. Indeed the sum total of know-how, both patentable and non-patentable, is often what gives the competitive edge, enabling the production of better products at affordable prices. Furthermore, trade secrets have the major advantage that they are unlimited in duration. For example, the secret process used for producing a well-known brand of Swiss spreading cheese goes back many generations, and the Swiss parent company goes to considerable lengths to ensure that its licensees around the world do not learn the secret. Thus, manufacturers will tend to disclose only to the extent that competitors could themselves reproduce the product were it not covered by a patent. It is this fact that weakens the utility of the patent systems as a source of information for developing countries.

As mentioned above, the disclosure of the origin of biological materials claimed in patent applications may have important economic implications. Such a disclosure would not be a necessary condition to but would facilitate claims of benefit sharing (under national access legislation in line with the CBD) by states from which the materials have been acquired. Many developing countries have significant expectations (albeit not confirmed in practice so far) about the income that compliance with benefit sharing obligations may generate.

Disclosure of the origin of biological materials may also facilitate the monitoring of patent grants in order to eventually challenge their validity, when states or other stakeholders consider that a misappropriation ("biopiracy") has taken place. A critical issue in relation to the disclosure of origin is the extent to which such disclosure, if made compulsory, would be deemed compatible with obligations under TRIPS, particularly if non-compliance may lead to the revocation of a patent.

---

[909] See also the IPR Commission recommendation (on p. 117 of the report) that "Developing countries should adopt the best mode provision to ensure that the patent applicant does not withhold information that would be useful to third parties."

25: Patents: Non-Voluntary Uses (Compulsory Licences)

> ### Article 31   Other Use Without Authorization of the Right Holder
>
> Where the law of a Member allows for other use* of the subject matter of a patent without the authorization of the right holder, including use by the government or third parties authorized by the government, the following provisions shall be respected:
>
> (a) authorization of such use shall be considered on its individual merits;
>
> (b) such use may only be permitted if, prior to such use, the proposed user has made efforts to obtain authorization from the right holder on reasonable commercial terms and conditions and that such efforts have not been successful within a reasonable period of time. This requirement may be waived by a Member in the case of a national emergency or other circumstances of extreme urgency or in cases of public non-commercial use. In situations of national emergency or other circumstances of extreme urgency, the right holder shall, nevertheless, be notified as soon as reasonably practicable. In the case of public non-commercial use, where the government or contractor, without making a patent search, knows or has demonstrable grounds to know that a valid patent is or will be used by or for the government, the right holder shall be informed promptly;
>
> (c) the scope and duration of such use shall be limited to the purpose for which it was authorized, and in the case of semi-conductor technology shall only be for public non-commercial use or to remedy a practice determined after judicial or administrative process to be anti-competitive;
>
> (d) such use shall be non-exclusive;
>
> (e) such use shall be non-assignable, except with that part of the enterprise or goodwill which enjoys such use;
>
> (f) any such use shall be authorized predominantly for the supply of the domestic market of the Member authorizing such use;
>
> (g) authorization for such use shall be liable, subject to adequate protection of the legitimate interests of the persons so authorized, to be terminated if and when the circumstances which led to it cease to exist and are unlikely to recur. The competent authority shall have the authority to review, upon motivated request, the continued existence of these circumstances;

(h) the right holder shall be paid adequate remuneration in the circumstances of each case, taking into account the economic value of the authorization;

(i) the legal validity of any decision relating to the authorization of such use shall be subject to judicial review or other independent review by a distinct higher authority in that Member;

(j) any decision relating to the remuneration provided in respect of such use shall be subject to judicial review or other independent review by a distinct higher authority in that Member;

(k) Members are not obliged to apply the conditions set forth in subparagraphs (b) and (f) where such use is permitted to remedy a practice determined after judicial or administrative process to be anti-competitive. The need to correct anti-competitive practices may be taken into account in determining the amount of remuneration in such cases. Competent authorities shall have the authority to refuse termination of authorization if and when the conditions which led to such authorization are likely to recur;

(l) where such use is authorized to permit the exploitation of a patent ("the second patent") which cannot be exploited without infringing another patent ("the first patent"), the following additional conditions shall apply:

(i) the invention claimed in the second patent shall involve an important technical advance of considerable economic significance in relation to the invention claimed in the first patent;

(ii) the owner of the first patent shall be entitled to a cross-licence on reasonable terms to use the invention claimed in the second patent; and

(iii) the use authorized in respect of the first patent shall be non-assignable except with the assignment of the second patent.

[Footnote]*: "Other use" refers to use other than that allowed under Article 30.

1. Introduction: terminology, definition and scope

Article 31 regulates the practice commonly known as compulsory licensing. A compulsory licence is an authorization granted by a government to a party other than the holder of a patent on an invention to use that invention without the consent of the patent holder. The patent itself is a charter from a government in favour of a particular person that gives that person certain rights. The compulsory licence acts to restrain the exercise of those private rights in the public interest. The compulsory licence is one mechanism through which governments limit the private power that resides in the grant of patents. It acknowledges that in various contexts the public interest in having technical knowledge more immediately accessible should take precedence over other patent interests.

Article 31 addresses "Other Use Without the Authorization of the Right Holder", and refers in its introductory clause to "other use [footnote: "Other use" refers to use other than that allowed under Article 30] of the subject matter of a patent without the authorization of the right holder". This awkward formulation reflects the effort by the drafters to distinguish between "limited exceptions" that are authorized under Article 30, and compulsory licensing authorized under Article 31. Article 31 (compulsory licensing) addresses the interests of patent holders in particular cases – a compulsory licence is directed to an identified patent and authorized party – while Article 30 exceptions may involve legislation of more general effect on patent holders and authorized parties.

Article 31 does not attempt to specify or limit in any way the grounds upon which such licences may be granted. It sets up procedures that governments are expected to follow when they grant a licence, and describes certain terms that compulsory licences should embody. The procedures and terms vary depending on the contexts in which the compulsory licence is employed.

The Declaration on the TRIPS Agreement and Public Health adopted at the Doha Ministerial Conference states:

> "Each Member has the right to grant compulsory licences and the freedom to determine the grounds upon which such licences are granted."[910]

2. History of the provision

2.1 Situation pre-TRIPS

Prior to TRIPS, countries throughout the world maintained legislation authorizing the grant of compulsory licences. The terms of this legislation varied considerably. A number of countries, such as Canada[911] and India,[912] provided for "licences of right" in certain subject matter areas, such as food and pharmaceutical patents, so that after a minimum time period prescribed by the Paris Convention, any person with an interest in exploiting a patent was automatically entitled to a compulsory licence.[913] The laws of most or all countries allowed the government to use any patent for national security purposes. Patent laws included various other public interest grounds on which compulsory licences might be granted. These grounds included non-working of the patent within the national territory, failure to meet demand for the patented invention on reasonable terms, and as remedy for anticompetitive practices. For instance, a large number of compulsory licences have been granted in the USA in order to remedy anticompetitive practices.[914]

---

[910] Declaration on TRIPS and Public Health, WTO Ministerial Conference, Fourth Session, Doha, 9–14 Nov. 2001, WT/MTN(01)/DEC/W/2, 14 Nov. 2001, at para. 5(b).

[911] See description of Canada's pre-1993 compulsory licensing system in *Canada – Patent Protection of Pharmaceutical Products*, Report of the Panel, WT/DS114/R, March 17, 2000 (hereinafter "*EC-Canada*"), at para. 4.6. See in particular Reichman, Hasenzahl, *The Canadian Experience*. See also the "Common Industrial Property Regime" (Decision 85) of the Andean Community.

[912] See Elizabeth Henderson, *TRIPs and the Third World: The Example of Pharmaceutical Patents in India*, 19 EUR J. INT. PROP. REV. 651, 658–59 (1997), discussing Patents Act of 1970. Note that since India did not grant food and pharmaceutical product patents, the licence of right related only to process patents in these areas.

[913] Canada's legislation was modelled on British patent law that provided for licences of right in the pharmaceutical and food sectors prior to amendment in 1977. See Cornish, 1998, pp. 7–43

[914] See, e.g., Carlos Correa, *Intellectual property rights and the use of compulsory licences: options for developing countries*, Trade-Related Agenda, Development and Equity, Working Papers,

The principal international agreement concerning patents, the Paris Convention, recognizes the right of its state parties to grant compulsory licences to remedy abuses of patent rights, including failure to work the patent (Paris Convention, Article 5A). Although the Paris Convention prescribes a minimum period of time before a compulsory licence may be applied for (3 or 4 years depending on the circumstances), it does not otherwise limit the grant of such licences, and does not establish a right of compensation on behalf of patent holders. Controversy over the appropriate scope of compulsory licensing is cited as one of the reasons TRIPS negotiations were initiated.[915] In the late 1970s and early 1980s, developing country demands for a New International Economic Order included greater access to technology. These demands were manifest in negotiations on revision of the Paris Convention. These negotiations broke down in 1982, in significant part because of competing demands concerning compulsory licensing. The failure of these negotiations convinced industry interests that they would not succeed in solving what they viewed as the "intellectual property problem" at WIPO. This led to a refocusing of IPR efforts towards the GATT.

2.2 Negotiating history

2.2.1 Early national proposals

The United States played a major role in the inclusion of the TRIPS negotiations in the Uruguay Round, and its initial November 1987 "Proposal for Negotiations on Trade-Related Aspects of Intellectual Property Rights" stated in regard to compulsory licensing:

> "Governments should generally not grant compulsory licenses to patents and shall not grant a compulsory license where there is a legitimate reason for not practicing the invention such as government regulatory review. If a government grants a compulsory license, it shall not discriminate against inventions in particular fields of technology and it shall provide for full compensation to the patentee for the license. No compulsory license shall be exclusive."[916]

In July 1988, the European Community submitted to the TRIPS Negotiating Group an alternate proposal regarding an agreement, stating in respect to compulsory licensing:

> "The granting of compulsory licences for lack or insufficiency of exploitation, compulsory licences in respect of dependent patents, official licences, and any

South Centre, Geneva 1999. See also UNCTAD-ICTSD, Jerome H. Reichman and Catherine Hasenzahl, *Non-Voluntary Licensing of Patented Inventions: Historical Perspective, Legal Framework under TRIPS, and an Overview of the Practice in Canada and the United States of America*, also available at <http://www.iprsonline.org/unctadictsd/projectoutputs.htm#casestudies>. See also the case study by the same authors specifically focusing on the U.S experience, forthcoming.

[915] *Id.*, at 3–17 to 3–18. See also Frederick Abbott, Thomas Cottier, and Francis Gurry, *The International Intellectual Property System: Commentary and Materials*, Kluwer Law 1998, pp. 717–718.

[916] Suggestion by the United States for Achieving the Negotiating Objective, United States Proposal for Negotiations on Trade-Related Aspects of Intellectual Property Rights, Negotiating Group on Trade-Related Aspects of Intellectual Property Rights, including Trade in Counterfeit Goods, MTN.GNG/NG11/W/14, 20 Oct. 1987, Nov. 3, 1987.

right to use patented inventions in the public interest shall, in particular in respect of compensation, be subject to review by a court of law."[917]

In July 1989, India submitted a detailed paper that proposed an approach to compulsory licensing that would authorize licensing for non-working, and licences of right in areas such as food, pharmaceuticals and agricultural chemicals.[918] Fair compensation under a licence of right would be determined as a matter of local law.[919]

At a meeting of the TRIPS Negotiating Group in July 1989, the subject of compulsory licensing was discussed extensively, particularly in relation to the issue of non-working of patents,[920] and it was further considered at a meeting in October-November 1989.[921]

2.2.2 The Anell Draft

Under the Anell Draft, the "A" text introductory clause on compulsory licensing stated: "PARTIES shall minimize the grant of compulsory licences in order not to impede adequate protection of patent rights".[922] It listed specific and limited grounds on which licences might be granted, including "On the grounds of the public interest concerning national security, or critical peril to life of the general public or body thereof".[923] This text specifically addressed the local working requirement, providing "Compulsory licences for non-working or insufficiency of working on the territory of the granting authority shall not be granted if the right holder can show that the lack or insufficiency of local working is justified by the existence of legal, technical or commercial reasons".[924] Compulsory licensees would have been allowed only to supply the local market ("Compulsory licences shall be granted to permit manufacture for the local market only").[925] At this stage, the authority that would be responsible for reviewing the grant was bracketed: ("Any decision relating to the grant and continuation of compulsory licences and the compensation provided therefore shall be subject to [judicial review] [review by a distinct higher authority]").[926]

---

[917] Guidelines and Objectives Proposed by the European Community for the Negotiations on Trade-Related Aspects of Substantive Standards of Intellectual Property Rights, Negotiating Group on Trade-Related Aspects of Intellectual Property Rights, including Trade in Counterfeit Goods, MTN.GNG/NG11/W/26, July 1988, at III.D.3.a(iv).

[918] Communication from India, Standards and Principles Concerning the Availability, Scope and Use of Trade-Related Intellectual Property Rights, MTN.GNG/NG11/W/37, 10 July 1989.

[919] At that stage in the TRIPS negotiations, India objected to the establishment of "any new rules and disciplines pertaining to standards and principles concerning the availability, scope and use of intellectual property rights."

[920] Note by the Secretariat, Meeting of Negotiating Group of 12–14 July 1989, Negotiating Group on Trade-Related Aspects of Intellectual Property Rights, including Trade in Counterfeit Goods, MTN.GNG/NG11/14, 12 September 1989.

[921] Note by the Secretariat, Meeting of Negotiating Group of 30 October–2 November 1989, Negotiating Group on Trade-Related Aspects of Intellectual Property Rights, including Trade in Counterfeit Goods, MTN.GNG/NG11/16, 4 December 1989, at para. 34.

[922] See document MTN.GNG/NG11/W/76, Section 5: Patents, 5A.1.

[923] Section 5A.2.2b.

[924] Section 5A.3.2.

[925] Section 5A.3.5.

[926] Section 5A.3.10.

In the Anell Draft, the only compulsory licensing text specifically designated "B" was the following:

"5B Nothing in this Agreement shall be construed to prevent any PARTY from taking any action necessary: (i) for the working or use of a patent for governmental purposes; or (ii) where a patent has been granted for an invention capable of being used for the preparation or production of food or medicine, for granting to any person applying for the same a licence limited to the use of the invention for the purposes of the preparation or production and distribution of food and medicines. (See also point 2.1B(c) above and Section 8 below)"

Records of the meeting of the TRIPS Negotiating Group subsequent to the Chairman's summary indicate substantial resistance on the part of developing countries to the strict limits suggested by the developed countries regarding grounds for compulsory licensing.

2.2.3 The Brussels Draft

The Brussels Ministerial Text[927] included an article on compulsory licensing (Article 34) that approximated the Dunkel Draft and final TRIPS Agreement text, but with several important differences.[928] The Brussels Draft eliminated any enumeration of permissible grounds for granting compulsory licences, and instead

---

[927] Draft Final Act Embodying the Results of the Uruguay Round of Multilateral Trade Negotiations, Revision, Trade-Related Aspects of Intellectual Property Rights, Including Trade in Counterfeit Goods, MTN.TNC/W/35/Rev. 1, 3 Dec. 1990.

[928] Article 34, Brussels Draft, provided:

"**Article 34: Other Use Without Authorisation of the Right Holder**

Where the law of a PARTY allows for other use[6] of the subject matter of a patent without the authorisation of the right holder, including use by the government or third parties authorised by the government, the following provisions shall be respected:

(a) Each case of such use shall be considered on its individual merits.

(b) Such use may only be permitted if, prior to such use, the proposed user has made efforts to obtain authorisation from the right holder on reasonable commercial terms and conditions and that such efforts have not been successful within a reasonable period of time. This requirement may be waived by a PARTY in the case of a national emergency or other circumstances of extreme urgency. In such situations, the right holder shall, nevertheless, be notified as soon as is reasonably practicable.

(c) The scope and duration of such use shall be limited to the purpose for which it was authorised.

(d) Such use shall be non-exclusive.

(e) Such use shall be non-assignable, except with that part of the enterprise or goodwill which enjoys such use.

(f) Any such use shall be authorised predominantly for the supply of the domestic market of the PARTY authorising such use.

(g) Authorisation for such use shall be liable to be terminated when the circumstances which led to it cease to exist and are unlikely to recur, subject to adequate protection of the legitimate interests of the persons so authorised. The competent authority shall have the authority to review, upon request, the continued existence of these circumstances.

(h) The right holder shall be paid fair and equitable adequate remuneration in the circumstances of each case, taking into account the economic value of the licence.

(i) The legality of any decision relating to the authorisation of such use shall be subject to judicial review or other independent review by a distinct higher authority in that PARTY.

(j) Any decision relating to the remuneration provided in respect of such use shall be subject to judicial review or other independent review by a distinct higher authority in that PARTY.

(k) Laws, regulations and requirements relating to such use may not discriminate between fields of technology or activity in areas of public health, nutrition or environmental protection or where necessary for the purpose of ensuring the availability of a product to the public at the lowest possible price consistent with giving due reward for the research leading to the invention.

focused on the processes by which such licences might be granted and the terms that such licences should contain.

In the Brussels Draft, "public non-commercial use" is addressed in a clause (Article 34(o)), separate from the provision regarding national emergency and circumstances of extreme urgency (compare Article 31(b), TRIPS Agreement). It was envisaged that public non-commercial use might provide exemption from at least some requirements of the compulsory licensing rules applicable in other contexts. Language intended to address U.S. legislation under which notice to the patent holder is not required was included.

The terms "fair and equitable" appeared before "adequate" in the general clause on remuneration of the patent holder (Article 34(h), Brussels Draft), as well as in the clause on public non-commercial use.

At the Brussels Draft stage, the principle that reviews would be undertaken either by a judicial authority or a distinct higher authority was accepted.

A provision on non-discrimination was at this stage incorporated directly in the draft article on compulsory licensing, rather than in the draft article on patentable subject matter (as it appears in the final TRIPS Agreement text). That clause of Article 34, Brussels Draft, provided:

> "(k) Laws, regulations and requirements relating to such use may not discriminate between fields of technology or activity in areas of public health, nutrition or environmental protection or where necessary for the purpose of ensuring the availability of a product to the public at the lowest possible price consistent with giving due reward for the research leading to the invention."

The language of draft clause (k) is ambiguous. For example, it is not clear what the phrase beginning "or where necessary for the purpose of ensuring the

---

(l) PARTIES are not obliged to apply the conditions set forth in sub-paragraphs (b) and (f) above where such use is permitted to remedy a practice determined after judicial or administrative process to be anti-competitive. Appropriate remuneration may be awarded in such cases.

(m) Where such use is authorised to permit the exploitation of a patent ("the second patent") which cannot be exploited without infringing another patent ("the first patent"), the following additional conditions shall apply:

  (i) the invention claimed in the second patent shall involve an important technical advance in relation to the invention claimed in the first patent and, where the invention claimed in the second patent is a process, such process shall be one of considerable economic significance;

  (ii) the owner of the first patent shall be entitled to a cross-licence on reasonable terms to use the invention claimed in the second patent; and

  (iii) the use authorised in respect of the first patent shall be non-assignable except with the assignment of the second patent.

(n) Authorisation by a PARTY of such use on grounds of failure to work or insufficiency of working of the patented product or process shall not be applied for before the expiration of a period of four years from the date of filing of the patent application or three years from the date of grant of the patent, whichever period expires last. Such authorisation shall not be granted where importation is adequate to supply the local market or if the right holder can justify failure to work or insufficiency of working by legitimate reasons, including legal, technical or economic reasons.

(o) Notwithstanding the provisions of sub-paragraphs (a)–(k) above, where such use is made for public non-commercial purposes by the government or by any third party authorised by the government, PARTIES are not obliged to apply the conditions set forth in sub-paragraphs ... above in such cases. Where it comes to the knowledge of the government that a patent is being exploited under the provisions of this sub-paragraph, the government shall ensure that the patent owner is informed and is fairly and equitably adequately compensated."

availability…" is directed toward. It might have been intended to prohibit the use of compulsory licensing to address pricing in particular fields, such as pharmaceutical products. Yet the combination of the phrase "may not discriminate" with "where necessary" produces a confusing result. Exceptions under Article XX, GATT 1947, were typically framed in the context of "necessity". The preclusion of "necessary" measures for public health would seem a result inconsistent with GATT practice. In the final TRIPS Agreement text, language requiring consistency of "necessary" public health measures with the terms of TRIPS appears in Article 8 (Principles).

Clause (l), Brussels Draft, provides in relation to remedying anticompetitive practices that Members "may" award appropriate remuneration. In Article 31(k), TRIPS, the need to correct anticompetitive practices "may be taken into account" in determining remuneration.

Clause (n), Brussels Text, expressly addressed non-working of patents, providing:

> "(n) Authorisation by a PARTY of such use on grounds of failure to work or insufficiency of working of the patented product or process shall not be applied for before the expiration of a period of four years from the date of filing of the patent application or three years from the date of grant of the patent, whichever period expires last. Such authorisation shall not be granted where importation is adequate to supply the local market or if the right holder can justify failure to work or insufficiency of working by legitimate reasons, including legal, technical or economic reasons."

This clause was not included in the Dunkel Draft or final TRIPS Agreement text. The first sentence would have essentially incorporated the time period prescribed by Article 5A(4), Paris Convention (which was effectively incorporated by reference in Article 2, Brussels Text, and Article 2, TRIPS Agreement text). The second sentence would have substantially affected "local working" requirements. The final TRIPS text, as discussed above, incorporates in Article 27.1 a rule that patent rights shall be enjoyable without discrimination as to whether products are imported or locally produced.

There were virtually no changes between the Dunkel Draft and the final TRIPS text on compulsory licensing.

As reflected in the statements by delegations, one of the main obstacles to conclusion of the text on compulsory licensing concerned debate over the right of governments to grant such licences on grounds of non-working. There were a number of negotiating texts on this subject proposed throughout the negotiations, but negotiators could not agree on a direct solution. The issue was indirectly addressed by Articles 27.1[929] and Article 70.6 of TRIPS.[930]

---

[929] See Chapter 18.

[930] This Article states that "Members shall not be required to apply Article 31, or the requirement in paragraph 1 of Article 27 that patent rights shall be enjoyable without discrimination as to the field of technology, to use without the authorization of the right holder where authorization for such use was granted by the government before the date this Agreement became known."

3. Possible interpretations

Article 31 does not purport to limit the grounds on which compulsory licences may be granted. If a WTO Member chooses to provide for such licences, then certain conditions must be fulfilled.

3.1 Individual merits

> (a) authorization of such use shall be considered on its individual merits;

The first of these conditions is that each licence should be considered on its individual merits (Article 31(a)). The ordinary sense of this would be that governments should not attempt to grant blanket authorizations of compulsory licences pertaining to types of technologies or enterprises, but instead should require each application for a licence to undergo a process of review to determine whether it meets the established criteria for the granting of a licence.

The practice of the United States in authorizing government use of patents, well known at the time of the adoption of Article 31 (and accounting for much of its peculiar language), indicates that the requirement of review of individual merits may be interpreted flexibly. Under U.S. law, the government may use any patented invention (or authorize its contractor to use such invention) without providing prior notification to the patent holder, subject only to the patent holder's right to initiate a proceeding before the Court of Claims for compensation. The U.S. patent holder may not obtain an injunction against such government use. This suggests that in cases of government use of a patent the consideration of individual merits can take place after the licence is granted and relate only to the question of compensation.

The requirement that licences be considered on their individual merits does not mean that presumptions may not be established in favour of granting licences in particular contexts, placing the burden on patent holders to overcome the presumptions. For example, a compulsory licensing statute might provide that the absence of supply on the local market of a patented product at an affordable price justifies the grant of a compulsory licence, placing the burden on the patent holder to demonstrate that there are adequate supplies of products on the local market at affordable prices.

The question of who must consider the individual merits of the licence is addressed below.

3.2 Prior negotiations

> (b) such use may only be permitted if, prior to such use, the proposed user has made efforts to obtain authorization from the right holder on reasonable commercial terms and conditions and that such efforts have not been successful within a reasonable period of time. This requirement may be waived by a Member in the case of a national emergency or other circumstances of extreme urgency

or in cases of public non-commercial use. In situations of national emergency or other circumstances of extreme urgency, the right holder shall, nevertheless, be notified as soon as reasonably practicable. In the case of public non-commercial use, where the government or contractor, without making a patent search, knows or has demonstrable grounds to know that a valid patent is or will be used by or for the government, the right holder shall be informed promptly;

Article 31 generally requires that a party seeking a compulsory licence first undertake negotiations with the patent holder for a voluntary licence on "reasonable commercial terms and conditions and that such efforts have not been successful within a reasonable period of time". This requirement is inherently flexible since the concept of reasonable terms and period of time will depend on context.

3.2.1 Commercial terms and conditions

If the applicant for a compulsory licence claims that it sought and failed to obtain a licence from the patent holder on reasonable commercial terms, the authority considering the application may need to decide whether the patent holder's position on compensation was reasonable.

Patent licences generally involve the payment of a royalty from the licensee to the patent holder. A royalty is a usage fee the amount of which may be calculated on different bases. As examples, a royalty may be payable based on the number of units of a licensed product made or sold, or it may be payable based on the licensee's net income from sales of the product. A royalty may be a fixed amount payable at periodic intervals.

The customary royalty for licensing of a patented product or process will vary from industry to industry, and within each industry, depending on the value of the particular technology involved. The royalty on a highly advanced new technology that was developed through substantial expenditures on research and development (R&D) is generally going to be higher than the royalty on a mature technology that might be nearing the end of its life-cycle. The level of royalty will also depend upon either the proven or anticipated success of the product in the market place.

Much of the global flow of patent royalties is internal to multinational enterprises that are transferring income and expenses among their operating units in different countries, and will often depend on factors such as minimization of tax burdens. In order to derive a reasonable royalty based on customary practices in an industry, it may be necessary to disregard evidence of intra-enterprise royalty payments.[931]

Royalty rates are discussed further below in regard to payment of compensation to patent holders.

---

[931] Typically, the negotiator seeking a commercial patent licence will seek to minimize the level of payments to the patent holder, and the patent holder will seek to maximize its stream of income. The patent holder might not seek the highest possible royalty rate since the aggregate amount of its income stream may depend on the level of sales of the patented product, and an excessive royalty might diminish its overall return.

The rate of royalty to be paid is not the only commercial term or condition that is important to a party seeking a licence. Other important elements include:

1. Duration of the licence term. The licensee must make sure that it will be able to use the technology for as long as is necessary to recover and earn a reasonable return on any investments it will be making.

2. Additional technology. Patent applications often do not disclose enough information to allow the practical exploitation of the technology without additional trade secret or other knowledge gained by the patent holder through practical experience. The extent to which the patent holder will aid in the implementation of technological solutions may substantially affect the value of the patent to the licensee.

3. Grant-backs. Patent licensees often develop improvements on inventions which have substantial commercial value. A patent licensor may seek to require that the licensee "grant back" to it any improvement on the invention. The extent of the licensee's obligations in this area will affect the value of the licence to both parties.

4. Tying Arrangements. Patent holders may seek to require licensees to purchase components of the patented product, ancillary products, unrelated products, or support services as conditions of granting a licence. Licensees risk being locked into higher than market commitments through these kinds of arrangements, and demands for undertaking such commitments will affect the value of a licence.

5. Export restrictions. Patent owners often impose on voluntary licences restrictions on the export of the licensed product. This may limit the ability of the licensee to achieve economies of scale in its production facilities.

3.2.2 Reasonable period of time

A patent holder that does not wish to licence its technology, but that also does not wish to see a compulsory licence granted, may well attempt to prolong negotiations using a variety of tactics. Such tactics may include appearing to be engaged in serious negotiations over detailed terms and conditions that do not reach a conclusion. Negotiators seeking licences on reasonable commercial terms are perfectly justified in setting an outer limit for successfully concluding licences, and refusing to negotiate beyond that point.

The reasonable time for negotiations may depend on the purpose for which the licence is sought. As example, a negotiator seeking to commence production of a life-saving pharmaceutical would be justified in seeking a more rapid conclusion of negotiations than a negotiator seeking to commence production of an improved fishing rod.

3.2.3 Waiver of prior negotiations

Under certain conditions, prior negotiation with the patent holder need not be pursued. These are the cases of:

1. "national emergency";
2. "other circumstances of extreme urgency"; or
3. "public non-commercial use".

The language used to define each of these cases leaves room for interpretation. Many countries have laws under which the executive or other authority may formally declare a situation of national emergency, and this declaration may lead to the suspension of certain otherwise applicable constraints. For example, in a situation of national emergency the executive may be able to rule by decree in areas that would normally require parliamentary assent. The terms "other circumstances of extreme urgency" make clear that a waiver of the prior negotiations requirement does not depend upon a formal declaration of national emergency. Even if a country's laws make specific provision for declarations of national emergency from which defined consequences flow, this does not mean that this specific provision needs to be invoked. As example, a government might declare the pandemic spread of a disease to constitute a national emergency, although it is not generally intending to alter the normal pattern of constitutional government.

The use of the term "extreme" in connection with "urgency" suggests that more than a preference to move quickly to authorize a licence is involved in invoking this waiver. The term "extreme" refers to the far end of the spectrum of urgency, but it is not possible to lay out a general rule as to what differentiates extreme urgency from moderate urgency.

The waiver of prior negotiations in the context of national emergency or extreme urgency applies to grants of compulsory licences for private commercial as well as public purposes.

The waiver of prior negotiations also applies when patents are used for public purposes. In many cases it will not be necessary to rely on "national emergency" or "extreme urgency" as the basis for a waiver. There are many ways that the terms "public non-commercial use" may be defined in good faith. The term "public" could refer to use by a government, as opposed to private, entity.[932] The term may refer also to the purpose of the use, that is, use for "public" benefit. A private entity could be charged with exploiting a patent for the benefit of the public.

"Non-commercial use" may be defined either in relation to the nature of the transaction, or in relation to the purpose of the use. Regarding the nature of the transaction, "non-commercial" may be understood as "not-for-profit" use. A commercial enterprise does not ordinarily enter the market without intending to earn a profit. Regarding the purpose of the use, "non-commercial" may refer to the supply of public institutions that are not functioning as commercial enterprises. The supply of a public hospital operating on a non-profit basis may be a "non-commercial" use of the patent.

"Public non-commercial use" is a flexible concept, leaving governments with considerable flexibility in granting compulsory licences without requiring

---

[932] For example, in the United States, a private contractor for the government may be authorized to use a third party's patent without prior negotiation.
There are many instances where the WTO Agreements refer to "governmental" use. For example GATT Article III:8(a) provides: "The provisions of this Article shall not apply to laws, regulations or requirements governing the procurement by governmental agencies of products purchased for governmental purposes and not with a view to commercial resale or with a view to use in the production of goods for commercial sale."
The Agreement on Government Procurement refers to identified "government" entities, not to "public" entities.

commercial negotiations in advance. Note, however, that the waiver of prior negotiations does not extinguish the requirement that adequate compensation in the
circumstances be paid to the patent holder (discussed later).

3.2.4 Notification

In cases of national emergency or extreme urgency, the government is obligated
to notify the patent holder of the grant of the compulsory licence as soon as reasonably practicable. Reasonable practicability will depend on the circumstances
of the case, and need not precede grant of the license. Regarding public non-
commercial use, Article 31(b) says: "where the government or contractor, without making a patent search, knows or has demonstrable grounds to know that
a valid patent is or will be used by or for the government, the right holder shall
be informed promptly." The peculiar wording derives from law and practice in
the United States that allows the government and its contractors to make use of
patents without advance notice to patent holders.[933] Although U.S. law does not
require that a patent holder be notified even if the government knows of a valid
patent, it would nonetheless appear that if a government or a private entity is
aware of the existence of a valid patent (without a patent search) when a compulsory licence is to be granted for public non-commercial use, it should notify the
patent holder.

3.2.5 Competition law remedy

It is important to note that, pursuant to Article 31(k), when compulsory licences
are used by the governments to remedy anticompetitive practices[934] (pursuant
to findings by judicial or administrative bodies) there is no requirement of prior
negotiations with or notification of the patent holders under Article 31(b).

3.3 Scope and duration

> (c) the scope and duration of such use shall be limited to the purpose for which
> it was authorized, and in the case of semi-conductor technology shall only be for
> public non-commercial use or to remedy a practice determined after judicial or
> administrative process to be anti-competitive;[935]

The purpose of the authorization is intended to determine the scope of the licence.
This suggests that compulsory licences should not necessarily provide the licensee
with an unencumbered field of application. A compulsory licence granted to an
aircraft parts supplier regarding military aircraft components might not, for example, authorize the supplier to sell the same patented parts for use in civilian
aircraft.

---

[933] But subsequently allowing the patent holders to seek compensation.

[934] On the relationship between competition law and intellectual property in developing countries,
see Carlos Correa, *The strengthening of IPRs in developing countries and complimentary legislation*
(2000), prepared upon the request of DFID (UK), available at <www.dfid.gov.uk>.

[935] The special provision regarding semiconductor technology is of limited application and not
discussed further here.

The duration of the licence should also be limited in terms of purpose, but this does not prevent a compulsory licensee from receiving a grant that is of sufficiently long duration to justify its investment in production from a commercial standpoint. A licence grant should in any case be long enough to provide adequate incentive for production. Otherwise the purposes of Article 31 will be frustrated.

3.4 Non-exclusivity

> (d) such use shall be non-exclusive;

In the ordinary commercial context, when a patent holder grants a licence for a particular territory, it may agree to refrain from conferring marketing rights over the product covered by the licence in that territory to other parties (i.e., it grants an exclusive licence). Otherwise, the licensee will face the risk of competition from other licensees that might reduce the value of the licence and any investment in exploiting it. The licensee may also face competition by the patent owner, unless he also agrees to exclude himself from the territory.

The requirement that a compulsory licence be non-exclusive raises difficulties from the standpoint of prospective compulsory licensees. They face the possibility that patent holders and possibly other licensees will seek to undercut them in the market, and this will reduce their incentive to invest.

In some contexts it may be possible to alleviate this concern by providing a government contract for assured purchase of the licensed product. In other contexts, the prospective licensee will have to assure itself, for example by negotiating commercial commitments in advance, that its investment in exploiting a compulsory licence will not involve an unreasonable level of risk.

3.5 Non-assignment

> (e) such use shall be non-assignable, except with that part of the enterprise or goodwill which enjoys such use;

The objective of this provision is to prevent the development of a market in compulsory licences as instruments with independent value. The creation of such a market would generally enhance the value of compulsory licences, and might encourage parties to seek them. This requirement does not prevent the sale or transfer of businesses that have obtained compulsory licences, and thereby allows investments in the licences to be sustained.

The reference to assignment of the goodwill means that there need not be any tangible assets constituting the party holding the licence. This adds an element of flexibility to the rule against non-assignment. If a party seeking a compulsory licence establishes a legal entity whose assets are largely comprised of the compulsory licence, it would be feasible to assign and transfer the entire entity ("goodwill") as part of a secondary market transaction.

3.6 Predominantly for the domestic market

> (f) any such use shall be authorized predominantly for the supply of the domestic market of the Member authorizing such use;

The word "predominantly" refers to the majority part, and would generally suggest that more than fifty percent of the production by a compulsory licensee should be intended for the supply of the domestic market.

It is clear that a government may authorize a compulsory licensee to produce for export, provided that the licence includes an undertaking to predominantly produce for the domestic market.

It is generally accepted that a country may issue a compulsory licence within its territory, and allow the licensee to fulfil the terms of the authorization through importation. Thus, if there are off-patent products available outside the country the compulsory licensee may import those products without the consent of the patent holder.

On August 30, 2003, the General Council of the WTO adopted the Decision on Implementation of Paragraph 6 of the Doha Declaration on the TRIPS Agreement and Public Health (the "Decision").[936] Adoption of the Decision was preceded by reading of a Chairperson's Statement that expressed certain "shared understandings" of the Members regarding the way it would be interpreted and implemented. The Decision establishes a mechanism under which the restriction of Article 31(f) will be waived for an exporting Member when it is requested by an eligible importing Member to supply products under compulsory license issued in the exporting country. Details regarding this waiver are discussed under New developments (Section 6.2 of this chapter).

It is important to note that, pursuant to Article 31(k), when compulsory licences are used by the governments to remedy anticompetitive practices (pursuant to findings by judicial or administrative bodies) there is no requirement that those licences be granted predominantly for supply of the domestic market.

3.7 Termination

> (g) authorization for such use shall be liable, subject to adequate protection of the legitimate interests of the persons so authorized, to be terminated if and when the circumstances which led to it cease to exist and are unlikely to recur. The competent authority shall have the authority to review, upon motivated request, the continued existence of these circumstances;

As noted above in regard to the terms and conditions of a licence, the compulsory licensee may be required to undertake substantial investment in connection with producing and distributing under a licence. If compulsory licensing

---

[936] Decision on Implementation of Paragraph 6 of the Doha Declaration on the TRIPS Agreement and Public Health WT/L/540, 2 September 2003 (hereinafter "Decision").

is going to be successful, it must provide sufficient economic incentive for the licensee.

There are a number of mechanisms that might be considered to allow for the termination of a licence under conditions that would adequately protect the legitimate interests of the licensee. For example, the initial grant of the licence could establish the minimum term necessary for the licensee to recover its costs and earn a reasonable return, and also provide for automatic extensions of the licence absent a showing by the patent holder that the conditions that led to the granting of the licence have ceased to exist and are unlikely to recur. The licence could not be terminated during the initial term in which protection of the licensee's interests is assured. Alternatively, the patent holder might be required to compensate the licensee for the remaining value of the licence if the patent holder desires to step in and supply the market in place of the licensee.

A country's compulsory licensing rules should include some mechanism by which the patent holder can petition for a review by the competent authority as to whether the circumstances leading to the granting of the licence have ceased and are unlikely to recur. The compulsory licensee may, of course, be permitted to present its own evidence and justifications for continuing the licence, and might well be entitled to appeal any decision on this matter to the courts.

3.8 Adequate remuneration

> (h) the right holder shall be paid adequate remuneration in the circumstances of each case, taking into account the economic value of the authorization;

The requirement of payment of adequate compensation was not part of the Paris Convention rules on compulsory licensing. The requirement applies to government use as well as private party use of the patent.

The TRIPS Agreement rules on compensation embody substantial flexibility as a consequence of use of the terms "in the circumstances of each case", indicating that factors relating to the underlying reasons for the grant of the licence may be taken into account in establishing the level of compensation. Granting authorities are instructed to "take into account the economic value of the authorization", but are not required to base the royalty payable to the patent holder on that value.

The term "adequate" generally is used to indicate something that is sufficient, or meets minimum standards, but not more than that.[937] In the context of payments to patent holders, adequate payment may be defined in a variety of ways.

Granting a compulsory licence is not the same as ordering forfeiture or revocation of a patent. Compulsory licences must be non-exclusive, and the grant of a compulsory licence to a third party (including the government) does not preclude the patent holder from exploiting the national market or exporting the patented product.

---

[937] A student who does "adequate" work is a student whose work meets the basic minimum standards, but whose work does not demonstrate qualities above that.

One way to approach adequacy of compensation is to ask what the licensee would have been required to pay as compensation to the patent holder for a commercial licence under ordinary circumstances. Assuming that there is a market for licences regarding the type of technology involved in the particular case, the market rate would provide an indication at least as to what patent holders might expect from licensing their technology.

However, the "market rate" may be difficult to determine or misleading for a number of reasons. First, in a market characterized by a limited number of patent-holder actors, there may be active or passive collusion among the patent holders that results in a market rate that is higher than would be the case if the market were functioning efficiently. Second, many, if not most, patent licences are granted among members of the same enterprise group. It may well be in a group's interest to charge high inter-enterprise patent royalties to reduce tax burdens, and it may be very difficult to disaggregate available data so as to establish what market rates would look like without reference to intra-group licences. Even in regard to transactions involving nominal competitors, there may be factors such as joint venture interests that affect what might otherwise be presumed to be market-rate transactions.

Another possible approach involves requiring each patent holder to present a detailed justification for its royalty request. The patent holder could be asked to provide specific data on its research and development costs (including any offsetting tax or accounting benefits), whether it received or made use of any government-supported research in developing its invention, its total global market for the patented invention, the percentage of the global market represented by the country granting the compulsory licence, the average rate of return on its patented products, and so forth. The granting authority could on the basis of this data determine what level of royalty would adequately reflect the patent holder's interest in the country in question.

An international organization might be relied upon to establish royalty guidelines on an industry or product/process basis that might be used as a benchmark by authorities granting compulsory licences.

The licensee's royalty obligation may be calculated as a percentage of its income from sales of the licensed product. That income may be represented, for example, by its wholesale sales, and may be net of tax liabilities.

The level of compensation depends on the circumstances of each case, and there are a number of factors that this potentially brings into play. If a compulsory licence is used to remedy an anticompetitive practice, the level of compensation may be adjusted to reflect the need to remedy past misconduct and to affirmatively promote the entry of new competitors in the market. Although Article 31 does not eliminate the requirement of compensation for compulsory licences to remedy anticompetitive practices, neither does it in any way suggest that this compensation may not be strictly limited to reflect governmental objectives. Article 31(k) expressly recognizes that "The need to correct anti-competitive practices may be taken into account in determining the amount of remuneration in such cases."

The authorities granting a compulsory licence may also take into account the public interest in effective exploitation of the licence as compared with the private interest in earning a particular level of return. For example, if a developing country government is granting a compulsory licence to address a public health crisis that affects a large segment of its population, the government could justify the payment of a minimal royalty on grounds that the public interest in the circumstances of the case warrants a reduced royalty.

The economic value of the authorization is to be "taken into account" in establishing the level of compensation. In cases where a compulsory licence is granted to achieve an industrial policy objective, the value of the licence in the hands of the licensee may be a significant factor in determining the level of payment. Where the licence is granted to address urgent public needs, the economic value of the licence to the licensee may be a much less significant factor.

The Decision on Implementation of Paragraph 6 of the Doha Declaration also provides for a waiver of the requirement for adequate remuneration in the eligible importing Member when remuneration is paid in the exporting Member (Decision, para. 3). This waiver was included to avoid the result that the patent holder would receive double compensation when the system established by the Decision is used. Paragraph 3 of the Decision states that remuneration in the export Member will be established "taking into account the economic value to the importing Member of the use that has been authorized in the exporting Member". The concept of economic value to the importing Member could be understood in a number of ways. The idea for avoiding double remuneration was that the level of compensation should be determined based on the level of economic development and financial capacity in the importing Member, and not the level of economic development and budget capacity in the exporting Member. The approach to remuneration taken by Canada in its implementation of the Decision, discussed in Section 6.1 of this chapter, illustrates one constructive approach to the remuneration issue.

3.9 Review by Judicial or Distinct Higher Authority

> (i) the legal validity of any decision relating to the authorization of such use shall be subject to judicial review or other independent review by a distinct higher authority in that Member;
>
> (j) any decision relating to the remuneration provided in respect of such use shall be subject to judicial review or other independent review by a distinct higher authority in that Member.

The procedures adopted for the review of decisions are likely to play a critical role in determining whether compulsory licences are applied for and used. No sensible enterprise deciding whether to seek a compulsory licence is interested in investing a large measure of resources in protracted court battles that represent not only a financial drain, but also a substantial imposition on managerial resources.

Because the legal institutions and procedures of nations differ fairly substantially, the requirements for review are set out in general terms, and provide substantial discretion to countries in implementation.

The review of grant and remuneration decisions may be undertaken by a court, or may be undertaken as an "independent review" by a "distinct higher authority".

Article 31 does not address the nature of the authority that may initially grant a compulsory licence or determine the level of compensation. This decision may be placed in the hands of an executive administrator. Since the WTO Agreements, including TRIPS, require transparency and basic fairness, governments should develop and publish regulatory procedures pursuant to which compulsory licences will be granted. However, since it is anticipated that governments may act to grant compulsory licences under conditions of urgency, there is nothing to prevent them from providing for waivers of generally applicable rules in such circumstances.

The use of a court as an independent review body is fairly self-explanatory. Court systems typically involve courts of first instance, and one or more levels of courts of appeal. Many legal systems employ specialized courts for particular subject matters, and this may include patent courts. Article 31 does not suggest a preference for the character of the court that is to review decisions regarding compulsory licences, and it may be preferable, because of the general-purpose objectives of this provision, that a court other than a specialized court be used for such review.

Article 31(i) and (j) also allow for "independent" review by a "distinct higher authority". "Independent" means that the reviewing person or body should not be subject to control by the person or body that initially grants the licence or determines the payment. Independence implies that the reviewer should be able to modify or reverse the initial decision without threat of political or economic reprisal. The term "higher authority" refers to a more senior level government person or body than the granting person or body. The term "distinct" could refer to a person or body within the same government agency that initially grants the licence, provided that there is adequate separation of personnel and function among the two persons or bodies. If the initial granting authority within a government is an administrator within the patent office, and the patent office is under the jurisdiction of the Minister of Economy and Trade, the Minister might serve as an authority "distinct" from the patent office administrator.

These provisions should be read in conjunction with Article 44.2, TRIPS Agreement, regarding injunctions. Article 44.2 provides in its first sentence that, with respect to government use licensing, remedies may be limited to the payment of remuneration. This means that the government may not be enjoined from using a patent without the consent of the patent holder, subject to the payment of remuneration, as long as it complies with the requirements as to government use licensing set out in Article 31. Since a government may use a patent without prior notice to or negotiations with the patent holder, this means that a patent holder need not have an opportunity to block the grant or use of a license. The drafting of this provision takes into account the U.S. approach to government use licensing.

The second sentence of Article 44.2 states "In other cases, the remedies under this Part shall apply or, where these remedies are inconsistent with a Member's law, declaratory judgments and adequate compensation shall be available." Once a compulsory license is granted, the licensee is not engaging in infringement of the patent holder's rights. Assuming the license is properly granted, there is no basis for injunctive relief. Nevertheless, before the grant of the license the patent holder might seek a court injunction to prevent the patent office from issuing it and, even after the grant, the patent holder might seek a temporary injunction pending a final determination by a court or distinct higher authority. The second sentence of Article 44.2 provides that injunctive remedies need not be available when they are "inconsistent with a Member's law". This is an ambiguous formula-tion. One interpretation is that injunctions need not be made available if they are not generally provided for in national law. This would be a strained interpreta-tion since Article 44.1 requires that injunction relief be made available in certain cases. A Member would not be in compliance with its general TRIPS obligations if it did not allow for such remedy in those cases. A second and more coherent interpretation is that a compulsory licensing statute need not allow for prelim-inary or temporary injunctions pending a determination whether the license is lawful. Instead, the courts or distinct higher authority may be asked to render a declaratory judgement, which means they will set out the rights of the parties without ordering relief, and to provide for compensation.

3.10 Remedies for anticompetitive practices

> (k) Members are not obliged to apply the conditions set forth in subpara-graphs (b) and (f) where such use is permitted to remedy a practice determined after judicial or administrative process to be anti-competitive. The need to cor-rect anti-competitive practices may be taken into account in determining the amount of remuneration in such cases. Competent authorities shall have the au-thority to refuse termination of authorization if and when the conditions which led to such authorization are likely to recur;

As previously discussed, when a compulsory licence is granted based upon a judi-cial or administrative finding of anticompetitive practices, the otherwise applica-ble requirements of prior negotiations, notice and limiting the licence to predom-inant supply of the domestic market do not apply. In addition, the finding may be reflected in the level of payment to the patent holder. Finally, if it is likely that the anticompetitive conditions that led to the initial grant will recur, competent authorities may refuse to terminate the licence.

In individual cases, authorities considering applications for compulsory li-cences may be presented with several potential grounds for granting them.[938] A finding of anticompetitive conduct on the part of the patent holder provides flexibility regarding the potential terms of a compulsory licence, and should be made when anticompetitive practices are evidenced.

3.11 Dependent Patents

> (l) where such use is authorized to permit the exploitation of a patent ("the second patent") which cannot be exploited without infringing another patent ("the first patent"), the following additional conditions shall apply:
>
> (i) the invention claimed in the second patent shall involve an important techni-cal advance of considerable economic significance in relation to the invention claimed in the first patent;

---

[938] A useful listing of potentially anticompetitive practices may be found in the *Set of Multilaterally Agreed Equitable Principles and Rules for the Control of Restrictive Business Practices*, adopted by the UN General Assembly.

(ii) the owner of the first patent shall be entitled to a cross-licence on reasonable terms to use the invention claimed in the second patent; and

(iii) the use authorized in respect of the first patent shall be non-assignable except with the assignment of the second patent.

Article 31(l) addresses the context in which a compulsory licence is granted to permit the exploitation of a second patented invention that depends upon rights to use an existing patented invention. It requires that the second invention involve an important technical advance of considerable economic significance, that the holder of the first patent be granted a cross-licence on reasonable terms to use the second patent, and that the compulsory licence not be assignable except with the assignment of the second patent.

The question whether an invention is an important technical advance involves a subjective judgment that necessarily involves a range of discretion. Patents are granted only if a claimed invention evidences a sufficient "inventive step" over prior art, so a second patent should not be granted in the first place unless there is an inventive step. The idea of an important technical advance is reminiscent of former German patent law that required a vaguely defined quantum of technical progress as a condition of patentability.[939] This idea was abandoned in European patent law because, among other reasons, it is exceedingly difficult to distinguish important and unimportant technical advances.

4. WTO jurisprudence

4.1 EC-Canada

As of today, there is no decision of a WTO dispute settlement panel or the Appellate Body that directly interprets Article 31. As noted above, in the *EC-Canada* decision, in the context of interpreting Article 30, the panel accepted the presumption of the EC and Canada that Article 31 is subject to the rule of non-discriminatory treatment of patents with respect to place of invention, field of technology and whether products are imported or locally produced.[940] Yet the panel in that case left a considerable degree of flexibility in the interpretation of Article 27.1. The panel said:

"The primary TRIPS provisions that deal with discrimination, such as the national treatment and most-favoured-nation provisions of Articles 3 and 4, do not use the term "discrimination". They speak in more precise terms. The ordinary meaning of the word "discriminate" is potentially broader than these more specific definitions. It certainly extends beyond the concept of differential treatment. It is a normative term, pejorative in connotation, referring to results of the unjustified imposition of differentially disadvantageous treatment."[941] [emphasis added]

---

[939] See Friedrich-Karl Beier, *The European Patent System*, 14 Vand. J. Transnat'l L. 1 (1981).

[940] The proposition that Article 31 is subject to Article 27.1 was accepted by the parties in the *EC-Canada* case, and the panel confirmed the parties' understanding. *EC-Canada* (WT/DS114/R), at paras. 7.90–7.91.

[941] *Id.*, para. 7.94.

The panel makes clear that the conduct prohibited by Article 27.1 is discrimination, and that "discrimination" is not the same as "differentiation". The panel suggests that governments are permitted to adopt different rules for particular product areas or locations of production, provided that the differences are adopted for *bona fide* purposes. The panel did not attempt to provide a general rule regarding what differences will be considered *bona fide*.

The panel's reasoning is of considerable importance in the implementation of Article 31 because it indicates that there may be distinctions regarding fields of technology, and distinctions regarding imported and locally produced products, made when adopting rules and granting compulsory licences. WTO Members are precluded from adopting or applying rules in a manner that "discriminate". This implies adopting or applying a rule for an improper purpose, such as solely to confer an economic advantage on local producers. There may, however, be *bona fide* reasons for drawing distinctions, such as assuring that compelling public interests are satisfied.

Strongly reinforcing the panel's view that Members may adopt *bona fide* distinctions among fields of technology are paragraphs 6 and 7 of the Doha Declaration on the TRIPS Agreement and Public Health. Paragraph 6 directs the TRIPS Council to specifically consider a situation affecting manufacturing capacity in the "pharmaceutical sector", and paragraph 7 specifically addresses the implementation and enforcement of TRIPS rules relating to "pharmaceutical products".

Moreover, it can be argued that Article 27 deals with patentable subject matter and that Article 31 is a self-standing Article. To affirm that Article 31 is *generally subject* to Article 27 could limit its application in ways that were not intended either by the negotiators or indeed by the text. In fact, the *EC-Canada* case was not about compulsory licensing and the panel's report cannot be considered as definite jurisprudence.[942]

4.2 United States – Brazil
On May 30, 2000, the United States requested consultations with Brazil under the WTO Dispute Settlement Understanding, stating:

> "[The United States] request[s] consultations with the Government of Brazil ... concerning those provisions of Brazil's 1996 industrial property law (Law No. 9,279 of 14 May 1996; effective May 1997) and other related measures, which establish a 'local working' requirement for the enjoyability of exclusive patent rights that can only be satisfied by the local production – and not the importation – of the patented subject matter.
>
> Specifically, Brazil's 'local working' requirement stipulates that a patent shall be subject to compulsory licensing if the subject matter of the patent is not 'worked' in the territory of Brazil. Brazil then explicitly defines 'failure to be worked' as 'failure to manufacture or incomplete manufacture of the product', or 'failure to make full use of the patented process'. The United States considers that such a

---

[942] In addition, the view of the panel was not shared by all Members, as reflected by the proceedings of the DSB meeting when the report was submitted for adoption.

requirement is inconsistent with Brazil's obligations under Articles 27 and 28 of the TRIPS Agreement, and Article III of the GATT 1994."[943]

The request for consultations was followed by a U.S. request for establishment of a panel.[944] The United States withdrew its complaint in this matter prior to the submission of written pleadings by either party.[945] However, the request for consultations illustrates that provisions authorizing compulsory licensing for "non-working" may be subject to challenge under Article 27.[946]

The Paris Convention authorizes the grant of compulsory licences for failure to work a patent. A major issue in a case such as that brought by the United States against Brazil is whether Article 27.1 was intended to prohibit WTO Members from adopting and implementing local working requirements, and effectively to supersede the Paris Convention rule. The negotiating history of TRIPS indicates that Members differed strongly on the issue of local working. Several delegations favoured a direct prohibition of local working requirements, but TRIPS did not incorporate a direct prohibition. Instead, it says that patent rights shall be enjoyable without discrimination as to whether goods are locally produced or imported. Under the jurisprudence of *EC-Canada*, this leaves room for local working requirements adopted for *bona fide* (*i.e.*, non-discriminatory) purposes.

5. Relationship with other international instruments

5.1 WTO Agreements

5.2 Other international instruments

Article 5.A.2 of the Paris Convention provides:

> "Each country of the Union shall have the right to take legislative measures providing for the grant of compulsory licences to prevent the abuses which might result from the exercise of the exclusive rights conferred by the patent, for example, failure to work."

Article 5.A.4 of the Paris Convention provides:

> "A compulsory licence may not be applied for on the ground of failure to work or insufficient working before the expiration of a period of four years from the date

---

[943] Request for Consultations by the United States, *Brazil – Measures Affecting Patent Protection*, WT/DS199/1, G/L/385, IP/D/23, 8 June 2000.

[944] Request for the Establishment of a Panel by the United States, *Brazil – Measures Affecting Patent Protection*, WT/DS199/39, January 2001.

[945] See Joint Communication Brazil-United States, June 25, 2001. Following notification of the U.S. decision to withdraw its complaint (without prejudice), the communication stated:

"the Brazilian Government will agree, in the event it deems necessary to apply Article 68 to grant a compulsory licence on a patent held by a U.S. company, to provide advance notice and adequate opportunity for prior talks on the matter with the United States. These talks would be held within the scope of the U.S.-Brazil Consultative Mechanism, in a special session scheduled to discuss the subject.

"Brazil and the United States consider that this agreement is an important step towards greater cooperation between the two countries regarding our shared goals of fighting AIDS and protecting intellectual property rights."

[946] Article 28, TRIPS Agreement, sets out the basic rights of patent holders. Article III of GATT 1994 is the national treatment provision applicable to trade in goods.

of filing of the patent application or three years from the date of the grant of the patent, whichever period expires last; it shall be refused if the patentee justifies his inaction by legitimate reasons. Such a compulsory licence shall be non-exclusive and shall not be transferable, even in the form of the grant of a sub-licence, except with that part of the enterprise or goodwill which exploits such licence."

The Paris Convention authorizes the grant of compulsory licences, and sets out limited conditions to be applied in cases of non-working.[947] The Paris Convention does not otherwise establish specific conditions or restrictions on the granting of compulsory licences.

6. New developments

6.1 National laws

The entry into force of TRIPS has resulted in the revision of patent laws by a substantial number of countries, including those that anticipate accession to the WTO. Many of these countries have consulted with the World Intellectual Property Organization (WIPO) concerning the terms of their revised intellectual property laws. The model patent law that is generally proposed by WIPO includes provision for compulsory licensing of patents taking into account the rules of Article 31.

6.1.1 Canada

Since the adoption of the Decision on Implementation of Paragraph 6, Canada and Norway have passed implementing legislation, and a number of other countries are proposing to do so. Canada's legislation prescribes a list of products eligible for export under license, but permits additions to the list by action of the executive (in consultation with an expert advisory committee).[948] Remuneration will be based on the level of economic development of the importing country, and royalties will range from less than one percent to four percent. Canada will authorize exports to non-WTO Member countries with an undertaking from the importing country to comply with the rules of the Decision. If exports are priced above a certain threshold in relation to Canadian prices, the patent holder will have the opportunity to challenge the grant and terms of the license.

6.1.2 Norway

The legislation and regulations adopted by Norway do not limit the products that may be exported, relying on the decision of the importing country.[949] Like Canada,

[947] Article 2.1 of the TRIPS Agreement states that the Agreement does not derogate from existing obligations of Members under the Paris Convention. If, for the sake of argument, Article 27.1 were to be construed to restrict or preclude compulsory licensing for non-working, this would derogate from a "right" of Members, not an "obligation". As such, this interpretation would not be precluded by Article 2.2 of TRIPS.

[948] Bill C-9, An Act to amend the Patent Act and the Food and Drugs Act (The Jean Chrétien Pledge to Africa), passed by the House of Commons, May 4, 2004, by the Senate without amendment, May 13, 2004, receiver Royal Assent, May 14, 2004).

[949] Regulations Amending The Patent Regulations (in accordance with the Decision of the WTO General Council of 30 August 2003, pursuant to sections 49 and 69 of the Act of 15 December 1967 No. 9 relating to patents, the Ministry of Justice and the Police laid down the following regulations by Royal Decree of 14 May 2004). See Consultation – Implementation of paragraph 6

Norway will permit exports to non-WTO Members with an appropriate commitment to abide by the rules of the Decision. Remuneration will be determined on a case-by-case basis.

6.2 International instruments

6.2.1 The decision on implementation of Paragraph 6 of the Doha Declaration on the TRIPS Agreement and Public Health[950]

Paragraph 6 of the Doha Declaration recognized the problem that countries with insufficient or no manufacturing capacity in the pharmaceutical sector have in making effective use of compulsory licensing, and directed the TRIPS Council to recommend an expeditious solution.[951] On August 30, 2003, following nearly two years of negotiations, the General Council adopted the Decision, preceded by the reading of a Chairperson's Statement. The Decision is intended to allow countries with manufacturing capacity to make and export pharmaceutical products to countries with public health needs, notwithstanding Article 31(f) of TRIPS that limits compulsory licensing predominantly to the supply of the domestic market. It does this by establishing a mechanism under which the restriction of Article 31(f) is waived for the exporting country, and Article 31(h) (remuneration) is waived for the importing country.

Paragraph 1 of the Decision defines "pharmaceutical product" broadly, and does not limit application of the solution to specific disease conditions. The definition expressly covers active pharmaceutical ingredients (APIs), and diagnostic kits. The definition is sufficiently broad to encompass vaccines. It requires Members other than least-developed country Members (which are automatically included) to submit a notification of their intention to use the system in whole or in part, which notification may be modified at any time. This notification establishes the Member as an "eligible importing Member", and several developed Members have opted out of the system in whole or in a limited way.

Paragraph 2 of the Decision establishes conditions for use of the waiver. The importing Member must notify the TRIPS Council of its needs, and (except for least developed country Members), must indicate that it has determined that it has insufficient or no manufacturing capacity for the product(s) in question. The latter determination is made in accordance with an Annex to the Decision. When there is a patent in the importing Member, it must indicate that it has issued, or intends to issue, a compulsory license (except for least developed country Members that elect not to enforce patents pursuant to Paragraph 7 of the Doha Declaration). The

of the Doha Declaration on the TRIPS Agreement and Public Health in Norwegian law, available at <http://www.dep.no/ud/engelsk/>.

[950] WT/L/540, the "Decision" (reproduced as Annex 1, including Chairperson's Statement).

[951] See Frederick M. Abbott, *The Containment of TRIPS to Promote Public Health: A Commentary on the Decision on Implementation of Paragraph 6 of the Doha Declaration*, manuscript with reference to be provided (forthcoming 2004); Carlos Correa, *Implementation Of The WTO General Council Decision on Paragraph 6 of the Doha Declaration on the TRIPS Agreement and Public Health*, WHO 2004 (forthcoming) (hereinafter "Correa 2004"), and; Paul Vandoren and Jean Charles Van Eeckhaute, *The WTO Decision on Paragraph 6 of the Doha Declaration on the TRIPS Agreement and Public Health*, 6 J. World Intell. Prop. 779 (2003).

exporting Member must notify the TRIPS Council of the terms of the export license it issues, including the destination, quantities to be supplied and the duration of the license. The products supplied under the license must be identified by special packaging and/or colouring/shaping. Before quantities are shipped, the licensee must post on a publicly accessible website the destination and means it has used to identify the products as supplied under the system.

Paragraph 3 provides for a waiver of the remuneration requirement for the importing country, discussed above in Section 3 of this chapter.

Paragraph 4 requires importing Members to implement measures proportionate to their means to prevent diversion of products imported under the system. Paragraph 4 does not specify the nature of such means, which might include mechanisms pursuant to which patent holders can obtain remedies.

Paragraph 5 requires other Members to take measures already provided for under TRIPS to prevent the importation of diverted products into their territories.

Paragraph 6 provides an additional waiver of Article 31(f) for regional trading arrangements in Africa (i.e., more than half of which were least developed countries when the Decision was adopted). This waiver allows a Member to export to countries throughout the region under a single compulsory license, although it does not expressly waive the requirement for licenses to be issued by importing countries of the region. The main benefit of the waiver may be to allow the import of APIs, formulation into finished products, and export throughout the African region.

Paragraph 7 refers in a general way to transfer of technology.

Paragraph 8 makes clear that the waiver does not require annual renewal.

Paragraph 9 indicates that the Decision is without prejudice to rights that Members may otherwise have under TRIPS (such as the potential for exports under Article 30).

Paragraph 10 precludes non-violation nullification or impairment causes of action with respect to the Decision.

Paragraph 11 provides that the waiver will remain effective for each Member until an amendment has come into effect to replace it there, and that Members will commence negotiations for an amendment to be based, where appropriate, on the waiver. Although the Decision stated that the negotiations would have a view to completion within six months following the end of 2003, in June 2004 the TRIPS Council extended that tentative completion date until the end of March 2005.

The Chairperson's Statement indicates, *inter alia*, that Members will act in good faith in using the Decision, providing:

> "First, Members recognize that the system that will be established by the Decision should be used in good faith to protect public health and, without prejudice to paragraph 6 of the Decision, not be an instrument to pursue industrial or commercial policy objectives."

This statement of good faith does not in any way preclude enterprises from acting for commercial gain. Since it is unlikely that a Member would use importation as the means to effect an industrial or commercial policy, it seems doubtful that this statement of good faith will inhibit use of the system.

6.2.2 Paragraph 5 of the Doha Declaration

Paragraph 5 of the WTO Doha Ministerial Declaration on the TRIPS Agreement and Public Health (Doha Declaration) states in its relevant part:

> "5. [...], while maintaining our commitments in the TRIPS Agreement, we recognize that these flexibilities [i.e. the ones contained in the TRIPS Agreement] include: [...]
>
> (b) Each Member has the right to grant compulsory licences and the freedom to determine the grounds upon which such licences are granted.
>
> (c) Each Member has the right to determine what constitutes a national emergency or other circumstances of extreme urgency, ..."

This statement does not provide for any substantive modifications of TRIPS but only reiterates what is already stipulated therein. Paragraph (b) relates to Members' discretion with regard to the grounds upon which compulsory licences are granted. Paragraph (c) refers to Article 31(b), making clear that the definition of the terms "national emergency" and "other circumstances of extreme urgency" is up to Members' discretion. This leaves Members considerable room for the pursuit of public policy objectives, especially those related to public health.

6.3 Regional context

6.3.1 FTAA

Countries of the western hemisphere have proposed to enter into a Free Trade Area of the Americas (FTAA) Agreement by 2005. A preliminary draft text of the FTAA includes a chapter on intellectual property rights.[952] That chapter includes a number of proposals regarding compulsory licensing.

6.3.2 The Andean Community

In September 2000, the Andean Community (Bolivia, Colombia, Ecuador, Peru and Venezuela) adopted Decision 486 establishing a new IPR system. This Decision contains a separate chapter on compulsory licensing.[953]

6.3.3 The Bangui Agreement

Finally, the African Intellectual Property Organization (OAPI) in 1999 revised the 1977 Bangui Agreement on the Creation of an African Intellectual Property Organization. Annex 1, Title IV to the 1999 Agreement regulates non-voluntary licenses.[954]

6.4 Proposals for review

As noted earlier, the Decision on Implementation of Paragraph 6 provides for negotiation of an amendment to be based, where appropriate, on the Decision. It

---

[952] FTAA – Free Trade Area of the Americas, Draft Agreement, Chapter on Intellectual Property Rights, Derestricted, FTAA.TNC/w/133/Rev.1, July 3, 2001.

[953] See <http://www.ftaa-alca.org/intprop/natleg/Decisions/dec486_e.asp>.

[954] See <http://www.oapi.wipo.net/en/textes/pdf/accord_bangui.pdf>.

is expected that some developing Members will propose changes to the Decision, but as of July 2004, no formal proposals to this effect had been made to the TRIPS Council.[955]

7. Comments, including economic and social implications

Compulsory licensing of patents is one of the most important economic instruments for developing countries attempting to address the technology gap with developed countries. In her classic 1951 work, *The Economics of the International Patent System*, Edith Penrose observed:

> "The second method of reducing the cost of the patent monopoly is that of compulsory licensing. This is by far the most effective and flexible method and enables the state to prevent most of the more serious restrictions on industry. It could be used very effectively to undermine the monopoly power of several of the more powerful international cartels whose position is largely based on their control of the patent rights to industrial processes in the larger industrial countries; and it could be used to ensure that patented new techniques developed abroad are available to domestic industries wishing to use them.
>
> The International [Paris] Convention places restrictions on the right of countries to subject patents to compulsory licensing. These restrictions should be eliminated and countries should be encouraged to use this device to break up some of the more serious of the monopolistic restrictions on the use of new techniques."[956]

Ownership of technology remains concentrated in the developed countries where large amounts of capital are invested in research and development (R&D). Industries in developing countries have great difficulty in competing in R&D because of persistent structural imbalances. Developed country enterprises are often reluctant to licence new technology on terms and conditions that will permit developing country enterprises to effectively compete in world markets. Although TRIPS makes a number of references to encouraging transfers of technology, there is little evidence that programmes to accomplish this are being implemented. Compulsory licensing, and the threat of compulsory licensing, are necessary to make transfer of technology a reality.

Developing countries that grant compulsory licences run the risk of economic retaliation by developed countries. For this reason, compulsory licensing should be undertaken in accord with international obligations. The adoption of the Doha Declaration has unambiguously confirmed the right of Members to define the grounds for granting compulsory licences.

---

[955] Note that as of August 2004, Members in the Council for TRIPS have not been able to agree on a common approach to amending Article 31, TRIPS Agreement. Main areas of controversy relate to the content of the amendment and its form. As to the content, delegations disagree whether the Chair's statement, issued together with the Decision of 30 August 2003, should be incorporated into the amendment of the TRIPS Agreement. Some Members have expressed concern about enhancing the Chair's statement's legal status by such incorporation. As to the legal form of the envisaged TRIPS amendment, some Members favour a footnote to Article 31 TRIPS, referring to the Decision as a separate document. Others support the inclusion into the TRIPS Agreement of the full text of the Decision, either under a new Article 31*bis*, or as an Annex, or as a footnote.

[956] Penrose.

The argument is made that compulsory licensing reduces incentives for developed country enterprises to engage in R&D, and that reduced R&D diminishes global welfare by lowering the future stock of useful inventions. However, the benefit to developing countries of increased R&D in the developed countries is often remote, and there is no evidence that the granting of compulsory licences has led to a reduction in R&D investment.[957] Compulsory licensing stresses the interest of developing countries in raising current standards of living.

---

[957] F. M. Scherer, *Comments* in Robert Anderson and Nancy Gallini (Eds.), *Competition policy and intellectual property rights in the knowledge-based economy*, University of Calgary Press, Alberta 1998.

Annex 1: The Decision on Implementation of Paragraph 6 of the Doha Declaration on the TRIPS Agreement and Public Health (the "Decision"), including Chairperson's Statement

Decision of 30 August 2003*

The General Council,

Having regard to paragraphs 1, 3 and 4 of Article IX of the Marrakesh Agreement Establishing the World Trade Organization ("the WTO Agreement");

Conducting the functions of the Ministerial Conference in the interval between meetings pursuant to paragraph 2 of Article IV of the WTO Agreement;

Noting the Declaration on the TRIPS Agreement and Public Health (WT/MIN(01)/DEC/2) (the "Declaration") and, in particular, the instruction of the Ministerial Conference to the Council for TRIPS contained in paragraph 6 of the Declaration to find an expeditious solution to the problem of the difficulties that WTO Members with insufficient or no manufacturing capacities in the pharmaceutical sector could face in making effective use of compulsory licensing under the TRIPS Agreement and to report to the General Council before the end of 2002;

Recognizing, where eligible importing Members seek to obtain supplies under the system set out in this Decision, the importance of a rapid response to those needs consistent with the provisions of this Decision;

Noting that, in the light of the foregoing, exceptional circumstances exist justifying waivers from the obligations set out in paragraphs (f) and (h) of Article 31 of the TRIPS Agreement with respect to pharmaceutical products;

Decides as follows:

For the purposes of this Decision:

(a) "pharmaceutical product" means any patented product, or product manufactured through a patented process, of the pharmaceutical sector needed to address the public health problems as recognized in paragraph 1 of the Declaration. It is understood that active ingredients necessary for its manufacture and diagnostic kits needed for its use would be included[958];

(b) "eligible importing Member" means any least-developed country Member, and any other Member that has made a notification[959] to the Council for TRIPS of its intention to use the system as an importer, it being understood that a Member may notify at any time that it will use the system in whole or in a limited way, for example only in the case of a national emergency or other circumstances of extreme urgency or in cases of public non-commercial use. It is noted that some Members will not use the system set out in this Decision as importing Members[960]

---

* This Decision was adopted by the General Council in the light of a statement read out by the Chairman, which can be found in JOB(03)/177. This statement will be reproduced in the minutes of the General Council to be issued as WT/GC/M/82.

[958] This subparagraph is without prejudice to subparagraph 1(b).

[959] It is understood that this notification does not need to be approved by a WTO body in order to use the system set out in this Decision.

[960] Australia, Austria, Belgium, Canada, Denmark, Finland, France, Germany, Greece, Iceland, Ireland, Italy, Japan, Luxembourg, the Netherlands, New Zealand, Norway, Portugal, Spain, Sweden, Switzerland, the United Kingdom and the United States.

and that some other Members have stated that, if they use the system, it would be in no more than situations of national emergency or other circumstances of extreme urgency;

(c) "exporting Member" means a Member using the system set out in this Decision to produce pharmaceutical products for, and export them to, an eligible importing Member.

2. The obligations of an exporting Member under Article 31(f) of the TRIPS Agreement shall be waived with respect to the grant by it of a compulsory licence to the extent necessary for the purposes of production of a pharmaceutical product(s) and its export to an eligible importing Member(s) in accordance with the terms set out below in this paragraph:

(a) the eligible importing Member(s)[961] has made a notification[959] to the Council for TRIPS, that:

(i) specifies the names and expected quantities of the product(s) needed[962];

(ii) confirms that the eligible importing Member in question, other than a least-developed country Member, has established that it has insufficient or no manufacturing capacities in the pharmaceutical sector for the product(s) in question in one of the ways set out in the Annex to this Decision; and

(iii) confirms that, where a pharmaceutical product is patented in its territory, it has granted or intends to grant a compulsory licence in accordance with Article 31 of the TRIPS Agreement and the provisions of this Decision[963];

(b) the compulsory licence issued by the exporting Member under this Decision shall contain the following conditions:

(i) only the amount necessary to meet the needs of the eligible importing Member(s) may be manufactured under the licence and the entirety of this production shall be exported to the Member(s) which has notified its needs to the Council for TRIPS;

(ii) products produced under the licence shall be clearly identified as being produced under the system set out in this Decision through specific labelling or marking. Suppliers should distinguish such products through special packaging and/or special colouring/shaping of the products themselves, provided that such distinction is feasible and does not have a significant impact on price; and

(iii) before shipment begins, the licensee shall post on a website[964] the following information:

– the quantities being supplied to each destination as referred to in indent (i) above; and

– the distinguishing features of the product(s) referred to in indent (ii) above;

---

[961] Joint notifications providing the information required under this subparagraph may be made by the regional organizations referred to in paragraph 6 of this Decision on behalf of eligible importing Members using the system that are parties to them, with the agreement of those parties.

[962] The notification will be made available publicly by the WTO Secretariat through a page on the WTO website dedicated to this Decision.

[963] This subparagraph is without prejudice to Article 66.1 of the TRIPS Agreement.

[964] The licensee may use for this purpose its own website or, with the assistance of the WTO Secretariat, the page on the WTO website dedicated to this Decision.

(c) the exporting Member shall notify[965] the Council for TRIPS of the grant of the licence, including the conditions attached to it.[966] The information provided shall include the name and address of the licensee, the product(s) for which the licence has been granted, the quantity(ies) for which it has been granted, the country(ies) to which the product(s) is (are) to be supplied and the duration of the licence. The notification shall also indicate the address of the website referred to in subparagraph (b)(iii) above.

3. Where a compulsory licence is granted by an exporting Member under the system set out in this Decision, adequate remuneration pursuant to Article 31(h) of the TRIPS Agreement shall be paid to that Member taking into account the economic value to the importing Member of the use that has been authorized in the exporting Member. Where a compulsory licence is granted for the same products in the eligible importing Member, the obligation of that Member under Article 31(h) shall be waived in respect of those products for which remuneration in accordance with the first sentence of this paragraph is paid in the exporting Member.

4. In order to ensure that the products imported under the system set out in this Decision are used for the public health purposes underlying their importation, eligible importing Members shall take reasonable measures within their means, proportionate to their administrative capacities and to the risk of trade diversion to prevent re-exportation of the products that have actually been imported into their territories under the system. In the event that an eligible importing Member that is a developing country Member or a least-developed country Member experiences difficulty in implementing this provision, developed country Members shall provide, on request and on mutually agreed terms and conditions, technical and financial cooperation in order to facilitate its implementation.

5. Members shall ensure the availability of effective legal means to prevent the importation into, and sale in, their territories of products produced under the system set out in this Decision and diverted to their markets inconsistently with its provisions, using the means already required to be available under the TRIPS Agreement. If any Member considers that such measures are proving insufficient for this purpose, the matter may be reviewed in the Council for TRIPS at the request of that Member.

6. With a view to harnessing economies of scale for the purposes of enhancing purchasing power for, and facilitating the local production of, pharmaceutical products:

(i) where a developing or least-developed country WTO Member is a party to a regional trade agreement within the meaning of Article XXIV of the GATT 1994 and the Decision of 28 November 1979 on Differential and More Favourable Treatment Reciprocity and Fuller Participation of Developing Countries (L/4903), at least half of the current membership of which is made up of countries presently on the United Nations list of least-developed countries, the obligation of that Member

---

[965] It is understood that this notification does not need to be approved by a WTO body in order to use the system set out in this Decision.

[966] The notification will be made available publicly by the WTO Secretariat through a page on the WTO website dedicated to this Decision.

under Article 31(f) of the TRIPS Agreement shall be waived to the extent necessary to enable a pharmaceutical product produced or imported under a compulsory licence in that Member to be exported to the markets of those other developing or least-developed country parties to the regional trade agreement that share the health problem in question. It is understood that this will not prejudice the territorial nature of the patent rights in question;

(ii) it is recognized that the development of systems providing for the grant of regional patents to be applicable in the above Members should be promoted. To this end, developed country Members undertake to provide technical cooperation in accordance with Article 67 of the TRIPS Agreement, including in conjunction with other relevant intergovernmental organizations.

7. Members recognize the desirability of promoting the transfer of technology and capacity building in the pharmaceutical sector in order to overcome the problem identified in paragraph 6 of the Declaration. To this end, eligible importing Members and exporting Members are encouraged to use the system set out in this Decision in a way which would promote this objective. Members undertake to cooperate in paying special attention to the transfer of technology and capacity building in the pharmaceutical sector in the work to be undertaken pursuant to Article 66.2 of the TRIPS Agreement, paragraph 7 of the Declaration and any other relevant work of the Council for TRIPS.

8. The Council for TRIPS shall review annually the functioning of the system set out in this Decision with a view to ensuring its effective operation and shall annually report on its operation to the General Council. This review shall be deemed to fulfil the review requirements of Article IX:4 of the WTO Agreement.

9. This Decision is without prejudice to the rights, obligations and flexibilities that Members have under the provisions of the TRIPS Agreement other than paragraphs (f) and (h) of Article 31, including those reaffirmed by the Declaration, and to their interpretation. It is also without prejudice to the extent to which pharmaceutical products produced under a compulsory licence can be exported under the present provisions of Article 31(f) of the TRIPS Agreement.

10. Members shall not challenge any measures taken in conformity with the provisions of the waivers contained in this Decision under subparagraphs 1(b) and 1(c) of Article XXIII of GATT 1994.

11. This Decision, including the waivers granted in it, shall terminate for each Member on the date on which an amendment to the TRIPS Agreement replacing its provisions takes effect for that Member. The TRIPS Council shall initiate by the end of 2003 work on the preparation of such an amendment with a view to its adoption within six months, on the understanding that the amendment will be based, where appropriate, on this Decision and on the further understanding that it will not be part of the negotiations referred to in paragraph 45 of the Doha Ministerial Declaration (WT/MIN(01)/DEC/1).

ANNEX [to the Decision]

Assessment of Manufacturing Capacities in the Pharmaceutical Sector Least-developed country Members are deemed to have insufficient or no manufacturing capacities in the pharmaceutical sector. For other eligible importing Members insufficient or no manufacturing capacities for the product(s) in question may be established in either of the following ways:

(i) the Member in question has established that it has no manufacturing capacity in the pharmaceutical sector;

   OR

(ii) where the Member has some manufacturing capacity in this sector, it has examined this capacity and found that, excluding any capacity owned or controlled by the patent owner, it is currently insufficient for the purposes of meeting its needs. When it is established that such capacity has become sufficient to meet the Member's needs, the system shall no longer apply.

The General Council's Chairperson's Statement

The General Council has been presented with a draft Decision contained in document IP/C/W/405 to implement paragraph 6 of the Doha Declaration on the TRIPS Agreement and Public Health. This Decision is part of the wider national and international action to address problems as recognized in paragraph 1 of the Declaration. Before adopting this Decision, I would like to place on the record this Statement which represents several key shared understandings of Members regarding the Decision to be taken and the way in which it will be interpreted and implemented. I would like to emphasize that this Statement is limited in its implications to paragraph 6 of the Doha Declaration on the TRIPS Agreement and Public Health.

First, Members recognize that the system that will be established by the Decision should be used in good faith to protect public health and, without prejudice to paragraph 6 of the Decision, not be an instrument to pursue industrial or commercial policy objectives.

Second, Members recognize that the purpose of the Decision would be defeated if products supplied under this Decision are diverted from the markets for which they are intended. Therefore, all reasonable measures should be taken to prevent such diversion in accordance with the relevant paragraphs of the Decision. In this regard, the provisions of paragraph 2(b)(ii) apply not only to formulated pharmaceuticals produced and supplied under the system but also to active ingredients produced and supplied under the system and to finished products produced using such active ingredients. It is the understanding of Members that in general special packaging and/or special colouring or shaping should not have a significant impact on the price of pharmaceuticals.

In the past, companies have developed procedures to prevent diversion of products that are, for example, provided through donor programmes. "Best practices" guidelines that draw upon the experiences of companies are attached to this statement for illustrative purposes. Members and producers are encouraged to draw from and use these practices, and to share information on their experiences in preventing diversion.

Third, it is important that Members seek to resolve any issues arising from the use and implementation of the Decision expeditiously and amicably:

• To promote transparency and avoid controversy, notifications under paragraph 2(a)(ii) of the Decision would include information on how the Member in question had established, in accordance with the Annex, that it has insufficient or no manufacturing capacities in the pharmaceutical sector.

• In accordance with the normal practice of the TRIPS Council, notifications made under the system shall be brought to the attention of its next meeting.

• Any Member may bring any matter related to the interpretation or implementation of the Decision, including issues related to diversion, to the TRIPS Council for expeditious review, with a view to taking appropriate action.

• If any Member has concerns that the terms of the Decision have not been fully complied with, the Member may also utilise the good offices of the Director General or Chair of the TRIPS Council, with a view to finding a mutually acceptable solution.

Fourth, all information gathered on the implementation of the Decision shall be brought to the attention of the TRIPS Council in its annual review as set out in paragraph 8 of the Decision.

In addition, as stated in footnote 3 to paragraph 1(b) of the Decision, the following Members have agreed to opt out of using the system as importers: Australia, Austria, Belgium, Canada, Denmark, Finland, France, Germany, Greece, Iceland, Ireland, Italy, Japan, Luxembourg, Netherlands, New Zealand, Norway, Portugal, Spain, Sweden, Switzerland, United Kingdom and United States of America. Until their accession to the European Union, Czech Republic, Cyprus, Estonia, Hungary, Latvia, Lithuania, Malta, Poland, Slovak Republic and Slovenia agree that they would only use the system as importers in situations of national emergency or other circumstances of extreme urgency. These countries further agree that upon their accession to the European Union, they will opt out of using the system as importers.

As we have heard today, and as the Secretariat has been informed in certain communications, some other Members have agreed that they would only use the system as importers in situations of national emergency or other circumstances of extreme urgency: Hong Kong China, Israel, Korea, Kuwait, Macao China, Mexico, Qatar, Singapore, Chinese Taipei, Turkey, United Arab Emirates.

Attachment:

"Best Practice" guidelines

Companies have often used special labelling, colouring, shaping, sizing, etc. to differentiate products supplied through donor or discounted pricing programmes from products supplied to other markets. Examples of such measures include the following:

• Bristol Myers Squibb used different markings/imprints on capsules supplied to sub-Saharan Africa.

• Novartis has used different trademark names, one (Riamet®) for an anti-malarial drug provided to developed countries, the other (Coartem®) for the same products supplied to developing countries. Novartis further differentiated the products through distinctive packaging.

• GlaxoSmithKline (GSK) used different outer packaging for its HIV/AIDS medications Combivir, Epivir and Trizivir supplied to developing countries. GSK further differentiated the products by embossing the tablets with a different number than tablets supplied to developed countries, and plans to further differentiate the products by using different colours.

• Merck differentiated its HIV/AIDS antiretroviral medicine CRIXIVAN through special packaging and labelling, i.e., gold-ink printing on the capsule, dark green bottle cap and a bottle label with a light-green background.

• Pfizer used different colouring and shaping for Diflucan pills supplied to South Africa.

Producers have further minimized diversion by entering into contractual arrangements with importers/distributors to ensure delivery of products to the intended markets.

To help ensure use of the most effective anti-diversion measures, Members may share their experiences and practices in preventing diversion either informally or through the TRIPS Council. It would be beneficial for Members and industry to work together to further refine anti-diversion practices and enhance the sharing of information related to identifying, remedying or preventing specific occurrences of diversion.

26: Process Patents: Burden of Proof

Article 34 Process Patents: Burden of Proof

1. For the purpose of civil proceedings in respect of the infringement of the rights of the owner referred to in paragraph 1(b) of Article 28, if the subject matter of a patent is a process for obtaining a product, the judicial authorities shall have the authority to order the defendant to prove that the process to obtain an identical product is different from the patented process. Therefore, Members shall provide, in at least one of the following circumstances, that any identical product when produced without the consent of the patent owner shall, in the absence of proof to the contrary, be deemed to have been obtained by the patented process:

(a) if the product obtained by the patented process is new;

(b) if there is a substantial likelihood that the identical product was made by the process and the owner of the patent has been unable through reasonable efforts to determine the process actually used. Any Member shall be free to provide that the burden of proof indicated in paragraph 1 shall be on the alleged infringer only if the conditions referred to in subparagraph (a) is fulfilled or only if the condition referred to in subparagraph (b) is fulfilled.

2. In adduction of proof to the contrary, the legitimate interests of the defendants in protecting their manufacturing and business secret shall be taken into account.

---

1. Introduction: terminology, definition and scope

Article 34 is concerned with patents the subject matter of which is a claim or claims to a process for the manufacture of a product, which may itself be the subject of a patent though it does not necessarily have to be.

Article 34 reverses the procedural principle under which the person asserting a fact must prove it. Its purpose is to meet the so called *"probatio diabolica"*: it is always difficult for a plaintiff owning a process patent to prove whether or not the process used by the alleged infringer to manufacture an identical product to the one resulting from the patented process infringes his exclusive right, unless the plaintiff gains access to the manufacturing process of the alleged infringer.[967]

The conditions on which the onus of proof should be reversed are as follows:[968]

1. The alleged infringer's product must be identical for material purposes to the product produced by the patented process.

2. If this is the case, Members should implement a presumption that such product has been obtained by the patented process if –

(a) the product obtained by the patented process is new; or

(b) if there is a substantial likelihood that the identical product (new or existing) was made by such process and the owner of the patent was unable through reasonable efforts to determine the process actually used, and the patent owner produces evidence that he/she has used reasonable efforts to try to determine the process used and was unable to do so.

2. History of the provision

2.1 Situation pre-TRIPS

The rule on the reversal of the burden of proof was introduced by the 1891 German patent law (Article 139). It was also incorporated in the patent laws of Italy, Belgium and Spain. It was also included in the Community Patent Convention (Article 35), as well as in the proposed WIPO treaty for harmonization of patent law (Article 24)[969] on terms substantially similar to the text adopted later on under TRIPS.

2.2 Negotiating history

Negotiations on this provision were based on the proposals submitted in 1990 by the European Communities, the USA and Switzerland. Equivalents of this provision existed in both the Brussels Draft of TRIPS and in the Anell Draft of July 23, 1990. The two conditions for the reversal of the *onus probandi* were similar in both drafts, but in its final version Article 34.2 makes it clear that Members may provide that the onus shall be on the alleged infringer if *either* of the conditions is fulfilled. During the negotiations the European Commission favoured the first condition and the United States the second.[970]

2.2.1 The Anell Draft

"2.3 <u>Reversal of Burden of Proof</u>

2.3A.1 If the subject matter of a patent is a process for obtaining a product, the same product when produced by any other party shall, in the absence of proof to

---

[967] See, e.g., Miguel Vidal-Quadras Trias des Bes, *Process patents on new products and reversal of the burden of proof: factors contributing to the interpretation of its scope*, European Intellectual Property Review 2002, vol. 24, No. 5, p. 237–243 (237) [hereinafter Vidal-Quadras Trias des Bes].

[968] See Gervais, p. 171.

[969] See WIPO, 1991, p. 32.

[970] See Gervais, p. 172.

the contrary, be deemed to have been obtained by the patented process in [at least one of] the following situation[s]:

(a) if the product is new, [or,

(b) where the product is not new, if there is a substantial likelihood that the product was made by the process [and the owner of the patent has been unable through reasonable efforts to determine the process actually used].

2.3A.2 In the adduction of proof to the contrary, the legitimate interests of the defendant in protecting his manufacturing and business secrets shall be taken into account.

2.3B Where the subject matter of a patent is a process for obtaining a product, whether new or old, the burden of establishing that an alleged infringing product was made by the patented process shall always be on the person alleging such infringement."

Alternative 2.3B, introduced by developing countries, was clearly intended to counter the proposals for reversal of the burden of proof. But this strategy was not successful, as is obvious from the text finally adopted.

2.2 The Brussels Draft

"Reversal of Burden of Proof

1. For the purpose of civil proceedings in respect of the infringement of the rights of the owner referred to in Article [28](1)(b), if the subject matter of a patent is a process for obtaining a product, PARTIES [shall] [may] provide in at least one of the following circumstances that any identical product when produced by any party not having the consent of the patent owner shall, in the absence of proof to the contrary, be deemed to have been obtained by the patented process:

(a) if the product obtained by the patented process is new;

(b) if there is a substantial likelihood that the identical product was made by the process and the owner of the patent has been unable through reasonable efforts to determine the process actually used.

2. In the adduction of proof to the contrary, the legitimate interests of the defendant in protecting his manufacturing and business secrets shall be taken into account."

3. Possible interpretations

> 1. For the purpose of civil proceedings in respect of the infringement of the rights of the owner referred to in paragraph 1(b) of Article 28, if the subject matter of a patent is a process for obtaining a product, . . .

The reversal of burden of proof logically applies to civil procedures only, since the presumption of innocence generally governs in criminal cases. The subject of the patent for the reversal to proceed should be a "patent for obtaining a process". It is left to Members, however, to determine whether such a process should be the *sole* object of the patent, or whether "hybrid" patents (including claims over both a process and a product) should also be subject to Article 34.

This Article only applies, further, in cases where an infringement of the acts described in Article 28.1(b) of TRIPS is alleged, that is, whenever the identical product has been directly obtained with the patented process. It is not enough, hence, to argue that the product is *obtainable* with such a process.

> ... the judicial authorities shall have the authority to order the defendant to prove that the process to obtain an identical product is different from the patented process.

Article 34.1 requires Members to empower their judicial authorities to order the reversal of the burden of proof. It is not an operative, self-executing provision, but requires positive action both by the Members and, in a particular case, the competent judge. The defendant can be obliged to prove that the process is different from the patented process, but cannot be obliged to prove that the process has not been infringed. If the defendant proves that the process used by himself on the one hand and the patented process on the other hand are different, the proof of infringement, which would normally require the application of the "doctrine of equivalents",[971] remains a plaintiff's burden, according to general principles of procedural law.[972]

> Therefore, Members shall provide, in at least one of the following circumstances, that any identical product when produced without the consent of the patent owner shall, in the absence of proof to the contrary, be deemed to have been obtained by the patented process:

Whether a product is "identical" to the product obtained by a patented process is to be determined on the basis of its structural composition. Similarity, therefore, is not sufficient to trigger the reversal of proof.[973]

---

[971] This doctrine provides a conceptual framework to determine if a violation of a patent exists when there is no literal infringement of patent claims. See, e.g., Correa, 2000a, p. 85.

[972] See the decision of the Barcelona Provincial Appellate Court of September 18, 2000, in *Enaaprile II*, according to which the defendant's burden of proving the contrary "is confined to disclosing the process actually used by the defendant (which would convert the proceedings into a mere comparison of both processes) and to show that the two processes are not identical, but not that the presumption also involves proof that the processes are not equivalent". See also the judgment of the German Federal Court of June 25, 1976, in *Alkylendiamine II*, which held that a similar rule under German law did not shift the responsibility for determining the scope of the plaintiff's right on the defendant; but merely required the defendant to provide sufficient proof of the process actually used in manufacturing the product. G.R.U.R 1997, p.103 (cases quoted in Vidal-Quadras Trias des Bes, p. 240).

[973] The German Federal Supreme Court in the *Alkylenediamine II* case clarified that the notion of "same substance" under the old Patents Act Section 47(3) applied also when established differences exist between two substances within the limits that technical experience shows to be attributable to a variation of the patented process, but not the application of a different process. See Straus, p. 820.

In addition to requiring that judges be empowered to order the reversal, Article 34 provides for the establishment of a *juris tantum* presumption that the patented process has been effectively used. This presumption admits proof to the contrary.

As mentioned, the conditions stipulated in Article 34.1 for the reversal to proceed constitute options for Members. They may opt for establishing one or the other,[974] at their discretion.

3.1 Article 34.1(a)

> (a) if the product obtained by the patented process is new;

This condition, probably inspired by European law, requires the "newness" of the product obtained through the protected process. In many cases, the product may be new but not inventive and, hence, not patentable. In the case of countries that did not grant product patent protection for pharmaceuticals or other products, there exist many instances in which the inventor was able to patent the process, but not the product. The rationale for this option is that when a product is new, it is unlikely that competitors had the time to develop alternative processes to obtain the same product. The older the product, the higher the possibility that such alternatives have been developed.[975]

For countries that opt for alternative (a), there is no obligation to order the reversal of the burden for products which are not new.

TRIPS does not determine when a product should be considered new for the purposes of this provision. Members enjoy considerable room for manoeuvre in this respect. They may, for instance, establish that newness be judged:

(1) according to the novelty requirement under the patent law on the date of the application (or the priority date). This solution is significantly advantageous to the patent owner: though a long period may have passed between that date and the date of infringement, the product would still be considered new for the purposes of the burden of proof. Under this approach the attribute of new is fixed once and forever ignoring that, as time passes, it may be reasonably presumed that other processes to obtain the product may have been developed.[976]

---

[974] A "TRIPS-plus" solution may obviously be to order reversal of the burden of proof when *any* of the conditions are met, as originally sought by the USA during TRIPS negotiations.

[975] Thus, it has been noted that "it seems to be reasonable to assume that, where subsequent processes have been described for obtaining the product resulting from the claimed patented processes to the extent that such processes may vary to a greater or lesser extent, bring different advantages or simply be practicable, when the patent invoked is close to expiry and alternative processes have been described, these circumstances must be taken into account in order to undermine the grounds for presuming that the patented process has been used" (Vidal-Quadras Trias des Bes, p. 242).

[976] The District Court of Munich considered (as long ago as 1963) that the "new product" characteristic required by the article of the Patent Law relating to the reversal of the burden of proof did not necessarily have to be interpreted as having the same meaning as novelty for the purpose of patentability. More recent German authors have taken the same view since such an interpretation

Or:

(2) at the time the product is introduced into the market. If other products obtained by non-infringing processes were available at that time, it would be *prima facie* proven that other processes existed for obtaining the product and, therefore, there would be no logical basis for the legal presumption to operate. This solution was proposed in one of the texts considered in the preparatory work of the WIPO Diplomatic Conference for the adoption of a Patent Law Treaty,[977] and has also been suggested by some authorities in Europe.[978]

3.2 Article 34.1(b)

> (b) if there is a substantial likelihood that the identical product was made by the process and the owner of the patent has been unable through reasonable efforts to determine the process actually used. Any Member shall be free to provide that the burden of proof indicated in paragraph 1 shall be on the alleged infringer only if the condition referred to in subparagraph (a) is fulfilled or only if the condition referred to in subparagraph (b) is fulfilled.

A "substantial likelihood" is more than the mere "possibility". The plaintiff must be able to prove that, in the circumstances of the particular case, the identical product is likely to have been obtained with his patented process. Under this option, the plaintiff would also have to prove that he has made reasonable and unsuccessful efforts to determine what process was used, for instance, by undertaking the chemical analysis of the product, requesting information from the product manufacturer (if known and different from the alleged infringer), or other measures that the owner could undertake at a reasonable cost and within a reasonable time.

3.3 Article 34.2

> 2. In adduction of proof to the contrary, the legitimate interests of the defendants in protecting their manufacturing and business secret shall be taken into account.

As noted, Article 34.2 makes it clear that the obligation to reverse the burden of proof may apply in *either* the circumstances specified in Article 34.1(a) or (b) set out above. If the product has in fact been produced by a different process, the alleged infringer will not want to disclose his process to competitors. Article 34.2

---

would be contrary to the purpose of the procedural rule contained in German law (Vidal-Quadras Trias des Bes, p. 242).

[977] Article 301(1)(b) of the 1987 Draft Patent Law Treaty disregarded the presumption of infringement "if, at the time of the alleged violation, an identical product emanating from a source other than the owner of the patent and the defendant was already known in commerce in the country in which the patent applies". See, e.g., Harold Wegner, *Patent Harmonization*, Sweet & Maxwell, London 1993, p. 334.

[978] See, e.g., authors quoted by Straus, p. 821.

provides that in the presentation of evidence to the contrary, the legitimate interests of the defendants in protecting their manufacturing and business secret shall be taken into account. Obviously, those legitimate interests include not disclosing the defendant's trade secrets to the other side, including technical and commercial information (e.g., the source of a given intermediate used in the process).

However, the defendant will be bound to disclose the process that has actually been used in order to rebut the *juris tantum* presumption. Otherwise, he will be deemed as infringing the patent. A possible strategy to protect the defendant's trade secrets is for the rules of court procedure of a Member to require the trade secrets to be disclosed only to an independent expert, who is under an obligation of secrecy, and who will advise the court under conditions of confidentiality. Another strategy which is perhaps more appropriate to adversarial (as opposed to inquisitorial) court procedures is to require the information to be disclosed to one member of the plaintiff's team who is similarly bound by an obligation of secrecy. That person will communicate the information to the plaintiff's independent lawyers (who are similarly under an obligation of confidentiality), who will then advise whether the proceedings are to continue or to be discontinued.

"Legitimate interests", as defined by the panel in *Canada-Patent protection of pharmaceutical products*, must be "construed as a concept broader than legal interests",[979] encompassing any business interest that the defendant may legitimately wish to protect.

4. WTO jurisprudence

There is no WTO jurisprudence on this provision. In a case settled between USA and Argentina after consultations, the Argentine government agreed to amend its patent law in order to comply with Article 34.1. The proposed amendment opts for the alternative provided for under Article 34.1 (a).[980]

5. Relationship with other international instruments

This provision has no counterpart in either the Paris Convention or the European Patent Convention, both of which leave the question of onus of proof to national law. However, Article 35 of the Community Patent Convention provides that

"1. If the subject-matter of a Community patent is a process for obtaining a new product, the identical product when produced by any other party shall, in the

---

[979] WT/DS114/R, 17 March 2000, at para 7.71.

[980] With regard to the definition of "new", the proposed amendment reads as follows: "[I]t shall be presumed that, in the absence of proof to the contrary, the product obtained by the patented process is not new if the defendant or if an expert appointed by the court at the request of the defendant is able to show that, at the time of the alleged infringement, there exists in the market a non-infringing product identical to the one produced by the patented process that originated from a source different from the right owner or the defendant". See WT/DS171/3, WT/DS196/4, IP/D/18/Add.1, IP/D/22/Add.1 of 20 June 2002.

absence of proof to the contrary, be deemed to have been obtained by the patented process.

2. In the adduction of proof to the contrary, the legitimate interests of the defendant in protecting his manufacturing and business secrets shall be taken into account".

6. New developments

In implementing the rule on reversal of burden of proof mandated by TRIPS, some countries opted for alternative (a),[981] others for alternative (b),[982] while many incorporated both conditions set out in Article 34.1.[983]

7. Comments, including economic and social implications

Process patents are a weak form of protection, because of the difficulties involved in proving infringement. As noted above, formerly some countries while barring the patenting of pharmaceutical products would allow the patenting of processes. The effect was that for practical purposes pharmaceutical products were not fully protected, because the key feature of a pharmaceutical product is usually its molecule, and in practice the composition of this is fairly easy to analyse, though the same molecule must be manufactured by an alternative method in order not to infringe the process patent. Article 34 attempts to ameliorate this weakness by reversing the onus of proof, so that if the defendant has produced an identical product to that produced by the process patent, the onus shifts to the defendant to show that the product was produced without use of the process covered by the patent. It is, of course, no defence in patent law that the defendant independently developed the identical process. Independent creation is a defence in copyright and trade secrets law, but a patent confers an exclusive right on the patentee.

The reversal of the burden of proof, hence, may be of particular importance in developing countries and economies in transition that did not recognize product patents for pharmaceuticals or in other fields of technology prior to the implementation of TRIPS. With the universal introduction of product patent protection for pharmaceuticals and chemical products under Article 27.1, the practical importance of such principle will diminish, since infringement of product patents would be easier to prove. However, Article 34 will provide a valuable procedural tool to patent holders that have only been able to obtain process and not product protection.

Those countries that opted, in implementing Article 34.1, for alternative (a) generally aimed at excluding the application of such a rule for products already in the market. The extent to which this will be achieved, however, would depend

---

[981] See, e.g., Argentine patent law 24.481 (Article 88).

[982] This alternative is often found, for instance, in bilateral agreements concluded between the USA and former centrally managed economies (Straus, p. 810).

[983] See, e.g., Indonesian patent law No. 14 of year 2000 (Article 119); Industrial Property Common Regime of the Andean Community, Decision 486 (Article 240).

on the way in which the concept of "new" is defined by law and jurisprudence. If "new" is assimilated to the "novelty" standard for patentability, and a product was new at the time of the patent application, it would remain "new" for the purposes of the reversal of the burden of proof until the patent expires, possibly many years after its introduction into commerce.

27: Integrated Circuits

Article 35   Relation to the IPIC Treaty

Members agree to provide protection to the layout-designs (topographies) of integrated circuits (referred to in this Agreement as "layout-designs") in accordance with Articles 2 through 7 (other than paragraph 3 of Article 6), Article 12 and paragraph 3 of Article 16 of the Treaty on Intellectual Property in Respect of Integrated Circuits and, in addition, to comply with the following provisions.

Article 36   Scope of the Protection

Subject to the provisions of paragraph 1 of Article 37, Members shall consider unlawful the following acts if performed without the authorization of the right holder:* importing, selling, or otherwise distributing for commercial purposes a protected layout-design, an integrated circuit in which a protected layout-design is incorporated, or an article incorporating such an integrated circuit only in so far as it continues to contain an unlawfully reproduced layout-design.

[Footnote]* The term "right holder" in this Section shall be understood as having the same meaning as the term "holder of the right" in the IPIC Treaty.

Article 37   Acts Not Requiring the Authorization of the Right Holder

1. Notwithstanding Article 36, no Member shall consider unlawful the performance of any of the acts referred to in that Article in respect of an integrated circuit incorporating an unlawfully reproduced layout-design or any article incorporating such an integrated circuit where the person performing or ordering such acts did not know and had no reasonable ground to know, when acquiring the integrated circuit or article incorporating such an integrated circuit, that it incorporated an unlawfully reproduced layout-design. Members shall provide that, after the time that such person has received sufficient notice that the layout-design was unlawfully reproduced, that person may perform any of the acts with respect to the stock on hand or ordered before such time, but shall be liable to pay to the right holder a sum equivalent to a reasonable royalty such as would be payable under a freely negotiated licence in respect of such a layout-design.

> 2. The conditions set out in subparagraphs (a) through (k) of Article 31 shall apply mutatis mutandis in the event of any non-voluntary licensing of a layout-design or of its use by or for the government without the authorization of the right holder.

Article 38   Term of Protection

1. In Members requiring registration as a condition of protection, the term of protection of layout-designs shall not end before the expiration of a period of 10 years counted from the date of filing an application for registration or from the first commercial exploitation wherever in the world it occurs.

2. In Members not requiring registration as a condition for protection, layout-designs shall be protected for a term of no less than 10 years from the date of the first commercial exploitation wherever in the world it occurs.

3. Notwithstanding paragraphs 1 and 2, a Member may provide that protection shall lapse 15 years after the creation of the layout-design.

---

1. Introduction: terminology, definition and scope

Integrated circuits (often called "chips") are the core components of the information technology industry. They are essential components in any digital equipment, and have been incorporated into a great variety of other industrial articles, ranging from machine tools to all kinds of household and consumer devices.

Integrated circuits consist of an electronic circuitry developed on the basis of a tri-dimensional design,[984] incorporated into a substrate, generally a solid sheet of semiconductor material,[985] typically silicon, and less commonly germanium or gallium arsenide.[986] Integrated circuits comprise a range of products (microprocessors, dynamic memories, programmable logic devices, etc.).

Both the design and, particularly, the production of such circuits require, because of the microscopic size of the transistors and other electronic components inserted into a chip, significant technical capabilities and heavy investments in plant facilities. The manufacturing technologies and production plants are under the control of a relatively small number of companies mainly from the USA and Japan. South Korea, Taiwan Province of China and Singapore have actively supported the development of a local semiconductor industry, while China, Ireland, Israel, Malaysia and, more recently, Costa Rica, have pursued investments of foreign semiconductor manufacturers.[987]

---

[984] For this reason, European legislation, as indicated below, opted for the term "topography" rather than "design".

[985] Because of the properties of the materials used, integrated circuits are also called "semiconductors". Materials other than semiconductors (such as sapphire) may also be used as a substrate.

[986] See, e.g., Jay Dratler, *Intellectual Property Law: Commercial, Creative, and Industrial Property*, Intellectual Property Series, Law Journal Seminars-Papers, Vol. 2, New York 1997, pp. 8–6 [hereinafter Dratler].

[987] See, e.g., Debora Sper, *Attracting high technology investment*. INTEL's Costa Rican Plant, FIAS/World Bank, Occasional Paper No. 11, Washington D.C. 1998.

TRIPS provides for the protection of the layout designs (or topographies) utilized in integrated circuits. Such protection extends to the integrated circuits that contain such designs or topographies, as well as, under certain conditions, to the industrial products that incorporate the integrated circuits. The Agreement heavily relies in this matter on the standards of protection provided for under the Washington Treaty on Intellectual Property in respect of Integrated Circuits (the "Washington Treaty"), despite the fact that this Treaty, adopted in 1989, never entered into force. The Agreement obliges Members to protect the layout-designs (topographies) of integrated circuits according to Articles 2 through 7 (except Article 6.3), Article 12 and Article 16.3 of the Washington Treaty, plus a number of additional obligations specified by the Agreement.

2. History of the provision

2.1 Situation pre-TRIPS

The protection of layout designs of integrated circuits as a specific subject matter was initiated in the United States in 1984, with the approval of the Semiconductor Chip Protection Act ("SCPA"). The decline of United States competitive advantages in chip production and trade during the 1980's prompted the U.S. Congress to adopt a *sui generis* protection. Industry was particularly concerned with the increasing strength of Japanese competitors and their ability to eventually copy American designs.

Though the U.S. Congress considered the possibility of protecting integrated circuits designs under copyright, the SCPA established a *sui generis* regime that provided for ten years' protection; registration was made compulsory within two years of the first "commercial exploitation" of a "mask work"[988]. A special provision allowing for "reverse engineering" was included, following the practices prevailing in the semiconductor industry. The SCPA, in addition, included a strict material reciprocity clause under which layout designs originating in other countries would be protectable in the United States only if those countries granted similar protection to U.S. designs.

This reciprocity clause forced Japan to rapidly adopt similar legislation,[989] followed by the European Communities[990] and other developed countries.

WIPO, shortly after the enactment of the SCPA, initiated studies and consultations in order to establish an international treaty on the matter. It convened a Diplomatic Conference which adopted the Washington Treaty based on the *sui generis* approach first introduced by U.S. law without excluding, however, the application of other forms of protection.

---

[988] This terminology corresponds to the technology used at the time of adoption of the SCPA, which was based on the utilization of "masks" for the reproduction of layouts. A mask was a template whose configuration controlled the deposition, doping, or etching of specific areas on each succeeding layer of a wafer. Where the mask had holes, new material was deposited or existing material was doped or etched. The manufacturer used a series of masks of different configurations in the proper order to build upon the wafer the collection of transistors and other components required for the electronic design (Dratler, pp. 8–7).

[989] "Act concerning the circuit lay-out of a semiconductor integrated circuit" (law No. 43).

[990] Council Directive on the Legal Protection of Topographies of Semiconductor Products, 87/54/EEC.

2.2 Negotiating history

The Washington Treaty was negotiated in parallel with TRIPS. Though adopted in 1989, the USA and Japan did not sign the Treaty, due to their dissatisfaction with some of its provisions, particularly those relating to compulsory licenses and acquisition of products containing infringing semiconductors.[991] These were precisely the main areas dealt with during the TRIPS Agreement negotiations.

The negotiations on this subject in the Uruguay Round were less difficult and controversial than in other areas, with the exception of the issue relating to the extension of protection to industrial goods and the imposition of payment obligations on *bona fide* acquirers (now under Article 37 of TRIPS). Developing countries were reluctant to accept these obligations, as they were during the Diplomatic Conference that drafted the Washington Treaty in 1989. The Anell Draft indicated the outstanding differences.

2.2.1 The Anell Draft

"SECTION 6: LAYOUT-DESIGNS (TOPOGRAPHIES) OF INTEGRATED CIRCUITS

1. Relation to Washington Treaty

1. PARTIES agree to provide protection to the layout-designs (topographies) of integrated circuits in accordance with the [substantive] provisions of the Treaty on Intellectual Property in Respect of Integrated Circuits as open for signature on 26 May 1989 [, subject to the following provisions].

2. Legal Form of Protection

2A The protection accorded under this agreement shall not prevent protection under other laws.

3. Scope of the Protection

3A Any PARTY shall consider unlawful the following acts if performed without the authorisation of the holder of the right:

3A.1 incorporating the layout-design (topography) in an integrated circuit;

3A.2 importing, selling, or otherwise distributing for commercial purposes a protected layout-design (topography), an integrated circuit in which a protected layout-design (topography) is incorporated or a product incorporating such an integrated circuit.

4. Acts not Requiring the Authorization of the Holder of the Right

4A.1 PARTIES may exempt from liability under their law the reproduction of a layout-design (topography) for purposes of teaching, analysis, or evaluation in the course of preparation of a layout-design (topography) that is itself original. This provision shall replace Articles (2)(a) and (b) of the Washington Treaty.

4A.2 The act of importing, selling, or otherwise distributing for commercial purposes [an unlawfully reproduced layout-design (topography),] [an integrated circuit incorporating an unlawfully reproduced layout-design (topography) or] a product incorporating an unlawfully reproduced layout-design (topography) [shall] [may] not

---

[991] See Carlos Correa, *Intellectual Property in the Field of Integrated Circuits: Implications for Developing Countries*, World Competition, vol.14, No.2, Geneva 1990.

itself be considered an infringement if, at the time of performance of the act in question, the person performing the act [establishes that he] did not know and had [no reasonable grounds to believe] that the layout-design (topography) was unlawfully reproduced. However, PARTIES [shall] [may] provide that, after the time [of receipt of notice] [that the person comes to know or has reasonable grounds to believe] that the layout-design (topography) was unlawfully reproduced, he may perform any of the acts with respect to the stock on hand or ordered before such time, but shall be liable to pay [a reasonable royalty] [an equitable remuneration] to the right holder.

4A.3a Non-voluntary licences shall not be granted for purposes or on terms which could result in a distortion of international trade.

4A.3b The conditions set out at point 5 of Section 5 above shall apply mutatis mutandis to the grant of any non-voluntary licences for layout-designs (topographies).

4A.3c Non-voluntary licences shall not be granted for layout-designs (topographies).

5. Term of Protection

5A (i) In PARTIES requiring registration as a condition of protection, layout-designs (topographies) shall be protected for a term of no less than 10 years from the date of [filing an application for registration] [registration] or of the first commercial exploitation wherever in the world it occurs, whichever is the earlier [, except that if neither of the above events occurs within 15 years of the first fixation or encoding there shall no longer be any obligation to provide protection].

(ii) In PARTIES not requiring registration as a condition for protection, layout-designs (topographies) shall be protected for a term of no less than 10 years from the date of the first commercial exploitation wherever in the world it occurs [, except that if a layout-design (topography) is not so exploited within a period of 15 years of the first fixation or encoding, there shall no longer be any obligation to provide protection].

[(iii) If registration is required by law, and no application is filed, the protection of the layout-design (topography) shall lapse after two years from the date of the first commercial exploitation wherever in the world it occurs.

(iv) Notwithstanding (i), (ii) and (iii) above, protection shall lapse 15 years after the creation of the layout-design (topography).]"[992]

2.2.2 The Brussels Draft

The Brussels draft provisions contained language very similar to the current version of Articles 35–38 of TRIPS. It provided:[993]

"PARTIES agree to provide protection to the layout-designs (topographies) of integrated circuits (hereinafter referred to as "layout-designs") in accordance with the substantive provisions of the Treaty on Intellectual Property in Respect of Integrated Circuits as opened for signature on May 26, 1989 and, in addition, to comply with the following provisions.

[992] Chairman's report to the Group of Negotiation on Goods, document MTN.GNG/NG11/W/76, of 23 July 1990.

[993] Draft Final Act Embodying the Results of the Uruguay Round of Multilateral Trade Negotiations, Revision, Trade-Related Aspects of Intellectual Property Rights, Including Trade in Counterfeit Goods, MTN.TNC/W/35/Rev. 1, 3 Dec. 1990.

Subject to the provisions of Article [37](1) below, PARTIES shall consider unlawful the following acts if performed without the authorization of the holder of the right: importing, selling, or otherwise distributing for commercial purposes a protected layout-design, an integrated circuit in which a protected layout-design is incorporated [, or an article incorporating such an integrated circuit. Rights extend to an article incorporating an integrated circuit only insofar as it continues to contain an unlawfully reproduced layout-design.]

Notwithstanding Article [36] above, no PARTY shall be obliged to consider unlawful the performance of any of the acts referred to in that paragraph in respect of an integrated circuit incorporating an unlawfully reproduced layout-design [or any article incorporating such an integrated circuit] where the person performing or ordering such acts did not know and had no reasonable ground to know, when acquiring the integrated circuit [or article incorporating such an integrated circuit], that it incorporated an unlawfully reproduced layout-design. [PARTIES shall provide that, after the time that such person has received sufficient notice that the layout-design was unlawfully reproduced, he may perform any of the acts with respect to the stock on hand or ordered before such time, but shall be liable to pay to the holder of the right a sum equivalent to a reasonable royalty in a freely negotiated licence in respect of the layout-design.]

The conditions set out in subparagraphs (a)–(l) and (o) of Article [31] above shall apply *mutatis mutandis* in the event of any non-voluntary licensing of a layout-design or of its use by or for the government without the authorization of the right holder.

[The final draft provision was essentially identical to Article 38, TRIPS Agreement]".

At the time of the Brussels Draft, delegations were still divided over the question whether to extend the coverage of the provision to articles incorporating integrated circuits which in turn incorporate unlawfully reproduced layout-designs. Under the final version of TRIPS, this extension was then agreed upon. Under TRIPS, the possibility of a *bona fide* acquisition exists therefore not only with respect to integrated circuits, but even as to products containing integrated circuits.

The reference in the Brussels Draft to Article 31(a)–(l) and (o) is slightly different from the current version in Article 37, TRIPS Agreement; the reason for this is that at the time of the Brussels Draft, the draft provision on compulsory licenses showed a slightly different structure than today.[994] As under the current version of TRIPS, the provision on dependent patents (i.e. paragraph (m) of the Brussels Draft provision on compulsory licenses) was excluded from non-voluntary licensing of layout-designs. The other exclusion referred to in the Brussels Draft above concerned the grant of compulsory licenses in case of non-working or insufficient working (i.e. paragraph (n) of the draft provision on compulsory licenses). This exclusion was not reproduced in the TRIPS text of Article 37.2, because the final version of Article 31 of TRIPS contains no reference to non-working.

---

[994] For details, see Chapter 25.

3. Possible interpretations

3.1 Definitions of products covered by the IPIC Treaty

An integrated circuit is, according to the Washington Treaty, "a product, in its final form or an intermediate form, in which the elements, at least one of which is an active element, and some or all of the interconnections are integrally formed in and/or on a piece of material and which is intended to perform an electronic function" (Article 2(i)).

This definition includes both products in their final and in intermediate forms. It covers "gate arrays" and other integrated circuits (e.g., programmable logic devices-PLDs), which cannot be considered "finished" products. In order to be protectable, integrated circuits should contain "at least" one active element. This means that "discrete" microelectronics components are not covered.

A "layout-design (topography)" is defined by the Treaty as "the three-dimensional disposition, however expressed, of the elements, at least one of which is an active element, and of some or all of the interconnections of an integrated circuit, or such a three-dimensional disposition prepared for an integrated circuit intended for manufacture" (Article 2(ii)).

Article 2(ii) of the Washington Treaty makes clear that protection refers to a three-dimensional layout-design. It covers both a design/topography incorporated in an integrated circuit as well as a layout-design/topography to be incorporated in an integrated circuit, that is, even before the actual manufacture took place. This means that the Washington Treaty does not require the *fixation* of the design/topography as a condition for protection (a requirement that existed, for instance, under the U.S. and Japanese laws at the time the Treaty was adopted).

The Treaty does not specify the type of material into which the layout-design/topography may be incorporated. Any country may, however, limit protection to *semiconductor* integrated circuits (Article 3.1.c), i.e. to integrated circuits built into silicon and other semiconductor materials. In fact, many laws (United States, Japan, European Union, Denmark, etc.) specifically refer to "semiconductor products".

3.2 Requirement for protection

Protection is conferred to "original" layout-designs/topographies, understanding "original in the sense that they are the result of their creators' own intellectual effort" (Article 3.2(a) of the Washington Treaty).

The Treaty combines the concepts of "originality" and of "intellectual effort" employed in the U.S. and in EC regulations, respectively. These concepts are qualified, as expressly provided for, for instance, in the U.S. and UK laws on the matter, by the condition that the layout/topography should not be "commonplace among creators of layout-designs (topographies) and manufacturers of integrated circuits at the time of their creation". Further, a layout-design that consists of a combination of elements and interconnections that are commonplace shall be protected only if the combination, taken as a whole, fulfils the condition of originality.

3.3 Form of protection

The Washington Treaty, as mentioned, followed the *sui generis* approach first developed by the U.S. law on the matter. However, neither the Treaty nor TRIPS precludes the application of one of the traditional forms of protection (e.g. copyright, patents) to the extent that the minimum standards set forth in the Treaty and in the Agreement are respected.

For instance, if copyright protection were applied, the minimum duration would be much longer than under a *sui generis* regime (e.g., 50 years *post mortem auctoris* or 50 years counted in accordance with Article 12 of TRIPS). If patent protection were applied, the designs/topographies would have to meet the requirements of novelty and inventive step, standards that layout-designs/topographies are unlikely to comply with in most cases.

Under Article 12 of the Treaty, a situation of cumulative protection may take place. The Treaty "shall not affect the obligations that any Contracting Party may have under the Paris Convention for the Protection of Industrial Property or the Berne Convention for the Protection of Literary and Artistic Works". According to the Director General of WIPO, the effect of this article is that

> "if a Contracting Party chose to implement its obligations under the Treaty through a law made, totally or partly, on the basis that layout-designs are works under the copyright law or are a subject matter of industrial property law, and that Contracting Party is a party not only to the proposed Treaty but also to the Berne Convention or the Paris Convention, the said law must be compatible not only with the proposed Treaty but also with that of those Conventions. For example, if a Contracting Party considered layout-designs to be works under its copyright law and was a party to both the proposed Treaty and the Berne Convention, layout-designs would have to be protected without formalities (even though the proposed Treaty admits formalities) and for 50 years after the death of the author (even though the proposed Treaty admits a shorter period of protection). Or, if the Contracting Party is party to both the proposed Treaty and the Paris Convention and protects layout-designs by patents for inventions or utility models, layout-designs would require the grant of a patent or other official certificate (even though the proposed Treaty admits protection without any procedure before a government authority)."[995]

3.4 National treatment

The application of the national treatment principle is subject, according to Article 5 of the Washington Treaty, to certain conditions and exceptions that were confirmed by TRIPS.[996]

The obligation to apply national treatment is limited to persons who have a "real and effective establishment"[997] for the "creation" of layout designs or for the

---

[995] See WIPO, Diplomatic Conference for the Conclusion of a Treaty on the Protection of Intellectual Property in Respect of Integrated Circuits, *Draft Treaty prepared under Rule 1(1) of the Draft Rules of Procedure*, by the Director General of WIPO, Washington D.C., 31 Jan. 1989, IPIC/DC/3, p. 66 [hereinafter WIPO].

[996] According to Article 3.1 of the TRIPS Agreement, the application of the national treatment principle is "subject to the exceptions" provided for, *inter alia*, by the Washington Treaty. See Chapter 4.

[997] This kind of requirement is not present in the Paris and Berne Conventions.

"production" of integrated circuits. A mere "commercial" establishment (e.g., for the distribution of integrated circuits designed and manufactured elsewhere) does not entail the right to claim national treatment.

A Party can elect, according to Article 5(2) of the Washington Treaty, not to apply national treatment as far as any obligations to appoint an agent or to designate an address for service, or as far as the special rules applicable to foreigners in court proceedings are concerned.

3.5 Exclusive rights

Article 36   Scope of the Protection

Subject to the provisions of paragraph 1 of Article 37, Members shall consider unlawful the following acts if performed without the authorization of the right holder:[footnote 9] importing, selling, or otherwise distributing for commercial purposes a protected layout-design, an integrated circuit in which a protected layout-design is incorporated, or an article incorporating such an integrated circuit only in so far as it continues to contain an unlawfully reproduced layout-design.

[Footnote 9]: The term "right holder" in this Section shall be understood as having the same meaning as the term "holder of the right" in the IPIC Treaty.

Article 6.1 of the Treaty enumerates the acts that require the titleholder's authorization. They include:

- total or partial reproduction by incorporation in an integrated circuit or otherwise (e.g., on a mask, on a computer tape, on paper, or by any other means including the manufacture of a microchip).[998]

- importing, selling or otherwise distributing for commercial purposes a protected layout-design/topography or an integrated circuit in which a protected layout-design/topography is incorporated.

Article 36, TRIPS, adds to the exclusive rights provided for under the Treaty, the right to import, sell or otherwise distribute an *article* incorporating such an integrated circuit. This obligation, however, only applies in so far as the article continues to contain an *unlawfully* reproduced layout-design.

3.6 Extension of protection to industrial products

Article 37   Acts Not Requiring the Authorization of the Right Holder

1. Notwithstanding Article 36, no Member shall consider unlawful the performance of any of the acts referred to in that Article in respect of an integrated circuit incorporating an unlawfully reproduced layout-design or any article incorporating such an integrated circuit where the person performing or ordering

---

[998] See WIPO, p. 30.

such acts did not know and had no reasonable ground to know, when acquiring the integrated circuit or article incorporating such an integrated circuit, that it incorporated an unlawfully reproduced layout-design. Members shall provide that, after the time that such person has received sufficient notice that the layout-design was unlawfully reproduced, that person may perform any of the acts with respect to the stock on hand or ordered before such time, but shall be liable to pay to the right holder a sum equivalent to a reasonable royalty such as would be payable under a freely negotiated licence in respect of such a layout-design.

According to Article 3.1(b) of the Washington Treaty, "the right of the holder of the right in respect of an integrated circuit applies whether or not the integrated circuit is incorporated in an article". This means that the rights relating to a layout-design/topography can be exercised even if it has been fixed in a chip which, in turn, has been incorporated into an industrial article. However, the right of the right holder is not extended to the *products* incorporating the integrated circuit.[999] This provision was included in the Washington Treaty as an alternative to the proposal by the United States and Japan to expressly extend the rights of title-holders to the industrial articles containing protected integrated circuits. This proposal was rejected by European and developing countries, particularly due to the difficulties that *bona fide* purchasers of electronic goods and of other goods containing semiconductors could face to establish whether such goods incorporated or not infringing semiconductors. The Washington Treaty includes a provision on "Sale and distribution of infringing integrated circuits acquired innocently" (Article 6(4)), which only provides that "no Contracting Party shall be obliged to consider unlawful" the acts of importing, selling or otherwise distributing for commercial purposes a protected layout-design/topography or an integrated circuit incorporating such protected layout-design/topography, if such acts were performed *bona fide*.

Article 37.1 of TRIPS differs from Article 6(4) of the Washington Treaty at least in two important aspects. First, instead of prescribing what the Members may do, as the Treaty does,[1000] Article 37.1 provides that Members "*shall not* consider unlawful" (emphasis added) acts relating to unlawfully reproduced layout-designs/topographies, thus indicating that TRIPS *obliges* WTO Members to consider lawful the acts mentioned in Article 36. Second, the Agreement prescribes royalty payments by the innocent infringer to the title-holder, an obligation that was not incorporated into the Treaty. Article 37.1, in effect, obliges the acquirer to pay a reasonable royalty with regard to goods on stock or ordered before the infringement notice by the title-holder. The criterion to determine what a "reasonable royalty" would be is to be based on what a voluntary license would have prescribed.[1001]

---

[999] In this respect, Article 36 of the TRIPS Agreement provides for an important extension of the exclusive rights of right holders in layout-designs.

[1000] By providing that "no Contracting Party shall be obliged to consider unlawful" the acts of importing, etc., the Treaty leaves parties the freedom to consider such acts unlawful.

[1001] The application of this criterion may pose considerable difficulties, particularly when the acquirer is just a commercial agent who trades with industrial articles that incorporate chips, but

Finally, the acts covered by Article 37.1 also relate to any *articles* incorporating unlawfully reproduced layout-designs, whereas Article 6(4) of the Washington Treaty is limited to acts in respect of integrated circuits and layout-designs. This difference is the logical consequence of the different scope of protection with respect to *articles incorporating* unlawfully made layout-designs.

3.7 Exceptions

Article 6(2) of the Washington Treaty allows for exceptions in relation to certain acts of *reproduction* of a layout design/topography of an integrated circuit performed by a third party. This article addresses, in particular, the issue of reverse engineering, that is, the evaluation of an existing integrated circuit in order to independently develop a competitive product, which may be similar or identical to the original one. Reverse engineering is common practice in the semiconductor industry.

Article 6.2(a) provides that no Contracting Party shall consider unlawful acts made, without the authorization of the title-holder, for "private purposes" or for the "sole purpose of evaluation, analysis, research or teaching". Article 6.2(b) further clarifies the extent of the reverse engineering exception. It states that as long as there is an independent effort involved (which is necessary to comply with the originality requirement) the rights of the title-holder of the reverse engineered design can not be exercised against the creator of the second design, even if identical. This means that the rights, as provided for by the Treaty and TRIPS confer exclusivity neither on the functionalities of the layout-design/topography nor on a specific expression thereof. They only protect, in essence, against slavish copying. Finally, Article 6.2(c) establishes that the reverse engineering exception applies even in cases where the second-layout design/topography is "identical" to a protected design, provided that the former was "independently created".

3.8 Compulsory licenses

Article 37.2   Acts not requiring the authorization of the right-holder

The conditions set out in subparagraphs (a) through (k) of Article 31 shall apply *mutatis mutandis* in the event of any non-voluntary licensing of a layout-design or of its use by or for the government without the authorization of the right holder.

The Washington Treaty, after intense negotiations, allowed the granting of a non-voluntary license only in two cases: (1) "to safeguard a national purpose deemed to be vital" by the national authority; and (2) "to secure free competition and to prevent abuses by the holder of the right". In addition, these licenses were available only for the domestic market (Article 6.3). Despite these limitations the provision on compulsory license was deemed too broad by the United States, and was one

not with chips as such. Chips producers do not normally grant voluntary licenses to commercial agents, but to other chips producers, or eventually, manufacturers of industrial goods that incorporate chips.

of the major reasons for the U.S. refusal to sign the Treaty. As indicated above, TRIPS declared the non-applicability of Article 6.3 of the Washington Treaty.

As stated by Article 37.2, the conditions laid down by TRIPS for the granting of compulsory licenses for patents (Article 31(a) to (k)), are applicable *mutatis mutandis* to the layout-designs of integrated circuits. Paragraph (l) of Article 31 (compulsory licenses in cases of dependency of patents) does not apply. The reason for this probably is that, in the case of integrated circuits, reverse engineering is explicitly permitted.[1002]

In addition, according to Article 31(c) of the Agreement, "semiconductor technology" may only be subjected to compulsory licenses for grounds relating to anticompetitive practices and for use by the governments for non-commercial purposes.[1003] Though this provision applies to compulsory licenses on patented inventions, the cross reference contained in Article 37.2 of the Agreement would seem to indicate that compulsory licenses of integrated circuits would only be admissible in those two cases.[1004]

3.9 Exhaustion of rights

Article 6.5 of the Washington Treaty explicitly introduced the exception of "exhaustion of rights", as an optional provision for Contracting States: after the titleholder or a third party with the title-holder's consent has put the products on the market, further acts on such products are no longer subject to the title-holder's authorization.

Article 6.5 of the Washington Treaty alludes to putting an integrated circuit "on the market", without limiting its effects to commercialization in the domestic market. Hence, according to this provision[1005] and to Article 6 of TRIPS, Members may provide for national, regional or international exhaustion of rights.[1006]

3.10 Term of protection

Article 38   Term of Protection

1. In Members requiring registration as a condition of protection, the term of protection of layout-designs shall not end before the expiration of a period of 10 years counted from the date of filing an application for registration or from the first commercial exploitation wherever in the world it occurs.

2. In Members not requiring registration as a condition for protection, layout-designs shall be protected for a term of no less than 10 years from the date of the first commercial exploitation wherever in the world it occurs.

[1002] See, e.g., Gervais, p. 179.

[1003] For any other technology, patents may be made subject to compulsory licenses based on the grounds determined by national legislation. See Article 31 of the Agreement and the referenced Doha Declaration on the TRIPS Agreement and Public Health (WT/MIN(01)/DEC/W/2, 14 November 2001).

[1004] See, e.g., Gervais, p. 179.

[1005] See WIPO, p. 6.

[1006] See also the Doha Ministerial Declaration on TRIPS and Public Health, para. 5(d) (WT/MIN(01)/DEC/W/2 of 14 November 2001).

> 3. Notwithstanding paragraphs 1 and 2, a Member may provide that protection shall lapse 15 years after the creation of the layout-design.

The Washington Treaty provides for a minimum term of protection of eight years. It is silent about the date from which the term was to be counted. That term was extended by TRIPS to a minimum of ten years.[1007] In addition, Article 38 specifies the dates from which such term is to be counted. In any case, Members may limit the duration of protection to 15 years after the creation of the layout-design.

3.11 Conditions for granting protection

The Washington Treaty sets out in Article 7.1 some conditions on which protection may be made conditional. It leaves freedom to grant protection from the creation of the design, or subject to "commercial exploitation" or registration.

Article 7.1 of the Treaty refers to "ordinarily" commercially exploited layout designs. It excludes cases in which a layout-design may be commercialized under confidential terms, without being apparent to the consumer public or to competitors.

Members may adopt any of the above-mentioned conditions for protection. They could even opt to require, for instance, commercialization plus registration within certain period of the latter, like in United States and Japan. However, Article 7.2(b) of the Treaty contains a limitation for those cases in which commercial exploitation and registration are cumulative requirements. Registration cannot be required before two years counted from the date of first commercialization anywhere in the world.

Finally, the applicant may be required to disclose the "electronic function that the integrated circuit is intended to perform", but is not obliged to submit information relating to the "manner of manufacture" of the integrated circuit, provided that the information supplied is sufficient for the identification of the layout-design (Article 7.2(a)).

4. WTO jurisprudence

There have been no cases decided on this subject matter.

5. Relationship with other international instruments

5.1 WTO Agreements

There are no other WTO agreements directly relevant to this subject matter.

5.2 Other international instruments

As discussed throughout in the text, TRIPS draws substantially on the Treaty on Intellectual Property in Respect of Integrated Circuits of 1989, the Washington Treaty.

[1007] In practice, ten years was the standard term set out by the SCPA and adopted by the regulations enacted in other developed countries at the time of the negotiation of the Washington Treaty.

6. New developments

6.1 National laws

The USA and Japan adopted, as mentioned, *sui generis* legislation on integrated circuits. Other developed and developing countries (e.g., Australia, Sweden, Austria, Poland, South Korea, Taiwan Province of China, Trinidad and Tobago and Mexico) also followed this approach. Many developing countries have not yet implemented any form of protection on this matter.

6.2 International instruments

6.3 Regional and bilateral contexts

6.3.1 Regional

The EC adopted, in December 1986, Council Directive 87/54/EEC on the Legal Protection of Topographies of Semiconductor Products, which establishes a *sui generis* regime on the matter, without prejudice to the application of other forms of protection.

The protection of integrated circuits is also provided for under NAFTA. Article 1710(1) to (8) of NAFTA parallels Articles 35 through 38 of TRIPS. The NAFTA provisions are virtually identical to those in the Agreement,[1008] with a significant exception: Article 1710(5) of NAFTA[1009] prohibits the granting of compulsory licenses on layout-designs of integrated circuits.

Articles 86 to 112 of Decision 486 of the Andean Group countries (2000) provide for a *sui generis* protection for integrated circuits.

6.4 Proposals for review

There have been no proposals for review on this matter.

7. Comments, including economic and social implications

The semiconductor industry is highly concentrated in industrialized countries. A few firms possess the technologies necessary for state-of-the-art semiconductor design and manufacture.

Though the *sui generis* regime on integrated circuit design allows for reverse engineering, the high investments required for semiconductor design and production, in an extremely competitive market, constitute formidable barriers for potential new entrants, particularly from developing countries. Hence, the impact of TRIPS Agreement rules are likely to be mainly felt in those countries with respect to the importation of semiconductors or, in most cases, of industrial products containing semiconductors.

It is unclear to which extent the *sui generis* regime promotes innovation in the semiconductor industry in developing countries. Technological advance in this sector is an interactive, cumulative process, where improvements are directly

---

[1008] See, e.g., Richard Neff and Fran Smallson, *NAFTA. Protecting and Enforcing Intellectual Property Rights in North America*, Shepard's,/McGraw Hill, Colorado Springs 1994, p. 96.

[1009] Article 1710(5): "No Party may permit the compulsory licensing of layout-designs of integrated circuits".

based on the pre-existing stock of knowledge. Studies on the role of IPRs in promoting innovation in this industry have shown that gaining lead time and exploiting learning curve advantages, rather than IPRs, are the primary methods for appropriating the returns of investments in research and development.[1010]

The very little litigation that has taken place in connection with the protection of integrated circuits[1011] seems to indicate that unlawful copying of layout-designs/topographies is not at all significant.[1012]

It should be recalled, finally, that TRIPS leaves freedom to determine the form of protection of integrated circuits, either under a *sui generis* regime or other existing modalities of intellectual property rights. In general, there will be few advantages in protecting integrated circuits via copyright or patent law. The flexibility apparently given on the form of protection is *de facto* limited by the need to comply with the Washington Treaty plus the TRIPS Agreement standards. The best option for a country implementing the Agreement probably is to establish a *sui generis* regime to deal with the specific features of integrated circuits as protectable subject matter.

[1010] See Richard Levin; Alvin Klovorick; Richard Nelson and Sidney Winter, *Appropriating the returns from industrial research and development*, Brooking Papers on Economic Activity, No 3, 1987, p. 788.

[1011] The legal controversies relating to semiconductors do not seem to relate to the layout-designs as protected by the Washington Treaty and the TRIPS Agreement, but to patents covering certain aspects of semiconductor technology. Patent protection in the field of the manufacture of integrated circuits is important. Literally thousands of patents have been granted in this field, and in general it is not possible to undertake semiconductor production by licensing technology from a single firm. Moreover, a few large firms control substantial blocks of patents and hence exercise considerable power over the terms on which technology is available.

[1012] See Daniel Siegel and Ronald Laurie, *Beyond microcode: Alloy v. Ultratek. The first attempt to extend copyright protection to computer hardware*, The Computer Lawyer, vol. 6, No. 4, April 1989, p.14, who described the SCPA as "a solution in search of a problem". In the USA only one case – *Brooktree Corp. v. Advanced Micro Devices Inc* (977 F2d. 1555, Fed. Circ. 1992) – is reported as litigated under the SCPA (see Mark Lemley; Peter Menell; Robert Merges and Pamela Samuelson, *Software and Internet Law*, Aspen Law & Business, New York 2000, p. 410).

28: Undisclosed Information

Article 39

1. In the course of ensuring effective protection against unfair competition as provided in Article 10bis of the Paris Convention (1967), Members shall protect undisclosed information in accordance with paragraph 2 and data submitted to governments or governmental agencies in accordance with paragraph 3.

2. Natural and legal persons shall have the possibility of preventing information lawfully within their control from being disclosed to, acquired by, or used by others without their consent in a manner contrary to honest commercial practices* so long as such information:

(a) is secret in the sense that it is not, as a body or in the precise configuration and assembly of its components, generally known among or readily accessible to persons within the circles that normally deal with the kind of information in question;

(b) has commercial value because it is secret; and

(c) has been subject to reasonable steps under the circumstances, by the person lawfully in control of the information, to keep it secret.

3. Members, when requiring, as a condition of approving the marketing of pharmaceutical or of agricultural chemical products which utilize new chemical entities, the submission of undisclosed test or other data, the origination of which involves a considerable effort, shall protect such data against unfair commercial use. In addition, Members shall protect such data against disclosure, except where necessary to protect the public, or unless steps are taken to ensure that the data are protected against unfair commercial use.

[Footnote*]: For the purpose of this provision, "a manner contrary to honest commercial practices" shall mean at least practices such as breach of contract, breach of confidence and inducement to breach, and includes the acquisition of undisclosed information by third parties who knew, or were grossly negligent in failing to know, that such practices were involved in the acquisition.

---

1. Introduction: terminology, definition and scope

"Undisclosed information" is one of the categories of "intellectual property" as defined in Article 1.2 of TRIPS (see Chapter 3). Though such information has often been referred to as "trade secrets" or "know-how", Article 39 does not use these terms nor does it provide a definition of "undisclosed information". The difficulty of finding a common and acceptable understanding of what those notions mean favoured the adoption of more neutral terminology that does not characterize the contents of the information, but only its "undisclosed" nature.

"Undisclosed information" covers any secret information of commercial value, including

• technical know-how, such as design, process, formula and other technological knowledge often resulting from experience and intellectual ability;

• data of commercial value, such as marketing plans, customers lists and other business-related information that provides an advantage over competitors;

• test and other data submitted for the approval of pharmaceutical and chemical products for agriculture.

The obligation established under Article 39.1 is limited to the protection of undisclosed information "against unfair competition as provided in Article 10*bis* of the Paris Convention".

The discipline of unfair competition provides a remedy against acts of competition contrary to honest business practices, such as confusing or misleading the customer and discrediting the competitor. An act of unfair competition may be defined as

> "any act that a competitor or another market participant undertakes with the intention of directly exploiting another person's industrial or commercial achievement for his own business purposes without substantially departing from the original achievement."[1013]

Unfair competition rules supplements in some cases the protection of industrial property rights, such as patents and trademarks. Unlike the latter, however, the protection against unfair competition does not entail the granting of exclusive rights. National laws must only provide for remedies to be applied in cases where dishonest practices have occurred.

Article 39.2 does not define what "undisclosed information" consists of. It only specifies the conditions that the information needs to meet in order to be deemed "undisclosed" and protectable: it should be secret, possess a commercial value and be subject to reasonable steps, under the circumstances, to be kept secret. The conditions set forth are substantially based on the U.S. Uniform Trade Secrets Act, as adopted by many states in the USA.[1014]

The scope of Article 39.3 is limited to undisclosed data which are required by a national authority as a condition for obtaining approval for the marketing of pharmaceutical or of agricultural chemical products "which utilize new chemical entities", provided that the origination of the data involved a "considerable effort".

[1013] WIPO, Protection against Unfair Competition, Geneva 1994, p. 55.

[1014] See, e.g., J. H. Reichman, *Universal minimum standards of intellectual property protection under the TRIPS component of the WTO Agreement*, The International Lawyer 1995, vol. 29, No. 2, p. 378 [hereinafter Reichman 1995].

This provision is, therefore, applicable, when:

a) There is an obligation to submit test data for obtaining marketing authorization for pharmaceuticals and agrochemicals;

b) The pertinent information is not publicly available;

c) The submission should refer to a "new chemical entity". Hence, there is no obligation with regard to new dosage forms, new uses or combinations of known products; and

d) In order to qualify as protectable the origination of the data should have involved a "considerable effort".

2. History of the provision

2.1 Situation pre-TRIPS

Trade secrets were protected under common law rules laid down by courts or under unfair competition statutes in many countries before the adoption of TRIPS. In some countries (e.g., the USA) specific statutes had been adopted.[1015] However, at the time of TRIPS negotiations there were significant differences in comparative law with regard to the scope and modalities of protection of undisclosed information of commercial value. Doubts about the availability of an effective protection for trade secrets in developing countries had also been raised.[1016]

Differences in pre-existing comparative law were even greater with regard to test data relating to pharmaceuticals and agrochemicals. Only a few countries had developed rules on the matter before the negotiation of TRIPS. Thus, the USA introduced a regulatory data protection regime for pesticides in 1972, and in 1984 adopted regulatory exclusivity provisions for medicines. The latter provided for five years of exclusivity for new chemical entities, and three years for data filed in support of authorizations based on new clinical research relating to chemical entities which have already been approved for therapeutic use. The EU member states provided exclusivity protection for the data filed in support of marketing authorization for pharmaceuticals since 1987.

TRIPS is the first international convention specifically imposing obligations on undisclosed information, including test data.

2.2 Negotiating history

2.2.1 Early national proposals

Trade secrets were initially included as part of a future agreement on IPRs in the U.S. proposal of 28 October 1987, as well as in the European and Swiss proposals.[1017] In their earlier positions in the negotiations, developing countries rejected any form of protection for know-how under a future agreement. In 1989,

---

[1015] See the Uniform Trade Secrets Act (1, 14 ULA 438 (1985), which has been widely adopted in the USA.

[1016] See R. Gadbaw and T. Richards, *Intellectual Property Rights – Global Consensus, Global conflict?*, Boulder 1988, p. 60.

[1017] EC Draft Text, Article 28; Switzerland Draft Text, Article 241(1), U.S. Draft Text, Article 31(1).

the Indian Government exposed, for example, that trade secrets were not a form of intellectual property right. It further held that the protection against unfair competition under Article 10*bis* of the Paris Convention would suffice, and that protection by contract and under civil law was to be preferred to intellectual property rules.[1018]

The EC insisted that the protection of trade secrets be subject to unfair competition rules as provided for under the Paris Convention.[1019] This conception finally prevailed over the consideration of undisclosed information as a form of "property", as suggested in informal submissions by the USA.[1020]

Developed countries were also the proponents of a specific provision for the protection of test data relating to pharmaceuticals and agrochemicals, which included the establishment of a minimum period of protection (five years). A precedent of such proposals may be found in the "Statement of Views of the European, Japanese and United States Business Communities", which influenced the drafting of several articles of TRIPS. This proposal clearly specified the obligation to establish a data exclusivity period:

"1. Information required by a government to be disclosed by any party shall not be used commercially or further disclosed without the consent of the owner.

2. Information disclosed to a government as a condition for registration of a product shall be reserved for the exclusive use of the registrant for a reasonable period from the day when government approval based on the information was given. The reasonable period shall be adequate to protect the commercial interests of the registrant".

The same approach was adopted in the U.S. proposal:

"Contracting parties which require that trade secrets be submitted to carry out governmental functions, shall not use the trade secrets for the commercial or competitive benefit of the government or of any person other than the right-holder except with the right holder's consent, on payment of the reasonable value of the use, or if a reasonable period of exclusive use is given to the right-holder".

2.2.2 The Anell Draft

"SECTION 7: ACTS CONTRARY TO HONEST COMMERCIAL PRACTICES INCLUDING PROTECTION OF UNDISCLOSED INFORMATION

1. Protection of Undisclosed Information

1A.1 In the course of ensuring effective protection against unfair competition as provided for in Article 10bis of the Paris Convention (1967), PARTIES shall provide in

---

[1018] Communication from India, MTN.GNG/NG11/W/37, 10 July 1989, p. 18, quoted in F. Dessemontet, *Protection of trade secrets and confidential information*, in C. Correa and A. Yusuf, Intellectual Property and International Trade, Kluwer Law International, London, 1998, p. 238 [hereinafter Dessemontet].

[1019] See, e.g., J. Reinbothe and A. Howard, *The state of play in the negotiations on TRIPS (GATT/Uruguay Round)*, European Intellectual Property Review 1991, vol. 13, No.5, p. 163; T. Cottier, *The prospects for intellectual property in GATT*, Common Market Law Review 1991, No.2, p. 396; A. Font Segura, *La protección internacional del secreto empresarial*, MONOGRAFIAS, Eurolex, Madrid 1999, p. 106.

[1020] These different approaches are mirrored in the Anell and Brussels Drafts, see below.

their domestic law the legal means for natural and legal persons to prevent information within their control from being disclosed to, acquired by, or used by others without their consent in a manner contrary to honest commercial practices insofar as such information:

1A.1.1 is secret in the sense that it is not, as a body or in the precise configuration and assembly of its components, generally known or readily accessible; and

1A.1.2 has actual [or potential] commercial value because it is secret; and

1A.1.3 has been subject to reasonable steps, under the circumstances, by the person in possession of the information, to keep it secret.

1A.2 "A manner contrary to honest commercial practice" is understood to encompass, practices such as theft, bribery, breach of contract, breach of confidence, inducement to breach, electronic and other forms of commercial espionage, and includes the acquisition of trade secrets by third parties who knew [or had reasonable grounds to know] that such practices were involved in the acquisition.

1A.3 PARTIES shall not limit the duration of protection under this section so long as the conditions stipulated at point 1A.1 exist.

2. Licensing

2Aa PARTIES shall not discourage or impede voluntary licensing of undisclosed information by imposing excessive or discriminatory conditions on such licences or conditions which dilute the value of such information.

2Ab There shall be no compulsory licensing of proprietary information.

3. Government Use

3Aa PARTIES, when requiring the publication or submission of undisclosed information consisting of test [or other] data, the origination of which involves a considerable effort, shall protect such data against unfair exploitation by competitors. The protection shall last for a reasonable time commensurate with the efforts involved in the origination of the data, the nature of the data, and the expenditure involved in their preparation, and shall take account of the availability of other forms of protection.

3Ab.1 PARTIES which require that trade secrets be submitted to carry out governmental functions, shall not use the trade secrets for the commercial or competitive benefit of the government or of any person other than the right holder except with the right holder's consent, on payment of the reasonable value of the use, or if a reasonable period of exclusive use is given to the right holder.

3Ab.2 PARTIES may disclose trade secrets to third parties, only with the right holder's consent or to the degree required to carry out necessary government functions. Wherever practicable, right holders shall be given an opportunity to enter into confidentiality agreements with any non-government entity to which the PARTY is disclosing trade secrets to carry out necessary government functions.

3Ab.3 PARTIES may require right holders to disclose their trade secrets to third parties to protect human health or safety or to protect the environment only when the right holder is given an opportunity to enter into confidentiality agreements with any non-government entity receiving the trade secrets to prevent further disclosure or use of the trade secret.

3Ac.1 Proprietary information submitted to a government agency for purposes of regulatory approval procedures such as clinical or safety tests, shall not be disclosed without the consent of the proprietor, except to other governmental agencies if necessary to protect human, plant or animal life, health or the environment. Governmental agencies may disclose it only with the consent of the proprietor or to the extent indispensable to inform the general public about the actual or potential danger of a product. They shall not be entitled to use the information for commercial purposes.

3Ac.2 Disclosure of any proprietary information to a third party, or other governmental agencies, in the context of an application for obtaining intellectual property protection, shall be subject to an obligation to hear the applicant and to judicial review. Third parties and governmental agencies having obtained such information shall be prevented from further disclosure and commercial use of it without the consent of the proprietor."[1021]

2.2.3 The Brussels Draft

"1A In the course of ensuring effective protection against unfair competition as provided in Article 10bis of the Paris Convention (1967), PARTIES shall protect undisclosed information in accordance with paragraphs 2 and 3 below and data submitted to governments or governmental agencies in accordance with paragraph 4 below.

2A PARTIES shall provide in their domestic law the legal means for natural and legal persons to prevent information lawfully within their control from being disclosed to, acquired by, or used by others without their consent in a manner contrary to honest commercial practices [footnote] so long as such information:

• is secret in the sense that it is not, as a body or in the precise configuration and assembly of its components, generally known among or readily accessible to persons within the circles that normally deal with the kind of information in question;

• has commercial value because it is secret; and

• has been subject to reasonable steps under the circumstances, by the person lawfully in control of the information, to keep it secret.

3A PARTIES shall not discourage or impede voluntary licensing of undisclosed information by imposing excessive or discriminatory conditions on such licenses or conditions which dilute the value of such information.

4A PARTIES, when requiring, as a condition of approving the marketing of new pharmaceutical products or of a new agricultural chemical product, the submission of undisclosed test or other data, the originator of which involves a considerable effort, shall [protect such data against unfair commercial use. Unless the person submitting the information agrees, the data may not be relied upon for the approval of competing products for a reasonable time, generally no less than five years, commensurate with the efforts involved in the origination of the data, their nature, and the expenditure involved in their preparation. In addition, PARTIES shall] protect such data against disclosure, except where necessary to protect the public.]

[Footnote]: For the purpose of this provision, "a manner contrary to honest commercial practices" shall [include] [mean] practices such as breach of contract,

---

[1021] Chairman's report to the Group of Negotiation on Goods, document MTN.GNG/NG11/W/76, of 23 July 1990.

breach of confidence and inducement to breach, and includes the acquisition of undisclosed information by third parties who knew, or were grossly negligent in failing to know, that such practices were involved in the acquisition."[1022]

As opposed to the final text of Article 39, the Brussels Draft proposed the establishment of a defined period (not less than five years) of data exclusivity, as illustrated by the bracketed text under paragraph 4A, above. According to this approach, data submitted for marketing approval for new pharmaceutical products or new agricultural chemical products could not be relied upon for the approval of competing products for a reasonable time, generally no less than five years, commensurate with the efforts involved in the origination of the data, their nature, and the expenditure involved in their preparation. This meant, in other words, that WTO Members would have been obligated to grant the originator of the data an exclusive right in his data. Such right would have entitled the right holder to prevent third parties from relying on the protected data in the context of obtaining marketing approval for competing products, or to subject use of such data to claims of compensation.

This approach differs considerably from the final version under Article 39, according to which Members arguably are not obligated to provide the originator of the data with exclusive property rights. Article 39 is based on the concept of unfair competition rules. According to this approach, data originators may prevent third parties from using their data only in the event that the third party has acquired the data through dishonest commercial practices. This enhances the possibilities of using existing data for the market entry of competing pharmaceutical products (see further discussion of this controversial issue under Section 3 of this chapter). In this context, it is important to note that the TRIPS flexibilities accorded to Members under the unfair competition approach are being rapidly narrowed down through bilateral and regional trade agreements (see below, Section 6 of this chapter).

3. Possible interpretations

3.1 Article 39.1

In the course of ensuring effective protection against unfair competition as provided in Article 10bis of the Paris Convention (1967), Members shall protect undisclosed information in accordance with paragraph 2 and data submitted to governments or governmental agencies in accordance with paragraph 3.

Article 39.1 establishes the main rule applicable in the field of undisclosed information. It also provides the context for the correct interpretation of paragraphs 2 and 3 of the same provision.

[1022] Draft Final Act Embodying the Results of the Uruguay Round of Multilateral Trade Negotiations, Revision, Trade-Related Aspects of Intellectual Property Rights, Including Trade in Counterfeit Goods, MTN.TNC/W/35/Rev. 1, 3 Dec. 1990.

The initial wording of Article 39.1 ("In the course of ensuring effective protection against unfair competition . . .") makes it clear that the protection to be conferred under paragraphs 2 and 3 is to be based on the discipline of unfair competition, as provided for in Article 10*bis* of the Paris Convention, which reads as follows:

"(1) The countries of the Union are bound to assure to nationals of such countries effective protection against unfair competition.

(2) Any act of competition contrary to honest practices in industrial or commercial matters constitutes an act of unfair competition.

(3) The following in particular shall be prohibited:

1. all acts of such a nature as to create confusion by any means whatever with the establishment, the goods, or the industrial or commercial activities, of a competitor;

2. false allegations in the course of trade of such a nature as to discredit the establishment, the goods, or the industrial or commercial activities, of a competitor;

3. indications or allegations the use of which in the course of trade is liable to mislead the public as to the nature, the manufacturing process, the characteristics, the suitability for their purpose, or the quantity, of the goods".

It is generally accepted that unfair competition is one of the disciplines of industrial property.[1023] Such protection requires, as mentioned, remedial action against "dishonest" commercial practices, but does not give rise to exclusive rights. The fact that the undisclosed information is deemed to be a "category" of intellectual property (Article 1.2 of the Agreement) does not imply the existence of "property" rights in undisclosed information. There is only "possession" or *de facto* "control" of that information. Thus, Articles 39.2 and 39.3 of the Agreement refer to a person who is "in control" of undisclosed information, in clear contrast to the ownership concept used in the sections relating to other categories of IPRs.[1024]

The ordinary meaning of "unfair" is "not equitable or honest or impartial or according to rules".[1025] The protection against unfair competition does not exclude the legitimate exploitation of externalities emerging from competition in the market, it does not deal with the protection of market interests, but rather of market behaviour. As noted by Kamperman Sanders:[1026]

"Where exploitation of another's achievements becomes inequitable, unfair competition law acts provide a remedy. This means that the mere fact that another's achievement is being exploited does not call for any impediment on the basis of unfair competition provisions. On the contrary, appropriating and building on others' achievements is the cornerstone of cultural and economic development. The axiom of freedom to copy epitomizes the principles of the free market system."

[1023] "Protection against unfair competition has been recognized as forming part of industrial property protection for almost a century", WIPO, *Intellectual property reading material*, Geneva 1998, p. 124.

[1024] See, e.g., Articles 16.1 and 28.1 which refer to the "owner" of a trademark and of a patent, respectively.

[1025] *The Concise Oxford Dictionary*, Seventh Edition, Oxford University Press, Oxford, 1989.

[1026] See, A. Kamperman Sanders, *Unfair Competition Law*, Clarendon Press, Oxford 1997, p. 7.

3.2 Article 39.2

> Natural and legal persons shall have the possibility of preventing information lawfully within their control from being disclosed to, acquired by, or used by others without their consent in a manner contrary to honest commercial practices so long as such information: . . .

The carefully drafted chapeau of this provision confirms the main elements of the framework of protection for undisclosed information as described above. The persons in control of undisclosed information "shall have the possibility of preventing" certain acts of disclosure, acquisition and use of information, but only when such acts have been made without their consent and "in a manner contrary to honest commercial practices". This clearly indicates that the right to prevent such acts only arises when the means used are condemnable. That is, there is not an absolute protection against non-authorized disclosure, acquisition and use of information, but only against acts made in a condemnable manner.

The concept of "honest" is relative to the values of a particular society at a given point in time. It varies among countries. As noted by one of the main commentators of the Paris Convention,

> "Morality, which is the source of the law of unfair competition, is a simple notion in theory only. In fact it reflects customs and habits anchored in the spirit of a particular community. There is no clear objective standard of feeling, instincts, or attitudes toward a certain conduct. Therefore, specific prescriptions involving uniform evaluation of certain acts are extremely difficult.

> The pressures existing in the various countries for the suppression of acts of unfair competition differ greatly. Generally, the development of law of unfair competition depends on active and intense competition in the marketplace by competing enterprises. It is the pressure of conflicting interests which leads to the establishment of clear rules of law. This pressure is not uniform in all countries and indeed it is evolving continuously . . . We look for a standard by which we may judge the act complained of. This is an objective standard: the honest practices in the course of trade in the particular community and at the particular time."[1027]

Given this diversity, different countries may judge certain situations differently. "Honest" is an inherently flexible notion, and this flexibility has been the cornerstone of unfair competition law in civil law systems.[1028]

The footnote to Article 39.2 indicates the practices that "at least" are to be considered as "contrary to honest practices", thus reducing the possible divergences in interpretation. The referred practices include those that may take place in the framework of or in relation to a contractual relationship (breach of a contract, breach of confidence and inducement to breach), as well as the acquisition by third parties of undisclosed information knowing – or being grossly negligent in failing to know – that such unfair practices are involved in the acquisition.

[1027] S. Ladas, *Patents, Trademarks, and Related Rights. National and International Protection*, vol. III, Cambridge 1975, pp. 1685–1686, 1689 [hereinafter Ladas].

[1028] See, e.g., A. Kamperman Sanders.

> ...as long as such information:
>
> (a) is secret in the sense that it is not, as a body or in the precise configuration and assembly of its components, generally known among or readily accessible to persons within the circles that normally deal with the kind of information in question;

This provision incorporates an objective standard of secrecy. In order to establish whether protection is to be conferred, it should be proven that the relevant information is "not generally known" or "readily accessible".

The established secrecy standard is relative[1029] in the sense that it does not require that the person seeking protection be the single one in control of the information. This may be available to other competitors (who also keep it as confidential) but should not be known to or readily accessible to most or every competitor in the circles that normally deal with that kind of information.

An important interpretive issue is whether this provision allows for reverse engineering[1030] as a means to obtain information embedded in products put in commerce by the person who is in control of the information. Article 39.2 (a) does not disallow the use of such method;[1031] to the extent that the secret information is "readily accessible", it would not be considered secret under such provision.

> (b) has commercial value because it is secret;

This requirement is an essential element for the protection of confidential information which, in order to be protectable, must have *actual* commercial value.[1032] The generality of this provision indicates that any business-related information is covered. National laws and courts should determine when a given information is deemed to possess "commercial value". In some countries,[1033] the basic test is the extent to which the information provides an opportunity to obtain an advantage over competitors who do not know or use it.

> (c) has been subject to reasonable steps under the circumstances, by the person lawfully in control of the information, to keep it secret.

[1029] See Dessemontet, p. 251.

[1030] "Reverse engineering" is the study of a product to understand its functional aspects and underlying ideas. It starts with the known product and works backwards to analyze how the product operates or was made.

[1031] See, e.g., Reichman 1995, p. 378. Reverse engineering is accepted in many jurisdictions (e.g., in the USA) as a legitimate means to obtain access to information embodied in the goods. See, e.g., R. Neff and F. Smallson, *NAFTA. Protecting and Enforcing Intellectual Property Rights in North America*, SHEPARD'S, Colorado 1994, p. 102.

[1032] Members may extend protection to information of *potential* commercial value, but this is not required by the Agreement.

[1033] See, e.g., the Mexican Industrial Property Law (1991) (R. Pérez Miranda *Propiedad Industrial y Competencia en México*, Editorial Porrúa, México 1999, p. 162).

The adoption of reasonable steps to preserve secrecy is one of the conditions of protection, inspired, like the other two conditions, by U.S. law. The provision does not identify the type of steps that could be taken, such as encryption, safes, division of work, contractual restrictions.

3.3 Article 39.3

Members, when requiring, as a condition of approving the marketing of pharmaceutical or of agricultural chemical products which utilize new chemical entities, the submission of undisclosed test or other data, the origination of which involves a considerable effort, shall protect such data against unfair commercial use. In addition, Members shall protect such data against disclosure, except where necessary to protect the public, or unless steps are taken to ensure that the data are protected against unfair commercial use.

3.3.1 Conditions for protection of data submitted for marketing approval

A basic premise for the application of Article 39.3 is that a Member imposes an obligation to submit data as a condition to obtain the marketing approval of pharmaceutical or agrochemical products. This provision does not apply when it is not necessary to submit such data, for instance, when marketing approval is granted by the national authority relying on the existence of a prior registration elsewhere.[1034]

The subject matter of the protection under this Article is *undisclosed* information contained in written material which details the results of scientific health and safety testing of drugs and agrochemicals, in relation to human, animal and plant health, impact on the environment and efficacy of use. This information is not "invented" or "created" but developed according to standard protocols. The protected data may also include manufacturing, conservation and packaging methods and conditions, to the extent that their submission is needed to obtain marketing approval.

The data to be protected must relate to a "new chemical entity". The Agreement does not define what should be meant by "new". Members may apply a concept similar to the one applied under patent law, or consider that a chemical entity is "new" if there were no prior application for approval of the same drug. Article 39.3 does not clarify either whether newness should be absolute (universal) or relative (local).[1035]

Based on the ordinary meaning of the terms used, Article 39.3 would not apply to new uses of known products, nor to dosage forms, combinations, new forms of administration, crystalline forms, isomers, etc., of existing drugs, since there would be no novel chemical entity involved.

[1034] In this case the authority does not require test data, but takes its decision on the basis of the registration granted in a foreign country.

[1035] See T. Cook, *Special Report: The protection of regulatory data in the pharmaceutical and other sectors*, Sweet & Maxwell, London 2000, p. 6.

Article 39.3 does not define any substantive standard for granting protection (like inventive step or novelty), but simply mandates protection when obtaining the data involved "a considerable effort". The text is vague about the type of effort involved (technical, economic?) and also with respect to its magnitude. (When would it be deemed considerable?) The wording used here is broader than that employed in Article 70.4 – where reference to "significant investment" is made. A reasonable understanding would be that the "effort" involved should not only be significant in economic terms but also from a technical and scientific point of view, including experimental activities.

3.3.2 Forms of protection of data submitted for marketing approval

The protection to be granted under Article 39.3 is twofold: against "unfair commercial use" and against disclosure of the relevant protected information.

Considerable controversy exists about the interpretation of the extent of the obligation to protect against "unfair commercial use". According to one view, the sole or most effective method[1036] for complying with this obligation is by granting the originator of data a period of *exclusive* use thereof, as currently mandated in some developed countries. Under this interpretation, national authorities would not be permitted, during the exclusivity period, to rely on data they have received in order to assess subsequent applications for the registration of similar products.[1037]

According to another view, Article 39.3 does not require the recognition of exclusive rights, but protection in the framework of unfair competition rules. Thus, a third party should be prevented from using the results of the test undertaken by another company as background for an independent submission for marketing approval, if the respective data had been acquired through dishonest commercial practices. However, under that provision a governmental authority would not be prevented from relying on the data presented by one company to assess submissions by other companies relating to similar products. If the regulatory body were not free, when assessing a file, to use all the knowledge available to it, including data from other files, a great deal of repetitive toxicological and clinical investigation will be required, which will be wasteful and ethically questionable. This position is also grounded on the pro-competitive effects of low entry barriers

---

[1036] See, e.g., the Communication from the EU and its Member States on *The relationship between the provisions of the TRIPS Agreement and access to medicines*, IP/C/W/280, 12 June 2001. A similar view is expressed by R. Kampf, *Patents versus Patients?* Archiv des Völkerrechts, vol. 40 (2002), pp. 90–234, on p. 120, 121.

[1037] The rationale behind this position is that "equity demands that protection be provided for data, which can cost the original submitter several million dollars to produce. Disclosing this data to the public or allowing its use by another applicant unfairly denies the compiler of the data the value of its efforts and grants an economic advantage to later applicants for marketing approval, enabling them to avoid the cost of developing test data for their own products. Countries that allow such unfair advantages to later applicants discourage developers of new pharmaceuticals and agricultural chemicals from seeking to introduce their state-of-the-art products in the country's market. So, not only is such protection required by the TRIPS Agreement, it is both equitable and wise from a public and health policy standpoint." See C. Priapantja, *Trade Secret: How does this apply to drug registration data?* Paper presented at "ASEAN Workshop on the TRIPS Agreement and its Impact on Pharmaceuticals", Department of Health and World Health Organization, May 2–4 2000, p. 4 [hereinafter Priapantja].

for pharmaceutical product. The early entry of generic competition is likely to increase the affordability of medicines at the lowest possible price.[1038]

On the other hand, protection is to be ensured against disclosure of the confidential data by governmental authorities, subject to the two exceptions mentioned in Article 39.3: a) when disclosure is necessary to protect the public; and b) when steps are taken to ensure that the data will not be used in a commercially unfair manner. Under these exceptions, disclosure may be permissible, for example, to allow a compulsory licensee to obtain a marketing approval, particularly when the license is aimed at remedying anti-competitive practices or at satisfying public health needs.

4. WTO jurisprudence

There is no WTO jurisprudence so far on this subject. However, the USA requested consultations under the DSU against Argentina in relation to, *inter alia*, Article 39.3 as applied to pharmaceuticals and agrochemicals.[1039] On 20 June 2002, the USA and Argentina notified the DSB of a mutually agreed solution.[1040] In their DSU notification, they stated that:

> "The Governments of the United States and Argentina have expressed their respective points of view on the provisions of Article 39.3 of the TRIPS Agreement, and have agreed that differences in interpretations shall be solved under the DSU rules. The Parties will continue consultations to assess the progress of the legislative process . . . and in the light of this assessment, the United States may decide to continue consultations or request the establishment of a panel related to Article 39.3 of the TRIPS Agreement."

> "In addition, the Parties agree that should the Dispute Settlement Body adopt recommendations and rulings clarifying the content of the rights related to undisclosed test data submitted for marketing approval according to Article 39.3 of the TRIPS Agreement, and should Argentinean law be inconsistent with Article 39.3 as clarified by the above-mentioned recommendations and rulings, Argentina agrees to submit to the National Congress within one year an amendment to Argentinean law, as necessary, to put its legislation in conformity with its obligations under Article 39.3 as clarified in such recommendations and rulings."[1041]

5. Relationship with other international instruments

As mentioned, Article 39 is based on and develops the disciplines on unfair competition contained in Article 10*bis* of the Paris Convention, for the particular case of

---

[1038] See Carlos Correa, *Protection of Data Submitted for the Registration of Pharmaceuticals. Implementing the Standards of the TRIPS Agreement*, South Centre, Geneva 2002 (available at <http://www.southcentre.org/publications/protection/toc.htm>).

[1039] See WT/DS 171/1; WT/DS 196/1. (Other controversial issues were the Argentinean provisions on compulsory licences; exclusive marketing rights; import restrictions; process patents, including the question of burden of proof; preliminary injunctions; patentability of micro-organisms and transitional patents.)

[1040] See WT/DS171/3.

[1041] Ibid., para. 9 ("Protection of Test Data Against Unfair Commercial Use").

undisclosed information. Hence, the interpretation of the Convention, including its negotiating history, is of relevance to the implementation of Article 39.[1042]

6. New developments

6.1 National laws

After the adoption of TRIPS, some countries have reportedly changed their legislation in order to implement Article 39.3. In some cases, the exclusivity approach, as applied in United States and Europe, has been followed. Thus, the U.S. government initiated in April 1996 an investigation under Special Section 301 of the U.S. Trade Act against Australia, where no exclusivity was granted and generic companies only had to demonstrate bio-equivalence[1043] in order to obtain marketing approval of a similar product. In addition, Australian authorities granted certificates of free sale that permitted generic companies to export to other countries where marketing approval was automatically granted on the basis of the Australian certificates. The USA argued that Australia was in contradiction with Article 39.3. This action led to an amendment to the Australian law. Under the Therapeutic Goods Legislation Amendment Act 1998 (No.34, 1998) test data have five (5) years of exclusivity. During this time, another company wishing to register a generic copy of the product will be required to seek the agreement of the originator company to use its data, or to develop its own data package.[1044]

Other countries have followed a non-exclusivity model. Thus, Argentina passed a law (No. 24.766) on the matter in 1996,[1045] according to which test data should only be submitted for the registration of *new* chemical entities. However, when a pharmaceutical product is already marketed in Argentina or in other countries that comply with certain standards defined by the law, the national health authority may rely on the prior registration. There is no need in these cases for the applicant to submit test data.

In Thailand, the Food and Drug Administration (FDA) established in 1989 a Safety Monitoring Program (SMP), according to which new drugs were approved conditionally and placed under the SMP for at least two years. During this period, those new drugs could only be available in either public or private hospitals/clinics where physicians would closely monitor adverse drug reactions. Producers were required to submit to the FDA substantial credible safety data of the products using proper statistical methodology during the SMP. Once the data satisfactorily supported safety of the products, an unconditional license was issued. Meanwhile, it was required that a bio-equivalence study be conducted for generic drugs to prove their quality and efficacy to be comparable with those of the original ones. No application for generic drugs could be made until the original product was released

---

[1042] See, in particular, Ladas.

[1043] Two pharmaceutical products are bioequivalent if they are pharmaceutically equivalent and their bioavailabilities (rate and extent of availability), after administration in the same molar dose, are similar to such a degree that their effects can be expected to be essentially the same.

[1044] Priapantja, p. 6.

[1045] The USA applied economic sanctions to Argentina in 1997, arguing insufficient protection of confidential information. As mentioned, the USA later on requested consultations under the DSU on, *inter alia*, Argentina's compliance with Article 39.3.

from the SMP and received unconditional licenses. Since the SMP delayed the entry of generic drugs into the market, the scheme led in some cases to high drug prices and limited drug accessibility to patients, particularly those suffering from such disease as HIV/AIDS. As a result, the Drug Committee decided to allow, as of January 2001, the bio-equivalence study to be done at any time regardless of whether or not the original products are under the SMP. However, if the original products are still under the SMP, those generic products must be under the SMP as well.

6.2 International instruments

Article 10*bis* of the Paris Convention, discussed above, provides the basic framework for the protection of trade secrets against unfair competition. In this context, WIPO has recommended a model provision to address the protection of secret information (see box). There are no other international instruments specifically dealing with the matter.

WIPO MODEL PROVISION ON UNFAIR COMPETITION IN RESPECT OF SECRET INFORMATION
Article 6

(1) [General Principle] Any act or practice, in the course of industrial or commercial activities, that results in the disclosure, acquisition or use by others of secret information without the consent of the person lawfully in control of that information (hereinafter referred to as "the rightful holder") and in a manner contrary to honest commercial practices shall constitute an act of unfair competition.

(2) [Examples of Unfair Competition in Respect of Secret Information] Disclosure, acquisition or use of secret information by others without the consent of the rightful holder may, in particular, result from

(i) industrial or commercial espionage;

(ii) breach of contract;

(iii) breach of confidence;

(iv) inducement to commit any of the acts referred to in items (i) to (iii);

(v) acquisition of secret information by a third party who knew, or was grossly negligent in failing to know, that an act referred to in items (i) to (iv) was involved in the acquisition.

(3) [Definition of Secret Information] For the purposes of this Article, information shall be considered "secret information" if

(i) it is not, as a body or in the precise configuration and assembly of its components, generally known among or really accessible to persons within the circles that normally deal with the kind of information in question;

(ii) it has commercial value because it is secret; and

(iii) it has been subject to reasonable steps under the circumstances by the rightful holder to keep it secret.

(4) [Use or Disclosure of Secret Information Submitted for Procedure of Approval of Marketing] Any act or practice, in the course of industrial or commercial

> activities, shall be considered an act of unfair competition if it consists or results in (i) an unfair commercial use of secret test or other data, the origination of which have been submitted to a competent authority for the purposes of obtaining approval of the marketing of pharmaceutical or agricultural chemical products which utilize new chemical entities; or (ii) the disclosure of such data, except where necessary to protect the public, or unless steps are taken to ensure that the data are protected against unfair commercial use."[1046]

6.3 Regional and bilateral contexts

6.3.1 Regional

6.3.1.1 The EU. The issue of data protection has been dealt with within the Union under the exclusivity approach, on the basis of Directive 65/65, as amended by Directive 87/21/EEC. Similar provisions for veterinary products are contained in Directive 81/851/EEC, as amended by Directive 90/676/EC. According to recently proposed legislation, new pharmaceutical products would be entitled to 8 years of data exclusively, 2 years of marketing exclusively (during which generic companies would be allowed to engage in "Bolar" – type activities) and an additional year of protection for new indications of existing products.[1047]

6.3.1.2 NAFTA. The NAFTA Agreement contains a specific provision on the matter (Section 1711). Though it is based on the concept of "trade secret" rather than "undisclosed information", it closely follows Article 39.3 with regard to the definition of protected subject matter.[1048] There are, nevertheless, two important differences with respect to TRIPS. First, the NAFTA provision does not include a text similar to paragraph 1 of Article 39, which clearly sets out the framework for the regulation of undisclosed information. Second, while para. 5 of section 1711 of NAFTA resembles paragraph 3 of Article 39 of the Agreement, paragraphs 6 and 7 add a "TRIPS-plus" obligation in terms of a minimum five-year period, as follows:

> "6. Each Party shall provide that for data subject to paragraph 5 that are submitted to the Party after the date of entry into force of this Agreement, no person other than the person that submitted them may, without the latter's permission, rely on such data in support of an application for the product approval during a reasonable period of time after their submission. For this purpose, a reasonable period shall normally mean not less than five years from the date on which the Party granted

---

[1046] WIPO, (1996), Model Provisions on Protection Against Unfair Competition, Geneva.

[1047] See Resolution of the European Parliament, Amendment 14, Article 1, Point 8 (17 December 2003). This Resolution is based on the recommendations of the European Parliament Committee on the Environment, Public Health and Consumer Policy. *Draft Recommendation for Second Reading on the Council Amending Directive 2001/83/EC on the Community Code Relating to Medicinal Products for Human Use* (28 November 2003), A5-0425/2003. See also Meir Perez Puzatch, *Intellectual Property and Pharmaceutical Data Exclusively in the Context of Innovation and Market Access* [hereinafter Puzatch], Third UNCTAD-ICTSD Dialogue on Development and Intellectual Property, 12–16 October 2004, Bellagio, Italy (paper available at <http://www.iprsonline.org/unctadictsd/bellagio/dialogue 2004/bell3_documents.htm>).

[1048] The NAFTA definition, however, covers information that "has or may have" commercial value.

approval to the person that produced the data for approval to market its product, taking account of the nature of the data and the person's efforts and expenditures in producing them. Subject to this provision, there shall be no limitation on any Party to implement abbreviated approval procedures for such products on the basis of bioequivalence and bioavailability studies.

7. Where a Party relies on a marketing approval granted by another Party, the reasonable period of exclusive use of the data submitted in connection with obtaining the approval relied on shall begin with the date of the first marketing approval relied on".

6.3.1.3 The Andean Community.

Provisions on the protection of business secrets are also established in the Common Regime on Industrial Property of the Andean Community. The definition of such secrets (Article 260) is based on Article 39.2. Though the regulation of business secrets is made separately from unfair competition, the prohibited acts are those contrary to proper commercial practices, including breach of contract. Decision 486 introduced an important amendment to the pre-existing regulation (Decision 344) in relation to the protection of data (Article 266): it eliminated an exclusivity period for the use of such data that Decision 344 had established.

6.3.1.4 CAFTA.

On 28 May 2004, the USA, Costa Rica, El Salvador, Guatemala, Honduras and Nicaragua signed the Central American Free Trade Agreement (CAFTA).[1049] This agreement considerably modifies the TRIPS approach toward protecting undisclosed information. In essence, it obligates Parties to introduce in their domestic laws exclusive rights to data submitted for marketing approval purposes.[1050] As opposed to the TRIPS approach of unfair competition law, the originator of the data in order to prevent third parties from relying on his data, does not have to prove unfair commercial practices on the part of the third party.[1051]

In addition, CAFTA establishes a link between the exclusive patent right and the marketing approval process by subjecting marketing approval for competing generic products to the consent or acquiescence of the patent holder:

> "3. Where a Party permits, as a condition of approving the marketing of a pharmaceutical product, persons, other than the person originally submitting safety or efficacy information, to rely on evidence or information concerning the safety and efficacy of a product that was previously approved, such as evidence of prior marketing approval in the Party or in another territory, that Party:
>
> shall implement measures in its marketing approval process to prevent such other persons from marketing a product covered by a patent claiming the product or its

---

[1049] For the text of the agreement, see <http://www.ustr.gov/new/fta/Cafta/final/index.htm>.

[1050] See Chapter 15, Article 15.10(1)(a). For a detailed legal analysis of CAFTA and the implications in the area of undisclosed information, see Frederick Abbott, *The Doha Declaration on the TRIPS Agreement and Public Health and the Contradictory Trend in Bilateral and Regional Free Trade Agreements*, Quaker United Nations Office, Geneva 2004 [hereinafter Abbott, *Contradictory Trend*]. Available at <http://www.geneva.quno.info/main/publication.php?pid=113>.

[1051] Considering that during the Uruguay Round negotiations, inclusion of a provision on data exclusivity was not feasible (see above, Section 2.2 of this chapter), CAFTA provides an opportunity to introduce such exclusivity "through the back door".

approved use during the term of that patent, unless by consent or acquiescence of the patent owner [...]."[1052]

In other words, the term of data protection is effectively extended to the full term of a patent, which is not required under TRIPS.[1053]

Next to the difficulties created for regulatory authorities to determine the validity of patents, this provision has been interpreted as possibly precluding governments' possibilities to use compulsory licensing as a means of making available low-priced pharmaceutical products.[1054] Since marketing approval is independent of patent law, the third party authorized to produce a patented product under compulsory license would arguably depend on the patentee's consent or acquiescence for the actual marketing of the product.

6.3.2 Bilateral

On the bilateral level, there have been similar trends as observed in the context of CAFTA, above. For instance, the FTA between the USA and Morocco provides for data exclusivity and, as under CAFTA, for the right of a patent holder to preclude marketing approval of medicines during the patent term.[1055] The Chile – USA FTA also includes a provision on data exclusivity.[1056]

6.4 Proposals for review

There are so far no proposals for review of Article 39. However, several countries, including the EU and its member states,[1057] developing countries[1058] and the USA have referred to the interpretation of Article 39.3 in written or oral submissions made on occasion of the Special Session on Intellectual Property and Access to Medicines held by the Council for TRIPS on 18–20 June, 2001.[1059] A number of developing countries have advocated that the establishment of exclusive rights – as is the case, e.g., in the USA and Europe – would delay the market entry of generic versions of products for which patents have expired, thereby unjustifiably limiting access to medicines.

7. Comments, including economic and social implications

Trade secrets protection covers business information of various natures, including mere commercial data as well as technical know-how. Such information may

---

[1052] See Chapter 15, Article 15.10(3)(a).

[1053] Abbott, *Contradictory Trend*, p. 8.

[1054] Ibid.

[1055] See Abbott, *Contradictory Trend*, p. 11.

[1056] For a detailed analysis of the USA – Chile FTA, see Roffe, 2004. This paper also provides an overview of other bilateral free trade agreements and their rules on undisclosed information.

[1057] See IP/C/W/288, 12 June 2001.

[1058] See IP/C/W/296, 19 June 2001.

[1059] See IP/C/M/31, 10 July 2001.

be of considerable economic value, particularly, but not exclusively, in process industries, such as chemicals production.[1060]

The protection of know-how and other business information may be of importance for large as well as small and medium enterprises, both in developed and developing countries. A distinct advantage of trade secrets protection is that no registration is necessary to acquire the relevant rights, and that protection lasts as long as the information is kept secret. These features make this form of protection particularly suitable to small/medium companies in developing countries. However, enforcement costs may be high.

Trade secrets protection may also be applied in relation to traditional knowledge. It has been noted that

> "The provisions against unfair competition may also be used to protect undisclosed traditional knowledge, for instance, traditional secrets kept by native and indigenous communities that may be of technological and economic value. Acknowledgement of the fact that secret traditional knowledge may be protected by means of unfair competition law will make it possible for access to that knowledge, its exploitation and its communication to third parties to be monitored. Control over the knowledge, and regulation of the manner in which it maybe acquired, used and passed on, will in turn make it possible to arrange contracts for the licensing of secret traditional knowledge and derive profits from its commercial exploitation. It is necessary to publicize more, within the sectors and communities concerned, the opportunities that the secrecy regime offers for controlling the dissemination and exploitation of traditional knowledge."[1061]

The protection of data submitted for the registration of pharmaceuticals and agrochemicals has been deemed of considerable economic importance by the so-called "research-based industry." The basic reasoning is that the manufacturer has invested, often heavily, in the research necessary to develop the relevant data, and where patent law fails to provide protection[1062] (for example, because the active component was shortly to be out of patent, or because the drug was based on a combination of known substances used in a novel manner) the secrecy of the testing work would provide the only barrier to a competitor rapidly producing and registering an exact copy of the drug. From a public health perspective, however, the early entry of generics competition is also seen as an important policy objective, whose realization is facilitated by regulations that allow health authorities to rely on existing test data to approve subsequent applications for generic products. Thus, developing country Members should be aware of recent developments on the regional and bilateral levels that limit existing TRIPS flexibilities in this respect.

[1060] According to a study by the USITC, for instance, trade secrets had gained growing importance in the 1980's. They were deemed of "great importance" by 43% of the surveyed U.S. industry (USITC, 1988, pp. 2–4).

[1061] GRULAC, *Traditional knowledge and the need to give it adequate intellectual property protection*, WO/GA/26/9, September 2000, 14. See also Graham Dutfield, *Protecting Traditional Knowledge and Folklore. A review of progress in diplomacy and policy formulation*, Issue Paper No. 1, UNCTAD-ICTSD, Geneva 2003.

[1062] The protection of test data is, in effect, particularly relevant when there is *no* patent protection. If the latter exists, the title-holder may exclude competitors on the basis of their exclusionary rights. See Puzatch.

29: Competition

Article 8.2   Principles

2. Appropriate measures, provided that they are consistent with the provisions of this Agreement, may be needed to prevent the abuse of intellectual property rights by right holders or the resort to practices which unreasonably restrain trade or adversely affect the international transfer of technology.

SECTION 8: CONTROL OF ANTI-COMPETITIVE PRACTICES
IN CONTRACTUAL LICENCES
Article 40

1. Members agree that some licensing practices or conditions pertaining to intellectual property rights which restrain competition may have adverse effects on trade and may impede the transfer and dissemination of technology.

2. Nothing in this Agreement shall prevent Members from specifying in their legislation licensing practices or conditions that may in particular cases constitute an abuse of intellectual property rights having an adverse effect on competition in the relevant market. As provided above, a Member may adopt, consistently with the other provisions of this Agreement, appropriate measures to prevent or control such practices, which may include, for example, exclusive grantback conditions, conditions preventing challenges to validity and coercive package licensing, in the light of the relevant laws and regulations of that Member.

3. Each Member shall enter, upon request, into consultations with any other Member which has cause to believe that an intellectual property right owner that is a national or domiciliary of the Member to which the request for consultations has been addressed is undertaking practices in violation of the requesting Member's laws and regulations on the subject matter of this Section, and which wishes to secure compliance with such legislation, without prejudice to any action under the law and to the full freedom of an ultimate decision of either Member. The Member addressed shall accord full and sympathetic consideration to, and shall afford adequate opportunity for, consultations with the requesting Member, and shall cooperate through supply of publicly available non-confidential information of relevance to the matter in question and of other information available

to the Member, subject to domestic law and to the conclusion of mutually satisfactory agreements concerning the safeguarding of its confidentiality by the requesting Member.

4. A Member whose nationals or domiciliaries are subject to proceedings in another Member concerning alleged violation of that other Member's laws and regulations on the subject matter of this Section shall, upon request, be granted an opportunity for consultations by the other Member under the same conditions as those foreseen in paragraph 3.

1. Introduction: terminology, definition and scope

Exploitation of Intellectual Property Rights (IPRs) could give rise to anticompetitive behaviour, whether by individual firms or by concerted practices or agreement among firms. An adequate definition and implementation of public policies to deal with this problem represents one of the most important criteria for the efficient functioning of any intellectual property system. IP laws aim at conferring exclusive rights on individuals to enable owners to appropriate the full market value of the protected subject matter. By promising that the intellectual property holder may obtain a full reward from the market, IPRs may serve as an incentive for the creation, use and exploitation of inventions, works, marks and designs. They may also provide, in a well-functioning market economy, a stimulus to competition to the extent that substitutes for the IPR protected product or service may be developed and marketed.

However, some IPR owners may exploit their legal rights to unreasonably block competition. They may do this, for example, by exploiting the unique characteristics of certain protected products that prevent rival firms from developing alternative products or entering certain markets, and refusing to grant licenses to prospective competitors.

According to one view, competition and IPRs should normally be seen as interdependent rather than contradictory. The efficiency of the intellectual property system, according to this view, is undermined when competition is distorted or artificially restrained. Moreover, a competitive market is likely to minimize the social costs resulting from the reality that IP protection cannot be adjusted to suit individual needs, notwithstanding the fact that over- or under-protection of IP are unavoidable from time to time.

Another view conceives competition law as a necessary limit to the legal powers conferred by IPRs on the basis that conflicts between the two are bound to arise given their different objectives. This view emphasizes the restrictions – especially from a static perspective – that IPRs impose on competition. Accordingly, "market economies only lead to efficient outcomes when there is competition, and intellectual property rights undermine the very basis of competition".[1]

---

[1] Joseph Stiglitz, *The roaring nineties. A new history of the world's most prosperous* decade, W.W. Norton & Company, New York-London, 2003, p. 208.

In safeguarding the efficient functioning of the market, competition policy seeks to deal with situations where the promotion of competitiveness is undermined by other factors. There are, in this context, three types of conflicts that may arise between the pursuit of competitiveness and IPRs. First, intellectual property may be used contrary to the objectives and conditions of its protection, a situation called misuse. Second, market power resulting from intellectual property may be used to extend the protection beyond its purpose, such as to enhance, extend or abuse monopoly power. Third, agreements on the use or the exploitation of intellectual property may be concluded in restraint of trade or adversely affecting the transfer or the dissemination of technology or other knowledge, a situation called restrictive contracts or concerted practice. In order to prevent or control such conflicts and to distinguish pernicious practices from competition-enhancing ones, many countries have enacted antitrust regulations or other competition legislation to respond to anticompetitive behaviour.[2] The approaches taken depend on the particular conditions of national markets, national legal traditions, and on public interest considerations. Competition rules are not designed to curb the functioning of the intellectual property system, but rather to safeguard its proper functioning.

Part 3 of this book covers the relationship between IPRs and the law of competition. This relationship involves the effects of intellectual property (which is inherently exclusionary) on economies whose functioning, in varying degrees, depends on the free movement of goods and services. The legislator may use an analysis of this relationship as the basis for specific rules (i.e., competition laws) that place boundaries on the use of IPRs (such as in the licensing context). However, in many instances the potential anticompetitive effect of IPRs is evaluated within more broadly applicable competition laws, and the analyst must then consider how IPRs should be evaluated within that broader framework. TRIPS has defined the scope of IPR protection that WTO Members should maintain bearing in mind its in-built flexibilities as analysed throughout this volume. TRIPS has, on the other hand, left largely open the way Members may address the potential anticompetitive effects of IPRs.

The relevant provisions of TRIPS in this respect are Article 8.2 and Article 40. Article 8.2 is part of the "General Provisions and Basic Principles" of Part I of the Agreement (see Part 1 of this book). It should be read as a complement to the first paragraph of Article 8, authorizing Members to adopt measures to protect public health and nutrition, and to promote the public interest in sectors of vital importance to their socio-economic and technological development. Part II, Section 8, on "Control of Anti-competitive practices in contractual licenses", consists of Article 40. Whereas paragraphs 1 and 2 of this provision deal with issues of substantive law relating to anti-competitive licensing practices, paragraphs 3 and 4 relate to matters of enforcement.

Another relevant competition provision of the Agreement is Article 31(k) dealing with compulsory licenses in the case of practices which have been determined,

---

[2] A large number of developing countries, however, have no competition law or little tradition and weak institutional mechanisms to apply competition policies.

after judicial or administrative process, to be anticompetitive and need to be remedied by the grant of compulsory licenses.[3]

2. History of the provision

2.1 Situation pre-TRIPS

TRIPS is the first international treaty to generally recognize the need to control anticompetitive IPR practices. Article 5A(2) of the Paris Convention for the International Protection of Industrial Property, though framed more broadly (". . . to prevent abuses which might result from the exercise of the exclusive right conferred by the patent. . . ."),[4] established a basis for remedying anticompetitive practices, but gave limited attention to defining the types of practices that would constitute abuse (beyond non-working). As regards abuses more generally, the provision relates only to patents. Article 10bis of the same Convention relates only to protection against acts of unfair competition, i.e., dishonest practices in business.[5] These are generally to be distinguished from restrictive trade practices, even though there may be some overlaps between the two sets of rules (e.g., boycott, discrimination, etc.).

The stillborn Havana Charter of 1948 on an International Trade Organization (ITO) contained in Article 46 an undertaking by Members to prevent restraints on competition (and to cooperate with the Organization in preventing such restraints), and permitted a Member to bring a complaint to the Organization on the

---

[3] Article 31(k) reads: "Members are not obliged to apply the conditions set forth in sub-paragraphs (b) and (f) above where such use is permitted to remedy a practice determined after judicial or administrative process to be anti-competitive. The need to correct anti-competitive practices may be taken into account in determining the amount of remuneration in such cases. Competent authorities shall have the authority to refuse termination of authorization if and when the conditions which led to such authorization are likely to recur". For a discussion of Article 31 see Chapter 25; Roffe, *Control of Anti-Competitive Practices in Contractual Licenses under the TRIPS Agreement*, in Correa, Yusuf (ed.), Intellectual Property and International Trade – The TRIPS Agreement, London 1998, 261 at 281 et seq. [hereinafter Roffe 1998].

[4] Article 5 A of the Paris Convention (1967) reads in relevant parts:
"(2) Each country of the Union shall have the right to take legislative measures providing for the grant of compulsory licenses to prevent the abuses which might result from the exercise of the exclusive rights conferred by the patent, for example, failure to work.
(3) Forfeiture of the patent shall not be provided for except in cases where the grant of compulsory licenses would not have been sufficient to prevent the said abuses. . . ."

[5] Article 10bis ("Unfair Competition") of the Paris Convention (1967) reads
"(1) The countries of the Union are bound to assure to nationals of such countries effective protection against unfair competition.
(2) Any act of competition contrary to honest practices in industrial or commercial matters constitutes an act of unfair competition.
(3) The following in particular shall be prohibited:
1. all acts of such a nature as to create confusion by any means whatever with the establishment, the goods, or the industrial or commercial activities, of a competitor;
2. false allegations in the course of trade of such a nature as to discredit the establishment, the goods, or the industrial or commercial activities, of a competitor;
3. indications or allegations the use of which in the course of trade is liable to mislead the public as to the nature, the manufacturing process, the characteristics, the suitability for their purpose, or the quantity, of the goods." See also the discussion on unfair competition in Chapter 28 of this book.

basis that another Member was failing to deal with a competition-related situation. The specific kinds of practices that the Organization's dispute settlement system would have addressed included commercial conduct:

> "3(e) preventing by agreement the development or application of technology or invention whether patented or unpatented;

> (f) extending the use of rights under patents, trademarks or copyrights granted by any Member to matters which, according to its laws and regulations, are not within the scope of such grants, or to products or conditions of production, use or sale of which are likewise not the subjects of such grants."[6]

The ITO would have had the authority to

> "request each Member concerned to take every possible remedial action, and ... recommend to the Members concerned remedial measures to be carried out in accordance with their respective laws and procedures."[7]

The Organization would have prepared, distributed to Members and made public a report on its decisions, and the remedial actions taken by Members.[8]

Attempts to establish general principles of public international law as regards the control of restrictive trade practices in general and, more particularly IPR-related anticompetitive conduct, such as a Code of Conduct on Transfer of Technology, have been suspended (see below Section 5.2). Therefore, the control of anticompetitive practices relating to IPRs has been a matter of national and regional law only. In this respect, the major industrialized countries, such as the USA, Japan, the European Union and some of its member states (in particular Germany), have well-developed rules and control practices, though these are by no means uniform.

2.2 Negotiating history

Industrialized countries with established rules for the control of intellectual property-related anticompetitive practices were not interested in establishing such rules in the TRIPS context. Instead they focused on the formulation of adequate standards of intellectual property protection. Thus, it was the developing countries, once it became clear that TRIPS negotiations would extend beyond matters of counterfeiting and piracy, who insisted on including the issue of anticompetitive practices in the Agreement.[9] In part they were of the opinion that restrictive trade practices were the only trade-related aspects of intellectual property protection,[10]

---

[6] Havana Charter for an International Trade Organization, United Nations Conference on Trade and Employment, held at Havana, Cuba, Nov. 21, 1947 to Mar. 24, 1948, Final Act and Related Documents (March 1948), at Chapter V, Restrictive Business Practices, Article 46. See Frederick M. Abbott, *Public Policy and Global Technological Integration: An Introduction*, in Public Policy and Global Technological Integration 3 (F. M. Abbott and D. Gerber eds. 1997) (Kluwer).

[7] Id. Articles 8 and 48(7).

[8] Id. Article 48(9) and (10).

[9] See Gervais, paras. 2.48, 2.182 *et seq.*; Cottier, *The prospects for intellectual property in GATT*, 28 CML Rev. 383, 409 et seq. (1991) [hereinafter Cottier]; Roffe 1998, at 278 *et seq.*

[10] See Communication from India of 10 July 1989 MTN.GNG./NG11/W/37 sub. 2 and VI.

but were also concerned about the pernicious effects of a number of contractual practices, opposition to which they had pursued unsuccessfully in negotiations on the Code of Conduct for the Transfer of Technology.[11] Their position was largely mirrored in the Anell Draft of 23 July 1990 (W/76)[12] by the two provisions that later became Articles 8.2 and 40.

2.2.1 The Anell Draft

The draft provision corresponding to the current Article 8.2 read as follows:

> "2B Each PARTY will take the measures it deems appropriate with a view to preventing the abuse of intellectual property rights or the resort to practices which unreasonably restrain trade or adversely affect the international transfer of technology. PARTIES undertake to consult each other and to co-operate in this regard."

The important difference with respect to the current version of Article 8.2 is that this provision did not expressly require the national measures to be consistent with the other provisions of the Agreement. Each Party was authorized to take any measure it deemed appropriate, according to its own discretion, without any express obligation to consider the effects of these measures on the substantive disciplines of IPR protection. This very wide language was later restricted.[13]

The Anell Draft article of what later became Article 40 provided that:

> "1B PARTIES may specify in their national legislation practices in licensing contracts deemed to constitute an abuse of intellectual property rights or to have an adverse effect on competition in the relevant market, and adopt appropriate measures to prevent or control such practices. [...]
>
> 2B PARTIES agree that practices which restrain competition, limit access to the technology or to markets or foster monopolistic control, and which are engaged in by licensors, may have harmful effects on trade and transfer of technology among their countries. Accordingly, each PARTY agrees upon the request of any other PARTY to consult with respect to any such practices and to co-operate with any other PARTIES with a view to ensuring that IPR owners, who are nationals or domiciliaries of its country, comply with the obligations prescribed in this respect by the national legislation of the PARTY granting them such rights."

The first paragraph largely corresponds to the current Article 40.2. Again, the difference is that the above draft provision did not require that the "appropriate" measures taken by Parties be consistent with the other provisions of the Agreement. The first sentence of the second draft paragraph is quite similar to the current paragraph 1 of Article 40. It acknowledges that certain licensing practices may harmfully affect trade and technology transfer. Other than Article 40.2, the above draft did not contain any exemplary list of possible IPR abuses.

---

[11] See Gervais, paras. 2.48, 2.182 et seq.; Cottier, at 409 et seq.; Roffe 1998, at 278 et seq. See also Communication from Brazil of 11 December 1989 MTN.GNG./NG11/W/57 sub. No. 29; Communication from Argentina, Brazil, Chile China, Colombia, Cuba, Egypt, India, Nigeria, Peru, Tanzania and Uruguay, of 14 May 1990, MTN.GNG/NG11/W/71, Article 15.

[12] Chairman's report to the Group of Negotiation on Goods, document MTN.GNG/NG11/W/76, of 23 July 1990.

[13] For an analysis of the consistency requirement, see Section 3, below.

The second sentence of the second draft paragraph contained a cooperation and consultation procedure like the current Article 40.3 of TRIPS. The latter is, however, more limited in scope in that while the draft provided an obligation to consult and to cooperate *with a view to ensuring compliance* of nationals or domiciliaries with domestic legislation, Article 40.3 does not refer to such final objective. On the contrary, it expressly provides that the obligation to consult does not affect the freedom of either Member to treat the alleged violation according to its own discretion. The obligation to cooperate is limited to the supply to the other Member of certain information. There is thus no obligation to undertake any concrete measures to stop the alleged violation.[14]

2.2.2 The Chairman's Draft of 23 November 1990 and the Brussels Draft

Article 8 (para. 2) and Article 43 of the Chairman's Draft Text on Trade Related Aspects of Intellectual Property Rights, Including Trade in Counterfeit Goods of November 23, 1990, came quite close to the current version of Articles 8.2 and 40. Thus, Article 8 (para. 2) recognized that

"appropriate measures [. . .] may be needed to prevent the abuse of intellectual property rights by right holders or the resort to practices which unreasonably restrain trade or affect the international transfer of technology."

Article 43 (para. 2 B) of the Chairman's Draft Text of November 23, 1990 listed a series of licensing clauses which members may deem to be abusive or anticompetitive. This provision read in relevant parts:

"1. PARTIES agree that some licensing practices or conditions pertaining to intellectual property rights which restrain competition may have adverse effects on trade and may impede the transfer and dissemination of technology.

2B. PARTIES may specify in their national legislation licensing practices or conditions that may be deemed to constitute an abuse of intellectual property rights or to have an adverse effect on competition in the relevant market, and may adopt appropriate measures to prevent or control such practices and conditions, including non-voluntary licensing in accordance with the provisions of Article 34 and the annulment of the contract or of those clauses of the contract deemed contrary to the laws and regulations governing competition and/or transfer of technology. The following practices and conditions may be subject to such measures where they are deemed to be abusive or anti-competitive: (i) grant-back provisions; (ii) challenges to validity; (iii) exclusive dealing; (iv) restrictions on research; (v) restrictions on use of personnel; (vi) price fixing; (vii) restrictions on adaptations; (viii) exclusive sales or representation agreements; (ix) tying arrangements; (x) export restrictions; (xi) patent pooling or cross-licensing agreements and other arrangements; (xii) restrictions on publicity; (xiii) payments and other obligations after expiration of industrial property rights; (xiv) restrictions after expiration of an arrangement".

Whilst Article 8 (para. 2) of the draft text required an assessment of the "unreasonableness" of a practice, Article 43 arguably allowed members to hold the listed

---

[14] For a detailed analysis of this provision, see under Section 3, below.

clauses to be unlawful *per se*. It is primarily because of this risk of a ruling of *per se* illegality that the draft text was not acceptable to industrialized countries. The same problem arose with respect to the Brussels Draft text, which was submitted to trade ministers meeting in Brussels soon after the Chairman's draft text of November 1990.[15] The Brussels Draft was essentially identical to the parts of the Chairman's draft as quoted above.

However, the industrialized countries conceded that, upon a circumstantial assessment of the effects of a licensing stipulation on competition, illegality may be found in individual cases.[16] Therefore, the final negotiations resulted in a more open-ended text.

3. Possible interpretations

3.1 Article 8.2

> ### Article 8.2   Principles
>
> 2. Appropriate measures, provided that they are consistent with the provisions of this Agreement, may be needed to prevent the abuse of intellectual property rights by right holders or the resort to practices which unreasonably restrain trade or adversely affect the international transfer of technology.

As indicated by its heading, Article 8.2 states a "principle", which is different from a mere "policy statement".[17] It constitutes a general rule of the treaty providing rights and duties for Members. The fact that it only states a "principle" rather than a specific rule mirrors the intention of the treaty-makers not to rule on the matter itself in any detailed form, but to leave Members broad discretion as regards its implementation. Article 8.2 purports, indeed, to recognize Members' authority to rule on IPR-related practices that are abusive, unreasonably restrain trade or adversely affect international transfer of technology. However, the provision does not simply spell out a "permissive" or, to the contrary, a "limiting" principle.[18] Rather, it positively recognizes that there "may be a need" to prevent the practices mentioned, and in that sense it represents an enabling provision: Members agree that there are such practices and that they have to be remedied. However, Article 8.2 also sets limits to Members' authority to prevent said practices: first, regarding the substance of preventive measures, and second, concerning the nature of the remedy. Thus, the measure must be "consistent with the provisions of this Agreement", and it must be "appropriate" to prevent the practices in question. It is in

---

[15] Draft Final Act Embodying the Results of the Uruguay Round of Multilateral Trade Negotiations, Revision, Trade-Related Aspects of Intellectual Property Rights, Including Trade in Counterfeit Goods, MTN.TNC/W/35/Rev. 1, 3 Dec. 1990.

[16] Reinbothe, Howard, *The State of Play in the Negotiations on TRIPS (GATT/Uruguay Round)*, (1991) Eur. Int. Prop. Rev. 157, 160; See also Cottier.

[17] For different views see Gervais, at 68, para. 2.49.

[18] For different views see Fox, *Trade, Competition and Intellectual Property – TRIPS and its Antitrust Counterparts*, 29 Vanderbilt J. Transnat'l. L 481, 484, 491, 494 (1996) [hereinafter Fox].

view of these limitations that the scope of Article 8.2 must be further explored including the precise meaning of its requirements.

3.1.1 Scope of application

The practices that Members may prevent relate to all disciplines of intellectual property dealt with in TRIPS as well as their differing forms of exploitation. The practices covered by Article 8.2 must be defined accordingly. They are of three kinds: the abuse of intellectual property rights by rights holders, practices which unreasonably restrain trade, and practices which adversely affect the international transfer of technology.

Since the practices that Members may prevent through domestic measures are listed in alternative form ("or"), they need to be distinguished. The distinctions are not obvious, since restrictive practices may cover both unilateral abuses of IPRs and contractual restraints of trade, and since contractual restraints may either affect trade or impair technology transfer.[19] However, in view of the twofold purpose of the provision to set forth a principle recognizing Members' power to act, and also in view of the multiple objectives of the Agreement as stated in Article 7, a broad construction of the practices in question seems to be justified. In particular, the meaning of the terms used may not be reduced to what they might mean according to the national laws of some Members or according to pre-determined concepts of antitrust laws. Any "national" reading of Article 8.2 would miss the international character of the Agreement and the underlying intention of the Article, which is precisely to largely maintain Members' sovereignty in the matter.[20]

As a general matter, Article 8.2 applies only to IPR-related abuses or practices. This means that the assessment of broader restrictive agreements or arrangements, which involve IPRs, but which, under general principles of competition law, are dealt with as separate categories of possible antitrust law violations, may not be subject to the limits set by Article 8.2. Thus, merger control (in particular, the sale and acquisition of enterprises) may involve ancillary licensing transactions, and authorization of a merger may be made conditional on certain licensing concessions by the merging firms either *inter se* or as regards third-party access to the technology in question. The provisions of Article 8.2 do not apply to merger control merely because of these IPR implications. The same holds true for merger control over the establishment of joint ventures.

Similarly, where the use or exploitation of IPRs is only indirectly related to the allegedly anticompetitive conduct, such as agreements between competitors on prices for their respective protected products, it is questionable whether Article 8.2 should apply. The question may not be important in the example given, since the application of Article 8.2 would hardly have any bearing on the outcome of the assessment of such a practice. However, it becomes important in cases of a territorial division of markets by competitors. As it does make a difference whether such horizontal market division that happens to relate to protected products is based on existing IPRs of the parties, or is agreed upon to solve IPR conflicts

---

[19] See Article 40.1 of the Agreement, and Subsection d) below.
[20] See also Fox at 485 *et seq.*

between the parties, it would seem that the dividing line between the applicability and the non-applicability of Article 8.2 must be drawn in accordance with where the centre of gravity of an agreement or of a transaction is. It is only where the practice is directly and essentially IPR-related that TRIPS may be deemed to require that Article 8.2 be taken into consideration. After all, it is an Agreement on intellectual property, not one on competition law. Therefore, the same prudence should be observed when research and development agreements, subcontracting arrangements or outsourcing agreements become subject to an antitrust control, which relates to the collusive or otherwise anticompetitive character of the practice rather than to the concomitant exploitation of IPRs, or which covers such exploitation only to the extent that it is subordinate to or instrumental for a more pervasive antitrust-relevant practice. Nonetheless an IPR-related restrictive practice is in no way "immunized" from competition law scrutiny and remedial action merely because it is part of a large scale transaction. It is for the national competition authorities to determine whether a particular practice will be addressed within the context of a transaction.

a) Abuse of intellectual property rights

For the reasons stated above, "abuses" of intellectual property must cover the illegitimate use of intellectual property. In particular, Members may consider a particular conduct of right holders to be abusive regardless of whether the enterprise in question dominates the market or not,[21] and regardless of whether there is an anticompetitive use or simply a use of an intellectual property right which defeats its purpose, e.g., the purpose of innovation or of dissemination of technology. Indeed, it is not Article 8.2 which defines the concept of abuse, but Members themselves through appropriate domestic measures. This is so because TRIPS uses the term "abuse" only to determine the connecting factor for Members' regulatory power. However, it follows from the very term that the use at stake must be illegitimate, i.e., contrary to the basis and/or the objectives of IPR protection. In that respect, it is the consistency requirement which defines the limits within which Members may determine both the basis and the objectives of domestic IPR protection and the abusive character of its use.

b) Practices which unreasonably restrain trade

Likewise, practices which "unreasonably" restrain trade are not only those, which, under a given concept of a "rule of reason" of antitrust law, would be held to be anti- rather than pro-competitive,[22] but any practice which "reasonably" may be held to be unreasonable. What Article 8.2 seeks to avoid is that Members outlaw practices that are inherently beneficial, such as contractual clauses facilitating the productive use of the intellectual property.[23] Conversely, the provision may

---

[21] See also: Fox at 482; abuse does not presuppose market domination, but may result from relational market power (e.g., discriminatory practices). However, abuse may also exist in the absence of market power, e.g., no challenge agreements.

[22] See text under Section 3.2.1 b) on Article 40.1.

[23] The distinction is not always easy, but typical examples are confidentiality requirements under trade secret agreements and licenses, or conditioning the grant of sub-licenses by the licensee on

not be read as excluding rules of *a priori* illegality of certain restrictive practices (so-called *per se* rules). It is true that, when negotiating the Agreement, Members did not wish to include such *per se* prohibitions in the Agreement.[24] But as many of them have such rules,[25] they did not wish to exclude them either as a matter of national law. This is the more true as Article 8.2 purports only to generally designate the practices upon which Members may rule autonomously, and not to rule itself on these practices other than by limiting Members' discretion. In that regard, however, the interpretation and the application of the requirement of consistency may not be anticipated by a narrow reading of the practices in question.

c) Practices which adversely affect the international transfer of technology

The third category of practices which Members may seek to prevent, namely practices which adversely affect the international transfer of technology, must be understood broadly as well. First, practices adversely affecting international technology transfer must be distinguished from practices which restrain trade. This is so because they are named separately in Article 8.2,[26] and because Article 7 of the Agreement singles out transfer of technology as one of the objectives of the Agreement. Thus practices which are not anticompetitive, but which do have an adverse effect on technology transfer, may be subject to specific national regulation.[27] Whether this is politically wise is another matter.[28] The consistency requirement already provides the necessary safeguards against truly counter-productive regulation of technology transfer. Second, compared to Article 40, which is ambiguously

---

the consent by the licensor. On the other hand, hardcore restrictions such as limiting a party's ability to determine its prices, do not fall under this category of beneficial practices, see Article 4 of Commission Regulation (EC) No. 772/2004 of 27 April 2004 on the application of Article 81 (3) of the Treaty to categories of technology transfer agreements, Official Journal of the European Union (OJEU) 2004 L 123/11 [hereinafter EU Regulation on Technology Transfer Agreements]; for another example see Court of Justice of the European Communities (CJEC) of April 19, 1988, case 27/87, *Erauw-Jacquery/La Hesbignonne*, Rep. 1988, 1919.

[24] See above, Section 2.

[25] See Article 3 of the EU Regulation on Technology Transfer Agreements, and the overviews of national antitrust law relating to IPRs exploitation by Anderson, *The Interface between Competition Policy and Intellectual Property in the Context of the International Trading System*, J. Int'l Ec. L. 1998, 655, 662 et seq. [hereinafter Anderson]; Marschall, *Patents, Antitrust, and the WTO/GATT: Using TRIPS as a Vehicle for Antitrust Harmonization*, 28 L. Pol'y Int'l. Bus. 1165, 1170 et seq. (1997) [hereinafter Marschall].

[26] It is true that Article 40.1 uses cumulative ("and") rather than alternative ("or") language, but Article 40.1 is a provision with a narrow meaning, and, most likely, needs corrective reading, see Subsection 3.2.1 below.

[27] Conversely, there are many possibly anti-competitive practices which do not affect technology transfer, e.g., restrictive licences concerning copyrights or trademarks.

[28] See the introductory contributions by the UNCTAD Secretariat, and the contribution in Part III of Patel, Roffe, Yusuf, *International Technology Transfer – The Origins and Aftermath of the United Nations Negotiations on a Draft Code of Conduct*, The Hague 2001, 3 et seq., 259 et seq. [hereinafter Patel, Roffe, Yusuf]; Stoll, *Technologietransfer – Internationalisierungs- und Nationalisierungstendenzen*, 1994, 365 et seq. [hereinafter Stoll]; Cabanellas, *Antitrust and Direct Regulation of International Transfer of Technology Transactions*, Munich 1982, 157 et seq. [hereinafter Cabanellas]. See also Section 5.2 below.

formulated in this respect, Article 8.2 clearly covers not only contractual practices affecting international transfer of technology, but also unilateral practices.[29]
Third, in accordance with the Agreement's rationale of improving international
trade relations, Article 8.2 covers all practices affecting international transfer
of technology, both inbound and outbound.

However, the provision concerns only international transfer of technology, not
domestic technology transfer, such as from the national science base to domestic
industry. This is a difference as compared to restrictive trade practices, whose
control is subject to Article 8.2 precisely whenever these practices affect domestic
markets. As a rule, TRIPS concerns the acquisition, use and exploitation of intellectual property in national markets. The difference means that the regulation
of domestic technology transfer is not subject to the requirements of consistency
and proportionality of measures taken against adverse practices.

3.1.2 Requirements for the application of appropriate measures

It is only once the scope of application of Article 8.2 has been defined properly
that the requirements limiting the exercise of national antitrust control, namely
the requirements of consistency with the Agreement and of proportionality of the
corrective measure, come into play.

a) The consistency requirement

The requirement of consistency may have two different meanings. It may be limited to the particular remedy taken; or it may apply more generally to the domestic
substantive rules of competition law that are at the basis of such remedies.

(i) A narrow interpretation: consistency as regards remedies
against unlawful practices

Read literally, the consistency requirement of Article 8.2 only refers to the nature
of the measures that may be taken as against practices that have been found to
constitute an abuse, a restrictive practice or a practice adversely affecting international technology transfer. Such a reading would appear to be confirmed by
similar language in Article 40.2, which clearly separates the qualification of anti-
competitive practices as a matter of substantive law (Article 40.2, first sentence)
from the remedies that may be taken against such measures (Article 40.2, second
sentence.). Such an understanding of the provision would make sense in that, for
instance, remedial measures ought not normally to result in public disclosure of
secret know-how or in frustration of the exclusivity of IP-protection by general

---

[29] Such as abusive refusals to license or to pre-disclose information on innovations affecting related
industries (spare parts, complementary equipment or services etc.), see Fox, at 487 et seq.; Ullrich,
*Intellectual Property, Access to Information, and Antitrust: Harmony, Disharmony, and International
Harmonization* [hereinafter Ullrich, *Intellectual Property, Access to Information, and Antitrust*], in
Dreyfuss et al. (ed.), Expanding the Boundaries of Intellectual Property, Oxford 2001, 365, 385 et
seq. [hereinafter Dreyfuss]; id., *Competition, Intellectual Property Rights, and Transfer of Technology*,
in Patel, Roffe, Yusuf, at 363, 375 et seq. [hereinafter Ullrich, *Competition, Intellectual Property
Rights, and Transfer of Technology*].

licensing requirements.[30] If the consistency requirement were limited to this meaning, its application presumably would largely overlap with the requirement of the proportionality of the measures taken. Another view is that the provision introduces a reservation against enforcement of national antitrust laws in a manner that would frustrate systematically the purpose and the operation of intellectual property protection in general.

(ii) A broad interpretation: consistency as regards the substance of IPR-related rules on competition

If the requirement of consistency of antitrust control over abusive and anticompetitive IP practices may have a broader meaning of requiring also consistency of the substantive rules of national competition law or antitrust law with the provisions of this Agreement,[31] it must nevertheless be clear that it does not justify an extensive application of the requirement. Since Article 8.2, read in conjunction with Article 8.1 and with Article 40.2 (first sentence), expressly authorizes Members to define and apply IPR-related rules of competition law, the consistency requirement may not be used to subject national antitrust laws to any TRIPS-supremacy, let alone to any specific antitrust standards of TRIPS origin, which TRIPS has not set forth anyway. Rather, the consistency requirement represents a reservation made to prevent an excessive application of national competition rules, which would bring the regular exercise and exploitation of IPRs, as they are assumed by TRIPS standards, within the ambit of and control by antitrust authorities. This understanding follows from two facts. First, competition law and intellectual property law are *in pari materiae* in that competition law is supposed to safeguard the kind of dynamic competition that should result from and is the basis for intellectual property protection.[32] Second, Members, in particular industrialized States, did and do follow different approaches as regards the assessment of potentially restrictive or anticompetitive IPR practices.[33] They cannot be presumed to have abandoned any of these approaches as a matter of contracting for and adopting TRIPS, because these approaches and the highly complex set of IPR-related antitrust rules, which they have produced, have not been made the object of any detailed negotiations.[34] It was only a general concern that some Members, in particular some major developing countries, might put too much reliance on competition, law with a view to limiting TRIPS concessions.[35]

---

[30] The relevant provisions of the TRIPS Agreement are Article 39 on trade secrets and Article 31 recognizing compulsory licenses, but subjecting their grants to certain pre-requisites.

[31] See also Heinemann, *Antitrust Law of Intellectual Property in the TRIPS Agreement of the World Trade Organization* [hereinafter Heinemann], in Beier, Schricker (ed.), From GATT to TRIPS, Weinheim 1996, 239, 242 et seq. [hereinafter Beier, Schricker]; implicitly Fox, at 492 et seq.

[32] See UNCTAD, *The TRIPS Agreement and Developing Countries*, Geneva 1996, 3 et seq. [hereinafter UNCTAD 1996]; Ullrich, *Intellectual Property, Access to Information, and Antitrust*, at 367 et seq.; id., *Competition, Intellectual Property Rights, and Transfer of Technology*, at 368 et seq.

[33] See Fox, at 486 et seq., 492 et seq.; UNCTAD 1996, at 55 et seq. (para 271 et seq.). See also Anderson; Marschall.

[34] See Cottier, at 410.

[35] See Section 2 above.

For these reasons, the consistency requirement neither adopts any of the various national approaches to or standards of antitrust assessment of IPR-related restrictive practices[36] nor establishes any standard of its own.[37, 38] Rather it must be understood as a negative limitation preventing an application of national competition rules that outlaw generally accepted methods of exploiting intellectual property that TRIPS recognizes through requiring the protection of IPRs. It is therefore the systematic development of national competition law as a general curtailment of intellectual property protection (as required by TRIPS) that the consistency requirement is intended to prevent. In other words, what it seeks to achieve is to contain national competition laws within the limits of their proper purpose, and to keep this purpose within limits: the safeguarding of competition, however defined.

(iii) Examples of non-compliance with the consistency requirement

It is difficult to specify in the abstract what might amount to inconsistencies with this requirement. As a general proposition, it may be said that antitrust rules which would tend to *systematically* invalidate the constitutive elements of intellectual property protection by exclusive rights, as distinguished from subjecting licensing obligations in *particular* circumstances to rules regulating anti-competitive

---

[36] According to Fox, at 492 et seq., the various existing approaches of national competition law, in particular, those of major industrialized countries (USA, EU) must be presumed not to violate the consistency requirement.

[37] Note that the variation of antitrust approaches to IPRs over time and the evolving insights into the operation of both IPR-systems and competition require a high degree of flexibility of international conventional law.

[38] In particular, it does not favour or disfavour the so-called scope-of-the-exclusivity test or the reasonable-reward test or a pure competition test or a profit maximizing efficiency test. For the various tests see Anderson; Marschall; and Ullrich, *Intellectual Property, Access to Information, and Antitrust*, at 367 et seq.. Basically, the scope-of-the-exclusivity test, which is still enshrined in Section 17 of the German Act Against Restraints of Competition, and the reasonable-reward test once followed by the USA, mean that all restrictive covenants in licensing agreements are justified, which only mirror the exclusivity or seek to secure to the IPRs-holder the profit due under his "legal monopoly". The profit-maximisation rationale of the efficiency test represents a modern variation in that it assumes that restrictions in licensing agreements between non-competitors (vertical restraints) generally are innocuous to the extent that they only mirror the market value of the licensed technology – a licensee will only accept restrictions that are justified by the value the technology has for him, provided that the market is itself competitive. All of these approaches present the following problems:
– they relate only to restrictions imposed on the licensee, not to those to which the licensor may be subject (e.g., exclusivity requirements, most-favoured-licensee clauses);
– they do not take account of either differences of bargaining power or of the fact that license transactions are negotiated on an overall-benefits basis;
– the horizontal/vertical distinction does not systematically apply (license transaction may be based on make-or-buy decisions by the licensee as a potential entrant);
– technology markets are not transparent;
– and competition is only interested in the answer to the question whether, in the absence of the restrictive agreement, competition would be enhanced or not, i.e., whether the agreement is pro- or anti-competitive in its results. Since the answer depends on the kind of competition a given competition policy wishes to favour, modern approaches do treat intellectual property as any property, i.e., they apply their general concepts to IPRs-related restrictions as well, see infra Section 6.1.

practice,[39] would be inconsistent with TRIPS.[40] Outlawing restricted licenses altogether and with no circumstantial qualification might be inconsistent with TRIPS to the extent that the exclusivity is divisible by nature and must be allowed to so be divided into different license rights (even though there is no specific TRIPS rule to this effect). Conversely, it may be said that competition rules, which equally apply to IPR-related and to non-IPR related conduct, that is, rules of general application, may hardly ever violate the consistency requirement.[41] Only antitrust rules that discriminate by singling out IPRs for treatment that is not justified by public policy concerns may be caught by the consistency requirement. Again, however, the dividing line may be narrow, since IPR-specific rules of competition law, which are designed to control the particular risks that IPR-related conduct may produce for competition, normally will satisfy the consistency requirement. Most national competition laws have developed such rules, either by legislative action, by administrative practice or through case law.[42]

Finally, the measures taken to prevent abuses and other unlawful IPR-related practices must be in conformity with the general principles of TRIPS. In particular, they must be non-discriminatory. They must provide national and most-favoured-nation treatment for the parties affected by the regulation. Normally, the consistency requirement will not raise problems in this respect; competition rules should be non-discriminatory by definition.

b) The proportionality requirement

The principle of proportionality, to which Article 8.2 subjects the application of antitrust remedies to IPR-related violations of national competition law, follows from the fact that Article 8.2 requires the measures to be "appropriate" and "needed" to prevent the abuses and practices covered by the provision. The principle seems to be less difficult to apply than the consistency requirement, since it is well known in many national competition laws. Again, however, due account must be taken of the fact that Article 8.2 leaves the control of the practices in question to domestic law. It is, therefore, national law which determines the nature of the available and applicable remedies, i.e., criminal law, administrative law and/or tort law or their cumulative application. TRIPS does not provide rules on these matters (except in Article 42 et seq. as regards infringement of IPRs).

The rigour of the remedies, e.g., criminal sanctions or other punitive or simple damages, would appear to be a matter of national law. Being merely an Agreement on intellectual property, TRIPS cannot interfere on these questions with the general sovereignty of Members. As a result, the proportionality requirement, as well, should be understood as imposing only a negatively defined limitation on national

---

[39] Which Article 31(k) of TRIPS accepts in principle.

[40] See Subsection 3.1.1 c) above on practices which unreasonably restrain trade.

[41] See the approach favoured by the U.S. Department of Justice, Federal Trade Commission, *Antitrust Guidelines for Licensing of Intellectual Property*, Washington D.C., April 6, 1995 (reprinted in 4 Trade Reg. Rep. (CCH) § 13.132 = 49 BNA – PTCJ 714/1995), sub. 2.0, 2.1; Ullrich, *Intellectual Property, Access to Information, and Antitrust*, at 375 et seq.

[42] See Anderson; Fox; Marschall; and UNCTAD 1996.

remedial action against abusive anticompetitive IPR-related practices. It outlaws clearly excessive remedies, which unnecessarily put the intellectual property altogether in jeopardy. More particularly, the proportionality requirement might be meant only to exclude generally excessive antitrust remedies for IPR practices, but does not control the remedies taken under the specific circumstances of individual cases. This should be a matter of discretion for the national judicial or administrative authorities.[43] Typically, the proportionality requirement will be disregarded if national competition rules provide for IPR-specific remedies that are not justified by the nature of an antitrust law violation,[44] or that arbitrarily discriminate against IPR-related violations as compared to similar, non-IPR-related anticompetitive conduct.

3.2 Article 40

3.2.1 Rules of substantive law
a) Relationship between Article 40 and Article 8.2

The relationship between Article 40 and Article 8.2 is not self-evident. Whilst some authors hold the view that Article 8.2 contains a policy statement, which is implemented by Article 40,[45] a more consistent interpretation seems to be that Article 40 represents a *lex specialis* provision. This is so, first, because Article 40 has a narrower scope of application than Article 8.2;[46] second, Article 8.2 is a rule of treaty law, not merely a policy statement.[47] Third, Article 40 contains rules which, with regard only to some of the conduct of IPR-holders listed in Article 8.2, may establish obligations on Members that are not mandated by Article 8.2. That is to say, Article 40.1 arguably imposes an obligation on Members to act on "licensing practices or conditions pertaining to intellectual property rights, which restrain competition".... if they "have adverse effects on trade and may impede the transfer and dissemination of technology", and it certainly requires Members to cooperate in accordance with Article 40.3 and 4, when and only when they enforce their national rules on competition with respect to practices mentioned in Article 40.1 and 2.

b) Article 40.1

> 1. Members agree that some licensing practices or conditions pertaining to intellectual property rights which restrain competition may have adverse effects on trade and may impede the transfer and dissemination of technology.

---

[43] This is the more true as Article 8.2 of the Agreement, by its very nature, is not directly applicable, i.e., may not be relied upon in litigation before national courts.

[44] As to the admissibility of compulsory licensing as an antitrust remedy, see Article 31(k).

[45] Gervais, at 68, para. 2.49.

[46] See below sub b) (ii).

[47] See above, Section 3.1.

(i) A minimum obligation to act

Article 8.2 only recognizes that there may be a need to prevent certain abuses and anticompetitive practices, thereby leaving it up to Members to act or not. Article 40.1, on the other hand, contains a definite though unspecific statement of Members' agreement that "some licensing practices or conditions... which restrain competition may have adverse effects ...". Although some authors[48] do not see the difference, the consensus of Members on the existence of licensing practices which, because they restrain competition, may have adverse effects on trade and technology transfer, creates a different legal situation. If Members have indeed agreed that certain licensing practices should be addressed, it is difficult to see why TRIPS would allow Members to remain inactive with respect to such practices, since these run directly contrary to the objectives of Article 7. Reading Article 40.1 in conjunction with Article 7 may well be understood as imposing an obligation on Members to address certain forms of anticompetitive practices in licensing agreements.

Article 40.1 is not worded as strictly as comparable provisions in other agreements of GATT/WTO, such as Articles VIII and IX of the GATS.[49] Therefore, it does not provide for a specific obligation of Members to actively enforce their rules on competition relating to matters covered by Article 40, each time these are violated. It is also true that, as a matter of principle, Article 40.1 and 2 leaves the definition of the anticompetitive practice in question to Members.[50] However, under Article 1.1 (first sentence), Members have obliged themselves "to give effect to the provisions of this Agreement". Anticompetitive practices, which adversely affect trade or impede technology transfer, may frustrate the very purpose of the protection of IPRs, as provided for by TRIPS. Therefore, a total absence of rules of competition even as regards such properly abusive practices may be considered as "inconsistent" with the provisions of the Agreement (Article 40.2,

---

[48] Gervais, at 191 (para. 2.184 *in fine*) considers Article 40.1 to be a non-binding "chapeau" of the section; Heinemann, at 245 also holds Article 40.1 to be non-committal.

[49] Article VIII and IX GATS-Agreement provide in relevant parts:

"Article VIII: Monopolies and Exclusive Service Suppliers

1. Each Member shall ensure that any monopoly supplier of a service in its territory does not, in the supply of the monopoly service in the relevant market, act in a manner inconsistent with that Member's obligations under Article II and specific commitments.

2. Where a Member's monopoly supplier competes, either directly or through an affiliated company, in the supply of a service outside the scope of its monopoly rights and which is subject to that Member's specific commitments, the Member shall ensure that such a supplier does not abuse its monopoly position to act in its territory in a manner inconsistent with such commitments."

"Article IX: Business Practices

1. Members recognize that certain business practices of service suppliers, other than those falling under Article VIII, may restrain competition and thereby restrict trade in services.

2. Each Member shall, at the request of any other Member, enter into consultations with a view to eliminating practices referred to in paragraph 1. The Member addressed shall accord full and sympathetic consideration to such a request and shall cooperate through the supply of publicly available non-confidential information of relevance to the matter in question. The Member addressed shall also provide other information available to the requesting Member, subject to its domestic law and to the conclusion of satisfactory agreement concerning the safeguarding of its confidentiality by the requesting Member."

[50] See below sub. c) on Article 40.2.

second sentence). Consequently, Members may be considered to contradict the spirit of Article 40.1 if they systematically abstain from taking measures against practices which directly offend the basis and the objectives of TRIPS provisions and/or principles, or if they systematically fail to enforce existing national rules on competition regarding such practices.

(ii) Restrictive licensing practices or conditions

Article 40.1 is only concerned with restrictive practices in contractual licensing, not with restrictive practices relating to other business transactions, such as assignments, joint ventures, subcontracting and outsourcing, regardless of how IPR- or technology transfer-related such transactions may be.[51] As licensing may occur in the context of some of the transactions referred to, the necessary distinction must be made in accordance with the overall nature of the arrangement as a business transaction and the centre of gravity of the restriction in question. Nonetheless, the fact that an abusive licensing practice takes place within the context of a transaction with a larger scope would not insulate that practice from being addressed by a Member. It is customary for competition authorities to address particular anti-competitive elements of large-scale arrangements such as mergers and acquisitions without necessarily seeking to prevent the conclusion of the arrangement.

Article 40.1 applies to licensing of any kind of intellectual property covered by TRIPS. This is so even though most of the practices mentioned in Article 40.2 seem to point to patents, or possibly also to trademarks. The reason is that, in a systematic perspective, Section 8 complements the rules of Part II on standards concerning the availability, scope and use of IPRs, which is to say, the "use" of *all* "intellectual property rights".

Although Section 8 relates only to "contractual" licenses, Article 40.1, by referring in general terms to "licensing practices or conditions", clarifies that it covers all conduct surrounding the grant and the execution of licenses. Thus, refusals to license, discriminatory grant of licenses as well as discriminatory license terms, and restrictive clauses in general, all fall within the scope of the provision. It is less clear whether, in addition to unilateral conduct and to restrictive contract terms, Article 40.1 also extends to multilateral licensing relations, such as cross-licensing or patent pools. While bilateral and multilateral licensing agreements may be distinguished for purposes of antitrust analysis under some national laws, the usual distinction, which is common to all competition rules, is between agreements among competitors (horizontal agreements) and agreements among non-competitors (vertical agreements), and this distinction cuts across all types of licensing. It would appear, therefore, that in the context of an international agreement which recognizes, as does Article 40, Members' authority to act on the basis of national law, the distinction between bilateral and multilateral licensing agreements is immaterial. Multilateral licensing agreements need the more to be

---

[51] The scope of application of Article 40.1 relates to a specific segment of the practices covered by Article 8.2 (see supra Subsection 3.1.1 b) – d), namely to license practices. As these are IPR-related by nature, the additional distinction to non-IPRs-related practices (see above 3.1.1e) is immaterial in the Article 40-context.

included in Article 40 as they may produce effects on trade and technology transfer at least as adverse as bilateral licensing agreements.

(iii) The particular link between the restriction of competition and the effects on trade or technology transfer

Article 40.1 must be interpreted from the perspective of Article 40.2. It constitutes the consensual recognition of the likely existence of harmful licensing practices and conditions, which Members may subject to control in accordance with Article 40.2. This consensual recognition means that Members will respect whatever measures other Members take pursuant to Article 40.2, because these are considered to be within the purpose and the spirit of TRIPS. Such general acceptance, however, only relates to "some" licensing practices or conditions, which "restrain competition" and may have "adverse effects on trade and may impede the transfer and dissemination of technology". These qualifications do not mean that Members may not act on other licensing practices, e.g., as regards their treatment under general rules of commercial law or under general or specific market regulations. It only means that the particular rules of Article 40 concern only practices which are potentially harmful for competition. The harm in question must result from the restrictive character of the practice or condition at issue, i.e., it must result from a restraint of competition, and it must consist of either an adverse effect on trade or of an impediment to the transfer or the dissemination of technology. The link between the restrictive nature of the licensing practice or condition and its effects on trade or technology transfer is important. It means that Article 40.1 does not recognize national measures, whereby Members subject technology transfer to a control in the abstract and regardless of their relationship to competition, or whereby they incriminate certain practices of technology transfer because of perceived general negative effects. Rather, it recognizes only those measures which address technology transfer, specifically cases of harmful effects resulting from a restraint of competition. In that sense, Article 40.1 enshrines a competition approach to the regulation of technology transfer, albeit not to the exclusion of other approaches.[52]

Article 40.1 takes into consideration only those licensing practices and conditions which have an "adverse" effect on trade or which constitute an impediment to technology transfer. Despite the express language ("and"), these negative criteria are meant to apply alternatively, not cumulatively. The reason is that Article 40.1 also relates to licensing of intellectual property which is not related to technology transfer.

Although referring to transfer or dissemination of technology in general, Article 40.1, like Article 8.2, only means international technology transfer. This is so because of the international character of the Agreement, and because of the procedural rules to which Article 40.3 and 40.4 subjects measures which Members take under Article 40.1 and 40.2. These rules make sense only with regard to licensing practices having some international component. However, there is no reason to apply a restrictive understanding to the requirement of an international element. For example, ownership of a local enterprise by a foreign direct investor

---

[52] For the various approaches to technology transfer, see Patel, Roffe, Yusuf; Stoll; and Cabanellas.

would provide a sufficient international element since ultimate control over the local activity would have an international character. Moreover, the harmful effects of such practices may concern national markets only, because TRIPS seeks to ensure adequate protection on national markets[53] and technology transfer to national markets.

Finally, Article 40.1 does not establish any degree of gravity or of harm caused by the negative effects of the practice. Any adverse effect on trade and any impediment to technology transfer suffices. Nor does Article 40.1 require that the practices and conditions produce an overall negative effect or are negative "on balance". Reading it in the context of Article 40.2, the provision merely provides for a threshold for Members' action to control potentially harmful licensing practices and conditions. The way and the standards by which Members determine which restrictive practices and conditions are so harmful as to require intervention and prevention, are left to their judgment. The proper yardstick for avoiding excessive control is the consistency requirement.

c) Article 40.2

> 2. Nothing in this Agreement shall prevent Members from specifying in their legislation licensing practices or conditions that may in particular cases constitute an abuse of intellectual property rights having an adverse effect on competition in the relevant market. As provided above, a Member may adopt, consistently with the other provisions of this Agreement, appropriate measures to prevent or control such practices, which may include, for example, exclusive grantback conditions, conditions preventing challenges to validity and coercive package licensing, in the light of the relevant laws and regulations of that Member.

Article 40.2 affirms Members' sovereign power to establish and define rules of competition law regarding licensing practices and conditions (first sentence), and then goes on to recognize Members' authority to take appropriate measures to prevent or control such practices consistent with other provisions of the Agreement (second sentence). Both sentences must be read as mutually complementary, and they must be read in the light of Article 40.1, because Article 40.2 describes the action which Article 40.1 invites Members to take, if they so wish.

(i) The concept of anti-competitive practices (Article 40.2, first sentence)

Article 40.2 (first sentence) is more narrowly worded than Article 40.1. It affirms each Member's sovereign power of "specifying in their national legislation licensing practices or conditions" only in view of "particular cases" in which they "constitute an abuse of intellectual property rights having an adverse effect on competition in the relevant market". Distinguished from Article 40.1, the negative effects seem to have to relate to competition rather than to trade, and impediments to

---

[53] For the territoriality principle underlying the TRIPS Agreement, see Ullrich, *Technology Protection According to TRIPS: Principles and Problems*, in Beier, Schricker, at 357, 361 et seq., 372 et seq.

the transfer or dissemination of technology are not mentioned at all. However, in view of the interrelationship between Article 40.1 and Article 40.2, and considering the link, which Article 40.1 establishes between the restrictive nature of licensing practices or conditions and its impact on trade or technology transfer, the difference seems to be one of wording rather than of substance. In particular, Article 40.2 confirms a competition law approach to the control of technology transfer, and does not elevate competition as such to the exclusion of promoting technology transfer, particularly in light of Article 7 and Article 8.2, which put particular stress on technology transfer as one of TRIPS' objectives.

The real difficulties of interpretation, which the first sentence of Article 40.2 raises, result from the fact that on the one hand, Article 40.2 fully confirms Members' sovereign power to specify in their national legislation which licensing practices or conditions they consider to be abusive and anti-competitive; and on the other, it seems to limit that discretion by stating that such practices or conditions "may in particular cases constitute an abuse of intellectual property rights having an adverse effect on competition in the relevant market". The difficulties of interpreting this limitation stem from the fact that the wording is both tautological and contradictory. Abuses always exist only in particular cases. Licensing practices that constitute an abuse of IPRs having an adverse effect on competition are always unacceptable. In all the cases where these two requirements are met, the licensing practice *must* be unlawful. Therefore, the provision seeks to ensure by its qualifying language that Members do not specify anticompetitive practices or conditions of licensing in general and in the abstract, but in reasonably detailed circumstantial form and by reference to their actual impact on the conditions of competition existing in the markets concerned.[54]

This particular understanding of Article 40.2 (first sentence) is confirmed by both the history of the provision[55] and by the literature.[56] It does not mean that Members may not, by their sovereign judgment, define what constitutes an abuse. Article 40.2 expressly refers to their national legislation. But they must do so on the competition merits of a practice as they see them. Nor does the provision exclude the establishment or the development of well defined *per se* prohibitions of licensing practices or conditions that have no redeeming virtues, i.e. which, as such, are *a priori* and under all foreseeable circumstances anticompetitive.[57] Members have and traditionally had such rules, and they have qualified the same licensing agreements differently.[58] The limits of such qualification may not be

---

[54] See Gervais, at 191 (para. 2.185) stressing that, contrary to the draft text submitted during negotiations, abuse and adverse effects on competition are cumulative ("and"), not alternative ("or") conditions, thus reaffirming the competition approach to the control of licensing practices, which Article 40.1 requires.

[55] See supra Section 2.2. In particular, Article 40.2 is intended to contain claims of developing countries to subject intellectual property and its exploitation as such to a pervasive competition test.

[56] See Heinemann, at 245 et seq.; Fox, at 492 et seq. (1996).

[57] Heinemann, at 246 considers that Article 40.2 (second sentence) itself lists examples of *per se* unlawful licensing practices.

[58] See Fox, 486 et seq., 492 et seq. A good example are the no-challenge clauses, which at least in principle are unlawful under U.S. law (see *Lear v. Adkins*, 395 U.S. 653 (1969) and for a critique

found in a preconceived notion of abuse or in its combination with adverse effects on competition, but only by reference to the purpose and the provisions of TRIPS, i.e., by reliance on a requirement of consistency.

(ii) The consistency and proportionality requirements (Article 40.2, second sentence)

Indeed, the first sentence of Article 40.2 must be read in conjunction with its second sentence, which specifies the measures Members may take to prevent or to control the practices mentioned in the first sentence. As in the case of Article 8.2, the requirement of consistency of such measures with the provisions of TRIPS concerns not only the nature of the remedy, but also the substance of the relevant rules on competition. In this regard the considerations and comments made with respect to Article 8.2 apply *mutatis mutandis* in the context of Article 40.2.

In particular, the examples given by the second sentence of Article 40.2, namely exclusive grant-back conditions, no-challenge clauses and coercive package licensing, refer only to practices which might be held to be abusive "in the light of the relevant laws and regulations of that Member". Thus, they may be qualified differently, just as other practices that are not mentioned may be deemed to be abusive.[59] In fact, the few practices listed are expressly referred to as mere examples, and they are in no way representative of the large number and variety of restrictive licensing practices and conditions, which may or may not be, depending on both their definition and their context, either pro- or anti-competitive.[60]

Finally, Article 40.2 (second sentence) requires Members to limit the measures to prevent anticompetitive practices to what is "appropriate". This requirement of proportionality must be understood similarly as the same requirement in Article 8.2. In particular, the appropriateness of the measure may only be assessed "in the light of the relevant laws and regulations of that Member". Therefore, TRIPS in no way precludes Members from establishing the forms of antitrust control they consider fit in view of their legal traditions and their socio-economic conditions. For example, they may establish an *ex-ante* control or an *ex-post* control by specific administrative agencies or by courts, and they may do so on the basis of administrative or of criminal law. The proportionality requirement means only that the measure must be suited to effectively address and deal with the risk and the harm for competition which a given licensing practice may entail.

Dreyfuss, *Dethroning Lear: Licensee Estoppel and the Incentive to Invent*, 72 Virg. L. Rev. 677 (1986)). On the other hand, they are perfectly lawful according to Section 17 (2) (Nr. 3) of the German Act Against Restraints of Competition. Consequently, even the clauses listed as examples by the second sentence of Article 40.2 are not necessarily good examples of bad clauses.

[59] For the listed examples, see Heinemann; for non-listed practices see Fox, at 488, as regards the treatment of territorial restrictions under EU competition law, and extensively Rey, Winter, *Exclusivity Restrictions and Intellectual Property* in Anderson, Gallini, Competition Policy and Intellectual Property Rights in the Knowledge-Based Economy, Calgary 1998, 153 [hereinafter Anderson, Gallini]; Anderson, Feuer, Rivard, Ronayne, *Intellectual Property Rights and International Market Segmentation in the North American Free Trade Area*, in Anderson, Gallini, at 397 et seq. [hereinafter Anderson, Feuer, Rivard, Ronayne].

[60] For the different treatment of such practices, see UNCTAD Secretariat, *Competition Policy and the Exercise of Intellectual Property Rights*, TD/B/COM.2 CLP/22 of 8 May 2001.

3.2.2 Procedural rules

a) Consultations and cooperation between Members (Article 40.3)

> 3. Each Member shall enter, upon request, into consultations with any other Member which has cause to believe that an intellectual property right owner that is a national or domiciliary of the Member to which the request for consultations has been addressed is undertaking practices in violation of the requesting Member's laws and regulations on the subject matter of this Section, and which wishes to secure compliance with such legislation, without prejudice to any action under the law and to the full freedom of an ultimate decision of either Member. The Member addressed shall accord full and sympathetic consideration to, and shall afford adequate opportunity for, consultations with the requesting Member, and shall cooperate through supply of publicly available non-confidential information of relevance to the matter in question and of other information available to the Member, subject to domestic law and to the conclusion of mutually satisfactory agreements concerning the safeguarding of its confidentiality by the requesting Member.

(i) The limited purpose of the provision

Article 40.3 provides for a consultation and cooperation procedure regarding the enforcement of measures of antitrust control, within the meaning of Article 40, by a Member A with respect to the nationals or domiciliaries of another Member B. This provision must be interpreted against the background of similar bilateral agreements, which were made or which were considered to be needed when TRIPS was negotiated.[61] As evidenced by the main obligation, which Article 40.3 imposes on Members, namely an obligation of information, its aim is to enhance effective control over potentially anticompetitive practices. Therefore, the consultation and cooperation procedure, which Article 40.3 establishes, has nothing to do and little in common with the consultation procedure of the WTO Dispute Settlement Mechanism.[62] In particular, the Article 40.3 mechanism is not aimed at preventing or settling disputes on whether the terms of Article 40, in particular, the requirements of consistency and proportionality, are complied with. The reason for this is that Article 40.3 provides for an obligation of information for the benefit of the enforcing State, and this obligation exists prior to the taking of any measures that might be inappropriate or inconsistent with TRIPS. The importance of Article 40.3 is that, for the first time in public international law, a duty of assistance in antitrust law enforcement has been established by a multilateral agreement,

---

[61] See UNCTAD Secretariat, *Experiences Gained so far on International Cooperation on Competition Policy Issues and the Mechanisms Used*, TD/B/COM.2/CLP/21 of 8 May 2001, annex 1 [hereinafter UNCTAD Secretariat, 2001]; Fullerton, Mazard, *International Antitrust Cooperation Agreements*, 24 (3) World Competition 405, 412 et seq. (2001) [hereinafter Fullerton, Mazard].

[62] But see Gervais, at 193 (para. 2.186).

albeit a duty limited to control over restrictive contractual licensing practices and conditions.[63]

(ii) Scope and obligation of consultation and cooperation

Article 40.3 is of limited scope in other respects as well. All it establishes is a basic obligation of consultation and cooperation. The obligation exists only if Member A has reason to believe that its competition laws and regulations regarding licensing practices or conditions have been violated by a national or domiciliary of Member B. This means that the latter may deny the request, if Member A does not provide a minimum of information on the alleged violation, thus substantiating the basis of its request both as regards the likelihood of such violation[64] and its involving a licensing practice or condition within the meaning of Article 40. There is no time set for the request nor is there a time limit set to Member B's reply to the request. There is no indication either as to what the reply should be other than that it must accord full and sympathetic consideration to the request, since the consultation must be held in such a spirit, and that it should accord adequate opportunity for such consultations. The main objective of the consultation seems to be to define the information needed by the Member requesting it, in particular, its nature and scope in view of the alleged violation.

The obligation of cooperation of the Member to which the request has been addressed is limited to an obligation to supply information to the Member making the request. This obligation in turn is limited to information which is relevant to the matter,[65] which is non-confidential and publicly available[66] or which is not publicly available and/or confidential, but available to Member B, provided that by giving such information Member B does not violate its domestic law, and provided, that "mutually satisfactory agreements concerning the safeguarding of its confidentiality by the requesting Member" are concluded either in an *ad hoc* form or more generally.

Neither the request for nor the reaction to the consultation and cooperation procedure bind Members as regards "any action under law and . . . . an ultimate decision" on the case. Thus, Members are free to abandon the enforcement activities subsequent to the request, whether it has been replied to their satisfaction or not, or to engage or not to engage in enforcement procedures of their own, if, due to the request or to the consultation, they have learned of an anticompetitive licensing practice falling within their jurisdiction. Likewise, they enjoy full freedom as to their ultimate decision on the matter. This means, on the one hand, that compliance with the requirement of consistency and of proportionality by the Member requesting the consultation is a separate matter, which may and must

---

[63] See above, Section 3; also in respect of similar provision in Article IX GATS.

[64] Such substantiation of the request is also necessary as a matter of establishing jurisdiction over the licensing practices in question, because Members may deny requests by Members not having jurisdiction.

[65] Such information might include the size of the domestic market and the share held by the enterprises in question, the turnover of such enterprises, their corporate affiliations, the ownership of registered IPRs, etc.

[66] By contrast, non-confidential information which is not publicly available need not be supplied, unless otherwise available to the Member to which the request has been addressed.

be dealt with in accordance with the general rules regarding consistency with TRIPS; and on the other, the Member to which the request has been addressed is under no duty to act or decide even if, due to the consultation procedure, it turns out that the licensing practice also or exclusively comes under its jurisdiction. This is so because Article 40.3 does not impose any duty of positive comity upon Members.[67]

(iii) Article 40.3 in the context of bilateral agreements on cooperation in antitrust law enforcement

Article 40.3 is, indeed, only a rudimentary provision on consultation and cooperation in matters of international antitrust law enforcement and differs substantially from more advanced bilateral agreements on the subject.[68] First, it is incomplete in the sense that practical matters such as formalities, time limits, designation of competent authorities, are not specified. Second, the connecting factor for a Member's obligation to enter into consultation and cooperation is the nationality or the domicile of the enterprise engaged in the licensing practices in question, rather than the fact of the practice in question and, consequently in most cases the remedy addressed to such conduct, also affects another Member's market. That, however, is normally the connecting factor for taking concurrent or conflicting jurisdiction by several States over international restraints of competition.[69] Thus, a Member may be obliged to cooperate and to supply information on grounds of personal jurisdiction only, and even in the absence of any anticompetitive conduct affecting its territory. This may be in conflict with domestic law, which may impair the efficacy of the cooperation.

Third, Article 40.3 provides for no obligation to inform other Members of anticompetitive conduct occurring on its territory, which may also in turn affect the territories of still other Members. Neither does it foresee any duty of coordination of enforcement activities of the Members concerned. Finally, the provision does not oblige Members to take account of the effects of their antitrust control measures on other Members' markets or on the competition policy of these other

---

[67] Positive comity agreements would oblige Members to intervene against anti-competitive practices over which they have jurisdiction, if such practices substantially affect competition on the markets of another Member. This has to be distinguished from general international (negative) comity which conversely requires States to take account of the negative impact which measures they take against anti-competitive practices occurring on their domestic markets might produce as regards the other Members' national interests and policies, see Article V (positive comity) and Article VI (negative comity) of the Agreement between the Government of the United States of America and the Commission of the European Communities regarding the application of their competition laws of September 23, 1991 as authorized by the Council of the EU on April 10, 1995, OJEC 1995 L 95, 45; Agreement between the European Communities and the Government of the United States on the application of positive comity principles in the enforcement of their competition laws of June 4, 1998, OJEC 1998 L 173, 28; Lampert, *International Cooperation Among Competition Authorities*, Eur. Comp. L. Rev. 1999, 214, 216 et seq. [hereinafter Lampert].

[68] See UNCTAD Secretariat, 2001; Fullerton, Mazard; Lampert.

[69] See Fullerton, Mazard, at 407 et seq.; for the EU: Ritter, Braun, Rawlinson, *European Competition Law*, 2nd ed. The Hague 2000, 61 et seq. [hereinafter Ritter, Braun, Rawlinson]; for the USA (and the EU compared): Sullivan, Grimes, *The Law of Antitrust: An Integrated Handbook*, St. Paul 2000, 968 et seq. [hereinafter Sullivan, Grimes].

Members. It is thus a weak provision on many accounts of both negative and positive comity in international antitrust law enforcement. Put positively, it is an invitation to enter into more elaborate bilateral or plurilateral agreements on the matter.

b) Opportunity for consultations (Article 40.4)

> 4. A Member whose nationals or domiciliaries are subject to proceedings in another Member concerning alleged violation of that other Member's laws and regulations on the subject matter of this Section shall, upon request, be granted an opportunity for consultations by the other Member under the same conditions as those foreseen in paragraph 3.

Article 40.4 provides that Members, whose nationals or domiciliaries are subject to competition law proceedings in another Member relating to restrictive licensing practices, in their turn, may request an opportunity for consultations by the other Member on the same conditions as foreseen in Article 40.3. *Prima facie*, the provision seems to be simply a counterpart to Article 40.3.[70] This, however, appears not to be the case given that Article 40.4 establishes only a claim to consultation, and not to cooperation and information. If that is the correct reading of Article 40.4, it cannot be aimed at allowing the Member making the request to institute antitrust law proceedings of its own with respect to possible adverse effects of the restrictive licensing practice on its domestic market.[71] Unless the referral to "the same conditions as those foreseen in paragraph 3" is construed broadly so as to include an obligation of information and cooperation, Article 40.4 seems to have a different meaning. It would allow Members to request only consultations with a view to "defending" their nationals and domiciliaries in foreign antitrust law proceedings. Arguably, such a reading of Article 40.4 may correspond to the pro-protection bias of TRIPS.

However, this interpretation may not be consistent, first, with the overall purpose of Article 40. Second, it is inconsistent with the system of TRIPS, which as regards potential disputes between Members, provides for specific procedures in Article 63, and, ultimately, refers Members to Dispute Settlement (Article 64). Third, such reading might be difficult to reconcile with the general principle of international competition law according to which States may generally apply fully their national competition rules to any conduct that affects domestic markets, provided that such adverse effects be sufficiently substantial to warrant control and prevention.[72] In brief, Article 40.4 would appear to be in need of clarification with a view to making it a real complement to an improved Article 40.3. At the very least, bilateral agreements implementing Article 40.3 should be used to make Article 40.4 properly operational.

---

[70] See Gervais, at 193 (para. 2.186); Heinemann, at 246.

[71] See also Heinemann, at 247.

[72] See Fullerton, Mazard; Ritter, Braun, Rawlinson; Sullivan, Grimes.

4. WTO jurisprudence

There is no WTO jurisprudence on disputes relating to either Article 8.2 or Article 40 or, more generally, to competition rules of Members concerning IPR-based restraints of competition. The USA-Japan dispute on *Measures Affecting Consumer Photographic Film and Paper* so far seems to be the only dispute at least indirectly related to matters of competition law. However, the complaint brought by the USA against Japan was not based on a violation of the GATT possibly resulting from the non-enforcement of domestic competition rules against a distribution system for certain photographic material, but on allegations that by various measures the Japanese Government had supported or tolerated the development and existence of a *de facto* closed distribution system, thus denying access to its market contrary to Article XXIII:1 (b) GATT. The Panel Report of March 31, 1998 dismissed the complaint mainly on the ground that it had not been established that market access had been impeded by government action.[73] The case thus is evidence of the difficulties of transposing on the GATT-WTO-level a dispute which essentially is one of litigation between private parties or between private parties and States on whether and how competition rules should be applied to private conduct that amounts to restrictions of access to national markets.[74]

5. Relationship with other international instruments

5.1 WTO Agreements

Whereas Articles 8.2 and 40 concern only IPR-related restrictive practices and business conduct, the WTO Agreements do not, as yet,[75] contain rules on restraints of competition or on anticompetitive practices in general. However, the GATS expressly covers antitrust matters in two provisions.[76] Thus, Article VIII GATS obliges Members to ensure that monopoly suppliers or exclusive service suppliers (Article VIII (5)) do not act in a manner inconsistent with the obligations and commitments of Members under the Agreement, and also that such monopolists or suppliers do not abuse their monopoly position in markets outside the scope of their legal monopoly. While Article VIII imposes a definite obligation on Members, Article IX, like Article 8.2, only recognizes that service suppliers may engage in restrictive practices, and that, therefore, under such circumstances, Members may intervene. In addition, Article IX (2) provides for an obligation of consultation and of cooperation of Members similar to that contained in Article 40.3 of TRIPS.

Since Articles VIII and IX GATS concern any service-related restrictive practice, they also cover such practices in cases where acquisition, use and exploitation of IPRs are involved. Such cases may occur in many service industries, in particular

---

[73] Panel Report *Japan-Measures Affecting Consumer Photographic Film and Paper* of March 31, 1998, WT/DS44/R; see also Furse, *Competition Law and the WTO-Report: "Japan-Measures Affecting Consumer Photographic Film and Paper"*, Eur. Comp. L. Rev. 1999, 9.

[74] See Drexl, *Trade-Related Restraints of Competition – The Competition Policy Approach*, in Zäch (ed.), Towards WTO-Competition Rules, Berne 1999, 225, 242 et seq. [hereinafter Zäch].

[75] As regards future inclusion of competition rules, see Section 6.2 below.

[76] See the text of Articles VIII, IX GATS, under 3.2.1 b) (i) above.

in the context of *de facto* or *de jure* standardization and interconnection. The Agreement on Telecommunications Services expressly points to the risks of misuse of information obtained from competitors and, conversely, the risks of undue withholding of essential information.[77] Obviously, in both situations, intellectual property, in particular trade secret protection (Article 39 of TRIPS), but also patent and copyright protection may raise particular problems.

5.2 Other international instruments

In the field of competition rules relating to restrictive business practices, the development of international instruments is marked by hesitancy.[78] There seem to be no other binding international[79] instruments directly dealing with competition rules that specifically apply to IPR-related restrictive practices. The Set of Multilaterally Agreed Equitable Principles and Rules for the Control of Restrictive Business Practices, which concerns anticompetitive conduct in general, was adopted by the United Nations General Assembly in 1980 as a non-binding resolution only.[80] It has the character of a recommendation addressed to Members, and, as such, may have guided the design of competition rules, which so many countries have adopted in recent years.[81]

Some instruments, such as the Paris Convention for the International Protection of Industrial Property,[82] refer indirectly to the existence of abusive practices by dealing with the grant of compulsory licences. The most ambitious effort to establish international rules of competition on IPR-related business practices was

---

[77] See Section 1 of the "Reference Paper" accepted by Members as "additional commitments" when signing the "Fourth Protocol to the General Agreement on Services" of February 15, 1997 (reprinted from 36 Int'l Leg. Mat. 354, 367 (1997):
"1. Competitive safeguards
1.1 Prevention of anti-competitive practices in telecommunications
Appropriate measures shall be maintained for the purpose of preventing suppliers who, alone or together, are a major supplier from engaging in or continuing anti-competitive practices.
1.2 Safeguards
The anti-competitive practices referred to above shall
include in particular:
a) engaging in anti-competitive cross-subsidization;
b) using information obtained from competitors with anti-competitive results; and
c) not making available to other services suppliers on a timely basis technical information about essential facilities and commercially relevant information which are necessary for them to provide services".

[78] For an overview and the various approaches to the establishment of international competition rules see Abdelgawad, *Jalons de l'internationalisation du droit de la concurrence: vers l'éclosion d'un ordre juridique mondial de la lex economica*, Rev. int. dr. écon. 2001, 161; Ullrich, *International Harmonisation of Competition Law: Making Diversity a Workable Concept*, in Ullrich (ed.), Comparative Competition Law: Approaching an International System of Antitrust Law, Baden-Baden, 1998, 43.

[79] For regional agreements see Section 6.3 below.

[80] Reprinted in 19 Int'l Leg. Mat. 813 (1980).

[81] See for an analysis of the set, its implementation and function in practice Dhanjee, *The Set of Multilaterally Agreed Equitable Principles and Rules for the Control of Restrictive Business Practices – an Instrument of International Law?* 28 (1) Leg. Iss. Int'l. Integr. 71 (2001); for a broad account of existing national competition laws, see UNCTAD, World Investment Report 1997, Geneva 1998, 189 et seq. and annex A 22 [hereinafter UNCTAD, WIR 1997].

[82] See also Section 2.1 above.

the International Code of Conduct on the Transfer of Technology, which was nego-tiated under the auspices of the United Nations.[83] However, the negotiations were suspended in 1985,[84] and have not been resumed since. The Draft Code[85] cov-ered both the contract law and the competition law aspects of technology trans-fer agreements, dealing specifically with restrictive business practices in Chap-ter 4. This chapter contained a detailed list of stipulations, which basically were deemed to be anticompetitive. Moreover, according to its preamble and its objec-tives and principles as stated in Chapter 2, the Code was transfer-oriented rather than competition-oriented. It is for these reasons, and due to the general change of circumstances[86] that Articles 8.2 and 40 relegate the issues to national law within the limits explained in this chapter.

6. New developments

6.1 National laws

The interface between intellectual property protection and competition rules re-lating to restrictive business practices is a matter of primary concern in most countries having and actually enforcing competition law. In general, the concern is more with technology-related intellectual property rights (patents, trade se-crets, copyright for computer programs and copyright-protected databases) than with distribution-related trademark protection (the matter is largely covered by general antitrust rules on vertical restraints regarding the various forms of distri-bution systems), or with copyright in general (though there are problems in the media industries and as regards the dominant position of collecting societies). Moreover, the concerns have varied over time, and so have the economic and le-gal analyses of restrictive practices and the resulting terms of the competition rules. These developments are bound to continue as economic insights evolve and technology advances, in particular in the information-based society.[87] In addition,

---

[83] For the historical development see the "Chronology" in Patel, Roffe, Yusuf, at p. XXVII, and Sell, *Negotiations on an International Code of Conduct for the Transfer of Technology*, ibid. at 151 et seq.; Fikentscher, et al., *The Draft International Code of Conduct on the Transfer of Technology*, Weinheim 1980, 5 et seq. [hereinafter Fikentscher].

[84] See references in the last footnote, and UNCTAD, Secretary-General, *Negotiations on an Inter-national Code of Conduct on the Transfer of Technology*, Doc. TD/Code TOT/60 of September 6, 1995.

[85] For the text of the Draft Code and commentaries relating to Chapter 4 see Fikentscher, at 39 et seq., 64 et seq., 151 et seq.; Patel, Roffe, Yusuf, Annex II (p. 417 et seq.); Thompson, *Overview of the Draft Code*, in Patel, Roffe, Yusuf, at 51, 62 et seq.

[86] See UNCTAD Secretariat, *The Status of Negotiations: A 1990 Evaluation*, in Patel, Roffe, Yusuf, at 139, 146 et seq.; Roffe, Tesfachew, *The Unfinished Agenda*, in Patel, Roffe, Yusuf, at 381 et seq.; Fikentscher, at 22 et seq.

[87] These new issues are discussed, *inter alia*, by Church, Ware, *Network Industries, Intellectual Property Rights and Competition Policy*, in Anderson, Gallini, at 227 et seq. [hereinafter Church, Ware]; Anderson, 655, 669 et seq.; De Santi, Cohen, *Competition to Innovate: Strategies for Proper Antitrust Assessments*, in Dreyfuss at 317 et seq. [hereinafter De Santi, Cohen]; Ullrich, *Intellectual Property, Access to Information, and Antitrust*, at 365 et seq.; OECD, *Competition Policy and Intel-lectual Property*, Paris 1998 [hereinafter OECD] (background note by Tom, p. 21 et seq.; special contributions by Barton, *The Balance between Intellectual Property Rights and Competition*, p. 295 et seq.).

the broadening scope and wider use of intellectual property protection as well as increased tolerance of and reliance on international inter-firm-cooperation may raise new issues both as a general matter and as regards intellectual property, e.g., pool-building, licensing exchanges, joint research and development, etc. It is not pertinent to examine these developments in an exhaustive manner in this book, and the less so as the general theoretical background of economic and legal analysis of antitrust law has changed and is continuously changing. Two examples (the USA, Subsection 6.1.1, and the EU, Subsection 6.3.1) of these important developments could illustrate the character of those changes as well as the evolving nature of competition policies.[88]

6.1.1 The United States

After many years of controversies resulting from the so-called antitrust revolution of the 1980's,[89] the antitrust law enforcement authorities of the USA have issued Guidelines for Licensing of Intellectual Property, which are based on the following express or implied principles:[90]

- Intellectual property is regarded as being essentially comparable to any other form of property, therefore no particular rules should apply to IPR-related restraints of competition.

- There is no presumption that intellectual property by itself creates market power.

- Unless licensing agreements are concluded between competitors (or at least actual-potential competitors), it is generally recognized that intellectual property allows enterprises to combine complementary factors of production and, therefore, is pro-competitive; this concerns in particular cross-licensing, but also field-of-use, territorial and other limitations on licenses.

- Unless the combined market shares of the parties to a license agreement exceed 20 % of the relevant markets, the antitrust authorities will not intervene (so called "safe haven").

---

[88] For an overview see Omer, *An Overview of Legislative Changes*, in Patel, Roffe, Yusuf, at 295 et seq.

[89] See Bowman, *Patents and Antitrust Law*, Chicago 1973. The "antitrust revolution" in the USA, emerging from the Chicago School, *inter alia* refers to the doctrinal shift under U.S. legal theory to approach vertical and horizontal restraints in licensing agreements. As opposed to earlier practice, *vertical* arrangements such as tying were no longer prohibited *per se*, but were increasingly regarded as causing pro-competitive effects. As a consequence of this approach, antitrust attention focused more on the way *horizontal* arrangements can harm competition and consumers. See *Vertical Restraints with Horizontal Consequences: Competitive Effects of "Most-Favored-Customer" Clauses* (1995), Remarks of Jonathan B. Baker, Director, Bureau of Economics, U.S. Federal Trade Commission, available at <http://www.ftc.gov/speeches/other/bakersp.htm>.

[90] See U.S. Department of Justice, Federal Trade Commission, *Antitrust Guidelines for Licensing of Intellectual Property*, Washington D.C., April 6, 1995 (reprinted in 4 Trade Reg. Rep. (CCH) §13.132 = 49 BNA – PTCJ 714/1995), sub. 2.0, 2.1; Ullrich, *Intellectual Property, Access to Information, and Antitrust*, at 375 et seq., and Gilbert, Tom, *Is Innovation King at the Antitrust Agencies? The Intellectual Property Guidelines Five Years Later*, 69 Antitrust L.J. 43 (2001); note that the Guidelines do not apply to trademark-related restrictive practices.

- With a few exceptions, license restrictions will not be subject to *per se* rules of unlawfulness, but will be examined on a "rule of reason" basis on the merits of each individual case, the test being whether a given restriction is efficiency-enhancing under the circumstances.

It is clear that such an approach is a far cry from the enforcement policy of the seventies,[91] and from the rules proposed in the Draft Code of Conduct on the Transfer of Technology.[92]

6.2 International instruments

The OECD Guidelines for Multinational Enterprises,[93] which contain a Chapter IX on Competition, and which have been revised and adopted in 2000, remain general and non-binding.

The outcome of ongoing work within the WTO on competition is difficult to predict.[94] For the time being, WTO Members do not agree on a common approach to the possible inclusion of competition rules in the WTO legal framework. The "Working Group on the Interaction Between Trade and Competition Policy", which was established by the WTO Ministerial Conference in December 1996, has discussed the interrelationship between the trade-related aspects of intellectual property and competition policy quite extensively.[95] However, it has only a preparatory role of gathering and defining the issues, not of suggesting solutions or rules.

6.3 Regional and bilateral contexts

6.3.1 The EU

On 1 May 2004, the new EU Regulation on Technology Transfer Agreements entered into force.[96] This Regulation is the result of the EU's overhauling and "modernizing" its entire enforcement system as well as reconsidering its policies *vis-à-vis* horizontal and vertical cooperation, and, in particular, its policy *vis-à-vis* licensing agreements.[97] By a "more economic approach" the Regulation clearly

---

[91] See Tom, Newberg, *U.S. Enforcement Approaches to the Antitrust-Intellectual Property Interface*, in Anderson, Gallini, at 343, 347 et seq.

[92] See Section 5.2.

[93] OECD, *Guidelines for Multinational Enterprises – Revision 2000–*, Paris 2000, at 26 (text), 53 et seq. (commentary).

[94] For the various approaches within the WTO see Jenny, *Globalization, Competition and Trade Policy: Issues and Challenges*, in Zäch, 3, 25 et seq.; Petersmann, *Competition-oriented Reforms of the WTO World Trade System – Proposals and Policy Options*, ibid. at 43 et seq.

[95] See WTO, Report of the Working Group on the Interaction Between Trade and Competition Policy to the General Council of December 8, 1998 (WT/WGTCP/2); WTO, Annual Report 1997, 72; Heinemann, *Problems of Intellectual Property Rights and Competition Policy – The Approach of the WTO Working Group on Trade and Competition*, in Zäch, at 299 et seq.

[96] See Official Journal of the European Union (OJEU) 2004 L 123/11. See also above, under Section 3 of this Chapter.

[97] See European Commission, Commission Evaluation Report of 20.12.2001 on the Transfer of Technology Block Exemption Regulation No. 240/96 (Technology Transfer Agreements under Article 81) (COM(2001) 786 final). See <http://europa.eu.int/eur-lex/en/com/rpt/2001/com2001_0786en01.pdf>.

distinguishes between licensing agreements concluded between competitors and those between non-competitors. A broadly defined (automatic) block exemption is granted, for competing undertakings, where the combined market share of the undertakings party to an agreement does not exceed 20% of the affected relevant technology and product market. For non-competing undertakings, the automatic block exemption is granted where the market share of each of the parties to the agreement does not exceed 30% of the affected relevant technology and product market.[98] Above these market shares even horizontal agreements would still benefit from a broad rule of reason analysis of each individual case,[99] the more economic approach being oriented toward an efficiency test similar to that applied in the U.S.[100] A further requirement is that the agreement does not fall under one of the specifically listed hardcore restrictions.[101] Finally, the Regulation provides for the possibility to refuse the block exemption to individual obligations in otherwise exempted agreements.[102]

In sum, the EU, though maintaining a critical stand as regards tight territorial restrictions, has approximated its enforcement policy to that of the USA. It remains to be seen what this convergence of the approaches of the two leading antitrust law systems means for the many countries which, upon invitation by the EU or the USA, by self interest and/or in the hope of the establishment of international competition rules, have given themselves competition rules of their own or have revised them recently with a view to enhancing their effectiveness.[103]

With respect to the EU's external relations, the EU has a regular practice of including the same or similar rules of competition, which it follows under Article 81, *et seq.* of the EC Treaty, in all multilateral or bilateral free trade treaties, such as the Agreement on the European Economic Area or the Europe Agreements concluded with Eastern European Countries in view of their accession to the Union.[104] In these cases, the Community's competition policy has to be accepted

---

[98] See Article 3, paragraphs 1 and 2 of the EU Regulation on Technology Transfer Agreements.

[99] The EC Commission has published guidelines on these case-by-case examinations, see *Commission Notice Guidelines on the application of Article 81 of the EC Treaty to technology transfer agreements*, OJEU C 101/2 of 27.04.2004.

[100] For the existing differences see Anderson; Marschall; Fox; UNCTAD 1996; and Gutterman, *Innovation and Competition Policy: A Comparative Study of the Regulation of Patent Licensing and Collaborative Research + Development in the United States and the European Community*, London 1997, 217 et seq.

[101] See Article 4 of the Regulation, referring, *inter alia*, to the restriction of a party's ability to determine its prices; the contractual limitation of output; and certain allocations of markets or customers.

[102] See Article 5 of the Regulation, referring, *inter alia*, to exclusive grant-back clauses.

[103] See the country reports in OECD and in Heath, Kung-Chung (ed.), *Legal Rules of Technology Transfer in Asia*, London 2002. Note also that Japan has already revised its competition policy regarding IPRs-related restrictive practices, see Arai, *Recent Developments of Japanese Antitrust Policy Regard Intellectual Property Rights*, 46 Antitrust Bull. 591 (2001).

[104] See Article 53 et seq. with Annex XIV EEA Agreement (OJEC 1994 L1, 1); the "acquis communautaire" listed in Annex XIV is continuously updated in accordance with the EU's secondary law on competition; for other EU free trade areas and the Europe Agreements see Bellis, *The Treatment of Dumping, Subsidies and Anti-competitive Practices in Regional Trade Agreements*, in Demaret, Bellis, Garcia Jimenez, *Regionalism and Multilateralism after the Uruguay Round*, Brussels 1997, 363, 364 et seq.

tel quel, including, in particular, the rules on technology transfer agreements. By contrast, in other trade and cooperation agreements only general principles of competition law are provided for.[105]

6.3.2 Other regional agreements

Other regional agreements, such as the North American Free Trade Agreement (NAFTA), oblige Parties to take appropriate action against anticompetitive practices; they are also not IPRs-specific, but of a general character.[106] Likewise, the Mercosul/r rules apparently are of a general nature and are not fully implemented.[107]

6.4 Proposals for review

There have been no proposals for review on this subject.

7. Comments, including economic and social implications

The relationship between intellectual property protection and competition policy raises complex issues, which have received different legislative solutions and produced a controversial and abundant literature.[108] In the context of TRIPS the following observations appear pertinent.

The design and the importance of competition policy concerning IPR-based restrictive business practices depend on how domestic law has defined intellectual property protection, and whether it has been well defined with respect to the economic conditions prevailing in the relevant market.[109] Competition-oriented systems of intellectual property protection leave less margin for abusive practices.

While the traditional problems of technology transfer in hardware industries persist, new problems have arisen in the service industries, and practices other than those relating to licensing have become more important, in particular, in regard to foreign direct investment,[110] cooperation agreements, outsourcing, standardization, interconnection, and access to information.[111]

---

[105] See e.g., Article 45 of the Partnership Agreement between the African, Caribbean and Pacific Group of States of the one Part, and the European Community and its Member States of the other Part of 23 June 2000 (ACP-EU Agreement of Cotonou, not yet in force, text available at <http://europa.eu.int/comm/development/cotonou/agreement_en.htm>).

[106] See Article 1501 et seq. of the North American Free Trade Agreement of December 17, 1992 (reprinted in 32 Int'l. Leg. Mat. 605, 663 et seq.); for relevant IPRs-related trade and competition issues see Anderson, Feuer, Rivard, Ronayne, at 397 et seq.

[107] See Tavares de Aranjo, Jr., Timeo, *Harmonization of competition policies among Mercosur countries*, 43 Antitrust Bull. 45, 57 et seq. (1998).

[108] See Church, Ware; Anderson; De Santi, Cohen; Ullrich, *Intellectual Property, Access to Information, and Antitrust*.

[109] See UNCTAD, 1996, 14 et seq.

[110] See UNCTAD, WIR 1997, 135 et seq., 163 et seq., 183 et seq.; Maskus, *Intellectual property rights, foreign direct investment and competition issues in developing countries*, 19 Int. J. Tech'y Management 22 (2000) [hereinafter Maskus].

[111] See Merges, *Antitrust Review of Patent Acquisitions: Property Rights, Firm Boundaries, and Organization*, in Anderson, Gallini, at 111 et seq.; Ullrich, *Competition, Intellectual Property Rights,*

Competition policy in itself raises considerable problems as concepts of competition vary over time and with respect to the nature and the needs of the markets concerned, in particular, the markets of developing countries.[112] One further complexity relates to the relative concept of markets in an economic system influenced by globalization. While Articles 8.2 and 40 clearly, albeit within limits, deem competition policy to be a matter of determination by Members, the new developments and the reduced control over domestic competition policy seem to invite Members to cooperate with regard both to the definition and the enforcement of competition policy. Regional approaches might be an important step in the evolution of international law in this sphere.[113]

It is not only the control of mere IPR-related restrictive business practices that matters. The control of other restrictive business practices that may involve intellectual property, and, foremost, the entire competitive environment, are significant factors.[114] Intellectual property, by its very nature and function, is competition-dependent. It will work properly only as a means of competition in competitively structured markets.[115] Therefore, one major concern should be to establish appropriate conditions of competition that might include, among others, effective regional integration.

In the above context, Articles 8.2 and 40 should not be understood as placing limitations on domestic law, but as invitations to establish an adequate competition policy.

Effective administration and enforcement of an IPR-related competition policy appear to be particularly important as, in view of the interdependency of intellectual property protection and competition, the costs of non-enforcement may be high. Where the efficient functioning of IPRs is impaired by restrictive practices, the market-oriented incentives decline and social costs rise. In this respect, a well-balanced design of intellectual property laws as regards, for example, exceptions for prior users, experimental or fair use, efficient and non-protectionist working requirements and misuse defences, may help both to unburden competition policy and encourage private action against undue claims for protection. Similarly, control of restrictive practices should be armed not only with administrative or criminal sanctions, but also with private remedies such as nullity of restrictive agreements, right to cancellation, and damages.

---

and Transfer of Technology, at 363, 375 et seq. See also Church, Ware; Anderson; De Santi, Cohen; Ullrich, *Intellectual Property, Access to Information, and Antitrust*.

[112] See as regards competition policy and developing countries in general Correa, *Competition Law and Development Policies*, in Zäch at 361 et seq.; UNCTAD, WIR 1997, at 183 et seq.; Godek, *A Chicago-school approach to antitrust for developing countries*, 43 Antitrust Bull. 261 (1998); as regards IPRs-antitrust and developing countries see Maskus; Primo Braga, Fink, *International transactions in intellectual property and developing countries*, 19 Int. J. Tech'y Management 35 (2000); as to the various and varying goals and concepts of competition policy see Anderson; Marschall; Fox; UNCTAD 1996; Ullrich, *Intellectual Property, Access to Information, and Antitrust*; and generally Ehlermann, Laudati (ed.), *The Objectives of Competition Policy*, Oxford 1998.

[113] See UNCTAD, WIR 1997, at 217 et seq.; Ullrich, *Competition, Intellectual Property Rights, and Transfer of Technology*, at 370 et seq.

[114] See UNCTAD, WIR 1997, at 210 et seq.; Zäch, *Competition Law as a Comparative Advantage* in Zäch, at 395 et seq.

[115] See Maskus; Ullrich, *Intellectual Property, Access to Information, and Antitrust*, at 371 et seq.

The complexities of the application of substantive competition policy rules relating to intellectual property mean that effective and legitimate control requires specialized and experienced enforcement bodies, both administrative agencies and courts. The task of distinguishing between restrictive practices or an abuse of market power and a reasonable practice to correct problems of risk management will require considerable expertise. A number of WTO Members provide for some administrative control by either advisory or enforcement agencies, whereas courts hear appeals about such agencies' decisions or direct actions by private parties. They may be either courts of general jurisdiction or of specialized jurisdiction, depending on national tradition. As regards specialized courts, it is important that they have experience in both competition matters and intellectual property law.

The establishment of enforcement agencies alongside private enforcement by action of competitors or dissatisfied parties to a restrictive agreement may entail considerable costs that may not, as in civil antitrust proceedings, be distributed between parties (although some of the costs may be compensated by charging them to enterprises violating the antitrust rules either as enforcement expenses or as fines levied on anticompetitive profits). But such administrative costs must be assessed in the light of the social costs resulting from non-enforcement. Experience shows that private enforcement of antitrust rules normally remains incomplete, both in general and in the specific area of the exercise of IPRs, so that administrative control is crucial for the effectiveness of competition policy.[116]

It appears important for developing countries to consider appropriate legal and economic responses to anticompetitive practices arising from the abuse or the misuse of IPRs. They can tailor applications of their competition laws as desired for this task, subject to the general requirements in TRIPS. Caution is in order, however, because overzealous use of competition law can increase uncertainty and limit incentives for investment, including by local firms, which, in turn, could also raise contracting costs in technology agreements. Again, a balance must be struck between promoting market incentives and the need to limit monopolistic and unfair business practices.

In sum, any implementation of TRIPS by substantive rules of competition policy must take account of a large number of complex factors, such as national and international market conditions and interdependencies and the goals and structure of national intellectual property (including its built-in competition rules such as experimental or fair use, exhaustion, patent or copyright misuse defences).[117] Other issues include the specific objectives of national antitrust policy, the adherence of Members to international economic organizations, and the impact TRIPS itself has on competition. This is certainly no easy task and not one that can be complied with by simple and hasty legislation. Rather this is a complex, challenging and time-consuming endeavour with objectives and emphases changing over time.[118]

---

[116] See UNCTAD 1996, paras. 279, 282, 283.

[117] See Ullrich, *TRIPS: Adequate protection, inadequate trade, adequate competition policy*, in: 1995 Pacific Rim Law & Policy Journal, Vol. 14, No. 1 (March), at 154–210.

[118] See UNCTAD 1996, para. 277.

30: Enforcement

1. Introduction, terminology, definition and scope

Part III of TRIPS (Articles 41–61) lays down minimum standards for the enforcement of intellectual property rights. Part IV (Article 62) does the same with respect to the acquisition and maintenance of such rights.

Both Parts thus complement the substantive minimum standards of the Agreement. From a right holder's perspective, substantive minimum rights are of little value if there are no effective procedures for the enforcement of such rights, or if a given WTO Member may render impossible the enjoyment of IPRs through certain acquisition and maintenance requirements. On the other hand, from a national government's perspective, it is important to retain its sovereignty to subject the acquisition and maintenance of IPRs to certain formalities and conditions, such as payment of registration and maintenance fees. Part IV of TRIPS addresses this kind of issue.

Due to the wide differences that existed in national laws with regard to enforcement rules, Part III of TRIPS does not attempt to harmonize such rules but to establish general standards to be implemented according to the method determined by each Member, in line with the general principle set forth in Article 1.1. Thus, the Preamble notes that the negotiating parties recognized "the need for new rules and disciplines concerning . . . (c) the provision of effective and appropriate means for the enforcement of trade-related intellectual property rights, taking into account differences in national legal systems". The Preamble also stresses "the need for a multilateral framework of principles, rules and disciplines dealing with international trade in counterfeit goods", an objective that had not been achieved during the Tokyo Round despite the attempts of the USA to establish rules on the matter.[1]

To "enforce" means, in this context, to execute a particular law, writ, judgment, or the collection of a debt or fine.[2] In the context of IPRs, in particular, it means to prevent or obtain remedies for infringement of conferred rights. An "infringement" occurs when acts under the exclusive control of the title holder (such as those defined in Articles 11, 14, 16, 26 and 28) and not subject to admissible exceptions (like those permitted by Articles 13 and 30), are performed by third parties without

---

[1] See, e.g., Bernard Hoekman, Michel Kostecki, *The Political Economy of the World Trading System, From GATT to WTO*, Oxford University Press, Oxford 1997, p. 151 See also Chapter 1 of this book.

[2] See *Black's Law Dictionary*, sixth edition, 1990, p. 528.

the authorization of the title holder or a competent authority (e.g., in the case of compulsory licenses).

The scope of the enforcement rules contained in Part III is broad: they include measures for the control of infringement domestically and at the border, and apply to *all* rights covered under the Agreement, without exception. However, some measures are only compulsory with regard to certain types of IPRs, such as border measures and criminal sanctions that are binding in relation to trademarks and copyright only.

Part III consists of five Sections: Section 1 (Article 41) deals with general obligations applying to all provisions of Part III. Section 2 (Articles 42–49) provides rules on civil and administrative procedures and remedies, while Section 3 (Article 50) covers provisional measures. Section 4 (Articles 51–60) contains rules on special requirements related to border measures, and Section 5 (Article 61) deals with criminal procedures.

More generally, Part III deals with remedies[3] and procedures).[4] (judicial and administrative).[5] These norms fall into three general categories: general procedures, right of appeal, and transparency.[6] The established obligations are not set out in detail, but they are rather result-oriented. This approach explains why this Part contains such vague phrases as "effective", "reasonable", "undue", "unwarranted" "fair and equitable" and "not.... unnecessarily complicated or costly".[7]

Part III contains mandatory provisions of different nature. While some establish outright obligations (e.g., Article 48.2), many provisions require Members to give judicial authorities (Articles 43.1, 44.1, 45.1 and 2, 46, 47, 48.1, 50.1, 2, 3 and 7) or other "competent" or "relevant" authorities (Articles 53, 56 and 59) the authority to take certain actions. While Members must *empower* their judicial authorities to order certain acts, such authorities are *not obliged* to do so, and can exercise discretion in applying the mandated rules. Even if a systematic refusal to use the authority conferred were proven, which may be difficult to demonstrate, the Member in question would have complied with the Agreement's obligations by empowering such authorities to take the prescribed action in a particular case,[8] where the courts have acted in accordance with the dominant practice in the Member in question. In addition, in order to assert violation it

---

[3] "Remedy" is "the means by which a right is enforced or the violation of a right is prevented, redressed, or compensated" (*Black's Law Dictionary*, sixth edition, 1990, p. 1294).

[4] "Procedure" is "the mode of proceeding by which a legal right is enforced, as distinguished from the substantive law which gives or defines the right" (*Black's Law Dictionary*, sixth edition, 1990, p. 1203).

[5] See Articles 50.8 and 49 as well as Article 61.

[6] See, e.g., Jay Dratler, *Intellectual property law, commercial, creative, and industrial property*, Law Journal Press, New York 1999, pp. 1A-115 [hereinafter Dratler].

[7] Dreier, *TRIPs and the enforcement of intellectual property rights* in F. Beier and G. Schricker, *From GATT to TRIPS*, Max Planck Institute/VCH, Weinheim 1996, p. 255 [hereinafter Dreier].

[8] Gervais, p. 202, argues that systematic refusal to apply their powers by the relevant authorities may constitute "non-violation". However, the applicability of Article 64.3 of TRIPS is still under discussion (the scope and modalities for complaints of that type have not been examined yet by the Council for TRIPS).

would be necessary to prove that the substantive standard of protection in relation to which an enforcement issue arises is sufficiently unambiguous to trigger the granting of certain enforcement measures.[9]

Part III also includes a number of optional provisions (e.g., application of border measures to rights other than copyright and trademarks) that Members may but are not obliged to adopt.

As a result, there are both mandatory and optional enforcement measures. Preliminary relief, injunctions, declaratory relief, damages, disposition or destruction of contraband, and criminal sanctions for wilful trademark counterfeiting and commercial copyright piracy, are mandatory in certain circumstances, while other remedies, including recovery of the infringer's profit, attorneys' fees and costs, statutory damages, and automatic (*"ex officio"*) border enforcement measures, are optional.[10]

The enforcement rules are subject to the general principle of fairness and equity.[11] There are also other standards to be applied, such as protection against abuses by right holders (Articles 41.1, 48.1, 50.3 and 53.1), the proportionality of the measure *vis-à-vis* the seriousness of the infringement (Articles 46 and 47), and the protection of confidential information (Articles 42, 43.1 and 57; see also Article 40.3 in Part II, Section 8).

While the objective of Part III is to ensure effective enforcement of IPRs in all Members, the Agreement allows for a broad exception for cases in which the remedies under this Part "are inconsistent with a Member's law", provided that declaratory judgments[12] and adequate compensation are available (see Article 44.2, second sentence).

Part IV (Article 62) concerns another important procedural aspect of IPRs, i.e., their acquisition and maintenance. The sole Article governing this issue is held in very general terms, leaving considerable discretion to Members as to its implementation. In essence, it authorizes Members to subject the acquisition and maintenance of IPRs to the compliance by the applicant or right holder with "reasonable" procedures and formalities (paragraph 1). As far as the granting or registration of IPRs is concerned, Members are obligated to make sure that such procedures are terminated within a "reasonable" time to allow the effective enjoyment by the right holder of the period of protection (paragraph 2). The general principles of fair and equitable procedures and reasoned decisions as applicable to the enforcement provisions in Part III shall also govern acquisition and maintenance rules in Part IV (Article 62.4). Finally, administrative decisions concerning procedures under Part IV are subject, on certain conditions, to judicial or quasi-judicial review (Article 62.5).

---

[9] See, e.g., Jerome Reichman, *Enforcing the enforcement procedures of the TRIPS Agreement*, Virginia Journal of International Law 1997, vol. 37, No. 2, p. 350 [hereinafter Reichman].

[10] See Dratler, p. 1A-100.

[11] See Articles 41.2 and 42.

[12] A "declaratory judgment" is a "binding adjudication of the rights and status of litigants even though no consequential relief is awarded" (*Black's Law Dictionary*, sixth edition, 1990, p. 409).

2. History of the provisions

2.1 Situation pre-TRIPS

One of the major innovations of TRIPS in relation to pre-existing IP treaties has been that it deals not only with the availability of rights, but also with their enforcement. This broad coverage was a specific objective of the proponents of an agreement on intellectual property rights in GATT, who complained about the lack of effective enforcement of the obligations under the Paris and the Berne conventions, particularly in developing countries. Adequate standards of IPR protection, they argued, were of little value if the conferred rights could not be effectively enforced.[13]

2.2 Negotiating history

The establishment of detailed rules on enforcement of IPRs was advocated in GATT negotiations by the USA[14] and the EC.[15] In independent submissions, the USA and the EC proposed texts that were in some cases very close or identical. In doing so, the United States and the EC reflected the views of the business community, as expressed in the joint position paper by the U.S. Japanese and European business associations (IPC, Keidanren and UNICE)[16] calling for the establishment of a set of "essential elements of enforcement procedures".[17]

Unlike other sections of TRIPS, and notwithstanding their importance and far reaching implications, the enforcement and maintenance provisions were subject to much less discussion and controversy than the substantive rules contained in the Agreement.[18] This was reflected in the fact that most provisions on the enforcement, acquisition and maintenance of IPRs in the final version of TRIPS are essentially identical to those in the Brussels Draft.[19,20]

---

[13] See, e.g., Trebilcock and Howse, p. 320–321.

[14] See, e.g., MTN.GNG/NG11/W/70 of May 11, 1990, Part 3.

[15] See, e.g., MTN.GNG/NG11/W/16 of November 20, 1987; MTN.GNG/NG11/W/31 of May 30, 1989.

[16] IPC is the (US) "Intellectual Property Committee"; Keidanren is the Japan Business Federation; and UNICE stands for the "Union of Industrial and Employers' Confederations of Europe".

[17] See IPC, Keidanren & UNICE (Eds.), *Basic Framework of GATT Provisions on Intellectual Property – Statement of Views of the European, Japanese and United States Business Communities*, June 1998.

[18] See, e.g., the submissions presented by India (MTN.GNG/NG11/W/40), Canada (MTN.GNG/NG11/W/42), (MTN.GNG/NG11/W/43), Switzerland (MTN.GNG/NG11/W/44), Korea (MTN.GNG/NG11/W/48), Australia (MTN.GNG/NG11/W/53), Hong Kong China (MTN.GNG/NG11/W/54), the Scandinavian Countries (MTN.GNG/NG11/W/58), and Austria (MTN.GNG/NG11/W/62); and the GATT Secretariat document MTN.GNG/NG11/W/33 Rev. 2 of February 1, 1990. See also Dreier, p. 257.

[19] Draft Final Act Embodying the Results of the Uruguay Round of Multilateral Trade Negotiations, Revision, Trade-Related Aspects of Intellectual Property Rights, Including Trade in Counterfeit Goods, MTN.TNC/W/35/Rev. 1, 3 Dec. 1990.

[20] For the same reason, the differences between the current text of the TRIPS Agreement, on the one side, and the EC and U.S. proposals as well as the Anell Draft (document MTN.GNG/NG11/W/76, of 23 July 1990), on the other side, do not seem to be substantial. Due to these circumstances, the treatment of the negotiating history in this part of the book deviates from that in other chapters. The differences in the various proposals that are relevant for the purposes of this book are highlighted throughout the discussion of the respective TRIPS provisions (see Section 3, below).

The comparatively uncontroversial nature of the negotiations stood in contrast to the fact that significant differences in enforcement rules existed amongst legal systems and national laws, and that many developing countries participating in the negotiations actually lacked the infrastructure and resources to apply higher standards for the enforcement of IPRs.

Since, in the light of such differences, the harmonization of enforcement rules seemed most unlikely, even among developed countries, the USA and the EC suggested a set of result-oriented rules, that is, rules that essentially define the objective to be attained (e.g., preventing infringement) rather than the specific details of the obligations to be assumed.

An analysis of the drafts and of the final adopted text[21] indicates that while many provisions were weakened and some measures were left at the discretion of the Members, the USA and the EC largely imposed their own conception of the subject. The extent to which the legitimate interests of developing countries received due attention in the course of the negotiations is still an open question.[22] Developing countries were able, based on an Indian proposal, to avoid any obligation to establish a special judicial system to enforce IPRs or to assign specific resources,[23] but did not influence otherwise very much the outcome of the negotiations.

3. Possible interpretations

3.1 Article 41

3.1.1 Article 41.1

> ### SECTION 1: GENERAL OBLIGATIONS
> ### Article 41
>
> 1. Members shall ensure that enforcement procedures as specified in this Part are available under their law so as to permit effective action against any act of infringement of intellectual property rights covered by this Agreement, including expeditious remedies to prevent infringements and remedies which constitute a deterrent to further infringements. These procedures shall be applied in such a manner as to avoid the creation of barriers to legitimate trade and to provide for safeguards against their abuse.

Section 1 of Part III lays down the general obligations relating to enforcement. It includes provisions on the availability of procedures to prevent and remedy infringement, on the basic conditions that such procedures should meet, on decisions and their review, and on the forum for infringement procedures. The obligations laid down in this Section apply to all types of IPRs covered by the Agreement.

---

[21] See generally, Reichman, pp. 335–356.

[22] See, e.g., Dreier, p. 257.

[23] See below Article 41.5.

Article 41 applies to judicial as well as to administrative procedures[24] relating to the enforcement of IPRs. Administrative enforcement procedures must be distinguished from those relating to the acquisition and maintenance of rights, which are dealt with in Part IV of TRIPS,[25] though, as mentioned below, in some cases the same procedural rules apply.

Article 41.1 states the basic obligation with regard to enforcement procedures: Members are bound to establish procedures that permit "effective" action against infringement. While the term "effective" is used in other provisions of the Agreement,[26] there is considerable room for interpretation in the particular context of this section.[27] The wording of Article 41.1 (which closely follows the original U.S. and EC proposals[28]), suggests that Members would comply with the Agreement's obligations if they make available the appropriate procedures as required in Part III, that is, the obligation to provide effective measures against infringement does not oblige them to introduce measures other than those stipulated in Part III.[29] Hence, any judgment about compliance should be objectively based on whether Members have made or not the required procedures available. In assessing whether a Member's enforcement procedures actually permit "effective action", a WTO panel or the Appellate Body would have to take into account that the effectiveness of measures may be differently assessed in different legal systems. There cannot be one single standard of what constitutes "effectiveness". This is confirmed by the TRIPS Preamble, which makes clear that the provision of effective and appropriate means for the enforcement of trade-related intellectual property rights needs to take into account "differences in national legal systems".

The requirement that Members provide effective enforcement procedures raises a question regarding the nature of the inconsistency that the DSB should examine. On the one hand, it could be argued that failure of a Member to provide an adequate remedy in an individual case is evidence of failure to provide effective enforcement procedures. On the other hand, the DSU is intended to provide a mechanism for addressing matters affecting the rights of Members, and not as a court of appeal for private litigants. It would appear more appropriate in evaluating the effectiveness of a Member's enforcement procedures that an inconsistency

---

[24] In some jurisdictions (e.g., Mexico, Peru) administrative bodies have been conferred powers to order injunctive relief, while in others this is an exclusive competence of judicial authorities.

[25] See below, Section 3.22.

[26] See Article 27.3 (b), Chapter 21 of this book.

[27] Under WTO jurisprudence the same word may be given different meanings when used in different provisions. See, for instance, the Appellate Body's analysis of the meaning of "like" in paragraphs 2 and 4 of Article III of GATT, in *European Union-Measures affecting Asbestos and Products Containing Asbestos*, WT/DS135. The Appellate Body held that "[i]n each of the provisions where the term "like products" is used, the term must be interpreted in light of the context, and of the object and purpose, of the provision at issue, and of the object and purpose of the covered agreement in which the provision appears" (para. 88).

[28] The original proposals submitted by the USA and the EC, however, referred to the obligation to "provide effective *procedures*" (emphasis added) (as opposed to "effective action" in the current text).

[29] See, e.g., Dreier, p. 260.

would be found when there is evidence of a *systemic* problem in the complaint against Member; that is, a problem that is likely to recur. A law or other measure that is intended to be applied as a matter of course might constitute the basis of a systemic problem. In respect to the operation of the courts or administrative authorities, a systemic problem could be evidenced by a series of decisions that are manifestly contrary to the effective enforcement of TRIPS obligations. Isolated "questionable decisions" should probably not constitute adequate evidence of failure to provide effective enforcement procedures.

Article 41.1 requires the establishment of two types of remedies: "expeditious remedies to prevent infringements", and "remedies which constitute a deterrent to further infringements". A Member should be deemed to provide "expeditious" preventive remedies if it complies with the obligations set forth in Article 50 (provisional measures) and Article 51 (border measures), and to comply with the obligation relating to remedies which constitute a deterrent to further infringements, if it provides for injunctions, damages and seizure to the extent mandated by the Agreement.[30]

Article 41.1 introduces the need for balancing the interest of title-holders, alleged infringers and the public interest. While the first sentence of the provision (as analysed above) mirrors the interests of rights holders, the second sentence takes account of the public interest in the availability of IPR-protected products: "procedures shall be applied in such a manner as to avoid the creation of barriers to legitimate trade and to provide for safeguards against their abuse". This provision indicates, in line with the Preamble[31] and Article 8.1[32] that in adopting and applying enforcement procedures Members *must* ensure that legitimate trade is not jeopardized, for instance, by injunctive measures adopted without sufficient justification. According to the panel report in *Canada-Pharmaceutical Products*,[33] "'legitimate' must be defined in the way that it is often used in legal discourse – as a normative claim calling for protection of interests that are 'justifiable' in the sense that they are supported by relevant public policies or other social norms" (para. 7.69).

The second sentence of Article 41.1 also requires[34] Members to take action to avoid abuses of enforcement procedures. Such abuses may equally create barriers to legitimate trade or impose other burdens on the public or competitors. For instance, there is evidence of "strategic litigation" by large companies (often based on weak or invalid titles) targeted at small and medium companies which cannot bear the high costs and lengthy procedures involved in IPR litigation.[35]

---

[30] See below Articles 44, 45 and 46.

[31] "Desiring . . . to ensure that measures and procedures to enforce intellectual property rights do not themselves become barriers to legitimate trade; . . . "

[32] "Appropriate measures, provided that they are consistent with the provisions of this Agreement, may be needed to prevent the abuse of intellectual property rights by right holders or the resort to practices which unreasonably restrain trade or adversely affect the international transfer of technology".

[33] WT/DS114/R, 17 March 2000.

[34] The language used is mandatory ("shall be applied . . .).

[35] See, e.g., Carlos Correa, *Internationalization of the patent system and new technologies*, Wisconsin International Law Journal 2002, vol. 20, No. 3, p. 543.

3.1.2 Article 41.2

> 2. Procedures concerning the enforcement of intellectual property rights shall be fair and equitable. They shall not be unnecessarily complicated or costly, or entail unreasonable time-limits or unwarranted delays.

Article 41.2 introduces a general clause relating to procedures concerning enforcement. It prescribes a rather general but important obligation: procedures concerning the enforcement of IPRs must be "fair and equitable". It then vaguely indicates undesirable elements that could presumably make a procedure unfair or inequitable, based on complexity, costs, time-limits and duration.[36] However, other elements may be taken into account to judge fairness and equity, such as the opportunity to be heard and to present evidence before a decision on the merits is adopted.[37]

The principle of fairness and equity applies to all the parties concerned in enforcement procedures, and not only to right holders. As mentioned below, there are several provisions in Part III specifically aimed at protecting the alleged infringer from false or abusive right holders' actions.

A violation of Article 41.2 might be claimed if "unnecessarily complicated or costly", or "unreasonable time-limits or unwarranted delays" were in-built features of such procedures, and not in relation to particular, isolated cases. If a dispute were to arise under the DSU, the complaining party would have the difficult burden of proving that a violation existed. In fact, cost and delays would be highly dependent on the way different national courts apply existing procedures. Moreover, it would be extremely difficult to set an objective international standard on these matters. For instance, in the USA, the costs of a typical infringement suit are estimated to run to $1–3 million; moreover, litigation is a lengthy process (one estimate suggests that the duration of the "average" patent suit in a District Court is 31 months), meaning that potential infringers are either paying royalties or risking costly infringement penalties for long periods until a final decision on the patent is reached.[38] High litigation costs are also common in other jurisdictions.[39] Given the broad room left to Members to determine the method to comply with the TRIPS obligations, it would be extremely difficult for a panel to determine when certain procedures may be deemed "unnecessarily" complicated or costly, or entail "unreasonable" time-limits or "unwarranted" delays.

---

[36] The adopted text does not include the condition "unnecessarily time-consuming" contained in the original proposals of the EC and the USA.

[37] See Article 42 on "Fair and Equitable Procedures".

[38] See, e.g., Stuart Graham and David Mowery, *Intellectual property in the U.S. software industry*, prepared for presentation at the NRC Board of Science, Technology and Economic Policy Conference "The Operation of the Patent System", Washington, D.C., October 22, 2001, available at <http://www4.nationalacademies.org/pd/step.nsf>.

[39] Litigation costs, according to some estimates, would amount to $1 million in the United Kingdom and $ 200,000 in Germany. See, e.g., John Orange, *Costs – an Issue for Whom?*, Paper submitted to the Conference on the International Patent System, World Intellectual Property Organization, Geneva, March 25–27, 2002.

Article 41.2 (as well as Article 41.3) also applies[40] to procedures concerning the acquisition or maintenance of IPRs and, where a Member's law provides for such procedures, administrative revocation and *inter partes* procedures such as opposition, revocation and cancellation.[41]

3.1.3 Article 41.3

> 3. Decisions on the merits of a case shall preferably be in writing and reasoned. They shall be made available at least to the parties to the proceeding without undue delay. Decisions on the merits of a case shall be based only on evidence in respect of which parties were offered the opportunity to be heard.

Article 41.3 requires that "decisions on the merits of a case shall *preferably* be in writing and reasoned". The original U.S. and EC proposals included the adverb "regularly". The change probably reflected the fact that even developed countries would have had to amend their legislation if the latter higher standard had been adopted.[42]

This Article also establishes a transparency obligation[43] with regard to the parties to a proceeding: decisions on the merits of a case shall be made available at least to them "without undue delay". Members have considerable leeway to establish how "undue" can be interpreted in this context.[44] Article 41.3 does not prevent decisions from being made known to third parties or, more generally, to the public.[45]

Finally, Article 41.3 prescribes that decisions on the merits of a case be based only on evidence in respect of which parties were offered the opportunity to be heard. This requires the establishment of a proper adversarial procedure for all evidence submitted by the parties or from any other source.[46]

The obligations established by Article 41.3 only apply to "decisions on the merits" and not to provisional measures, which are governed by other rules in the Agreement.[47] However, this Article is not necessarily limited to *final* decisions on the merits.

---

[40] See Article 62.4 of TRIPS.

[41] These types of procedure are undertaken by the Patent and Trademark Offices in many jurisdictions, such as the by the European Patent Office and the U.S. Patent and Trademark Office.

[42] See, e.g., Dreier, p. 260.

[43] See also Article 63 of the TRIPS Agreement, Chapter 31.

[44] The terminology of the Agreement relating to procedural delays is not uniform. Article 41.2 refers to "unwarranted delays" and Article 50.4 to "without delay". It is unclear whether the use of "undue" and "unwarranted" may lead to different solutions ("undue" is "excessive, disproportionate"; "unwarranted" means "unauthorized; unjustified", *The Concise Oxford Dictionary*, 8th edition, Oxford, 1990, pp. 1334 and 1348). The expression "without delay" in Article 50.4 seems to establish a higher standard, requiring authorities to take prompt action. Note also that Articles 44.1 and 50.1(a) require that action be taken "immediately".

[45] In general, judicial decisions, whether officially published or not, are available to any interested party.

[46] See, e.g., Gervais, p. 198.

[47] As examined below (see analysis of Article 50.4) in the case of provisional measures adopted *inaudita altera parte*, the parties affected shall be given notice, "without delay after the execution of the measures at the latest".

3.1.4 Article 41.4

> 4. Parties to a proceeding shall have an opportunity for review by a judicial authority of final administrative decisions and, subject to jurisdictional provisions in a Member's law concerning the importance of a case, of at least the legal aspects of initial judicial decisions on the merits of a case. However, there shall be no obligation to provide an opportunity for review of acquittals in criminal cases.

Article 41.4 requires that the proceedings be made available for review of final administrative decisions relating to enforcement of IPRs, and that such a review be specifically made by "a judicial authority".[48] However, Article 62.5 of the Agreement provides that in case of procedures relating to the acquisition and maintenance of rights rather than to their enforcement, final administrative decisions shall be subject to review "by a judicial or quasi-judicial authority".[49] On the other hand, there shall be no obligation to provide an opportunity for such review of decisions in cases of unsuccessful opposition or administrative revocation, provided that the grounds for such procedures can be subject to invalidation procedures.[50]

Article 41.4 also mandates the judicial review of "initial judicial decisions". There are three important possible limitations to the right of appeal enshrined in this Article. First, it must be conferred at least in relation to "the legal aspects" of such decisions, thereby reflecting the fact that in many jurisdictions appeals do not address findings of fact. Second, the right to appeal may be excluded in cases of minor economic importance, as also provided for in many national laws, according to "jurisdictional provisions in a Member's law".[51] Finally, there shall be no obligation to provide an opportunity for review of an acquittal (that is, the legal and formal certification of the innocence of a person) in criminal cases.

3.1.5 Article 41.5

> 5. It is understood that this Part does not create any obligation to put in place a judicial system for the enforcement of intellectual property rights distinct from that for the enforcement of law in general, nor does it affect the capacity of

---

[48] In contrast, Article 31(j) of the Agreement (on "Other Use Without Authorization of the Right Holder") only requires that "any decision relating to the remuneration provided in respect of such use shall be subject to judicial review or other independent review by *a distinct higher authority* in that Member" (emphasis added).

[49] The Agreement leaves Members the opportunity to define what "quasi-judicial authority" means. This concept may include, for instance, the board of appeals established in many countries to review decisions by patent and trademark offices, such as the Board of Patent Appeal and Interferences and the Trademark Trial and Appeal Board of the USA. See, e.g., Dratler, pp. 1A-118.

[50] For more details on Article 62.5, see below.

[51] Such provisions may be, in the case of federal states, of federal or state (provincial) nature.

> Members to enforce their law in general. Nothing in this Part creates any
> obligation with respect to the distribution of resources as between enforcement
> of intellectual property rights and the enforcement of law in general.

The last paragraph of Article 41 was not suggested in the original U.S. and EC
proposals. It was included in order to address the concerns of developing countries, based on a proposal by the Indian delegation.[52] This was in fact one of the
few provisions in Part III where developing countries' views made a difference.
Article 41.5 makes it clear that Members are not obliged to establish a special
court to deal with intellectual property issues, nor to allocate special funds to this
area. Such a special jurisdiction has been established, for instance, in the USA,
and its creation is often regarded as one of the key factors that contributed to the
strengthening of IPR protection in that country since the 1980's.[53] Many developing countries (e.g., China) have also established special courts in the area of IPRs,
even though they are not obliged to do so.

3.2 Article 42

> ### SECTION 2: CIVIL AND ADMINISTRATIVE PROCEDURES AND REMEDIES
> #### Article 42   Fair and Equitable Procedures
>
> Members shall make available to right holders* civil judicial procedures concern-
> ing the enforcement of any intellectual property right covered by this Agreement.
> Defendants shall have the right to written notice which is timely and contains
> sufficient detail, including the basis of the claims. Parties shall be allowed to
> be represented by independent legal counsel, and procedures shall not impose
> overly burdensome requirements concerning mandatory personal appearances.
> All parties to such procedures shall be duly entitled to substantiate their claims
> and to present all relevant evidence. The procedure shall provide a means to
> identify and protect confidential information, unless this would be contrary to
> existing constitutional requirements.
>
> [Footnote]* For the purpose of this Part, the term "right holder" includes federations and
> associations having legal standing to assert such rights.

Article 42 applies directly only to *civil judicial* procedures.[54] As suggested by its
title, this Article develops the general obligations spelled out in Article 41.2 examined above. The wording used to describe some of these obligations ("timely",
"sufficient detail", "overly burdensome") leaves considerable leeway to Members
for their implementation.

---

[52] See MTN.GNG/NG11/W/40, at 3, No. 4(e).

[53] See, e.g., John Barton, *Adapting the intellectual property system to new technologies*, International
Journal of Technology Management 1995, vol. 10. No. 2/3, p. 163 [hereinafter Barton, 1995].

[54] By way of reference in Article 49, Article 42 also applies to administrative procedures. See below,
Section 3.9.

The footnote clarifies the concept of "right-holder" for the purposes of this Article and the whole Part III, by specifying that it includes federations and associations. The purpose of this footnote is to enable copyright collecting societies and other entities that have recognized legal standing, according to national law, to file joint actions. This footnote, however, does not clarify whether the concept of "right holder" may include not only the "owner"[55] of IPRs, but also other parties legally authorized to exercise such rights. Since TRIPS is not intended to harmonize IPRs and related procedures (see Article 1.1), it is up to each Member to determine its own concept of "right holder".[56] Voluntary licensees,[57] for instance, may under certain circumstances initiate enforcement procedures under some national laws.[58] This broad understanding of "right holders" under Article 42 has even been widened in a recent report by the WTO Appellate Body: according to the AB, the procedural rights under Article 42 are not limited to the established owner of an IPR, but extend as well to all other persons "who claim to have the legal standing to assert rights".[59] In other terms, a presumptive owner equally benefits from the rights under Article 42, as long as a court has not made a determination that the claimant is in fact not the owner of the respective right.

The basic obligation under Article 42 is to make available civil procedures. This should not pose any problem to Members. It also indicates several elements that such procedures must provide for:

(a) Defendants shall have the right to written notice which is timely and contains sufficient detail, including the basis of the claims. This obligation is intended to give the defendant an effective opportunity to argue his case.

(b) Parties shall be allowed to be represented by independent legal counsel. No exception is provided for this obligation, thereby indicating that parties may be represented in all acts in judicial proceedings by the legal counsel of their choice.

(c) Procedures shall not impose "overly burdensome" requirements concerning mandatory personal appearances. The wording used in this provision indicates that there is nothing wrong with mandatory personal appearances, even if they are cumbersome. Only excessively cumbersome requirements are banned.

---

[55] The concept of "right-holder" is also used in the Agreement in relation to integrated circuits. Footnote 9 to Article 36 clarifies that "the term 'right holder' in this Section shall be understood as having the same meaning as the term 'holder of the right' in the IPIC Treaty". However, the concept of "owner" is used in relation to copyrights (Article 14.3), trademarks (e.g., Article 16.1), industrial designs (Article 26.1) and patents (e.g., Article 28.1).

[56] See, for example, the British unregistered design right, under which a person can qualify for protection either as the author, employer, commissioner or the first marketer of the design work (Ss. 215, 217 et seq., Copyright, Designs and Patents Act 1988, U.K.). On this issue, see Chapter 16 (Industrial Designs).

[57] Despite some submissions during the negotiation of this Article, a reference to exclusive licensees was not incorporated.

[58] See, e.g., Article 38 (2) of the WIPO Secretariat "Draft Industrial Property Act".

[59] See United States – Section 211 Omnibus Appropriations Act of 1998 (hereinafter Havana Club); WTO document WT/DS176/AB/R of 2 January 2002, p. 63, paragraphs 217, 218, partly referring to the panel that had decided the case in the first place (WT/DS176/R of 6 August 2001). In the report, the Appellate Body limited its interpretation to the case of trademarks. But there is no reason why this interpretation of Article 42 should not equally apply to other intellectual property rights covered by the TRIPS Agreement. For a more detailed analysis of the Appellate Body report, see Section 4, below.

(d) All parties shall be duly entitled to substantiate their claims and to present all relevant evidence. This provision applies to all types of civil and administrative procedures, including for the adoption of provisional measures.

(e) Finally, Article 42 establishes that the procedure shall provide a means "to identify and protect confidential information", unless this would be contrary to existing constitutional requirements. This protection may apply, for instance, when an expert is appointed by the court to determine the damages arising from infringement.[60] It is interesting to note that, while Article 39.3 refers to "undisclosed information", Articles 40.3, 42, 43.1, 57 and 63.4 allude instead to "confidential" information. The latter term is much wider than the notion of "undisclosed information": Article 39.3 refers to a narrowly defined subset of commercial data (regarding certain new chemical entities). There is a great deal more involved in "confidential information" of a business, for example, the elements of a trade secret that parties might be required to submit to a judge or expert but not disclose to the other party in the course of litigation.[61] Thus, there is clearly a distinction between what is referred to in Article 39.3 and other confidential information as to which more general rules are applied.

The obligation to identify and protect confidential information does not apply if it is "contrary to existing constitutional requirements". The exception reflects the fact that in some countries types of secrecy in civil judicial procedures may be prohibited as a matter of constitutional law. In these cases, a contradiction with a national law not having the status of a constitutional provision or principle may not be sufficient to justify non-compliance. Questions may arise as to whether constitutional rules introduced after the entry into force of the Agreement would fall within the category of "existing" requirements. Since the Agreement does not include a temporal reference (especially with regard to its entry into force in a particular Member), it should be interpreted in the sense that "existing" simply means applicable at the time where a particular enforcement measure is requested or applied.

3.3 Article 43

3.3.1 Article 43.1

Article 43   Evidence

1. The judicial authorities shall have the authority, where a party has presented reasonably available evidence sufficient to support its claims and has specified evidence relevant to substantiation of its claims which lies in the control of the

---

[60] See, e.g., Mireille Buydens, *L'Accord ADPIC (TRIPS) et les dispositions destinées à assurer la mise en oeuvre effective des droits de propriété intellectuelle*, IR DI, Mys & Breess Ed., 1997, p. 9 [hereinafter Buydens].

[61] Note that in the absence of a specific definition in the Agreement, the scope of "confidential information" under Articles 42, 43.1 and 57 may be determined by national laws, and it may encompass information that does not strictly comply with the standards under Article 39.3, such as information of potential commercial value, or which is not "secret" as defined in Article 39.2(a). For a detailed analysis of Article 39, see Chapter 28.

> opposing party, to order that this evidence be produced by the opposing party, subject in appropriate cases to conditions which ensure the protection of confidential information.

The purpose of this obligation is to secure, under certain conditions, access to evidence[62] under control of the opposing party.[63] Like other provisions in Part III, Article 43 does not provide for a straightforward obligation, but mandates Members to empower the judicial authorities to order the production of evidence by the opposing party. It will be up to such authority to exercise or not such a power in a particular case. According to this provision, the judicial authority may order one of the parties to produce evidence which lies in its control, provided that the following conditions are met:

(a) The complaining party has presented reasonably available evidence sufficient to support its claims. Prior to ordering the opposing party to produce evidence, the judicial authority must verify that the complaining party has provided its own "reasonably available" evidence. Large discretion is left to judges to assess when this condition has been met. It is unclear, however, at what stage of the procedures this may take place, since often the evidence is only assessed by the court after it has been substantiated in its totality by both parties. In some countries, however, the right to request the other party to submit evidence under its control is not subject to the condition imposed under Article 43.1.

(b) The complaining party has specified evidence relevant to the substantiation of its claims. The evidence is in the control of the opposing party. This condition imposes on the complaining party the burden to concretely specify the evidence that the opposing party possesses. A general statement about evidence under the opponent's control would not suffice to meet this condition. Implicit in this requirement is that the order to produce evidence under this Article is to be made upon request of one of the parties, and not *ex officio*.

(c) The evidence in the control of the opposing party may include information (e.g., distribution channels used) or means (e.g., infringing articles, machinery used, etc.).

(d) Conditions which ensure the protection of confidential information are adopted in appropriate cases. The protection of "confidential information" is not subject, unlike in Article 42, to an examination of consistency under constitutional law, although if this were the case the latter would normally prevail in case of conflict.

The obligation to produce evidence applies to any of the parties. Though the right holder may be presumed to be the main beneficiary of this provision, the defendant may equally request the court to order the right holder to supply evidence that

---

[62] "Evidence" includes "testimony, writings or material objects offered in proof of an alleged fact or proposition" (*Black's Law Dictionary*, sixth edition, 1990, p. 555).

[63] This provision reflects "the camel's nose in the tent for discovery, long sought by advocates from English-speaking countries abroad" (Dratler, p. 1A-116).

would support his claims (e.g., reports of foreign patent offices referring to the patentability of an invention).

3.3.2 Article 43.2

> 2. In cases in which a party to a proceeding voluntarily and without good reason refuses access to, or otherwise does not provide necessary information within a reasonable period, or significantly impedes a procedure relating to an enforcement action, a Member may accord judicial authorities the authority to make preliminary and final determinations, affirmative or negative, on the basis of the information presented to them, including the complaint or the allegation presented by the party adversely affected by the denial of access to information, subject to providing the parties an opportunity to be heard on the allegations or evidence.

Article 43.2 provides that Members may accord to judicial authorities the authority to make preliminary and final determinations, affirmative or negative, on the basis of the information presented to them, in three different situations:

a) A party to a proceeding voluntarily and without good reason refuses access to necessary information within a reasonable period. The authority must determine that there is no justified reason for refusal, as well as that the information is effectively necessary to make a determination. The simple convenience to get additional information would not be sufficient to exercise this authority. Further, though not explicitly indicated in Article 43.2, this Article must be read in conjunction with Article 43.1, leading to the interpretation that the information a party may be required to submit must be under its control. It would be contrary to everyone's basic right to defend his/her rights in court to require information that is not controlled by him/her.

b) A party "otherwise does not provide" necessary information within a reasonable period. "Otherwise" should be interpreted here in relation to "access" and not to "good reason". If not, this sentence would contradict the condition indicated in a) above, since it would seem to empower the judge to adopt a determination even if the requested party had "good reasons" not to provide access. Such an interpretation would put an excessive and unfair burden on the requested party.

c) A party "significantly impedes" a procedure relating to an enforcement action. This last situation goes well beyond the refusal to provide information and leaves open a "Pandora's box", since it would be up to the judicial authority to establish when a party has "significantly" impeded an enforcement procedure. To "impede", however, means to "retard by obstructing; hinder",[64] and not simply to articulate defences that make it difficult for the other party to advance. In any case, the applicability of this rule is quite hypothetical, since under civil enforcement procedures the parties are subject to specified terms and obligations, and it might be difficult to prove that a party has been able to *impede* a procedure.

---

[64] *The Concise Oxford Dictionary*, 1990, p. 591.

It should be noted that Article 43.2 refers to "information" and not to "evidence" like Article 43.1. In addition, this rule, which in any case is non-binding on Members, does not authorize the drawing of inferences from resistance to discovery, since in any case the decision must be based on "the information presented to them", including "the complaint or the allegation presented by the party adversely affected by the denial of access to information". In addition, both parties, including the party required to produce evidence, must be given "an opportunity to be heard on the allegations or evidence".

3.4 Article 44

3.4.1 Article 44.1

Article 44   Injunctions

1. The judicial authorities shall have the authority to order a party to desist from an infringement, *inter alia* to prevent the entry into the channels of commerce in their jurisdiction of imported goods that involve the infringement of an intellectual property right, immediately after customs clearance of such goods. Members are not obliged to accord such authority in respect of protected subject matter acquired or ordered by a person prior to knowing or having reasonable grounds to know that dealing in such subject matter would entail the infringement of an intellectual property right.

Article 44 deals with injunctions to be adopted when an infringement has been established. It also follows the "judicial authorities shall have the authority" formulation, in this case to order a party to desist from an infringement. This provision, in tone with the general approach under Part III, does not define the nature of the measure to be adopted, but only its purpose. Unlike Article 50, which essentially aims to prevent an infringement from occurring, Article 44 applies to an infringement that has already been determined.

This Article further mentions the particular case in which an injunction is necessary to prevent the entry into the channels of commerce of imported goods that involve the infringement of *any* type of intellectual property right, *immediately after* customs clearance of such goods. Though remedies may also be obtained under Article 51 of the Agreement, the latter is only binding in respect of trademark counterfeiting and copyright piracy, and applies before the release by the customs authorities of the infringing goods.[65]

An important exception to the rule established in Article 44.1 is that Members are not obliged to accord judges the authority to grant injunctions in respect of protected subject matter acquired or ordered by a person prior to knowing or having reasonable grounds to know that dealing in such subject matter would entail the infringement of an intellectual property right.[66] This means that where

---

[65] See the analysis of Article 50 below.

[66] The U.S. and EC original proposals did not contain this limitation. The Anell Draft as of July 23, 1990, read as follows: "1A. The judicial authorities shall have the authority to issue upon request

infringing matter is innocently acquired, Members are free to refuse an injunction and allow the *bona fide* acquirer to use or further dispose of the infringing subject matter.[67]

3.4.2 Article 44.2

> 2. Notwithstanding the other provisions of this Part and provided that the provisions of Part II specifically addressing use by governments, or by third parties authorized by a government, without the authorization of the right holder are complied with, Members may limit the remedies available against such use to payment of remuneration in accordance with subparagraph (h) of Article 31. In other cases, the remedies under this Part shall apply or, where these remedies are inconsistent with a Member's law, declaratory judgments and adequate compensation shall be available.

Inspired by U.S. law and practice,[68] Article 44.2 explicitly excludes the granting of injunctions for cases of government use[69] and other uses permitted by the government without the authorization of the right holder, such as compulsory licenses.[70] This provision makes it clear that the title holder cannot prevent in these cases the exploitation of the respective subject matter, and that his sole right would be to claim payment of a remuneration in accordance with subparagraph (h) of Article 31.[71] This is subject to compliance of the "provisions of Part II specifically addressing use by governments, or by third parties authorized by a government". The only provisions addressing such issue refer to patents (Article 31) and layout designs of integrated circuits (Article 37.2).[72] Therefore, Article 44.2 (first sentence) does not apply to cases of government use or non-voluntary licenses in respect of IPRs covered by TRIPS other than patents and integrated circuits.[73]

an order that an infringement be refrained from or discontinued, irrespective of whether the defendant has acted with intent or negligence" (W/76).

[67] According to Dratler, p. 1A-103, the exception operates like a "sort of compulsory license by refusing an injunction and remitting the claimant to a damage remedy". See also Article 45, below.

[68] The text of Article 44.2 was included in the US proposal, but not in the EC submission for the enforcement part of TRIPS (see, e.g., Dreier, p. 262). The US law limits the right of holders of patents and copyrights to seeking "reasonable and entire compensation" from the US federal government where it has used their rights without authorization (see, e.g., Dratler, p. 1A-104).

[69] See Chapter 25.

[70] Ibid. See also Jerome Reichman and Catherine Hasenzahl, *Non-voluntary Licensing of Patented Inventions: Historical Perspective, Legal Framework under TRIPS, and an Overview of the Practice in Canada and the United States of America* (UNCTAD-ICTSD 2002), available at <http://www.ictsd.org/iprsonline/unctadictsd/docs/reichman_hasenzahl.pdf>.

[71] See Chapter 25.

[72] Article 21 of the Agreement establishes that "the compulsory licensing of trademarks shall not be permitted" (see Chapter 14).

[73] On compulsory licenses relating to copyright and other IPRs, see e.g., Carlos Correa, *Intellectual property rights and the use of compulsory licenses: options for developing countries*, South Centre, Geneva 1999.

For these latter cases, Article 44.2 (second sentence) provides that "the remedies under this Part shall apply", but "where these remedies are inconsistent with a Member's law, declaratory judgments and adequate compensation shall be available". It is to be noted that this provision broadly refers to "remedies under this Part" and not only to injunctions, which is the subject matter of Article 44. Most importantly, whenever other remedies are inconsistent with national laws, this provision expressly allows Members to limit remedies to declaratory judgment and "adequate" compensation.

When may certain remedies covered by Part III be deemed inconsistent with national law? This may occur when the Member does not provide for such a covered remedy, or when it would be contrary to national law provisions regarding, for instance, license of rights or compulsory licenses. The inconsistency standard in Article 44.2 (second sentence) does not require contravention of constitutional law (as required in the case of Article 42). In sum, subject to the availability of declaratory relief and adequate compensation, Article 44.2 (second sentence) preserves Members' freedom to establish compulsory licenses and government use for copyrights, industrial designs and undisclosed information.

Finally, Members have considerable leeway to determine when the compensation would be deemed adequate under Article 44.2. The compensation in this context is intended to remunerate for the exploitation of the protected subject matter and not to compensate for the injury caused to the right holder, like in the case of damages.[74] A payment equivalent to a reasonable royalty as would be payable under a freely negotiated contract would be "adequate" in this case. The compensation may also be based on the recovery of costs. For instance, under U.S. law (28 USCS 1498), whenever an invention covered by a patent is used or manufactured by or for the United States without consent of the patent owner, the owner's sole remedy is an action against the United States "for the recovery of his reasonable and entire compensation. Reasonable and entire compensation shall include the owner's reasonable costs, including reasonable fees for expert witnesses and attorneys, in pursuing the action …".

3.5 Article 45

3.5.1 Article 45.1

Article 45   Damages

1. The judicial authorities shall have the authority to order the infringer to pay the right holder damages adequate to compensate for the injury the right holder has suffered because of an infringement of that person's intellectual property right by an infringer who knowingly, or with reasonable grounds to know, engaged in infringing activity.

The availability of damages and the amount of the award varies under national laws, often according to the type of intellectual property involved. Article 45

[74] See Article 45 below.

imposes damages as a mandatory remedy. It requires the judicial authorities to have the power to order the infringer to pay the right holder damages adequate to compensate for the injury the right holder has suffered. Members may define when compensation is to be deemed "adequate".[75]

However, an infringer who did not know, or had no reasonable grounds to know, that he engaged in infringing activity is not required to pay damages, whatever the nature of his offence.[76] It is to be noted that there is only one provision in the Agreement that specifically mandates payment of a compensation by the *bona fide* acquirer: in the case of infringing integrated circuits, the *bona fide* acquirer is bound to pay the title holder a sum equivalent to a reasonable royalty such as would be payable under a freely negotiated license in respect of the protected layout-design (Article 37.1).[77]

3.5.2 Article 45.2

> 2. The judicial authorities shall also have the authority to order the infringer to pay the right holder expenses, which may include appropriate attorney's fees. In appropriate cases, Members may authorize the judicial authorities to order recovery of profits and/or payment of pre-established damages even where the infringer did not knowingly, or with reasonable grounds to know, engage in infringing activity.

Article 45.2 (first sentence) contains another "the judicial authorities shall also have the authority" type of provision. It requires Members to empower the judges to order the infringer to pay the right holder expenses, which may include "appropriate" attorney's fees.[78] This obligation will be satisfied if judges are authorized to impose on the infringer the payment of expenses made in relation to the judicial action, but are not obliged to include attorney's fees, which is an exceptional measure in many jurisdictions.[79]

Lastly, Article 45.2 (second sentence) includes a further optional provision, according to which, in appropriate cases, Members may authorize the judicial authorities to order recovery of profits and/or payment of pre-established damages. Unlike Article 45.1, this provision specifically indicates that damages may be calculated so as to allow for the "recovery of profits",[80] or be based on damages set

---

[75] "Adequate" means "sufficient, satisfactory (often with the implication of being barely so)", *The Concise Oxford Dictionary*, 1990, p. 14.

[76] See, e.g., Dratler, p. 1A-108.

[77] See Chapter 27. Note, however, that this liability arises only once the acquirer has lost his/her *bona fide* status. This is the prerequisite for his/her liability to arise.

[78] The facultative nature of this provision is in line with US law, under which it is discretionary to a US court to allow the recovery of costs and attorney's fees by the prevailing party. See, e.g., W. Herrington and G. Thompson, *Intellectual property rights and United States international trade laws*, Oceana Publications Inc., USA 2002, p. 7–20.

[79] See, e.g., Gervais, p. 207.

[80] When the loss of profits is difficult to calculate, courts often admit compensation based on the amount of net profits made from infringement.

by national laws ("pre-established damages"). This provision further indicates that this may apply even where the infringer did not knowingly, or had no reasonable grounds to know s/he did, engage in infringing activity, that is, in respect of a *bona fide* acquirer or user of protected subject matter.[81]

Members may provide measures for damages and other remedies that are more extensive than those required by TRIPS,[82] but in doing so they need not necessarily comply with the conditions set forth in Article 45.2 (second sentence). Hence, a Member may provide for the recovery of profits or pre-established damages but limit these measures to culpable and negligent infringers only. It should also be noted that TRIPS is intended (per the Preamble) not only to protect IPRs, but also to prevent distortions of international trade that may result from overprotection. Aricle 41.1 reiterates this general principle and may be used as a basis for evaluating whether overly aggressive remedies constitute a barrier to legitimate trade.

3.6 Article 46

> ### Article 46   Other Remedies
>
> In order to create an effective deterrent to infringement, the judicial authorities shall have the authority to order that goods that they have found to be infringing be, without compensation of any sort, disposed of outside the channels of commerce in such a manner as to avoid any harm caused to the right holder, or, unless this would be contrary to existing constitutional requirements, destroyed. The judicial authorities shall also have the authority to order that materials and implements the predominant use of which has been in the creation of the infringing goods be, without compensation of any sort, disposed of outside the channels of commerce in such a manner as to minimize the risks of further infringements. In considering such requests, the need for proportionality between the seriousness of the infringement and the remedies ordered as well as the interests of third parties shall be taken into account. In regard to counterfeit trademark goods, the simple removal of the trademark unlawfully affixed shall not be sufficient, other than in exceptional cases, to permit release of the goods into the channels of commerce.

With the same approach as used in most provisions in Part III, Article 46 obliges Members to give the judicial authorities additional powers "to create an effective

---

[81] The Anell Draft of July 23, 1990 contained the following provision: "8A The right holder shall be entitled to [obtain] [claim] from infringement [adequate] [full] compensation for injury he has suffered because of a [deliberate or negligent] infringement of his intellectual property right. The right holder shall also be entitled to claim remuneration for costs, including attorney fees, reasonably incurred in the proceedings. In appropriate cases, PARTIES may provide for recovery of profits and/or pre-established damages to be granted even where the infringer has not acted intentionally or negligently" (W/76).

[82] Article 1.1 of TRIPS (see Chapter 2).

deterrent to infringement" where goods have been effectively found to be infringing. The measures that such authorities may have the power to adopt "without compensation of any sort" to the infringer, include:

a) To remove the infringing goods from commercial circulation. Such a removal would not apply, however, if the commercialization did not cause harm to the right holder (for instance, if distributed in local markets not supplied by the right holder and leakage to markets of interest to him is unlikely to occur);

With regard to counterfeit trademark goods, Article 46 establishes that the simple removal of the trademark[83] unlawfully affixed shall not be sufficient to permit release of the goods into commerce. The aim of this provision is to fight professional counterfeiting by avoiding that trademarks be unlawfully fixed again to the goods if released into commerce. However, simply removing the trademark may be possible "in exceptional cases" that Article 46 does not define, thereby leaving Members freedom to determine when such cases may arise (e.g., cases of non-professional infringement).[84]

b) To destroy the infringing goods, unless this would be contrary to existing constitutional requirements. This is a quite strong sanction, since in the absence of requirements set forth in the constitution itself, destruction may be deemed mandatory and may lead to significant economic waste and be socially questionable, especially in developing countries. The infringing goods may be supplied to charities or to government (if not involved in commercial activities for the legitimate goods).[85] However, judicial authorities (who are given the authority but are not obliged to order this measure) can adopt less disruptive measures.

c) To dispose of outside the channels of commerce materials and implements used in the creation of the infringing goods. This measure would apply when the "predominant" use of such materials and implements was to create infringing goods, and when disposition is necessary "to minimize the risks of further infringements".

Lastly, Article 46 subjects the adoption of these measures to a proportionality test under which the seriousness of the infringement and the remedies ordered, as well as the interests of third parties, need to be taken into account. This means that judicial authorities need to balance the interests at stake and, at their discretion, can refuse the granting of the measures described in the first and second sentences of Article 46. One of the considerations that such authorities can make relates to the effects of the mandated remedies on third parties, for instance, distributors who may have ordered and paid for the infringer's merchandise without knowing that these were counterfeit goods.

---

[83] It is interesting to note that the Anell Draft extended (though in a bracketed text) the same treatment to affixed geographical indications.

[84] See, e.g., Gervais, p. 209.

[85] These alternatives to destruction have been utilized, for instance, in the United States. See, e.g., Dratler, p. 1A-109.

3.7 Article 47

> ### Article 47   Right of Information
>
> Members may provide that the judicial authorities shall have the authority, unless this would be out of proportion to the seriousness of the infringement, to order the infringer to inform the right holder of the identity of third persons involved in the production and distribution of the infringing goods or services and of their channels of distribution.

The right to obtain information from the infringer is a "may" provision, that is, Members are not obliged to stipulate it in national law. This provision only refers to orders by judicial authorities, and applies in civil and in administrative procedures.

The provision assumes that an infringement has been established: the obligation may be imposed on an "infringer", and not generally on a "defendant". Moreover, the rule introduces a proportionality test, that is, this obligation would only apply in cases of serious infringements. Should a Member country choose to establish this obligation, the courts would have considerable leeway to determine when an infringement is sufficiently serious to justify this measure.

Since the infringer would be obliged to inform the right holder and not directly the court, it may be assumed that the information is not indispensable for the court's decision, and that the judicial authorities should only order it upon request of the right holder.

The content of the obligation is limited to providing information on:

a) The identity of third persons involved in the production and distribution of the infringing goods or services.

The obligation to provide information about third parties is limited to their identity. The infringer would not be obliged to provide other information such as the type of business or commercial activities of such parties, methods or technologies used, etc.

b) The channels of distribution of such third parties.

The limits of the obligation to inform about "channels of distribution" are more difficult to establish, since information about such channels may include data on persons, places of storage and sale, destination of infringing products, etc. This obligation does not seem to include upstream information about suppliers. Given the territoriality of IPRs, it would be reasonable to interpret that it only refers to distribution channels in the jurisdiction where infringement took place, but this point is unclear.

An obligation of the type established in Article 47 may be important to deal with professional infringers, so as to help the right holder to locate and take action against the infringers' accomplices.[86]

Though Article 47 does not refer to the protection of confidential information, the general rule of Article 41 should apply.

---

[86] See, e.g., Gervais, p. 209.

3.8 Article 48

3.8.1 Article 48.1

Article 48   Indemnification of the Defendant

1. The judicial authorities shall have the authority to order a party at whose request measures were taken and who has abused enforcement procedures to provide to a party wrongfully enjoined or restrained adequate compensation for the injury suffered because of such abuse. The judicial authorities shall also have the authority to order the applicant to pay the defendant expenses, which may include appropriate attorney's fees.

The risk of liability in enforcement procedures is a two-edged-sword.[87] Right holders may knowingly and in bad faith use IPRs to block legitimate competition. In these cases, the defendant is likely to suffer an important economic injury, such as when a provisional measure forces him out of the market.

Article 48.1 addresses these issues in the typical "the judicial authorities shall have the authority" format. It requires Members to empower judicial authorities to order a plaintiff who has "abused" enforcement procedures to provide to a defendant "wrongfully enjoined or restrained adequate compensation for the injury suffered because of such abuse". This provision thus focuses on the abuse of enforcement procedures. The concept of abuse is also employed in several other provisions of TRIPS (Articles 8.2, 40.2, 41.1, 50.3, 53.2, 63.1, and 67), thereby strongly indicating the Agreement's search for a balance between the protection of IPRs and the interests of third parties. Of course, when IPRs are abused not only the particular competitor whose activity has been restrained suffers, but also the general public unduly deprived of access to a competitive product or service.

An important interpretive issue is to determine when the exercise of enforcement proceedings may be deemed abusive. This would certainly be the case when the intention of the plaintiff has been to deliberately exclude an innocent competitor. But also in the absence of bad faith, abuse may take place when a serious departure from the reasonable use of enforcement proceedings is found.[88]

Article 48.1, which gives content to the general provisions contained in Articles 8.2[89] and, more specifically, Article 41.1,[90] applies when a party has been "wrongfully enjoined or restrained", for instance, due to the adoption of a preliminary injunction. The plaintiff is required in these cases to pay an "adequate compensation for the injury suffered".[91]

---

[87] See, e.g., Dratler, p. A-108.

[88] See, e.g., Gervais, p. 211.

[89] "Appropriate measures, provided that they are consistent with the provisions of this Agreement, may be needed to prevent the abuse of intellectual property rights by right holders ...". See Chapter 29 of the Resource Book.

[90] See the analysis of this Article above.

[91] See above the analysis on the concept of "adequate compensation".

Under a provision that mirrors Article 45.2,[92] the judicial authorities shall also have the authority to order the applicant to pay the defendant expenses, which may include "appropriate attorney's fees".

According to the language of Article 48.1, first sentence, one of the prerequisites of a possible indemnification of the defendant is the abuse by the plaintiff of enforcement procedures. For example, if the plaintiff initiates infringement proceedings in bad faith, knowing that the defendant is actually not infringing his/her rights, there would be abuse as required under Article 48.1. An important question arises as to whether Members may also provide for the compensation for the injury suffered by a defendant when there is no abuse on the part of the plaintiff, but at the same time, an infringement on the part of the defendant cannot be established. Examples would include controversial cases in patent litigation, where the application of the doctrine of equivalents[93] has led to a conclusion of non-infringement. In such cases, the plaintiff cannot be expected to refrain from the initiation of proceedings in the first place, because the exact scope of the patent claim is not obvious and can only be established through thorough examination of the infringement claim by a court. Thus, the plaintiff has not abused the procedures, but the defendant, if enjoined or restrained, may nevertheless have suffered an injury which is due to the initiation of infringement procedures by the plaintiff.

TRIPS does not prevent a Member from requiring the plaintiff to compensate the defendant in these cases. It is true that Article 48 refers to the indemnification of the defendant only in cases of abuse on the part of the plaintiff. But independently of Article 48, TRIPS is not intended to modify a Member's domestic rules on the distribution of expenses of a court proceeding between the parties, unless this would disregard the TRIPS minimum standards for IP protection in that Member. If a Member chooses to impose on the losing party in a court proceeding an order to cover the expenses of the winning party, such expenses may include the costs arising from any enforcement procedure, including compensation for the injury suffered through injunctions.[94] This is a matter of domestic law and is not limited to IP issues but concerns enforcement proceedings for any kind of right. TRIPS would only affect Members' sovereignty in this respect if its minimum standards on IP were threatened. But this is not the case. It is true that the prospect of a

---

[92] See above.

[93] For an explanation of this doctrine, see Chapter 17, Section 1. In actual practice, the operation of this doctrine is quite complex, and its scope under U.S. law has been the object of a recent U.S. Supreme Court ruling (see *Festo Corp. v. Shoketsu Kinzoku Kogyo Kabushiki Co.*, partly overruling a decision of the U.S. Court of Appeals for the Federal Circuit (CAFC) in the context of an amended patent claim). For the purpose of this part of the book, it suffices to note that in patent cases involving the doctrine of equivalents, the outcome of an infringement proceeding is far from certain, due to the complex question whether a given element of a product/process may actually be considered "equivalent" to another element of a patented product/process. Under such circumstances, the initiation by the right holder of infringement proceedings cannot be considered to constitute "abuse" in the sense of Article 48.1, first sentence, of the TRIPS Agreement, even if eventually, the court comes to the conclusion that the infringement claim is not justified.

[94] See, for example, § 945 of the German Code of Civil Procedure.

possible indemnification of the opposing party could deter a right holder from enforcing his right, especially in controversial cases where the outcome is not obvious. But the risk of having to bear the opposition's expenses (including the damage incurred through provisional measures) is inherent in any initiation of court proceedings against a third party. It is a risk that is not particularly related to the enforcement of IPRs and therefore, TRIPS is not intended to liberate IPR holders from such risk.

Thus, it may be stated that in cases where there is no abuse of enforcement proceedings on the part of the plaintiff and no infringement of any IPR on the part of the defendant, it is up to the domestic law of Members to provide for a possible indemnification of the expenses borne and the injury suffered by the defendant.

Further, under Article 48.1, second sentence, the judicial authorities shall also have the authority to order the applicant to pay the defendant's expenses, which may include appropriate attorney's fees. This provision mandates a treatment to the defendant, who was the victim of abusive enforcement proceedings, equivalent to that conferred to the plaintiff under Article 45.1.

3.8.2 Article 48.2

> 2. In respect of the administration of any law pertaining to the protection or enforcement of intellectual property rights, Members shall only exempt both public authorities and officials from liability to appropriate remedial measures where actions are taken or intended in good faith in the course of the administration of that law.

Article 48.2 establishes an obligation with regard to the administration of any law pertaining to the protection or enforcement of IPRs. The purpose of the provision is to ensure that public authorities and officials are subject to liability where actions have been taken or intended in bad faith.

"Law" may be understood in the context of this provision, either in a formal sense, as legislation adopted by a national or regional parliament, or in a material sense, as any regulation dealing with the enforcement of IPRs. To the extent that the provision refers to "any" law, both federal and sub-federal legislation would be included. Further, no distinction is made between civil and criminal, or administrative and judicial procedures.

Article 48.2 prevents Members from exempting public authorities and officials from liability to appropriate remedial measures, except "where actions are taken or intended in good faith in the course of the administration of that law". Public authorities of any kind, whether judicial or administrative, and their officials are subject to this provision, which requires a judgment about the intention with which a measure has been adopted. Actions not conforming to the law, but adopted in good faith, may be exempted from the remedial measures mandated in this Article.

The Article leaves open to Members' decision the kind of remedial measures that may be applied.[95] This provision applies whether actions were taken upon request by the interested party or *ex officio*, to the extent that such actions were made in the normal course of administration of enforcement-related laws. The burden of proof that actions were not taken or intended in good faith would rest with the party that alleges misconduct; in other words, *bona fide* would be presumed.

Though Article 48.2 does not differentiate with regard to the party that may claim remedial action, it is included under the title "Indemnification of the Defendant". This indicates that it is intended to protect the defendant from abuses committed with the intervention of public authorities, in logical connection to Article 48.1.

3.9 Article 49

Article 49   Administrative Procedures

To the extent that any civil remedy can be ordered as a result of administrative procedures on the merits of a case, such procedures shall conform to principles equivalent in substance to those set forth in this Section.

Article 49 extends the application of the rules on procedures and civil remedies dealt with in Articles 41–48 to administrative procedures on the merits of the case. The rules applied, however, need not be identical but "conform to principles equivalent in substance" to those contained in Section 2 of Part III. Conformity with the "principles" and not with the "provisions" is required, thereby suggesting that there is considerable room to adapt the provisions set forth in that Section to the characteristics (e.g., informalism) of administrative procedures. The determination of what the principles are may certainly give rise to different opinions. Further, the equivalence required is "in substance" and not in detail.

As noted above, administrative procedures are also subject to the general obligations set forth in Article 41.

In some countries, administrative enforcement procedures are of particular importance. In China, for instance, there is a "dual-track" system of enforcement of IPRs, involving judicial or administrative authorities.[96] It has been estimated that around 90% of all patent litigation in China has involved the administrative authorities.[97]

---

[95] In contrast, the Anell Draft referred to "compensation" only: "PARTIES may provide for the possibility that such parties [may] [shall] be entitled to claim compensation from [authorities] [public officers] in appropriate cases, such as negligent or deliberate improper conduct. [they shall provide for such possibility in the case of administrative *ex officio* action.]").

[96] See, e.g., Liu Xiaohai, *Enforcement of intellectual property rights in the People's Republic of China*, IIC 2001, vol. 32, No. 2, p. 141.

[97] See, e.g., Matthew Murphy, *Patent litigation in China. How does it work?*, Patent World, June/July 2001, p. 19.

3.10 Article 50

3.10.1 Article 50.1

> **SECTION 3: PROVISIONAL MEASURES**
> **Article 50**
>
> 1. The judicial authorities shall have the authority to order prompt and effective provisional measures:
>
> (a) to prevent an infringement of any intellectual property right from occurring, and in particular to prevent the entry into the channels of commerce in their jurisdiction of goods, including imported goods immediately after customs clearance;
>
> (b) to preserve relevant evidence in regard to the alleged infringement.

Article 50 is the sole Article in Part III dealing with "Provisional measures". It contains important procedural rules to deal with infringements that are taking place or that are imminent (Article 50.3).[98]

This Article sets forth the minimum requirements to be met by proceedings for provisional measures. Like other provisions in Part III, it establishes the obligation to empower judicial authorities (in this case, to grant provisional measures) and defines the results to be achieved rather than the conditions to do so. This leaves Members considerable leeway to implement the granting of provisional measures and, particularly, to determine the requirements to be imposed in accordance with each national legal system. There may be different views with respect to the question if Article 50 contains all the required elements to make it directly operative ("self-executing"). In order to be self-executing, a provision needs to provide a sufficient basis to apply in a concrete case, and to be intended by the parties to be self-executing.[99] It could be argued, on the one hand, that Article 50 lacks precision as to the conditions for the granting of provisional measures. Judicial authorities, in order to enter an order of the type referred to, would arguably depend on additional legislative measures in this respect. On the other hand, the view that Article 50 is sufficiently precise for direct application seems equally defendable: the provision states that the judicial authorities shall have certain competences, and that such competences may be exercised in two clearly defined cases, as stated in Article 50.1 (a) and (b) (see the quoted text, above). These provisions arguably provide sufficient details on the conditions to be met for the granting of provisional measures.[100]

---

[98] Note that Article 50.7 also refers to the "threat" of infringement of an intellectual property right.

[99] For more details on self-executing provisions, see Chapter 2.

[100] Note that, in some countries, Article 50 TRIPS has been deemed self-executing by case law. See, e.g., Carlos Correa, *Medidas cautelares en material de patentes de invención*, Lexis Nexis Jurisprudencia Argentina, JA-2002-IV, No. 8, p. 21–28 [hereinafter Correa, Medidas cautelares]. In the law of the European Community (EC), the European Court of Justice (ECJ) has repeatedly denied the self-executing character of the provisions of the TRIPS Agreement (and all other WTO

In any case, it appears useful to note that self-execution might not be favourable to developing Members in various contexts, including this one, leaving them less freedom as to the implementation of the provision.

As to the notion of "provisional measures" that aim at restraining a party from engaging in a particular act, these are generally known as "preliminary", "interlocutory" or "interim" injunctions.[101]

The provisional measures, which should be "prompt and effective", must be available to address two situations:

a) To prevent an infringement of any intellectual property right from occurring and, in particular, to prevent the entry into the channels of commerce in their jurisdiction of goods, including imported goods immediately after customs clearance.[102] This provision only applies to acts concerning commercialization within the jurisdiction of the Member,[103] and would not apply immediately upon exportation of infringing goods.[104] As to the notion of "intellectual property rights", TRIPS does not provide an express definition. Instead, it refers, in Article 1.2, to all categories of IPRs that are the subjects of Part II, Sections 1 through 7. The European Court of Justice (ECJ) in its *Dior* decision has observed that TRIPS leaves WTO Members the freedom to specify in detail

> "the interests which will be protected under TRIPS as intellectual property rights and the method of protection, provided always, first, that the protection is effective, particularly in preventing trade in counterfeit goods and, second, that it does not lead to distortions of or impediments to International trade."[105]

Agreements). See its judgment of 14 December 2000 (*Parfums Christian Dior SA v TUK Consultancy BV and Assco Gerüste GmbH and Rob van Dijk v Wilhelm Layher GmbH & Co. KG and Layher BV*, joined cases C-300/98 and C-392/98, European Court Reports 2000, p. I-11307 [hereinafter Dior]). However, the ECJ in Dior also decided that in fields that do not fall within the scope of EC law but within the competence of the EU member states (such as rules on industrial designs), national legislation may confer upon individuals the right to directly rely on the provisions of Article 50 (*in casu* its paragraph 6) before national courts (see Dior, paragraphs 48, 49). Thus, the ECJ does not follow a uniform approach with respect to Article 50 TRIPS. This confirms that different views on the self-executing character of this provision are admissible.

[101] See, e.g., *Interim relief. A worldwide survey*, Managing Intellectual Property, November 1997, p. 35–44 [hereinafter Managing Intellectual Property].

[102] The same approach as examined above is adopted in Article 44. The difference between Article 44 and Article 50.1(a) is that in cases of Article 44, an infringement of IPRs has already occurred, while the procedure under Article 50.1(a) is supposed to prevent such a thing in the first place. Both Articles 44 and 50 have in common that they apply *after* customs clearance, as opposed to Article 51 (suspension of release by customs authorities), which applies to measures to be adopted *before* customs clearance.

[103] The Brussels Convention on Jurisdiction in the Enforcement of Judgements in Civil and Commercial Matters, applicable within the European Community, allows a provisional measure to be requested in the jurisdiction of a State even in cases where the jurisdiction of another State is competent to take a decision on the merits of the case (Article 24). For instance, cross border injunctions have been granted by courts in the Netherlands with respect to cases in Germany (see, e.g., Managing Intellectual Property, p. 35).

[104] See, e.g., Dreier, p. 264.

[105] ECJ, *Dior*, paragraph 60.

This means that Article 50.1 accords Members the discretion to decide whether the term "intellectual property rights" encompasses not only national laws relating specifically to intellectual property, but equally general provisions of national law covering wrongful acts, in particular unlawful competition, that confer upon individuals the right to sue third parties for the alleged infringement of IPRs.[106]

b) The second situation to be addressed under Article 50.1 refers to the preservation of relevant evidence with regard to the alleged infringement. The scope of the preliminary relief, according to this provision, embraces the preservation of any evidence relevant to establish the infringement, and not only of the infringing products. "Anton Piller" orders have ordinarily been granted in common law countries for this purpose.[107]

In many countries injunctions are difficult to obtain in intellectual property disputes, particularly those involving patent infringement, because in most cases damages are a sufficient remedy until the issues of infringement and (validity) are settled at trial. Thus, in the USA the judge would normally consider whether:

– there is a reasonable likelihood that the patent, if challenged by the defendant as being invalid, be declared valid;

– any delay in granting such measures will cause an irreparable harm to the patent holder;

– the harm that may be caused to the title holder exceeds the harm that the party allegedly infringing the patent will suffer in case the measure was wrongly granted; and whether

– there is a reasonable likelihood that the patent is infringed; and granting of the measure would be consistent with the public interest.[108]

Preliminary injunctions have been characterized in the USA as the exception rather than the rule, including in trademark cases; the granting of such injunctions is deemed an exercise of a very far-reaching power, not to be ordered except in a case clearly demanding it.[109]

In Canada and Australia, a "balance of convenience" must also be in favour of granting the injunction; this means that in case a provisional measure is ordered, the inconveniences of both parties should be balanced in the sense that the measure should be adequate to its purpose (thus serving the interest of the

---

[106] See ECJ, Dior, paragraph 62, with respect to the Dutch Civil Code and Code of Civil Procedure, which may be invoked, *inter alia*, for the prevention of illegal copying of industrial designs.

[107] An "Anton Piller order" may be adopted so as to require the defendant to permit plaintiff's representatives to enter the defendant's premises and remove infringing items or obtain other evidence (photocopies, photographs, etc.) to be used to prove that an infringement has occurred.

[108] See, e.g., J. Reichman and M. Zinnani, *Las medidas precautorias en el derecho estadounidense: el justo balance entre las partes*, Lexis Nexis Jurisprudencia Argentina, JA 2002-IV, No. 8, p. 15–21 [hereinafter Reichman/Zinnani].

[109] See, e.g., Thomas McCarthy, *McCarthy on Trademarks and Unfair Competition*, 4th. Edition, Thomson, West, USA 2002, vol. 5, pp. 30–59 [hereinafter McCarthy].

plaintiff), but should not be any more restrictive than absolutely necessary (thus serving the interest of the defendant).[110] The court would also consider the age of the patent and whether the validity of the patent is an issue, and would generally refuse an injunction if the defendant undertakes to keep an account of profits and appears likely to be able to meet an award against a final trial.[111] The balance of convenience is also applied in the United Kingdom, among other countries.[112]

Similarly, in order to obtain interlocutory injunctions (*référés d'interdiction provisoire*) in France, the patent must not obviously be null and void and the infringement must appear serious; in Germany such measures are granted where infringement and validity are clearly beyond doubt, and normally in cases of literal infringement and not where questions of equivalence arise; in Mexico, injunctions in patent infringement hardly ever take place, and an official expert must determine whether the patent is likely to be used by the person allegedly infringing the patent before a measure is granted; in the United Kingdom, it is also generally difficult to obtain an injunction because courts have taken the view that damages are quantifiable and would only proceed if damages are not an adequate remedy, taking the balance of convenience into account.[113]

3.10.2 Article 50.2

> 2. The judicial authorities shall have the authority to adopt provisional measures *inaudita altera parte* where appropriate, in particular where any delay is likely to cause irreparable harm to the right holder, or where there is a demonstrable risk of evidence being destroyed.

Article 50.2 requires that the judicial authorities also have the authority to adopt provisional measures *inaudita altera parte*.[114] This provision does not provide a general rule to establish when such measures are justified, but vaguely refers to its application "where appropriate" and in two particular cases:

(a) where any delay is likely to cause irreparable harm to the right holder, or

(b) where there is a demonstrable risk of evidence being destroyed.

In case (a) the critical element is the *delay* as a cause of an "irreparable harm".[115] The latter would exist if the right holder were unlikely to obtain an adequate compensation for damages (for instance, because the infringer had no permanent

---

[110] See the Canadian Competition Tribunal of 22 March 1991, *Director of Investigation and Research v. Southam Inc.*, CT-901_4, paragraph (c) (may be consulted at <http://www.canlii.org/ca/cas/cact/1991/1991cact11.html>).

[111] See, e.g., Managing Intellectual Property, p. 36.

[112] Idem, pp. 37 and 43.

[113] Idem, pp. 38, 39, 42 and 43.

[114] Latin for "Without hearing the other Party".

[115] An example of this type of measure is the *"Mareva"* injunction allowed under common law to temporarily freeze the defendant's assets (generally bank deposits) that are required to satisfy a judgement in order to prevent their dissipation or removal from the jurisdiction.

business activity in the country). The mere possibility of producing harm to the right holder would not be sufficient to ignore the defendant's basic right to be heard before an injunction or other relief is granted.

In case (b) an *ex parte*[116] provisional measure would proceed if the risk of evidence being destroyed is demonstrable. The applicant must duly substantiate his request.

It is up to Members to determine whether there are other cases in which *ex parte* provisional measures would be appropriate, but a prudent approach is advisable. In fact, in developed countries *ex parte* measures are only exceptionally granted. This is the case, for instance, in the USA,[117] Germany and France.[118] In Canada, patent infringement matters are not deemed to be of extreme urgency, and "it is difficult to imagine the circumstances where a Canadian court would consider it appropriate to grant relief without notice where there was only an allegation of patent infringement".[119]

3.10.3 Article 50.3

> 3. The judicial authorities shall have the authority to require the applicant to provide any reasonably available evidence in order to satisfy themselves with a sufficient degree of certainty that the applicant is the right holder and that the applicant's right is being infringed or that such infringement is imminent, and to order the applicant to provide a security or equivalent assurance sufficient to protect the defendant and to prevent abuse.

Article 50.3 reflects the "check and balances" approach adopted in many provisions of Part III. The judicial authorities must have the authority to impose a number of requirements on the applicant of a provisional measure:

(a) to provide any reasonably available evidence in order to satisfy the authorities with a sufficient degree of certainty that the applicant (i) is the right holder and that (ii) the applicant's right is being infringed or that such infringement is imminent;

(b) to provide a security or equivalent assurance "sufficient to protect the defendant and to prevent abuse". The amount of the security or other assurance is to be determined by the national authority. It must be sufficient not only to compensate the defendant for losses generated, but also to prevent the abusive use of provisional measures to interfere with legitimate competition.

---

[116] Latin for "one-sided" (i.e., where the judge mainly bases his decision on the assertions of the plaintiff, if these appear substantiated. Details vary according to domestic laws.). The reason for this procedure is that the court has to act quickly, due to the danger of irreparable harm or a possible destruction of evidence.

[117] See, e.g., Reichman/Zinnani, p. 19.

[118] See, e.g., Joseph Straus, *Reversal of the burden of proof, the principle of 'fair and equitable procedures' and preliminary injunctions under the TRIPS Agreement,* The Journal of World Intellectual Property 2000, Vol. 3., No. 6., p. 815–820.

[119] Managing Intellectual Property, p. 37.

3.10.4 Article 50.4

> 4. Where provisional measures have been adopted *inaudita altera parte*, the parties affected shall be given notice, without delay after the execution of the measures at the latest. A review, including a right to be heard, shall take place upon request of the defendant with a view to deciding, within a reasonable period after the notification of the measures, whether these measures shall be modified, revoked or confirmed.

The same balancing approach as applied under Article 50.3 (see above) inspires Article 50.4, with regard to provisional measures adopted *ex parte*. The parties affected (that is, the alleged infringer, distributors, etc.) shall be given notice, without delay after the execution of the measures *at the latest*. As drafted, this provision implies that notice may be given *before* the execution of the provisional measure. In addition, a review, including a right to be heard, shall take place upon request of the defendant with a view to deciding, within a reasonable period after the notification of the measures, whether these measures shall be modified, revoked or confirmed. This review may take place either before or after the execution of the measure, depending on the date of notification. If revoked, the compensation established in Article 50.7 would apply.

3.10.5 Article 50.5

> 5. The applicant may be required to supply other information necessary for the identification of the goods concerned by the authority that will execute the provisional measures.

Article 50.5 contains a non-mandatory provision indicating that the applicant may be required to supply other information necessary for the identification of the goods concerned by the authority that will execute the provisional measures. This provision assumes that the authority that executes the measure may not be the (judicial) authority that ordered it, for instance, when the police or customs authorities intervene upon request of the latter.

3.10.6 Article 50.6

> 6. Without prejudice to paragraph 4, provisional measures taken on the basis of paragraphs 1 and 2 shall, upon request by the defendant, be revoked or otherwise cease to have effect, if proceedings leading to a decision on the merits of the case are not initiated within a reasonable period, to be determined by the judicial authority ordering the measures where a Member's law so permits or, in the absence of such a determination, not to exceed 20 working days or 31 calendar days, whichever is the longer.

Paragraphs 6 and 7 of Article 50 refer in certain detail to obligations that must be imposed on the applicant of provisional measures. They aim at establishing safeguards to protect the alleged infringer from misconduct or abuses.[120]

Article 50.6 protects the party affected by a provisional measure from actions that are not effectively pursued in courts by the applicant. It establishes the right of the affected party to request that the provisional measure be revoked or otherwise cease to have effect, if proceedings leading to a decision on the merits of the case are not initiated within a reasonable period. This period is to be determined by the judicial authority ordering the measures where a Member's law so permits. In the absence of such a determination, the period shall not exceed 20 working days or 31 calendar days, whichever is the longer. The judicial authority or the national law may certainly establish a shorter period for the applicant to initiate proceedings.[121]

3.10.7 Article 50.7

> 7. Where the provisional measures are revoked or where they lapse due to any act or omission by the applicant, or where it is subsequently found that there has been no infringement or threat of infringement of an intellectual property right, the judicial authorities shall have the authority to order the applicant, upon request of the defendant, to provide the defendant appropriate compensation for any injury caused by these measures.

Article 50.7 requires Members to grant the judicial authorities the power to order the applicant, upon request of the defendant, to provide the defendant appropriate compensation for any injury caused by a provisional measure, in three cases:

(a) where the provisional measures are revoked. Revocation may take place on occasion of the review contemplated in Article 50.4.

(b) where the provisional measures lapse due to any act or omission by the applicant; or

(c) where it is subsequently found that there has been no infringement or threat of infringement of an intellectual property right.

It is to be noted that this provision uses the term "appropriate"[122] and not "adequate" like Articles 44.2 and 48.1, as examined above. It is unclear whether this difference was deliberate and intended to introduce a different standard.[123] In any case, the defendant should receive a compensation commensurate to "any" injury caused, including lost benefits and expenses incurred.

---

[120] See Article 41.1, above.

[121] Note that in the *Dior* case, the ECJ denied individuals in the EU the right to directly rely on Article 50.6 before domestic courts with respect to areas of law in which the EC has passed internal legislation. For more details, see above, under Article 50.1.

[122] "Appropriate" is "suitable or proper", *The Concise Oxford Dictionary*, 1990, p. 53.

[123] As argued, e.g., by Gervais, p. 205.

3.10.8 Article 50.8

> 8. To the extent that any provisional measure can be ordered as a result of administrative procedures, such procedures shall conform to principles equivalent in substance to those set forth in this Section.

Finally, Article 50.8 provides that to the extent that any provisional measure can be ordered as a result of administrative procedures, such procedures shall conform to "principles equivalent in substance" to those set forth in other paragraphs of Article 50. This provision makes it clear ("[T]o the extent . . .") that Members[124] are not obliged to empower administrative authorities to grant provisional measures. It employs the same wording as in Article 49, that is, administrative procedures need not be identical to those applicable by judicial authorities, but respond to the same principles, in substance and not in detail.

3.11 Article 51

> ## SECTION 4: SPECIAL REQUIREMENTS RELATED TO BORDER MEASURES*
> ### Article 51   Suspension of Release by Customs Authorities
>
> Members shall, in conformity with the provisions set out below, adopt procedures** to enable a right holder, who has valid grounds for suspecting that the importation of counterfeit trademark or pirated copyright goods*** may take place, to lodge an application in writing with competent authorities, administrative or judicial, for the suspension by the customs authorities of the release into free circulation of such goods. Members may enable such an application to be made in respect of goods which involve other infringements of intellectual property rights, provided that the requirements of this Section are met. Members may also provide for corresponding procedures concerning the suspension by the customs authorities of the release of infringing goods destined for exportation from their territories.
>
> [Footnote]*: Where a Member has dismantled substantially all controls over movement of goods across its border with another Member with which it forms part of a customs union, it shall not be required to apply the provisions of this Section at that border.
>
> [Footnote]**: It is understood that there shall be no obligation to apply such procedures to imports of goods put on the market in another country by or with the consent of the right holder, or to goods in transit.
>
> [Footnote]***: For the purposes of this Agreement:
> (a) "counterfeit trademark goods" shall mean any goods, including packaging, bearing without authorization a trademark which is identical to the trademark validly registered in respect of such goods, or which cannot be distinguished in its essential aspects from such a trademark, and which thereby infringes the rights of the owner of the trademark in question under the law of the country of importation;

---

[124] Administrative authorities have the power to adopt provisional measures in some countries (e.g., Peru, Mexico, China) but in others such measures can only be conferred by judicial authorities.

(b) "pirated copyright goods" shall mean any goods which are copies made with-out the consent of the right holder or person duly authorized by the right holder in the country of production and which are made directly or indirectly from an Article where the making of that copy would have constituted an infringement of a copyright or a related right under the law of the country of importation.

Section IV introduces the first set of international rules on counterfeiting and copyright piracy, thereby materializing a major objective of the proponents of TRIPS.[125] This Section has been largely modelled on the national laws[126] existing in developed countries at the time of the Uruguay Round negotiations. According to this Section, the customs authorities' intervention should take place after the merchandise has been transported into the territory of a Member, but before it is released for consumption.[127] The obligations established therein only apply with regard to the importation of counterfeit trademark or pirated copyright goods. Members may also provide for corresponding procedures for infringing goods destined for exportation, as provided for in some countries[128] and in recent bilateral free trade agreements,[129] but this is a "TRIPS-plus" requirement that Members are not obliged to implement.

Border measures are required because enforcement against infringement at the source of the imported goods has failed. An important feature of the procedures under Section IV is that they involve two separate steps. Customs authorities' intervention is required only with regard to the execution of a specific provisional measure, while it is up to the "competent authorities, administrative or judicial" (Article 51) to decide on the merits of a particular case, that is, to determine whether the goods at stake are or not counterfeit trademark or pirated copyright goods.

According to Article 51, the application to suspend the release of goods must also be lodged with the "competent authorities, administrative or judicial". An "administrative authority" in this context may be the customs authority itself, as established in some countries.[130] However, there is no obligation under Article 51 to empower such authority to directly adopt provisional measures, and in many countries this is an exclusive competence of the judicial authorities.

---

[125] The Preamble of the TRIPS Agreement recognizes "the need for a multilateral framework of principles, rules and disciplines dealing with international trade in counterfeit goods". See Chapter 1.

[126] For an analysis of national border regulations, see *Border control of intellectual property rights* Sweet & Maxwell, Hampshire 2002.

[127] See, e.g., Fabio Ponce Lopez, *Observancia de los Derechos de la Propiedad Intelectual en Aduanas. Procedimientos, acciones y competencias (Parte III, Seccion 4 de los ADPIC)*, WIPO seminar for the Andean Community on the observation of intellectual property rights at the border, Bogota, D C; July 11, 2002, p. 2 [hereinafter Ponce Lopez].

[128] See, e.g., Article 246 (c) of Decision 486 (Andean Community Common Regime on Industrial Property).

[129] See, e.g., Article 17.11.20., Free Trade Agreement between Chile and the USA.

[130] E.g., Spain, Panama. See Ponce Lopez, p. 9.

Members are obliged to adopt procedures as mandated in Article 51 only with regard to counterfeit trademark or pirated copyright goods, and not in respect of other types of infringement concerning trademarks (e.g., "passing off", improper use of a trademark)[131] or copyright (e.g., substantial similarity, adaptation without the author's permission).[132] This provision does not apply either to other types of intellectual property rights. The reason for this differentiation is that infringement in the case of trademark counterfeiting and copyright piracy may generally be determined with certain ease, on the basis of the visual inspection of an imported good, since infringement will be apparent "on its face".

In order to obtain the suspension of release, the right holder must prove that he "has valid grounds for suspecting" that infringing goods covered by Article 51 are being imported. He must show that there is *prima facie* an infringement. Unlike Article 50, however, this provision does not impose an "irreparable harm" standard, despite that the measures at the border are adopted *inaudita altera parte*. Therefore, the likelihood of an infringement would be sufficient to trigger the procedures under Section 4.

It should be noted that Article 51 does not impose on custom authorities any obligation to inspect imported goods. In fact, such authorities routinely inspect a small fraction of such goods.[133] Moreover, there is no obligation to intervene *ex officio*. Article 51 requires a specific request by the right holder for the custom authority to take action.

The first footnote, quite logically, exempts Members that form part of a customs union from the application of Section 4, provided they have dismantled substantially all controls over the movement of goods across its border with other Members of the union, like, for instance, the member states of the European Union.

---

[131] In this context, it is important to clarify the difference between "counterfeit trademark goods" as covered by Article 51 and "passing off", which is not encompassed by this provision. The notion of "counterfeit trademark goods" as defined in footnote 14 to Article 51 (see below) requires the existence of a registered trademark, which is used by an unauthorized third party, thereby infringing the exclusive right of the trademark owner. By contrast, the doctrine of passing off (also called sometimes "palming off") is much wider, referring to unfair competition more generally, applying also to cases where no trademarks or other IPRs are involved (see <http://www.intellectual-property.org.uk/std/resources/other_ip_rights/passing_off.htm>). "Passing off" broadly refers to causes of action based on the injury that is suffered by a business through a false representation by a competitor that its product comes from the same source. Thus, passing off is a broader category than trademark counterfeiting, encompassing the latter, but going beyond such cases. Those cases of passing off that do not involve trademarks are therefore not covered by Article 51. On the common law doctrine of passing off, see W. R. Cornish, *Intellectual Property: Patents, Copyright, Trade Marks and Allied Rights* (4th ed. 1999), at Chapter 16. See also Chapter 15 of this book on geographical indications.

[132] It appears useful to highlight the difference between the copyright cases covered by Article 51 and the situations that fall outside the scope of this provision. Copyright piracy within the meaning of Article 51 and its footnote 14 (see below) requires the *copying* of a copyrighted good, as opposed to the above mentioned cases where a third person produces a work that is not a copy of, but substantially similar to the protected work, or that modifies the protected work without the right holder's authorization. Such cases do not fall within the category of "pirated copyright goods".

[133] See the commentary on Article 58, below.

The second footnote of this Article addresses the issue of parallel imports in the context of trademark and copyright protection. It indicates that the obligation to suspend the release of goods contained in Article 51 would not apply when the products have been put in commerce "by or with the consent of the right holder". Parallel trade in trademarked goods (often called the "grey market") is admitted in many countries. This is the case, for instance, in the USA, where a Supreme Court Decision of June 1989 allowed retailers to import trademarked foreign-made watches, cameras, perfumes, and other goods from foreign independent distributors.[134]

It could be argued that the second footnote may also have interpretive value with regard to parallel trade in goods protected by other IPRs, particularly patents. If so, this would imply that parallel trade would not be legitimate when products are introduced in a foreign market without the consent of the right holder, for instance, by a compulsory license. However, the footnote clearly applies to certain cases of infringement of trademark and copyright only, and there is no solid basis to extend it into other fields in a manner that would limit the rights conferred on Members under Article 6 of the Agreement, as confirmed by the Doha Declaration on the TRIPS Agreement and Public Health.[135]

The second footnote also clarifies that it is not mandatory to apply border measures with regard to "goods in transit". Some countries, however, have extended those measures to such products.[136]

The third footnote contains definitions for the purposes of the Agreement of "counterfeit trademark goods" and of "pirated copyright goods". Reference to counterfeiting goods is made, in addition to Article 51, in the Preamble and in Articles 46, 59, 61 and 69, while pirated copyright goods or piracy are only referred to in Articles 61 and 69, as examined below. These definitions clarify that the possible existence of infringement is to be considered in accordance with the law of the country of importation. Trademark counterfeiting is not limited to the case of the unauthorized use of a trademark identical to the trademark validly registered in respect of such goods, but also includes cases where it "cannot be distinguished in its essential aspects from such a trademark". Copyright piracy, on the other hand, includes copies made "directly or indirectly" from a copyrighted

---

[134] To get around the 1989 Supreme Court ruling, many manufacturers tried copyrighting the packaging on their goods. The Coalition to Protect the Integrity of American Trademarks (COPIAT) articulated this argument in the case *Parfums Givency, Inc. v. Drug Emporium, Inc.*, 38 F.3d 477 (9ᵗʰ Cir. 1994), but in March 1998 the Supreme Court defeated this legal strategy. See Paul R. Paradise, *Trademark Counterfeiting: Product Piracy and the Billion Dollar Threat to the U.S. Economy*, Quorum Books, Westport, Connecticut 1999, p. 30 [hereinafter Paradise].

[135] "The effect of the provisions in the TRIPS Agreement that are relevant to the exhaustion of intellectual property rights is to leave each member free to establish its own regime for such exhaustion without challenge, subject to the MFN and national treatment provisions of Articles 3 and 4" (para. 5.d). See "Doha Ministerial Declaration on the TRIPS Agreement and Public Health" (hereinafter "the Doha Declaration"), WT/MIN(01)/DEC/W/2, 14 November 2001. See also Chapter 25.

[136] EC Regulation 3295/94, for instance, applies to goods in "external transit", that is, non-Community goods moving within the Community or exceptionally Community goods destined for export and for which custom procedures are complied with. See, e.g., Buydens, p. 13.

article, thereby including not only the first but subsequent copies of a protected work.

3.12 Article 52

> ### Article 52   Application
>
> Any right holder initiating the procedures under Article 51 shall be required to provide adequate evidence to satisfy the competent authorities that, under the laws of the country of importation, there is *prima facie* an infringement of the right holder's intellectual property right and to supply a sufficiently detailed description of the goods to make them readily recognizable by the customs authorities. The competent authorities shall inform the applicant within a reasonable period whether they have accepted the application and, where determined by the competent authorities, the period for which the customs authorities will take action.

A right holder willing to obtain a border measure of the type established under Article 50 must comply with two basic requirements:[137]

(a) to provide "adequate evidence" to satisfy the competent authorities that, under the laws of the country of importation, there is *prima facie* an infringement. This means that the evidence provided must satisfy the competent authorities that there is a likely infringement of IPRs.

(b) to supply a sufficiently detailed description of the goods to make them readily recognizable by the customs authorities. This provision only requires information for the customs authorities to identify the allegedly infringing goods, but their inspection to determine whether *prima facie* infringement exists or not can be made by a different authority, e.g., by a court.

Finally, Article 52 requires the competent authorities to inform (whether in written form or not)[138] the applicant "within a reasonable period" whether they have accepted the application and, where determined by the competent authorities, the period for which the customs authorities will take action. Only a "reasonable period", to be determined by the Member's national law is required. Notification need not be immediate or "without delay" as provided for, for instance, under Article 50.4. The notification may include information about the period for which the customs authorities will detain the goods, where the competent authority has established such a period.[139]

---

[137] See also Article 53 with regard to securities or equivalent assurances.

[138] The requirement to inform in a written form applies, as discussed above, to decisions on the merits of the case (Article 41.3) and in respect of notices to the defendant (Article 42).

[139] The Anell Draft of July 23, 1990, indicated in a bracketed text that was not finally adopted, the applicant's obligation to specify the length of the period for which the customs authorities would be requested to take action (W/76).

3.13 Article 53

3.13.1 Article 53.1

> ### Article 53　Security or Equivalent Assurance
>
> 1. The competent authorities shall have the authority to require an applicant to provide a security or equivalent assurance sufficient to protect the defendant and the competent authorities and to prevent abuse. Such security or equivalent assurance shall not unreasonably deter recourse to these procedures.

Article 53.1 is drafted in the typical "the competent authorities shall have the authority to" format and is intended to avoid abuses[140] by requiring the applicant of border measures to provide a security or equivalent assurance sufficient to protect the defendant and the competent authorities. The protection to be provided under this Article is for the defendant (though at this stage of the procedures there may be none) and the customs authorities as such, which may be liable in case they adopt measures that unjustifiably interfere with the legal activities of traders. The obligation to provide a security, thus, should act as a deterrent to anticompetitive practices.

Article 53.1, however, cautions that the security or equivalent assurance that is requested "shall not unreasonably deter recourse to these procedures", that is, it should not be of such an unreasonable amount that would inhibit interested parties from applying for border measures. This provision leaves significant latitude to Members to determine what "unreasonable" means in this context.

3.13.2 Article 53.2

> 2. Where pursuant to an application under this Section the release of goods involving industrial designs, patents, layout-designs or undisclosed information into free circulation has been suspended by customs authorities on the basis of a decision other than by a judicial or other independent authority, and the period provided for in Article 55 has expired without the granting of provisional relief by the duly empowered authority, and provided that all other conditions for importation have been complied with, the owner, importer, or consignee of such goods shall be entitled to their release on the posting of a security in an amount sufficient to protect the right holder for any infringement. Payment of such security shall not prejudice any other remedy available to the right holder, it being understood that the security shall be released if the right holder fails to pursue the right of action within a reasonable period of time.

Article 53.2 addresses the case in which the release of allegedly infringing goods into free circulation has been suspended by customs authorities on the basis

---

[140] The Anell Draft referred to "avoid border enforcement procedures being abused by means of unjustified or frivolous applications" (W/76).

of a decision other than by a judicial or other independent authority. This is, hence, a specific safeguard that applies when a court or an authority independent from the customs has not had an opportunity to consider the case and order the suspension.

Article 53.2 only applies in relation to industrial designs, patents, layout-designs and undisclosed information, and not trademarks, copyright and geographical indications. It is a "slightly unusual provision",[141] since it regulates measures that Members are *not* obliged to order under Article 51, which, as examined above, is only mandatory with regard to counterfeit trademarks and pirated copyrights.

This Article applies where the period provided for in Article 55 has expired[142] without the granting of the provisional measure by the "duly empowered authority" (which may be a court or another administrative authority independent from customs), and where all other conditions for importation (that is, the *normal* requirements imposed in the importing country) have been complied with.

Subject to these conditions, the owner, importer, or consignee of the allegedly infringing goods shall be entitled to their release on the posting of a security. No reference is made in this Article to securing an "adequate" or "appropriate" compensation, like in other provisions of Part III, but simply to "an amount sufficient to protect the right holder for any infringement". Members are free to determine the criteria to determine such an amount. However, payment of the security shall not prejudice "any other remedy available to the right holder". The security shall be released if the right holder fails to pursue the right of action within a "reasonable" period of time, to be also determined by national law.

3.14 Article 54

Article 54   Notice of Suspension

The importer and the applicant shall be promptly notified of the suspension of the release of goods according to Article 51.

Both the importer and the applicant must be notified if the suspension of the release of goods has been decided by the competent authority. This should be done "promptly". Though this may be interpreted as equivalent to "undue delay"[143] or "immediately",[144] there is also some latitude here to determine the exact period. Of course, given the economic consequences that an unjustified suspension may entail, it would be to the benefit of both the applicant and of the importer (and also of the competent authority) that notice be given as soon as feasible.

---

[141] See Dreier, p. 266, who notes that a similar provision was not in the original U.S. and EC proposals, and that it was included because of the U.S. concern that border measures could be abused in some developing countries as a device to obstruct the importation of U.S. goods.

[142] See the commentary on this provision, below.

[143] See Article 41.3.

[144] See Articles 44.1 and 50.1(c).

3.15 Article 55

Article 55   Duration of Suspension

If, within a period not exceeding 10 working days after the applicant has been served notice of the suspension, the customs authorities have not been informed that proceedings leading to a decision on the merits of the case have been initiated by a party other than the defendant, or that the duly empowered authority has taken provisional measures prolonging the suspension of the release of the goods, the goods shall be released, provided that all other conditions for importation or exportation have been complied with; in appropriate cases, this time-limit may be extended by another 10 working days. If proceedings leading to a decision on the merits of the case have been initiated, a review, including a right to be heard, shall take place upon request of the defendant with a view to deciding, within a reasonable period, whether these measures shall be modified, revoked or confirmed. Notwithstanding the above, where the suspension of the release of goods is carried out or continued in accordance with a provisional judicial measure, the provisions of paragraph 6 of Article 50 shall apply.

Article 55 explicitly applies to both imports and exports. Unlike other provisions commented above, it contains a specific time period for action by the competent authority. Within a period not exceeding 10 working days after the applicant has been notified of the suspension, the allegedly infringing goods shall be released if the customs authorities have not been informed that:

(a) proceedings leading to a decision on the merits of the case have been initiated by a party other than the defendant, or

(b) the competent authority has taken provisional measures prolonging the suspension of the release of the goods.

The condition under (a) requires that the applicant or another party initiated a case in order to obtain a decision on the merits of the case. If it is the defendant himself who has initiated such procedures, the release should be ordered. Article 55 seems to assume that the title holder should request that a decision on the merits be taken by the same authority that adopted the provisional measure.

Like in the case of Article 53.2, release is subject to compliance with "all other conditions" for importation or exportation". In "appropriate cases" (to be determined by Members' regulations), the ten-day period may be extended by another 10 working days.

Article 55 specifies that if proceedings leading to a decision on the merits of the case have been initiated, a review, including a right to be heard, shall take place upon request of the defendant with a view to deciding, within a reasonable period, whether these measures shall be modified, revoked or confirmed. It is to be noted that, unlike Article 50.4, the right to review is subject according to Article 55 to the initiation of proceedings on the merits of the case. However, where the suspension of the release of goods is carried out or continued in accordance with a provisional judicial measure, the provisions of Article 50.6 shall apply. As a result, a period not exceeding 20 working days or 31 calendar days, whichever is the longer, would apply. If a decision on the merits has been requested, the title holder may also request that the provisional measure (that is, the suspension of release) be maintained until such decision is taken.

3.16 Article 56

Article 56   Indemnification of the Importer and of the Owner of the Goods

Relevant authorities shall have the authority to order the applicant to pay the importer, the consignee and the owner of the goods appropriate compensation for any injury caused to them through the wrongful detention of goods or through the detention of goods released pursuant to Article 55.

Article 56 empowers the authorities that are competent according to the national law to order the applicant to pay the importer, the consignee and the owner of the goods an "appropriate" compensation if the suspension of the release of goods was "wrongful" or where procedures to obtain a decision on the merits of the case was not initiated in accordance with Article 55.

The compensation must be sufficient to cover "any injury caused", which may include lost benefits due to the detention, and expenses incurred (e.g., attorneys' fees). Compensation is to be paid to the importer, the consignee *and* the owner of the goods, that is, the applicant is liable to indemnify all those who may have suffered an economic loss because of the border measure.[145]

It is to be noted, finally, that the obligation to indemnify under this Article creates an objective liability, since it is not dependent on the bad faith or otherwise malicious intent of the applicant.

3.17 Article 57

Article 57   Right of Inspection and Information

Without prejudice to the protection of confidential information, Members shall provide the competent authorities the authority to give the right holder sufficient opportunity to have any goods detained by the customs authorities inspected in order to substantiate the right holder's claims. The competent authorities shall also have authority to give the importer an equivalent opportunity to have any such goods inspected. Where a positive determination has been made on the merits of a case, Members may provide the competent authorities the authority to inform the right holder of the names and addresses of the consignor, the importer and the consignee and of the quantity of the goods in question.

---

[145] There may also be other affected parties (e.g., carriers, distributors, retailers) who may potentially claim damages as well, but under general principles and rules of national law.

Article 57 provides (under the "Members shall provide the competent authorities the authority" formulation) for two different kinds of rights in border
procedures:

(a) the right of inspection: both the right holder and the importer must be given
"sufficient opportunity" to have any goods detained inspected in order to substantiate the right holder's claims or to articulate the defence, respectively;

(b) the right of information: Members may provide the competent authorities the
authority to inform the right holder of the names and addresses of the consignor,
the importer and the consignee, and of the quantity of the goods in question. The
obvious purpose of this provision (which is not mandatory) is to allow the right
holder to act against all those that were possibly involved in the infringement;
this is despite the fact that they may have acted in good faith and without having
reason to know that the goods were infringing. This right only arises (if established
by the national law) where a positive determination has been made on the merits
of a case.

Both the right of inspection and the right of information (if conferred) are subject
to the protection of "confidential information".[146] Article 57 does not clarify to
whose benefit this protection should be established, thereby suggesting that any
party may invoke it and that the competent authorities must not confer such rights
when a violation of such information may occur.

3.18 Article 58

Article 58   *Ex Officio* Action

Where Members require competent authorities to act upon their own initiative
and to suspend the release of goods in respect of which they have acquired
prima facie evidence that an intellectual property right is being infringed:

(a) the competent authorities may at any time seek from the right holder any
information that may assist them to exercise these powers;

(b) the importer and the right holder shall be promptly notified of the suspension. Where the importer has lodged an appeal against the suspension with the
competent authorities, the suspension shall be subject to the conditions, *mutatis
mutandis*, set out at Article 55;

(c) Members shall only exempt both public authorities and officials from liability
to appropriate remedial measures where actions are taken or intended in good
faith.

The provisions in Articles 51–60 do not entail specific inspection obligations for
customs authorities with regard to IPR-protected goods, nor to act *ex officio*. If
they opt to do so, they must comply with the conditions set forth in Article 58. In
general, customs authorities only inspect *ex officio* a small proportion of all trade,

---

[146] See the commentary on Article 42 above.

notably in order to verify the valuation of goods for the purpose of applying tariffs and other charges.[147]

Article 58 applies only "where Members require competent authorities to act upon their own initiative and to suspend the release of goods in respect of which they have acquired *prima facie* evidence that an intellectual property right is being infringed". This means that (a) the said Article is not binding in cases where national law does not provide for an *ex officio* intervention and for the power to suspend release, and (b) that establishing such a form of intervention is entirely left to Members' discretion.

Article 58(a) is formulated as a facultative provision, but a correct reading thereof would indicate that whenever the competent authorities seek information that may assist them to exercise these powers, the right holders would be obliged to provide it. Failure to do so may obviously lead to a decision by the authorities not to take action in the particular case.

The obligation to notify the suspension applies equally with regard to the importer and the right holder. Quite logically, Article 58(b) requires that the same conditions be applied to an appeal by the importer as established in Article 55.

Article 58 (c), finally, does not contain conditions for *ex officio* measures but limits, like Article 48.2, Members' right to exempt public authorities and officials from liability to appropriate remedial measures to cases where actions were taken or intended in good faith in the course of the administration of that law.[148]

3.19 Article 59

Article 59   Remedies

Without prejudice to other rights of action open to the right holder and subject to the right of the defendant to seek review by a judicial authority, competent authorities shall have the authority to order the destruction or disposal of infringing goods in accordance with the principles set out in Article 46. In regard to counterfeit trademark goods, the authorities shall not allow the re-exportation of the infringing goods in an unaltered state or subject them to a different customs procedure, other than in exceptional circumstances.

In the usual "competent authorities shall have the authority to" format, this clause requires Members to empower the authorities (judicial or administrative) to order the destruction or disposal of infringing goods. This is subject

(a) to the right of the defendant to seek review by a judicial authority;

(b) to the "principles" set out in Article 46, that is,

– without compensation of any sort;

– in order to avoid any harm caused to the right holder;

– if not contrary to existing constitutional requirements.

---

[147] In the USA, for instance, customs examiners usually inspect about 5% of the goods entering the country, looking for contraband, contaminated food products, diseased animals, and goods that are either illegal or pose a danger to the public. See, e.g., Paradise, p. 29.

[148] See Article 48.2 above.

In addition, counterfeit trademark goods cannot be re-exported in "an unaltered state" but may be exported if somehow altered or subject to a different customs procedure, other than in exceptional circumstances. The Agreement is not explicit about the extent of the alteration, which is to be determined by national law. A reasonable standard would be an alteration that is sufficient to differentiate those products from those legitimately commercialized, for instance, by removing the infringing trademark.

3.20 Article 60

Article 60   De Minimis Imports

Members may exclude from the application of the above provisions small quantities of goods of a non-commercial nature contained in travellers' personal luggage or sent in small consignments.

"De minimis" clauses can be found in other components of the WTO system.[149] Article 60 is also a *may* provision which reflects not only the difficulty that customs authorities face in controlling imports in small quantities, but also the fact that title holders will not normally be interested in bearing the costs of enforcement procedures in such cases. The "above provisions" refer to the other provisions in Section 4.

3.21 Article 61

SECTION 5: CRIMINAL PROCEDURES
Article 61

Members shall provide for criminal procedures and penalties to be applied at least in cases of wilful trademark counterfeiting or copyright piracy on a commercial scale. Remedies available shall include imprisonment and/or monetary fines sufficient to provide a deterrent, consistently with the level of penalties applied for crimes of a corresponding gravity. In appropriate cases, remedies available shall also include the seizure, forfeiture and destruction of the infringing goods and of any materials and implements the predominant use of which has been in the commission of the offence. Members may provide for criminal procedures and penalties to be applied in other cases of infringement of intellectual property rights, in particular where they are committed wilfully and on a commercial scale.

Article 61 creates an obligation to provide for criminal procedures and penalties for cases of wilful trademark counterfeiting or copyright piracy on a commercial scale. Several aspects of this provision need to be highlighted.

First, though during the negotiations some delegations argued for a comprehensive application of criminal procedures and sanctions, this provision does not

---

[149] See, e.g., Article 5.8 of the Antidumping Agreement, Article 11.9 of the Agreement on Subsidies and Countervailing Measures.

oblige Members to apply the same rule in other fields of intellectual property. Members are, however, free to do so, and many do in fact provide for such remedies and penalties in other areas, notably patents.

Second, criminal procedures and penalties are only required in relation to specific types of trademark and copyright infringement: trademark counterfeiting and copyright piracy, as defined in Article 51 of the Agreement. The provision, hence, does not cover other forms of violation, such as atypical uses of trademarks or reprography.

Third, Article 61 only covers "wilful" infringement, thereby excluding acts done without knowing or having reasonable grounds to know that an infringement was taking place.

Lastly, infringement that cannot be deemed "on a commercial scale" (e.g., isolated acts of infringement even if made for profit) is not subject to this provision.

The second and third sentences of Article 61 specify the content of criminal remedies, without going, however, into details. Penalties must include imprisonment or monetary fines, while Members may apply both measures and other criminal penalties if they wish. The standard to assess compliance with Article 61 is based on two elements: (a) remedies must be "sufficient to provide a deterrent" to infringement, and (b) the level of penalties applied in these cases must be consistent with that applied for crimes of "a corresponding gravity". Members have considerable discretion to determine how to apply these standards and, particularly, to establish which are the crimes of comparable gravity in the national context.

In "appropriate cases" (to be determined by the national law), remedies available shall also include the seizure, forfeiture and destruction of the infringing goods and of any materials and implements the predominant use of which has been in the commission of the offence. Unlike Articles 46 and 59, which subject the destruction of goods to existing constitutional requirements, Article 61 does not contain this limitation. Though the difference may be justified by the criminal nature of the offence, it is also true that destruction of goods may represent a significant economic loss and be regarded as socially unacceptable.[150]

Article 61, last sentence, contains a "may" provision emphasizing the Members' faculty to adopt a "TRIPS-plus" approach, in particular, where infringement is committed wilfully and on a commercial scale. This sentence refers to other types of infringement in the field of trademark and copyright law, as well as to violations of other types of IPRs.

It must be noted that countries have had very different approaches with regard to the application of criminal penalties in cases of IPR infringement. In the USA, for instance, criminal penalties and stiff civil remedies are available under federal law (and some state laws) for intentionally dealing in goods or services knowingly using a counterfeit mark.[151]

---

[150] In the case of conflict between a constitutional provision and the mandate in Article 61, an interesting case about the extent to which WTO rules limit national sovereignty may arise.

[151] Federal criminal penalties include: (a) fines for individuals up to $2,000,000 ($5,000,000 for subsequent offences), or imprisonment not exceeding ten years (twenty years for subsequent offences), or both; and fines for corporations or partnership up to $5,000,000 ($15,000,000 for subsequent

In many developing countries criminal penalties apply in cases of patent infringement as well. This may constitute an important deterrent for companies, especially small and medium enterprises, willing to operate around patented inventions. A criminal accusation carries out many negative effects (in terms of prestige, defence costs, restrictions to travel abroad, etc.). Even if the defendants can prove to be innocent, the risk of facing criminal actions may often be strong enough to dissuade a firm from activities that the title holder may argue are infringing. Unlike the case of trademark counterfeiting or copyright piracy, a patent infringement cannot be established without an expert investigation, including determining whether there is "equivalence" or not. This may explain why in countries that are deemed to confer a high level of patent protection, such as the USA, there are no criminal penalties for patent infringement under federal law. In the USA two civil remedies are available: an injunction against future infringement, and compensatory damages (at least equal to a reasonable royalty), which may be trebled.[152]

Often, criminal sanctions are graduated according to the subject matter involved, the importance of the infringement, and whether subsequent offences take place. For instance, the U.S. Copyright Act, as amended in 1992, stipulates that an infringement with regard to phonorecords becomes a felony depending on the number of infringing copies made or distributed and their retail value. The penalty may be up to five years' imprisonment, or a fine, or both, in case of reproduction or distribution of at least 10 copies above a minimum retail value during six months. Imprisonment of up to 10 years may apply in case of a second or subsequent infringement.[153]

3.22 Article 62

3.22.1 Article 62.1

PART IV   ACQUISITION AND MAINTENANCE OF INTELLECTUAL PROPERTY RIGHTS AND RELATED *INTER-PARTES* PROCEDURES
Article 62

1. Members may require, as a condition of the acquisition or maintenance of the intellectual property rights provided for under Sections 2 through 6 of Part II, compliance with reasonable procedures and formalities. Such procedures and formalities shall be consistent with the provisions of this Agreement.

Article 62 is the sole provision making up Part IV of TRIPS. Its first paragraph takes account of the fact that in many domestic laws, the acquisition and maintenance of

---

offences); and (b) destruction of articles bearing the counterfeit mark. See Paradise, p. 8 and 18.

[152] See, e.g., Paradise, p. 14. It has been noted that the treble damages procedures for wilful infringement may deter those within a firm even from reading patents which may be relevant to their technologies. See John Barton, *Issues Posed by A World Patent System*, Journal of International Economic Law 2004, Volume 7, Issue 2, p. 341–357.

[153] See, e.g., Paradise, p. 11.

IPRs are subject to certain procedures and formalities, such as registration. These formalities often serve certain public policy purposes.[154] Article 62 safeguards Members' sovereignty to apply such measures, but at the same time makes sure that they do not prevent the effective protection of IPRs and respect certain due process standards.

The Members' right recognized in Article 62.1 to provide for certain acquisition and maintenance procedures does not cover all IPRs contained in TRIPS. It only applies to Sections 2 through 6 of Part II, thus excluding the areas of copyright and related rights and the protection of undisclosed information. This is so because in these two areas, protection does not require any registration.[155]

According to Article 62.1, the procedures and formalities that a Member may require for the acquisition and the maintenance of IPRs have to be reasonable. TRIPS does not provide for a definition of what is "reasonable". Thus, Members enjoy some flexibility as to the implementation of this requirement. In general terms, "reasonable" may be interpreted as letting Members impose formalities that are adequate to their purpose, but on the other hand not overly restrictive on the applicant. In other words, there should be a balance between the operation of the formalities, on the one hand, and the availability of IPRs, on the other. Such availability of rights may only be restricted to the extent permitted by the substantive rules of TRIPS, as made clear by the second sentence of this paragraph (which requires procedures and formalities to be consistent with the provisions of TRIPS). But since these substantive rules contain only minimum standards, and are themselves subject to exception clauses, there appears to be some room for Members to interpret the term "reasonable" according to their domestic policy objectives.

3.22.2 Article 62.2

> 2. Where the acquisition of an intellectual property right is subject to the right being granted or registered, Members shall ensure that the procedures for grant or registration, subject to compliance with the substantive conditions for acquisition of the right, permit the granting or registration of the right within a reasonable period of time so as to avoid unwarranted curtailment of the period of protection.

Article 62.2 seeks to prevent overly long examination or registration procedures. The significance of this rule may be illustrated by means of Article 33: the term of patent protection (at least 20 years) is to be counted from the date of filing. This means that the time needed for examination as to whether a patent may be granted will be deducted from the effective term of protection, to the detriment of

---

[154] For example, the registration of IPRs serves the purposes of transparency and legal certainty: third parties may easily verify whether a product is protected by an IPR and who the owner of this right is.

[155] As far as copyright is concerned, Article 5(2) of the Berne Convention actually prohibits to subject its enjoyment and its exercise to any formality. As to undisclosed information, registration would defeat the objective of keeping such information secret.

the right holder. In order to prevent an "unwarranted curtailment" of the period of protection, the present provision obligates Members to permit the granting or registration of a right within a reasonable period of time. Again, there is no definition of "reasonable", and the above considerations (see Article 62.1) equally apply in the context of this paragraph. In particular, this provision should not discourage patent offices from carrying out thorough examinations of patent applications. If a Member considers that in the pursuit of certain policy objectives, a detailed and time-consuming granting procedure is required, the amount of time taken would seem reasonable as long as any shorter time frame would not suffice for the realization of the respective policy objective.[156]

3.22.3 Article 62.3

> 3. Article 4 of the Paris Convention (1967) shall apply *mutatis mutandis* to service marks.

Article 4 of the Paris Convention concerns the right of priority, which plays a decisive role in the acquisition of patents, trademarks, industrial designs, utility models and inventors' certificates.[157] The purpose of Article 62.3 is to bring service marks into the realm of trademark law. This provision complements Article 16.2 and 3, which extend the application of typical trademark rules (i.e., on well-known marks) to service marks. Article 62.3 does the same, with respect to another typical trademark rule (i.e., the right of priority). The reason for this extension is that prior to TRIPS, Parties to the Paris Convention were not obliged to protect service marks through trademark law. Instead, they could opt for other means of protection outside the IPR system, such as rules on unfair competition.[158]

The right of priority is particular to trademark law (and the other industrial property rights under the Paris Convention). It has nothing to do with the non-IPR means of protection of service marks admitted under the Paris Convention. By subjecting service marks to the right of priority, Article 62.3 accords service marks specific trademark protection and takes them out of the realm of non-IPR means of protection.

---

[156] For instance, in order to keep pharmaceuticals at affordable prices, developing country patent offices should subject patent applications to a detailed patentability examination before granting the patent. According to a report by Médecins Sans Frontières (MSF, *Drug patents under the spotlight. Sharing practical knowledge about pharmaceutical patents.* Geneva, May 2003, p. 17/18) a number of national patent offices (including in developed countries) do not examine each application in depth, but merely check that the right papers have been filed and that the fees have been paid. Such practice is favourable to patent applicants, but it defeats the public policy purpose of access to affordable medicines. A longer time frame for a more detailed examination would therefore not constitute an unreasonable period of time in the sense of Article 62.2.

[157] See Chapter 17.

[158] See Article 6*sexies*, Paris Convention, which leaves Parties the freedom not to register service marks as trademarks. For a detailed discussion of Article 16 and the relevant provisions of the Paris Convention, see Chapter 14.

3.22.4 Article 62.4

> 4. Procedures concerning the acquisition or maintenance of intellectual property rights and, where a Member's law provides for such procedures, administrative revocation and *inter partes* procedures such as opposition, revocation and cancellation, shall be governed by the general principles set out in paragraphs 2 and 3 of Article 41.

This provision refers to some of the key rules governing Part III of TRIPS on enforcement. Thus, the obligations of Members to provide for fair and equitable procedures (Article 41.2) and for reasoned decisions (Article 41.3) are made applicable in the context of acquisition and maintenance procedures.[159] Depending on the domestic law of the respective Member, the same obligations apply also to administrative revocation and *inter partes* procedures. Administrative revocation procedures in this context concern the *ex officio* revocation of an intellectual property right. Such procedure involves only the administration and the right holder. *Inter partes* procedures, on the other hand, involve a third party, usually the one opposing the registration of an IPR or requesting the administration to revoke or cancel a granted right.

3.22.5 Article 62.5

> 5. Final administrative decisions in any of the procedures referred to under paragraph 4 shall be subject to review by a judicial or quasi-judicial authority. However, there shall be no obligation to provide an opportunity for such review of decisions in cases of unsuccessful opposition or administrative revocation, provided that the grounds for such procedures can be the subject of invalidation procedures.

Like Article 41.4 in the context of enforcement procedures, this provision obligates Members to provide for the possibility of reviewing final administrative decisions in any of the procedures referred to under paragraph 4.[160] Such availability of review is a basic civil right under the principle of the rule of law.[161] The second sentence contains a conditioned exception to this obligation. "Unsuccessful opposition" refers to an *inter partes* procedure, where a third party has unsuccessfully attempted to prevent the granting of a right by the administration. "Administrative revocation" is a procedure involving only the right holder and an administrative authority (usually identical with the one responsible for the original grant of a

---

[159] For details on Article 41.2 and 3, see above, in this Section.

[160] Note that under Article 41.4, the authority carrying out the review has to be a *judicial* authority. Article 62.5 is wider in this respect, allowing also the review by *quasi*-judicial authorities (i.e., not a judge but usually an administrative body independent of the body granting the right in the first place).

[161] The idea is that every citizen may challenge before the courts any administrative acts that possibly affect unfavourably his/her rights.

right). The case of an unsuccessful revocation under Article 62.5 refers to the situation where the administrative authority first considers revocation of a right, but eventually decides not to do so.

In the case of an unsuccessful opposition, there is no need for the separate review of the administrative rejection of the opposition, provided that under domestic law, the unsuccessful third party may challenge invalidation procedures before a court the grounds used in the administrative rejection. This means that the party opposing the grant of a given IPR is expected to tolerate the establishment of such right (instead of preventing this in the first place through successful opposition), but will subsequently have a chance to challenge the right in invalidation proceedings. In such proceedings, the judge will examine whether the grounds for rejection used by the administration were justified. The same rule applies when administrative revocation procedures are unsuccessful. Any third party may later initiate invalidation procedures on the same grounds as invoked by the administrative authority. Thus, the fact that the administrative authority rejected the revocation of the right does not preclude third parties from challenging the same right before a court.

4. WTO jurisprudence

4.1 Havana Club

On 2 January 2002, the Appellate Body issued its report on the *Havana Club* case,[162] a complaint by the EC with respect to Section 211 of the U.S. Omnibus Appropriations Act of 1998.[163] In this complaint, the EC had alleged several inconsistencies of U.S. Section 211 with TRIPS and the Paris Convention.[164]

U.S. Section 211 has the objective of protecting trademarks, trade names and commercial names that are "the same or substantially similar to a mark, trade name, or commercial name that was used in connection with a business or assets" confiscated by the Cuban government on or after 1 January 1959.[165] Section 211 is intended to prevent unauthorized third parties from benefiting from this confiscation by using an affected trademark, trade name or commercial name. For this purpose, Section 211 makes the registration of such trademark, trade name or

---

[162] *United States – Section 211 Omnibus Appropriations Act of 1998* – WTO document WT/DS176/AB/R. This report as well as the panel report (WT/DS176/R of 6 August 2001) were adopted by the WTO Dispute Settlement Body (DSB) on 1 February 2002. The texts of both reports are available at <http://www.wto.org>.

[163] Section 211 of the Department of Commerce Appropriations Act, 1999, as included in the Omnibus Consolidated and Emergency Supplemental Appropriations Act 1999, Public Law 105–277, 112 Stat. 2681, which became law in the USA on 21 October 1998 [referred to hereinafter as "Section 211"]. The relevant parts of Section 211 are quoted in paragraph 3 of the Appellate Body report.

[164] The following analysis is limited to those parts of the Appellate Body report dealing with the TRIPS obligations on enforcement procedures. The Appellate Body also examined the compatibility of Section 211 with the general TRIPS obligations of National Treatment and Most-Favoured-Nation Treatment as well as with certain trademark provisions of the TRIPS Agreement and the Paris Convention. For an analysis of those parts of the report dealing with trademark law, see Chapter 14.

[165] See Section 211(a)(1).

commercial name dependent on the express consent of the original owner[166] of the mark, trade name or commercial name, or of the *bona fide* successor-in-interest.[167]

Section 211 further provides that:

> "[a] (2) No U.S. court shall recognize, enforce or otherwise validate any assertion of rights by a designated national based on common law rights or registration [...] of such a confiscated mark, trade name, or commercial name.
>
> (b) No U.S. court shall recognize, enforce or otherwise validate any assertion of treaty rights by a designated national or its successor-in-interest [...] for a mark, trade name, or commercial name that is the same as or substantially similar to a mark, trade name, or commercial name that was used in connection with a business or assets that were confiscated unless the original owner of such mark, trade name, or commercial name, or the bona fide successor-in-interest has expressly consented."

The EC contended that these provisions were inconsistent with Article 42 TRIPS, because they "expressly deny [...] the availability of [U.S.] courts to enforce the rights targeted" by Section 211.[168]

The panel followed the EC's argumentation and considered Section 211(a)(2) to be inconsistent with Article 42. According to the panel, this provision effectively prevents a right holder "from having a chance to substantiate its claim", which would contradict Article 42:

> "effective civil judicial procedures mean procedures with the possibility of an outcome which is not pre-empted a priori by legislation."[169] (footnote omitted)

The Appellate Body did not disagree on this interpretation of Article 42. However, it reversed the panel's finding, based on a different assessment of the legal situation in the USA.[170]

As to the term "right holders" in Article 42 (first sentence), the AB agreed with the interpretation of the Panel, confirming that the beneficiaries of this provision are not only parties who have been established as owners of trademarks, but equally parties who claim to have legal standing to assert rights. In other terms, a presumptive owner is to be treated as a "right holder":

> "Consequently, in our interpretation, this presumptive owner must have access to civil judicial procedures that are effective in terms of bringing about the

---

[166] I.e., the owner of the *Cuban* trademark used in connection with confiscated assets.

[167] See Section 211(a)(1), providing that in such cases, the payment of registration fees by the applicant shall not be accepted, unless there is such an express consent. Without payment, however, registration will not be effectuated. Thus, the failure by the applicant to prove the original owner's (or his *bona fide* successor's-in-interest) *express consent* to the registration will practically result in the denial of trademark registration.

[168] See the report of the panel, at paragraphs 4.91 and 4.147.

[169] Ibid., paragraph 8.100, as quoted in paragraph 210 of the report of the Appellate Body. The panel rejected the EC's claim with respect to Section 211(b), due to the EC's failure to substantiate its claim (paragraph 8.162 of the panel report).

[170] According to the Appellate Body, Section 211 is not a provision that pre-empts *a priori* the possibility for a party to enforce its rights. See paragraphs 227 and 229 of the report.

enforcement of its rights until the moment that there is a determination by the court that it is, in fact, not the owner of the trademark that it has registered [...]"[171]

In other words, a party may benefit from the procedural rights under Article 42 as long as, according to the applicable national law, it cannot be excluded that such party is the right holder.[172] In support of this interpretation, the AB referred to the term employed under Article 42 ("right holders") in comparison with the term "owner" in Article 16.1, arguing that where TRIPS limits rights exclusively to the "owner", it does so in express terms.[173] In addition to that, the AB draws on the fact that the fourth sentence of Article 42 refers to "parties" (plural) and not to "party" (singular), thus including not only the true right holder, but equally the party that will eventually be determined to have no right in the respective IPR.[174]

However, the Appellate Body stressed that Article 42 is of procedural character,[175] thus leaving the determination of who is the owner of a right to the domestic substantive intellectual property laws.[176] The AB went on to state that Section 211 constitutes a substantive provision on the determination of ownership.[177] The EC conceded that, despite Section 211, persons seeking to register a trademark did have access to judicial procedures, based on other U.S. laws (i.e., the pertinent procedural provisions of the Lanham Act and the U.S. Federal Rules of Civil Procedure).

The crucial point of controversy was that once a party has been given the opportunity to substantiate its claims under the latter provisions, and the court finds that ownership has to be denied on the substantive grounds under Section 211, Section 211 obligates U.S. courts to abstain from the examination of any further substantive conditions that may be required for the recognition of an intellectual property right.[178]

According to the EC, the decision whether to examine any other of such cumulative substantive conditions has to be left to the discretion of the courts. The EC expressed the view that Article 42 is violated if domestic law prevents a plaintiff from pursuing all issues or claims that arise and from presenting all relevant evidence in this context.[179]

---

[171] See paragraph 8.99 of the report of the panel, as endorsed by the Appellate Body in paragraph 218 of its report.

[172] The Appellate Body and the panel focussed on the "owner" of the trademark. As observed above (Section 3 on Article 42), the term "right holder" is not limited to ownership, but may include other parties authorized to make use of an intellectual property right (depending on domestic law).

[173] See paragraph 217 of the report of the Appellate Body.

[174] Ibid.

[175] See paragraph 221 of the report.

[176] Ibid, paragraph 222.

[177] Ibid.

[178] Apart from the question of ownership, other substantive requirements that are typically relevant in trademark law include issues such as use of the trademark; alleged deficiency of a registration; identity or similarity of signs in general; class of goods or services covered by the trademark; existence and scope of a licence. See paragraph 213 of the Appellate Body report, footnote 148.

[179] See paragraph 213 of the report of the Appellate Body.

The AB disagreed on this interpretation. Stating the procedural character of Article 42, it held that:

> "In our view, a conclusion by a court on the basis of Section 211, after applying the Federal Rules of Civil Procedure and the Federal Rules of Evidence, that an enforcement proceeding has failed to establish ownership – a requirement of substantive law – with the result that it is impossible for the court to rule in favour of that claimant's or that defendant's claim to a trademark right, does not constitute a violation of Article 42. There is nothing in the *procedural* obligations of Article 42 that prevents a Member, in such a situation, from legislating whether or not its courts must examine each and every requirement of substantive law at issue before making a ruling. (emphasis in the original)

> With this in mind, we turn to the alleged inconsistency of Section 211(a)(2) with Article 42. Section 211(a)(2) does not prohibit courts from giving right holders access to fair and equitable civil judicial procedures and the opportunity to substantiate their claims and to present all relevant evidence. Rather, Section 211(a)(2) only requires the United States courts not recognize, enforce or otherwise validate any assertion of rights by designated nationals or successors-in-interest who have been determined, after applying United States Federal Rules of Civil Procedure and Federal Rules of Evidence, not to own the trademarks referred to in Section 211(a)(2). As we have said, Section 211(a)(2) deals with the substance of ownership. Therefore, we do not believe that Section 211(a)(2) denies the procedural rights that are guaranteed by Article 42."[180]

To summarize, Article 42 is of procedural character, which leaves Members the discretion to determine their concept of right holders and ownership. Article 42 does not require Members to provide in their national rules on civil procedure an obligation of courts to examine each of several cumulative substantive criteria for the recognition of an intellectual property right, if one of those criteria is definitely not met.

4.2 Complaints United States v. Sweden and Unites States v. Argentina

Complaints submitted by the USA under the WTO Dispute Settlement Understanding in relation to provisional measures were settled during consultations. This was the case of a complaint against Sweden (WT/DS86/1, 2 June 1997)[181] and another one against Argentina (WT/DS196, 30 May 2000).[182]

---

[180] See paragraphs 226, 227 of the report. On the same grounds, the Appellate Body then also denied an inconsistency of Section 211(b) with Article 42 TRIPS (paragraph 229).

[181] The USA, the EC and Sweden notified an agreed solution to the DSB, based on the approval by the Swedish Parliament of an amendment to several intellectual property laws authorizing the judicial authorities to grant provisional measures, including *ex parte* in cases of risk of destruction or disappearance of materials and documents (WT/DS86/2, December 11, 1998). The amendment entered into force on January 1, 1999.

[182] As an outcome of the consultations, the government of Argentina agreed to propose an amendment to Article 83 of the patent law so as to incorporate the following provision on preliminary measures: "The judicial authorities shall have the authority to order provisional measures in relation to a patent granted in conformity with Articles 30, 31 and 32 of the Law, in order to:
1) prevent an infringement of the patent and, in particular, to prevent the entry into channels of commerce of goods, including imported goods, immediately after customs clearance;
2) preserve relevant evidence in regard to the alleged infringement,

4.3 EC – Protection of Trademarks and GIs

Following separate requests by Australia[183] and the USA,[184] the WTO Dispute Settlement Body (DSB) at its meeting on 2 October 2003 established a single panel[185] to examine complaints with respect to EC Council Regulation (EEC) No. 2081/92 of 14 July 1992[186] on the protection of geographical indications and designations of origin for agricultural products and foodstuffs. The complaints are based, *inter alia*, on alleged violations of Articles 41.1, 41.2 (general obligations on fair and equitable IPR enforcement procedures), 41.4 (review of final administrative decisions), 42 (fair and equitable IPR enforcement procedures), and 44.1 (injunctions).[187] The complainants contend that the above EC Regulation does not provide adequate enforcement procedures.[188]

5. Relationship with other instruments

5.1 WTO Agreements

5.2 Other international instruments

The introduction of a detailed set of enforcement rules as part of TRIPS has been, as mentioned, one of the major innovations of this Agreement. Earlier conventions only contain a few provisions relating to enforcement. For instance, the Paris Convention includes Article 9 (seizure upon importation of goods bearing infringing trademarks and trade names), Article 10 (false designation of source

---

whenever the following conditions are met:
a) there is a reasonable likelihood that the patent, if challenged by the defendant as being invalid, shall be declared valid; b) it is summarily proven that any delay in granting such measures will cause an irreparable harm to the patent holder; c) the harm that may be caused to the title holder exceeds the harm that the alleged infringer will suffer in case the measure was wrongly granted; d) there is a reasonable likelihood that the patent is infringed. Provided that the above conditions are met, in exceptional cases such as when there is a demonstrable risk of evidence being destroyed, the judicial authorities can grant such measures inaudita altera parte.

In all cases, before granting a provisional measure, the judicial authority shall request that an expert appointed ex officio examine items a) and d) above within a maximum period of 15 days.

In the case of granting of any of the measures provided for under this article, the judicial authorities shall order the applicant to provide a security or equivalent assurance sufficient to protect the defendant and to prevent abuses".

[183] WT/DS290/18 of 19 August 2003.

[184] WT/DS174/20 of 19 August 2003.

[185] *European Communities – Protection of Trademarks and Geographical Indications for Agricultural Products and Foodstuffs* [hereinafter *EC – Protection of Trademarks and GIs*], WT/DS174/21 and WT/DS290/19 of 24 February 2004, Constitution of the Panel Established at the Requests of the United States and Australia.

[186] See above, Section 2.1.

[187] See the above requests by Australia and the USA for the establishment of a panel. The alleged violation of Article 44.1 was invoked solely by the USA, whereas Australia referred more generally to Articles "41 and/or 42" of the TRIPS Agreement. Note that the same complaint was also based on other TRIPS provisions, in particular those relating to the national treatment and most-favoured nation treatment obligations and to the protection of trademarks and geographical indications. See Chapters 4, 14 and 15.

[188] See the U.S. request for the establishment of a panel, p. 1. Australia in its request (p. 1) merely referred to the asserted diminished legal protection for trademarks as being contrary, *inter alia*, to Articles 41 and/or 42, TRIPS Agreement.

or geographic origin), Article 10*bis* (protection against unfair competition), and Article 10*ter* (general requirement for "appropriate legal remedies effectively to repress" acts prohibited under Articles 9, 10, and 10*bis*).

The Berne Convention also contains some provisions on enforcement (Articles 13(3) and 15), while they are absent in other important treaties such as the Rome Convention, the Geneva Phonograms Convention, the Universal Copyright Protection and the Washington Treaty.[189]

6. New developments

6.1 National laws

As mentioned, Part III of TRIPS is not intended to harmonize national enforcement rules, but to ensure a minimum level of effectiveness of IPRs, subject to the legal methods and practices applied in each Member. Given that the provisions in this section are oriented to results and do not provide detailed obligations, most of the provisions in Part III are likely to be deemed as non self-executing even in countries where the direct application of international treaties is admitted under constitutional law.

The need to implement legislation to make the provisions in Part III operational is unambiguously suggested by the wording of those provisions that are addressed explicitly to the Members (Members "shall ensure," "shall make available," or "shall provide for"; "judicial authorities" or "competent authorities" "shall have the authority" to order certain measures pursuant to Article 43.1; Article 44.1, first sentence; Article 45; Article 46; Article 48.1; Article 50.1–3 and 7; Article 53.1; Article 56; Art 57, second sentence; Article 59).

In some jurisdictions (e.g., Germany) Part III provisions have been deemed not directly applicable,[190] while elsewhere some courts (e.g., in Argentina) have admitted the direct application of some of such provisions, such as Article 50 on provisional measures.[191]

In many countries adaptation of national laws to Part III was not deemed necessary. In the USA, for instance, it was considered that no amendment to national law was required to comply with TRIPS in this area,[192] thereby suggesting that the USA, one of the main proponents of enforcement rules during the Uruguay Round, was able to obtain the adoption of rules essentially inspired by and consistent with its own legal system.

Issues of compatibility between national enforcement provisions and TRIPS have arisen, for instance, in the context of the European Community. The

---

[189] See, e.g., Dreier, p. 250–251.

[190] Idem, p. 270.

[191] See, e.g., Correa, *Medidas cautelares*, at. 93.

[192] See e.g., *Nimmer on Copyright*, Sec. 18.06 (b) (2), No. 17. The U.S. "Uruguay Agreements Act" (1994), which amended various aspects of U.S. law to comply with obligations emanating from the Uruguay Round Final Act, only include amendments in relation to substantive rules applicable to certain areas of copyright, trademarks geographical indications, and patent (Public law 103–465, December 8, 1994).

European Court of Justice (ECJ) was required to judge whether provisional measures (*"kort geding"*) as provided for by the Dutch law (Article 289 of the Code of Civil Procedures) were compatible with Article 50.6 of the Agreement. The compatibility of national provisions was upheld in this case.[193]

However, in other Members, particularly developing countries, national laws have been more or less extensively amended in order to conform to the new regulatory framework, often directly importing the language from particular provisions of the Agreement.[194]

The examination of the TRIPS-consistency of the national provisions on enforcement is normally a significant chapter in the review of national laws conducted by the Council for TRIPS in discharging its duty to monitor the operation of TRIPS and, in particular, of Members' compliance with their obligations thereunder (Article 68). However, no systematic review of changes introduced in national laws in order to conform to Part III is so far available.

6.2 International instruments

6.3 Regional and bilateral contexts

6.3.1 Regional

Enforcement obligations on IPRs have been included in several regional trade agreements that deal with intellectual property, such as the North American Free Trade Agreement (NAFTA)[195] and the Agreement of the Group of Three,[196] which include provisions substantially similar to those in Part III of TRIPS. Proposals for enforcement rules have also been made in the negotiation of a Free Trade Area for the Americas.

A detailed chapter on enforcement rules, clearly inspired by Part III of TRIPS, is also incorporated into Decision 486 of the Andean Community. The Decision allows member states, in some cases,[197] to apply levels of protection higher than those established by the Decision and TRIPS.

6.3.2 Bilateral

Many bilateral agreements signed by the USA,[198] including free trade agreements, contain provisions on IPR enforcement, which generally establish TRIPS-plus

---

[193] See *Hermes v. FHT*, ECJ, 16 June 1998, case C 53/96.

[194] See, e.g., Decision 486 of the Andean Community Common Regime on Industrial Property.

[195] In fact, NAFTA obliged Mexico to provide for remedies that already existed in the USA. Some have characterized these provisions as an "Americanization" of Mexican law. See R. Neff and F. Smallson, *NAFTA: Protecting and enforcing intellectual property rights in North America*, Shepard's/McGraw-Hill, 1994, p. 127.

[196] Established by Colombia, Mexico and Venezuela. In contrast, the ASEAN Free Trade Area (AFTA) does not include intellectual property provisions.

[197] Such as the *ex officio* granting of provisional and border measures (Articles 246 and 250).

[198] See, e.g., the USA-China Agreement on Protection of Intellectual Property, February 26, 1995.

standards. The USA-Jordan Free Trade Agreement (FTA) signed in 2002,[199] for instance, obliges the parties to comply with the following:

– Article 24 makes payment of lost profits mandatory, and provides that the retail price of the legitimate product be considered to calculate damages.

– Article 25 does not establish the level of fines to be applied, but obliges each Party to "ensure that its statutory maximum fines are sufficiently high to deter future acts of infringement with a policy of removing the monetary incentive to the infringer", and also requires that the judicial and other competent authorities have the authority "to order the seizure of all suspected pirated copyright and counterfeit trademark goods and related implements the predominant use of which has been in the commission of the offence, and documentary evidence".

– Each Party shall provide, at least in cases of copyright piracy or trademark counterfeiting, that its authorities may initiate criminal actions and border measure actions *ex officio*, without the need for a formal complaint by a private party or right holder (Article 26).

– Article 16 stipulates presumptions (not provided for under TRIPS) for civil cases involving copyright or related rights. Each Party shall provide that the natural person or legal entity whose name is indicated as the author, producer, performer or publisher of the work, performance or phonogram in the usual manner shall, in the absence of proof to the contrary, be presumed to be the designated right holder in such work, performance or phonogram. It shall be presumed, in the absence of proof to the contrary, that the copyright or related right subsists in such subject matter. Moreover, such presumptions shall also apply in criminal cases until the defendant comes forward with credible evidence putting in issue the ownership or subsistence of the copyright or related right.

– Finally, the Agreement expands the concept of copyright piracy "on a commercial scale" to encompass cases of "significant wilful infringements that have no direct or indirect motivation of financial gain" (Article 28).

The USA-Singapore Trade Agreement has gone much farther than the TRIPS approach. It includes detailed provisions which significantly expand the obligations existing under Part III of TRIPS:[200]

– Article 1609.3 requires both Parties to publicize their enforcement efforts including making available enforcement statistics that a country might keep.

– Article 1609.4 provides that decisions by a country on how to distribute enforcement resources among different areas, including intellectual property enforcement does not excuse a country from meeting its "deterrence" and related obligations under the agreement.

---

[199] See also the USA-Vietnam Trade Agreement, July 13, 2000.

[200] The following summary is substantially based on *The U.S.-Singapore Free Trade Agreement (FTA) The Intellectual Property Provisions*, Report of the Industry Functional Advisory Committee on Intellectual Property Rights for Trade Policy Matters (IFAC-3), Advisory Committee Report to the President, the Congress and the United States Trade Representative on the U.S.-Singapore Free Trade Agreement Prepared By the Industry Functional Advisory Committee on Intellectual Property Rights for Trade Policy Matters (IFAC-3), February 28, 2003, p. 14–15 [hereinafter *USA-Singapore Free Trade Agreement*].

– Article 1609.6 includes detailed presumptions that must be implemented in national law concerning the subsistence and ownership of copyright in all protected subject matter. A side letter to the agreement spells out in detail how these presumptions will operate in practice in Singapore.

– Article 1609.8 also introduces a TRIPS-plus standard for civil damages, at least in the area of copyright piracy and trademark counterfeiting. Such damages must compensate the right holder for the damages suffered, including payment to the right holder of the profits realized by the party that has infringed the right. The Agreement also requires the judicial authorities to consider the suggested retail price of the legitimate product being infringed upon as a measure of the loss to the right holder.

– Article 1609.9 makes it mandatory to provide for statutory (or "pre-established") damages at least with respect to copyright piracy and trademark counterfeiting.

– Articles 1609.10–13 elaborate on and make mandatory many discretionary remedies from TRIPS including: payment of reasonable attorney's fees to the prevailing party; the authority of judicial authorities to order the seizure of all suspected infringing goods, implements, other materials and documents used in the commission of the infringement; the destruction of infringing goods, except in exceptional circumstances; the destruction of implements used in the commission of an infringement even if the predominant use may have been for legitimate purposes; that the removal of a trademark from infringing goods will never be sufficient to permit their release back into commerce; and that the courts shall have the authority to order the infringer to identify accomplices, suppliers and other third parties involved in the infringement, at the risk of fines or imprisonment for failure to do so.

– Article 1609.14 requires that *ex parte* provisional relief in civil cases be issued "expeditiously."

– Article 1609.15 provides that any security required of the plaintiff shall be "reasonable" and not "deter" recourse to these procedures, and adds that, if expert witnesses are required by the court and must be paid for by the right holder, the charges be related to the work performed and not deter recourse to such relief.

– Article 1609.18 requires that the competent authorities have the power to order infringers to provide the right holder with information regarding the consignee, consignor and importer of infringing goods.

– Article 1609.19 requires Parties to provide for enforcement at the border without any formal complaint filing requirements, that the competent authorities shall have the authority to initiate actions *ex officio* relating to suspect shipments being imported, exported or consigned to a local party. It also allows for enforcement actions against trans-shipped infringing goods that are not consigned to a local party.

– Article 1609.20 mandates that counterfeit and pirated goods shall be destroyed except in exceptional circumstances. The simple removal of unlawfully affixed trademarks shall not be sufficient to permit release into channels of commerce and in no event shall authorities permit export of counterfeit or pirated goods.

– Article 1609.21(a) expands the concept of "on a commercial scale" to include infringing acts without a profit-motive or commercial purpose but which cause damage "on a commercial scale".

– Article 1609.21(b) includes an "encouragement" that deterrent fines be imposed in the case of trademark counterfeit and copyright piracy. The Agreement requires the two governments to have a "policy to remove the monetary incentive to the infringer."

– Article 1609.21(c) authorizes seizure by authorities not only of products named in a search order but also of all products within the "general categories" indicated in such order.

– Article 1609.21(d) expands on TRIPS and requires destruction of counterfeit and pirated goods, except in exceptional cases, and with respect to copyright piracy, any implements or other materials used in accomplishing the infringement.

– Article 1609.21(e)(i) requires criminal authorities to act *ex officio* against piracy and counterfeiting.

– Article 1609.21(e)(ii) provides that the "fiat" prosecution system applied in Singapore shall not be the "primary means" to ensure effective enforcement. A side letter to the agreement outlines changes in that system.

A similar approach to the agreement with Singapore is the one followed in the bilateral free trade agreement between the USA and Chile, which entered into force on 1 January 2004.[201]

6.4 Proposals for review
No proposals for review of Part III have been submitted so far.

7. Comments, including economic and social implications

As described in this chapter, TRIPS places much emphasis on enforcement. However, Members are not required to put in place a judicial system for enforcing IPRs separate from that for the enforcement of law in general. Moreover, TRIPS creates no obligation to shift resources away from general law enforcement toward the enforcement of IPRs. Nonetheless, resource-poor countries may face a difficult dilemma when determining how to allocate their scarce resources.[202]

The economic value of IPRs strongly depends on the ability to effectively enforce them, and on the costs associated with the applicable procedures, whether

---

[201] The enforcement provisions of the FTA between Chile and the USA follow the same structure as the TRIPS Agreement. Accordingly, the FTA contains provisions dealing with General Obligations; Civil and Administrative Procedures; Provisional Measures; Border Measures; and Criminal Procedures. For the USA, probably the most important achievement in this area was to make mandatory many of the discretionary remedies included under TRIPS. The important novelty of the FTA, as far as TRIPS and the WIPO Internet Treaties are concerned, is that it provides for "Limitations on Liability of Internet Service Providers". See Article 17.12.23 of the Chile – USA FTA. See also Roffe, 2004.

[202] For a discussion on challenges for developing countries in the national enforcement and administration of TRIPS standards, see UNCTAD-ICTSD, *Intellectual Property Rights: Implications for Development*, Policy Discussion Paper Geneva, 2003.

administrative or judicial. Enforcement rules are crucial for companies highly dependent on intellectual property rights, both in developed and developing countries.[203]

Copyright piracy and trademark counterfeiting emerged as a key concern in the Uruguay Round negotiations, but it was not a new phenomenon. Copyright piracy was already common in the 19th century, including in the USA, where weakened protection was offered to foreigners.[204] As strong copyright-based industries (such as the software, music industry and the motion picture industry) developed in the USA and became more vulnerable to piracy, the U.S. government turned into an active proponent of international enforcement rules.

Global trademark counterfeiting has been fostered in the last 20 years by advances in technology and the globalization of the economy. Though originally ignored because of the poor quality of copies, trademark counterfeiting increased dramatically since the late 1960s, and became a major concern for trademark-based industries. The U.S. industry, for instance, has claimed, and continues to do so despite the adoption of TRIPS, billions of dollars in losses[205] due to counterfeiting and other infringements of the rights provided in TRIPS, particularly due to the continued development of new technologies, such as the Internet, and the accompanying greater ease with which piracy and counterfeiting can be accomplished.[206]

The economics of litigation shapes the effective scope of IPR protection. Rights that title holders are unable to defend are worthless.[207] Though enforcement measures are, in principle, available to all IPRs holders, high litigation costs, as noted above, may constitute a deterrent to their effective use by individual right holders and small and medium enterprises (SMEs). For this reason, patents have been found of little relevance to the majority of SMEs as a means of appropriation of returns on innovation.[208]

It is also important to note that, like in other areas of TRIPS, a balanced approach is necessary in the application of Part III. While enforcement rules should ensure the protection of the legitimate interests of right holders, they should also protect against possible abuses. Patent suits, in particular, may be misused to

---

[203] In the United States, for instance, anywhere from 5 to 15% of all videos rented are counterfeit. See Paradise, p. 135.

[204] "[T]he early Americans were notorious for pirating English literary works. New York City became the piracy centre of the world. The English were powerless, because under the U.S. Copyright Act of 1790 only American nationals were afforded copyright protection. Book piracy produced revenue and culture for the early Americans. The works of Charles Dickens were freely pirated" (Paradise, p. 131). See also Doron S. Ben-Atar, *Trade Secrets: Intellectual Piracy and the Origins of American Industrial Power*, Yale University Press, New Haven & London 2004; B. Zorina Khan, *Does Copyright Piracy Pay? The Effects of US International Copyright Laws on the Market for Books, 1790–1920*. National Bureau of Economic Research Working Paper W10271, 2004.

[205] See Pury Tang, *The social and economic effects of counterfeiting*, IPI, London 2001.

[206] See, e.g., *The USA-Singapore Free Trade Agreement*.

[207] See, e.g., Barton, 1995, p. 163.

[208] See, e.g., Carlos Correa, *Do small and medium enterprises benefit from patent protection?*, in Carlo Pietrobelli and Árni Sverrisson (eds.), *Linking Local and Global Economies. Organisation, Technology and Export Opportunities for SMEs*, Routledge, London and New York 2003.

impede legitimate competition.[209] The weak infrastructure available in patent granting offices to examine patent applications, and the low standards applied to assess inventive step, permit the grant of patents which are often found invalid when subject to a more rigorous scrutiny in courts. While in some developed countries the abusive use or misuse of patents may lead to antitrust sanctions,[210] in most developing countries there are no rules to control strategic or "sham"[211] litigation practices.

In sum, while implementing Part III Members should carefully balance all interests at stake, including the right holders' interest in protecting his property against wilful infringement, the competitors' legitimate right to freely use or build on knowledge in the public domain and, more broadly, the society's interest in securing the functioning of efficient markets.

---

[209] For instance, a local company was sued in Chile in 1993 accused of infringement of a patent on a process for producing fluconazole (an important drug to treat certain types of meningitis, often associated to HIV infection). The title-holder obtained a preliminary injunction to ban the commercialization of the drug of the alleged infringer, which allowed the patent holder to effectively exclude competition for several years, during which the price of the corresponding medicine increased significantly. The case, however, was finally dismissed, since no infringement was found.

[210] See, for instance, the U.S. Supreme Court decision in *Walker Process Equipment Inc. vs. Food Machinery & Chemical Corp.* (1965) and subsequent case law on antitrust liability when there is an attempt to enforce invalid patents. See, e.g., Arun Chandra, *Antitrust liability for enforcing a fraudulent patent in the United States*, Patent World, April 1999. See also J. H. Reichmann, with C. Hasenzahl, *Nonvoluntary Licensing of Patented Inventions: The Law and Practice of the United States*, forthcoming at <http://www.ictsd.org/iprsonline/unctadictsd/projectoutputs.htm#casestudies>.

[211] The doctrine on "sham" litigation applies in the USA when a lawsuit is baseless and there is an intent to use it as a tool for monopolization.

31: Transparency

Article 63   Transparency

1. Laws and regulations, and final judicial decisions and administrative rulings of general application, made effective by a Member pertaining to the subject matter of this Agreement (the availability, scope, acquisition, enforcement and prevention of the abuse of intellectual property rights) shall be published, or where such publication is not practicable made publicly available, in a national language, in such a manner as to enable governments and right holders to become acquainted with them. Agreements concerning the subject matter of this Agreement which are in force between the government or a governmental agency of a Member and the government or a governmental agency of another Member shall also be published.

2. Members shall notify the laws and regulations referred to in paragraph 1 to the Council for TRIPS in order to assist that Council in its review of the operation of this Agreement. The Council shall attempt to minimize the burden on Members in carrying out this obligation and may decide to waive the obligation to notify such laws and regulations directly to the Council if consultations with WIPO on the establishment of a common register containing these laws and regulations are successful. The Council shall also consider in this connection any action required regarding notifications pursuant to the obligations under this Agreement stemming from the provisions of Article 6ter of the Paris Convention (1967).

3. Each Member shall be prepared to supply, in response to a written request from another Member, information of the sort referred to in paragraph 1. A Member, having reason to believe that a specific judicial decision or administrative ruling or bilateral agreement in the area of intellectual property rights affects its rights under this Agreement, may also request in writing to be given access to or be informed in sufficient detail of such specific judicial decisions or administrative rulings or bilateral agreements.

4. Nothing in paragraphs 1, 2 and 3 shall require Members to disclose confidential information which would impede law enforcement or otherwise be contrary to the public interest or would prejudice the legitimate commercial interests of particular enterprises, public or private.

1. Introduction: terminology, definition and scope

The notion of transparency in Article 63 basically refers to the obligation of Members to provide other Members with information regarding the ways intellectual property is protected in their territories. This obligation is executed through official publications (paragraph 1), notifications to the TRIPS Council (paragraph 2), and bilateral requests for information and access (paragraph 3). It is subject to a security exception (paragraph 4).

In the context of international trade in IPR-protected goods and services, transparency of national IP legislation serves the purpose of making foreign economic operators familiar with the domestic rules, thus making international transactions in IPR-related products more predictable.

2. History of the provision

2.1 Situation pre-TRIPS

Transparency was a central element of the GATT 1947 system. The legal basis was Article X GATT 1947, which continues to apply to trade in goods under the new GATT 1994. Article X is divided into three paragraphs:

(a) Paragraph 1 contains Members' obligation to publish promptly all laws, regulations, judicial decisions and administrative rulings of general application that affect the subject matter of the GATT (trade in goods). The stated objective is to enable governments and traders to become acquainted with those new rules.

(b) Paragraph 2 stipulates that any rules of the kind referred to in paragraph 1, which render more burdensome the importation of goods, must not be enforced before they have been officially published according to paragraph 1.

(c) Paragraph 3 lays down certain requirements for the administration of the rules referred to in paragraph 1:

(aa) This administration has to be carried out in a uniform, impartial and reasonable manner.

(bb) Each Member must maintain or establish independent authorities for the review of administrative action relating to customs matters. Formal independence of the customs authority is not required as long as objectiveness and impartiality of the review are factually guaranteed.

2.2 Negotiating history

2.2.1 The Anell Draft

This draft[1] provided:

> "1.1.1 [National (73)] laws, regulations, judicial decisions and administrative rulings [of general application (86, 70, 74)] [of precedential value (73)], [and all

---

[1] See composite text of 23 July 1990, circulated by the Chairman (Lars E. R. Anell) of the TRIPS Negotiating Group, document MTN.GNG/NG11/W/76.

international agreements and decisions of international bodies (73)] [made effective by any PARTY, (70, 74)] pertaining to [the availability, scope, acquisition and enforcement of (68)] [the protection of (74)] intellectual property [rights (68, 74)] [laws (73)] (68, 70, 73, 74)] [the application of the principles and norms prescribed at points 9 and 11 of Part I and point 2A.1 of Part IV above (71)] shall be:

- published promptly by PARTIES. (73)
- [published, or where such publication is not practicable, (74)] made [publicly (74)] available [promptly (74)] in such a manner as to enable governments [of the PARTIES (74)] and [traders (68)] [other interested parties (74)] to become acquainted with them. (68, 74)
- shall be subject to the provisions of Article X of the General Agreement. (70)
- made publicly available in the official language of the PARTY adopting such texts and, shall be provided, upon request, to any other PARTY. (71)

1.1.2 Agreements concerning the protection of intellectual property rights which are in force between the government or governmental agency of any PARTY and the government or a governmental agency of any other PARTY to the Agreement shall also be published or made publicly available. The provision of this paragraph shall not require PARTIES to disclose confidential information which would impede law enforcement or otherwise be contrary to the public interest or would prejudice the legitimate commercial interests of particular enterprises, public or private. (74)

(Notification)

1.2A PARTIES shall notify the laws and regulations referred to above to the Committee on Trade Related Intellectual Property Rights in order to assist the Committee in its review of the operation of this Annex. The Committee shall enter into consultations with the World Intellectual Property Organisation in order to agree, if possible, on the establishment of a common register containing these laws and regulations. If these consultations are successful, the Committee may decide to waive the obligation to notify such laws and regulations directly to the Committee. (68)

1.2B.1 The Committee established under point 1B of Part VIII below shall ensure, in co-operation with the World Intellectual Property Organization and other international organizations, as appropriate, access to all international agreements, decisions of international bodies, national laws, regulations, judicial decisions and administrative rulings of a precedential value, related to the intellectual property laws of the PARTIES. (73)

1.2B.2 PARTIES shall promptly notify all international agreements, national laws and regulations, judicial decisions and administrative rulings of a precedential value relying upon an exception of the principles of National Treatment and Most-Favoured Nation Treatment through the Committee to the other PARTIES. (73)

1.2C PARTIES shall inform the TRIPS Committee, established under point 1C of Part VIII below, of any changes in their national laws and regulations concerning the protection of intellectual property rights (and any changes in their administration). PARTIES engaged in a special arrangement as stipulated in point 8B.2C.2 of Part II above shall inform the TRIPS Committee of the conclusion of such a special arrangement together with an outline of its contents. (74)

(Information on Request)

1.3A A PARTY, having reason to believe that a specific judicial decision, administrative ruling or bilateral agreement in the area of intellectual property rights affects its rights under this Annex, may request in writing to be given access to or be informed in sufficient detail of such specific judicial decisions and administrative rulings or bilateral agreement. (68)

1.3B PARTIES shall, upon request from other PARTIES, provide information as promptly and as comprehensively as possible concerning application and administration of their national laws and regulations related to the protection of intellectual property rights. PARTIES shall notify the TRIPS Committee of the request and the provision of such information and shall provide the same information, when requested by other PARTIES, to the TRIPS Committee. (74)"

At the time of the Anell Draft, the details of the publication requirement were quite controversial, as indicated by the heavily bracketed text of paragraph 1.1.1. As to the notification requirement, the proposal under 1.2B.1 did not refer to any notification to the "TRIPS Committee" (i.e., what later became the TRIPS Council) of IPR-related laws. Instead, it proposed that the TRIPS Committee "shall ensure" in cooperation with WIPO, access to IPR-related national and international laws. This language is much stronger than the corresponding proposal under 1.2A, which in very careful terms ("enter into negotiations", "to agree, if possible, on the establishment") refers to cooperation with WIPO.

2.2.2 The Brussels Draft

With respect to transparency, this draft[2] was essentially similar to the final Uruguay Round text, thus indicating that at this stage of the negotiations, there was no longer much controversy about the necessity of the publication and notification requirements. The language of Article 63.1 draws on Article X:1 of GATT 1947 (see above) and in that sense is not new.

3. Possible interpretations

3.1 Article 63.1

---

1. Laws and regulations, and final judicial decisions and administrative rulings of general application, made effective by a Member pertaining to the subject matter of this Agreement (the availability, scope, acquisition, enforcement and prevention of the abuse of intellectual property rights) shall be published, or where such publication is not practicable made publicly available, in a national language, in such a manner as to enable governments and right holders to become acquainted with them. Agreements concerning the subject matter of this Agreement which are in force between the government or a governmental agency of a Member and the government or a governmental agency of another Member shall also be published.

---

[2] Document MTN.TNC/W/35/Rev. 1 of 3 December 1990.

This paragraph contains the basic principle, i.e., the obligation of Members to make known to the other Members their IPR-related rules. The objective is to keep foreign governments and private right holders informed about possible changes in a Member's legislation on intellectual property rights in order to ensure and contribute to a stable and predictable legal environment.[3] However, it follows from the terms "made effective" that the obligation to notify arises only after the respective act has entered into force. An obligation to notify pure draft regulations would probably conflict with the sovereign discretion of Members' decision-making bodies.

The obligation to publish applies to IPR-related laws, regulations, final judicial decisions and administrative rulings of general application, as well as to IPR-related bilateral or regional agreements. As indicated by the first sentence of the first paragraph, the publication requirement is not limited to rules on IPRs as such, but applies also to any rules with respect to their acquisition, enforcement and abuse prevention.

3.1.1 Laws
In the sense used in this provision, "laws" should be understood as enforceable rules of general application promulgated by parliamentary or legislative bodies, as distinguished from "regulations" adopted by administrative agencies.

3.1.2 Regulations
The term "regulation" could be understood in a very general sense, encompassing all sorts of rules, *inter alia* laws as referred to above. However, Article 63.1 refers to laws "and" regulations, thus indicating that those terms should be distinguished from each other.

Regulations, like laws, are acts of general application (see above). Unlike laws, however, regulations are not passed by a legislative body, but originate in the administration. Regulations are often more detailed than laws. The legislature may choose not to provide a high level of detail in a law, but to authorize the executive administration to implement the law by means of regulations. Typically regulations do not undergo the same constitutionally mandated adoption procedures as laws (i.e., majority voting in parliament, including possible conciliation committees) and may be more appropriate to deal with a rapidly changing environment.

3.1.3 Final judicial decisions
To complete the picture of how IP is handled in a given WTO Member, not only acts of the legislative and the executive powers, but also of the third power, the judiciary, have to be published in case they are final.[4] In common law jurisdictions, judicial decisions have a precedential effect, thus influencing posterior jurisprudence, which is not the case in continental law countries. Final judicial decisions

---

[3] Thus, the ultimate goal of this basic obligation to notify TRIPS-related rules can be described as to stimulate the trade in IPRs-protected goods by contributing to the predictability of the trading system.

[4] Note that it is not clear from the language of Article 63.1 whether the obligations to publish encompasses *any* final judicial decision, or just those that are *of general application*. The latter qualification clearly applies to administrative rulings.

are an important indication of the approach a society takes toward the protection of IP and the extent to which rights holders' interests prevail or not over the general interest in the availability of IPR-affected goods or services.

The question when a judicial decision is "final" may be rather complex. In some legal systems, an essentially equivalent claim may be pursued in different parts of the judicial system (e.g., civil, administrative or constitutional) so that the finality of a decision in one area may be questioned in another. The issue of when appeals are exhausted even within a single court hierarchy is not always easily resolved. However, for most purposes a decision should be considered final when the highest court with responsibility for the subject matter has rendered a decision in the case (which may include rejecting the hearing of an appeal), or when the time period for filing an appeal from a decision by a lower court has expired without notice of appeal. Thus, a final decision in a case may be the decision of a court of a lower instance that is not subject to any further appeal, according to domestic law.[5] In other words, "final" decisions do not necessarily have to emanate from the highest instance of the judiciary.

3.1.4 Administrative rulings of general application

Next to regulations (see above), administrative rulings are the second instrument of the executive power that is subject to the publication requirement, provided they are of general application. The term "administrative rulings of general application" derives directly from the GATT 1947 and can still be found under Article X.1 of the GATT 1994. It has been interpreted by a WTO panel as follows:

> "We note that Article X:1 of GATT 1994, which also uses the language "of general application", includes "administrative rulings" in its scope. The mere fact that the restraint at issue was an administrative order does not prevent us from concluding that the restraint was a measure of general application. Nor does the fact that it was a country-specific measure exclude the possibility of it being a measure of general application. *If, for instance, the restraint was addressed to a specific company or applied to a specific shipment, it would not have qualified as a measure of general application.* However, to the extent that the restraint affects an *unidentified number of economic operators*, including domestic and foreign producers, we find it to be a measure of general application."[6] (emphasis added)

The Appellate Body confirmed this interpretation by stating that:

> "The Panel found that the safeguard restraint measure imposed by the United States is "a measure of general application" within the contemplation of Article X:2. We agree with this finding. While the restraint measure was addressed to particular, i.e., named, exporting Members, including Appellant Costa Rica, as contemplated by Article 6.4, ATC, *we note that the measure did not try to become specific as to the individual persons or entities* engaged in exporting the specified

---

[5] For instance, in Germany until 2002 certain rulings of the civil courts of second instance could not be appealed, despite the existence, in general, of a third instance.

[6] See *United States – Restrictions on Imports of Cotton and Man-made Fibre Underwear*, Report of the Panel of 8 November 1996, WTO document WT/DS24/R, at para. 7.65.

textile or clothing items to the importing Member and hence affected by the proposed restraint."[7] (part of the emphasis added)

As illustrated by the above decisions, a characteristic element of an "administrative measure of general application" is that it is addressed to an unlimited number of (natural or juridical) persons. However, the same is true in the case of administrative "regulations" that also fall under Article 63.1 (see above). Thus, these notions cannot be distinguished by looking at the respective circles of addressees. In that sense, both regulations and administrative rulings are of a general character (as opposed to administrative acts that address one or several particular individuals). However, there is another element in respect of which the two instruments do differ: this is the number of cases to which the measure applies. A regulation is like a law (the only difference being its different origin, see above), generally applying to an unlimited number of economic operators, and also to an unlimited number of cases. Typically a regulation addresses an unlimited number of situations in the abstract, providing a particular consequence whenever certain factual requirements are met. In this sense, the regulation precedes the actual cases to which it will then be applied. By contrast, a "ruling" within the meaning of Article 63.1 (and Article X GATT) is a reaction to something that has already happened. It therefore concerns the particular facts of one specific case (even though it is not limited to a particular addressee).

This may be illustrated by the example of the above-mentioned case *United States – Restrictions on Imports of Cotton and Man-made Fibre Underwear*. The measure at issue was considered an administrative ruling, not a regulation. It concerned a transitional safeguard measure in respect of cotton and man-made fibre underwear imports from Costa Rica.[8] This restriction specifically addressed the particular case of imports of a number of defined products into the United States. It was valid for a limited (but renewable) period of 12 months, and it was a reaction to a particular situation (in which the total number of cotton imports from certain countries was considered harmful to the U.S. domestic cotton industry). The measure did not apply to an unlimited number of cases, but was based on a comparison of the actual figures on cotton imports and domestic production.[9] It was a reaction to the calculated ratio of imported and domestically made products (which allegedly seriously damaged the domestic industry).

3.1.5 Agreements

IPR-related agreements in force between one Member's government or government agency and another Member's government or government agency also have to be published. Economic operators and governments in other Members are thus given the opportunity to be updated on the current developments of IP protection outside their territories. This is important with respect to the most-favoured nation obligation (MFN): according to Article 4, any IPR-related advantage, favour,

---

[7] See *United States – Restrictions on Imports of Cotton and Man-made Fibre Underwear*, Report of the Appellate Body of 10 February 1997, WTO document WT/DS24/AB/R, p. 19.

[8] For an overview of the facts of this case, see the Report of the Appellate Body, p. 2 *et seq.*

[9] See paras. 2.8 and 2.9 of the panel report.

privilege or immunity granted by a Member to the nationals of any other country shall be accorded immediately and unconditionally to the nationals of all other Members. Thus, if two or more Members agree on certain forms of IP protection that go beyond the minimum standards of TRIPS, these Members have to grant the same preferences to nationals from all other WTO Members. The publication requirement in this context serves the purpose of informing third country nationals of their rights arising from IPR-related agreements.

3.2 Article 63.2

2. Members shall notify the laws and regulations referred to in paragraph 1 to the Council for TRIPS in order to assist that Council in its review of the operation of this Agreement. The Council shall attempt to minimize the burden on Members in carrying out this obligation and may decide to waive the obligation to notify such laws and regulations directly to the Council if consultations with WIPO on the establishment of a common register containing these laws and regulations are successful. The Council shall also consider in this connection any action required regarding notifications pursuant to the obligations under this Agreement stemming from the provisions of Article 6ter of the Paris Convention (1967).

This paragraph concerns a specific issue, i.e., the cooperation of Members with the Council for TRIPS.[10] The objective of the notification requirement is to assist the Council in its task to review the operation of TRIPS. The provision has to be read in conjunction with Article 68 TRIPS, according to which the Council shall monitor the operation of the Agreement, and Article 71.1 TRIPS, which authorizes the Council to review both the implementation of the TRIPS provisions by Members and the provisions of the Agreement itself.[11] In order to effectively comply with this task, the Council for TRIPS depends on the communication from Members of information on domestic IP laws and regulations. Review of domestic legislation in the Council in turn serves the objective of transparency and predictability, making governments acquainted with the rights their nationals enjoy in other Members. As opposed to the first paragraph, the notification requirement applies only to "laws and regulations", but not to final judicial decisions, administrative rulings of general application and bilateral or regional IPR-related agreements (see para. 1, above).

As to judicial decisions, they are not subject to the review because of the division of powers, which makes the judiciary independent of a national government's control.

As to administrative rulings, it should be noted that the transparency requirement under Article 63 is supposed to update Members on the general IP practice prevailing in other Members. Due to their limited scope (see above), administrative rulings may not be considered to represent the general IP practice of a

---

[10] For more details on the TRIPS Council, see Chapter 35.

[11] For more details on these provisions, see Chapters 35 (Article 68) and 37 (Article 71).

given Member. They respond to the particular facts of a specific case, and do not necessarily indicate a general line of action.

Finally, IPR-related bilateral or regional agreements do not fall under the notification requirement, because they are in any case not subject to a review by the Council. According to Article 71.1 of TRIPS, the Council's review exercise is limited to TRIPS and domestic implementing legislation. Consequently, the notification requirement under Article 63.2 covers only such legislation.

In order to ensure Members' cooperation with the Council (and thus the latter's efficiency in reviewing the implementation of TRIPS disciplines), the second sentence of the paragraph seeks to reduce the administrative burden placed on Members by the requirement laid down in the first sentence. Direct notification to the Council for TRIPS is not required if a Member has already notified its IPR-related laws and regulations to the International Bureau (secretariat) of WIPO and if transmission of this notification from the WIPO secretariat to the Council is assured through the establishment of a common register. This register was set up in an Agreement between WIPO and the WTO,[12] which lays down, *inter alia*, the right of the WTO to request free of charge copies of such notifications from WIPO.[13] Consequently, Members will have met their obligation under Article 63.2 not only by direct communication of their laws and regulations to the Council, but equally by notifying the WIPO secretariat, thus avoiding a double effort.

The last sentence of the paragraph relates to Article *6ter* of the Paris Convention. Under this provision, countries must communicate state emblems and official signs and hallmarks, flags etc. that they wish to protect. There is also the possibility of receiving objections with regard to these. In sum, the WIPO-WTO Cooperation Agreement provides that WIPO will act as a registration office and that communications under Article *6ter* shall constitute notification under Article 63.2.[14]

3.3 Article 63.3

> 3. Each Member shall be prepared to supply, in response to a written request from another Member, information of the sort referred to in paragraph 1. A Member, having reason to believe that a specific judicial decision or administrative ruling or bilateral agreement in the area of intellectual property rights affects its rights under this Agreement, may also request in writing to be given access to or be informed in sufficient detail of such specific judicial decisions or administrative rulings or bilateral agreements.

This paragraph contains another specific application of the general transparency obligation under paragraph 1. It refers to two obligations. The first sentence completes the publication requirement of the first paragraph (see above). Members

[12] Agreement Between the World Intellectual Property Organization and the World Trade Organization, see at <*http://www.wto.org/english/tratop_e/trips_e/wtowip_e.htm*>.

[13] Article 2 (3) of the WIPO-WTO Agreement.

[14] Article 3 of the WIPO-WTO Agreement.

shall not only publish IPR-related laws, regulations, judicial decisions, administrative rulings and agreements; they shall also be ready to actively supply other Members with information on these matters. As opposed to paragraph 2, this obligation does not concern multilateral cooperation within the Council for TRIPS, but the bilateral relationship between two Members.

The second sentence appears to go beyond the mere obligation to provide information under the first sentence. It refers to Members' right to ask other Members to be given access to IP-related specific judicial decisions or administrative rulings or bilateral agreements that allegedly affect their rights under TRIPS. This provision somewhat complements the notification requirement under the second paragraph by referring to those instruments that are not covered by that requirement. However, the extent of the obligation under this sentence is not obvious: reference is made only to a Member's right to request access, but there is no express mentioning of a corresponding obligation of the requested Member to actually follow the request. By contrast, the first sentence expressly refers to the obligation to "supply... information". On the other hand, it should be noted that the judicial decisions, administrative rulings and bilateral agreements under consideration are in any case subject to the publication requirement under the first paragraph.

3.4 Article 63.4

> 4. Nothing in paragraphs 1, 2 and 3 shall require Members to disclose confidential information which would impede law enforcement or otherwise be contrary to the public interest or would prejudice the legitimate commercial interests of particular enterprises, public or private.

This last paragraph provides for the typical public interest exception by recognizing that there are certain areas where transparency may be unduly burdensome. The language of this provision is based on Article X:1 of the GATT 1994. Similar wording can also be found in Article XVII:4(d) GATT (State Trading Enterprises). As to the exception of "public interest", this is a very broad notion giving WTO Members substantial discretion to determine what they consider to fall under this term. The same is true for the "legitimate commercial interests" of enterprises.[15] As with other elements of the WTO agreements, a Member would be expected to exercise its discretion in this area in good faith so as to avoid abuse of the right.

In practice, paragraph 2 has turned out to be the most relevant provision contained in Article 63. This is due to the fact that the review exercise has proven to be the most important task of the Council for TRIPS.[16]

---

[15] It has been stated that the prejudice to these interests includes the damage to a firm's bargaining position. See *D. Gervais*, p. 246, fn. 50, referring to the fourth review under the Protocol of Accession on Trade with Hungary, Basic Instruments and Selected Documents (BISD) 29S/139-140.

[16] For details, see Chapter 35.

4. WTO jurisprudence

4.1 India – Patent Protection

In *India – Patent Protection for Pharmaceutical and Agricultural Chemical Products*,[17] the panel took the view that India had violated its obligation under Article 63 by failing to publish the details of its system for receiving and holding patent applications.[18] In fact, the Indian Patent Act of 1970 excluded pharmaceutical and agricultural chemical products from patent protection. Under TRIPS, India among others is authorized to delay product patent protection in these areas until 1 January 2005, but must provide for a system of registration of applications for such patents prior to that date ("mailbox system", Article 70.8).[19] In addition, countries benefiting from the above transitional period have to grant to patent applicants, prior to 1 January 2005, exclusive marketing rights (EMRs) in defined circumstances (see Article 70.8).[20]

With a view to meeting its obligations under Article 70.8 and 9, the Indian Government promulgated in 1994 the Patents Ordinance to amend the 1970 Patents Act until the entry into force of a corresponding parliamentary law. In accordance with Article 70.8 and 9, this Ordinance provided for the filing and handling of patent applications for pharmaceutical and agricultural chemical products prior to the date as of which India would have to implement TRIPS rules on product patent protection. The Ordinance also provided for the grant of EMRs for patent applicants. However, at the time this transitory Ordinance lapsed in 1995, the Indian Parliament had not been able to conclude its discussions on a law amending the 1970 Patents Act, so that at that time, there was no legal basis in India for the operation of the mailbox system and the granting of EMRs. In order to ensure consistency with Article 70.8 and 9, the Indian executive authorities decided to instruct the patent offices to continue the application of these two instruments. However, no public notice of this administrative decision was issued, nor was it communicated to the TRIPS Council. The only public statement in this matter made on behalf of the Indian government was a written response by the Minister of Industry to a question asked by a Member of the Indian Parliament. The Minister confirmed that the mailbox system continued to apply on the sole basis of the administrative decision.[21]

In reaction to the U.S. complaint, India advanced two major substantive arguments.[22] First, it argued that the transitional provision of Article 65.2 also covered the obligation under Article 63, which would consequently not apply before 2000.

---

[17] WTO document WT/DS50/R (Report by the Panel) [hereinafter *India – Patent Protection*]. The report was later reversed by the Appellate Body on procedural grounds. See WTO document WT/DS50/AB/R (Report of the Appellate Body), at paras. 85–96.

[18] Note that the dispute concerned predominantly the alleged violations by India of Articles 70.8 and 9. For more details on this dispute, see Chapter 36, Section 4.

[19] See in detail Chapters 33 and 36.

[20] Ibid.

[21] See para. 2.7 of the panel report.

[22] India also relied on a procedural argument concerning the scope of jurisdiction of the Panel. This does not directly concern Article 63, though, and is therefore irrelevant for the purposes of this chapter.

Second, India contended that the obligation under Article 63.1 did not apply to single administrative acts of the kind at issue, because those were not laws and regulations or administrative rulings of general application within the meaning of Article 63.1.[23]

The panel rejected both arguments. With respect to the first argument, it observed:

"0.1 The issue before the Panel is whether this exemption should be understood to cover the transparency obligations under Article 63 or whether such a procedural obligation to publish and notify national laws and regulations should be understood as becoming applicable at the time that a Member is obliged to start applying a substantive provision of the TRIPS Agreement, i.e., that the timing of the transparency obligation is a function of the timing of the substantive obligation. In the former case, India would not be under an obligation to publish and notify, as from 1 January 1995, laws and regulations giving effect to the requirements of Article 70.8(a). In examining this matter, we note that the TRIPS Agreement contains a range of procedural and institutional provisions, relating not only to transparency but also to dispute settlement, the establishment of the Council for TRIPS and international cooperation, which have to be understood, and have been understood in the practice of the Council for TRIPS, as applying either from 1 January 1995 or from the time that the corresponding substantive provision has to be met consistently with the provisions of Part VI and Article 70. An example is Part V of the TRIPS Agreement on "Dispute Prevention and Settlement", which includes both transparency provisions (Article 63) and dispute settlement provisions (Article 64). If transparency provisions were not applicable to India by virtue of Article 65.2, then the logical conclusion would be that dispute settlement provisions are equally not applicable. This clearly cannot be the case and we reject the Indian argument on this point.

0.2 We also note that the WTO Members have confirmed this understanding in the actions taken by the Council for TRIPS. The Council has considered Article 63.2 as requiring that "as of the time that a Member is obliged to start applying a provision of the TRIPS Agreement, the corresponding laws and regulations shall be notified without delay".[24] Moreover, the Preparatory Committee for the World Trade Organization, which met in 1994, noted that "one substantive obligation, Article 70.8, which comes into force as of the date of entry into force of the WTO Agreement was referred to and there was acceptance that, under Article 63.2, national laws and regulations should be notified as of the time that the corresponding substantive obligation applies. [...]"

Turning to the second of the above arguments, the panel made clear that *any* mechanism for receiving mailbox applications constitutes a measure of "general application" in the sense of Article 63.1, whether made effective by law or through administrative practices. The panel considered that India had not met its

---

[23] See para. 4.22, last indent of the panel report.

[24] *Procedures for Notification of, and Possible Establishment of a Common Register of, National Laws and Regulations under Article 63.2*, Decision of the Council for TRIPS of 21 November 1995 (see document IP/C/2).

obligation under Article 65.1 to make this measure publicly available, because a written answer from the government to a question posed by a Member of Parliament could not be considered as a sufficient means of publicity within the meaning of Article 63.[25] Consequently, India was held to have acted inconsistently with Article 63.1.

Since India had not notified its administrative measures to the TRIPS Council, the panel also stated an infringement of Article 63.2.[26]

It is important to note that the Appellate Body reversed the panel's findings regarding Article 63 on procedural grounds (i.e., the United States had not included a claim based on Article 63 in its request for establishment of a panel and such claim was not included in the panel's terms of reference). In light of the AB's rejection of other parts of the panel's legal analysis in this case, the foregoing legal analysis should be treated with some caution.

4.2 United States – Restrictions on Imports of Cotton and Man-made Fibre Underwear

As noted above, the panel in *United States – Restrictions on Imports of Cotton and Man-made Fibre Underwear* analysed the term "administrative rulings of general application" under Article X:1 of the GATT 1994.[27] Since Article 63.2 contains the same term, the panel's analysis is also relevant in the context of that provision (see Section 3).

4.3 EC – Protection of Trademarks and GIs

Following separate requests by Australia[28] and the USA,[29] the WTO Dispute Settlement Body (DSB) at its meeting on 2 October 2003 established a single panel[30] to examine complaints with respect to EC Council Regulation (EEC) No. 2081/92 of 14 July 1992[31] on the protection of geographical indications and designations of origin for agricultural products and foodstuffs. The complaints are based, *inter alia*, on alleged violations of Articles 63.1 and 63.3. The complainants contend that the above EC Regulation is not applied in a transparent manner.[32]

---

[25] Para. 7.48.

[26] See para. 7.49.

[27] See report of the panel of 8 November 1996, WTO document WT/DS24/R. Note that the Appellate Body upheld the panel's interpretation.

[28] WT/DS290/18 of 19 August 2003.

[29] WT/DS174/20 of 19 August 2003.

[30] *European Communities – Protection of Trademarks and Geographical Indications for Agricultural Products and Foodstuffs* [hereinafter *EC – Protection of Trademarks and GIs*], WT/DS174/21 and WT/DS290/19 of 24 February 2004, Constitution of the Panel Established at the Requests of the United States and Australia.

[31] See above, Section 2.1.

[32] See the U.S. request for the establishment of a panel, p. 1, and the Australian request at p. 2. Note that the same complaint was also based on other TRIPS provisions, in particular those relating to the national treatment and most-favoured nation treatment obligations and to the protection of trademarks and geographical indications. See Chapters 4, 14 and 15.

5. Relationship with other international instruments

5.1 WTO Agreements

There is no expressly defined relationship between Article 63 and the provisions on transparency in other WTO Agreements.[33]

5.2 Other international instruments

6. New developments

6.1 National laws

6.2 International instruments

On 21 November 1995, the Council for TRIPS adopted a Decision on "Procedures for Notification of, and Possible Establishment of a Common Register of National Laws and Regulations Under Article 63.2."[34] This Decision basically establishes rules in respect of two categories of national laws and regulations: first, those dedicated to IPRs as such; and second, *inter alia* those "not dedicated to intellectual property rights as such but which nonetheless pertain to the availability, scope, acquisition, enforcement and prevention of abuse of intellectual property rights (notably laws and regulations in the areas of enforcement and the prevention of abusive practices)."[35] In respect of the latter category, the Council also adopted a Decision setting up a format (i.e., a model) for their listing.[36] Finally, the Council agreed on a Decision establishing a checklist of issues on enforcement of IPRs.[37]

6.3 Regional and bilateral contexts

6.4 Proposals for review

So far, there have been no proposals to modify Article 63.

7. Comments, including economic and social implications

The requirement for Members to make their IP legislation available to other Members contributes to the predictability and security of international trade relations.

---

[33] For example, Articles X GATT (see above), III GATS, 7 SPS Agreement, 10 TBT Agreement, and XVII of the Agreement on Government Procurement. Also, the WTO Trade Policy Review Mechanism (Annex 3 to the WTO Agreement) is based on the idea of enhancing transparency.

[34] See WTO document IP/C/2 of 30 November 1995.

[35] Ibid., para. 9.

[36] See IP/C/4 of 30 November 1995.

[37] See IP/C/5 of 30 November 1995.

32: Dispute Settlement

1. Introduction: terminology, definition and scope

1.1 General observations concerning the WTO Dispute Settlement System

In the WTO context, the need for dispute settlement arises whenever a Member considers that any benefits accruing to it under the WTO agreements are being impaired through measures taken by another Member.[38] Since the WTO agreements are based on the idea of reciprocal and mutually advantageous economic

---

[38] See Article 3:3 of the Understanding on Rules and Procedures Governing the Settlement of Disputes (DSU) as well as Article XXIII:1 GATT. Note that a Member has broad discretion in deciding to bring a case against another Member under the DSU, as is made clear by the Appellate Body in *EC – Regime for the Importation, Sale and Distribution of Bananas* [hereinafter *EC – bananas*] WTO document WT/DS27/AB/R, para. 135, basing its argumentation on the language in Article XXIII GATT 1994 ("If any Contracting Party should consider that any benefit [. . .] is being nullified or impaired [. . .]") and Article 3:7 DSU ("Before bringing a case, a Member shall exercise its judgement as to whether action under these procedures would be fruitful.").

benefits through trade liberalization,[39] it is the principal objective of WTO dispute settlement to reinstall, as quickly as possible, a situation in which every Member can fully enjoy the benefits it is entitled to under the various agreements.[40] For the realization of this objective, the DSU provides a very detailed and rules-based procedure, which consists of several different phases, each of which is subject to mandatory time frames. In the following, this procedure will briefly be described. The methods of interpretation under the DSU are discussed in Annex 1 at the end of this chapter.

1.2 Overview of the procedure

1.2.1 The consultations
As a first step, the Members involved in the dispute are supposed to enter into consultations, which consist of legally non-binding, diplomatic negotiations with a view to reaching a mutually satisfactory solution. In this context, the traditional methods of good offices, conciliation and mediation may be employed.[41]

1.2.2 The panel phase
In case the consultations do not arrive at a solution within 60 days, or in case the party complained against refuses to engage in consultations in the first place, the complaining party may request the WTO's Dispute Settlement Body (DSB) to establish a dispute settlement panel.[42] The defendant may refuse such a request once, but if the request is renewed, it may only be rejected through the DSB by unanimity (i.e., including the Member that requested the establishment of the panel).[43] For this reason, the complainant may be said to have an actual right to a panel once the time limits described above have elapsed. The panels are normally composed of three independent trade experts,[44] who examine the dispute

---

[39] See the third para. of the preamble of the Marrakesh Agreement as well as Article 3:3 DSU, which stresses the importance for the effective functioning of the WTO of the "maintenance of a proper balance between the rights and obligations of Members".

[40] See Article 3:7 DSU.

[41] This is expressly provided for by Article 5 DSU. Requests for consultations shall be notified to the WTO's Dispute Settlement Body (DSB), containing the reason for the request, i.e., an identification of the measure at issue and an indication of the legal basis for the complaint, Article 4:4 DSU.

[42] See Article 4:7 DSU, which also refers to the possibility to request the establishment of a panel *before* the 60 days have passed if both parties jointly consider that the consultations have failed.

[43] See Article 6:1 of the DSU: "If the complaining party so requests, a panel shall be established at the latest at the DSB meeting following that at which the request first appears as an item on the DSB's agenda, unless at that meeting the DSB decides by consensus not to establish a panel." [footnote omitted]

[44] See Article 8:3 DSU, which in principle excludes the participation as panelists of individuals whose governments are parties to the dispute or third parties. Under current WTO practice, the panel's chair is usually given to an experienced panelist, who will be assisted by a Geneva-based negotiator and an academic with a legal background (see also Article 8:1 DSU). The nomination of the panelists is up to the parties, who in more than 50% of the cases cannot find three persons who are acceptable to both of them. In that case, it is the WTO Director-General who appoints the panelists, in consultation with the chairman of the DSB and the chairman of the relevant Council or Committee, as stipulated in Article 8:7 DSU.

according to certain terms of reference[45] in order to find out whether the measures complained of have actually impaired the complaining party's benefits.[46] The terms of reference serve the important function of defining the scope of the panel's jurisdiction. The panel will only have the authority to adjudicate on those provisions explicitly mentioned in the terms of reference.[47] In order for a claim to be inserted into the terms of reference, it must have been referred to in the request for the establishment of the panel (see above).[48] This highlights the importance of a careful drafting of the request for a panel. Indirectly, this request determines the scope of the later panel report. According to Article 6:2 DSU, the request has to contain an identification of the specific measure complained of as well as the legal basis which the complainant considers affected.[49] It is important to note that the complaining party may at any time request the panel to suspend the proceedings.[50] Once the panel has come to its conclusions, it issues an interim report to the parties, including both the descriptive section and the panel's findings and

---

[45] The terms of reference are either the standard ones expressly provided for in Article 7:1 DSU, or specific ones agreed upon by the parties, Article 7:1 DSU.

[46] This is usually the case if a violation of any WTO obligation on the part of the party complained against is established. For further details, see below, Section 3.

[47] See Appellate Body Report on *India – Patent Protection for Pharmaceutical and Agricultural Chemical Products*, WT/DS50/AB/R, para. 92: "[. . .] A panel may consider only those claims that it has the authority to consider under its terms of reference. A panel cannot assume jurisdiction that it does not have. In this case, Article 63 was not within the Panel's jurisdiction, as defined by its terms of reference. Therefore, the Panel had no authority to consider the alternative claim by the United States under Article 63."

[48] See Appellate Body Report on *Brazil – Measures Affecting Desiccated Coconut*, (fn. 9), p. 22. See also the Appellate Body Report on *India – Patent Protection for Pharmaceutical and Agricultural Chemical Products*, WT/DS50/AB/R, paras. 88, 89 (partly quoting the *EC – bananas* decision): "[. . .] Article 6.2 of the DSU requires that the claims, but not the arguments, must all be specified sufficiently in the request for the establishment of a panel in order to allow the defending party and any third parties to know the legal basis of the complaint. If a claim is not specified in the request for the establishment of a panel, then a faulty request cannot be subsequently "cured" by a complaining party's argumentation in its first written submission to the panel or in any other submission or statement made later in the panel proceeding. Thus, a claim must be included in the request for the establishment of a panel in order to come within a panel's terms of reference in a given case [. . .]"

[49] According to the Appellate Body in the *EC – bananas* case, the complaining party, in order to meet the requirements in Article 6:2 DSU, has to "list the provisions of the Agreements alleged to have been violated without setting out detailed arguments as to which specific aspects of the measures at issue related to which specific provisions of those agreements. In our view, there is a significant difference between the *claims* identified in the request for establishment of a panel, which establish the panel's terms of reference under Article 7 of the DSU, and the *arguments* supporting those claims, which are set out and progressively clarified in the first written submissions, the rebuttal submissions and the first and second panel meetings with the parties." (para. 141 of the report; emphasis in the original). Consequently, panels may not, in their examination, go beyond the legal claims expressly advanced by the complainant. However, they are by no means bound by the legal arguments put forward by the parties.

[50] Article 12:12 DSU. This might be the result of successful diplomatic consultations between the parties (see above), which may be continued while the panel process proceeds, Article 5:5 DSU. If the panel's work has been suspended for more than 12 months, the authority for establishment of the panel shall lapse, Article 12:12 DSU.

conclusions.[51] The parties may request the review of precise aspects of the interim report, after which the panel circulates the final report to the parties and to the DSB (i.e., all other WTO Members). The report is then adopted by the DSB, unless a party to the dispute appeals to the Appellate Body (or in the unlikely event that the DSB decides by consensus not to adopt the report).[52] According to Article 20 DSU, the period between the date of establishment of the panel by the DSB and the date the DSB considers the panel or appellate report for adoption shall as a general rule not exceed nine months where the panel report is not appealed or 12 months where the report is appealed.

1.2.3 The appellate phase

Contrary to the panels, whose members are appointed on a case-by-case basis, the Appellate Body is a standing organ whose task is limited to the review of legal issues.[53] Its members are persons of recognized authority, with demonstrated expertise in law, international trade and the subject matter of the WTO agreements in general.[54] The appellate review is subject to tight deadlines: in general it is supposed not to exceed 60 days from the date a party to the dispute formally notifies its decision to appeal to the date the Appellate Body circulates its report. Even in exceptional circumstances the final report must absolutely be circulated to the DSB within 90 days. In case the AB reaches the conclusion that the measure at issue is inconsistent with a WTO obligation, it recommends that the Member concerned bring the measure into conformity with that obligation.[55] Here again, the report is adopted by the DSB (unless in the unlikely event of a consensus among Members not to adopt it).[56]

1.2.4 The implementation of DSB decisions

Once adopted, the phase of implementation of the panel or Appellate Body report begins. 30 days after the adoption, the Member concerned shall inform the DSB of its intentions in respect of implementation of the report.[57] The DSB monitors the effective implementation by that Member.[58] The original panel can be re-established in order to assess whether the implementing measures taken by the defendant meet the relevant WTO obligations.[59]

---

[51] See Article 15, paras. 2 and 3 DSU. For the panel work's timetable, see para. 12 of the Working Procedures (Appendix 3 to the DSU) and the graphical overview in Box 1 at the end of this section, below.

[52] Article 16:4 DSU. This also requires the consent of the winning party not to adopt the report.

[53] See Article 17, in particular paras. 1 and 6.

[54] Article 17:3 DSU.

[55] See Article 19:1 DSU.

[56] Article 17:14 DSU, again implying the consent of the winning party.

[57] Article 21:3 DSU.

[58] The Member concerned is granted a "reasonable period of time" to implement the rulings of the DSB. This period can be determined through binding arbitration, Article 21:3 c) DSU.

[59] Article 21:5 DSU. This procedure was employed, for instance, against the EC's implementing measures in the *EC – bananas* case (concerning the WTO-irregularity of the EC's import regime for bananas).

1.2.5 The case of non-compliance

In case the Member concerned fails to implement an adopted report, the parties to the dispute shall enter into negotiations with a view to developing mutually acceptable compensation.[60]

If these negotiations fail, any party having invoked the dispute settlement procedures may request authorization from the DSB to suspend the application to the Member concerned of concessions or other obligations under the WTO Agreements.[61] Should the complaining party consider the suspension of concessions from the same sector or the same multilateral agreement as that in which a violation has been found to be impracticable or ineffective, it may also, on some carefully defined conditions, suspend concessions or other obligations under another of the covered agreements ("cross-retaliation").[62] Thus, if country "A" is found to be in contravention of TRIPS by nullifying benefits accruing to country "B" in the area of intellectual property, the latter country could suspend concessions to country "A" in another area such as tariffs or services.

1.2.6 The scope of the dispute settlement procedure

Finally, it should be noted that with respect to trade in goods and services, the above procedure is not only applicable where the complaining party asserts a violation of any WTO obligation ("violation complaints", see Article XXIII:1 a GATT), but comes equally into play when one Member's measure, without violating any WTO rule, still results in factual nullification or impairment of benefits accruing to another Member ("non-violation complaints", see Article XXIII:1 b GATT; Article XXIII:3 GATS), or when the "existence of any other situation" leads to the same result ("situation" complaints, see Article XXIII:1 c GATT). The peculiarity of the notion of non-violation is that it does not, like many other international treaties, focus on the legality of an action, but rather on the protection of expectations arising from reciprocal tariff and market access concessions (in the GATT context)[63] or from a Member's specific commitments (in the GATS context). These might be affected even by measures that are not prohibited by GATT/GATS rules and therefore have to be addressed through non-violation complaints.[64] Finally, "situation" complaints were introduced in the GATT 1947 as a catch-all category to deal with unforeseen new developments.[65] In the TRIPS context, neither non-violation nor "situation" complaints are currently applied (see below, Section 3).

---

[60] Article 22:2 DSU. Note that the full implementation of the DSB rulings is the preferred option; see Article 22:1 DSU.

[61] Article 22:2 DSU.

[62] See Article 22:3 DSU with further details.

[63] See Petersmann, *The GATT/WTO Dispute Settlement System. International Law, International Organizations and Dispute Settlement*, Kluwer Publishers, 1997, p. 73 and especially pp. 142 ff [hereinafter Petersmann]. According to this author, this approach goes back to the pre-World War II U.S. bilateral trade agreements.

[64] For example, some domestic legislation of country "A" which, even though fully respecting the WTO most-favoured-nation (MFN) and national treatment obligations, influences in a negative way the conditions of sale for certain products irrespective of their origin. Country B, which has negotiated lower tariffs with country A in order to enhance marketing opportunities for its products, considers these efforts frustrated and seeks to challenge country A's domestic legislation.

[65] In this context, Petersmann (p. 73) mentions worldwide monetary crises or depressions with widespread unemployment.

Box 1 Graphical overview of the WTO dispute settlement procedure[66]

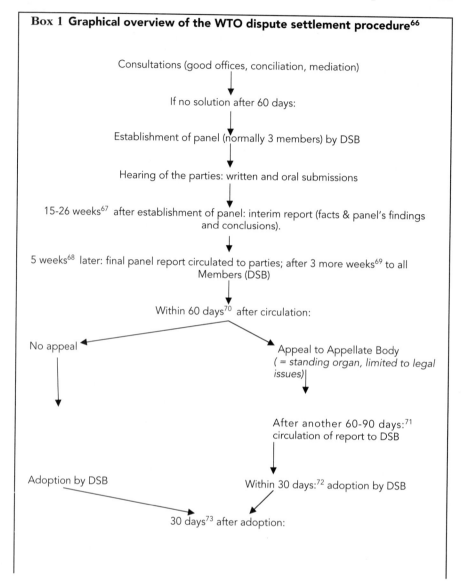

Consultations (good offices, conciliation, mediation)

If no solution after 60 days:

Establishment of panel (normally 3 members) by DSB

Hearing of the parties: written and oral submissions

15-26 weeks[67] after establishment of panel: interim report (facts & panel's findings and conclusions).

5 weeks[68] later: final panel report circulated to parties; after 3 more weeks[69] to all Members (DSB)

Within 60 days[70] after circulation:

No appeal

Appeal to Appellate Body (= standing organ, limited to legal issues)

After another 60-90 days:[71] circulation of report to DSB

Adoption by DSB   Within 30 days:[72] adoption by DSB

30 days[73] after adoption:

[66] The concept of this overview is modeled upon Gervais, *The TRIPS Agreement. Drafting History and Analysis*, London, 1998, p. 251.

[67] See para. 12 (g) of Appendix 3 (Working Procedures) to the DSU.

[68] Ibid., para. 12 (j).

[69] Ibid., para. 12 (k).

[70] Article 16:4 DSU.

[71] Article 17:5 DSU.

[72] Article 17:14 DSU.

[73] Article 21:3 DSU.

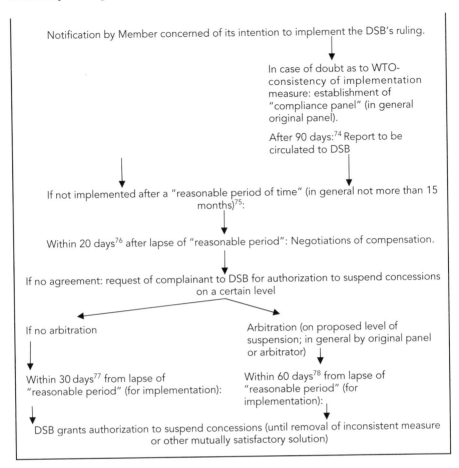

Notification by Member concerned of its intention to implement the DSB's ruling.

In case of doubt as to WTO-consistency of implementation measure: establishment of "compliance panel" (in general original panel).

After 90 days:[74] Report to be circulated to DSB

If not implemented after a "reasonable period of time" (in general not more than 15 months)[75]:

Within 20 days[76] after lapse of "reasonable period": Negotiations of compensation.

If no agreement: request of complainant to DSB for authorization to suspend concessions on a certain level

If no arbitration

Within 30 days[77] from lapse of "reasonable period" (for implementation):

Arbitration (on proposed level of suspension; in general by original panel or arbitrator)

Within 60 days[78] from lapse of "reasonable period" (for implementation):

DSB grants authorization to suspend concessions (until removal of inconsistent measure or other mutually satisfactory solution)

2. History of the provision

2.1 Situation pre-TRIPS

It is usually thought that intellectual property rights and related dispute settlement were brought into the ambit of the GATT/WTO for the first time after the conclusion of the Uruguay Round. This is largely true in the sense that TRIPS introduces, for the first time, common minimum standards for the protection of intellectual property rights. The international treaties for the protection of IPRs (e.g., the Paris Convention), on their part, provide certain intellectual property protection

---

[74] Article 21:5 DSU.

[75] To be determined upon proposal of the Member concerned, through mutual agreement between the parties or through binding arbitration. See Article 21:3 DSU, in particular lit. (c).

[76] Article 22:2 DSU.

[77] Article 22:6 DSU (first sentence).

[78] Article 22:6 DSU (third sentence).

disciplines, but they do not contain their own dispute settlement mechanism. Instead, reference is made to the settlement of disputes before the International Court of Justice (ICJ).[79]

The dispute settlement system under the GATT 1947 was considerably different from that of the WTO. The detailed DSU did not exist, but parties relied on the rather general provisions of Article XXIII GATT.[80] This Article contained both provisions on consultations (in paragraph 1) and dispute settlement (in paragraph 2). The major difference consists of the shift of the dispute settlement system from a diplomatic forum to a rules-based, court-like procedure.[81]

This "legalization" of the dispute settlement system is best illustrated by the fact that under the GATT 1947, panel reports could only be adopted if all Contracting Parties, including the losing one, agreed to do so. This was in fact the exact opposite of the quasi-automatic adoption of reports under the DSU of the WTO. In other words, under the old GATT, it used to be considerably easier for the party found in violation of a GATT obligation to block the adoption of the report. It sufficed simply to vote against its adoption in the GATT Council, whereas nowadays a Member would have to convince every other Member, including the complainant, to vote against the adoption of the report.[82]

The second major element of the "legalization" of the dispute settlement system referred to above is the creation of the Appellate Body. Under the GATT 1947, by contrast, there was no means of reviewing the legal aspects of panel recommendations. Due to the quasi-automatic adoption of panel reports under the DSU, the possibility of review is more important than under the GATT 1947.

As far as the GATT 1947 case law is concerned, one of the most famous disputes was indeed one involving intellectual property rights, albeit indirectly. This was the panel report on *United States: Section 337 of the Tariff Act of 1930*.[83] This dispute brought by the EC against the USA concerned the claim by the EC that for the purpose of enforcing intellectual property rights in the USA, the imported

---

[79] See for instance Article 28(1) of the Paris Convention and Article 33(1) of the Berne Convention, both of which read in their relevant part: "(1) Any dispute between two or more countries of the Union concerning the interpretation or application of this Convention, not settled by negotiation, may, by any one of the countries concerned, be brought before the International Court of Justice by application in conformity with the Statute of the Court, unless the countries concerned agree on some other method of settlement. [. . .]"

[80] Article XXIII GATT continues to be relevant for the WTO dispute settlement procedure: Article 3:1 DSU makes it clear that Members adhere to the principles developed under that provision and that the DSU in fact further elaborates and modifies Articles XXII, XXIII GATT.

[81] Note that this shift did not occur all at once with the adoption of the DSU. Rather, it took place gradually under the GATT 1947. By the time of the Uruguay Round most of the current DSU rules were part of existing customary practice, except for the establishment of the Appellate Body and the quasi-automatic adoption of dispute settlement rulings, see below.

[82] This is what is usually referred to as "negative consensus" under the DSU in contrast to the "positive consensus" under Article XXIII GATT 1947. The same kind of automaticity now applies to the establishment of a panel (see above, Section 1), which was not the case under the GATT 1947 before the 1989 improvements of the GATT dispute settlement procedures. See Petersmann, p. 182.

[83] Basic Instruments and Selected Documents (BISD) 36S/345, adopted by the GATT Contracting Parties on 7 November 1989.

goods were subjected to a separate and distinct procedure solely by virtue of their non-American origin. The EC therefore considered that the different rules applicable under Section 337 amounted to a denial of national treatment within the meaning of Article III of the GATT and could not be justified under the intellectual property-related provision of Article XX (d) GATT. After a detailed examination of the issues raised by both parties, the panel came to the conclusion that Section 337 of the U.S. Tariff Act of 1930 was in fact inconsistent with Article III:4 GATT (national treatment) and that this inconsistency could not be justified under Article XX (d) GATT.

As to the different sorts of complaints under Article XXIII GATT, over 90 percent of the actual disputes during the era of the GATT 1947 were violation complaints over nullification and impairment, whereas the number of non-violation complaints over nullification and impairment as well as of situation complaints was negligible.[84]

2.2 Negotiating history

At least until 1989, most developing countries were opposed to the inclusion of intellectual property rights on the Uruguay Round negotiating agenda. In addition, Members under the new DSU would be unable to block the adoption of panel or Appellate Body reports. For these reasons developing countries were rather hesitant, during the Uruguay Round negotiations, about applying the dispute settlement mechanism to any eventual agreement on intellectual property rights. Their idea was to keep this subject outside the scope of the new dispute settlement mechanism, mainly because a number of developing countries were not fully aware of the consequences. In particular, they rejected the possibility of enforceable dispute settlement decisions as a threat to national sovereignty. Such concerns were exacerbated by the fact that, just before the Uruguay Round negotiations, developing countries had faced considerable pressure to conform to strong IPRs by means of changing their domestic legislation.[85] The TRIPS negotiations on dispute settlement must be seen against this background.

2.2.1 The Anell Draft

"2A PARTIES shall make reasonable efforts within the framework of their constitutional systems to inform and, upon request, to consult with the other PARTIES on possible changes in their intellectual property right laws and regulations, and in the administration of such laws and regulations relevant to the operation of this Annex. (68)

2B.1 Whenever laws, regulations and practices relevant to, and affecting, the protection and enforcement of intellectual property rights are under review or

---

[84] See Petersmann, pp. 73/74. As to the notions of non-violation and "situation" complaints, see above, Section 1 and below, Section 3.

[85] It was particularly in the period from 1984 to 1990 that the USA threatened to apply higher tariffs to products from those developing countries that would not adopt higher intellectual property standards.

intended to be introduced by a PARTY to this Agreement, such PARTY shall

• publish, in an official GATT language, a notice in a publication at an early appropriate stage that it proposes to introduce, amend or abolish legislation or regulation; (73)

• promptly provide, upon request, draft legislation and draft regulations, including explanatory materials, to such PARTIES; (73)

• allow, without discrimination, reasonable time of no less than [X] months for other PARTIES to submit comments in writing on the basis of the General Agreement; (73)

• consult with interested PARTIES, upon request, on the basis of comments submitted. (73)

2B.2 None of these obligations is meant to limit the sovereignty of PARTIES to legislate, regulate and adjudicate in conformity with international obligations. (73)

3. Dispute Settlement (68, 71, 73); Consultation, Dispute Settlement (74)

3A Contracting parties agree that in the area of trade related intellectual property rights covered by this Annex they shall, in relation to each other, abide by the dispute settlement rules and procedures of the General Agreement, and the recommendations, rulings and decisions of the CONTRACTING PARTIES, and not have recourse in relation to other contracting parties to unilaterally decided economic measures of any kind. Furthermore, they undertake to modify and administer their domestic legislation and related procedures in a manner ensuring the conformity of all measures taken thereunder with the above commitment. (68)

3B (i) Disputes arising under this PART shall be settled on the basis of Article XXII and Article XXIII and in accordance with the consolidated instrument [name]. (73)

(ii) Non-compliance with obligations under this PART shall be deemed to cause nullification and impairment of advantages and benefits accruing under the General Agreement on Tariffs and Trade. (73)

(iii) PARTIES shall refrain from taking any measure against another PARTY other than those provided for under the rules on dispute settlement within the General Agreement on Tariffs and Trade. (73)

3C A PARTY shall not suspend, or threaten to suspend, its obligations under the Agreement without abiding by the procedures for settlement of disputes set out in this section. (74)

3D.1 Consultations (71)

(a) Where a dispute arises concerning the interpretation or implementation of any provision of this Agreement, a PARTY may bring the matter to the attention of another PARTY and request the latter to enter into consultations with it. (71)

(b) The PARTY so requested shall provide promptly an adequate opportunity for the requested consultations. (71)

(c) PARTIES engaged in consultations shall attempt to reach, within a reasonable period of time, a mutually satisfactory solution to the dispute. (71)

3D.2 Other Means of Settlement (71)

If a mutually satisfactory solution is not reached within a reasonable period of time through the consultations referred to at point 3D.1, PARTIES to the dispute may agree to resort to other means designed to lead to an amicable settlement of their dispute, such as good offices, conciliation, mediation and arbitration. (71)

(See also point 11 of Part II above)"[86]

This draft in paragraph 2 referred to measures that should be taken in an effort to make domestic IP laws transparent to other countries. This provision on transparency was later separated from the rules on dispute settlement. Under the current version of TRIPS, there is an independent provision on transparency (Article 63).[87]

As far as the settlement of IPR-related disputes was concerned, the Anell Draft in paragraph 3 contained four different proposals (see above, 3A–D). In this context, two issues were of particular importance: whether there should be a dispute settlement system for trade-related IPRs in the first place; and the question of unilateral trade measures.

As to the former, proposals A and B both referred to the GATT 1947 dispute settlement system as the means of addressing TRIPS disputes. Proposal C also referred to "procedures for the settlement of disputes". By contrast, the D proposal did not contain any such reference. Instead, it was limited to consultations (D.1) and other non-binding means of settlement (D.2). The purpose of this proposal was to exclude IPRs from the scope of the GATT-like dispute settlement system.

As far as unilateral trade measures were concerned, proposal A made express reference to "unilaterally decided economic measures of any kind". These express terms were kept in the Brussels Draft (see below), but disappeared later on. The B and C proposals also subjected trade measures directed against other parties to the pertinent dispute settlement rules. The D proposal did not refer in any way to unilateral measures. As it intended to avoid binding dispute settlement, there was logically no way of strictly prohibiting such measures. They could only be addressed through consultations and other non-binding means (see above).

2.2.2 The Brussels Draft

"PARTIES shall not have recourse in relation to other PARTIES to unilaterally decided economic measures of any kind. Furthermore, they undertake to modify and administer their domestic legislation and related procedures in a manner ensuring the conformity of all measures taken thereunder with the above commitment.

Note:

In regard to dispute settlement procedures, see the Annex to this text."[88]

[for a discussion of this Annex, see below]

The Brussels Draft reproduced part of the A proposal under the Anell Draft (see above, paragraph 3A). Like the latter, the Brussels Draft also had clear language

---

[86] Document MTN.GNG/NG11/W/76, of 23 July 1990.

[87] For details of this provision, see Chapter 31.

[88] Draft Final Act Embodying the Results of the Uruguay Round of Multilateral Trade Negotiations, Revision, Trade-Related Aspects of Intellectual Property Rights, Including Trade in Counterfeit Goods, MTN.TNC/W/35/Rev. 1, 3 Dec. 1990.

against unilateral measures and required those countries resorting to such practices to modify their domestic legislation in a manner ensuring the conformity of all action with the commitment not to resort to unilateral measures.[89]

As far as the applicability to trade-related IPRs was concerned, the Brussels text of December 1990 indicated clearly that there was no consensus on this issue. Thus, the Brussels text in an Annex (see above) provided three options. The first one was to make the dispute settlement procedures apply "as far as possible" but to put it outside the ambit of "cross-retaliation."[90] The second option was to admit the GATT-type panel procedure but without any trade sanctions. The TRIPS Committee (later "Council for TRIPS") was supposed to monitor the implementation of any ruling or recommendation by a panel. The third option (which was later adopted under TRIPS) was to bring trade-related IPRs fully under the binding dispute settlement of the Uruguay Round, including the recourse to cross-retaliation.

2.2.3 The Dunkel Draft

"Article 64

Dispute Settlement

The provisions of Articles XXII and XXIII of the General Agreement on Tariffs and Trade and the Understanding on Rules and Procedures Governing the Settlement of Disputes under Articles XXII and XXIII of the General Agreements on Tariffs and Trade as adopted by the CONTRACTING PARTIES shall apply to consultations and the settlement of disputes under this Agreement except as otherwise specifically provided herein. [footnote]

[Footnote:] This provision may need to be revised in the light of the outcome of work on the establishment of an Integrated Dispute Settlement Understanding under the Agreement Establishing the Multilateral Trade Organisation."[91]

Between the Brussels Draft of December 1990 and the Dunkel Draft of December 1991, there were further efforts on the part of industrialized countries to convince their developing country counterparts to agree to full coverage of dispute settlement with regard to TRIPS. When the GATT Director-General put forward his draft he laid emphasis on the point that this area was to be fully covered by the new dispute settlement system. In order to seek a modification of the

---

[89] Arguably, this was primarily aimed at the USA and its Section 301–310 legislation, according to which the U.S. Trade Representative (USTR) may determine, even before the conclusion of multilateral dispute settlement proceedings, that another WTO Member has not met its WTO obligations and may thus be exposed to U.S. trade sanctions. Note that in a later dispute, a WTO panel upheld Section 301–310 against EC claims of WTO-inconsistency (See *US – Sections 301–310 of the Trade Act of 1974* – Report of the panel of 22.12.1999, WTO document WT/DS 152/R). However, the panel made clear that the sole reason why it considered Section 301–310 as being in line with Article 23 of the DSU (i.e., the prohibition of certain unilateral action) was because through administrative measures, the statutory discretion of the USTR as described above was limited to the effect that the USTR would not be permitted to make any unilateral determinations before the exhaustion of DSU proceedings. The panel stressed that, should this limitation of the USTR's discretionary powers be lifted, Sections 301–310 would be rendered inconsistent with Article 23 of the DSU (paras. 7.126, 7.136).

[90] Thus, retaliatory action would have been possible only with respect to obligations under TRIPS, but not under other covered agreements.

[91] See document MTN.TNC/W/FA of 20 December 1991.

draft, a country had to assure consensus, which proved impossible for most, if not all, developing countries.[92] From the industrialized countries' point of view, the insistence on dispute settlement in the Dunkel Draft was only logical: it would have made no sense to adopt such an agreement and then leave it to Member countries to comply on a voluntary basis. What is important to note, though, is that the express reference to unilateral measures, included in the Brussels Draft, was absent in the Dunkel Draft. It was only later that some language which may be interpreted as being directed against unilateral measures (but without mentioning the word "unilateral") was incorporated in the DSU (Article 23) and in the Marrakesh Agreement establishing the WTO (Article XVI:4). It is particularly Article 23 DSU that can be considered as responding to developing countries' concerns about unilateral measures on the part of industrialized Members. This provision clearly establishes Members' obligation to have recourse to the DSU rules and procedures, and not to determine unilaterally whether another Member has nullified or impaired any benefits accruing under a WTO agreement.

Finally, the Dunkel Draft did not address the question of whether non-violation complaints[93] should apply to TRIPS. This issue only arose in the Legal Drafting Group in 1992–93. Some countries argued that TRIPS was substantially different from either the GATT tariff type commitments or the specific commitments undertaken by Members in the GATS context.[94] TRIPS was not about such commitments but about minimum standards. So, these countries took the view that non-violation should not apply to TRIPS at all, or at least it was not clear how non-violation would apply to TRIPS. The rationale behind this view was some Members' concern that the applicability of non-violation complaints to TRIPS might eventually lead to *de facto* intellectual property standards higher than those actually agreed to during the negotiations.[95]

Other Members, on the other hand, were concerned that the absence of non-violation complaints would enable governments to undermine their TRIPS obligations by resorting to lawful, but narrow interpretations of the TRIPS protection standards.[96] After discussing the matter thoroughly, parties agreed on a

---

[92] When introducing his draft, the GATT Director-General insisted that this was a "take it or leave it" document, thus requiring GATT Parties to support any modifications through unanimity.

[93] For a definition see above, Section 1.

[94] Note that the objective behind "non-violation complaints" in the GATT is to assure the benefits from reciprocal tariff concessions. See above, Section 1.

[95] Cottier/Nadakavukaren Schefer, *Non-Violation Complaints in WTO/GATT Dispute Settlement: Past, Present and Future* [hereinafter Cottier/Nadakavukaren Schefer], in: Petersmann (ed.), International Trade Law and the GATT/WTO Dispute Settlement System, London, The Hague, Boston, 1997, pp. 145 (156). Note that this position was not only taken by developing countries but also by the EC. The latter was concerned that its market access restrictions in the audio-visual sector might be challenged by the USA through non-violation complaints. See Abbott, *Dispute Settlement Under the WTO Agreement on Trade-Related Aspects of Intellectual Property Rights (TRIPS Agreement)*, draft paper for the UNCTAD Handbook on WTO Dispute Settlement, 2002, p. 32 [hereinafter Abbott, UNCTAD Handbook].

[96] Ibid. In the same context, see also Roessler, *The Concept of Nullification and Impairment in the Legal System of the World Trade Organization* [hereinafter Roessler], in: Petersmann (ed.), International Trade Law and the GATT/WTO Dispute Settlement System, London, The Hague,

moratorium concerning the applicability of non-violation to TRIPS. This compromise is reflected in the second paragraph of Article 64, which provides for a moratorium for five years during which non-violation shall not apply to TRIPS. Whether or not it applies after this period is a controversial issue.[97]

3. Possible interpretations

3.1 Violation complaints, Article 64.1

The provisions of Articles XXII and XXIII of GATT 1994 as elaborated and applied by the Dispute Settlement Understanding shall apply to consultations and the settlement of disputes under this Agreement except as otherwise specifically provided herein.

The part of Article XXIII GATT relevant for the present purpose reads:

"If any contracting party should consider that any benefit accruing to it directly or indirectly under this Agreement is being nullified or impaired or that the attainment of any objective of the Agreement is being impeded as the result of

(a) the failure of another contracting party to carry out its obligations under this Agreement, [...]"

On this basis, paragraph 1 of the same Article then provides for consultations between the parties, whereas paragraph 2 establishes the GATT 1947 dispute settlement system, on which the current and more detailed DSU is based.

The first paragraph of Article 64 clarifies that the dispute settlement mechanism as developed in the Uruguay Round will apply fully to the Agreement. The only exception to this is the issue of non-violation and its applicability to TRIPS, which is discussed below. Thus, Article 64.1 makes violation complaints applicable to the Agreement.

The full applicability of the DSU means that TRIPS is justiciable before the WTO. It is the automatic and binding character of the dispute settlement mechanism (see Section 1 above) which makes the provisions of TRIPS fully enforceable.

According to long-established GATT practice as confirmed by the Appellate Body,[98] violation complaints (Article XXIII:1 (a) GATT) follow the purpose of protecting Members' expectations as to the *competitive relationship* between their own and foreign products. In case this competitive relationship is upset, there is nullification or impairment of the benefits accruing to that Member

---

Boston, 1997, p. 125 (138), who gives the example of prohibitively high fees for patent registration or non-binding, purely informal state action as something not specifically covered by TRIPS. The same author, however, argues that such cases could be addressed as violation complaints.

[97] See below, Sections 3 and 7.

[98] See *India – Patent Protection for Pharmaceutical and Agricultural Chemical Products* – complaint by the United States, Report of the Appellate Body of 19 December 1997, WTO document WT/DS50/AB/R [hereinafter *India – Patent Protection*].

whose nationals, products or services suffer from a deterioration of competitive conditions.[99]

The competitive relationship is reflected in the legal obligations as set up by GATT/WTO rules.[100] It is upset

- if one Member violates one of its WTO obligations (e.g., the national treatment principle, or a substantive intellectual property right),

- if this violation cannot be justified (e.g., through one of the substantive exceptions such as Articles 30 in the area of patents; or Article XX GATT 1994 in a trade in goods-context)

- and if, in addition, this has an adverse impact on the Member whose right has been violated (Article 3:8 DSU).

For one Member to convince a panel or the Appellate Body that the competitive relationship has been upset (i.e., that there is a nullification of its competitive benefits), it needs to provide evidence for an infringement of a WTO rule on the part of the respondent. Once this infringement is established, there is a *prima facie* presumption that the respondent has nullified or impaired benefits accruing to the complainant.[101] In the language of Article 3:8, second sentence of the DSU:

> "This means that there is normally a presumption that a breach of the rules has an adverse impact on other Members parties to that covered agreement, and in such cases, it shall be up to the Member against whom the complaint has been brought to rebut the charge."[102]

It follows from the language of this provision that a "breach of the rules" alone is not sufficient, but that there has to be an "adverse impact" of the respondent's action on the complaining Members. This "adverse impact" consists of a nullification or impairment of the competitive relationship. However, as the cited provision stipulates, the complaining Member is not required to demonstrate this nullification/impairment. All it needs to show is that there is a violation of a

---

[99] In other words, in the context of violation complaints, the "benefits" in the sense of Article 3:3 of the DSU and Article XXIII:1 of the GATT 1994 consist of an undistorted competitive relationship between domestic and foreign intellectual property right holders, products or services.

[100] E.g., the disciplines of most-favoured-nation treatment and national treatment, assuring equal treatment of equal products and thus a fair competitive relationship between domestic and imported goods/services. In the TRIPS context, it is Article 3 (national treatment) and Article 4 (most-favoured-nation treatment) that reflect the right of Members to have their nationals abroad treated as favourably as the nationals from other Members. Also, the obligation to respect substantive IPRs such as patents and trademarks is part of the competitive relationship under TRIPS as established in the Uruguay Round negotiations. Substantive IPR rules, for instance on patents, make sure that inventors can still market their products, despite high R&D costs. Note that, according to the TRIPS preamble, intellectual property rights are private rights. Therefore, TRIPS obligations on substantive IPRs apply not only *vis-à-vis* other states, but equally with respect to individuals.

[101] See Article 3:8. (first sentence) of the DSU.

[102] Before the entry into force of the DSU, the same rule applied to the GATT 1947, as decided by the Contracting Parties in 1960, see GATT, BISD, 11S/99-100.

WTO rule, which again results in an automatic presumption of nullification or impairment.[103]

If the respondent intends to remove the presumption of nullification or impairment, it is up to the respondent to rebut the charge.[104] It has to show that despite a violation of WTO law, there is no "adverse impact"[105] on the complainant.

At this point, GATT/WTO practice differs considerably from the language of Article 3:8 DSU or the analogous previous decision of the GATT Contracting Parties. In the history of GATT/WTO dispute settlement, there has not been a single case where the respondent could successfully rebut the presumption of impairment by denying an adverse impact of its measure on other Parties/Members.[106] In other words, despite the language employed in Article 3:8 DSU, the presumption established by the violation of a WTO rule is practically not rebuttable, it is in fact an irrefutable presumption.[107]

Consequently, the only way for the respondent to win the case is to convince the panel or the Appellate Body that there is no violation in the first place; either by addressing the asserted violation as such, or by providing evidence that the violation is justified under an exception clause. Once an unjustifiable violation

---

[103] Note that, in order for the violation to be established and to activate the presumption of nullification/impairment as stipulated under Article 3:8 of the DSU, the violation must not be justifiable under any of the exception clauses of the pertinent agreement, such as TRIPS Article 30 (general exception to patent rights), or Article 31 (compulsory licenses). In other words, the responding Member has the possibility of preventing the presumption of nullification or impairment by showing that the infringement of WTO law is justified. Only if the panel/Appellate Body comes to the conclusion that the measure at issue is not justifiable, the infringement is actually established and the presumption under Article 3:8 DSU comes into play.

[104] See Article 3:8 of the DSU as cited above.

[105] See Article 3:8 of the DSU.

[106] See Roessler, pp. 125 (127 ff.), with several examples of GATT panel reports.

[107] Idem., p. 129, quoting the panel in US – Taxes on Petroleum and Certain Imported Substances (Superfund case), BISD 34S/156–158. For an explanation of this approach, this author points out, inter alia, parts of the same report (154–159), where the panel states that a violation of GATT Article III:2 first sentence results ipso facto in a nullification of benefits, rejecting the U.S. argument of a missing negative trade impact of the measure at issue. This view was confirmed by the Appellate Body in EC – Regime for the Importation, Sale and Distribution of Bananas, WT/DS27/AB/R, at section IV, C, 6 (d), para. 253. The reluctance to take into account any demonstration of an absence of an "adverse impact" (see Article 3:8 DSU) can be explained by the fact that the GATT and now the WTO do not protect any expectations concerning export volumes, but expectations with respect to the competitive relationship between domestic and imported products (or, in the case of GATS and TRIPS, between national and foreign service suppliers or intellectual property rights holders). For example, if Member A violates a WTO rule to the detriment of Member B, the mere fact that there is a violation upsets the competitive relationship established by this rule (e.g., the most-favoured-nation or national treatment, or substantive rules on intellectual property protection). In that case, the conditions of competition for products or nationals from Member B have certainly been negatively affected, even though this might not right away be mirrored in actual trade volumes. Trade volumes might not be affected by actions that only minimally disfavour foreign production, because foreign producers might consider it worthwhile to continue selling the same amount of products on a given market, in spite of slightly higher costs. However, the competitive conditions would always be modified to the detriment of the foreign IPR holder (or product or service supplier in a GATT or GATS context), because prices for products or services on the given market would be slightly lower for domestic rights holders. In other words, the "adverse impact" required in Article 3:8 of the DSU is caused by the violation itself, upsetting the carefully negotiated balance of competitive conditions as expressed in WTO rules.

has been established, previous GATT practice indicates that the respondent has no more possibilities to prevent the panel/Appellate Body from definitely affirming a case of nullification or impairment.[108]

Article 22:2 DSU provides for retaliatory action in the form of suspension of concessions if the defendant fails to bring the measure found to be inconsistent with a WTO agreement into compliance therewith. In case the inconsistency arises in the TRIPS area, several problematic issues requiring further thought have been observed.[109] These issues will be dealt with in the following paragraphs.

3.1.1 Retaliation in the same sector

As a general rule, retaliation will be authorized to take place in the same sector[110] where the TRIPS violation has occurred. For example, if Member A has failed to bring a national measure into conformity with the TRIPS provisions on patents, the affected Member B will be authorized, on the conditions laid down in Article 22:2 DSU, to equally disregard its TRIPS patent obligations with respect to nationals from Member A. However, neither TRIPS nor the DSU clarifies the exact scope of this retaliation. Thus, it is not clear what becomes of the patents that have been granted by Member B's authorities to nationals from Member A. For instance, many domestic producers manufacture the patented products without compensating the patent holder from Member A? In the case of trademarks, would the owner be refused the right to demand royalties for their utilization, and in addition, would he be refused the right to control the quality of his trademarked products when these are sold in the market of Member B? As to copyright, would it be legal, *after* the suspension has been lifted, to recopy without consent of the right holder those copies that could be made without the latter's consent *during* the period of suspension of the copyright?

3.1.2 Retaliation in a different sector or a different WTO Agreement

If the complaining party considers that retaliation in the same sector is not practicable or effective, it may seek the suspension of concessions or other obligations in other sectors under the same agreement (see Article 22:3(b) of the DSU). In case the complainant considers even this remedy to be impracticable or ineffective, and if it also considers that the circumstances are sufficiently serious, the complainant may seek to suspend concessions or other obligations under another WTO agreement covered by the DSU (see Article 22:3(c) of the DSU: note that it is

---

[108] Thus, the burden of proof first lies with the complainant, who has to show that the respondent has not respected a substantive WTO rule. In case the respondent intends to invoke an exception clause, the burden of showing that the requirements of the exception are met is shifted to the respondent. As to the burden of proof, see also the 1997 Appellate Body Report on *India – Woven Wool Shirts and Blouses*, WT/DS33/AB/R, under Section IV.

[109] See Abbott, *WTO Dispute Settlement and the Agreement on Trade-Related Aspects of Intellectual Property Rights* [hereinafter Abbott, *WTO Dispute Settlement*], in: Petersmann (ed.), International Trade Law and the GATT/WTO Dispute Settlement System, London, The Hague, Boston, 1997, p. 415 (432, 433).

[110] According to Article 22:3 (f) (iii) of the DSU, the term "sector" indicates one category of intellectual property rights covered under the TRIPS Agreement, such as section 1 (Copyright and Related Rights), section 2 (Trademarks), section 3 (Geographical Indications), etc.

up to the complainant to determine the seriousness of the situation that justifies retaliation under another agreement).

For example, the failure on the part of one Member (A) to bring its inconsistent measure into conformity with, for instance, the TRIPS patent provisions may be responded to by the suspension of concessions to Member A in the area of, for example, trademarks (i.e., a different TRIPS sector) or even trade in goods (i.e., a different WTO Agreement).[111]

This gives rise to the same problems as in the case of retaliation in the same sector (see above), but there is another particularly complicated issue in the case of cross-retaliation. According to Article 22:4 of the DSU, the level of the suspension of concessions authorized by the DSB shall be equivalent to the level of nullification or impairment.[112] For this purpose, the DSB has to make a factual assessment of the actual level of impairment caused by the defendant's measure and then ensure that the proposed retaliation does not go beyond this economic impact. Such assessment is a rather complex task, especially when the DSB has to compare the economic impacts of two measures in completely different areas such as, for instance, patents on the one hand and trade in bananas on the other. At this point, there is a risk of the retaliation having a disproportionately greater impact on the respondent than the original measure has on the complainant.[113]

3.2 Non-violation and situation complaints, Article 64.2 and 3

2. Subparagraphs 1 (b) and 1 (c) of Article XXIII of GATT 1994 shall not apply to the settlement of disputes under this Agreement for a period of five years from the date of entry into force of the WTO Agreement.

3. During the time period referred to in paragraph 2, the Council for TRIPS shall examine the scope and modalities for complaints of the type provided for under subparagraphs 1 (b) and 1 (c) of Article XXIII of GATT 1994 made pursuant to this Agreement, and submit its recommendations to the Ministerial Conference for approval. Any decision of the Ministerial Conference to approve

---

[111] According to Article 22:3 (b), (c), these two forms of retaliation may be authorized by the DSB if the complainant considers that the simple form of retaliation (see above) is not practicable or effective and that the circumstances are serious enough. The question whether it is the complainant's prerogative to determine if simple retaliation is practicable or effective is not clearly answered in the DSU. Article 22:6 DSU just authorizes the respondent to request the establishment of an arbitration panel in case "principles and procedures set forth in paragraph 3 [i.e., the requirements for the suspension of concessions] have not been followed". WTO jurisprudence has clarified that such an arbitration panel does have the authority to review and reverse the complainant's assessment of impracticability or ineffectiveness. The respective panel also ruled that cross-retaliation is only admissible to the extent that simple retaliation is insufficient to reach the level of nullification or impairment. See *EC – Regime for the Importation, Sale and Distribution of Bananas, Recourse to Article 22.6 DSU*, WTO documents WT/DS27/53, WT/DS27/ARB/ECU. In this case Ecuador, as the first developing country ever, was authorized to cross-retaliate against the EC and to suspend its obligations under the TRIPS Agreement in response to violations of the GATT 1994 by the EC. See in more detail below, Section 7.

[112] This level can be determined through binding arbitration, Article 22:6, 7 of the DSU.

[113] See Abbott, *WTO Dispute Settlement*, p. 433.

> such recommendations or to extend the period in paragraph 2 shall be made only by consensus, and approved recommendations shall be effective for all Members without further formal acceptance process.

Subparagraphs 1 (b) and 1 (c) of Article XXIII of the GATT 1994 provide that:

> "If any contracting party should consider that any benefit accruing to it directly or indirectly under this Agreement is being nullified or impaired or that the attainment of any objective of the Agreement is being impeded as the result of
>
> [...]
>
> (b) the application of another contracting party of any measure, whether or not it conflicts with the provisions of this Agreement, or
>
> (c) the existence of any other situation [...]"

On this basis, paragraph 1 of the same Article then provides for consultations between the parties, whereas paragraph 2 establishes the GATT 1947 dispute settlement system, on which the current and more detailed DSU is based.

Paragraph 2 of Article 64 TRIPS constitutes a limitation of paragraph 1, excluding (at least for a certain period) TRIPS from non-violation and situation complaints. In the following, the concepts of both remedies are explained in general terms (see 3.2.1, 3.2.2), before turning to the controversial issue of their application to TRIPS (see 3.2.3).

3.2.1 Non-violation complaints, Article XXIII:1 (b) of the GATT

Like under violation complaints, the cause of action in this context is the nullification or the impairment of benefits accruing to a Member under a covered agreement. Like under violation complaints, these benefits consist of a competitive relationship between domestic and imported products;[114] and like under violation complaints, nullification or impairment is caused by upsetting the competitive relationship between domestic and imported products.

The difference between the two remedies is that, under violation complaints, the competitive relationship is upset through the violation by one Member of a WTO obligation, whereas under non-violation complaints, this competitive relationship is upset through WTO-*consistent* action on the part of one Member, rendering the results of certain market access concessions made by that Member less beneficial for other Members.[115] Non-violation complaints are perceived as introducing the

---

[114] See v. Bogdandy, *The Non-Violation Procedure of Article XXIII:2 of GATT: Its Operational Rationale*, in: 26 Journal of World Trade 1992, 95 (98): "A benefit is a competitive relationship between a foreign and a domestic product, established by the binding of the relevant tariff position."

[115] See above, Section 1. Cottier/Nadakavukaren Schefer, p. 161, observe that WTO-consistent action giving rise to non-violation may consist of action as well as of non-action (non-kept promise). For the former, these authors cite the Panel in the *Australian Subsidy on Ammonium Sulphate* case (BISD II/188, adopted 3.3.1955); for the latter they refer to the panel in the *German Import Duties on Starch* case (BISD 3S/77, 1955). The same authors (on p. 160, quoting Petersmann) note that, even though the language used in the non-violation provisions (Article 26:1 of the DSU, Article XXIII:1(b) of the GATT: "any benefit accruing to it directly or indirectly") is broad and could theoretically cover the impairment of a multitude of various benefits, GATT panels have in practice limited non-violation complaints to market access related benefits expected from tariff

notion of "equity" to international trade relations in goods.[116] It is considered a valid cause of action if one Member by some purely domestic measure frustrates the legitimate expectations of other Members as to the competitive advantages their products can draw from a negotiated tariff concession. However, such legitimate expectations may not be invoked if the complainant could *anticipate*, at the time of negotiating the concession, the possible adoption of future domestic measures by the respondent that would cancel out the complainant's competitive advantage resulting from the negotiated concession.[117] This requirement serves the purpose of ensuring that non-violation complaints are actually used in case of the frustration of legitimate expectations and not merely on grounds of a negative economic development.[118]

Under the DSU, non-violation complaints are specifically dealt with in Article 26:1. According to this provision, non-violation complaints differ from violation complaints in three crucial respects:

a) The burden of proof (Article 26:1 (a) of the DSU)

Under violation complaints the complainant, having demonstrated an infringement of a WTO obligation on the part of the respondent, may take advantage of the *prima facie* presumption of nullification or impairment as stipulated in Article 3:8. DSU (see above). With respect to non-violation, Article 26:1 (a) requires that

> "the complaining party shall present a detailed justification in support of any complaint relating to a measure which does not conflict with the relevant covered agreement;"

This means that, as opposed to violation complaints, the nullification or impairment (of benefits) itself has to be shown by the complainant.[119] There is no *prima*

---

concessions in the context of Article II GATT. In other words, non-violation typically comes into play when the negotiated balance of tariff concessions between Members is upset by one Member's domestic measures, as confirmed by the Appellate Body in *India – Patent Protection*, paragraphs 36–42. For a detailed survey of GATT case law on non-violation complaints, see Petersmann, pp. 150 ff.

[116] According to Cottier/Nadakavukaren Schefer, p. 151, the introduction to international trade relations of non-violation complaints as an expression of equity (protection of legitimate expectations) was necessitated by two factors: First, trade agreements of the 1920s were exclusively concerned with tariff reductions and quantitative restrictions and did not address domestic measures such as taxes, subsidies and technical regulations, which could thus easily be employed to undermine binding tariff concessions. Second, legal positivism prevailing before World War II rendered impossible any attempts to integrate equity into international trade law: states could do anything which was not expressly ruled out in the text of an agreement, even if such action frustrated other parties' legitimate expectations as to the competitive situation of their products in foreign markets. Since the frustration of legitimate expectations could thus not be addressed as a violation of international law, a specific remedy for state action that did not violate the law had to be introduced.

[117] This qualification has been emphasized by a number of GATT panels, see Cottier/Nadakavukaren Schefer, p. 162, quoting the *Australian Ammonium Sulphate* case.

[118] Cottier/Nadakavukaren Schefer, p. 163. The same authors note on p. 160 that non-violation complaints are a means of protecting a balanced competitive relationship, but never a Member's expectation of a concrete amount of trade flows.

[119] Idem (p. 162), quoting, *inter alia*, the panel in *Japan – Trade in Semi-Conductors*, BISD 35S/116 (1989).

facie presumption to assist him in this task as under violation complaints (see Article 3:8 DSU). On the contrary, it is the complaining Member itself that has to set up the *prima facie* presumption of nullification or impairment. In order to do so, it is not sufficient for the complainant to merely assert a frustration of legitimate expectations. On the contrary, it must provide detailed reasoning as to why the disputed action on the part of the respondent has come unexpectedly.[120] It is only after this presumption of nullification or impairment has been successfully established by the complainant that the respondent has to take action, i.e. rebut the presumption by showing that the measure at issue was in fact foreseeable.

b) The available remedies (Article 26:1 (b) of the DSU)

Under violation complaints Article 22:1 DSU provides for the obligation of the respondent to withdraw the illegal measure. With respect to non-violation complaints, on the other hand, Article 26.1 (b) stipulates:

> "where a measure has been found to nullify or impair benefits under, or impede the attainment of objectives, of the relevant covered agreement without violation thereof, there is no obligation to withdraw the measure. However, in such cases, the panel or the Appellate Body shall recommend that the Member concerned make a mutually satisfactory adjustment;"

This means that the remedies available under non-violation complaints are limited to the negotiation of a mutually satisfactory compensation or, in case this proves impossible, to the right of the complainant to ask authorization from the DSB to suspend the application to the respondent of concessions under the WTO agreements. Contrary to violation complaints, the respondent is under no obligation to withdraw the measure.

c) The final character of compensation (Article 26:1 (d) of the DSU)

In the case of violation complaints, Article 22:1 of the DSU provides that the withdrawal of the (WTO-inconsistent) measure at issue should normally be given priority over the other available remedies. This means that compensation or the suspension of concessions are only temporary measures.[121] Since under non-violation complaints, the respondent is not obliged to withdraw the (WTO-consistent) measure (see above), Article 26:1 (d) of the DSU provides that

---

[120] See the 1990 panel report on *US Restrictions on Importation of Sugar and Sugar-Containing Products Applied Under the 1955 Waiver and Under the Headnote to the Schedule of Tariff Concessions*, BISD 37S, para. 5.21: "A complaint under Article XXIII:1(b) must therefore be supported by a justification that goes beyond a mere characterization of the measure at issue as inconsistent with the General Agreement", quoted by Cottier/Nadakavukaren Schefer, p. 159. However, the same authors point to the fact that not all GATT panels have always been equally strict: "While in some cases the panels set out an extensive account of why the complainant would reasonably have expected an adherence to the status quo, in others the panels seem almost to assume a nullification of the benefits by the mere action of the respondent."

[121] Article 22.1 of the DSU provides: "Compensation and the suspension of concessions or other obligations are temporary measures available in the event that the recommendations and rulings are not implemented within a reasonable period of time. However, neither compensation nor the suspension of concessions or other obligations is preferred to full implementation of a recommendation to bring a measure into conformity with the covered agreements. Compensation is voluntary and, if granted, shall be consistent with the covered agreements."

mutually agreed compensation may constitute a *final* measure for the settlement of disputes.

3.2.2 Situation complaints, Article XXIII:1 (c) of the GATT

This remedy (for the text of the provision, see above) has rarely been argued and has never constituted the basis of a decision throughout the entire GATT 1947 and WTO history of dispute settlement. This has led to the observation that situation complaints "seem to have fallen into disuse."[122]

The principal reason why neither the GATT Contracting Parties nor WTO Members have relied on this remedy is its impracticability. According to Article 26.2 of the DSU, panel reports based on a situation complaint may only be adopted by consensus, which would require the approval by the responding Member.

In addition, this complaint may only be invoked if neither violation nor non-violation complaints apply, as indicated by the language employed in the same provision.[123] It appears difficult to define the exact scope of application of such remedy. It has been observed that situation complaints refer to a general depression, bringing with it the collapse of commodity prices, high unemployment, etc.[124] Since a given Member cannot be held responsible for a general economic slowdown, situation complaints may be invoked against a given Member only if that Member could have prevented the economic crisis from arising in the first place, but failed to take the necessary measures.[125] In addition to that, the complaining Member would have to show that it could reasonably expect the respondent to apply those measures.

The application of these requirements in practice would be likely to cause considerable problems with respect to legal certainty. A panel would have to assess whether the complainant could reasonably have expected the respondent to take concrete measures to prevent a certain situation from arising. In this context, there is no agreement between WTO Members concerning any criteria for government intervention.[126]

For these reasons, it appears more than doubtful that situation complaints will become more relevant in the future.[127]

---

[122] Petersmann, p. 74, welcomes this development, considering the unclear concept behind the notion of "situation" complaints.

[123] Article 26:2 of the DSU reads in relevant part: "Where the provisions of paragraph 1(c) of Article XXIII of GATT 1994 are applicable to a covered agreement, a panel may only make rulings and recommendations where a party considers that any benefit accruing to it directly or indirectly under the relevant covered agreement is being nullified or impaired or the attainment of any objective of that Agreement is being impeded *as a result of the existence of any situation other than those to which the provisions of paragraphs 1(a) and 1(b) of Article XXIII of GATT 1994 are applicable.*" (emphasis added).

[124] See Petersmann, above, Section 1. For the following, see Roessler, p. 139.

[125] Roessler, noting that in case the crisis is brought about by the *application* of a measure (as opposed to the *failure* to apply a measure, see above), recourse to "situation" complaints would not be necessary, because this case would already be covered by non-violation complaints (Article XXIII:1(b) refers explicitly to "the application... of any measure...").

[126] Ibid.

[127] Considering their limited relevance, situation complaints will not be dealt with separately in this book. In the following, references to non-violation complaints will equally cover situation complaints.

3.2.3 Are non-violation complaints applicable in the TRIPS context?

Non-violation complaints as outlined above have traditionally applied in the GATT context. If applicable in the TRIPS context, non-violation complaints could be brought against another Member's domestic measures as allegedly depriving the market access advantages that right holders could reasonably expect as a result of the Uruguay Round negotiations on TRIPS. For instance, the recourse by Member countries to price controls, particularly in the area of pharmaceutical products, could be considered as impairing marketing expectations on the part of foreign patent holders.[128]

3.2.3.1 Interpretation of the language in Article 64 TRIPS. During the Uruguay Round negotiations, delegations were split over the question whether non-violation complaints should also apply to TRIPS (see Section 2.2 above). This division of opinions persisting, the final text of Article 64 paragraphs 2 and 3 appears to accommodate both views, due to its vague language. Recall that these provisions read as follows:

> "2. Subparagraphs 1(b) and 1(c) of Article XXIII of GATT 1994 shall not apply to the settlement of disputes under this Agreement for a period of five years from the date of entry into force of the WTO Agreement.
>
> 3. During the time period referred to in paragraph 2, the Council for TRIPS shall examine the scope and modalities for complaints of the type provided for under subparagraphs 1(b) and 1(c) of Article XXIII of GATT 1994 made pursuant to this Agreement, and submit its recommendations to the Ministerial Conference for approval. Any decision of the Ministerial Conference to approve such recommendations or to extend the period in paragraph 2 shall be made only by consensus, and approved recommendations shall be effective for all Members without further formal acceptance process."

As made clear by paragraph 2, non-violation complaints did not apply to TRIPS for a period of five years from the date of entry into force of the WTO Agreement, i.e., until 1 January 2000. During this period, the Council for TRIPS was supposed to make recommendations to the Ministerial Conference with respect to the scope and modalities for non-violation complaints under TRIPS (paragraph 3). However, Members of the Council for TRIPS have so far been unable to make such recommendations. Under this new scenario, which was not foreseen by the drafters of TRIPS, the meaning of paragraph 3 and its relationship with paragraph 2 is not entirely clear.[129] Paragraph 2 seems to imply that once the five-year moratorium on dispute settlement has lapsed, non-violation complaints should automatically apply. This seems to be supported by the requirement under paragraph 3 that the dispute settlement moratorium may only be extended by consensus.

---

[128] For more examples of possible non-violation complaints and their implications for developing countries see below, under Section 7.

[129] See, for instance, Note by the WTO Secretariat, *Non-Violation Complaints and the TRIPS Agreement*, IP/C/W/124 of 28 January 1999; see also Summary Note by the WTO Secretariat, *Non-Violation Complaints and Situation Complaints* IP/C/W/349 of 29 June 2002.

Such view (i.e., an automatic applicability of non-violation complaints after 1 January 2000) was supported by a number of delegations,[130] arguing that the five-year delay in the application of non-violation complaints already constituted a concession, and that any further delay would upset the equilibrium of concessions reached at the Uruguay Round negotiations.[131]

On the other hand, paragraph 3 of Article 64 makes the decision whether or not to admit non-violation complaints in the TRIPS context contingent upon a unanimous approval by the Ministerial Conference (based on a recommendation by the Council for TRIPS). The view that the lapse of time indicated in paragraph 2 automatically triggers the applicability of non-violation complaints arguably disregards this consensus requirement under paragraph 3.

Thus, there is a contradiction between the consensus requirement concerning the extension of the dispute settlement moratorium on the one hand, and the consensus requirement with respect to the introduction of non-violation complaints on the other.

This contradiction is due to the above-mentioned failure by Members to reach agreement with respect to the scope and modalities of non-violation complaints under TRIPS. Article 64 was drafted under the presumption that Members would reach agreement before the lapse of the dispute moratorium provided under paragraph 2. It is against this background that the Appellate Body in a 1997 report stated that:

> "Whether or not 'non-violation' complaints should be available for disputes under the *TRIPS Agreement* is a matter that remains to be determined by the Council for Trade-Related Aspects of Intellectual Property (the 'Council for TRIPS') pursuant to Article 64.3 of the *TRIPS Agreement*. It is *not* a matter to be resolved through interpretation by panels or by the Appellate Body."[132]

The Appellate Body did not address the question of what would happen if Members in the Council for TRIPS failed to reach consensus. However, its insistence that the issue of non-violation be decided by the Members (in other words, through unanimity) arguably supports the view that non-violation complaints should not be admitted automatically in case the dispute settlement moratorium is not extended by consensus.

Such view would also be in line with the expression in the literature of serious concerns about the basic compatibility of non-violation complaints with TRIPS.[133] According to these critics, non-violation complaints were intended for the typical GATT situation of one Member frustrating, by domestic measures, the expectations of other Members concerning the competitive relationship between domestic and imported products as laid down in Members' tariff concessions. The situation

---

[130] See in particular Non-Paper from the United States of America, *Non-Violation Nullification or Impairment under the TRIPS Agreement*, JOB (99)/4439 of 26 July 1999.

[131] Ibid., page 3.

[132] *India – Patent Protection for Pharmaceutical and Agricultural Chemical Products*, Report of the Appellate Body of 19 December 1997, WTO document WT/DS50/AB/R, at para. 42 (emphasis in the original).

[133] See Roessler, p. 135 et seq.; Abbott, *WTO Dispute Settlement*, p. 434; Petersmann, p. 149 et seq. The following is largely based on these contributions.

under TRIPS, it is argued, is entirely different and may therefore not serve as a model. As opposed to the GATT, where non-violation complaints are meant to protect legitimate expectations (of competitive marketing conditions) that go beyond the pure respect of the GATT obligations, it has been observed that TRIPS does not protect any expectations that go beyond the respect of the substantive intellectual property standards. The main purpose of TRIPS is to promote certain public policy objectives (such as the transfer of technology, see Article 7) through effective intellectual property protection. This objective is entirely met by the respect of the legal obligations as stipulated in the substantive provisions. The non-respect of these obligations is to be addressed through violation complaints. Any further expectations as to the commercial exploitation of these IPRs (i.e., beyond the pure respect of the law) are in no way covered by TRIPS.[134] Such market access benefits, which could be protected through non-violation complaints, accrue under the GATT and the GATS, but not under TRIPS. Applying non-violation to TRIPS in order to protect marketing benefits expected by intellectual property rights holders would thus amount to a transformation of IPRs from negative to positive rights.[135]

Thus, the concept of non-violation is extraneous to IPRs. As a matter of policy, it might therefore be suggested that the incorporation of such concept into an agreement on intellectual property rights would constitute an exceptional move and should have to be agreed upon in express terms. The mere lapse of a delay should not represent a sufficient basis for such a fundamental change in the area of IPRs.

Members would be justified to interpret the language in Article 64 paragraphs 2 and 3 as leaving Members the discretion to reject the applicability of non-violation complaints to TRIPS. Yet there is substantial uncertainty regarding how the Appellate Body will interpret the relationship between Article 64.2 and 64.3 in the event Members are unable to reach a consensus on "scope and modalities".

3.2.3.2 Later developments at Doha and Cancun. Having interpreted the language of Article 64, paragraphs 2 and 3, it appears useful to highlight some recent developments and their possible impact on the treatment of non-violation complaints under TRIPS.

Members of the Council for TRIPS were unable to agree on any recommendations with respect to non-violation complaints before the mandated deadline of 1 January 2000 (see Article 64.3). However, at the Doha Ministerial Meeting in 2001, WTO Members extended this deadline as well as the express moratorium on non-violation complaints. They decided that:

> "The TRIPS Council is directed to continue its examination of the scope and modalities for complaints of the types provided for under subparagraphs 1 (b)

---

[134] Roessler, p. 136, illustrates this with the following example: authors may legitimately rely on protection against *illicit copying* of their books in the territory of WTO Members. However, the TRIPS Agreement provides for no *marketing rights* with respect to the protected books, the sale of which could be prohibited under other laws (for example, for public interest reasons).

[135] Abbott, *WTO Dispute Settlement*, p. 434. "Negative" right in this context refers to the typical function of intellectual property rights to prohibit the unauthorized use of the protected products. "Positive" right consequently refers to an extension of the protected right beyond that prohibition, covering claims regarding business opportunities.

and 1 (c) of Article XXIII of GATT 1994 and make recommendations to the Fifth Session of the Ministerial Conference. It is agreed that, in the meantime, Members will not initiate such complaints under the TRIPS Agreement."[136]

Despite this extension, Members in the TRIPS Council were not able to agree on any recommendations to the Fifth Ministerial Conference at Cancun in September 2003. In addition, there is no express extension of the moratorium on non-violation complaints for the time after the Cancun Ministerial. Therefore, the uncertainty caused by contradictory consensus requirements (see above) persists.[137]

Since there is no consensus to extend the moratorium, it could be argued that it has expired with the end of the Cancun Ministerial Conference, so that non-violation complaints would be admissible since September 2003.

However, such approach would neglect another possible interpretation of the language of Article 64; i.e., that a decision to admit non-violation complaints in the TRIPS context is contingent upon a consensus-based decision by the Ministerial Conference (Article 64.3). The fact that the moratorium as extended in the Doha Declaration (see above) expressly covers only the period up to the Cancun Ministerial Conference did not alter this requirement. When drafting the Doha Declaration, delegations acted under the assumption that by the time of the Fifth Ministerial Meeting, Members would be able to come to a consensus agreement with respect to the scope and modalities of non-violation complaints. The current situation with contradictory consensus requirements was not altered by Members at the time of the Doha Ministerial. Given the important concerns that some Members have had with respect to such complaints, neither the reference to the Fifth Ministerial Conference nor the failure to renew the express moratorium should be interpreted as implicitly waiving Members' sovereign right to reject the applicability of non-violation in the TRIPS context. Had there been a consensus at Doha that after the Cancun meeting, non-violation should apply, Members should have provided so in express terms. It may be argued that any other interpretation would not only disregard Members' sovereignty; it would equally reduce the consensus requirement in Article 64.3 to redundancy, which is contrary to the principle of effectiveness of treaty interpretation.[138]

---

[136] See Decision on Implementation-Related Issues and Concerns, WT/MIN(01)/W/10, at para. 11.1.

[137] Note that after completion of this volume, the WTO General Council decided to extend the dispute settlement moratorium with respect to non-violation complaints under TRIPS up to the Sixth WTO Ministerial Conference in December 2005. See *Decision Adopted by the General Council on 1 August 2004*, WT/L/579 of 2 August 2004, para. 1.h.

[138] This principle is embodied in Article 31 of the Vienna Convention on the Law of Treaties. In the terms employed by the Appellate Body: "One of the corollaries of the 'general rule of interpretation' in the Vienna Convention is that interpretation must give meaning and effect to all the terms of the treaty. An interpreter is not free to adopt a reading that would result in reducing whole clauses or paragraphs of a treaty to redundancy or inutility." (See *United States-Standards for Reformulated and Conventional Gasoline*, Report of the Appellate Body, WT/DS2/AB/R, 29 April 1996, p. 23.) For an analysis of the rules on treaty interpretation in the context of the TRIPS Agreement, see Annex 1 to this Chapter.

This being said, there is nevertheless a substantial risk[139] that with the failure by Members to expressly extend the Doha moratorium on non-violation, such complaints are now more likely to be initiated. On the particular implications for developing countries, see below (Section 7).

4. WTO jurisprudence

Apart from the case *India – Patent Protection for Pharmaceutical and Agricultural Chemical Products*,[140] there has been no WTO jurisprudence specifically concerning Article 64 as such.

5. Relationship with other international instruments

5.1 WTO Agreements
According to Appendix 1 of the DSU, the DSU applies to all WTO multilateral agreements (i.e., Annexes 1A through 1C to the Marrakesh Agreement). As to the plurilateral agreements, (i.e., Annex 4 to the Marrakesh Agreement), the applicability of the DSU shall be subject to the adoption of a decision by the parties to each plurilateral agreement setting out the terms for the application of the DSU to the individual agreement, including any special or additional rules or procedures.

5.2 Other international instruments

5.2.1 The WIPO-administered conventions
The state – state dispute settlement system provided by the WIPO-administered intellectual property protection treaties has in the past proved less efficient than the DSU.[141] There is a WIPO Draft Treaty on the Settlement of Disputes between States in the Field of Intellectual Property.[142] The utility of such treaty is rather controversial. Some states have insisted that, after the entry into force of TRIPS, there would be no further need to pursue the creation of a WIPO dispute settlement system.[143] On the other hand, it may be argued that the establishment of such system in parallel to the WTO DSU would bring certain, particularly political, advantages.[144]

---

[139] Abbott, *Non-Violation Nullification or Impairment Causes of Action under the TRIPS Agreement and the Fifth Ministerial Conference: A Warning and Reminder*, Quaker United Nations Office, Occasional Paper 11, Geneva, July 2003, p. 1 [hereinafter Abbott, *A Warning*].

[140] Report of the Appellate Body of 19 December 1997, WTO document WT/DS50/AB/R.

[141] See Section 2.1, above.

[142] WIPO document SD/CE/V/2 of 8 April 1993 as cited by Abbott, *WTO Dispute Settlement*, p. 434, fn. 80.

[143] Abbott, *WTO Dispute Settlement*, p. 435, referring to the U.S. delegation to the WIPO Committee of Experts.

[144] Ibid., referring to the possible preference by some states of a dispute settlement system not linked to trade sanctions. The same author also points out the fact that not all intellectual property rights-related issues can be brought before a WTO panel. Finally, he also notes that not all parties to international intellectual property rights conventions are WTO Members.

In case the draft treaty should materialize, important issues as to the relationship between the two dispute settlement systems would arise. The three following main problems have been highlighted, namely:

a) Once either the WTO or WIPO have been chosen by the complainant as the forum for dispute settlement, would the other organization be excluded to pronounce itself on the same subject matter? If so, would such exclusion apply only during the actual proceedings or permanently?[145]

b) How does one forum's decisions influence the work of the other dispute settlement body? Should they be legally binding, serve as an orientation or be irrelevant?[146]

c) If both forums pronounced themselves on the same subject-matter and came to opposing conclusions, what consequences would this entail for the relationship between intellectual property rights and trade liberalization?

6. New developments

6.1 National laws

6.2 International instruments
Possible ways of interpreting the Doha Declaration with respect to non-violation complaints are analyzed in Section 3, above. With respect to the attempts to reform the DSU provisions in general, see Section 6.4, below.

6.3 Regional and bilateral contexts

6.3.1 Regional

6.3.1.1 The status of DSB decisions in the EC legal order. In a number of highly controversial cases, the European Court of Justice (ECJ) has decided that, even though the EC is legally bound by the WTO agreements and the decisions of the DSB, neither the EU member states nor EU citizens may invoke WTO rules or DSB decisions to challenge the validity of EC legislative acts.[147] This approach has been confronted with strong criticism among legal scholars.[148]

---

[145] Idem, p. 436, supporting a proposal submitted by the EC to the WIPO Committee of Experts, according to which the election of one organization as dispute settlement forum should foreclose recourse to the other one.

[146] Ibid., advocating the accordance of "great weight" to decisions of the other respective dispute settlement organ, but refusing a legally binding effect.

[147] ECJ – *Portugal/Council*, C-149/96 – European Court Reports (ECR) 1999, I-8395 [hereinafter *Portugal/Council*]; ECJ – *OGT Fruchthandelsgesellschaft mbH/Hauptzollamt Hamburg-St. Annen*, C-307/99 – ECR 2001, I-3159; specifically for the TRIPS Agreement, see ECJ – *Dior and Layher*, joint cases C-300/98 and C-392/98 – ECR 2000, I-11307, and ECJ – *Schieving-Nijstad vof and others/Robert Groeneveld*, C-89/99 – ECR 2001, I-5851. All decisions are also available on the ECJ's website at <http://curia.eu.int>.

[148] For an overview of the different opinions see Cottier/Nadakavukaren Schefer, *The Relationship between World Trade Organization Law, National and Regional Law*, in: Journal of International Economic Law 1998, 91ff.; Peers, *Fundamental Right or Political Whim? WTO Law and the*

The ECJ advances two reasons for its denial of direct effect of WTO law in the EC's legal order: First, the necessity to maintain the EC's discretionary power to negotiate compensation instead of immediately implementing the DSB rulings.[149] Second, the fact that neither the USA, nor Japan, have so far accorded direct effect to WTO law and DSB decisions in their domestic legal systems would lead to an imbalance in the implementation of WTO law.[150]

However, the ECJ does admit two exceptions under which WTO rules may be used to challenge the validity of EC legislation:[151]

- where the contested EC legislative act is intended to implement a WTO obligation;
- or where the EC act refers to specific WTO provisions.

In those cases, the EC has waived its discretion and made a commitment to implement its WTO obligations.

In addition to that, there is a third possibility of WTO law influencing EC law. The ECJ has consistently stressed the requirement to interpret EC legal measures and national legislation as far as possible in the light of GATT/WTO rules (obligation of "consistent interpretation").[152]

Finally, it can be observed that it is easier for an individual EU citizen to challenge the measures of third states on grounds of alleged WTO-inconsistency than to challenge measures of the EC. EC Council Regulation No. 3286/94,[153] as modified by Regulation No. 356/95[154] foresees the possibility for individuals, companies, or EU member states to request the EC Commission to initiate WTO dispute

---

European Court of Justice, in: de Burca/Scott (ed.), The EU and the WTO, 2001, 111–130 (footnotes 1, 14, 15); Rosas, Case C-149/96, *Portugal v. Council. Judgment of the Full Court of 23 November 1999, nyr.*, Common Market Law Review 2000, 798 et seq., especially footnotes 11 and 12.

[149] The (merely temporary) option of compensation is authorized under Article 22 DSU, with the purpose of avoiding retaliation when the infringing measure cannot be withdrawn within the foreseen time frame. Note that this gives a WTO Member the possibility to maintain, on a temporary basis, a WTO-inconsistent measure. If the ECJ permitted WTO rules to be directly enforceable before national courts throughout the EU, affected individuals or EU member states could obligate the EC to immediately withdraw its WTO-inconsistent measures. Thus, the temporary possibility offered by Article 22 DSU would be void. The radical changes direct effect would introduce may be illustrated by the dispute on the EC's import regime of bananas: if the WTO decisions as to the inconsistency of this regime had been directly enforceable before national courts, European banana importers would have been able to challenge successfully the relevant EC regulations before their domestic courts and the ECJ. This would have been a way to avoid the lengthy legal battle over bananas before the WTO.

[150] While the EC could be forced to immediately respect WTO obligations (see above), both the USA and Japan would not be exposed to the same pressure.

[151] See ECJ – *Fediol*, C-70/87 – ECR 1989, 1781 and ECJ – *Nakajima*, C-69/89 – ECR 1991, I-2069. Both decisions concerned the GATT 1947, but the ECJ confirmed their applicability to the new WTO rules in its *Portugal/Council* judgement (see above).

[152] For the GATT 1947: ECJ – *Interfoods*, C-92/71 – ECR 1972, 231; for the TRIPS Agreement: ECJ – *Hermès International*, C-53/96 – ECR 1998, I-3603, at para. 28; ECJ – *Schieving-Nijstad vof and others/Robert Groeneveld*, C-89/99 – ECR 2001, I-5851, at paras 35, 36, 55. The ECJ employs a balancing test concerning the requirement of liberal trade on the one hand and intellectual property protection on the other.

[153] Official Journal of the European Communities 1994, No. L 349, p. 71 ff.

[154] Official Journal of the European Communities 1995, No. L 41, p. 3.

settlement proceedings against third countries whose trade practices violate WTO rules. The Commission has the discretionary power to decide whether the request should be granted. So far, such requests have always been treated favourably.[155]

6.3.2 Bilateral

A recent trend in bilateral and regional free trade agreements has been to declare non-violation complaints applicable to the respective provisions on IPRs. In most cases, these non-violation clauses do not appear in the intellectual property chapter of the agreement, but in a separate dispute settlement chapter.[156]

6.4 Proposals for review

In a 1994 *Decision on the Application and Review of the Understanding on Rules and Procedures Governing the Settlement of Disputes*,[157] Ministers agreed on a full review of WTO dispute settlement rules and procedures by 1 January 1999. Although the Dispute Settlement Body in special sessions started this review in 1997 and extended the deadline until 31 July 1999,[158] Members could not agree on possible amendments of the DSU.[159]

On the same issue, the 2001 Doha Declaration provided:

"We agree to negotiations on improvements and clarifications of the Dispute Settlement Understanding. The negotiations should be based on the work done thus far as well as any additional proposals by Members, and aim to agree on improvements and clarifications not later than May 2003, at which time we will take steps to ensure that the results enter into force as soon as possible thereafter."[160]

However, the May 2003 deadline also passed without Members' coming to an agreement. On 24 July 2003, the General Council acknowledged that the DSB special session needed more time to conclude its work and extended the deadline for the special session until May 2004.[161]

7. Comments, including economic and social implications

7.1 Non-violation complaints

The legal analysis of Article 64, paragraphs 2 and 3 (see Section 3, above) has led to the conclusion that the current situation concerning non-violation complaints

---

[155] See Nowak, *Der Rechtsschutz von Beschwerdeführern im EG-Wettbewerbs- und EG-Außenhandelsrecht*, in: Europäische Zeitschrift für Wirtschaftsrecht 15/2000, 453 (456).

[156] See, for instance, Annex 22.2 of the Chile – USA FTA; and Annex 20.2 of the Central American Free Trade Agreement (CAFTA). For an overview of non-violation complaints at the regional and bilateral levels, see South Centre/CIEL IP Quarterly Update: First Quarter 2004. *Intellectual Property and Development: Overview of Developments in Multilateral, Plurilateral, and Bilateral Fora*, available at <http://www.ciel.org/Publications/IP_Update_Spring04.pdf>. For a detailed analysis of the USA – Chile FTA, see Roffe 2004.

[157] See at <http://www.wto.org/english/docs_e/legal_e/53-ddsu.pdf>.

[158] See the DSB decision WT/DSB/M/52 of December 1998.

[159] See at <http://www.wto.org/english/tratop_e/dispu_e/dispu_e.htm#negotiations>.

[160] See Ministerial Declaration of 14 November 2001, WT/MIN(01)/DEC/W/1, para. 30.

[161] See <http://www.wto.org/english/tratop_e/dispu_e/dispu_e.htm#negotiations>.

under TRIPS is unclear. This is due to contradictory consensus requirements with respect to both the extension of the moratorium and the introduction of non-violation complaints. Under this scenario, there is a substantial risk that some Members will attempt to resort to non-violation complaints in the future, based on the assertion that with the lapse of the express moratorium, such complaints have generally become admissible.[162]

The implications for developing countries would be manifold. Before going into some details, it is important to emphasize that from a legal point of view, the risk of a developing country being exposed to a successful claim of non-violation before the WTO is currently very low.[163] It is highly unlikely that the Appellate Body will depart from its usual strong reliance on the express text of the pertinent agreement[164] for the sake of enforcing some very vague expectations that go well beyond the express TRIPS obligations.

This being said, the fact that developing country Members might be forced to defend non-violation claims constitutes a considerable challenge, taking account of the legal expenses caused by such action. Even more importantly, the uncertainty as to the outcome inherent in any legal action might have a chilling effect on developing countries' domestic legislative activities. Members bringing non-violation cases might argue that certain public policies restricting market access of IPR-protected products deprive right holders of certain expectations arising from the TRIPS substantive rules on IPRs (see Section 3 above). This can be illustrated through several examples.[165] For instance, the recourse by developing countries to price controls, particularly in the area of pharmaceutical products, could be considered as impairing marketing expectations on the part of foreign patent holders.[166] Also, the use by governments of other TRIPS flexibilities such as the general exceptions clause to patent rights (Article 30), the granting of compulsory licenses (Article 31), fair use exceptions to copyright, or even the narrow design of patentability criteria could be the target of non-violation complaints. In addition, although TRIPS grants considerable discretion with respect to the enforcement of IPRs, Members could seek to challenge another Member's choice of remedies as not being sufficiently stringent. Finally, public policy choices pursued through internal taxes, packaging and labelling requirements, consumer protection rules and environmental standards may affect the profitability of IPRs and thus nullify or impair benefits expected from such rights.

---

[162] Note, however, the 1 August 2004 Decision by the General Council to extend the moratorium until the Sixth Ministerial Conference in December 2005. See above, Section 3 of this chapter.

[163] See Abbott, *A Warning*, p. 3.

[164] For an example of this strong reliance of the express text, see *India – Patent Protection for Pharmaceutical and Agricultural Chemical Products*, AB-1997-5, WT/DS50/AB/R of 19 December 1997.

[165] See Abbott, *A Warning*, p. 2, 3.

[166] See Abbott, *UNCTAD Handbook*, p. 33, who, however, underlines the improbability of such a non-violation complaint to succeed: no Member could reasonably expect price controls not to be used, for they were already in many governments' use at the time of the negotiation of the TRIPS Agreement. In addition, TRIPS does not contain any rules concerning price controls and can thus not create any reasonable expectations that such controls will not be used.

Such restrictions of each Member's right to regulate in the common interest would affect not only developing countries, but should equally be of major concern to developed Members. After all, it was the EC that during the Uruguay Round negotiations expressed doubts about non-violation under TRIPS in view of its market access restrictions in the audio-visual sector (see Section 2.2 above). The negotiated rules in TRIPS on substantive IPRs represent a carefully weighted balance between the interests of private right holders and the public. The admission of non-violation complaints in the TRIPS context would upset this balance to the detriment of those public policy goals, the promotion of which is one of the core objectives of TRIPS.

7.2 The issue of cross-retaliation

The fact that the TRIPS disciplines are subject to binding dispute settlement decisions constitutes an important novelty for all WTO Members, but especially for developing countries. As opposed to industrialized Members, developing Members' domestic IPR systems are far less developed, so their adjustment to the TRIPS standards requires a considerably higher effort, not only on the financial side. If Members fail to meet their obligations, they risk being exposed to trade sanctions in the form of suspension of concessions.

The availability of cross-retaliation[167] means that developing countries, when not meeting their TRIPS obligations, may see the withdrawal of concessions in areas essential for their own industries, like the exports of certain goods (textiles, agricultural products). From an industrialized Member's perspective, this is a valuable and powerful tool to ensure developing Members' efforts as to the improvement of their IP protection systems, which, in turn, is essential for the industrialized Members' advanced industries. From a developing (and especially a least-developed) Member's perspective, however, enhanced intellectual property protection might not always represent the optimal (short and medium term) policy choice, as illustrated in several chapters of this book. Thus, developing countries might feel compelled to engage in something they consider contrary to their national interests.

7.3 The consequences of the binding force of the WIPO-administered conventions

In addition to that, the incorporation by TRIPS of the most important previous intellectual property conventions[168] automatically obliges developing countries to respect these conventions' disciplines, whether or not they ever adhered to the respective convention itself. In this context, it has been observed that not only the conventions themselves, but equally the related state practice has deliberately

---

[167] See above, Section 1.

[168] See Article 2(1) as to the Paris Convention, Article 9(1) as to the Berne Convention and Article 35 as to the Treaty on Integrated Circuits. Note, however, that this does not apply to the Rome Convention for the Protection of Performers, Producers of Phonograms and Broadcasting Organizations. Those WTO Members that are no parties to this treaty shall not be obligated by its disciplines; see Article 2.2 of TRIPS and Chapter 3 of this book.

been incorporated into TRIPS.[169] This includes judicial decisions, executive actions and legislative measures.[170] At this point, the question arises whether these judicial interpretations of intellectual property protection, developed in the limited context of mainly industrialized countries, may without any alteration be transposed into the TRIPS context, with the majority of WTO Members being developing countries.[171] It has been observed that not all interpretations given to the WIPO intellectual property conventions by domestic courts in developed countries have necessarily adopted the status of customary international law.[172] In fact, those customary practices of some Members that have never been followed by other Members (e.g., because of their different economic and social preferences) do not bind the latter.[173] Consequently, where a developing country Member's intellectual property legislation or practice is challenged because of an alleged infringement of one of the WIPO intellectual property conventions, that Member should verify whether the complaining party's view can directly be based on the wording of the respective agreement or whether it is merely the result of the interpretation of the issue by a domestic court.

7.4 Development-related provisions under the DSU

In order to accommodate some of the concerns developing countries have with respect to WTO dispute settlement, the DSU contains some specific developing/least developed countries provisions:[174]

- Article 3:12 DSU

"Notwithstanding paragraph 11, if a complaint based on any of the covered agreements is brought by a developing country Member against a developed country Member, the complaining party shall have the right to invoke, as an alternative to the provisions contained in Articles 4, 5, 6 and 12 of this Understanding, the corresponding provisions of the Decision of 5 April 1966 (BISD 14S/18), except that where the Panel considers that the time-frame provided for in paragraph 7 of that Decision is insufficient to provide its report and with the agreement of the complaining party, that time-frame may be extended. To the extent that there is a difference between the rules and procedures of Articles 4, 5, 6 and 12 and the corresponding rules and procedures of the Decision, the latter shall prevail."

The 1966 Decision provides for expedited dispute settlement procedures as an alternative to the DSU provisions. Since the entry into force of the WTO Agreements, no developing country has had recourse to this 1966 Decision.[175]

---

169 See Abbott, *WTO Dispute Settlement*, p. 421/422.

170 Ibid.

171 See Petersmann, p. 214.

172 See Abbott, *UNCTAD Handbook*, p. 35.

173 Ibid.

174 For an overview of those DSU provisions see The South Centre, *Issues Regarding the Review of the WTO Dispute Settlement Mechanism*, Working Papers, Geneva, February 1999, p. 18 *et seq.* [hereinafter The South Centre] and Kongolo, *The WTO Dispute Settlement Mechanism. TRIPS Rulings and the Developing Countries*, in: The Journal of World Intellectual Property, vol. 4, March 2001, 257 *et seq.* [hereinafter Kongolo].

175 See The South Centre, p. 19.

- Article 4:10 DSU

"During consultations Members should give special attention to the particular problems and interests of developing country Members."

It has been observed that there is no possibility of assessing Members' compliance with this rule, because it does not specify what exactly is meant by "special attention".[176] This provision is thus of declaratory nature and of very limited practical use.[177]

- Article 8:10 DSU

"When a dispute is between a developing country Member and a developed country Member the panel shall, if the developing country Member so requests, include at least one panelist from a developing country Member."

In the cases *India – Shirts and Blouses*[178] and *Argentina – Textiles*[179] all three panelists were nationals of developing countries.[180]

- Article 12:10 DSU

"In the context of consultations involving a measure taken by a developing country Member, the parties may agree to extend the periods established in paragraphs 7 and 8 of Article 4. If, after the relevant period has elapsed, the consulting parties cannot agree that the consultations have concluded, the Chairman of the DSB shall decide, after consultation with the parties, whether to extend the relevant period and, if so, for how long. In addition, in examining a complaint against a developing country Member, the panel shall accord sufficient time for the developing country Member to prepare and present its argumentation. [. . .]"

So far, the DSB chairman has never taken a formal decision concerning the extension of consultation periods.[181]

- Article 12:11 DSU

"Where one or more of the parties is a developing country Member, the panel's report shall explicitly indicate the form in which account has been taken of relevant provisions on differential and more-favourable treatment for developing country Members that form part of the covered agreements which have been raised by the developing country Member in the course of the dispute settlement procedures."

This provision has so far never been expressly referred to in any panel report.[182]

---

[176] Ibid.
[177] Ibid.
[178] WTO document WT/DS33, report of the panel.
[179] WTO document WT/DS56, report of the panel.
[180] See The South Centre, p. 19.
[181] Ibid., p. 20.
[182] Ibid.

- Article 21:2 DSU

"Particular attention should be paid to matters affecting the interests of developing country Members with respect to measures which have been subject to dispute settlement."

Like Article 4.10, this provision is of limited practical use due to the vagueness of the term "particular attention".

- Article 21:7 DSU

"If the matter is one which has been raised by a developing country Member, the DSB shall consider what further action it might take which would be appropriate to the circumstances."

Complaining developing country Members have never had recourse to this provision.[183] One of the reasons might be the vagueness of words such as "might" and "appropriate."

- Article 21:8 DSU

"If the case is one brought by a developing country Member, in considering what appropriate action might be taken, the DSB shall take into account not only the trade coverage of measures complained of, but also their impact on the economy of developing country Members concerned."

So far, the DSB has never made use of this provision.[184]

- Article 24 DSU

"1. At all stages of the determination of the causes of a dispute and of dispute settlement procedures involving a least-developed country Member, particular consideration shall be given to the special situation of least-developed country Members. In this regard, Members shall exercise due restraint in raising matters under these procedures involving a least-developed country Member. If nullification or impairment is found to result from a measure taken by a least-developed country Member, complaining parties shall exercise due restraint in asking for compensation or seeking authorization to suspend the application of concessions or other obligations pursuant to these procedures.

2. In dispute settlement cases involving a least-developed country Member, where a satisfactory solution has not been found in the course of consultations the Director-General or the Chairman of the DSB shall, upon request by a least-developed country Member offer their good offices, conciliation and mediation with a view to assisting the parties to settle the dispute, before a request for a panel is made. The Director-General or the Chairman of the DSB, in providing the above assistance, may consult any source which either deems appropriate."

Since no LDC has ever been involved in a WTO dispute, an assessment of this provision is not possible for the time being.

---

[183] Ibid., p. 21.

[184] Ibid., proposing a careful analysis of the reasons for the "apathy" on the part of developing countries to have recourse to the differential treatment provisions.

- Article 27:2 DSU

"While the Secretariat assists Members in respect of dispute settlement at their request, there may also be a need to provide additional legal advice and assistance in respect of dispute settlement to developing country Members. To this end, the Secretariat shall make available a qualified legal expert from the WTO technical cooperation services to any developing country Member which so requests. This expert shall assist the developing country Member in a manner ensuring the continued impartiality of the Secretariat."

It has been observed that despite this important support, developing countries are nevertheless inclined to ask for costly legal advice from abroad. WTO legal experts are obliged to keep their impartiality with respect to all the parties to the dispute. It cannot be their objective to argue a case in favour of one of the parties.[185]

7.5 General implications of the rules-based system of the DSU

While it is clear that the possibility of enforcing TRIPS disciplines through the DSU constitutes a major challenge for developing countries, there are at the same time possible advantages. The DSU may actually be seen as seeking to put WTO Members on an equal footing despite their very different levels of development and very different economic and political powers. All Members are subject to the same rules. Those rules are, in theory, enforceable against any Member, irrespective of its political or economic power. In the absence of the DSU, the only means available for the settlement of disputes would be traditional diplomatic procedures, with all their possibilities for the exercise of unilateral economic or political pressure. Under the DSU, the only decisive criterion for the outcome of the dispute is the law, which applies equally to every Member. Article 23:2 (a) DSU makes it clear that Members are not allowed to determine unilaterally whether another Member has violated WTO rules. The only way to arrive at this conclusion is through recourse to the DSU procedures (see Article 23:1 of the DSU).

For developing countries, this aspect should not be underestimated. Considering the very different levels of domestic IPR systems, there will certainly be a lot of disagreement between industrialized and developing country Members as to the TRIPS legality of certain domestic legislation. In that case, however, developing countries are no longer confronted with a unilateral assessment of their legislation by their developed country counterparts. WTO panels and the Appellate Body are construed as impartial adjudicative bodies (see Article 8:2 of the DSU for the panels; Article 17:3 for the AB). Their obligation to base their findings only on questions of law (as opposed to political considerations) contributes to the predictability and transparency of the dispute settlement system.

There are a number of examples in the GATT/WTO dispute settlement history of developing countries successfully defending their WTO-compatible interests against powerful global players. In the *Tuna-Dolphin I* dispute,[186] Mexico successfully challenged U.S. legislation banning the imports of tuna caught with certain fishing techniques. The panel held that unilateral action with extraterritorial

---

[185] Ibid., p. 23.
[186] BISD 39S/155–205.

effects violated GATT rules and was generally not justifiable under Article XX GATT. Under the old GATT, it was possible for the losing party to block the adoption of the report. With the introduction of the quasi-automatic adoption of panel reports, such blocking would no longer be possible. Thus, the further "legalization" of dispute settlement procedures under the new DSU cannot necessarily be considered as opposed to developing countries' interests.

In the *Shrimps-Turtle* dispute, India, Malaysia, Pakistan and Thailand brought a complaint against a U.S. law prohibiting the importation of shrimp caught with a certain fishing technique. The Appellate Body[187] considered the application by the USA of that domestic law as constituting an "unjustifiable discrimination" under Article XX GATT 1994. The reason for this assessment was the failure on the part of the USA to enter into serious multilateral negotiations to settle disagreements over fishing techniques before imposing unilateral action on other WTO Members.[188] Since this case was brought under the new DSU, the USA was unable to block the adoption of the report.

7.6 Some shortcomings of the DSU with respect to developing countries

7.6.1 The limited power to make use of retaliation

Even the legalistic approach to dispute settlement under the DSU cannot cancel out the factual differences in economic power among WTO Members. This becomes most apparent in the phase of implementation of DSB rulings, as illustrated in the *bananas* case.[189] Pursuant to the EC's failure to bring its banana regime into WTO-conformity, Ecuador, as the first developing country in GATT/WTO history, requested the authorization by the DSB to suspend concessions to a developed WTO Member, the EC. This request was granted by the DSB, as recommended by an arbitration panel, in the amount of US$ 201.6 million.[190] However, in the course of the proceedings, Ecuador had to recognize that the adverse economic effects of an actual suspension of concessions would rather be felt by Ecuador itself than by the EC.[191] This was so for the following reasons:

In the goods area, higher tariff barriers would prevent EC products from supplying the Ecuadorian market, which was highly dependent on them. Thus, the economic crisis would be exacerbated. On the other hand, a closing of the relatively small Ecuadorian market would hardly be felt by European companies,

---

[187] See *US – Import Prohibition of Certain Shrimp and Shrimp Products*, Report of the Appellate Body of 12 October 1998, WTO document WT/DS58/AB/R.

[188] Idem, under Section VI. C. 2., paras. 165–180.

[189] See *European Communities – Regime for the Importation, Sale and Distribution of Bananas*, Report of the Appellate Body, WT/DS27/AB/R. For a detailed overview of the complex procedural issues involved in this case, see Jackson/Grane, *The Saga Continues: An Update on the Banana Dispute and its Procedural Offspring*, in: Journal of International Economic Law 2001, 581 et seg. [hereinafter Jackson/Grane].

[190] See WTO documents WT/DS27/53, WT/DS27/ARB/ECU. Ecuador was authorized to apply cross-retaliation (for a definition, see above, Section 1).

[191] Jackson/Grane, p. 589, note in this context that even the arbitrators realized that the actual implementation by Ecuador of the authorized retaliation might not be realistic.

whose main export targets are the large markets of the EU itself, of the USA and of Japan.

In the TRIPS area, Ecuador intended to export phonograms to third countries without the consent of the European right holders, thus suspending its obligations towards the EC under Article 14 TRIPS (i.e., protection of performers, producers of phonograms and broadcasting organizations). However, this attempt to improve Ecuador's export volume proved illusory. The arbitration panel clarified that all other WTO Members remained bound by their TRIPS obligations towards the EC. Consequently, any third WTO Member country into which Ecuador would seek to export EU phonograms in the above described manner would have to apply Article 51 TRIPS Agreement, obligating Members' customs authorities to suspend the release into free circulation of those phonograms. In other words, the authorization of Ecuador to have recourse to cross-retaliation proved rather counterproductive, partly because of Ecuador's comparative economic weakness *vis-à-vis* the EC.

7.6.2 The high cost of dispute settlement

Due to the lack of domestic human resources, many developing countries for the purpose of dispute settlement need recourse to foreign experts. This implies high costs and often obliges those countries to refrain from making use of their right to invoke the DSU procedures against other states. It has been proposed that the WTO develop methods to reduce such financial burdens on developing countries.[192]

7.6.3 The lack of information between the government and the private sector

In many developing countries, there is a lack of effective mechanisms to ensure the flow of information between the government on the one side and the private sector on the other side. Given that only governments are authorized to launch a WTO dispute, this has important repercussions on the ability of governments to defend their domestic industry's interests. If private business is not informed about WTO rules, it will not be able to identify violations of those rules by other governments. Thus, the domestic industry will not ask their government to intervene in their favour before the WTO. The government, for its part, depends on information from the private sector in order to know whether there are any violations of WTO rules in foreign countries that limit the marketing opportunities of the domestic exporting industry.[193]

7.6.4 The DSU approach to compensation

According to Article 22:2 DSU, the effective payment of compensation for the non-implementation of DSB rulings depends on a common agreement between the parties to the dispute. If no such agreement can be reached, the complaining party will not be compensated, but authorized to suspend concessions or other obligations towards the respondent. As stated above, trade retaliation is of very

---

[192] See Kongolo, p. 261.
[193] See Kongolo, p. 261.

limited value to developing countries. Their interests would be better served if they could claim compensation instead, which would constitute an actual benefit. This is why it has been proposed that the DSB should exercise pressure on developed countries to compensate the respective developing country.[194] Otherwise, the DSU might be conceived as a system largely ignoring the relative economic weakness of developing countries.

---

[194] Kongolo, p. 263, referring to Petersmann.

Annex 1 Methods of Interpretation under the DSU

1. Introduction

TRIPS does not contain any specific provision dealing with treaty interpretation. However, it is listed in Annex 1 of the Dispute Settlement Understanding (hereinafter DSU) as one of the "covered agreements" to which the DSU applies (Article 1:1 DSU).

Article 3:2 of the DSU provides that the dispute settlement system serves

> "to preserve the rights and obligations of Members under the covered agreements, and *to clarify the existing provisions of those agreements in accordance with customary rules of interpretation of public international law*" . . . (Emphasis added).

Article 3:2 of the DSU also provides that

> "[R]ecommendations and rulings of the DSB [Dispute Settlement Body] cannot add to or diminish the rights and obligations provided in the covered agreements."

A similar provision can be found in Article 19:2 in connection with panel and Appellate Body reports.

This means that the role of the DSB, the Appellate Body and the panels is limited to clarifying Members' rights and obligations under the WTO Agreements. Authoritative interpretation of the covered agreements is reserved to the WTO Members, as stated in Article IX:2 of the WTO Agreement:

> "The Ministerial Conference and the General Council shall have the exclusive authority to adopt interpretations of this Agreement and of the Multilateral Trade Agreements. [. . .]"

In its ruling on *Japan – Taxes on Alcoholic Beverages*, the Appellate Body found that Articles 31 and 32 of the Vienna Convention on the Law of Treaties constituted customary rules of interpretation of public international law for the purposes of Article 3:2 DSU.[195] In addition, the Appellate Body made it clear in its first ruling that WTO law could not be considered in isolation from public international law.[196]

It has been observed that among the WTO Agreements, TRIPS is "probably the most difficult to interpret".[197] This is due to the following factors:[198]

a) Intellectual property rights are perceived differently by societies according to levels of economic development and technological prowess. Given this divergent perception, WTO panels and the Appellate Body will be watched closely in the perspective of not to "add to or diminish the rights and obligations provided in

---

[195] *Japan-Taxes on Alcoholic Beverages*, Report of the Appellate Body, WT/DS8, 10, 11/AB/R, 4 October 1996, at 9, citing *United States-Standards for Reformulated and Conventional Gasoline*, Report of the Appellate Body, WT/DS2/AB/R, 29 April 1996. Note that GATT panels already applied customary methods on treaty interpretation. See E.-U. Petersmann, *The Dispute Settlement System of the World Trade Organization and the Evolution of the GATT Dispute Settlement System since 1948*, 31 Common Market Law Review, 1994, p. 1188.

[196] *United States-Standards for Reformulated and Conventional Gasoline*, WT/DS2/9, p. 19.

[197] See O. Cattaneo, *The Interpretation of the TRIPS Agreement: Considerations for the WTO Panels and Appellate Body*, Journal of World Intellectual Property, September 2000, volume 3, number 5, pp. 627–681 (p. 679) [hereinafter Cattaneo].

[198] Ibid.

the . . . agreement". For the panels and the AB, this demands a delicate balancing exercise.

b) TRIPS incorporates pre-WTO intellectual property rights conventions (usually WIPO-administered). Membership of these agreements is not necessarily identical to membership of the WTO. This raises the question whether WTO panels and the Appellate Body have the power to adopt binding interpretations of these conventions. Also, it would be important to know if under TRIPS, those WIPO conventions should be subject to the same interpretations as customarily used or whether the different membership under TRIPS and the changing nature of IPRs should be taken into account.

c) The language of TRIPS, especially as far as the exceptions are concerned, is extremely vague. This makes it even more important for the panels and the AB to rely on clear, internationally agreed rules of treaty interpretation like the Vienna Convention.

2. Historical overview

2.1 Situation pre-TRIPS

WTO panels are not obliged to apply the rules of treaty interpretation laid down in Articles 31 and 32 of the Vienna Convention on the Law of Treaties[199], although some panels have actually referred to them in some circumstances. But the provisions of the Vienna Convention are not mandatory.

2.2 Negotiating History of Articles 31 and 32 of the Vienna Convention[200]

It is at least dubious that any rule of interpretation of treaties existed before the conclusion of the Vienna Convention on the Law of Treaties.[201] Adjudicative

---

[199] Vienna Convention on the Law of Treaties, 1969, 1155 *United Nations Treaty Series*, 331.

[200] These provisions read as follows:
"Article 31 General Rule of Interpretation
1. A treaty shall be interpreted in good faith in accordance with the ordinary meaning to be given to the terms of the treaty in their context and in the light of its object and purpose.
2. The context for the purpose of the interpretation of a treaty shall comprise, in addition to the text, including its preamble and annexes:
(a) any agreement relating to the treaty which was made between all the parties in connection with the conclusion of the treaty;
(b) any instrument which was made by one or more parties in connection with the conclusion of the treaty and accepted by the other parties as an instrument related to the treaty.
3. There shall be taken into account, together with the context:
(a) any subsequent agreement between the parties regarding the interpretation of the treaty or the application of its provisions;
(b) any subsequent practice in the application of the treaty which establishes the agreement of the parties regarding its interpretation;
(c) any relevant rules of international law applicable in the relations between the parties.
4. A special meaning shall be given to a term if it is established that the parties so intended."
"Article 32 Supplementary means of interpretation
Recourse may be had to supplementary means of interpretation, including the preparatory work of the treaty and the circumstances of its conclusion, in order to confirm the meaning resulting from the application of Article 31, or to determine the meaning when the interpretation according to Article 31:
(a) leaves the meaning ambiguous or obscure; or
(b) leads to a result which is manifestly absurd or unreasonable."

[201] See, in general, V.D. Degan, *L'interprétation des accords en droit international*, Martinus Nijhoff, The Hague, 1963.

international bodies resorted to several principles of interpretation that generally contradicted or cancelled each other out, but there was no mandatory rule as to how to interpret treaties.

These pre-Vienna principles responded to three diverse approaches to treaty interpretation. First, for the "intention of the parties" school the only legitimate intention of interpretation is to ascertain and to give effect to the intentions, or the presumed intentions, of the parties.[202] This method is analogous to common law contract interpretation, based on the principle that the most important value is to protect a party's reasonable expectations,[203] and admits liberal recourse to *travaux préparatoires* and to other evidence of the intention of the contracting States as means of interpretation. Second, for the "meaning of the text" school, the prime object of interpretation is to establish what the text means according to the ordinary or apparent signification of its terms. Finally, for the "teleological" school, it is the general purpose of the treaty itself that counts, considered to the same extent "as having an existence of its own, independent of the original intentions of the framers."[204]

Article 31 of the Vienna Convention on the Law of Treaties is based on the view that the text must be presumed to be the authentic expression of the intention of the parties; and that, in consequence, the starting point of interpretation is the elucidation of the meaning of the text, not an investigation *ab initio* into the intentions of the parties.[205] The ordinary meaning of a term is not to be determined in the abstract but in the context of the treaty and in the light of its object and purpose.

Article 31.2 seeks to define what is comprised in the "context" for the purposes of the interpretation of the treaty. According to this paragraph, two classes of acts should be so regarded:

a) any agreement relating to the treaty which was made between all the parties in connection with the conclusion of the treaty; and

b) any instrument which was made in connection with the conclusion of the treaty and accepted by the other parties as an instrument related to the treaty.[206]

---

[202] See McDougal, S. Myres et al., *The Interpretation of Agreements and World Public Order* 90, 1967. For a criticism to McDougal's approach to treaty interpretation, see Sir G. Fitzmaurice; *Vae Victis or Woe to the Negotiators! Your Treaty or Our Interpretation of It?*, American Journal of International Law, vol. 65, 1971, p. 358 et seq.

[203] Peter C. Maki, *Interpreting GATT Using the Vienna Convention on the Law of Treaties: A Method to Increase the Legitimacy of the Dispute Settlement System*, Minnesota Journal of Global Trade 2000, vol. 9, pp. 343–360. However, it must be noted that the majority of authors in international law do not study the principles of interpretation as they exist in domestic law, as they consider that interpretation problems arising from international and domestic law are different and require the application of different principles. Exceptionally, Kelsen has pointed out that there is nothing in treaties that calls for different principles of interpretation as applied to other legal instruments (H. Kelsen, *Principles of International Law*, New York, Holt Rinehart and Winston, 1966, p. 321).

[204] For a detailed description of these three approaches to treaty interpretation, see G. Fitzmaurice, *The Law and Procedure of the International Court of Justice: Treaty Interpretation and Certain Other Treaty Points*, British Yearbook of International Law, 1951, p. 1 ff.

[205] United Nations Conference on the Law of Treaties, Official Records, First and Second sessions (Vienna, 26 March–24 May 1968 and 9 April–22 May 1969), p. 40, para. 11.

[206] Ibid. p. 41, para. 13.

Article 31. 3(a) embodies the well-settled principle that when an agreement as to the interpretation of a provision is established as having been reached before or at the time of the conclusion of the treaty, it is to be regarded as forming part of the treaty.[207]

Paragraph 3(b) specifies that any "subsequent practice in the application of the treaty" by its parties may constitute objective evidence of the understanding of the parties as to the meaning of the treaty.

Paragraph 3 (c) sets up the principle of "contemporaneity" or "evolutionary" interpretation, by stating that "any relevant rules of international law applicable in the relations between the parties" have to be taken into account when interpreting the treaty. There is controversy about how this provision is to be interpreted. While advocates of "contemporaneity" stress the necessity of any interpretation to closely keep to the understanding of the respective rules at the time of their adoption, proponents of an "evolutionary" interpretation argue that legal rules cannot be detached from societal, political and economic changes and will only remain relevant if these changes are taken into account.

Finally, Article 31.4 provides for the somewhat exceptional case where, notwithstanding the apparent meaning of a term in its context, it is established that the parties intended it to have a special meaning.

Although Article 31 sets up different principles of treaty interpretation, it cannot properly be regarded as laying down a hierarchy of norms for the interpretation of treaties. The preparatory work of the Vienna Convention on the Law of Treaties (VCLT) reveals that the connection underlying the different paragraphs intended to indicate that the application of the means of interpretation in this provision would be a single combined operation. All the various elements, as they were present in any given case, would be seen as a whole and their interaction would provide the legally relevant interpretation. It was emphasized that the process of interpretation is a unity and that the provisions of the Article form a single, closely integrated rule.[208]

Article 32 contemplates the possibility of resorting to the preparatory work of a treaty when, after applying Article 31, the result is ambiguous or obscure, or manifestly absurd or unreasonable. It must be noted that the word "supplementary" emphasizes that there is no room for considering Article 32 as an alternative or autonomous means of interpretation, but only as a means to aid an interpretation governed by the principles contained in Article 31.[209]

3. The interpretation of the TRIPS Agreement

Before turning to the methods of interpretation actually applied by the Appellate Body,[210] some general observations concerning the interpretation of TRIPS appear useful.[211]

---

[207] Ibid. p. 41, para. 14.

[208] Ibid. p. 39, para. 8.

[209] Ibid. p. 43, para. 19.

[210] See below, Section 4 of this Annex.

[211] For more details on possible interpretations of each TRIPS provision see the respective chapters of this book.

It is a common feature of TRIPS that its obligations are worded in a very broad manner, leaving considerable discretion to WTO Members for their domestic implementation.[212] In addition to that, these obligations represent only minimum standards.[213] For instance, Article 15.1 does not contain an exhaustive list of criteria for the registrability of trademarks; it merely sets up minimum rules for the eligibility of a trademark for registration, leaving it up to WTO Members to deny the registration on other grounds determined under domestic law.

Consequently, the general approach to the interpretation of TRIPS obligations must be a broad one, leaving considerable discretion to Members for their implementing legislation. For the panels and the Appellate Body, this implies the exercise of judicial self-restraint.[214]

As far as the exceptions are concerned, their interpretation might have to follow a different concept. As a general rule, exceptions are to be interpreted in a narrow manner in order to prevent them from rendering the basic obligations ineffective.[215] On the other hand, this should not prevent Members from relying on these exceptions for the pursuit of important policy objectives. It is thus the difficult task of the panels and the Appellate Body to make sure that the exceptions meet their objective without blocking IPR holders from exercising their rights. Like the obligations, the exceptions are expressed in very broad and vague language. This makes it important to develop some general guidelines for their interpretation.[216]

Under the various intellectual property rights conventions administered by WIPO, Member countries have adopted their own and sometimes conflicting interpretations of the exceptions contained in these instruments. Thus, WTO panels and the Appellate Body have to make sure that these provisions, which are incorporated into TRIPS by reference, are interpreted in a uniform way. Another way of promoting uniformity is to use the same interpretation for several different exceptions. In the *Canada – Patent* case, the panel used the negotiating history and the text of Article 9(2) of the Berne Convention (i.e., a copyright-related exception) for the interpretation of the patent-related exception under Article 30.[217] This may be explained by the fact that the language

---

[212] See TRIPS Article 1.1, third sentence: "Members shall be free to determine the appropriate method of implementing the provisions of this Agreement within their own legal systems and practice."

[213] See Article 1.1, second sentence: "Members may, but shall not be obliged to, implement in their law more extensive protection than is required by this Agreement, provided that such protection does not contravene the provisions of this Agreement."

[214] J. H. Jackson, *Dispute Settlement and the WTO. Emerging Problems*, 1 Journal of International Economic Law 1998, pp. 329, 342, observes a trend in the jurisprudence of the Appellate Body toward more deference to national law.

[215] In accordance with this rule of interpretation, the WTO panels and the Appellate Body have so far taken a narrow approach to the various TRIPS exceptions, see below, under Section 4 of this Annex.

[216] For the following, see Cattaneo, p. 638 et seq.

[217] *Canada – Patent Protection of Pharmaceutical Products*, Report of the panel of 17 March 2000, WT/DS114/R, paras. 7.70–7.72.

of Article 9(2) of the Berne Convention[218] more or less reappears in several of the TRIPS exceptions, not only in Article 13 (exceptions to copyrights: "normal exploitation", "do not unreasonably prejudice the legitimate interests"), but also partly in Article 17 (exception to trademarks: "limited exceptions", "legitimate interests"), and Article 30 (exception to patents: "limited exceptions", "do not unreasonably conflict with a normal exploitation", "do not unreasonably prejudice the legitimate interests"). This means that the same criteria may be employed for the interpretation of these similar terms. What actually constitutes a "normal exploitation", "legitimate interests" and an "unreasonable prejudice" obviously depends on the respective intellectual property right and on each individual case. However, the common denominator of all these different exceptions is their basic purpose to prevent the abuse of such rights.[219] This is an expression of the basic structure of TRIPS, as made clear in its preamble and in Articles 7 and 8. Instead of a one-sided protection of IPRs, the Agreement aims to strike a balance between the protection of private rights and trade liberalization and various public policy objectives (such as the preservation of public health, for example). This means that the "normal exploitation" of any intellectual property right is one which does not restrain international trade or the pursuit of public policy objectives. "Legitimate interests" are those not colliding with legitimate trade or with other public policy objectives, and a "prejudice" to an intellectual property right is "unreasonable" when the limitation of such right is either not necessary for the attainment of a public policy objective or disproportionate.

4. WTO jurisprudence

4.1 The particular nature of the TRIPS Agreement

The complexities of the negotiations of TRIPS are reflected in its rather vague provisions, particularly in the field of exceptions. As Hudec pointed out,

> "...[W]hen a government is unable to secure true protection of certain interests, the first form of temporizing will usually be the imperfect legal commitment. [...] International litigation can provide for second-stage temporizing."[220]

In *India – Patent Protection* the question arose as to whether TRIPS should be interpreted by applying the same principles applicable to the other covered agreements. The panel decided that

> "We must bear in mind that the TRIPS Agreement, the entire text of which was newly negotiated in the Uruguay Round and occupies a relatively self-contained, sui generis, status in the WTO Agreement, nevertheless is an integral part of the WTO system, which itself builds upon the experience of nearly half a century

---

[218] This Article reads as follows: "It shall be a matter for legislation in the countries of the Union to permit the reproduction of such works in certain special cases, provided that such reproduction does not conflict with a *normal exploitation of the work* and does not *unreasonably prejudice the legitimate interests* of the author."(emphasis added).

[219] See Cattaneo, p. 640.

[220] R.E. Hudec, *Transcending the Ostensible: Some Reflections on the Nature of Litigation Between Governments*, 72 Minnesota Law Review 211, 1987, at. 218.

under the GATT 1947 [. . .] Indeed, in light of the fact that the TRIPS Agreement was negotiated as a part of the overall balance of concessions in the Uruguay Round, *it would be inappropriate not to apply the same principles in interpreting the TRIPS Agreement as those applicable to the interpretation of other parts of the WTO Agreement.*"[221] (Emphasis added).

4.2 The principle of effectiveness

The first principle of interpretation embodied in Article 31 of the VCLT is the principle of effectiveness. In the *United States – Gasoline case*, the Appellate Body has recognized this principle as applying in connection with the "covered agreements", and therefore to TRIPS. The AB held that:

> "One of the corollaries of the 'general rule of interpretation' in the Vienna Convention is that interpretation must give meaning and effect to all the terms of the treaty. An interpreter is not free to adopt a reading that would result in reducing whole clauses or paragraphs of a treaty to redundancy or inutility."[222]

This strong reliance by the Appellate Body on the terms of a treaty reappeared in the *India – Patent Protection case*, where the AB reversed the panel's findings concerning the issue of good faith interpretation. In the panel's opinion, good faith interpretation within the meaning of Article 31(1) of the Vienna Convention necessitated the protection of WTO Members' legitimate expectations as to TRIPS.[223] Such protection is not expressly required in TRIPS, but, according to the panel, the obligation to provide such protection can be derived from the fact that the Agreement serves the protection of IPRs in general.[224] The AB refused this interpretation of the Agreement as being too detached from the actual terms used in that Agreement. It observed:

> "The Panel misapplies Article 31 of the Vienna Convention. The Panel misunderstands the concept of legitimate expectations in the context of the customary rules of interpretation of public international law. The legitimate expectations of the parties to a treaty are reflected in the language of the treaty itself. The duty of a treaty interpreter is to examine the words of the treaty to determine the intentions of the parties. This should be done in accordance with the principles of treaty interpretation set out in Article 31 of the Vienna Convention. But these principles of interpretation neither require nor condone the imputation into a treaty

---

[221] *India – Patent Protection for Pharmaceutical and Chemical Agricultural Products* (complaint by the United States), WT/DS50/R, Report of the panel, 5 September 1997, para. 7.19.

[222] *United States – Standards for Reformulated and Conventional Gasoline*, Report of the Appellate Body, WT/DS2/AB/R, 29 April 1996, p. 23.

[223] In the TRIPS context, such legitimate expectations would concern the competitive relationship between Members' respective nationals. See *India – Patent Protection for Pharmaceutical and Chemical Agricultural Products*, Report of the panel, 5 September 1995, WT/DS50/R, paras. 7.21, 7.22.

[224] Ibid., para. 7.18: "In our view, good faith interpretation requires the protection of legitimate expectations derived from the protection of intellectual property rights provided for in the Agreement."

of words that are not there or the importation into a treaty of concepts that were not intended."[225]

In other words, the Appellate Body expressed the opinion that the clear language of a treaty imposes a definite limit to any teleological interpretation. For developing country Members, this interpretation applied by the AB has important implications. If the AB had condoned the panel's view on the protection of legitimate expectations under TRIPS, Members could actually initiate WTO proceedings against other Members for alleged frustration of legitimate expectations on the part of their nationals. Thus, even if the defendant Member had respected all its TRIPS obligations, it could still be sued before the WTO if some of its public policy objectives had upset the competitive relationship between national and foreign right holders, without however violating any TRIPS rules. Such claims would amount to non-violation complaints, which are currently not admitted under TRIPS.[226] By stating that the legitimate expectations of a party to a treaty are reflected in the treaty language itself, the AB has made clear that TRIPS-related complaints before the Dispute Settlement Body may only be based on allegations of violations that are reflected in the express terms of the Agreement. The AB has thus rejected the introduction through the back door of TRIPS-related non-violation complaints. Members therefore remain free to adopt certain public policy objectives to pursue their development goals, as long as they respect their express obligations under TRIPS. In that case, a possible impact of domestic policy measures on the economic expectations of foreign IP right holders does not expose the respective host country Member to any valid claims before a WTO dispute settlement panel.

4.3 The context of the treaty terms and the object and purpose of the treaty

According to Article 31, paragraph 2, of the Vienna Convention, the context to be taken into account for the purposes of interpretation includes the preamble and the annexes of the treaty, and any other agreement or text concluded by the parties in connection with that treaty. In the TRIPS Preamble, WTO Members express the desire

> "to ensure that measures and procedures to enforce intellectual property rights do not themselves become barriers to legitimate trade."

This is certainly guidance also for the determination of the object and purpose of TRIPS. In *Canada-Patent*, the Panel took a view in perfect line with Article 31, paragraph 2, of the Vienna Convention:

> "In the framework of the TRIPS Agreement, which incorporates certain provisions of the major pre-existing international instruments on intellectual property, *the context to which the Panel may have recourse for the purposes of interpretation of specific TRIPS provisions [. . .] is not restricted to the text, Preamble and Annexes to*

---

[225] *India – Patent Protection for Pharmaceutical and Chemical Agricultural Products*, Report of the Appellate Body, 19 December 1997, WT/DS50/AB/R, para. 45.

[226] See above, Chapter 32.

the TRIPS Agreement itself, but also includes the provisions of the other international instruments on intellectual property incorporated into the TRIPS Agreement, as well as any agreement between the parties relating to these Agreements within the meaning of Article 31:2 of the Vienna Convention on the Law of Treaties. Thus [...] Article 9:2 of the Berne Convention for the Protection of Literary and Artistic Works [...] is an important contextual element for the interpretation of Article 30 of the TRIPS Agreement."[227] (Emphasis added).

4.4 Subsequent state practice and the status of prior panel reports in WTO law

Article 31, paragraph 3 (b) of the Vienna Convention provides that "any subsequent practice in the application of the treaty which establishes the agreement of the parties regarding its interpretation" should be taken into account for the purpose of interpretation together with the context. "Subsequent practice" was, in the view of the Panel in *Japan – Taxes on Alcoholic Beverages,* previously adopted panel reports. The AB overruled this conclusion, arguing that previous panel reports were no binding precedents and thus did not have sufficient force and consistency to constitute "subsequent practice" within the meaning of Article 31 (3) (b) of the Vienna Convention. According to the AB, adopted panel reports should be taken into account for the settlement of a specific dispute, without however obliging the panel to follow the same reasoning. Even unadopted panel reports provide guidance for the interpretation of the WTO Agreements. But the exclusive authority to adopt generally binding interpretations of the WTO agreements lies with the Ministerial Conference, as the AB pointed out. It held:

> "Generally, in international law, the essence of subsequent practice in interpreting a treaty has been recognized as a "concordant, common and consistent" sequence of acts and pronouncements which is sufficient to establish a discernible pattern implying the agreement of the parties regarding its interpretation. An isolated act is generally not sufficient to establish subsequent practice; it is a sequence of acts establishing the agreement of the parties that is relevant.

> Although GATT 1947 panel reports were adopted by decisions of the CONTRACTING PARTIES, a decision to adopt a panel report did not under GATT 1947 constitute agreement by the CONTRACTING PARTIES on the legal reasoning in that panel report. The generally-accepted view under GATT 1947 was that the conclusions and recommendations in an adopted panel report bound the parties to the dispute in that particular case, but subsequent panels did not feel legally bound by the details and reasoning of a previous panel report.

> We do not believe that the CONTRACTING PARTIES, in deciding to adopt a panel report, intended that their decision would constitute a definitive interpretation of the relevant provisions of GATT 1947. Nor do we believe that this is contemplated under GATT 1994. There is specific cause for this conclusion in the WTO Agreement. Article IX:2 of the WTO Agreement provides: "The Ministerial Conference and the General Council shall have the exclusive authority to adopt interpretations of this Agreement and of the Multilateral Trade Agreements". Article IX:2 provides

---

[227] *Canada – Patent Protection of Pharmaceutical Products,* WT/DS114/R, Report of the panel, 17 March 2000, at para. 7.14.

further that such decisions "shall be taken by a three-fourths majority of the Members". The fact that such an "exclusive authority" in interpreting the treaty has been established so specifically in the WTO Agreement is reason enough to conclude that such authority does not exist by implication or by inadvertence elsewhere.

Historically, the decisions to adopt panel reports under Article XXIII of the GATT 1947 were different from joint action by the CONTRACTING PARTIES under Article XXV of the GATT 1947. Today, their nature continues to differ from interpretations of the GATT 1994 and the other Multilateral Trade Agreements under the WTO Agreement by the WTO Ministerial Conference or the General Council. This is clear from a reading of Article 3:9 of the DSU, which states:

> The provisions of this Understanding are without prejudice to the rights of Members to seek authoritative interpretation of provisions of a covered agreement through decision-making under the WTO Agreement or a covered agreement which is a Plurilateral Trade Agreement.

Article XVI:1 of the WTO Agreement and paragraph 1(b)(iv) of the language of Annex 1A incorporating the GATT 1994 into the WTO Agreement bring the legal history and experience under the GATT 1947 into the new realm of the WTO in a way that ensures continuity and consistency in a smooth transition from the GATT 1947 system. This affirms the importance to the Members of the WTO of the experience acquired by the CONTRACTING PARTIES to the GATT 1947 – and acknowledges the continuing relevance of that experience to the new trading system served by the WTO. Adopted panel reports are an important part of the GATT acquis. They are often considered by subsequent panels. They create legitimate expectations among WTO Members, and, therefore, should be taken into account where they are relevant to any dispute. However, they are not binding, except with respect to resolving the particular dispute between the parties to that dispute. In short, their character and their legal status have not been changed by the coming into force of the WTO Agreement.

For these reasons, we do not agree with the Panel's conclusion in paragraph 6.10 of the Panel Report that "panel reports adopted by the GATT CONTRACTING PARTIES and the WTO Dispute Settlement Body constitute subsequent practice in a specific case" as the phrase "subsequent practice" is used in Article 31 of the Vienna Convention. Further, we do not agree with the Panel's conclusion in the same paragraph of the Panel Report that adopted panel reports in themselves constitute "other decisions of the CONTRACTING PARTIES to GATT 1947" for the purposes of paragraph 1(b)(iv) of the language of Annex 1A incorporating the GATT 1994 into the WTO Agreement.

However, we agree with the Panel's conclusion in that same paragraph of the Panel Report that unadopted panel reports "have no legal status in the GATT or WTO system since they have not been endorsed through decisions by the CONTRACTING PARTIES to GATT or WTO Members". Likewise, we agree that "a panel could nevertheless find useful guidance in the reasoning of an unadopted panel report that it considered to be relevant".[228]

---

[228] *Japan – Taxes on Alcoholic Beverages*, WT/DS8/AB/R, WT/DS10/AB/R, WT/DS11/AB/R, Report of the Appellate Body, 1 November 1996, p. 13 ff. (under section "E. Status of Adopted Panel Reports"; footnotes omitted).

India – Patents raised the specific question as to whether GATT subsequent practice is to be taken into account for interpreting TRIPS. The panel categorically concluded that

> "Since the TRIPS Agreement is one of the Multilateral Trade Agreements, we must be guided by the jurisprudence established under GATT 1947 in interpreting the provisions of the TRIPS Agreement unless there is a contrary provision . . ."[229]

This conclusion is in line with the provision of Article XVI:1 of the WTO Agreement, providing that

> " . . . the WTO must be guided by the decisions, procedures and customary practices followed by the CONTRACTING PARTIES to GATT 1947 and the bodies established in the framework of GATT 1947".[230]

Article 3, paragraph 1, of the DSU, for its part, states that

> "[M]embers affirm their adherence to the principles for the management of disputes heretofore applied under Articles XXII and XXIII of GATT 1947, and the rules and procedures as further elaborated and modified therein."

4.5 The principle of evolutionary interpretation

Article 31, paragraph 3 (c), of the Vienna Convention, has been interpreted as referring either to the so-called principle of contemporaneity or to the principle of evolutionary interpretation (see above, in the introduction to this Annex).

Article 31, paragraph 3 (c) is a key provision for dealing with the interrelationship between WTO law and other international law rules and for the interpretation of certain provisions of TRIPS, such as Article 27, paragraph 2 which stipulates that

> "Members may exclude from patentability inventions, the prevention within their territory of the commercial exploitation of which is necessary to protect *ordre public* or morality, including to protect human, animal or plant life or health, to avoid serious prejudice to the environment, provided that such exclusion is not made merely because the exploitation is prohibited by their law."

The same goes for the interpretation of Article 31(b) that allows for compulsory licensing in case of national emergency, or other cases of extreme emergency or in cases of public non-commercial uses. Such concepts as *ordre public*, morality, national emergency or extreme urgency are likely to call for the application of this principle of interpretation. The same is true for determining what is "necessary" in order to protect human, animal or plant life or health, or to avoid serious prejudice to the environment. On the one hand, it could be argued that any interpretation should be guided by the understanding of those terms at the time of their negotiation. Such approach would put much emphasis on the sovereignty of the

---

[229] *India – Patent Protection for Pharmaceutical and Chemical Agricultural Products* (complaint by the United States), WT/DS50/R, Report of the panel, 5 September 1997, para. 7.19.

[230] Similarly, Article 1, paragraph (b) (iv), of the GATT 1994, establishes that "other decisions of the CONTRACTING PARTIES to GATT 1947"are part of the GATT 1994.

parties to a treaty and leave changes in interpretation up to express modifications of a treaty's text.

On the other hand, it could be argued that the above concepts are evolutionary by nature. A treaty may only serve its purpose of effectively regulating the relationship between states if it takes account of important legal, political, economic and societal developments. The *Shrimp-Turtle* case is the leading example of the application of this approach by the Appellate Body. In referring to the International Court of Justice Advisory Opinion on *Namibia (Legal Consequences)*, the AB upheld the view that

"[Concepts embodied in a treaty are] by definition, evolutionary, [their] interpretation cannot remain unaffected by the subsequent development of the law [...] Moreover, an international instrument has to be interpreted and applied within the framework of the entire legal system prevailing at the time of interpretation."[231]

In another case, the Appellate Body stated that

"WTO rules are not so rigid or so inflexible as not to leave room for reasoned judgments in confronting the endless and ever-changing ebb and flow of real facts in real cases in the real world. They will serve the multilateral trading system best if they are interpreted with that in mind."[232]

4.6 Recourse to preparatory work, to the intention of the parties and to teleological interpretation

In the *India – Patent case* (complaint by the EC), the panel referred to the negotiating history of TRIPS in accordance with Article 32 of the VCLT, "only to confirm the meaning resulting from the application of the rules set out in Article 31 of the Vienna Convention."[233] Similarly, in *Canada – Patent*, the panel referred to the preparatory work of Article 11*bis* of the Berne Convention in the understanding that interpretation may go beyond the negotiating history of TRIPS proper and also inquire into that of the incorporated international instruments on intellectual property.[234]

It may be stated that the rules of interpretation embodied in Article 31 of the VCLT, although they give preeminence to the principle of textuality, leave certain room for searching into the intention of the parties or for teleological interpretation. The limits of such a margin of manoeuvre of the judge depend, to some extent, on its judicial policy. A conservative tribunal is likely to stick almost exclusively to the terms of the text, whereas a more activist tribunal is likely to give more room to the object and purpose of the treaty or to further research into the intentions of the parties.

---

[231] *United States – Import Prohibition of Certain Shrimp and Shrimp Products*, WT/DS58/AB/R, Report of the Appellate Body, 12 October 1998, at para. 130. See Ph. Sands, *Vers une transformation du droit international*, Cours de l'IHEI, Droit International 4, Pedone, 2000, pp. 179 and ff.

[232] *Japan – Taxes on Alcoholic Beverages*, WT/DS8, 10, 11/AB/R, p. 34 (section H(2)c).

[233] *India – Patent Protection for Pharmaceutical and Chemical Agricultural Products*, Complaint by the European Communities, Report of the panel, 24 August 1998, WT/DS79/R, p. 60, para. 7.40, note 110.

[234] *Canada – Patent Protection of Pharmaceutical Products*, WT/DS114/R, Report of the panel, 17 March 2000, p. 150, para. 7.15

These subjective approaches to treaty interpretation appear mainly in connection with multilateral treaties. As Thirlway has noticed, in analyzing the case law of the International Court of Justice:

> "at least in multilateral treaties, it has been the 'intention' or object of the treaty which has been taken as starting-point, either explicitly or implicitly".[235]

Divergent perceptions of WTO Members regarding intellectual property protection may lead them to present different approaches to interpretation of TRIPS in disputes before the organs for the settlement of disputes. While developing countries might take a narrower view in interpreting their obligations and an expansive (evolutionary) view of the exceptions contained in TRIPS, developed countries might wish, on the contrary, to narrow the scope of these exceptions in order to avoid undermining the protection of private rights. The WTO panels and Appellate Body have so far interpreted the exceptions contained in TRIPS in a narrow way,[236] and they will have in the future the challenging task of achieving a balance among these different views when interpreting the Agreement.

4.7 The interpretation of national law

In the *India – Patent* case, the Appellate Body upheld the panel's approach to the interpretation of Indian domestic law for the implementation of the "mailbox rule" under Article 70.8.[237] While acknowledging that WTO Members were in principle free to determine the appropriate method of implementing the TRIPS obligations (Article 1.1), the AB insisted that a WTO panel has to have the possibility to examine whether a Member has violated those obligations. It is solely for this purpose, and not for the examination of the respective domestic law "as such" that a panel may verify the compatibility of national law with TRIPS obligations. The Appellate Body held:

> 64. "India asserts that the Panel erred in its treatment of India's municipal law because municipal law is a fact that must be established before an international tribunal by the party relying on it. In India's view, the Panel did not assess the Indian law as a fact to be established by the United States, but rather as a law to be interpreted by the Panel. India argues that the Panel should have given India the benefit of the doubt as to the status of its mailbox system under Indian domestic law. India claims, furthermore, that the Panel should have sought guidance from India on matters relating to the interpretation of Indian law.
>
> 65. In public international law, an international tribunal may treat municipal law in several ways. Municipal law may serve as evidence of facts and may provide evidence of state practice. However, municipal law may also constitute evidence of compliance or non-compliance with international obligations. For example, in

---

[235] H.W.A. Thirlway, *The Law and Procedure of the International Court of Justice 1960–1989*, British Yearbook of International Law, 1992, p. 19.

[236] C. Correa, *The WTO Dispute Settlement Mechanism*, The Journal of World Intellectual Property, vol. 4, March 2001, 251, 253, second para [hereinafter Correa].

[237] Article 70.8 requires Members that do not, for a transitional period, provide patent protection to pharmaceutical and agricultural chemical products to establish a mechanism for the receipt and the preservation of patent applications (the so-called "mailbox"). For more details on this case, see Chapter 2 on Article 1.1 and Chapter 36 on Article 70.

Certain German Interests in Polish Upper Silesia, the Permanent Court of International Justice observed:

> It might be asked whether a difficulty does not arise from the fact that the Court would have to deal with the Polish law of July 14th, 1920. This, however, does not appear to be the case. From the standpoint of International Law and of the Court which is its organ, municipal laws are merely facts which express the will and constitute the activities of States, in the same manner as do legal decisions and administrative measures. The Court is certainly not called upon to interpret the Polish law as such; but there is nothing to prevent the Court's giving judgment on the question whether or not, in applying that law, Poland is acting in conformity with its obligations towards Germany under the Geneva Convention.

66. In this case, the Panel was simply performing its task in determining whether India's "administrative instructions" for receiving mailbox applications were in conformity with India's obligations under Article 70.8(a) of the TRIPS Agreement. It is clear that an examination of the relevant aspects of Indian municipal law and, in particular, the relevant provisions of the Patents Act as they relate to the "administrative instructions", is essential to determining whether India has complied with its obligations under Article 70.8(a). There was simply no way for the Panel to make this determination without engaging in an examination of Indian law. But, as in the case cited above before the Permanent Court of International Justice, in this case, the Panel was not interpreting Indian law "as such"; rather, the Panel was examining Indian law solely for the purpose of determining whether India had met its obligations under the TRIPS Agreement. To say that the Panel should have done otherwise would be to say that only India can assess whether Indian law is consistent with India's obligations under the WTO Agreement. This, clearly, cannot be so."

67. Previous GATT/WTO panels also have conducted a detailed examination of the domestic law of a Member in assessing the conformity of that domestic law with the relevant GATT/WTO obligations. For example, in United States – Section 337 of the Tariff Act of 1930, the panel conducted a detailed examination of the relevant United States' legislation and practice, including the remedies available under Section 337 as well as the differences between patent-based Section 337 proceedings and federal district court proceedings, in order to determine whether Section 337 was inconsistent with Article III:4 of the GATT 1947. This seems to us to be a comparable case.

68. And, just as it was necessary for the Panel in this case to seek a detailed understanding of the operation of the Patents Act as it relates to the "administrative instructions" in order to assess whether India had complied with Article 70.8(a), so, too, is it necessary for us in this appeal to review the Panel's examination of the same Indian domestic law.[238]"

5. Conclusion

Given the considerable vagueness of many TRIPS provisions, legal interpretation plays a decisive role in the definition of Members' rights and obligations. Depending on whether a panel stresses more the purpose of intellectual property

---

[238] Report of the Appellate Body, paras. 64–68.

protection or of certain public policies such as the transfer of technology, the TRIPS obligations will become more burdensome either on developing or on developed countries. Here, it is important to have recourse to methods of interpretation acceptable to all Members.[239] Since a purely textual interpretation will not always clarify the extent of a right or an obligation, it has to be combined with an analysis of the respective provision's object and purpose (teleological interpretation). It is in this context that the interests of developing countries may be taken into account. Panels should stress the developmental and technological objectives of TRIPS as articulated in the preamble as well as in Articles 7 and 8. This of course should not contradict the clear language of a certain provision; an effective protection of intellectual property rights has to be secured, and a balance of interests needs to be struck. But it is important to acknowledge that TRIPS, in its present form, considerably enhances the protection of intellectual property rights and thus serves the interests of technologically more advanced economies.[240] On the other hand, an efficient worldwide protection of intellectual property is only possible with the cooperation of developing countries. In order to assure a cooperative attitude on the part of those countries, their concerns about high-level intellectual property protection and TRIPS-plus approaches have to be taken seriously. Given the considerable differences in the level of development of WTO Members, it is important to give the weakest countries the possibility to accede to a higher economic level. This is possible through an interpretation that has regard for the developmental objectives of TRIPS. Once developing countries have had the chance to establish their own industries, it will be in their own interest to shift from the promotion of public policy objectives to a more efficient protection of intellectual property.[241] This shift of preference may be reached by a combined textual and teleological interpretation, based on both the in-built flexibility of the Agreement and its objectives and principles.

---

[239] See Cattaneo, p. 636.

[240] The main elements of this enhanced protection *vis-à-vis* the traditional WIPO conventions are the establishment of (relatively high) minimum standards of protection (Article 1.1) as well as the obligation to establish a mechanism for the receipt and preservation of patent applications under Article 70.8. Finally, the decisive advantage offered to IP holders under the TRIPS Agreement is the existence of the binding dispute settlement procedures under the DSU.

[241] For more details on the relationship between enhanced protection of intellectual property rights and technology transfer, see Chapter 34.

33: Transitional Periods

Article 65   Transitional Arrangements

1. Subject to the provisions of paragraphs 2, 3 and 4, no Member shall be obliged to apply the provisions of this Agreement before the expiry of a general period of one year following the date of entry into force of the WTO Agreement.

2. A developing country Member is entitled to delay for a further period of four years the date of application, as defined in paragraph 1, of the provisions of this Agreement other than Articles 3, 4 and 5.

3. Any other Member which is in the process of transformation from a centrally-planned into a market, free-enterprise economy and which is undertaking structural reform of its intellectual property system and facing special problems in the preparation and implementation of intellectual property laws and regulations, may also benefit from a period of delay as foreseen in paragraph 2.

4. To the extent that a developing country Member is obliged by this Agreement to extend product patent protection to areas of technology not so protectable in its territory on the general date of application of this Agreement for that Member, as defined in paragraph 2, it may delay the application of the provisions on product patents of Section 5 of Part II to such areas of technology for an additional period of five years.

5. A Member availing itself of a transitional period under paragraphs 1, 2, 3 or 4 shall ensure that any changes in its laws, regulations and practice made during that period do not result in a lesser degree of consistency with the provisions of this Agreement.

Article 66   Least-Developed Country Members

1. In view of the special needs and requirements of least-developed country Members, their economic, financial and administrative constraints, and their need for flexibility to create a viable technological base, such Members shall not be required to apply the provisions of this Agreement, other than Articles 3, 4 and 5, for a period of 10 years from the date of application as defined under

paragraph 1 of Article 65. The Council for TRIPS shall, upon duly motivated
request by a least-developed country Member, accord extensions of this period.

2. [...]

1. Introduction: terminology, definition and scope

The notion of transitional periods in the WTO needs to be understood as the time
necessary for a WTO Member to bring itself into full conformity with the obligations set out by an Agreement. It has been argued that transitional periods are
an important component of Special and Differential Treatment in favour of developing countries. However, it may be borne in mind that in the various WTO
agreements, it is not just the developing countries that are given transitional periods. Thus, in the Agreement on Textiles and Clothing, it is the developed countries
that are in effect entitled to a transition period of 10 years for the elimination of
quotas. Nevertheless, in the context of TRIPS, transition periods basically constitute the amount of time available for a WTO Member (developed, developing
or least-developed) to bring itself into full conformity with the obligations of the
Agreement.

2. History of the provision

2.1 Situation pre-TRIPS

Under the predecessor of the WTO, the GATT 1947,[1] there were no transitional
periods for any Contracting Party, be it developed or not.[2] This may be explained
by the fact that the GATT is mainly about the reduction of tariffs. This has considerably less effect on a country's internal legal system than the TRIPS disciplines, which require the introduction of minimum standards, border controls
and domestic enforcement procedures along with the setting up of the respective
authorities. Instead of transitional periods, Part IV of the GATT (Trade and Development, Article XXXVI) seeks to boost developing countries' and least-developed
countries' (LDCs) export earnings by obligating developed states to open their
markets for primary products from those countries[3] and to waive reciprocity for
tariff reduction commitments.[4]

2.2 Negotiating history

Since TRIPS is a new and unprecedented Agreement in the WTO, and since it
was clear that the adjustment of the internal legal regimes of developing and

---

[1] In the framework of the WTO, the GATT 1947 is replaced by the identical GATT 1994.

[2] On the other hand, the GATT admits grandfather clauses allowing countries that accede to
it to maintain pre-existing domestic legislation inconsistent with GATT provisions. In addition,
the GATT in Part IV (Trade and Development) contains some provisions on special treatment
for developing countries. For instance, according to Article XXXVI:8 of the GATT, "developed
contracting parties do not expect reciprocity for commitments made by them in trade negotiations
to reduce or remove tariffs and other barriers to the trade of less-developed contracting parties".

[3] See Article XXXVI:4 of GATT 1994.

[4] See Article XXXVI:8 of GATT 1994.

least-developed countries would require a very substantial effort,[5] the question of transition periods assumed enormous importance for those countries. It was not settled until the very end of the TRIPS negotiations. The reason for this was that the developing countries did not agree to the introduction of substantive IPR standards until late in the negotiations. Without having agreed on the substance, there was no question of agreeing to transition periods.

When formal negotiations in the Uruguay Round began in early 1987, about 14 developing countries led by Brazil, India and Argentina resisted the mandate to develop substantial IPR standards. However, it can be stated that the negotiating draft submitted by the Trade Negotiations Committee (TNC) meeting in Geneva in April 1989 for the mid-term review of the Uruguay Round signalled a success for the interests of the developed countries and a setback for those developing countries which had opposed the inclusion of substantive IPR standards. The text agreed to by Ministers specifically mentioned transition periods. This was the first time that ministers explicitly took note of the issue of transition periods in TRIPS. The text makes clear, albeit implicitly, that some transition period would be required if the full participation of all countries in the results of the negotiations was to be ensured.

Following the above-mentioned mid-term review, important changes were made in the negotiating texts between July 1989 and December 1990. However, with respect to the issue of transition periods, neither the Anell Draft nor the Brussels Draft brought about a final agreement.[6] The differences between those drafts and the final versions of TRIPS Articles 65 and 66.1 will now be analysed.[7]

2.2.1 The Anell Draft[8]

"1. Transitional Period (68); Transitional Arrangements for Developing Countries and Technical Cooperation (73); Transitional Arrangements (74)

1A PARTIES shall take all necessary steps to ensure the conformity of their laws, regulations and practice with the provisions of this Annex within a period of not more than [-] years following its entry into force. The Committee on Trade Related Intellectual Property Rights may decide, upon duly motivated request, that developing countries which face special problems in the preparation and implementation of intellectual property laws, dispose of an additional period not exceeding [-] years, with the exception of points 6, 7 and 8 of Part II, in respect of which this additional period shall not apply. Furthermore, the Committee may, upon duly motivated request, extend this additional period by a further period not exceeding [-] years in respect of least developed countries. (68)

1B.1 Developing Countries (73)

(i) With a view to achieve full and successful adjustment and compliance with levels of protection and enforcement set forth in Parts III and IV above, and provided

---

[5] This is because many legal systems in developing countries or LDCs do not have a comparable tradition of IP protection.

[6] Such agreement was only expressed in the Dunkel Draft of December 1991 (see below).

[7] For this purpose, the draft articles that later became two independent TRIPS provisions (i.e., Articles 65 and 66.1) will be discussed together.

[8] See composite text of 23 July 1990, circulated by the Chairman (Lars E. R. Anell) of the TRIPS Negotiating Group, document MTN.GNG/NG11/W/76.

that existing levels of protection and enforcement are not reduced, developing PARTIES may not apply such standards for a period of a total of [X] years beginning with the date of acceptance or accession of such PARTY, but not later than the year [Z]. (73)

(ii) Delay in implementation of obligations under Parts III and IV above may be extended upon duly motivated request for a further period not exceeding [X] years by the Committee established under point 1B of Part VIII below. Such decision shall take into account the level of technological and commercial development of the requesting PARTY. (73)

(iii) Non-application of levels óf protection set forth in Parts III and IV above after final expiration of the transitional period agreed shall entitle other PARTIES, without prejudice to other rights under the General Agreement, to suspend the application points 7 and 8 of Part II above and grant protection of intellectual property rights on the basis of reciprocity. (73)

1B.2 Least-Developed Countries (73)

(i) With a view to achieve full and successful adjustment and compliance with levels of protection and enforcement set forth in Parts III and IV above, least developed PARTIES are not expected to apply such standards for a period of a total of [X + Y] years. (73)

(ii) Delay of implementation of obligations may be further extended upon request by the Committee established under point 1B of Part VIII below. (73)"

The above proposals differ considerably from each other and from the final version of Articles 65 and 66.1. Compared to TRIPS, the proposal under 1A imposed tighter requirements on both developing countries and LDCs with respect to an initial period of transition and also a possible extension thereof.

As to developing countries, the proposal under 1A made an initial transition period subject to two conditions: first, the given developing country had to "face special problems in the preparation and implementation of intellectual property laws"; and second, the same country was supposed to submit a "duly motivated request" to the Committee on Trade Related Intellectual Property Rights (i.e., the body that later became the Council for TRIPS).[9] Once this request was submitted, it was entirely in the discretionary power of the Committee to allow or to reject the request. There was no possibility of further extending a transitional period in favour of a developing country.[10]

With respect to LDCs, the "A" draft provided a specific, longer transitional period, which was added to the period available for developing countries. But as opposed to the current Article 66.1 (which accords an unconditional right), this required a duly motivated request and, like in the case of developing countries,

---

[9] By contrast, Article 65.2 TRIPS accords developing countries an unconditional right of transition of four years (see Section 3, below).

[10] Under TRIPS, in general, there is no such possibility, either. However, Article 65.4 authorizes such an additional period with respect to product patent protection in areas of technology not so protectable in the territory of the respective developing country Member on the general date of application of the TRIPS Agreement (see Section 3, below). Also, an extension of a transition period may be granted as a waiver of a WTO obligation pursuant to Article IX.3 of the WTO Agreement.

depended on the Committee's discretion. Also, the "A" proposal did not provide for a possibility to extend this LDC-specific period.[11]

Compared to the "A" proposal, the proposal under 1B contained an unconditional right for developing countries to benefit from an initial transition period (see 1B.1(i)), like under Article 65.2. Also, there was a general possibility to further extend this initial period in favour of developing countries (see 1B.1(ii)), unlike under TRIPS.

With respect to LDCs, the "B" proposal contained a specific (longer) period, which was to be enjoyed unconditionally (see 1B.2(i)), as under Article 66.1. Also, provision was made of a possibility to extend this LDC-specific period (see 1B.2(ii)), again as under Article 66.1.

Finally, the third paragraph under 1B.1 is worth noting. It addressed the situation of non-compliance with substantive IPR obligations after the expiry of the transitional periods. The proposed remedies for non-compliance included the suspension of the most-favoured nation (MFN) obligation[12] and the reciprocal withdrawal of IP protection with respect to nationals of the country found in non-compliance. On the other hand, there was no express reference to any dispute settlement procedures to bring the respective national law or practice into conformity with the relevant substantive IP standard.

2.2.2 The Brussels Draft[13]

As late as the Brussels meeting in December 1990, the Chairman of the TRIPS Negotiating Group circulated a report stating that there were differences in substance, among other things, in the transition period to be provided for developing countries and LDCs. Developing countries were interested in a transition period of at least 10 years. The USA, on the other hand, favoured the idea of "pipeline protection" which went in the opposite direction.[14] Another reason for the deadlock in the negotiations was the fact that the issue of agriculture and textiles still remained unresolved. For developing countries, there was a link between what happened in the negotiations on the Agriculture and Textiles Agreements on the one hand and TRIPS on the other.[15] At Brussels itself, there was consequently no breakthrough with respect to the determination of actual time frames.

---

[11] By contrast, such possibility exists under TRIPS Article 66.1, second sentence (Section 3, below).

[12] Points 7 and 8 in the quoted proposal above referred to the MFN principle and certain exceptions; now under Articles 4 and 5 of TRIPS.

[13] Document MTN.TNC/W/35/Rev. 1 of 3 December 1990.

[14] The U.S. position can be found in the patent section 7 of the Anell Draft. "Pipeline protection" refers to a method of protection that would deny any transition periods by obligating countries to protect foreign patents from the date they were granted in the country of origin. For more details, see Chapter 36 (Transitional provisions).

[15] This position was based on the developing countries' hope to gain in the field of textiles and agriculture what they feared to lose in the new areas such as TRIPS and Services. Indeed, there was a negotiating linkage between the expiry of the transitional period of the Textiles Agreement and the expiry of the transitional period for providing product patent protection for pharmaceuticals, i.e., both periods expire on 1 January, 2005. Note, however, the more favourable situation for LDCs in the pharmaceutical sector, where those countries have until 2016 to implement the TRIPS disciplines on patents and undisclosed information. See in detail under Section 6.2, below.

In the following, the pertinent provisions of the Brussels Draft will be analysed. The immediate antecedent to Article 65 TRIPS provided:

"1. Subject to the provisions of paragraphs 2 and 3 below, PARTIES shall not be obliged to apply the provisions of this Agreement before the expiry of a period of [...] years following the date of entry into force of this Agreement for that PARTY.

2. A developing country PARTY may delay for a period of [...] years the date of application, as defined in paragraph 1, of the provisions of this Agreement other than Articles 3, 4 and 5 [, insofar as compliance with those provisions requires the amendment of domestic laws, regulations or practice.]

3. Any other PARTY which is undertaking structural reform of its intellectual property system and faces special problems in the preparation and implementation of intellectual property laws, may also benefit from a period of delay as foreseen in paragraph 2 above.

4. *No provision*

[5.] Any PARTY availing itself of a transitional period under paragraphs 1, 2 or 3 shall ensure that any changes in its domestic laws, regulations and practice made during that period do not result in a lesser degree of consistency with the provisions of this Agreement.

5. Any PARTY availing itself of a transitional period in accordance with paragraph 2 or 3 above shall provide, on accession, a schedule setting out its timetable for application of the provisions of this Agreement. [This timetable shall be without commitment.] [The Committee established under Part VII below may authorise, upon duly motivated request, departures, consistent with provisions of paragraphs 2 or 3 above, from the timetable.]"

Paragraphs 1 and 2 of the above draft were essentially similar to TRIPS Article 65.1 and 2. However, paragraph 1 determined as the base for the computing of the transitional period the date on which the Agreement entered into force *for the respective Party*. This differs from Article 65.1, according to which the decisive date is the general entry into force of the WTO Agreement. This difference has important consequences for countries acceding to the WTO at a later point in time (see Section 3 below).

Draft paragraph 3 was construed wider than its current counterpart. It applied to "any" country undertaking structural reforms of its IP system, whereas Article 65.3 is limited to transition economies. An important difference exists with respect to paragraph 4: the specific transition period for product patent protection in certain areas of technology (see Section 3 below) was not yet contained in the Brussels Draft. This appeared only in the Dunkel Draft text of 1991 (see below). Finally, paragraph 5 appeared twice in the Brussels Draft (see above). The text containing a bracketed numbering ([5]) is what later became the final version of paragraph 5. It states that any changes in domestic laws, regulations or practice made during a transitional period shall not result in a lesser degree of consistency with the provisions of the agreement.

The second text numbered as draft paragraph 5 represented an idea that was eventually dropped. According to this proposal, each country taking advantage of a transitional period was supposed to submit to the other Parties a timetable indicating as of when it would fully apply the substantive IPR disciplines. The purpose of this provision was to increase transparency. Since the end of a country's transition period was to be computed on an individual basis (i.e., on the respective date of entry into force of the Agreement in the country in question, see draft paragraph 1, above), the dates of full applicability of the Agreement could have varied from country to country, depending on the length of domestic ratification procedures. Under such circumstances, countries could not be expected to be aware of the multitude of different dates of application of the Agreement in other countries. However, with the abandonment of individual time frames and the introduction of a commonly applicable base for the computing of the transitional periods (i.e., the date of entry into force of the WTO Agreement, see below), the above provision was no longer necessary and therefore did not reappear in the final text of TRIPS.

Finally, the Brussels Draft contained an extra provision on least-developed countries (the provision that later became Article 66.1), which provided:

"1. In view of their special needs and requirements, their economic, financial and administrative constraints, and their need for flexibility to create a viable technological base, least-developed country PARTIES shall not be required to apply the provisions of this Agreement, other than Articles 3, 4 [and 5, insofar as compliance with those provisions requires the amendment of domestic laws, regulations or practices for a period of [...] years from the date of application as defined under paragraph 1 of Article [65] above. The Committee shall, upon duly motivated request by a least-developed country PARTY, accord extensions of this period.] The requirement of paragraph 5 of Article [65] above shall not apply to least-developed country PARTIES."[16]

This draft paragraph is quite similar to Article 66.1. The time frame for the transition period was still bracketed. So was the possibility of extending the initial period upon duly motivated request. The last sentence of the above paragraph appears to refer to the non-bracketed draft paragraph 5 regarding submission of timetables since (a) it is likewise non-bracketed, and (b) it appears in any case to be more consistent with the first sentence that refers also to paragraph 5 in a context apparently related to fixing a transition period. This last sentence reappeared neither in the Dunkel Draft nor in the final version of TRIPS.[17]

2.2.3 The Dunkel Draft[18]

The issue of transitional periods in TRIPS was essentially settled in 1991. The final time frames were agreed upon and reflected in the Dunkel Draft of December 1991, which contained the same provisions on transition periods that we find today in TRIPS. In particular, and in contrast to the Brussels Draft (see above), paragraph 1 of draft Article 65 referred to the date of the entry into force of "this Agreement",

---

[16] Paragraph 2 of this draft provision was essentially the same as Article 66.2, which is not the subject of this chapter (see Chapter 34).

[17] As to the treatment of LDCs in this respect under the current version of TRIPS, see below, Section 3.

[18] Document MTN.TNC/W/FA of 20 December 1991.

and thereby introduced a common basis for the computing of the transitional periods, irrespective of the date on which the Agreement becomes binding for an individual country (TRIPS maintains this objective approach, referring to the "WTO Agreement" instead of to TRIPS alone).

The Dunkel Draft Article 65 contained an important additional paragraph 4, providing:

> "4. To the extent that a developing country Party is obliged by this Agreement to extend product patent protection to areas of technology not protectable in its territory on the general date of application of this Agreement for that Party, as defined in paragraph 2 above, it may delay the application of Section 5 of Part II of this Agreement to such areas of technology for an additional period of five years."

The reason for the inclusion of this paragraph was the fact that many developing countries, at the time of the Uruguay Round, did not provide patent protection in the areas of agricultural and pharmaceutical products. In fact, for most developing countries the issue of product patent protection in these sensitive areas was the most problematic feature of TRIPS. Paragraph 4 was therefore introduced to address such concerns. However, the extra transitional period was made subject to the mailbox provision under Article 70.8 and the obligation to provide exclusive marketing rights (EMRs) under Article 70.9 (see Section 3 below).[19]

3. Possible interpretations

Article 65 contains the transition period available for developed (para. 1), developing (para. 2) and economies in transition countries (para. 3). Article 66.1 contains the transition period for LDCs. These transition periods are effective automatically and do not have to be specifically requested or reserved.

3.1 Article 65.1

> 1. Subject to the provisions of paragraphs 2, 3 and 4, no Member shall be obliged to apply the provisions of this Agreement before the expiry of a general period of one year following the date of entry into force of the WTO Agreement.

This provision lays down a general transition period that applies to all WTO Members, irrespective of their status. Accordingly, no Member was obligated to fully apply the provisions of TRIPS until one year after the entry into force of the Agreement (1 January 1995), i.e., until 1 January 1996. Note that this general transition period is made subject to the provisions of paragraphs 2, 3 and 4 of Article 65.

---

[19] In brief, the mailbox rule obliges Members benefiting from a transition period to register incoming patent applications for later examination, thus preserving priority and novelty of the relevant inventions. An exclusive marketing right (EMR) has to be granted *in lieu* of a patent during the transition period, provided that certain important preconditions are met. Note that the obligation to provide EMRs does not apply to LDCs, see below, Section 6.2. For more details on the mailbox rule and on the notion of EMRs, see Chapter 36 (Transitional Provisions).

On the one hand, those paragraphs further extend the general transition period in favour of developing countries and economies in transition. On the other hand, the general extension in paragraph 2 does not relieve Members of their obligations with respect to the national treatment and MFN disciplines (see below).

3.2 Article 65.2

> 2. A developing country Member is entitled to delay for a further period of four years the date of application, as defined in paragraph 1, of the provisions of this Agreement other than Articles 3, 4 and 5.

This paragraph deals with the transition period specifically available for developing countries. It extends the general transition period of paragraph 1 by four years. Thus, for developing countries the transition period generally available was five years from the date of the entry into force of TRIPS, i.e., 1 January 2000.

There is a very important exception to this rule. The additional transition period under paragraph 2 does not apply to Members' obligations under Articles 3, 4 and 5 (National Treatment, MFN and Multilateral Agreements on Acquisition or Maintenance of IPRs). These disciplines fall therefore under the first paragraph of Article 65 and have to be implemented by developing countries from 1 January 1996.[20]

The reason for singling out national treatment and MFN for immediate implementation by all WTO Members is based on the perceived overall importance of those rules for the functioning of TRIPS.[21] From a developed country perspective, immediate implementation of national treatment and MFN secures a level playing field in developing countries for IP holders with respect to domestic firms and third country foreigners. As a general rule, developing country governments may no longer treat foreigners less favourably than domestic IP holders, e.g., with a view to promoting the economic development of domestic infant industries.[22] With respect to MFN, developed country governments may now be sure that in developing countries, the nationals of other developed countries are not treated more favourably than their own nationals with respect to the protection of IPRs.[23]

---

[20] The same applies to economies in transition and LDCs, based on Articles 65.3 and 66.1, see below.

[21] The WTO Appellate Body has qualified the national treatment and MFN obligations as "cornerstones" of the world trading system, including the TRIPS Agreement (see WTO Appellate Body, *United States – Section 211 Omnibus Appropriations Act of 1998*, WT/DS176/AB/R, 2 January 2002 (*U.S. – Havana Club*), at para. 297). For more details on the national treatment and MFN disciplines, see Part 1 of this Resource Book (Chapter 4).

[22] See the relevant part of Article 3 TRIPS: "Each Member shall accord to the national of other Members *treatment no less favourable* than that it accords to its own nationals with regard to the protection [footnote omitted] of intellectual property, [...]" (emphasis added).

[23] See the relevant part of Article 4: "With regard to the protection of intellectual property, any advantage, favour, privilege or immunity granted by a Member to the nationals of any other country shall be accorded immediately and unconditionally to the nationals of all other Members." Note that prior to the establishment of TRIPS, there was growing concern among trade negotiators that due to bilateral pressure, some developing countries were granting certain IPR privileges to foreigners from selected countries only, to the detriment of both their own nationals and the

3.3 Article 65.3

> 3. Any other Member which is in the process of transformation from a centrally-planned into a market, free-enterprise economy and which is undertaking structural reform of its intellectual property system and facing special problems in the preparation and implementation of intellectual property laws and regulations, may also benefit from a period of delay as foreseen in paragraph 2.

The same period of five years available for developing countries (para. 2) applies to countries in transition. Contrary to paragraph 2, paragraph 3 does not automatically accord a transitional period, but makes this dependent on further conditions. The Member in question must undertake structural reforms of its intellectual property system and must face problems in implementing IP laws and regulations. There is no specification as to what are "special problems" in the preparation and implementation of intellectual property laws and regulations. It may be assumed, however, that the transition from a centrally-planned economy to a system of free markets constitutes *per se* a major challenge, not only in economic respects. The establishment of an IP system that is tailored to free market requirements would therefore appear to provide a strong *prima facie* case of "special problems" in the above sense. The reference to paragraph 2 makes clear that transition economies like developing countries had to comply with national treatment and MFN obligations as early as 1 January 1996.

3.4 Article 65.4

> 4. To the extent that a developing country Member is obliged by this Agreement to extend product patent protection to areas of technology not so protectable in its territory on the general date of application of this Agreement for that Member, as defined in paragraph 2, it may delay the application of the provisions on product patents of Section 5 of Part II to such areas of technology for an additional period of five years.

This is an important additional transition period on top of the five years generally provided to developing countries. As opposed to the general transitional periods in paragraphs 1 through 3, which apply to all types of IPRs, this additional period is limited to the obligation to extend product patent protection to areas of technology not so protectable in a Member's territory on the date of application of TRIPS (i.e., 1 January 2000). It applies to areas such as, for instance, pharmaceutical or agricultural chemical products where many developing countries did not grant patent protection at the time of entry into force of TRIPS. However, this provision

---

nationals of third countries. Such practices do not constitute an infringement of the national treatment obligation. Hence, the call for an incorporation of the MFN principle into the TRIPS Agreement. (For details, see Chapter 4.)

should be read in conjunction with Article 70.8 and 9, which obligates developing countries invoking Article 65.4 to provide, during the transition period, for a means of registering applications for the above patents as well as for exclusive marketing rights.[24]

3.5 Article 65.5

> 5. A Member availing itself of a transitional period under paragraphs 1, 2, 3 or 4 shall ensure that any changes in its laws, regulations and practice made during that period do not result in a lesser degree of consistency with the provisions of this Agreement.

This is essentially a provision which prevents WTO Members from "rolling back" during the transition period, i.e., from providing a reduced degree of IP protection in their domestic laws. On the other hand, this provision also makes sure that, if under a bilateral arrangement some developing countries choose to go "TRIPS-plus", the Agreement does not prevent them from rolling back to the common TRIPS standards. This issue would exclusively be governed by the respective bilateral agreement.

In this context, the question arises whether paragraph 5 also applies to LDCs. The reference in paragraph 5 is only to the transitional periods under Article 65, but not to the special LDC period under Article 66.1. In Article 66.1, there is no mention of any prohibition comparable to the one under Article 65.4, nor is there any reference to this provision. The obligation under Article 70.2 to protect existing subject matter does not apply to LDCs for the time indicated in Article 66.1 (see below). For these reasons, LDCs are not bound by Article 65.5 and may actually "roll back" on their IPR laws during the 10-year transition period. This obviously does not alter the fact that once their TRIPS obligations do begin, LDCs have to make sure that their IP laws are fully TRIPS-consistent.

3.6 Article 66.1

> 1. In view of the special needs and requirements of least-developed country Members, their economic, financial and administrative constraints, and their need for flexibility to create a viable technological base, such Members shall not be required to apply the provisions of this Agreement, other than Articles 3, 4 and 5, for a period of 10 years from the date of application as defined under paragraph 1 of Article 65. The Council for TRIPS shall, upon duly motivated request by a least-developed country Member, accord extensions of this period.

This provision pertains to LDC Members. It may be noted that only one LDC at the time, i.e., Tanzania, participated actively in the TRIPS negotiations. The provision in Article 66 acknowledges that there are special needs and requirements of LDC

---

[24] For details, see Chapter 36 (Transitional provisions).

Members[25] and allows them ten years to implement TRIPS, except the national treatment and most-favoured nation obligations (Articles 3–5). This means that LDCs will, in general, have to comply with TRIPS obligations as of 1 January 2006. Until then, Article 70.8 and 9 obliges them, like developing countries, to provide for a system of registration (mailbox) of patent applications for pharmaceutical and agricultural chemical products and for exclusive marketing rights (EMRs). However, LDCs have been exempted through a WTO waiver from the obligation to grant EMRs for pharmaceutical products until 2016.[26] Article 66.1 also provides that a duly motivated request for further extension of the transition period can be made by an LDC Member in the TRIPS Council and that the latter shall follow the request. In this regard, attention may be drawn to the Decision of the TRIPS Council to implement paragraph 7 of the Doha Declaration on the TRIPS Agreement and Public Health, according to which LDCs shall be free to disregard the TRIPS disciplines on patents and undisclosed information with respect to pharmaceutical products until 2016.[27] The above-mentioned waiver from the obligation to grant EMRs has to be seen in conjunction with this extension of the transition period. Such extension would be of little use if LDCs nevertheless had to provide for EMRs, which presumptively give their holder the right to exclude others from the marketing of pharmaceutical products.[28]

Finally, it should be noted that all of the above provisions for the computing of the time frame refer to paragraphs 1 or 2 of Article 65 (i.e., the date of the entry into force of the WTO Agreement). This means that with respect to countries acceding to the WTO at a later point in time, the same deadlines will apply. For instance, developing countries joining the WTO after 1 January 2005 will not be authorized to claim any transitional period with respect to product patents. LDCs acceding after 1 January 2006 will not automatically be granted a general transitional period comparable to the one available to LDCs under Article 66.1. Note that the situation would have been different under the Brussels Draft, according to which newly acceding Members would have been accorded the same time frames as original Members.[29]

---

[25] Note that the TRIPS Preamble equally recognizes the special needs of the least-developed country Members in respect of maximum flexibility in the domestic implementation of laws and regulations in order to enable them to create a sound and viable technological base.

[26] The waiver was approved by the WTO General Council on 8 July 2002. For more details, see below, Section 6.2.

[27] See the Decision of the Council for TRIPS on the *Extension of the Transition Period under Article 66.1 of the TRIPS Agreement for Least-Developed Country Members for Certain Obligations with Respect to Pharmaceutical Products*, IP/C/25 of 27 June 2002. For details on this Decision and the Doha Declaration, see below, Section 6.2.

[28] Note that under TRIPS, there is no definition of EMRs. Even though Members therefore have some flexibility as to the national design of EMRs, it follows from the term as such that there has to be some degree of exclusivity at least with respect to the marketing of the covered products. For more details on EMRs, in particular their distinction from patent rights, see Chapter 36.

[29] See above, Section 2.2, paragraph 1 of the draft Article that later became Article 65 TRIPS. This draft provision for the computing of transitional periods relied on the respective date of the entry into force of the Agreement for each individual country, and not on the general date of the entry into force of the WTO Agreement.

4. WTO jurisprudence

4.1 EC – Protection of Trademarks and GIs

Following separate requests by Australia[30] and the USA,[31] the WTO Dispute Settlement Body (DSB) at its meeting on 2 October 2003 established a single panel[32] to examine complaints with respect to EC Council Regulation (EEC) No. 2081/92 of 14 July 1992[33] on the protection of geographical indications and designations of origin for agricultural products and foodstuffs. The complaints are based, *inter alia*, on alleged violations of Article 65.[34] The complainants contend that since the above EC Regulation is not in conformity with certain substantive TRIPS provisions (in particular those on national treatment, MFN treatment, trademarks and geographical indications),[35] the EC does not respect its obligation under Article 65.1 to apply TRIPS as of 1 January 1996.

5. Relationship with other international instruments

5.1 WTO Agreements

5.2 Other international instruments

The transitional periods contained in Articles 65, 66.1 refer only to TRIPS obligations. An LDC Member by benefiting from Article 66.1 or from paragraph 7 of the Doha Declaration on TRIPS and Public Health does not infringe the Agreement, but could, at the same time and through the same action, infringe non-TRIPS obligations such as the patent disciplines of the Paris Convention (provided it is a Party to this Convention).[36] However, such non-WTO agreements are not enforceable through trade sanctions, due to the lack of a dispute settlement system comparable to the DSU of the WTO.

6. New developments

6.1 National laws

6.2 International instruments

6.2.1 The Doha Declaration

6.2.1.1 The extension in paragraph 7. The Doha Ministerial Conference agreed to extend until 2016 the transition period for LDC Members to implement their

---

[30] WT/DS290/18 of 19 August 2003.

[31] WT/DS174/20 of 19 August 2003.

[32] *European Communities – Protection of Trademarks and Geographical Indications for Agricultural Products and Foodstuffs*[hereinafter *EC – Protection of Trademarks and GIs*], WT/DS174/21 and WT/DS290/19 of 24 February 2004, Constitution of the Panel Established at the Requests of the United States and Australia.

[33] See above, Section 2.1.

[34] See the above requests by Australia and the USA for the establishment of a panel.

[35] See Chapters 4, 14 and 15. The complaints are principally based on those provisions.

[36] For a list of the Parties to the Paris Convention, among which there is a considerable number of LDCs, see <http://www.wipo.org/treaties/documents/english/pdf/d-paris.pdf>.

obligations in the areas of patents and undisclosed information with respect to pharmaceutical products. The relevant part of paragraph 7 of the Declaration reads as follows:

> "[. . .] We also agree that the least-developed country Members will not be obliged, with respect to pharmaceutical products, to implement or apply Sections 5 and 7 of Part II of the TRIPS Agreement or to enforce rights provided for under these Sections until 1 January 2016, without prejudice to the right of least-developed country Members to seek other extensions of the transition periods as provided for in Article 66.1 of the TRIPS Agreement. We instruct the Council for TRIPS to take the necessary action to give effect to this pursuant to Article 66.1 of the TRIPS Agreement."[37]

Even though the legal character of this Declaration is controversial,[38] it clearly indicates Members' will to extend the transitional period contained in Article 66.1 beyond 1 January 2006, i.e., until 1 January 2016. Consequently, LDC Members may, until that date, disregard substantive TRIPS provisions on patents and undisclosed information with respect to pharmaceutical products.

LDC Members may equally engage in exports and imports of generic drugs among themselves.[39] Finally, as far as the importation into LDC Members of drugs from non-LDC Members is concerned, two situations need to be distinguished.[40] If a drug is off-patent in the non-LDC exporting Member (either because the patent there has expired or because the exporting Member is a developing country that does not have to honour patent rights until 2005, in line with Article 65.4), importation of low-priced medicines into the respective LDC Member will be possible. On the other hand, if the drug is on-patent in the exporting country (in particular after 1 January 2005, when developing country Members like India have to introduce patent protection for pharmaceutical products), generic producers there will no longer be permitted to the same extent as before to supply LDCs with low-priced copies of patented drugs. The fact that as of 1 January 2005, major developing country exporters of pharmaceuticals have to provide for product patent protection does not mean that from that date, the production of any generics will be prohibited. Patent protection will apply only to those pharmaceuticals for which

---

[37] See the Declaration on the TRIPS Agreement and Public Health, WTO document WT/MIN(01)/DEC/W/2, under para. 7.

[38] See F. Abbott, *The Doha Declaration on the TRIPS Agreement and Public Health: Lighting A Dark Corner at the WTO*, in: Journal of International Economic Law (2002), 469–505 [hereinafter Abbott, *Doha Declaration*]. As opposed to the position taken by the authors of this book, it could be argued that the Doha Declaration is not legally binding, because it was not adopted pursuant to the formalities laid down for authoritative interpretations in Article IX:1 of the WTO Agreement, i.e., not based on a recommendation by the TRIPS Council. This interpretation would be too formalistic, though, and would not only disregard the clear language of the Declaration (especially in the quoted para. 7), but also the rule of treaty interpretation in Article 31 of the Vienna Convention on the Law of Treaties, which considers the language of an agreement (in the context of its object and purpose) to be the essential criterion of interpretation.

[39] See Abbott, *Doha Declaration*, p. 503.

[40] Ibid.

a patent application was filed after 1 January 1995,[41] and which actually meet the national patentability criteria. Other drugs will not benefit from patent protection and may thus be further available as low-priced generics. Those drugs on-patent after 1 January 2005 may nevertheless be exported to qualifying importing Members at low prices under a compulsory license, according to the 2003 Decision on Implementation of Paragraph 6 of the Doha Declaration on the TRIPS Agreement and Public Health.[42]

6.2.1.2 Paragraph 7 and the mailbox obligation. Apart from the above, there are further aspects limiting the benefits LDC Members can draw from paragraph 7 of the Doha Declaration. In particular, it has been observed that paragraph 7 does not expressly refer to the obligations under Article 70.8 and 9 of Part VII.[43] Therefore, a strict interpretation of paragraph 7 would lead to the conclusion that this paragraph does not relieve LDC Members from the obligation to provide for mailbox protection and to grant EMRs before 2016.[44] While the issue of EMRs has been settled through a 2002 WTO General Council waiver (see below), there has been no clarification on the part of the TRIPS Council concerning the mailbox obligation. According to Article 31.1 of the Vienna Convention on the Law of Treaties, a treaty is to be interpreted in accordance with the ordinary meaning of the terms of the treaty in their context and in the light and the objective of the treaty's object and purpose. The terms of paragraph 7 do not refer to Part VII of TRIPS. However, the purpose of paragraph 7 is to prevent the TRIPS patent rules to become an obstacle to Members' efforts to protect public health. On these lines, it could be argued that the extension of the transitional period only makes sense if LDC Members are not at the same time obliged to provide for mailbox protection. It is true that such obligation would not affect the LDC Members' right as such to disregard patents for pharmaceutical products until 2016. But it would require them to install and maintain mechanisms that permit the receipt and retention of pharmaceutical patent applications for the purpose of later examination (i.e., from 2016). This implies considerable financial and administrative efforts that will place an additional burden on a given country's health budget. More importantly, the mailbox obligation entails a considerable problem for the affordability of low-priced drugs after the expiry of the transition period in 2016. Provided they

[41] See Article 70.8 ("mailbox"), and Chapter 36 for details. See also *Implementing the paragraph 6 decision and Doha Declaration: Solving practical problems to make the system work*, Report of a seminar organised by the Quaker United Nations Office 21–23 May 2004, Jongny-sur-Vevey, Switzerland, Section I.

[42] For details, see Chapter 25. In essence, this Decision of 30 August 2003 (WTO documents IP/C/W/405 or WT/L/540 as adopted by the General Council) authorizes WTO Members with drug manufacturing capacities to make and export pharmaceutical products to countries with public health needs, despite the requirement in Article 31(f) that products made under compulsory licences shall be predominantly for the domestic market of the country of production. For a critical analysis of this "paragraph 6 solution", see C. Correa, *Recent International Developments in the Area of Intellectual Property Rights*, paper submitted to the Second ICTSD-UNCTAD Bellagio Series on Development and Intellectual Property, 18–21 September 2003, available at <http://www.iprsonline.org/unctadictsd/bellagio/docs/Correa_Bellagio2.pdf>.)

[43] Abbott, *Doha Declaration*, p. 502.

[44] Ibid.

meet the patentability requirements, the patent applications received during the transition period will turn into enforceable patents after 1 January 2016. Without a mailbox system in place, by contrast, the novelty of inventions made before 2016 will not be preserved for the time after 1 January 2016, with the result that after that date, a patent may not be issued and drugs remain available as generics.[45]

From the above point of view, paragraph 7 of the Doha Declaration could therefore be interpreted as also relieving LDC Members from the mailbox obligation. However, it is by no means certain that a WTO panel or the Appellate Body would endorse the interpretation offered above. It could be argued that such interpretation would be contrary to the clear language of paragraph 7, which does not refer to Article 70. In addition, the free availability of generics would only be affected *after* the expiry of the transitional period. These effects could therefore be considered as falling outside the intended scope of protection of paragraph 7. Finally, the fact that the waiver issued by the General Council (see below) refers expressly only to EMRs, but not to the mailbox obligation, is very likely to be read as a sign that the mailbox obligation was intended to be maintained.

6.2.1.3 Paragraph 7 and pharmaceutical process patents. Another interpretative uncertainty persisted with respect to the question whether paragraph 7 extends to pharmaceutical process patents. The language directly refers to pharmaceutical "products".[46] But this does not necessarily exclude process patents. It has been observed that paragraph 7 could be interpreted as covering those process patents that have been issued with respect to pharmaceutical products.[47] This would include processes employed for the production of a pharmaceutical product.

The TRIPS Council Decision of 30 August 2003 (WT/L/540) on the implementation of paragraph 6 of the Doha Declaration on TRIPS and Public Health contains a definition of "pharmaceutical product", providing that:

"1. For the purposes of this Decision:

(a) "pharmaceutical product" means any patented product, or product manufactured through a patented process, of the pharmaceutical sector needed to address the public health problems as recognized in paragraph 1 of the Declaration. [...]"

This definition does not completely clarify the interpretive issue highlighted above. It includes process patents to the extent they are necessary to produce a covered product. In any case, the definition was adopted in the particular context of paragraph 6 and does not necessarily apply to paragraph 7.

---

[45] Abbott, *Doha Declaration*, p. 502/503.

[46] "[...] We also agree that the least-developed country Members will not be obliged, with respect to pharmaceutical products, to implement or apply Sections 5 and 7 of Part II of the TRIPS Agreement [...]" (see above).

[47] Abbott, *Doha Declaration*, p. 504, footnote 102, referring to TRIPS Article 28.1(b) as covering process patents that are arguably related to the subject matter of "pharmaceutical products" within the meaning of paragraph 7 of the Doha Declaration.

6.2.1.4 Implementing paragraph 7 on the domestic level. It is important to note that paragraph 7 concerns only obligations Members have toward other WTO Members. Thus, one Member will not be able to successfully challenge an LDC Member for not implementing, applying or enforcing patent rights in its territory before 2016. However, if an LDC Member does not take advantage of its right under paragraph 7 and provides in its domestic law for product patent protection before 2016, a patent holder may invoke his patent right under local law and sue generic producers for infringement of this right.[48]

Therefore, in case a domestic law of an LDC Member already provides for patent protection, one way of giving effect to the paragraph 7 extension would be to modify such law by internal legislation before authorizing third parties with the production of generic drugs. As noted above (Section 3), LDC Members are not prevented under TRIPS to adopt during the transition period new laws showing a lesser degree of TRIPS-consistency. Instead of modifying domestic law, LDC Member governments could alternatively take steps to allow their enforcement authorities, whether those are administrative authorities or courts, to reject requests for patent right enforcement. In fact, such authority need not be granted until the time it is exercised, and may even be granted "after the fact". As in most legal matters, however, by acting in advance the government can save itself and its procurement authorities from the potential delay and expense involved in legal battles with IPR holders, and potential political pressure from the home governments of IPR holders.

Because the political and constitutional arrangement in each country is somewhat different, it is difficult to offer general guidance regarding the specific steps LDC governments should take to pave the way for avoiding IPR-based obstacles to procuring generic medicines and supplies. If the executive and parliament (or legislature) cooperate in adopting a grant of authority for the procurement authority to disapply IPRs in order to promote and protect public health, this should in most or all LDCs be adequate to accomplish the objective. Other procedures are certainly possible and acceptable.[49] The government should, however, avoid discriminating among IPR holders of different nationalities so as to comply with the TRIPS requirements of national treatment and MFN treatment.

6.2.2 The TRIPS Council Decision implementing the extension
On 27 June 2002, the TRIPS Council adopted a decision implementing paragraph 7 of the Doha Declaration on TRIPS and Public Health, as instructed by the

---

[48] This is independent of the question whether in the respective country WTO law may be directly relied upon by individuals before local courts. The local patent right at issue would not derive directly from WTO law, but from local law, which may usually be invoked directly.

[49] Action by the executive or parliament alone may well be adequate (depending on the constitutional arrangement), and the courts might have authority to act on their own to disapply patent protection taking into account TRIPS Agreement principles. Among all possible ways, the most reliable one appears to be the actual modification of the law that the courts then apply (see above). The downside of this solution, on the other hand, is that this process might be time consuming. In addition, legislation would have to be amended again at the end of the transition period, provoking the risk of delayed implementation of TRIPS rules.

Fourth Ministerial Conference in the same paragraph (see above). This decision provides:

> "Having regard to paragraph 1 of Article 66 of the TRIPS Agreement;
>
> Having regard to the instruction of the Ministerial Conference to the Council for TRIPS contained in paragraph 7 of the Declaration on the TRIPS Agreement and Public Health (WT/MIN(01)/DEC/2) (the "Declaration");
>
> Considering that paragraph 7 of the Declaration constitutes a duly motivated request by the least-developed country Members for an extension of the period under paragraph 1 of Article 66 of the TRIPS Agreement;
>
> Decides as follows:
>
> 1. Least-developed country Members will not be obliged, with respect to pharmaceutical products, to implement or apply Sections 5 and 7 of Part II of the TRIPS Agreement or to enforce rights provided for under these Sections until 1 January 2016.
>
> 2. This decision is made without prejudice to the right of least-developed country Members to seek other extensions of the period provided for in paragraph 1 of Article 66 of the TRIPS Agreement."[50]

Paragraphs 1 and 2 of the decision essentially repeat the language employed in paragraph 7 of the Doha Declaration on TRIPS and Public Health. There is no clarification with respect to the interpretive uncertainties left by paragraph 7 (as discussed above).[51] The third introductory clause of the decision ("Considering that...") confirms that the extension of the transition period under paragraph 7 is based on Article 66.1, second sentence.

6.2.3 The waiver of the obligation to provide EMRs
On 8 July 2002, the WTO General Council approved a draft waiver submitted by the TRIPS Council concerning the obligation of LDC Members to provide exclusive marketing rights during the extended transitional period.[52] The waiver provides:

> "The General Council,
>
> Having regard to paragraphs 1, 3 and 4 of Article IX of the Marrakesh Agreement Establishing the World Trade Organization (the "WTO Agreement");
>
> Conducting the functions of the Ministerial Conference in the interval between meetings pursuant to paragraph 2 of Article IV of the WTO Agreement;
>
> Noting the decision of the Council for TRIPS on the Extension of the Transition Period under Article 66.1 of the TRIPS Agreement for Least-Developed Country Members for Certain Obligations with respect to Pharmaceutical Products

---

[50] Decision of the Council for TRIPS on the *Extension of the Transition Period under Article 66.1 of the TRIPS Agreement for Least-Developed Country Members for Certain Obligations with Respect to Pharmaceutical Products*, WTO document IP/C/25 of 27 June 2002.

[51] Note, however, that the issue of EMRs has been settled through a waiver adopted by the General Council. See below.

[52] The draft waiver was adopted by the TRIPS Council on 27 June 2002. The text of the waiver is available at <http://www.wto.org/english/news_e/pres02_e/pr301_e.htm>.

(IP/C/25) (the "Decision"), adopted by the Council for TRIPS at its meeting of 25–27 June 2002 pursuant to the instructions of the Ministerial Conference contained in paragraph 7 of the Declaration on the TRIPS Agreement and Public Health (WT/MIN(01)/DEC/2) (the "Declaration");

Considering that obligations under paragraph 9 of Article 70 of the TRIPS Agreement, where applicable, should not prevent attainment of the objectives of paragraph 7 of the Declaration;

Noting that, in light of the foregoing, exceptional circumstances exist justifying a waiver from paragraph 9 of Article 70 of the TRIPS Agreement with respect to pharmaceutical products in respect of least-developed country Members;

Decides as follows:

1. The obligations of least-developed country Members under paragraph 9 of Article 70 of the TRIPS Agreement shall be waived with respect to pharmaceutical products until 1 January 2016.

2. This waiver shall be reviewed by the Ministerial Conference not later than one year after it is granted, and thereafter annually until the waiver terminates, in accordance with the provisions of paragraph 4 of Article IX of the WTO Agreement."

This waiver fulfils an important complementary function with respect to paragraph 7 of the Doha Declaration. As noted before, paragraph 7 leaves some interpretive uncertainty as to its precise extent, in particular with respect to EMRs and mailbox application systems. The waiver makes clear that the obligation of LDC Members with respect to EMRs in the area of pharmaceutical products shall be waived until 2016 (subject to annual review).

This considerably enhances the practical value of the extension of the transitional period under paragraph 7. If LDC Members had to honour EMRs, the availability of less costly generic copies of a drug would be seriously put into question. Depending on local law, the patent applicant might not be able to invoke EMRs against the making or the importation of the covered drugs. But the patent applicant would presumptively have the right to prevent the marketing of the less costly copies throughout the respective LDC Member.[53]

On the other hand, the language employed in the waiver refers expressly to Article 70.9, thus arguably indicating that the waiver is not intended to cover the obligation of LDC Members to provide for mailbox application systems (Article 70.8) during the extended transitional period.

6.3 Regional and bilateral contexts

6.4 Proposals for review

There is no formal review of the transitional periods contained in Article 65 and 66.1.

---

[53] Abbott, *Doha Declaration*, p. 502, footnote 99, noting also that absent any clarification in the domestic law, EMRs might not be subject to the same limitations as patents (such as the general exception clause under Article 30, or the compulsory licensing provision in Article 31 TRIPS) and therefore be even more burdensome to a public health policy that seeks to promote the availability of low-priced medicines. Note, however, that India in its domestic law has subjected EMRs to compulsory licenses.

7. Comments, including economic and social implications

Considering the enormous adaptation efforts that need to be made in order to implement the TRIPS obligations in developing and least-developed countries, transitional periods are of vital importance to those Members. If a transition period of five years in the case of developing countries or even 10 or 20 years (for pharmaceuticals) in the case of LDCs seems long at first sight, it needs to be noted that these countries very often do not have a culture of IP protection like their industrialized country counterparts. The examples of the Republic of Korea[54] and Japan have shown that, in order for a country to develop an IPR-based industry that could engage in innovation and inventive activity it is essential for that country to have the human resources, the entrepreneurial capacity, the institutions and policies that are at the centre of a sound and viable technological base. It is only at that point that strong IP protection becomes relevant. If, on the other hand, a strong IP protection system prevents the domestic industry from engaging in legitimate imitation and innovation, developing countries will depend on the willingness of foreign right holders to share their knowledge. In that sense, transitional periods constitute an important tool for developing countries to set up that sound and viable base and thus develop their own IP-based industries.

---

[54] For a detailed analysis of the Korean experience with IPRs and their impact on technology transfer, see Linsu Kim, *Technology Transfer and Intellectual Property Rights: Lessons from Korea's Experience*, UNCTAD-ICTSD, Geneva 2003 (available at <http://www.iprsonline.org/unctadictsd/docs/Kim2002.pdf>.)

34: International and Technical Cooperation and Transfer of Technology

Article 69   International Cooperation

Members agree to cooperate with each other with a view to eliminating international trade in goods infringing intellectual property rights. For this purpose, they shall establish and notify contact points in their administrations and be ready to exchange information on trade in infringing goods. They shall, in particular, promote the exchange of information and cooperation between customs authorities with regard to trade in counterfeit trademark goods and pirated copyright goods.

Article 67   Technical Cooperation

In order to facilitate the implementation of this Agreement, developed country Members shall provide, on request and on mutually agreed terms and conditions, technical and financial cooperation in favour of developing and least-developed country Members. Such cooperation shall include assistance in the preparation of laws and regulations on the protection and enforcement of intellectual property rights as well as on the prevention of their abuse, and shall include support regarding the establishment or reinforcement of domestic offices and agencies relevant to these matters, including the training of personnel.

Article 66   Least-Developed Country Members

1. [. . .]
2. Developed country Members shall provide incentives to enterprises and institutions in their territories for the purpose of promoting and encouraging technology transfer to least-developed country Members in order to enable them to create a sound and viable technological base.

1. Introduction: terminology, definition and scope

The above-cited provisions of TRIPS create the basis for an international regime between its Members concerning international cooperation, technical cooperation and incentives for technology transfer. These three elements differ from each other and therefore need to be clearly distinguished.

International cooperation (Article 69) has the purpose of eliminating international trade in IPR-infringing goods. The provision makes explicit reference to trade in counterfeit trademark goods and pirated copyright goods and thus responds to the main concern voiced by industrialized countries prior to the Uruguay Round negotiations. According to Article 69, trade in IPR-infringing goods is to be eliminated through international cooperation. This is to be achieved by way of the establishment of contact points within Members' administrations, which will be notified to the other Members, and whose purpose is to exchange information on trade in infringing goods. In particular, the Members shall promote the exchange of information and cooperation between customs authorities with regard to trade in counterfeit trademark goods and pirated copyright goods. This provision applies to all Members regardless of their level of development. It aims to tighten up international procedures for cooperation in this field.[55]

By contrast, the other provisions that contribute to this regime of cooperation are addressed specifically to developed country Members and aim to remedy particular problems experienced by developing and least-developed country Members. Two policy strands are covered: technical cooperation (Article 67) and the encouragement of technology transfer (Article 66.2). Under Article 67, developed country Members are obliged, under certain conditions,[56] to provide for technical and financial cooperation in favour of both developing country and least-developed country Members. Despite this obligation, the overall purpose of technical cooperation under Article 67 corresponds to developed countries' interests in that technical cooperation is to be provided "in order to facilitate the implementation of this Agreement".

The second policy strand applies only to the LDC Members, as expressed by Article 66.2. As opposed to the above provisions on international and technical cooperation, this provision promotes the interests of the LDCs. By obliging developed country Members to provide for incentives for the promotion and the encouragement of technology transfer to LDCs, this provision takes account of concerns that the benefits of TRIPS might bypass the world's poorest nations.

Transfer of technology may be realized through formal as well as informal means. Informal technology transfer is carried out by imitation, and is typically not based on any monetary transaction or legal agreement.[57] Formal technology

---

[55] Note that the rather general terms of this provision are complemented by detailed minimum requirements with respect to the enforcement, acquisition and maintenance of intellectual property rights (Articles 41–62; Article 51 referring to border measures concerning counterfeit trademark and pirated copyright goods.). For details, see Chapter 30 of this Resource Book.

[56] These conditions will be examined in detail below, Section 3.

[57] See UNCTAD-ICTSD, *Intellectual Property Rights: Implications for Development*, Policy Discussion Paper, Geneva 2003, chapter 5 [hereinafter UNCTAD-ICTSD Policy Discussion Paper].

transfer is a commercial operation, based on a legal arrangement that involves monetary transaction. It includes foreign direct investment (FDI), joint ventures, whollyowned subsidiaries, licensing, technical-service arrangements, joint research and development (R&D) arrangements, training, information exchanges, sales contracts and management contracts.[58]

2. History of the provisions

2.1 Situation pre-TRIPS

Prior to the adoption of TRIPS, the prevailing concern as regards IPR regimes in developing countries was the perceived lack of adequate protection. In particular, developed countries with advanced IPR protection, and the transnational corporations (TNCs) headquartered in such countries, expressed worries about the adverse effects on trade and investment stemming from inadequate IPR protection and enforcement in developing countries leading to the extensive copying of goods protected by such rights in their home countries. These copies could then be traded with ease across borders, thereby undermining the protection afforded to its owner by the IPR in question. Stronger cooperation in the elimination of such trade was therefore a major objective for the advocates of TRIPS.

On the other hand, while developing countries were perceived as having weak IPR regimes, they were also perceived as having very real problems obtaining technology that would be useful to their development. In response to such concerns, the Draft UN Code on the Transfer of Technology contained *inter alia* provisions that exhorted developed countries to implement policies aimed at encouraging technology transfer to such countries.[59] Equally, the OECD Guidelines for Multinational Enterprises, concluded in 1976, contained a chapter on "Science and Technology" which exhorted TNCs to co-operate in the science and technology policies of the countries in which they operated.[60] Furthermore, at the national level, special technology transfer regimes were adopted by many developing, and some developed, countries to regulate the terms and conditions of inward technology transfer transactions.[61] Thus, prior to TRIPS, there was wide recognition of the special problems of developing countries in relation to technology transfer in both national laws and international deliberations.

2.2 Negotiating history

The negotiating history of these provisions suggests that the Agreement did not undergo any major changes. The most significant differences are outlined below.

---

[58] See also Keith Maskus, *Encouraging International Technology Transfer*, UNCTAD-ICTSD, Geneva 2004, available at <http://www.iprsonline.org/unctadictsd/projectoutputs.htm#casestudies>. [hereinafter Maskus, 2004]

[59] See S. Patel/P. Roffe/A. Yusuf, *International Technology Transfer. The Origins and Aftermath of the United Nations Negotiations on A Draft Code of Conduct*, Kluwer Law International, The Hague, 2001 [hereinafter Patel/Roffe/Yusuf]. See also UNCTAD, *International Investment Agreements: A Compendium* (New York and Geneva 1996, United Nations) Vols. I–III (See in particular chapters 2, 6 and 7 of Vol. I. at pp. 184–6, 195–8) [hereinafter UNCTAD, Compendium (IIAS)].

[60] UNCTAD, Compendium (IIAS), Vol. II. at p. 192.

[61] See Michael Blakeney, *Legal Aspects of the Transfer of Technology to Developing Countries* (Oxford 1989, ESC Publishing).

2.2.1 Article 69

2.2.1.1 The Anell Draft[62]

"4. International Cooperation (68)

PARTIES agree to cooperate with each other with a view to eliminating international trade in goods infringing intellectual property rights. For this purpose they shall establish and notify contact points in their national administrations, and shall be ready to exchange information on trade in infringing goods. They shall, in particular, promote the exchange of information and cooperation between customs authorities with regard to trade in counterfeit goods. (68) (See also point [–] of Part IX below.)"[63]

2.2.1.2 The Brussels Draft[64]

"PARTIES agree to cooperate with each other with a view to eliminating international trade in goods infringing intellectual property rights. For this purpose, they shall establish and notify contact points in their administrations and be ready to exchange information on trade in infringing goods. They shall, in particular, promote the exchange of information and cooperation between customs authorities with regard to trade in counterfeit goods."

As regards Article 69 the main change involves an extension of the types of illicit trade in IPRs that are to be covered by the duty of cooperation and exchange of information introduced by this provision. Thus, while the Anell Draft and the Brussels Draft specified only "trade in counterfeit goods", the final version refers to trade in "counterfeit trademark goods and pirated copyright goods".

2.2.2 Article 67

2.2.2.1 The Anell Draft

"2. Technical Assistance (68); Technical Cooperation (73); International Co-operation, Technical Assistance (74)

2A Developed PARTIES shall, if requested, advise developing PARTIES on the preparation and implementation of domestic legislation on the protection and enforcement of intellectual property rights covered by this Annex as well as the prevention of their abuse, and shall grant them technical assistance on mutually agreed terms and conditions, regarding the establishment of domestic offices and agencies relevant to the implementation of their intellectual property legislation, including the training of officials employed in their respective governments. (68)

2B PARTIES to this Agreement shall provide for technical cooperation to developing and least-developed PARTIES upon co-ordination by the Committee

---

[62] Document MTN.GNG/NG11/W/76, of 23 July 1990.

[63] Note that the referenced section of Part IX provided: "*Desirous* of providing for adequate procedures and remedies to discourage international trade in counterfeit and pirated goods while ensuring an unimpeded flow of trade in legitimate goods;"

[64] Draft Final Act Embodying the Results of the Uruguay Round of Multilateral Trade Negotiations, Revision, Trade-Related Aspects of Intellectual Property Rights, Including Trade in Counterfeit Goods, MTN.TNC/W/35/Rev. 1, 3 Dec. 1990.

established under point 1B of Part VIII below in collaboration with the World Intellectual Property Organization, and other international organizations, as appropriate. Upon request, such cooperation includes support and advice as to training of personnel, the introduction, amendment and implementation of national laws, regulations and practices, and assistance by the Committee for settlement of disputes. (73)"

2.2.2.2 The Brussels Draft. This draft was essentially identical to the final version of Article 67.

Two main changes can be noted between the Anell Draft and the final version of Article 67. The first change involves the scope of the duty to provide technical assistance in the preparation of IPR laws and regulations. The Anell Draft used the term "shall grant them technical assistance ..." (proposal 2A, above), suggesting a degree of compulsion in the discharge of this obligation. The final version has dropped the word "grant" and simply states that "[s]uch cooperation shall include assistance ...". This suggests a less directed approach to the carrying out of the assistance obligation, implying that assistance in this area may be part of a wider policy adopted by the developed country Member and may, in fact, be granted as a matter of discretion and judgment, as opposed to mandatory obligation. The second change involves the omission, from the final draft, of a proposed second paragraph to Article 67 (above, proposal 2B). This provision outlined an institutional process through which cooperation under this provision would take place. It involved the co-ordination of technical cooperation with developing and least-developed Parties through a Committee set up for this purpose in collaboration with the World Intellectual Property Organization. This draft paragraph had been dropped by the time of the Brussels Draft.

2.2.3 Article 66.2

Article 66.2 was not envisaged in the Anell Draft. It appears in the Brussels Draft in a form essentially identical to that of the final version of the provision. Like the final version of Article 66.2 TRIPS, the Brussels draft provision was addressed exclusively to LDCs.

3. Possible interpretations

3.1 Article 69

According to this provision ("Members agree to co-operate ... "), WTO Members are committed to cooperate. The language suggests a compulsory method of cooperation through the contact points in the Members' national administrations. The existence of these contact points must be notified to the other Members.

They must also be "ready to exchange information ... ". Thus there is no positive duty to volunteer information to other Members, but relevant information must be made available upon request.

Finally, promotion and cooperation between customs authorities is specified in relation to trade in counterfeit trademark goods and pirated copyright goods.

3.2 Article 67

There are no mandatory rules or methods of cooperation imposed on developed country Members under this provision. However, the duty on developed countries to cooperate is activated upon the receipt of a request for cooperation by a developed country member from a developing or least developed country Member, followed by the conclusion of mutually agreed terms and conditions that will govern the cooperation process.

The nature of the cooperation is described as "technical and financial". In view of the freedom to request cooperation on the part of the developing or least-developed country Member, and the concomitant freedom of the developed country Member to whom the request is made, to determine by mutual agreement the nature and scope of the cooperation so requested, that cooperation could involve technical and/or financial cooperation. The parties are free to determine this in the course of their negotiations.

The remaining parts of Article 67 add three further possible avenues of cooperation that shall be considered by the developed and developing or least-developed cooperating Members:

– assistance in the preparation of laws and regulations on the protection and enforcement of IPRs;

– assistance in the prevention of the abuse of laws and regulations on the protection and enforcement of IPRs (a matter related to the more general aims of Article 69);

– support regarding the establishment or reinforcement of domestic offices and agencies relevant to these matters, including the training of personnel.

3.3 Article 66.2

This provision places a duty on developed country Members to provide incentives to enterprises and institutions in their territory for the purpose of promoting and encouraging technology transfer to least-developed country Members with the aim of creating a sound and viable technological base.

The precise scope and nature of that duty is not defined in any detail. Thus there would appear to be considerable discretion on the part of the developed country Member on how to discharge this duty.[65] However, it is clear that the duty exists and must be discharged. This reading is consistent with the general objectives of TRIPS, as laid out in Articles 7 and 8, where the protection of IPRs is seen as having to contribute to the promotion of technological innovation and the transfer and dissemination of technology, to the mutual advantage of producers

---

[65] Note, however, that some precision has been added to this provision through the decision by the Council for TRIPS concerning the implementation of Article 66.2 of the TRIPS Agreement. For details, see below, Section 6.2.3.

and users of technological knowledge and in a manner conducive to social and economic welfare, and to the balance of rights and obligations. Moreover, the Doha Ministerial Declaration expressly reaffirmed the mandatory nature of the provisions under Article 66.2.[66]

Finally, the obligation to encourage technology transfer includes proprietary technology and not only technology in the public domain.[67] The latter is more easily accessible, whereas the transfer of the former is in the exclusive discretion of the holder of the respective right.

3.4 The combined effect of these provisions

Thus, these provisions together create a model of cooperation between TRIPS Members, especially developed and developing or least-developed country Members which aims to:

– control international trade in counterfeit goods (Article 69);

– establish an effective legal and administrative regime for the protection of IPRs in developing and least-developed countries (Articles 69 and 67);

– encourage enterprises and institutions in developed country Members to transfer technology to least developed country Members to help in the development of a sound and viable technological base (Article 66.2).

In the light of these provisions, the Council for TRIPS regularly receives numerous notifications from developed countries of their technical cooperation programmes.

4. WTO jurisprudence

To date no dispute concerning these provisions has been brought before the dispute settlement body of the WTO.

5. Relationship with other international instruments

5.1 WTO Agreements

The WTO agreements specify, in numerous provisions,[68] the need to offer technical assistance to developing and LDC Members.[69] Each of those provisions relates specifically to the particular subject matter of the respective agreement.

---

[66] For details, see below, Section 6.2.2.

[67] See C. Correa, *Can the TRIPS Agreement Foster Technology Transfer to Developing Countries?* Draft of March 2003, submitted to a Conference at Duke University [hereinafter Correa, Draft].

[68] For a detailed overview of these provisions, see UNCTAD (2001), *Compendium of International Arrangements on Transfer of Technology. Selected Instruments*, New York and Geneva, p. 52 et seq. [hereinafter Compendium (TOT)].

[69] A generally flexible approach to the obligations of, in particular, the least-developed country Members is advocated by the terms of the Decision on Measures in Favour of Least Developed Countries appended to the Final Act of the Uruguay Round of 1994.

In particular, reference can be made to Articles 11, 12 TBT Agreement; Article IV GATS; Article 9 of the Agreement on the Application of Sanitary and Phytosanitary Measures; and Article 20.3 of the Agreement on Implementation of Article VII of the GATT 1994 (Customs Valuation Agreement).

5.2 Other international instruments

Other multilateral instruments contain provisions offering an opportunity to negotiate commitments for home country measures beneficial to developing countries.[70]

6. New developments

6.1 National laws

6.2 International instruments

6.2.1 The WIPO-WTO agreement on technical cooperation

In 1996 the WTO and the World Intellectual Property Organization (WIPO) entered into a technical cooperation agreement. Of particular relevance to the provisions under discussion is Article 4 of that Agreement, which deals with "Legal-Technical Assistance and Technical Cooperation":

> "(1) [*Availability of Legal-Technical Assistance and Technical Cooperation*] The International Bureau shall make available to developing country WTO Members which are not Member States of WIPO the same legal-technical assistance relating to the TRIPS Agreement as it makes available to Member States of WIPO which are developing countries. The WTO Secretariat shall make available to Member States of WIPO which are developing countries and are not WTO Members the same technical cooperation relating to the TRIPS Agreement as it makes available to developing country WTO Members.
>
> (2) [*Cooperation Between the International Bureau and the WTO Secretariat*] The International Bureau and the WTO Secretariat shall enhance cooperation in their legal-technical assistance and technical cooperation activities relating to the TRIPS Agreement for developing countries, so as to maximize the usefulness of those activities and ensure their mutually supportive nature.
>
> (3) [*Exchange of Information*] For the purposes of paragraphs (1) and (2), the International Bureau and the WTO Secretariat shall keep in regular contact and exchange non-confidential information."

Thus the secretariats of both organisations will offer the same technical and legal assistance to developing countries so long as those belong to at least one of the two organisations.

---

[70] Due to the great number of relevant agreements, a discussion of these would go beyond the scope of this book. For an overview of international instruments on technology transfer, see the Compendium (TOT). For a detailed analysis of home country measures for the promotion of foreign direct investment (FDI) and technology transfer to developing countries in international agreements see UNCTAD, *Home Country Measures: Facilitating the Transfer of Technology to Developing Countries*. UNCTAD Series on issues in international investment agreements, New York and Geneva (forthcoming, 2005).

In addition, reference should be made to the WTO-WIPO joint initiative of 14 June 2001 to provide technical assistance to the least-developed countries aimed at helping those countries to comply with their obligations under TRIPS. The joint initiative builds on existing cooperation between WIPO and WTO[71] and on each organization's own technical assistance programmes. It is also similar to a joint WIPO-WTO project[72] launched in 1998 to help all developing countries, particularly those that are not least developed, which had to comply with TRIPS by 2000.[73] Least-developed countries have until 1 January 2006 to comply with TRIPS. They have to bring their laws on copyright, patents, trademarks and other areas of intellectual property into line with TRIPS.[74] They also have to provide ways of enforcing the laws effectively in order to deal with various forms of intellectual property infringement. To help these countries meet their obligations, the technical assistance available under the joint initiative includes cooperation with preparing legislation, training, institution-building, modernizing intellectual property systems and enforcement.[75] All LDCs can participate in the technical assistance offered. They do not need to be WIPO or WTO Members.[76]

Technical cooperation is an important instrument to facilitate developing countries' adequate integration into the multilateral trading system. It should also be a vehicle for exploring the flexibilities inherent in TRIPS as highlighted throughout this book.

6.2.2 The Doha mandate on Article 66.2 TRIPS

At the WTO Ministerial Conference at Doha in November 2001, Members agreed, *inter alia*, on a Decision concerning implementation-related issues and concerns.[77] This Decision addresses several developing Members' preoccupations about the implementation of the WTO agreements into their domestic laws.[78] As to TRIPS, paragraph 11.2 of the Decision provides that:

---

[71] Agreement between the World Intellectual Property Organization and the World Trade Organization, see at <http://www.wto.org/english/tratop_e/trips_e/intel3_e.htm>.

[72] See the WTO press release of 21 July 1998, at <http://www.wto.org/english/news_e/pres98_e/pr108_e.htm>.

[73] Note that under Article 65.4 of TRIPS, this deadline is extended until 1 January 2005 concerning the obligation to provide product patents in areas not so protectable in a developing country Member on the general date of application of TRIPS (i.e., 1 January 1996).

[74] Note that on certain conditions, this deadline is extended under para. 7 of the Doha Declaration on the TRIPS Agreement and Public Health (WT/MIN(01)/DEC/W/2): Members agreed that "least-developed country Members will not be obliged, with respect to pharmaceutical products, to implement or apply" the TRIPS disciplines on patent rights and on the protection of undisclosed information until 1 January 2016 (independently of their right to seek further extension of transition periods as provided under Article 66.1 TRIPS). For details, see Chapter 33.

[75] Of the 50 countries defined by the UN as least developed, 31 are Members of the WTO (another nine are negotiating WTO membership). See <http://www.wto.org/english/thewto_e/whatis_e/tif_e/org7_e.htm>.

[76] World Intellectual Property Organisation (WIPO)/World Trade Organisation (WTO) *Press Release* (Press/231) 14 June 2001 *WIPO and WTO launch new initiative to help world's poorest countries*.

[77] Decision on Implementation-Related Issues and Concerns, WTO document WT/MIN(01)/17 of 20 November 2001.

[78] See the third consideration of the Decision, reading as follows: "*Determined* to take concrete action to address issues and concerns that have been raised by many developing-country Members regarding the implementation of some WTO Agreements and Decisions, including the difficulties

"Reaffirming that the provisions of Article 66.2 of the TRIPS Agreement are mandatory, it is agreed that the TRIPS Council shall put in place a mechanism for ensuring the monitoring and full implementation of the obligations in question. To this end, developed-country Members shall submit prior to the end of 2002 detailed reports on the functioning in practice of the incentives provided to their enterprises for the transfer of technology in pursuance of their commitments under Article 66.2. These submissions shall be subject to a review in the TRIPS Council and information shall be updated by Members annually."

According to the second sentence of the Decision, developed country Members shall report on the "functioning in practice" of their respective incentive regimes for the transfer of technology. It has been suggested that this language could be interpreted as committing developed country Members to establish an incentives regime that actually promotes successful technology transfer.[79]

6.2.3 Recent developments in the Council for TRIPS

Pursuant to the Doha Decision on Implementation-Related Issues and Concerns, the WTO Council for TRIPS adopted, on 19 February 2003, a Decision concerning the implementation of Article 66.2.[80] In essence, it lays down an obligation for developed country Members to submit reports on actions taken or envisaged (including any specific legislative, policy and regulatory framework) to provide incentives to enterprises and institutions in their territories for the promotion of technology transfer to LDC Members. Such reports are to be updated annually, and new detailed reports have to be submitted every third year. The reports are to be reviewed by the Council for TRIPS at its end of year meeting with a view to providing other Members with the opportunity to pose questions and request additional information. Developed country Members are obliged to disclose certain information concerning their incentive regimes, particularly on the functioning in practice of these incentives.[81] Finally, the arrangements contained in this Decision are subject to a review after three years by the Council with a view to improving them.

This Decision constitutes an important step forward in the attempt to operationalize Article 66.2. It considerably reduces developed Members' discretion as to their implementation of it.

---

and resource constraints that have been encountered in the implementation of obligations in various areas;"

[79] See Correa, Draft.

[80] See WTO document IP/C/28.

[81] According to paragraph 3(d) of the Decision such information includes:

"– statistical and/or other information on the use of the incentives in question by the eligible enterprises and institutions;

– the type of technology that has been transferred by these enterprises and institutions and the terms on which it has been transferred;

– the mode of technology transfer;

– least-developed countries to which these enterprises and institutions have transferred technology and the extent to which the incentives are specific to least-developed countries; and

– any additional information available that would help assess the effects of the measures in promoting and encouraging technology transfer to least-developed country Members in order to enable them to create a sound and viable technological base."

6.2.4 The WTO Working Group on Trade and Technology Transfer

In paragraph 37 of the Doha Ministerial Declaration, Members agreed to establish a Working Group on Trade and Technology Transfer. Its mandate is as follows:

"37. We agree to an examination, in a Working Group under the auspices of the General Council, of the relationship between trade and transfer of technology, and of any possible recommendations on steps that might be taken within the mandate of the WTO to increase flows of technology to developing countries. The General Council shall report to the Fifth Session of the Ministerial Conference on progress in the examination."

6.2.5 The Conference of the Parties to the Convention on Biological Diversity

At its seventh meeting in February 2004, the Conference of the Parties (COP) to the Convention on Biological Diversity (CBD) decided to invite the Secretariat of the CBD, WIPO, UNCTAD and other relevant organizations to prepare:

"technical studies that further explore and analyse the role of intellectual property rights in technology transfer in the context of the Convention on Biological Diversity and identify potential options to increase synergy and overcome barriers to technology transfer and cooperation, consistent with paragraph 44 of the Johannesburg Plan of Implementation. The benefits as well as the costs of intellectual property rights should be fully taken into account."[82]

6.3 Regional and bilateral contexts

6.3.1 Regional context

6.3.1.1 Agreements between developed and developing country Members. The 2000 Cotonou Agreement[83] is intended to encourage developing country parties to integrate more fully into the global economy. To this end, cooperation between the EC and developing contracting parties in the field of economic sector development includes the development of scientific, technological and research infrastructure and services, including the enhancement, transfer and absorption of new technologies (see Article 23(j) of the Agreement).

Of particular relevance is the commitment of all parties, in Article 46, to ensuring an adequate and effective level of protection of IPRs and other rights covered by TRIPS. This includes, *inter alia*, an agreement to strengthen cooperation on the preparation and enforcement of laws and regulations in this field, the setting up of administrative offices and the training of personnel.

---

[82] See UNEP/CBD/COP/7/L.20 of 19 February 2004, page 11.

[83] European Commission (EC) (2000), *Partnership Agreement between the Members of the African, Caribbean and Pacific Group of States of the one part, and the European Community and its Member States, of the other part, signed in Cotonou, Benin on 23 June 2000.* (See <http://www.acpsec.org/gb/cotonou/accord1e.htm>.)

In a similar vein, agreements concluded between the EC and Latin American economic integration groups contain a commitment to economic cooperation that includes the encouragement of technology transfer.[84]

6.3.1.2 Agreements between developing country Members. Certain intra-regional economic integration agreements among developing and least-developed country Members contain provisions encouraging the development and transfer of technology by enterprises operating within the region. These may be divided into two main groups: general provisions stressing cooperation in areas relevant to the development and transfer of technology within the region, and specialized provisions establishing regional multinational enterprises, which, in turn, serve the purpose of developing technology and transferring it across the region.[85]

6.3.2 Bilateral context

Although almost all bilateral investment treaties (BITs) are silent on the question of technology transfer, it should be noted that the Dutch model agreement of 1997 states, in its Preamble, that "agreement upon the treatment to be accorded to investments [by the nationals of one Contracting Party in the territory of the other Contracting Party] will stimulate the flow of capital and technology and the economic development of the Contracting Parties".[86] Thus the Dutch model agreement makes a clear connection between the promotion and protection of investors and their investments (arguably including IPRs) and the stimulation of technology transfer. However, it is far from certain that enhanced IPR protection will automatically result in more transfer of technology (see the discussion under Section 7 below).

7. Comments, including economic and social implications

7.1 Technical cooperation

Considering the lack of experience and expertise in IP issues prevailing in many developing and least-developed country Members, the need for technical assistance for those countries is obvious. It is of crucial importance in this respect that

---

[84] See Framework Agreement for Cooperation Between the EC and the Cartagena Agreement and its Member Countries, 1993, Article 3 (UNCTAD, *International Investment Agreements: A Compendium* (New York and Geneva, 2000) [hereinafter UNCTAD, 2000], Vol. V, p. 187); and EC-MERCOSUL/R Interregional Framework Cooperation Agreement, 1993, Articles 11(2) and 16(2)(b) (UNCTAD, World Investment Report 2001, pp. 162–164).

[85] For the general provisions, see, e.g., the Treaty Establishing the African Economic Community of 1991 that calls upon the Community to harmonize national policies on science and technology and to promote technical cooperation and the exchange of experience in the field of industrial technology and implement technical training programmes among member States (Articles 4(2)(e) and 49(h), in UNCTAD 2000, Vols. IV–V, in Vol. V, pp. 16–18). A similar commitment can be found in Article 26 (3)(i) of the Revised Treaty of the Economic Community of West African States (ECOWAS) of 1993 (UNCTAD, 2000a, Vol. V, p. 40), and in Articles 100 (d) and 103 (2) of the Treaty Establishing the Common Market for Eastern and Southern Africa (COMESA) of 1993 (UNCTAD Compendium (IIAS), Vol. III, p. 102). For the specialized provisions, see, e.g., Article 101 (2) (iv.) of the COMESA Treaty (UNCTAD Compendium (IIAS), Vol. III, p. 103).

[86] UNCTAD, 2000, Vol. V, p. 333.

policy makers and providers of technical cooperation are fully aware of the TRIPS-inherent flexibilities that may be used for the realization of development goals. Concerns have been voiced in this respect as to the appropriateness and nature of the technical assistance offered to developing countries.[87] In particular, any organization or institution involved in technical IP assistance should take account of the different levels of development of their target countries, and those countries' different needs with respect to IP implementation.

Another important aspect of technical assistance is the facilitation of active participation of developing countries in the ongoing negotiations in Geneva and their ability to be represented by experts to international meetings on IPRs. Here, two lines of assistance have been identified:[88] first, the expansion of funding schemes of international organizations to cover the related costs; second, the improvement of the quality of developing country participation through permanent advice in the area of intellectual property rights.

7.2 Technology transfer

Given the increasing dependence of a country's wealth and competitiveness on its ability to produce high technology products for the world market, the technological gap between developed and developing countries has become one of the main obstacles to a successful integration of developing nations into the globalized economy.[89] Considering that most developing countries are net importers of new technologies, incoming technology transfer is a critical source of technical change.[90] Article 66.2 takes account of this by obliging Members to provide incentives for the promotion and encouragement of technology transfer to least-developed country Members.

However, the effect of Article 66.2 on the encouragement of technology transfer to the LDCs, and on the development of a sound technological base in those

---

[87] Such criticism comes not only from many NGOs, but has also been expressed by the IPR Commission (see p. 158 of the Report): "We recognise that WIPO has a role to play in promoting IPRs. However, we believe that it needs to do so in a much more nuanced way that is fully consistent with the economic and social goals to which the UN, and the international community are committed. A more balanced approach to the analysis of IPRs, and, in consequence WIPO programmes, would be beneficial to both the organisation and the developing world, which forms the majority of its membership." See also p. 161 of the Report: "There is also evidence that, in cases where WIPO's assistance has been acknowledged, the result has not incorporated all TRIPS flexibilities. For instance, the revised Bangui Agreement for the OAPI countries, where WIPO's assistance is acknowledged, has been criticised in various quarters for going further than TRIPS. It obliges LDC members (the majority of OAPI members) who ratify it to apply TRIPS in advance of need; it restricts the issuance of compulsory licences to a greater extent than required by TRIPS; it does not explicitly allow parallel imports; it incorporates the elements of UPOV 1991 in the agreement and it provides for a copyright term of 70 years after the death of the author." See also S. Musungu/G. Dutfield, *Multilateral agreements and a TRIPS-plus world: The World Intellectual Property Organisation (WIPO)*, TRIPS Issue Paper 3, Quaker United Nations Office, Geneva 2003 (available at <http://www.geneva.quno.info/pdf/WIPO(A4)final0304.pdf>).

[88] Ibid., p. 165.

[89] The importance of this gap may be illustrated by the following figures from 2000: only 10 developed countries accounted for 84% of global R&D annually, received 91% of global cross-border technology licence fees and royalties, and took out 94% of the patents granted in the USA between 1977 and 2000. Figures from Correa Draft, Table 1.

[90] See Policy Discussion Paper, chapter 5, and Maskus, 2004.

countries, has been very limited.[91] This raises concerns as to the appropriateness not only of Article 66.2, but of TRIPS in general to foster effective transfer of technology.[92] The decisive issue is whether enhanced IPR protection in developing countries and LDCs, as promoted by TRIPS, will actually result in increased technology transfer to these countries. Opinions differ widely in this respect, and the available empirical evidence is inconclusive.[93]

---

[91] See Keith Maskus, *Intellectual Property Rights in the Global Economy* (Washington DC, Institute for International Economics, 2000), p. 225. See also the IPR Commission, p. 26.

[92] See IPR Commission, p. 26. See also Correa, Draft, in his conclusions: "The TRIPS Agreement was essentially conceived as a means of strengthening the control by titleholders over the protected technologies, and not with the objective of increasing the transfer and use of technology globally. The transfer of technology was not, in fact, a concern of TRIPS proponents, and the possible effects of the new protectionist standards on such transfer were never seriously considered during the negotiations."

[93] See Policy Discussion Paper, Chapter 5, and Maskus, 2004.

35: Council for TRIPS

Article 68   Council for Trade-Related Aspects of
Intellectual Property Rights

The Council for TRIPS shall monitor the operation of this Agreement and, in particular, Members' compliance with their obligations hereunder, and shall afford Members the opportunity of consulting on matters relating to the trade-related aspects of intellectual property rights. It shall carry out such other responsibilities as assigned to it by the Members, and it shall, in particular, provide any assistance requested by them in the context of dispute settlement procedures. In carrying out its functions, the Council for TRIPS may consult with and seek information from any source it deems appropriate. In consultation with WIPO, the Council shall seek to establish, within one year of its first meeting, appropriate arrangements for cooperation with bodies of that Organization.

1. Introduction: terminology, definition and scope

The Council for TRIPS is charged with the monitoring of WTO Members' compliance with their obligations under TRIPS.[94] The legal base for its establishment is Article IV:5 of the WTO Agreement, which stipulates that the Council "shall oversee the functioning" of TRIPS. With a view of understanding the role of the Council within the general institutional structure of the WTO, a brief account is presented below.

a) The Ministerial Conference is the main body of the WTO, being composed of the representatives of all WTO Members at a ministerial level meeting at least once every two years. According to Article IV:1 of the WTO Agreement, the Ministerial Conference "shall have the authority to take decisions on all matters under any of the Multilateral Trade Agreements" including TRIPS. It is the Ministerial Conference that has the exclusive authority to adopt generally binding interpretations of the Multilateral Trade Agreements (Article IX:2 of the WTO Agreement).

b) The General Council is composed of representatives of all WTO Members who are generally Geneva-based ambassadors accredited to the WTO, meeting as appropriate (Article IV:2 of the WTO Agreement). According to the same provision,

---

[94] For more details on the functions of the Council, see below, under Section 3.

the General Council shall conduct the functions of the Conference in the intervals between the meetings of the ministers. In other words, the decision-making authority of the Conference is most of the time delegated to the General Council. In addition to this, the General Council has two other functions: it also meets, under different rules, as the Dispute Settlement Body (as such responsible for the adoption of reports by dispute settlement panels and the Appellate Body) and as the Trade Policy Review Body (see Article IV:3 and 4 of the WTO Agreement).

c) The Council for TRIPS, the Council for Trade in Goods and the Council for Trade in Services operate "under the general guidance of the General Council" (Article IV:5 of the WTO Agreement). According to the same provision, membership in these Councils shall be open to the representatives of all WTO Members.

2. History of the provision

2.1 Situation pre-TRIPS

As explained elsewhere in this book, the trade-related aspects of intellectual property rights are a new and complex subject in the new structure of GATT-WTO and it was thus considered necessary to establish a new organ responsible to deal with the operation and implementation of the new Agreement.

2.2 Negotiating history

The negotiating history of Article 68 was intertwined with the substantive aspects of the negotiations. Since the idea of substantive standards in TRIPS itself was not commonly accepted until the mid-term review of the Uruguay Round in April 1989, not much consideration was given to what kind of body would supervise the operation of an agreement in this area. Adding to this complication was the debate on what exactly the successor organization to the GATT would be.

Developing countries, in general, insisted for a long time after the Uruguay Round was launched that both TRIPS and the Services Agreement should be on separate tracks and not on a par with negotiations in the goods area. Their idea was to make these two subjects non-justiciable under any possible dispute settlement rules. While this did not happen, it constituted the main reason for the developing countries' entertaining the idea of a separate organ for supervision of TRIPS.

2.2.1 The Anell Draft

This draft provided:[95]

> "Committee on Trade-Related Intellectual Property Rights (68); The Committee on Trade-Related Aspects of Intellectual Property Law (73); The TRIPS Committee (74)
>
> 1A PARTIES shall establish a Committee on Trade Related Intellectual Property Rights composed of representatives from each PARTY. The Committee shall elect its own chairman, establish its own rules of procedures and shall meet not less

---

[95] See composite text of 23 July 1990, circulated by the Chairman (Lars E. R. Anell) of the TRIPS Negotiating Group, document MTN.GNG/NG11/W/76.

than once a year and otherwise upon request of any PARTY. The Committee shall monitor the operation of this Annex and, in particular, PARTIES' compliance with their obligations hereunder, and shall afford PARTIES the opportunity of consulting on matters relating to trade related intellectual property rights. It shall carry out such other responsibilities as assigned to it by the CONTRACTING PARTIES, and it shall, in particular, provide any assistance requested by them in the context of procedures under Articles XXII and XXIII of the General Agreement. In carrying out its functions, the Committee may consult with and seek information from any source they deem appropriate. (68)

1B (i) All PARTIES shall be represented in the Committee on Trade-Related Aspects of Intellectual Property Rights (hereinafter the Committee). It shall elect its Chairman annually and meet as necessary, but not less than once a year. It shall carry out its responsibilities as assigned to it under this PART or by the PARTIES. It may establish working groups. (73)

(ii) The Committee shall monitor the implementation and operation of this PART, taking into account the objectives thereof. It shall examine periodical country reports prepared by the GATT Secretariat on laws, regulations, practices and international agreements related to, and affecting, the protection of intellectual property rights. It shall make recommendations, as appropriate, to the PARTIES concerned. (73)

(iii) The Committee shall periodically agree upon a schedule of country reports. It shall adopt a work programme and coordinate activities of PARTIES in the field of technical cooperation. (73)

(iv) The Committee shall annually report to the CONTRACTING PARTIES. It may submit recommendations. (73)

(v) The Committee is entitled to elaborate and adopt guidelines for the interpretation, in particular of Parts III and IV above. It shall take into account relevant findings of adopted panel reports. (73)

1C The TRIPS Committee composed of representatives of the PARTIES shall be established. The TRIPS Committee shall carry out functions under this Agreement or otherwise assigned to it by the PARTIES. (74)

Joint Expert Group (68), Joint Group of Experts (73)

2A In order to promote co-operation between the Committee on Trade Related Intellectual Property Rights and bodies under the World Intellectual Property Organization, the latter shall be invited by the Committee to serve together with the GATT Secretariat as Secretariat for a joint Expert Group which shall consist of representatives of the CONTRACTING PARTIES and of the Member States of the Paris and Berne Unions. The Expert Group shall, when requested to do so by the Committee, advise the Committee on technical matters under consideration. (68)

2B In order to promote co-operation between the Committee and bodies under the World Intellectual Property Organization, the Committee may establish, as appropriate, Joint Groups of Experts consisting of representatives of the PARTIES and of the Member States of the Unions created by the Paris Convention (1967) and the Berne Convention (1971), respectively. Upon request of the Committee, the Joint Groups of Experts shall give advice on technical matters under consideration. (73)"

Both proposals "A" and "B" had a broader coverage than the final version of Article 68. The latter is limited to the substantive functions of the Council for TRIPS, whereas the proposals under the Anell Draft additionally contained some provisions on the organizational structure of this body (in particular with respect to its composition, its chairperson and its rules of procedure). Such organizational rules were subsequently removed from the specific TRIPS context and incorporated into the WTO Agreement (see Article IV:5 and 6). Contrary to the Anell Draft, however, the WTO Agreement does not expressly refer to the election of the Chairperson. As to the actual functions of the "Committee" (i.e., the body that later became the Council for TRIPS), the final version is closer to proposal "A" than to proposal "B". The latter contained more details than the former. In the context of the Committee's monitoring function, it referred expressly to the objectives of the Agreement that should be taken into account. These objectives at the time of the Anell Draft were contained in a provision that later became Article 7. This draft provision provided:

> "1B PARTIES recognize that intellectual property rights are granted not only in acknowledgement of the contributions of inventors and creators, but also to assist in the diffusion of technological knowledge and its dissemination to those who could benefit from it in a manner conducive to social and economic welfare and agree that this balance of rights and obligations inherent in all systems of intellectual property rights should be observed.
>
> 2B PARTIES agree that the protection and enforcement of intellectual property rights should contribute to the promotion of technological innovation and enhance the international transfer of technology to the mutual advantage of producers and users of technological knowledge."[96]

The reference to these objectives in the context of the Committee's monitoring task highlights the concerns of some developing countries relating to the loss of flexibility in handling IP issues. A comparable reference is missing under the current Article 68.

Finally, both draft proposals contained, in a separate provision, reference to cooperation with WIPO. The "A" and the "B" proposal did not differ much from each other, in particular with their reference to the advice that the Committee should receive from the joint GATT-WIPO group of experts. In this respect, both draft proposals were more detailed than the final version of Article 68, which only makes a general reference to establishing "appropriate arrangements for cooperation" with WIPO bodies (see below, Section 3).

2.2.2 The Brussels Draft
Once the agreement of all countries to negotiate on substantive IPRs standards was secured in April 1989, discussions began on the institutional arrangements

---

[96] Note that the final version of Article 7 is closer to the second of the quoted paragraphs.

and by the time the meeting took place in 1990 in Brussels, the draft[97] contained the following provision:

"PARTIES shall establish a Committee on Trade Related Intellectual Property Rights composed of representatives from each PARTY. The Committee shall elect its own chairperson, establish its own rules of procedures and shall meet not less than once a year and otherwise upon request of any PARTY. The Committee shall monitor the operation of this Agreement and, in particular, PARTIES' compliance with their obligations hereunder, and shall afford PARTIES the opportunity of consulting on matters relating to the trade-related aspects of intellectual property rights. It shall carry out such other responsibilities as assigned to it by the PARTIES, and it shall, in particular, provide any assistance requested by them in the context of dispute settlement procedures. In carrying out its functions, the Committee may consult with and seek information from any source they deem appropriate. In consultation with the World Intellectual Property Organization, the Committee shall seek to establish, within one year of its first meeting, appropriate arrangements for co-operation with bodies of that Organization.[a]

Note: (a) This provision depends on the decision to be taken regarding the institutional arrangements for the international implementation of this Agreement."

This draft Article was in essence quite similar to today's Article 68. There are three minor differences. First, the draft Article in its two first sentences contained a reference to the organizational structure of the Committee (which is now to be found in Article IV:5 and 6 of the WTO Agreement). Second, the terminology used in the draft differed slightly in employing the terms "Committee" (instead of "Council for TRIPS") and "Parties" instead of "Members". The latter may be explained by the fact that the GATT 1947 lacked legal personality, as it was not an international organization but only an agreement. Consequently, it did not have "Members", but only "Contracting Parties". Likewise, "Committee" reflected the usage in the GATT and its various agreements. Third, the note at the end of the draft provision was not maintained in Article 68. The Cooperation Agreement with WIPO was subsequently established in 1995 (see Section 3 below).

2.2.3 The Dunkel Draft
When the Dunkel Draft[98] was submitted by December 1991, the term "Council" was used rather than "Committee". This was because intensive negotiations had taken place prior to the issuance of the Dunkel Draft on institutional matters. Apart from this, Article 68 of the Dunkel Draft was essentially identical to the current TRIPS provision.

Briefly, it was during this period that the following issues were settled: first, that the results of the Uruguay Round were a single undertaking, i.e., either a country could accept all the agreements or none at all; second, that there was to be an international organization called MTO (Multilateral Trade Organization, later

---

[97] Document MTN.TNC/W/35/Rev. 1 of 3 December 1990.
[98] Document MTN.TNC/W/FA of 20 December 1991.

changed to World Trade Organization) which would be the successor to the GATT; and third, that there would be an integrated dispute settlement mechanism, i.e., binding dispute settlement rules would apply across the board.[99] Finally, there was to be a General Council at the apex and there would be three Councils directly under it (Goods Council, Services Council and TRIPS Council).

3. Possible interpretations

3.1 The functions of the Council

> The Council for TRIPS shall monitor the operation of this Agreement and, in particular, Members' compliance with their obligations hereunder, [...]

The monitoring of Members' compliance with their obligations is the predominant task of the Council. In order to facilitate such action, Article 63.2 lays down Members' obligation to notify to the Council their TRIPS-related laws and regulations.[100] This is a way of reducing the necessity for Members to have recourse to the dispute settlement procedures for breaches of the Agreement.[101] The reference in the first sentence of Article 68 to the term "in particular" indicates that this monitoring does not exclusively consist of the review of Members' compliance with their TRIPS obligations. In more general terms, the Council is supposed to monitor the "operation" of the Agreement, a term that refers to the overall objective of ensuring a smooth functioning of the Agreement, including its objectives and principles. Besides the compliance monitoring, the Council also fulfils other functions, as indicated below.

> [...] and shall afford Members the opportunity of consulting on matters relating to the trade-related aspects of intellectual property rights. [...]

The Council equally provides a forum for consultations on IPR-related matters. This is an important contribution to the building of mutual trust and cooperation, which ideally prevents Members from having recourse to dispute settlement proceedings.

> [...] It shall carry out such other responsibilities as assigned to it by the Members, and it shall, in particular, provide any assistance requested by them in the context of dispute settlement procedures. [...]

---

[99] This implies the possibility of cross-retaliation (for a definition of that notion, see Chapter 30).

[100] For more details, see Chapter 31.

[101] Note, however, that the obligation to notify TRIPS-related domestic rules applies only after their entry into force (see Chapter 31).

In case there is no room for a settlement of a dispute between the parties, it is an important responsibility of the Council to provide assistance in dispute settlement procedures before a WTO panel or the Appellate Body.

> [...] In carrying out its functions, the Council for TRIPS may consult with and seek information from any source it deems appropriate. [...]

The Council has considerable discretion as to the procurement of relevant information necessary to carry out its main functions properly.

> In consultation with WIPO, the Council shall seek to establish, within one year of its first meeting, appropriate arrangements for co-operation with bodies of that Organization.

The cooperation agreement between the WTO and WIPO was established in 1995 and entered into force on 1 January 1996.[102] In essence, it concerns three different areas of cooperation. First, WIPO agrees to make available to WTO Members, WTO Member nationals, the WTO Secretariat and the Council laws and regulations contained in the WIPO database and to provide to the same parties access to computerized databases of the International Bureau containing laws and regulations. Second, both organizations agree on the procedures regarding the implementation of Article *6ter* of the Paris Convention for the purposes of TRIPS. This concerns the communication from WTO Members to the International Bureau of state emblems that shall not be used as trademarks.[103] Third, and most importantly for developing country and LDC Members that are Members of the WTO or of WIPO but not of both, the organizations agree to make available to these countries the legal-technical assistance/technical cooperation relating to TRIPS that Members are entitled to even if it is the other organization that they belong to. Likewise, the organizations agree to enhance cooperation in their technical assistance activities with a view to maximizing the usefulness of those activities.

Apart from the functions expressly provided for in Article 68, the Council is equally entrusted with other tasks that are referred to in other TRIPS provisions:[104]

- Various exceptions provided for in different parts of the TRIPS Agreement have to be notified to the Council, in particular the ones in Articles 1.3, 3.1, 4(d), and 63.2.[105]

---

[102] The text of this agreement is available at <http://www.wto.org/english/tratop_e/trips_e/wtowip_e.htm>.

[103] Article *6ter* of the Paris Convention prohibits, *inter alia*, the registration of trademarks consisting of, or incorporating, state emblems.

[104] For more detailed information on these provisions, see the respective chapters in this book.

[105] Detailed technical information on the notification procedures can be found in the Technical Cooperation Handbook on Notification Requirements, WTO document WT/TC/NOTIF/TRIPS/1, which is available in the documents online section of the WTO Website (<http://www.wto.org)>.

• Under Article 23.4, the Council shall undertake negotiations concerning the establishment of a multilateral system of notification and registration of geographical indications for wines and spirits.[106]

• Under Article 24.2, the Council is given the authority to review the application of the provisions on geographical indications.

• Under Article 63.2, the Council shall receive notifications from WTO Members concerning their TRIPS-related legislation.

• Article 66.1 authorizes the Council to accord, upon motivated request by an LDC Member, an extension of the transition period after the expiry of which the TRIPS disciplines become fully binding on LDC Members.

• Under Article 71, the Council is charged with the review of the implementation of the TRIPS Agreement at two-year-intervals.

3.2 The Council in actual practice

3.2.1 The meetings
According to Article IV:5 of the WTO Agreement, the Council "shall meet as necessary" to carry out its functions. The Council has followed this suggestion in practice. The number of meetings is decided upon by the Chairman in consultation with Members and is based on the workload that is expected in the year which lies ahead. In other words, the TRIPS Council meets as appropriate. Four to five formal meetings have been the norm in the recent past. The main purpose of these meetings is to monitor the operation of TRIPS. In addition, the Council for TRIPS also meets in "special sessions" for the negotiations on a multilateral system for the registration and the notification of geographical indications for wines and spirits under Article 23.4 (see above).

3.2.2 The decision-making process
In accordance with Article IV:5 of the WTO Agreement, the Council has established its own rules of procedures, which have been approved by the General Council. The rules of procedure for the Council are essentially the same as for the General Council, with adjustments.

As in other WTO bodies, the decisions in the Council are always taken by consensus. In case of no agreement, the Council will refer the matter to the General Council, which will then take the decision. This means that when decisions are adopted by the Council, no Member present at the meeting should formally object. In theory, this means that any country not agreeing to a proposed decision has the right to block it. In practice, of course, there would be a need to justify such a position and the country doing so can be expected to come under pressure from other Members wanting to move forward. Negotiations in the WTO

See also the WTO's IP gateway page at <http://www.wto.org/english/tratop_e/trips_e/trips_e.htm> ("Notifications under the TRIPS Agreement").

[106] Note that according to para. 18 of the Doha Ministerial Declaration (WTO document WT/MIN(01)/DEC/1 of 20 November 2001), Members agreed to negotiate such multilateral system "by the Fifth Session of the Ministerial Conference". However, by the time of the fifth Ministerial Conference, which took place from 10–14 September 2003 in Cancun, Mexico, no agreement was reached on the multilateral register (for details, see Chapter 15).

follow the same pattern in the various bodies. When a delegation raises an issue it considers important, it usually convenes an informal meeting (which could be outside the ambit of the TRIPS Council) among what it believes are like-minded delegations who are likely to support the issue. Once a certain critical mass is reached, the delegation could approach the Chairperson and request the matter be included on the agenda of the next formal TRIPS Council meeting. If the issue is straightforward, the Chairperson might do so without further consultations. On the other hand, if the issue is likely to be a contentious one, then the Chairperson is likely to call what are known as small group informal meetings to seek an agreed compromise.

3.2.3 The compliance review

The Council in actual practice has devoted a lot of time to this task. Those notifications that Members are obliged to make to the Council according to Article 63.2 constitute the basis for reviews of the implementing legislation.[107] Obviously, the precondition of this exercise is that a Member's obligation to implement the TRIPS Agreement has already commenced.[108] Thus, the Council one year after the entry into force of the Agreement started the review of the legislation of the developed countries whose transitional period ended on 1 January 1996. This exercise has now been completed. At present, the TRIPS Council is involved in reviewing the national legislation of the vast majority of developing countries.[109] Concerning LDC Members, the review has not yet begun, taking into account the fact that their obligations to implement the Agreement are yet to be activated (in general, as of 1 January 2006, see Article 66.1).

As far as the review exercise itself is concerned, it is carried out as follows. The Member notifies the laws and regulations, preferably in full but if not, even in part.[110] Then, an opportunity is given to other interested WTO Members to ask questions in writing; after that the concerned WTO Member whose legislation is being reviewed answers in writing, preferably ahead of the meeting of the Council. Often, there are further questions on the answers provided by the Member and these would have to be answered at a subsequent meeting of the Council. In order for the answers to be of satisfying substance, the Member whose legislation is being reviewed should bring in its experts and officials from its capital.

It may be observed that the time period and deadlines provided for the questions and answers are quite flexible. This is the reason why the reviews could spread over two or more meetings lasting from six to nine months. Another reason for the length of this procedure is the fact that some developing countries and LDC Members do not have the resources to bring all the experts they have for all the meetings.

[107] Article 63.2 states in relevant part: "Members shall notify the laws and regulations referred to in paragraph 1 to the Council for TRIPS in order to assist that Council in its review of the operation of this Agreement. [. . .]" See in detail under Chapter 31.

[108] See the transition periods as laid down in Articles 65 and 66. For more details, see Chapter 33.

[109] For a list of those countries whose legislation is currently under review, see the WTO's IP gateway page at <http://www.wto.org/english/tratop_e/trips_e/trips_e.htm> ("Review of members' implementing legislation").

[110] This was designed to motivate Members to notify relevant legislation even if the latter has only been partly elaborated.

Finally, it should be stressed that the review exercise is without prejudice to the rights and obligations of the WTO Member whose legislation is being reviewed. Such Member remains free to maintain the relevant legislation, even if another Member expresses doubts about the WTO compatibility of these provisions. The only way of possibly forcing a Member to modify its domestic laws is through the remedies available under the DSU (in particular, the suspension of concessions). But this may only be authorized after the adoption of a panel or Appellate Body dispute settlement report. This procedure is entirely independent of the review exercise in the Council for TRIPS. The opinion expressed by a WTO Member in the context of this review about another Member's domestic law does not anticipate the conclusion of a relevant examination conducted by a panel or the Appellate Body.

4. WTO jurisprudence

Article 68 does not contain any substantive obligations and thus far has not been the specific object of a dispute before the WTO. However, panels or the Appellate Body, while reviewing the TRIPS-compliance of a Member's legislation, might draw on the comments provided by Members during the review procedure before the Council.

5. Relationship with other international instruments

5.1 WTO Agreements

The Council has specifically been set up for the purpose of monitoring the operation of TRIPS. There is no other WTO organ that could take over this function, except for the General Council in the specific case when a decision needs to be taken and the Members of the Council have not been in a position of reaching such decision.

When compared, for example, to the GATS Council, it can be noted that the powers conferred to the Council for TRIPS are considerably greater. Contrary to Article 68, Article XXIV GATS does not authorize the GATS Council to monitor Members' compliance with their GATS obligations. This difference in the attribution of powers is due to the fact that under TRIPS there are common (minimum) standards that have to be respected by every Member. The extent of GATS obligations, by contrast, depends on each Member's schedule of specific commitments and thus varies from Member to Member. From a practical point of view, a monitoring of such commitments appears much more complicated than the review of the common standards under TRIPS.

5.2 Other international instruments

6. New Developments

6.1 National laws

6.2 International instruments

The Chairperson's Statement accompanying the 2003 General Council Decision on Implementation of Paragraph 6 of the Doha Declaration on the TRIPS Agreement and Public Health contained several references to the work and competencies of the Council for TRIPS:

"[...] Third, it is important that Members seek to resolve any issues arising from the use and implementation of the Decision expeditiously and amicably:

• To promote transparency and avoid controversy, notifications under paragraph 2(a)(ii) of the Decision would include information on how the Member in question had established, in accordance with the Annex, that it has insufficient or no manufacturing capacities in the pharmaceutical sector.

• In accordance with the normal practice of the TRIPS Council, notifications made under the system shall be brought to the attention of its next meeting.

• Any Member may bring any matter related to the interpretation or implementation of the Decision, including issues related to diversion, to the TRIPS Council for expeditious review, with a view to taking appropriate action.

• If any Member has concerns that the terms of the Decision have not been fully complied with, the Member may also utilise the good offices of the Director General or Chair of the TRIPS Council, with a view to finding a mutually acceptable solution.

Fourth, all information gathered on the implementation of the Decision shall be brought to the attention of the TRIPS Council in its annual review as set out in paragraph 8 of the Decision.

[...]"[111]

6.3 Regional and bilateral contexts

6.4 Proposals for review

There are no proposals to modify the functions of the Council.

7. Comments, including economic and social implications

For delegates from developing and least-developed countries, formal and informal participation in Council meetings presents an opportunity to better familiarize themselves with the review exercise. Thus, when their turn comes, they will be able to cooperate more efficiently with the Council and its Members. In this context, it should be stressed again that the review of national IP laws does not constitute a pre-stage of dispute settlement proceedings (see above, under Section 3). To the contrary, this exercise should be understood as a means of avoiding recourse to the DSU through cooperation and dialogue between Members. With respect to the review exercise the written records of those reviews provide for a source of highly valuable information.[112]

The issue of the proper participation of developing countries in a highly technical body such as the Council for TRIPS deserves further consideration. It is

---

[111] Reproduced in the minutes of the General Council, WT/GC/M/82.

[112] The records of the introductory statements made by delegations, the questions put to them and the responses given are made public, six months after their circulation, in the WTO on-line database (at <http://www.wto.org>). In this context, see also the WTO's IP gateway page at <http://www.wto.org/english/tratop_e/trips_e/trips_e.htm> ("Review of members' implementing legislation").

not always the case that the Council is attended by experts on TRIPS matters but by trade diplomats that normally cover a wide variety of subjects. This is not the case of developed countries that participate, in general, with technical support from capitals. This issue deserves the attention of not just policy-decision makers in developing and least-developed countries, but also of international organizations and NGOs. In order to improve the situation, the first step to be taken is to create awareness among the aforementioned institutions of the importance of informed and efficient participation of developing and least-developed countries in the Council deliberations. It should be noted, however, that in recent years a number of activities are being organized back to back to the Council's meetings to precisely support developing countries' proper participation in those discussions.

36: Transitional Provisions

Article 70   Protection of Existing Subject Matter

1. This Agreement does not give rise to obligations in respect of acts which occurred before the date of application of the Agreement for the Member in question.

2. Except as otherwise provided for in this Agreement, this Agreement gives rise to obligations in respect of all subject matter existing at the date of application of this Agreement for the Member in question, and which is protected in that Member on the said date, or which meets or comes subsequently to meet the criteria for protection under the terms of this Agreement. In respect of this paragraph and paragraphs 3 and 4, copyright obligations with respect to existing works shall be solely determined under Article 18 of the Berne Convention (1971), and obligations with respect to the rights of producers of phonograms and performers in existing phonograms shall be determined solely under Article 18 of the Berne Convention (1971) as made applicable under paragraph 6 of Article 14 of this Agreement.

3. There shall be no obligation to restore protection to subject matter which on the date of application of this Agreement for the Member in question has fallen into the public domain.

4. In respect of any acts in respect of specific objects embodying protected subject matter which become infringing under the terms of legislation in conformity with this Agreement, and which were commenced, or in respect of which a significant investment was made, before the date of acceptance of the WTO Agreement by that Member, any Member may provide for a limitation of the remedies available to the right holder as to the continued performance of such acts after the date of application of this Agreement for that Member. In such cases the Member shall, however, at least provide for the payment of equitable remuneration.

5. A Member is not obliged to apply the provisions of Article 11 and of paragraph 4 of Article 14 with respect to originals or copies purchased prior to the date of application of this Agreement for that Member.

6. Members shall not be required to apply Article 31, or the requirement in paragraph 1 of Article 27 that patent rights shall be enjoyable without discrimination

as to the field of technology, to use without the authorization of the right holder where authorization for such use was granted by the government before the date this Agreement became known.

7. In the case of intellectual property rights for which protection is conditional upon registration, applications for protection which are pending on the date of application of this Agreement for the Member in question shall be permitted to be amended to claim any enhanced protection provided under the provisions of this Agreement. Such amendments shall not include new matter.

8. Where a Member does not make available as of the date of entry into force of the WTO Agreement patent protection for pharmaceutical and agricultural chemical products commensurate with its obligations under Article 27, that Member shall:

(a) notwithstanding the provisions of Part VI, provide as from the date of entry into force of the WTO Agreement a means by which applications for patents for such inventions can be filed;

(b) apply to these applications, as of the date of application of this Agreement, the criteria for patentability as laid down in this Agreement as if those criteria were being applied on the date of filing in that Member or, where priority is available and claimed, the priority date of the application; and

(c) provide patent protection in accordance with this Agreement as from the grant of the patent and for the remainder of the patent term, counted from the filing date in accordance with Article 33 of this Agreement, for those of these applications that meet the criteria for protection referred to in subparagraph (b).

9. Where a product is the subject of a patent application in a Member in accordance with paragraph 8(a), exclusive marketing rights shall be granted, notwithstanding the provisions of Part VI, for a period of five years after obtaining marketing approval in that Member or until a product patent is granted or rejected in that Member, whichever period is shorter, provided that, subsequent to the entry into force of the WTO Agreement, a patent application has been filed and a patent granted for that product in another Member and marketing approval obtained in such other Member.

1. Introduction: terminology, definition and scope

TRIPS significantly alters the rights and obligations of states regarding the treatment of intellectual property. One major issue in determining the extent of change was how the new agreement would affect subject matter existing when it entered into force, or that would come into being during relevant transition periods. Because TRIPS has been in force since 1995, it might appear that most of the questions likely to arise in connection with the protection of existing subject matter have already been asked and answered. However, since the duration of some forms of protection is lengthy, and since some transition arrangements have not expired (and some have been extended), it is important to address the implications of Article 70.

Because TRIPS negotiations were promoted by developed country parties to GATT 1947 that were seeking to oblige other parties to the new WTO to enhance protection of IP, it would logically follow that *demandeur* countries would seek to maximize the extent to which existing subject matter came under the protective umbrella of the new TRIPS Agreement. By the same logic, developing countries would seek to preserve the *status quo ante* with respect to existing subject matter. The greater the extent of existing subject matter that came under the new regime, the higher would be the static rent payments flowing to the preponderant new IP holders.

2. History of the provision

2.1 Situation pre-TRIPS

Article 70 concerns the protection of IP subject matter existing when TRIPS entered into force, or that will come into being during transition periods. Its provisions are therefore unique to the agreement, and the product of particularized negotiation. This does not mean that prior treaties addressing IP failed to include provisions regarding pre-existing subject matter. They typically did. So, for example, the Berne Convention provides:

> "Article 18:
>
> [*Works Existing on Convention's Entry Into Force:* 1. Protectable where protection not yet expired in country of origin; 2. Non-protectable where protection already expired in country where it is claimed; 3. Application of these principles; 4. Special cases]
>
> (1) This Convention shall apply to all works which, at the moment of its coming into force, have not yet fallen into the public domain in the country of origin through the expiry of the term of protection.
>
> (2) If, however, through the expiry of the term of protection which was previously granted, a work has fallen into the public domain of the country where protection is claimed, that work shall not be protected anew.
>
> (3) The application of this principle shall be subject to any provisions contained in special conventions to that effect existing or to be concluded between countries of the Union. In the absence of such provisions, the respective countries shall determine, each in so far as it is concerned, the conditions of application of this principle.
>
> (4) The preceding provisions shall also apply in the case of new accessions to the Union and to cases in which protection is extended by the application of Article 7 or by the abandonment of reservations."

The Berne Convention formula requires state parties to extend protection to works that are not in the public domain in the "country of origin" (a term of art in the Convention) through "expiration of the term of protection" when the Convention enters into force. Berne countries may, however, exclude protection for the same works to the extent they are in the public domain within their territory, also by virtue of expiration of the term of protection. Note these provisions apply to new accessions. So, for example, when the United States acceded to the Berne

Convention in 1989, it was required to grant copyright protection to foreign works whose copyright term had not expired in their countries of origin, unless those works had previously been protected by copyright in the United States (and had lost protection by expiration of the copyright term).

The Paris Convention makes limited reference to the protection of existing subject matter. This is not surprising considering that the Convention does not define the subject matter of protection for patents and trademarks. Article 4*bis* provides with regard to its rule of independence of patents that:

"(3) The provision shall apply to all patents existing at the time when it comes into effect.

(4) Similarly, it shall apply, in the case of the accession of new countries, to patents in existence on either side at the time of accession."

A panel and the WTO Appellate Body have interpreted Article 70 as it relates to pre-existing patents.[113] There is no discussion in those reports of the Paris Convention treatment of pre-existing subject matter.[114]

2.2 Negotiating history

2.2.1 The Anell Draft
The Anell Draft included the following on the subject of existing subject matter ("A" developed and "B" developing country proposals):[115]

"SECTION 1: COPYRIGHT AND RELATED RIGHTS

9. Protection of Works Existing at Time of Entry into Force

9A A PARTY shall provide protection, consistent with this agreement, for all works not yet in the public domain in its territory at the time of entry into force of this agreement. In addition, a PARTY that has afforded no effective copyright protection to works or any class of works of other PARTIES prior to its entry into force in its territory shall provide protection, consistent with this agreement, for all works of other PARTIES that are not in the public domain in their country of origin at the time of entry into force of this agreement in its territory.

SECTION 5: PATENTS

7. Transitional Protection

7A.1 PARTIES shall provide transitional protection for products embodying subject matter deemed to be unpatentable under its patent law prior to its acceptance of this Agreement, where the following conditions are satisfied:

(a) the subject matter to which the product relates will become patentable after acceptance of this Agreement;

(b) a patent has been issued for the product by another PARTY prior to the entry into force of this Agreement; and

---

[113] See Section 4, below.

[114] There is a reference in the Appellate Body report to the terms of the Paris Convention, but in another context. *Canada, Term of Patent Protection*, Report of the Appellate Body, AB-2000-7 WT/DS170/AB/R, 18 Sept. 2000, at para. 40.

[115] MTN.GNG/NG11/W/76, 23 July 1990.

the product has not been marketed in the territory of the PARTY providing such transitional protection.

7A.2 The owner of a patent for a product satisfying the conditions set forth above shall have the right to submit a copy of the patent to the PARTY providing transitional protection. Such PARTY shall limit the right to make, use, or sell the product in its territory to such owner for a term to expire with that of the patent submitted."

The developed country "A" proposal regarding copyright would have effectively required each Member to extend copyright protection consistent with the agreement for all works already under protection within their territory (that is, works not yet in the public domain). This is similar to the result achieved in Article 70.2 through incorporation of Article 18 of the Berne Convention, although it lacks explicit reference to expiration of the copyright term. The proposal would have required that countries which had not provided effective copyright protection to foreign works provide such protection "consistent with this agreement" for works that were not in the public domain in their country of origin.[116]

The developed country "A" proposal regarding patent is directed to providing protection to subject matter previously unpatentable based on existing patents in other Members. This is a form of so-called "pipeline protection" under which a country that has not provided patent protection undertakes to give effect to patents and/or patent applications from another country(s), notwithstanding circumstances that might otherwise have precluded late-patenting within the former country's territory. This is a substantially more ambitious proposal from the developed country side than was ultimately adopted because it would effectively have required all Members to extend protection to existing patents granted in other Members (with some limitation). Article 70 as adopted did not require Members to grant patents based on those previously granted in other Members. Its effect is prospective.

2.2.2 The Brussels Draft
The Brussels Ministerial Text of December 1990 provided:[117]

"Article 15: Protection of Works Existing at Time of Entry into Force

The provisions of the Berne Convention (1971) concerning the protection of works existing at the time of entry into force shall apply in respect of the rights secured under that Convention.

Article 16: Protection of Performers, Producers of Phonograms (Sound Recordings) and Broadcasts

Any PARTY to this Agreement may, in relation to the rights conferred under paragraphs 1–3 above, provide for conditions, limitations, exceptions and reservations

---

[116] Article 7(8) of the Berne Convention provides that regarding the term of copyright where protection is claimed, "unless the legislation of that country otherwise provides, the term shall not exceed the term fixed in the country of origin of the work." It is not clear whether the proposal in the Anell text was intended to modify this rule.

[117] MTN.TNC/W/35/Rev.1, 3 Dec. 1990.

to the extent permitted by the Rome Convention. However, the provisions of Article 15 of this Section shall also apply *mutatis mutandis* to the rights of performers and producers of phonograms in phonograms.

Article 73: Protection of Existing Intellectual Property

1. PARTIES shall apply the provisions of Articles 3, 4 and 5 of Part I, of Sections 2, 3, 7 and 8 of Part II, of Part III and of Part IV to subject matter under protection in a PARTY on the date of application of the provisions of this Agreement for that PARTY as defined in Part VI above.

2. PARTIES are not obliged to apply the provisions of Sections 1, 4, 5 and 6 of Part II to subject matter under protection in a PARTY on the date of application of the provisions of this Agreement for that PARTY, subject to the provisions of Articles 15 and 16.6. Subject matter in respect of which the procedures for the acquisition of rights have been initiated as of that date for which, however, the intellectual property title has not yet been granted shall not benefit from the provisions of this Agreement. Nothing in this Agreement shall affect other subject matter covered by these Sections which is already in existence and not under protection in a PARTY on the date of application of the provisions of this Agreement for that PARTY, subject to the provisions of Articles 15 and 16.6.

3. The application of Articles 2 and 6 of this Agreement to existing intellectual property shall be governed by paragraphs 1 and 2 of this Article, as appropriate to the intellectual property right in question."

In respect to copyright, the Brussels Text began to approximate the final Article 70 text by shifting focus for protection of traditional copyright subject matter to the Berne Convention. Since the Berne Convention does not cover producers of phonograms and performers, it was necessary to address this subject matter separately, although by cross reference to Berne. Article 73.1 of the Brussels Text would have extended protection to existing subject matter in the areas of trademark, geographical indications, undisclosed information and competition law, while Article 73.2 would have exempted layout-designs of integrated circuit, industrial designs and patents. Article 73.3 would have subjected rules on application of other IP treaties and exhaustion to the provisions of Article 73.1-2. With respect to the sensitive subject of patents, negotiators had not yet agreed in Article 68 of the Brussels Text on a general approach to the implementation of patent protection, and this accounts for the absence of special treatment such as later appears in Article 70.8-9 of TRIPS for pharmaceutical and agricultural chemical products. The commentary by the Chair of the TRIPS Negotiating Group to the Brussels Ministerial reflects that transition arrangements remained a major point of contention.

Article 73 of the Brussels Text was largely abandoned in favour of a new Article 70 appearing in the Dunkel Draft. There are no material differences between the Dunkel Draft text and the final TRIPS text, with the exception of subparagraph 9, which adds the phrase "notwithstanding the provisions of Part VI". Part VI addresses "Transitional Arrangements", and appears directed to clarifying that exclusive marketing rights (EMRs) are to be granted in respect of mailbox applications (and when relevant criteria are met) notwithstanding the absence of an obligation to provide patent protection as to relevant subject matter. By broadly referring to Part VI, the clarification appears to extend to least developed Members enjoying a transitional exemption. Note, however, that least developed countries were granted a waiver as to compliance with Article 70.9 EMR rules by action taken pursuant to Paragraph 7 of the Doha Declaration on the TRIPS Agreement and Public Health (discussed below).

3. Possible interpretations

3.1 Article 70.1

> 1. This Agreement does not give rise to obligations in respect of acts which occurred before the date of application of the Agreement for the Member in question.

"obligations"

Article 70.1 provides that the Agreement does not give rise to *obligations* [emphasis added] with respect to certain acts. This raises the threshold question of what parties might have obligations under the agreement. From a dispute settlement standpoint, only Members are the subject of disputes, so it may appear that only Members have obligations. Yet TRIPS is unique among WTO agreements in stating that IPRs are private rights. If TRIPS at least indirectly creates private rights, it might also indirectly create "private obligations". This suggests at least two possible interpretations of "obligations" in Article 70.1. A first interpretation is that Members as government entities are not liable for acts which they may have taken before TRIPS became applicable to them. A second interpretation is that private parties within Members are not liable for acts they may have undertaken before TRIPS became applicable within the subject territory.

This threshold question of interpretation is important because it may affect the extent to which Members are (or were) required to provide remedies with respect to conduct that occurred before the agreement became applicable. If Article 70.1 only addresses the obligations of Members, it might not address the question whether conduct by private parties taking place before application of the agreement should be subject to potential liability. If Article 70.1 is more broadly interpreted to encompass both public and private obligations, then remedies for conduct preceding TRIPS need not be provided. The latter view appears to be more consistent with the "private rights" character of the agreement. That is, TRIPS did not directly or indirectly establish private obligations predating its application in a Member.

"acts"

The term "act" is defined as a noun by the New Shorter Oxford English Dictionary as "a thing done; a deed". In its common meaning, Article 70.1 excludes from obligation things that were done by a party prior to application of the agreement.

In the *Canada – Patent Term* case, Canada argued that the term "act" extended to the granting of a patent prior to the application of TRIPS. Canada argued that when Article 33 extended the term of patents to 20 years from the date of grant, this did not affect Canada's "act" of granting a patent prior to TRIPS, and did not oblige Canada to extend the term of patents previously granted.

The Appellate Body disagreed, finding that the term "acts" referred to things that had already been completed or ended. It said that if "acts" were interpreted to apply to the continuing results of "acts" (that is, rights that had been created by "acts"), this would effectively negate the extension by Article 70.2 of protection to subject matter existing when TRIPS became applicable.

"date of application of the Agreement"

Article 65.1 draws a distinction between the date of application of TRIPS for a Member and the date of entry into force of the Agreement. Various transition periods establish different dates of application.[118] Article 70.1 is most logically interpreted not to impose obligations prior to the date of application of relevant provisions for a Member. Otherwise, a Member would incur responsibility for acts occurring during a transition period, and this would be contrary to the spirit of affording such transition periods.

On the whole, Article 70.1 appears most reasonably interpreted to exclude a Member from obligation (that is, from taking steps to provide a remedy) for acts by that Member or by private parties taking place within its territory prior to the date of application of the relevant TRIPS provisions in that Member.

3.2 Article 70.2

> 2. Except as otherwise provided for in this Agreement, this Agreement gives rise to obligations in respect of all subject matter existing at the date of application of this Agreement for the Member in question, and which is protected in that Member on the said date, or which meets or comes subsequently to meet the criteria for protection under the terms of this Agreement. In respect of this paragraph and paragraphs 3 and 4, copyright obligations with respect to existing works shall be solely determined under Article 18 of the Berne Convention (1971), and obligations with respect to the rights of producers of phonograms and performers in existing phonograms shall be determined solely under Article 18 of the Berne Convention (1971) as made applicable under paragraph 6 of Article 14 of this Agreement.

The introductory clause indicates that the general rule stated in Article 70.2 may be varied by other terms of TRIPS. This may, of course, give rise to the interpretive question of whether a particular other provision is intended to vary the general rule, but it is difficult to approach this question in the abstract, that is, without identifying a particular provision.

---

[118] For more details on the TRIPS transitional periods, see Chapter 33.

"all subject matter existing"

As TRIPS is concerned with "intellectual property", it is reasonable to assume that the "subject matter" referenced by this second clause is intangible subject matter protectable by intellectual property. Thus, an invention meeting applicable patentability criteria would be subject to the grant of a patent, following appropriate review of an application, from the date the relevant patent provisions of TRIPS become applicable in the Member in question. However, this rule must be understood in the context of the criteria for IPR protection. For example, an invention that has been disclosed to the public and therefore is no longer novel[119] is not patentable subject matter in the sense of meeting the criteria for patentability recognized by Article 27.1. So TRIPS does not retroactively protect subject matter that may have been protectable at some stage but was no longer protectable IPR subject matter when the TRIPS provisions became applicable. (Article 70.8 addresses the situation of subject matter that might otherwise have become non-patentable as a result of the operation of the patent transition period and mailbox rules.)

"and which is protected in that Member on the said date,"

The third clause indicates that if subject matter is already protected in a Member when TRIPS provisions take effect, then the rules of TRIPS apply to that subject matter. Of course, the application of these new rules may have significant consequences. And, this was the issue raised by Canada in its challenge to application of Article 33 (20-year patent term) to previously granted patents. Canada argued that the intent of Article 70.2 was not to extend previously granted rights, but only to cause them to be recognized. The Appellate Body disagreed, saying that the intent of Article 70.2 was to apply new rules to existing patented subject matter, thereby effectively extending the term of patents in many cases.

"or which meets or comes subsequently to meet the criteria for protection under the terms of this Agreement."

The fourth clause provides that when subject matter existing in a Member becomes eligible for protection, that subject matter will be accorded the benefits of TRIPS Agreement rules. So, for example, an invention reduced to practice following the date TRIPS provisions become applicable will be subject to patent rules that are TRIPS-consistent.

"In respect of this paragraph and paragraphs 3 and 4, copyright obligations with respect to existing works shall be solely determined under Article 18 of the Berne Convention (1971), and obligations with respect to the rights of producers of phonograms and performers in existing phonograms shall be determined solely under Article 18 of the Berne Convention (1971) as made applicable under paragraph 6 of Article 14 of this Agreement."

---

[119] Subject to certain exceptions, such as the one-year grace period in the United States.

Article 70.3 refers to subject matter that has already fallen into the public domain. Article 70.4 refers to the limitation of remedies regarding pre-existing situations that become infringing. These paragraphs, as well as Article 70.2, are governed by Article 18 of the Berne Convention with respect to copyright subject matter, including the rights of phonogram producers and performers "in existing phonograms".

Article 18.1 of the Berne Convention provides that works that have not entered the public domain in the country of origin through the expiry of the term of protection will become protectable at the moment the Convention enters into force. There is a proviso in Article 18.2 that a country in which a copyright on the subject matter has already expired does not need to restore protection. Article 18.3 subjects the general principle to special conventions on this subject that might be concluded by the Berne Union, and further provides: "In the absence of such provisions, the respective countries shall determine, each in so far as it is concerned, the conditions of application of this principle." Article 18.4 subjects new adherents to the Convention to these rules. It should be noted that Article 7.8 of the Berne Convention limits the duration of copyright term to that prescribed in the country of origin, unless a country has otherwise provided.

The foregoing provisions were the subject of a dispute between the United States (and later the European Community) on one side, and Japan on the other.[120] The United States asserted that Japan was obliged to provide protection to sound recordings made in the United States before 1972 that were in the public domain in the United States not as a result of expiration of the term of copyright, but because of an absence of copyright protection. U.S. federal copyright protection for sound recordings was initiated only in 1972. Japan had initiated protection for sound recordings as of 1971. The USA argued that Japan was obliged to provide a minimum 50-year term for sound recordings of U.S. origin from 1946 since those recordings were not in the public domain as a result of expiration of the copyright term, even though U.S. legislation only granted protection for the same recordings from 1972. (The term of protection would commence from the fixation of the work in the United States.)

Japan argued that Article 18.3 of the Berne Convention allowed it flexibility with respect to the manner in which it implemented Articles 18.1 and 18.2. It argued that granting protection for works back to 1971 was a good faith application of the retroactivity rule. It seemed anomalous that the result of applying Article 18 of the Berne Convention would be that Japan would grant copyright protection to U.S. sound recordings more extensive than that provided by the United States. Yet, Japan agreed to adopt the measures proposed by the United States, and the complaints against Japan were withdrawn.[121]

---

[120] *Japan-Measures Concerning Sound Recordings*, Request for Consultations by the United States, WT/DS28/1, 14 Feb. 1996; *Japan-Measures Concerning Sound Recordings*, Request for Consultations from the European Communities, WT/DS42/1, 28 Feb. 1996. See Stephen Obenski, *Retroactive Protection and shame Diplomacy in the US-Japan Sound Recordings Dispute, or, How Japan Got Berne-d*, 4 Minn. Intell. Prop. Rev. 183 (2002).

[121] See notifications of mutually agreed solutions, WT/DS28/41, 24 Jan. 1997; WT/DS42/4 (17 Nov. 1997).

3.3 Article 70.3

> 3. There shall be no obligation to restore protection to subject matter which on the date of application of this Agreement for the Member in question has fallen into the public domain.

When an intangible is in the public domain, this means that it is the common property of the people, with the consequence that it may not be appropriated to the exclusive control of any person or people. Typically, intellectual property that has lost its legal effect in the sense of conferring a right to exclude others from use, commonly at the end of the term of protection, falls into the public domain. Generally speaking, once an intangible has fallen into the public domain, it remains open to use by any person. However, as noted in respect to Japan's decision to retroactively provide copyright protection to sound recordings that were already in the public domain, it is possible that intangibles within the public domain may be restored to private ownership.

Intangibles do not enter the public domain only as a consequence of the expiration of a term of IPR protection. For intangibles to qualify as "intellectual property" they must meet the criteria of protection. If they do not, they do not benefit from exclusive rights as intellectual property and may be part of the public domain.[122] Also, IPRs may be lost other than through the expiration of the term of protection. For example, trademark holders may lose their exclusive rights through non-use of the mark, and the sign that constituted the mark may fall into the public domain.

Article 70.3 uses the term "restore", which means to return something to a position it previously held. This implies that the option not to provide IPR protection to otherwise qualifying subject matter applies only to subject matter which at some point *was* protected as intellectual property, but for some reason lost that protection.[123]

It is important to note that Article 70.2 and Article 18 of the Berne Convention draw an express distinction between subject matter that has fallen into the public domain as a consequence of the expiration of a term of protection, and subject matter that has fallen into the public domain for other reasons. This clearly implies that, outside the specific context of copyright protection covered in Article 70.2, the Article 70.3 option *not* to provide protection for subject matter that has fallen into the public domain applies equally to subject matter which fell into the public domain for reasons other than expiration of a term of protection (as well as by reason of expiration of a term of protection).

It is also important to note that Article 70.3 provides Members with the option to not restore protection. It is not mandatory, and Members may decide to grant

---

[122] Whether an intangible that is not "intellectual property" may also fall outside the public domain is an important theoretical question that cannot be adequately addressed here. Consider, for example, the situation of databases that are not "intellectual property" in the generally accepted sense, but may be protected by *sui generis* rights in data (e.g., in the European Union). Is the data in the database in the public domain?

[123] This interpretation is consistent with Article 70.2 which says that subject matter qualifying for protection on the date of application of TRIPS provisions shall be protected.

protection to subject matter that fell into the public domain for whatever reason. This is not to suggest that such a decision would be good public policy.

3.4 Article 70.4

> 4. In respect of any acts in respect of specific objects embodying protected subject matter which become infringing under the terms of legislation in conformity with this Agreement, and which were commenced, or in respect of which a significant investment was made, before the date of acceptance of the WTO Agreement by that Member, any Member may provide for a limitation of the remedies available to the right holder as to the continued performance of such acts after the date of application of this Agreement for that Member. In such cases the Member shall, however, at least provide for the payment of equitable remuneration.

Article 70.4 uses the "date of acceptance of the WTO Agreement by that Member" as the point at which the exceptional treatment it provides may be based. For original Members of the WTO, this date is 1 January 1995.[124] For later acceding Members it will differ.

Article 70.4 effectively allows for the establishment of a "prior user's right" as to all forms of IPRs protected by the Agreement. In other words, if a third party was making use of subject matter prior to its becoming subject to protection (per the terms of Article 70.2), the law of a Member does not need to allow the new IPR holder to exclude the third party user from the market. However, it must provide for the payment of "equitable remuneration". TRIPS does not define "equitable remuneration". The term is used in Article 14.4 with respect to phonogram rentals. The term differs from that used in connection with Article 31(h) (compulsory licensing) providing for "adequate remuneration in the circumstances of each case, taking into account the economic value of the authorization".

To benefit from an exception, the third party user should have "commenced" otherwise infringing acts regarding the specific object of protection, or made a significant investment regarding the specific object of protection, before the date the WTO Agreement was accepted. The date of commencement of IPR-contravening acts may not be so easily determined because this requires a clear delimitation of the scope of an IPR, as well as an evidentiary determination regarding the date of an occurrence. There is interpretive flexibility in the term "made a significant investment", *inter alia*, because what is "significant" will vary in relation to the financial situation of the investor, the country that investor is investing in, and the industry in which the investment is being undertaken. In sum, rule makers and enforcement authorities have some discretion in developing and applying the Article 70.4 prior user's right rule.

---

[124] Although an argument could be made that a Member "accepted" the WTO Agreement on the date it conveyed its acceptance to the WTO Director General, and not the date of entry into force for the Member, it seems unlikely that negotiators intended to draw such a fine distinction. Instead, this appears as discussed above as a means to distinguish between Members accepting the WTO Agreement as original Members, and Members that subsequently accede to the WTO.

3.5 Article 70.5

> 5. A Member is not obliged to apply the provisions of Article 11 and of paragraph 4 of Article 14 with respect to originals or copies purchased prior to the date of application of this Agreement for that Member.

Article 11 establishes rental rights with respect to computer programs and cinematographic works (i.e., videos). Paragraph 4 of Article 14 extends equivalent rights to producers of and other right holders in phonograms. The qualifications and conditions associated with these rights are discussed in Chapters 10 and 13 of this book.

Article 70.5 provides Members with the option not to provide rental rights as against those who purchased the subject works prior to the date of application of this Agreement for that Member. Recall from discussion of Article 70.1 that the date of application refers to the date when the provisions regarding the subject matter became effective, and are subject to the transition provisions of the Agreement.

A Member that decides not to grant rental rights regarding purchasers of originals or copies is effectively providing that the copyright holder's right is exhausted at the point of first sale. The former holder does not have the right to control the buyer's decision to rent out the object of the purchase. Articles 11 and paragraph 4 of Article 14 are qualified in the extent to which they require the grant of rental rights. There are other circumstances in which Members may provide for the exhaustion of rights in computer programs, videos and phonograms (i.e., without providing a rental right).

A copyrighted work may be an original, or it may be a copy or reproduction of the original. Article 70.5 does not distinguish between authorized and unauthorized copies. If a work was protected by copyright prior to application of TRIPS, and a copy was made without the consent of the copyright holder, that copying would have violated local law. Generally, the sale of a counterfeit copy would not exhaust the copyright holder's right in the work. If, however, the object was not protected by copyright, then the initial sale would not have been unlawful. Thus, the absence of reference to authorization with respect to copying does not appear to affect the rights of the holder of a copy.[125]

3.6 Article 70.6

> 6. Members shall not be required to apply Article 31, or the requirement in paragraph 1 of Article 27 that patent rights shall be enjoyable without discrimination as to the field of technology, to use without the authorization of the right holder where authorization for such use was granted by the government before the date this Agreement became known.

---

[125] Except perhaps in cases of good faith purchasers in due course without notice.

Article 70.6 adds yet another effective date, "the date this Agreement became known." It is perhaps fair to attribute knowledge of TRIPS to any Member that was part of the Uruguay Round negotiations. Yet a Member could not have known of the Agreement in the sense of security as to its terms until the signing of the WTO Agreement by Ministers in Marrakesh on 15 April 1994. While an argument might be made in favour of relating the date of knowledge back to the approval of the texts (the Final Act Embodying the Results of the Uruguay Round of Multilateral Trade Negotiations) on 15 December 1993,[126] at that stage the agreements still required the approval of the Ministers. No cases appear to have arisen in which a compulsory license was granted in the period between 15 December 1993 and 15 April 1994, and as to which controversy might arise concerning the date of knowledge of the Agreement. It is very doubtful that such a case might arise at this late stage, so there is little practical reason to explore this interpretive issue further. Suffice it to say that the drafters of Article 70.6 appear to have had in mind a date prior to the entry into force of the WTO Agreement (and TRIPS Agreement), or application of TRIPS in the subject Member.

Article 70.6 effectively provides that a Member must apply the provisions of Article 31 to any compulsory license that was granted after the Agreement became known. However, by virtue of Article 70.1 (providing that no obligations arise in respect to acts occurring prior to the date of application of the Agreement), this could only mean with prospective effect after the provisions become applicable. In other words, licenses granted after the Agreement became known and that did not comply with the Agreement (for example, by not including provision for adequate remuneration) would have to be brought into compliance, but only after Article 31 became applicable. For developing Members, Article 31 became applicable on 1 January 2000.

The second clause of Article 70.6 provides that the Article 27.1 rule that patent rights shall be enjoyable without discrimination as to the field of technology need not be applied to compulsory licenses granted before the Agreement became known. By logical implication, Members are required to apply Article 27.1 to compulsory licenses granted after the Agreement became known. The panel in the *Canada-Generic Pharmaceuticals* case interpreted Article 70.6 this way.[127]

---

[126] GATT Doc. MTN/FA, 15 Dec. 1993.

[127] See *Canada – Patent Protection of Pharmaceutical Products*, Report of the Panel, WT/DS114/R of 17 March 2000. In the context of interpreting Article 30, the panel accepted the presumption of the EC and Canada that Article 31 is subject to the rule of non-discriminatory treatment of patents with respect to place of invention, field of technology and whether products are imported or locally produced. The panel concluded by implication that Article 27.1 also applies to Article 30, but this conclusion does not necessarily follow since Article 30 and Article 31 are drafted differently and directed to different purposes. As to the applicability of the non-discrimination requirement of Article 27.1 to compulsory licensing, it has been observed that the panel in the *Canada – Generic Pharmaceuticals* case may be interpreted as making a distinction between "discrimination" and "differentiation" for *bona fide* purposes (see Chapter 25). Moreover, the argument has been made that Article 27 deals with patentable subject matter and that Article 31 is a self-standing Article. To affirm that Article 31 is generally subject to Article 27 could limit its application in ways that were not intended either by the negotiators or indeed by the text. In fact, the *EC-Canada* case was not about compulsory licensing and the panel's report cannot be considered as definite jurisprudence.

This peculiar drafting of Article 70.6 almost certainly reflects specific concerns between the United States and Canada. The United States pressured Canada to amend its compulsory licensing legislation for pharmaceuticals in connection with negotiation of the NAFTA, concluded in 1993. Canada had issued a substantial number of compulsory licenses under its previous regime that, for example, treated pharmaceutical inventions differently from other fields of technology.[128] The United States was unable to persuade Canada to modify licenses that had been issued while its pre-NAFTA regime was in effect, but wanted to assure that Canada did not grant post-NAFTA licenses that did not comply with its new TRIPS obligations. Any such licenses that were granted would have to be brought into conformity with Article 31 upon the application of that Article on 1 January 1996. This is not to suggest that Article 70.6 will not affect other Members, but only to account for the obtuse drafting, and specifically to the reference concerning the date the Agreement became known.

3.7 Article 70.7

> 7. In the case of intellectual property rights for which protection is conditional upon registration, applications for protection which are pending on the date of application of this Agreement for the Member in question shall be permitted to be amended to claim any enhanced protection provided under the provisions of this Agreement. Such amendments shall not include new matter.

Article 70.7 concerns IPRs for which protection is conditional upon registration. Under the Berne Convention, protection of copyrighted works may not be conditioned on registration, and for that reason Article 70.7 would not generally be relevant to copyright subject matter. Patents are "granted" following a review of an application. The term "registration" is not ordinarily associated with the field of patents, and it is doubtful whether this Article 70.7 has relevance to patent applications. In most countries, trademark rights are conferred by registration, and registration is also a predicate to protection for industrial designs, geographical indications, plant varieties and layout-designs of integrated circuits, depending on the national system for conferring IPRs.

However, in some countries Article 70.7 was invoked by applicants that under pre-TRIPS law were denied the possibility of obtaining product patent protection for pharmaceuticals. The argument was that Article 70.7 would give a right to the "conversion" of applications relating to processes into product applications, to the extent (as was often the case) that the product had been described in the original application (and, therefore, would not constitute "new matter"). In the case of Argentina, several lower courts accepted this interpretation. Nevertheless, the Supreme Court[129] correctly dismissed it, arguing that accepting such a

---

[128] See Jerome H. Reichman and Catherine Hasenzahl, *Non-Voluntary Licenses of Patent Inventions: The Canadian Experience*, UNCTAD/ICTSD, Oct. 2002 (available at <http://www.iprsonline.org/ unctadictsd/docs/reichman_hasenzahl_Canada.pdf>).

[129] *Pfizer Inc. c/ Instituto Nacional de la Propiedad Industrial s/ denegatoria de patente*, 21 May 2002.

theory would contradict the prospective character of the Agreement and, in particular, render meaningless Article 70.8, which established a special regime to recognize patent protection for pharmaceutical products, provided that applications were filed after January 1, 1995 (or January 1, 1994 if a priority right was invoked).

Article 70.7 allows for the amendment of applications pending at the date of application of the Agreement to claim any enhanced protection provided under the provisions of this Agreement, as qualified by the restriction that "Such amendments shall not include new matter." In most cases, the protection accorded to a particular form of IPR will not be "claimed" in an application because the scope of protection is determined as a matter of national IP legislation, not by the applicant by virtue of a claim on an application form. In other words, when registration is granted, the applicant enjoys the rights conferred by national law. When that is combined with the restriction against including "new matter", the scope of this provision is narrowed further.

TRIPS Agreement rules (Article 18) on trademarks, by way of illustration, require that the term of protection conferred by an initial application will be a minimum 7 years. If a Member, prior to application of the trademark rules, conferred only a five-year term and that term was referenced (i.e., "claimed") in the form of application, then the application could be amended to claim an initial term of 7 years. TRIPS also established trademarks and service marks on the same footing from the standpoint of registration.[130] Whether a trademark application, as to the same mark, could be amended to claim service mark protection (in a Member that previously did not allow registration of service marks) is not clear, since service mark protection might be considered to cover "new matter". That is, the provision of a service is different from the sale of goods, and a mark covering services might be said to claim "new matter" in comparison to a trademark. However, because the mark is unchanged, that might be construed not to involve a claim of new matter.

The question of applicability of Article 70.7 can be properly evaluated only in light of particular national legislation because the question whether rights are conditioned on registration will vary, and the types of claims asserted in an application will vary.

3.8 Article 70.8

> 8. Where a Member does not make available as of the date of entry into force of the WTO Agreement patent protection for pharmaceutical and agricultural chemical products commensurate with its obligations under Article 27, that Member shall:
>
> (a) notwithstanding the provisions of Part VI, provide as from the date of entry into force of the WTO Agreement a means by which applications for patents for such inventions can be filed;

---

[130] Effectively modifying the rule of Article 6*sexies* of the Paris Convention. See Chapter 14.

> (b) apply to these applications, as of the date of application of this Agreement, the criteria for patentability as laid down in this Agreement as if those criteria were being applied on the date of filing in that Member or, where priority is available and claimed, the priority date of the application; and
>
> (c) provide patent protection in accordance with this Agreement as from the grant of the patent and for the remainder of the patent term, counted from the filing date in accordance with Article 33 of this Agreement, for those of these applications that meet the criteria for protection referred to in subparagraph (b).

"Where a Member does not make available as of the date of entry into force of the WTO Agreement"

The WTO Agreement entered into force on 1 January 1995. The first clause of Article 70.8 makes that date its initial reference point.

"patent protection for pharmaceutical and agricultural chemical products commensurate with its obligations under Article 27,"

Article 27 requires that patents shall be available in all fields of technology, subject to exceptions otherwise allowed in Article 27.2 and 27.3.[131] Article 27.1 states, *inter alia,*

"Subject to paragraph 4 of Article 65, paragraph 8 of Article 70 and paragraph 3 of this Article, patents shall be available and patent rights enjoyable without discrimination as to the place of invention, the field of technology and whether products are imported or locally produced." [italics added]

Since Article 65.4 allows a developing Member that did not previously grant product patent protection in an area of technology to delay its availability until 1 January 2005,[132] and since that right is recognized in Article 27, it is a poor semantic choice to refer to that Member's "obligations under Article 27". Despite the poor choice of words, it seems clear that Article 70.8 refers to Members that did not provide patent protection for pharmaceutical and agricultural chemical products when the WTO Agreement entered into force (even if they did not have an "obligation" to do so at that time).

"(a) notwithstanding the provisions of Part VI,"

Part VI of TRIPS addresses Transitional Arrangements, and addresses both developing and least-developed Members. It relieves developing Members of an

---

[131] In Chapter 17 the extent to which Article 27 mandates patent protection for pharmaceutical products is considered, including the extent to which Articles 27.2 and 27.3 might allow exceptions to such patentability. That discussion will not be repeated here.

[132] Paragraph 65.4 provides, as discussed in Chapter 6.1:
"4. To the extent that a developing country Member is obliged by this Agreement to extend product patent protection to areas of technology not so protectable in its territory on the general date of application of this Agreement for that Member, as defined in paragraph 2, it may delay the application of the provisions on product patents of Section 5 of Part II to such areas of technology for an additional period of five years."

obligation to provide pharmaceutical and agricultural chemical product patent protection until 1 January 2005 (where such protection was not earlier provided), and it relieves least-developed Members of any obligation to provide such protection until at least 1 January 2006 (which period was extended as to pharmaceutical products by action taken under the Doha Declaration until 1 January 2016).

> *"provide as from the date of entry into force of the WTO Agreement a means by which applications for patents for such inventions can be filed;"*

As noted above, the date of entry into force of the WTO Agreement was 1 January 1995. The requirement to "provide" arose as of that date. The Member must provide a "means by which applications...can be filed". This would suggest at least the designation of a receiving point for applications, such as a designated administrative authority within the government. The term "filed" implies that the application is recorded and stored in some manner. "Applications for patents" is a term of art that refers to a form on which the applicant for a patent sets out its claims and related specification or description, as well as prior art references where applicable, as a request for the grant of a patent. Article 70.8 does not refer to preliminary documents or statements of intent to file, but to "applications". Therefore, a Member should allow for the filing of complete applications.

Because Article 70.8(a) requires that Members without patent coverage provide a means for filing applications, but not for granting patents, Article 70.8(a) applications have commonly been referred to as "mailbox" applications.

The term "patents for such inventions" appears to refer to patents for pharmaceutical and agricultural chemical products.[133] The definition of "pharmaceutical...products" and "agricultural chemical products" is subject to interpretation. This was much discussed in the context of more recent negotiations regarding implementation of Paragraph 6 of the Doha Declaration on the TRIPS Agreement and Public Health.

The Oxford New Shorter English Dictionary defines "pharmaceutical" by cross reference to "medicinal drug".[134] It defines "medicinal" as "1 Having healing or curative properties or attributes; therapeutic"[135] and "drug" as "1. Any substance that affects the physical or mental functioning of a living organism; *esp.* one used for the treatment or prevention of an ailment or disease".[136] The term "pharmaceutical products" can be given a broader or narrower interpretation depending on the context.

"Agricultural chemical" may encompass chemical products with multiple uses, and it would appear that a Member might restrict applications to those claiming uses of chemicals specifically in the field of agriculture, so as to avoid the prospect

---

[133] It will be interesting to examine the practice of the pharmaceutical companies with respect to these applications. The Decision on Implementation of Paragraph 6 of the Doha Declaration refers to pharmaceutical products, and there may be interpretative issues with respect to the scope of coverage.

[134] "Pharmaceutical" is defined as an adjective, as "Pertaining to or engaged in pharmacy; pertaining to the preparation, use, or sale of medicinal drugs". As a noun, it is defined as "A pharmaceutical preparation; a medicinal drug." (at page 218 2)

[135] *Id.*, at page 1730.

[136] *Id.*, at page 756.

of applicants attempting to extend the scope of Article 70.8 protection to "multiple uses" of the same chemicals outside the field of agriculture.

> *"(b) apply to these applications, as of the date of application of this Agreement, the criteria for patentability as laid down in this Agreement as if those criteria were being applied on the date of filing in that Member or, where priority is available and claimed, the priority date of the application; and"*

The date of application of this Agreement for developing Members is up until 1 January 2005, at latest, in respect of newly covered areas of technology. If a developing Member elects to extend the scope of patent protection prior to 1 January 2005 (as most such countries have done) that date should logically be considered "the date of application of this Agreement" for the purposes of this provision.[137] There is no apparent reason why patent protection for pharmaceutical and agricultural chemical products cannot be extended by a developing Member at different times prior to 1 January 2005. For least-developed Members, the relevant end-point date for pharmaceutical products is 1 January 2016 (per paragraph 7 of the Doha Declaration), and for agricultural chemical products until 1 January 2006.[138]

The phrase "apply to these applications, as of the date of application of this Agreement" is relevant to the question when applications filed under Article 70.8(a) should be processed. A patent application is typically processed by a patent office over a period of between 18 and 36 months from the filing date, depending on a variety of factors such as the volume of applications in the patent office, the complexity of an application, the exchange of correspondence with the applicant, and so forth. The first two clauses of Article 70.8(b) might be interpreted in two ways. First, it might be interpreted to require that when applications are taken out of the mailbox on the date of application of the Agreement (e.g., 1 January 2005), the applications should be processed in the customary manner (that is, subject to procedural and substantive review), with the determination as to the grant of a patent made in due course. Because the phrase is followed by an instruction as to patentability criteria (that is, to apply "the criteria for patentability as laid down in this Agreement as if those criteria were being applied on the date of filing in that Member"), a natural interpretation is that the phrase is an instruction to the patent examiner regarding patentability standards to apply when the applications are ultimately processed. From this perspective, the phrase "apply to these

---

[137] A developing Member might argue that early extension of scope was "voluntary" because it might have taken advantage of further delay, and therefore it was not applying the TRIPS Agreement when it extended the scope. However, in light of the obligation in Article 65.5 that consistency with TRIPS should not be reduced during the transition period, it would be difficult to argue in favour of withdrawing an action that established such consistency. In this regard, the "date of application of this Agreement" is most reasonably understood as the date on which the developing Member extends patent protection to pharmaceutical or agricultural chemical products, respectively.

[138] Also, because least developed Members are not subject to Article 65.5, they may withdraw patent protection for agricultural chemical (and other) products until 1 January 2006, and for pharmaceutical products up until 1 January 2016. Thus, in theory, least developed Members might suspend the processing of applications under Article 70.8(b) after initiating their processing and until the date when protection is mandated.

applications, as of the date of application of this Agreement," is an instruction to the Member that applications must be withdrawn from the mailbox and their processing initiated on a certain date.

A second interpretation would place greater emphasis on the phrase, "as of the date of application of this Agreement", and oblige a Member to actually make a decision regarding patentability on that date, taking into account the rule regarding patentability criteria stated in the subsequent phrase. This interpretation is implausible and would be inconsistent with the general structure of Article 70.8 and patent law as it is customarily applied. Recall that Article 70.8(a) obliges a Member to provide a means to file a patent application. It does not obligate a Member to put in place a mechanism for the substantive review of patent applications, including corresponding with patent applicants, and so forth. There is good reason why patent offices do not grant patents immediately on the filing of applications. These are highly technical documents requiring research into prior art, evaluation of claims, correspondence with applicants, and so forth. Unless a Member were obliged to process and review applications prior to the date of application of the Agreement, it would simply be implausible (if not impossible) to grant patents as of that date. On the assumption that the negotiators of TRIPS did not intend an implausible or absurd result, the interpretation that applications must be reviewed and acted upon on the date of application of the Agreement should not prevail.

Article 27.1 lays down three traditional criteria of patentablity, that inventions must be "new, involve an inventive step and are capable of industrial application". Article 29 lays down a fourth criterion, "an applicant for a patent shall disclose the invention in a manner sufficiently clear and complete for the invention to be carried out by a person skilled in the art and may require the applicant to indicate the best mode for carrying out the invention known to the inventor at the filing date or, where priority is claimed, at the priority date of the application."

Article 70.8 provides that the Member will apply the criteria of patentability "as if those criteria were being applied on the date of filing in that Member or, where priority is available and claimed, the priority date of the application". When a patent application is first filed in a member country of the Paris Union (as made applicable also under TRIPS), the applicant thereby secures a priority date. From this priority date, a one-year period is counted during which that applicant may file in other countries of the Paris Union (Article 4, Paris Convention), and such applications "shall not be invalidated by any acts accomplished in the interval, in particular, another filing, the publication or exploitation of the invention, ... and such acts cannot give rise to any third party right or any right of personal possession."

The filing date and priority date for an application will typically be different (except in the country of first filing) with the priority date being earlier outside the country of first filing. A Member that has not provided pharmaceutical or agricultural product patent protection is likely to have initial filings only from its own nationals (if those),[139] with the preponderance of applications from inventors

---

[139] An inventor outside a country with no patent protection would have little reason to make its first filing in that country. An inventor within that country might have reason for filing an Article 70.8

that first filed abroad. Most holders of applications under Article 70.8 will therefore be relying on the priority date as the date of application, since the earlier date cuts off claims of subsequent applicants.

Article 70.8 (b) refers to "where priority is available and claimed." Unless a filing under Article 70.8(a) is within the priority period established by the Paris Convention (that is, within 12 months of the initial filing), the criteria for patentability will be based on the filing date, and not an earlier priority date. If a patent applicant neglects to file its application under Article 70.8(a) during its priority period, its invention might not be novel (by virtue of disclosure) when its filing is made.

Patent examination authorities in the Member that is reviewing applications under Article 70.8(b) are instructed to apply the criteria of patentability as of the earlier of the filing or priority date. This means that events or acts that occur after that date are not to be considered in the review of the application. Ordinarily, a patent application will be published approximately 18 months after the date of initial application, and the invention becomes known to the public at least as of that date (it may have been introduced and made public earlier).

When an application is filed in a country that provides patent protection, the application may not be substantively reviewed for a number of months (since patent offices are backlogged), but when the patent examiner does evaluate the application he or she considers circumstances as they existed as of the initial filing or priority date.[140] The inventor is held to a standard of knowledge at or before the date of application.

If an inventor does not file a patent application in a country prior to expiration of the priority period,[141] the inventor is not protected against disclosures made in connection with publication of the application abroad or putting the invention on the market. In the ordinary case, failure to file a patent application during the priority period will make it impossible to obtain a patent later on since the invention will have been disclosed, and it will no longer be considered new or novel. (In some cases, countries have granted retroactive patent protection, or "pipeline protection", to inventions that would not ordinarily meet novelty standards, but this is an exception from generally applicable patenting criteria.)

Article 70.8(b) addresses this situation. If a Member that does not provide patent protection for a particular subject matter, a patent application claiming such an invention would be rejected, and the inventor would not enjoy a right of priority. Publication of the patent application in a foreign country, or availability of the product on the market (at least in the subject country) would negate the novelty of the invention if patent protection subsequently became available. By requiring a preservation of priority even without the availability of patent protection, Article 70.8(b) guards against this result. By specifying that the determination as

---

application there because, for example, of domestic laws requiring national security review of patent applications.

[140] See, e.g., *Biogen v. Medeva*, U.K. House of Lords, [1997] RPC 1, 31 Oct. 1996.

[141] The rule is modified by operation of the Patent Cooperation Treaty, which deems applications incorporating designated countries to be filed within the priority period, but that technical matter does not affect this discussion.

to criteria of patentability relates back to the priority (or filing) date, Article 70.8(b) avoids doubt as to whether the application would be subject to later acts or events, such as marketing of the product in the subject country. If an application is filed in 1996, it might not be reviewed until 2005, and there might be concerns about the preservation of patentability criteria for such an extended period. Since the drafters of the provision were dealing with a unique legal situation, there were reasonable grounds for specifying the intended result; that is, patentability will be evaluated as of the date of the filing or priority date, whichever is earlier.

> *"(c) provide patent protection in accordance with this Agreement as from the grant of the patent and for the remainder of the patent term, counted from the filing date in accordance with Article 33 of this Agreement, for those of these applications that meet the criteria for protection referred to in subparagraph (b)."*

The first clause of subparagraph (c) requires the Member where Article 70.8 applications are processed to provide patent protection "as from the grant of the patent." Recall from discussion under subparagraph (b) that the grant of the patent will be made following a substantive review of the application. Article 70.8(c) imposes no obligation on the Member granting the patent to relate protection back to a date earlier than the grant, or to provide provisional protection during the period following the filing date (but see Article 70.9 below).

Although criteria of patentability are evaluated as of the earlier of the filing or priority date, the term of the patent is expressly based on the filing date of the application. (Recall that unless the filing was within the priority period established by the Paris Convention, that is, within 12 months of the initial filing, the criteria for patentability will be based on the filing date, and not an earlier priority date.) Article 33 establishes a minimum patent term of 20 years "counted from the filing date". The "remainder of the patent term" will therefore relate back to the filing date (under Article 70.8(a)) in the Member processing the application. This date may be as early as 1 January 1995 (the date of entry into force of the WTO Agreement). And, of course, patent protection will only be granted for those applications that meet the criteria of patentability applicable under Article 70.8(b).

Doha Concerns

When the TRIPS Council made its recommendations to the General Council concerning implementation of Paragraph 7 of the Doha Declaration on the TRIPS Agreement and Public Health, concern was expressed by least-developed Members that the requirement to accept the filing of mailbox applications and subsequently to grant patents based upon them (for example, after 1 January 2016), would reduce the incentive for commencement of medicines production within their territories. While the TRIPS Council recommended, and the General Council waived, the obligation to provide exclusive marketing rights under Article 70.9 (see discussion below), it did not waive the obligation on least-developed Members to accept mailbox applications, or to grant patents based on such applications following the entry into force of patent protection.

3.9 Article 70.9

> "9. Where a product is the subject of a patent application in a Member in accordance with paragraph 8(a), exclusive marketing rights shall be granted, notwithstanding the provisions of Part VI, for a period of five years after obtaining marketing approval in that Member or until a product patent is granted or rejected in that Member, whichever period is shorter, provided that, subsequent to the entry into force of the WTO Agreement, a patent application has been filed and a patent granted for that product in another Member and marketing approval obtained in such other Member."

"Where a product is the subject of a patent application in a Member in accordance with paragraph 8(a),"

Article 70.9 applies only with respect to patent applications filed in a Member under Article 70.8(a). Article 70.8(a) is discussed in the preceding section. Recall that the definition or scope of "pharmaceutical product" and "agricultural chemical product" is not fixed, and there may be questions regarding the inventions which qualify for coverage under Article 70.8 and, by extension, Article 70.9.

"exclusive marketing rights shall be granted"

From the moment the term "exclusive marketing rights" was agreed upon in the TRIPS Negotiating Group there has been uncertainty concerning its meaning. The language was used to effectuate a compromise between the countries demanding early patent protection for pharmaceutical and agricultural chemical products, and countries demanding a full 10-year transition period for those products.[142] The term was not known in intellectual property law generally, or patent law specifically. Its use permitted each side to the negotiations to give it the meaning that suited their immediate purpose of concluding the negotiations. While a mechanism for allowing TRIPS negotiations to be brought to a conclusion, those implementing the phrase are not guided by customary practices.

It may be useful to start with what exclusive marketing rights are *not*. They are not the equivalent of patent rights. Were that the intent of the negotiators, a reference to the rights ordinarily conferred by patent could readily have been used.

The Oxford New Shorter Dictionary defines "exclusive" as an adjective: "5. Of a right, privilege, quality, etc.: possessed or enjoyed by the individual(s) specified and no others; confined or restricted to." The term marketing is defined as a verb as "1 b *spec.* The action, business, or process of promoting and selling a product etc., including market research, choice of product, advertising, and distribution." The term "right" is defined as a noun as "5 A legal, equitable, or moral title or

---

[142] The author bases this observation on conversations with TNG negotiators that took place shortly following agreement on the text, and in which he queried several negotiators regarding the intended meaning of the phrase. The reply can be paraphrased as "no one knows". India and the United States were said to be the principal parties at odds over this matter.

claim to the possession of property or authority, the enjoyment of privileges or immunities, etc."

Article 28 gives the patent holder the right to prevent third parties without its consent from making, using, offering for sale, selling or importing the product covered by the patent. The term "marketing" does not appear to encompass the right to prevent others from "making" a product, or to prevent others from "using" a product except in the sense of promoting and selling the product. Based on the dictionary definition, the term "marketing" appears to apply to the acts a business enterprise undertakes in connection with selling products that are already manufactured; that is, acts associated with placing the products into sales channels. A reasonable interpretation of the term marketing in the context of pharmaceutical and agricultural chemical products is that the holder of the patent application may not prevent third parties from producing the product within the territory of the Member, but may prevent third parties from advertising, offering or selling the product to a person other than the patent applicant.

If the patent applicant is in a position to supply the market with a product, whether through local manufacturing or importation, an exclusive right to sell may have the effect of curtailing potentially competing local producers just as effectively as the grant of a patent, although it would not preclude such manufactures from exporting and selling the products in foreign countries where patent protection was not in force.

Questions also arise concerning how exceptions to the grant of exclusive marketing rights should be treated. Exclusive marketing rights are not patents, so they are not subject to the rules of Part II, Section 5, of TRIPS regarding patents. They are a *sui generis* creation of Article 70.9. As Members implement EMRs, they will need to consider the extent to which the public interest will require allowing use by third parties without the consent of the holder of the exclusive marketing rights. They may look to the exceptions allowed with respect to patents, including prior user rights, compulsory licensing and so forth, but are not restricted to these. Per Article 1.1, it will be up to Members to "determine the appropriate method of implementing the provisions of this Agreement within their own legal system and practice".

"for a period of five years after obtaining marketing approval in that Member or until a product patent is granted or rejected in that Member, whichever period is shorter,"

Before a pharmaceutical or agricultural chemical product is placed on the market within a country, its marketing must be approved by regulatory authorities. As noted by the panel in the *Canada-Generic Pharmaceuticals* case, the period for approval in the case of new pharmaceutical products is commonly over 6 years.

The substantive and procedural conditions to putting a pharmaceutical or agricultural chemical product on the market, and the terminology with respect thereto, vary among countries. Marketing approval should be understood to refer to the final action by regulatory authorities that allows the entry of a product into circulation and use within a Member.

Article 70.9 refers to the time when a product patent is granted or rejected in that Member. If marketing approval had been granted, and led to the grant of exclusive marketing rights, those rights would terminate on the date of rejection of the patent application. Such a rejection would typically take place by official action of the patent office. When a patent is granted, EMRs terminate and patent protection begins. The grant of a patent likewise typically takes place by official action of the patent office.

The maximum period of EMR protection is five years. If that period expires before the grant or rejection of a patent, EMR protection will end. IPR protection may subsequently be initiated upon the grant of a patent, considering that patentability criteria will have been preserved under Article 70.8(b).

> *"provided that, subsequent to the entry into force of the WTO Agreement, a patent application has been filed and a patent granted for that product in another Member and marketing approval obtained in such other Member."*

There is an important precondition to the grant of exclusive marketing rights. First, a patent application must have been filed and a patent granted for the subject product in another Member. This condition was to assure that a Member was not required to grant EMRs with respect to a product that would not ultimately be subject to patent protection. The condition refers not only to a patent grant, but to the filing of a patent application. A patent application contains the claims and description defining the scope of an invention and enabling its production. Article 29 requires an enabling disclosure as a condition to granting a patent. The requirement in Article 70.9 to file an application was presumably intended to prevent an applicant for EMRs to rely on a patent granted by a Member with inadequate patenting standards, although it is not clear that the mere requirement of an application would meet that objective.

Second, marketing approval must have been granted in that same "other Member". Marketing approval for a pharmaceutical or agricultural chemical product is typically granted significantly later than a patent. Patents are applied for when a new molecule is created and may show promise in application. Approval for such molecule to be used by humans involves years of refinement and testing. A Member is not expected to grant exclusive marketing rights until a pharmaceutical or agricultural chemical product has completed its development and testing cycle and been approved for marketing. There are no express grounds for preventing a less scrupulous private enterprise from obtaining a patent in a country where minimal review is undertaken, and where marketing approval is not the subject of a rigorous review process. However, the Member country where EMRs are sought still controls the process because such rights need not be granted until it has internally approved the marketing of the product. Moreover, there is a general obligation of good faith in all legal systems, and a Member would not need to grant EMRs on the basis of a manifestly inadequate or "sham" foreign patent and marketing approval.[143]

Doha Developments

Finally, the application of Article 70.9 to least-developed Members with respect to pharmaceutical products was waived by the General Council in connection with

---

[143] In this context, the question arises whether a patent that has been granted without examination should be considered a "patent" in terms of Article 70.9.

implementation of Paragraph 7 of the Doha Declaration on the TRIPS Agreement and Public Health.[144] That waiver provides:

> "1. The obligations of least-developed country Members under paragraph 9 of Article 70 of the TRIPS Agreement shall be waived with respect to pharmaceutical products until 1 January 2016.
>
> 2. This waiver shall be reviewed by the Ministerial Conference not later than one year after it is granted, and thereafter annually until the waiver terminates, in accordance with the provisions of paragraph 4 of Article IX of the WTO Agreement."

4. WTO jurisprudence

4.1 Canada – Term of Patent Protection ("Canada – Patent Term")[145]

In *Canada – Patent Term* the Appellate Body interpreted Articles 70.1 and 70.2 regarding subject matter existing prior to its application in a Member. This case involved a complaint by the United States against Canada for an alleged failure to apply the minimum 20-year patent term requirement of Article 33 to patents that were granted under pre-TRIPS patent legislation.

Canada argued that it was not required to extend the term of patents that had been granted under an act that applied to patents granted up until 1989 (and which patents remained in force when Article 33 became applicable), because Article 70.1 excluded application of TRIPS to "acts" which occurred before the date of application. In Canada's view, the grant of a patent was an "act" that occurred before Article 33 became applicable. Canada argued that Article 70.2, which establishes obligations regarding "subject matter existing at the date of application . . . and which is protected in that Member on the said date" covered patents granted prior to application of the Agreement, but did not obligate it to extend the patent term, which was excluded under Article 70.1 as prior "acts".

The decision of the panel and Appellate Body in this case focused on the plain meaning of Articles 70.1 and 70.2. Neither the panel nor the AB found Canada's attempt to distinguish the act of setting out a patent term (as within Article 70.1), and the general "existing" nature of the patented invention under Article 70.2, persuasive. The Appellate Body found that Article 70.2 required the application of Article 33 to the term of existing patents based on the express language of the Agreement.

4.2 India – Patent Protection for Pharmaceutical and Agricultural Chemical Products ("India – Mailbox")[146]

The first case brought under TRIPS was a claim by the United States alleging that India had failed to implement its obligations to provide an adequate mailbox

---

[144] General Council, Decision of 8 July 2002, Least-Developed Country Members – Obligations Under Article 70.9 of the TRIPS Agreement with Respect to Pharmaceutical Products, WT/L/478, 12 July 2002.

[145] *Canada – Term of Patent Protection*, WT/DS170/AB/R, 18 Sept. 2000 (*Canada – Patent Term*).

[146] India – Patent Protection for Pharmaceutical and Agricultural Chemical Products, AB-1997-5, WT/DS50/AB/R, 19 Dec. 1997 (*India – Mailbox*).

mechanism to receive and preserve applications pending the availability of patent protection for pharmaceutical and agricultural chemical products (Article 70.8, TRIPS Agreement), and that India had failed to establish a legal mechanism for the granting of exclusive marketing rights (Article 70.9, TRIPS Agreement). India argued that it met its mailbox obligations by virtue of administrative instructions given by the executive to the patent commissioner. The United States claimed that those instructions were inconsistent with express terms of the India Patents Act that required the patent commissioner to reject patent applications for pharmaceutical and agricultural chemical products, and that the Indian Constitution did not permit the executive to override the terms of the Patents Act in this manner. Regarding EMRs, India claimed that it had no obligation to establish a mechanism for granting them until the need arose. The United States said that the obligation was not contingent on future events, and that India had an explicit obligation to immediately establish a legal mechanism.

The panel and Appellate Body held that India had failed to act consistently with its obligations under Articles 70.8 and 70.9. However, the AB rejected a key element of the panel's legal approach (and also differed on a minor procedural issue). The panel held that India's approach to providing a legal means for implementing its mailbox obligation did not satisfy the "legitimate expectations" of the United States and private patent holders, and that India should have adopted a system that would allay reasonable doubts the parties might have concerning the security of patent mailbox applications.

The AB faulted the panel for what, in its view, was lack of sufficient attention to the express terms of TRIPS. The AB said that the concept of "legitimate expectations" derived from GATT 1947 jurisprudence on adverse treatment of imported products. It was typically applied to assess conditions of competition after finding of a *prima facie* violation of GATT rules, and in the context of a Member seeking to disprove nullification or impairment of benefits. In the AB's view, the panel had instead used the concept of "legitimate expectations" in the sense of a non-violation nullification or impairment cause of action alleging the undermining of benefits expected from negotiated concessions in the absence of a rule violation. Used in this sense, the panel had exceeded the scope of its authority because Article 64.2–3 precluded non-violation causes of action as of the date of the proceeding. Thus, to the extent that the panel had suggested that it should interpret TRIPS in light of the legitimate expectations of the United States or its patent holders, or had placed on India a burden to relieve them of "reasonable doubts", the panel was in error.

The AB emphasized that India's textual obligation under TRIPS was to provide a "means" to implement its mailbox obligations, and analogized this obligation to providing a "sound legal mechanism". India was under no further obligation. The AB concurred with the panel that India had not done this since it appeared from the evidence that the Indian Constitution did not permit the executive to override a statutory requirement in the manner alleged by India. The AB rejected India's assertion that it alone should decide on what means were adequate within its legal system, noting that legal rules could be treated as matters of fact by international judicial bodies, and referring to the fact that the United States had been subject to just such an inquiry in the *U.S. – Section 337*[147] case under GATT 1947. The AB went on to hold that the plain language of TRIPS required India to provide a mechanism for granting EMRs from its entry into force. It said that Article 70.9 operates in tandem with Article 70.8(a), which clearly takes effect from the entry into force of the WTO Agreement, and that India's argument that its obligation was contingent on the need for granting an EMR was not supported by the text of the agreement.

In the *India – Mailbox* decision, the AB stressed the importance of adhering to the text of the TRIPS Agreement in the process of interpretation, and of avoiding the addition of new obligations based on broad concepts such as removing reasonable doubts. Such an approach can hardly be faulted, particularly since Members may have very different views regarding their expectations as to TRIPS.

4.3 Japan – Measures Concerning Sound Recordings[148]

The United States and European Communities requests for consultations regarding Japan's alleged failure under Article 70.2 to provide retroactive protection for sound recordings in the public domain (but not by virtue of expiration of the term of copyright) is discussed above at Section 3.2.

5. Relationship with other international instruments

Article 70 is specifically directed to obligations surrounding its entry into force. Generally speaking, these obligations are not related to the provisions of other WTO agreements or other international instruments. However, because TRIPS, including Article 70, incorporates by reference provisions of the Paris, Berne and other IPR conventions, it necessarily bears a relationship to those instruments. As seen in the *Japan – Sound Recordings* request for consultations, interpretation of Article 70 may depend upon incorporated provisions of WIPO Conventions. This is not a feature unique to Article 70.

As with all other elements of TRIPS, interpretation of Article 70 must take into account the Doha Declaration on the TRIPS Agreement and Public Health, and the agreement by Members that TRIPS should be interpreted in a manner supportive of access to medicines for all.

6. New developments

6.1 National laws

Each Member of the WTO takes into account the provisions of Article 70 in the implementation of its TRIPS obligations, and we will not undertake to review that panoply of Member action. However, it may be useful to consider an example of

---

[147] United States – Section 337 of the Tariff Act of 1930 Panel Report, adopted 7 November 1989, BISD 36S/345 (*U.S. – Section 337*).

[148] *Japan-Measures Concerning Sound Recordings*, Request for Consultations by the United States, WT/DS28/1, 14 Feb. 1996; and *Japan-Measures Concerning Sound Recordings*, Request for Consultations from the European Communities, WT/DS42/1, 28 Feb. 1996.

legislation adopted to establish an Article 70.8 patent application mailbox and an Article 70.9 mechanism for the grant of EMRs.

6.1.1 The India 1999 Patents Amendment Act

Following the decision of the Appellate Body in the *India – Mailbox* case, India amended its Patents Act in 1999 to add a mechanism for the filing of patent applications with respect to pharmaceutical products,[149] as well as a mechanism for the grant of exclusive marketing rights.[150] It added a new Chapter IVA to the Patents Act titled "Exclusive Marketing Rights". That new Chapter provided that the Controller General of Patents would not refer an application regarding a medicine or drug to a patent examiner until December 31, 2004. However, if an application was made for the grant of EMRs, it would be referred to an examiner for the purposes of preparing a report as to whether it fell within the scope of claimed inventions otherwise excluded from patentability in India,[151] such as the mere discovery of a scientific principle,[152] or an invention claiming a new use for a known substance.[153] If the report does not conclude that the invention should be rejected as outside the subject matter scope of patenting (this report is *not* an examination as to whether the claimed invention satisfies the criteria of patentability), then the Controller may grant exclusive marketing rights under the specified conditions.[154] The 1999 Amendment Act enumerated the preconditions set out in Article 70.9 (i.e., that a patent was filed for and granted in a Paris Convention country on or after 1 January 1995, a patent had been granted in that country, and "the approval to sell or distribute the article or substance on the basis of appropriate tests conducted on or after the 1st day of January, 1995, in that country has been granted on or after the date of making a claim for a patent covered under [the provision referring to medicines or drugs]." If those conditions are met, and marketing approval for the medicine or drug has been granted in India,

> "then, he shall have the exclusive right by himself, his agents or licensees to sell or distribute in India the article or substance on and from the date of approval granted by the Controller in this behalf till a period of five years or till the date of grant of patent or the date of rejection of application for grant of patent, whichever is earlier."[155]

The 1999 Amendment Act provides for a prior user's right in the following terms:

---

[149] India's Patents Act did not at that time exclude patenting of agricultural chemical products. Also, the Patents Act permitted the patenting of processes relating to pharmaceutical products. See Patents Act, 1970, Sec. 5, pre-amendment.

[150] The Patents (Amendment) Act, 1999 (No. 17 of 1999), 26th March, 1999, to amend the Patents Act, 1970 (India) (hereinafter "1999 Amendment Act"). Note that the India Patents Act has also been amended by the Patents (Amendment) Act, 2002, No. 38 of 2002, 25th June 2002. The mechanism excluded "intermediate" chemical substances used in the production of medicines. 1999 Amendment Act, sec. 2.

[151] *Id.*, sec. 3, at 24A(1).

[152] Patents Act, sec. 3(c).

[153] Patents Act, sec. 3(d).

[154] 1999 Amendments Act, sec. 3, 24A(3).

[155] *Id.*, sec. 24B(1).

"24B(2) Where, the specifications of an invention relatable to an article or a substance covered under sub-section (2) of Section 5 [i.e., medicines and drugs] have
been recorded in a document or the invention has been tried and used, or, the
article *or the substance has been sold, by a person, before a claim for a patent of that
invention is made in India or in a convention country, then, the sale or distribution
of the article or substance by such person, after the claim referred to above is made,
shall not be deemed to be an infringement of exclusive right to sell or distribute* under
sub-section (1)." [emphasis added]

Thus, a third party that has sold a medicine prior to the earlier of the filing date
in India or the priority date may continue to sell and distribute the product.[156]
And, since exclusive marketing rights do not address the manufacture of pharmaceutical products, the prior user's right effectively allows producers to make,
sell and distribute medicines in India *provided that* they were producing and selling such products prior to the applicant's filing or priority date. This right would
not permit generic producers that commenced production *after* originators filed
patent applications to continue their activities, and in that sense is not an extensive grant of rights. The prior user's right is consistent with exceptions to patent
rights customarily applied, for example, in Europe. The European Commission
proposal for a Community Patent Regulation expressly incorporates a prior user's
right.[157]

The Indian exclusive marketing rights legislation applies the compulsory licensing provisions of the Patents Act *mutatis mutandis* to those new rights, exchanging
the rights under patent for "exclusive right to sell and distribute". In addition, the
legislation authorizes government use of medicines or drugs covered by exclusive
marketing rights, as follows:

"24D(1) Without prejudice to the provisions of any other law for the time being
in force, where, at any time after an exclusive marketing right to sell or distribute
any article or substance has been granted under sub-section (1) of section 24B, the
Central Government is satisfied that it is necessary or expedient in public interest
to sell or distribute the article or substance by a person other than a person to
whom exclusive right has been granted under sub-section (1) of section 24B, it
may, by itself or through any person authorized in writing by it in this behalf, sell
or distribute the article or substance.

---

[156] This is so because the patent in such cases lacks novelty: the third party has already sold the
product before the priority date of the patent.
[157] "*Article 12*
Right based on prior use of the invention
1. A Community patent may not be invoked against a person who, in good faith and for business
purposes, had used the invention in the Community or had made effective and serious preparations
for such use before the filing date or, where priority has been claimed, the priority date of the
application on the basis of which the patent is granted (hereinafter referred to as "the prior user");
the prior user shall have the right, for business purposes, to continue the use in question or to use
the invention as planned during the preparations.
2. The right of the prior user may not be transferred either during the user's lifetime or following
his death other than with the user's undertaking or that part of the undertaking in which the use or
the preparations for use took place."
Proposal for a Council Regulation on the Community patent, Brussels, 1.8.2000, COM(2000) 412
final 2000/0177 (CNS).

(2) The Central Government may, by notification in the Official Gazette and at any time after an exclusive right to sell or distribute an article or a substance has been granted, direct, in the public interest and for reasons to be stated, that the said article or substance shall be sold at a price determined by an authority specified by it in this behalf."

The government use right is an especially important feature of the Indian approach to exclusive marketing rights because it will allow the government to manage the introduction of pharmaceutical patents in a manner that protects the public interest. Because, as discussed earlier, EMRs are not patents, and are not governed by the patent rules of TRIPS, India is entitled to provide for more extensive exception to such rights than might be permitted with respect to patents. For example, government use of exclusive marketing rights does not require payment of remuneration to the holder of the rights.

6.2 International instruments
Article 70 is a transitional mechanism under TRIPS. It has not been the subject of other international instruments.[158]

6.3 Regional and bilateral contexts

6.3.1 Regional

6.4 Proposals for review
To the extent that Article 70.8-9 implicate the availability of pharmaceutical products, they are the subject of ongoing study. More generally, as a provision relating to subject matter existing upon entry into force of its provisions, Article 70.1-7 is not the subject of proposals for review.

7. Comments, including economic and social implications

The extension of intellectual property protection to subject matter existing in a Member as of the date of the application of TRIPS necessarily changes the balance between public access to ideas and expression, and the interests of private claimants to such ideas and expressions. Negotiators might have decided that TRIPS Agreement rules would apply only to subject matter arising after the date of its application, and this would have resulted in a less dramatic shift in the balance. At least in the short run, the decision to protect existing subject matter worked in favour of the preponderant creators of IPR subject matter, which are enterprises from OECD countries. However, this decision by now is largely in the category of "old business", and the focus of attention for developing countries is whether the present TRIPS Agreement balance, in its many forms, is in their interests. And, if not, what changes should be sought.

Articles 70.8 and 70.9 continue to be important to those few developing Members that have yet to implement pharmaceutical product patent protection, and

---

[158] On the WTO waiver for least-developed country Members with respect to Article 70.9 see above, Section 3.9 ("Doha Developments").

Article 70.8 remains important to least-developed Members. On 1 January 2005, India will initiate pharmaceutical product patent protection and should then begin the review of mailbox applications. The extent to which patents and/or EMRs granted on the basis of those applications impedes the manufacture and sale of generic medicines in India and for export markets may have dramatic consequences for public health in many developing countries. It will be important for the WHO and other multilateral organizations, including the WTO, to pay close attention to the impact of the end of the pharmaceutical product transition period on medicines pricing and availability.

37: Review and Amendment

> ### Article 71   Review and Amendment
>
> 1. The Council for TRIPS shall review the implementation of this Agreement after the expiration of the transitional period referred to in paragraph 2 of Article 65. The Council shall, having regard to the experience gained in its implementation, review it two years after that date, and at identical intervals thereafter. The Council may also undertake reviews in the light of any relevant new developments which might warrant modification or amendment of this Agreement.
>
> 2. Amendments merely serving the purpose of adjusting to higher levels of protection of intellectual property rights achieved, and in force, in other multilateral agreements and accepted under those agreements by all Members of the WTO may be referred to the Ministerial Conference for action in accordance with paragraph 6 of Article X of the WTO Agreement on the basis of a consensus proposal from the Council for TRIPS.

1. Introduction: terminology, definition and scope

Article 71 deals with two distinctive issues: the review and the amendment of the Agreement. While paragraph 1 refers mainly to review, paragraph 2 provides a (simplified) procedure for amendments adjusting the TRIPS standards of IPRs to higher levels of protection. In general, a review does not necessarily have to result in an amendment of a given agreement; it may also confirm the agreement as it is. Despite this distinction of subject matter, it follows from paragraph 1 that review and amendment are closely interlinked: the purpose of a TRIPS review is not limited to an examination of Members' implementation efforts (see first sentence of para. 1); it may equally be undertaken with a view to accommodating relevant new developments warranting modification or amendment of the Agreement (see third sentence of para. 1).

1.1 Review
The purpose of the first paragraph of Article 71 is to monitor the operation of TRIPS in practice with a view to ensuring a successful realization of

its objectives.[159] To this end, paragraph 1 provides for three different review procedures:

a) Its first sentence refers to the review of the implementation by Members of the TRIPS Agreement. This review is mandatory ("The Council for TRIPS shall...") and must take place after the expiration of the transitional period referred to in Article 65.2, i.e., as of 1 January 2000.

b) By contrast, the second sentence refers to the review of the provisions of the TRIPS Agreement itself. This review is also mandatory ("The Council shall...") and must be commenced two years after the expiration of the transitional period under Article 65.2 (i.e., as of 1 January 2002) and every two years thereafter. In reviewing the TRIPS Agreement, the Council for TRIPS shall have "regard to the experience gained in its implementation".

c) Finally, the third sentence of paragraph 1 equally refers to a review of the TRIPS provisions. As opposed to the above review exercises, though, this review is optional ("The Council may...") and may expressly result in a modification or an amendment of the TRIPS Agreement, in case such developments merit an amendment to the treaty. Unlike for the other two cases of review, there is no reference to any date as of when this review may be commenced (see Section 3 for details of all three kinds of review).

1.2 Amendment

Amendments are dealt with under Article 71 paragraph 1, third sentence (see above) as well as under paragraph 2. Contrary to a review, an amendment will necessarily result in the changing of the text of an agreement. It may be (but does not have to be) the consequence of a review, as illustrated by the third sentence of Article 71.1.

The latter provision refers to "modification or amendment" of TRIPS. Due to this language, it could be argued that amendment and modification of a treaty must be distinguished from one another. While an "amendment" seeks to change the treaty between *all* the parties to it, a "modification" operates *inter partes* between two or more parties to the treaty. It seeks to modify that treaty on the basis of an agreement authorized, or conversely not prohibited, by the treaty which neither affects the rights of third parties nor the objectives and purposes of the agreement.[160]

2. History of the provision

2.1 Situation pre-TRIPS

Neither the review nor the amendment or modification of a treaty is specific to TRIPS. Amendment and modification of treaties have been traditional

---

[159] For the objectives of TRIPS and the rationales underlying its adoption see Section 7. For a detailed analysis, see Chapter 6 (in particular on Article 7) and Chapter 1 (on the preamble).

[160] See Article 41 of the Vienna Convention on the Law of Treaties. It is doubtful, however, if this provision is directly applicable to the TRIPS Agreement. In any case, in the TRIPS context, such modification could occur where a vote among WTO Members does not result in unanimity. In that case, the proposed modifications of the Agreement would apply only to those Members supporting it.

instruments under public international law and are reflected in Part IV of the Vienna Convention on the Law of Treaties (Articles 39-41). Both revision and amendment are provided for in the most important pre-TRIPS conventions on IPR protection, namely the Paris and the Berne Conventions.

2.1.1 The Paris Convention

The Paris Convention for the Protection of Industrial Property in its Article 17 grants state parties the possibility to propose amendments to a number of organizational provisions. Article 18 of the same Convention constitutes the legal basis for revision conferences to be held successively in one of the countries of the Union. Such revisions concern, *inter alia*, the substantive provisions of the Paris Convention. Each revision has the stated purpose of introducing amendments "designed to improve the system of the Union" (Article 18.1). Accordingly, the Paris Convention has been revised at a series of conferences between its entry into force in 1883 and the latest revision in 1967.[161]

2.1.2 The Berne Convention

The Berne Convention for the Protection of Literary and Artistic Works follows the same approach as the Paris Convention. Its Article 26 accords any party the right to propose the amendment of certain organizational provisions.[162] Article 27 provides for the possibility of holding successive revision conferences with a view to introducing "amendments designed to improve the system of the Union" (Article 27.1). These amendments concern, *inter alia*, the substantive provisions of the Berne Convention.[163]

2.2 Negotiating history

2.2.1 The Anell Draft

This draft provided:[164]

> "7. Review and Amendment (68); Amendments (73)
>
> 7A PARTIES shall review the implementation of this Annex after the expiration of the transitional period referred to at point 1 of Part VII above. They shall, having regard to the experience gained in its implementation, review it [-] years after that date, and at identical intervals thereafter. The PARTIES shall also undertake reviews in the light of any relevant new developments which might warrant modification or amendment of this annex. (68)
>
> 7B (i) Amendments to this part shall take effect in accordance with the provisions on entry into force and on provisional application. (73)

---

[161] The Paris Convention Revision Conferences were held in 1911 (Washington), 1925 (The Hague), 1934 (London), 1958 (Lisbon), and 1967 (Stockholm).

[162] Accordingly, the Berne Convention was amended in 1979.

[163] The 1886 original text of the Berne Convention has undergone revisions or completions in 1896 (Paris), 1908 (Berlin), 1914 (Berne), 1928 (Rome), 1948 (Brussels), 1967 (Stockholm), and 1971 (Paris).

[164] See composite text of 23 July 1990, circulated by the Chairman (Lars E. R. Anell) of the TRIPS Negotiating Group, document MTN.GNG/NG11/W/76.

(ii) Amendments merely serving the purpose to adjust to higher levels of protection of intellectual property rights achieved, and in force, in other multilateral agreements and accepted by all PARTIES may be adopted by the Committee. (73)"

Comparing these proposals, there is a striking similarity between the proposal under "A" and the final version of Article 71.1. The proposal refers to the same kinds of review as mentioned earlier (see 1.1 above). The only substantive difference is that under the proposal, the Parties were *obliged* to undertake reviews in case of relevant new developments, whereas under Article 71.1, the TRIPS Council *may* do so. By contrast, this proposal did not contain a separate paragraph dealing with amendment as Article 71.2.

The "B" proposal differed from Article 71 in two important respects: first, it did not make any provision for the review of domestic implementation laws. Second, the "B" proposal did not contain a specific legal basis for "spontaneous" reviews of the Agreement in the light of relevant new developments. Finally, the "B" proposal with respect to the introduction of higher levels of IP protection was essentially similar to Article 71.2 TRIPS.

2.2.2 The Brussels Draft

This draft[165] came very close to the current Article 71. It provided:

"1. PARTIES shall review the implementation of this Agreement after the expiration of the transitional period referred to in paragraph 2 of Article [65]. They shall, having regard to the experience gained in its implementation, review it [-] years after that date, and at identical intervals thereafter. The PARTIES may undertake reviews in the light of any relevant new developments which might warrant modification or amendment of this Agreement.

2. Amendments merely serving the purpose of adjusting to higher levels of protection of intellectual property rights achieved, and in force, in other multilateral agreements and accepted by all PARTIES may be adopted by the Committee."

The first paragraph derived from the "A" proposal under the Anell Draft and thus established the obligation of Members to have their domestic legislation reviewed by the TRIPS Council (referred to as the "Committee" in the Brussels draft).[166] The second paragraph was directly taken from the "B" proposal in the Anell Draft (see above).

3. Possible interpretations

3.1 Article 71.1

1. The Council for TRIPS shall review the implementation of this Agreement after the expiration of the transitional period referred to in paragraph 2 of Article 65. The Council shall, having regard to the experience gained in its implementation,

---

[165] Document MTN.TNC/W/35/Rev. 1 of 3 December 1990.

[166] For an historical overview of the Uruguay Round negotiations on the establishment of the Council for TRIPS, see Chapter 35.

> review it two years after that date, and at identical intervals thereafter. The Council may also undertake reviews in the light of any relevant new developments which might warrant modification or amendment of this Agreement.

As stated in the introduction, this provision establishes three distinct forms of review:

a) The first sentence refers to the *mandatory* review of WTO Members' domestic implementing legislation. It has to be read in conjunction with Articles 65.2 and 63.2. The former provides the basis for computing the actual date for the commencement of the review of the TRIPS implementation in the Council, which is at the same time the date of the expiration of the transitional period after which developing country Members are obliged to comply with TRIPS (i.e., 1 January 2000).[167] Article 63.2 obliges Members to notify the Council about their intellectual property-related laws and regulations for the purpose of assisting the Council in its review of the operation of the Agreement.[168] Such review is one of the core competencies of the Council for TRIPS, as stipulated under Article 68.[169] Seen from a larger perspective, necessity for the review exercise under Article 71.1 arises from each Member's obligation to ensure the conformity of its laws, regulations and administrative procedures with its obligations under the covered agreements (see Article XVI:4 of the WTO Agreement).[170]

The five-year transitional period referred to in Article 65, paragraph 2, expired on 1 January 2000. Therefore, the first review of developing countries' TRIPS legislation started in 2000.[171] As far as developed country Members are concerned, review of their implementing legislation by the Council started as early as 1996.[172] This earlier date is not expressly referred to in Article 71.1. However, it may be inferred from that provision that the review of a Member's implementing legislation may start after the expiry of the transitional period applying to that Member. For developed country Members, that was 1 January 1996 (see Article 65.1).

Article 71 does not define "implementation". However, according to Article 63.2, Members shall notify to the Council their laws and regulations pertaining to the subject matter of TRIPS (i.e., the availability, scope, acquisition, enforcement and prevention of the abuse of IPRs) with a view to assisting the Council in its review of the operation of the Agreement. Thus, review of a Member's implementation encompasses domestic legislation passed by parliament as well as regulations adopted by the administration. On the other hand, the Article 71.1 review does not extend to a Member's final judicial decisions and administrative rulings of general application. This follows from Article 63.2 that refers only to laws and

---

[167] For details, see Chapter 33.

[168] For more details on Article 63 TRIPS, see Chapter 31.

[169] For more details on Article 68 TRIPS, see Chapter 35.

[170] Article XVI:4 of the Marrakesh Agreement establishing the World Trade Organization reads as follows: "Each Member shall ensure the conformity of its laws, regulations and administrative procedures with its obligations as provided in the annexed Agreements."

[171] For a list of those developing country Members whose legislation is currently being reviewed, see the IP gateway page at <http://www.wto.org/>.

[172] Ibid, with an overview of the reviewed IPR categories.

regulations as the objects of the review. As to judicial decisions, they are not subject to the review because of the division of powers, which makes the judiciary independent of a national government's control. Concerning "administrative rulings of general application", they need to be distinguished from "regulations" that according to Article 63.2 are subject to review by the Council. Both are instruments of the administration, and both are addressed to an undetermined number of people (as opposed to one single party). The difference is that regulations of any sort apply to a multitude of cases, whereas administrative rulings of general application, even though addressed to the public at large, concern only particular facts of one particular case. This follows from the term "ruling". Such ruling is of general application in the sense that it is not addressed to one single party only (like an administrative act), but to an undetermined number of addressees. This limitation to one particular case is the reason why such administrative rulings are not subject to the review by the Council under Articles 63.2 and 71.1. Contrary to laws or regulations that apply to an indefinite number of cases, a case-specific administrative ruling, even though addressed to the public at large, does not represent a generally valid application of the law and therefore cannot be considered as a Member's implementation of TRIPS for the purpose of Article 71.1.

In this context, it is important to stress that the review of domestic laws and regulations by the Council is neither related to, nor a first phase of, the WTO dispute settlement procedures. In case other Members during the review express doubts about the TRIPS compatibility of the legislation under review, this will not lead to an automatic establishment of a WTO panel. For this purpose, the Dispute Settlement Understanding (DSU) provides for a separate set of procedural rules to be followed.[173] A possible panel would have to assess the case before it independently of some views expressed in the Council during the review exercise. Thus, the review of domestic legislation should rather be considered as a means of multilateral consultations with a view to making the recourse to dispute settlement procedures unnecessary. This is confirmed by the title of Part V of TRIPS that refers to "Dispute Prevention and Settlement". Part V consists of only two Articles, 63 and 64. The latter is on "Dispute Settlement". Thus, the reference in the title to dispute prevention can only be to Article 63, which deals, *inter alia*, with the review by the Council of domestic laws.

b) The second sentence obliges the Council to review TRIPS itself ("review it"). This exercise is not to be commenced at the same time as the review of the national implementing legislation, but two years later (i.e., as of 1 January 2002). This time frame appears very ambitious considering that in actual practice, the Council so far has not started reviewing the provisions of TRIPS under the Article 71.1 mandate. This is due to the fact that the review of the domestic implementing legislations (see above) has not yet been concluded. As the Council when reviewing TRIPS shall have "regard to the experience gained in its implementation", it would be against the spirit of this provision to engage in a substantive TRIPS review before such experience has fully been acquired.

Article 71 contains a general mandate for the review of all TRIPS provisions. In particular cases, other TRIPS provisions that contain a more specific review

---

[173] For more details on WTO dispute settlement in the context of TRIPS, see Chapter 32.

mandate concerning a particular provision will prevail over Article 71. For instance, as far as the review of the TRIPS rules on the protection of biological material is concerned, Article 27.3(b) represents a *lex specialis*, prevailing over Article 71.1.[174]

With respect to the authorization of the Council to review TRIPS under Article 71, the question arises if such review would be limited to the formulation of non-binding recommendations (concerning the interpretation of certain TRIPS provisions), or if it would authorize the TRIPS Council to actually propose legally binding amendments to the Ministerial Conference according to Article X:1 of the WTO Agreement.[175] In this respect, the view has been expressed that Article 71.1 does not provide the TRIPS Council with a mandate to propose any amendments to TRIPS.[176] In this vein, it could be argued that such mandate would be referred to in express terms, like under Articles 23.4,[177] 64.3[178] and 71.2 (see below). On the other hand, Article X:1 expressly authorizes the GATT, GATS and TRIPS Councils to "submit to the Ministerial Conference proposals to amend the provisions of the corresponding Multilateral Trade Agreements ... the functioning of which they oversee." In addition, it should not be overlooked that according to the third sentence of Article 71.1, the Council may undertake reviews "in the light of any relevant new developments which might warrant modification or amendment" of TRIPS. This kind of review implies an authorization by the Council to propose amendments (or modifications) to the Ministerial Conference (see below). The purpose behind this provision is to ensure that TRIPS addresses in an efficient way current trends in actual IP practice. The same reasoning applies to the second sentence. By stating that the review of TRIPS shall be guided by the experience gained in its implementation, this provision shows Members' intention to adapt the TRIPS provisions to actual needs and practices, including the amendment of provisions that have proven difficult to implement. Efficiency of TRIPS with respect to its objectives can only be ensured if its provisions may actually be amended in case they turn out to be contrary to what is practicable on the domestic level. Therefore, it appears logical to consider the mandate given to the Council under the second sentence of Article 71.1 as encompassing the possibility of proposing substantive amendments to the Ministerial Conference.[179] While the

---

[174] Note that the special review of the provisions under Article 27.3(b) should have commenced in 1999. Due to disagreement between Members concerning the scope of the review, this exercise was delayed. For more details on the Article 27.3(b) review, see Chapter 21.

[175] Pursuant to this provision, the TRIPS Council may propose amendments of the TRIPS Agreement to the Ministerial Conference. The final acceptance of any proposed amendment is up to the WTO Members.

[176] See Communication of Australia of 3 October 2000, WTO document IP/C/W/210, page 5.

[177] This provision obligates the TRIPS Council to undertake negotiations concerning the establishment of a multilateral register for geographical indications for wines.

[178] Article 64.3 obliges the TRIPS Council to submit to the Ministerial Conference recommendations with respect to the applicability of non-violation complaints in the context of TRIPS.

[179] Such proposals would then follow the procedure laid down in Article X:1 of the WTO Agreement: the Ministerial Conference would have to decide by consensus to submit the proposed amendment to the Members for acceptance.

review exercise as such is mandatory ("The Council shall [...] review it [...]"), the Council is free to actually make proposals for amendment.

c) The third sentence authorizes the Council to conduct reviews in the light of any relevant new development that might warrant amendment or modification of the Agreement. Contrary to the other forms of review (see above), this review is not mandatory and may be undertaken any time. As mentioned above, the TRIPS Council is expressly authorized, under the third sentence, to propose amendments of TRIPS to the Ministerial Conference.

Summing up, the sequential logic of actions to be taken by WTO Members under Articles 63.2 and 71.1 includes:

- notification of relevant laws and regulations by Members implementing TRIPS (Article 63.2);

- collective review of Members' intellectual property systems (Article 71.1, first sentence);

- collective review of the provisions of the TRIPS Agreement (Article 71.1, second and third sentence);

- consideration of possible amendments and modifications in the light of the experience of implementation (second sentence) or relevant new developments (third sentence);

- possible formulation of proposals for modification or amendment to be submitted to the Ministerial Conference (second and third sentence).

3.2 Article 71.2

> 2. Amendments merely serving the purpose of adjusting to higher levels of protection of intellectual property rights achieved, and in force, in other multilateral agreements and accepted under those agreements by all Members of the WTO may be referred to the Ministerial Conference for action in accordance with paragraph 6 of Article X of the WTO Agreement on the basis of a consensus proposal from the Council for TRIPS.

Article X:6 of the WTO Agreement provides:

"Notwithstanding the other provisions of this Article, amendments to the Agreement on TRIPS meeting the requirements of paragraph 2 of Article 71 thereof may be adopted by the Ministerial Conference without further formal acceptance process."

The purpose of Article 71.2 of TRIPS is to facilitate the adoption of certain amendments by exempting them from the lengthy acceptance process provided under Article X:1 of the WTO Agreement. Amendments falling under Article 71.2 may be adopted directly by the Ministerial Conference, and do not have to be submitted, by consensus, to the Members for acceptance.[180]

---

[180] Acceptance through a Member usually means that the proposed amendment has to be approved by the respective national parliament, depending on constitutional requirements. This might take

As to the multilateral agreements referred to in Article 71.2, there does not seem to be any of that kind in force at present. The WIPO-sponsored Copyright Treaty (WCT) and the Performers and Phonograms Treaty (WPPT) have some potential eventually to fall under this provision. However, Article 71.2 requires the acceptance by all WTO Members of the higher IPR standards under the respective agreements.

Finally, the case of amending TRIPS for the purpose of adjusting the Agreement to higher levels of IP protection has to be distinguished from the case where higher levels of IP protection are agreed upon in a separate treaty by a limited number of WTO Members and subsequently have to be extended to all other Members on the basis of the most-favoured-nation principle (MFN). MFN requires any Member granting higher IP protection to the nationals of any other country (not necessarily a WTO Member) to accord the same TRIPS-plus protection to the nationals of all other WTO Members (Article 4 TRIPS). But such obligation only applies to those Members that are parties to the relevant TRIPS-plus agreement. Non-party WTO Members are not obliged to grant the same level of TRIPS-plus protection, even though they are entitled to claim such protection for their nationals. By contrast, an amendment of TRIPS binds all WTO Members. The WCT and WPPT may serve to illustrate this point. Those WTO Members that are parties to these treaties have to accord any TRIPS-plus IP protection deriving from the WIPO treaties to all other WTO Members, even those that are not parties to the WIPO treaties.[181] But those non-parties in their territories do not have to grant the same rights. If, by contrast, the higher levels of protection were agreed upon in an amendment to TRIPS, they would have to be complied with by all WTO Members.

4. WTO jurisprudence

So far, there have been no cases before a panel or the Appellate Body dealing specifically with Article 71.

5. Relationship with other international instruments

5.1 WTO Agreements

As mentioned above, Article X:6, WTO Agreement, refers to Article 71 in the context of simplified adoption procedures. Another WTO provision also dealing with

---

a considerable amount of time. In comparison, acceptance by the Ministerial Conference will be much speedier.

[181] Note that according to Article 5, the MFN obligation does not apply in the case of the WIPO treaties on acquisition or maintenance of IPRs. These encompass the Madrid Agreement (and Protocol) Concerning the International Registration of Marks, the Hague Agreement Concerning the International Deposit of Industrial Designs, the Patent Cooperation Treaty, the Trademark Registration Treaty and the Budapest Treaty on the International Recognition of the Deposit of Microorganisms for the Purposes of Patent Procedure, and certain provisions of the Lisbon Agreement for the Protection of Appellations of Origin and their International Registration. The list of such agreements is not fixed, and new multilateral acquisition and maintenance agreements adopted under WIPO auspices would also qualify for national and MFN treatment exemption under Article 5 of the TRIPS Agreement. For details, see Chapter 4.

amendments is Article XXX of the GATT 1994, but it is limited to the trade in goods sector.

5.2 Other international instruments

As indicated above (Section 2.1), provisions on review and amendment are not particular to TRIPS, but also exist, *inter alia*, under the Paris and Berne Conventions. Since these Conventions have to be respected by all WTO Members (see Articles 2.1 and 9.1), any amendments to their texts are automatically binding, even for those Members not parties to the respective Convention. This does not apply vice versa, in that TRIPS amendments will not be binding on countries that are Paris/Berne Convention parties, but not WTO Members.

6. New developments

6.1 National laws

6.2 International instruments

In February 2000 the WTO General Council agreed that mandated reviews should address the trade and development impact on developing countries of the agreement concerned.[182] Even more importantly, at the 2001 Ministerial Conference at Doha, Members in the Ministerial Declaration referred to the Article 71.1 review as follows:

> "We instruct the Council for TRIPS, in pursuing its work programme including under the review of Article 27.3(b), the review of the implementation of the TRIPS Agreement under Article 71.1 [. . .], to examine, *inter alia*, the relationship between the TRIPS Agreement and the Convention on Biological Diversity, the protection of traditional knowledge and folklore, and other relevant new developments raised by Members pursuant to Article 71.1. In undertaking this work, the TRIPS Council shall be guided by the objectives and principles set out in Articles 7 and 8 of the TRIPS Agreement and shall take fully into account the development dimension."[183]

By referring to the development dimension/impact, both of the above instruments make an important contribution to the clarification of the criteria according to

---

[182] WT/GC/M/53, paragraph 39.

[183] See para. 19 of the Ministerial Declaration of 14 November 2001, WTO document WT/MIN(01)/DEC/W/1. Article 7 of the TRIPS Agreement reads:
"The protection and enforcement of intellectual property rights should contribute to the promotion of technological innovation and to the transfer and dissemination of technology to the mutual advantage of producers and users of technological knowledge and in a manner conducive to social and economic welfare, and to the balance of rights and obligations."
Article 8 establishes the principles that underpin the TRIPS Agreement:
"1. Members may, in formulating or amending their laws and regulations, adopt measures necessary to protect public health and nutrition, and to promote the public interest in sectors of vital importance to their economic and technological development, provided that such measures are consistent with the provisions of this Agreement.
2. Appropriate measures, provided they are consistent with the provisions of this Agreement, may be needed to prevent the abuse of intellectual property rights by right holders or the resort to practices which unreasonably restrain trade or adversely affect the international transfer of technology."

which TRIPS reviews under Article 71 should be undertaken. In addition, the Doha Declaration as quoted above obliges the Council to take into account the public policy objectives in Articles 7 and 8, i.e., *inter alia*, technological innovation and the transfer and dissemination of technology, the protection of public health and nutrition, the promotion of the public interest in sectors of vital importance to socio-economic and technological development, and the control of IPR abuses and other restrictive behaviour. This means that when reviewing national implementing legislation, compliance with TRIPS minimum standards shall not be considered an objective in itself, but rather a means of promoting the non-IP policy goals referred to above (see Section 7 below).

The Doha Declaration as cited above also contains some concrete proposals for topics to be examined under the Articles 27.3(b) and 71.1 reviews (i.e., with respect to the Convention on Biological Diversity, traditional knowledge and folklore, and other relevant new developments). Even though these topics are not expressly assigned to one particular review, Article 27.3(b) is the *lex specialis* in the area of biodiversity, traditional knowledge and folklore, whereas the "other relevant new developments" are a reference to the review under the third sentence of Article 71.1.

6.3 Regional and bilateral contexts

6.3.1 Regional

6.4 Proposals for review
There have been no proposals to review Article 71 itself.

7. Comments, including economic and social implications

As observed above, Article 71 serves the purpose of ensuring that national implementing legislation is in conformity with TRIPS, and that the TRIPS provisions themselves correspond to the actual needs and trends in trade-related IPRs. Article 71 is supposed to ensure the efficiency of the Agreement with respect to the attainment of its objectives. These objectives set the criteria according to which the Council for TRIPS examines national implementing legislation as well as possible amendments to TRIPS. The assessment of the current state of domestic laws and of TRIPS provisions, and consequently the possible need for changes, will vary according to what is considered the main objective of the Agreement. Developed country Members tend to emphasize the private property nature of IPRs, whereas developing country Members put more emphasis on the public policy objectives of the Agreement. The former position is partly supported by the TRIPS preamble that refers to the promotion of "effective and adequate protection" of IPRs. In addition, the provisions on substantive and procedural IPRs standards as spelled out in TRIPS are very detailed, whereas the public policy objectives are held in very general terms. In this vein, it has been observed that

> "The TRIPS Agreement was essentially conceived as a means of strengthening the control by titleholders over the protected technologies, and not with the objective of increasing the transfer and use of technology globally. The transfer of technology

was not, in fact, a concern of TRIPS proponents, and the possible effects of the new protectionist standards on such transfer were never seriously considered during the negotiations."[184]

TRIPS is actually the result of a political compromise. In order to make the Agreement more acceptable to developing countries, some rather broad provisions on technology transfer and other public policy objectives were included in the Agreement.[185]

On the other hand, the broad formulation of these objectives provides Members with discretion as to the interpretation of the TRIPS disciplines. Also, the TRIPS objectives are recognized in the preamble as underlying the national systems for the protection of IP. Article 7 refers to certain societal benefits as objectives to be attained through the protection and enforcement of IPRs.[186] In addition to that, the Doha Ministerial Declaration has expressly stated that TRIPS reviews are to be guided by the objectives and principles in Articles 7 and 8,[187] taking full account of the development dimension. Finally, the General Council agreed that reviews should address the trade and development impact on developing countries of the agreement concerned (see above, Section 6.2).

In this vein, the review of the national implementing legislation and of the TRIPS provisions would have to be directed at assessing the suitability of those rules for the promotion of public policy goals as stipulated under Articles 7 and 8. Also, the review exercise should be conducted with a view to assessing the impact of IPR standards on the realization of non-IP development goals, seeking to reconcile possible collisions of interest between these two areas.

Thus, IPR standards in TRIPS should be conceived as a means for the promotion of non-IP public policy objectives, and not as running counter to them. As a result, any review under Article 71 should take account of both public policy goals and the protection of private rights. On the one hand, Members have to examine whether national implementing legislation complies with the TRIPS standards. On the other, the review will have to address the question of whether these standards leave sufficient leeway for the realization of certain non-IPR-related objectives.

Addressing the development dimension while reviewing TRIPS would include considering the implementation of TRIPS in key sectors of concern to developing countries, such as technology transfer,[188] measures to counter anti-competitive abuse of intellectual property rights under Article 40,[189] the digital environment,[190]

---

[184] See C. Correa, *Can the TRIPS Agreement Foster Technology Transfer to Developing Countries?* Draft of March 2003, submitted to a Conference at Duke University [hereinafter Correa, Draft].

[185] For an historical overview of the TRIPS negotiations and the position of developing countries, see UNCTAD-ICTSD Policy Discussion Paper, Part I, Chapter 2 ("The emergence of TRIPS"). For a detailed analysis of the public policy objectives of the TRIPS Agreement, see Chapter 6 (Articles 7 and 8 of this book).

[186] For the text of Article 7 see above, Section 6.2.

[187] For the text of Article 8, as well as the relevant part of the Doha Declaration, see above, Section 6.2. It should be noted that Articles 7 and 8 constitute the "object and purpose" of the Agreement for the purposes of its interpretation, according to Article 31 of the Vienna Convention on the Law of Treaties.

[188] See Chapter 34.

[189] See Chapter 29.

[190] See, Chapter 7.

IPRs in traditional and indigenous contexts[191] and compulsory licensing.[192] It would also include consideration of extending the moratorium of the application to the Agreement of the non-violation complaint remedy[193] and a debate as to whether it is necessary to include general exceptions clauses in TRIPS.[194]

[191] See Chapter 21.

[192] See Chapter 25.

[193] See Chapter 32.

[194] See The South Centre, *Review of TRIPS Agreement under Article 71.1*, Occasional Papers No. 3 by M. Stilwell and C. Monagle, December 2000, also covering the other sectors referred to above.

38: Reservations

Article 72   Reservations

Reservations may not be entered in respect of any of the provisions of this Agreement without the consent of the other Members.

1. Introduction: terminology, definition and scope

Article 72 provides that a Member may not enter a reservation to all or part of the Agreement without the consent of the other Members. A reservation is a statement by which a party to a treaty undertakes to modify its obligations when it becomes party to the treaty (see VCLT, Articles 2(d), 19–23). The allowance of reservations to TRIPS may have created a situation in which different rules applied to different Members. This would not be so different from the situation in which Members enter exceptions in GATS Schedules of Commitments. This is not the approach followed by TRIPS.

2. History of the provision

2.1 Situation pre-TRIPS

The Vienna Convention on the Law of Treaties expressly addresses reservations to treaties and their effect (see Articles 19–23). There is an extensive legal literature on the nature and effect of reservations,[195] and there are decisions of international tribunals that address them. Generally, a reservation to a treaty may be entered by a state adhering to it provided that the treaty does not expressly exclude this, or if this would be inconsistent with the object and purpose of the treaty. If other state parties to the treaty do not object to the reservation, it will take effect. If a party objects to a reservation, it does not take effect with respect to that party. The result for the adhering (i.e., reserving) party's treaty obligations in that situation will vary depending on the circumstances (see Article 21.3 of the VCLT).

---

[195] See generally, Parliamentary Participation in the Making and Operation of Treaties: A Comparative Study (S. A. Riesenfeld & F. M. Abbott, eds. 1994: Martinus Nijhoff/Kluwer).

2.2 Negotiating history

There is no analogue to Article 72 in negotiating texts prior to the Brussels Ministerial Text of December 1990. Up through the Montreal Mid-Term Ministerial in
1988, developing countries on the whole had not accepted that TRIPS would be
binding on all Members, and the question of reservations was not especially relevant until the decision to accept the concept of the single undertaking was made.[196]
Throughout the TRIPS negotiating process, issues concerning permissible exceptions to obligations, and later on the issue of transitional arrangements, were
discussed extensively. These discussions considered differences in developmental
circumstances among prospective Members to the agreement. The prospect of
differentiated obligation on a Member-by-Member basis does not appear to have
been considered in any detail, though this would have been one way to take into
account different developmental circumstances.

2.2.1 The Brussels Draft

The Brussels Ministerial Text[197] included a predecessor to Article 72 that would
have permitted reservations under limited conditions:

> "Article 75: Reservations:
>
> A PARTY may only enter reservations in respect of any of the provisions of this
> Agreement at the time of entry into force of this Agreement for that PARTY and
> with the consent of the other PARTIES."

By referring to reservations in an affirmative way (that is, by indicating when
Members may enter them), the Brussels Draft provision implied that Members
at least contemplated the possibility of bargaining toward differentiated TRIPS
commitments on a Member-by-Member basis. If the negotiating parties had bargained toward acceptable sets of reservations prior to the conclusion of TRIPS,
the Agreement might ultimately have taken on a substantially different character
than that ultimately achieved.[198] Article 75 of the Brussels Ministerial Text reflects
the fact that the "single undertaking" concept embodied in the WTO Agreement
was not settled as of late 1990.

2.2.2 The Dunkel Draft

The Dunkel Draft text of late 1991 amended the reservations clause of the Brussels
Ministerial Text, substituting for it a "no reservations without consent" clause.[199]

---

[196] On the TRIPS Agreement negotiating process, see Silvia Ostry, *The Uruguay Round North-South
Grand Bargain: Implications for future negotiations*, at 285; J. Michael Finger, *The Uruguay Round
North-South bargain: Will the WTO get over it?*, at 301; Frederick M. Abbott, *The TRIPS-legality
of measures taken to address public health crises: Responding to USTR-State-industry positions
that undermine the WTO*, at 311, and; T.N. Srinivasan, *The TRIPS Agreement*, at 343, each in The
Political Economy of International Trade: Essays in Honor of Robert E. Hudec (eds. D. Kennedy
and J. Southwick 2002)(Cambridge University Press).

[197] Document MTN.TNC/W/35/Rev. 1 of 3 December 1990.

[198] TRIPS takes account of differences in the level of development among Members principally,
though not exclusively, through its transition provisions (Articles 65, 66 and 70, see Chapters 33,
36).

[199] Recall the final text of Article 72, which provides: "Reservations may not be entered in respect
of any of the provisions of this Agreement without the consent of the other Members."

Though seemingly admitting for the possibility of reservations, the negative drafting of the Dunkel Draft and final TRIPS Agreement reservations text appeared to signal an important distinction between TRIPS and the GATT and GATS. Although neither the GATT nor GATS specifically provides for reservations, commitments on tariff bindings and services market access are made on a Member-by-Member basis, and these commitments are made in the context of individualized reciprocal negotiations. In practical effect, this is similar to the allowance of reservations. The WTO Agreement does not permit reservations to its own terms, and provides that "Reservations in respect of any of the provisions of the Multilateral Trade Agreements [including TRIPS] may only be made to the extent provided for in those Agreements" (Article XVI: 5, WTO Agreement).

3. Possible interpretations

Article 72   Reservations

Reservations may not be entered in respect of any of the provisions of this Agreement without the consent of the other Members.

There is limited practical scope for interpretative disagreement as to the meaning of Article 72 precluding the entry of reservations absent the consent of the other Members. Under the VCLT and customary international law, reservations may only be entered upon adherence to a treaty.[200] No Member attempted to enter a reservation to TRIPS when the WTO Agreement was initially concluded. This leaves little possibility that an issue with respect to Article 72 might surface in connection with original WTO membership. An interpretive issue theoretically might arise upon accession of a new Member to the WTO.[201] However, as a practical matter this is unlikely because a new Member accedes to the WTO (and TRIPS Agreement) on the basis of an accession agreement (a Protocol of Accession), and this agreement is concluded by consensus (absent exceptional circumstances). If there were a consensus among Members as to a waiver or modification of a TRIPS Agreement obligation in an accession agreement, this would be the

---

[200] Article 19, VCLT. Technically, a reservation may be formulated "when signing, ratifying, accepting, approving or acceding to a treaty", *id.*

[201] A question might arise whether the consent of the other Members to a reservation must take place by some affirmative act, or might be tacit or passive (i.e., by lack of formal objection to a reservation). Article 72 does not specify the form by which acceptance of other Members must take place, and there is room to argue that the lack of an objection by any of the other Members to a reservation could constitute its acceptance. Article 20(1) of the VCLT provides that if a treaty allows for a particular reservation, no acceptance is required by other parties. Otherwise, acceptance is required. In general (unless the treaty provides otherwise) acceptance will be presumed if the party does not object within 12 months following notification (Article 20(5), VCLT). Article 20(5) of the VCLT makes clear that a reservation must be "notified" to other Members for it to be subject to tacit or passive acceptance, and Article 23(1) indicates that a reservation must be in written form. Since it must be "notified" as a reservation in written form, it is unlikely that a reservation made by an acceding Member could be inadvertently accepted by other Members by failing to object to it.

substantive equivalent of a reservation with the consent of the other Members. It seems doubtful that such a waiver or modification would be legally framed as a "reservation" but, if it was, the consent of the other Members would be present and an interpretive issue would not arise.[202] It is difficult to foresee the context in which an acceding Member might propose to modify the terms of TRIPS by entering a reservation outside its Protocol of Accession.

4. WTO jurisprudence

There have been no WTO disputes on Article 72.

5. Relationship with other international instruments

5.1 WTO Agreements

The WTO Agreement provides at Article XVI:5:

> "5. No reservations may be made in respect of any provision of this Agreement. Reservations in respect of any of the provisions of the Multilateral Trade Agreements may only be made to the extent provided for in those Agreements. Reservations in respect of a provision of a Plurilateral Trade Agreement shall be governed by the provisions of that Agreement."

Article 72, pursuant to Article XVI:5 of the WTO Agreement, governs the extent to which reservations may be entered in respect of TRIPS.

5.2 Other international instruments

The Vienna Convention on the Law of Treaties prescribes rules regarding reservations at Articles 19–23.

6. New developments

6.1 Proposals for review

No proposals have been made to review Article 72.

7. Comments, including economic and social implications

TRIPS does not permit reservations absent the consent of the Members. The same rules generally apply to all Members. Transitional mechanisms are intended to ease potential economic and social dislocations. TRIPS negotiators might have

---

[202] The question might be asked whether consent of the "other Members" means "all" of the other Members, or might mean only "some" or "a few" of the other Members. If negotiators had intended that a limited number of Members might among themselves agree on a reservation, this might better have been made explicit. There might have been reference to a reservation accepted by "another Member". The consequences of such an individuated arrangement (e.g., from an MFN standpoint) might have been addressed. Absent some persuasive evidence that negotiators intended a fairly dramatic break with the general application of the TRIPS Agreement, there is little reason to suggest that less than all Members might accept a reservation as among themselves.

taken another approach and allowed each Member to negotiate its own intellectual property commitments based on its particular situation. If negotiators had followed this alternative approach, they probably would not have employed the legal formula of allowing reservations. More likely they would have adopted schedules of commitments along the lines of the GATS. Article 72 is significant largely for confirming the single undertaking approach adopted in TRIPS.

39: Security Exceptions

> ### Article 73   Security Exceptions
>
> Nothing in this Agreement shall be construed:
>
> (a) to require a Member to furnish any information the disclosure of which it considers contrary to its essential security interests; or
>
> (b) to prevent a Member from taking any action which it considers necessary for the protection of its essential security interests;
>
> (i) relating to fissionable materials or the materials from which they are derived;
>
> (ii) relating to the traffic in arms, ammunition and implements of war and to such traffic in other goods and materials as is carried on directly or indirectly for the purpose of supplying a military establishment;
>
> (iii) taken in time of war or other emergency in international relations; or
>
> (c) to prevent a Member from taking any action in pursuance of its obligations under the United Nations Charter for the maintenance of international peace and security.

1. Introduction: terminology, definition and scope

Although there is a relatively widespread tendency among scholars to perceive international trade law as a concept differing from the classical idea of state sovereignty and to regard national security, borders and territory as state interests difficult to reconcile with liberalization of markets,[203] the provision of Article 73, almost identical to Article XXI of the GATT and Article XIV *bis* of the GATS, proves that these traditional state interests continue to be a major concern of WTO Members.[204]

---

[203] See, for instance, D.M. McRae, *The Contribution of International Trade Law to the Development of International Law*, Collected Courses of The Hague Academy of International Law, 1996, v. 260, pp. 99–238, at pp. 130–131.

[204] For a more detailed analysis as to whether international trade law challenges the existing paradigm of public international law, see Mariano Garcia-Rubio, *On the Application of Customary Rules of State Responsibility by the WTO Dispute Settlement Organs – A General International Law Perspective* – Geneva, Studies and Working Papers, Graduate Institute of International Studies, 2000, p. 100, particularly Chapter 1 [in the following: Garcia-Rubio].

There was a clear reluctance among the former Contracting Parties of the GATT 1947 (which still exists as the "GATT 1994" among WTO Members) to activate the institutionalized dispute settlement mechanisms to deal with disputes involving the interpretation of the national security exceptions. The WTO is not perceived as an adequate forum for dealing with national security issues. Under the GATT 1947, only four such cases reached the level of formalized dispute settlement, while no panel established since the creation of the WTO for dealing with these kinds of disputes has succeeded in producing a report.[205] Tacit agreement seems to exist among states to exclude the trade distortions originating from unilateral economic sanctions imposed for alleged security reasons from the scope of disputes to be solved through the compulsory dispute settlement system of the WTO.[206]

Article 73 allows states to take three kinds of measures contrary to their normal obligations under TRIPS: to preserve undisclosed security-sensitive information (para. a); to act in pursuance of obligations flowing from the Charter of the United Nations (para. c); or to take "any action" they "consider [. . .] necessary for the protection of [their] essential security interests (para. b) relating to nuclear materials (sub-para. i), trade in arms, ammunition and the like (sub-para. ii), or to redress war and other emergencies in international relations (sub-para. iii).

No dispute has been brought before the WTO dispute settlement organs regarding economic sanctions imposed by the Security Council of the United Nations under Chapter VII of the Charter. Although paragraph (c) of Article 73 is in line with Article 103 of the UN Charter, the compatibility of the adopted measures with the UN Security Council orders they are meant to serve could have potentially been the object of a WTO dispute. However, this situation has never arisen.[207]

2. History of the provision

2.1 Situation pre-TRIPS

At the outset of the negotiations on the establishment of the International Trade Organization, the suggested Charter, as proposed by the United States in 1946, as well as the first draft prepared by the Preparatory Committee in London in October and November of 1946 and the draft prepared by a technical drafting committee in New York in January and February of 1947, provided for national security exceptions only as a part of the general exceptions of the chapters on commercial policy and commodity agreements.[208] Only at the meeting of the Preparatory Committee in Geneva from April to October 1947 was it decided to transfer the security

---

[205] See below, Section 4.

[206] To illustrate this point, see for instance the list of unilateral economic sanctions adopted by the Council of the European Union (which have never been the object of a dispute before the WTO dispute settlement organs) in Ramses Wessel, *The European Union's Foreign and Security Policy – A Legal Institutional Perspective*, The Hague, Kluwer Law International, 1999, p. 340 and ff.

[207] Nevertheless, we share the doubts of Schloemann and Ohloff as to the competence of WTO panels to deal with such cases. See Hannes L. Schloemann, and Stefan Ohloff, *'Constitutionalization' and Dispute Settlement in the WTO: National Security as an Issue of Competence*, American Journal of International Law, v. 93, no. 2, 1999, pp. 424–451, at p. 431 [hereinafter Schloemann/Ohloff]. Also Garcia-Rubio, at p. 52.

[208] GATT, *Analytical Index: Guide to GATT Law and Practice* (6th. rev. ed., 1995), at 608 [hereinafter Analytical Index].

exceptions from the general exceptions to a separate article at the end of the Charter, which was practically identical with the present text of GATT Article XXI.[209]

Concerns were raised at the Geneva meeting about the applicability of the dispute settlement mechanism to the security exceptions. By placing Article XXI between the general exceptions (Article XX) and the dispute settlement provision (Article XXIII), the Contracting Parties to the GATT 1947 made it clear that the dispute settlement mechanism would apply to the new article.

Countries imposing economic sanctions on Argentina after the Falkland/Malvinas events were of the view that they were exercising an inherent right existing under general international law, which was merely reflected by Article XXI of the GATT. This situation led Argentina to request an interpretation of such Article and the then Contracting Parties, although they did not interpret Article XXI, adopted a Decision Concerning Article XXI of the General Agreement.[210]

Article 73 is essentially identical to Article XXI of the GATT 1947 (1994). By contrast, the major pre-TRIPS intellectual property instruments, the Berne and Paris Conventions, do not contain any provision on security exceptions.

2.2 Negotiating history
Neither the Anell Draft[211] nor the Brussels Draft[212] contained a provision on security exceptions. The Dunkel Draft,[213] by contrast, did provide for security exceptions. This provision was essentially the same as the current Article 73.

3. Possible interpretations

The lack of a general interpretation of the meaning and scope of the provision of Article XXI of the GATT gains relevance when it comes to the analysis of the

---

[209] *Ibid.*

[210] GATT Doc. L/5426 (1982), GATT B.I.S.D. (29th Supp.), at 23 (1983). The text of the decision reads as follow:

"Considering that the exceptions envisaged in Article XXI of the General Agreement constitute an important element for safeguarding the rights of contracting parties when they consider that reasons of security are involved;

Noting that recourse to Article XXI could constitute in certain circumstances, an element of disruption and uncertainty for international trade and affect benefits accruing to contracting parties under the General Agreement;

Recognising that in taking action in terms of the exceptions provided in Article XXI of the General Agreement, contracting parties should take into consideration the interests of third parties which may be affected;

That until such time as the Contracting Parties may decide to make a formal interpretation of Article XXI it is appropriate to set procedural guidelines for its application;

The Contracting Parties decide that:

1. Subject to the exception in Article XXI:a, contracting parties should be informed to the fullest extent possible of trade measures taken under Article XXI.

2. When action is taken under Article XXI, all contracting parties affected by such action retain their full rights under the General Agreement.

3. The Council may be requested to give further consideration to this matter in due course."

[211] See composite text of 23 July 1990, circulated by the Chairman (Lars E. R. Anell) of the TRIPS Negotiating Group, document MTN.GNG/NG11/W/76.

[212] Document MTN.TNC/W/35/Rev. 1 of 3 December 1990.

[213] Part of document MTN.TNC/W/FA of 20 December 1991.

possible interpretations of Article 73. By stating that it is for the WTO Members to decide what information is essential for their essential security interests[214] and to define which are those essential security interests,[215] Article 73 places itself at the core of the tensions between a traditional decentralized legal order and the institutionalized dispute settlement mechanism embodied in the Dispute Settlement Understanding (DSU) of the WTO.[216] What is the role left for the dispute settlement organs, if any, when a Member invokes national security as a justification for the failure to comply with its obligations under the "covered agreements"?

One interpretation of Article 73 is to consider it not only as a justification, but also as a procedural jurisdictional defence, making a dispute inadmissible *ipso facto* by the mere invocation of the clause. However, there seem to be no grounds either in the negotiating history of the provision at issue or in their textual and contextual interpretation for upholding such a view.[217] Article 1 of the DSU states that it "shall apply to disputes brought pursuant to the consultation and dispute settlement provisions of the Agreement listed in Appendix 1", "subject to such special or additional rules and procedures on dispute settlement contained in the covered agreements as are identified in Appendix 2". No mention is made in such Appendix of any dispute settlement provision applying particularly to disputes concerning the national security exceptions. Therefore, the DSU itself is not subject to a national security exception and no particular rule applies to disputes on the application or interpretation of Article 73 or the analogous provisions in GATT and GATS. Furthermore, if Members were able to circumvent the application of the DSU merely by invoking the national security exception of GATT 1994, GATS or TRIPS, the purpose of strengthening the system that underlies Article 23 of the DSU could not be achieved.[218]

What is, then, the scope of review that panels and the Appellate Body can exercise over measures taken under Article 73 or its analogous provisions in GATT and GATS? It appears that the political qualification of what constitutes a "national security" issue remains a right reserved for the Members themselves. However, the respect of the objective limits imposed on the exercise of that right by Article 73 is a matter of interpretation and, therefore, subject to judicial review.

One of those objective limits is that neither Article 73 nor its analogous provisions in GATT and GATS serves to protect economic security interests.[219] In

---

[214] Paragraph (a) of Article 73 of the TRIPS Agreement.

[215] Paragraph (b) of Article 73 of the TRIPS Agreement.

[216] One of the main features of international law is that "each state establishes for itself its legal situation *vis-à-vis* other states". See *Air Services Agreement* case, 18 R.I.I.A., Vol. XVIII, p. 443, para. 81. See also Abi-Saab, Georges; '*Interprétation*' *et* '*Auto-Interprétation*': *Quelques réflexions sur leur rôle dans la formation et la résolution du différend international*, in Recht zwischen Umbruch und Bewahrung, Festschrift für Rudolf Bernhardt, Springer Verlag, Berlin, 1995, pp. 9–19.

[217] We refer to the negotiating history of the provision in first place because it was already dealt with in this chapter. However, it must be noted that a correct application of Articles 31 and 32 of the Vienna Convention on the Law of Treaties would call for an analysis of the text in its context before making reference to the preparatory work.

[218] Schloemann/Ohlhoff, p. 439.

[219] Article XXI GATT requires a rather delicate balance. As expressed by one of the drafters of the provision: "We have got to have some exceptions. We cannot make it too tight, because we cannot

some cases, however, it may be particularly difficult to establish a clearly cut bor-
derline between commercial purposes and security reasons. As illustrated by the
debate on IPRs and access to essential medicines, pandemics such as HIV may
pose fundamental threats to the very existence of vulnerable societies. In such
cases, it might be possible to invoke the Article 73 security exception for the protection of a nation's essential security interests. Arguably, pandemics such as HIV
could be qualified as "emergencies in international relations" as provided under
Article 73(b)(iii) (the international relations component being the failure to obtain
adequate supplies of medicines within the framework of the multilateral institutional structure). This being said, the issue requires further thought.

Another example in this context refers to Sweden's introduction of a quota for
a certain type of shoes in 1975, arguing that a decrease in its domestic capacity
to produce footwear, qualifying as a "vital industry", threatened the country's economic defence strategy and thus its security interests. Many Contracting Parties
took the view that this was precisely the kind of justification not available under
Article XXI. Sweden terminated the quotas imposed on leather and plastic shoes
as of 1 July 1977.[220]

The compatibility with Article 73 of a measure allegedly adopted for national
security reasons may also involve a test of reasonableness and an interpretation of
whether the measure is "necessary" to protect the invoked security interests. This
was the view taken by the International Court of Justice in the *Nicaragua* case by
stating that

> "[T]he concept of essential security interests certainly extends beyond the concept
> of armed attack, and has been subject to very broad interpretations in the past.
> The Court has therefore to assess whether the risk run by these 'essential security
> interests' is reasonable, and secondly, whether the measures presented as being
> designed to protect these interests are not merely useful but 'necessary'".[221]

Whether a security threat reasonably exists is also a matter of interpretation,
and the margin of discretion given to Members under Article 73 to define their
national interests can by no means be considered as an absolute discretion.[222]
Some delegates noted, in discussing the embargo measures brought by the United
States against Nicaragua, that it "was not plausible that a small country with small
resources could constitute an extraordinary threat to the national security of the
United States".[223]

---

prohibit measures which are needed purely for security reasons. On the other hand, we cannot
make it so broad that, under the guise of security, countries will put on measures which really
have a commercial purpose." Cited in GATT, Analytical Index, p. 600.

[220] GATT, Analytical Index, p. 603.

[221] *Case Concerning Military and Paramilitary Activities in and against Nicaragua*, ICJ Reports,
1986, p. 117, para. 224.

[222] On the concept of "reasonableness" in international law, see Olivier Corten, *L'utilisation
du "raisonnable" par le juge international: discours juridique, raison et contradictions*, Brussels,
Bruylant: Ed. de l'Université de Bruxelles, 1997.

[223] GATT Council, *Minutes of the Meeting Held May 29, 1985*, GATT Doc. C/7/188 (restricted), at p.
7, as cited by M. Hahn, '*Vital Interests in the Law of GATT: An Analysis of GATT's Security Exception*,
Michigan Journal of International Law, v. 12, 1991, p. 558.

Therefore, "security interests" that are "essential" must be defined by WTO Members in good faith and preventing any abuse of the right.[224] This requires a minimum degree of proportionality between the threatened individual security interest and the measure taken in response to that threat that is clearly subject to judicial review, according to general international law standards, by the competent WTO organs for the settlement of disputes.[225]

4. GATT and WTO jurisprudence

Four cases involving the security exception can be said to have reached the level of formalized dispute settlement under Article XXIII of the GATT 1947:

Shortly after the creation of the GATT, in 1949, the United States, through a system of export licenses, imposed a ban on the export of certain products to Czechoslovakia. Czechoslovakia, in turn, resorted to dispute settlement under Article XXIII and the United States invoked, *inter alia*, Article XXI, not as a procedural defence but as a substantive one. Although the Contracting Parties "decided to reject the contention of the Czechoslovak delegation that the Government of the United States had failed to carry out its obligations under the Agreement through its administration of the issue of export licences",[226] they did not altogether deny their formal Article XXIII jurisdiction over matters involving Article XXI of the GATT 1947.

The Reagan administration's Central American policy gave rise to two cases relating to Article XXI. In 1983, the United States decided to drastically reduce the share of sugar imports allocated to Nicaragua. The United States did not block either the establishment of the panel or the adoption of its report. Neither did it invoke Article XXI or attempted to defend its actions in GATT terms. According to the 1984 panel report, "The United States stated that it was neither invoking any exceptions under the provisions of the General Agreement nor intending to defend its actions in GATT terms ... [and that t]he action of the United States did of course affect trade, but was not taken for trade policy reasons".[227] Consequently, the panel did not examine whether the action could be justified under the security exception because it had not been invoked. However, this fact did not prevent the panel from finding that the United States was in violation of Article XIII (2).[228]

In 1985, the United States decided to impose a complete import and export embargo on Nicaragua, which requested the establishment of a panel again. The position of the United States in this case was considerably different to that adopted in the first dispute with Nicaragua. It managed to exclude from the terms of reference of the panel the possibility "to examine or judge the validity of or motivation

---

[224] See, in general, Robert Kolb, *La bonne foi en droit international public – Contribution à l'étude des principes généraux de droit*, Paris, PUF, 2000, particularly pp. 429 et seq.

[225] See J. Delbrück, *Proportionality*, in R. Bernhardt (ed), *Encyclopedia of Public International Law*, v. 7, 1984, p. 396.

[226] Decision of June 8, 1949, 2 GATT B.I.S.D. 28 (1952).

[227] *United States – Imports of Sugar from Nicaragua*, March 13, 1984, GATT B.I.S.D. (31st. Supp.), at para. 3.10.

[228] Ibid. paras. 4.3, 4.5 and 4.7.

for the invocation of Article XXI:(b)(iii) by the United States...".[229] Some other GATT Contracting Parties, such as Canada and the European Communities agreed with the United States that Article XXI issues were political questions not subject to panel scrutiny.[230] The panel nevertheless referred to the question in the following terms:

> "If it were accepted that the interpretation of Article XXI was reserved entirely to the contracting party invoking it, how could the CONTRACTING PARTIES ensure that this general exception to all obligations under the General Agreement is not invoked excessively or for the purposes other than those set out in this provision? If the CONTRACTING PARTIES give a panel the task of examining a case involving an Article XXI invocation without authorizing it to examine the justification of that provision, do they limit the adversely affected contracting party's right to have its complaint investigated in accordance with Article XXIII:2?"[231]

In 1991, as a consequence of the civil war in the former Socialist Federal Republic of Yugoslavia, the European Communities decided to restrict trade explicitly on the grounds of Article XXI.[232] Yugoslavia requested the establishment of a panel and argued that the requirements of neither Article XXI(b) nor (c) were met. This could have been the first case in which a panel could have properly analyzed the scope of Article XXI. However, given the uncertainties about the status of Serbia and Montenegro (FRY) as Party to the GATT, the proceedings were suspended by a Council decision in 1993.

Two other situations relating to Article XXI during the GATT era deserve to be mentioned, although they did not reach the level of a formalized dispute under GATT Article XXIII. One is the situation arising out of the sanctions imposed on Argentina in 1982 referred to above (Section 2.1). The other relates to the boycott of Portuguese goods imposed by Ghana in 1961. The particularity of this case resides in the fact that Ghana invoked Article XXI, arguing that each contracting party was the sole judge of what was necessary in its essential security interests and, therefore, there could not be an objection to the boycott.[233]

After the establishment of the WTO, there has been no dispute related to Article 73. However, disputes related to the national security exception under other WTO agreements arose in connection with the extra-territorial effects of some U.S. legislation, notably the *Cuban Liberty and Democratic Solidarity Act* of 1996,[234] and the *Iran and Libya Sanctions Act*.[235]

---

[229] GATT Doc. C/M/196, at 7 (1986).

[230] Such interpretation is based on the view that the mere invocation of a clause relating to security exceptions makes a dispute inadmissible, see above, Section 3.

[231] *United States – Trade Measures Affecting Nicaragua*, 13 October 1986 (unadopted), GATT Doc. L/6053, par. 5.17.

[232] GATT, Analytical Index, p. 604.

[233] Ibid., p. 600.

[234] Generally referred to as the "Helms-Burton Act", International Legal Materials 1996, pp. 357 et seq.

[235] Generally referred to as the "D'Amato-Kennedy Act", International Legal Materials 1996, pp. 1274 et seq. For a study on this issue, see, among others, Andrea Giardina, *The Economic Sanctions of the United States against Iran and Libya and the GATT Security Exception*,

With regard to the *Cuban Liberty and Democratic Solidarity Act*, the European Communities requested consultations with the United States in connection with trade sanctions imposed on Cuba. The EC claimed that U.S. trade restrictions on goods of Cuban origin, as well as the possible refusal of visas and the exclusion of non-U.S. nationals from U.S. territory, were inconsistent with the U.S. obligations under the GATT 1994 and the GATS. The Dispute Settlement Body (DSB) established a panel at its meeting on 20 November 1996[236] but, at the request of the EC, dated 21 April 1997, the panel suspended its work. The panel's authority lapsed on 22 April 1998, pursuant to Article 12.12 of the Dispute Settlement Understanding (DSU).

More recently, Honduras and Colombia instituted proceedings against the trade sanctions imposed by Nicaragua as a result of a maritime delimitation dispute.[237] The dispute has been at the consultations stage since 26 June 2000, in respect of Law 325 of 1999 whereby a tax is established on goods and services coming from or originating in Honduras and Colombia as well as implementing Decree 129–99 and Ministerial Order 041–99. Honduras considered that Law 325 of 1999 and implementing Decree 129–99 are incompatible with Nicaragua's obligations under the GATT 1994, and in particular Articles I and II thereof, and that the aforementioned measures as well as Ministerial Order 041–99 are incompatible with Nicaragua's obligations under Articles II and XVI of the GATS.[238]

5. Relationship with other international instruments

5.1 WTO Agreements

There is no particular relationship between Article 73 and the provisions on security exceptions under other WTO agreements. As mentioned above (Section 1), the text of Article 73 was modelled upon Article XI of the GATT 1947 and is almost identical to Article XIV *bis* of the GATS.

5.2 Other international instruments

There is no particular relationship between Article 73 and the provisions on security exceptions under other international instruments.

---

in G. Hafner and others (eds), *Liber Amicorum Professor Seidl-Hohenveldern – in Honour of his 80th Birthday*, the Netherlands, Kluwer Law International, 1998; R. Dattu, and J. Boscariol, *GATT Article XXI, Helms-Burton and the Continuing Abuse of the National Security Exception*, Canadian Business Law Journal, v. 28, No. 2, 1997, pp. 198–221; K.J. Kuilwijk, *Castro's Cuba and the U.S. Helms-Burton Act – An Interpretation of the GATT Security Exemption*, Journal of World Trade, v. 31, No. 3, 1997, pp. 49–62; A. Perez, *WTO and U.N. Law: Institutional Comity in National Security*, Yale Journal of International Law, v. 23, No. 2, 1998, pp. 302–381; K. Alexander, *The Helms-Burton Act and the WTO Challenge: Making a Case for the United States under the GATT Security Exception*, Florida Journal of International Law, v. 11, No. 3, 1997, pp. 487–516.

[236] WT/DS38.

[237] WT/DS201/1. The EC requested to join the consultations, see WT/DS201/2.

[238] See <http://www.wto.org>.

6. New developments

6.1 National laws

6.2 International instruments

6.3 Regional and bilateral contexts

6.4 Proposal for review

There are no proposals so far to review Article 73.

7. Comments, including economic and social implications

The rare recourse to security exceptions in the context of international economic relations illustrates the limited importance of such exception for developing countries. The problems these countries will face in the intellectual property area are usually of an economic and a social nature, rather than security-related.

Index